COMMUNICATION YEARBOOK 6

COMMUNICATION YEARBOOK 6

edited by
MICHAEL BURGOON
Associate Editor NOEL E. DORAN

an Annual Review Published for the
International Communication Association

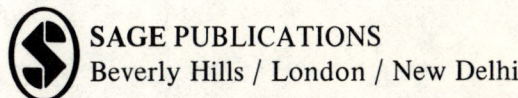

SAGE PUBLICATIONS
Beverly Hills / London / New Delhi

Copyright © 1982 by the International Communication Association.

All rights reserved. No part of this book may be reproduced or utilized in any form or by any means, electronic or mechanical, including photocopying, recording, or by any information storage and retrieval system, without permission in writing from the publisher.

For information address:

        SAGE Publications, Inc.
        275 South Beverly Drive
        Beverly Hills, California 90212

SAGE Publications India Pvt. Ltd.   SAGE Publications Ltd
    C-236 Defence Colony   28 Banner Street
    New Delhi 110 024, India   London EC1Y 8QE, England

Printed in the United States of America

Library of Congress: 76-45943
ISBN: 0-8039-1862-3

FIRST PRINTING

CONTENTS

Preface   11
Acknowledgments   13
Overview   15

PART I. COMMUNICATION REVIEWS AND COMMENTARIES

1. The Mass Media and Critical Theory: An American View
    James W. Carey   18
2. Language and Speech Communication
    Donald G. Ellis   34
3. Nonverbal Cues as Linguistic Context:
    An Information-Processing View
    Joseph P. Folger and W. Gill Woodall   63
4. Communication Between Handicapped and Nonhandicapped
    Persons: Toward a Deductive Theory
    Gordon L. Dahnke   92
5. Oral Communication Apprehension: A Reconceptualization
    James C. McCroskey   136
6. Does Communication Theory Need Intersubjectivity? Toward
    an Immanent Philosophy of Interpersonal Relations
    Lawrence Grossberg   171
7. Privacy and Communication
    Judee K. Burgoon   206
8. Direct Satellite Broadcasting: Selected Social Implications
    Rolf T. Wigand   250
9. Public Communication and Televised Presidential Debates
    Dennis K. Davis and Sidney Kraus   289
10. Social Judgment Theory
    Donald Granberg   304
11. Cognitive Schemata and Persuasive Communication:
    Toward a Contingency Rules Theory
    Mary John Smith   330

PART II. INFORMATION SYSTEMS

12. Attitude Change and Attitudinal Trajectories:
    A Dynamic Multidimensional Theory
    Stan A. Kaplowitz and Edward L. Fink 364
13. An Unequal Speaking Linear Discrepancy Model:
    Implications for Polarity Shift
    *Franklin J. Boster, Jan E. Fryrear,
    Paul A. Mongeau, and John E. Hunter* 395
14. Measuring Aspects of Information Seeking: A Test of a
    Quantitative/Qualitative Methodology
    *Brenda Dervin, Thomas L. Jacobson,
    and Michael S. Nilan* 419

PART III. INTERPERSONAL COMMUNICATION

15. Accuracy in Detecting Deception: Intimate
    and Friendship Relationships
    Mark. E. Comadena 446
16. The Affective Perspective-Taking Process: A Test of
    Turiel's Role-Taking Model
    Brant R. Burleson 473
17. Marital Interaction: Perceptions and Behavioral
    Implications of Control
    Donavan Emery 489
18. Reciprocity of Self-Disclosure: A Sequential Analysis
    Kathryn Dindia 506

PART IV. MASS COMMUNICATION

19. International Mass Communication Research: A Critical
    Review of Theory and Methods
    K. Kyoon Hur 531
20. Television Rules of Prepartum New Families
    Thomas R. Lindlof and Gary A. Copeland 555
21. Contextual Age and Television Use: Reexamining a
    Life-Position Indicator
    Rebecca B. Rubin and Alan M. Rubin 583
22. Children's Realities in Television Viewing: Exploring
    Situational Information Seeking
    *Rita Atwood, Richard Allen, Ralph Bardgett,
    Susanne Proudlove, and Ronald Rich* 605

PART V. ORGANIZATIONAL COMMUNICATION

23. Communicative Strategies in Organizational Conflicts: Reliability and Validity of a Measurement Scale
    Linda L. Putnam and Charmaine E. Wilson   629
24. The Compliance Interview: Negotiating Across Organizational Boundaries
    James A. Gilchrist   653
25. Office Technology: A Report on Attitudes and Channel Selection from Field Studies in Germany
    Arnold Picot, Heide Klingenberg, and Hans-Peter Kränzle   674

PART VI. INTERCULTURAL COMMUNICATION

26. The Television Environment in Black and White
    Richard L. Allen and Benjamin F. Taylor   694
27. Attribution Theory: Implications for Intercultural Communication
    Peter Ehrenhaus   721

PART VII. POLITICAL COMMUNICATION

28. News Media Use in Adolescence: Implications for Political Cognitions
    Steven H. Chaffee and Albert R. Tims   736
29. Public Opinion, Communication Processes, and Voting Decisions
    Carroll J. Glynn and Jack M. McLeod   759
30. The Successful Communication of Cognitive Information: A Study of a Precinct Committeeman
    David A. Bositis and Roy E. Miller   775

PART VIII. INSTRUCTIONAL COMMUNICATION

31. Teacher Communication and Student Learning: The Effects of Perceived Solidarity with Instructor and Student Anxiety Proneness
    Gregory S. Andriate   792
32. Sugar or Spice: Teachers' Perceptions of Sex Differences in Communicative Correlates of Attraction
    Cynthia Stohl   811

PART IX. HEALTH COMMUNICATION

33. Coping with Occupational Stress: Relational and Individual
    Strategies of Nurses in Acute Health Care Settings
    Terrance L. Albrecht — 832
34. The Advertising and Alcohol Abuse Issue: A Cross-Media
    Comparison of Alcohol Beverage Advertising Content
    T. Andrew Finn and Donald E. Strickland — 850

PART X. HUMAN COMMUNICATION TECHNOLOGY

35. Teleconferencing, Concern for Face,
    and Organizational Culture
    Glen Hiemstra — 874
36. Computer-Mediated Communication: A Network-Based
    Content Analysis Using a CBBS Conference
    James A. Danowski — 905
37. Communication Networking in Computer-Conferencing
    Systems: A Longitudinal Study of Group Roles and
    System Structure
    Ronald E. Rice — 925

Author Index — 945
Subject Index — 964
About the Editor — 968

COMMUNICATION YEARBOOK 6

EDITOR
Michael Burgoon, *Michigan State University*

Associate Editor
Noel E. Doran, *Michigan State University*

THE INTERNATIONAL COMMUNICATION ASSOCIATION

Communication Yearbook is an annual review. The series is sponsored by the International Communication Association, one of several major scholarly organizations in the communication field. It is composed of 2,500 communication scholars, teachers, and practitioners.

Throughout its 33-year history, the Association has been particularly important to those in the field of communication who have sought a forum where the behavioral science perspective was predominant. The International Communication Association has also been attractive to a number of individuals from a variety of disciplines who hold communication to be central to work within their primary fields of endeavor. The Association has been an important stimulant to the infusion of behavioral concepts in communication study and teaching, and has played a significant role in defining a broadened set of boundaries of the discipline as a whole.

The International Communication Association is a pluralist organization composed of eight subdivisions: information systems, interpersonal communication, mass communication, organizational communication, intercultural communication, political communication, instructional communication, and health communication.

In addition to *Communication Yearbook,* the Association publishes *Human Communication Research,* the *ICA Newsletter,* and *ICA Directory,* and is affiliated with the *Journal of Communication.* Several divisions also publish newsletters and occasional papers.

INTERNATIONAL COMMUNICATION ASSOCIATION
EXECUTIVE COMMITTEE

President
Erwin P. Bettinghaus, *Michigan State University*

President-Elect
James A. Anderson, *University of Utah*

Past President
Steven H. Chaffee, *Stanford University*

Executive Director
Robert L. Cox (ex officio), *ICA Headquarters*

BOARD OF DIRECTORS

Members-at-Large
Joseph N. Cappella, *University of Wisconsin—Madison*
Sue DeWine, *Ohio State University*
James C. McCroskey, *West Virginia University*
Thomas Scheidel, *University of Washington*
Carol Wilder, *San Francisco State University*

Division Chairpersons
Information Systems
Edward L. Fink, *University of Maryland*

Interpersonal Communication
Mary Anne Fitzpatrick, *University of Wisconsin—Madison*

Mass Communication
Thomas R. Donohue, *University of Kentucky*

Organizational Communication
Raymond Falcione, *University of Maryland*

International (and Development) Communication
Nobleza Asuncion-Lande, *University of Kansas*

Political Communication
Sidney Kraus, *Cleveland State University*

Instructional Communication
Robert Norton, *Purdue University*

Health Communication
Loyd Pettegrew, *Vanderbilt University*

Student Members
Marsha Stanback, *University of Massachusetts*
Cynthia Stohl, *Purdue University*

Special Interest Groups
Larry Grossberg, Philosophy of Communication, *University of Illinois*
Maureen Beninson, Human Communication Technology, *Upjohn Co., Kalamazoo, Michigan*

PREFACE

Communication Yearbook 6 represents more than just the sixth volume of a series published by the International Communication Association. In many ways, this volume represents new beginnings for the association and the series.

First, this volume is composed entirely of refereed manuscripts. Most of the manuscripts that open this book were selected from submissions of people who read a call for papers in January 1981. In the past, the editor of *Communication Yearbook* has solicited, cajoled, and sometimes even begged people to supply articles to open the volume. It was my thought that these opening pieces were a very important part of past volumes and that steps should be taken to open up this section to anyone who thought he or she had something important to say. People were encouraged to submit longer, theoretical pieces and to say what they had to say. This discipline needs a publication outlet for high-risk scholarship that does not fit journal formats limiting length and content. Overall, I was satisfied with the response of people to the call. I wish that the volume of submissions had been greater, but, in my opinion, we received some very important scholarly works for publication here.

Second, the division overviews have been dropped in *Communication Yearbook 6*. This change was promised in *Yearbook 5* because I thought that such an action should be taken. Simply stated, the division overviews were an idea whose time had come and gone. When Professor Ruben began this series, these overviews served a very useful purpose in updating the subareas within the discipline. Some divisions took these reviews to the next step and continued to provide editors with excellent state-of-the-art reviews in specific areas of import to the study of human communication. However, other divisions simply did not get with the program, and the quality of the reviews diminished over the years. This year, division chairs were encouraged to solicit manuscripts to be reviewed for potential publication, but no promises were made in advance that such pieces ultimately would be published.

Third, all "top three" papers were reviewed independently prior to acceptance for publication in *Communication Yearbook 6*. Several divisions submitted papers in addition to their top-ranked papers and, in some cases, those papers were selected for publication instead of the "top three" submissions. The editor must be responsible for the overall quality of this volume, and the divisions are not equivalent in terms of their quality standards. In my opinion, this review process benefits the book and the authors whose manuscripts are accepted for publication. Unfortunately, because of the deadlines associated with publication of this rather large book, it is really not possible to suggest major revisions to individual researchers. Therefore, some articles were rejected this year that might well have been publishable had there been time to work with the authors to accomplish needed revisions.

There was no attempt made this year to balance the space allocated to divisions. Papers were accepted when, in my opinion, they merited publication. Three papers were accepted from the Technology Interest Group even though they have not yet met the requirements for divisional status; I thought that each paper deserved publication and included their submissions. I fought for the right to exercise such editorial discretion with the full understanding that such prerogatives on the part of an editor make him or her fully responsible for the final product. I, of course, accept such responsibility and will take whatever criticism or praise is associated with such an editorial style.

Finally, this volume marks the beginning of a relationship with a new publisher. The enthusiasm for this project at Sage Publications is encouraging. Let us hope that this relationship is mutually beneficial to the association and the publisher.

— Michael Burgoon
East Lansing, Michigan

ACKNOWLEDGMENTS

This volume ends my tenure as editor of *Communication Yearbook*. I am sure that the transition to a new editor will be welcomed by some with much enthusiasm. Frankly, I too look forward to completing this task; however, I do want to say that I have enjoyed it. About the only rewards available to one who has been promoted as many times as he can and assured lifelong employment as long as the assembly lines roll are those that come from his colleagues. I appreciate those of you who made a special effort to tell me that you thought *Communication Yearbook 5* was good. I appreciate the fact that the Board of Directors and officers of the International Communication Association supported my policies during this period of change in the *Yearbooks*. Frankly, I would have done it anyway, but I am glad you people came along for the ride.

The person who deserves my thanks the most is Noel Doran, who is listed as Associate Editor in this volume. He really cared about these books and he also cared about the authors and their work. He is a very special person and, as mentioned in my acknowledgments for *Yearbook 5,* those of you who chair faculty search committees out there would do well to pay attention to my comments about him. He is still here in part because of the *Yearbook* series. Carol Doran got us organized and moving even when we would rather not have moved. I thank her for her editorial assistance. Erv Bettinghaus provided the necessary financial support and constant encouragement for two full years; we should all appreciate his service to the Association.

I appreciate the fact that I work with people like Gerry Miller, who continues to believe in substance over form. Michael Hourani continues to keep me whole. Judee Burgoon continues to get me out of the trouble I still get into, and all of you who care about me and human communication, in whichever order, provide me with reasons for getting up each morning.

M. B.

OVERVIEW OF THE COMMUNICATION YEARBOOK SERIES

This is the sixth in a series of annual volumes providing yearly reviews and syntheses of developments in the evolution of the science of communication. Each volume in the series provides (1) disciplinary reviews and commentaries on topics of general interest to scholars and researchers no matter what their specialized interest in communication studies, (2) current research in a variety of topics that reflect the scholarly concerns of persons working in designated areas, and (3) subject and author indexes that offer convenient reference for each volume. Reviews and commentaries for this volume were solicited by the series editor and chapters presenting current research were selected through processes of competitive judging. Final acceptance of *all* chapters was based upon refereeing processes established by the editor.

Reviews and Commentaries

Review and Commentary chapters are general discussions and critiques of substantive matters of generic interest and relevance that transcend the more specialized concerns of scholars working in the highly diversified discipline of communication science. This section provides a unique outlet for discussions of issues and ideas not readily adaptable to more restrictive journal formats.

Selected Studies

Communication Yearbook is also a means of publishing edited versions of representative current research that has been selected competitively for presentation at annual conferences of the International Communication Association. *Yearbook 6* presents studies selected for the 32nd Annual Conference held in Boston, Massachusetts, in May 1982. These studies represent the papers chosen by competitive evaluation by each of the ICA's divisions and by the *Yearbook* editor and selected reviewers. The papers represent research from the following divisions: information systems, interpersonal communication, mass communication, organizational communication, intercultural communication, political communication, instructional communication, health communication, and the communication technology interest group.

10 ● COMMUNICATION REVIEWS AND COMMENTARIES

1 ● The Mass Media and Critical Theory: An American View

JAMES W. CAREY

University of Illinois—Urbana

THE task of hermeneutics is to charm hermetically sealed-off thinkers out of their self-enclosed practices and to see the relations among scholars as strands of a conversation, a conversation without presuppositions that unites the speakers, but "where the hope of agreement is never lost so long as the conversation lasts" (Rorty, 1979, p. 318). In other words, on this view scholars are not locked in combat over some universal truth, but united in society: "persons whose paths through life have fallen together, united by civility rather than by a common goal, much less a common ground."

This hermeneutic intent is nowhere more needed than in theoretical discussions of the mass media. Of all the areas or subareas within communications, that of the mass media has proven to be the most fiercely resistant to adequate theoretical formulation — indeed, even to systematic discussion. The concepts and methods, which if not adequate are at least not embarrassing, when applied to interpersonal communication prove hapless and even a little silly when applied to the mass media. There is more than a matter of complexity involved here, though complexity is part of it. Many matters concerning interpersonal communication can be safely encysted from the surrounding world and treated with relatively simple models and straightforward methods. Not so with the mass media, where questions of political power and institutional change are inescapable and usually render hopelessly ineffective the standard cookbook recipes retailed by the graduate schools.

AUTHOR'S NOTE: This chapter is an edited transcript of an address delivered at the International Communication Association meeting in Minneapolis, Minnesota, May 1981.

Correspondence and requests for reprints: James W. Carey, 119 Gregory Hall, University of Illinois, Urbana, IL 61801.

In this chapter, I would like to make a modest attempt at argument, or at least to make an entry into this perpetually unsatisfying discussion about the mass media. First, let me anticipate a conclusion. In a recent paper on the history of the telegraph I tried to show how that technology — the major invention of the mid-nineteenth century — was the driving force behind the creation of a mass press. I also tried to show how the telegraph produced a new series of social interactions, a new conceptual system, new forms of language, and a new structure of social relations. In brief, the telegraph extended the spatial boundaries of communication and opened the future as a zone of interaction. It also gave rise to a new conception of time as it created a futures market in agricultural commodities and permitted the development of standard time. It also eliminated a number of forms of journalism — for example, the hoax, and tall tale — and brought other forms of writing into existence — for example, the lean "telegraphic" style Hemingway learned as a correspondent. Finally, the telegraph brought a national, commercial middle class into existence by breaking up the pattern of city-state capitalism that dominated the first half of the nineteenth century. The point of repeating conclusions arrived at elsewhere is that here I am attempting to elucidate a theoretical structure that will support and give generality to detailed historical-empirical investigation. But the path from the theoretical vacuity surrounding the media to concrete investigations must proceed by way of a number of detours.

OBJECTIVISM VERSUS EXPRESSIVISM

The ragged ambulating ridge dividing the Enlightenment from the Counter-Enlightenment — Descartes from Vico, if we need names — has surfaced in contemporary media studies as an opposition between critical and administrative research. The ridge that Descartes's action and Vico's reaction carved as an engram in the Western imagination has among its features three peaks.

1. *The noncontingency of starting points.* There is a given place to begin to unravel any problem and a given place where it is unraveled.
2. *Indubitability.* In unraveling problems there are available certain concepts and methods of universal standing and applicability, and insofar as there are not, one can make no claim to knowledge.
3. *Identity.* The world of problems is independent of and accessible to the mind of the knowing observer.

In short, if you begin at the beginning, if you are armed with indubitable concepts and methods, if you stand as an observer gazing upon an independent reality, then there is a path to positive knowledge. Taken together they described and secured the way to positive knowledge, and yielded up an epistemologically centered philosophy. Most importantly, they made science paradigmatic for culture as a whole — discrediting or at least reducing other human activities that did not conform to the Cartesian paradigm.

The reaction from the Italian side of the Alps settled all those divides that are with us to this day: Science versus the humanities, objective versus subjective, Rationalism versus Romanticism, analysis versus interpretation. There are three aspects of Vico's reaction worth noting and, I will admit, twisting somewhat to the purpose here. First, the world as such has no essence and therefore no real independence. The "real" is continuously adapted and remade to human purposes, including the remaking of man himself. It is this world of human activity we can understand with greatest clarity. Second, Cartesian science ought not be viewed as paradigmatic for culture as a whole, but as one more form of human expression, a new suburb of the language in Wittgenstein's phrase. Science, on this view, is one more voice in the conversation of mankind, one more device of self-expression, of communication with other humans. It must be understood, as we would say today, hermeneutically, as part of an extended conversation. Third, there are, then, no timeless invariant methods, concepts, or principles by which things are grasped; only the bounded symbols and knowledge, more or less unique to a people, through which the world is rendered intelligible.

I have painted a misleading and exceedingly two-dimensional portrait. The ridge of the Enlightenment does not neatly divide people. Some dextrous scholars try to stand on both sides at once; others are on different sides in different books or at different stages of their careers. Others attempt to save what is valuable in both traditions. Still others, some modern literary critics are examples, assimilate Descartes to Vico and make positive science but one more literary genre; others assimilate Vico to Descartes and scientize all of culture. And finally, some like William James find the whole argument bootless and just walk away from the discussion leaving nothing in its place.

I do not wish to debate any of these issues I have raised but merely to sharpen one of the distinctions, a distinction in Charles Taylor's (1976) terms, between "objectivism" and "expressivism."

Taylor characterizes Descartes' vision as an objectionist one. Descartes saw humans as subjects who possessed their own picture of the world (as opposed to a picture determined by God) and an endogenous motivation. Along with this self-defining identity went an objectification of the world. That is, the world was not seen as a cosmic order but as a domain of neutral, contingent fact to which man was related only as an observer. This domain was to be mapped by the tracing of correlations and ultimately manipulated for human purposes. Furthermore, this vision of an objectified neutral world was valued as a confirmation of a new identity before it became important as the basis of the mastery of nature. Later this objectification was extended beyond external nature to include human life and society (Taylor, 1976, p. 539).

This objectivist view not only collided with deeply held religious beliefs but with secular ones as well. Most people most of the time have felt that reality expressed something; that it was an inscription or a resemblance. Most commonly, this expressiveness was seen as spiritualism or animism; reality expressed spirit, the divine and transcendent. It was the doctrine of expressivism that Descartes most thoroughly discredited. On his view reality expressed nothing. It was neutral, contingent, concatenated.

However, expressivism did not go away merely because Descartes attacked it. It reappeared in various forms of romanticism. More importantly, the notion that reality expressed something reappeared in Hegel as the *Geist:* the growth of rational freedom. Finally, in Charles Taylor's useful phrase, "Marx anthropologized the *Geist:* He displaced it onto man" (Taylor, 1976, p. 546). In Marx and much of Marxism reality is not neutral and independent of man. Rather, it expresses man in the sense that it is a product of human activity. In William James's lovely phrase, the "mark of the serpent is overall." Reality expresses at any historical moment the purposes and objectives, intentions and desires of humans. Technology, social relations, and all artifacts are social hieroglyphics. Reality is expressive not because it reveals any nature, human or divine, or any eternal essence of any kind, but rather because it is a product of human action in and upon the world.

It is this distinction between objectionist and expressivist views of the world, not between administrative and critical research, that constitutes the fundamental divide among scholars. But I accept this distinction only as a prelude to modifying it. I agree, at least to a limited extent, that reality is a product of human activity. But the claim is neither philosophical nor meta-scientific but a simple historical one. Reality has been made — has been progressively made — by human activity. This is through a process, celebrated by structuralists, whereby nature is turned into culture, and by a similar, but inverse, process whereby culture penetrates the body of nature. The first process is revealed by the simple Levi-Strauss examples of vegetation transformed into cuisine or animals into totems. The second by the mind ulcerating the stomach, or the more menacing moment when an equation splits the atom. The point is general: The history of the species is simultaneously the history of the transformation of reality. There is now virtually no reach of space, of the microscopic or macroscopic, that has not been refigured by human action. Increasingly, what is left of nature is what we have deliberately left there. But if this is true, then reality is not objective, contingent, and neutral. To imagine such an objectivist science is in fact to imagine a world in which, as Lewis Mumford has argued, humans did not exist. And so did Galileo imagine it (Mumford, 1970, pp. 57-65). But if all that is true, it has a philosophical consequence: There are no given starting points, no Archimedian points or indubitable concepts, or privileged methods. The only basing point we have is the historically varying nature of human purposes.

In presenting the expressionist position I have deliberately glossed over the serious, even fundamental, disagreements within this tradition. The fault line — often described by the terms materialism and idealism — pivots on the question of whether reality should be seen as an expression of the human mind — "the place of the mind in nature," in Ernst Cassirer's useful phrase — or of human activity, human labor power. However important the debate on this question, it is possible to agree to the following on either a materialist or idealist reading. The mind — the associative, cooperative mind — its extension in culture, and realization in technique is the most important means of production. The most important product of the mind is a produced and sustained reality.

I want now to leave the savannah of continental philosophy for the rather more secure village of American studies. I shall not refer in what follows to these preliminary matters but, to steal Stuart Hall's lovely phrase, "their absent presence will lay across the route like the sky-trail of a vanished aircraft" (Hall, 1977, p. 18).

PUBLIC OPINION AND THE MASS MEDIA

I want to locate the distinction between administrative and critical research — now transformed into a distinction between objectivism and expressivism — outside the European tradition and within American studies. Inevitably, when this subject comes up, critical and administrative research are identified with those two emigrés from the fall of Weimar, T. W. Adorno and Paul Lazarsfeld. The context of the discussion is thus fixed in advance by the type of research and sponsorship identified with Lazarsfeld and by the research and "Hegelianized" version of Marxism identified with Adorno. Indeed the term "critical" did not so much describe a position as a cover under which Marxism might hide during a hostile period in exile. It is useful, however, to resituate the distinction between administrative and critical research within the conversation of American culture, and, in particular, in an exchange during the 1920s between Walter Lippmann and John Dewey. I do this not to dramatize the importance of Lippmann or Dewey, but rather, to underscore the point that you cannot grasp a conversation elsewhere until you can understand one at home. If we accept the contingency of starting points (the time and place where we reside) "we accept our inheritance from and our conversation with our fellow human beings as our only source of guidance" (Rorty, 1979). To attempt to evade this contingency is to hope to become a properly programmed machine, which is what graduate education is so often. In short I turn to Dewey and Lippmann to see if I can grasp their conversation within the tradition we have inherited and shaped. Once having grasped it we can use it as an entrance to other conversations — foreign, strange, and elliptical.

Walter Lippmann's *Public Opinion* (1922) is, I believe, the founding book in American media studies. It was not the first book written about the mass media in America, but it was the first serious work to be philosophical and analytical in confronting the mass media. The title of his book may be *Public Opinion,* but its subject and central actor is the mass media, particularly the news media. The book founded or at least clarified a continuous tradition of research as well. Finally, the book self-consciously restated the central problematic in the study of the mass media.

In earlier writing on the mass media the central problematic, true to the utilitarian tradition, was freedom. Utilitarianism assumes that, strictly speaking, the ends of human action are random or exogenous. Rational knowledge could not be gained of human values or purposes. The best we can do is rationally judge the fitting together of ends and means. One can attain rational knowledge of the primal allocation of resources among means and toward given ends, but one can gain no rational knowledge of the selection of ends. Apples are as good as oranges, baseball as good as poetry. All that can be determined is the rational means to satisfy subjective and irrational desire. Truth in this tradition is a property of the rational determination of means. In turn, the rationality of means depended upon freedom and the availability of information. More precisely, it was freedom that guaranteed the availability of perfect information and perfect information that guaranteed the rationality of means. In summary then: If men are free they will have perfect information; if perfect information, they can be rational in choosing the most effective means to their individual ends, and if so, in a manner never quite explained, the social good will result. So the problem that concerned writers about the press in the Anglo-American tradition was how to secure the conditions of freedom against the forces that would undermine it. These forces were considered to be political and institutional, not psychological. Once freedom was secured against these forces, truth and social progress was guaranteed.

Lippmann changed this problematic. He argued that a free system of communication will not guarantee perfect information and, therefore, there are no guarantees of truth even when the conditions of freedom are secure. Moreover, the enemies of freedom were no longer the state and the imperfections of the market but in the nature of news and news gathering, in the psychology of the audience, and in the scale of modern life. It is important to note the following: Lippmann redefined the problem of the press from one of morals and politics to one of epistemology. The consequence of that move was to radically downplay the role of state and class power, indeed to contribute, paradoxically in a book about politics, to the depolitization of the public sphere.

The very title of Lippmann's introductory chapter, the most famous chapter in the book, "The World Outside and the Pictures in Our Heads," reveals his basic assumptions. We can know the world if we can represent accurately what is outside our mind. The possibility and nature of knowledge is determined by the way in which the mind is able to construct representations. The philosophical side of Lippmann is arguing for a general theory of representation that divides culture up into the areas that represent reality well (such as science), those that represent it less well (such as art), and those that do not represent it at all (such as journalism), despite their pretense of doing so (Rorty, 1979, p. 3). Lippmann's view is that reality is picturable, and truth can be achieved by matching an independent, objective, picturable reality against a language that corresponds to it. News, however, cannot picture reality or provide correspondence to the truth. News can only give — like the blip on a sonar scope — a signal that something is happening. More often it provides degenerate photographs or a pseudo-reality of stereotypes. News can approximate truth only when reality is reducible to a statistical table: sport scores, stock exchange reports, births, deaths, marriages, accidents, court decisions, elections, economic transactions such as foreign trade and balance of payments. Lippmann's major argument is this: Where there is a good machinery of record, the news system works with precision; where there is not, it disseminates stereotypes. What is needed is an official, quasi-governmental intelligence bureau that will reduce all the contestable aspects of reality to table.

One does not have to rehearse the well-known phenomenological and ethnomethodological critiques of official records and tables to see in Lippmann the classic fallacy of the Cartesian tradition, to wit: the belief that metaphors of vision, correspondence, mapping, picturing, and representation that apply to small routine assertions — the rose is red, the Cubs lost 7-5, IBM is selling at 67½ — will apply equally to large debatable ones. Numbers may picture the stock market but they will not tell you what is going on in Central America or, alas, what we should do about Poland.

There are a number of subsidary assumptions and doctrines in *Public Opinion* and let me mention but a couple. The basic metaphor of communication is vision. Communication is a kind of seeing things aright. Because communication is seen within the requirements of epistemological exactness, it is similarly a method of transmitting that exactness. Ideally, communication is the transmission of a secured and grounded truth independent of power. Because such conditions of truth cannot be achieved outside of Cartesian science, it is necessary to employ cadres of scientists to secure exact representations that can then permit the newspaper to correctly inform public opinion.

Lippmann left an intellectual legacy that is still influential, despite the fact he refuted many of his views in subsequent works. He particularly furthered a set of beliefs shared with large stretches of the progressive movement. Lippmann endorsed the notion that it was possible to have a science of society such that scientists might constitute a new priesthood: the possessors of truth as a result of having an agreed upon method for its determination. The mass media could operate as representatives of the public by correctly informing public opinion. Public opinion is merely the statistical aggregation of the private opinions informed by the news media. The effects of mass communication derive from the epistemological inadequacy of the system of news, as well as the prior stereotypes, prejudices, and selective perceptions of the audience. Intellectual-political activity had to be professionalized if truth was to be produced. Finally, and in summary, Lippmann implied that the ground for discussion of the mass media had to be shifted from questions of the public, power, and freedom to questions of knowledge, truth and stereotypes.

John Dewey reviewed *Public Opinion* in the May 3, 1922 issue of the *New Republic*. He admitted to the virtues of the book but his sharpest conclusion was that it was the greatest indictment of democracy yet written. Dewey answered Lippmann in lectures given four years later at Antioch College and published in 1927 as *The Public and Its Problems* (Dewey, 1927). It is a maddeningly difficult book and so rather than trying to summarize it, let me quote from the last three pages of it, a quotation I have mercifully shortened and improved without impairing its meaning:

> The generation of democratic communities and an articulate democratic public carries us beyond the question of intellectual method into that of practical procedure. But the two questions are not disconnected. The problem of securing diffused and seminal intelligence can be solved only in the degree in which local communal life becomes a reality. Signs and symbols, language, are the means of communication by which a fraternally shared experience is ushered in and sustained. But conversation has a vital import lacking in the fixed and frozen words of written speech. Systematic inquiry into the conditions of dissemination in print is a precondition of the creation of a true public. But it and its results are but tools after all. Their final actuality is accomplished in face-to-face relationships by means of direct give and take. Logic in its fulfillment recurs to the primitive sense of the word: dialogue. Ideas which are not communicated, shared, and reborn in expression are but soliloquy, and soliloquy is but broken and imperfect thought. It, like the acquisition of material wealth, marks a diversion of the wealth created by associated endeavor

and exchange to private ends . . . expansion of personal understanding and judgment can be fulfilled only in the relations of personal intercourse in the local community. The connections of the ear with vital and out-going thought and emotion are immensely closer and more varied than those of the eye. Vision is a spectator: hearing is a participator. Publication is partial and the public which results is partially informed and formed until the meanings it purveys pass from mouth to mouth. There is no limit to the intellectual endowment which may proceed from the flow of social intelligence when that circulates by word of mouth from one to another in the communications of the local community. That and that only gives reality to public opinion. We lie, as Emerson said, in the lap of an immense intelligence. But that intelligence is dormant and its communications are broken, inarticulate and faint until it possesses the local community as its medium. (Dewey, 1927, pp. 217-219)

There is much that might be noted about that quotation and much that is implied in it. Let me draw out just enough to focus Dewey's conflict with Lippmann and to set the stage for the argument I wish to advance. What is most sharply etched in the quotation is Dewey's espousal of the metaphor of hearing over that of seeing. While his language is mindful of arguments that were to resurface over subsequent decades with Harold Innis and Marshall McLuhan, it is important to note that Dewey is attacking the doctrine of representation in both its political and epistemological forms. He chooses the metaphor of hearing over seeing in order to argue that language is not a system of representations but a form of activity, and speech captures this action better than the more static images of the printed page. As an instrument of action, language cannot serve a representative function. Truth is, in William James's happy phrase, what "it is better for us to believe" and the test of the truth of propositions is their adequacy to our purposes (Rorty, 1979, p. 10).

In Dewey's view words take on their meanings from other words and in their relations to activity rather than by virtue of their representative character. As a corollary vocabularies acquire their privilege from the men who use them, not from their transparency to the real. Science, rather than a privileged, grounded set of representations, is merely part of the conversation of our culture, though an exceedingly important part of it. Science is a pattern of discourse adopted for various historical reasons for the achievement of objective truth, where objective truth is no more and no less than the best idea we currently have about how to explain what is going on.

Dewey is, in other words, proposing that conversation, not photography, is the ultimate context within which knowledge is to be understood. Science is one, but only one, strand of that conversation. Science is to be commended not because of the privilege of its representations but because of its method, if we understand method not to refer to technique but to certain valued habits: full disclosure, willingness to provide reasons, openness to experience, an arena for systematic criticism. Dewey did not want a science *of* society presided over by a priesthood, but a science *in* society: a means of getting our thinking straight by improving the conversation. In this sense, everyone is a scientist. Dewey did not want a new science of communications that would objectify society and propose to improve it, but a science that would clarify our purposes and the advance of mutual understanding. News is not to be judged on such a view as a degenerate form of science, trading in stereotypes, but as the occasion of public discussion and action. Another voice to be heard.

Finally, if reality is what we will to believe in support of our shared purposes, then it is proper to claim that reality is constituted by human action, particularly symbolic action, particularly associative action. Therefore reality has no essence to be discovered but rather a character to be, within limits, constituted. The instrument of political action, of the generation of a democratic political order, is the form of collective life we call the public. Therefore if the public is atomized, eclipsed, made a phantom, democracy is impossible.

Let me summarize Lippmann and Dewey. First, Lippmann. You have an effective public opinion when the individual minds that make up the public possess correct representations of the world. The newspaper serves its democratic function when it transmits such representations to individual members of the public. An effective public opinion then can be formed as the statistical aggregation of such correct representations. This is at present impossible because of censorship, the limited time and contact available to people, a compressed vocabulary, certain human fears at facing facts, etc. But the greatest limitation is in the nature of news, which fails to adequately represent, at best signals events, and implants and evokes stereotypes. Therefore the formation of a correct public opinion requires the formation of independent cadres of social scientists working in quasi-public bureaucracies, (the Bureau of Standards was his model) using the latest statistical procedures to produce veridical representations of reality — representations to be in turn transmitted to the waiting individuals who make up the public.

Dewey's response takes a number of turns. Public opinion is not formed when individuals possess correct representations of the environment, even if correct representations were possible. It is formed only in discussion, when it is made active in community life. While news suffers from many of the deficiencies Lippmann cites, its major deficiency is not its failure to represent. The line between an adequate image and a stereotype is impossible to draw anyway. The purpose of news is not to represent and inform but to signal, tell a story, and activate inquiry. Inquiry, in turn, is not something other than conversation and discussion but a more systematic version of it. What we lack is the vital means through which this conversation can be carried on: institutions of public life through which a public can be formed and can form an opinion. The press, by seeing its role as that of informing the public, abandons its role as an agency for carrying on the conversation of our culture. We not only lack an effective press but certain vital habits: the ability to follow an argument, grasp the point of view of another, expand the boundaries of understanding, debate the alternative purposes that might be pursued.

Behind Dewey's surface-level critique is a deeper one directed at the problem of representation in both its epistemological and political-journalistic sense. It is here that Dewey is in the most acute conflict with Lippmann. He sees in Lippmann a manifestation of what he most argued against: the spectator theory of knowledge. Lippmann views the public as a second-order spectator: a spectator of the spectator. Scientists observe reality and represent it. This correct representation is then transmitted to the audience who receives it as a correct representation. Dewey expresses this dissatisfaction in ordinary language with a visual metaphor. We associate knowledge with vision in order to emphasize that we are spectators rather than participants in the language game through which knowledge is made or produced. We associate politics with vision and the spectator in order to deny the public any political role other than to ratify a political world already represented — a depoliticized world in which all the critical choices have been made by the experts. We are not, however, he would insist, observors or spectators of a given world but participants in its actual making. How we constitute the world is dependent on our purposes and on our skill at foresight, at imagining the possible states of a desirable politics.

COMMUNICATION AS ACTION

There was much that was flawed in Dewey's thought, as I tried to point out on a number of occasions: a congenital optimism, a romance with the small town, a disastrously simple-minded view of technology. I do think he had the best of this argument, however. Rather than blissfully repeating his insights or unconsciously duplicating his errors, I tried in a group of papers to extend, however gently, Dewey's pragmatist conception of mass communication. Let me summarize that earlier argument, though with a modification of emphasis here and there. In the concluding section I want to repair or at least patch up certain deficiencies in the earlier presentations.

I can summarize the earlier argument with a series of assertions that are not quite propositions. I believe with Dewey that one must begin the analysis of mass communication from within a genuine crisis in culture, a crisis of community life, of public life. This crisis of community life derives from a loss or better a failure to realize the most active principles of associative life in the Western tradition, namely a democratic social order. While the roots of this crisis may be described in a variety of compatible ways, for disciplinary purposes, if no other, they can be traced to certain models of communication that dominate everyday life, models through which we create social relationships precluding the possibility of community life. These models, in turn, derive from a commitment to a science of society that paradigmatically describes the essence of communication as a process in which men alternatively pursue influence or flee anxiety, essences that derive from social science models of causality and functionalism, respectively. Indeed the crisis comes in part from the model of communication, knowledge, and culture one finds in *Public Opinion*. These models not only undergird news but all our cultural productions, the discussions and arguments about these productions, and the media that carry them. To put this both more colloquially and philosophically, language — the fundamental medium of human life — is increasingly defined as an instrument for manipulating objects, not a device to establish the truth but to get others to believe what we want them to believe. As Albert Camus says "dialogue and personal relations have been replaced by propaganda or polemic" (Pitkin, 1972, p. 329). Or as Hannah Arendt argues, the result of this view of language is that we no longer recognize as a serious possibility the truth — revealing function of language, so cut off are we from its power to establish genuine relationships or to create "public space": an institutional arena in which shared public deliberation and free political action are possible (Pitkin, 1972). Or to return it to Dewey, though the language is Arendt's: "There is an intimate link between speech and political life. Speech is what makes man a political being and wherever the relevance of speech is at stake matters become political by definition. The *polis* was a way of life in which speech and only speech made sense and where the central concerns of all citizens was to talk to each other" (Pitkin, 1972, p. 331). What I take all these arguments to converge on is this: The divorce of truth from discourse and action — the instrumentalization of communication — has not merely increased the incidence of propaganda; it has disrupted the very notion of truth and therefore the sense by which we take our bearings in the world is destroyed.

If this diagnosis is even approximately correct, it requires that we reformulate our conception of communication not as mere reflection but as action. That is, if communication is, in Wittgenstein's terms, among our central forms of life, then to change the models that describe the terms of communication would open up the possibility of changing this form of life; in fact, it is to change it not merely as a form of talk but as a form of associative life.

Let me reiterate, then, the direction this reformulation must take. We must discard first of all the view of language as reference, correspondence, and representation and the parallel view that the function of language is primarily to express assertions about the world, and substitute the view that language — communication — is a form of action, action or better interaction, that not merely represents or describes but actually molds or constitutes the world.

In examining communication as a process by which reality is constituted, maintained, and transformed I am trying to stress that communication as such has no essence, no universalizing qualities; it cannot be represented in nature. Communication simply constitutes a set of historically varying practices and reflections upon them. These practices bring together human conceptions and purposes with technological forms in sedimented social relations. Of the essence of communication we can only say with Heidegger (1968, p. 277): "We — mankind — are a conversation. . . . The being of man is found in language . . . by which mankind continually produces and contemplates itself a reflection of our species being." I call this approach cultural studies and its central problem that of meaning in order to contrast it with versions of communication that search for laws and functions and to focus on the hermeneutic side of the task. Meaning in this view is not representation but a constituting activity whereby humans interactively endow an elastic though resistant world with enough coherence and order to support their purposes. The agency by which they do this is certainly representation but not representations simply of the world. It is the great power of symbols to portray that which they pretend to describe. That is, symbols have an "of" and "for" side. It is this dual nature that allows us to produce the world by symbolic work and then take up residence in the world so produced. This is a ritual view of communication emphasizing the production of a coherent world that is then presumed — for all practical purposes — to exist. It is to emphasize the construction and maintenance of paradigms rather than experiments, presuppositions rather than propositions, the frame not the picture. The objective of doing all this — of looking at the practices that organize communications, the concepts such practices presuppose and the social relations they bring into existence — is a hermeneutic one: to try to find out what other people are up to or at least what they think they are up to; to render transparent the concepts and purposes that guide their actions and render the world coherent to them; to extend the human conversation, to incorporate other actors tending other dramas into our world by comprehending what they are saying. Understanding another person or culture, which is the first-order goal and wasting resource of the study of communication, is akin to understanding a scientific theory. You look at the practices people engage in, the conceptual world embedded in and presupposed by those practices and the social relations and forms of life that they manifest.

Communication is an ensemble of social practices into which ingress, to use Whitehead's favorite term, conceptions, forms of expression, and social relations. These practices constitute reality (or alternatively deny, transform, or merely celebrate it). Communication naturalizes the artificial forms that human relations take by merging technique and conception in them. Each moment in the practice coactualizes conceptions of the real, forms of expression, and the social relations anticipated and realized in both. One can unhinge the practice at each of the points. The social forms and relations technology makes possible are themselves imagined in and anticipated by the technology. Technique is vectoral and not merely neutral in the historical process. A building, its precise architecture, anticipates and imagines the social relations that it permits and desires. So does a television signal. Social relations of class, status, and power demand both a conceptual structure of persons and a technology to effectuate them. Conceptual structures, in turn, never float free of the expressive forms that realize them or the social relations that make them active agents.

Communication is at once a structure of human action — activity, process, practice — an ensemble of expressive forms, and a structured and structuring set of social relations. To describe communication is not merely to describe a constellation of enshrined ideas; it is also to describe a constellation of practices that enshrine and determine those ideas in a set of technical and social forms. As Clifford Geertz has recently argued, it should not be necessary, at least since Wittgenstein, to insist that such an assertion involves no commitment to idealism, to a subjectivist conception of social reality, to a belief that men act in circumstances of their own making and choosing, to a naive faith in the power of ideas, or to the romantic notion that the creative imagination can willfully triumph over all the forces sedimented in nature, in society, in the economy, or in the unconscious — biological, collective, lived (Geertz, 1981, p. 134). Reality is not, as Americans are so quick to make it, a form of private property or a matter of taste. It is not the eternal given either merely waiting about to be accurately represented in the individual mind once that mind is emptied of history and tradition or the veil of false consciousness is lifted or a better technology of communication is perfected. Reality is a product of work and action, collective and associated work and action. It is formed and sustained, repaired and transformed, worshipped and celebrated in the ordinary business of living. To set the matter up in this way is neither to deny, ignore, or mystify social conflict; in fact, it is an attempt to locate such conflict and make it intelligible.

Reality is, above all, a scarce resource. Like any scarce resource it is there to be struggled over, allocated to various purposes and projects, endowed with given meanings and potentials, spent and conserved, rationalized and distributed. The fundamental form of power is the power to define, allocate, and display this resource. Once the blank canvas of the world is portrayed and featured it is also preempted and restricted. Therefore the site where artists paint, writers write, speakers speak, filmmakers film, broadcasters broadcast is simultaneously the site of social conflict over the real. It is not a conflict over ideas as disembodied forces. It is not a conflict over technology. It is not a conflict over social relations. It is a conflict over the simultaneous codetermination of ideas, technique, and social relations. It is above all not a conflict over the effects of communication but of the acts and practices that are themselves the effects.

Conflict over communications is not, however, undifferentiated. It occurs at the level of paradigms and theories, formulas and stereotypes, recipes and programs; that is, conflict occurs over the general determination of the real as well as at the points of exclusion, repression, and denial, where forms of thought, technique and social relations are cast beyond the glow of the real into the darkness of unintelligibility, subversion, and disgrace. In our time reality is scarce because of access: so few command the machinery for its determination. Some get to speak and some to listen, some to write and some to read, some to film and some to view. It is fine to be told we are the species that actively creates the world and then simultaneously to be told that we are part of the subspecies denied access to the machinery by which this miracle is pulled off. There is no irony intended in saying we have to accept both those independent clauses. But it reveals as well, and the thought is deliberately allusive, that there is not only class conflict in communication but status conflict as well. Everyone these days seems willing to testify to class domination and to describe it in elegant detail. Alas, we are less willing to describe the internal divisions within dominant classes and the access of dominant and dominated intellectuals to the machinery of reality production: classrooms, journals, books — even newspapers, film, and broadcasting. Status only seems less real than class for those who possess too much of the latter and too little of the former.

John Dewey's notion of public life is naive because in retrospect he seems so innocent of the role of class, status, and power in communication. Lippmann's views seem sophisticated, even if objectionable, because he both understood and accepted the new media and the forms of class power they embodied. Dewey's image of a democratic community was that of a community of equals using the noblest procedures of rational thought to advance their shared purposes. His emphasis on the community of inquirers, the public, was designed to highlight the process of the codetermination of reality in the medium of maximum equality, flexibility, and accessibility. We can all talk. He saw more clearly than most the decline and eclipse of public life, the rise of a new breed of professional experts, and the models of communication they were embodying in the new mass media. With the noise of an even angrier and uglier world in our heads we can scarcely follow him, let alone believe him.

We are all democrats, in communication as in everything alse, but we are also more than a little in love with power. In *Penguin Island* Anatole France remarked that "in every society wealth is a sacred thing; in a democracy it is the only sacred thing." He is wrong of course. Let us substitute power for wealth. Modern thought about communication — both that which affirms and that which critiques — reveals the same lust. A critical theory of communication must affirm what is before our eyes and transcend it by imagining, at the very least, a world more desirable.

REFERENCES

Dewey, J. *The public and its problems.* New York: Henry Holt, 1927.
Geertz, C. *Negera.* Princeton, NJ: Princeton University Press, 1981.
Hall, S. The hinterland of science: Ideology and "The sociology of knowledge." In Centre for Contemporary Cultural Studies, *On ideology.* London: Hutchinson, 1977.
Heidegger, M. *Existence and being.* Chicago: Henry Regnery, 1968.
Lippmann, W. *Public opinion.* New York: Macmillan, 1922.
Mumford, L. *The pentagon of power.* New York: Harcourt Brace Jovanovich, 1970.
Pitkin, H. F. *Wittgenstein and justice.* Berkeley: University of California Press, 1972.
Rorty, R. *Philosophy and the mirror of nature.* Princeton, NJ: Princeton University Press, 1979.
Taylor, C. *Hegel.* Cambridge: Cambridge University Press, 1975.

… COMMUNICATION REVIEWS AND COMMENTARIES

2 ● Language and Speech Communication

DONALD G. ELLIS
Michigan State University

THE unique human ability to use language has captured the imagination of philosophers, scientists, and scholars ever since the first meaningful sounds were uttered. Opinions about language run to extremes; language is credited with either structuring all experience or denying us access to the "real" world. But wherever the truth lies, there is no escaping the centrality of language to the human experience. Ancient scholars were well aware of this. Power came with literacy and it is no accident that early statesmen and religious leaders were highly literate and adept at using their language. Members of contemporary society are even more dependent on linguistic skills. Because of certain economic and social developments, a large number of citizens have access to information, mass media, and new technologies. Moreover language continues to occupy the interests of philosophers, psychologists, sociologists, anthropologists, and academics of all callings.

Interestingly, the role of language in the tradition of speech communication is a bit strange. Researchers certainly recognize the centrality of language to any communicative experience, but they tend to neglect it. A close examination of our scholarly work will underscore just how much we have overlooked the study of language. Even though there are some understandable reasons for this neglect, it remains an oddity for a discipline that identifies "spoken symbolic behavior" as its central concern. Actually, the scholarly literature in speech communication has addressed language-related issues, but in a very limited sense. The purpose of this essay is to explore the character of language as treated by speech communication scholars and then suggest some future directions. My intent is to describe briefly how research in speech communication has dealt with language and then offer a perspective for thinking about and conducting research into language and communication. The greatest portion of this

Correspondence and requests for reprints: Donald G. Ellis, Department of Communication, Michigan State University, East Lansing, MI 48824.

chapter will be devoted to exploring problems and proposing a perspective for future research.

The act of describing how speech communication scholars have treated language is a difficult one. After all, when a discipline carves out "spoken symbolic behavior" as its intellectual territory, there remains little human activity that cannot somehow be related to the central concern of the discipline. I became even more convinced of this after reviewing books and journals in the preparation of this chapter. Below is a description of two general trends with respect to language and speech communication. The word "description" is important because my intent is not to classify and evaluate all the perspectives on language; rather, what follows is more of a report on the tendencies of people who identify with the field of speech communication and publish within its confines. The orientations are the result of asking the question, "When people in speech communication write or report research about language, what do they write about and what is the primary function of language?" The unadorned answer to this question is that language is used as either a variable that influences some outcome or a philosophical tool for the justification of a particular perspective or approach to research.

THE VARIABLE-ANALYTIC ORIENTATION

It is clear that the research tradition of communication is rooted in the social psychological model, where a communication variable is presumed to have a psychological or behavioral effect on a receiver. The elements of communication (source, message, channel, receiver) are assumed to be variable, and the manipulation of their particular values is responsible for the observed effect of a message. There are some slight modifications of this perspective such that the active role of the receiver can be emphasized to underscore the receiver's influence on how a message is ultimately interpreted. But this modification is rare in actual research practice and, even when it is included, the receiver's role is segmented into variable attributes that can be manipulated and controlled. There is nothing new about this characterization of research practices in speech communication. It has been called the variable-analytic approach by Delia (1977), the directive approach by Lin (1977), and the mechanistic approach by Fisher (1978).

A large portion of language research emerges from the variable-analytic orientation. The typical research project begins with an assessment of subject attitudes, exposes them to a message where a language variable has been manipulated, and then takes postexposure measures to ascertain any change in subject attitudes. My point is not that this approach is "wrong," just that it is quite limited and fails to account for much of the richness language infuses into communication. There are three problems that emerge from this research tradition, and I would like to review the research in the context of these problems. The first problem is that language is almost always examined out of context and considered a static phenomenon. A second limitation is that our models for research force us to concentrate on the lexicon at the expense of other forms. Finally, our discipline fails to investigate the formal nature of language.

Context Specification

The failure to consider social context when studying language might be the most damning criticism that can be levied in this area. Contexts bring language use (communication) into existence and are extremely important. Since language does not take place in isolation, it must be related to people, a background of events, and scenarios. "Real" language use, and by that I mean naturally occurring interaction that is situated in a pattern of communicative events, is not an abstracted form but a correlate of the situation. One level of communication is a structural level and pertains to the elements and abstract qualities that are present in all communication activities. All interaction, for example, is composed of speakers, turn exchanges, linguistic rules, a medium, methods for organizing the interaction, etc. Below I will argue for the importance of these qualities, but for now the important point is that the study of language *in situations* (communication), as opposed to primary structural qualities of language, is inescapably tied to a social context, and speech communication research typically ignores or glosses the notion of context. Moreover research practices often unjustifiably generalize across context without specifying contextual similarities. Although the structural and constitutive aspects of communication are context-free, meanings and cognitive states that presumably result from exposure to messages cannot be separated from contexts.

Consider the research on language intensity and verbal immediacy (Bradac, Bowers, & Courtright, 1979). The process of "norming" lexical items so that a word receives a categorical classification as either intense or not intense is conceptually akin to abstracting similarities. Bradac, Bowers, and Courtright (1979, p. 258), in their review article, claim that this line of research attends to actual utterances and is not concerned with "abstract properties of grammar." True, they are not interested in the abstract properties of a grammar, but they continue to abstract commonalities of some linguistic phenomena (lexical items) and treat it as applicable across a variety of contexts. The authors are quite aware of this problem, because they spend time disclaiming the variations in operationalizations (p. 259);

nevertheless, they continue to generalize on the assumption that the lexical items used in their studies "contain" levels of intensity independent of context.

There is an elaboration of this criticism that is even more penetrating. Even the notion that grammars are abstract and context-free continues to crumble under close scrutiny. That is, grammarians are beginning to take dimensions of context into account when describing a grammar. There are any number of examples where knowledge of social features is necessary to understand grammatical functioning (e.g., Bruner, 1975). Even the acquisition of grammar has been related to communicative needs rather than considered simply an "object" of a child's knowledge (Bruner, 1975). Searle (1969) has been especially persuasive with respect to how language functions as a response to performance needs, such as asking a question or making a statement. The perception of lexical intensity, like any other feature of language and communication, is embedded in contextual constraints, and our research almost uniformly neglects this feature of communication. Again we will see where it is useful to discuss structures of communication that are relatively context-free, but this is not the case when examining lexical items and meaning. Moreover it is true that some lexical items can be considered "generally" more intense than certain alternatives, but the conditions under which this is true are not specified in the research (Bowers, 1963; Burgoon & Miller, 1971). I can, for example, describe something as "brilliant" (positive intensity in Bowers, 1963) and in the appropriate situation mean the exact opposite.

The literature on verbal immediacy is even more problematic. Wiener and Mehrabian (1967) pose an interesting conceptualization of what it means to be verbally immediate, but their examples of utterances that illustrate immediacy have limited value because context specifications are absent. It is fairly simple to offer alternative accounts of how a supposedly immediate utterance can be interpreted. Bradac, Bowers, and Courtright (1979) provide an example of a sequence of utterances in descending order of immediacy. The following is the most immediate utterance: "We certainly will enjoy the party." The least immediate utterance is "I think you must enjoy the beef wellington at that party with me." The utterances are immediate or not to the extent that they represent an association or a disassociation between a source and a receiver. The first utterance is immediate because it theoretically expresses mutuality and a future orientation. The least immediate utterance is supposed to symbolize tentativeness ("I think"), distance (adjectival "that" rather than "this," which indicates closeness), and obligation rather than voluntarism (e.g., "you must"). This approach violates even the simplistic platitude that meanings are in people, not words. The most immediate utterance could easily be interpreted as a condescending order where "will" not only implies futurity but inevitability. The pronoun "we" reads less like mutuality between speaker and hearer than like an editorial "we." The "must" in the least immediate utterance could easily communicate the speaker's commitment to the hearer's pending enjoyment of the beef wellington. And by distancing the party ("*that* party") the interactants might be creating a bond between themselves because the party represents some external event in which they will participate together. In any event, these utterances could easily mean something other than what they appear to mean. Such research approaches render language a bit static rather than the malleable social entity that it is.

In addition to language intensity and verbal immediacy there are a number of other research practices that emanate directly from the variable analytic approach; that is, where some language feature is abstracted from contexts and used as a variable whose impact on a dependent variable is presumed to be understood. The methods and theoretical logic remain constant across research interests; only the nature of the content changes. For example, the attitudinal consequences of exposure to various dialects have received considerable attention. Again, the research strategy is to gloss contextual matters and presume that features of a dialect are relatively static and have a singular effect on attitude formation. Miller (1975) examined the effects of dialect and ethnicity on communicator effectiveness. Other studies have focused on Mexican-American evaluations of Spanish and English (de la Zerda Flores & Hopper, 1975), teacher ratings of ethnic group speech (Williams & Naremore, 1974), and language attitude scale development and testing (Whitehead, Williams, Civikly, & Albino, 1974; Mulac, 1976; Mulac, Hanley, & Prigge, 1974). This same theoretical perspective has guided research on the effects of obscene language (Mulac, 1976), perceptions of maleness and femaleness (Bradley, 1981), and style characteristics as predictors of credibility attributions (Carbone, 1975).

In some respects the above approach to language research has misled us about the actual influence of certain language features. Most of the work cited in the preceding paragraphs identifies lexical aspects of a language style and notes the attitudinal consequences of exposure to the style. But a somewhat overlooked article by Giles, Bourhis, Trudgill, and Lewis (1974) would lead us to a different conclusion. These authors were interested in why one style of speech gains superiority over another. In an earlier study Giles and his associates proposed two possible answers to this question, which they termed the "imposed norm" hypothesis or the "inherent value" hypothesis. The inherent value hypothesis holds that a style of speech (e.g., a dialect) achieves prestige because it is inherently superior; that is, the quality of grammar and modes of expression permitted in the style are linguistically more sophisticated. The imposed norm hypothesis argues that a style gains prestige because it is associated with certain cultural norms. That status and prestige are a function of the qualities of the social group who use the style. Giles et al. tested these competing hypotheses and found clear support for the imposed norm hypothesis. The implications are that the specific linguistic choices associated with a style are *not* responsible for variations in attitudes about the style. They would, of course, be correlated with attitudes about the style but cannot be considered out of context (see Piché, Michlin, Rubin, & Sullivan, 1977). The Giles et al. study suggests the importance of more microscopic analyses of contexts. Not a single study cited in the above paragraphs included discussions of speakers, listeners, relationships, topics, settings, purposes, or subject matter and how they combine to form a social context that brings communication into existence.

Lexical Items

A second limitation of the research that has developed from the variable-analytic approach is the almost complete preoccupation with lexical items at the expense of other linguistic qualities. In other words, almost all of the research in this area conducted by speech communication scholars is primarily concerned with single words or combinations of words and how their meanings can be manipulated to create an effect. Except for a few isolated cases (Goss, 1972; Powers, 1975; Cummings & Renshaw, 1979), no researcher has given serious attention to phonetics, syntax, or, until more recently, pragmatics.

There are plausible historical reasons for this overconcern with lexical items and meaning, but recent developments and theorizing make the traditional research protocol problematic if not unacceptable. One reason for the inordinate emphasis on lexical items is the rather restrictive view of language that has characterized our thinking. John Stewart (1972) reviewed over 400 journal articles and thirty-six speech communication textbooks and found that the overwhelming conception of language was as a system of symbols that "represent something." Most authors maintain that language is composed of "representational elements" or "symbols that direct attention to things" or "symbols that substitute for objects, ideas, and experience." The first function of language, according to these authors, was to "point to concepts we have acquired." All of these definitions emphasize words and their meaning referents. There are no references to language as a *system,* that is, a system of symbols with relationships among them such as combination rules (syntax), function rules (grammatical elements), and rules of usage (pragmatics).

The general semanticists were the principal proponents of this account of language. They argued that words were signs that named objects and concepts and served as vehicles by which people developed attitudes. This process of using words to form attitudes was presumably related to "thinking" and cognitive behavior. But the general semanticists were not alone in this endeavor. Psychology was also interested in the relationship between cognition and the spoken word, because Bloomfield had earlier relegated linguistics to the task of describing the structural characteristics of languages. Bloomfield (1933) had very early warned that the study of meaning should be outside the domain of linguistics, and psychology was most often cited as the appropriate place to conduct the study of meaning.

The behavioral approach to meaning was the prevailing perspective for both psychologists and speech communication theorists. This approach stated that meaning was conveyed by words that acted like stimulus signs and conditioned responses (Mowrer, 1952). Osgood, Suci, and Tannenbaum (1957) encouraged this approach by providing an instrument for measuring meaning. The instrument, known as the semantic differential, was a mechanism for rating words on a scale. Although Osgood shifted to other means of studying meaning, his theoretical position remains unchanged. He argues that people acquire the meaning of words by making mediating representational responses to the words; words are signs for the stimuli to which people respond. The major theoretical advantage, according to Osgood, is that meaning is no longer considered a simple relationship between a symbol and its referent; meaning is not the thing it refers to. Rather, meaning is a psychological process where a symbol elicits an internal response and directs the individual to behave in a specified manner. This internal response instructs the individual on how to perceive a symbol, how to interpret it, how to think about it, and what to do with it.

The behavioral approach to meaning informs, either explicitly or implicitly, most of the empirical work on language and communication. In almost all cases subjects encounter symbols, which have been manipulated for an experimental purpose (immediacy, obscenity, intensity, diversity, density, status, dialect type, etc.), and then indicate their "meaning" for these symbols by completing semantic differential scales. There are two problems with this approach: The first is simply that it is narrow and directs attention away from any number of interesting issues in language and communication. But the other problem is related to the theoretical shortcomings of the behavioral approach to meaning. Any cracks in this approach have implications for the stability of the work it stimulates.

Although alternatives to the behaviorist approach to meaning were slow to come, a number of linguists, psycholinguists, and cognitivists have recently advanced sophisticated theories about how meaning is created and used by people. Much of this theorizing speaks directly to the problems with the theory and practice of language research in speech communication. For example, the typical research design for a language intensity study utilizes treatment messages that vary only the intensity of selected lexical items. Consider the following example from a study by Bradac, Hosman, and Tardy (1978, p. 8).

> *High intensity* . . . My *fabulous* friend Joan and I *actually* got together in a bar. I was working at this *enormous* nightclub just on the outskirts of Chicago . . . a *fantastic* set-up. . . .
>
> *Low intensity* . . . My girlfriend Joan and I got together in one. I was working at this nightclub just on the outskirts of Chicago . . . a nice set-up.

The "intense" language in the first passage is designed to signal the speaker's strong affect and a departure from attitudinal neutrality (Bowers, 1963). But the problem becomes whether or not the two messages are experimentally "equal" except for the intensity level of the manipulated lexical items. In other words, do subjects actually establish equivalent meanings for the two passages and recognize differences as *only* one of more or less intensity. If by varying intensity the semantic message of the string of utterances is altered, then the experimenter is left with two different messages, not the same message with different intensity levels.

There is considerable research that suggests some disparity between the above two messages. As early as 1967 Miller and McNeill, discussing psycholinguistics in the *Handbook of Social Psychology,* explained a feature theory of semantics that poses problems for the type of research conducted by speech communication scholars. The basic idea of feature theory is that the meaning of words is composed of bundles of features. These features are basic semantic units that represent the internal structure of a word. Words such as "mother," "father," "boy," etc. are not the most basic semantic units. Analyzing words is known as lexical decomposition, and the decomposition process is analogous to the cognitive activity of a person who encounters a word. Clark and Clark (1968) propose that when people listen to a discourse (any string of sentences), they extract semantic distinction or features that are partially responsible for the "meaning" of the discourse. Consider the following example:

Definition of "boy": HUMAN(X) and MALE(X) and NOT-ADULT(X)

The words in capital letters are semantic components that make up the meaning of the world "boy." So the two sentences below are equivalent:

1. He is a boy.
2. He is a human male who is not an adult.

Words that are opposites have every component in common except for one. So to decompose the word "girl" we would have:

Definition of "girl": HUMAN(X) and FEMALE(X) and NOT-ADULT(X)

It is possible to identify basic semantic units and pose relationships among these units such that words of all grammatical types can be decomposed.

Markedness is a related principle of feature analysis. Markedness refers to one member of a pair that has a feature distinguishing it from the other member of the pair. The marked version of a pair has all but one feature in common with the unmarked item. In phonetics /p/ and /b/ are a pair of phonemes that share all phonetic properties except for one: /b/ is voiced or marked for voicing. Grammatically, "boy" and "boys" are equivalent, except that "boys" is marked for plurality. In semantics the unmarked member of a word pair denotes neutral meaning. So in "deep:shallow" the word "deep" is unmarked because it can be used with neutral meaning without connoting the actual depth of a thing. I can say "How deep is the water?" in an earnest attempt to ascertain the depth of the water. But "How shallow is the water?" presupposes knowledge that the water is shallow. Any time a linguistic feature is uniquely descriptive of a linguistic unit, it is said to *mark* the unit: A rising intonation marks questioning behavior, tag questions might mark a powerless speech style, "be" deletion marks Black English, high-status address terms (e.g., doctor, professor) mark asymmetrical status relationships, and so on.

The above passages from the Bradac et al. (1978) study might not be "communicating" the same message. A more rigorous test of the effects of intense language would generate messages where the manipulated lexical items vary only on the basis of an intensity marker. Moreover, individual words do not operate in a vacuum; the emergent meaning of a message results from the combination rules that are operating within the message. "Fabulous" friend and "girl" friend, for example, do not imply the same relationship between the speaker and Joan where intensity is the only difference. Many of the manipulated words in these messages do not even have counterparts (e.g., "actually" and "enormous"). It is unclear, for example, why the size of the nightclub increases the intensity of the resultant message.

Speech communication studies typically ignore the polysemous nature of language. Polysemy is how a single word can express a variety of concepts. The most often cited example is Katz's (1964) example of "good," which can mean "sharp" if modifying knife, "comfortable" when used with chair, "skillful" when used with violinist, "tasty" when coupled with food, or "healthful" when coupled with food and other contextual information. Words depend on their relationships with other words for meaning. In the "good" example it is the functional information in the head noun that determines the meaning of good. A construal rule (Miller, 1981, p. 104) would be that the combination of an evaluative adjective and a noun should be construed to mean that the entity denoted by the noun has a greater or lesser degree of the properties required for the activity, use, or appearance of the noun. It is this rule that allows "good" to acquire the appropriate meaning for an infinite number of nouns. Therefore it is difficult, if not impossible, to simply replace isolated words for experimental reasons and assume that the meaning of a message has been left in tact. This criticism is applicable to most of the research I have cited.

A somewhat different orientation toward meaning is the relationship between semantics and knowledge. Much of our research implicitly assumes that language is a tool for an exchange of knowledge between a speaker and a listener. While this is true, it is more accurate to consider language as a verbal *cue* that must be integrated into a hearer's conceptual system. Meanings of words are only partially recovered by bundles of features. Instead, meaning is constructed from linguistic utterances by a speaker-listener relationship within a context of use. Ambiguous language or intense language or language that communicates immediacy does not result from different dictionary definitions, but from specification of a referent from a set of available alternatives. The word "fantastic" in the phrase "a fantastic set-up" is a cue for a listener to differentiate among possible meanings. The word combines with other textual and contextual information to establish a meaning. But what meaning presents itself to a subject who encounters the message? Does "fantastic" mean that the bar is "large," "exciting," "unreal," "strange in appearance," "extravagant," "bizarre," "a great place to pick up girls," "fun," "architecturally unique," or "novel"? Such specifications are neglected in research that manipulates lexical items.

Barclay, Bransford, Franks, McCarrell, and Nitsch (1974) elaborate on the importance of semantic context and knowledge through a series of experiments. They convincingly demonstrate that lexical meaning is effective only if it is relevant to a semantic context. If, for example, you hear the sentence, "The man lifted the piano," you are more likely to recall the word "piano" if you are cued with "something heavy," because that is the relevant semantic context for the sentence. However, if the sentence is "The man tuned the piano," then the cue "something with a nice sound" is more likely to stimulate recall of the word "piano." These data, along with others, indicate the importance of an activated semantic context for the proper interpretation of linguistic input. The sentence, "The man lifted the piano," is a statement about strength and the weight of an object and provides a semantic context for "something heavy" because the man lifted something heavy, not a nice-sounding instrument. Daniels and Whitman (1981) report a related study of the advance organizer. The advance organizer is a concept that derives from Ausubel (1960), who argued that meaning resulted from integrating a linguistic string (sentence, phrase, etc.) into a hierarchically organized conceptual system. If an individual has a conceptual scheme that can work as background material for a message, then the message will be interpreted within the schematic framework, and this will facilitate the extraction of the appropriate meaning. The advance organizer interacts with the subject variables and message structure to influence the comprehensibility of a message. Again my purpose is not to explicate this material but to show how it weakens the foundation of much of the research I have been discussing. Simply to label sentences or words as immediate or nonimmediate or intense, without anchoring them to a relevant semantic context, is to lose the multifaceted nature of language and introduce error into a subject's semantic responses.

At this point I have identified what I believe to be two limitations of typical speech communication research, namely, a lack of adequate context specifications and a preoccupation with the lexicon. The third problem is a sin of omission rather than commission; that is, speech communication scholars never examine the interaction system itself as the object of study. Almost all the research treats language as a medium for affecting other individuals or accomplishing source-oriented goals. This point is conceptually akin to the distinction between language *(langue)* and speaking *(parole)*. Language is a formal and idealized symbol system; it is what we all have in common and is composed of a set of operation rules. Speaking is what we do individually; it is a social phenomenon that varies according to time, place, context, ethnic identification, etc. Historically, speech or speech communication has been identified with the act of speaking in some situation — *parole*. The seeds of pragmatism in our discipline spawned research where prescriptions for how to communicate in some setting are the ultimate goal. In fact, most people would classify their professional association, their courses, or their departments into dyads, groups, organizations, public speaking, advertising, etc. All of these categories are based on a desire for knowledge about how to communicate on particular occasions.

A general theory of communication will come only when there is some understanding of the basic structure of the phenomenon we examine. Our theories and models will remain isolated and detached from one another as long as researchers fragment their interests on the basis of various settings. All language and language use (speaking) is "structured" and composed of entities that are organized according to a set of rules. One approach to communication must be to study these structural entities and determine how they form an underlying calculuslike system that governs the activity we call communication. While a concern for structural characteristics of interaction might sound contrary to the above discussion of context, it is really relatively independent of it. Structural analyses are analogous to the rules of the game, where contextual specifications are concerned with strategies, tactics, and meaning in the here and now. The rules of chess, for example, are independent of the various ploys and strategies that a player uses during the actual game. The nature and structure of the communication system becomes the phenomenon of interest, not the effects of the system. I will develop this point in the following section.

A PERSPECTIVE ON LANGUAGE AND COMMUNICATION

Below is an alternative to typical speech communication research. The purpose of what follows is to make a case for a particular perspective on language and communication and to try to show how it can increase our conceptual sophistication. The first section draws on structuralism and the general linguistic model as a basis for investigating some formal qualities of communication. The second is a conceptual scheme for studying language and situation.

Structuralism and Communication

In a sense structuralism serves as a metaphor for a perspective on studying communication, a structural metaphor because the assumptions of one apply to the other. A structural perspective is important to the development of speech communication because we failed to accomplish much of the early descriptive work that characterizes most mature sciences. All advanced sciences can articulate a reasonably agreed-upon set of assumptions about the nature and compositional structure of the phenomenon of interest: Physicists operate according to a set of laws, zoologists have well established categories for organizing and classifying forms of life, and linguists have identified the properties of language and posed rules that account for their operation. A structural perspective asks what all communicative experiences have in common: What are the elements and rules operating that constitute the activity called communication? If, for example, a husband and wife are arguing over the family budget, how is this communicative activity the *same* as when a superior and a subordinate are interacting in an organization. The issue is *not* whether their experiences, or feelings, or emotions, or the subject matter, or strategies, or goals, or purposes, or styles, or the words they use are the same; the issue is how the forms and the compositional nature of the activity are the same. Consider another chess example. If a finely crafted wooden king from a chess set is removed and replaced with a piece of cardboard with a large K inscribed on it, the game can still be played and nothing has changed. The form and structural relationships among the pieces remain the same, only the matter changes. Linguistics has retained this distinction between form and matter. A word has both a phonic and a conceptual element, a sound and a thought. The "formal" nature of this relationship is primary. The actual sound and what it relates to are less important than the structural nature of the relationship.

The early work in linguistics can be useful. Linguistic procedures and techniques were valuable for describing and classifying the elements of language. Linguistics was a sort of verbal botany. A linguistic model can be useful to speech communication if we borrow certain techniques and perspectives. Because the linguist identified the elements of language (phonemes, morphemes, etc.), it was possible to account for and explain the structure of any language. But these early techniques had limitations because, while it was possible to classify a finite set of phonemes and morphemes, structural linguistics did not work well with sentences. Although Chomsky attacked structural linguistics in *Syntactic Structures* (1957) and reset the direction of the study of language, the fact remains that this early structural classification work was essential and still forms the foundation of linguistics, at least to the extent that any language can be decomposed into its basic elements (phonemes, morphemes, and syntactic structures).

The classification and identification of the elements of communicative behavior are mandatory if speech communication is going to develop theoretically. A structure emerges from an arrangement of entities, and this arrangement has three ideals. The first is the notion of *wholeness,* or internal coherence. Structures have parts that are related to one another, and the nature of these relationships is primary, not the parts. A second aspect of structures is that of *transformation.* This point emerges from Chomsky's contributions to understanding the linguistic system; it was impossible to account for sentences that were grammatically correct but had two possible meanings. The sentence, "The shooting of the hunters is terrible," can mean that the hunters are poor shots or that killing hunters is bad. Chomsky's formulations of various deep structures, which can be transformed into the same surface structures, accounts for the double meaning. Another way to think of structures is as entities through which new material can be processed. The third principle is *self-regulation,* or that a structure need only refer to itself for viability. A language does not establish words and form useful relations among them by reference to "reality." Rather, its correctness is on the basis of an internal rule system. The word "chair" exists and functions within the structure of language without regard to any four-legged object that people sit on. While these principles have worked well enough for language systems, the question remains how they apply to a communication system, say dyadic communication. These structural systems develop hierarchically from sound units through the relationships among strings of sentences (discourses). Perhaps an example will help clarify this hierarchical development. Consider the following sentence:

A tree fell to the ground.

This entire structure (the sentence) is whole and coherent because each entity is organized according to a set of "acceptable" relationships. The phonemic structure, for example, represents a sequence of sounds that are recognizable to the reader. The sounds are organized according to phonetic rules in English. The same is true of the more general levels of organization, the morphemic and grammatical structures. The grammatical structure is general and stable enough to process any content through it. The sentence is a sequence of *indefinite article, noun, verb, preposition, definite article, and noun.* This sequence represents a relational structure that is appropriate for an infinite variety of content. The particular noun that is "falling" can change without altering the grammatical structure, so that one could say, "the apple fell to the ground"; or we might change the verb and say, "the tree crashed to the ground." In either case the structure can process a variety of content. And since language allows for new aspects of itself as new experiences are encountered, the sentence above can be transformed into a negative statement, a metaphorical one, a more or less complex one, a different voice or tense, and so on. Moreover, the self-regulating nature of language means that the sentence above does *not* depend on empirical reality for its own correctness. The sentence is a correct and well-formed sentence according to the rules of the structure, and whether or not some tree actually fell to the ground is another matter.

Now the task for the communication theorist is to detail the elements and organizational rules that constitute not morphemes or sentences but communicative exchanges. Where traditional linguistics stops at the organization of words into well-formed sentences, the communication theorists must go beyond sentences to *relationships among sentences, phrases, and sentence groups.* Any and all instances of communication involve the stringing together of word groups, phrases, or sentences; and whether this string is long or short, contained in one utterance or many, or realized in monologue or between speakers is irrelevant. The husband and wife discussing the family budget, the superior-subordinate interaction in an organization, the actor reciting lines in a play, the members of a group, and the author writing a novel are all stringing sentences together to make meaning. In short they are encoding verbal or written texts that are a unified whole and organized according to structural mechanisms. The communication theorist must turn attention toward the communication system itself and work to identify its governing principles. What stable structures can process the talk of the husband and wife, or the superior and the subordinate, or the group members, and so on.

The term "text" is appropriate here because any communicative experience results in a text. A text refers to any passage, spoken or written, of any length, that forms a unified whole (Halliday & Hasan, 1976). A text is a whole that is organized and made meaningful on two levels. The first level — the one being discussed here — rests on the stable structural mechanisms that allow the text to cohere. There are some objective factors involved in constituting a text, factors that are characteristic of the text but not found elsewhere. These objective factors that make a text work are linguistic, and, like most linguistic phenomena, they are common to the native speaker even though the speaker is not "aware" of them. The second level that organizes and makes a text meaningful is the con-textual level, or the extralinguistic factors that speakers use to interpret and produce linguistic texts. The environment, interpersonal relationships, the medium employed, and general situational characteristics are the extralinguistic features that are related to texts, but not part of the actual linguistic text.

Traditional communication research has neglected this first level of analysis and devoted most of its energy to the meaning of single words rather than to how these meanings are organized into a text. The primary purpose of this first level of structural analysis should be to discover what mechanisms are responsible for text production and operation. Halliday and Hasan (1976) illustrate how text coherence is probably the most basic issue with respect to text operation. They are concerned with the internal structure of a text, and references to people and situations are secondary. Any communication must solve the problem of relating one part of a message to another. Just as sentences must agree in tense or case, texts must agree with respect to logic and topical structure. Coherence is the fundamental issue. Coherence is a correspondence or a congruity arising from some principle common to a sequence. Coherence is what makes a sequence of words, or clauses, or sentences, or paragraphs, or utterances sensible; it ties the elements of the sequence together. Suppose we encounter the following simple two utterance exchange:

A: Where are the pencils?
B: They are on your desk.

It is clear that "they" in the second utterance refers back to "the pencils" in the first utterance. "They" is an anaphoric mechanism and lends coherence to the two utterances so we interpret them as a whole. The particular functions are primary. There are any number of mechanisms for tying a text together, but it is important to understand that these mechanisms are the resources in the language for creating the textual system.

Classifying and categorizing the mechanisms that organize an interaction is no small matter. Halliday and Hasan (1976) present an extremely insightful and detailed account of cohesion mechanisms; but they still have limitations, because not all mechanisms for organizing a text are apparent within the text. It is very often necessary to turn to socially agreed-upon conventions. This is true of the following example:

A: Did you go to the game last night?
B: Terrific, just terrific.

In this example there are no direct linguistic ties to the prior utterance. Coherence is accomplished by pragmatic presuppositions. The development of conversation involves knowledge of social rules such as Grice's (1975) cooperative principle. This principle states that a conversational contribution should be in accordance with the purpose of the talk exchange. It should be, in addition to other things, relevant. The utterance by B is understood and organizes the conversation by conversational implicature. An implicature is a supposition by A that is necessary to preserve the cooperative principle. Person A must presume that B's utterance is designed to maintain the cooperative principle; that is, B is responding in earnest. So, assuming all of the conditions for a normal conversation are met — focused encounter, turn exchanges, normal speaking and listening conditions — the implicature directs A to assume that B's utterance is relevant to the just prior utterance and the text can be understood as whole.

The adjacency pair is another structural mechanism that organizes the above text (Sacks, Schegloff, & Jefferson, 1974; Jackson & Jacobs, 1980). Adjacency pairs consist of related speech acts that imply one another (e.g., request-grant or refusal; question-answer; offer-accept or reject). Textual unity is accomplished because the utterance of the first pair part (e.g., question) establishes the next turn (answer). It also establishes an interpretive scheme for understanding the second part of the pair. The nature of the second pair part is so firmly established that its absence will be interpreted with reference to the first pair part. In the example above, B's utterance is understood as related to A's, thereby forming a coherent text, partially on the basis of presupposition and partially on the basis of A's turn. A asked if B attended the game. The utterance was in question form (the auxiliary verb "did" is to the left of the subject group), so B's statement about some affective reaction he experienced can be interpreted as an answer to the question. It was A's utterance that allowed B's utterance to be taken as an answer.

One additional example will help clarify how various structural mechanisms work in interaction. It is possible to expand on sentence ties and two-turn exchanges and pose techniques for ordering larger conversations. Jefferson and Schenkein (1978) explain how an action sequence can be expanded. One form can be schematized as follows:

    A: Wanna buy a book?   (appeal)
    B: Yes/No.   (accept/reject)
    C: OK.   (acknowledgment)

This sequence is an example of a common structure that is useful for accomplishing a variety of interaction work. The goal in explicating the textual nature of a communicative encounter is to identify how the structure is organized according to various mechanisms that combine in such a way as to establish the semantic content of the structure. In other words, what is it that makes the above three-turn exchange "count as" a complete "sales appeal"? The descriptions in parentheses classify the function of each utterance, and these descriptions emerge from linguistic and contextual features. It is possible to analyze each utterance (e.g., by syntactic, semantic, speech act analyses) and make a determination as to its function, but given the propositional force of each utterance, the three coterminous utterances form a common sequential structure that is useful for any type of context. The structure can be expanded with, for example, a "pass" that delays acceptance or rejection.

    A: Wanna buy a book?   (appeal)
    B: Well, uh, ask my wife.   (processing pass)
    A: Wanna buy a book, mam?   (redirected appeal)
    C: Yes/No.   (accept/reject)
    A: OK.   (acknowledgment)

This processing pass, which shifts the responsibility of accepting or rejecting to someone else, is an example of one mechanism available to the competent language user. It expands the basic structure in some organizationally acceptable manner and maintains the unity of the text.

My argument is that the text of a natural discourse is analogous to a story narrative. It is a mechanical structure where meaning is at least partially dependent on the parts and their relationship toward one another. These parts cohere and provide a framework for processing content. The anaphoric "they" in the above example about pencils is pure mechanics and functions as an organizational device only. Any symbol other than the word "they" can perform the same operation, as long as its structural relationship to the previous noun phrase, "the pencils," is the same. Moreover, this anaphoric mechanism is obviously appropriate for any type of content. It can refer to any other phenomenon and does not depend on empirical reality for its correctness.

At the risk of sounding repetitive, I want to reiterate the distinction between a structural level of analysis and a contextual one, because I think that future work in language and communication must consider both levels. I am really drawing less on the formal structuralism of, say, Levi-Strauss or Barthes or Derrida than I am on structuralism as a model for entering the study of interaction at a certain level. In short it is important that our scholarship attend to the organizational features of our conceptual domain *and* the multifaceted situational expressions. This structural level is a basic descriptive level where the "tools" of communication rest; communicators utilize these tools to make meaning. These tools are part of our linguistic and interactional toolbox and not variable according to situational needs. But given a line of research directed toward the structure of communication, how do people use language *in situations,* and how might research proceed so that language as a social resource is the object of inquiry?

Language and Situation

The language and situation perspective is quite different from the structural approach discussed above. It serves as an alternative for thinking about communication research and as a conceptual anchor for a number of the limitations of current research. While the structural and situational approaches are fundamentally different, they complement one another. It is possible and necessary to study the role of language as a context-free mechanism for producing interaction, but it is also important to understand how people use language to accomplish goals and define relationships. The language and situation perspective is rooted in sociolinguistics, where the concern is with the conditions under which there are correlations among language, people, and contexts. But the perspective I want to present is a little more than this. If language is the fundamental resource of communication and if the basic goal of communication is to make meaning, then the primary functional unit of communication must be the semantic unit, the text. The text must be the focal point of all the other elements that constitute a communication situation.

Any number of authors have detailed the key components in an interactional setting. In brief these are the participants and the setting, although both can be broken down further. Figure 2.1 (Brown & Fraser,

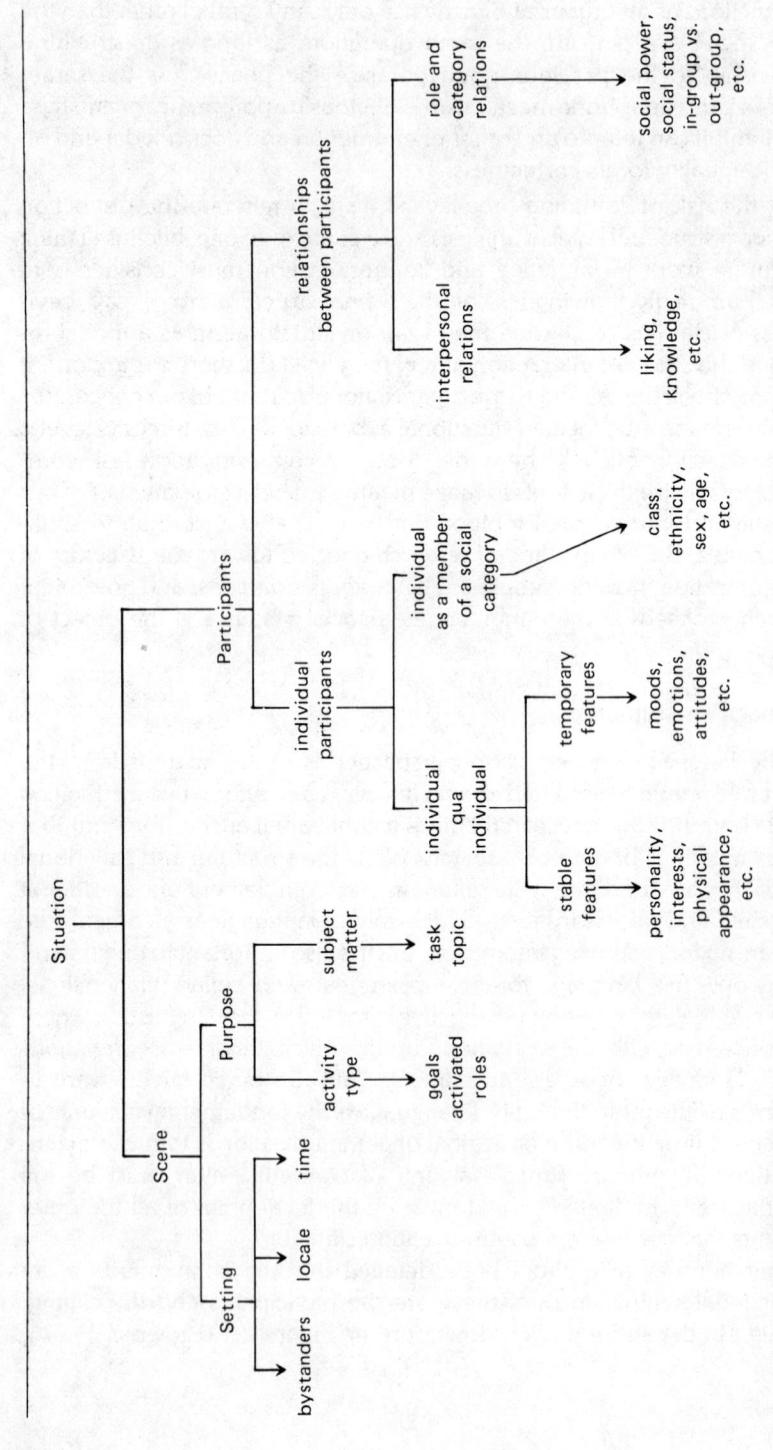

Figure 2.1. Components of a situation (Brown & Fraser, 1979).

1979) illustrates the details of the communicative situation and the components that form it. The participants are the individuals and their relationships with others. Any number of individual characteristics, either stable or temporary, social or private, can influence the communication. The setting assumes the physical environment and the purposes and intentions of the participants.

The role of language becomes more than a lexical, grammatical, or phonological system of structures. Language relates the participants in the communicative activity to the environment and the operational instance of this relation is the text. If the text functions properly as a common social meaning system, then the words and their combinations are functioning as expressions of the "living" environment. Unlike the structural relations that organize a text and form its framework, meaning is not fixed or stable. The participants in an interaction are making linguistic choices, and these choices are encoded in grammatical and lexical options. Although meaning results from language-in-use, participants soon recognize regular correlations between linguistic and sociological phenomena. To say that a linguistic feature correlates with a sociological feature and that this correlation has meaning requires an intermediary concept linking language to the social world. A code is just such a concept.

Codes

A code is a set of rules for converting one sign system into another. Alphabetic writing is a code where the sounds of a language are converted into written symbols. Morse developed a code that converts alphabetic letters into sounds. In the social world an interactant "codes" when he or she translates sense impressions or cognitive activity into linguistic or extralinguistic (nonverbal) output. A code is a strategy or plan of linguistic use. An individual codes when the linguistic text is tied to the social world and meaning develops according to the nature of this tie. A code can embody a wide range of meanings and linguistic forms, and these are determined by the relationship between the individual and the social structure.

The concept of code holds considerable potential for research in communication. Bernstein's (1975) interesting and controversial work is an example of research where codes are central. He showed how meaning was organized according to the type of relationship into which a person enters. Given a primary socialization experience where a child is assigned a rigid and binding role with others and the environment, the child codes messages in accordance with this relationship. Bernstein then set about the task of detailing the linguistic and semantic consequences of this coding. But the key point is that codes are ever-present orientations toward language behavior, and understanding communication in some setting is a matter of breaking the code. Whenever a researcher can correlate linguistic and social features and these relationships obtain for a community or group of people across a period of time, then the researcher has identified a code. Code determines the verbal behavior and range of styles a person can possess. If meaning is a matter of language-in-use, and language-in-use is obviously related to the social features that require it, then a code determines the range of meanings that an individual can express through linguistic behavior. A code is a use strategy and determines how a situation will be interpreted. Labov's (1972) work with Black English is another example of research with verbal codes. It relates the features of language use to a social environment and describes how meaning is actualized in communication.

An emphasis on the details of symbols and their organization is the crucial distinction. Speech communication, by its very nature, has always been concerned about messages and how they work in various social settings. But the research often generated artificial situations and focused on one message and one effect; or the variable of interest (immediacy, diversity, etc.) was abstracted from a concrete context and made a discrete variable that was either present or not. A discrete-continuous dimension is one aspect of codes and language use. Some variables might be discrete such that speakers either use them or not (for example, curse words or passive syntactical constructions). But most variables are continuous, with not only degrees of the feature in question, but also the value of the feature in one setting is different than in another setting: Phonological features (e.g., an accent), the level of formality, and syntactical complexity are a few obvious examples. Language intensity is probably just such a continuous variable. The authors of language intensity studies are certainly aware of the continuous nature of the variable, but they do not treat a subject's use of a lexical item as continuous. Given a subject's coding requirements, a word may "count as" intense in one environment but not in another. This point is especially applicable to verbal immediacy. What counts as immediate is a function of the relationship between speakers, not the generalized use of a term. By concentrating on codes, or how linguistic qualities are relevant to social qualities, it is possible to specify linguistic functions more completely.

Another aspect of code is the strength of the relationship between linguistic behavior and the situation (Giles, Scherer, & Taylor, 1979). A particular use of language might be always associated with some other social variable or probabilistically associated with it. Distinct languages and ethnic varieties are extremely stable. The copula "be" combined with an adjective, as in "he be good," is an extremely strong marker of a Black dialect; it is a stable feature of the code. Private terms, shop talk, and intimate talk (Knapp, Hopper, & Scott, 1981) are probably all examples of permanent markers of a code. Probabilistic correspondences between language and a social variable occur when a linguistic feature acquires a certain meaning and functions some percentage of the time. A larger percentage of women use tag questions, and these are usually associated with powerless speech, but not necessarily.

The importance of relating language to situation is underscored by a third distinction, which is whether or not a linguistic feature can be related to a single social condition or any number of them. Using an address status marker (e.g., doctor or professor) can signal an asymmetrical relationship where power and authority are clearly established, or it can be a ploy to poke fun at the differences in the relationship and thereby reduce the status distance. Similarly, a curse word can mean that one speaker is uncouth, hostile, angry, or strongly committed to something. How this behavior is being coded rests on situational distinctions.

Situated language use is a form of primary data the communication theorists can work with and call their own. Communication is a form of exchange, and the text is the fundamental expression of this exchange. Although communication theorists should be adept at conducting research into any type of language behavior, verbal interaction is the arena that has received most theoretical attention. It is here where interactants create, improvise, and make meaning with the skill of a musical virtuoso. The language behavior (text) is a product of the interplay between language, the environment, and the multitude of choices available to the participants. Although it is easy enough to cite the complexities of interaction, research is only useful if it allows us to describe and explain specific instances. Interactants do not haphazardly go about communication. There is a systematic relationship between language and the environment, and codes function to organize this relationship. Halliday (1978) and Halliday and Hasan (1976) suggest that a meaningful text is brought into existence in accordance with three general principles, which are characteristics of codes, that tie a situation to a text to render it meaningful. These concepts interpret the social context of the language use. They are the field of discourse, the tenor of discourse, and the mode of discourse.

Field

The field of discourse is the subject matter of the text. It is related to the ideational function of language and helps determine what the text is about. Interactants make an early decision about the field of discourse and then classify the interaction accordingly. If I begin a conversation with a statement about how the basketball team did last night, the ensuing text will vary in accordance with this particular subject matter. But the field of discourse can also be more abstract. If two strangers are having a "polite" conversation about the weather, the field of discourse would be "phatic" communication. Field refers not only to subject matter but also to what is happening, or the nature of the social action that is taking place. Technical and nontechnical conversation would be another example. The discussion of two psychologists and a classroom lecture on multivariate statistics are instances where very specific textual variations reflect the ideational dimension of the social activity. How difficult would it be to guess the field of discourse for the following passage if one knew nothing else about it: "Thy money perish with thee, because thou hast thought that the gift of God's blessedness may be purchased with money. O Repent therefore of this thy wickedness, and pray if perhaps the thought of thine heart may be forgiven. Amen."

It is evident that the above passage is from the Bible and the field of discourse is Christian religion. It is the nature of the text that makes this so evident. Lexical items such as "blessedness," "perish," and "repent" and archaic terms like "thy" and "thine" mark the period of time and the subject matter of the passage. Moreover, the acts of "repenting," "forgiving," and "perishing" combined with "God's blessedness," and the distinction between this world and the next clearly relates the text to Christian religion. The ease with which one can recognize the passage is testimony to the systematic variation in the text.

Tenor

Texts not only impart information or ideas, but also are used to talk about or convey information about relationships between people. The expression to a friend, "You idiot," says more about the state of the speaker and how he or she is feeling about another person than it does about the intellectual prowess of the other person. This dimension of the text-environment relationship is called the tenor of discourse. It refers to the nature of the participants, their status and roles, and the relationships among the participants. The tenor of a text results from the mutual relations between the language and the relationships among the participants in the communication event. Greetings are prototypical examples of when a speaker is using language to say something about relationships rather than ideational information. The ritualistic "Hi, how are you doing?" and the response "OK, and you?" have nothing to do with an earnest inquiry about the state of the other person. They are greeting rituals designed to express recognition of the other person and the speaker's relationship with him or her. Any role relationship that affects linguistic behavior is an example of the tenor of discourse. In the course of a day one shifts relationships with relative ease, and all of these have linguistic reflections. I will interact in the role of husband, then professor, then colleague, then father, then group leader, and so on. A woman who demands to be referred to as Ms. rather than Miss or Mrs. is saying something about how she wants others to relate to her.

The social and interpersonal dimensions of communication are important and should not be overlooked. Speaking the "right" language might mean inclusion in and recognition from a social group, and speaking the "wrong" language can mean exclusion. Language shapes and identifies relationships; it can express commonality, intimacy, formality, comradeship, or any number of role relationships. The private and idiomatic expressions of in-groups mark membership in the group and establish identities. This is also true of technical fields of discourse; the users not only interpret and understand the interaction on the basis of subject matter, but also communicate a social relationship and establish cohesiveness. Often the restricted language of members of a group develops as a result of tenor, not field. If we reexamine the above example from the Bible, the tenor markers are apparent. They are the words of the lord to his flock, and the tenor is one of authority. "Repenting" and "praying" are not only activities typical of the Christian religion, but also are formulated in the imperative mood. The receiver of this message is "instructed" to repent and pray. The lexical items "forgiven" and "wickedness" symbolize the power of the authority to prescribe proper behavior and to absolve transgressions. The modal "may" signifies the authority and right of the speaker to allow forgiveness and the possibility that forgiveness will not be granted.

Mode

The third category is the mode of discourse. Initially, this is simply the relationship between the language user and the medium of transmission: written, verbal, or electronically mediated. But it is necessary to make more specific distinctions about what the language is doing in the situation, what the participants are expecting it to do, and what is being achieved rhetorically, i.e., whether the language is designed to be didactic, persuasive, forensic, or the like. Language is organized and takes shape partially as a function of the medium of transmission. Expressions such as "he writes like he talks" or "he sounds like a book" are explicit realizations of the differences attributable to the mode of discourse. A mode is also a customary method or form, which is usually recognizable by the language user, and is associated with a series of choices about how to make the language do what the user wants it to do. Consider the lecture mode versus the conversation mode. The lecture mode, regardless of the field of discourse, is designed for an uninterrupted flow of talk where it is difficult for another person to take the floor. Halliday and Hasan (1976) demonstrate how lectures are more lexically cohesive, have more intratextual pronoun references, rely less on assumed experience, and are phonologically uniform. Conversations, on the other hand, stimulate participation from others and rely on a variety of incomplete and shorthand verbal forms.

Another interesting example of mode differences is written language that has vocal delivery in mind. Gregory (1967) shows how the difference between speaking what is written to be spoken and actual, spontaneous speech is that one is planned and designed as a coherent experience and the other is fragmented. If actors on stage actually included all of the sentence fragments, digressions, and false starts of a spontaneous conversation, the audience would have trouble following the pattern of the performance. Scripts, sermons, and political speeches all have vocal delivery in mind, in addition to other mode constraints. Returning to the biblical example, the vocative O, the italicized *Amen* (indicating audience response), and the punctuation pattern all indicate that the passage was written to be spoken. This should not obscure the fact that the written mode has its own resources: punctuation marks, quotes, and performance directions such as "she screamed," "he argued," or "John whispered" are all cues about how something was said and do not have a counterpart in the spoken mode.

SOME FINAL COMMENTS

One of the prime purposes of this chapter is to show how the study of language and language behavior can have important implications for communication theory. It is clear that there is a growing interest in language, discourse, and conversation analysis. The past couple of years have witnessed an increase in publications that pertain to linguistic mechanisms for organizing interaction (Ellis, Hawes, & Avery, 1981), structural variables for organizing a story text and responding to it (McLaughlin, Cody, Kane, & Robey, 1981), various sequencing rules that establish conversations (Jackson & Jacobs, 1980), conceptual paradigms for language use (Frentz & Farrell, 1976), structuralism (McGuire, 1977; Warnick, 1979), ethnography (Philipsen, 1976; Lull, 1980), and any number of papers and convention presentations on speech acts and rhetorical mechanisms. One excellent line of work that has been consistently published in speech communication journals but has gone relatively unheralded is Mike Motley's work with spoonerisms (Motley, 1973; Motley & Baars, 1975) and cognitive editing (Motley, Camden, & Baars, 1981). True, his work is less related to social interaction, but it remains as a paradigmatic example of a long-term research program that has explored the relationship between psychological conditions and linguistic behavior. Nevertheless, if we examine most textbooks and articles published by speech communication scholars, there is a conspicuous lack of language-related research. Linguists, psycholinguists, and sociolinguists have had relatively little impact on our field.

Language can serve an important conceptual function for much speech communication research; it is both a fixed entity with a stubborn structure and a public instrument that adopts the fashions of usage. The interplay between these two qualities should be our area of exploration. The hierarchical organization of linguistic phenomena lends a unity to the perspective. The building blocks of language are phonemes and their various expressions (allophones). These are highly rule-governed entities that combine in specified ways to form meaning units — morphemes. Here there is a basic relationship between the phonic and the conceptual. Strings of morphemes are called sentences, and they have their own system of rules for acceptability. The next level in the hierarchy is the one most related to speech communication. Until this point the rules governing language emerged from the system itself and are relatively (not completely) free from social constraints. But when language is used as a device for symbolizing the environment, when it functions as a reflection of individual or sociological conditions, then language is performing its communicative function and speaks to the interests of speech communication scholars. Beyond the sentence level is the discourse level. Any sequence of sentences or phrases that are related to one another in a context is a discourse. Discourse relies on both the "said" and the "unsaid." Phonology, syntactic structure, and lexical choice are the "said;" background, unspoken presuppositions, and context are the "unsaid" (see Hopper, 1981). Monologues, conversations, public speeches, essays, poems, lectures, stories, group meetings, and radio shows are all discourses that rely on situated language use. The speech communication scholar can contribute much to an understanding of these areas.

The study of what our discipline calls "nonverbal" communication can also benefit from renewed attention to language. The term "nonverbal" is a little misleading and unfortunate because it directs attention away from vocal activity, which is, of course, an integral part of any communication. Much of the behavior that accompanies natural conversation might be better termed paralinguistic and integrated into the general language model. There are qualities of language that make it "linguistic" (e.g., unbound, nondiscrete, infinite combination rules; see Hockett, 1960; Chomsky, 1966) that do not pertain to what we typically consider "nonverbal" communication. Much of what we term nonverbal communication accompanies the linguistic and certainly cannot be separated from it. Rather than research that relies on listing and categorizing "nonverbal" behavior, a language perspective can be useful for integrating the linguistic and the "para" linguistic into a coherent framework that shows how meaning is a function of the interplay between linguistic and extralinguistic behavior.

It is impossible to do justice to this subject matter in an essay of this size, but I have tried to clarify the contradiction between speech communication's commitment to symbolic behavior and our imprudent neglect of language. True, Chomsky and the syntacticians have scared people in the last few years; they relegated language to a level of technicality beyond the layperson and removed it from the social world. Although Chomsky's revolution in language is real, it is not without its critics and certainly does not negate the centrality of language to the human experience. Personally, I believe that language can function as the primary organizing theory of communication. And while it is fashionable to call for more theory, this does not deny its importance. Those of us who identify with speech communication have often congratulated ourselves on our tolerance for research and theoretical diversity, but real progress comes when a small army of researchers are working within a consistent theoretical perspective. Language can be that perspective.

REFERENCES

Ausubel, D. P. The use of advance organizers in the learning and retention of meaningful verbal material. *Journal of Educational Psychology,* 1960, *51,* 267-272.

Barclay, J. R., Bransford, J. D., Franks, J. J., McCarrell, N. S., & Nitsch, K. Comprehension and semantic flexibility. *Journal of Verbal Learning and Verbal Behavior,* 1974, *13,* 471-481.

Bernstein, B. *Class, codes, and control.* New York: Schocken, 1975.

Bloomfield, L. *Language.* New York: Henry Holt, 1933.

Bowers, J. W. Language intensity, social introversion, and attitude change. *Speech Monographs,* 1963, *30,* 345-352.

Bradac, J. J., Bowers, J. W., & Courtright, J. A. Three language variables in communication research: Intensity, immediacy, and diversity. *Human Communication Research,* 1979, *5,* 257-269.

Bradac, J. J., Hosman, L. A., & Tardy, C. H. Reciprocal disclosures and language intensity: Attributional consequences. *Communication Monographs,* 1978, *45,* 1-17.

Bradley, P. H. The folk-linguistics of women's speech: An empirical examination. *Communication Monographs,* 1981, *48,* 73-90.

Brown, P., & Fraser, C. Speech as a marker of situation. In K. R. Scherer & H. Giles (Eds.), *Social markers in speech.* Cambridge: Cambridge University Press, 1979.

Bruner, J. S. The ontogenesis of speech acts. *Journal of Child Language,* 1975, *2,* 1-19.

Burgoon, M., & Miller, G. R. Prior attitude and language intensity as predictors of message style and attitude change following counterattitudinal advocacy. *Journal of Personality and Social Psychology,* 1971, *20,* 246-253.

Carbone, T. Stylistic variables as related to source credibility: A content analysis approach. *Speech Monographs, 1975, 42,* 99-106.

Chomsky, N. *Syntactic structures.* The Hague: Mouton, 1957.

Chomsky, N. *Cartesian linguistics.* New York: Harper & Row, 1966.

Clark, H. H., & Clark E. V. Semantic distinctions and memory for complex sentences. *Quarterly Journal of Experimental Psychology,* 1968, *20,* 129-138.

Cummings, H. W., & Renshaw, S. L. SLCA III: A metatheoretic approach to the study of language. *Human Communication Research*, 1979, *5*, 291-300.

Daniels, T. D., & Whitman, R. F. The effects of message introduction, message structure, and verbal organizing ability upon learning of message information. *Human Communication Research*, 1981, *7*, 147-160.

de la Zerda Flores, N., & Hopper, R. Mexican Americans' evaluations of spoken Spanish and English. *Speech Monographs*, 1975, *42*, 91-98.

Delia, J. G. Alternative perspectives for the study of human communication: Critique and response. *Communication Quarterly*, 1977, *25*, 46-62.

Ellis, D. G., Hawes, L. C., & Avery, R. K. Some pragmatics of talking on talk radio. *Urban Life*, 1981, *10*, 155-177.

Fisher, B. A. *Perspectives on human communication*. New York: Macmillan, 1978.

Frentz, T. S., & Farrell, T. B. Language-action: A paradigm for communication. *Quarterly Journal of Speech*, 1976, *62*, 333-349.

Giles, H., Scherer, K. R., & Taylor, D. M. Speech markers in social interaction. In K. R. Scherer & H. Giles (Eds.), *Social markers in speech*. Cambridge: Cambridge University Press, 1979.

Giles, H., Bourhis, R., Trudgill, P., & Lewis, A. The imposed norm hypothesis: A validation. *Quarterly Journal of Speech*, 1974, *60*, 405-410.

Goss, B. The effect of sentence context on associations to ambiguous, vague, and clear nouns. *Speech Monographs*, 1972, *39*, 286-289.

Gregory, M. J. Aspects of varieties differentiation. *Journal of Linguistics*, 1967, *3*, 177-198.

Grice, H. P. Logic and conversation. In P. Cole & J. L. Morgan (Eds.), *Syntax and semantics. Volume 3: Speech acts*. New York: Academic Press, 1975, 41-58.

Halliday, M.A.K. *Language as social semiotic: The social interpretation of language and meaning*. London: Edward Arnold, 1978.

Halliday, M.A.K., & Hasan, R. *Cohesion in English*. New York: Longman, 1976.

Hockett, C. The origin of speech. *Scientific American*, 1960, *203*, 88-96.

Hopper, R. The taken-for-granted. *Human Communication Research*, 1981, *7*, 195-211.

Jackson, S., & Jacobs, S. Structure of conversational argument: Pragmatic bases for the enthymeme. *Quarterly Journal of Speech*, 1980, *66*, 251-265.

Jefferson, G., & Schenkein, J. Some sequential negotiations in conversation: Unexpanded and expanded action sequences. In J. Schenkein (Ed.), *Studies in the organization of conversational interaction*. New York: Academic Press, 1978.

Katz, J. J. Semantic theory and the meaning of "good." *Journal of Philosophy*, 1964, *61*, 739-766.

Knapp, M. L., Hopper, R., & Scott, L. Couples' personal idioms: Exploring intimate talk. *Journal of Communication*, 1981, *31*, 23-33.

Labov, W. The logic of nonstandard English. In P. P. Giglioli (Ed.), *Language and social context*. New York: Penguin, 1972.

Lin, N. Communication effects: Review and commentary. In B. Rueben (Ed.), *Communication yearbook 1*. New Brunswick, NJ: Transaction Books, 1977.

Lull, J. The social uses of television. *Human Communication Research*, 1980, *6*, 197-209.

McGuire, M. Mythic rhetoric in *Mein Kampf*: A structuralist critique. *Quarterly Journal of Speech*, 1977, *63*, 1-13.

McLaughlin, M. L., Cody, M. J., Kane, M. J., & Robey, C. S. Sex differences in story receipt and story sequencing behaviors in dyadic conversations. *Human Communication Research*, 1981, *6*, 99-116.

Miller, D. T. The effects of dialect and ethnicity on communicator effectiveness. *Speech Monographs*, 1975, *42*, 69-74.

Miller, G. A. Semantic relations among words. In M. Halle, J. Bresnan, & G. Miller (Eds.), *Linguistic theory and psychological reality*. Cambridge: MIT Press, 1981.

Miller, G. A., & McNeill, D. Psycholinguistics. In G. Lindzey & E. Aronson (Eds.), *Handbook of social psychology* (Rev. ed.). Reading, MA: Addison-Wesley, 1967.

Motley, M. T. An analysis of spoonerisms as psycholinguistic phenomena. *Speech Monographs*, 1973, *40*, 66-71.

Motley, M. T., & Baars, B. J. Encoding sensitivities to phonological markedness and transitional probability: Evidence from spoonerisms. *Human Communication Research*, 1975, *1*, 353-361.

Motley, M. T., Camden, C. T., & Baars, B. J. Toward verifying the assumptions of laboratory-induced slips of the tongue: The output-error and editing issues. *Human Communication Research*, 1981, *8*, 3-15.

Mowrer, O. H. The autism theory of speech development and some clinical applications. *Journal of Speech and Hearing Disorders*, 1952, *17*, 263-268.

Mulac, A., Hanley, T. D., & Prigge, D. Y. Effects of phonological speech foreignness upon three dimensions of attitude of selected American listeners. *Quarterly Journal of Speech*, 1974, *60*, 411-420.

Mulac, A. Assessment and application of the revised speech dialect attitudinal scale. *Communication Monographs*, 1976, *43*, 238-245.

Osgood, C. E., Suci, G. J., & Tannenbaum, P. H. *The measurement of meaning.* Urbana: University of Illinois Press, 1957.

Philipsen, G. Places for speaking in Teamsterville. *Quarterly Journal of Speech*, 1976, *62*, 15-25.

Piché, G. L., Michlin, M., Rubin, D., & Sullivan, A. Effects of dialect-ethnicity, social class and quality of written compositions on teachers' subjective evaluations of children. *Communication Monographs*, 1977, *44*, 60-72.

Powers, W. G. A research note on "the effect of sentence context on association to ambiguous, vague, and clear nouns." *Speech Monographs*, 1975, *42*, 80-82.

Sacks, H., Schegloff, E. A., & Jefferson, G. A simplest systematics for the organization of turn-taking for conversation. *Language*, 1974, *50*, 696-735.

Searle, J. R. *Speech acts: An essay in the philosophy of language.* Cambridge: Cambridge University Press, 1969.

Stewart, J. Concepts of language and meaning: A comparative study. *Quarterly Journal of Speech*, 1972, *58*, 123-133.

Warnick, B. Structuralism vs. phenomenology: Implications for rhetorical criticism. *Quarterly Journal of Speech*, 1979, *65*, 250-261.

Wiener, M., & Mehrabian, A. *Language within language: Immediacy, a channel in verbal communication.* New York: Appleton-Century-Crofts, 1967.

Whitehead, J. L., Williams, F., Civikly, J. M., & Albino, J. W. Latitude of attitude in ratings of dialect variations. *Speech Monographs*, 1974, *41*, 397-407.

Williams, F., & Naremore, R. C. Language attitudes: An analysis of teacher differences. *Speech Monographs*, 1974, *41*, 391-396.

3 ● Nonverbal Cues as Linguistic Context: An Information-Processing View

JOSEPH P. FOLGER ● W. GILL WOODALL

University of Michigan–Ann Arbor ● University of New Mexico–Albuquerque

IN concluding a recent work on *Language and Perception*, George Miller and Phillip Johnson-Laird (1976, p. 690) address those interested in studying how people process language when they caution that "a psychology of language should be psychological." Their point is that "if we hope to create something recognizable as a psychological theory of human language, psychological methods and principles should be applied in the same way they are applied to other mental and behavioral phenomena" (p. 691). For communication researchers the statement is a reminder that there are a considerable number of psychological principles emerging from research in cognitive psychology that can prove useful in providing information-processing explanations of communicative phenomena. If communication researchers tackle processing questions, these principles need to be invoked.

Several communication theorists (Planalp & Hewes, 1981; Hewes & Planalp, in press) have offered integrative analyses of a wide variety of cognitive functions and information-processing principles to help explain fundamental social processes like the reduction of uncertainty in social encounters. Other researchers have demonstrated the utility of these information-processing principles in examining such issues as the understanding of metaphor (Whiting, 1975), the attitude-behavior inconsistency (Cappella & Folger, 1981), and turn-taking in interaction (Planalp & Tracy, 1980).

AUTHORS' NOTE: An earlier version of this chapter was presented at the annual conference of the Speech Communication Association, November 1979.

Correspondence and requests for reprints: Joseph P. Folger, Department of Communication, University of Michigan, Ann Arbor, MI 48109.

Even the most cursory survey of recent developments in information processing and cognitive psychology suggests the important place context seems to hold in people's ability to process information (Miller, Heise, & Lichten, 1951; Denes, 1963; Bransford & Johnson, 1973; Andersen, 1976; Watkins, Ho, & Tulving, 1976; Rumelhart, 1977; Palmer, 1975). Increasing attention has been given to the input environments of language, to those cues in encoding conditions that influence how people make inferences about, comprehend, store, and retrieve language. For the most part this research has focused on the contextual cues of either written discourse or verbal language that is removed from its social environment (i.e., subjects read or have words or passages read to them). This focus has provided valuable knowledge about the mental operations governing our ability to process symbolic information in what Anderson (1976, p. 390) calls "impoverished stimulus situations." It has not, however, prompted systematic research or even speculation about the contextual impact of cues such as nonverbal behaviors that ordinarily accompany language in social encounters.

Markel (1975, p. 189) has coined the term *coverbal behavior* to include "the behavior of interlocutors which occurs in association with or accompanying words but which is not essential for the articulation of grammatical functioning of words." Coverbal behaviors are one subset of nonverbal behaviors; they are nonverbal cues which co-occur with speech. From an information-processing perspective coverbal behaviors can be seen as contextual cues that normally accompany language in its social environment. At present the potential theoretical and empirical consequences of viewing these behaviors as part of the input conditions remain largely unexplored. Although some attempt has been made to determine how nonverbal communication might mediate persuasive outcomes (Mehrabian & Williams, 1969; Woodall & Burgoon, 1981) or allow subjects to reproduce visual figures (Graham & Argyle, 1975), only one study has considered whether nonverbal factors might affect the processing of linguistic information per se. Rogers (1978) reports that kinesic illustrators can contribute to the comprehension of verbal behavior.

We believe that any attempt to examine the role of nonverbal cues in the processing of human language should begin with what is known about cognitive functioning. In this chapter we draw upon principles that have emerged in cognitive psychology to raise several theoretical and empirical issues that might guide a systematic study of the contextual impact of nonverbal cues on language processing.

More specifically, we have found the recent distinction that Ortony (1978) has drawn between comprehension and recall useful in understanding how nonverbal cues are processed in conversational settings. This distinction offers a strong theoretical basis for clarifying the empirical steps necessary to understand how coverbal behaviors could influence the processing of messages in social encounters. In this chapter we will (1) clarify the distinction between comprehension and recall and show how it applies to the processing of coverbal behavior; (2) specify the conditions under which nonverbal cues can aid in comprehension; (3) point to a strong theoretical and empirical basis for arguing that nonverbal cues can influence the recall of communicative events, and (4) suggest the likely problems that occur in operationalizing decoding measures when the distinction between comprehension and recall is ignored in nonverbal research.

DISTINGUISHING COMPREHENSION AND MEMORY

Ortony (1978) argues that any model of human cognition should include a distinction between two important cognitive capacities — the capacity to understand and the capacity to remember. He maintains that although one can comprehend and retrieve the same set of information, the processes involved in comprehending information are different from those involved in recalling it.

Comprehension

Ortony's explanation of comprehension is built on recent network models of long-term memory (Quillian, 1968; Collins & Loftus, 1975; Rumelhart, Lindsay & Norman, 1972). These models suggest that the storehouse of knowledge a person holds in long-term memory (words, concepts, properties, and their interrelationships) can be represented by a network of associated nodes. Each node in the network is a concept or proposition held in one's total data base of stored information. The link between the nodes can be characterized by labeled relations. The node "concerto," for example, would be linked in memory to the node "composition" by a class relationship: "a concerto is a composition." Concerto might be linked to other concepts such as "music," "piano," "notes," "orchestra," etc. by different relationships (Norman & Rumelhart, 1975; Lindsay & Norman, 1972). Rather elaborate network models have been developed to capture both the structural and dynamic aspects of knowledge representations (Tulving & Donaldson, 1972).

Comprehension, according to Ortony, involves the utilization of knowledge that is already stored in long-term memory. In comprehending linguistic information an interaction occurs between the input (for our purposes, the language and its contextual information) and a set of concepts held in memory that are relevant to the input. Some set of nodes is activated in the memory network by the input: "The process of comprehension involves activating concepts related to those of the input and the context and engaging in inferences based primarily on those concepts" (Ortony, 1978, p. 59). Like Ortony, Hewes and Planalp (in press) emphasize that *integration* and *inference making* are both central in comprehension processes. Integration is the process of combining new data with prior knowledge; inference making refers to the deductions one makes based on existing and newly integrated information. Deductions involve the activation of further memory nodes at input so that these inferences are seen as legitimate contributions to the comprehension process. Hewes and Planalp suggest that, as a lay scientist, an individual's intuitive theories about the social information being processed influence what gets integrated and what inferences get made when information is incorporated into memory.

According to this account of comprehension, someone who hears a musicologist say that "Mahler's First Symphony is nothing less than a concerto for orchestra" may activate a set of semantic concepts related to "concerto" that would allow him or her to understand the (somewhat metaphorical) meaning of this sentence. The most likely candidates for activation would be those nodes signifying structural, musical properties of a concerto composition. Less likely candidates may be those nodes associated with historical knowledge about particular concerto compositions that the individual has in memory. Presumably, the person would make a set of inferences about the Mahler symphony based on the concept nodes that were activated by the sentence and any contextual information surrounding it.[1] One might, for example, infer that Mahler exaggerates the use of the French horn in the first movement to achieve a concertolike effect. This proposition would be an inference because the speaker made no explicit statements about the role of any particular instrument in the piece. The activation of a set of information already held by the listener (namely that the horn is used in the first movement) is integrated with the musicologist's statement to *infer* that the horn is given prominence in a way that resembles the structure of a concerto.[2]

Ortony emphasizes that the crucial component in comprehension is the spread of activation through the semantic network, but he is not entirely clear on which factors stop activation or spread. He suggests that some restraining principle is probably in operation so that "if a concept does not receive sufficient activation to exceed its threshold, then it does not transmit activation to neighboring concepts" (p. 55). The factors that set threshold points for activation are not specified, but Ortony does indicate that the activation process is sensitive to (1) contextual information and (2) the depth to which stimulus information is processed. Different contextual conditions surrounding the stimulus information can contribute to the "final activated subgraph" (i.e., all nodes activated after the input has been comprehended). Cues at the time of input besides those from the target sentence can trigger the activation of nodes in memory and thus enter the trace.

Besides the contextual conditions, the depth at which information is processed can influence what gets activated at input. Craik and Lockhart (1972) suggest that the mental operations performed on what is being encoded influence the depth to which information is processed (i.e., determine how elaborate a memory trace is established). The mental operations performed on stimulus information vary according to how much semantic involvement they entail. Operations that require greater levels of semantic involvement produce deeper levels of processing and, in Ortony's terms, would result in more extensive activation of nodes in memory.

Craik and Lockhart (1972), Craik and Tulving (1975), and Hyde and Jenkins (1973) studied depth-of-processing by asking subjects to answer different types of questions about words or passages. Questions that were intended to evoke shallow encodings included queries about the typescript of words or the occurence of certain letters of the alphabet in the words. Intermediate encodings were elicited by questions about rhymes or parts of speech. Deeper levels of processing were induced by asking subjects to rate the pleasantness of a word or to determine whether the word fit into a given category or sentence context. These questions varied in the amount of semantic involvement they required of the subject. Deeper encodings were found to take longer to process and, in general, resulted in better recall and recognition of the material. The explanation for this finding was that a more elaborate encoding was established at input for the deeper processing conditions and therefore there was more information in the trace that could be accessed at recall. Bower and Karlin (1974) replicated these findings with visual stimulus information. In their research subjects were asked either to label faces as male or female (shallow encoding) or to rate faces on a pleasantness-unpleasantness scale (deep encoding). Memory for the faces was better when they were more deeply processed.

The depth-of-processing analysis is consistent with Ortony's conception of comprehension because it establishes that comprehension is not an all-or-nothing phenomenon. Spread of activation is a function of how deeply one processes incoming information; more nodes in memory are activated when information is processed in greater depth. Although there is considerable evidence in support of a depth-of-processing stance, Craik and Lockhart's analysis has been criticized on several important grounds (Baddeley, 1978; Eysenck, 1978). Baddeley, for example, has raised three major concerns about this analysis. First, he argues that Tulving has failed to develop "a satisfactory independent measure of processing depth"

(Baddeley, 1978, p. 141). He notes that the one index that has been employed (processing time) has not stood as a suitable indicator of depth-of-processing. Decisions that were made more slowly about processed information did not result in better retention. Baddeley contends, therefore, that processing time cannot be equated with processing depth.

Second, Baddeley argues that the levels-of-processing explanation may be an inaccurate representation of cognitive functioning because it assumes a *continuum* of semantic involvement. He suggests that there are different processing *domains* rather than levels on a continuum of semantic processing. He posits, for example, that visual information may be in a different domain of processing than linguistic information. "It seems probable that subjects adopting a strategy of elaborating a visual image are processing information in a different way from those attempting to generate associative links (Paivio, 1971), but is unclear how one would describe these differences in terms of a levels-of-processing approach" (p. 142).

Finally, Baddeley criticizes the depth-of-processing argument by claiming that deeper encodings may not be necessary for establishing more durable memory traces. Once again Baddeley turns to studies in visual information processing to support his position. Work by Kirsner (1973) and Rothkopf (1971) suggests that visual features (considered in a depth-of-processing view as superficial aspects of the stimulus may be retained over substantial periods of time. In addition, Baddeley argues that studies that *have* demonstrated significant differences in recall for various levels of processing are seriously flawed. The tasks given to the subjects are often irrelevant to the subsequent recall procedures: "For example, the instruction to decide whether a given word is printed in upper- or lowercase does not require the subject to process the word at all; one letter would be sufficient. Hence it is hardly surprising that a subject's ability to remember words processed in this way is poor" (p. 145).

Baddeley's criticisms suggest that a depth-of-processing analysis may be an inaccurate approach to explaining how people comprehend *visual* cues. We will argue, however, that Baddeley's second and third criticisms overlook the possibility that some visual features entail semantic involvement. His explanation may only be valid for visual cues that contain no inherent inducement of semantic processing at input. We cannot rule out a depth-of-processing explanation for how people process coverbal behavior, because some coverbal cues can induce semantic involvement; the role they play in the production of a message requires semantic processing. These cues have been found to yield higher levels of recall and thus could suggest that a more elaborate memory trace is constructed when these cues are processed.

Memory

While *comprehension* processes are tied to the utilization of knowledge in long-term memory, *memory* "involves the retrieval, recognition and in some cases even the regeneration of representations of knowledge" (Ortony, 1978, p. 57). One creates a memory representation for information and can access that representation *after* comprehension occurs: "Comprehension is a process prior to and distinct from the creation of a memory representation." Comprehending language is not, then, synonymous with creating a memory representation for the information; recall involves the reconstruction of information that was activated at the time of comprehension.

Ortony's major objective is to characterize how memory representations for comprehended language are constructed at recall. He suggests that in constructing memory representations we draw upon those nodes that were activated at the time of comprehension to encode "a record of the experienced meaning of the input" (p. 58). Omission or distortion of the nodes results in memory failures. Ortony indicates that there are three parts to memory representations that work in combination to overcome memory lapses and help create faithful reconstructions of the language that was understood (or misunderstood) at the time of input. The three levels of information included in memory representations are: (1) syntactic information about the surface structure of the sentence, (2) underlying semantic information, and (3) contextual cues associated with the context in which the input occurred. Information is subject to decay at all three levels, but the information retrieved at any one level can help to trigger that at another in an attempt to reconstruct the originally encoded information. As Ortony (1978, p. 58) puts it:

> Each level, however, provides some reconstructive potential for the more rapidly decaying level next to it. Thus, if the surface structure has decayed, the semantic structure still provides the possibility of reconstructing it in whole or part, although more often than not, this reconstruction results in a paraphrase rather than a verbatim recall. More interesting, however, is what happens if details have been lost from the second level, the semantic structure. If, for example, the value assigned to a particular variable has decayed, the bottom level provides a list of candidate concepts for regenerating or reconstructing the semantic representation.

Someone attempting to recall how a certain music critic described Mahler's First Symphony may, for example, first access the underlying semantic content that he or she took away from reading the review. One might recall that the critic was suggesting that every instrument is treated at some point in the work as a solo instrument or that an inference was made about the use of the French horn. This meaning (which was comprehended at the time of encoding) may then help the reader cue the terms actually used by the critic (i.e., "concerto") and ultimately the exact syntactic structure of the entire input sentence.

Thus Ortony's discussion of memory centers on those processes involved in reconstructing the concept nodes in semantic memory that were activated at the time of comprehension. What needs to be examined, Ortony says, are the factors that cause distortion and omission of nodes and the way in which one level of information (syntactic, semantic, or input associates) helps generate information at other levels during reconstruction of the experienced meaning of the input.

For our purposes, two points from Ortony's discussion of comprehension and recall need to be emphasized. First, he contends that comprehension and memory processes are distinct in reality (i.e., we can remember things we did not understand and can understand things that we do not remember) and therefore must be distinguished in accounts of how people process language. Second, although Ortony does distinguish between these two cognitive capacities, there are important points of overlap. It is assumed, for instance, that greater levels of activation in comprehension at input entail a greater likelihood of retrieval (Craik & Lockhart, 1972). Retrieval depends on a matching between the retrieval cues generated and those in the trace (Flexser & Tulving, 1978). Elaboration is assumed to increase the likelihood of recall for the item in question because when activation in the trace is greater, there is a greater chance of matching at recall. Greater recall is evidence for a more elaborate trace. It is also assumed that contextual information is employed in both comprehension and memory processes. Contextual cues can activate nodes in semantic memory to aid comprehension; they also play a role in creating memory representations by providing cues for the semantic information that was encoded at the time of comprehension.

Since nonverbal cues are part of the contextual information that accompanies spoken language, these cues may play a role in both the comprehension and retrieval of language. Ortony's distinction suggests the possibility that nonverbal cues may affect memory and comprehension in different ways and that a particular nonverbal cue may be important for one or the other process. At least one recent finding suggests that people may deal differently with nonverbal contextual cues in comprehension and recall.

Woodall and Burgoon (1981) compared the effects of synchronous (nonverbal activity such as hand-gesturing and facial-head movement coordinated to the rhythmic pattern of speech) and dissynchronous (uncoordinated) nonverbal cues on recall and recognition of spoken messages. Subjects were exposed to either a synchronized or unsynchronized version of a message. The recall measure in this study was clearly a memory task. Subsequent to message exposure, subjects were requested to "list everything they could remember about the content of the message." The recognition task, however, was a test of message comprehension. Subjects were asked to answer multiple-choice questions about the messages they had heard. These questions required subjects to integrate argument subpoints in order to respond correctly. Thus this measure tested whether subjects had used information in semantic memory to make correct inferences about the spoken language they heard. Woodall and Burgoon found a significant difference between synchronous and dissynchronous nonverbal cues on recall (recall was greater for synchronized than dissynchronized messages) but no significant difference for the recognition (comprehension) task. Other analyses of these data (Woodall, 1979) indicated that recall and recognition scores were not highly correlated ($r = .37$). These researchers concluded that recognition and recall may be different processes involving different methods of access to, storage and retrieval of information.

The Woodall and Burgoon finding, coupled with Ortony's discussion of the information-processing differences between comprehension and recall, indicate that a closer examination of the cognitive processes governing the contextual impact of nonverbal cues is warranted. In the next section we turn our attention to the cognitive operations involved in comprehension and examine the role nonverbal cues could play in the understanding of language.

COMPREHENSION AND THE PROCESSING OF COVERBAL BEHAVIORS

It is clear from Ortony's discussion of comprehension that two processes — integration and inference-making — need to be considered in any analysis of the possible impact of coverbal behaviors on comprehension. Both of these processes are seen as central components of comprehension. Based on these dual processes, two questions will guide our analysis in this section: (1) Under what conditions do coverbal behaviors trigger greater spread of activation in memory networks when they are *integrated* at input? and (2) In processing messages with co-occurring nonverbal cues, when are *inferences* made on the basis of the coverbal behavior?

Integration

As speakers, we often assume that coverbal behaviors may aid the listener in comprehension. Studies by Cohen and Harrison (1973) and

Cohen (1977) have examined the use of hand gestures in various communicative contexts. These studies indicate that speakers use significantly more illustrative gestures in face-to-face settings than in situations where the listener is not physically present (e.g., over an intercom or into a tape recorder). Cohen suggests that the most plausible explanation for these findings is that speakers use illustrative gestures in an attempt to facilitate listener comprehension. Although it seems unlikely that speakers would produce substantially more cues in face-to-face encounters if these cues did not aid processing, these studies say little about whether or when nonverbal cues activate further links in memory and thereby assist comprehension.

If we accept the depth-of-processing claim that greater levels of recall are due to more elaborate traces at input, there is substantial indirect evidence that nonverbal cues might assist in comprehension. Research on processing differences for words and pictures, for example, demonstrates that memory for pictures is often better than memory for words and sentences (Shepard, 1967; Standing, Conezio, & Haber, 1970; Gehring, Toglia, & Kimble, 1976). Similarly, concrete words, those that can easily evoke images, are better recalled than abstract words (Paivio, 1971). Baddeley might challenge the depth-of-processing explanation for these findings, however, and argue that the visual stimuli may not be processed more deeply but instead are in a different domain of processing entirely. While it may be true that many or all visual cues are in a different processing domain than linguistic stimuli, visual cues *can* require or induce semantic involvement in much the same way that linguistic stimuli can.

Linguistic stimuli can be processed at the level of auditory forms (sound characteristics of spoken words) or visual shapes (graphic features of written words). Typically, however, language induces semantic involvement because it is intended to convey standardized meanings. In the depth-of-processing studies, subjects had to be restrained from engaging in semantic processing of the language; they were instructed to process only formal features of the cues so that normal semantic processing would not occur in the weak depth-of-processing conditions. Under normal processing conditions of language, far more semantic than formal processing occurs. For some visual cues, such as certain types of coverbal behaviors, both levels of processing (formal and semantic) are also available; the formal features of the cues can be processed (i.e., the visual characteristics of a gesture or facial expression can be noted) or the shared semantic meaning of these gestures can be encoded, i.e., the meaning "three" can be encoded when a speaker raises three fingers as she says: "There have been a few attempts to trace the systematic influence of Mozart's work on Mahler's harmonic innovations." Clearly, not all coverbal behaviors carry semantic cues. We would argue, however, that in cases where coverbal behaviors have the potential for semantic encoding, these visual stimuli carry the same inducement for semantic processing that linguistic stimuli carry. In addition, because listeners can turn to coverbal behavior for assistance in comprehension when language seems insufficient, coverbal behaviors carrying no immediately recognizable semantic information can be assigned semantic significance (or at least be scanned for possible semantic cues) because of the social context in which they are produced. Our point is that coverbal behaviors can carry more or less inducement for semantic involvement and thus could result in more or less trace elaboration at input. The depth-of-processing analysis cannot be ruled out as a possible explanation for how coverbal behaviors function in comprehension.

Consider, for example, Freedman's (1972) distinction between speech primacy and motor primacy movements. Speech primacy movements include any gesture or action that has no clear representational or semantic properties; these movements occur as an "overflow from the emphatic aspect of speech" (p. 158). Gestures that emphasize or accent co-occuring speech would fall in this category. Ekman and Friesen (1969) called these gestures "baton illustrators." In contrast, motor primacy movements are gestures or actions that carry some semantic relationship to their co-occurring language. They offer some visual representation of the idea that the speaker is trying to convey. Ekman and Friesen have called these behaviors emblems or pictographs because they provide kinesic motor expression for words or phrases. Based on Craik and Tulving's (1975) analysis of the factors that influence trace elaboration, we suggest (Woodall & Folger, 1981) that speech primacy and motor primacy cues differ in their ability to elaborate a trace when messages are comprehended.

Craik and Tulving specify that the degree of elaboration or activation is a function of three stimulus characteristics: the number of features available, the qualitative nature of these features, and, in the case of contextual cues for language, the extent to which these cues are integrated with the target information. Motor primacy cues offer greater potential for trace elaboration on all three counts. Emblems and pictographs carry more features than speech primacy cues because they contain semantic cues as well as the spatial cues of motion that any coverbal behaviors display. In addition, motor primacy movements are qualitatively richer than speech primacy cues in that they offer more vivid information. Nisbett and Ross (1980) note that information vividness is in part a function of how concrete a stimulus is. More detail and more specificity produce more concrete and thus more vivid information. In offering pictorial representation, emblems and pictographs present a more vivid image than emphasizing gestures or gestures that simply accentuate the rhythmic patterns of speech. Motor primacy movements depict length, width, and shape in representing some object or idea and thus offer a richer image than speech primacy cues. Finally, as contextual cues for "target" linguistic information, motor primacy behaviors are integrated more closely with co-occuring language. There is a clear semantic link between these gestures and co-occurring speech. The spoken message is, in many cases, dependent on the motor primacy gesture to complete the sense of the intended utterance (e.g., the three-finger gesture accompanying the statement about attempts to analyze Mahler's harmonic innovations). This close integration with spoken language increases the likelihood that motor primacy gestures will contribute to the elaboration of a trace at comprehension.

Because motor primacy gestures hold more potential for trace elaboration than speech primacy cues along all three of Craik and Tulving's criteria, we hypothesized that the presence of motor primacy cues would result in greater levels of recall and recognition for co-occuring speech than accentuating or emphasizing gestures. We found support for this hypothesis in a recent study that compared the use of speech and motor primacy hand gestures (Woodall & Folger, 1981). Our research and analysis suggest that Baddeley's position on the depth-of-processing issue may need modification. We can accept Baddeley's claim that the cognitive operations involved in processing visual cues may be different from those involved in processing language and that visual cues can create durable memory traces. Baddeley's position fails to acknowledge, however, that there are sets of visual cues, like coverbal behaviors, whose elements may or may not induce semantic processing. Some cues within the set have this potential while others do not. For these sets of visual cues, the particular stimuli that foster semantic involvement have a greater potential for trace elaboration than cues within the set that do not induce semantic processing. The whole set of visual cues may be processed differently than linguistic information because they are visual (e.g., additional transformations of the stimulus might be necessary) and any member of the set may contribute to the durability of a trace because a visual marker is present at input, but differences in trace elaboration appear to emerge when comparisions are drawn across cues that do and do not carry an inducement for semantic processing. It appears that deeper processing occurs when there is some semantic involvement with a visual cue.

While some coverbal behaviors carry an inherent inducement for semantic processing because they contain semantic features that can contribute to the sense of the entire utterance, coverbal behaviors that do not contain these semantic markers can also be processed at a deeper semantic level. A listener can turn to the coverbal behavior to obtain further information that can contribute to one's understanding of a message even though there are no semantic features present in the cue. A listener can, in other words, engage in semantic processing of nonverbal cues that do not carry a strong inducement for this deeper level of involvement. The conditions that might evoke deeper processing of cues carrying no clear semantic features have not been identified. We suspect, however, that ambiguous or anomalous encoding conditions act as the primacy source of encouragement for deeper processing of these behaviors.

There are several types of evidence that would suggest deeper processing of anomalous or incongruent coverbal behaviors. Hastie (1980) found, for example, that behavioral information incongruent with implicit personality expectations is better recalled and more deeply processed. In his research subjects were first presented with five to seven implicit personality traits (Rosenberg & Sedlak, 1972) and were asked to integrate them into an impression of a person. Subjects were then presented with a series of sentences or film clips depicting a character (the same person that subjects had formed an impression of) engaged in a variety of behavioral episodes. Some of these episodes were incongruent with the impression formed from the traits. After exposure to the behavioral episodes, subjects evaluated the target person on a set of personality rating scales and recalled as much of the information presented in the episodes as possible. In general, information incongruent with the initial impressions was recalled more often than congruent information. In addition, subjects offered commentary about incongruent impressions that required deeper levels of processing than comments offered about congruent input.

Other research in information processing indicates that we rely heavily on contextual information to clarify messages and eliminate alternative meanings (Tulving & Gold, 1963; Bransford & Johnson, 1973). As perhaps the most common and immediate contextual cues for spoken messages in face-to-face settings, coverbal behaviors are likely targets for assistance when the co-occuring language is ambiguous or the message is anomalous. The likelihood of seeking such assistance has been noted in cognitive analyses of social behavior that point to interactants' strong motivation to reduce uncertainty or clarify ambiguity in social encounters (McCall & Simmons, 1978; Berger & Calabrese, 1975; Hewes & Planalp, in press).

There are at least three ambiguous contexts that might induce semantic processing of coverbal cues carrying no clear semantic features.[3] First and most obvious are instances where the spoken message has more than one possible meaning (e.g., metaphors, double entendres, ironic statements). If a gesture or facial expression accompanies this type of message, it may be examined for evidence that could reduce ambiguity or eliminate an alternative meaning.

Second, coverbal behaviors that are rhythmically out of sync with the verbal stream may evoke deeper processing. Because rhythm provides an important connection between coverbal behavior and language utterances, rhythmic relationships may be an important factor to consider in how face-to-face messages are processed. Research by Dittmann (1972), Kendon (1970), and Boomer (1978) indicates that speakers coordinate nonverbal cues with the rhythm and flow of the verbal stream and that in most cases synchronization occurs at the phonemic clause level. If the nonverbal activity is not in sync with the rhythmic pattern of speech and people's normal expectations for the occurrence of these nonverbal cues are violated, there is reason to believe that there will be not only more attention to but also more semantic involvement with these contextual cues.

In one sense the dissynchronous cues can be looked at as distractions from the verbal message if they capture the attention of the listener in a way that they normally would not. But beyond attention, dissynchrony may heighten the semantic involvement with the nonverbal cues (and thus be processed more deeply). The listener may spend more time interpreting the semantic content of a gesture or may seek alternative interpretations of any dissynchronous activity. One might, for example, question whether the speaker was being deceitful, was nervous, or even had some slight physical disorder. A consideration of these alternatives entails a greater involvement with the meaning of the coverbal behavior. Dissynchronous cues carrying semantic information relevant to the verbal message may actually enhance accuracy of comprehension. We would not expect accuracy of comprehension to be enhanced for dissynchronous bodily movements or gestures that, by themselves, activate no concepts in memory relevant to the spoken message. Nonetheless, both types of cues can contribute to a final activated subgraph at comprehension regardless of whether these contributions result in more accurate understanding. When the cues are dissynchronous, we expect deeper involvement to occur.

A third ambiguous context in which coverbal behaviors may be processed more deeply is found when the coverbal behaviors suggest that the spoken message cannot be taken at face value. Coverbal behaviors that carry no clear semantic features can nevertheless reveal information about the emotional state or intent of the speaker (e.g., that the speaker is anxious, joking, deceptive). When the listener feels that there is some incongruence between the utterance and coverbal cues, these cues may be consulted to determine, for example, if the speaker is being deceptive or if the speaker has some emotional reaction to what he or she is saying that is not being expressed in the utterance. While we will further specify in the next section how coverbal cues affect processing in these situations, we expect an elaboration and deepening of processing under such conditions.

It seems clear that coverbal behaviors carrying semantic cues or those having no inherent semantic features can be processed at greater depths (i.e., with some degree of semantic involvement) when the communicative situation warrants such involvement. We have suggested that there are inducements in face-to-face encounters for processing these cues at deeper levels: Inherent semantic cues in some coverbal behaviors evoke semantic involvement to help the listener understand messages, and a variety of ambiguous or anomalous encoding conditions can also evoke greater involvement with cues that may ordinarily be processed only as visual shapes or motions. Our specification of contexts that induce semantic involvement of nonverbal cues may be a conservative estimate of the extent to which nonverbal cues contribute to the comprehension of messages. Research by Archer and Akert (1977) that examined the effects of full (verbal and nonverbal) and partial (verbal) channel stimuli on the accuracy of interpretations suggests that nonverbal cues have significant effects on subjects' processing of unambiguous messages. These researchers go so far as to claim that nonverbal cues appear to provide "a qualitative 'script' without which verbal cues cannot be interpreted accurately" (p. 449). While this research provides clear support for the role of nonverbal cues in comprehension, we believe that there must be clearer specification of the contexts and factors that make coverbal behaviors likely contributors to comprehension.

In any context where deeper processing of coverbal cues occurs, further inferences can be made with the interpretations that have been assigned to these behaviors. In the next section we examine the inference-making processes that occur when coverbal behaviors are processed as potential contributors to comprehension.

Inference Making

An analysis of how coverbal cues prompt inference making by observers needs to consider how inferences are made in at least two information stores: (1) semantic information memory stores that underlie language production and comprehension, and (2) social information memory stores that hold information about social concepts, events, processes, and persons (Hastie & Carlston, 1980). Whether these two domains constitute distinct subsystems within a cognitive model, or simply specialized subnetworks within a larger global network store, is undetermined. We will assume, however, that social and semantic information domains are interrelated and that inferences made about the meaning of messages (implications of what was said, comprehension of the utterance) can be affected by inferences of a social nature about the source (impressions of the source, the source's intentions, situation and context in which the utterance was made). Further, we shall argue that coverbal cues can affect inferences made in both semantic and social information domains. Inferences can be made about the substance of what is being said as well as about the person, social interaction, and social situation in which the message is being produced. Although researchers have begun to document clearly the impact that nonverbal cues have on person impressions, the potential for coverbal cues to affect inferences about receiver's understanding of language has largely been ignored.

There are several different situations where we would expect nonverbal cues to play a major role in prompting inference making by observers. One such situation occurs during everyday interactions when actors form impressions of others. A substantial amount of evidence suggests that nonverbal cues are an important source of information in impression formation. In a recent review of this research, Burgoon (1980) suggests three general contexts where nonverbal cues have been shown to be important in impression information: (1) when sociological and personality judgements are made, (2) when judgments of credibility and attraction are made, and (3) when judgments of veracity and deception are made. Research has shown, for example, that vocal cues and physical appearance affect judgments of age, socioeconomic status, education, and personality traits; that eye contact, smiling and headnodding, postural and gestural activity, and interpersonal distance and touch cues affect judgments of status, credibility, liking and attraction; and that certain hand gestures, leg and feet behaviors, vocal cues, and self-touching affect judgments of truthfulness or deception by observers (for a review of this literature, see Burgoon, 1980; Burgoon & Saine, 1978; Harper, Wiens & Matarazzo, 1978; Knapp, 1978).

From our point of view, what characterizes all these situations is that nonverbal cues trigger inferences about others and thus contribute to what gets activated in social information stores. Regardless of the type of judgment a receiver makes, all such judgments involve inferences that are based on coverbal information. Thus, coverbal cues may act to elaborate information at input and prompt deeper processing of social information by activating nodes within the social information memory store. Everyday impression formation and judgmental tasks may be based on such cognitive reactions to nonverbal cues.

Beyond impression formation there are at least three other contexts where the encoding of nonverbal cues during interaction is likely to result in social and semantic inferences. As noted earlier, situations where an actor's behavior is anomalous, ambiguous, or incongruent may result in deeper processing of coverbal behaviors at input. Such conditions result in more elaborate activation of information in both semantic and social domains and a deeper and more extensive set of inferences about the content of a message and the person and situation in which it is made. When verbal information is inadequate to allow an overall understanding of an actor's communicative behavior, coverbal information is more deeply processed to assist comprehension. Recent research on the effects of messages that contain inconsistent verbal and nonverbal cues points to the role nonverbal cues play in inference making.

McMahan (1976), for example, conducted a study in which subjects were exposed to one of four videotaped messages where (1) nonverbal cues conveyed dominance and the verbal message conveyed submissiveness, (2) nonverbal cues conveyed submissiveness and the verbal message conveyed dominance, (3) nonverbal cues as well as the verbal message conveyed dominance, or (4) nonverbal cues as well as the verbal message conveyed submissiveness. After viewing a videotape subjects were asked to indicate their written impressions of the speaker and to provide a written reconstruction of the message. McMahan then coded the references to either verbal or nonverbal information in these accounts. In addition, subjects rated attitudes conveyed by the message and the speaker and indicated agreement with a series of questions designed to measure discrimination of overt statements and speaker intentions. The results of this study indicated that impressions of the *speaker* were dominated by the nonverbal cues, while the reconstructions of the *message* were dominated by references to verbal information. Of more importance, however, was the finding that in answering items about overt statements in the message and speakers' perceived intentions, the subjects in the inconsistent conditions rated the speaker as being less sincere in communicative intent than in the sincerity of the statements themselves. McMahan notes that this result "lends support to the theory that perceivers discriminate between statement and intention, and they attribute intentions to the person which are used to reinterpret the verbal message when the incongruent verbal and nonverbal cues are received" (1976, p. 202). McMahan's results and conclusion are consistent with our analysis that anomalous encoding conditions, such as verbal-nonverbal incongruity, result in deeper and more elaborate processing and more extensive inference making in both social and semantic information domains. Inferences made about the message are affected by inferences linked to the source, the source's communicative behavior, and the source's intentions. As a result, a more elaborate, extensive, and different understanding is obtained when incongruent messages are sent.

A number of other researchers (Mehrabian, 1970; Mehrabian & Ferris, 1967; Mehrabian & Wiener, 1967; Argyle, Salter, Nicholson, Williams, & Burgess, 1970; Rosenthal, Hall, DiMatteo, Rogers, & Archer, 1979; Bugental, 1974; Bugental, Kaswan, & Love, 1970; Bugental, Love, Kaswan, & April, 1971) have also investigated reactions to discrepant or contradictory messages. In general these studies have found that receivers rely primarily on visual nonverbal cues to clarify inconsistent messages, although this conclusion is qualified by several factors, including gender of receiver, extremity of discrepancy, and age of the receiver.

A second context where nonverbal cues play a role in inference making is in those situations where detection of deception is at issue. The most recent studies in deception research suggest that there is an interaction between the use of nonverbal and verbal information when veracity judgments are made (Bauchner, Kaplan, & Miller, 1980). It appears that in making attributions of veracity, observers first recognize or detect that the message cannot be taken at face value and then draw inferences from both verbal and nonverbal cues to come to some overall assessment of the truth of the statement. Such inference making represents processing at a greater-than-usual depth in both semantic and social information domains. A receiver can make sense of messages in such situations through more involved processing that combines both verbal and nonverbal information in order to make inferences and judgments.

A final area of study that illustrates how nonverbal cues are utilized in inference making is that concerned with violations of expectations. Studies by Burgoon (1978), Burgoon and Jones (1976), and Burgoon, Stacks, and Woodall (1979) have shown how violations of personal space expectations by interactants affect social judgments of attractiveness and credibility. Recent evidence indicates that rewarding interactants (those perceived as high status or providing positive feedback) may increase favorable reactions through violations of conversational distance expectations in either the close or far direction. This finding suggests again that there is no one-to-one relationship between nonverbal behaviors and social judgments based on them. Rather, such evidence suggests that violations may lead to inferences that are specific to certain social contexts and that integrate both verbal and nonverbal behavior. When expectations about nonverbal behavior are violated, inferences are drawn about the possible meaning of the violations, and this information is incorporated into a final interpretation of the message.

RETRIEVAL AND NONVERBAL CUES OF LANGUAGE

Ortony's proposed account of the processes involved in the retrieval of language suggests that, apart from their impact on comprehension, nonverbal cues may serve an important function in the construction of memory representations. In creating a record of the experienced meaning at input, recall of the contextual information that came at the time of encoding can aid in the recall of semantic information, which, in turn, may trigger syntactic constructions.

Since nonverbal cues provide prominent contextual information for verbal messages in face-to-face encounters, these cues may be useful retrieval mechanisms. We have relied on one recent line of theory and research to make an initial determination of whether nonverbal cues can contribute to the recall of co-occurring verbal messages.

Tulving and his colleagues have found that subjects can fail to recognize words that they are able to recall. Working within a list-learning paradigm, Tulving and Thomson (1973) studied the encoding conditions under which words in a to-be-remembered list are learned. Their purpose was to determine whether words encoded as context act as retrieval mechanisms. In the first series of studies, subjects were given lists of target (to-be-remembered) words that were paired with "weak" input cue words. The target item "cold," for example, was paired with "ground." The target "day" was paired with the input cue "sun," "cut" with "blade," etc. Subjects were told that their task was to remember the target words and that paying attention to the cue words might help them at the time of the memory test. After the list of paired words was presented, subjects were given a set of "strong" cues that were not presented at the time the target words were encoded. These cues were words like "hot" (for the target "cold"), "night" (for "day") and "scissors" (for "cut"). Each of these strong cue words had a strong semantic association with one of the target words. The subjects were asked to write down all the words they could generate as free associates to these strong, extralist words. Roughly 74 percent of the to-be-remembered target words were found in the free associations made to the extralist strong cues. When subjects were asked to circle all the words in their freely associated list that they recognized as target words, only 24 percent were recognized. Subsequently, when given the weak input cues that had been paired with the target items at the time of encoding, subjects could surprisingly, recall 63 percent of the target words.

This "recall without recognition" finding suggested to Tulving and Thomson that it is not the target word or its semantic characteristics that are critical in retrieval. If this were the case, then surely recall of the target words would have been facilitated by seeing an exact copy of the targets in the free associated list. Rather, the authors conclude, it is the encoding conditions that are critical in retrieval: "Given the fact that the target words can be more readily recalled in the presence of the input cue than in the presence of its own literal copy, it is possible to think of the input cue as a 'control element' or code that governs the access to the complex of stored information about the target word" (Tulving & Thomson, 1973, p. 368).

Watkins and Tulving (1975) made a number of changes in the design of this research (including omitting the free association task and presenting subjects with forced-choice recognition tasks) to determine if the original findings were a methodological artifact. In general, the results of these studies replicated the original findings. And, despite challenges to and suggested limitations of the phenomena (Light, Kimble, & Pellegrino, 1975), Anderson (1976, p. 380) concludes that the effects are "in some sense, real."

Tulving has posited the encoding specificity principle and a feature extraction hypothesis to explain the recall-without-recognition finding. The encoding specificity principle claims that retrieval cues can provide access to information in memory if and only if they have been stored as part of the specific memory trace of the event. The memory trace is defined simply as the "encoding operations on what is stored" and thus, according to this principle, "encoding determines the trace and the trace determines the effectiveness of retrieval cues" (Tulving & Thomson, 1973, pp. 369-370). In short, the encoding specificity principle acknowledges that contextual information can aid in retrieval if this information is stored at input.

In a further analysis of the results of over thirty studies, Flexser and Tulving (1978) posit a feature extraction hypothesis to explain how recognition failure occurs. According to their analysis, any memory trace (the trace that both the recognition and recall cue must access) is constructed of some subset of features encoded by a subject out of the total possible set of features in the entire stimulus. Similarly, when a recognition or recall cue is presented, a subset of features from these cues is encoded by the subject. Retrieval will result if there is sufficient matching between those features which were encoded in the memory trace of the original stimulus and those extracted from the retrieval cue. Since different cues can be extracted from the recognition cue (exact copy) than are extracted from the recall (context) cue, recall can occur without recognition. It is possible, in other words, that sufficient matching can occur with the context cue but not the exact copy. In these situations recognition failure of recallable words occurs.

Most of the research on encoding specificity has been tied to the rather narrow list-learning paradigm described above. However, one study conducted by Watkins, Ho, and Tulving (1976) provides some support for the contextual effects of visual information on subsequent recognition of visual targets. In this research, subjects studied pairs of pictures of unfamiliar faces. When tested, subjects were more likely to recognize target faces when they were accompanied by the same context face rather than one that was not presented with the target at encoding. In a second study, faces were paired with descriptive phrases. Re-presentation of the study context once again enhanced recognition, thereby demonstrating that linguistic contextual information can assist in the recall of visual targets.

Encoding specificity and the recall-without-recognition finding are consistent with Ortony's account of how memory representations are reconstructed. The input cues given in the list-learning contexts provide the "input associates" that can aid at recall in the reconstruction of a semantic or syntactic representation. Since coverbal behaviors are contextual cues for language, we hypothesized that these cues may be employed in the reconstruction of messages sent in face-to-face settings.

In a recent study (Woodall & Folger, 1981), we adopted Tulving's basic paradigm in an initial attempt to determine whether nonverbal cues such as hand gestures could act as effective retrieval cues for co-occurring language. The specific objectives of the research were twofold: (1) to determine if the encoding specificity principle would be supported when coverbal behaviors that ordinarily accompany spoken messages are the contextual cues for target, linguistic information, and (2) to test whether different types of kinesic behaviors (specifically, speech primacy and motor primacy gestures) have different effects on recall or recognition failure.

In this research subjects saw videotaped segments of spoken messages that were accompanied by either motor primacy or speech primacy gestures. After the presentation of the segments, subjects were given a written recognition test of the verbal messages on the tape. Contextually cued recall was then tested by playing the videotaped segments back to the subjects in random order without the sound. Subjects were asked to recall the target messages by relying on the co-occurring gesture.

Instances of recognition failure were found in this research when either speech primacy or motor primacy hand gestures were employed as the contextual cues for spoken language. This result supports Tulving's general thesis that visual contextual cues can provide access to target information even when an exact copy of the target fails to trigger recognition. Although recognition failure rates were lower in these studies then in Tulving's word pair research,[4] these studies demonstrate that the encoding specificity principle is generalizable to contextual cues that are part of natural communicative settings.

As we noted in our earlier discussion of trace elaboration and depth-of-processing, this research also revealed that motor primacy cues produced significantly higher levels of recall for co-occurring language than emphasizing (speech primacy) gestures. This difference was attributed to the greater trace elaboration potential of gestures carrying semantic cues. Motor primacy cues have more encodable features, contain more vivid information, and are well integrated with the semantic content of their co-occurring verbal messages. The important point for this discussion, however, is that both types of cues aided in the reconstruction of linguistic target information.

Tulving's analysis of the role of contextual information in recall and our initial study of the effects of gestures on the retrieval of language suggest that coverbal behaviors have at least the potential to reconstruct semantic representations encoded at comprehension. At this point, however, we can make no firm claims about the strength of this potential in everyday conversational settings. In Tulving's list-learning paradigm (and our modification of it), subjects were instructed to use the contextual information to help them recall target items and to rely on this information shortly after encoding to reconstruct a semantic representation. The extent to which coverbal behaviors are encoded as potential retrieval cues in natural encoding conditions, such as face-to-face conversations, is still unknown. The conditions or conversational characteristics that "instruct" receivers to encode contextual features need to be specified, and the relative strength of coverbal cues to reconstruct decaying representations over time needs to be assessed.

MEASURING MEMORY AND UNDERSTANDING

The memory/understanding distinction is important not only because it clarifies how nonverbal cues can aid in both of these cognitive processes but also because it has important implications for the construction of operational measures of recall and comprehension. A careful evaluation must be made of what measures can stand as adequate indicants of recall and comprehension in information-processing studies. Communication researchers have not always distinguished between these processes. Often the term "comprehension" stood for measures of both recall and understanding. As a result, it is difficult in some cases to determine whether reported research could draw valid claims about either memory or understanding.

For example, research examining the effects of various vocal cues, such as rate and pitch, on listener comprehension did not draw clear operational distinctions between recall and comprehension (see Orr, 1968; Foulke & Sticht, 1969, for reviews of this research). In two investigations of the effects of time-compressed speech on comprehension, Fairbanks, Guttman, and Miron (1957a, 1957b) used multiple-choice questions that were queries about the factual content of a presented message. Although these items were used to seek recall of stimulus material, the measures were offered as indicants of listener comprehension. Similarly, Diehl, White, and their colleagues (Diehl, White, & Burk, 1959; Diehl, White, & Satz, 1961) used a question-completion test based on presented lecture material to draw conclusions about the effects of vocal parameters on comprehension. Finally, Beighley (1952) used multiple-choice tests and immediate and delayed recall measures to assess listener comprehension. Although the tests in the above studies are offered as measures of comprehension, the items used may actually be memory-related recognition tests, since they appeared to access factual information presented in the stimulus messages.[5] These investigations may in fact say very little about comprehension of the presented material. As Ortony points out, words and phrases can be remembered verbatim but may not be integrated in currently held knowledge stores or may not be used to spark further inferences as they are integrated. As a result, we are left with a muddled picture of what these investigations measured and what cognitive processes the vocal parameters under investigation affected. The same problem arises in other areas of communication research that involve comprehension as a variable of interest (cf. Woodall, Davis, & Sahin's 1981 discussion of television news comprehension).

Operational measures of recall and comprehension must follow Ortony's theoretical distinction to ensure that valid claims are made about these cognitive processes. Memory measures are based on retrieval processes and attempt to determine whether subjects can reconstruct information presented to them in some stimulus. As Brown (1976) notes, there are two principle tests that are used to measure memory: recall tests and recognition tests. The essence of a recall test is that the subject generates the target or to-be-remembered information. In a recognition test, subjects are given one or more potential targets and are then asked to choose the target information from a list of target and lure items. Although differences between recall and recognition as retrieval processes exist, both types can be legitimately viewed as memory measures.

Measures of understanding, on the other hand, are based on the integration of information and inference-making processes. They attempt to determine how subjects integrate new information with information held in memory stores and to assess whether previously stored information is activated and used to make inferences that go beyond the information given. In cases where the researcher cannot assume that subjects hold similar information about the topic at hand in memory stores, comprehension tests may require some assessment of what information each subject currently holds in memory to determine if this information is activated when the input message is processed. Questions that require inference making in order to generate an answer provide clear measures of comprehension. These items cannot be collapsed with simple recall questions that require no clear integration or cognitive use of the input message. Further research on comprehension will require the development of measures that can adequately assess depth-of-processing. As Baddeley notes in his critique of the depth-of-processing research, recall of information provides only indirect evidence for deeper levels of processing. Prompted or open-ended responses that can be coded for semantic-involvement or inference making may be a more promising method for assessing processing depth.

It should be noted that the format of an item has little to do with whether the measure seeks evidence for recall or understanding. A multiple-choice question format may tap either memory or understanding, depending on what the subject is required to do in answering the question. If the items require a subject to recognize a target item from several alternatives, it is a memory test. If the items require subjects to integrate information given at input and make inferences beyond information given in order to select a correct response, the measure taps understanding. Free response and open-ended questions can demonstrate simple recall or comprehension, depending on what coding criteria the researcher employs in analyzing the responses.

Finally, there may be an overemphasis on accuracy in constructing measures of both recall and comprehension. Ortony's analysis suggests a broad view of comprehension and recall that seeks information about these cognitive processes apart from any accuracy criterion. Comprehension measures that reflect what gets activated in social or semantic memory stores or what inferences are drawn may provide the most valuable insights about how messages in social contexts are processed. Simple measures of accuracy may miss important information about how the activation of memory nodes occurs and what prompts deeper processing of verbal and nonverbal messages.

CONCLUSION

The relationship between verbal and nonverbal components of messages remains an important concern in therapy, conversational analysis, and studies of impression formation and relationship definition. There are several reasons why we feel the distinction between comprehension and memory discussed here provides a sound basis for examining the potential impact of coverbal behaviors in a wide variety of social contexts.

First, this approach can focus the study of coverbal behaviors on important and well-researched cognitive capacities. Comprehension and retrieval processes are central cognitive antecedents to almost any context in which the interplay between verbal and nonverbal behavior is of interest. It is unlikely that any study of coverbal behavior could be conducted without making at least some implicit assumptions about memory representations, assigned interpretations and inferences, or the reconstruction of conversational episodes. Recognizing the theoretical distinction between comprehension and retrieval and constructing operational measures that reflect differences in these cognitive processes can allow researchers to invoke information-processing principles in explaining how messages are exchanged and interpreted in interpersonal settings. In turn, studies of coverbal behavior can contribute to our understanding of comprehension and retrieval processes; they can reveal how co-occurring visual and linguistic cues activate concepts in memory and serve as the basis for the retrieval of conversational events. New light can be shed on theoretical controversies like the depth-of-processing issue if coverbal behaviors are examined within an information-processing framework.

Second, this analysis of comprehension and retrieval offers new inroads into the study of verbal and nonverbal cues as *interrelated* channels. The analysis suggests that, as contextual cues for language, coverbal behaviors can be expected to play an important role in how co-occurring language is incorporated in memory and reconstructed at retrieval. The account of retrieval, for example, begins with the recognition that contextual information plays an active role in cueing semantic representations that in turn trigger surface-level or syntactic constructions of target information. This proposed link between contextual cues and the construction of semantic representations at retrieval raises challenging research issues for those interested in the effects of coverbal behaviors. In many instances, the coverbal contextual cues may be more vivid than the actual language used in constructing a message. If the coverbal cues are used to reconstruct some decaying semantic representation, these cues may be a significant source of distortion in retrieval processes. If support is found for this possibility, it would suggest that nonverbal cues have a greater influence on message interpretation as time elapses.

Finally, research examining coverbal behaviors from an information-processing perspective is consistent with the broad, cognitive approaches to the study of interpersonal behavior that are now being developed. Hewes and Planalp (in press), for example, portray social actors as lay scientists who make sense of interpersonal behaviors by employing intuitive theories about the social events at hand. A major objective of this work is to characterize cognitive functions that define actors' intuitive theories and that ultimately influence how messages are integrated in cognitive representations of social knowledge. The study of nonverbal cues can be integrated into this broader cognitive approach to the study of interpersonal behavior if researchers begin with clear theoretical and operational conceptions of important cognitive capacities.

NOTES

1. This example is a somewhat atypical and thus interesting sentence, because a person might activate memories of musical themes, melodies, or motifs (from Mahler's symphony and familiar concertos) that would have no representation in a semantic network but could allow them to comprehend the meaning of the utterance. Clearly, there

is nonsemantic, sensory information stored in long-term memory that can also disambiguate language.

2. It should be noted that comprehension, in the sense in which Ortony discusses it, is not synonymous with accuracy of understanding. Links in memory can be activated (as, for example, when inferences are made at input) that take the listener far from the speaker's intended meaning. Comprehension is *what* gets recorded and makes no claim to the accuracy or inaccuracy of this imprint. To say one has comprehended a message is not, in Ortony's terms, to say that one has understood it accurately.

3. In all of these contexts, the information encoded may be seen by the receiver as part of the message being sent; it may, in other words, be simply integrated with knowledge currently held in memory as a representation of the intended message. It is likely, however, that in anomalous or ambiguous contexts, the listener will need to make inferences that allow for a more satisfying interpretation of the stimulus message. Because ambiguous messages appear incomplete, listeners have some awareness that they must make inferences that go beyond "what is there" to gain a satisfying interpretation of the message. There is, then, some overlap between this discussion of integration and the following section where we examine the inference-making process in more detail.

4. The differences in recognition failure were explained by differences in the number of available features in the recognition (exact copy of the phrase) or recall (hand gesture) cues. If the phrases have significantly more features that *could* be encoded than the visual contextual cues, then recognition rates would increase, because there would be a greater chance of sufficient matching in the recognition task than in the recall task. Higher recognition rates, by definition, reduce recognition failure levels. This explanation for the reduced recognition failure rates was supported by our research because we found higher rates of recognition failure when motor primacy gestures (visual cues that carried semantic information and thus more possible encodable features) were employed as contextual cues.

5. It is difficult to know for sure if all of the items on the multiple-choice tests assessed recall, since the content of all of the items is not reported in the investigations. It is possible that some questions could have required subjects to draw inferences from the presented material.

REFERENCES

Andersen, J. *Language, memory and thought.* Hillsdale, NJ: Lawrence Erlbaum, 1976.

Archer, D., & Akert, R. M. Words and everything else: Verbal and nonverbal cues in social interpretation. *Journal of Personality and Social Psychology,* 1977, *35,* 443-449.

Argyle, M., Salter, V., Nicholson, H., Williams, M., & Burgess, P. The communication of inferior and superior attitudes by verbal and nonverbal signals. *British Journal of Social and Clinical Psychology,* 1970, *9,* 222-231.

Baddeley, A. The trouble with levels: A reexamination of Craik and Lockhart's framework for memory research. *Psychological Review,* 1978, *85,* 439-450.

Bauchner, J. E., Kaplan, E. A., & Miller, G. B. Detecting deception: The relationship of available information to judgmental accuracy in invited encounters. *Human Communication Research,* 1980, *6,* 253-264.

Beighley, K. C. An experimental study of the effect of four speech variables on listener comprehension. *Speech Monographs,* 1952, *19,* 249-258.

Berger, C., & Calabrese, R. Some explorations in initial interactions and beyond. Toward a developmental theory of interpersonal communication. *Human Communication Research,* 1975, *1,* 99-112.

Boomer, D. The phonemic clause: Speech unit in human communication. In A. W. Siegman & S. Feldstein (Eds.), *Nonverbal behavior and communication.* Hillsdale, NJ: Lawrence Erlbaum, 1978.

Bower, G. H., & Karlin, M. B. Depth of processing: Pictures of faces and recognition memory. *Journal of Experimental Psychology,* 1974, *103,* 751-757.

Bransford, J. D. & Johnson, M. K. Considerations of some problems of comprehension. In W. G. Chase (Ed.), *Visual information processing.* New York: Academic Press, 1973.

Brown, J. An analysis of recognition and recall and of problems in their comparison. In J. Brown (Ed.) *Recall and recognition.* New York: John Wiley, 1976.

Bugental, D. E. Interpretation of naturally occurring discrepancies between words and intonation: Modes of inconsistency resolution. *Journal of Personality and Social Psychology,* 1974, *30,* 125-133.

Bugental, D. E., Kaswan, J. W., & Love, L. R. Perception of contradictory meanings conveyed by verbal and nonverbal channels. *Journal of Personality and Social Psychology,* 1970, *16,* 647-655.

Bugental, D. E., Love, L. R., Kaswan, J. W., & April, C. Verbal-nonverbal conflict in parental messages to normal and disturbed children. *Journal of Abnormal Psychology,* 1971, *77,* 6-10.

Burgoon, J. K. A communication model of personal space violations: Explication and an initial test. *Human Communication Research,* 1978, *4,* 129-142.

Burgoon, J. K. Nonverbal communication research in the 1970s: An overview. In D. Nimmo (Ed.), *Communication yearbook 4.* New Brunswick, NJ: Transaction, 1980.

Burgoon, J. K. & Jones, S. B. Toward a theory of personal space expectations and their violations. *Human Communication Research,* 1976, *2,* 131-146.

Burgoon, J. K., & Saine, T. J. *The unspoken dialogue: An introduction to nonverbal communication.* Boston: Houghton-Mifflin, 1978.

Burgoon, J. K., Stacks, D. W., & Woodall, W. G. A communicative model of violations of distancing expectations. *Western Journal of Speech Communication,* 1979, *43,* 153-167.

Cappella, J. N., & Folger, J. P. An information processing explanation of the attitude-behavior inconsistency. In D. P. Cushman & R. McPhee (Eds.), *The attitude behavior controversy.* New York: Academic Press, 1981.

Cohen, A. A. The communicative function of hand illustrators. *Journal of Communication,* 1977, *27,* 54-63.

Cohen, A. A., & Harrison, R. P. Intentionality in the use of hand illustrators. *Journal of Personality and Social Psychology,* 1973, *28,* 276-279.

Collins, A. M., & Loftus, E. F. A spreading-activation theory of semantic processing. *Psychological Review,* 1975, *82,* 407-428.

Craik, F., & Lockhart, R. S. Levels of processing: A framework for memory research. *Journal of Verbal Learning and Verbal Behavior,* 1972, *11,* 671-684.

Craik, F., & Tulving, E. Depth of processing and the retention of words in episodic memory. *Journal of Experimental Psychology: General,* 1975, *104,* 268-294.

Denes, P. B. On the statistics of spoken English. *Journal of the Acoustical Society of America,* 1963, *35,* 892-904.

Diehl, C. F., White, R. C., & Burke, K. Rate and communication. *Speech Monographs,* 1959, *26,* 229-232.

Diehl, C. F., White, R. C., & Satz, P. H. Pitch change and comprehension. *Speech Monographs,* 1961, *28,* 65-68.

Dittmann, A. T. *Interpersonal messages of emotion.* New York: Springer, 1972.

Ekman, P., & Friesen, W. Nonverbal leakage and clues to deception. *Psychiatry,* 1969, *32,* 88-106.

Eysenck, M. W. Levels of processing: A critique. *British Journal of Psychology,* 1978, *69,* 157-169.

Fairbanks, G., Guttman, N., & Miron, M. S. Auditory comprehension in relation to listening rate and selective verbal redundancy. *Journal of Speech and Hearing Disorders,* 1957, *22,* 23-32. (a)

Fairbanks, G., Guttman; N., & Miron, M. S. Auditory comprehension of repeated high speed messages. *Journal of Speech and Hearing Disorders,* 1957, *22,* 20-22. (b)

Flexser, A., & Tulving, E. Retrieval independence in recognition and recall. *Psychological Review,* 1978, *85,* 153-171.

Foulke, E., & Sticht, T. G. Review of research on the intelligibility and comprehension of accelerated speech. *Psychological Bulletin,* 1969, *72,* 50-62.

Freedman, M. The analysis of movement behavior during the clinical interview. In A. Siegman & B. Pope (Eds.), *Studies in Dyadic Communication.* New York: Pergamon Press, 1972.

Gehring, R. E., Toglia, M. P., & Kimble, G. A. Recognition memory for words and pictures at short and long retention intervals. *Memory and Cognition,* 1976, *4,* 256-260.

Graham, A., & Argyle, M. A cross-cultural study of the communication of extraverbal meanings in gestures. *International Journal of Psychology,* 1975, *1,* 21-28.

Harper, R. G., Wiens, A. M., & Matarazzo, J. D. *Nonverbal communication: The state of the art.* New York: John Wiley, 1978.

Hastie, R. Memory for behavioral information that confirms or contradicts a personality impression. In R. Hastie, T. Ostrom, E. Ebbesen, R. Wyer, D. Hamilton, & D. Carlston (Eds.), *Person memory: The cognitive basis of social perception.* Hillsdale, NJ: Lawrence Erlbaum, 1980.

Hastie, R., & Carlston, D. Theoretical issues in person memory. In R. Hastie, T. Ostrom, E. Ebbesen, R. Wyer, D. Hamilton, & D. Carlston (Eds.), *Person memory: The cognitive basis of social perception.* Hillsdale, NJ: Lawrence Erlbaum, 1980.

Hewes, D., & Planalp, S. "There is nothing as useful as a good theory . . . ": The influence of social knowledge on interpersonal communication. In C. Berger & M. Roloff, *Social cognition.* Beverly Hills, CA: Sage, in press.

Hyde, T. S., & Jenkins, J. J. Recall for words as a function of semantic, graphic and syntactic orienting tasks. *Journal of Verbal Learning and Verbal Behavior,* 1973, *12,* 471-480.

Kendon, A. Movement coordination in social interaction: Some examples described. *Acta Psychologica,* 1970, *32,* 100-125.

Kirsner, J, An analysis of the visual component in recognition memory for verbal stimuli. *Memory and Cognition.* 1973, *1,* 449-453.

Knapp, M. L. *Nonverbal communication in human interaction.* New York: Holt, 1978.

Light, L., Kimble, G., & Pellegrino, J. Comments on episodic memory: When recognition fails. *Journal of Experimental Psychology: General,* 1975, *104,* 30-36.

Lindsay, P. H., & Norman, D. A. *Human information processing.* New York: Academic Press, 1972.

Markel, N. Coverbal behavior associated with conversation turns. In A. Kendon, R. Harris, & M. R. Key (Eds.), *Organization of behavior in face-to-face interaction.* The Hague: Mouton, 1975.

McCall, G. & Simmons, J. L. *Identities and interactions* (revised edition). New York: Free Press, 1978.

McMahan, E. M. Nonverbal communication as a function of attribution in impression formation. *Communication Monographs,* 1976, *43,* 287-294.

Mehrabian, A. When are feelings communicated inconsistently? *Journal of Experimental Research in Personality,* 1970, *4,* 198-212,

Mehrabain, A., & Ferris, S. R. Inference of attitudes from nonverbal communication in two channels. *Journal of Consulting Psychology,* 1967, *31,* 248-252.

Mehrabian, A., & Wiener, M. Decoding of inconsistent communications. *Journal of Personality and Social Psychology,* 1967, *6,* 109-114.

Mehrabian, A., & Williams, M. Nonverbal concomitants of perceived and intended persuasiveness. *Journal of Personality and Social Psychology,* 1969, *13,* 37-58.

Miller, G. A., Heise, G. A., & Lichten, W. The intelligibility of speech as a function of the context of the test materials. *Journal of Experimental Psychology,* 1951, *41,* 329-335.

Miller, G. A., & Johnson-Laird, P. *Language and perception.* Cambridge: Cambridge University Press, 1976.

Nisbett, R., & Ross, L. *Human inference: Strategies and shortcomings of social judgment.* Englewood Cliffs, NJ: Prentice-Hall, 1980.

Norman, D. A. & Rumelhart, D. *Explorations in cognition.* San Francisco: W. H. Freeman, 1975.

Orr, D. B. Time compressed speech — a perspective. *Journal of Communication*, 1968, *18*, 288-292.
Ortony, A. Remembering, understanding and representation. *Cognitive Science*, 1978, *2*, 53-69.
Paivio, A. *Imagery and verbal processes*. New York: Holt, 1971.
Palmer, S. E. The effects of contextual scenes on the identification of objects. *Memory and Cognition*, 1975, *3* (5), 519-526.
Planalp, S., & Hewes, D. A cognitive approach to communication theory: Cogito ergo dico? In M. Burgoon (Ed.), *Communication yearbook 5*. New Brunswick, NJ: Transaction, 1981.
Planalp, S., & Tracy, K. Not to change the topic but: A cognitive approach to the management of conversation. In D. Nimmo (Ed.), *Communication yearbook 4*. New Brunswick, NJ: Transaction, 1980.
Quillian, M. R. Semantic memory. In M. L. Minsky (Ed.), *Semantic information processing*. Cambridge: MIT Press, 1968.
Rogers, W. T. The contribution of kinesic illustrators toward the comprehension of verbal behavior within utterances. *Human Communication Research*, 1978, *5*, 54-62.
Rosenberg, S., & Sedlak, A. Structural representations of implicit personality theory. In L. Berkowitz (Ed.), *Advances in experimental social psychology* (Vol. 6). New York: Academic Press, 1972.
Rosenthal, R., Hall, J. A., DiMatteo, M. R., Rogers, P. L., & Archer, D. *Sensitivity to nonverbal communication: The PONS test*. Baltimore: Johns Hopkins University Press, 1979.
Rothkopf, E. Z. Incidental memory for location of information in text. *Journal of Verbal Learning and Verbal Behavior*, 1971, *10*, 608-613.
Rumelhart, D. *Introduction to human information processing*. New York: John Wiley, 1977.
Rumelhart, D., Lindsay, P. H., & Norman, D. A. A process model for long-term memory. In E. Tulving & W. Donaldson (Eds.), *Organization of memory*. New York: Academic Press, 1972.
Shepard, R. N. Recognition memory for words, sentences and pictures. *Journal of Verbal Learning and Verbal Behavior*, 1967, *6*, 156-163.
Standing, L. Conezio, J., & Haber, R. N. Perception and memory for pictures: Single-trial learning of 2500 visual stimuli. *Psychonomic Science*, 1970, *19*, 73-74.
Tulving, E., & Gold, C. Stimulus information and contextual information as determinants of tachistoscopic recognition of words. *Journal of Experimental Psychology*, 1963, *66*, 319-327.
Tulving, E., & Thomson, D. Encoding specificity and retrieval processes in episodic memory. *Psychological Review*, 1973, *80*, 352-373.
Watkins, M., Ho, E., & Tulving, E. Context effects in recognition memory for faces. *Journal of Verbal Learning and Verbal Behavior*, 1976, *15*, 505-517.
Watkins, M. J., & Tulving, E. Episodic memory: When recognition fails. *Journal of Experimental Psychology: General*, 1975, *103*, 5-29.
Whiting, G. *Comprehension and metaphor*. Paper presented at the annual conference of the Speech Communication Association Convention, 1975.
Woodall, W. G. *The effects of nonverbal synchronization and vocal rate on receiver attention, comprehension and yielding*. Paper delivered at the Eastern States Communication Association, May 1979.
Woodall, W. G., & Burgoon, J. K. The effects of nonverbal synchrony on message comprehension and persuasiveness. *Journal of Nonverbal Behavior*, 1981, *5*, 207-223.
Woodall, W. G., Davis, D. K., & Sahin, H. *From the boob tube to the black box: Televised news comprehension from an information processing view*. Paper presented at the annual convention of the Association for Education in Journalism, East Lansing, 1981.
Woodall, W. G., & Folger, J. P. Encoding specificity and nonverbal cue context: An expansion of episodic memory research. *Communication Monographs*, 1981, *49*, 39-53.

COMMUNICATION REVIEWS AND COMMENTARIES

4 ● Communication Between Handicapped and Nonhandicapped Persons: Toward a Deductive Theory

GORDON L. DAHNKE
Universidad Anáhuac, Mexico City

A RECENT survey conducted by the President's Committee on Employment of the Handicapped indicates that one in eleven Americans has some disability. These persons constitute a minority group that is subject to adverse educational, economic, and employment discrimination. A significant segment of this minority is involuntarily relegated to a dependency role in which they become wards of the state. The plight of the handicapped is exacerbated by attitudinal factors that impede meaningful social discourse with nonhandicapped persons, and communication problems tend to restrict their complete integration into the productive mainstream of society.

Recent literature addressing problems encountered by physically handicapped persons (e.g., Goffman, 1963; Comer & Piliavin, 1975; Park, 1975) differentiates physical and psychological barriers that inhibit such individuals during interactions with nonhandicapped persons. Physical barriers such as architectural impediments are relatively easy to remove. Psychological barriers may arise in (1) the handicapped person's perception of him- or herself, (2) the handicapped person's perception of nonhandicapped counterparts, and (3) the nonhandicapped person's perception of the handicapped. These mutual perceptions appear to influence the manner in which handicapped and nonhandicapped persons interact (Goffman, 1963). Their interactions may, in turn, reinforce or alter existing attitudes of both parties. Similar effects may also accrue from a decision not to interact.

Correspondence and requests for reprints: Gordon L. Dahnke, 4812 Nakoma Drive, Okemos, MI 48864.

Two general research foci are apparent in the literature: (1) assessment of attitudes held by each group of persons and (2) investigation of the interaction process between these two types. Review of the literature suggests that considerable attention has been devoted to the former issue. For example, extensive attitudinal studies by Siller, Chipman, Ferguson, and Vann (1967) conclude that current attitudes toward handicapped persons contribute to a serious problem involving "strain in social interaction" during face-to-face encounters. The strain may result from both participants being uncertain about the most appropriate communication strategy to employ in order to maximize the quality of their interactions. The implication of this research is that "reduction of the 'sticky' problems in initial and subsequent encounters would be a major help in reducing anxiety about dealing with the handicapped" (Siller et al., 1967, p. 65).

Regarding the interaction process more limited research to date indicates that during interactions with the handicapped, nonhandicapped persons tend to (1) increase their physical distance (Kleck, 1969; Worthington, 1974); (2) terminate the interaction more quickly and exhibit less variance in verbal behavior (Kleck, Ono, & Hastorf, 1966); (3) demonstrate greater motoric inhibition — that is, restrict their nonverbal behavior (Kleck, 1968); and (4) exhibit more anxiety (Marinelli & Kelz, 1973; Marinelli, 1974). Furthermore, nonhandicapped individuals report more emotional discomfort following interaction (Kleck, 1966).

Four of eleven different areas suggested for future research by Richardson (1976) concern the problem of strain between handicapped and nonhandicapped persons during social interaction. Specifically, little is known about factors influencing various behavioral distortions which develop on the part of both participants during such interactions. Moreover, it is intuitively reasonable to expect that identification of specific anxiety-producing (or anxiety-reducing) communication behavior which may originate with either party would be a significant first step toward elimination of these problematic distortions. Siller et al. (1967) report anecdotal evidence indicating the heuristic promise of this approach.

Among the host of relevant variables, few communication scholars will deny that interpersonal transactions largely depend on the effectiveness of verbal/nonverbal cues exchanged. Furthermore, certain nonverbal cues (e.g., illustrators, regulators, and affect displays) are believed to be closely associated with, and auxiliary to, linguistic behavior (Harrison, 1974; Ekman & Friesen, 1969). Under normal circumstances these nonverbal counterparts of language may serve to repeat, substitute for, complement, accentuate, contradict, or regulate verbal communication (Burgoon & Saine, 1978). Assuming their validity in this context, these assertions have serious implications for physically handicapped persons who may also be communicatively handicapped particularly in the nonverbal realm — that is, they may be unable to encode appropriate nonverbal cues effectively as a result of impairment. Consequently, handicapped persons with normal verbal capabilities may frequently display nonverbal behaviors that are perceived to be incongruous with their verbal communication. Such verbal versus nonverbal discrepancies, as well as the sheer absence of supporting nonverbal cues in some instances, may be major determinants of communication problems arising when handicapped and nonhandicapped persons interact.

Previous research indicates that visible impairments per se tend to provoke anxious reactions from nonhandicapped interactants (Marinelli & Kelz, 1973; Marinelli, 1974). This anxiety may be manifest via the verbal (Dibner, 1956) or the nonverbal (Mehrabian, 1969) channel of communication. For example, the nonhandicapped individual may exhibit verbal nonfluencies, nervous fidgeting, anxious facial affects, and restricted body movements.

Given the transactional nature of human communication, anxiety revealing cues and/or discrepant verbal/nonverbal messages emitted by either interactant may be perceived as betraying the source's ambivalent emotional state, negative social evaluations, or communicative uncertainty toward the counterpart. In turn, these perceptions are expected to affect the level of ambivalence, social evaluation, and uncertainty experienced by the counterpart and thus to elicit a similar affect-revealing response. Ongoing transactions of this type may result in an escalation process that continues until a termination threshold has been reached by one or both interactants.

Theoretically, such an escalation process provides an explanation reasonably consistent with several previous findings (e.g., Kleck et al., 1966; Kleck, 1968, 1969; Worthington, 1974; Marinelli, 1974). Obviously this line of reasoning assumes, for example, that discrepant verbal/nonverbal behaviors are perceived and interpreted by both participants in the general manner described above. It further suggests that the exhibition of negative or ambiguous communicative behaviors is more probable, at an accelerated pace, in interactions with handicapped persons who are restricted in their ability to encode nonverbal cues.

As a result of atypically high uncertainty, it is also conceivable that handicapped and nonhandicapped interactants tend to monitor the nonverbal channel more intensely than the verbal, in order to assess the emotional states of the counterpart. While there is general support for the dominant impact of nonverbal information, particularly when discrepant messages occur simultaneously (e.g., Argyle, Alkema, & Gilmour, 1971; Fujimoto, 1971; McMahan, 1976), nonverbal messages are not always preeminent. Situational factors, personality types, and the type and degree of message components apparently tend to complicate this issue (e.g., Fujimoto, 1971; Shapiro, 1968; VandeCreek & Watkins, 1972).

To date, little empirical research has attempted to determine which major channel exerts the greater impact on transactions of the present type. Knowledge of the verbal/nonverbal relationship and the extent to which these channels differ as salient sources of information would likely prove invaluable for development of effective communication strategies in the context of handicapped/nonhandicapped interactions. More specifically, the ensuing discussion anticipates development and use of such strategies to address the pressing problem of unequal employment opportunities for handicapped persons.

Two methodological impulses that guided the writing of this chapter deserve comment. First, it should not be necessary to argue the general need for substantive, deductive theory in our discipline — certainly not in this area. Social scientists are well aware that facts do not explain themselves. If observations are to be interpretable, sound theoretical information is necessary (Heise, 1975). Moreover, there is an obvious need for a *testable* theory which is sufficiently complex to provide informative insights that supersede those gleaned from common sense and practical experience. Hence, this chapter represents an initial attempt to build theory defined as a set of interrelated "systematically organized, lawlike propositions" that can be supported or falsified via empirical evidence (Zetterberg, 1965, p. 22).

Second, the attempt to build a sufficiently complex yet testable, deductive theory poses a serious problem, particularly in the context of a young science. To develop such a theory, the builder must begin with relatively simple sets of relationships that serve as first approximations of deductive theory. Typically, the model includes only a few variables (at best) and is far too simple to represent the complexities of the real world under study. Moreover, at this stage it is extremely difficult not to prioritize those variables and relationships that are more easily observed or tend to "fit" conveniently into the simple theory while eliminating relevant others that do not (Blalock, 1969). The theoretical statement to follow attempts a happy medium between the goals of complexity and testability. It is a first approximation of deductive theory that invites reformulation toward more realistic representations of the real world via inductive research processes.

Given prior seminal ideas, the subsequent theoretic formulation addresses this general research question:

In an initial employment interview, what effects do varying levels of verbal and nonverbal communication, emitted simultaneously by handicapped interviewees, have on the nonhandicapped interviewer's (1) communicative uncertainty, (2) state anxiety level, (3) interpersonal attraction toward the interviewee, (4) perception of the interviewee's state anxiety level, and (5) perception of the interviewee's interpersonal attraction toward the interviewer?

While present interests focus on an employment interview context, the theoretical statement developed to address this question is sufficiently general to apply to any initial encounter between handicapped and nonhandicapped persons.

A word about the road ahead is in order. Theorists and researchers alike may well view the circuitous itinerary of this essay with a jaundiced eye. Its organization was simply dictated by mental processes through which I was pressed, in reverse order. I tried to begin, as I suspect rookie theorists often do, at the end of the matter — that is, formulating defensible propositions that relate relevant variables. But how does one decide from the legions in our literature which are relevant and which are defensible? It depends, at least in part, on how explicitly we answer prior conceptual questions. For example, what specific class of events qualifies for inclusion under labels such as "verbal" and "nonverbal communication"? In turn, that depends on how clearly we distinguish communication per se from other forms of behavior.

The attitude of many researchers toward theoretical issues "is not unlike the attitude of most citizens toward the sewage system. They know it is there, they assume that it works, and they question the good sense of anyone who goes poking around in it" (McClelland, 1975, p. 18). Yet, however unconsciously, most of us do poke around in theoretical areas, by bemoaning the dearth of competent research, if in no other sense. Our explanations for this sad state of affairs usually boil down to blatant defects in others' theory or method. The divorce of these two bedfellows is, of course, still pending.

In sum, it is necessary to define the domain and relevant subcategories within which a given theory is designed to operate. Hence, Part I specifies four types of verbal/nonverbal acts which circumscribe the subject matter of subsequent theoretical statements. This section represents a serious attempt to distinguish communication from other types of human behavior. Part II moves to a lower level of abstraction in an effort to reduce the number of relevant variables (within the specified domain) based on prior research. Factor-analytic studies are reviewed to identify those underlying referent behaviors known, on existing empirical evidence, to determine social interaction. This review, in effect, tells us where to place our theoretical bets in selecting the relevant independent variable(s).

Part III explicates, and provides the rationale for adopting, an uncertainty reduction paradigm based on current theoretical developments in interpersonal communication. Adoption of this perspective recommends the uncertainty concept as a promising, primary dependent variable. Axiomatic propositions are then formulated in light of previous research. Finally, in Part IV a limited number of possible theorems are deduced from prior axioms.

I. THE DOMAIN

This discourse presupposes an interdependent relationship between verbal and nonverbal components in ordinary human communication. It does not imply a subordinate role for either channel; nor does it deny that each can function effectively alone. Their ordinary interdependence does imply that selection of appropriate variables for comparison across the two channels will depend partly on a conceptual view of communication theoretically capable of consistent application in both verbal and nonverbal areas.

Communication per se, in distinction from other human behavior, minimally requires (1) a socially shared signal system — that is, a code; (2) an encoder actively making some experience public via that code; and (3) a decoder able to respond systematically to the same code (Wiener, Devoe, Rubinow, & Geller, 1972; Burgoon & Saine, 1978). While this definition provides a useful point of departure, it leaves several key questions unanswered, particularly in the nonverbal realm.

First there is the *sign* versus *symbol* issue. For some scholars signs are distinguished as a natural extension of the events they herald. Thus, the occurrence of cumulus clouds is considered a sign of impending rain, or a flushed face may naturally signal an underlying emotional state. On the other hand, symbols have arbitrarily assigned, socially shared, referent meanings. While verbal symbols such as "cumulus cloud" are clearly understood by English speakers, their association with the real event is neither natural nor necessary. Nonverbal symbols are believed to serve essentially the same communicative function. Although complex differences between verbal/nonverbal systems are becoming increasingly apparent, these distinctions are not relevant here.

Another approach allows the term "sign" to represent any attribute or human behavior from which an observer can infer some significance or glean any information about the source. Presumably, "sign" may then include such diverse and idiosyncratic behaviors as lint-picking, head-scratching, or weight-watching activity. The nonverbal literature is replete with similar examples. Signs, in this latter sense, do not qualify as communicative events by present definition. While they may be informative in some broad sense, idiosyncratic behaviors and more general stimuli serving only as a basis for inference are excluded here. However, the pathological interest of this chapter recommends inclusion of nonverbal signs as well as symbols which meet either of two criteria: (1) natural behaviors that reflect underlying emotional states, provided they are known to bear socially shared meanings, and (2) learned behaviors that reflect the enculturation process and are known to bear socially shared referent meanings.

Second, *intentionality* in the nonverbal area is equally problematic. Who decides what is intentional and the required level of consciousness involved are closely related, complicating issues. Several prominent investigators (e.g., Ekman & Friesen, 1969; Wiener et al., 1972) insist on conscious intent by the message source as a prerequisite for communicative events. Others are willing to relax this stipulation to include messages that are perceived as intentional by either the receiver, an outside observer, or the source (Miller & Steinberg, 1975). Still others accept an even broader view involving messages that are either (1) subconsciously or unintentionally sent, if interpreted as intentional by any observer, or (2) subconsciously received by an observer, if consciously and intentionally sent (Burgoon & Saine, 1978).

This already complex issue is exacerbated in the context of interactions with handicapped persons who may be unable, due to physical impairment, to encode their intentions appropriately via the nonverbal stream. Previous research suggests the extraordinarily high information potential of affect-revealing cues when handicapped/nonhandicapped persons interact. Nonverbal signs of this type, whether natural or learned, which may occur at a relatively low level of awareness are germane to present concerns.

The following discussion is a modest attempt to avoid some of the confusion extant in nonverbal literature by establishing clear conceptual parameters for the class of events under study here and the terminology used to describe it.

Wiener et al. (1972) expose conceptual problems associated with the now prevalent decoding perspective and argue convincingly for greater emphasis on the encoding subject in current conceptualizations of nonverbal communication. In that regard, the authors offer a useful distinction between informative *nonverbal behavior,* which may be emitted at a relatively low level of awareness, and *nonverbal communication,* which they define as a more distinctly intentional act by the message source.

Although use of the term *"behavior"* is eventually eliminated as a label for informative events here, the prior conceptual distinction proposed by Wiener et al. (1972) suggests that theory construction involving both verbal and nonverbal communication might ideally begin at a higher level of abstraction, using a larger generic category that will allow consistent classification of informative events across the two channels. That class of events, to be defined momentarily, is labeled "information transfer." The more familiar term, "information exchange," would have been preferred. However, as the introductory comments warn, it is imperative to begin with simple models. The term "exchange" implies a dynamic, nonrecursive process with which the present formulation is not designed to deal. The genre labeled "information transfer" here will require careful definition.

The concept "information" is drawn from general information theory. It is defined as any observation, perception, or cognition that reduces uncertainty for the observer. A more thorough explication of this notion is provided later. Basically, uncertainty arises in a communication context when an interactant is confronted with several alternatives, either for encoding or decoding a message, and does not know which to choose. Information eliminates alternatives from the response field, reducing the probability of error proportionately and, thus, the level of uncertainty associated with the choice. For present purposes, information also necessarily involves a socially shared set of referent meanings. That is, uncertainty-reducing behaviors based on rules or referent meanings unique to a specific interacting dyad do not qualify as informative actions by this definition.

The term "transfer" refers to mediated or face-to-face transmission of signs or symbols, with some awareness, from a human source to a human receiver. Consistent with the recursive communication model (see Figure 4.1) under consideration here, transfer implies only a one-way flow of signs or symbols from source to receiver at a single point in time.

Information transfer, then, minimally requires a source manipulating signs or symbols with socially shared referent meanings in the presence of an interacting receiver. That is, information associated with the signs and symbols must be common to some specifiable set of individuals who systematically interpret them in a similar manner (Ekman & Friesen, 1969). Hence, the observation, perception, or cognition of these signs and/or symbols must be informative—that is, they must reduce the interacting receiver's uncertainity.

As suggested earlier, an informative act implies some decoded meaning. It does not mean that the act of the source in question was intended to convey any information at all, although it does in fact do so. The source must, however, be aware that he or she has performed the act. This raises a critical distinction between intentionality and awareness, most germane to the classification of informative acts to be proposed below.

Much of the ensuing discussion relies largely on the seminal work of Ekman and Friesen (1969), who attempted to order the nebulous realm of nonverbal communication. In order to avoid a potentially unproductive entrenchment in problematic issues involving intentionality, the authors simply argue that a source can be aware of his or her nonverbal behavior whether or not he or she engages in the act with intent to communicate a specific message. In support of this contention, the following definitions are provided. *Awareness* or internal feedback refers to the person's knowledge that he or she is engaging in a particular nonverbal act at the moment it is done, or the ability to recall with ease what he or she has done (1969, p. 53). Relevant examples are provided later. *Intentionality* implies deliberate use of a nonverbal act to communicate a specific message. This definition does not include behavior considered subconsciously intended. Intentional nonverbal acts must be within awareness and the source must purport to send a message via those acts (1969, pp. 53-54).

Obviously, prior definitions and distinctions do not solve all problems associated with levels of intentionality, particularly with respect to operationalization in the nonverbal realm. Grey areas remain between those nonverbal acts which are clearly intentional and those which lie somewhere within the source's stream of awareness but fall short of a conscious effort to communicate. One example is the flushed face. Neither has the line been definitively drawn between acts that occur within and those that occur without awareness. I contend that these modest conceptual beginnings will enable a clear identification of many, though by no means all, informative nonverbal acts.

Thus far discussion has necessarily focused primarily on conceptual problems arising in the nonverbal area. My intent from the outset was to provide a set of parameters sufficiently general to be applied with relative consistency to the verbal domain as well. Given prior criteria, it seems intuitively reasonable to subsume at least four types of informative events under the conceptual umbrella labeled "information transfer": (1) verbal communication, (2) informative verbal acts, (3) nonverbal communication, and (4) informative nonverbal acts. These four categories will be defined primarily in terms of the previous intentionality/awareness distinction and the type of information conveyed in each case. Two additional types, verbal and nonverbal behavior, will be defined in general terms to clarify their exclusion via parameters established for the domain of events being described.

Verbal communication is defined as use of an elaborate code system or language by which an encoding source is actively and with deliberate intent attempting to make his or her experience known to some other person(s). Use of a code system means manipulation of written or spoken word symbols with arbitrarily assigned, socially shared meanings. It is assumed that these symbols are addressed to receivers who are privy to the code system and thus able systematically to interpret them.

Informative verbal acts refer to implicit characteristics exhibited by a source in the process of encoding a verbal message. They support and contribute to, but do not independently constitute, verbal communication by our definition. While these implicit dimensions of the encoded message are ordinarily produced without deliberate intent to inform, the source is usually aware of his or her actions at the moment of execution or is able to recall them at a later time. Verbal immediacy (Wiener & Mehrabian, 1968) illustrates the type of implicit verbal characteristics to which this category refers; for example systematic use of the first person plural pronoun "we" as opposed to "you and I." Brief vocalizations expressing agreement or understanding (e.g., "uh-huh," "hmm"), called "vocal reinforcers" (Mehrabian, 1971a), provide another example. Limited evidence to date suggests that verbal characteristics of this type are informative regarding attitudes or emotional states of the source (e.g., Mehrabian, 1971a; Mehrabian & Ksionzky, 1972).

Similar to its verbal counterpart, *nonverbal communication* involves deliberate use of an elaborate code that functions much the same as any ordinary language system. Accordingly, the more rigorous definition adopted here restricts nonverbal communication to highly stylized gestural movements called "emblems" (Ekman & Friesen, 1969). Emblems are defined as "those nonverbal acts which have a direct verbal translation or dictionary definition, usually consisting of a word or two, or perhaps a phrase. This verbal definition or translation of the emblem is well known by all members of a group, class or culture" (1969, p. 63). These gestures may serve to repeat, substitute for, or contradict some part of the accompanying verbal message.

Emblems are used in an intentional effort to communicate. The source knows when he or she is using an emblem, can repeat it if asked to do so, and will accept communicative responsibility for it. Many emblems are arbitrarily coded, such as the sign language used by the deaf. Others are iconically coded (visually resembling their meaning), as illustrated in signal systems used by officials during sports events. While emblems may be exhibited in any area of the body, they are expressed primarily via the hands and face in this culture. The projected thumb of a hitchhiker is a familiar example of the former.

Informative nonverbal acts have several characteristics in common with their verbal couterparts. They are intrinsically related to the concomitant verbal message, are emitted quite spontaneously, and ordinarily occur within the source's awareness. Similarly, they support and contribute to, but do not ordinarily constitute, nonverbal communication. This class of events includes use of three additional gesture types described by Ekman and Friesen (1969): illustrators, affect displays, and regulators. In common with all informative acts previously defined, these nonverbal signs have agreed-upon, decoded meanings that elicit similar interpretations from a specifiable set of observers.

Illustrators are defined as body movements which directly accompany and serve to illustrate what is being said verbally — for example, gestures which (1) time out, accent, or emphasize a particular word or phrase; (2) sketch a path or direction of thought; (3) point to a present object; (4) depict a spatial relationship; or (5) draw a picture of the referent. Illustrators augment the verbal band "on a moment-to-moment basis; they are directly tied to content, inflection, loudness, etc." (1969, p. 69).

Affect displays are movements which reveal the state of one's emotions. While some bodily motions such as trembling are considered affective, the site of these nonverbal acts is more specifically the face. Distinctive movements of facial muscles are generally associated with the primary affects believed to be universal: happiness, surprise, fear, sadness, anger, disgust, and interest (e.g., Tomkins, 1962, 1963; Tomkins & McCarter, 1964; Ekman & Friesen, 1967; Frijda & Philipszoon, 1963; Izard, 1968). These affective states are easily distinguished by observers in this culture; hence, it is assumed that they bear socially shared, decoded meanings. Affect displays may accompany use of the verbal channel or they may meaningfully occur alone. The former usage is of central concern here.

Regulators are nonverbal acts used to maintain or regulate the back-and-forth flow of speaking/listening behavior between two or more interactants. They indicate that the speaker should continue, repeat, elaborate, increase speech rate, give up the floor, and so on. Regulators may also signal the listener to give special attention, wait, or assume the encoding role.

The most common regulator is the head nod; others include eye contact, slight movements forward, small postural shifts, and eyebrow raising. Regulators carry no message content independent of the verbal conversation. Rather, they convey control messages necessary for pacing the exchange of information via the verbal band (Ekman & Friesen, 1969).

Thus I have defined illustrators, affect displays, and regulators in terms of their primary functions for the purpose of setting some parameters on the class of events termed "informative nonverbal acts." These subcategories can, and likely do, overlap in actual conversation. Affect displays, for example, can also serve as regulators. As Mahl (1966) has suggested, the fact that a particular nonverbal act may exert some influence on the verbal flow does not mean that regulation is its sole or even primary purpose. Hence, the term "regulator" is reserved here for those behaviors that do not conceptually fit into other categories, such as illustrators or affect displays. The latter categories were also defined in terms of their major functions. In short, regulators appear only to regulate and tend to occur at a relatively low level of awareness.

In sum, prior discourse defines the domain of events with which subsequent theoretic statements are concerned. Four types of action were subsumed under the rubric of information transfer: verbal communication informative verbal acts, nonverbal communication, and informative nonverbal acts. This choice of nomenclature deliberately reserves the term "behavior" for reference to verbal/nonverbal actions that are uninformative by prior definition.

Verbal behavior, as opposed to communicative/informative verbal acts, will refer to unintentional linguistic innovations (Sturtevant, 1947) — that is, articulatory or performance errors that do not contribute to, and may actually inhibit, information exchange. Boomer and Laver provide a useful definition in this regard: "A slip of the tongue . . . is an involuntary deviation in performance from the speaker's current phonological, grammatical or lexical intention" (1968, p. 4). Behaviors of this type include, for example, nonfluencies such as meaningless combinations of phonemes or morphemes that occur during a lapse in the encoding process, whole words of semantic context, repetition of syllables, spoonerisms, omissions, and mispronunciations. While these behaviors may occur within the encoder's awareness, they fail to meet the criterion of agreed-upon decoded meaning.

Similarly, *nonverbal behavior,* as opposed to communicative/informative nonverbal acts, will refer to what appear (on present knowledge) to be more random, idiosyncratic movements which specific individuals develop over time. The conceptualization of *adaptors* provided by Ekman and Friesen serves well as a general description of the type of activity intended here. Adaptors are believed to be movements learned in childhood as part of adaptive efforts to satisfy bodily needs, manage emotions, learn instrumental activities, or develop and maintain prototypical interpersonal contacts. While adaptors represent behaviors first learned "as part of a total adaptive pattern where the goal of the activity was obvious, when these actions are emitted by the adult, particularly during social conversation, only a fragment of the original adaptive behavior is seen. These fragments or reductions of previously learned adaptive acts are maintained by habit. . . . By this reasoning, adaptors when emitted by the adult are habitual, not intended to transmit a message, and usually without awareness" (1969, pp. 84-85).

Examples of this behavioral type are hand-to-face (or head) movements such as grooming the hair with one's hands in public, wiping the lips with the tongue or hands, picking or scratching the scalp, and wiping the brow or nose with the back of the hand. Restless movements such as bouncing the lower leg and foot in a seated position also exemplify this category. While these movements on occasion can provide a basis for attitudinal inferences, Ekman and Friesen argue that their interpretation "is difficult, often speculative and uncertain" (1969, p. 87).

II. BEHAVIORAL DETERMINANTS OF SOCIAL INTERACTION

This section reviews basic research in pursuit of heuristically promising independent variables. Social intercourse in general has been the subject of considerable study. Investigation of this area has had at least two emphases: (1) description and measurement of specific behaviors that determine social interaction, and (2) examination of effects situational and individual differences may have on these behaviors (Mehrabian & Ksionzky, 1972). This essay relies on findings in the former area to develop a theory of the latter type.

Prior research repeatedly demonstrates that two or three basic factors can be used to describe and measure social interaction. Several studies using Bales's (1950) Interaction Process Analysis (e.g., Carter, 1954; Couch, 1960; Bales, 1950, 1968) consistently produced three underlying dimensions identified as affection (positive/negative evaluation), power, and contribution to group tasks. Others have obtained two major factors (e.g., Borgatta, 1962): sociability, similar to affection, and assertiveness relating to power.

Mehrabian and Ksionzky (1972) used twenty-six reliably scored verbal/nonverbal cues with previously demonstrated social significance (cf. Mehrabian, 1972a) to measure behaviors of participants in live interaction. Factor analysis of their observations yielded a six-factor solution: (1) affiliative behavior, related to the affection factor above; (2) responsiveness, an index of activity or reaction to the counterpart; (3) relaxation, believed to imply dominance and thus related to the power factor identified earlier; (4) ingratiation; (5) distress or active avoidance; and (6) intimate position, an index of physical proximity. The authors note that the first three factors are most important in characterizing social interaction.

The foregoing research confirmed original factor-analytic work by Williams and Sundene (1965) and Osgood (1966) which identified essentially the same three factors as major referents of nonverbal communication. Similar analyses (Osgood, Suci, & Tannenbaum, 1957; Snider & Osgood, 1969) on verbal cues using semantic differential scales likewise obtained factors labeled "evaluation" (liking or preference), "dominance" (power), and "activity" (responsiveness). Mehrabian (1972b) used these three referent meanings to characterize nonverbal comminication and demonstrated their relevance across a wide range of social situations.

An early review (Foa, 1961) of factor-analytic studies in this area indicated that two factors consistently emerge: love-hostility and dominance-submission. In a therapeutic context, Lorr and Suziedelis (1969) factor analyzed ratings of social behavior across patient/normal groups; the resulting structure included essentially the same two factors—sociability (or affiliation) and control (or power). Cross-cultural factor-analytic studies on group behavior of children (Longabaugh, 1966) and role perceptions, behavioral intentions, and perceptions of social behavior (Triandis, Vassiliou, & Nassiakou, 1968) have produced comparable results.

Summarily, research attempting to characterize social interaction via factor-analytic techniques indicates that three factors are consistently identified: *affiliation, potency* (or status), and *responsiveness*. The first factor, typically identified as affiliation (sociability, love-hostility, or affection), appears more tentatively to be the dominant dimension across a variety of social settings.

Effects of situational and personality correlates on the characteristic dimensions of social interaction reported in factor-analytic research have been examined less extensively. Two experiments in this area (Mehrabian, 1971a; Mehrabian & Ksionzky, 1972) have had considerable influence on the present work. These studies, based on a model of affiliative behavior by Mehrabian and Ksionzky (1970), were primarily designed to explore effects of social reinforcement and individual differences on nonverbal and implicit verbal behaviors exhibited by pairs of strangers interacting in a waiting situation. Their proposed model hypothesized that affiliation increases as a function of positive (and decreases as a function of negative) reinforcement by an interacting counterpart. The main experimental factors introduced in both studies were (1) degree of positive reinforcement and (2) degree of negative reinforcement received prior to or during interaction. The second, more comprehensive study introduced four levels of reinforcement (positive, negative, mixed, and neutral) and included anticipated cooperation versus competition with the target person as an additional independent variable. Five individual difference variables — affiliative tendency, sensitivity to rejection, achieving tendency, sex, and birth order — were measured by questionnaire.

Dependent measures, taken on each subject during spontaneous interactions with an experimental confederate, were twenty-six nonverbal/implicit verbal behaviors drawn from prior factor-analytic research. Scoring criteria for each dependent measure are reported in Mehrabian (1972b, Appendix A). The observations were factor analyzed, and a principal component solution yielded the following six factors: affiliative behavior, responsiveness, relaxation, ingratiation, distress, and intimacy. Table 4.1 reports specific behaviors subsumed under the first factor, which is the most relevant here. Variables are listed in order according to the magnitude of their loadings (highest to lowest). Direction of the loading for each variable is also indicated in parentheses.

Table 4.1
Nonverbal and Implicit Verbal Behaviors
Defining Affiliation, a Primary
Dimension of Social Interaction*

FACTOR I: Affiliative Behavior	
Total number of statements per minute	(+)
Number of declarative statements per minute	(+)
Percent duration of eye contact with confederate	(+)
Percent duration of subject's speech	(+)
Percent duration of confederate's speech**	(+)
Positive verbal content	(+)
Head nods per minute	(+)
Hand and arm gestures per minute	(+)
Pleasantness of facial expressions	(+)

*From Mehrabian and Ksionzky (1972, p. 591).
**The only item that did not pertain to subject's behavior.

Additional analyses related each of the six factors (via composite indices for each subject) as dependent measures to the eight independent variables listed above. Significant main effects were found, as expected, for affiliative behavior as a function of affiliative tendency and anticipated cooperation. The direction was positive in both cases. Several significant interaction effects, particularly when positive/negative reinforcements were included, provide refinements on these single-variable relationships.

First, subjects who scored high on the affiliative tendency measure exhibited more affiliation *only* when they did not receive negative reinforcement from the confederate prior to interaction, regardless of whether or not positive evaluations were also involved (i.e., via mixed reinforcements). Second, a significant third-order interaction effect was found in one of the four evaluation conditions. Subjects who received mixed evaluations (i.e., high positive and high negative reinforcements) affiliated significantly less when anticipating competition rather than cooperation.

In sum, these findings were largely consistent with the authors' original model of affiliative behavior. They also support the primacy of affiliation as a basic dimension of social interaction and suggest the following conclusions. First, the Mehrabian and Ksionzky (1970) model provides a useful framework for investigating the special type of interaction at hand. Second, results of that study are intuitively consistent with early research on communication with handicapped persons (e.g., Kleck et al., 1966; Kleck, 1969; Worthington, 1974) and encourage an initial approach to this area focusing primarily on affiliation as a promising source of further insight. Third, the interaction effects reviewed above clearly indicate that mixed or discrepant evaluative cues (emitted by a counterpart via only a single channel) tend to reduce affiliative effort even in relatively "normal" social situations, most notably among persons with strong tendencies to affiliate. It is reasonable, then, to expect that this negative effect will increase if discrepancies in affiliative communication occur across the two major channels when handicapped and nonhandicapped persons interact.

III. THEORETICAL MOORINGS

If the interpretation of empirical data depends on theory (Heise, 1975), it is also the case that sound theory must be grounded in empirical data (Glaser & Strauss, 1967). Typically, the researcher attempts to formulate the best theoretical statement possible in light of existing evidence (Blalock, 1969). It seems reasonable, then, to approach the problem of handicapped/nonhandicapped communication from the vantage point of current theoretical developments and prior research on interpersonal relationships in general. Results of research on the handicapped reviewed earlier (e.g., Kleck, 1966; Marinelli & Kelz, 1973; Marinelli, 1974) suggest that atypically high levels of uncertainty are present when nonhandicapped persons initially interact with the handicapped. Hence, the general uncertainty reduction paradigm outlined below was adopted as the most promising theoretical point of departure.

Human beings have a strong innate need to make sense out of their environment (Heider, 1958). We strive for certainty and have perhaps more tolerance for ignorance than ambiguity. The theoretical perspective to follow rests on the assumption that when unfamiliar persons initially interact, they are primarily concerned to reduce their own uncertainty in order to predict, explain, and ultimately control the effects of their respective communication behaviors (Jones, Kanouse, Kelley, Nisbett, Valins, & Weiner, 1972; Kelley, 1973; Berger & Calabrese, 1975).

Prior to choosing a course of action, interacting persons attempt to predict the most likely alternative among possible responses their counterpart might make (Miller & Steinberg, 1975). This predictive process is conceptually analogous to the strategy-planning forethought of a chess player who anticipates the counterpart's response alternatives before each move. In fact, probable outcomes for several reciprocal moves will likely be predicted in advance. Such predictions are assumed to be more or less certain depending on the amount of relevant information available to the predictor.

Information is defined as any observation, perception, or cognition that reduces uncertainty. Generally, uncertainty arises when one is confronted with several alternatives and does not know which to choose. The level of uncertainty in a given situation is defined by the probability of error inherent in the number of *plausible* and *desirable* options from which one must choose. In theory, information eliminates alternatives from the response field, reducing the probability of error proportionately. Consequently, the level of uncertainty associated with the choice is also reduced. In short, to the extent that one's choice is informed, the number of plausible options is decreased and prediction is made with greater certainty. Information, so defined, is the complement of uncertainty (Krippendorff, 1975) and the stock-in-trade of uncertainty reduction.

Following recent attribution theory, Berger and Calabrese (1975) provide a useful distinction between two types of uncertainty. First, the *proactive type* is associated with prediction as described above; it occurs prior to the actual behavior in question. Proactive uncertainty is a function of the amount of information available to participants during interaction enabling them (1) to predict the most likely response their counterpart may make and (2) to choose an appropriate strategy from their own repertoire so as to maximize likelihood of a desired response (Miller & Steinberg, 1975).

Second, *retroactive uncertainty* is associated with the problem of explaining or interpreting a particular behavior after its occurrence. Several theorists (e.g., Jones et al., 1972; Kelley, 1973) hold that in addition to predicting responsive actions, human interactants are equally concerned to explain or validate social behavior, their own as well as that of others. Typically, a number of plausible attributions can be made from a particular social act. In this regard, Schachter and Burdick (1955) demonstrated that recipients of ambiguous messages tend to engage in intensive social contact for the purpose of reducing uncertainty of this type.

Similarly, humans are often as uncertain about events within themselves as they are about events in their environment. Considerable research on the link between the need for self-evaluation and affiliative behavior has shown that human beings desire to identify or confirm their own reactions to specific situations (e.g., Fromm-Reichman, 1959; Schachter, 1959). This research is supportive of Festinger's (1954) social comparison theory which suggests that persons seek out similar others with whom to confer when they experience high levels of uncertainty regarding the appropriateness of their own behavior and/or their perceptions of a particular situation.

More specifically, retroactive uncertainty is a function of the amount of information available to participants during interaction enabling them (1) to select the most likely explanation for a counterpart's behavior and (2) to identify or confirm their own reactions to that behavior. In addition, information exchange (or transfer, in this context) is regarded as the primary means interacting persons use to minimize the number of alternatives from which they must choose for both predictive and explanatory purposes.

According to Blalock (1969), a deductive theory contains both axioms and theorems. Axioms are those propositions assumed to be true while theorems are logically derived or deduced from the axioms. Moreover, axioms should be causal assertions that are, strictly speaking, "untestable because of the fact that it will never be possible to control for all 'relevant' variables" (1969 p. 11). This is tantamount to saying that axioms should be causal, "lawlike" probability statements for which there is substantial evidence.

By these criteria, the axioms to be proposed momentarily do not qualify this formulation for deductive theory status. It is my judgment that the following propositions should be considered associational, rather than lawlike causal statements, in lieu of additional support. They were formalized in light of the preceding rationale and additional evidence to be cited. Each axiom pertains to initial interaction between strangers and thus assumes a high level of uncertainty at the outset (Lalljee & Cook, 1973).

> *Axiom 1:* As level of information transfer generated by either interactant increases, level of communicative uncertainty experienced by the counterpart will decrease. Conversely, increasing levels of communicative uncertainty experienced by the counterpart will accompany decreasing levels of information transfer generated by either interactant.

Axiom 1 relates the two primitive terms with which our formal theory begins. It is logically true in terms of prior complementary definitions provided for information transfer and uncertainty. This proposition might simply have been stated as the pivotal a priori assumption underlying the entire theory. It was formalized here in the interest of clarity. Subject to future refinements, Axiom 1 may also prove useful beyond present definitional constraints.

In addition, Axiom 1 expresses a theoretical relationship between highly abstract concepts. Even before these concepts are operationalized via specific observables, a second important inferential leap is logically required. In the interest of experimental control (i.e., testability), information transfer must be reduced to a lower level of abstraction. The necessary reduction can be accomplished by assuming that the *amount* of information transferred in a given interaction is approximately coterminous with the *number* of communicative/informative acts (as defined above) transmitted from source to receiver. This assumption is formalized in the next two propositions.

> *Axiom 2:* As number of communicative/informative verbal acts emitted by either interactant increases, level of information transfer will increase.

Conversely, decreases in level of information transfer will accompany decreases in number of communicative/informative verbal acts emitted by either interactant.

Axiom 2 is a crucial step in the logical process at hand for at least two reasons. First, the informative value of any given verbal act will likely vary in actual performance depending on the context, information levels held prior to interaction, individual differences reflected in the encoding process, and so on. Second, it is highly unlikely that discrete verbal acts (even of the same type), to be quantified as a means of measuring information transfer, will be equally informative. For example, several declarative sentences expressed by a given source may have less informative value than the smaller number expressed by a counterpart. Nor can it be taken for granted that discrete verbal acts regularly function in a linear, additive fashion — that is, without interactive effects.

Hence, the *number* of discrete verbal acts produced by interactants is assumed to be a gross index of the actual *amount* of information transferred in a given context. The preceding proposition makes this assumption explicit. The following rationale is offered in support of Axiom 2.

Lalljee and Cook (1973), in a study allowing two-way communication, found that as interactions between strangers progressed, the number of words spoken per minute increased significantly over a nine-minute period. The present formulation suggests that as the number of informative verbal acts exchanged in this study increased, the amount of information available to each person also increased, resulting in uncertainty reduction for both persons. In turn, reduced uncertainty encouraged the production of verbal acts by each participant at an accelerating rate.

Conversely, Berger and Larimer (1974) found that when feedback was not allowed in a similar context, the number of words spoken per minute decreased significantly over a four-minute period. My theory suggests that restricting feedback in this instance interrupted the flow of information by introducing a significant decrease in the number of informative verbal acts emitted by at least one person at a given point or over time. Intuitively, the absence of an appropriate verbal response can be expected to impede exchange of information by increasing retroactive *uncertainty* dramatically. That is, little or no feedback would seem to be the least informative, and may be the most ambiguous, of plausible response alternatives when an uncertain interactant initially solicits or discloses information.

Indeed, the absence of verbal feedback can be expected to increase the number of possible interpretations open to the receiver and to render the next response virtually unpredictable. If interacting strangers are primarily concerned to reduce uncertainty, then initial attempts to communicate that result in greater uncertainty likely appear to elicit negative reinforcement or even punishment. If deprivation of feedback is viewed in either manner (via increased uncertainty), we would expect a reduction in the subsequent number of verbal acts generated by the unrequited source, hence the decrease in number of words per minute observed by Berger and Larimer. Following the prior line of reasoning, it is assumed that level of information transfer and number of informative verbal acts will covary in the same direction as stated in Axiom 2.

By extension of the preceding rationale, a similar positive association is posited between information transfer and informative nonverbal acts.

> Axiom 3: As number of communicative/informative nonverbal acts emitted by either interactant increases, level of information transfer will increase. Conversely, decreases in level of information transfer will accompany decreases in number of communicative/informative nonverbal acts emitted by either interactant.

Introductory comments alluded to the common assumption that certain nonverbal cues are closely associated with, and auxiliary to, linguistic behavior (e.g., Harrison, 1974; Ekman & Friesen, 1969). Under normal circumstances, these nonverbal counterparts of language function to repeat, substitute for, complement, accentuate, contradict, or regulate verbal communication (Burgoon & Saine, 1978). Although the processes involved may differ considerably, the present claim is that verbal and nonverbal actions (within the domain defined above) serve essentially the same general purpose — exchange of information — hence the parallel relations posited in preceding propositions.

The rationale offered in support of Axioms 2 and 3 attempts to provide some theoretical justification for reducing the concept, information transfer, to an experimentally manageable level of abstraction. This move has considerable bearing on available options from which relevant, observable variables can subsequently be selected. However, the domain of eligible communicative/informative events that might be used to index information transfer (across the two major channels) is still extremely large. Thus, an important question rises at this juncture. Given our theoretical concern with uncertainty reduction, what type of information is most relevant — that is, most likely transferred — during initial interactions? The following pair of propositions and supporting rationale address this issue. Both axioms express *reciprocal* relationships.

> Axiom 4: As level of verbal affiliation increases, level of information transfer will increase. As level of information transfer increases, level of verbal affiliation will further increase. Decreases in level of information transfer will accompany decreases in level of verbal affiliation.
>
> Axiom 5: As level of nonverbal affiliation increases, level of information transfer will increase. As level of information transfer increases, level of

nonverbal affiliation will further increase. Decreases in level of information transfer will accompany decreases in level of nonverbal affiliation.

Axioms 4 and 5 are based on the following summary discussion of Part II.

Prior factor-analytic research on behavioral determinants of social interaction indicated that three factors consistently emerge. The first factor, typically identified as affiliation (sociability, love-hostility or affection), appears to be the dominant referent dimension of social interaction across a variety of settings (Mehrabian, 1971a). Two such studies in particular (Mehrabian, 1971a; Mehrabian & Ksionzky, 1972), exploring relationships among nonverbal/implicit verbal behaviors of strangers in a waiting situation, suggest several associations of theoretical interest here. The model under study hypothesized that affiliation is encouraged by positive verbal and nonverbal reinforcement while it is discouraged by negative reinforcement of both types. Significant positive correlations were found in both studies between indicators of the *amount* of verbal communication and several measures of positive reinforcement. Both sets of indicators showed strong positive loadings on the first factor, labeled "affiliative behavior."

Affiliation is a useful construct in this context for two reasons. First, it is akin to the concept of "approach-avoidance" as discussed by Mehrabian (1971b) and thus suggests the tendency for individuals to decrease their physical distance in order to interact. In terms of the present formulation, affiliation is then a logical precondition for increased interaction and uncertainty reduction via information transfer. Second, affiliation is generally identified with positive reinforcement, which serves to encourage both physical and social proximity during interaction. Thus, affiliation may be considered a fundamental (positive), source-oriented stimulus which is expected to foster the exchange of similar (as well as other) types of information.

Factor-analytic studies cited above indicate that positive reinforcement is exchanged via nonverbal as well as verbal cues. Approximately half of the variables loading on the affiliative factor in both studies (Mehrabian, 1971a; Mehrabian & Ksionzky, 1972) were nonverbal measures. The latter study in particular provides evidence recommending two constructs of theoretical interest for purposes of examining verbal/nonverbal relationships in the context of handicapped/nonhandicapped communication. Division of the affiliative factor (see Table 4.1) into its verbal and nonverbal components yields a composite set of positive indicators for both verbal and nonverbal reinforcement. For reference purposes here, the composite set of verbal measures is labeled "verbal affiliation"; their nonverbal counterparts, "nonverbal affiliation."

Theoretically, both constructs represent the prerequisite type of reinforcement by which social interaction is initiated and continues to develop. Defined in terms of specific behaviors identified by Mehrabian and Ksionzky (1972), affiliation is the logical first step in our uncertainty reduction model presented in Figure 4.1. Based on prior discussion, both verbal and nonverbal affiliation are expected to occupy a direct, positive, and reciprocal relationship with the broader class of events defined previously as information transfer. These relations were formalized in Axioms 4 and 5.

Observed correlations among empirical indicators of verbal and nonverbal affiliation (Mehrabian, 1971a) suggest a strong association between these variables. Fifteen of sixteen relevant intercorrelations were significant ($\alpha = .01$) in a positive direction; the single exception approached significance at this level in the same direction. These data, collected exclusively from observation of target subjects, imply that interacting strangers ordinarily encode their affiliative messages with a high degree of consistency across the two channels. On this account, levels of verbal and nonverbal affiliation emitted simultaneously by a single source are expected to covary in the same direction.

> *Axiom 6:* As level of verbal affiliation increases, level of nonverbal affiliation from the same source will increase. Decreases in level of nonverbal affiliation will accompany decreases in level of verbal affiliation from the same source.

A major concern of this chapter is the potentially serious problem the previous discussion implies for handicapped persons with normal verbal skills who may be unable to encode appropriate nonverbal cues in a manner consistent with Axiom 6. As noted earlier, physically impaired persons may frequently exhibit nonverbal signals that are perceived to be incongruous with their verbal communication. Axiom 6 provides a theoretical basis for the following conceptual distinction between congruent and incongruent verbal/nonverbal messages. *Incongruent messages* are defined as those in which the level of a specific type of information conveyed via the verbal channel is perceived to be significantly different from the accompanying level of the same type of information conveyed via the nonverbal channel by the same source. Conversely, *congruent messages* are those in which levels of a given type of information emitted simultaneously across the two channels (by a single source) are not perceived to be significantly different.

In this connection, it is postulated that *when incongruency occurs between simultaneous verbal/nonverbal cues emitted by the same source, the nonverbal portion will dominate in determination of the total message impact.* Direct empirical support for this prediction was found in two

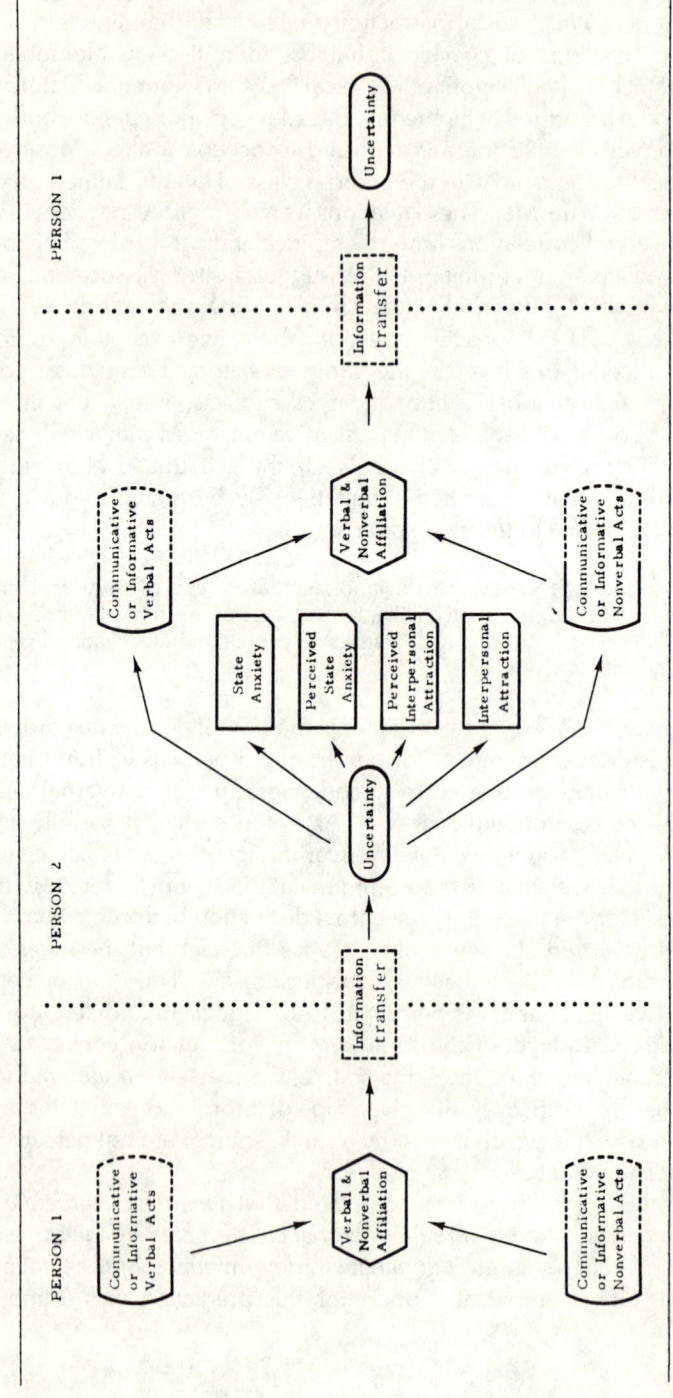

Figure 4.1. Flowchart illustrating a logical model of the theory proposed to represent initial interactions between handicapped and non-handicapped persons from an uncertainty reduction perspective.

experimental studies (Mehrabian & Ferris, 1967; Mehrabian & Wiener, 1967). These authors' findings indicate that the combined effect of verbal, vocal, and facial cues which convey liking attitudes is a weighted sum of their independent effects as represented in the following equation (Mehrabian, 1971b):

$$\text{Total liking} = 7\% \text{ verbal liking} + 38\% \text{ vocal liking} + 55\% \text{ facial liking}$$

More recently, two studies confirmed the former finding (Argyle, Salter, Nicholson, Williams, & Burgess, 1970; Argyle et al., 1971). Subsequent research suggests that attitudes conveyed through various channels may interact to determine the total message impact (Bugental, Kaswan, Love, & Fox, 1970; Lampel & Anderson, 1968). Hence, while the equation above represents only a first-order approximation (Mehrabian, 1972b), it does provide general support for the dominant effect of the nonverbal band. With regard to affiliative cues in this case, when incongruency occurs across the two channels, the nonverbal component is expected to exert a greater influence on the sum total of information conveyed. This expectation is formally stated in the following proposition.

> *Axiom 7:* Given incongruent levels of verbal/nonverbal affiliation emitted simultaneously by a single source, level of nonverbal affiliation will exercise the dominant influence on level of information transfer.

Since affiliation is only one of three basic determinants of social interaction consistently identified in prior research, it seems reasonable to assume that other factors involving different types of information (e.g., potency) will also influence uncertainty reduction and contribute to the receiver's ultimate perception of how he or she is being evaluated. Hence, the present model (see Figure 4.1) suggests that level of information transfer will mediate the effects of verbal/nonverbal affiliation on communicative uncertainty. The latter construct, communicative uncertainty, is logically associated in this model with attitudes inferred by, and other responses of, the receiver as reasoned below.

In support of Axiom 6, it was argued that interacting strangers ordinarily encode their affiliative messages with a high degree of consistency across the two major channels. If this is the case, it is reasonable to expect that less congruent messages will introduce greater ambiguity into the decoding process than more congruent levels of the same verbal/nonverbal cues (Mehrabian & Reed, 1968). That is, incongruent messages are expected to be more difficult to decode, since they tend to increase the number of plausible, alternative interpretations from which a receiver must choose. Assuming that some degree of cancellation occurs when conflicting bits of information emanate from the two channels, the combined informative impact of incongruent verbal/nonverbal messages is expected to be lower and, consequently, to have less uncertainty-reducing effect than congruent messages. They may, in fact, increase the receiver's uncertainty depending on the degree of discrepancy between the two channels. While some degree of ambiguity may be characteristic of all human communication, as discrepancy across the two channels increases, recipients of incongruent messages are expected both to experience less uncertainty reduction and to attribute greater uncertainty to the source. More specifically, perceived verbal/nonverbal incongruency in single-source messages should be inversely related to information transfer (and, in turn, to the level of certainty experienced by the receiver). Hence, the following formal proposition is advanced.

> *Axiom 8:* As level of verbal/nonverbal incongruency in single-source messages increases, level of information transfer will decrease. Increases in level of information transfer will accompany decreases in level of verbal/nonverbal incongruency perceived in single-source messages.

Several theorists have advanced the notion that "response-matching" behavior (Argyle, 1969; Brooks & Emmert, 1976) or a reciprocity norm functions to control exchange of information in interpersonal transactions (Gouldner, 1960; Jourard, 1960; Berkowitz, 1968; Berger & Calabrese, 1975). According to Argyle, "During social interaction it is very common for an act by A to be followed by a similar act from B. This we call response matching" (1969, p. 171). Numerous studies between 1950 and 1969 have verified this phenomenon with regard to length of utterances (Matarazzo, Wiens, & Saslow, 1965; Argyle & Kendon, 1967), interruptions and silences (Argyle & Kendon, 1967), type of utterance (Bales, 1950), gesture and posture (Rosenfeld, 1967), and self-disclosure (e.g., Jourard, 1960). It is also likely that response matching occurs with regard to emotional states — that is, an "emotional contagion" takes place (Argyle, 1969; Brooks & Emmert, 1976). The latter area may be particularly important in the context of communication with handicapped persons where high stress has been observed repeatedly.

It should be noted that the term "response matching" as used in this context implies only that increases or decreases in a particular behavior by a given source tend to be reciprocated via changes in the same type of behavior moving in the same direction by the respondent. Response matching does not imply that the reciprocal changes are quantitatively equal or symmetrical (cf. Matarazzo et al., 1965).

It has been argued that the reciprocity or response-matching construct is of limited theoretical value since theorists have been unable to explain the phenomenon adequately (Altman & Taylor, 1973). In response to this claim, Berger and Calabrese (1975) advance a general rationale for reciprocity based on Goffman's (1959) notion that people prefer smooth-running rather than stressful interactions. Utilizing an uncertainty-reduction paradigm similar to the present formulation, these authors contend that the "easiest way to reduce mutual uncertainty would be to ask for and give the same kinds of information at the same rate of exchange. In this way, no one interactant in the system would be able to gain *information power* over the other" (1975, p. 105).

While the former explanation moves in a heuristically promising direction, I find it inadequate for two reasons. First, to assert a human preference for less stressful interactions and to assume that reciprocity is the "easiest way" to reduce uncertainty does not advance our understanding of the phenomenon much more than the assertion of a reciprocity norm ipso facto explains its presence. Second, the explanation as stated seems not to account for response-matching behavior that involves stress itself. For example, in situations such as those under analysis here, stressful interactions frequently do occur and anxious reactions per se appear to be reciprocated. The notion of "information power" is, in my view, a more promising idea for development of useful theory to explain reciprocity within the uncertainty-reduction perspective.

If it is assumed, as several influential theorists argue (e.g., Homans, 1961; Thibaut & Kelley, 1959; Miller & Steinberg, 1975), that the basic function of communication is to control one's environment so as to realize certain rewards, information that enables a communicator to predict the effect of his or her own behavior with greater certainty becomes a powerful means of such control. Possession of information, required by either interactant to reduce uncertainty, represents potential power to direct the interaction toward one's own desired end. Given the transactional nature of human communication (Miller & Steinberg, 1975), exchange of information can be conceptualized as a kind of bartering process in which the interactants attempt to relinquish as little information as possible in quest of maximum returns.

On this account, unfamiliar persons are expected to exercise considerable caution in their release of and requests for relevant information. In effect, they may initially engage in a mutual testing exercise to determine "supply and demand" characteristics of the situation. That is, during early stages of the encounter, interactants may be willing to risk only minimal amounts of relatively superficial information while attempting to reduce their own uncertainty regarding the counterpart's willingness to reciprocate in kind. Indeed, several studies have shown that the amount of demographic (low intimacy) information requested and disclosed is highest during the earliest stages of interaction. Significant decreases in the amount of demographic information exchanged occur rapidly after the first minute of interaction (e.g., Berger, 1973; Cozby, 1972; Sermat &

Smyth, 1973; Taylor, Altman, & Wheeler, 1973). At the same time requests for, and disclosures of, more intimate information (e.g., personal attitudes and opinions) were observed to increase significantly.

Altman and Taylor (1973) contend that intimacy level of communication content tends to increase over time as the relationship becomes more rewarding and less costly. The Miller-Steinberg (1975) distinction between psychological and sociological information suggests an explanation more consistent with the present formulation. They argue that predictive (or proactive) uncertainty is reduced more efficiently by psychological level data — that is, predictive error can be greatly reduced by basing one's forecast on information that distinguishes the counterpart as a unique person. Given the basic control function of communication and assuming that control depends on predictive accuracy, interacting strangers should prefer to reduce their uncertainty as rapidly and efficiently as possible. Hence, each will be inclined to pursue the more idiosyncratic information his or her counterpart may be willing to disclose. At the same time, while personal information represents increased potential for control and is therefore in greater demand, it also involves greater risk to the discloser.

On the prior rationale, response matching is even more likely to occur and/or continue as the interaction moves toward psychological level data — in other words, as more intimate information is exchanged. Thus, the early "demographic stage" may serve to initiate the preliminary prediction-making process via exchange of low-risk information; it may also function to establish the response-matching rule by which exchange of more personal information will be regulated. Indeed, several investigators have observed the response-matching phenomenon at high levels of self-disclosure (e.g., Jourard, 1960; Cozby, 1972; Sermat & Smyth, 1973).

The present formulation posits an inverse relationship between a source's level of uncertainty and his or her self-disclosure. As uncertainty is initially reduced, particularly with regard to the counterpart's willingness to respond in kind (which greatly facilitates predictive accuracy), more intimate self-disclosure is expected to increase. As intimacy increases, response matching is expected to become more definitive due to potentially negative consequences which accrue with intimate self-disclosure — for example, risk of rejection, abuse, or loss of control in the interaction. Indeed, as intimacy level increases, response matching may also increase within certain parameters appropriate for a given stage of relational development. That is, a high intimacy threshold can be reached so as to violate social norms for initial encounters and/or place the receiver under an unacceptable obligation to respond in kind. At this extreme, response matching may begin to decrease as suggested by Miller and Steinberg (1975) and observed by Cozby (1972). Ordinarily, interacting strangers are not expected to violate such intimacy norms.

This account attempts to explain response matching, as observed in prior research, at various levels of information exchange. It diverges considerably from the Berger and Calabrese (1975) formulation, which postulates that high levels of uncertainty produce high rates of reciprocity while low levels of uncertainty produce low rates of reciprocity. The authors do not clearly define reciprocity rate. However, their view does not appear to take account of the increased potential for uncertainty reduction, predictive accuracy, and control involved in the exchange of more salient, idiosyncratic information. Neither does it explain the response-matching phenomenon observed repeatedly when highly intimate information is being exchanged. The contention here is that response matching continues to influence the type and flow of information well beyond initial interactions and is particularly critical when high-risk information is being disclosed. On present evidence, it is conceivable that the decline in reciprocity rate associated with decreasing uncertainty by Berger and Calabrese does not occur until well-established interpersonal relationships have developed over time.

Three specific associations reflecting prior research on response matching can be meaningfully integrated with the theoretical framework proposed thus far. First, in a series of experimental studies by Matarazzo et al. (1965) significant increases in length of interviewee speech duration were observed to follow increases in length of utterances by the interviewer. The associated increases were not quantitatively symmetrical. Observed ratios of interviewee to interviewer speech duration were, however, remarkably constant at five or six to one across several studies.

Admittedly, length of utterance alone is not likely a very reliable index of informative value as, for example, in the case of a congressional filibuster. It is intuitively reasonable to assume for theoretic purposes that speech duration and number of communicative verbal acts (as defined above) will ordinarily covary in the same direction. By extrapolation, the response-matching pattern observed by Matarazzo et al. might also be expected to occur regarding number of communicative verbal acts as well as other informative events within the domain of theoretical interest here. Hence on the assumption expressed in Axiom 2, gross levels of information transfer generated by interactants in initial dyadic encounters are expected to covary in the same direction. Formally stated, the following proposition refers to the combined impact of verbal/nonverbal acts (emitted by a single source) previously defined as either communicative or informative events.

> *Axiom 9:* As level of information transfer generated by either interactant increases, level of information transfer generated by the counterpart will increase. Decreasing levels of information transfer will be reciprocated with deceasing levels of the same variable.

Second, response matching has repeatedly been found to occur with regard to communication content or type of verbal message exchanged.

Worthy, Gary, and Kahn (1969), in addition to several studies cited earlier, provide empirical evidence in support of matching message types involving self-disclosure. Given the influence, for example, of psychological-level data on uncertainty reduction as discussed above, it is reasonable to assume that reciprocal content-matching messages will have a direct bearing on information transfer, mutual levels of uncertainty reduction, and the outcome of an interaction. For present purposes, this reciprocal relationship focuses exclusively on verbal components of the interaction. In general, levels of a given type of verbal content generated by individual interactants are expected to covary in the same direction. For example, increases in positive verbal reinforcement produced by a given interactant will accompany increases of the same verbal type from the counterpart. It is further assumed that specific types of verbal content are usually conveyed via the standardized use of a relatively specific symbol set. For example, self-disclosure may involve increased use of the first person singular pronoun. On these accounts, the following response-matching association extends to all verbal acts previously included within the larger domain labeled information transfer.

Axiom 10: As level of a specific type of verbal information transferred by either interactant increases, level of the same type of verbal information transferred by the counterpart will increase. Decreasing levels of a specific type of verbal information will be reciprocated with decreasing levels of the same variable.

Third, primarily by extrapolation from research on related variables, interactants will tend to adopt and reflect what they perceive to be the counterpart's emotional state as inferred from affect displays and other relevant nonverbal cues. Bales (1950) provides indirect evidence for this hypothesis from his analysis of response sequences observed in small groups. For example, stimulus joking behaviors were frequently followed by joking responses. In dyadic contexts, Condon and Ogston (1966) produced evidence for "interactional synchrony" between source and receiver in terms of small movements of hands, head, and eyes. Kendon (1968) observed listeners giving continuous kinesic commentary on a speaker's performance, consisting of nods and changes in facial expression. Nonverbal response matching has also been observed in psychotherapeutic dyads with respect to smiling, gestures, and posture (e.g., Rosenfeld, 1967; Scheflen, 1965).

Nonverbal messages are of central theoretical import in this context due to the type of information they convey. Bettinghaus (1973) suggests that nonverbal communciation serves most effectively to reveal information about the communicator per se, rather than about ideas he or she may espouse. Of the five gestural categories classified by Ekman and Friesen

(1969), affect displays are particularly important here because they provide access to private emotional states. Hence, they represent a potentially critical form of self-disclosure. Theoretically, then, we would expect affect displays to convey valuable information primarily at the psychological level and to be an integral part of the information transfer/uncertainty reduction paradigm under consideration. By the same token, response-matching patterns involving other informative nonverbal acts can be expected to play a crucial role in the management, control, and transfer of salient interpersonal information.

The argument here is that response-matching patterns observed on several types of nonverbal cues (as reviewed above) warrant the theoretical expectation that reciprocity occurs with respect to all communicative/informative nonverbal acts included by definition in the larger domain — information transfer. The proposition to follow implies that the number of specific emblems, illustrators, affect displays, and regulators emitted by individual interactants in initial dyadic encounters will covary in the same direction.

> *Axiom 11:* As level of a specific type of nonverbal information transferred by either interactant increases, level of the same type of nonverbal information transferred by the counterpart will increase. Decreasing levels of a specific type of nonverbal information will be reciprocated with decreasing levels of the same variable.

At this juncture, focus of the present theoretical development turns more directly to handicapped/nonhandicapped interactions. Reference was made earlier to a series of programmatic studies indicating the serious "strain in social interaction" present during initial face-to-face encounters between these types. This strain is believed to result from prior attitudes of participants toward each other which give rise to uncertainty about the most appropriate communicative strategy for maximizing the quality of their transactions. For instance, Siller et al. (1967) found that nonhandicapped persons participating in their research invariably reported

> uncertainty about how to comport themselves, e.g., whether to take notice of the disability or not. Frequently and readily, people admit a compulsion to stare, fully realizing that the disabled person would be made uncomfortable by this, and that they, in turn, would be branded as cruel or socially inconsiderate for indulging their curiosity. (p. 64)

Goffman (1963) discusses interpersonal interactions with stigmatized persons such as the visibly handicapped in terms of the "pathology of interaction-uneasiness." He describes this condition as

> accompanied by one or more of the familiar signs of discomfort and stickiness: the guarded references, the common everyday words sud-

denly made taboo, the fixed stare elsewhere, the artificial levity, the compulsive loquaciousness, the awkward solemnity. (p. 19)

In a similar vein, Davis (1961) noted that this type of personal interaction gives rise to anxiety resulting from an imputation of the handicapped person which expresses itself "in the embarrassment of the normal by which he conveys the all too obvious message that he is having difficulty in relating to the handicapped person as he would to 'just an ordinary man or woman'" (p. 121). Limited research to date examining handicapped/nonhandicapped interactions generally agrees with the previous citings (Fontes, Miller, & Kaminski, 1978).

As reported at the outset, nonhandicapped individuals tend to increase their physical distance (Kleck, 1969; Worthington, 1974), terminate the interaction sooner and exhibit less variance in their verbal behavior (Kleck et al., 1966), demonstrate greater motoric inhibition — that is, restrict their nonverbal behavior (Kleck, 1968), and manifest more anxiety (Marinelli & Kelz, 1973; Marinelli, 1974) when interacting with handicapped persons. The nonhandicapped also report more emotional discomfort following this type of interaction (Kleck, 1966).

On present evidence, it is conceivable that the uneasiness, apparent ambivalence, and strain observed repeatedly when handicapped and nonhandicapped persons interact are essentially akin to, and have their source in, communicative uncertainty as described theoretically above with reference to initial interactions in general. Consequently, it is assumed that the uncertainty reduction perspective proposed earlier can be applied to, and will facilitate basic research on, interactions involving handicapped persons. Differences observed between this type of interaction and the general case are expected to be quantitative rather than qualitative.

If communicative uncertainty is ordinarily high at the outset whenever strangers interact (Berger & Calabrese, 1975), this condition should be exacerbated when either person bears a visible disability. On that assumption plus prior evidence, the following proposition seems tenable.

Axiom 12: Initial interactions between handicapped and nonhandicapped persons are characterized by atypically high levels of communicative uncertainty.

Extending the preceding rationale, it is reasonable to assume further that high uncertainty gives rise to the high anxiety previously observed (e.g., Marinelli, 1974) in interactions of this type, hence the expectation that uncertainty and state anxiety (Marinelli & Kelz, 1973; Spielberger, 1966) will covary in the same direction. The following proposition refers specifically to initial interactions between handicapped and nonhandicapped persons.

Axiom 13: As level of communicative uncertainty experienced by either interactant decreases, level of state anxiety experienced by the same interactant will decrease. Increasing levels of state anxiety will accompany increasing levels of communicative uncertainty experienced by the same interactant.

In support of Axiom 11, evidence was cited suggesting that the number of specific affect displays emitted by individuals in dyadic encounters will tend to covary in the same direction. This presupposes, of course, that a given set of nonverbal cues are perceived and identified with a particular emotional state by the counterpart, perhaps at a low level of awareness. Thus, to the extent that anxiety is typically accompanied by observable and interpretable affect displays, one would expect the level of state anxiety experienced by a given interactant to covary with the counterpart's perception of these anxiety-revealing cues. That is, changes in level of state anxiety experienced by either person should be accompanied by similar directional changes in the counterpart's attribution of this emotional state to the source.

Further research in this area would likely enlighten our understanding of the anxiety syndrome that apparently occurs when handicapped/nonhandicapped dyads initially interact. In conjunction with Axiom 13, the prior association between state anxiety and level of that affect perceived by the counterpart (hereafter labeled "perceived state anxiety") leads to the following proposition:

Axiom 14: As level of communicative uncertainty experienced by either interactant decreases, level of perceived state anxiety (by the counterpart) will decrease. Increasing levels of perceived state anxiety will accompany increasing levels of communicative uncertainty experienced by either interactant.

In support of Axioms 4 and 5, it was reasoned that affiliation is a prerequisite type of positive reinforcement through which social interaction is initiated and ongoing relationships involving other types of information exchange are encouraged. Intuitively, affiliative information might then be considered a particularly important source of uncertainty reduction in initial encounters, determining whether or not the interaction will continue. More specifically, as affiliative information from a given source increases, the receiver's uncertainty should be reduced, particularly with respect to how he or she is being evaluated by the source. Assuming that affiliative cues normally signal a favorable disposition, as they increase we would expect the receiver to perceive him or herself as more interpersonally attractive to the source.

Essentially, foregoing arguments amount to the assertion that affiliation is (1) a *necessary* precondition for uncertainty reduction, in general, involving other types of information and (2) a *sufficient* condition for reducing receiver uncertainty with specific reference to his or her evaluation by the source. On these accounts, an inverse relationship is posited between uncertainty and *perceived interpersonal attraction* for initial encounters in handicapped/nonhandicapped dyads. The latter variable refers to the extent to which a given interactant perceives him or herself as interpersonally attractive to the counterpart.

> *Axiom 15:* As level of communicative uncertainty experienced by either interactant decreases, the same interactant's perceived interpersonal attraction to the counterpart will increase. Decreasing levels of perceived interpersonal attraction will accompany increasing levels of communicative uncertainty experienced by the same interactant.

Contrary to the rationale advanced in support of Axiom 15, it may be argued that negative reinforcement or nonaffiliative (as well as affiliative) cues can be equally effective in reducing receiver uncertainty in the opposite direction with regard to how he or she is being evaluated. In that case, lower levels of perceived interpersonal attraction would logically accompany lower levels of uncertainty (i.e., the recipient of nonaffiliative cues could be *certain* of a negative evaluation). Thus a *curvilinear* relation is suggested. Axiom 15 is linear for two theoretic reasons.

First, the rudimentary concept of approach — avoidance underlying present use of the term "affiliation" does not imply an overtly negative counterpart for affiliative behavior. That is, casual observation suggests that *avoidance* can usefully be defined as simply a failure to approach. Likewise, nonaffiliation can meaningfully refer to the absence of affiliative cues when unfamiliar persons meet. In such a case, nonaffiliation would not ordinarily reduce uncertainty and could conceivably increase it.

Second, I suspect that nonaffiliation (or the absence of affiliative cues), as opposed to overt negative communication, frequently occurs in initial encounters, particularly those involving handicapped and nonhandicapped persons. There is some evidence suggesting that overt negative reactions such as straightforward verbal rejection of the handicapped are culturally inhibited (e.g., Siller et al., 1967; Kleck, 1966) and do not ordinarily occur in interactions of this type. More likely, meaningful interactions fail to develop, and termination occurs prematurely (Kleck et al., 1966) due to the absence of an appropriate level of affiliative information rather than the presence of distinctly negative information. Hence, Axiom

15 seems the more theoretically sound, heuristically promising approach. One additional proposition completes the propositional framework from which a limited number of possible hypotheses will be generated in Part IV.

On the common assumption that people tend to like those who like them (Brooks & Emmert, 1976), it is reasonable to expect that people are also initially attracted to others who appear to be attracted to them. More specifically, as a receiver's perception of his or her attractiveness to a message source increases, that source will become more interpersonally attractive to the receiver. Thus, perceived interpersonal attraction (i.e., the attractiveness of R to S as perceived by R) and interpersonal attraction (i.e., the attractiveness of S to R) are expected to covary in the same direction. Consequently, given the inverse association posited in Axiom 15, an inverse relationship between uncertainty and interpersonal attraction is also logically warranted.

> *Axiom 16:* As level of communicative uncertainty experienced by either interactant decreases, the same interactant's interpersonal attraction to the counterpart will increase. Decreasing levels of interpersonal attraction will accompany increasing levels of communicative uncertainty experienced by the same interactant.

IV. TESTABLE THEOREMS

> Science does not aim, primarily, at high probabilities. It aims at high informative content, well backed by experience. But a hypothesis may be very probable simply because it tells us nothing, or very little. (Popper, 1955, p. 146)

Presumably, Popper does not mean that the theorist can or should avoid all concern with probability. Axiomatic foundations in Part III rely heavily on existing theory and prior evidence. To that extent, the following hypotheses do aim at high probabilities. Given current literature in this area, they relate fundamental variables most likely to inform development of more effective communication strategies for both handicapped and nonhandicapped persons. In other words, these basic relationships should be examined empirically first, then discarded if necessary, before search is made for additional and/or other relevant variables. In the latter sense, theorems to follow are primarily concerned with informative content rather than high probability.

Since this theory focuses specifically on handicapped/nonhandicapped dyads, at least three independent variables are implied: (1) verbal/nonverbal affiliation, (2) verbal/nonverbal congruency, and (3) type of dyadic interaction. In addition, prior axioms express relationships involving five dependent variables: (1) communicative certainty/uncertainty, (2) state anxiety, (3) perceived state anxiety, (4) perceived interpersonal attraction, and (5) interpersonal attraction. Minimally, then, the theory will allow generation of fifteen first-order predictions relating three independent variables to each of five dependent variables. Fifteen second-order (A × B) and five third-order (A × B × C) interaction effects are also possible. In the interest of brevity, the sample of fifteen theorems below provides first- and second-order examples from which additional hypotheses can easily be constructed. It also reflects that set of theorems with which the writer expects to begin testing the present theory.

Theorems 1 through 5 specify main effects predicted from the primary independent variable, verbal/nonverbal affiliation (abbreviated as V/NV affiliation). Each theorem was deduced from two or more of the prior axioms identified in parentheses. All hypothesized relations to follow presuppose Axiom 1 and refer to initial dyadic encounters between handicapped and nonhandicapped persons.

Theorem 1: Interactants exposed to increasing levels of V/NV affiliation will report increasing levels of *communicative certainty* (Axioms 4 and 5).

Theorem 2: Interactants exposed to increasing levels of V/NV affiliation will report decreasing levels of *state anxiety* (Axioms 4, 5, and 13).

Theorem 3: Interactants exposed to increasing levels of V/NV affiliation will report decreasing levels of *perceived state anxiety* (Axioms 4, 5, and 14).

Theorem 4: Interactants exposed to increasing levels of V/NV affiliation will report increasing levels of *perceived interpersonal attraction* from the message source (Axioms 4, 5, and 15).

Theorem 5: Interactants exposed to increasing levels of V/NV affiliation will report increasing levels of *interpersonal attraction* toward the message source (Axioms 4, 5, and 16).

Similar hypotheses predicting main effects from the second independent variable can be generated by substituting "V/NV congruency" for "V/NV affiliation" in Theorems 1 through 5. Relevant axioms, in this case, are 1, 8, 13, 14, 15, and 16. Theorems 6 through 10 below identify main effects (holding affiliation constant) predicted as a function of the specific type of dyadic interaction to which this theory applies (i.e., as a consequence of the fact that one interactant is handicapped). In essence, given similar amounts of information transfer, the theory predicts proportionately less uncertainty reduction in handicapped/nonhandicapped dyads since interactions of this type are characterized by atypically high levels of uncertainty at the outset (Axiom 12). Theoretically, other variables depending on uncertainty reduction are expected to follow suit in either a positive or negative direction according to prior predictions. Again, all subsequent theorems presuppose Axiom 1.

Theorem 6: Nonhandicapped persons will report more *communicative certainty* when exposed to the same level of V/NV affiliation generated by a nonhandicapped, as opposed to a handicapped, source (Axiom 12).

Theorem 7: Nonhandicapped persons will report less *state anxiety* when exposed to the same level of V/NV affiliation generated by a nonhandicapped, as opposed to a handicapped, source (Axioms 12 and 13).

Theorem 8: Nonhandicapped persons will report less *perceived state anxiety* when exposed to the same level of V/NV affiliation generated by a nonhandicapped, as opposed to a handicapped, source (Axioms 12 and 14).

Theorem 9: Nonhandicapped persons will report more *perceived interpersonal attraction* (from the counterpart) when exposed to the same level of V/NV affiliation generated by a nonhandicapped, as opposed to a handicapped, source (Axioms 12 and 15).

Theorem 10: Nonhandicapped persons will report more *interpersonal attraction* (toward the counterpart) when exposed to the same level of V/NV affiliation generated by a nonhandicapped, as opposed to a handicapped, source (Axioms 12 and 16).

These five theorems focus on reactions of the nonhandicapped interactant. However, given Axiom 12, there is no reason to attribute these reactions to one interactant more so than the other. Hence the theory allows generation of parallel predictions focusing on reactions of the handicapped participant by reversing the terms "handicapped" and "nonhandicapped" in Theorems 6 through 10.

Five additional theorems complete the present sample. Theorems 11 through 15 posit second-order interaction effects predicted from the two independent variables for which main effects were formalized in prior theorems (i.e., level of V/NV affiliation and type of dyadic interaction). In lieu of additional information, our theory leads to the expectation that these predictors will interact in an *ordinal* manner (see Keppel, 1973), producing conjoint effects on communicative certainty and other theoretically related variables. This general interaction hypothesis is advanced on two counts.

First, systematic differences between two types of dyads (Theorems 6 through 10) were predicted primarily on account of atypically high levels of uncertainty expected when handicapped and nonhandicapped persons initially interact. Holding V/NV affiliation constant, we reasoned that proportionately less uncertainty reduction would occur in contexts where uncertainty is characteristically higher at the outset. Second, Axiom 4 posits a reciprocal relationship between verbal affiliation and information transfer. Axiom 5 posits a similar reciprocal association for nonverbal affiliation. In combination, Axioms 4 and 5 imply a reciprocal association between level of V/NV affiliation and information transfer. Thus, as information transfer initially increases, further concomitant increases in V/NV affiliation are also expected to occur.

| Type of | Level of V/NV Affiliation | | |
Interaction	high	medium	low
NH/NH	1	2	3
H/NH	4	5	6

Figure 4.2. Representation of a factorial design crossing three levels of verbal/nonverbal affiliation with two types of dyadic interaction.

If this is the case, information transfer should increase at an accelerating rate over time, particularly in initial interactions. As a result, given Axiom 1, uncertainty reduction should also occur at an accelerating rate. On this rationale, anticipated conjoint effects of the predictors at hand are twofold: (1) A given input of V/NV affiliation will initially result in proportionately less uncertainty reduction for handicapped and nonhandicapped interactants; and (2) given similar rates of acceleration and proportionately higher levels of uncertainty, overall uncertainty reduction should occur *less rapidly* in handicapped/nonhandicapped dyads (as opposed to nonhandicapped dyads) during a comparable period of time. In turn, main effects predicted from V/NV affiliation on other dependent variables previously related to uncertainty should increase or decrease less rapidly in dyads involving the handicapped.

Ordinal interactions predicted in Theorems 11 through 15 will be clarified by means of the matrix presented in Figure 4.2. Suggestive of a factorial design, this matrix illustrates the simultaneous crossing of three levels of V/NV affiliation with two levels of the second independent variable, type of interaction.

The pattern of mean differences in effect size predicted via each theorem will be identified symbolically where:

$\bar{X}_1$ = mean for nonhandicapped persons exposed to a *high* level of V/NV affiliation generated by a nonhandicapped source;

$\bar{X}_2$ = mean for nonhandicapped persons exposed to a *medium* level of V/NV affiliation generated by a nonhandicapped source;

$\bar{X}_3$ = mean for nonhandicapped persons exposed to a *low* level of V/NV affiliation generated by a nonhandicapped source;

$\bar{X}_4$ = mean for nonhandicapped persons exposed to a *high* level of V/NV affiliation generated by a handicapped source;

$\bar{X}_5$ = mean for nonhandicapped persons exposed to a *medium* level of V/NV affiliation generated by a handicapped source;

$\bar{X}_6$ = mean for nonhandicapped persons exposed to a *low* level of V/NV affiliation generated by a handicapped source;

Handicapped and Nonhandicapped Persons

These theorems assume the same rank order of effects predicted previously in Theorems 1 through 10. Each presupposes Axiom 1.

> As nonhandicapped persons are exposed to increasing levels of V/NV affiliation generated by handicapped versus nonhandicapped sources...
>
> *Theorem 11:* Their reported levels of *communicative certainty* will increase more rapidly when the source is a nonhandicapped person (Axioms 4, 5 and 12).
>
> $$(\bar{X}_1 - \bar{X}_2) > (\bar{X}_4 - \bar{X}_5)$$
> $$(\bar{X}_2 - \bar{X}_3) > (\bar{X}_5 - \bar{X}_6)$$
>
> *Theorem 12:* Their reported levels of *state anxiety* will decrease more rapidly when the source is a nonhandicapped person (Axioms 4, 5, 12, and 13).
>
> $$(\bar{X}_2 - \bar{X}_1) > (\bar{X}_5 - \bar{X}_4)$$
> $$(\bar{X}_3 - \bar{X}_2) > (\bar{X}_6 - \bar{X}_5)$$
>
> *Theorem 13:* Their reported levels of *perceived state anxiety* will decrease more rapidly when the source is a nonhandicapped person (Axioms 4, 5, 12, and 14).
>
> $$(\bar{X}_2 - \bar{X}_1) > (\bar{X}_5 - \bar{X}_4)$$
> $$(\bar{X}_3 - \bar{X}_2) > (\bar{X}_6 - \bar{X}_5)$$
>
> *Theorem 14:* Their reported levels of *perceived interpersonal attraction* (from the counterpart) will increase more rapidly when the source is a nonhandicapped person (Axioms 4, 5, 12, and 15).
>
> $$(\bar{X}_1 - \bar{X}_2) > (\bar{X}_4 - \bar{X}_5)$$
> $$(\bar{X}_2 - \bar{X}_3) > (\bar{X}_5 - \bar{X}_6)$$
>
> *Theorem 15:* Their reported levels of *interpersonal attraction* (toward the counterpart) will increase more rapidly when the source is a nonhandicapped person (Axioms 4, 5, 12, and 16).
>
> $$(\bar{X}_1 - \bar{X}_2) > (\bar{X}_4 - \bar{X}_5)$$
> $$(\bar{X}_2 - \bar{X}_3) > (\bar{X}_5 - \bar{X}_6)$$

The rank order of effects and ordinal interactions predicted in Theorems 11 through 15 are graphically illustrated as shown in Figures 4.3 and 4.4.

In sum, we have no theoretical reason to attribute prior interaction effects exclusively to nonhandicapped interactants. In fact, investigation of the transactional nature of the apparent strain characterizing initial encounters with the handicapped, as suggested earlier in this chapter, will require examination of similar hypotheses casting the handicapped interactant in the receiver's role. Comparison of reactions to similar stimuli experienced by interactants of these two types should shed considerable light on the present issue. In principle, investigation of this critical social problem

130 COMMUNICATION REVIEWS AND COMMENTARIES

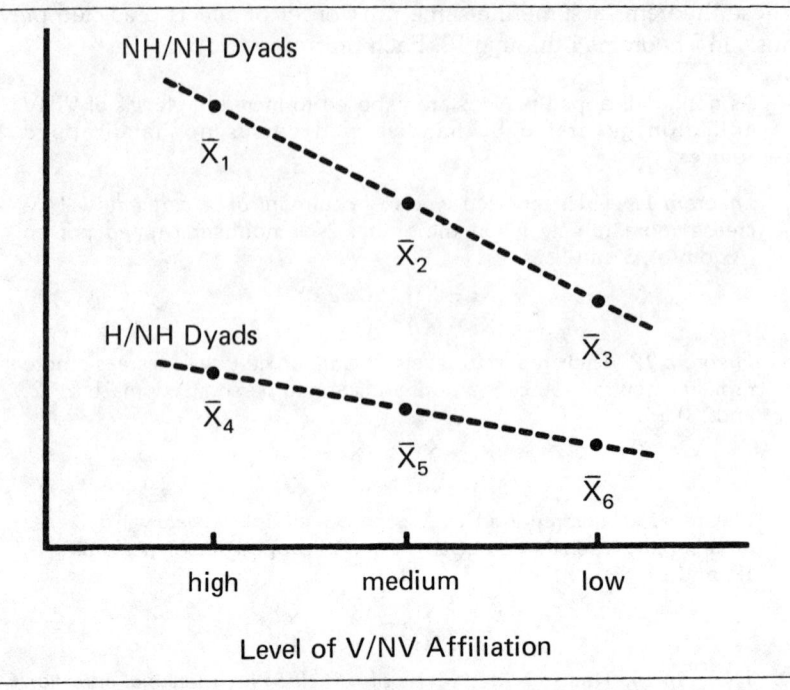

Figure 4.3. Pattern of means showing rank order of effects and interactions predicted in Theorems 11, 14, and 15.

should proceed on the assumption that participants in any communication event are mutually responsible for the outcome of that event. Resorting to the trite, it takes at least "two to tango."

This discourse may most appropriately end, as it began, with emphasis on the need for empirical research in this area. That need is evident in the following summary of findings gleaned from a conference sponsored by Johns Hopkins Medical Institutions (Richardson, 1976), which may serve to suggest other queries:

1. Initial reactions toward those who are physically handicapped are less favorable than toward those who are not handicapped.
2. Emotional arousal and anxiety occur in varying degrees in an initial encounter with a handicapped person.
3. The physical disability initially dominates the attention of the nonhandicapped person. The salience of the handicap leads to inattention to the other attributes of the handicapped person — attributes which normally would be included in initial interpersonal evaluation and used in guiding the initial stage of the interpersonal relationship.

Handicapped and Nonhandicapped Persons

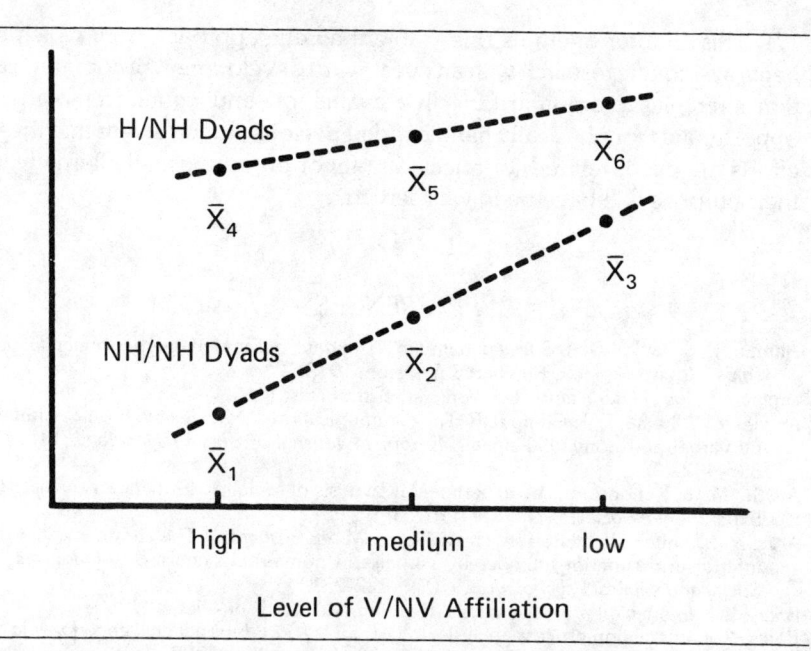

[Figure: Graph showing H/NH Dyads (upper dashed line with points $\bar{X}_4$, $\bar{X}_5$, $\bar{X}_6$) and NH/NH Dyads (lower dashed line with points $\bar{X}_1$, $\bar{X}_2$, $\bar{X}_3$), x-axis labeled "Level of V/NV Affiliation" with high, medium, low.]

Figure 4.4. Pattern of means showing rank order of effects and interactions predicted in Theorems 12 and 13.

4. The initial interaction frequently includes a feeling of ambivalence on the part of the nonhandicapped person. For fear of revealing the negative aspect of the ambivalence, the nonhandicapped person is more formal and controlled in the behavior he or she exhibits.
5. Depending on the experience in the initial social encounter, the ambivalence felt may later be expressed as denigration of the handicapped or as giving overly favorable impressions.
6. There is inhibition of nonverbal behavior, such as gesture, and a tendency to come less close physically.
7. The nonhandicapped exhibit less variability in their behavior, and they distort their opinions in the direction they feel is more acceptable to the handicapped person.
8. The nonhandicapped tend to terminate the initial social encounter more quickly with a handicapped than with a nonhandicapped person. (pp. 20-21)

Findings reported by the same author relative to reactions of the physically handicapped typically complement foregoing statements.

As the reader may long since have suspected, theoretical efforts of the present type never really end. As Quine said, "In science all is tentative, all admits to revision, right down to the law of the excluded middle" (1957, p.

17). This chapter attempts one viable theoretic approach from which to begin systematic research with an eye toward development of communication strategies promoting objective evaluation and equal employment opportunities for physically handicapped persons. To the extent that these efforts are used, revised, or rejected in favor of more useful alternatives, their purpose will have been well served.

REFERENCES

Altman, I., & Taylor, D. A. *Social penetration: The development of interpersonal relationships.* New York: Holt, Rinehart & Winston, 1973.

Argyle, M. *Social interaction.* New York: Atherton Press, 1969.

Argyle, M., Alkema, F., & Gilmour, R. The communication of friendly and hostile attitudes by verbal and nonverbal signals. *European Journal of Social Psychology,* 1971, *1,* 385-402.

Argyle, M., & Kendon, A. The experimental analysis of social performance. *Advances in Experimental Social Psychology,* 1967, *3,* 55-98.

Argyle, M., Salter, V., Nicholson, H., Williams, M., & Burgess, P. The communication of inferior and superior attitudes by verbal and nonverbal signals. *British Journal of Social and Clinical Psychology,* 1970, *9,* 222-231.

Bales, R. F. *Interaction process analysis.* Reading, MA: Addison-Wesley, 1950.

Bales, R. F. Interaction process analysis. In D. L. Sills (Ed.), *International encyclopedia of social sciences.* New York: Crowell-Collier and Macmillan, 1968.

Berger, C. R. *The acquaintance process revisited: Explorations in initial interaction.* Paper presented at the meeting of Speech Communication Association, New York, November 1973.

Berger, C. R., & Calabrese, R. J. Some explorations in initial interaction and beyond: Toward a developmental theory in interpersonal communication. *Human Communication Research,* 1975, *1,* 99-112.

Berger, C. R., & Larimer, M. W. *When beauty is only skin deep: The effects of physical attractiveness, sex and time on initial interaction.* Paper presented at the meeting of the International Communication Association, New Orleans, April 1974.

Berkowitz, L. Responsibility, reciprocity, and social distance in help-giving: An experimental investigation of English social class differences. *Journal of Experimental Social Psychology,* 1968, *4,* 46-63.

Bettinghaus, E. P. *Persuasive communication.* New York: Holt, Rinehart & Winston, 1973.

Blalock, H. M. *Theory construction: From verbal to mathematical formulations.* Englewood Cliffs, NJ: Prentice-Hall, 1969.

Boomer, D. S., & Laver, J. D. M. Slips of the tongue. *British Journal of Disorders of Communication,* 1968, *3,* 1-12.

Borgatta, E. F. A systematic study of interaction process scores, peer and self-assessments, personality and other variables. *Genetic Psychology Monographs,* 1962, *65,* 219-291.

Brooks, W. D., & Emmert, P. *Interpersonal communication.* Dubuque, IA: William C. Brown, 1976.

Bugental, D. E., Kaswan, J. W., Love, L. R., & Fox, M. N. Child versus adult perception of evaluative messages in verbal, vocal and visual channels. *Developmental Psychology,* 1970, *2,* 367-375.

Burgoon, J. K., & Saine, T. *The unspoken dialogue: An introduction to nonverbal communication.* Boston: Houghton Mifflin, 1978.

Carter, L. F. Evaluating the performance of individuals as members of small groups. *Personnel Psychology,* 1954, *7,* 477-484.

Comer, R. J., & Piliavin, J. A. As others see us: Attitudes of physically handicapped and normals toward own and other groups. *Rehabilitation Literature,* 1975, *36,* 206-221, 225.

Condon, W. S., & Ogston, W. D. Sound film analysis of normal and pathological behavior patterns. *Journal of Nervous and Mental Disease,* 1966, *143,* 338-347.

Couch, A. S. *Psychological determinants of interpersonal behavior.* Unpublished doctoral dissertation, Harvard University, 1960.

Cozby, P. C. Self-disclosure, reciprocity and liking. *Sociometry,* 1972, *35,* 151-160.

Davis, F. Deviance disavowal: The management of strained interaction by the visibly handicapped. *Social Problems,* 1961, *9,* 121-132.

Dibner, A. S. Cue-counting: A measure of anxiety in interviews. *Journal of Consulting Psychology,* 1956, *20,* 475-478.

Ekman, P., & Friesen, W. V. Head and body cues in the judgment of emotion: A reformulation. *Perceptual and Motor Skills,* 1967, *24,* 711-724.

Ekman, P., & Friesen, W. V. The repertoire of nonverbal behavior: Categories, orgins, usage, and coding. *Semiotica,* 1969, *1,* 49-98.

Festinger, L. A theory of social comparison processes. *Human Relations,* 1954, *7,* 117-140.

Foa, U. G. Convergences in the analysis of the structure of interpersonal behavior. *Psychological Review,* 1961, *68,* 341-353.

Fontes, N. E., Miller, G. R., & Kaminski, E. P. *Communication barriers between handicapped and nonhandicapped interactants: Identification and removal.* Unpublished manuscript, Department of Communication, Michigan State University, 1978.

Frijda, N. H., & Philipszoon, E. Dimensions of recognition of expression. *Journal of Abnormal and Social Psychology,* 1963, *66,* 45-51.

Fromm-Reichmann, F. In D. M. Bullard (Ed.), *Psychoanalysis and psychotherapy: Selected papers of Freida Fromm-Reichmann.* Chicago: University of Chicago Press, 1959.

Fujimoto, E. K. *The comparative power of verbal and nonverbal symbols.* Unpublished doctoral dissertation, Ohio State University, 1971.

Glaser, B., & Strauss, A. *The discovery of grounded theory.* Chicago: Aldine, 1967.

Goffman, E. *The presentation of self in everyday life.* Garden City, Doubleday, 1959.

Goffman, E. *Stigma: Notes on the management of spoiled identity.* Englewood Cliffs, NJ: Prentice-Hall, 1963.

Gouldner, A. W. The norm of reciprocity: A preliminary statement. *American Psychological Review,* 1960, *25,* 161-178.

Harrison, R. P. *Beyond words: An introduction to nonverbal communication.* Englewood Cliffs, NJ: Prentice-Hall, 1974.

Heider, F. *The psychology of interpersonal relations.* New York: John Wiley, 1958.

Heise, D. R. *Causal analysis.* New York: John Wiley, 1975.

Homans, G. C. *Social behavior: Its elementary forms.* New York: Harcourt Brace Jovanovich, 1961.

Izard, C. E. The emotions and emotion constructs in personality and culture research. In R. B. Cattell (Ed.), *Handbook of modern personality theory.* Chicago: Aldine, 1968.

Jones, E. E., Kanouse, D. E., Kelley, H. H., Nisbett, R. E., Valins, S., & Weiner, B. (Eds.) *Attribution: Perceiving the causes of behavior.* Morristown, NJ: General Learning Press, 1972.

Jourard, S. Knowing, liking, and the "dyadic effect" in men's self-disclosure. *Merrill Palmer Quarterly of Behavior and Development,* 1960, *6,* 178-186.

Kelley, H. H. The processes of causal attribution. *American Psychologist,* 1973, *28,* 107-128.

Kendon, A. *Some observations on interactional synchrony* (preliminary report). Unpublished manuscript, Cornell University, 1968.

Keppel, G. *Design and analysis: A researcher's handbook.* Englewood Cliffs, NJ: Prentice-Hall, 1973.

Kleck, R. Emotional arousal in interactions with stigmatized persons. *Psychological Reports,* 1966, *19,* 1226.

Kleck, R. Physical stigma and nonverbal cues emitted in face-to-face interactions. *Human Relations,* 1968, *21,* 19-28.

Kleck, R. Physical stigma and task oriented interactions. *Human Relations,* 1969, *22,* 53-60.

Kleck, R., Ono, H., & Hastorf, A. The effects of physical deviation upon face-to-face interaction. *Human Relations,* 1966, *19,* 425-436.

Krippendorff, K. Information theory. In G. J. Hanneman & W. J. McEwen (Eds.), *Communication and behavior.* Reading, MA: Addison-Wesley, 1975.

Lalljee, M., & Cook, M. Uncertainty in first encounters. *Journal of Personality and Social Psychology,* 1973, *26,* 137-141.

Lampel, A. K., & Anderson, N. H. Combining visual and verbal information in an impression-formation task. *Journal of Personality and Social Psychology,* 1968, *9,* 1-6.

Longabaugh, R. The structure of interpersonal behavior. *Sociometry,* 1966, *29,* 441-460.

Lorr, M., & Suziedelis, A. Modes of interpersonal behavior. *British Journal of Social and Clinical Psychology,* 1969, *8,* 124-132.

Mahl, G. F. *Gestures and body movements in interviews.* Paper presented at the Third Research in Psychotherapy Conference, Chicago, 1966.

Marinelli, R. P. State anxiety in interactions with visibly disabled persons. *Rehabilitation Counseling Bulletin,* 1974, *18,* 72-77.

Marinelli, R. P., & Kelz, J. W. Anxiety and attitudes toward visibly disabled persons. *Rehabilitation Counseling Bulletin,* 1973, *17,* 198-205.

Matarazzo, J. D., Wiens, A. N., & Saslow, G. Studies of interview speech behavior. In L. Krasner & L. P. Ullman (Eds.), *Research in behavior modification: New developments and implications.* New York: Holt, Rinehart & Winston, 1965.

McClelland, P. D. *Causal explanation and model building in history, economics, and the new economic history.* Ithaca, NY: Cornell University Press, 1975.

McMahan, E. M. Nonverbal communication as a function of attribution in impression formation. *Communication Monographs,* 1976, *43,* 287-294.

Mehrabian, A. Methods and designs: Some referents and measures of nonverbal behavior. *Behavioral Research Methods and Instrumentation,* 1969, *1,* 203-207.

Mehrabian, A. Verbal and nonverbal interaction of strangers in a waiting situation. *Journal of Experimental Research in Personality,* 1971, *5,* 127-138. (a)

Mehrabian, A. *Silent messages.* Belmont, CA: Wadsworth, 1971. (b)

Mehrabian, A. Nonverbal communication. In J. K. Cole (Ed.), *Nebraska symposium on motivation* (Vol. 20). Lincoln: University of Nebraska Press, 1972. (a)

Mehrabian, A. *Nonverbal communication.* Chicago: Aldine, 1972. (b)

Mehrabian, A., & Ferris, S. E. Inference of attitudes from nonverbal communication in two channels. *Journal of Consulting Psychology,* 1967, *31,* 248-252.

Mehrabian, A., & Ksionzky, S. Models for affiliative and conformity behavior. *Psychological Bulletin,* 1970, *74,* 110-126.

Mehrabian, A., & Ksionzky, S. Some determiners of social interaction. *Sociometry,* 1972, *35,* 588-609.

Mehrabian, A., & Reed, H. Some determinants of communication accuracy. *Psychological Bulletin,* 1968, *70,* 365-381.

Mehrabian, A., & Wiener, M. Decoding of inconsistent communications. *Journal of Personality and Social Psychology,* 1967, *6,* 109-114.

Miller, G. R., & Steinberg, M. *Between people: A new analysis of interpersonal communication.* Chicago: Science Research Associates, 1975.

Osgood, C. E., Dimensionality of the semantic space for communication via facial expressions. *Scandinavian Journal of Psychology,* 1966, *7,* 1-30.

Osgood, C. E., Suci, G. J., & Tannenbaum, P. H. *The measurement of meaning.* Urbana: University of Illinois Press, 1957.

Park, L. D. Barriers to normality for the handicapped adult in the United States. *Rehabilitation Literature,* 1975, *36,* 108-111.

Popper, K. Degree of confirmation. *British Journal for the Philosophy of Science,* 1955, *5,* 143-149.

Quine, W. V. The scope and language of science. *British Journal for the Philosophy of Science,* 1957, *8,* 1-17.
Richardson, S. A. Attitudes and behavior toward the physically handicapped. In D. Bergsma & A. Pulver (Eds.), *Development disabilities: Psychologic and social implications.* New York: Alan R. Liss, 1976.
Rosenfeld, H. M. Nonverbal reciprocation of approval: An experimental analysis. *Journal of Experimental Social Psychology,* 1967, *3,* 102-111.
Schachter, S. *The psychology of affiliation: Experimental studies of the sources of gregariousness.* Stanford: Stanford University Press, 1959.
Schachter, S., & Burdick, H. A field experiment on rumor transmission and distortion. *Journal of Abnormal Social Psychology,* 1955, *50,* 363-371.
Scheflen, A. E. Quasi-courtship behavior in psychotherapy. *Psychiatry,* 1965, *28,* 245-257.
Sermat, V., & Smyth, M. Content analysis of verbal communication in the development of a relationship: Conditions influencing self-disclosure. *Journal of Personality and Social Psychology,* 1973, *26,* 332-346.
Shapiro, J. G. Responsivity to facial and linguistic cues. *Journal of Communication,* 1968, *18,* 11-17.
Siller, J., Chipman, A., Ferguson, L., & Vann, D. H. *Attitudes of the nondisabled toward the physically disabled.* New York: New York University School of Education, 1967.
Snider, J. G., & Osgood, C. E. (Eds.) *Semantic differential techniques.* Chicago: Aldine, 1969.
Spielberger, C. D. (Ed.). *Anxiety and behavior.* New York: Academic Press, 1966.
Sturtevant, E. H. *An introduction to linguistic science.* New Haven, CT: Yale University Press, 1947.
Taylor, D. A., Altman, I., & Wheeler, L. Self-disclosure in isolated groups. *Journal of Personality and Social Psychology,* 1973, *26,* 39-47.
Thibaut, J. W., & Kelley, H. H. *The social psychology of groups.* New York: John Wiley, 1959.
Tomkins, S. S. *Affect, imagery, consciousness* (Vol. 1). New York: Springer, 1962.
Tomkins, S. S. *Affect, imagery, consciousness* (Vol. 2). New York: Springer, 1963.
Tomkins, S. S., & McCarter, R. What and where are the primary affects? Some evidence for a theory. *Perceptual and Motor Skills,* 1964, *18,* 119-159.
Triandis, H. C., Vassiliou, V., & Nassiakou, M. Three cross-cultural studies of subjective culture. *Journal of Personality and Social Psychology,* 1968, *8,* (Monograph Supplement, No. 4).
VandeCreek, L., & Watkins, J. T. Responses to incongruent verbal and nonverbal emotional cues. *Journal of Communication,* 1972, *22,* 311-316.
Wiener, M., Devoe, S., Rubinow, S., & Geller, J. Nonverbal behavior and nonverbal communication. *Psychological Review,* 1972, *79,* 185-214.
Wiener, M., & Mehrabian, A. *Language within language: Immediacy, a channel in verbal communication.* New York: Appleton-Century-Crofts, 1968.
Williams, F., & Sundene, B. Dimensions of recognition: Visual vs. vocal expression of emotion. *Audio Visual Communications Review,* 1965, *13,* 44-52.
Worthington, M. E. Personal space as a function of the stigma effect. *Environment and Behavior,* 1974, *6,* 289-294.
Worthy, M., Gary, A. L., & Kahn, G. M. Self-disclosure as an exchange process. *Journal of Personality and Social Psychology,* 1969, *13,* 59-64.
Zetterberg, H. L. *On theory and verification in sociology* (3rd ed.). Totowa, NJ: Bedminster Press, 1965.

COMMUNICATION REVIEWS AND COMMENTARIES

5 ● Oral Communication Apprehension: A Reconceptualization

JAMES C. McCROSKEY
West Virginia University

COMMUNICATION apprehension (CA) has been the subject of over 200 reported studies during the decade of 1970-1980. From the limited concern of a few U.S. scholars in speech communication, interest in CA has spread to other disciplines[1] and to other nations and cultures.[2] Reports of such research have appeared in most of the journals devoted to communication as well as many diverse publications in other fields of scholarship.[3] There are two published booklets devoted to CA, one directed to teachers (McCroskey, 1977b) and the other to basic course students (McCroskey & Richmond, 1980). CA has even received attention from the popular press[4] and spawned a newsletter.[5]

It is not an exaggeration to suggest that this area of interest has generated more research over the past decade than almost any other in the communication field. If we include research concerning related constructs such as reticence and shyness, this volume of research is even more substantial. When so much attention is directed in a single area it is vital that the conceptualizations in the area be strong enough to support such efforts.

The purpose of this chapter is to reexamine the conceptualization of CA. This reexamination has led me to conclude that the original conceptualization of CA lacks sufficient clarity and specificity for continued use. A reconceptualization of CA will be provided.

THE ORIGINAL CONCEPTUALIZATION

The original conceptualization of CA that I advanced (McCroskey, 1970) viewed CA as "a broadly based anxiety related to oral communica-

Correspondence and requests for reprints: James C. McCroskey, Department of Speech Communication, West Virginia University, Morgantown, WV 26506.

tion." Subsequent writings have made only apparently minor modifications of this definition. My more recent papers present the view that CA is "an individual's level of fear or anxiety associated with either real or anticipated communication with another person or persons" (McCroskey, 1977a, 1978).

This seeming consistency across time may be more apparent than real. Two conceptual modifications occurred. The first concerned the oral communication focus of CA and the other concerned whether CA was restricted to a trait conceptualization.

The Oral Focus of CA

In the original article in which I advanced the construct of CA, the focus clearly was on oral communication (McCroskey, 1970). Although in this article "communication" frequently was used without the "oral" qualifier, the earlier work in the areas of stage fright and reticence were acknowledged as the foundations upon which the CA construct was developed. Both of these areas focused exclusively on oral communication at that time.

In some subsequent writings the oral context of CA received less emphasis. Of particular importance were two research programs that were conducted under the general rubric of communication apprehension but that did not focus on speaking. The first was the research concerned with apprehension about writing (Daly & Miller, 1975). This stream of research, led by Daly and his associates, continues currently and has received considerable attention in the field of English. The measure developed by Daly and Miller, the Writing Apprehension Test (WAT), has been employed widely and has been found to have only a moderate correlation with my CA measures. The second research area was that concerned with apprehension about singing. While receiving far less attention than the articles and measures concerned with speaking and writing, research involving the Test of Singing Apprehension (TOSA) also discovered low correlations between the TOSA and CA measures (Andersen, Andersen, & Garrison, 1978).

Clearly, talking, writing, and singing are all forms of communication. Just as clearly, apprehension about one is a poor predictor of apprehension about any other one. The emergence of research concerning apprehension about writing and singing requires a reevaluation of the original definition of the construct "communication apprehension." My revised definition, noted above, satisfactorily overcomes this problem. It permits apprehension about talking, writing, or singing to fall comfortably within its boundaries. However, it should be recognized that no measure currently exists that even claims to tap this broadly conceived construct of CA. The

Personal Report of Communication Apprehension (PRCA; McCroskey, 1970, 1978, 1982) taps the talking component, the WAT taps the writing component, and the TOSA taps the singing component. While generation of a general CA instrument probably would be possible, efforts in that direction might not be particularly useful. The research indicating that the three measures currently available have little association with each other clearly indicates the multidimensional nature of the general construct. Thus dimension scores of the new instrument would be the product of major concern. Since satisfactory measures of those dimensions already exist, little would be gained by generating additional ones. If a unidimensional measure could be generated, it would, of necessity, have to be composed of items so general as to make the likelihood almost certain that the ultimate measure would be nothing more than a new general anxiety measure. Several of these already are available.

In sum, over the decade since the CA construct has been advanced it has been broadened substantially. While originally it was restricted to talking, it now encompasses all modes of communication. Consequently, it should be recognized that current instruments labeled as CA measures are restricted to oral CA, specifically apprehension about talking to or with others. My focus in the remainder of the chapter is on this form of CA, and when I use the term "CA" this will be my referent. I believe that most of what will follow will apply equally well to other forms of CA, however.

The Trait Conceptualization of CA

The original article that advanced the construct of CA included no explicit mention of whether it is a trait of an individual or a response to the situational elements of a specific communication transaction. However, the implication is clear that the construct was viewed from a trait orientation. Not only was the discussion directed toward a response generalized across situations and time, but the measures advanced clearly focused on a traitlike pattern.

The overwhelming majority of the research studies employing the CA construct have taken a trait approach (McCroskey, 1977a). Many have referred to CA with terms such as "a traitlike, personality-type variable." More recently, the CA construct has been expanded explicitly to encompass both trait and situational views (McCroskey, 1977a). Some research has been reported that has investigated CA in both the trait and state form (eg., Richmond, 1978; Prisbell and Dallinger, 1981).

In sum, over the decade since the CA construct has been advanced it has been broadened substantially. While originally it was restricted to a trait orientation, it is now viewed as representing both trait and state approaches. While the original definition of CA restricts the construct to a trait perspective, the revised definition noted above is consistent with the broader view. It should be recognized, however, that the most popular measures of CA are restricted to a trait conceptualization. Research based on more situational perspectives must employ other instruments.

RELATED CONSTRUCTS

As noted above CA currently is viewed as a person's level of fear or anxiety associated with any form of communication with other people, experienced either as a traitlike, personality-type response or as a response to the situational constraints of a given communication transaction. A number of other constructs have been advanced that have, or at least appear to have, similarities to the CA construct. Two of these appeared in the literature prior to the generation of the CA construct: stage fright and reticence. Four others have come into prominence more recently: unwillingness to communicate, predispositions toward verbal behavior, shyness, and audience anxiety. An examination of these constructs in comparison to the CA construct will help place all of these constructs in clearer perspective.

Stage Fright

Stage fright is the oldest of the conceptualizations related to CA. Empirical research has been directed toward stage fright for almost half a century (Clevenger, 1959). Since the attention of the field of speech during the early days of the work with stage fright was directed almost exclusively to public speaking, it is not surprising that stage fright was examined in this context. From our contemporary vantage point, then, we can view the construct of stage fright as representing CA in the public speaking context.

During the early years of research on stage fright, our sister disciplines of personality, social, and behavioral psychology also were in their developmental years. Many of the insights we now find so useful in understanding the CA phenomenon were yet to be generated. Most importantly, the distinction between trait and state anxiety had yet to be made. Thus different researchers studying stage fright approached it from different vantage points, while assuming that they were studying the same thing. Lomas (1934) and Gilkinson (1942), for example, worked from a trait, self-report orientation. In contrast, Henning (1935) studied state anxiety as manifested through observer ratings, while Redding (1936) was examining state anxiety as manifested in a physiological arousal measure. Great concern was expressed because high correlations were not obtained between trait self-report measures and such state measures as observer ratings and physiological arousal measures (Clevenger, 1959).

In retrospect it is clear that such concern was misplaced. Measures of traits should not be expected to be highly correlated with state measures restricted to a given situation at a given time (Jaccard & Daly, 1980). Trait measures should only be expected to be predictive generally across situations, across time. In any event, it is clear that stage fright can be viewed as either a traitlike orientation of an individual that has impact across public speaking situations or as a state response of an individual to a given public speaking situation. Viewed in this way, stage fright is a subset of the broader construct of CA. Sibling constructs relating to other broad types of communication contexts (small group, meetings, dyads, etc.) would be analogues of stage fright and also subsets of the broader CA construct.

Reticence

The construct of reticence has evolved and changed over the fifteen years it has been discussed in the literature. As originally conceived reticence and CA were virtually interchangeable (Phillips, 1968). Reticence grew out of the earlier work with stage fright and represented an expansion of that construct to include other communication contexts. The work of Phillips with reticence is acknowledged specifically as the immediate antecedent of CA (McCroskey, 1970, 1980).

Over the decade of the 1970s, however, the constructs of reticence and CA became quite divergent. While CA was and remains a cognitive construct (although with presumed behavioral impact), reticence moved from being viewed as a cognitive construct to being viewed from a strict behavioral perspective. The contemporary view of reticence is the reverse of communication competence (Phillips, 1980). Reticent communicators are, simply, people who do not communicate competently. While CA is acknowledged as one of the elements that may lead an individual to be reticent, it is not considered the only, nor even necessarily the most important, contributing factor.

Although reticence and CA once were twin constructs, their relationship today is markedly different. Reticence is the much broader of the two constructs. If reticence is viewed as a construct representing the broad range of communicative incompetence, as it currently is viewed by Phillips, then CA is a subset of that broad construct. CA relates to communicative incompetence stemming from anxiety or fear. Its sibling constructs would include such things as inadequate communication skills and cultural divergence (McCroskey & Richmond, 1980).

Unwillingness to Communicate

The unwillingness-to-communicate construct focuses exactly on what its name implies, the unwillingness of an individual to communicate with others. This construct was advanced by Burgoon (1976) in an explicit attempt to broaden concern about noncommunicative behavior beyond the narrower focus of CA and reticence (as conceived at that time).

This construct views the sources of noncommunication to be, in addition to CA, low self-esteem, introversion, and anomia and alienation. All of these factors, presumed to lead to noncommunication, are cognitively based. Thus this construct can be viewed as intermediary between CA and the contemporary view of reticence. More simply, reticence is concerned with people who do not communicate effectively; unwillingness to communicate is concerned with one of the reasons that people may not do so (i.e., they do not want to); and CA is concerned with one of the reasons that people may be unwilling to communicate. The validity and usefulness of this construct is suggested by the results of research employing the unwillingness-to-communicate measure. This measure includes two factors, one of which is highly associated with CA, the other of which is uncorrelated with CA.

At this point research employing the unwillingness-to-communicate construct is very limited and the measure of the construct needs further development, since it lacks isomorphism with the construct. However, its intermediary position between CA and reticence is particularly helpful for understanding the distinctions between the two latter constructs.

Predispositions Toward Verbal Behavior

The construct of predispositions toward verbal behavior (PVB; Mortensen, Arntson, & Lustig, 1977) is very similar to the unwillingness-to-communicate construct, with two important exceptions. First, PVB appears to be the logical opposite of unwillingness to communicate. A person scoring highly on an appropriate measure of PVB would be expected to be very willing to communicate. In short, PVB could be called "willingness to communicate." In this sense, then, the constructs can be viewed as isomorphic; they are only discussed in differing ways.

The second distinction between the PVB construct and that of unwillingness to communicate is more important. While unwillingness is viewed cognitively, PVB is viewed behaviorally. Although the only PVB measure available at present is a self-report scale (thus cognitively mediated), the construct views people behaving in a consistent manner across communication contexts in terms of the amount they talk. Although

PVB is a behavioral construct, it should not be confused with the contemporary view of reticence. While reticence is concerned with the quality or competence of communication, PVB is concerned only with the amount.

The conceptual distinctions between CA and PVB and unwillingness to communicate, and the association between the latter constructs, have received some empirical support. In research reported by Daly (1978), a measure of PVB was found to correlate with CA at .66, while the dimensions of unwillingness, labeled reward ($r = .01$) and approach ($r = .88$), had widely differing correlations. However, PVB correlated significantly with both the reward factor (.36) and the approach factor ($r = .91$) of the unwillingness-to-communicate measure. PVB, like unwillingness to communicate, should be viewed as a construct holding an intermediary position between CA and reticence. Variability in CA may lead to variability in predispositions toward verbal behavior, which may lead to variability in reticence or communication competence.

Shyness

As Zimbardo (1977), the leading writer in the area of shyness, says, "Shyness is a fuzzy concept." Careful reading of the literature in the area of shyness indicates that there is no consensual definition of the construct. Zimbardo carefully and explicitly avoids defining what he means by "shyness." However, a careful reading of his book on shyness indicates that he is referring to a feeling of discomfort in a variety of communication situations. Thus Zimbardo can be considered to be approaching shyness primarily from a cognitive orientation. He also acknowledges the trait/state distinction in shyness when he notes that some people are generally shy while others experience situational shyness. If we restrict our view of shyness to that enunciated by Zimbardo, there appears to be no meaningful distinction between this construct and that of CA.

In contrast, Pilkonis (a former student of Zimbardo and a major participant in the well-known Stanford shyness research program) sees shyness as "a tendency to avoid other people [unwillingness to communicate? negative PVB?], to fail to respond appropriately to them [reticence?] . . . and to feel nervous and anxious during interactions with them [CA?]" (Pilkonis, Heape, & Klein, 1980).

In behavioral terms, Pilkonis et al. (1980) suggest that shy people "are characterized by avoidance of social interaction, and when this is impossible, by inhibition and an inability to respond in an engaging way; they are reluctant to talk, to make eye contact, to gesture, and to smile." As suggested by my bracketed questions, this view does not seem amenable to classification within any one of the previously discussed construct categories. Rather, it seems to fall at least partially into several of them. Of particular note, however, is Pilkonis et al.'s apparent restriction of shyness to the interpersonal context. This restriction distinguishes their construct from all others we have discussed, but the distinction is implied rather than explicit and may not represent the actual view of these authors.

Of all the writers in the area of shyness, Buss (1980) makes the clearest distinctions between shyness and other constructs. Buss is concerned with a more general construct, which he calls "social anxiety," that refers to discomfort in the presence of others. He identifies four categories of this general construct. Two of these, embarrassment and shame, are not of concern here. The third, audience anxiety, will be discussed in the next section. His fourth category is shyness, which he views as "the relative absence of expected social behaviors" (Buss, 1980, p. 184). This conceptualization of shyness is explicitly restricted to dyadic and small group communication contexts. His operationalization of the construct focuses on discomfort in such contexts, and when viewed in this way can be seen as a subset of the larger CA construct. When viewed from his behavioral definition, however, shyness can be seen as a subset of the reticence construct.

The confusion in the literature concerning the construct of shyness is illustrated by the conflicting positions I have advanced. In 1977, after attempting to distinguish between reticence and CA, and referencing Zimbardo's book, I concluded that the shyness construct is "essentially similar to the CA construct" (McCroskey, 1977a). Only four years later, however, I presented a different view. After examining factor-analytic results in a study designed to simplify CA measurement and finding two distinct factors, I labeled one CA and the other shyness (McCroskey, Andersen, Richmond, & Wheeless, 1981). The dimension labeled shyness is composed of items essentially similar to those included on the PVB scale. Thus, seemingly at least, shyness was equated with PVB. The correlation between this shyness scale and CA is also very similar to that between CA and PVB.

What then is the nature of the shyness construct? Shyness does not represent a single construct. It is a label that has been applied to a variety of disparate constructs. Most importantly, the construct does not seem to have any property that is either universal across writers in this area or that is unique from the constructs discussed previously. Thus I caution people who read the shyness literature to be aware of the inconsistent use of this label and advise against assuming that shyness is a unique construct. All writings in the area of shyness I have examined are amenable to translation to the constructs of reticence, PVB or unwillingness to communicate, or CA as these constructs have been outlined above. I believe such translation will lead to increased understanding of the literature and avoidance of the conceptual confusion currently present.

Audience Anxiety

The newest conceptualization related to CA, audience anxiety, is highly similar to the oldest conceptualization, stage fright. Audience anxiety is viewed as "fear, tension, and disorganization in front of an audience" (Buss, 1980, p. 165). This construct is almost the same as the original stage fright construct. The only meaningful distinction is that anxiety felt in talking in meetings is included in the new construct, while generally it was excluded in the older version. They both include anxiety about public speaking.

Audience anxiety, clearly, is a subset of the CA construct. Buss's shyness and audience anxiety constructs represent a two-part subdivision of CA. Taken together they represent an approximation of the generalized trait view of CA, although, as I will note later, I believe these are inadequate subdivisions.

When we consider all of the constructs discussed in this section we can see that the CA construct is neither the largest nor the smallest of the group. Communication competence, or reticence, seems to be the broadest construct. Unwillingness to communicate and PVB, seen as parallel but not fully isomorphic constructs, are viewed as constructs purporting to explain part of what is seen as reticence. CA is seen as one of the elements leading to unwillingness to communicate or negative PVB. Stage fright and audience anxiety are seen as representative subconstructs of CA. Shyness, depending on how the label is employed in a given case, can be employed as an equivalent term for constructs at each of the descending conceptual levels.

CROSS-CULTURAL FOUNDATION

The CA construct was developed within the general U.S. culture and most of the research concerning CA has been restricted to that culture. Given this cultural context, it is reasonable to question whether the resulting construct and the research based on that construct are culturally biased. The data available suggest that if such a bias is present, it probably is minimal.

To analyze the relevance of culture to the CA construct, one must first recognize that within the general U.S. culture communication is valued quite highly. The bulk of high-status and high-income occupations are dependent on effective communication. Lest we make too much of this fact, however, we should recognize that the U.S. culture is not greatly deviant in this regard. While some cultures place an even higher value on communication, notably the Israeli culture, others place a somewhat lower value on it, notably some Asian and African cultures. Thus, in terms of a value placed on communication, the U.S. culture should be viewed as approximating a mainstream position. The rewards obtainable and punishments avoidable by effective communication in the culture are, by and large, similar to those in most other cultures.

To argue that the CA construct can be generalized beyond the general U.S. culture, two considerations are of particular importance. These are the degree to which representative samples of people from other cultures report levels of CA comparable to those reported by U.S. samples and the degree to which reduced communicative output (one of the presumed impacts of CA) has comparable effects in other cultures compared to the effects in the United States.

Distribution of CA

Several studies have been directly concerned with comparing the distribution of CA in other cultures with that found within the general U.S. culture. In general, the results have indicated comparability across cultures.

In the most extensive cross-cultural comparison reported to date, Hansford and Hattie (1979) compared data from 1784 Australians with data from five American samples (total n = 4542). They found no significant differences between the U.S. and Australian samples, nor did they find any differences attributable to either sex or age. In addition, confirmatory factor analysis indicated that the structure of the CA measure was the same whether applied in the United States or Australia. Klopf and Cambra (1979) report similar findings with regard to the distribution of CA among Australians compared to the general U.S. norms. In addition, they found that Hawaiian Americans reported CA higher than the mainland norms, as did a sample of Japanese. In contrast, they found that a sample of Koreans reported lower CA than the mainland norms. In other phases of this same research program it was found that Guamanians (Bruneau, Cambra, & Klopf, 1980) and mainland Chinese (Klopf & Cambra, 1980) did not differ from mainland U.S. norms.

In his research with shyness, Zimbardo (1977) has also examined the comparability of other cultures with U.S. norms. In most instances no meaningful differences attributable to culture were observed. However, as with the CA studies, Zimbardo found a higher proportion of shys among Hawaiians and Japanese. He also found Israelies and Jewish Americans to report significantly less shyness than any other groups. No comparable data for CA have yet been reported.

The general conclusion from these cross-cultural investigations, then, is that people in the U.S. culture are not greatly deviant from people in other cultures. However, cultures do exist in which the normative level of

CA is both higher and lower than in the general U.S. culture. Direct generalization to these cultures, therefore, must be done with extreme caution.

Reduced Communication

In a wide variety of studies conducted within the U.S. culture, it has been observed that lowered levels of talking are associated with less positive perceptions on the part of other people. People who talk more generally are stereotypically perceived as more credible, attractive, competent, and the like (Hayes & Meltzer, 1972; McCroskey & Richmond, 1976). Recently, Hayes and Meltzer (1979) have conducted similar investigations in a variety of cultures. The results in England, Chile, and Mexico have been consistent with those obtained within the U.S. culture.

The tentative conclusion I draw from the investigations that have been conducted in non-U.S. cultures is that the conceptualization of CA is not seriously culture bound. Nevertheless, people wishing to generalize to other cultures must keep in mind the particular communication orientations peculiar to those cultures. CA may be more or less of a problem, depending on the cultural communication norms of the society in which it exists. In addition, sexual norms and expectations may interact with CA in greatly differential ways as we move from culture to culture.

A RECONCEPTUALIZATION OF CA

Minor changes in the conceptualization of CA over the past decade have been noted. Such changes have appeared in the literature in a nonsystematic manner. In addition, some elements of the CA construct have never been spelled out clearly. In the following sections the conceptualization of CA will be enunciated in three major areas: (1) types of CA, (2) causes of CA, and (3) effects of CA.

Considerable attention has been directed toward the distinction between trait and situational or state CA. This distinction has been quite helpful to researchers in the CA area in their attempt to distinguish older from newer approaches to this subject. Unfortunately, this distinction has come to be viewed as a dichotomy, a false dichotomy. To view all human behavior as emanating from either a traitlike, personality orientation of the individual or from the statelike constraints of a situation ignores the powerful interaction of these two sources. No element of personality yet isolated by psychologists or others has been found to have universal predictability across all situations for all individuals. Similarly, no situation has yet been identified in which we can predict a universal behavior from all individuals. Even in life-threatening situations, people do not all behave alike. Thus it is important that we reject this false state/trait dichotomy and view the sources of CA on a continuum. This continuum can be viewed as ranging from the extreme trait pole to the extreme state pole, although neither the pure trait nor pure state probably exists as a meaningful consideration. Four points along this continuum can be identified. Each of these points represents a distinct type of CA.

Traitlike CA. The term "traitlike" is used intentionally to indicate a distinction between this view of CA and one that would look at CA as a true trait. A true trait, as viewed here, is an invariant characteristic of an individual, such as eye color or height. No personality variable, and traitlike CA is viewed as a personality-type variable, meets this strict interpretation of "trait." After achieving adulthood, true traits of an individual are not subject to change. Traitlike personality variables, although highly resistant to change, can be and often are changed during adulthood. That CA is subject to such change is indicated clearly in the substantial research on treatment of people identified as having high CA (e.g., McCroskey, 1972).

Traitlike CA is viewed as *a relatively enduring, personality-type orientation toward a given mode of communication across a wide variety of contexts.* Three varieties of this type of CA have been addressed in the literature — CA about oral communication, CA about writing, and CA about singing. The primary measures of these (PRCA, WAT, and TOSA) are presumed to be traitlike measures, by which is meant that it is assumed that scores for an individual on any one of these measures will be highly similar across an extended period of time, barring an intervention program designed to alter the relevant CA level or a demand characteristic introduced in the CA measurement.[6] This is the type of CA to which most of the research has been directed over the past decade (McCroskey, 1977a).

Generalized-Context CA. Generalized-context CA is one step further removed from pure trait than traitlike CA. CA viewed from this vantage point represents orientations toward communication within generalizable contexts. Fear of public speaking, the oldest of the CA conceptualizations, is illustrative of this type of CA. This view recognizes that people can be highly apprehensive about communicating in one type of context while having less or even no apprehension about communicating in another type of context.

Generalized-context CA is viewed as *a relatively enduring, personality-type orientation toward communication in a given type of context.* Although no taxonomy for generalized-context CA yet has received consensual acceptance in the literature, the one advanced by McCroskey and Richmond (1980), which is based on types of communication settings, appears quite adequate. From this view there are four varieties of this type of CA — CA about public speaking, CA about speaking in meetings or classes, CA about speaking in small group discussions, and CA about speaking in dyadic interactions.

The first CA measure to receive wide acceptance by researchers, the Personal Report of Confidence as a Speaker (PRCS) developed by Gilkinson (1942), is illustrative of an instrument designed to tap this type of CA. Subsequent instruments for measuring public speaking anxiety reported by Paul (1966), and McCroskey (1970; the Personal Report of Public Speaking Apprehension — PRPSA) also fall within this area. More recently, McCroskey and Richmond (1980) have offered instruments to measure each of the four varieties of generalized-context CA that they describe. As was the case with the traitlike CA measures noted in the previous section, it is assumed that scores for an individual on any one of these measures will be highly similar across an extended period of time, barring an intervention program designed to alter the relevant CA level or a demand characteristic in measurement. These measures are distinguished from the previously noted traitlike measures in that they focus more narrowly on communication within a given type of context rather than on communication across contexts. It should not be surprising, however, to find moderate to moderately high correlations between the two types of measures. To the extent that a traitlike orientation toward communication actually exists, an appropriate measure of that orientation should be at least somewhat predictive of orientations within generalized contexts.

Person-Group CA. This type of CA represents the reactions of an individual to communicating with a given individual or group of individuals across time. People viewing CA from this vantage point recognize that some individuals and groups may cause a person to be highly apprehensive while other individuals or groups can produce the reverse reaction. For some people more apprehension may be stimulated by a peer or group of peers. For others, more apprehension may be stimulated by unfamiliar individuals or groups. A school teacher, for example, may be highly apprehensive about talking to her or his principal, but have no apprehension about talking to a student in her or his own class.

Person-Group CA is viewed as *a relatively enduring orientation toward communication with a given person or group of people.* It is not viewed as personality-based, but rather as a response to situational constraints generated by the other person or group. Although presumed to be relatively enduring, this type of CA would be expected to be changed as a function of changed behavior on the part of the other person or group. Although people with high traitlike CA or high generalized-context CA would be expected to experience high CA with more persons and groups, knowledge of the levels of neither of these should be expected to be predictive of CA experienced with a given individual or group. In short, this type of CA is presumed to be more a function of the situational constraints introduced by the other person or group than by the personality of the individual. Length of acquaintance should be a major consideration here. While in early stages of acquaintance the personality orientations should be somewhat predictive, in later stages the situational constraints should be expected to overpower these orientations (Richmond, 1978).

Few attempts to measure this type of CA have appeared in the literature. However, the state anxiety measure developed by Spielberger (1966), particularly as modified for this purpose by Richmond (1978), appears to be an excellent tool. It can be adapted readily for use with any person or group within any communication context.

Situational CA. This type of CA represents the reactions of an individual to communicating with a given individual or group of individuals at a given time. This is the most statelike of the types of CA. When we view CA from this vantage point we recognize that we can experience CA with a given person or group at one time but not at another time. For example, a student may experience little or no apprehension when going to a teacher to ask a question about an assignment, but be terrified if the teacher instructs the student to stay after class to meet with her or him.

Situational CA is viewed as *a transitory orientation toward communication with a given person or group of people.* It is not viewed as personality-based, but rather as a response to the situational constraints generated by the other person or group. The level of this type of CA should be expected to fluctuate widely as a function of changed constraints introduced by the other person or group. Although people with high traitlike CA or high generalized-situation CA would be expected to experience high CA in more individual situations than would other people, knowledge of the levels of neither of these should be expected to be highly predictive of CA experienced by an individual in any given situation. On the other hand, level of person-group CA should be expected to be moderately highly related to situational CA. Person-group CA primarily is a function of the prior history of the individual with the given person or group. Such a history can be assumed to produce expectations that would influence the level of CA in the given situation involving communication with that person or group.

Measurement of situational CA has received little attention in the previous research. However, the Spielberger (1966) instrument as modified by Richmond (1978), as noted in the previous section, appears to be a very satisfactory tool for this purpose.

Figure 5.1 illustrates the four types of CA. As indicated in that figure, the three components of this conceptualization are context, receiver (person/group), and time. Time should be taken to represent more than

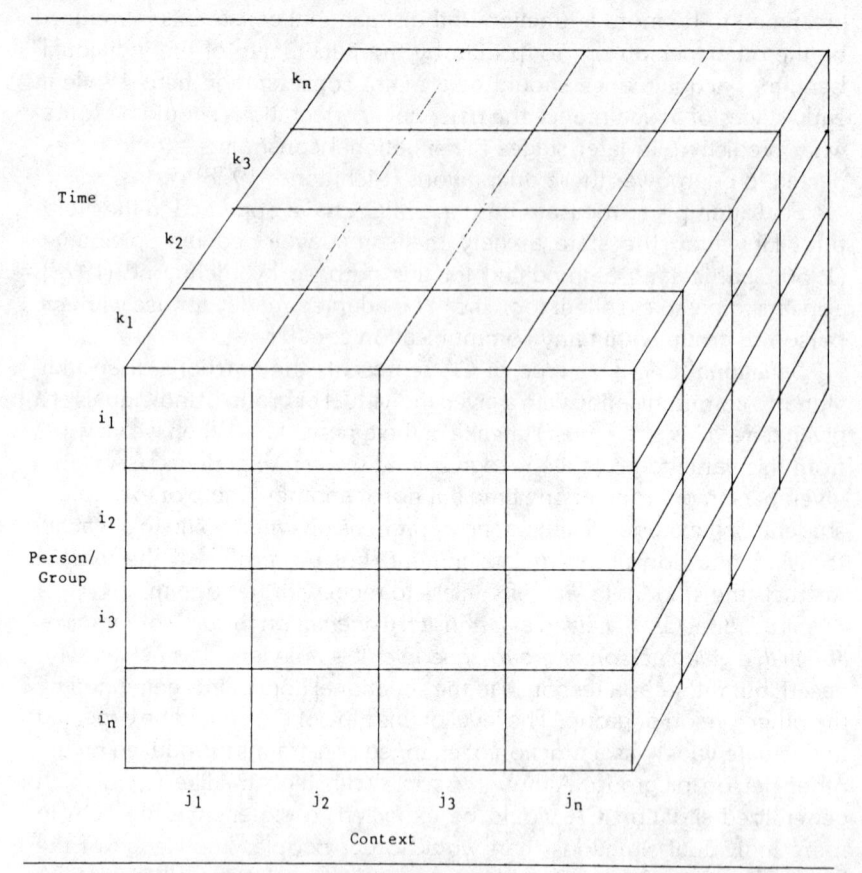

Figure 5.1. Illustration of types of CA. Traitlike = grand sum of all i_x j_x k_x cells; Generalized-Context = j_x across time and context; Person-Group = i_x across time and context; Situational = each i_x j_x k_x cell.

just the hour or day of the communication. As conceived here this element includes the variability associated with topic, mood, health, and the like that are seen as changeable over time, as well as the literal element of time itself. Traitlike CA is seen as that which cuts across context, receiver, and time. Generalized-context CA is seen as that which is associated with a single type of communication context cutting across receiver and time. Person-group CA is seen as that which is associated with a single receiver or group of receivers cutting across context and time. Situational CA is seen as that which is specific to a given context with a given receiver at a given time. It should be recognized that the three components in this model could be combined to generate additional types of CA. However, at present, I do not believe such combinations provide useful insights.

Pathological CA

It is important that we recognize that the four types of CA discussed above do not reference different types of people. Rather, every individual is affected by each type of CA to either a greater or lesser degree. It is a truly rare individual, if one actually exists, that never experiences CA in any communication situation. Such an individual would be seen as evidencing pathological behavior, since fear is a natural human response to a truly threatening situation. Similarly, it is comparatively rare individual who experiences CA in all communication situations, although some such people do exist. With the exception of these rare individuals, even people with very high traitlike CA find some situations in which they can communicate comfortably. The most common of these situations involve communication with close friends. It is not so much that close friends produce less apprehension as it is that people who produce less apprehension are allowed to become close friends, while more threatening individuals are avoided.

Since in the previous literature much has been made of the pathological nature of high CA, high reticence, and high shyness, we need to consider what we should view as pathological, or abnormal, levels of CA. This distinction can be made both conceptually and empirically, although the distinctions are not fully isomorphic.

At the conceptual level, we view abnormal behavior to be that which is nonadaptive, nonresponsive, or nonfunctional in the environment in which it is engaged. Normal individuals are sensitive to their environment, respond to its demands, and adapt their behavior so that they are a functional part of that environment. Experiencing fear or anxiety in a threatening situation and adapting by withdrawing or avoiding the threatening situation is normal. Experiencing no fear or anxiety in a nonthreatening environment and continuing to function in that environment is normal. The reverse responses are abnormal. Experiencing low CA in the face of real danger and experiencing high CA when no real danger is present are both abnormal responses. If such responses become characteristic of the individual, the individual may be regarded as pathological and in need of professional help. The question, of course, is one of degree. Abnormal responses in one or a few circumstances certainly should not generate a judgment of "pathological." Only when such behavior is a consistent pattern of the individual would such a judgment seem warranted. Most importantly, such judgments should not be restricted to only one end of the CA continuum. Extremely low CA can be just as abnormal as extremely high CA.

Empirically, the distinction between normal and abnormal is a bit more easily determined. I strongly endorse the empirical distinction made most frequently in the previous research. This distinction is based on the normal curve, an approximation of which is generated by scores on most of the common CA measures. People with scores beyond one standard deviation above or below the mean score of the population are identified as high or low in CA. In normally distributed scores, approximately 68 percent of the population falls within one standard deviation of the mean, with 16 percent scoring over one standard deviation higher and 16 percent scoring over one standard lower. The latter two groups are, in fact, statistically significantly different at alpha = .05.

For research purposes this is a particularly good distinction. The researcher can be reasonably assured that the people classified as "high" are truly different from those classified as "low." These two groups are the ones that theoretically should manifest differential behaviors related to the measure. Those in the middle, the "normals," actually may have no consistent pattern of behavior, particularly if the measure is a personality-type measure. The middle scores most likely indicate that this is a facet of personality not highly associated with the behavior of these individuals. Other personality elements, or situational constraints, may completely dominate their behavior to the exclusion of this particular personality variable.[7]

I originally introduced this system of classification into the literature as a function of observing groups of students brought into rooms for treatment of traitlike CA. I observed that groups of students composed entirely of individuals with scores beyond one standard deviation from the mean simply did not talk. The behavior of individuals in groups composed of people with scores between one-half and one standard deviation above the mean did not have such a consistent pattern. Some were totally noncommunicative, but others were willing to interact.[8] Thus this classification scheme is not purely arbitary. It does seem to have a behavioral justification.

Two cautions should be stressed, however. First, some samples may not be representative of the overall population. Therefore the classification-by-standard-deviation procedure should be sensitive to the mean and standard deviation of the population norms rather than the particular sample studied. A sample of successful salespersons, for example, probably would include few people with high CA. Second, while this procedure is excellent for research involving comparatively large samples and based on aggregate data analyses, such a procedure is far too subject to measurement error to be applied to single individuals. Judgments about individuals should never be based on a single score or any scale. Rather, such a score should be only one of many factors to be considered. This is particularly important for people to recognize when developing or implementing intervention programs designed to alter high or low CA.

Causes of CA

The etiology of CA has received comparatively little attention in the literature. Varying writers have presented different views. The differences, however, are not so much a function of disagreement as they are of desperation. The best method of isolating causes of subsequent events generally is considered to be carefully controlled experimentation. Unfortunately, for ethical reasons, this method is highly restricted for investigations of the causes of CA. While we might ethically employ experimentation to investigate situational CA, almost no one would approve such experimentation with traitlike CA. The other types of CA fall within the gray area between these two types. Consequently, most research directed toward the etiology of CA has been performed in naturalistic environments. Such research is useful for establishing correlational associations, but it is fraught with potential error when attempting to infer causality. Much of the writing in this area is based more on speculation than on research. Regretably, the following causal analysis will also have this characteristic. It is hoped that future research will provide insight into the validity of my speculations.

Previous causal analyses generally have been restricted to viewing either traitlike CA or situational CA. I will first present my positions in each of these areas and then advance an etiological explanation that I believe may be applied to all types of CA.

Causes of Traitlike CA. Throughout the social sciences only two major explanations of the differential traitlike behaviors of individuals hold sway: heredity and environment. Simply put, we can be born with it or we can learn it. I believe that both of these explanations can contribute to our understanding of the etiology of CA.

Although most early writers discounted heredity as a cause of traitlike CA out of hand, recent writers have grudgingly acknowledged that there indeed may be a hereditary contribution. Although no one has yet argued that there is a "CA gene," the work of social biologists, particularly their research with twins, has provided compelling evidence that something other than environmentally based learning is having an impact on human behavior tendencies. McCroskey and Richmond (1980, p. 6) summarize the thrust of this research:

> Researchers in the area of social biology have established that significant social traits can be measured in infants shortly after birth, and that infants differ sharply from each other on these traits. One of these traits is

referred to as "sociability," which is believed to be a predisposition directly related to adult sociability — the degree to which we reach out to other people and respond positively to contact with other people. Research with identical twins and fraternal twins of the same sex reinforces this theoretical role of heredity. Identical twins are biologically identical, whereas fraternal twins are not. Thus, if differences between twins raised in the same environment are found to exist, biology (heredity) can be discounted as a cause in one case but not in the other. Actual research has indicated that biologically identical twins are much more similar in sociability than are fraternal twins. This research would be interesting if it were conducted only on twin infants, but it is even more so because it was conducted on a large sample of adult twins who had the opportunity to have many different and varied social experiences.

It is important we recognize that the work of the social biologists does not support the argument that heredity is the only cause of sociability, much less of CA, but rather suggests that heredity may be one of the contributing causes. Children, it seems, are born with certain personality predispositions or tendencies. No one has yet argued, not even the most ardent social biologists, that these predispositions or tendencies are unchangeable. Thus what happens in the child's environment will have some impact on the predispositions and tendencies the child carries over into later life. However, because children are born with different predispositions and tendencies they will react differently to the same environmental conditions. This interaction of heredity and environment, then, is seen as the precursor of adult predispositions and tendencies such as CA.

Although heredity appears to be a meaningful contributor to traitlike CA, most writers allege that reinforcement patterns in a person's environment, particularly during childhood, are the dominant elements. Although most of the views supporting reinforcement as a cause are based primarily on speculation or analogy, some available research is supportive (e.g., McCroskey & Richmond, 1978).

We can view the causal impact of reinforcement in at least two ways. The first is a fairly narrow, behaviorist view. If the child is reinforced for communicating, the child will communicate more. If the child is not reinforced for communicating, the child will communicate less. While this is a rather simple application of the general theory of reinforcement, and may serve to explain many communication behaviors, since it does not address the cognitions of the individual and CA is viewed as a cognitive variable, this explanation is less than satisfactory for our purpose.

The second way we can view the impact of reinforcement is as an adjunct of modeling. Modeling theory suggests that children (and to some extent adults) observe the communication behavior of others in their environment and attempt to emulate it. If their attempts are reinforced, they continue to behave in a similar manner. If they are not reinforced, they alter their behavior. Such an explanation seems to be a very good way of looking at the development of many communication behaviors, such as accent, dialect, and use of nonverbal behaviors. However, this explanation also ignores the cognitive element and thus does not address CA as conceived here.

While I agree that reinforcement is a central component in the development of CA, I do not believe that the behavioristic approaches outlined above can account for this relationship. My view of the place of reinforcement as a causal element in the development of CA will be outlined below when I consider the theory of learned helplessness.

Causes of Situational CA. While causal attributions for elements leading to the development of traitlike CA are based primarily on speculation and rather tenuous analogies, the causes of situational CA appear much clearer. In some cases they have been the subject of direct research, in others strong analogies with similar fears or anxieties can be drawn. I find the causal elements outlined by Buss (1980) particularly insightful. Buss suggests that the major elements in the situation that can result in increased CA are: novelty, formality, subordinate status, conspicuousness, unfamiliarity, dissimilarity, and degree of attention from others. In most instances the opposite of each of these factors would be presumed to lead to decreased CA in the situation. Let us examine each of these briefly.

The novel situation presents the individual with increased uncertainty about how he or she should behave. If one almost never has an interview, going to an interview would be novel and the individual might not be sure how to behave and thus might become more apprehensive. For most people giving a speech is a novel experience, not something they do every day (or for many, every year). Approaching such a situation would be likely to increase CA sharply.

Formal situations tend to be associated with highly prescribed appropriate behaviors, with comparatively little latitude for deviation. Less formal situations have less rigid behavior rules and much wider latitudes of acceptable behavior. CA is increased in formal situations because of the narrower confines for acceptable behavior. A similar impact results from interacting from a subordinate position. In such situations appropriate behavior is defined by the person holding higher status. This is particularly important in evaluative settings, which are common in superior/subordinate communication situations.

Probably nothing can increase CA more than being conspicuous in one's environment. Giving a public speech is a prime example of being conspicuous; so is standing up to make a comment in a meeting or classroom. Similarly, being the new person in a social setting or meeting a new person can make a person feel conspicuous. Generally, the more conspicuous people feel, the more CA they are likely to experience.

Although not all people react to unfamiliarity in the same way, many people feel much more comfortable when communicating with people they know than when communicating with people they do not know. In general, as the degree of familiarity increases, the degree of CA decreases. To some extent similarity has the same kind of impact. For most people, talking to others who are similar to themselves is easier than talking to people who are greatly different. There are major exceptions to this rule, however. Some people are the most uncomfortable when communicating with similar peers, because they are more concerned with the evaluations such people make than they are with those of people who are very different from themselves.

A moderate degree of attention from others is the most comfortable situation for most people. When people stare at us or totally ignore us when we are communicating, our CA level can be expected to rise sharply and quickly. In addition, if people become overly intrusive into our private feelings and thoughts, we can become very uncomfortable.

In recent work, Daly and Hailey (1980) have noted two elements that go beyond those advanced by Buss as causes of situational CA. These are degree of evaluation and prior history. When we are evaluated we tend to be more anxious than otherwise. For example, a student giving a talk in a public speaking class for a grade may be more apprehensive than the same student would be if he or she were giving the same talk to the same people at a meeting in the dorm. Of course, not everyone responds to evaluation in the same way. As Daly and Hailey have noted, good writers do better when being evaluated, but poor writers do worse. This may also be true for oral communication, but no research addressing this issue is available.

The final causative element, prior history, may be the most important of all, as we will note when we consider learned helplessness in the next section. If one has failed before it is increasingly likely that one will fear that one will fail again, hence be more apprehensive. On the other hand, success breeds both success and confidence, hence less apprehension.

In sum, there are a variety of elements in communication situations that can cause our CA to increase — whether we are high, moderate, or low in traitlike CA. Their absence, likewise, can lower our CA. Most of these elements are at best only marginally under our control. Thus situational CA is produced by others in our communication environment, and to a large extent controlled by them. Often, then, the only method of avoiding the unpleasant aspects of situational CA is to withdraw from or avoid such communication situations.

Learned Helplessness and Learned Responsiveness. Although the above causal explanations are useful in developing a fuller understanding of the etiology of CA, none of them are fully satisfactory. Work in the area of expectancy learning, particularly that concerning learned helplessness (Seligman, 1975), permits a causal explanation that can be applied to all types of CA since it takes into account both traits of the individual and the variety of situational demands the individual can confront.

My approach is a cognitive one. My underlying assumption is that people develop expectations with regard to other people and with regard to situations. Expectations are also developed concerning the probable outcomes of engaging in specific behaviors (such as talking). To the extent that such expectations are found to be accurate, the individual develops confidence. When expectations are found to be inaccurate, the individual is confronted with the need to develop new expectations. When this continually recurs, the individual may develop a lack of confidence. When no appropriate expectations can be developed, anxiety is produced. When expectations are produced that entail negative outcomes that are seen as difficult or impossible to avoid, fear is produced. When applied to communication behavior, these latter two cases are the foundation of CA.

Reinforcement is a vital component of expectancy learning. Organisms form expectations on the basis of attempting behaviors and being reinforced for some and either not reinforced or punished for others. The most gestalt expectancy is that there is regularity in the environment. This forms the basis for the development of other, more specific expectations. When no regularity can be discovered in a given situation, either because none exists or there is too little exposure to the situation to obtain sufficient observation and reinforcement, the organism is unable to develop a regular behavioral response pattern for that situation which will maximize rewards and minimize punishments. Anxiety is the cognitive response to such situations, and the behavior is unpredictable to a large extent. However, nonbehavior such as avoidance or withdrawal is probable, since even though this does not increase probability of obtaining reward, it decreases probability of receiving punishment in many instances. The organism essentially becomes helpless.

In the early animal research concerning helplessness, dogs were placed in an environment in which rewards and punishments were administered on a random schedule. After attempting behaviors to adapt to this environment, but receiving no regular response from the environment, the dogs retreated to a corner and virtually stopped behaving. They became helpless, and some actually died (Seligman, 1975).

An analogy may be drawn here with human communication behavior. We learn our communicative behavior by trying various behaviors in our environment and receiving various rewards and punishments (or absence of rewards or punishments) for our efforts. Over time and situations we develop expectations concerning the likely outcomes of various behaviors within and across situations. Three things can occur from this process. All can occur for the same individual; however, they may occur to greatly different degrees for different individuals. All are environmentally controlled. The three things that can occur are positive expectations, negative expectations, and helplessness. Let us consider each.

When we engage in communication behaviors that work (i.e., are reinforced, we achieve some desired goal), we develop positive expectations for those behaviors and they become a regular part of our communicative repertoire. While in the early childhood years much of this occurs through trial and error, during later stages of development cognition becomes much more important. We may think through a situation and choose communication behaviors that our previous experience suggests we should expect to be successful. Formal instruction in communication adds to our cognitive capacity to develop such expectations and choose appropriate behaviors. To the extent that our behaviors continue to be reinforced, we develop stronger positive expectations and our communication behavior becomes more regularly predictable. In addition, we develop confidence in our ability to communicate effectively. Neither anxiety nor fear, the core elements of CA, is associated with such positive expectations.

The development of negative expectations follows much the same pattern as the development of positive expectations. We discover that some communication behaviors regularly result in punishment or lack of reward and we tend to reduce those behaviors. During later stages of development, we may make cognitive choices between behaviors for which we have positive and negative expectations, the former being chosen and the latter rejected. However, we may find situations for which we have no behaviors with positive expectations for success. If we can avoid or withdraw from such situations, this is a reasonable choice. However, if participation is unavoidable, we have only behaviors with negative expectations available. A fearful response is the natural outcome. Consider, for example, the person who has attempted several public speeches. In each case, the attempt resulted in punishment or lack of reward. When confronted with another situation that requires the individual to give a public speech, the person will fear that situation. The person knows what to expect, and the expectation is negative.

The development of helplessness occurs when regularity of expectations, either positive or negative, is not present. Helplessness may be either spontaneous or learned. Spontaneous helplessness occurs in new situations. If the person has never confronted the situation before, he or she

Oral Communication Apprehension

may be unable to determine any behavioral options. While this is much more common for young children, adults may confront such situations. For example, visiting a foreign country where one does not know the language may place one in a helpless condition. Similarly, some people who are divorced after many years of marriage report that they find themselves helpless in communication in the "singles scene." Such spontaneous helplessness generates strong anxiety feelings, and the behavior of people experiencing such feelings often is seen by others in the environment as highly aberrant.

Learned helplessness is produced by inconsistent receipt of reward and punishment. Such inconsistency may be a function of either true inconsistency in the environment or the inability of the individual to discriminate among situational constraints in the environment that produce differential outcomes. For example, a child may develop helplessness if the parent reinforces the child's talking at the dinner table some days and punishes it on other days. If the child is unable to determine why the parent behaves differently from day to day, the child is helpless to control the punishments and rewards. Similarly, the child may be rewarded for giving an answer in school but punished for talking to another child in the classroom. If the child is unable to see the differences in these situations, the child may learn to be helpless. When helplessness is learned, it is accompanied by strong anxiety feelings.

Learned helplessness and learned negative expectations are the foundational components of CA. The broader the helplessness or negative expectations, the more traitlike the CA. Inversely, the more situationally specific the helplessness or negative expectations, the more situational the CA. It should be stressed that helplessness and negative expectations (as well as positive expectations) are the product of an interaction of the behaviors of the individual and the responses of the other individuals in the environment. The development of the cognitive responses of the person, then, may be heavily dependent on the behavioral skills of that person, partly dependent on those skills and partly dependent on the responsiveness of the environment, or almost entirely a result of the environment. Thus any hereditary component that may exist may have either a large or small impact on later cognitions, depending on the type of environment in which the hereditarily predisposed behaviors are performed.

Learned responsiveness is seen as the opposite of learned helplessness. When the individual is able to discern differences in situations and has developed positive expectations for communication behaviors between and across differing situations, the individual has learned to be communicatively responsive. Learned responsiveness is associated with neither fear nor anxiety, thus it presents a circumstance antithetical to CA. Learned responsiveness can be the product of unsystematic learning in the natural environment or the direct result of formal communication instruction.

Treatment of CA

This explanation of the etiology of CA has taken a cognitive perspective. Before turning attention to possible treatments for CA, I should stress a distinction between what I will call "rational" CA and "nonrational" CA.

Rational levels of CA are produced by combinations of positive and negative expectations and helplessness or responsiveness that are consistent with views of an outside, objective observer's perceptions of reality. That is, the individual, for example, has a positive expectation for a behavior and an outside observer would agree that such a behavior should be expected to produce positive outcomes. Or, as another example, the individual feels helpless and knows of no behavior that would result in a desired outcome, and an outside observer would agree that that individual has no behavioral choice that would result in a positive outcome. Nonrational CA, on the other hand, is seen as the unjustified expectations and helplessness or responsiveness of the individual, as viewed from the perspective of an outside, objective observer. For example, the individual may have negative expectations for a behavior, but an outside observer would see the behavior as highly likely to produce a desired outcome. Or the individual feels very responsive, but the observer sees the person's behavior as nonfunctional in the situation.

I stress this distinction in order to emphasize the fact that some people feel CA in situations where there is no objective reason for them to do so, while others may not experience CA even in situations in which they should. Past approaches to treatment, for the most part, have failed to make this distinction. It was presumed unreasonable to hold high levels of CA but reasonable to hold low levels of CA, thus only those people with high CA were seen as in need of treatment.

In my view, there are two major classifications of treatments, and they should be applied differentially depending on whether the CA level is rational or nonrational. Let me explain.

Treatments may be directed either toward communication behaviors or toward cognitions about communication behaviors. That is, our treatment focus can be on communication skills within or across contexts or on the apprehension about engaging in communication within or across contexts.

Four general conditions are illustrated in Figure 5.2. The figure represents two levels of communication skill, satisfactory and unsatisfactory, and two levels of CA, low and high. Both low CA/satisfactory skills and high CA/unsatisfactory skills are seen as rational conditions. Low CA/un-

Oral Communication Apprehension

		Communication Skill Level	
		Satisfactory	Unsatisfactory
Communication Apprehension Level	Low	Rational I	Nonrational II
	High	Nonrational III	Rational IV

Figure 5.2. Rational and nonrational CA levels.

satisfactory skills and high CA/satisfactory skills are seen as nonrational conditions. Each condition provides different requirements for effective treatment.

Condition I, low CA/satisfactory skills, requires no treatment. People in this condition have rational cognitions, and most likely are reasonably effective communicators. The goal of all treatments is to move people from the other three conditions to this one.

Condition IV, high CA/unsatisfactory skills, also includes people with rational cognitions. They have unsatisfactory communication skills and are apprehensive about their communication. They have two problems, one behavioral and the other cognitive. No single solution is likely to overcome these problems and move these people to Condition I. If only their skills are improved, they will move to Condition III but still suffer from high CA. If only their CA is improved, they will move to Condition II but still suffer from inadequate skills. Thus both their skill deficiencies and their CA require treatment. An analogy with basketball may help to clarify this point. People in Condition IV are poor foul shooters (say, 30 percent in practice) and are very anxious about shooting foul shots in a game. If we overcome only the anxiety, they still can only shoot 30 percent in a game. If we only improve their shooting ability in practice, their anxiety will still cause them to miss in a game. To produce a good foul shooter, then, we need both to improve shooting accuracy and to reduce anxiety. Returning to communication, people in this condition must develop better skills and reduce their apprehension to become more effective communicators.

Condition II, low CA/unsatisfactory skills, includes people with nonrational cognitions. These are people who should experience high CA but do not. We could increase their CA, thus making their cognitions more rational, but that would only move them to Condition IV, certainly not solving a problem but only making it worse. The treatment for people in this condition is directed toward improving communication skills. If skill levels are raised, people in this condition move to Condition I, the desired condition. To employ our basketball analogy, these people are poor foul shooters but they are not anxious about it. If we raise their skill level (say, from 30 percent to 70 percent), we will produce good foul shooters in the regular games.

Condition III, high CA/satisfactory skills, also includes people with nonrational cognitions. These are people who should not experience high CA but do. The treatment for people in this condition is directed toward reducing their CA level, thus moving them into Condition I. In our basketball analogy, these are people who shoot well in practice (say, 70 percent) but choke and shoot poorly in the game (say, 30 percent). If we overcome their anxiety, we will produce good foul shooters in the regular games.

Treatment programs intended to produce effective communicators, then, are of two general types, those directed toward improving communication skills and those directed toward reducing CA. The different types of treatment programs are different solutions to different problems and should not be expected to have major effects on problems to which they are not directed. Reducing CA, for example, should not be expected to be associated with major increases in skill levels. Similarly, improving skills should not necessarily be expected to reduce CA, since CA level may be either rational or nonrational. For people with one problem, one treatment should be chosen. For people with both problems, two treatments should be chosen.

The specific nature of treatment programs is beyond my focus here. However, for skill deficiencies regular classroom instruction in communication, individualized skills training, and rhetoritherapy (Phillips, 1977) are recommended. For CA problems, systematic desensitization (McCroskey, 1972) and cognitive restructuring (Fremouw & Scott, 1979) seem to be most appropriate. Various combinations of these treatments are possible. The choice of one should not be taken to exclude use of another.

Effects of CA

The effects of CA have been the target of extensive research, particularly concerning traitlike CA, and have been summarized elsewhere (McCroskey, 1977a). My focus here will not be on such specific variable research, but rather I will direct my attention toward theoretically more global effect patterns. The previous research, although extremely valuable for generating an understanding of how CA is manifested in ongoing communicative relationships of individuals, has been subject to considerable overinterpretation, if not misinterpretation. Effects observed in aggregate data analyses often are seen as regular behavioral and outcome patterns for individual people with high or low CA. Such interpretations fail to recognize the high potential for the individual to deviate from the aggregate norm and the possibility of choosing from numerous behaviors, all of which would be theoretically consistent with the individual's CA level. My concern here, therefore, will be directed toward the internal impact of CA, possible external manifestations of CA, and the role CA plays as a mediator between communicative competence and skill and ultimate communicative behavior.

Internal Impact of CA. As I have noted previously, CA is viewed from a cognitive rather than a behavioral perspective. Although CA indeed may have some behavioral implications, as I will note below, it is experienced by the individual internally. *The only effect of CA that is predicted to be universal across both individuals and types of CA is an internally experienced feeling of discomfort.* The lower the CA, the less the internal discomfort. Since people's cognitions are imperfectly related to their levels of physiological arousal, no physiological variable is predicted to be associated universally with CA across people or across types of CA.

The implications of this conceptualization of CA for both research and treatment cannot be overemphasized. Since CA is experienced internally, the only potentially valid indicant of CA is the individual's report of that experience. Thus self-reports of individuals, whether obtained by paper-and-pencil measures or careful interviews, obtained under circumstances in which the individual has nothing to gain or avoid losing by lying, provide the only potentially valid measures of CA. Measures of physiological activation and observations of behavior can provide, at best, only indirect evidence of CA and thus are inherently inferior approaches to measuring CA. Thus physiological and behavioral instruments intended to measure CA must be validated with self-report measures, not the other way around. To the extent that such measures are not related to self-report measures, they must be judged invalid. Currently available data indicate that such physiological measures and behavioral observation procedures have low to moderately low validity.[9]

External Impact of CA. As noted above, there is no behavior that is predicted to be a universal product of varying levels of CA. Nevertheless, there are some externally observable behaviors that are more likely to occur or less likely to occur as a function of varying levels of CA. When examining behavioral outcomes of CA, we must keep in mind the distinction among the types of CA discussed earlier. Traitlike CA, for example, will be manifested in behavior in a given situation only as it interacts with the constraints of that situation. A person with high traitlike CA, for example, may behave in a manner no different from anyone else in a quiet conversation with a good friend. Similarly, a person with low traitlike CA may behave in a manner no different from anyone else if called to a meeting to be reprimanded by a superior. The behavioral manifestations of high CA we will discuss here, therefore, presuppose that CA actually is present to a sufficient degree in a given situation to trigger the behavior. The link is most direct for the most situational type of CA. For traitlike CA the link is most tenuous. The behavioral prediction should only be assumed to be correct when considering aggregate behavioral indicants of the individual across time and across contexts.[10]

Three patterns of behavioral response to high CA may be predicted to be generally applicable and one pattern can be described as sometimes present, but an atypical response pattern. The three typical patterns are communication avoidance, communication withdrawal, and communication disruption. The atypical pattern is excessive communication. Let us consider each.

When people are confronted with a circumstance that they anticipate will make them uncomfortable, and they have a choice of whether or not to confront it, they may decide either to confront it and make the best of it or avoid it and thus avoid the discomfort. Some refer to this as the choice between "fight" and "flight." Research in the area of CA indicates the latter choice should be expected in most instances. In order to avoid having to experience high CA, people may select occupations that involve low communication responsibilities, pick housing units that reduce incidental contact with other people, choose seats in classrooms or in meetings that are less conspicuous, and avoid social settings. At the lowest level, if a person makes us uncomfortable, we may simply avoid being around that person. Avoidance, then, is a common behavioral response to high CA.

Avoidance of communication is not always possible. In addition, one can find oneself in a situation that generates a high level of CA with no advance warning. Under such circumstances, withdrawal from communication is the behavioral pattern to be expected. This withdrawal may be complete, i.e., absolute silence, or partial, i.e., talking only as much as absolutely required. In a public speaking setting, this response may be represented by the very short speech. In a meeting, class, or small group discussion, it may be represented by talking only when called upon. In a dyadic interaction, it may be represented by only answering questions or supplying agreeing responses, with no initiation of discussion.

Communication disruption is the third typical behavioral pattern associated with high CA. The person may have disfluencies in verbal presentation or unnatural nonverbal behaviors. Equally as likely are poor choices of communicative strategies, sometimes reflected in the after-the-fact "I wish I had (had not) said . . ." phenomenon. It is important to note, however, that such behaviors may be produced by inadequate communication skills as well as by high CA. Thus inferring CA from observations of such behavior is not always appropriate.

Overcommunication is a response to high CA that is not common but is the pattern exhibited by a small minority. This behavior represents overcompensation. It may reflect the "fight" rather than the "flight" reaction, the attempt to succeed in spite of the felt discomfort. The person who elects to take a public speaking course in spite of her or his extreme stage fright is a classic example. Less easily recognizable is the individual with high CA who attempts to dominate social situations. Most of the time people who employ this behavioral option are seen as poor communicators but are not recognized as having high CA; in fact, they may be seen as people with very low CA.

To this point we have looked at the typical behaviors of people with high CA levels. We might assume that the behaviors of people with low CA would be the exact reverse. That assumption might not always be correct, however. While people with low CA should be expected to seek opportunities to communicate rather than to avoid them, and to dominate interactions in which they are members rather than to withdraw from them, people with low CA may also have disrupted communication and overcommunicate. The disruptions may stem from pushing too hard rather than from tension, but the behaviors may not always be distinctly different to the observer. Similarly, the person who overcommunicates engages in very similar behavior whether the behavior stems from high or low CA. While future research may permit us to train observers who can distinguish disrupted communication resulting from high CA from that resulting from low CA and possibly distinguish between overcommunication behaviors stemming from the two causes, these behaviors are, and probably will remain, indistinguishable by the average person in the communication situation.

CA and Communication Behavior. Without discounting a possible role for hereditary predispositions, I view communication behavior, as other human behavior, as a learned response to one's environment. Since I wish to explore the role of CA as it relates to human communication behavior more generally, it is important to enunciate my assumptions about human learning. Following the lead of contemporary writers in educational psychology, I view human learning as composed of three domains. These are the cognitive (understanding or knowing),[11] affective (feeling of liking or disliking), and psychomotor (the physical capability of doing) domains.

Because of inconsistent and confused use of terms within the communication literature, when I apply these domains to communication learning it is important that I make a distinction between communication *competence* and communication *skill.* I see communication competence as falling within the cognitive domain and communication skill as falling within the psychomotor domain. More specifically, communication competence is "the ability of an individual to demonstrate knowledge of the appropriate communicative behavior in a given situation" (Larson, Backlund, Redmond, & Barbour, 1978, p. 16). Communication competence, then, can be demonstrated by observing a communication situation and identifying behaviors that would be appropriate or inappropriate in that situation. Communication skill, on the other hand, involves actual psychomotor behavior. Communication skill is the ability of an individual to perform appropriate communicative behavior in a given situation. To be judged skilled, then, a person must be able to physically engage in appropriate behaviors.

The three components of desired communication learning, then, are communication competence (knowing and understanding appropriate communication behaviors), communication skill (being able physically to produce appropriate communication behaviors), and positive communication affect (liking and wanting to produce appropriate communication behaviors). Any desired impact on long-term behavior of the individual requires that production of all of these types of learning be achieved, whether by the "natural" environment or by a formal instructional system, or by some combination of the two.

CA can have a major impact in all three areas of communication learning, and, consequently, on the long-term behavior of individuals. High CA is seen as a potential inhibitor of the development of both communication competence and communication skill and as a direct precursor of negative communication affect. Low CA, on the other hand, is seen as a facilitator of the development of communication competence and communication skill and as a precursor of positive communication affect.

With regard to communication competence, high CA is projected as a barrier to accurate observation of the natural environment and sufficient experience within it and as a barrier to the formal study of communication. Not only do people try to avoid studying things that cause them discomfort, but such discomfort may inhibit their learning when they do study it. The projected pattern for learning communication skills is seen in the same way. A major facet of psychomotor learning is practice. High CA will lead to less practice and possible misinterpretations of the outcomes of what practice is attempted. The impact of CA in terms of communication affect is even more direct. If we are fearful or anxious about something, we are not given to liking it. On the other hand, things that are not threatening are more likely to generate positive affect.

A major conclusion we can draw from this conceptualization of CA and communication learning is that high CA is highly associated with ineffective communication. As such, CA must be considered a central concern of any instructional program concerned with more effective communication as a targeted outcome, whether the program is labeled a program in communication competence or a program in communication skill. Basic competencies and basic skills cannot be separated from the problem of high CA.

CONCLUSION

CA has received extensive attention from many researchers over the past decade and currently is the target of many educationally based programs designed to help both children and adults. The purpose of this chapter has been to analyze what we have learned over the past decade and provide a revised conceptualization of the CA construct. It is hoped that this effort will clarify directions for future research in this area and help both researchers and practitioners avoid the pitfalls encountered by their predecessors.

NOTES

1. Some of these include personnel psychology, business administration, behavioral psychology, English, education, general psychology, and pharmacy.
2. CA research has been reported in Australia, Canada, China, Guam, Korea, and Japan. Projects are under way in Finland, West Germany, India, Puerto Rico, the Soviet Union, and South Africa.
3. For example, *The Australian Journal of Education, Psychological Reports, Journal of Pharmaceutical Education, Cross Currents, Korea Journal, Journal of Psychology, Journal of Counseling Psychology, Research in the Teaching of English, Journal of Consulting and Clinical Psychology, Behavior Therapy,* and *Journal of Personality.*
4. CA was the topic of a "People Quiz" column by John E. Gibson in *Family Weekly* in November 1979. CA has also been the topic of discussion on numerous radio talk shows. Both shyness and reticence have been the subject of interviews on the Johnny Carson and Phil Donahue shows as well as other television interview shows.
5. The *Communication Apprehension Newsletter* was begun in 1980. To be included on the mailing list, write to Mrs. Arden Watson, Department of Communication and Theatre, Western Kentucky University, Bowling Green, KY 42101.
6. Criticisms of the twenty- and twenty five-item PRCA instruments have been directed toward a heavy emphasis on items relating to public speaking in those instruments. This problem has been overcome in the most recent form of the measure, PRCA-24 (McCroskey, 1982). For this reason the new form is to be preferred over the earlier versions. This instrument permits four subscores as well as an overall score. The reliability of the instrument (internal) is estimated at .94 and the total score correlates with the earlier

forms above .90. Data from over 10,000 subjects indicates the scores form a normal distribution with a mean of 65.6 and a standard deviation of 14.1.

7. It has been demonstrated repeatedly in the personality literature that any given personality variable may be relevant to behavioral prediction for some people but not for all people. People scoring in the midrange of the measure are least predictable. For such people the variable may be irrelevant and their behavior may be controlled by the situation and/or other personality characteristics. For a discussion of these problems, see Bem and Allen (1974) and Bem and Funder (1978).

8. These observations were made during data collection for the study reported by Ertle (1969).

9. For earlier research, see Clevenger (1959). More recently, it has been found that although self-reported traitlike CA, as measured by the PRCA, is not highly correlated with physiological arousal, as measured by heart rate, the two combined are able to predict over 80 percent of the variance in self-reported state apprehension, as measured by a modification of the Spielberger state anxiety measure. The beta weights for the two predictors are nearly equal with little colinearity. See Behnke and Beaty (1981).

10. For suggestions for testing this type of prediction, see Jaccard and Daly (1980). Recent research reports validity coefficients in the neighborhood of .50 for the PRCA and a measure of shyness when tested in this way. See McCroskey and Richmond (1981).

11. My use of "cognitive" previously referred to the distinction made in psychology between "cognitivists" and "behaviorists." This is a broader use of the term than the one relating to the domains of learning. The reader should avoid confusing the two usages.

REFERENCES

Andersen, P. A., Andersen, J. F., & Garrison, J. P. Singing apprehension and talking apprehension: The development of two constructs. *Sign Language Studies,* 1978, *19,* 155-186.

Behnke, R. R., & Beaty, M. J. A cognitive-physiological model of speech anxiety. *Communication Monographs,* 1981, *48,* 158-163.

Bem, D. J., & Allen, A. On predicting some of the people some of the time: The search for cross-situational consistencies in behavior. *Psychological Review,* 1974, *81,* 506-520.

Bem, D. J., & Funder, D. C. Predicting more of the people more of the time: Assessing the personality of situations. *Psychological Review,* 1978, *85,* 485-501.

Bruneau, T., Cambra, R. E., & Klopf, D. W. *Communication apprehension: Its incidence in Guam and elsewhere.* Paper presented at the Communication Association of the Pacific Convention, Agana, Guam, 1980.

Burgoon, J. K. The unwillingness-to-communicate scale: Development and validation. *Communication Monographs,* 1976, *43,* 60-69.

Buss, A. H. *Self-consciousness and social anxiety.* San Francisco: W. H. Freeman, 1980.

Clevenger, T., Jr. A synthesis of experimental research in stage fright. *Quarterly Journal of Speech,* 1959, *45,* 134-145.

Daly, J. A. The assessment of social-communicative anxiety via self-reports: A comparison of measures. *Communication Monographs,* 1978, *45,* 204-218.

Daly, J. A., & Hailey, J. L. *Putting the situation into writing research: Situational parameters of writing apprehension as disposition and state.* Paper presented at the National Council of Teachers of English Convention, Cincinnati, 1980.

Daly, J. A., & Miller, M. D. The empirical development of an instrument to measure writing apprehension. *Research in the Teaching of English,* 1975, *9,* 242-249.

Ertle, C. D. *A study of the effect of homogeneous grouping on systematic desensitization for the reduction of interpersonal communication apprehension.* Unpublished doctoral dissertation, Michigan State University, 1969.

Fremouw, W. J., & Scott, M. D. Cognitive restructuring: An alternative method for the treatment of communication apprehension. *Communication Education*, 1979, *28*, 129-133.

Gilkinson, H. Social fears as reported by students in college speech classes. *Speech Monographs*, 1942, *9*, 141-160.

Hansford, B. C., & Hattie, J. A. *Communication apprehension: An assessment of Australian and United States data.* Unpublished manuscript, University of New England, Australia, 1979.

Hayes, D. P., & Meltzer, L. Interpersonal judgments based on talkativeness, I: Fact or artifact? *Sociometry*, 1972, *33*, 538-561.

Hayes, D. P., & Meltzer, L. *Interpersonal judgments based on talkativeness, II.* Unpublished manuscript, Cornell University, 1979.

Henning, J. H. *A study of stage fright through the comparison of student reactions and instructor observations during the speech situation.* Unpublished master's thesis, Northwestern University, 1935.

Jaccard, J., & Daly, J. A. Personality traits and multiple-act criteria. *Human Communication Research*, 1980, *6*, 367-377.

Klopf, D. W., & Cambra, R. E. Communication apprehension among college students in America, Australia, Japan, and Korea. *Journal of Psychology*, 1979, *102*, 27-31.

Klopf, D. W., & Cambra, R. E. Apprehension about speaking among college students in the People's Republic of China. *Psychological Reports*, 1980, *46*, 1194.

Larson, C. E., Backlund, P. M., Redmond, M. K., & Barbour, A. *Assessing communicative competence.* Falls Church, VA: Speech Communication Association and ERIC, 1978.

Lomas, C. W. *A study of stage fright as measured by student reactions to the speech situation.* Unpublished master's thesis, Northwestern University, 1934.

McCroskey, J. C. Measures of communication-bound anxiety. *Speech Monographs*, 1970, *37*, 269-277.

McCroskey, J. C. The implementation of a large-scale program of systematic desensitization for communication apprehension. *Speech Teacher*, 1972, *21*, 255-264.

McCroskey, J. C. Oral communication apprehension: A summary of recent theory and research. *Human Communication Research*, 1977, *4*, 78-96. (a)

McCroskey, J. C. *Quiet children and the classroom teacher.* Falls Church, VA: Speech Communication Association and ERIC, 1977. (b)

McCroskey, J. C. Validity of the PRCA as an index of oral communication apprehension. *Communication Monographs*, 1978, *45*, 192-203.

McCroskey, J. C. On communication competence and communication apprehension: A response to Page. *Communication Education*, 1980, *29*, 109-111.

McCroskey, J. C. *An introduction to rhetorical communication* (4th ed.). Englewood Cliffs, NJ: Prentice-Hall, 1982.

McCroskey, J. C., Andersen, J. F., Richmond, V. P., & Wheeless, L. R. Communication apprehension of elementary and secondary students and teachers. *Communication Education*, 1981, *30*, 122-132.

McCroskey, J. C., & Richmond, V. P. The effects of communication apprehension on the perception of peers. *Western Speech Communication Journal*, 1976, *40*, 14-21.

McCroskey, J. C., & Richmond, V. P. Community size as a predictor of development of communication apprehension: Replication and extension. *Communication Education*, 1978, *27*, 212-219.

McCroskey, J. C., & Richmond, V. P. *The quiet ones: Communications apprehension and shyness.* Dubuque, IA: Gorsuch Scarisbrick, 1980.

McCroskey, J. C., & Richmond, V. P. *Communication apprehension and shyness: validation of two constructs and measures.* Paper presented at the International Communication Association Convention, Minneapolis, 1981.

Mortensen, C. D., Arntson, P. H., & Lustig, M. The measurement of verbal predispositions: Scale development and application. *Human Communication Research*, 1977, *3*, 146-158.

Paul, G. L. *Insight versus desensitization in psychotherapy.* Stanford, CA: Stanford University Press, 1966.

Phillips, G. M. Reticence: Pathology of the normal speaker. *Speech Monographs,* 1968, *35,* 39-49.

Phillips, G. M. Rhetoritherapy versus the medical model: Dealing with reticence. *Communication Education,* 1977, *26,* 34-43.

Phillips, G. M. On apples and onions: A reply to Page. *Communication Education,* 1980, *29,* 105-108.

Pilkonis, P. A., Heape, C., & Klein, R. H. Treating shyness and other relationship differences in psychiatric outpatients. *Communication Education,* 1980, *29,* 250-255.

Prisbell, M., & Dallinger, J. Trait and state communication apprehension and level of uncertainty over time. Paper presented at the Western Speech Communication Association Convention, San Jose, California, 1981.

Redding, C. W. *The psychogalvanometer as a laboratory instrument in the basic course in speech.* Unpublished master's thesis, University of Denver, 1936.

Richmond, V. P. The relationship between trait and state communication apprehension and interpersonal perceptions during acquaintance stages. *Human Communication Research,* 1978, *4,* 338-349.

Seligman, M. E. *Helplessness: On depression, development and death.* San Francisco: W. H. Freeman, 1975.

Spielberger, C. D. Theory and research on anxiety. In C. D. Spielberger (Ed.), *Anxiety and behavior.* New York: Academic Press, 1966.

Zimbardo, P. G. *Shyness: What it is and what to do about it.* Reading, MA: Addison-Wesley, 1977.

COMMUNICATION REVIEWS AND COMMENTARIES

6 ● Does Communication Theory Need Intersubjectivity? Toward an Immanent Philosophy of Interpersonal Relations

LAWRENCE GROSSBERG
University of Illinois—Urbana

IT IS by now commonplace to think of theories as linguistic constructs. I would propose two emendations to this view. First, theories consist of a vocabulary with particular relationships between the terms. The structure of these relationships is like that of a house of cards: It is significant that each card is just where it is, but no one card supports or is the acme of the entire edifice. Second, theories are never entirely linguistic; there are always connections between a theory's vocabulary and particular features of material existence. Thus, one describes a theory by mapping out the relations that exist among its terms, and between these relations and the reality with which it is concerned.

This metaphor suggests an approach to meta-theorizing different from that normally taken in the study of communication. Philosophers of communication commonly begin by granting "communication" a privileged status in the theoretical house of cards. They assume that communication is a transcendental term, either the most fundamental fact in the constitution of the human or the most problematic. In either case, communication becomes the essential statement of the contemporary human condition. The result is that the concept of "communication" remains impervious to philosophical scrutiny. I have argued recently that this status may be connected to particular social institutions of power (Grossberg, 1982).

An alternative strategy, built upon the metaphor of the house of cards, would draw the lines between communication and, on the one hand, other terms within our theoretical vocabularies and, on the other hand, particular aspects of our material existence. This chapter, building upon earlier

Correspondence and requests for reprints: Lawrence Grossberg, Department of Speech Communication, University of Illinois, Urbana, IL 61801.

research (Grossberg, 1979, in press), will address the relationships among the concepts of meaning, communication, and intersubjectivity, proceeding in the following manner: I shall present three "ideal types" of vocabularies beginning with conceptions of meaning and providing answers to the question: Communication is the _____ of meaning between individuals through _____. The form of the question obviously assumes that communication involves meaning processes that result in particular relationships among individuals. Furthermore, my argument assumes that one can adequately summarize the diversity of responses that have been given to the question of communication with three phrases: (1) correspondence through exchange, (2) sharing through emergence, and (3) constitution through interpretation. Each of these solutions permits a limited range of concrete descriptions of the communicative process, depending on different details in the "meaning of meaning."

In addition, each of these three vocabularies defines a relationship between communication and intersubjectivity. The second section of this chapter will attempt to describe the role and significance of "intersubjectivity" within each of the three structures. Finally, I will suggest that the conceptual relation between intersubjectivity and interpersonal relationships underlying the three vocabularies of communication has made it more difficult, if not impossible, for us to account for the increasingly pervasive feeling that interpersonal relationships are problematic.[1] What is necessary therefore is an alternative way of talking about interpersonal relationships without the assumption of intersubjectivity. I will briefly contrast two alternative strategies for developing such a discourse: deconstruction and rhizomatics. But if the product of communication — in the form of interpersonal relations — is described differently, then we must presumably find a radically new vocabulary for an account of communication itself.

MEANING AND COMMUNICATIVE RELATIONSHIPS[2]

Correspondence Through Exchange

Probably the most common view of meaning is that it exists as entities, as isolatable and identifiable units. Something "has" a meaning, then, insofar as it refers to a particular unit. Of course one must still ask the question, units of what? While there have been a large number of answers given to this question, philosophers generally agree that there are two major schools of such atomistic views of meaning, although there are disagreements about how to describe them. I shall call them *physicalism* and *mentalism*. A physicalist sees meaning as units of some physical world that exist independently of any uniquely human activity. Meanings may be conceived of, for example, as atomic facts, sense data (taken nonphenomenally), behaviors, or information. A mentalist, on the other hand, argues that meaning exists as units but only within the uniquely human domain of consciousness. Meanings are bits of human mental existence that may be seen as sense impressions, concepts, intentions, or ideas, for example.

While these two views diverge on a number of points, they seem to imply a common view of the fundamental terms with which communication is described: Communication is a process whereby two individuals are related by virtue of having the same meaning. There is a correspondence between the meaning-entities in the possession of the two individuals, that is, at least, the product of communication. Communication itself is the process by which the same meaning exists in two places, for two people. Furthermore, the process itself must be causally determinative of this resulting state of affairs. There must be, then, some sort of exchange by which the meaning-entity of one person is made to correspond to an already existing meaning-entity in the possession of another person. It is obvious that "correspondence" and "exchange" have provided the dominant framework within which most communication theorists have operated — the so-called linear or transmission view of communication.

However, there are significant differences in one's view of communication depending upon whether this exchange is understood in the terms of a physicalist or a mentalist conception of meaning. A physicalist view of communication (e.g., Berlo, 1960) gives meaning a status independent of the consciousness of the subject. This is not merely to say that meanings are located within publicly available signs, for if the meaning ultimately refers to something located within individual consciousness, then its status is not inherently objective. That is, in addition to the public availability of meaning in signs or behavior, a physicalist view maintains that the very nature of meaning can be explicated without reference to consciousness. For example, if meaning is itself nothing but behavior or patterns of behavior, then communication is describable as a specific instance of the more general process of learning and hence, persuasion. This is what is commonly referred to as the *effects model*. Alternatively, if meaning is taken to be information, then its physicality lies in the real world that it refers to or represents. In such a model, communication is described as the exchange of information and it is accounted for as an achievement of the elimination of all subjective interpretations or inputs from the information exchange itself. Only in this way can information be exchanged and come to correspond. The attractiveness of a physicalist or linear view is due in part to the fact that it opens up the study of communication to quantitative analyses, with research programs built upon the observation, measurement, and testing of the exchange and correspondence of meaning in communication processes. On the other hand, there is a serious disadvantage to such views from the perspective of communication theorists: namely, that such views deny the particularity of communication. In fact, they reduce communication to simply another example of a more general process (e.g., learned response to stimuli, information processing) with little or no way of distinguishing communication from other forms of interaction and interpersonal relationships. Finally, physicalist theories have no way of describing the uniquely human forms of such processes other than by an appeal to degrees of complexity.

The mentalist account of communication (e.g., Mortenson, 1972) has the advantage of seeming so commonsensical, of appearing to accurately represent our experience of communication. Such a view assumes that meanings ultimately refer to and are describable as nonlinguistic entities that are the "private" property of individual subjects, located within consciousness. If meanings belong in some essential way to individual consciousness, to subjects isolated from each other not only in their physical but in their psychical lives as well, one seems inevitably locked into a position of viewing meaning as private. The question of communication must then be seen in terms of the need to free meanings from the individual, to exchange them and to cause two individuals to have the same meaning. This is traditionally known as the egocentric predicament, in which humans are seen as prisoners of their own minds isolated from others. The question of communication involves the nature of the connections that enable us to escape the egocentric predicament: Through what medium of exchange can there be the causal production of a correspondence between individual meanings?

Mentalism as a foundation for communication theory requires that one posit an objective medium through which individuals can connect in such a way as to causally determine the contents of each other's consciousness. This objective medium of exchange provides the possibility of bridging the radical gap between individual consciousnesses. But if communication is to be accounted for, meaning itself must be located in this objective (i.e., stable and public) medium as well as in the consciousness of the individual. This is the function of the concept of the sign in such theories, for it gives stability and identifiability — and hence the possibility of identification and correspondence — to particular meanings that would otherwise be individualized and unknowable by the other. But in order to accomplish this, the mentalist must postulate a second type of meaning — the meaning of a sign — which itself may or may not correspond to the mental entity of a particular person. The only alternative would be to allow the physicalist the position that signs are stimuli that elicit particular behavioral responses, in which case the mentalist's subjective meaning-entities seem unnecessary.

Thus, if the mentalist is to defend her or his claim that signs are an objective medium of exchange by which subjective meanings are made to correspond, he or she is forced to postulate a meaning carried in the sign itself. This sign-meaning cannot be said to exist in any individual's consciousness. The sign must involve a nonindividually constituted connection between a material vehicle and a meaning, a meaning that is present in the sign itself as a socially shared entity and hence, available to any number of individuals, however isolated they are as consciousnesses. This sign-meaning cannot be entirely dependent on the individual; it is the link through which exchange can be made and correspondence accomplished. The mentalist then, in order to account for communication as the correspondence of individual meanings, is forced to introduce a notion of a social meaning and, furthermore, to assume some necessary correspondence between individual (subjective) and social (sign) meanings. It is here, as I shall argue shortly, that the concept of intersubjectivity first enters into the vocabulary of communication, for it is used to postulate a transcendence of the separation between individuals into another realm — that of the social.

Sharing Through Emergence

I have argued that accounts of communication that begin with a conception of meaning as an entity find themselves operating with a number of dualisms: subjective meaning and objective medium, individual and social meaning. The second dualism, in fact, seems to result inevitably from the first. It is not surprising, therefore, to find an alternative conception of meaning that refuses to locate meaning outside of its medium of objective existence, without reducing it to the physicalist's entity. In fact, such views attempt to avoid altogether the issue of whether meaning is physically or mentalistically existent. The status of meaning is given, instead, in its relationship to the medium of its articulation. Meaning is an emergent and epiphenomenal product of the relations among the elements of the medium itself. By claiming that all meaning emerges out of the system of its articulation, such views are able to suggest that meaning is more akin to a process than to an entity that can exist as such. Differences arise within such "systemic" views of meaning over the the issue — crucial in this case — of the nature of the medium of articulation itself. In any case, the medium must be described as having some sort of objective or material existence: for example, the system of linguistic units or rules, the observable system of human interactions or speech acts, etc. The question that then arises is the status of the meaning that emerges out of the system — its epiphenomenality. As long as meaning always has one status and that status is not a mentalistic one, such views would appear to avoid the egocentric predicament and to lay the groundwork for an adequate account of the process of communication.

The importance of the epiphenomenal status can be seen if we begin by asking what it is that distinguishes communication from other forms of the emergence of meaning from a system of, e.g., language or language use. The systemic theorist is threatened on the one side with having everything human be a form of communication and, on the other side, with having disallowed the possibility of a failed communicative interaction. The uniqueness of communication for such views resides once again in the particular result of emergence in communication processes: that the same meaning is possessed by the two interactants. But this no longer requires two entities that correspond. The epiphenomenality of meaning allows it to exist apparently as one meaning that is possessed by two individuals. It is the same meaning that is shared, where same now refers to a strict, self-identity. Thus, communication requires that emergent meanings, despite their epiphenomenality, must be "real" and capable of being possessed by individuals. However, emergent meanings have the additional property of a commodity that can belong simultaneously to multiple individuals. The fact is that, on such views, there is a real emergence of meaning from the medium of articulation. That which emerges is different from the articulation itself. There is in fact a *meaning* that emerges and is shared. Communication is no longer seen in terms of individual meanings being exchanged through a medium of social meaning; rather it involves interactions among individuals within a system of articulation out of which shared meaning emerges. However, the vocabulary of a systemic view must also allow for the possibility of communication processes that result in something other than the sharing of the same meaning. The possibility of miscommunication must be allowed. In attempting to incorporate failure, emergent theories of communication are forced to deviate somewhat from the original power of the notion of an emergent epiphenomenal meaning.

Obviously, the understanding of the individual has changed significantly. It is no longer a subject or isolated consciousness but an actor engaged in interactions with other individuals and with the environment. No longer the absolute origin and locus of meanings, the individual is now the active and practical agent who serves as both initiator of and respondent to particular actions. The individual is not isolated from others but exists within a field of active agents who are already related to one another and constantly engaged in processes of interaction. Furthermore, such concrete interactions always occur within an already existing context or system of articulation that makes them possible. It is this context that takes the place of the objective or social within these views. This system is not reducible to individuals or their actions; it is the already present structure of shared meaning within which individuals live out their lives. That is, at any moment, it appears to be a structure of stability and transindividuality because emergence itself cannot be accounted for in individual terms. The existence of the system must be taken for granted, its origin unquestioned.

However, these descriptions are to some extent inadequate because, while both the individual and the system of articulation have apparently discrete and separable properties, their natures are also inherently interwoven with each other. While the system has its own stability and its own possibilities for change, it exists only insofar as it is continuously reaffirmed by individuals in particular interactions. Individuals are responsible in part for the continued existence of the system and for its continuous development and change. Similarly, the nature of the individual must be understood in terms of its relation to the system of articulation. While continuing to exist outside of the system as an origin of intentions, projects, and actions, the individual simultaneously exists in relation to the system as a competent social actor, where competence is defined by the particular nature of the system itself. Finally, it is the stability of the system that allows the individual to act in ways that reaffirm and change the system itself.

Consequently, the question of communication is asked within systemic theories of meaning in terms of the possibilities of shared meanings emerging within an already constituted context of shared, historically emergent meanings. Sharing is itself the emergent product of interactions among individuals located within a constantly rearticulated system. Privacy is no longer central to an understanding of communication because individual meaning is already shared since it itself must presumably have emerged from some interaction. Communication is the emergence of shared meaning out of individual interactions within an ongoing context of shared social meanings.

Communication is, then, an ongoing contextualized process of interaction in which shared meaning emerges from the relationship of the individual interaction and the system of articulation. As I have said, these terms — individual and system — can be neither radically separated nor totally identified if one is to account for both the emergence of sharedness and the possibility of failure. The system has a stability to which the individual must acquiesce if interactions are to be possible, but the individual must have an identity apart from the system (or the particular context) if creativity and change are inevitable. By beginning with a system of relations within which individuals are able to engage in creative and original actions with others, the question of communication is one of contextualization and emergence, systematization and innovation. The question of communication is not that of accounting for a correspondence between subjective meanings, but rather of describing the relations between individuals as a continuous immersion within and transcendence of an ongoing context of already shared meanings. Consequently, communication is located in an always and already ongoing context of a communication community. The "sameness" of meaning that linear views of communication see as the achievement of correspondence is instead the continuous recreation and change of our common social reality. It is both the original, given context within which meanings exist to be appropriated by individuals and the process by which that appropriation renews and changes that context. The view that communication accomplishes a sharing of the same, emergent meaning appeals to a context of meaning in which individuals already find themselves in relations, as socialized into a community. Communication as sharing opens up the interinvolvement of creativity and tradition, of act and structure.

The particular descriptions of communication arising from the discourse of sharing and emergence can be divided according to whether they begin with structures or acts. The former I will call a *structural* view of communication; it often draws heavily upon semiotics, linguistics, and rule theories. The latter I will call an *interactional* view of communication; it is closely tied with symbolic interactionism, ethnography, and a particular reading of speech act theory.

The structural view of communication (e.g., Nofsinger, 1975) focuses on a description of the objectivity and stability of the system within which particular communicative interactions take place. It describes this context as a structure that pre-exists and constitutes the possibility of concrete interactions. Particular events of communication — the concrete emergence of a shared meaning — are merely the expression of the structure within which they are articulated. The uniqueness and appropriateness of a message is the result of the structure's being competently used. While communication is always an act, it is defined by the structured context within which it functions. Communication, then, points to our continued existence within a structure that has already located the individual within a context of shared meanings and/or a system of rules prescribing the appropriate action. We are able to communicate only because we exist as potential communicators, and that potentiality is the expression of our already existing in a relation with others, i.e., within a common structure. That common structure is self-sufficient and objectively describable. Communication does not involve individuals using the system of articulation to exchange something existing outside of the system itself, but rather the emergence of a meaning that is the common possession of the interactants. The success of communication is located within the structure itself; it does not demand any appeal to either a subjective locus of meaning or an objective world to which meanings refer. Meaning is the product of the system itself and as such, exists only within the system. It does not demand any appeal to something outside of the system. Communication is merely the reassertion of our condition as already coexisting with others within the structure. To understand a message is not to bring something to or take anything away from it, but rather, it is the fact that we are able to continue using the structure itself in appropriate ways. According to a structural view, then, the individual is merely defined as the user of the system: Anything else that may be a feature of the identity of the individual is itself a product of the articulation of the system itself.

If the communicative event is merely the concrete manifestation of a structure within which individuals already exist with each other and which defines the unique perspective of the individual, then the task of communication theory is to describe the operation of the structures involved. However, one can also approach the question of the emergence of shared meaning by focusing on the ongoing actions of the individuals. The context within which individuals are already located is not that of a given stable structure, but is rather that of the ongoing concrete interactions among the members of a community. The interactions themselves define and constitute the continuous existence of the community and it is within this context that the emergence of meaning is an ongoing occurrence.

The interactional view (e.g., Rommetveit, 1974) appeals only to the concretely given emergence of shared meaning within particular situated interactions. Communication is described as an ongoing series of active engagements between individuals within a historically existing context of shared meaning. The interaction is itself the site of shared meaning, both as given and as emergent. It is the concrete communicative interaction that reaffirms and represents the individual's existence wtihin a context of shared meaning. Thus, the context is both the locus of the emergence of new meaning and the rearticulation of that meaning as already shared. The context of interaction as the locus of meaning is the source of both creativity and tradition; in fact, creativity and tradition always and only exist together within concrete interactional contexts. Consequently, the context of interaction has little stability except that which it articulates for itself. It is constantly emerging and hence, constantly changing. Its stability is merely the product of the ongoing emergence of meaning, even as the very possibility of the emergence of meaning requires a stable context of shared meaning already existing. Consequently, communication is the ongoing interactional production and reproduction of shared meaning.

The power of a systemic view of communication rests upon an unacknowledged paradox, however, for it assumes both that meaning is always shared and that meaning is always the possession of and manipulatable by the individual. I have tried to suggest that systemic views inevitably assume a domain of individual meaning that, if not mentalistic, at least exists independently of the systemic determination of shared meaning. The individual as a competent interactant or user of the system must bring his or her own intentions and projects into particular interactions. These individual structures of meaning are different from the shared meanings that emerge from the interaction itself. The crucial question is whether they can be accounted for totally within the terms of the system of emergent shared meaning itself. If not, a dichotomy exists that reproblematizes the possibility of communication at just the same point that plagued atomistic theories: the relation between individual and shared (social) meanings. If emergent meanings are real and are still the possessions of individuals, the question remains whether the meanings brought into the interaction are shared. Are they merely the product of a history of interactions? If they are, then communication appears no more than a social ritual through which social reality is maintained, and it is difficult to account for creativity and motivated change. In fact, systemic theories of communication inevitably seem to fall back into a dichotomized theory of meaning in which the individual is endowed with structures and meanings that precede not only particular interactions, but the possibility of interaction itself. The obvious solution also appears unacceptable. One could assume that all meanings are shared, and therefore, that there is no such thing as a domain of individual meaning; the individual is merely a product of the system, not even a manipulator of it. However, such a strategy leaves little room for creativity, change, or even miscommunication. The individual is simply and entirely eliminated from the discourse as a significant influence in the interactional process according to his or her intentions and projects. This paradox is glossed over in the discourse of systemic views by the notion of the epiphenomenality of meaning, for it is this that allows meaning to be both shared and individually possessed. And it is here that we can locate the second point at which the notion of intersubjectivity enters into discourses about communication. This time it is more obviously carried within the idea of the *same* meaning than in the relation of the individual to the social.

Constitution Through Interpretation

A transcendental view of meaning assumes that meaning is the environment within which human individuals live out their lives as human beings. Meaning is neither subjective (the possession of individual consciousness) nor objective (part of the physical world). It cannot be described either as entities or as an emergent product of a system of articulation. It is the "given" of human existence. To be human is precisely to live in an already meaningful world. Rather than beginning with some objective context (a physical world or a context of interactions) into which the individual is inserted, the transcendentalist starts with a meaningful world in which an active individual exists. Consequently, such a view of meaning talks about experience or phenomena rather than reality, where experience is always and already meaningful.

The transcendentalist adds, significantly, that the meaningfulness of experience — always given — is also always structured. Human reality is always organized, patterned, constituted as a system of relations among meanings. This constituted reality is the result of a particular process that defines the essential nature of human existence. The most general name given to this process is "interpretation." The question of meaning is superseded by a question of the interpretation of meanings to produce a structured or constituted reality, what we normally think of as experience. Transcendental views of meaning differ, however, over the question of the relationship between the process of interpretation and the individual. The phenomenologist argues that interpretation is something that individuals do and consequently, that constitutions are, in some essential way, individual. The most common expression of this view is that which sees the individual as a subject, and interpretation as the basic nature of consciousness. On the other hand, hermeneutics suggests that constitutions are not individual but rather, that individuals themselves exist only as constituted within the process of interpretation. The process itself precedes the individual and is the ground of the individual's existence. Interpretation is not a social process either, however, because the social is also constituted within the process.

On either of these transcendental views of meaning, the task of accounting for communication changes because one now questions the interpretive processes by which a particular experience is constituted as communicative. This is, however, not as radical a shift as it may appear. The transcendental view of meaning starts with experience and accounts for its particular constitution by describing interpretive processes or practices. The experience itself remains unexamined insofar as it is taken as the given. Consequently, the question of communication becomes how interpretive processes constitute interactions so as to produce the experience of communication. The description of the experience, however, is taken directly from the discourses of the atomistic and systemic views; it still involves the possession of the same meaning by two individuals; it is now understood, however, as an experience rather than as a fact. At the same time, although such views deny the reality — beyond that as a constituted reality — of the relation of sameness between meanings, they do not question the reality of the meanings themselves. Communication involves a set of ongoing interpretive processes that constitute human existence as constructed of individuals possessing meanings that can be compared and related to the meanings of other individuals. The question of communication directs us to the constitution of the sense of sameness as a product of either individual or transindividual processes.

The difference between a phenomenological and a hermeneutic theory of communication can be understood in terms of the description of the "same" that is accomplished in communication, either as correspondence or sharing. In a phenomenological discourse on communication (O'Keefe, Delia, & O'Keefe, 1981), where interpretive processes and the resulting constitutions or meaning-structures belong to the individual, communication is an imputed or constituted accomplishment of an apparent correspondence between individual constitutions that are, for all intents and purposes, real. Communication is a product of individuals engaged in public and routinized performances of coordinated action, for example. On the other hand, in a hermeneutic discourse of communication (e.g., Hawes, 1977), one starts with the sense or experience of the reality of a shared meaning that precedes the uniqueness of and separation between individually experienced meanings. One must be careful to avoid identifying this domain of shared constitutions with any actual system of experientially shared meaning, for this would lead to the reduction of hermeneutics to a systemic view (Hawes, 1977). The hermeneutic concern is for a transcendental realm in which individuals necessarily and already coexist and it is only out of this givenness of community that the experience of the individuality of meanings (which can then be compared or mediated) is constituted. The transcendental moment of sharing, described as the event of understanding, is neither individual nor social for it is the event itself that is the ground of the constituted sense of both individuality and of social systems (e.g., systems of articulation). It is in the event of understanding, carried out in the process of interpretation, that we come to see ourselves as individuals sharing meanings through social systems of articulation. This experience is constituted by processes over which we have no control.

Let me expand on these two transcendental views of communication, once again drawing heavily upon some earlier work (Grossberg, in press). In a phenomenological view of communication, where interpretive practices belong to the individual, the individuality of meaning-structures is assumed and communication is only the accomplishment of the sense of correspondence between the individual constitutions (which are themselves taken as real). As we shall see, the phenomenological account of communication replaces "correspondence" with the notion of "coordination" and it questions the reality of the "sameness" that characterizes communication; instead, it settles for the constitution of a sense of sameness in the form of coordinated activity. Such a view challenges the "reality" of the product of communication but not its character. Communication is accomplished by individuals engaged in particular interpretive practices by which they constitute a particular relationship between themselves and the other.

Obviously, once again, the description of the individual has changed from that of the previous views. The individual is neither an isolated consciousness nor merely an actor within a context of interactions. It is an organism constantly related and oriented to its environment and hence, it is the locus of particular interpretive processes by which that orientation is accomplished. Meanings are not located within some privileged domain of consciousness but are that toward which the individual is oriented. The individual is constantly engaged in practices that structure the meaningfulness of experience in particular ways. Thus "reality" is constituted in a continuous process of interpretation by which the individual makes sense of and acts in the world. A phenomenological view focuses on the ways in which the individual acts in the world by organizing and making sense of the already meaningful world in particular, structured ways. The phenomenologist examines the practices by which we interpret the world and our engagements with it.

These individual processes of interpretation are the constitutive source of meaning-structures (and of their apparent stability), including that of the apparent correspondence between individual constitutions in communication. The reality of the correspondence of meaning as the defining product of communication is describable as an accomplishment of individuals interpreting the world in ways that appear to correspond with the interpretations of others. Hence, the "sameness" purportedly achieved in communication is always and only an imputation, constituted by individual, interpretive processes. What we achieve in communicative interaction is not some transcendent or real correspondence but the experience of sameness. Through an ongoing process of interpretation, we achieve a kind of satisfaction that there is some correspondence between individual meaning-structures.

However, the phenomenologist cannot rest with this articulation of the position, for the question of how individuals accomplish this sense of correspondence remains unanswered. And without some specific answer, the phenomenologist is threatened with a new form of solipsism: If constitutions themselves are the possessions of individuals, then the sense of sameness that is accomplished in communication is itself merely a "private" meaning-structure with no necessary relation to the actions or interpretations of the other. The phenomenological response to the predicament is to suggest that interpretive processes depend not only on cognitive operations, but also upon actions through which the individual engages the world. That is, modes of action are themselves interpretive practices that bear a complex relationship to the more cognitive processes. Individuals' actions in the world are in fact processes by which they make sense of the world as they act within it and upon it. Consequently, the question of the apparent correspondence between meaning-structures can be seen in terms of the relationship between individual actions. Communication becomes, then, a process of interpreting the actions of others according to the concrete need to coordinate lines of action so as to accomplish particular individual projects. The notion of a correspondence of meaning-structures is replaced by that of a coordination of lines of action.

Communication can now be described as a practical and situated management of interpretive practices producing "coordinated" action. The accomplishment of this new understanding of the "same" of communication is the constitutive product of our public performance of particular actions. We act in ways that are constitutive of this sense. Communication is still explicated as the achievement of a state of correspondence but understood pragmatically rather than intentionally. Communication is not merely constituted in individual perspectives and cognitive processes; it is also a feature of the routine practices with which we act in the world so as to coordinate our projects with those of the other. The investigation of communication requires a study of the social organization of routine interpretive practices that, while always manifested in individual action, have a public character. Individuals are engaged in a constant process of the strategic manipulation and management of such practices to accomplish a coordination of action defined by their own projects. Thus communication is constituted by the possibilities and implications of the routine practices available to us.

The notion of "routine practices," however, is itself problematic, for the phenomenologist must deny them an objectivity juxtaposed to the subjectivity of individual projects and intentions. Their apparent objectivity must itself be an accomplishment of interpretive practices; the sense that such practices exist to be used is constituted by the ongoing and successful situated management of the sense-making practices themselves. Nevertheless, they must have a status that makes them, to some extent, public and social; they are available to the individual and not merely created by individuals. To some extent, the notion of routine practices has replaced the notion of the sign in atomistic views, and the problem remains of describing the relations between individual intentions and the routine practices by which they are accomplished publicly. The phenomenological view that communication is a situated performance of individuals engaged in a reciprocal coordination of perspectives through the practical management of socially available practices recreates many of the dilemmas and dichotomies of the mentalistic view. The phenomenological view problematizes the reality of the accomplishment of a sameness of meaning and substitutes a pragmatic criterion of coordination.

A hermeneutic view of communication, on the other hand, starts with the givenness of "sameness" as a transcendental condition of the individuality of meaning-structures. The "event of understanding" precedes the constitution of either individual meaning or of the particular ways in which that sameness is interpreted (as correspondence or sharing). The event of understanding is the essential moment of human existence, an event in which both the individual and the social are constituted as existing in a continuously changing, albeit necessary, relation. The sense of communication as a relationship between individual meanings is a product of the event of understanding embodied within particular concrete human practices. Neither communication nor communicative practices can be understood as an accomplishment or project of individuals. Communication is not merely a purposive activity; the correspondence or sharing of meaning, as well as the coordination of lines of action, are always constitutions of the a priori fact of communication itself. Communication is not reducible to individual processes, nor can it be accounted for in terms of a domain of social meanings within which individuals live and act. It is, rather, in communication that individual and social, creativity and tradition, are reciprocally constituted. Communication is an ongoing historical context of events of understanding within which individuals are constituted in a relationship to one another and to a social system of articulation.

If the phenomenological view accounts for the sense of communication as the achievement of a correspondence of individual meanings, the hermeneutic view describes the constitution of a sense of sharing, i.e., that there is one meaning that is possessed by two individuals. It does so, however, by locating the moment of sharing before a moment in which individuals are present to each other. Individuals are constituted out of the event of understanding as a transcendental moment of shared meaning-structures. Similarly, the relationship between the individual and a social context of meaning is only the product of the interpretive activity that is the event of understanding. Thus these two relationships — individual to individual and individual to social — are parallel. They are both constituted moments of an a priori event of shared meaning-interpretation.

The hermeneutic view describes this constituted structure as a fusion of horizons, but the term is somewhat misleading since the fusion precedes the existence of the horizons as separated or even separable. In order to explain this notion of a fusion of horizons, I will use the relation of the individual and the social as my example. The reality of both of these domains is only their existence within concrete events of understanding in which they appear to be mutually constitutive. This constitution places the individual in a particular, structured relation to the social: The individual both participates in and is alienated from the social. The individual is neither independent of nor an immediate expression of social systems of articulation. Individuality (i.e., the individuality of meaning) is constituted by interpretative events as existing within social domains of meaning precisely by virtue of being distanced from it. Similarly, social systems are constituted as having their own objectivity precisely in their distance from the individual. Each is constituted both in relation to and independent of the other.

The individuality constituted in the hermeneutic event of communication is, however, neither the psychological nor the practical subject of earlier views. It is rather a perspective or horizon constituted within the ongoing events of communication. It is not that the individual strategically manipulates communicative practices to create a sense of coordination but rather, that in communicative events the individual is constituted in a mediated relationship to another horizon of meaning.

Events of communication as interpretation always take the form of an interpretation of something, and it is this form that is described as the fusion of horizons. Communication is a process in which sharedness of meaning-structures constitutes itself as a mediation of one horizon into another. Thus, communication appears to involve an already existing meaning (sign-meanings, tradition, social meanings, etc.), which the individual appropriates as his or her own. But that original meaning exists only in being appropriated, and the individual as a perspective from which such appropriation is accomplished is itself an accomplishment of the appropriation itself. Communication thus has the appearance of two perspectives fusing into a common or shared meaning. But it is the originary sharedness that is the source of the apparent structure of the event. The fusion of meanings or perspectives is not a mediation of two independent domains but the constitution of them within the unity of the event of communication itself.

Thus while affirming the gap between the individual and the other (individual or social) as a unique perspective or domain of meaning, a hermeneutic view argues that it is the gap itself — as the event of communication — that is the locus within which the two horizons are constituted as different but united in a moment of sharing. Communication is constituted as a mediation of one horizon into another or as the appropriation of a particular meaning-structure into a particular perspective on that meaning-structure. Yet in this event the other appears to shape and define the individual precisely because he or she appropriates it as his or her own. The other is both alienated from and embedded within the individual as a horizon of meaning. And this is possible only because they both exist within their mutual constitution within the event of communication itself.

Communication opens up a shared, fluid world that is constantly changing as its meanings are "played out" in further concrete events of communication. Creativity and tradition, individual meaning and shared meaning, individuality and social systems of articulation are merely the constituted structures of the communicative event itself. The apparent oppositions come to have an existence and stability only in the continuous "happening" of communication.

It is significant that neither transcendental view questions the basic assumption that communication involves a relationship between independent (e.g., individual) meanings or meaning-structures. Communication still involves a comparison between two terms, and its product is the conclusion that the two terms are the same. The phenomenologist, apart from the problem of the relation between individual projects and routine practices, makes the fact of sameness depend upon the constitutive activity of individuals seeking to accomplish coordinated interaction. The hermeneutic view locates the relation of identity as the transcendental source of the individual terms to be compared. Thus both continue to maintain the reality of something transcending but not entirely accounting for individuality. Correlatively, both affirm a dichotomy between this transcendental moment (e.g., routine practices, the event of communication) and the individual as a possessor of meaning in the form of either a source of intentions or as a unified, albeit constituted, horizon of or perspective on meaning. In fact, both see the individual as actively engaged in the process of interpretation in a way that defines an essential and universal human nature: a subject distinct from either the physical world or the ongoing context of the articulation/constitution of meaning. The individual as the possessor and/or mediator of meaning is always the necessary condition of all interpersonal relationships; communication exists when the meanings possessed are or have been constituted as the same.

COMMUNICATION AND INTERSUBJECTIVITY

Thus far I have presented six different vocabularies for describing communication (mentalist, physicalist, interactional, structural, phenomenological, and hermeneutic) derived from three distinct views of meaning (atomistic, systemic, and transcendental). I wish now to consider the relation between these accounts of communication and the notion of intersubjectivity. The question of communication is frequently linked to that of intersubjectivity. For example, Rommetveit (1978) has cautioned theorists against identifying communication with "perfect intersubjectivity." The question is what this identification consists of and entails, and what solutions are available to the different vocabularies of communication.

The relationship between the concepts of communication and intersubjectivity can initially be located in the fact that both seem to refer to the transcendence of individuality. In the case of communication, as I have tried to demonstrate, this takes the form of asking how it is possible that different individuals come to possess the *same* meaning, and this is true of all six views. Thus communication always involves a transcendence of the individuality of meaning into a relationship of identity: Two meanings, possessed by different individuals, are nevertheless the same. Moreover, in each case, the question of the relationship between individuals is answered by postulating a mediating third term — e.g., sign-meaning, systems of articulation, or interpretation. The question of the relationship between individuals is replaced with the question of the relation between the individual and the mediating terms taken as a social dimension. As I have argued, even the transcendental views, while problematizing the reality of the social as a mediation between individuals, do not question the mediation itself. There is still a moment of transcendence or identity mediating between the individual differences.

There is no universally accepted definition of intersubjectivity, but one can perhaps begin by asserting that intersubjectivity also involves a process of the transcendence of individuality. In communication this transcendence is accomplished for and through particular meanings. Thus communication is but one form of the more general process of intersubjectivity; it is one way in which intersubjectivity is accomplished. Intersubjectivity is not merely the result, furthermore, of interactions or of any relationships among individuals. It involves something more — a mediation through which individuality is transcended in a moment of identity with the other. Thus whether one conceives of intersubjectivity as Schutz's (1967) "we-relation," Dewey's (1925) "community," or Gadamer's (1975) "dialogue," the concept seems to involve a movement beyond the particular differences (identities) of individuals into a new moment of identity. Intersubjectivity embodies the claim that this new, transcendent identity is more general than the momentary and specific identity produced in communicative interactions.

The question to be raised then is what intersubjectivity means and how it functions within each of the three general forms of the question of communication. I shall attempt to demonstrate that each type of discourse about communication assumes an image of intersubjectivity that, rather than addressing directly the question of interpersonal relationships, deals with a mediated relation between the individual and the social. And in each case this third term, embodied in intersubjectivity, plays a transcendental role within the theory of communication; intersubjectivity is the *Ursprung* (ground), *telos* (goal), or *eidos* (essence) of both communication and human existence.

The first image of intersubjectivity, associated with atomistic and especially mentalist views of meaning and communication, is that of the union of essentially opposed terms. Individuals are isolated consciousnesses and the achievement of some identity among them requires the mediation of a third term, an objective term that cannot be reduced to the possession of an individual because it is the same for both individuals. Intersubjectivity is the result of a sharing of a common object of consciousness. In the case of communication, it is a sign-meaning. In the broader case of intersubjective relationships, it is any object with which two individuals are simultaneously involved resulting in an identity of consciousness. As Schutz (1964) puts it, they grow older together. It is this sharing that provides the measure of correspondence in particular instances of, for example, communication. Schutz's we-relation is an excellent example of this image of intersubjectivity. The we-relation is not something that we merely experience or assume; it is real for Schutz although it may simply be that the social theorist has to assume its reality in order to account for everyday social life. More importantly, the we-relation is not the result or product of some process of interaction, including communication. It is that which makes communication possible. Intersubjectivity on this view is the *Ursprung* of communication and interaction, that out of which communication originates. Such a view cannot question the nature of this relationship of sharing; it cannot problematize the relation between the individual and the shared object of consciousness.

The second image of intersubjectivity begins with the assumption that although individuals are unique and separated from each other, they are always interacting with each other. Furthermore, it is in this interaction that they manifest and reassert their existence as human individuals. This ongoing context of interaction is not reducible to the actions or intentions of individuals; it exists as a unique domain that is both related to and separated from the actions of individuals. Thus the relation between the individual and the social recreates that which exists between individuals: different yet belonging together. Although each has an independent identity, they exist only in their interaction. On first glance, it appears that intersubjectivity is the process of the continuous reaffirmation of our social nature, but this is actually misleading. For what is being reaffirmed in such interactions is our competence to achieve intersubjectivity. As I have argued elsewhere (Grossberg, 1982), systemic theories must presuppose an innate and universal competence to engage in just those sorts of interactions that articulate our social existence. If we distinguish this sense of social competence — that the individual is already a social actor — from the notion of intersubjectivity, then we can see that the latter notion serves a particular function: It is the *telos* of our social existence. Intersubjectivity functions as the image of the fullest expression of the structures, already present in primitive form in our social competencies, of human existence as interactional. Furthermore such views of intersubjectivity often give communication a special role: It is the primary means by which the goal of intersubjective existence can be accomplished. To be fully human, then, is to be intersubjective, and this is realized through communicative interaction. Through communication individuals maximize the possibilities of social interaction and realize their own potential. Buber's (1958) image of the dialogue and Dewey's (1925) "community" provide, I think, clear examples of intersubjectivity as *telos*, as an achievement rather than the ground of interaction. Rommetveit (1978, p. 3) is clearly operating with such a view when, after denying the identification of communication and perfect intersubjectivity, he asserts that we can only concretely achieve "partial intersubjectivity": "We must, naively and unreflectively take the possibility of perfect intersubjectivity for granted in order to achieve partial intersubjectivity in real-life discourse with our fellow men [sic]."

The third image of intersubjectivity is built upon the transcendental turn that questions the reality or substantiality of the transcendence that is claimed in the notion of intersubjectivity. Nevertheless, the issue of the relationship between individuals is translated into a question of their relation to a third term for which one cannot provide an account in purely individualistic terms. In a phenomenological view, this involves the domain of "coordinated action," which serves as a nonsubstantial or pragmatic definition of the social. In a hermeneutic view, it involves the event of understanding as the transcendental domain from which both the individual and the social emerge. In either case, the question of intersubjectivity becomes that of accounting for our experience of the world in terms of self and other, either in the form of individuals related to individuals or of individuals related to the social. That we appear to live in a world in which individuals have corresponding or shared meanings, in which in fact individuals transcend their separation in a momentary but ongoing unity of social existence, remains nonproblematic. One must ask how human practices are able to maintain the sense of transcendence as a necessary and ongoing part of our reality, either in the form of a social world that transcends the particular interaction or of a relation between individuals and social systems that transcends the immediate context of understanding. The function, then, of the concept of intersubjectivity within a transcendental framework is neither that of the ground of particular forms of transcendence nor the full and perfect expression of what are always only partially realized human potentials. Rather, it is an essential structure or a constitutive moment of human existence, an *eidos*. It expresses the fact that we are always acting in ways built upon and manifesting this particular experience of transcendence as an aspect of human nature. To put it simply, to be human necessarily involves that we are intersubjective. Of course it is quite possible (and probably true) that we no longer recognize this feature of our existence, that our theories of human existence hide or ignore it. The function of transcendental theorizing must be, in part, to reassert intersubjectivity as a significant, operative, and necessary feature of human existence. The status of intersubjectivity as an eidetic structure may of course vary among transcendental theorists: for Sartre (1969), it is an a posteriori observation; for Heidegger (1962), an a priori discovery; and for Gadamer (1975), a sufficient condition of our humanity. However, for any transcendental view, while intersubjectivity is a basic structure, it may not be sufficient by itself to account for any particular form of concrete human activity. Nevertheless, intersubjectivity is not something to be sought or achieved; it is already and always there. For example, neither Gadamer's (1975) image of the dialogue nor Heidegger's (1962) structure of *Mitsein* (being-with) is intended to suggest some goal for human action. They are rather descriptions of one necessary and constitutive moment of human existence.

I have endeavored to identify three views of intersubjectivity that roughly correspond to the three views of meaning presented above. Moreover, I have suggested that within each of the views the concept of intersubjectivity serves a different function. I want now to reiterate and summarize the commonalities that exist among these three images. All three images assume that individuals are, in some way, the possessors and manipulators of meaning, and consequently, that there is a real separation, beyond the trivial physical one, between individuals. In philosophical terms, all three images operate with a theory of meaning that locates the individual within a theory of subjectivity. Intersubjectivity then becomes the moment of transcendence, a leap into an identity or sameness out of difference and separation. Furthermore all three seem to make this transcendence into a substantial fact; that is, this structural moment of identity cannot be described within the terms of individual differences and existence. It has a nature all its own. The substantiality of intersubjectivity means that it must be located outside of the concrete contexts of everyday interactions and relations. It defines a transcendental measure or framework in terms of which all relationships are to be described. This is most obvious in the case of communication, which appears to be little more than a special case of the structure of intersubjectivity. Communication involves the transcendence of the individuality of meaning rather than the transcendental notion of the transcendence of individuality itself.

INTERPERSONAL RELATIONS WITHOUT INTERSUBJECTIVITY

According to my argument thus far, the concept of intersubjectivity has played an important role in our accounts of communication and interpersonal relationships. It is — as *Ursprung, telos,* or *eidos* — a transcendental assumption. It is a foundation upon which we have built our understanding of relationships and, one might add, it underlies the forms of social practice dominating such spheres. Furthermore it functions as a transcendental condition of our understanding of relationships (including communication) precisely by virtue of the fact that it embodies the assumption of the transcendence of individuality. That is the content, or more accurately, the form that it has imposed on all of our conceptions of the nature of interpersonal relationships.

For a number of reasons, this situation has become problematic. First, it does not allow us to explain and cope with the increasingly pervasive concern with, and the sense of the problematicity of, interpersonal relationships in contemporary society. Somehow this feature of our everyday lives is tied to the second, more academic reason: The concept of transcendence has itself become problematic. Recent theoretical work (Coward & Ellis, 1977) has attempted to articulate approaches to various philosophical issues within the terms of a philosophy of immanence, i.e., without any assumption of transcendence. Derrida (1976), Barthes (1974), and Kristeva (1980), for example, have all written about problems of subjectivity, meaning, texts, and interpretation. Foucault (1979, 1980) and Deleuze and Guattari (1977) have explored questions of psychology, history, and society. Although there are significant differences among these authors, they follow the common strategy of offering new models of description to replace the traditional structures of explanation and causation built upon transcendence. These philosophers of immanence argue that one can think of traditional descriptive models as binary, implying a movement from a to b (e.g., from individuality to intersubjectivity) in which b represents the transcendence of a. To this they oppose an immanentist description that is not merely the critique of the second, transcendental term b. Since both terms are involved in the transcendental structure, both must be subjected to a radical rethinking. Thus the concept of individuality is already so intertwined with the assumption of intersubjectivity that it remains trapped within a particular discourse of the individual, namely that of the subject.

A philosophy of immanence assumes that experience itself is a transcendental category within traditional philosophy. This is evident in the above description of transcendental views of communication. Hence any appeal to experience in order to establish the categories of description must itself be rejected. Experience itself is insufficient as the foundation of a theoretical analysis. For example, the fact that we experience ourselves as subjects — as creators and manipulators of meaning — does not itself justify our using the category of subjectivity in an account of human existence. Experience is itself the product of other determining forces working within the space of our environment. Consequently, one must ask how experience is produced and why it is produced in particular forms (Grossberg, 1982). Part of the task of a philosophy of immanence must be critical; it asks how a particular fact has come to be interpreted in transcendental terms and what functions this particular transcendental discourse serves in relation to other social and discursive structures. The second task of a philosophy of immanence is to seek a more adequate (i.e., non-transcendental) discourse within which to describe particular facts of our existence. Thus one might give an account of individuality without assuming any universal human nature (in the form of the individual's relation to meaning). Or one might attempt to describe interpersonal relations without the mutually dependent assumptions of subjectivity and intersubjectivity. It is this latter question that will direct my arguments in this concluding section: What is an adequate, immanent description of social aggregations?

Three Strategies of Discursive Description

Let me begin by describing and contrasting three alternative strategies for constructing discursive descriptions, drawing upon the work of Deleuze and Guattari (1981). The three forms of description are root structures, radicle structures, and rhizomes. To describe some fact or event within a root structure is to locate it in a centered, expressive system. The particular event becomes a reflection or direct causal product of some other, core phenomenon. A radicle structure, on the other hand, denies the existence of any center that can serve as an origin or sufficient definition of the nature of the event to be described. The particular event is located within an "indefinite multiplicity of elaborate secondary roots" (Deleuze & Guattari, 1981, p. 51). And yet the radicle structure still assumes a unity, a moment of transcendence. This becomes clearer if one considers the notion of an "indefinite multiplicity," for it implies a never-ending possibility of fragmentation. Any term can be multiplied by fragmenting it into its concrete constitutents or determinants. The indefiniteness of this process is reflected inversely in the activity of the elaboration itself. Such "deconstruction" is a free play that comes back upon itself as a subject. In a radicle discourse, "unity is endlessly thwarted and impeded in the object, while a new type of unity triumphs in the subject . . . a higher unity of ambivalence or of overdetermination, in a dimension always supplementary to that of its object" (Deleuze & Guattari, 1981, p. 52). That is, discursive fragmentation as a strategy leaves the trace of the deconstructed unity within its own discourse as either a constantly deferred future or an irretrievable past.

Finally, rhizomes are made through subtraction rather than multiplication: "write to the power of n − 1" (Deleuze & Guattari, 1981, p. 52). Rhizomatics always subtracts the unique, the individual, the transcendent from the multiplicity. Deleuze and Guattari elaborate this strategy for the description of a particular situation in a series of principles. First, any point can and must be connected to any other. That is, every relation must be drawn. Second, any multiplicity (or "assemblage") is defined by its exterior, by the lines connecting it with other registers. For example, a book is defined by its connections not only to other books and forms of discourse but to various nondiscursive domains as well. Third, "it is only when the multiple is effectively treated as a substantive . . . that it loses all relationship to One as subject or as object" (Deleuze & Guattari, 1981, p. 53). Fourth, an assemblage has no privileged lines or constitutive relations; how it is ruptured or fragmented at any moment in its description does not depend upon some inherent significant or signifying structure. In fact, lines of signification ("semiotic flows") work along with material and social connections. Fifth, rhizomatics is always concerned with the assemblage as it is connected to the real or actual; it is concerned with performance rather than competence. And finally, rhizomes are not amenable to any structural or generative modeling because both of these strategies would reduce the assemblage to the "idea of a traced fatality" (Deleuze & Guattari, 1981, p. 58). That is, both structural and generative models reduce the assemblage to a mere trace of a predetermined history. Rhizomes render maps connected to the real rather than being infinitely repeatable tracings.

These principles may be somewhat misleading, however, for the first suggests that the starting point of a rhizomatic description is points that are then connected. Actually, rhizomatics is always a return to the concrete, material, and substantive reality of relations. There are no points, only lines. What exists are lines and assemblages of lines. The priority of lines or connections means that any fact (a point) is only its existence within a network of relations. To ask what a particular event, fact, or assemblage is, is to ask how it is made, with what, and how it functions. Lines then are merely the fact of connection, of the effects of one point transmitted to another. What Deleuze and Guattari describe as the "transmission of intensities through lines" is the existence of any point as its effectivity. This latter term, introduced by Foucault (1980), refers to effects but with three significant revisions of the traditional notion of effects. First, it is always a multiple; second, it works in multiple directions; and third, it cannot be defined outside of a particular assemblage. It includes what might normally be conceived of as potential as well as actual effects. Rhizomatics is then a strategy in which something is described in terms of an assemblage of interwoven effects. Effects, understood as described above, are the real. Consequently, points do not exist outside of the lines that define their determination and effectivity. Something is what it is only by virtue of the lines connecting it to what is outside and beyond it, to that which acts upon it and upon which it may act. Furthermore any particular intensity or effect is transmitted at a particular rate, and different effects travel at different rates. Thus rhizomatics not only describes effectivities but measures their rates without assuming that there exists a universally applicable unit of measurement. The way in which one measures effects is dependent upon the particular assemblage that one is measuring.

Rhizomatics then claims to be a philosophy of immanence, a monism that assumes only one term, but that term itself is a plural one rather than the singular term with which deconstruction begins (e.g., Derrida's *differance*). A rhizome is "an acentred, nonhierarchical and nonsignifying system" (Deleuze & Guattari, 1981, p. 65) of multidirectional and multidimensional effects. However, rhizomes do not exist; they are made. Lines are drawn; unities are subtracted. The metaphor that seems most appropriate, a metaphor that must be taken literally, is that of crabgrass. At best, one can have some crabgrass.

There are, generally speaking, two major kinds of effects, two forms of intensities corresponding to different lines. Lines of articulation define boundaries and hence, produce identities within differences. They hierarchize and centralize, bringing lines back onto themselves so as to produce relations of power. Lines of articulation constitute root-structures. On the other hand, lines of flight deterritorialize by connecting assemblages with their exteriors; they cut across and dismantle unities, identities, centers, and hierarchies. They are lines of desire rather than lines of power. Rhizomes must be made precisely because there are always lines of articulation that must be crossed or subtracted by drawing lines of flight. That is to say, in understanding a particular assemblage, one must subtract all of the relations that deny its relations to other assemblages, and draw the lines connecting it to whatever is outside of the particular assemblage. Rhizomes are not found, they are made; one constructs "true fictions" (Foucault, 1980, p. 193).

Rhizomatics is, in conclusion, an alternative strategy to either the addition (through some transcendental argument) of a core identity or origin, or the fragmentation of unities into dispersed and displaced systems. It is the mapping of a network of effects: Something is where its effectivities are. Rather than beginning with independent terms or facts and asking what their effects are, rhizomatics maps out a world of effects and locates the terms at the points of particular conjunctions of effects and effectivities. The "objects" we normally think of as the agents or passions of effects are merely the places of the effects themselves, with no other identity. Hence there can be no privileged terms of description or units of measurement. If relations (effects) precede the existence or identity of the terms related (a position first systematized by Heidegger and Saussure), then the nature of the terms cannot be assumed before the relation itself is concretely described.

These three strategies have significantly different consequences for the description of interpersonal relations. Briefly, a root description locates intersubjectivity — the transcendence of individuality — as the transcendental condition of any relationship. This is the tradition I have described in the first part of this chapter. A deconstruction of intersubjectivity, as I shall describe it shortly, denies any universal human nature (subjectivity) to the individual. Instead, it talks about the determination of different subject-positions; different forms of individual identity are produced within different structures of relations or forms of social practice. Relations place the individual in different positions vis-a-vis the other and consequently, one cannot appeal to an identity transcending the particular context. For example, I have argued in another article (Grossberg, 1982) that communicative practices position the individual in a particular relation to the signifying system (as the cause of the connection between the signifier and signified) and to another individual as coequals. The failure of such an approach from the perspective of a philosophy of immanence is that the unit is predefined as the individual. A deconstruction of intersubjectivity maintains the identity of the individual because it is always the individual who has an identity in the form of a position determined within a particular contextual relation. While deconstruction fragments the concept of subjectivity, it leaves its trace in the structure of individuality. A rhizomatics of interpersonal relations argues that it is not always individuals, even as hierarchized totalities with indefinite possibilities of identities, who are related to each other. Rhizomatics looks instead at the concrete effects of interpersonal relations in order to decide what it is that is being related, i.e., what the particular relation is is measured in terms of its effectivities. For example, Foucault (1973, 1977, 1978,) has argued that the interpersonal relations characteristic of modern systems of penology, medicine, and to some extent, education, are locatable within an emerging system of disciplinary relations and strategies. The significant fact or terms within such relations are not individuals; rather, they are relations between the eyes of one and the body of the other. Rhizomatic descriptions of relations always involve partial objects, objects from which unity and identity have been subtracted.

The Deconstruction of Interpersonal Relationships

I will continue by expanding the summaries of both the deconstruction and the rhizomatics of interpersonal relations and intersubjectivity. Although deconstructionists are likely to disagree, one can see deconstruction as a continuation of the phenomenological discourse of Heidegger. Heidegger (1962) recognized that meaning or signification is the context of human existence, but he did not go far enough. The deconstructionist explicitly locates *Existenz* in discourse and provides a different description of discourse in terms of "textual processes." Rather than talking about interpretation and hermeneutic processes, deconstruction sees all human experience as an ongoing "reading" within which the individual is implicated and determined. The ongoing reading, the "textuality" of existence, is a semiotization of experience: the experience of signification. The context of experience is replaced by the ongoing production of an intertextuality. That is, the process of signification no longer involves a relation between two discrete domains (the signifiers and the signifieds). Rather, it is a process, within discourse, of the continuous articulation — a laying out as a production — of differences. Meaning is merely the trace of difference, but because that trace is always a supplement as well, since it is constantly dispersed into the discursive process, meaning is always undecidable. A process in which difference is constantly deferred (and deferred to) is the deconstructionist's notion of discourse as "differance." Thus everything, including the individual's identity, is an effect of textuality or discourse. What does it mean to say that the individual is an effect of discourse? The deconstructionist says that discourse "positions" the individual. The identity of the individual is dispersed or fragmented into a context of determining discourse: the individual as intertext. Moreover, the form of one's identity as an individual is determined by the place in which one is positioned or located by and in relationship to the reading. Thus our existence as subjects — the fact that we experience ourselves as subjects and act from such a position — is the product of the way in which various discourses locate us within an essentially discursive context. Subjectivity is a particular relationship to particular discourses (i.e., as the origin and possessor of meaning and manipulators of discourse standing outside of discourse) produced within discourse. And while different discourses fill the place in which the individual is positioned differently (hence the unique identities and histories of individuals is itself a textual production), and the reality of our subjectivity is only the residue of discourse, discourse *necessarily* positions the individual as a subject. That is how it is able to "have" a meaning and avoid the possibility of an infinite generation of meaning (Eco, 1976). Thus there is always necessarily an individual involved who is articulated as a discursive subject. The individual is a unity existing outside of discourse but his or her identity and effectiveness as an agent depends upon discursive determinations. The subject/other distinction is replaced by an individual/discourse dichotomy that always locates the former at some place within the latter.

The problem with this view is that there is no way to account for, on the one hand, what might be called a politically oppositional subject and, on the other hand, the psychologically deviant subject. Furthermore there can be no account given of the origin of the individual as a subject: How is it that language positions the individual as a subject and how does the individual gain access to language? Foucault (1979) has argued that the problem exists because deconstruction excludes the "other." There is nothing effective outside of difference. All determination is discursive.

The deconstructionist's solution to this problem is to revise the notions of signification and individuality. The individual is defined as the locus of desires or drives, as if desire were only individual. Kristeva (1975) refers to the semiotic chora, Lacan (1977) to the originary need (*petit objet a*), which is constantly displaced into a desire worked over by discourse. Thus, while the individual is always "subjected" by discourse, there are also processes contradicting and constantly erupting into discourse, semiotic processes of desire. This is the source of the oppositional subject, but it is still the effect of textuality. Textuality or discourse must be understood now, according to Kristeva, precisely as a relation between the semiotic (drives) and the symbolic, a process referred to as "signifiance" rather than as signification. The latter applies to the narrower case of the symbolic discourse. While such "psychoanalytic deconstruction" does seem to have an other in the form of a psychoanalytic subject, that subject is always located within textual practices. Signifying practices articulate the individual as the discursive subject, but signification is merely a limit case of the practices of signifiance in which the semiotic erupts through the signifying. Signifiance brings together the discursive subject and the oppositional subject of desire in such a way that they still continue to exclude anything outside of discourse, because the semiotic (desire) is itself called into existence by the discursive. Desire, for Lacan and Kristeva, is a retrospective constitution (*Nachtraglichkeit*) of some originary need that can never be recuperated, a constitution that gives it a discursive form. In fact, neither the symbolic nor the semiotic can exist without the other; they exist only together, each serving to prop up (anaclisis) the other.[3]

The transition from talking of textual processes to practices is a significant and valuable one, however, for it rejects the claim that there is a totally unified articulation characteristic of all discourse. It makes discourse a concrete material event rather than merely an abstract (i.e., idealist) construct. It thus allows both Kristeva and Barthes (1975) to describe different textual or reading practices that implicate the individual in different positions. Barthes even goes so far as to suggest that there are reading practices that, perhaps, position the individual as something other than the unified subject of discourse. Thus the possibility exists that the subject is worked over by discursive practices in contradictory ways and exists, not as a homogeneous subject, but as a fractured unity of potentially contradictory moments. But there remains something that is an essential unity involved in all discursive relations: the individual as the locus of some needs or drives; and there remains the impossibility of locating anything outside of the discursive practices of reading.

The deconstructionist then sees intersubjectivity as the product of particular forms of discursive practices that implicate the individual as subject and place him or her in a relation to another individual positioned as subject. Intersubjectivity — the transcendence of individuality — is real only as a residue of these practices. That is to say, the experience of transcendence is a textually produced relation between individuals within discourse. One might describe it further by saying that intersubjectivity is a trace of a discursive process that locates two individuals in the *same* place within the reading. There appears to be an identity — even more, a unity — between two individuals in the form of an intersubjectivity, a tracing of one onto the place of the other. Intersubjectivity is a particular form of intertextuality. If we remember that for the deconstructionist traces have their effects, the positioning of the subject as an intersubject is itself a determined identity from which the individual may act, sometimes in contradiction with other subject-positionings.[4]

Deconstruction seems to address a particular sort of question. It asks how this particular discursive effect is produced and what function it serves within a larger context of discursive practices and discursive reality. But in the end we may note that the deconstruction of intersubjectivity still postulates a moment of identity — a subject-position that is the same for two distinct individuals existing within discourse. Deconstruction then does not provide a description of interpersonal relations that does not assume intersubjectivity. In fact, deconstruction as a descriptive strategy can never accomplish such a task because it begins with the categories of experience and proceeds to demonstrate that they are the determined contextual effects of discourse. Experience is questioned and its innocence and priority rejected, but it remains as an originary discourse that leaves its traces on the discourse of deconstruction.

A Rhizomatics of Social Aggregates

The distinction between deconstruction and rhizomatics as strategies of description can be summarized in one sentence: If deconstruction excludes the other of discourse, rhizomatics asserts that there are only others. Deconstruction starts with discourse as a singular term; rhizomatics starts with the plurality of effectivities or lines. Rhizomatics is built upon a rejection of the phenomenological traces that remain within the deconstructionist's discourse: individuality and discursivity. Within deconstruction, the unity of the individual remains, traced upon the surface of its fragmentation. At the very least, for psychoanalytic deconstruction, desire remains individual even if it is always worked over by and in discourse. Rhizomatics argues that there are no individuals, only lines of intensities or effectivities and the assemblages that they compose. Consequently, desire belongs not to an individual but to an assemblage, and since assemblages are always connected to the other, desire always belongs to an aggregate. In more common terms, desire is always social.

If the deconstructionist is confronted with the task of describing the relations between social (discursive) production and individual desire, rhizomatics does not draw such a boundary. Instead, the former are institutions of desire and desire itself is part of the infrastructure of social production. Both desire and social production are forms of effectivities, operating in different regimes and always infiltrated by the other. There are always lines of flight connecting the regimes (Deleuze & Guattari, 1977).

If desire is not individual, and if it is part of the institutions of social production, then it has clearly taken on a different meaning or function. In psychoanalysis and psychoanalytic deconstruction, the unconscious is the seat of desire; the unconscious is the site (theater) for the enactment or expression of already constituted desires. Deleuze and Guattari (1977) argue that this view forces desire into a centered structure (under the domination of lack, law, and/or signifier). Psychoanalysis reduces the unconscious to a system of representation, a stage for the performance of Oedipus, a site for the incorporation of the family, or the writing pad of a magical discourse. Rhizomatics deterritorializes desire into effectivity — desire as production. The unconscious is an assemblage of the lines or effectivities of desiring production; it is a machine that produces, among other things, itself, a factory drawing the lines between partial objects. That is, the objects of desire exist only because of their intensities or effectivities; a bit of material (a hand, an eye, a small mark, a piece of clothing, or part of a toy) exists with its own identity as an object of desire only within a particular assemblage of mutual effects. The psychoanalytic notion of "libidinal energy" is merely an identification of a particular regime of effects and production, for energy itself exists only in its effectivity.

Effectivity, to reiterate, is a description of the continuous production of multiple lines and assemblages connecting points or (partial) objects whose identity is the product of the lines themselves. However, we must not make the mistake of thinking that all lines are of the same form. The connections of effects that exist between partial objects are not all manifestations of some unified process of production. Effectivity is not meant to replace the deconstructionist's discourse or *differance*. On the other hand, the task is not merely to fragment production into an indefinite multiplicity but rather, to describe the kinds of connections that one can make. Again, using Deleuze and Guattari, one can distinguish "connective," "disjunctive," and "conjunctive" linkages between partial objects or assemblages. Connections are direct links between assemblages along the paths of energy flows. They are what is commonly thought of as desire, i.e., attraction. Because attraction is always operating again in a redirected way, connections reproduce desire as production. And since the unconscious is the factory assembling connections, connections produce the unconscious itself. Of course connections exist not only in the regime of the unconscious but in other regimes, including the social.

The second linkage is disjunction as the production of differences. Disjunction is the inscription or articulation of boundaries upon the surface of that which connections produce. Disjunction is territorialization, which produces a grid or tracing, disconnected from and placed on top of the real. This grid is disconnected from the real because it defines a circuit through which intensities are now distributed, and this circuit, by imposing structures on desiring production, acts against the deterritorialization of connections. Obviously, the error of deconstruction is to reduce all effectivities to disjunctions.

The third effectivity is conjunction, which draws lines between the grid that traces out the real (desiring production) and the surface upon which it is inscribed. If disjunctions produce tracings, conjunction produces maps, always connected to the real. Conjunction is a reconciliation of sorts because it is a deterritorialization (of the grid), which is also a reterritorialization. It reterritorializes, not by articulating a system of difference but by producing a sort of partial object that appears to exist outside of the concrete lines of an assemblage. Such products — a "residue" or "quality" — have no fixed identity; they are not confined to circulating within the grid of disjunction. They wander over the surface of reality, apparently independent of desire. While they may flow through the circuit of distribution, they exist adjacent to it and to desire as well. They escape the mere tracing of reality while they travel through that tracing, reterritorializing it. Capital and the subject are obvious examples of residues; meaning and desire may be less obvious examples. Conjunction reterritorializes by giving a unity to a particular assemblage, which can then become the transcendental condition defining the measure of both production and distribution. Using an economic example, one might think of qualities as the regime of consumption. Thus the subject is neither an experience nor a discursive effect but the residue produced by particular conjunctions. It is always "nomadic" and "polyvocal." Rhizomes themselves may be qualities as well. Rhizomes must always be made, but as soon as one has some rhizome, it is already reterritorialized. Deleuze and Guattari describe (1981, p. 53) a rhizome as an "abstract machine" that is nevertheless the most concrete.

Interpersonal relations cannot be understood in terms of individuals existing outside of relations, nor as some opposition between individual desire and social discourse. Individuality already presupposes the connections of partial objects of desire, and the production of residues in conjunctions. In fact, interpersonal relations must be described without the benefit of either individuality (e.g., subjectivity) or intersubjectivity. So-called interpersonal relations are linkages between particular assemblages, and these are just as likely to be subindividuals or groups of individuals. For example, my relationship to my colleague may be a connection between my own writing and his or her intellectual voice, or a connection between particular physical assemblages.

Once connections are made, they are articulated into a network of relationships in which they are territorialized (boundaries and divisions are made), valued, and excluded. The connections of desire become located and interpreted within codes of social interaction, practices, and discourse. It is the coding that limits the validity and production of some connections in favor of others.

Finally, there is a reconciliation between the social aggregations of desire and the social relationships of discourse in the production of qualities providing the measure and justification of the circuit of distribution, even as they transcend it. Subjectivity is such a moment, for it defines an identity with which to divide social assemblages. Moreover, intersubjectivity is such a quality for it provides the measure valorizing those aggregations already legitimated by the codes themselves. Thus intersubjectivity is not a concrete moment of unity but the residue of particular effects that, in providing a measure of the circulation of our desires in relations, reterritorializes and rationalizes particular structures of circulation or codes of relations.[5]

Conclusion

Given the difficulty of the discourse involved in the preceding argument concerning deconstruction, rhizomatics, and intersubjectivity, it seems reasonable to conclude by questioning the advantages of rhizomatics as a strategy of description. There are, I think, three: philosophical, practical, and scientific. The movement of contemporary philosophy, from neo-Kantianism through pragmatism, linguistic philosophy and phenomenology to post-structuralism, brings together two concerns. The first is the desire to escape Cartesian dualism, which has led to the critique of transcendence and the attempt to articulate a philosophy of immanence. The second concern begins with the recognition that human reality is, at least in part, always meaningfully mediated. Rhizomatics attempts to carry these developments even further, and must be judged by the philosophical criteria of consistency, parsimony, and reflexivity. The second advantage is the possibility that rhizomatics can provide at least an explanation of the problematicity of interpersonal relationships in the contemporary world. Such an account might talk about the contradiction that has developed between desire and codes (a distinction not corresponding to an individual/social distinction) and the changing historical assemblage within which the quality of intersubjectivity no longer seems to be effectively produced as a measure.

The final advantage may strike the reader as odd, and I can present it only vaguely and tentatively. It concerns the question of doing science after Kuhn (1970). Of course Kuhn's work, building upon others, is a philosophy of science reflecting the twentieth-century concern with the meaningfulness and determination of human reality. One of the most common objections to contemporary philosophy as the foundation for an empirical investigation of human existence — extending from symbolic interactionism to hermeneutics and poststructuralism — is that every researcher becomes an interpreter of meaning-structures, a critic of individual discourses with no clear-cut way to join his or her research with others' in a common, generalized description. The problems of an epistemology of social science have been rehearsed over and over, with little suggestion of any reconciliation between the so-called interpretivists and those committed to a more materialist, scientific description. Rhizomatics, however, presents a postinterpretivist discourse that reconnects with the materialism — albeit a reconceptualized materialism — of more traditional scientific discourses. This connection between apparently opposed regimes of discourse[6] may seem more reasonable if one recognizes the metaphorical similarity between rhizomatics and the process of crystal formation — both involve a constant drawing of lines of multidirectional and multidimensional effects. Recent developments in systems theory and, in particular, the notion of auto-/allopoetic systems (Zeleny, 1981) suggests interesting parallels with rhizomatics. Together these two discourses raise the possibility of a new, theoretically and methodologically sophisticated approach to the study of human existence. Their convergence remains, at present, only a distant notion but one that may at least enable us to seek new understandings of what would constitute a scientific discourse on human existence.

NOTES

1. The fact that interpersonal relationships have become increasingly problematic is evident in much contemporary writing, both fiction and non-fiction. It is also obvious from even the most cursory glance at popular culture, including music and films. Are there any movies being made that do not have or in which we do not see at least a subtext about relationships?

2. The summary of the six views draws heavily upon my earlier presentation of these views in Grossberg (in press) although there are significant differences in the presentation of some of the views.

3. The terms "anaclisis" and "*Nachtraglichkeit*" are crucial, albeit difficult, concepts in Freud's elaboration of psychoanalysis. Anaclisis refers to the notion of "propping," and is

used by Freud to describe the relation between the sexual instincts and the self-preservative instincts; the former arise by "leaning upon" the latter. *Nachtraglichkeit* is the idea of deferred action, and expresses Freud's view of psychical temporality and causality. Thus, the significance of a particular event in early childhood may be revised at a later stage in development and given a sexual or oedipal effect. (see Laplanche & Pontalis, 1973, pp. 29-33 and 111-114, respectively).

4. The deconstruction of intersubjectivity that is presented here is my own construction since, for the most part, they have avoided these issues. Only Coward and Ellis (1977) have touched upon questions of communication and interpersonal relations.

5. For a good summary of *Anti-Oedipus*, see Stivale (1981). The presentation of a rhizomatics of intersubjectivity given here is obviously quite sketchy. I hope to extend this work directly into the areas of communication and interpersonal ethics in future work. Although he takes a very different theoretical perspective and is concerned with the question of action rather than relations, Giddens (1979) attempts a comparable reconceptualization of the foundations of social theory and research.

6. The connection drawn between rhizomatics and systems theory is reinforced by Deleuze and Guattari's (1981, p. 61) discussion of contemporary developments in information science. One must distinguish between the critique of scientific approaches to human life based on its theoretical foundations and the measures that it subsequently proposes, and a critique based on its claim to power in which "science" is a disjunctive domain rather than the connective possibilities opened by rhizomatics (see Foucault, 1980, pp. 78-108.)

REFERENCES

Barthes, R. [*S/Z: an essay*] (Richard Howard, trans.). New York: Hill & Wang, 1974.
Barthes, R. [*The pleasure of the text*] (Richard Miller, trans.). New York: Hill & Wang, 1975.
Berlo, D. *The process of communication.* New York: Holt, 1960.
Buber, M. [*I and thou*] (R. G. Smith, trans.). New York: Scribner's, 1958.
Coward, R., & Ellis, J. *Language and materialism: Developments in semiology and the theory of the subject.* London: Routledge & Kegan Paul, 1977.
Dewey, J. *Experience and nature.* La Salle, IL: Open Court, 1925.
Deleuze, G., & Guattari, F. [*Anti-oedipus: Capitalism and schizophrenia*] (R. Hurley, M. Seem, & H. R. Lane, trans.). New York: Viking, 1977.
Deleuze, F., & Guattari, D. Rhizome. *I & C,* 1981, (8), 49-71.
Eco, U. *A theory of semiotics.* Bloomington: Indiana University Press, 1976.
Foucault, M. [*The birth of the clinic: An archeology of medical perception*] A. M. Sheridan Smith, trans.). New York: Pantheon, 1973.
Foucault, M. [*Discipline and punish: the birth of the prison*] (Alan Sheridan, trans.). New York: Pantheon, 1977.
Foucault, M. [*The history of sexuality, Volume 1: An introduction*] (R. Hurley, trans.). New York: Pantheon, 1978.
Foucault, M. My body, this paper, this fire. *Oxford Literary Review,* 1979, *4,* 9-28.
Foucault, M. *Power/knowledge: Selected interviews and other writings* (C. Gordon, Ed.). New York: Pantheon, 1980.
Gadamer, H-G. *Truth and method.* New York: Seabury, 1975.
Giddens, A. *Central problems in social theory: Action, structure and contradiction in social analysis.* Berkeley: University of California Press, 1979.
Grossberg, L. Language and theorizing in the human sciences. In Norman K. Denzin (Ed.), *Studies in Symbolic Interaction* (Vol. 2). Greenwich, CT: JAI Press, 1979.
Grossberg, L. The ideology of communication. *Man and World,* 1982, *15,* 83-101.
Grossberg, L. Intersubjectivity and the conceptualization of communication. *Human Studies,* in press.
Hawes, L. C. Toward a hermeneutic phenomenology of communication. *Communication Quarterly,* 1977, *25,* 30-41.
Heidegger, M. [*Being and time*] (J. Macquarrie & E. Robinson, trans.). New York: Harper & Row, 1962.

Kristeva, J. The subject in signifying practice. *Semiotexte,* 1975, *1,* 19-26.
Kristeva, J. [*Desire in language: A semiotic approach to literature and art*] (T. Gora, A. Jardine, & L.S. Roudiez, trans.). New York: Columbia University Press, 1980.
Kuhn, T. *The structure of scientific revolutions.* Chicago: University of Chicago Press, 1970.
Lacan, J. [*Ecrits: A selection*] (A. Sheridan, trans.). New York: W.W. Norton, 1977.
Laplanche, J., & Pontalis, J-B. [*The language of psychoanalysis*] (D. Nicholson-Smith, trans.). New York: W.W. Norton, 1973.
Mortensen, C.D. *Communication: The study of human interaction.* New York: McGraw-Hill, 1972.
Nofsinger, R.E., Jr. The demand ticket: A conversational device for getting the floor. *Speech Monographs,* 1975, *42,* 1-9.
O'Keefe, B., Delia, J.G., & O'Keefe, D. Interaction analysis and the analysis of interactional organization. In Norman K. Denzin (Ed.), *Studies in Symbolic Interaction* (Vol. 3). Greenwich, CT: JAI Press, 1981.
Rommetveit, R. *On message structure: a framework for the study of language and communication.* New York: John Wiley, 1974.
Rommetveit, R. On negative rationalism in scholarly studies of verbal communication and dynamic residuals in the construction of human intersubjectivity. In M. Brenner, T. Marsh, & M. Brenner (Eds.), *The social context of method.* London: Croon Helm, 1978.
Sartre, J-P. *Being and nothingness* (Hazel Barnes, trans.). London: Methuen, 1969.
Schutz, A. Making music together. In *Collected papers 2: Studies in social theory.* The Hague: Martinez Nijhoff, 1964.
Schutz, A. The phenomonology of the social world (G. Walsh & F. Lehnert, trans.). Evanston: Northwestern University Press, 1967.
Stivale, G. Gilles Deleuze and Felix Guattari: Psychoanalysis and the literary discourse. *Journal of Substance,* 1981, *29,* 46-57.
Zeleny, M. *Autopoiesis: a theory of living organization.* Amsterdam: Elsevier, 1981.

… COMMUNICATION REVIEWS AND COMMENTARIES

7 ● Privacy and Communication

JUDEE K. BURGOON
Michigan State University

THE past few decades have seen a rapidly growing awareness of issues related to privacy. From consumer advocates and politicians who express concern over infringements on privacy rights by computerized information banks, to environmental design experts who anticipate escalating pressures on physical privacy from spiraling urban density, to penologists trying to solve the problems of the country's overcrowded prisons, there is wide recognition of the fundamental importance of privacy. This vital issue should be a concern to communication scholars as well. Given the status accorded privacy in this culture and the profound implications of privacy loss for interpersonal transactions, the communicational facet of privacy needs to be more fully analyzed and integrated with the perspectives offered by other disciplines. Beyond the social utility of such analysis, privacy has promise as a useful construct in theories of interpersonal communication. Its interrelatedness with many other communication variables may place it in a superordinate role; as an overarching concept it may offer more parsimonious explanations of many motives and observed communication patterns.

In analyzing privacy's relevance to communication, several questions need to be addressed. First, just what is privacy? What distinguishes private from nonprivate communication settings? Second, are there different kinds of dimensions of privacy that have implications for communication? Third, is privacy a major goal of our interpersonal behavior? How essential is it to individual and group functioning? Fourth, how is privacy expressed? What strategies and messages have as their explicit or implicit purpose the achievement or restoration of privacy?

AUTHOR'S NOTE: The author wishes to acknowledge the significant contributions of Martie Parsley to early conceptualizations of the dimensionality of privacy.

Correspondence and requests for reprints: Judee K. Burgoon, Department of Communication, Michigan State University, East Lansing, MI 48824.

Privacy and Communication

This chapter is an initial attempt to address some of these questions. Literature from other disciplines that has a bearing on these issues is reviewed, along with communication literature that can be recast in privacy terms. The formulations presented are intended to offer a fuller representation of the complex nature of privacy and to provide a communication-oriented perspective missing in most previous analyses.

DEFINING PRIVACY

Reflecting the diverse disciplines that have studied privacy, conceptualizations of it vary widely. Following are just a few of the ways in which it has been defined:

1. Ability to exert control over self, objects, spaces, information, and behavior (Wolfe & Laufer, 1974).
2. Autonomy of action within an unviolated living-space (Conklin, 1976).
3. Interpersonal boundary process by which a person or group regulates interaction with others (Derlega & Chaikin, 1977).
4. Selective control of access to the self or one's group (Altman, 1975).
5. Control of stimulus inputs from other people; control of mutual separateness and degree of knowledge about one another (Simmel, 1950).
6. Desire to be an enigma to others; desire to control others' perceptions of and beliefs about self; self-concealment (Jourard, 1966).
7. Consensually agreed-upon right to maintain boundaries and deny access to others (Warren & Laslett, 1977).
8. Control of movement of information across a boundary to and from individuals and groups (Shils, 1966).
9. Individual independence and reduced vulnerability to the power and influence of others (Kelvin, 1973).
10. Individual freedom of choice in a particular situation to control what, how, and to whom the person communicates information about the self (Proshansky, Ittleson, & Rivlin, 1970).
11. The claim of individuals, groups, or institutions to determine for themselves when, how, and to what extent information about them is communicated to others (Westin, 1970).

Beyond these explicit definitions of privacy, a number of familiar communication constructs appear to relate to privacy. Communication reticence (Phillips, 1968), predispositions toward verbal behavior (Mortensen, Arntson, & Lustig, 1977), and unwillingness to communicate (Burgoon, 1976) all concern a person's inclination to avoid or withdraw from face-to-face interaction, a disposition that may indicate a greater need or desire for privacy. Similarly, such personality variables as shyness (Zimbardo, 1975) and introversion (Eysenck & Eysenck, 1969) are suggestive of privacy in terms of greater separation from others and greater self-concealment. The relational dimension of inclusion-exclusion (Schutz, 1958) also reflects the degree to which one person chooses to be open or closed to another. Finally, intimacy (Derlega & Chaikin, 1975) can be conceived of as involving low privacy for those within the intimate relationship and high privacy for those outside it.

If one extracts the kernel elements underlying these various conceptualizations of privacy, it becomes apparent that privacy is a complex phenomenon, involving multiple levels of analysis. It is useful to parse out these different analytic perspectives, because they have important implications for communication study.

First, the definitions differ on the *unit experiencing the privacy*. In the case of definitions such as Conklin's (1976), Simmel's (1950), Jourard's (1966), and Kelvin's (1973), the unit is seen as the individual; that is, privacy is conceived of as the individual maintaining some kind of freedom from contact, surveillance, and/or social pressure from others. This is the same perspective that would be taken when analyzing personality types or communication avoidance syndromes. In other definitions, such as Derlega and Chaikin's (1977), Altman's (1975), Shils's (1966) and Westin's (1970), there is recognition that a dyad or group may also seek privacy from others. Intimacy presupposes such relational privacy. From a communication vantage point, it seems essential to recognize both forms of privacy. The inclusion-exclusion concept nicely satisfies this requirement. Within an interaction, one individual may attempt to exclude others, or a group may attempt to exclude others while maintaining high inclusiveness among themselves. Presumably the more tightly controlled the boundaries between those who are included and those who are excluded, the more privacy is achieved.

A second distinction evident in the various conceptualizations is that which Altman (1975) has described as between *"desired" and "achieved" privacy*. Some definitions specify the ideal state that is desired (e.g., right to deny access), while others specify the actual end state realized (e.g., reduced vulnerability). This distinction proves useful in analyzing under what conditions people might communicate the need for more or less privacy and what forms those "messages" might take.

A third, related distinction is that between the *conditions conducive to privacy and the actual experience of privacy*. Many definitions and conceptualizations specify the prerequisites for achieving privacy (e.g., the right to maintain boundaries), as opposed to what actually constitutes privacy (e.g., freedom from surveillance). Both are useful because the former provide a starting point for elaborating what communication mechanisms need to be operative to gain privacy, while the latter specify the goals to be met.

A fourth valuable distinction has also been noted by Altman (1975, 1976). He points out that many definitions emphasize seclusion or withdrawal from interaction, while others center on notions of control and freedom of choice. This can be characterized as a *reactive versus proactive distinction.* Implicit in the withdrawal version is the notion of passive retreat in response to undesired incoming stimili; it is more a stimulus-response approach. The latter interpretation allows for both approach and avoidance. As Altman (1975, 1976) has argued, defining privacy as involving "selective control" is preferable because it takes into account the input-output nature of privacy (it is a bidirectional process involving receipt of stimuli from others as well as outputs from the self) and it recognizes the dynamic, dialectic nature of the process (privacy involving a continous readjustment of boundaries to satisfy changing needs). It also underscores the active role played by the seeker of privacy. This preference for a control orientation is echoed by Proshansky et al. (1970, p. 176), whose thesis is that "privacy serves to maximize freedom of choice, to permit the individual to feel free to behave in a particular manner or to increase his range of options by removing certain classes of social constraints." From a communication standpoint, the inclusion of the concepts of choice and control also seem preferable, so as to distinguish privacy, which is considered a desirable state, from such undesirable states as social isolation and alienation, both of which imply lack of choice and personal control.

A fifth distinction might be cast as the *relative legitimacy of privacy demands.* Whereas some definitions appear to imply that the individual must lay claim to privacy and take responsibility for its maintenance, others make more explicit the consensual and often legal basis of privacy. Warren and Laslett (1977), in distinguishing between secrecy and privacy, emphasize the public endorsement of the "right to privacy" in many areas of life, noting that privacy, unlike secrecy, involves concealment of behavior that is morally valued or regarded neutrally by society. This recognition of privacy as a right rather than a tenuous privilege means not only that the rules governing privacy should be relatively well understood within a given society, but also that sanctions against violations of privacy should be relatively explicit. From a research standpoint, this should make "messages" of privacy more accessible to study.

A final distinction implicit in the conceptualizations of privacy is that of *different types of privacy.* Westin (1970) has delineated four types of privacy, all of which are evident in the definitions cited earlier. The first type, *solitude,* exists when a person is completely isolated from others, free from observation and alone. The second, *intimacy,* exists when a dyad or group minimizes sensory inputs from "outsiders" so as to maximize personal relationships. The third, *anonymity,* involves freedom from recognition and from direct, personal surveillance while in a public setting. The final type, *reserve,* involves the ability to erect a psychological barrier against "unwanted intrusion" and to keep from revealing personal or embarrassing information about the self. These dimensions have been confirmed by Marshall (1972) in a factor-analytic study of privacy preferences, along with two additional dimensions: *not neighboring,* or a preference for noninvolvement with neighbors, and *seclusion,* the desire for a home removed from the sight and sound of neighbors and traffic.

Conklin (1976) offers a different typology. He identifies *informational privacy,* which refers to freedom from outside knowledge being gathered and stored about oneself; *remote observational privacy,* which is freedom from observation by another who is not physically present (as through wiretapping); *direct observational privacy,* which is freedom from observation by a physically present other who gathers information about self directly through the senses of sight, sound, and smell; and *contact privacy,* or the freedom from touch, restraint, and interference by others (including denial of privileges, economic manipulation, verbal commands, and behavior modification, as well as actual physical contact).

While these typologies are useful in highlighting the multifaceted nature of privacy, they are somewhat confusing because they tend to overlap without being exhaustive. Solitude, seclusion, and observational privacy (direct and remote) all seem highly related, for instance, in their emphasis on freedom from surveillance and aloneness. At the same time, they have not been adequately explicated to distinguish those that apply to the individual from those that apply to the group, those that are more physical in nature from those that are more psychological, those that are manifested through communication patterns from those that merely impinge on the communication process, and so forth. For purposes of studying communication, it may be more useful to delineate four broadly defined, interdependent dimensions of privacy, all of which have implications for communication. These are discussed in detail here.

DIMENSIONS OF PRIVACY

Physical Privacy

It's just like packing sardines in a can. If you keep stuffing them in there, the pressure builds up inside and pretty soon the top's going to blow. (Quoted from an inmate during the Michigan prison riots, *Detroit Free Press,* May 31, 1981, p. 4B.)

Implicit in almost all definitions of privacy and particularly those of Altman (1975), Conklin (1976), Derlega and Chaikin (1977), and Warren and Laslett (1977) is the notion of physical privacy, or the degree to which one is physically inaccessible to others. If personal space invasion or crowding can be seen as one end of a distancing continuum, then physical privacy is the opposite end, since it involves freedom from intrusion on one's self-defined "body buffer zone" and freedom from the discomfiture of too many people for the available space. At its extreme, it may entail complete isolation from others.

Its salience to communication becomes evident when we consider the essential role of physical privacy in the organization of human life. Not only is there abundant literature to suggest that humans, like other mammalian species, are territorial and depend on interpersonal spacing to organize the social system (e.g., Ardrey, 1970; Edney, 1976; Esser, 1967; Hall, 1973; Leyhausen, 1971; Washburn, 1961); innumerable experiments on personal space invasions and crowding document serious negative consequences from the loss of physical privacy. Summaries of such research and related theorizing consistently conclude that overcrowding, spatial intrusions, and surveillance cause such stress-related reactions as physiological indications of arousal and anxiety, illness, feelings of helplessness, impaired cognitive functioning, loss of self-identity, withdrawal, and other behavioral, architectural, and psychological responses designed to restore physical comfort and insulation (Altman, 1975; Calhoun, 1969; Davis, 1971; Desor, 1972; Dosey & Meisels, 1969; Esser, 1976; Evans & Eichelman, 1976; Greenberg & Firestone, 1977; Paulus, 1980; Stokols, 1972a, 1976). By implication, then, physical privacy is a requisite for maintaining optimal functioning of the individual within society and of society itself. Given this pervasive if subtle influence on day-to-day living, it must have significant communication implications, both in terms of how privacy messages are interwoven into the text of normal interpersonal transactions and how different environmentally defined levels of privacy affect communication patterns within those contexts.

In elaborating on the nature of physical privacy, it would be ideal if the concept had a precise, objective definition. Unfortunately, it is not that simple. According to Altman's (1975) analysis at least, what constitutes privacy is individualized and subjective, based on what inputs and outputs the person desires compared to what is actually achieved. That is, privacy only exists when the degree to which an individual is accessible and has access to others matches what is preferred. The degree of privacy in any given situation is therefore dependent on each individual's interpretation of the situation.

Reflecting this same philosophical perspective on privacy, Wapner et al. (1973, p. 258) underscore the individual's cognitively active manner of dealing with the physical environment:

> Man seeks to make sense out of his surroundings and to define and locate himself with respect to these surroundings. . . . Striving and acting in a world, he defines among the objects of his environment (indeed makes a distinction between things and persons) in terms of what it is that he wants to have or avoid.

Definitions of crowding (e.g., Baum & Greenberg, 1975; Desor, 1972; Esser, 1973; Stokols, 1972a, 1972b) and personal space (e.g., Dosey & Meisels, 1969; Leibman, 1970; Sommer, 1969) similarly stress psychological components. What is experienced as crowding, a personal space invasion, or a privacy violation depends on personal and social factors in addition to the actual physical density, distance, or nonverbal correlates of distance (such as eye contact) that are involved. Thus total seclusion for one individual may be perceived as the ultimate in privacy, while for another it may be experienced as involuntary social isolation or boredom. Conversely, actual physical contact for the person seeking affiliation may be seen as intimacy, while for another desiring reclusion it may constitute a serious encroachment on privacy.

From a methodological standpoint, this emphasis on subjective factors could make privacy difficult to assess empirically, a point aptly made by Willems and Campbell (1976). However, if social norms are assumed to serve as a barometer of general privacy preferences, then individual desires may be deduced with some accuracy from the aggregate patterns of behavior. More important, nonverbal messages may signal individual deviations from the general preference pattern by expressing a need for greater or lesser privacy. This makes analysis of the communication patterns associated with privacy all the more important. What constitutes physical privacy is also made somewhat more explicit by laws on human rights. For instance, the right to sanctuary — maintaining a protected zone within which one can withhold certain things from the scrutiny of others — is guaranteed by the Fourth Amendment to the U.S. Constitution (Latin, Bostwick, & Ratner, 1976).

The nature of physical privacy can be further understood through application of Hall's (1973) model for analyzing cultures, which entails identifying sets, isolates, and patterns. Using a linguistic analogy, sets are like words, isolates like the sounds that constitute the words, and patterns like grammar or syntax linking the words to one another. Hall (1973, p. 102) explains: "The sets (words) are what you perceive first, the isolates (sounds) are the components that make up the sets, while the patterns (syntax) are the way in which sets are strung together in order to give them meaning." Using this approach, it is possible to delineate the various levels of physical privacy (the sets), the distinguishing characteristics that set them apart (the isolates), and the communication patterns associated with a given level or kind of privacy. Potential sets and isolates will be discussed at this point; a discussion of communication patterns will be reserved for the last section of this chapter, where the four kinds of privacy and their respective communication patterns are discussed together.

One typology that can be reconceptualized as physical sets is that offered by Lyman and Scott (1967) in their analysis of four types of territory: public, interactional, home, and body. *Public territory* is any locale that has open access to all, such as a park or public sidewalk. It obviously is the opposite of physical privacy. *Interactional territory* is designed for social activity, with access restricted to approved participants (such as ticket holders in a movie theater or members of a private country club). Access is typically regulated through implicit social sanctions. Groups may experience privacy in such territories, but opportunities for individual privacy are limited. *Home territory* (which may be one's neighborhood, an office, an automobile, or even a favorite chair) involves more restricted access, which is under the control of those who own or occupy the territory. Physical force or explicit sanctions are permissible in defense of a home territory. Because access is often controlled through physical barriers, home territories afford considerable privacy for their occupants, whether individuals or groups. Marshall's (1972) category of seclusion most closely corresponds to this type of privacy. Finally, *body territory* is the human body itself and the space immediately surrounding it, what has been typically defined as personal space or a body buffer zone. As the most inviolate of territories, access is typically only granted a select few, with violations invoking strong sanctions. In contrast to the other types of territory, which may create individual or group privacy, body territory necessarily offers only individual privacy.

These four types of territory may be considered the points defining a privacy continuum. They may be regarded as sets because they are readily apparent to members of Western culture as separate kinds of privacy.

Another analysis that has implications for physical privacy sets comes from Latin et al. (1976). In their legal elaboration of types of privacy, they distinguish between the *privacy of repose* and the *privacy of sanctuary*. The former is the freedom from anything that excites or disturbs; the latter is the freedom to maintain a protected zone that keeps others from seeing, hearing, or knowing what transpires within. Rephrased, repose involves the right not to have annoyances or distressing events penetrate one's boundaries, while sanctuary involves the right to a physical refuge free from the surveillance of others. These two types of privacy seem to offer a qualitative distinction as opposed to the more quantitative (i.e., amount of privacy) distinction represented in the territory typology.

Apparent in these typologies (which by no means exhaust the possible sets) and in the definitions of privacy are several isolates that distinguish one kind of physical privacy from another. Two of the most basic, alluded to earlier, are the twin features of *controlled access* and *choice*. To the degree that one can personally control the physical boundaries and choose who is to be included or excluded, the individual has more physical privacy. A prime example of how the absence of these qualities translates into a lack of privacy comes from Ramsey's (1976, p. 44) observations on prison life:

> An integral part of the punishment procedure is the control of space. Not only is the size of the living space a factor, but freedom of access to environmental space and people as well. Inmates have no control over who they will live next to and little control over who they will socialize with. . . . one's cell is the only claim to privacy available. . . . Any uninvited intrusion into the cell is considered a direct assault.

As is evident from this quotation, a closely related isolate is the *degree of stress*. Glass and Singer's (1972) work has demonstrated that perceived lack of control leads to psychological stress. Privacy, then, serves to reduce stress.

Fourth, physical privacy usually implies some *degree of seclusion*. The more remote and insulated an area, the more private it is typically perceived to be. As an extension of the seclusion feature, a fifth factor distinguishing different levels of privacy is the *degree of freedom from surveillance,* which is the same concept as expressed in Conklin's (1976) direct and remote observational privacy, the former referring to in-person and the latter to mechanical information gathering. The greater the opportunity for any kind of surveillance, the less the privacy. A sixth, related factor is the *number of sensory channels through which access is possible.* Kira (1966) enumerated four combinations: (1) privacy of being heard but not seen, (2) privacy of being seen but not heard, (3) privacy of not being seen or heard, and (4) privacy of not being seen, heard, or sensed (i.e., other people are not aware of where you are or your intended behavior). This schema needs to be expanded to account for other channels, such as touch and smell, and for all the combinations of channels. It also must be recognized that these channels not only operate to make one's outputs accessible or inaccessible to others, but also provide the possibility of one being exposed to inputs from others. Hence, cooking odors or the sounds of an argument emanating from a neighboring apartment reduce one's physical privacy as much as does the neighbor's ability to overhear one's intimate conversations through an adjoining wall. The degree of physical privacy, then, should be some function of how many channels are open to others. The more channels involved, presumably the less privacy. Given that privacy loss through crowding or personal space invasion leads to greater stress and that such conditions, by definition, mean high sensory involvement, the reduction of channels available for input-output exchange should reduce stress, reduce the potential for information overload, and consequently increase the privacy experienced. Based on this analysis, it is clear why seclusion is equated with privacy: because it makes the individual inaccessible through most channels (the exceptions being remote visual or auditory surveillance). What remains to be clarified is how the channels and their combinations might be rank ordered in terms of providing the most to least privacy.

A seventh isolate of privacy concerns the *amount and nature of territory under one's control*. Physical privacy and territory seem almost synonymous. As Edney (1976, p. 38) attests, one function of territory is to provide privacy: "Among many animal species there is a broad recognition of a territory holder's rights — his claim to privacy and his relative immunity to arbitrary challenge and interruption when he is on home ground." Within one's territory, one has enhanced control over priority of access, initiation of behavior, choice in behavior type, and ability to resist the control of others (Edney, 1975, 1976). The more or qualitatively better territory one occupies and the greater the undisputed control, the greater the privacy. These features of quantity of territory, quality of territory (e.g., a more expensive, better-insulated, or more "imposing" home) and unquestioned control are treated here as part of the same isolate because they are so interrelated. Amount of territory may determine whether there will be any jurisdictional dispute, economic value of the territory may compensate size, and so forth. Applying this isolate to distinctions among the levels of privacy, it becomes evident that what separates a home territory, say, from an interactional one is that the owner/occupant can legitimately claim personal control of the space and has the resources to reject any attempts at usurpation.

Three final isolates that appear to determine the degree of privacy within as well as across sets are the *probability of a violation*, the *humanness of the violator*, and the *relationship of the violator to self*. The lower the probability that a violation can occur from any quarter, the greater the felt privacy. Thus, home territories accord more privacy because they physically preclude many types of intrusions compared to a public territory. By the same token, if one is in an empty public territory, a well-partitioned restaurant, or any social situation in which decorum dictates that people maintain great distances from one another, one senses greater physical privacy because the likelihood of an intrusion or surveillance is reduced. The humanness of the potential violator similarly makes a difference.

People appear to be much less bothered by an intrusion on their privacy by a pet than by another person. There are also many public situations, such as a football game or riding in an elevator, in which it is customary to treat others as nonpersons and so reduce one's sense of violation. To the extent that the violator is nonhuman or can be treated as an inanimate object, the experience of privacy loss should be minimized. Sommer (1969) makes the point that servants, maids, and other service personnel are typically treated as nonpersons and that their presence in the midst of otherwise private circumstances is therefore ignored. Related to this last point, the relationship of violator to self should affect felt privacy. Just as nonpersons pose little threat to one's privacy, one's most intimate relatives and friends should cause minimal reductions in one's sense of physical privacy. It is possible that some kind of curvilinear relationship exists between degree of regard and privacy loss, such that those held in the highest or lowest esteem create the least sense of privacy violation, while those in the middle ranges — acquaintances and strangers who cannot be relegated to nonperson status — have the greatest potential to create felt privacy loss by violating one's physical territory.

Social Privacy

The alternative to privacy is the ant heap. (Kelvin, 1973, p. 260)

Related to the physical dimension of privacy, and often a natural consequence of it, is social privacy. Inasmuch as privacy presupposes the existence of others, a fundamental facet of privacy is the ability to withdraw from social intercourse. Consonant with Rapoport's (1975) concept of controlling unwanted interaction, Westin's (1970) notion of limited and protected communication, Proshansky et al.'s (1970) view of privacy as the maximization of behavioral options in social activities, and Altman's (1976) concept of regulating interpersonal boundaries, this dimension of privacy centers directly on the communicational aspects of privacy.

Social privacy is best understood as both an individual and a group state. Just as individuals frequently opt to remove themselves from contact with others, so do groups of people frequently set themselves apart from the larger social unit in order to achieve greater intimacy within the group or to shelter themselves from involvement with the larger group. In this regard, the relational concept of inclusion-exclusion captures well the nature of this dual role of social privacy — to foster closeness among some individuals while simultaneously creating distance from others. The dating couple is a case in point. Actions designed to create a greater sense of togetherness between the two at the same time signal to outsiders that they are excluded from the relationship. The perception of social privacy applies to the feelings of intimacy and protection within the pair as well as the sense of remoteness and inaccessibility from outsiders. By the same token, each person may occasionally withdraw from the relationship to seek individual solitude; this, too, is social privacy. Any efforts to control one's degree of social contacts on an individual, dyadic, or group level relate to social privacy.

Just as physical insularity may be essential to the functioning of the individual, so may social privacy be essential to the functioning of society. According to Merton (1957), group life presupposes some leeway in conforming to role expectations. Without the benefit of privacy, which makes allowances for situational exigencies and individual differences in training or ability to fulfill role responsibilities, the full surveillance of group activities would lead to dysfunction through fear of discovered dereliction and inability to punish all such failures. In other words, effective social structure is dependent on some nonobservability of behavior so that all infractions against the norms need not be detected or enforced.

Implicit in this view is the normative foundation of social privacy, a point made explicit by Kelvin (1973, p. 257):

> Privacy is only relevant to situations or behaviour where laws or norms, including 'private' norms as in a family, constrain (and/or interfere with) the behaviour of the individual. . . . I suggest, speculatively, that areas of privacy arise within a context of well-established norms; the emergence, and acceptance, of a higher-order norm of privacy then introduces freedom of choice which had previously been inhibited by the original, basic norms.

The significance of this normative basis to social privacy and the behaviors it shields from public sanctions is that it makes privacy more accessible to empirical scrutiny. Because there are consensually agreed-upon patterns of contact and withdrawal, rule adherence, rule violations, and sanctions against violations can be readily identified and studied. Seen through a communication lens, patterns of social interaction can be examined for their role in safeguarding individual and group privacy and thereby maintaining social order.

Beyond its role in preserving social structure, social privacy appears to be necessary for individual well-being. Milgram (1970), Calhoun (1970), and Desor (1972), among others, have argued that humans need a manageable number of meaningful social encounters so that gratifications from such relationships can be maximized while annoyances and conflicts are kept to a minimum. When the number of social contacts becomes excessive, the amount of stimulation "overloads" the system, causing stress and a motivation to seek greater distance or privacy. A similar view is expressed in the writings of animal behaviorists (e.g., Leyhausen, 1971; McBride, 1971; Schneirla, 1965), who support the reinforcing value of affiliative interactions for vertebrate species and note that affiliative drives lead to tendencies to approach conspecifics, but who also note that such tendencies are tempered by dominance and self-protective needs leading to countertendencies to withdraw. Schneirla (1965), in fact, has proposed that animal spacing is a function of these two vectors of approach and withdrawal; as one changes, so does the other, constantly bringing distance back to a state of equilibrium. Interestingly, a nearly identical analysis comes from theories of affiliative conflict (e.g., Argyle & Dean, 1965; Knowles, 1980), which begin with the similar though more psychological premise that approach and avoidance tendencies represent conflicting desires to affiliate with others and to maintain separateness or privacy. The theories likewise posit that people strive to keep these two desires in balance and that excessive intimacy or isolation, being stressful, prompts efforts to restore equilibrium. Interpreted from a privacy perspective, people oscillate between lesser and greater degrees of social involvement. The same principle is echoed in Simmel's (1950) conception of privacy as a dialectic process whereby people alternate between opening themselves up to others and closing themselves off, a perspective that more recently has been embraced by Altman (1975, 1977). While the communication syndromes of reticence (Phillips, 1968), unwillingness to communicate (Burgoon, 1976), and predispositions toward verbal behavior (Mortensen, et al., 1977) are by design more traitlike than situational in nature, they, too, underscore the differential involvement in human interaction that people seek — unwillingness to communicate even has as one of its dimensions approach-avoidance — and are recognized as showing some situational variability. Social privacy, then, reflects these apparently universal fluctuations in interpersonal advance and retreat.

The elemental value of social privacy can be better understood through the functions it serves. Two of its more obvious ones are *managing social interactions* and *establishing plans and strategies for interacting with others* (Altman, 1976, 1977). The freedom to engage and disengage in interaction allows one to exercise control over social relationships; the respites from social engagement allow one to plan for future contacts. In the same vein, social privacy permits one to rehearse roles, to gain temporary release from roles, and to evade institutional rules (Chapin, 1951; Goffman, 1959; Merton, 1957). Applying Goffman's (1959) dramaturgic perspective, one is able to withdraw from "frontstage" performance of socially prescribed roles to the "backstage," where role requirements are not in force and rules can be broken with impugnity. As expressed by

Chapin (1951, p. 164), "there is often need to escape from the compulsions of one's social role, to be able to retire from the role of parent, spouse, relative, or child, as the case may be." It is also backstage where one is free to engage in emotional release (Westin, 1970). The tensions of role and rule conformity give way to idiosyncratic and cathartic behavior.

In his analysis of privacy and the family, Berardo (1974) elaborates on functions satisfied by the invisibility of the backstage. One is to *provide a buffer* between pressures on the marital couple and their responses to those pressures. The pair is able to experiment, make mistakes, disclose feelings, and engage in acts that otherwise might draw criticism or punishment from others. Another is to *provide latitude in conforming to social norms* regarding family behavior. Privacy permits parents to adjust to their own personal values and abilities the ways in which they exercise their responsibilities in socializing their children and fulfilling adult roles. A third is to *create protection for the family unit from outside interference or scrutiny* while it works out its difficulties. The autonomy granted by privacy improves the family's ability to survive crises intact. A fourth is an *"ameliorative" function,* offering a haven within which to recover from the strains of life in general and assaults on one's self-esteem in particular. The privacy associated with the backstage region enables one to recuperate from the traffic of day-to-day living and to regenerate energy and initiative. The metaphor of the backstage thus gives social privacy a spatial and temporal dimension. It is seen as a place — a "behind-the-scenes" hideaway where people go to escape from the demands of daily social transactions, to heal after stressful encounters, to rehearse and prepare for future contacts — and also as a duration of time — a "grace" period during which the normal rules of conduct can be suspended. Conceiving of social privacy this way clarifies why intimate relationships are regarded as private, because they permit, even encourage, nonconformity and emotional purgation while creating a protective shield against outside interference.

Two additional functions pertinent to social privacy have been suggested by Schwartz (1968): *removal from irritation* and *maintenance of status divisions.* It is his thesis that "excessive contact is the condition under which Freud's principle of ambivalence most clearly exercises itself, when intimacy is most likely to produce open hostility as well as affection" (Schwartz, 1968, p. 741). Withdrawal into privacy therefore offers necessary distraction and respite from the tensions, annoyances, and resentments that arise from frequent and multiple social contacts; it is the palliative of unbearable relationships. By providing escape, social privacy preserves what Schwartz refers to as the "horizontal order" of society; and, because privacy is a scarce resource, its possession becomes associated with status, thereby reinforcing the "vertical order" of society as well.

Social privacy, then, according to this analysis, is a key force in stabilizing the social system. The obvious corollary is that communication patterns that promote social privacy are important stabilizing influences on social relationships.

As a further analysis of social privacy, it is possible to identify sets and isolates, as was done with physical privacy. One potentially applicable set of categories comes from Hall (1970), who identified four distance zones, each with a near and a far phase: intimate, personal, social, and public. *Intimate distance* is zero to eighteen inches, close enough to touch, to reach extremities, to distort the visual system, and to detect heat and odor from another. *Personal distance,* eighteen inches to four feet, is the distance typically separating numbers of non-contact species; it is close enough to produce kinesthetic involvement while limiting the possibility of actual touch. *Social distance,* four to twelve feet, is the distance usually occurring for impersonal or casual exchanges and greatly reduces sensory involvement with another's presence. *Public distance,* ranging from twelve feet and beyond, is reserved for public occasions and is such a great distance that it reduces fine visual detail of another and typically evokes an increase in vocal volume. While these four categories apply specifically to distances, they can just as easily be adapted to serve as categories of social privacy. Not only do these categories reflect perceptual differences in each range, they also entail differences in conversational content and the formality of the interaction. They do not, however, adequately distinguish kinds of social privacy that may occur at a public distance or nonprivate situations that may occur at close range, which is to say privacy does not correlate closely with actual physical distance.

A more useful set of social privacy categories comes from the typologies outlined earlier. Those that show the closest kinship to social privacy are Westin's (1970) anonymity, reserve, and intimacy and Marshall's (1972) not neighboring. *Anonymity,* as the label implies, is the lack of personal identification and correspondent freedom from observation in a public setting. Its relevance to social privacy is that one can be in the midst of a crowd and yet have minimal probability of communicating with others in any but a most superficial way. Hence physical privacy may be at a minimum, but social privacy is quite high. The pedestrian on a public street, for example, will be aware of the presence of others, and to that extent will not have total social privacy, but will feel no pressure to interact with passersby and will probably feel at ease because of the limited likelihood of being watched, approached, or spoken to. This type of privacy seems most applicable to an individual rather than a group, since two or more people together are by definition no longer completely anonymous. However, it is possible to talk about degrees of anonymity felt by a pair or group in the midst of a larger group. Mob action, after all, is often explained as a sense of anonymity among participants, despite the fact that many are acquainted with one another. The key to anonymity is the relative absence of personal identification and responsibility coupled with low probability of communication with others.

Reserve, by contrast, implies some degree of interaction with others and refers to the manner in which one communicates so as to limit others' knowledge of oneself. It is also applicable to the remaining two dimensions of privacy to be discussed, but in regard to social privacy it suggests a pattern of infrequent or more formalized conversations. The introverted personality, for example, gains social privacy by virtue of reducing the number and frequency of his or her social contacts; most would describe such a person as reserved. Again, this type of privacy seems to describe an individual more appropriately than a group state, but it is possible to conceive of, say, clique groups in any large organization exhibiting reserve so as to maintain their social distance and power.

Intimacy as a description of a communication style could be considered the polar opposite of reserve in that it involves maximizing knowledge and "personalness" among members of a dyad or larger group, except that it also connotes a high level of reserve toward those outside the intimate relationship. Embedded in the concept of intimacy is minimization of sensory inputs, human or physical, from outside the boundaries of the intimate setting. Intimacy is clearly a dyad or group form of privacy and corresponds closely with the concept of the backstage — the intimate relationship itself becomes the private retreat.

Not neighboring captures a final kind of social privacy in which the opportunity for interaction is limited. While Marshall's (1972) measure for this type of privacy referred specifically to preferences for noninvolvement with neighbors and a dislike for people who drop in without warning, the concept can be widened to cover all those circumstances in which one is able to control and restrict the amount of interaction with others. This category of social privacy can be seen to parallel physical privacy, in that physical seclusion within a home territory offers maximum control over social interactions by eliminating the opportunity for them, while public or interactional territories in which one is known and recognized provide little if any control over who may approach and when.

These four kinds of social privacy may not be exhaustive, but they at least describe circumstances that run the gamut from a high-density social environment to one in which few or no other people are present and from complete freedom from communicative involvement to little or no control over one's social accessibility to others. The isolates that distinguish different degrees of social privacy include, for starters, (1) *control of who the participants of an interaction are*, (2) *control of the frequency of interaction*, (3) *control of the length of interaction*, and (4) *control of the content of interactions*. Anonymity, for example, leaves one little control over who might choose to approach, but it involves low probability of contact actually being made, so that there is greater control over the latter three factors. Intimacy, on the other hand, implies that one has decided with whom one will have an intimate relationship, but there is less personal control over the when and what of interaction because it is mutually negotiated and there are tacit obligations to maintain high levels of involvement. Of course, the degree to which an intimate pair can successfully insulate itself from others' interruptions will determine how much control they have as a unit over the number, duration, and topics of conversation with others. In other words, intimacy may minimize individual control but maximize unit control over the probability of contact with others. All four complementary facets of interaction control seem to be implied in Kelvin's (1973) conception of privacy as reducing constraints on, interruptions of, and interference with social behavior.

Another isolate of social privacy appears to be the *degree of formality of the situation*. The more formal the communication context in terms of the physical arrangement and/or the behavioral patterns adapted by participants, the greater the individual's ability to maintain reserve. Formality invokes social norms of politeness and decorum. With such norms governing the situation, each participant has greater freedom to terminate an unwanted interaction and to keep topics at an impersonal level without being held personally responsible for circumscribing the conversation. Greater informality, by contrast, invites longer, more intimate interactions and may precipitate more frequent contacts.

In a similar vein, degree of social privacy can be distinguished by the *degree of personalness of conversational topics and language*. Just as nonverbal behaviors may signal formality, so may the verbal content create an impersonal situation. The more immediate and involving the language and nonverbal cues are, and the more personalized and self-disclosive the topics of discussion are, the more intimate the situation becomes, which means less individual privacy in the reserve sense but more dyadic or group privacy in the intimacy sense of social privacy.

Two more isolates come from the earlier analysis of the backstage region: *degree of rule nonconformity and backstage behavior* and *freedom to engage in emotional release*. The freedom to step out of expected role behavior, to give vent to one's emotions, to engage in actions and language that derogate or invalidate the frontstage performance, and to behave in a generally uninhibited way all translate into a greater sense of social privacy. Anonymity can be seen to create this experience of social privacy, because one feels that, despite the presence of others, one's performance is not being watched or evaluated and therefore need not conform to the usual standards. Similarly, role figmentation, the *modus operandi* of singles bars, whereby people adopt a new, false identity, fits this concept of social privacy because the person can play with a new persona and behavioral repertoire with low risk. By the same token, settings that allow one to break the rules, to engage in socially undesirable behaviors such as nonverbal adaptors (e.g., scratching, yawning, belching), or to rehearse new roles are seen as private contexts because they temporarily remove the individual from the binding social order. A key motivation for desiring physical privacy is the social privacy that accompanies it. As a corrollary, the "removal of the mask" in the presence of others fosters a greater sense of intimacy and privacy within the group.

One final isolate that bridges social privacy with the next dimension to be discussed is *reduced vulnerability of one's behavior to the power and influence of others.* As expressed by Kelvin (1973, p. 251),

> It is a necessary condition of privacy (though not sufficient to define 'privacy') that the individual is free from the power or influence of other people; he enjoys privacy, as it were, to the extent to which the probabilities of his behavior are *not* causally affected by others.

The same principle is expressed by Johnson (1974) as behavior selection control; one has privacy to the extent that one is able to control one's own actions indirectly by controlling interactions with others. One way privacy enables greater control over one's own behavior is by limiting opportunities for social sanctions to be applied. As Warren and Laslett (1977, p. 46) have noted, the restricted access and observability that accompanies privacy limits opportunities for various audiences to control behavior: "Sanctions, whether their bases are legal or moral, cannot be applied by others when the behavior to which they might be attached is hidden from public view."

Social privacy, then, entails being free not only from actual interaction with others but also from any perceived pressures on one's own course of action. As an example, the physical appointments of a church sanctuary and the hushed behavior of those participating in a worship service might foster a sense of physical privacy and some degree of intimacy, but a total sense of social privacy would be lacking to the extent that one felt compelled to contribute to the collection plate because of the surveillance of neighbors. Any threat to the autonomy of action of an individual or group is a threat to social privacy.

Psychological Privacy

> *Just as material property is, so to speak, an extension of the ego, and any interference with our property is, for this reason, felt to be a violation of the person, there is also an intellectual private property whose violation effects a lesion of the ego in its very center.* (Simmel, 1950, p. 322)

This dimension of privacy is intricately related to the previous one and may even be regarded by many as part of it. But just as it is possible to have freedom of thought apart from freedom of action, so it is possible to consider the psychological side of privacy apart from its interactional aspect.

Basically, psychological privacy concerns one's ability to control affective and cognitive inputs and outputs. On the input side, it involves the ability to think, to formulate attitudes, beliefs, and values, to develop an individual identity, to assimilate personal experiences with one's understanding of the world and its problems, and to engage in emotional catharsis free from outside impediments or interferences. On the input side, it entails determining with whom and under what circumstances one will share thoughts and feelings, reveal intimate information and secrets, extend emotional support, and seek advice. By its nature, psychological privacy pertains only to the individual and not to groups. The communication constructs of self-disclosure (Jourard, 1971a, 1971b) and the social psychology theory of social penetration (Altman & Taylor, 1973) have direct relevance to this dimension of privacy.

The existence of a psychological dimension to privacy is evident in Laufer et al.'s (1973) own dimensional analysis of privacy. Among the nine they identified, three have psychological overtones. The *self-ego dimension* addresses the role of privacy in nurturing and enhancing the independence of self from the social and physical environment. The *control dimension* concerns the ability to exert control over self, information, and behavior (as well as objects and spaces) so as to maximize choices, limit access, and observation, and control amount of sensory stimulation. The aims that are specified for such control — self-enhancement, self-protection, and functional (e.g., eliminating distractions) — reveal the psychological underpinnings of this dimension. The *phenomenological dimension* is the most explicit: In referencing the affects and cognitions associated with the concept of privacy, it takes the experience out of the realm of being merely behavioral and into a uniquely psychological domain.

The importance of psychological privacy to communication may be seen in the functions it performs. There are six that have been tacitly or directly recognized. One is the *development of self-identity and relational definitions with others*. Altman (1975), among others, regards privacy as central to self-definition and self-identity. As many developmental psychologists have observed, it is through the cyclical process of interacting and withdrawing from social interactions that the child learns to separate self from the surrounding world, to develop a sense of identity or ego apart from other objects and people in the environment. As Altman (1975, p. 46) puts it,

> Self-identity is partly dependent on the ability of a person to define his or her own limits and boundaries. . . . This happens as a result of interaction with others, when mutual contact is controlled and regulated, when one's own behavior is separable from others' behavior, and when contacts with others are paced and regulated.

Privacy allows a person to create and maintain boundaries between self and others and, in so doing, not only aids the development of self-definition but also a definition of his or her relationship to others. Through the process of engagement and disengagement, a person comes to discover how he or she connects with other people and what makes the self unique. It is also through this dialectic process of approach and avoidance that one comes to define self *relative* to others — as dominant or submissive, as liked or disliked, as open or closed, and so forth. In this manner the individual develops a mental picture of his or her role within, and separate from, an interpersonal network and is able to achieve greater clarity about personal identity. This psychological aspect of privacy is dependent on one's opportunity to retreat physically and/or socially; without it, the sense of identity is jeopardized. As Evans and Eichelman (1976, p. 110) speculate, "close exposure to aggregates may be a threat to our individual sense of self and ego boundary. Perhaps personal space functions as a concrete expression of ego boundary in addition to a check on stress due to intraspecific aggression." When this function of psychological privacy is not fulfilled, stress results. In simulated prison experiments, Haney, Banks, and Zimbardo (1973) found that prisoners manifested pathological reactions to the perceived loss of personal identity that resulted from the invasion of privacy.

A second function that is closely related is *self-evaluation and observation*. Drawing an analogy with a religious retreat, Westin (1970) sees the opportunity for self-reflection and evaluation as one goal of privacy. Privacy allows a person to review his or her own behavior, to pass judgment on it, and to adjust future thoughts and actions accordingly. Altman (1975) considers this function of privacy to correspond with Festinger's (1954) social comparison theory, which argues that people need to compare themselves to others, especially in ambiguous or uncertain situations. Psychological privacy can be seen as the opportunity to interpret and internalize the comparisons that are made, using them as a framework for evaluating one's present and future actions.

A third function is *self-protection through control over outputs,* or what some have referred to as concealment (Goffman, 1959; Jourard, 1966, 1971b). A key reason for psychological insulation and withdrawal is to bolster and restore self-esteem. This requires hiding from view one's weaknesses and faults and putting one's best "face" forward in social situations. Jourard (1966, 1971b) has described this as desiring to be an enigma to others and controlling others' perceptions of self by withholding information about past, present, and future actions and intentions. It is the concealment of negative information about self (i.e., the controlling of outputs) that allows one to rationalize one's own behavior in the most favorable way without risk of contradictory feedback or interpretations from others. Simmel (1950) has contended that some degree of concealment is not only healthy but also necessary. Derlega and Chaikin (1975) agree; they point out that while some self-disclosure is good, too much can have negative consequences and may be associated with maladjustment. The point is succinctly put by Westin (1970, p. 36):

> The most serious threat to an individual's autonomy is the possibility that someone may penetrate the inner zone and learn his secrets . . . [which] would leave him naked to ridicule and shame and would put him under the control of those who know his secrets.

Privacy spares the individual embarrassment and humiliation (Kira, 1970).

A companion fourth function is *self-protection through control over inputs.* Just as psychological security is influenced by how much a person divulges to others about the self, so it is also affected by the amount and nature of sensory inputs from other people and the environment. A key value of psychological privacy is to protect the self from undue mental strain and fatigue and to gain relief from excessive sensory stimulation (Plant, 1930; Westin, 1970). Latin, Bostwick and Ratner (1976) call this the privacy of "repose," or the freedom from anything that disturbs or excites. In Kelvin's (1973, p. 259) words, "It could well be at times that the need to be alone is no more than a response to sheer satiation with the particular type of stimulation which is provided by other people." To the extent that such stimulation is physically tiring or emotionally draining, it impinges on psychological privacy. Dosey and Meisels (1969), who have advanced a view of personal space as a mechanism for achieving protection from psychological as well as physical threats, similarly consider threats to one's self-esteem and feeling states as insidious as physical ones, a view repeated by Stokols (1976). Psychological privacy, then, provides a temporary buffer against outside sources of stimulation that may cause emotional, mental, or psychosomatic stress.

A fifth function, hinted at in Westin's statement (quoted above) is *personal autonomy.* Kelvin (1973), Plant (1930), Warren and Laslett

(1977), and Westin (1970) have all commented on the importance to humans of independence and freedom from the influence of others. Encompassed in Kelvin's (1973) theory of privacy as freedom from power and influence is the belief that freedom of thought, as well as freedom of social action, is necessary to achieve personal responsibilty and to "feel truly oneself." From a legal standpoint, a similar concept is expressed in Latin, Bostwick, and Ratner's (1976) "zone of intimate decision," which refers to an area in which a person must be allowed to apply his or her own value systems in making essential decisions without the injection of disruptive factors by the state. They characterize this as less "freedom from" and more "freedom to."

A final function extends beyond autonomy to *personal growth*. Psychological privacy may contribute to an individual's intellectual, emotional, and spiritual maturation by providing freedom to fantasize, to meditate, to plan, and to think creatively (Chapin, 1951; Jourard, 1966; Kira, 1966; Plant, 1930). While individual development certainly profits from interaction with others, it also requires occasions for reflective thought, interpretation, and evaluation, whether that occurs in a state of solitude or in the midst of a group. The key to this function of privacy, then, is not necessarily physical separation but time and opportunity to develop one's own ideas, to think divergently without penalty, to experiment, and to come to grips with one's own emotions, values, and abilities as they relate to future goals and development.

In analyzing psychological privacy from a sets and isolates perspective, it appears that all four of Westin's (1970) types of privacy are salient to this dimension. *Solitude* offers the maximum freedom of thought and emotional insularity; *intimacy* provides the least, because of the pressures to open oneself up, to self-disclose, and to make oneself vulnerable to others. *Anonymity* and *reserve* offer intermediate degrees of psychological privacy, the former offering great control over outputs but little over inputs, and the latter offering just the reverse.

As for isolates that distinguish different levels and kinds of psychological privacy, all those have been identified for the social and physical dimensions of privacy are again applicable here, because they set the stage for experiencing psychological privacy. Additionally, there are some isolates implicit in the functions of psychological privacy. A central one is the *ability to conceal thoughts and feelings*. The more transparent one is to others, the less felt privacy. In this regard, hypnosis constitutes a serious infringement on psychic privacy because of the loss of control over disclosure of potentially risky information. In a similar vein, *freedom from the influence of others on one's thoughts and feelings* (which parallels the social isolate of reduced vulnerability of one's *behavior* to the power and influence of others) expresses the importance of control over inputs as a distinguishing feature of psychological privacy. Whereas in social privacy it is nearly impossible to be totally free from the influence of others unless one is physically isolated (because of the power of conversational norms to govern behavior, if nothing else), psychological privacy seems to connote virtual freedom from external interference. The opposite extreme would be brainwashing.

A final isolate appears to be *amount of sensory stimulation*. It was noted earlier that crowding, as one form of excess stimulation, impairs cognitive functioning and produces stress. The pressure of too many people in one's environment, regardless of whether they are involved in any kind of mutual social activity or not, can overload the system, causing mental and emotional fatigue. Under such circumstances, the probability of engaging in creative thinking, assimilation of experiences, or critical self-analysis is greatly reduced. By the same token, excessive stimulation from one's physical surroundings can distract and annoy. And when environmental complexity overlies an emotionally charged communication context, as in the case of an angry encounter between two intimates, psychological privacy all but vanishes. On the other hand, understimulation may be equally threatening to psychological privacy. To the extent that sensory deprivation leads the individual to desire more human contact or physical stimulation, the negative emotions that such a state engenders — boredom, lethargy, frustration — will likewise interfere with effective mental functioning and so limit the amount of psychological privacy that is experienced. Based on a wealth of literature on mammalian responses to stimulus complexity and novelty (e.g., Berlyne, 1970; Kahneman, 1973; Parr, 1966; Wohlwill, 1966, 1974), which indicates optimal functioning typically at an intermediate level of stimulation, it seems reasonable to surmise that psychological privacy will also usually be maximized under moderate levels of stimulation.

Informational Privacy

> The old, the poor, the disabled and others in need of various life support services must usually barter away their privacy in exchange for these services. The bartering typically revolves around disclosure of certain personal information such as money, personality and/or the body. (Pastalan, 1974, p. 73)

This last dimension of privacy is closely allied to psychological privacy, but its legalistic and technological implications, coupled with its significance beyond the individual to the soiety as a whole, warrant treating it separately. Shil's (1966) and Westin's (1970) definitions of privacy relate to its informational aspect and correspond with Carroll's (1975, p. 277) definition of "the right of an individual to determine how, when, and to what extent data about oneself are released to another person" (p. 277). In a seminar on privacy rights, the Council of State Governments (1975, p. 41) amplified the definition:

> Protection of privacy is largely concerned with assuring that accurate, relevant, and timely information about people is used only for stated purposes and in the best interests of each individual. It includes giving the individual both control over how information about him is used and a mechanism for making corrections to the record.

Because information about a person, group, or organization can be gathered and disseminated without their knowledge, informational privacy goes beyond that which is under personal control. In that regard, it can be distinguished from the self-disclosive aspect of psychological privacy.

A plethora of books, government agencies, law review articles, and public and private seminars have addressed the issue of the serious erosion of privacy that is occurring from increased data gathering on private citizens and organizations by governmental agencies, political groups, and private industry; from computerized data banks that have few safeguards on who can access information; and from technological advances that have made electronic eavesdropping easy (see, for example, Carroll, 1975; Clarke, 1972; Council of State Governments, 1975; Ernst & Schwartz, 1977; Gerety, 1977; Lippmann, 1977; Miller, 1971; Smith, 1979; U.S. Congress, 1976). The sheer volume of information that is gathered from and about the typical citizen — through credit card applications, insurance applications, medical records, school records, military records, tax returns, financial statements, voter registrations, license applications, newspaper publicity, warranty registrations, mail-order purchases, police records and even information on personal checks — means that the minutest details of a person's daily habits and personal history are potentially accessible to others without the person's direct permission or knowledge. For instance, responding to a product refund offer may earn you a position on a catalogue mailing list; information supplied for a credit application may find its way into a collection agency dossier. The problem is compounded by the use of computers for data storage and retrieval; inaccurately or maliciously reported information, human errors in data entry and processing, systems failures during data transfers, inadequacies in physical security over who can tap into data banks, and poorly developed legal restrictions over the right to gather, share, or sell such information make the individual highly vulnerable. The situation is exacerbated by illegal wiretaps, searches and seizures, and governmental, political, and industrial espionage using sophisticated technology to acquire additional knowledge secretly. A recent 654-page report from a two-year study by a federal commission confirmed that the problem has reached mammoth proportions.

Beyond the societal issue of what protections are needed and what responsibilities communication-related industries have to provide such protections, this assault on privacy has ramifications for individual functioning in social and communicational contexts. The key consideration is whether the individual perceives any threat to his or her privacy. That experience should depend on several factors, which may be regarded as the isolates defining the degree of informational privacy. The first one is degree of *control* that the individual can exercise, not only over the initial release of the information but also over its subsequent distribution and use. Most people have no qualms about providing what they consider to be public information about their place of residence, marital status, occupation, and the like when such information is requested on application forms. But if such information is forwarded to a marketing department or political group and becomes the basis for a barrage of literature and telephone calls, the individual may experience a loss of privacy due to lost control over who has access to self and when. In Pastalan's (1974) estimation, the element of control is what is crucial to privacy. Indeed, the involuntary nature of information giving and disposal among the indigent and institutionalized, for example, is what makes their dependency on others such an indignity.

A second isolate is the *amount of information in the hands of others*. If one perceives that very little is known about oneself, there is little sense of susceptibility. Closely tied to this consideration is the *number of people who have access to information about oneself or one's group*. Even a few trivial facts, if spread to many others, create more of a sense of risk because of the possibility of their distortion or misuse. The combination of a large quantity of data about oneself and one's associates in the possession of a large number of people or organizations over whom one has no control creates a multiplicative threat to privacy.

A fourth isolate is the actual *content* of the information. Although Pastalan (1974) discounts its importance, it seems obvious that knowledge of innocuous demographic characteristics such as age and educational history constitutes much less of an intrusion on privacy than, say, knowledge of one's sexual habits, political activities, or financial status. What matters is the degree of risk involved if someone else possesses the information. The more intimate and sensitive the information, the more vulnerable the individual becomes to the power and influence of others. Certain kinds of data — such as past brushes with the law — may also subject the person to continued surveillance, thereby curtailing physical and social privacy. The kinds of personal details that people are most reluctant to disclose to others — moral and religious views, sexual practices, fantasies, personal failings and idiosyncracies, embarrassments, illegal activities, hygiene habits, and so forth — seem to be the kinds of knowledge that would cause the greatest sense of a privacy violation if obtained and shared by other than one's most intimate friends and relatives.

This raises the fifth and final isolate, the *nature of the relationship with those possessing the information*. Lewin (1936) hypothesized that subjective privacy is a function of the various kinds of information that others have about oneself and one's relationship to the information holders. He believed that an invasion of privacy results when another gains access to facts more personal than the intimacy of the interpersonal relationship itself. Hence, highly personal information known by strangers or enemies would constitute an invasion of privacy. Simmel (1950) has noted an exception to this: people's willingness, on occasion, to divulge highly intimate information to total strangers (the stranger-on-the-bus phenomenon). Under such circumstances, there seems to be no sense of informational privacy loss, because of the anonymity of the situation. Thus the least risk occurs when knowledge is gained by strangers who do not know one's identity and whom one does not expect to encounter again. By extension, the more familiar the information holder and the greater the likelihood of future contacts, the greater the potential for felt privacy loss (the exception being highly intimate relationships in which highly personal information is freely divulged without fear of it being abused).

As for sets of informational privacy, the two extreme conditions of *anonymity* and *status as a public figure* help to identify the continuum underlying this dimension. Anonymity permits total freedom of expression and no misuse of any information gained from or about the individual, because there is no personal identity to which to attach it. Being identified as a public figure (for example, a celebrity, politician, or criminal), by contrast, means that not only will a great deal of information be actively gathered about the self, but it will no doubt also be publicized and the individual will have little recourse unless what is disseminated is libelous or slanderous. Between these two poles are varying degrees of informational privacy, but no typology of privacy to date offers categories that reflect them.

These four dimensions of privacy — physical, social, psychological, and informational — are all clearly interrelated, as has been evident in the discussion so far. However, each has different implications for communication, both in terms of mechanisms used to signal what state of privacy exists and strategies used to restore privacy or express the desire for more. The last section of this monograph analyzes these "messages" of privacy and how they relate to the four dimensions.

PRIVACY MESSAGES AND STRATEGIES

In creating and refining their favorite concepts, psychologists often neglect to anchor their models in the level of primary pay-off — what persons do. In fact, we would not even be interested in how crowded persons feel or how much control of access to themselves they perceive unless it could be shown that these phenomena actually account for what persons do in their everyday habitats and everyday lives. (Willems & Campbell, 1976, p. 136)

Many analyses of privacy have speculated on the ways in which people cognitively and affectively regard privacy and cope with privacy loss. They may make reference, for instance, to psychological withdrawal or changed evaluations of situations and associates. While understanding the psychological correlates of privacy is certainly useful in gaining a fuller understanding of the entire privacy construct, the Willems and Campbell quote astutely underscores the importance of ultimately focusing on the behavioral component. This is particularly true for the communicologist, who needs to know to what extent privacy demands and needs eventuate in recognizable messages and to what extent different communication patterns alter states of privacy. The analysis that follows comports with this view. While it is recognized that individuals and groups have psychological strategies for adapting or reacting to changes in privacy level, the emphasis here is on behavioral manifestations of privacy and privacy loss. It also should be noted at this point that even though this author subscribes to Altman's (1975) view of privacy as an interpersonal boundary control process involving matching of desired levels of privacy with achieved levels, no attempt will be made to detail those communication strategies that are used to increase affiliation (i.e., when achieved privacy exceeds desired privacy), since affiliative behavior has received considerable attention elsewhere.

Among those writings that have analyzed privacy mechanisms, perhaps the most salient to communication are Altman's (1975, 1976). He identifies three categories: environmental, nonverbal, and verbal. This division is a good starting point but can be further refined into the following categories: (1) environmental and artifactual, (2) spatial and haptic, (3) temporal, (4) kinesic and vocalic, (5) physical appearance, and (6) verbal. Such a division makes it easier to differentiate those behaviors that define privacy states from those that are responses to privacy loss, and to identify which dimensions of privacy the behaviors most affect. To date, little

Privacy and Communication

systematic research has verified the messages and strategies of privacy, so much of what is to be presented is speculative or anecdotal.

Environment and Artifacts

Included in this category are all those aspects of fixed and semifixed feature space (Hall, 1970), as well as the use of objects, that are responsible for defining a locale as private or public. Because environmental designs evolve out of a culture's customs and expectations, these elements serve as messages to their occupants about what rules of conduct are to be followed; in designating what the situational definition is and what roles are to be performed, they dictate what behavioral programs, including communication patterns, are appropriate (Goffman, 1967, 1974; Scheflen, 1974). While they most strongly relate to physical privacy, they not only make possible the other dimensions of privacy but may also have direct implications for social and psychological privacy.

Elements within this category can be divided further into architectural design, furnishings and artifacts, and gatekeepers. *Architectural design* determines the degree of physical privacy first through the use of barriers and insulation. The amount of visual, auditory, olfactory, and bodily protection afforded by a setting is dependent on how many physical impediments there are (walls, fences, partitions) and how well insulated against sound, sight, and smell it is (Altman, 1975; Derlega & Chaikin, 1977; Marshall, 1972; Sommer, 1974). For instance, solid doors, blinds on windows, and white noise to mask distracting sounds all contribute to greater physical privacy. Simultaneously they reduce accessibility to social contact. One particularly significant form of barrier, according to Schwartz (1968, p. 747) is the door, which has been referred to as "a human event of significance equal to the discovery of fire." He notes not only its use in regulating physical and social intrusion and its entailment of choice, in that it can be opened or closed from either side, but also its value in providing psychological self-definition:

> Doors provide boundaries between ourselves (i.e., our property, behavior, and appearance) and others. Violation of such boundaries implies a violation of selfhood. Trespassing or housebreaking, for example, is unbearable for some not only because of the property damage that might result but also because they represent proof that the self has lost control of its audience. (Schwartz, 1968, p. 747).

The door's utility in establishing privacy has been corroborated by Vinsel, Brown, Altman, and Foss (1980), who found 92 percent of their first-year college student respondents reported shutting their dorm room doors as a way of avoiding contact with others. As one of Hall's (1966, p. 127)

German subjects said, "If there hadn't been doors, I would always have been in reach of my mother."

A second way architectural design influences privacy is through the number of enclosures it creates. The more rooms or partitioned areas in a locale and the smaller the volume of space in them, the greater the sense of physical and psychological security (Kira, 1966, 1970). Social intimacy is also fostered by such spaces: Simonds (1961) has suggested that smaller enclosures produce more informal, relaxed conversation, and Marshall (1972) found that the number of rooms and bedrooms per person in a house corresponds to greater perceived intimacy. By contrast, large, open spaces create a sense of vulnerability.

Design may also determine amount of privacy by difficulty of access to a particular setting (Izumi, 1970; Schwartz, 1968; Stea, 1970). Corporate offices, for example, are often designed so that people in top management are hidden in the recesses of a building, with winding corridors, layers of offices, and many floors buffering them against unwanted physical and social intrusions. Similarly, expensive estates, with their enormous expanses of lawn and tree-lined perimeters, are less approachable. The more remote or difficult it is to find, the greater privacy a setting affords.

The state of privacy is also expressed through functional differentiation (Kira, 1966). In Western cultures, it is common for different territories to be designated for different activities, such as sleeping, eating, playing, and copulating (Edney, 1976). The functional properties of the setting, then, dictate what kind of activities are expected. Kira (1970), who has done extensive analyses of bathrooms, notes that the relatively private nature of elimination and hygiene activities in many cultures makes the bathroom one of the most physically private of territories. Because of its smallness and association with highly personal activities, however, it may also be a location for great intimacy. In the same way, the bedroom has become a location for intimate conversation (Goffman, 1963). In circumstances where a living area fails to provide this differentiation of function, interpersonal strife can result (Lewis, 1970). One solution has been to set aside other locations where physical retreat or protection from social involvement is possible, as in the case of creating meditation and study rooms in dormitories.

A fifth way that design elements foster privacy is through symbolism. Massive and expensive-looking properties in choice locations should be much more "forbidding" of physical and social invasion than cheaply constructed, squalid buildings in rundown areas. The nature of the structure communicates something about the status and power of its owner/occupants and thus invokes social norms about the approachability of such people. The only exception to qualitatively better territories creating greater privacy might be the invitation they pose to vandalism and theft.

All of these architectural elements contribute to an essential facet of physical privacy, the designation of territories (Stea, 1970). Altman and Chemers (1980), Edney (1976), Edney and Buda (1976), and Goffman (1961) have commented on the importance of territories as a means of regulating social interaction, creating a sense of personal identity, and promoting group identity and bonding, beyond their utility in warding off physical intrusions. These points are made in Edney's (1976, pp. 37-38; 40) functional analysis of human territories:

> Among many animal species there is broad recognition of a territory holder's "rights" — his claim to privacy and relative immunity to arbitrary challenge and interruption when he is on home ground. The complementary restrictions on a visitor on another organism's territory — his circumspection, inhibition, and restraint — seem to be a tacit recognition of those rights. . . . The geographic separation of individuals into personal territories gives those individuals physical distinctiveness, but the effects of this spacial distinctiveness also appear on a psychological level. . . . To the extent that it reduces ambiguity of anonymity, this presumably also contributes to a person's subjective sense of order. . . . Territory is also likely to facilitate social bonding through a cognitive sense of similarity, and it may also help to preserve bonds because a person has to lose his territorial identity if he leaves the group.

The second subcategory of environmental elements is *furnishings and artifacts,* which complement fixed design elements in providing barriers and insulation. Drapes, room dividers, bookcases, tall lamps, and the like help to carve spaces into smaller territories, block visual access, and cushion noise. Filing cabinets are commonly used for this purpose in small or overcrowded offices (Stea, 1970), as are book stacks in the library (Sommer, 1970). Additionally, personal possessions may be used to "mark" territories. Patterson (1978), in a study of territorial behavior among the elderly, found that the use of such territorial markers as "no tresspassing" signs, welcome mats, and external surveillance devices reduced a person's fear of property loss and personal assault. Sommer (1970) has empirically verified that people wishing to minimize physical or social advances use personal possessions to demark a territory as their own, along with other territorial defense behaviors, such as choice of a seating position that permits surveillance of entrances (as in a library study room) and bodily postures that discourage infringement on their space. Territorial markers also have psychological significance. The more personalized the environment, the more the individual expresses uniqueness and autonomy. Vinsel et al. (1980) also found the amount and diversity of personalization of a dorm room through such things as posters, pictures, and other mementos were associated with the student's likelihood of staying in school. Decorations, then, may reveal an individual's sense of comfort and identification with an environment.

Furnishings may also be used to create sociopetal or sociofugal environments (Osmond, 1957). In the former, chairs and other objects are arranged in a way that encourages interaction, such as small conversational groupings facing each other; in the latter, arrangements inhibit interaction, as in placing all chairs along the walls in an institutional setting. The arrangement therefore signals whether social encounters are permissible and expected.

Finally, artifacts and furnishings may have symbolic value. Lavishly or expensively appointed interiors, like prized locations or impressive exteriors, invoke status and power and the greater inaccessibility accompanying them. People are inclined to show greater formality and restraint when surrounded by furniture and objects of high value. Artifacts may also be responsible for defining what kind of behavior is acceptable in a setting, as in the case of religious icons eliciting a quiet and reverent attitude.

The third category of environmental elements, *gatekeepers,* refers to the use of electronic, animal, or human means of controlling physical access. Keycards for gated parking lots, watchdogs, and office receptionists are all designed to bar entrance by unwelcome visitors and intruders. Their presence clearly signals that one cannot enter at will. In this regard, they are an extension of the difficulty of access imposed by design elements. The difference is that boundaries set by gatekeepers are permeable, whereas certain architectural structures, such as walls and fences, are not.

When the privacy made available by a given setting is insufficient, its occupants may communicate their need for more through a variety of behaviors. To escape physical/biological stress, Esser (1976) suggests that people will resort to prosthetic devices, or what Stokols (1976) refers to as architectural intervention; that is, they may erect more barriers or retreat to a more physically secure locale. If the threat to privacy comes from social sources, they may put out more territorial markers, increase the collective defense of group boundaries (as in cruising a neighborhood to deter criminals), augment their space (as in annexing a piece of private property or claiming more tables for a group in a bar), or withdraw from the setting entirely (Lyman & Scott, 1967; Stokols, 1976; Sundstrom & Sundstrom, 1977). These actions, then, can be viewed as messages of a desire for greater privacy.

Personal Space and Touch

This class of nonverbal privacy mechanisms concerns the use of informal space (Hall, 1970) and the opportunities for proximity and physical contact. It should be evident from the preceding discussions of crowding and personal space that these behaviors relate to three dimensions of privacy: physical, social, and psychological. All of the following have been associated with greater physical insularity, social nonintimacy, and psychological protection: (1) *large conversational distances,* (2) *seating positions at tables that are less proximate and permit less surveillance,* (3) *indirect body orientation,* (4) *extreme sideways or backward lean,* and (5) *absence of touch.* Conversely, the following behaviors correspond with greater social and psychological intimacy: (1) *close distances,* (2) *side-by-side or adjacent seating at a table,* (3) *direct body orientation* (except at the closest of distances), (4) *moderate degrees of leaning and reclining,* (5) *frequent use of touch,* and (6) *touch of more intimate body zones* (Bond & Shiraishi, 1973; Burgoon, Buller, Hale, & deTurck, 1982; Cooper & Bowles, 1973; Derlega & Chaikin, 1977; Evans & Howard, 1973; Henley, 1977; Little, 1965; Jourard & Friedman, 1970; Mehrabian, 1967, 1969; Morris, 1971; Patterson, 1976; Rosenfeld, Kartus, & Ray, 1976; Sommer, 1969; Willis, 1966). It is also likely that spatial and haptic behaviors associated with status may reinforce the privacy of their users. For example, having access to a lot of space, particularly space possessed by others (e.g., the company president who can walk into anyone's office), and intruding on others' territories or personal space may psychologically intimidate others and signal dominance, thereby assuring the interloper greater freedom from approach by others.

The proxemic and haptic codes may also be used to communicate privacy loss. When a person feels physically or psychologically threatened, he or she will often exhibit a fight or flight response. While physical aggression occasionally occurs, the most common response is flight — complete departure from the situation (Baum, Riess, & O'Hara, 1974; Elman, Schulte, & Bukoff, 1977; Felipe & Sommer, 1966; Ginsburg, Pollman, Wauson, & Hope, 1977; Hayduk, 1978; Konečni, Libuser, Morton, & Ebbesen, 1975; Loo & Smetana, 1978; Matthews, Paulas, & Baron, 1979; Smith & Knowles, 1979; Stokols, 1976; Sundstrom & Sundstrom, 1977). Lesser forms of escape may also appear, especially if the privacy loss is due to excess social involvement. Often referred to as compensation behaviors, the proxemic ones include increased distance, more indirect body orientation, more leaning away from the source of disturbance, and movement to a more distal seating position, all of which increase one's ability to avoid or withdraw from a social encounter (Argyle & Dean, 1965; Baum & Greenberg, 1975; Felipe & Sommer, 1966; Hayduk, 1978; Knowles, 1972; Patterson, Mullens, & Romano, 1971; Patterson & Sechrest, 1970; Stokols, 1976; Sundstrom & Sundstrom, 1977). These occur with such regularity, along with other compensation behaviors to be discussed below, that they can be taken as clear indications that a person is trying to regain some degree of privacy. Whether such behaviors qualify as messages or should better be taken as indications of stress and arousal is open to question. However, since people may elect to use these same behaviors as an intentional message to others of their displeasure or desire to reduce social interaction, it seems reasonable to include them within the set of possible moves to restore privacy.

Chronemics

A little-recognized means of establishing privacy is the use of time. There appear to be three ways in which time manipulations may be used to regulate privacy: (1) by permitting territories to overlap spatially but to be segregated by time use (as occurs in the animal kingdom, with several species making use of the same pathways but at different times), a sort of *regulation of traffic by time* (Leyhausen, 1971); (2) by *avoiding use of public and interactional territories during peak times* and using them more frequently during nonpeak times — for example, avoiding dorm bathrooms when they are most crowded (Vinsel et al., 1980); and (3) by *designating functions for a given space by time,* such as using a poorly enclosed toilet in a one-room home when meals are not being served or prepared (Kira, 1967) or using communal living areas for study during certain hours, for television viewing during other hours, and for entertaining visitors during yet other hours.

When existing patterns of time-space use accord insufficient privacy, two chronemic mechanisms for coping seem to be a change in schedule — shifting to use of particular locales when they are least crowded — and a change in the "rules" governing what activities are permissible at what time within a territory.

Kinesics and Vocalics

Included in this category are all those body movements and vocal cues that have been variously labeled as immediacy, inclusion-exclusion, affiliation, dominance, and threat cues. These behaviors are particularly important in availing social and psychological privacy, though they may also serve as a deterrent or invitation to physical contact.

One class of behaviors might be called *turf defense and exclusion cues.* These are behaviors designed primarily to protect physical privacy and secondarily to minimize social contact. Included in this category are (1) threat displays, such as tongue showing and the threat stare (Burgoon & Saine, 1978; Ellsworth & Carlsmith, 1973; Ellsworth, Carlsmith, & Henson, 1972; Ellsworth & Langer, 1976), (2) dominance displays, such as expansive postures and louder vocal volume (Henley, 1977), (3) body blocks and face covering (Argyle & Dean, 1965), (4) emblems such as "go away," that signal unapproachability (Ekman, 1976), (5) postures and body orientations in dyads that create a closed unit, excluding others from participation (Scheflen, 1974), (6) silences (Bruneau, 1973), and (7) avoidance of eye contact, which prohibits another person from "entering" the communication channel (Duncan, 1972).

A second class of behaviors serves the opposite function of inviting approach and creating social and psychological intimacy. These are *immediacy and affiliation cues*. Included in this group (besides distance, body orientation, lean, and touch, which have already been discussed) are (1) increased eye gaze (Argyle, 1967; Burgoon et al., 1982; Mehrabian, 1969, 1971, 1972; Mehrabian & Williams, 1969; Patterson, 1973, 1976), (2) increased smiling (Argyle, 1967; Burgoon et al., 1982; Mehrabian, 1971, 1972; Mehrabian & Williams, 1969), (3) relaxed and asymmetrical trunk and limb postures (Mehrabian, 1967, 1969), (4) greater mirroring — the matching of postures and gestures by members of an interaction (Charney, 1966; Mach, 1972; Mansfield, 1973), (5) emblems signaling approach, including the eyebrow flash (Eibl-Eibesfeldt, 1972; Ekman, 1976), and (6) "warm," soft, and varied vocal tones (Argyle, 1967; Scheflen, 1974).

A third class of behaviors has been discussed at length earlier: *role violations and backstage behaviors* (Goffman, 1959). Intimate situations permit individuals to use adaptor behaviors, reveal idiosyncracies, and violate the normal behavioral repertoire associated with their social roles. By the same token, engaging in these role "releases" normally signals to another that one considers the situation to be a private one.

A fourth indication of the degree of privacy is the *behavior patterns of others*. Goffman (1963) speaks of "civil inattention" as a means of granting greater privacy to others, which is to say we avoid watching or eavesdropping on others when it might prove embarrassing. Pretending not to notice when a person has invalidated his or her role or is engaged in a highly private act serves to maintain the other person's sense of privacy. A good example is showing lack of recognition of members of the opposite sex who share the same toilet facilities in some mideastern and oriental cultures. Edney (1976) also refers to the deferent behaviors of visitors in someone else's territory. Their restrained and polite behavior similarly reinforces the privacy of the occupant/owner of the territory.

One final kinesic means of guarding psychological and informational privacy is the *proxemic shift* (Erickson, 1975), which is used to signal changes in conversational topic. One may use this behavior to indicate to another that the current discussion is now closed and that a new one must be introduced.

When people experience violations of privacy, whether it be through proxemic invasions, abnormal surveillance, overstimulation from the environment, or excessively intimate topics, their kinesic and vocalic patterns may reveal efforts to compensate for the heightened arousal (Argyle & Dean, 1965; Patterson, 1973), to deescalate the intimacy of the interaction, or to retreat from the encounter, what Stokols (1976) refers to as psychological "cocooning." They may increase their use of exclusion and threat displays and may show evidence of anxiety and negative affect. Specifically, all of the following have been found to occur: (1) aggressive gestures, glares, and threat stares; (2) body blocks, such as extending the elbows forward, and face covering; (3) reduced gaze or facial regard; (4) reduction of other immediacy and affiliation cues, such as lowered vocal volume and reduced smiling; (5) increased indications of anxiety and arousal, including use of more self-adaptors, more object manipulations, and more postural shifts; and (6) increased negative affect (Baum & Greenberg, 1975; Greenberg & Firestone, 1977; Hayduk, 1978; Maines, 1977; McCauley, Coleman, & DeFusco, 1978; Patterson, 1973; Patterson et al., 1971; Sunstrom, 1975, 1978; Westin, 1970).

Physical Appearance and Attire

Little analysis has been done on the role of these nonverbal cues in establishing privacy. Altman (1975) mentions three that relate chiefly to social privacy: *signaling status, signaling approachability,* and *defining the context and role behavior.* Occupational uniforms connote different levels of status — the office manager wearing more formal dress than the garage mechanic, and the physician's smock identifying its wearer as holding a respected position in society. Similarly, military and institutional uniforms symbolically express status. As suggested earlier, persons of higher status are accorded more privacy and deference from others; hence clothing indirectly determines social inaccessibility. It may also directly communicate approachability. Veils worn by women in many cultures express a prohibition against advances by strangers, while the near-nudity of a bikini invites approach (and possibly physical contact). As for clarifying the nature of the interactional setting and the roles that are expected, the manner of dress of other people in the setting conveys what kind of interaction is anticipated — work-related, recreational, social — and, by implication, what kinds of communication behaviors are expected. If everyone is dressed in suits, this will create a more formal, polite interaction, which will result in greater privacy for the participants.

A fourth possible way in which appearance effectuates privacy, this time on the psychological dimension, is through *creating personal identity or anonymity.* A prime example of how an individual can be stripped of his or her identity comes from Goffman (1961), who described mental patients in institutions as restricted on the use of toiletry items, forced to have their hair cut according to the institution's schedule, and often required to wear hospital garb. The military and prisons, as two other institutions, similarly work to create a mass rather than individual identity by requiring identical uniforms, forbidding facial hair, instituting regulation haircuts, and controlling other facets of personal grooming. While such enforced appearance standards undermine the self-identity facet of psychological privacy, they do provide some degree of psychological privacy through anonymity. Political groups may also opt for identical appearance as a way of preserving anonymity, the Ku Klux Klan being a prime example.

A fifth possible use of attire to establish privacy might be as a form of *insulation.* Since clothing is often viewed as an outer extension of the inner self, use of many layers of clothing, conservative costumes, or unrevealing dress may create a sense of psychological and physical protection. This use of clothing occasionally surfaces in psychiatric discussions.

Lyman and Scott (1967) contend that when spatial privacy is violated, people may respond through various forms of bodily manipulation, including both adornment and penetration. Ramsey (1976) offers an example of how adornment is used in noting that prisoners often wear sunglasses and earrings as a way of creating their own identity within the crowded and anonymous confines of the prison. Other ways of restoring privacy through use of clothing or adornment might include increased insulation, use of clothing to make a person appear larger and therefore more dominant, and use of clothing as a symbolic status cue.

Verbal Mechanisms

This last category includes language choice, topic choice, and more macroscopic verbal strategies, all of which may ensure informational, social, and psychological privacy. While it is possible to request directly to be left alone, to chastise someone for getting too personal, or to refuse to give information, these explicit verbal responses are apparently strategies of last resort. People are much more inclined to resort to subtler messages first.

Altman (1975) identifies as one major subcategory the *linguistic features* of speech, including language immediacy, vocabulary diversity, and language style (which would include adverbial intensity). Immediate language, as defined by Weiner and Mehrabian (1968), expresses the degree of psychological distance between speaker and listener. It includes temporal aspects of language (past tense being more nonimmediate than present tense), spatial aspects ("here" versus "there"), use of possessives and personal pronouns, determinacy of referents, use of negation, and so forth. The more nonimmediate and ambiguous the language, the greater distance that is created and, consequenly, the greater opportunity for privacy. Kuiken (1981) found that people forced to make public statements contrary to their private beliefs expressed them in more nonimmediate language. Burgoon, Hale, and Garrison (1981) similarly found that people who are high communication avoiders, apprehensive about communication, and/or less expressive nonverbally (which might be a privacy mechanism in itself) used less intense language, more diverse and complex vocabulary, and less comprehensible verbalizations, all of which should make for a less straightforward, more enigmatic presentation. Bradac, Bowers, and Courtright (1979), in formulating propositional statements about language intensity, immediacy, and diversity, indicated inverse relationships between these variables and cognitive stress. Language choice, then, may be a clear sign of one's desire to distance self from others and to be more "opaque."

A second class of verbal behaviors revolves around *self-disclosure* — controlling the depth, breadth, and intimacy level of sensitive information revealed about the self (Altman & Taylor, 1973; Argyle, 1967; Derlega & Chaikin, 1975, 1977; Jourard, 1971a, 1971b; Morton, 1978). According to social penetration theory (Altman & Taylor, 1973), as a relationship becomes more personal and intimate, people reveal more about themselves, expanding the topics about which they share information, going into greater depth on those topics, and divulging increasingly riskier information. A key indicator, then, of personal privacy or interpersonal intimacy is the amount and kind of self-disclosure that occurs.

A third class of behaviors is *polite or formal communication patterns* (Westin, 1970). As noted earlier, formality produces greater privacy. Polite forms of address (use of a title for example, rather than a first name), avoidance of indelicate topics, conformity to social etiquette, and the like contribute to a sense of remoteness and inscrutability. In many oriental cultures such decorous communication behavior is mandated and is considered a key means of achieving personal privacy.

Yet a fourth subcategory of verbal behaviors includes what Lyman and Scott (1967) have called *linguistic collusion*. Groups attempting to protect themselves against interference or influence from others may resort to the use of a private code or in-group language. Not only does this linguistic maneuver effectively keep others from understanding verbal exchanges among group members; it also helps to cement their social bond with one another and reinforces their sense of a separate, unique identity. Parents who adopt "pig Latin" around their children are displaying this same verbal strategy.

Some additional verbal strategies that have not been discussed elsewhere but seem likely to communicate a desire to withhold information or to maintain psychological privacy are *changing the topic of conversation* (a not-so-subtle way of saying that no more is to be revealed on the previous topic), *brevity or verbosity of replies, references to one's possessions or territory* (as an attempt to evoke more deferent behavior), and *invocation of laws and consensually agreed-upon rights* (as a way of implicating social or legal sanctions).

As for verbal moves used to reassert informational and psychological privacy, Greenberg and Firestone (1977) and Sundstrom (1975, 1978) have found that in response to increased surveillance, spatial intrusions, or psychological intrusions, people reduce the depth and breadth of their self-disclosure. Esser (1976) has also suggested that greater reliance on role playing might be a response to behavioral constraints. Similarly, psychological constraints might elicit role figmenting. Other possible verbal parries are less intense language, nonimmediate language, greater lexical diversity and complexity, more formal and polite communication patterns, more topic changes, shorter replies (or possibly the opposite — increased verbosity) as a means of obfuscation, more references to one's personal possessions in the immediate vicinity, and more references to one's rights to privacy.

CONCLUSION

Throughout this analysis of privacy much of what has been presented has been speculative. Even where empirical findings have been presented, they have often been gathered for purposes other than studying privacy and have been imported here because they appear applicable. What is now needed is more systematic empirical exploration of the dimensions of privacy — their interrelatedness, the characteristics that distinguish them, the levels that are recognized within cultures — and the actual communication strategies people are most likely to employ in expressing and recovering privacy states. Investigations currently under way will address these issues.

REFERENCES

Altman, I. Ecological aspects of interpersonal functioning. In A. H. Esser (Ed.), *Behavior and environment.* New York: Plenum Press, 1971.
Altman, I. *The environment and social behavior.* Belmont, CA: Wadsworth, 1975.
Altman, I. Privacy: A conceptual analysis. *Environment and Behavior,* 1976, *8,* 7-29.

Altman, I. Privacy regulation: Culturally universal or culturally specific? *Journal of Social Issues*, 1977, *33*, 66-84.
Altman, I., & Chemers, M. M. *Culture and environment.* Monterey, CA: Brooks/Cole, 1980.
Altman, I., & Taylor, D. A. *Social penetration: The development of interpersonal relationships.* New York: Holt, Rinehart & Winston, 1973.
Ardrey, R. *African genesis.* New York: Dell, 1970.
Argyle, M. *The psychology of interpersonal behavior.* Baltimore: Penguin, 1967.
Argyle, M., & Dean, J. Eye-contact, distance and affiliation. *Sociometry*, 1965, *28*, 289-304.
Baum, A., & Greenberg, C. I. Waiting for a crowd: The behavioral and perceptual effects of anticipated crowding. *Journal of Personality and Social Psychology*, 1975, *32*, 671-679.
Baum, A., Riess, M., & O'Hara, J. O. Architectural variants of reaction to spatial invasion. *Environment and Behavior*, 1974, *6*, 91-100.
Berardo, F. M. Marital invisibility and family privacy. In S. T. Margulis (Ed.), *Privacy.* Stony Brook, NY: Environmental Design Research Association, 1974.
Berlyne, D. E. Novelty, complexity, and hedonic value. *Perception and Psychophysics*, 1970, *8*, 279-286.
Bond, M. H., & Shiraishi, D. The effect of interviewer's body lean and status on the nonverbal behavior of interviewees. *Japanese Journal of Experimental Social Psychology*, 1973, *13*, 11-21.
Bradac, J. J., Bowers, J. W., & Courtright, J. A. Three language variables in communication research: Intensity, immediacy, and diversity. *Human Communication Research*, 1979, *5*, 257-269.
Bruneau, T. J. Communicative silences: Forms and functions. *Journal of Communication*, 1973, *23* (1), 17-46.
Burgoon, J. K. The unwillingness-to-communicate scale: Development and validation. *Communication Monographs*, 1976, *4*, 13-21.
Burgoon, J. K., Buller, D. B., Hale, J. L., & deTurck, M. A. *Relational messages associated with immediacy behaviors.* Paper presented at the International Communication Association Convention, Boston, April 1982.
Burgoon, J. K., Hale, J. L., & Garrison, S. S. *Dimensions of communication avoidance and their impact on verbal encoding.* Paper presented at the International Communication Association Convention, Minneapolis, May 1981.
Burgoon, J. K., & Saine, T. *The unspoken dialogue.* Boston: Houghton Mifflin, 1978.
Calhoun, J. B. The role of space in animal sociology. *Journal of Social Issues*, 1969, *22*, 46-58.
Calhoun, J. B. Space and the strategy of life. *Ekistics*, 1970, *29*, 325-437.
Carroll, J. M. *Confidential information sources: Public and private.* Los Angeles: Security World, 1975.
Chapin, F. S. Some housing factors related to mental hygiene. *Journal of Social Issues*, 1951, *7*, 164-171.
Charney, E. J. Psychosomatic manifestations of rapport in psychotherapy. *Psychosomatic Medicine*, 1966, *28*, 305-315.
Clarke, C. F. O. *Private rights and freedom of the individual.* Oxfordshire, England: Ditchley Foundation, 1972.
Conklin, K. R. Privacy: Should there be a right to it? *Educational Theory*, 1976, *26*, 263-270.
Cook, M. Experiments on orientation and proxemics. *Human Relations*, 1970, *23*, 61-76.
Cooper, C. L., & Bowles, D. Physical encounter and self-disclosure. *Psychological Reports*, 1973, *33*, 451-454.
Council of State Governments. *Privacy: A summary of a seminar on privacy, December 15-17, 1974, Washington, D.C.* Lexington, KY: Author, 1975.
Davis, D. E. Physiological effects of continued crowding. In A. H. Esser (Ed.), *Behavior and Environment.* New York: Plenum Press, 1971.
Derlega, V. J., & Chaikin, A. L. *Sharing intimacy: What we reveal to others and why.* Englewood Cliffs, NJ: Prentice-Hall, 1975.

Derlega, V. J., & Chaikin, A. L. Privacy and self-disclosure in social relationships. *Journal of Social Issues,* 1977, *33,* 102-122.

Desor, J. A. Toward a psychological theory of crowding. *Journal of Personality and Social Psychology,* 1972, *21,* 79-83.

Dosey, M. A., & Meisels, M. Personal space and self-protection. *Journal of Personality and Social Psychology,* 1969, *11,* 93-97.

Duncan, S., Jr. Some signals and rules for taking speaking turns in conversations. *Journal of Personality and Social Psychology,* 1972, *23,* 283-292.

Edney, J. J. Territoriality and control: A field experiment. *Journal of Personality and Social Psychology,* 1975, *38,* 1108-1115.

Edney, J. J. Human territories: Comment on functional properties. *Environment and Behavior,* 1976, *8,* 31-47.

Edney, J. J., & Buda, M. A. Distinguishing territoriality and privacy: Two studies. *Human Ecology,* 1976, *4,* 283-296.

Eibl-Eibesfeldt, I. Similarities and differences between cultures in expressive movements. In R. A. Hinde (Ed.), *Non-verbal communication.* Cambridge: Cambridge University Press, 1972.

Ekman, P. Movements with precise meanings. *Journal of Communication,* 1976, *26*(3), 14-26.

Ellsworth, P., & Carlsmith, J. M. Eye contact and gaze aversion in an aggressive encounter. *Journal of Personality and Social Psychology,* 1973, *28,* 280-292.

Ellsworth, P., Carlsmith, J. M., & Henson, A. The stare as a stimulus to flight in human subjects. *Journal of Personality and Social Psychology,* 1972, *21,* 302-311.

Ellsworth, P., & Langer, E. J. Staring and approach: An interpretation of the stare as nonspecific activation. *Journal of Personality and Social Psychology,* 1976, *33,* 117-122.

Elman, D., Schulte, D. C., & Bukoff, A. Effects of facial expression and stare duration on walking speed: Two field experiments. *Environmental Psychology and Nonverbal Behavior,* 1977, *2,* 93-99.

Erickson, F. One function of proxemic shifts in face-to-face interaction. In A. Kendon, R. Harris, & M. Key (Eds.), *Organization of Behavior in Face-to-Face Interaction.* The Hague: Mouton, 1975.

Ernst, M. L., & Schwartz, A. U. *Privacy — The right to be left alone.* Westport, CT: Greenwood Press, 1977.

Esser, A. H. Experiences of crowding: Illustration of a paradigm for man-environment relations. *Representative Research in Social Psychology,* 1973, *4,* 207-218.

Esser, A. H. Theoretical and empirical issues with regard to privacy, territoriality, personal space and crowding. *Environment and Behavior,* 1976, *8,* 117-124.

Eysenck, H. J., & Eysenck, S.B.J. *Personality structure and measurement.* San Diego: Robert R. Knapp, 1969.

Evans, G. W., & Eichelman, W. Preliminary models of conceptual linkages among proxemic variables. *Environment and Behavior,* 1976, *8,* 87-116.

Evans, G. W., & Howard, R. B. Personal space. *Psychological Bulletin,* 1973, *80,* 334-344.

Felipe, N., & Sommer, R. Invasions of personal space. *Social Problems,* 1966, *14,* 206-214.

Festinger, L. A. A theory of social comparison processes. *Human Relations,* 1954, *7,* 117-140.

Gerety, T. Redefining privacy. *Harvard Civil Rights & Civil Liberties Review,* 1977, *12*(2), 233-296.

Ginsburg, H. J., Pullman, V. A., Wauson, M. S., & Hope, M. L. Variation of aggressive interaction among male elementary school children as a function of changes in spatial density. *Environmental Psychology and Nonverbal Behavior,* 1977, *2,* 67-75.

Glass, D. C. and Singer, J. E. *Urban stress.* New York: Academic Press, 1972.

Goffman, E. *The presentation of self in everyday life.* Garden City, NY: Doubleday, 1959.

Goffman, E. *Asylums.* Garden City, NY: Doubleday, 1961.

Goffman, E. *Behavior in public places.* New York: Macmillan, 1963.

Goffman, E. *Interaction ritual.* Garden City, NY: Doubleday, 1967.

Goffman, E. *Frame analysis.* New York: Harper & Row, 1974.

Greenberg, C. I., & Firestone, I. J. Compensatory responses to crowding: Effects of personal space intrusion and privacy reduction. *Journal of Personality and Social Psychology*, 1977, 35, 637-644.

Hall, E. T. *The hidden dimension*. Garden City, NY: Doubleday, 1966.

Hall, E. T. The anthropology of space: An organizing model. In H. M. Prohansky, W. H. Ittleson, & L. G. Rivlin (Eds.), *Environmental psychology: Man and his physical setting*. New York: Holt, Rinehart & Winston, 1970.

Hall, E. T. *The silent language*. Garden City, NY: Doubleday, 1973.

Haney, C., Banks, C., & Zimbardo, P. Interpersonal dynamics in a simulated prison. *International Journal of Criminology and Penology*, 1973, 1, 69-97.

Hayduk, L. A. Personal space: An evaluative and orienting overview. *Psychological Bulletin*, 1978, 85, 117-134.

Henley, N. M. Power, sex and nonverbal communication. In Z. Rubin (Ed.), *Doing unto others: Joining, molding, conforming, helping, loving*. Englewood Cliffs, NJ: Prentice-Hall, 1974.

Henley, N. M. *Body politics: Power, sex and nonverbal communication*. Englewood Cliffs, NJ: Prentice-Hall, 1977.

Izumi, K. Psychosocial phenomena and building design. In H. M. Proshansky, W. H. Ittleson, & L. G. Rivlin (Eds.), *Environmental psychology: Man and his physical setting*. New York: Holt, Rinehart & Winston, 1970.

Johnson, C. A. Privacy as personal control. In S. T. Margulis (Ed.), *Privacy*. Stony Brook, NY: Environmental Design Research Association, 1974.

Jourard, S. M. Some psychological aspects of privacy. *Law and Contemporary Problems*, 1966, 31, 307-318.

Jourard, S. M. *Self-disclosure*. New York: John Wiley, 1971. (a)

Jourard, S. M. *The transparent self*. New York: Van Nostrand Reinhold, 1971. (b)

Jourard, S. M., & Friedman, R. Experimenter-subject "distance" and self-disclosure. *Journal of Personality and Social Psychology*, 1970, 15, 278-282.

Kahneman, D. *Attention and effort*. Englewood Cliffs, NJ: Prentice-Hall, 1973.

Kelvin, P. A social psychological examination of privacy. *British Journal of Social and Clinical Psychology*, 1973, 12, 248-261.

Kira, A. *The bathroom: Criteria for design*. New York: Center for Housing and Environmental Studies, Cornell University, 1966.

Kira, A. Privacy and the bathroom. In H. M. Proshansky, W. H. Ittleson, & L. G. Rivlin (Eds.), *Environmental Psychology: Man and His Physical Setting*. New York: Holt, Rinehart, & Winston, 1970, pp. 269-275.

Knowles, E. S. Boundaries around social space: Dyadic responses to an invader. *Environment and Behavior*, 1972, 4, 437-445.

Knowles, E. S. An affiliative conflict theory of personal and group spatial behavior. In P. B. Paulus (Ed.), *Psychology of Group Influence*. Hillsdale, NJ: Lawrence J. Erlbaum, 1980.

Konečni, V. J., Libuser, L., Morton, H., & Ebbesen, E. B. Effects of a violation of personal space on escape and helping responses. *Journal of Experimental Social Psychology*, 1975, 11, 288-299.

Kuiken, D. Nonimmediate language style and inconsistency between private and expressed evaluations. *Journal of Experimental Social Psychology*, 1981, 17, 183-196.

Latin, H., Bostwick, L., & Ratner, D. A taxonomy of privacy: Repose, sanctuary and intimate decision. *California Law Review*, 1976, 64, 1447-1483.

Laufer, R. S., Proshansky, H. M., & Wolfe, M. *Some analytic dimensions of privacy*. Paper presented at the Third International Conference in Architectural Psychology, Lund, Sweden, June 1973.

Leibman, M. The effects of sex and race norms on personal space. *Environment and Behavior*, 1970, 2, 208-246.

Lewin, K. *Principles of topological psychology*. New York: McGraw-Hill, 1936.

Lewis, O. Privacy and crowding in poverty. In H. M. Proshansky, W. H. Ittelson, & L. G. Rivlin (Eds.), *Environmental psychology: Man and his physical setting*. New York: Holt, Rinehart & Winston, 1970.

Leyhausen, P. Dominance and territoriality as complemented in mammalian social structure. In A. H. Esser (Ed.), *Behavior and environment*. New York: Plenum Press, 1971.
Lippmann, L. Commentary: Privacy. *International Journal of Epidemiology*, 1977, *6*, 305-308.
Little, K. B. Personal space. *Journal of Experimental Social Psychology*, 1965, *1*, 237-247.
Loo, C., & Smetana, J. The effects of crowding on the behavior and perception of 10-year-old boys. *Environmental Psychology and Nonverbal Behavior*, 1978, *2*, 226-249.
Lyman, L. M., & Scott, M. B. Territoriality: A neglected sociological dimension. *Social Problems*, 1967, *15*, 236-249.
Mach, R. S. *Postural carriage and congruency as nonverbal indicators of status differentials and interpersonal attraction*. Unpublished doctoral dissertation, University of Colorado, 1972.
Maines, D. R. Tactile relationships in the subway as affected by racial, sexual, and crowded seating situations. *Environmental Psychology and Nonverbal Behavior*, 1977, *2*, 100-108.
Mansfield, E. Empathy: Concept and identified psychiatric nursing behavior. *Nursing Research*, 1973, *22*, 525-530.
Marshall, N. J. Privacy and environment. *Human Ecology*, 1972, *1*, 93-110.
Matthews, R. W., Paulus, P. B., & Baron, R. A. Physical aggression after being crowded. *Journal of Nonverbal Behavior*, 1979, *4*, 5-17.
McBride, G. Theories of animal spacing: The role of flight, fight and social distance. In A. H. Esser (Ed.), *Behavior and environment*. New York: Plenum Press, 1971.
McCauley, C., Coleman, G., & DeFusco, P. Commuters' eye contact with strangers in city and suburban train stations: Evidence of short-term adaptation to interpersonal overload in the city. *Environmental Psychology and Nonverbal Behavior*, 1978, *2*, 215-225.
Mehrabian, A. Orientation behaviors and nonverbal attitude communication. *Journal of Communication*, 1967, *17*, 324-332.
Mehrabian, A. Significance of posture and position in the communication of attitude and status relationships. *Psychological Bulletin*, 1969, *71*, 359-373.
Mehrabian, A. Verbal and nonverbal interaction of strangers in a waiting room. *Journal of Experimental Research in Personality*, 1971, *5*, 127-138.
Mehrabian, A. *Nonverbal communication*. Chicago: Aldine, 1972.
Mehrabian, A., & Williams, M. Nonverbal concomitants of perceived and intended persuasiveness. *Journal of Personality and Social Psychology*, 1969, *13*, 37-58.
Merton, R. K. *Social theory and social structure*. New York: Macmillan, 1957.
Milgram, S. The experience of living in cities. *Science*, 1970, *167*, 1461-1468.
Miller, A. *The assault on privacy*. Ann Arbor: University of Michigan Press, 1971.
Morris, D. *Intimate behavior*. New York: Random House, 1971.
Mortensen, C. D., Arntson, P. H., & Lustig, M. The measurement of verbal predispositions: Scale development and application. *Human Communication Research*, 1977, *3*, 146-158.
Morton, T. L. Intimacy and reciprocity of exchange: A comparison of spouses and strangers. *Journal of Personality and Social Psychology*, 1978, *36*, 72-81.
Osmond, H. Function as the basis of psychiatric ward design. *Mental Hospitals*, 1957, *8*, 23-29.
Parr, A. E. Psychological aspects of urbanology. *Journal of Social Issues*, 1966, *22*, 39-45.
Pastalan, L. A. Privacy preferences among relocated institutionalized elderly. In S. T. Margulis (Ed.), *Privacy*. Stony Brook, NY: Environmental Design Research Association, 1974.
Patterson, A. H. Territorial behavior and fear of crime in the elderly. *Environmental Psychology and Nonverbal Behavior*, 1978, *2*, 131-144.
Patterson, M. L. Compensation in nonverbal immediacy behaviors: A review. *Sociometry*, 1973, *36*, 236-252.
Patterson, M. L. An arousal model of interpersonal intimacy. *Psychological Review*, 1976, *83*, 235-245.

Patterson, M. L., Mullens, S., & Romano, J. Compensatory reactions to spatial intrusion. *Sociometry,* 1971, *34,* 114-121.

Patterson, M. L., & Sechrest, L. B. Interpersonal distance and impression formation. *Journal of Personality,* 1970, *38,* 161-166.

Paulus, P. B. Crowding. In P. B. Paulus (Ed.), *Psychology of group influence.* Hillsdale, NJ: Lawrence J. Erlbaum, 1980.

Phillips, G. M. Reticence: Pathology of the normal speaker. *Speech Monographs,* 1968, *35,* 39-49.

Plant, J. Some psychiatric aspects of crowded living conditions. *American Journal of Psychiatry,* 1930, *9,* 849-860.

Proshansky, H. M., Ittelson, W. H., & Rivlin, L. G. Freedom of choice and behavior in a physical setting. In H. M. Proshansky, W. H. Ittelson, & L. G. Rivlin (Eds.), *Environmental psychology: Man and his physical setting.* New York: Holt, Rinehart & Winston, 1970.

Ramsey, S. J. Prison codes. *Journal of Communication,* 1976, *26*(3), 39-45.

Rappoport, A. Toward a redefinition of density. *Environment and Behavior,* 1975, *7,* 133-158.

Rosenfeld, L. B., Kartus, S., & Ray, C. Body accessibility revisited. *Journal of Communication,* 1976, *26,* 27-30.

Scheflen, A. E. *How behavior means.* Garden City, NY: Doubleday, 1974.

Schneirla, T. C. Aspects of stimulation and organization in approach/withdrawal processes underlying vertebrate behavior development. *Advances in the Study of Behavior,* 1965, *1,* 1-74.

Schutz, W. C. *FIRO: A three dimensional theory of interpersonal behavior.* New York: Holt, Rinehart & Winston, 1958.

Schwartz, B. The social psychology of privacy. *American Journal of Sociology,* 1968, *73,* 741-752.

Shils, E. Privacy: Its constitution and vicissitudes. *Law and Contemporary Problems,* 1966, *73,* 741-752.

Simmel, G. [Secrecy and group communication.] In K. H. Wolff (Ed. and trans.), *The sociology of George Simmel.* New York: Macmillan, 1950.

Simonds, J. O. *Landscape architecture.* New York: McGraw-Hill, 1961.

Smith, R. E. *Privacy: How to protect what's left of it.* Garden City, NY: Doubleday, 1979.

Smith, R. J., & Knowles, E. S. Affective and cognitive mediators of reactions to spatial invasions. *Journal of Experimental Social Psychology,* 1979, *15,* 437-452.

Sommer, R. *Personal space: The behavioral basis of design.* Englewood Cliffs, NJ: Prentice-Hall, 1969.

Sommer, R. The ecology of privacy. In H. M. Proshansky, W. H. Ittelson, & L. G. Rivlin (Eds.), *Environmental psychology: Man and his physical setting.* New York: Holt, Rinehart & Winston, 1970.

Sommer, R. *Tight spaces: Hard architecture and how to humanize it.* Englewood Cliffs, NJ: Prentice-Hall, 1974.

Stea, D. Space, territory and human movements. In H. M. Proshansky, W. H. Ittelson, & L. G. Rivlin (Eds.), *Environmental psychology: Man and his physical setting.* New York: Holt, Rinehart & Winston, 1970.

Stokols, D. A social-psychological model of human crowding phenomena. *Journal of the American Institute of Planners,* 1972, *38,* 72-83. (a)

Stokols, D. On the distinction between density and crowding: Some implications for future research. *Psychological Review,* 1972, *79,* 275-277. (b)

Stokols, D. The experience of crowding in primary and secondary environments. *Environment and Behavior,* 1976, *8,* 49-85.

Sundstrom, E. An experimental study of crowding: Effects of room size, intrusion, and goal blocking on nonverbal behavior, self-disclosure, and self-reported stress. *Journal of Personality and Social Psychology,* 1975, *32,* 645-654.

Sundstrom, E. A test of equilibrium theory: Effects of topic intimacy and proximity on verbal and nonverbal behavior in pairs of friends and strangers. *Journal of Nonverbal Behavior,* 1978, *3,* 3-16.

Sundstrom, E., & Sundstrom, M. G. Personal space invasions: What happens when the invader asks permission? *Environmental Psychology and Nonverbal Behavior,* 1977, *2,* 76-82.

U.S. Congress. *Interception of nonverbal communications by federal intelligence agencies: Hearings before a subcommittee of the committee on government.* Washington, DC: U.S. Government Printing Office, 1976.

Vinsel, A., Brown, B. B., Altman, I., & Foss, C. Privacy regulation, territorial displays, and effectiveness of individual function. *Journal of Personality and Social Psychology,* 1980, *39,* 1104-1115.

Wapner, S., Kaplan, B., & Cohen, S. B. An organismic-developmental perspective for understanding transactions of men and environments. *Environment and Behavior,* 1973, *5,* 255-289.

Warren, C., & Laslett, B. Privacy and secrecy — conceptual comparison. *Journal of Social Issues,* 1977, *33,* 43-51.

Washburn, S. L. (Ed.) *Social life of early man.* New York: Wenner-Gren Foundation, 1961.

Weiner, M., & Mehrabian, A. *Language within language: Immediacy, a channel in verbal communication.* New York: Appleton-Century-Crofts, 1968.

Westin, A. *Privacy and freedom.* New York: Atheneum, 1970.

Willems, E. P., & Campbell, D. E. One path through the cafeteria. *Environment and Behavior,* 1976, *8,* 125-140.

Willis, F. N. Initial speaking distance as a function of the speaker's relationship. *Psychonomic Science,* 1966, *5,* 221-222.

Wohlwill, J. F. The physical environment: A problem for psychology of stimulation. *Journal of Social Issues,* 1966, *22,* 21-38.

Wohlwill, J. F. Human adaptation to levels of environmental stimulation. *Human Ecology,* 1974, *2,* 127-147.

Wolfe, M., & Laufer, R. The concept of privacy in childhood and adolescence. In S. T. Margulis (Ed.), *Privacy.* Stony Brook, NY: Environmental Design Research Association, 1974.

Zimbardo, P. G. *Shyness: What it is and what to do about it.* Reading, MA: Addison-Wesley, 1975.

COMMUNICATION REVIEWS AND COMMENTARIES

8 ● Direct Satellite Broadcasting: Selected Social Implications

ROLF T. WIGAND

Arizona State University

SATELLITE communication has become an integral part of the communications industry in less than twenty years. Merely ten years ago countries depended on undersea cables and high frequency radio. Today over one hundred nations rely on communication satellites to meet their broadcast and information transmission needs. Satellites are a most desirable means to bridge long distances. Costs for terrestrial facilities are proportional to the length of the distance to be covered. This implies that the longer the distance, the higher the cost to provide the desired linkage. Satellites, however, are independent of the length of the route, i.e., connecting two facilities thirty miles apart costs as much as connecting them 4,000 miles apart. Satellites, therefore, are cost-effective as well as efficient to bridge long distances (Rice & Parker, 1979; Wigand, 1980a). The key advantages of communication satellites over terrestrial systems include: local autonomy, flexibility, growth and coverage, improved signal quality, cost, and reliability.

In October 1957 the Soviets launched Sputnik into orbit, thus marking the beginning of the space age. Since this date more than 25,000 satellites and space probes have been launched by governments, as well as by various civilian organizations. Today's satellites can carry 7,000 two-way messages on twelve simultaneous color channels. In 1960 NASA launched its ECHO I satellite into a 1,000 mile-high orbit. It was followed by AT&T's TELSTAR satellite in 1962 that was generally considered the first active communication satellite. TELSTAR was engineered to operate on solar power batteries. The satellites that followed required enormous ground

AUTHOR'S NOTE: This research was supported by a grant from the International Social Science Council, Paris. The author gratefully acknowledges the assistance received from scholars and organizations in over twenty countries, too numerous to recognize individually.

Correspondence and requests for reprints: Rolf T. Wigand, Center for Public Affairs, Arizona State University, Tempe, AZ 85287.

transmitters to function effectively. Subsequently, a generation of active wideband systems could carry a television picture or its equivalent. The first geostationary satellites were launched through the SYNCOM program. By the time EARLYBIRD was placed into orbit in 1965, artificial satellites had become a most valuable tool for the field of communication.

Transatlantic commercial transmission of television first became a reality with the INTELSAT system and other satellites providing more bandwidth. In addition, it is relatively uncomplicated to connect, disconnect, and interconnect a number of disparate points when compared with conventional terrestrial systems. This versatility no doubt represents one of the key advantages of satellite communications since the geography, such as mountains or oceans, can readily be overcome, and at the same time signals can now be received by remote and less-developed regions.

Communication satellites have been used successfully for voice, video, and data transmissions in numerous situations. Newspaper printing, medical care, peace missions, teleconferencing, Olympic Games, teaching/education, as well as emergency disaster and rescue services have all been carried out successfully via satellite communication. Today there exist at least two international systems, more than five regional systems, six military systems, and a handful of satellite systems for specific purposes such as broadcast, data relay, maritime, as well as aeronautical purposes.

With the accession of Fiji, 102 nations are presently participating in the INTELSAT agreement, and still more are scheduled to become signatories to the agreement. At the same time, several nations have or are now planning national (domestic) communication systems via satellites. National satellite communication systems are now in operation in Brazil, Canada, Indonesia, Saudi Arabia, the Sudan, the United States, the USSR, and in part, Japan. Several Western European countries, as well as China, India, Iran, the Middle East, and Nigeria are in advanced planning stages. Australia, Brazil, the Andean nations, and several Scandinavian countries are presently studying the investment in satellites (Henderson, 1979; Grey & Gerard, 1978; "Global Communications," 1978). Algeria, Brazil, Norway, Saudi Arabia, the Sudan, and Zaire use rented capacity from INTELSAT. The Phillippine Islands use PALAPA 1, rented from Indonesia. The Government of India signed a contract in 1978 with Ford Aerospace for the manufacture of two satellites for its domestic system, expected to be operational in 1982. An Arab regional satellite system (ARABSAT) is on the drawing boards (Kader, 1979), and an African satellite system (AFROSAT) is being considered by the thirty-eight-member Panaftel group. The Andean satellite system was proposed by Aseta, a regional organization of the countries of Brazil, Chile, Colombia, Ecuador, and Peru, and there is also the Nordic system (NORD-SAT), proposed by the five Nordic countries. For additional information, see Wigand (1980a).

New generations of communication satellites are presently under construction or in the planning stages. They will establish new communication systems or expand existing ones. Numerous actors are involved in these developmental efforts. Among them are: Satellite Business Systems (SBS), a partnership of Comsat General Corporation, International Business Machines, and Aetna Life and Casualty; and the Western Union advanced WESTAR system, in combination with the data relay and tracking system of NASA. There is also the Canadian TELESAT system that launched the first commercial geosychronous domestic communication satellite. The Federal Republic of Germany is presently building its series of TV-SAT satellites as a joint venture among the firms of AEG-Telefunken, Erno, Dornier-System, Messerschmitt-Bölkow-Blohm, and SEL. Additional organizations are referred to later on in conjunction with specific developments in the field of Direct Broadcast Satellites (DBS).

At present there is indeed no shortage of application possibilities. A satellite can see all of its designated surface area; distance and isolation have been removed as obstacles to the field of communication. There are very few technological hurdles that could possibly constitute serious difficulties for future telecommunication systems. Although there appear to be no technological difficulties, problems do arise with regard to social, legal, and policy implications. Within just a few years, satellites will be broadcasting television signals directly into many homes around the world. One may be impressed with such technological accomplishments, but many nations are very concerned about the psychological and, indirectly, the sociological and political impacts that such broadcasts could have on their people (Wigand, 1981a, 1980b).

Since its formation in 1959, the UN Committee on the Peaceful Uses of Outer Space has been concerned with these issues. In 1968 the committee formed a working group to study DBS. In 1972 the USSR tabled a draft international convention before the UN General Assembly to govern direct television broadcasting. Based on this event, the General Assembly requested the Committee on Peaceful Uses of Outer Space to study the "principles governing the use by states of artificial earth satellites for direct television broadcasting, with a view to concluding an international agreement or agreements." The Working Group on Direct Broadcast Satellites and the Legal Sub-Committee of the Outer Space Committee have been investigating these issues since 1972. Discussions and agreements have moved at a slow pace. Interested readers may want to review the *Current Report of the Legal Sub-Committee on the Work of its Eighteenth Session* (United Nations, 1979).

Differences with regard to philosophical, social, and cultural concerns stem largely from differences in ideologies as well as in legal principle — viewed in some countries as human rights — e.g., the right to freedom of opinion. The underlying assumption for such a position is a concrete form of freedom of expression and, consequently, free dissemination of information and ideas. Other countries, such as those in Eastern Europe, place greater importance on the right of states to protect their national sovereignty together with their social, cultural, and political values.

The delineation of and relationship between the free dissemination of information and ideas and the sovereign rights of states constitute one of the most difficult legal issues in an effort to regulate DBS. This complicated issue becomes readily apparent when one considers freedom of expression as an absolute right. In this situation broadcasters would be entitled to have an unrestrained right to broadcast over a foreign state. On the other hand, if one subscribes to the sovereignty principle, then the consent of a state exposed to intentional broadcasting from a foreign state is mandatory. Otherwise its sovereign rights can be infringed upon by foreign broadcasts. This area has been reviewed extensively by Dauses (1975). Various other legal aspects that may influence social, cultural, and economic conditions have been addressed by Frutkin (1975), Galloway (1975), and Pikus (1975).

On the following pages key developments in the field of DBS are examined that may offer insights to students of communication, as well as to communication policymakers. More specifically, the potential social implications of DBS are explored with respect to:

1. the possibilities of using DBS for governmental, administrative, private, and commercial communications; and
2. the potential effects and uses such possibilities may have.

These explorations are made in terms of DBS in worldwide and regional settings for direct-to-home and point-to-multipoint situations. Their implications for cable televison (CATV) and word, data, and management systems are examined. Finally, forthcoming technological developments and applications, as well as policy implications, are discussed.

DEFINITIONS OF DIRECT SATELLITE BROADCASTING

Distinguishing between direct broadcasting satellites and other broadcasting satellite systems is a complicated process. For present purposes direct broadcasting by satellites is defined as the transmission of broadcast signals via high-powered satellites that permit direct reception of television or radio programs by means of small antennae. This definition should be viewed in contrast to transmission via satellites in point-to-point or point-to-multipoint systems for networking, transmission of television and radio programs, telephone service, data, etc. It becomes readily apparent that a precise delineation between these two types of satellite transmission is not quite possible. It is conceivable that a large magazine publisher may transmit copy from headquarters via satellite to numerous regional locations simultaneously. The copy is received directly by the regional printing plant that will then insert the copy into its own regional edition of the magazine. Similarly, a live television program may be transmitted via satellite to various regional cable television or microwave systems that then disseminate these live programs *directly* to the local viewer (Wigand, 1980a).

The International Telecommunication Union (ITU) recognized this difficulty in defining DBS. It adopted the 1977 World Administrative Radio Conference for Space Telecommunications' (WARC-ST) definitions for DBS, stating that "in the broadcasting satellite service, the 'direct reception' shall encompass both individual reception and community reception" (International Telecommunication Union, 1971). Individual reception is defined as "the reception of emissions from a space station in the broadcast satellite service by simple domestic installations and in particular those possessing small antennae" (International Telecommunication Union, 1971). Community reception is defined as:

> the reception of emissions from a space station in the broadcast satellite service by receiving equipment, which in some cases may be complex and have antennae larger than those used for individual reception, and intended for use:
> — by a group of the general public at one location; or
> — through a distribution system covering a linked area.

These definitions do not refer exclusively to physically or technically distinct concepts. Mixtures of several systems are possible, as indicated earlier. The crucial difference between these definitions is not of a technical but rather an organizational nature (Wigand, 1980a). From this perspective it becomes important to note whether or not some controllable link exists between the satellite and the receiver. For the present purposes these delineations will suffice.

WORLDWIDE AND REGIONAL COMMUNICATION VIA DIRECT SATELLITE BROADCASTING

For nations to play their proper role in world affairs, they must share with each other their health, agricultural, educational, cultural, and indus-

Direct Satellite Broadcasting

trial knowledge. Modern transportation and communication are key factors in enhancing this role. Until twenty years ago, the regular exchange and sharing of such knowledge was difficult and cumbersome because of the vast distances involved. In addition, using various transportation methods to move people was expensive, time-consuming, and tiring. Transmitting information was slow and, depending on the circumstances, rather expensive. Today, with the development of satellites, this sharing has become fully possible, no matter how remote the location on earth. International meetings can be brought to local participants, possibly even into their homes, and travel may no longer be necessary. The advent of direct broadcasting via satellites has provided the opportunity for people separated by continents and oceans, ideological as well as language differences, and cultural discrepancies to work together to improve communication and to progress toward common goals. In this context the key advantage of satellite communication over its main competitors, telephone and cable, is the potential that if n earth terminals are visible from one or several satellites, then $n(n-1)/2$ two-way communication circuits exist.

Several of the experimental and demonstration satellites are prime examples of how worldwide communication was facilitated, though only for specific purposes. Today, 102 members belong to the International Telecommunications Consortium that launched the INTELSAT series of satellites providing communication services among major cities of the world. It is predicted that all countries will be linked via satellite by 1985. In 1978 world communication was made possible by eight INTELSAT 4 and 4a satellites providing 80,000 voice channels via 165 earth stations in eighty countries. At present, major world capitals are linked by satellites, but a high priority need for improved communications lies with the geographically remote and sparsely populated areas. INTELSAT reports that the 1978 World Cup Soccer Championship was the world's biggest satellite event: A total of more than 3,200 transmission and reception hours and an estimated viewing audience of about one billion people surpassed the comparative statistics of the 1976 Olympic Games. By March 31, 1979 INTELSAT functioned as the carrier for national domestic services in fifteen countries (Algeria, Brazil, Chile, Colombia, France, Malaysia, Nigeria, Norway, Oman, Peru, Saudi Arabia, Spain, the Sudan, Uganda, and Zaire). Other countries that will soon join or are presently considering INTELSAT's use for their domestic services are Denmark, Egypt, India, and Iraq.

Worldwide communication is made possible also by reducing the cost of needed ground stations. One example of this type of satellite was NASA's ATS-6, launched in May 1974. ATS-6 differed from previous satellites because the high transmission power was built into the satellite itself rather than into the ground station. Previously, ground stations were required that cost from $100,000 to several million dollars each; now, such a ground station could be acquired for about $5,000 or less. In this way, isolated communities as well as populated areas can receive satellite signals at a much lower cost, at least when considering the specific local situation. ATS-6 was used in the United States for one year and then given to India on loan for the next year. While the satellite was in use in India, ATS-6 successfully reached thousands of isolated villages in remote areas of that country. Programs on family planning, agriculture, health, and education were broadcast.

EUTELSAT, the European consortium of seventeen member countries, has its own experimental satellite, the Orbital Test Satellite (OTS), with 6,000 voice channels. Further plans include the European Communications Satellites, intended for digital communications, and Eurovision in the 1980s. Other large systems are in operation or in various advanced planning stages in Canada (TELSAT/ANIK), the USSR (INTERSPUTNIK/MOLNIYA-2), and Japan (BSE 14/12). Similarly, the Federal Republics of Germany and France made their jointly financed and controlled SYMPHONIE 1 and 2 satellites (launched in 1974 and 1975) available to other countries interested in getting to know this technology. Egypt, India, Indonesia, Iran, and the People's Republic of China have all explored the possibilities that these satellites can provide to establish modern communication services needed for economic and educational improvement, as well as for industrialization. Indonesia has chosen to develop its own domestic satellite system rather than rely on cable and microwave links. Cable and microwave hardware would have been too expensive, as well as physically difficult to install over thousands of miles of oceans, hills, and forest. Two satellites, PALAPA 1 and 2, now provide communication services to the multitude of inhabited islands in Southeast Asia.

MARISAT, another communication satellite, provides ship-to-shore telephony and telex services in the Pacific. Similarly, the European Space Agency (ESA) is operating MAROTS, the Maritime Orbiting Test Satellite. An International maritime satellite organization, INMARSAT, has been in existence since 1979. Over one hundred countries are now users of information from LANDSAT satellites. This series of satellites was designed to observe and report information on water, minerals, and ground cover, as well as the earth's surface. Much of this information was previously not available. LANDSAT satellites provide a most useful service for national development and for urban and rural planning in all parts of the world.

In 1975 the Public Service Satellite Consortium was created. Originally this organization was to serve primarily organizations in the United States, but today public service organizations from Canada and Australia have also joined the Consortium. The organization was founded with the expressed purpose to ensure that satellite communication and its related technology would develop and be put to use in the public service. The membership varies greatly: several prestigious universities and school districts from the state of Maine to Hawaii, the American Medical Association, the American Hospital Association, as well as the American College of Physicians and Surgeons. Several states work with professional organizations such as the American Bar Association, the American Library Association, and various religious organizations.

In Europe the interest in DBS has increased considerably since the 1977 WARC-ST. New geostationary positions and frequencies were allocated to the twenty-five European entities transmitting television programs, and several studies were undertaken to explore the possibilities provided by direct broadcasting satellites. Most European countries are considering the use of DBS

- for economic reasons;
- to provide for additional television programs, especially when there are limited frequencies in the VHF and UHF bands; and
- to permit coverage of population segments with television programs in isolated and poor reception areas.

Communication satellites provide easy access to reliable radio, television, and telephone services for small, isolated communities. These amenities may attract professionals, skilled workers, and technicians who are familiar with metropolitan living and conveniences into small, possibly remote communities. Access to these communication means will enhance the attractiveness of these communities and at the same time enhance the growth and development of industry and business in these locations.

DBS could provide a desirable service to people living in isolated and remote areas. Most city-dwellers have access to broadcasting services from many stations. Many isolated and rural areas, however, are less fortunate. In the case of Canada, e.g., six million citizens live in rural areas. A large proportion of these country-dwellers have spotty reception of AM radio at best. In all, 20 percent cannot be reached by their nearest television station. In addition, a mere 35 percent are able to get FM radio. One might initially speculate that the solution to such a problem is CATV, but here the missing economic incentive makes the difference. Cable systems need about twelve to eighteen customers per mile to enjoy a profit. Commercial broadcasters also have a financial disincentive to enlarge their rural broadcasting service, since advertisers look for markets in high-density urban areas. Canada has looked to other alternatives, such as fiber optics, in lieu of expensive copper cable.

Satellite communication could improve the situation of the rural inhabitant by ensuring easier delivery of high-quality television reception in conjunction with community antenna systems or head ends. Government communications in remote areas are handled in many situations by private telecommunications networks, and high-frequency radio networks are frequently utilized. If the various government departments would share satellite facilities, the proliferation of private systems would cease. Such a step would also increase substantially the reliability of government communications in several remote areas of Canada. Furthermore, this switch would improve the social services offered to residents in these areas, a stated priority of the Canadian Federal Government. The Canadian Department of Communications is planning a direct-to-home television program delivery pilot project using ANIK B satellite services provided by Telesat Canada (Golden, 1979). In Latin America efforts are underway by Argentina, Bolivia, Chile, Colombia, Ecuador, Paraguay, Peru, Uruguay, and Venezuela to develop a regional system for educational, cultural, and developmental purposes.

At the present time it seems unlikely that a comprehensive and integrated international DBS system will develop. Such a system could provide member nations with a full range of satellite communication services, including DBS. At one point such a system was proposed by the Twentieth Century Fund; it would have been internationally owned and operated by INTELSAT. Eventually, it could have been linked with INTERSPUTNIK, the Russian-proposed international satellite system that connects the Eastern European countries, Cuba, and Mongolia. It is much safer to predict a large number of national or regional satellite systems for domestic purposes. In this organizational form, satellite systems might become — at least functionally — part of the various national broadcasting organizations. The USSR already has such a large point-to-point domestic network and, as indicated, many other countries are planning satellite systems that will broadcast to community receiving stations.

The present trend, then, is toward the development of about twenty separate systems that are global, regional, or national in nature, not all of which will be used for broadcast purposes. Each system would function as a self-contained, discrete entity. Each receiving station would be set on only those frequencies through which signals could be received from satellites in a given country's own system. This design would largely reduce problems with regard to spillover of the signal into neighboring territories. Eventually, interconnections may stretch between national and regional satellite systems via terrestrial connections, and future plans provide for a linkage between satellite systems without the terrestrial connection. A French earth station has already made such a linkage possible with its basic INTELSAT design and the MOLNIYA system on an experimental basis.

DIRECT-TO-HOME AND POINT-TO-MULTIPOINT SATELLITE TELEVISION RECEPTION

Today's television signals still enter home sets from a local or regional earth-based transmitter. This way of receiving signals would change rather drastically if the cost of ground installations could be reduced by receiving signals directly from a geostationary satellite. In order to make low-cost ground receiving terminals feasible, the transmitter power must be increased so that the size and cost of the ground receiving installation is reduced.

The most promising, but presently hotly debated area of direct satellite broadcasting is direct-to-home television reception. This form of distribution of television programs has only been seriously discussed in Japan, North America, and Western Europe.

Japan. This country encounters the problem of overcoming geographical barriers posed by the large number of islands. In addition, the mountainous character of the country and the tall urban structures present shadow problems interfering with high-quality television reception from ground-based diffusion points. DBS would make reception possible for Japanese citizens without regard to their respective geographical isolation or urban shadow. Japan is scheduled to launch its first domestic communication satellite in 1982 and a domestic broadcasting satellite in 1983. The Diet is presently considering a new bill that calls for a Communications/Broadcast Satellite Organization to own and manage these satellites. This organization would be financed 50 percent by the government and 50 percent by nongovernmental backers.

North America. The Canadian Department of Communications is planning a direct-to-home television delivery project using the ANIK B satellite under contract with Telesat Canada (Golden, 1979). Canada has a long-term interest in DBS, manifesting itself in past experiments utilizing its HERMES satellite. Consequently, Canada is not presently involved in direct-to-home television program delivery. In the United States, a few firms have started to offer dish antennae to private individuals. One such firm, Homesat, a subsidiary of Scientific-Atlanta, is offering such a system to private individuals. Homesat viewers can enjoy the high quality of satellite color reception and have access to a large variety of programs. The price for such a setup amounts to more than $15,000, an extremely high price due to the large dish antenna, 4.6 m in diameter. The price — not including shipping and installation costs — covers the following:

- 4.6 m dish antenna;
- all cable, two twelve-channel amplifiers, and a switch;
- a remote receiver that converts the satellite signal to a television picture;
- an adapter that adapts the television picture to a normal television set using a spare channel;
- frequency coordination;
- Federal Communications Commission (FCC) license and construction permit; and
- pay television fees.

These costs are unusually high for a large-scale, direct-to-home television distribution effort. With higher-powered satellites, smaller dish antennae would be adequate and should drastically reduce the cost of required private earth stations.

COMSAT, the Communications Satellite Corporation, is proposing to offer subscription television service to millions of U.S. homes using rooftop antennae. The service offers subscribers programming on several channels simultaneously with no commercial interruptions and an emphasis on first-run movies, sports events, educational and cultural programs, as well as data and text transmissions. Subscribers will pay a monthly charge that covers the total service, including the use and maintenance of a rooftop antenna. COMSAT estimates the monthly cost to be no more than many families pay now for a single night at the movies. The service could be introduced as early as 1983.

COMSAT has conducted demonstration experiments using a Canadian satellite and COMSAT-developed dish-type antennas suitable for rooftop installation. The FCC decided on October 18, 1979, to drop its licensing requirements for satellite receiving stations. The agency took the action to eliminate the cost of the licensing process for builders of receiving stations and to end delays in obtaining a license. Of course, operators of receiving stations will still have to obtain permission from the operators of the sending satellites to receive their transmissions.

On July 16, 1981 the FCC received a flood of applications for DBS. Due to the FCC's inclination to loosely regulate this new television service, a wide range of applications was received. Applicants proposed to provide direct-to-home pay and advertiser-supported television, the leasing of transponders on satellites to independent service providers, and the distribution of high-definition television for retransmission by terrestrial broadcasters. A total of thirteen additional applications were received,

Direct Satellite Broadcasting

implying that at least thirty-five satellites will have to be launched if all applications are to be approved. These thirteen applicants that will have to be considered by the FCC are listed and described in Table 8.1. COMSAT's Satellite Television Corporation (STC) was already formally accepted by the FCC. The most innovative application came from CBS utilizing DBS technology for the conversion of the conventional NTSC television system to a still-to-be-specified system of high-definition television, including stereophonic sound and wide-screen pictures.

The frequency plans submitted by the DBS applicants request that a minimum of forty channels be utilized by each applicant in each time zone. The maximum number of channels over which transmissions are possible in each time zone is about forty. This licensing and allocation dilemma has been placed before the U.S. Congress. Indications are that this dispute will not become a stumbling block delaying the new service, in spite of considerable opposition from the National Association of Broadcasters. In October 1981 the FCC narrowed the field of applicants to nine. The FCC cannot grant any permanent licenses before 1983 when another international WARC conference is to be held to determine which frequencies and orbital positions can be used. Conventional broadcasters claim that DBS will merely provide the same type of television programming that viewers are familiar with today by cable television. In the long run, such DBS efforts would undercut the entire American system based on local broadcasters serving the needs of local audiences (Wigand, 1981b).

Western Europe. Direct-to-home service is still in its infancy in North America and Japan. Western European nations, however, have already developed large-scale, fixed plans for direct-to-home television and radio broadcast services. Fully operational satellite systems are anticipated in the next one or two years. The European Space Agency (ESA) will serve as a carrier's carrier, and the services themselves will be marketed by Eutelsat, the consortium of Western European ministries of post, telephone, and telegraph (PTT) covering Belgium, Denmark, Ireland, France, Italy, Netherlands, Spain, Sweden, Switzerland, the United Kingdom, and the Federal Republic of Germany. The European Communications System (ECS) is intended primarily to carry television programs, but can also handle telephone and data transmissions. By 1984, European PTTs plan to provide service between small earth stations. The current thrust of European communication satellite development is clearly toward the higher frequencies.

The ESA has been engaged for a number of years in an extensive program of reseach and development that has considerably strengthened European-based space technology. European firms such as West Germany's Messerschmitt-Bölkow-Blohm (MBB) have been negotiating with

Table 8.1
DBS Applicants with the FCC and Their Plans

Applicant	Number of Satellites (spares)	Number of Channels per Satellite	Downlink Power (watts)	Channel Bandwidth mhz	Total Satellite Power (watts)	EIRP[f] (dbw)	Satellite Design Life (years)	Orbital Slot (degrees west longitude)	Weight of Satellite in Orbit (lbs)	Type of Service
Advance	*	*	*	*	*	*	*	*	*	A,C,H
CBS	4(2)	3	400	27	4,000	60-65	7	*	2,317	A,C,D,E,G,I,J
DBSC	3(1)	14[b]	200[b]	22.5	4,600	56	7	103,123 143	2,987	H,I,G,J
Focus Broadcast Satellite[e]	3, 4 or 5	*	*	*	*	*	*	*	*	A,B,C,D,E,F, G,I,J
Graphic Scanning	2(1)	2	300	18	2,000	53.7-56.7	*	143,115	*	A,B,G,J
Home Broadcasting	1	*	19.7	*	*	*	*	110	*	K
Television Partners										
RCA	4(2)	6	230	24[c]	4,770	58	7	*	2,415	H,I
Satellite Development Trust	4(2)	3	150-250	*	*	*	*	115,135 155,175	*	H
STC	4(2)	3	185	16	1,700	55-60	7	115,135	1,430	A,B,E,G,I,J

Unitel	*	*	*	*	*	100	*	K
USSB (Hubbard)	2(1)	6[a]	230	16	4,000	57	7	115,135	2,300	A,C,D,F,I
Video Satellite Systems	2(1)	2	150-190	18	1,000[d]	54-58	8	115,135	1,201	A,C,D,E,H,I
Western Union[e]	4(2)	4	100	16	*	55.5-58	7	80,100	1,175[d]	H

a. USSB's six channels will be divided between two time zones served by each satellite. A seventh low-power (20 watts) transponder is also contained on the satellite for feeding programming to the main distribution uplink.
b. Each satellite contains six 200-watt broadbeam channels and eight low-power spot beam channels.
c. Two of the six transponders can be switched to pass 72 mhz for HDTV transmission.
d. At the end of the design life.
e. In addition to its DBS application, FBS also has requested authorization to use an Advanced Westar Satellite, slated for launch in January 1984, to offer one channel of direct-to-home service to four distinct areas of the country.
f. Effective Isolated Radiated Power—the higher the EIRP (expressed in decibel watts), the stronger the signal received on the ground and the smaller the antenna needed to receive it.
*Not specified in the application.

Key to proposed DBS service offerings:

A—Direct to home (or business)
B—Pay television
C—Advertiser-supported
D—Terrestrial retransmission by broadcasters
E—Terrestrial retransmission by cable systems
F—Terrestrial Transmission by LPTV stations
G—Electronic text services
H—Leased-channel system
I—High definition TV
J—Additional audio services
K—Unspecified

Source: *Broadcasting*, 1981, 101(3), 25.

several European and Asiatic countries for the production of satellites. During the spring of 1979, China signed an agreement with MBB for a joint production program to deliver a total of seven television satellites. In the past, France and Germany cooperated in the development of SYMPHONIE, an experimental satellite that is in operation in several programs over the Atlantic and Indian Oceans. SYMPHONIE is used to link France with French-speaking areas in Africa, the Carribean, and North America. Another joint venture by France and West Germany is scheduled for 1983 to provide direct television to homes.

France's proposed TELECOM-1 will serve metropolitan France (including Corsica) and her overseas *Départements* (Guadelupe, Guyana, Martinique, Mayotte, Réunion, and Saint-Pierre-et-Miquelon). TELECOM-1 — with a second satellite on a standby basis — will provide television and telephone transmissions, but also digital wideband, high-speed connections between 3 m dishes installed on the premises of major users. TELECOM-1 will have two main objectives:

1. A service providing "links with overseas *Départements*" for handling traffic (telephone and television); and
2. An "intracompany link" service providing digital wideband high-speed links between different branches of an organization.

Initially, TELECOM-1 will serve well-defined users; hence, the cost of earth stations will be within the reach of large-scale users only. This satellite — via the use of mobile earth stations — will provide temporary links for the transmission of television programs. TELECOM-1 will be launched by means of the European launcher Ariane and will be the first of a new system of European satellites to be placed into orbit during the second half of the 1980's (Wigand, 1980a).

In December 1978 the Ministry for Research and Technology of the Federal Republic of Germany, along with MBB, ordered a television satellite, TV-SAT, that could transmit three television programs directly into every West German home from a geostationary orbit starting in 1983. All that television consumers would need would be a parabolic antenna exactly 69 cm in diameter and a frequency converter at an estimated cost of $280 to $560 when mass-produced. The TV-SAT project is financed with a budget of approximately $147 million. As suggested earlier, to provide direct-to-home transmission of television programs via satellite, a new generation of satellites is needed with increased electric power, i.e., 3 kW. The transmitter power received in orbit is 235 watts per channel, compared with the 5 to 20 watts needed in conventional communication satellites. TV-SAT will be operated at first on an experimental basis from its

Direct Satellite Broadcasting

35,800-kilometer distant position. Its funnellike beam will project a *footprint* on the Federal Republic of Germany in an ellipselike shape that will include West Berlin.

Direct-to-home satellite broadcasting would make it possible to receive a high-quality signal in all parts of the Federal Republic. Until today, 3 percent of the population still cannot receive television due to various difficulties, from broadcasting into valleys to blockage by high-rise buildings. With the advent of TV-SAT, transmitting towers and relay stations become dispensable and are probably only of use for strictly regional or supplementary broadcasting. Furthermore, West Germans could then receive more than their present three television channels: ARD, ZDF, and the regional Third Program.

During the 1977 WARC-ST in Geneva, an agreement was reached to utilize the frequencies of 11.7 to 12.5 GHz. These shortwaves were previously unassigned due to their susceptibility through rain and mountains for terrestrial broadcasting. This frequency range only lends itself to forty television channels, and their broadcasting powers and *footprint* areas were distributed via computer analysis to various countries so that the broadcast target areas would not disturb each other. In the case of the Federal Republic, channel 2, e.g., was reserved, but the same channel was also reserved for North Sweden and South Ireland, as well as Rumania, parts of India, Algeria, China, Australia, and nineteen other countries, including the Cook Islands. The ellipselike footprints, however, are geographically so far apart that no spillover will be possible. Some of the *footprint*, however, will penetrate the borders of neighboring countries. In the case of West Germany, channel 2, as well as the four other channels of the Federal Republic, may not be used by neighboring countries, and thus it is possible to receive it in some portions of those countries. Similarly, TV-SAT may not be broadcast on channels reserved for other countries.

It will be possible to receive West German television broadcasts in portions of Austria, Belgium, CSSR, Denmark, France, the German Democratic Republic, Italy, Luxembourg, the Netherlands, and Switzerland. Similarly, some portions of West Germany will be able to receive television broadcasts from these countries on different channels. When a larger dish antenna with a diameter of approximately 1.80 m is utilized, the programs from neighboring countries could be received all over West Germany. This is possible since some of the above-mentioned countries (Austria, Belgium, France, Italy, Luxembourg, Netherlands, Switzerland) use the same satellite position as West Germany, although they use different channels. If the dish antennas become flexible such that they could be directed to a different satellite position, viewers could also receive the programs of Scandinavia, the German Democratic Republic, and the CSSR.

The first series of TV-SAT is presently being constructed and will be placed in orbit by the end of 1982 or the beginning of 1983. It is planned for a two-year test period until 1985 with three channels. In 1985 a fully operational TV-SAT 1 will be launched with the five channels utilizing solar power from 4:00 a.m. until 2:00 a.m. A complete malfunctioning of all channels is virtually impossible, since replacement channels will be available. In addition, a co-orbiting twin satellite can start transmitting any time when necessary.

Radio-Télé Luxembourg, the only wholly privately-owned broadcasting company in Europe, has announced that it would like to use its spillover portion of its footprint to direct commercial television programs to West Germany. Presently, there is no commercial television in the Federal Republic. For several years, however, certain German publishing houses have expressed considerable interest in starting a private, commercial television program. There has even been some talk of joint ventures between Radio-Télé Luxembourg and West German media companies and publishing houses. It appears that once again the confrontation between the issues of private versus public control of the airwaves, as well as the function of television — i.e., the desirable interplay between information/education/cultural programs versus entertainment — will have to be addressed by policymakers. The question of what type of programming is to be shown on the five West German channels is still being debated. West Germany's ARD has proposed to use one of the channels for an attractive Eurovision program.

Direct broadcasting satellites reach entire nations and connect peoples and continents. In the case of Europe, DBS does not lend itself well to local or regional programs, neither for feedback programs nor for those that require audience participation. This is due in part to the proximity of neighboring countries with their own channel allocations. In the case of North America, DBS lends itself ideally to overcome large distances and — by proper delay — time zones. As local and regional programming and transmission become desirable, feedback and audience participation become possible and have been used successfully in past demonstration experiments.

SATELLITE BROADCASTING AND CABLE TELEVISION

The distinction between satellite and cable transmissions is artificial because functionally the choice of mode of transmission is not dictated by technological requirements. Satellite and cable television broadcasts, when used as combined transmission means, have been explored, among other areas (Johansen, 1977), through teleconferencing. In 1979, for example, Arizona hospital personnel saw and heard portions of the American Hospital Association convention held in Chicago, Illinois. Portions of the convention were broadcast to KAET-TV, Arizona State University's Public Broadcasting Service station, via domestic satellite and CATV. The system is called Cable-Med. The signals were picked up from SATCOM 1 satellite by a local CATV company, American Cable, and transmitted via microwave to KAET-TV's studios. In the studio large viewing screens were installed and a special toll-free telephone system enabled Arizona hospital personnel to see and hear convention speakers and to discuss topics with them. Through these broadcasts, hospital personnel were able to contribute to the national convention without having to leave the state. Other experimental system connections have shown that meetings somewhere on one continent can be shared with their professional, scientific, or business colleagues gathered on another continent. The current question is whether the advantages of combining several systems warrant the costs.

The combined efforts of satellite technology and cable television have made an astonishing impact on the use of satellites for the distribution of television programs. U.S. viewers not only receive a higher quality picture but have a larger choice among programs (Wigand, 1980c, 1979). In 1976, Home Box Office (HBO), a private corporation that offers television programs via cable subscribers and a subsidiary of Time, Inc., had about 500,000 subscribers throughout the United States. Of this number a total of 75,000 were served by a network of forty-five satellite-earth stations (Topol, 1978). At that time the minimum diameter permitted by the FCC for a CATV receive-only dish antenna was 9 m. In December 1976 the FCC permitted earth terminals with a diameter permissible to 4.5 m, thus decreasing significantly the cost of a receive-only earth station. HBO now has over 1,000,000 subscribers, and over 64 percent receive their programming by satellite. This example in itself demonstrates to what extent such growth was related to satellite distribution of programs.

Another development is the growth of so-called superstations. Since 1976 Southern Satellite Systems, Inc. has provided satellite common-carrier service for WTBS, channel 17, Atlanta, Georgia, to cable operators. This service includes all of WTBS programming as well as live major league sports broadcasts, syndicated programs, and selections from a library of over 3,000 films. WTBS is now seen in over three million homes. Through the use of satellites, the once-local Atlanta station has its programs picked up by CATV systems throughout the United States. This enables the owners to sell advertising on a national basis. In addition to HBO and WTBS, the cable operator can select from a good number of satellite alternatives. These include such services as Showtime Plus,

Warner's Star Channel, and Fanfare, as well as religious programming by the Christian Broadcasting Network, Praise the Lord, and the Trinity Broadcasting Network. Other alternatives are Nickelodeon and Calliope for children, the Satellite Program Network and Home Box Office Take 2 for family viewing, as well as C-SPAN's live daily broadcasts from the floor of the U.S. House of Representatives. In addition, satellite broadcasting from the Spanish International Network and special events from New York City's Madison Square Garden are available. Other so-called superstations are based in San Francisco, Chicago, and New York.

WTBS's owner, Mr. Ted Turner, has started his own television news network (CNN) just for CATV subscribers. Start-up costs were estimated at $20 million, with another $12 million in monthly operating costs (Weintraub, 1979). The cable news network is on the air twenty-four hours a day to broadcast news from a Washington, D.C. bureau and five other bureaus in major U.S. cities. In addition, bureaus operate in London, the Middle East, Latin America, and elsewhere. This allows for the reporting of news in greater depth and length. Viewers can watch news whenever they feel like it rather than the short segments — about twenty-two minutes for national news and from twenty-two to about forty-five minutes for local and regional news — at noon, early evening, and late at night.

One particular application of this new technology, namely, combining satellite communications with CATV, involves the regional and national networking of cable broadcasters via satellite. Such networks no doubt accelerate the availability of variety and diversity in television programming for many communities (Wigand, 1979). Presently, CATV service is available to over fourteen million homes in the United States. With multiple sources of programming available to even small CATV systems, the economical employment of satellite program services has now become an integral part of viewers' home information and entertainment package in the United States. It remains to be seen if in other countries without privately owned broadcast and program distribution systems, and where these systems are run by the PTT, similar growth of CATV will occur. This unique relationship between satellites and CATV may not necessarily imply that "the sky — or space — is the only limit to the future" in all situations as proposed by Hill (1978, p. 25).

THE FUTURE OF DIRECT SATELLITE BROADCASTING

Word, Data, and Management Communications via Satellite. New communication networks are planned that promise to greatly extend the speed, reach, and reaction time of business executives through the use of DBS. The following plans of several organizations and corporations will

Direct Satellite Broadcasting

give some indication of what to expect in the future. Although the plans of several U.S. corporations are described, it should be noted that several other countries expect similar developments (e.g., France's TELECOM-1 system, described earlier).

Satellite Business System (SBS), a joint venture of International Business Machines Corporation, Comsat General Corporation, and Aetna Life and Casualty Company, has made a major contribution to revolutionize current business practices and develop the office of the future. SBS's communication network via satellite is geared to large and geographically dispersed organizations.

In today's organizations it is not uncommon to find a warehouse-to-store network, as well as an order-entry network. Separate terminals are used for each network. It would be highly desirable to allow one terminal to operate all networks in existence. In addition, there may be other networks in operation (distribution of memoranda, letters; distribution of information via the telephone, computer, etc.) that are not formalized. The SBS and other communication networks plan to integrate such communication activities via four broad areas of communications: data communications, voice communications, facsmile, and teleconferencing. All of these areas are presently used rather sparingly and as separate entities, while each uses different and more conventional communication means and channels. SBS's efforts have brought these four areas together conceptually and offer an integrated service that permits widespread use. For over twenty years, computer data in relatively limited quantities have been transmitted by voice-grade telephone lines as well as by microwave. SBS's communication network, is no longer dependent upon the services of the Bell telephone system, but rather links computers together at on-line speeds over long distances. The resulting high-speed service (at up to 6.3 megabits per second) is fast enough to transmit in one minute a file or data base that today still takes an entire hour. Similarly, a one-billion byte file or eight billion bits — an amount of information of a magnitude that would have to be delivered by truck — could be distributed to one or multiple locations simultaneously anywhere in the United States in thirty minutes. These channels will also be capable of carrying voice. The actual user will not be aware of it, but the voice will be digitized before transmission and then reassembled. The voice signals can be received internally within the organization through its own system or it will be possible to simply switch the voice signal over to outside telephone lines at *local* call rates.

With regard to facsimile transmission, SBS claims that its network allows one to transmit "hard copy" two to twenty times faster than current facsimile transmission methods. This resulting low rate may suggest that business may want to use facsimile transmission as an alternative to intracompany mail.

The fourth element of such communication networks will allow a relatively new application of technology that will become financially attractive — at least in part — due to DBS teleconferencing. The uniqueness of this integrated network will make it possible for business and government executives to hold conferences across a continent that will not only enable the participants to see and hear each other, but to transmit and exchange conveniently the visuals, data, and hard copy that are needed in their conference discussion points. SBS will supply earth stations as well as clients with computer terminals, video screens, facsimile machines, etc. at each participating location. Earth station antennas are 5-7 m in diameter and can be installed on the user's parking lot, roof top, etc.

Such a system is not inexpensive. SBS is marketing its efforts toward a target customer base of the top 200 U.S. corporations and large governmental entities. The typical company has a network of fifteen to twenty earth stations. Earth stations alone cost $500,000. SBS claims that by providing a total communications service (integrating voice, data, and image transmission) on the same system, these large corporations will benefit beyond direct cost savings.

SBS faces a major challenge in 1982, since, only after spending six years and $600 million to plan, market, and build its satellite-based network, the first revenues were generated. Industry analysts report that these revenues amounted to a trickle of $5 million in 1981. That same year SBS was granted a $400 million loan from a sixteen-bank consortium headed by the Bank of America. SBS development plans have not quite progressed as anticipated: The first marketing plan focused on providing high-speed data communication networks for the nation's largest one hundred companies. By January 1982 ("SBS's Services," 1982) only twenty five corporations had signed up for this service. For the present, SBS is emphazising the lucrative voice-only market in direct competition with the American Telephone & Telegraph Company and independent carriers, expecting to tap the high-speed data market at a later point. It is claimed that 80 percent of all business communications is voice communication and that data communications amount to only 20 percent. SBS is handling about one million phone calls a month for seven corporate customers and is planning to pursue the lucrative long-distance telephone market vigorously. It anticipates offering a competitive service to Bell's Wide Area Telephone Service (WATS) at rates 10 to 20 percent lower. In addition, SBS plans to offer a residential, long-distance discount service similar to MCI's Execunet. The SBS satellite is presently operating at only 25 percent of its capacity. Based on the company's confidence in increasing usage of its services, SBS is planning to launch another satellite by 1983. Expansion plans also include the accommodation of U.S. companies with overseas offices, which would mean SBS's entry into the

Direct Satellite Broadcasting

international satellite market. Industry analysts think that the odds are high for the FCC to approve SBS's international satellite service ("SBS's Services," 1982).

Newspaper and magazine publishers, as well as the various news services, are interested in the development of facsimile equipment capable of receiving reproduction-quality materials. Publishers, of course, would also be interested in receiving via fascimile transmission high-quality advertising materials, as well as the accompanying billing and scheduling information from national advertisers and their agencies. Matsushita of Japan, for example, has developed a high-quality graphic receiver. This company intends to provide a terminal at a cost of about $25,000 that can produce a newspaper page in about four minutes with a scan rate of 650 lines per inch.

Another corporation that has been using satellite communication, Western Bancorporation, transmits and receives data on bank accounts and transactions and provides all data processing needs for its system members. This system connects twenty-two member banks in eleven western U.S. states, a region covering one-third of the nation's land area and housing 17.5 percent of its people. With 797 domestic banking offices in 405 western communities, Western Bancorporation has the widest geographical coverage of any U.S. banking company. This system has been called Teller Information Processing System (TIPS) and is expected to save $1 million in leased-line costs during its first three years of operation, a savings of 40 percent (Tabussi, 1979). Western Bancorporation is presently experimenting with other communication methods by satellite, namely video conferencing, electronic mail, and high-speed facsimile transmission.

Data are transmitted as rapidly as possible every night and updated computer files are returned to the banks via satellite. Some of the key advantages of using this satellite-based system are as follows:

- *Speed.* Eight satellite circuits can transmit at 56,000 bits per second, and the circuits are used at 97 percent capacity. This enables TIPS to transmit data at twice the speed of conventional telephone circuits.
- *Reliability.* Advanced network control centers continually monitor nearly every component of this data communication network. Backup systems are available if needed, but satellite "up-time" is very high.
- *Security.* Western Bancorporation controls both endpoints of the transmission system. All satellite circuits are protected by newly developed data encryption devices that make it virtually impossible to break a code.

American Satellite Corporation (AmSat), the Fairchild Industries subsidiary, actually installed the Western Bancorporation network, surprising the communications industry by completing a total of three private communication networks between September 1978 and January 1979. A roof-to-roof linkage exists now between the Minnesota and Pennsylvania development centers of Sperry Rand Corporation's Univac Division. Boeing Computer Services now enjoys a satellite link between Seattle, Witchita, and Washington, D.C. Lastly, AmSat placed a 13.8 m dish antenna at Texas Instruments, Inc.'s Dallas headquarters to relay data via a double-satellite connection to London. RCA American Communications, Inc. also offers similar services. This company has been busy promoting satellite distribution of television programs. RCA teamed up with Western Union and launched their WESTAR and SATCOM satellites. Once the satellite was in its 36,000 km-high orbit, a surplus capacity was realized that gave AmSat the opportunity to engage in its lease business at bargain rates.

In 1978 AmSat developed the important satellite delay composition unit that is designed to overcome the time lag in getting signals between an earth station and the satellite. The delay previously amounted to merely half a second, but with regard to efficient computer operations this amounts to an eternity. Previously, data were sent in short bursts, after which the system had to wait for acknowledgment from the other end. Such a delay constituted an efficiency problem of such a magnitude that some experts even thought that satellites for business data were not even viable (Belitz, 1979). AmSat's device provides a buffer that fools the computer into functioning as if it were "talking" to a local terminal.

Several problem areas still lie ahead. The technology itself is not a problem per se; what is new is the scale in which it will be applied. An additional question arises with regard to how favorably the corporate and government worlds receive these new communication networks. This, of course, cannot be answered until the firms have signed on a number of customers. Some market research indicates that the predicted demand exists. SBS, together with Comsat Laboratories, conducted an experiment — Project Prelude — in late 1977 and early 1978 for satellite business applications (Barna, 1979). The researchers used (with NASA's permission) the most powerful communications satellite in orbit, the Communications Technology Satellite (CTS). Earth stations, newly developed terminal equipment and business machines, were placed at three host companies (Rockwell International, Texaco, and Montgomery Ward). The transmission of high-speed data, high-speed facsimile, and voice and video communications was tested. 1,476 respondents from the three firms gave their reactions in a questionnaire. The participants were grouped into the following activity areas: administration ($N=353$), marketing ($N=216$), data processing ($N=310$), engineering ($N=120$), and other

Direct Satellite Broadcasting

areas (N = 477). Among the findings were the following generalizations (Barna, 1979, p. 83):

- *Time Savings.* Time saving — in terms of both reduced travel time and quicker decisionmaking — was perceived as the most important benefit from holding teleconferences. Together, the two were mentioned ten times more often than was the reduced direct cost of travel.
- *Cost Savings.* Forty-three of those who participated estimated that they saved as much as $15,000 per teleconference, with most savings in the $10,000 range. This same group estimated that manpower savings ranged from two hours to twenty-five man-days per conference. These results varied, of course, with the size of the sessions and the distances involved.
- *Personal Involvement.* One-fourth of the participants said they would personally operate desk terminals to store and retrieve information and that they would use the equipment five or more times per week. A total of 40 percent stated that they would use high-speed facsimile equipment five or more times a week if it were available.
- *Preferred Mode of Communication.* Of the participants, 75 percent agreed that teleconferencing was better than traveling as a way to conduct business meetings; 15 percent said they would move immediately to put in teleconferencing systems if they had authority. Only 2 percent stated they would not use the teleconferencing at all.

The general reactions to Project Prelude indicate that the participants qualified their responses with "depending on cost." This tenor is consistent with spokespersons of the industry: The corporate world is ready to use the new, more efficient and effective technology if the price is right. The potential will be created to coordinate and control large and dispersed organizations to a degree unknown today. Within the next ten years, corporate offices will be connected to an integrated digital communication network for the transmission of voice, video, facsimile, and other devices. As in the past, information technology inventors will be presenting their new devices and gadgets long before man has fully adapted to the device to be replaced. This is further reflected in worldwide efforts in the WARC conferences, as well as in the various legal implications and social effects that still need to be explored (Wigand, 1981a; 1980a and b).

There is no doubt, however, that technology — and DSB in particular — will reduce the importance of location. It will make it easier to start a business enterprise and will encourage competition. There are definite indications that during the next 25 years top management may be *remote management* and that these managers will not have a need to see their subordinates on a daily basis. Subordinates can be contacted by a touch of the button. The advent of satellites advances geography, and many persons will be able to work in areas distant from their office or factory. Widespread information systems will provide instant information. Flexibility will no longer be an issue as it is known today. Specialization is bound to increase in conjunction with the technological developments described earlier. This specialization may require more work and career changes and places additional emphasis on continuing education, training, and development. Many workers might have computer terminals in their homes and work from there. This author knows a couple, for instance, both computer consultants for the New Jersey Institute of Technology's Electronic Information Exchange System (EIES), working from their terminal in a cabin located in the Oregon forest some 3,000 miles away. A large Chicago bank has a word processing department partly staffed by women who work at home using a terminal. Managers operating in such an environment must be trained to learn how to manage people at distant locations. This implies new management techniques in addition to new criteria for productivity. As can be seen from this discussion, there will be an increased emphasis on communication in business during the years to come.

Technological Developments and New DBS Applications. The rapidly increasing and expanding use of satellites in conjunction with cable, microwave, computers, and other technologies is drastically changing the uses and applications of broadcasting. In many cases the advent of satellite-related technology can free the user of the constraints of previous lifestyles. Homes, schools, and hospitals, as well as businesses and governments, are gaining access to numerous channels for a multitude of services. Satellites can widen opportunities for television program distribution by linking with diverse media to meet joint functional and geographical needs. It appears that satellites have become the universal link for broadcasting and related technologies in a wireless world.

New applications for direct broadcast satellites have been explored by NASA through its series of Applications Technology Satellites (ATS) 1, 3, 5, and 6, the joint NASA and Canadian Department of Communications CTS experimental and commercial satellites ("Business Communications," 1978; Bargellini, 1977; Engler, Strange, and Hein, 1976). The main new and promising DBS applications are:

- direct broadcast television and radio;
- teleducation;
- telemedicine;
- transportable emergency terminals;
- newspaper facsimile transmissions;
- simultaneous, multilanguage translation between two continents;
- high-speed facsimile transmissions;

Direct Satellite Broadcasting

- electronic mail;
- electronic newspapers (Videotext);
- electronic shopping and funds transfer.

Satellite communication is a prime example of technology advancing more rapidly than concurrent uses and applications in terms of political constraints, ideological issues, legal complications, economic considerations, etc. The applications referred to earlier, as well as others, are not dependent on future breakthroughs in technology. Today's satellite technology is fully operational and practical using existing terminals and sender and receiver stations.

DBS have also been utilized as a new distribution method for spot commercials. On March 18, 1979 twelve commercial television stations in the United States took part in a first test by John Blair & Company ("TV Commercials," 1979). This national television and radio sales representative firm uses a nationwide system for the distribution of spot television commercials via satellite. The test was coordinated by the Hughes Television Network for a thirteen-week period. It is well known that in North America the traffic in commercials constitutes a nightmare of coordination, with about 30,000 new spots being produced by agencies each year. The potential for missing deadlines, due to slow mail, bad weather conditions, and errors of various types, is high. This new distribution method allows for the following advantages:

- Reduction of the problem of "make-goods" for television stations when spots arrive too late.
- Topical commercials can be distributed quickly in response to idiosyncratic needs of specific markets.
- Drastically change the speed with which commercials and traffic instructions are disseminated.
- Reduction in advertising agencies' overhead in trafficking commercials.
- Allows agencies to skip an entire generation of taping and dubbing master commercials.
- Enhances the lead time for agency media and creative departments.
- Cuts out the use of expediting firms or forces them to adopt the new technology.

Using the WESTAR rate card, one industry spokesperson indicated that the cost, on an occasional basis, for a thirty-minute transmission at 4 a.m. is $45 plus $12.50 for each reception ("TV Commercials," 1979, pp. 43-44). Assuming the commercial was distributed to twenty stations, the cost would amount to $295. In comparison, distributing a duplicate by mail to twenty stations would amount to about $340 ($15 for the dub and $2 for shipping costs). Transmitting the commercial during prime time, however, would increase the cost to about $1,200 on an occasional-use basis ($225 for the thirty minutes' use plus $45 per reception).

Industry spokespersons estimate that these developments will take anywhere from three to five years before spot commercials distribution via DBS becomes widespread in North America. It remains to be seen how this new application of DBS will effect print houses, duplication companies, film laboratories, and the shipping industry once spot commercials distribution systems become a fait accompli.

Of course, many other application possibilities exist. In 1974 the Canadian Broadcasting Corporation used TELESAT to demonstrate how modifications in remote television stations would allow radio programs originating in the south — or any other location — to be received simultaneously with television signals. TELESAT's transportable earth stations allow for a maximum of flexibility, enabling broadcasters to disseminate live television programs from locations without permanent transmission facilities (Wigand, 1981b). A number of other experiments have already demonstrated the potential of providing various types of message services such as teletype, telephony, facsimile, and data transmission in numerous settings, ranging from emergency and disaster situations to off-shore oil rigs. One of the major uses of the new ANIK-C series of TELESAT, Canada's domestic satellites, is that of digital voice communications traffic between ten major Canadian cities (Sauve, 1978).

Technological Developments in Space. Research scientists will soon be able to carry out much of their work directly in space. Numerous scientists are already predicting that with the advent of the Space Shuttle and other new technology in the 1980's the construction, assembly, placement, checkout, repair, maintenance, retrieval, and stabilization of satellites in space will be made possible (Disher, 1979). Others are planning on the construction of large space platforms for building structures 50 to 70 meters long, so-called orbital antenna farms (Disher, 1979; Press, 1979; Goodwin, 1978; Edelson & Morgan, 1977). The key to all of these endeavors is the Space Shuttle, NASA's space transportation system. The present trend is somewhat of an inversion of past practices, in that previously, scientists had made every effort to produce satellites as small and as cost-efficient as possible, whereas current trends are increasing satellite antenna size and power. Utilizing the old type of satellite implied that very large and expensive earth stations had to be built. The new generation of satellites with increased antenna size, power, and sophistication, however, makes it possible to reduce the power and antenna size of the earth terminals, which in turn leads to lower construction and operating cost. At the same time, this savings will make it possible to build more earth stations for numerous purposes. The future — at least from the distribution, consumption, and technical side — of DBS looks bright indeed: Experiments have beamed color television through earth dish antennas as small as 0.6 m. Presently, a receiver station as small as 1 m costs under $1,000 (Eastland, 1977). The West German-produced receiver stations, with a diameter of 0.69 m, are said to cost between $280 and $560 when mass produced.

In October 1982, NBC will become the first commercial television network to experiment with the distribution of programs by satellite using facilities of the American Telephone & Telegraph Company. Presently, NBC uses RCA's Americom satellite to distribute a limited number of programs, mainly the *Today Show* and the *Tonight Show*. Some of these programs are shipped from one coast to the other where timing is a consideration. The American Telephone & Telegraph Company announced on September 25, 1981 that ABC, CBS, the National Entertainment Network Inc., and Robert Wold Communications are the next four customers scheduled to use the satellite service. The Public Broadcasting Service has transmitted its programs by satellite since 1978.

The three largest commercial U.S. television networks (ABC, CBS, NBC) have argued that one of the reasons that they object to an all-satellite broadcasting system, is the presently very expensive set-ups for *uplinks*, requiring a dish antenna of about 10 m in diameter. This equipment is rather inflexible and difficult to move, and costs approximately $200,000 to $400,000 (Taylor, 1978). In comparison, a 3 m-model used by TELESAT costs about $20,000 (Eastland, 1977). This difficulty and inflexibility in disseminating news and sports events from the point of origin in the field to headquarters via an all-satellite system remains a drawback for the broadcaster. What he needs to overcome this problem is a strong uplink signal for which large earth antennas are necessary. It also necessitates a modification of presently known satellites that are equipped with a relatively wide beam width of receiving antennas. The satellite receiving beam, however, should be rather narrow so that a "spot" beam focused on the transmitting point could be applied (Taylor, 1978).

Given such requirements, smaller earth-based antennas could be effectively and efficiently utilized in the direct field transmission via an all-satellite system. Such developments can be expected with the third generation of satellites to be launched in the late 1980s. Smaller uplink antennas could be readily mounted on trucks from where a spot beam could be transmitted directly to the receiving satellite. Furthermore, a dish antenna of such a size would be sufficiently small to be permanently installed atop buildings or sports complexes from which broadcasts frequently originate. The price of such small uplinks could certainly be afforded by most stations and networks.

There are a number of other technological developments that will alter the use of satellites. Among these innovations are the use of multibeam signals and on-board switching capabilities. They can also be expected with the third generation of satellites. The third-generation satellites will have to be planned during the 1983-1986 period. Considering parallel developments at the present time, it does not seem very likely that all the various kinds of social, political, legal, technical, economic, and other problem areas will be solved satisfactorily to the point that satellites can be used at an international level to their full capabilities. Taylor (1978) and others speculate that it will be the fourth generation of satellites in the mid-1990's that eventually will put satellites to their full use.

This fourth generation of satellites has aroused considerable interest. It is largely believed that this generation will be of a very different kind of satellite than are known at the present time. Several researchers (Disher, 1979; Press, 1979; Goodwin, 1978; Taylor, 1978; Edelson & Morgan, 1977) predict that there will be large platforms 50 to 70 meters long, so-called orbital antenna farms. Such structures are too large to be launched in their final shape. Various parts and pieces will be transported by several flights via the Space Shuttle and they will be assembled in space. Maintenance is to occur either by an on-board crew or by regular visits of maintenance personnel. The Shuttle will have reached parking orbit 300 km or 182 miles above earth. Edelson and Morgan (1977) describe how the cargo bay doors would open and the various prefabricated sections of the space platform could then be connected. A cranelike structure, the "cherry picker," will aid in this process (Goodwin, 1978) by allowing for the mounting of antennas with a diameter of up to 33 m, together with smaller antennas, transponders, switchers, and other equipment. Most of the equipment will be modular to facilitate maintenance and repair, as well as the addition of equipment to the platform. Such large platforms will have numerous advantages: Economies of scale, maintenance, etc. can be shared by all services on the platform, interconnections between systems, reductions in launch costs per transponder and in interference caused by crowding in orbit, smaller earth stations, savings due to sharing of antennas, power, and equipment, an increase in flexibility, and others.

Edelson and Morgan (1977) describe one such gigantic platform that could fill all the communication needs for the Western hemisphere. The capacity of such a proposed antenna farm is most impressive: It would include seventeen separate systems, would generate 20 kW, and would be the equivalent (in bandwidth) of 927 transponders as they are known today. Only eighteen of these are designated for television distribution, only one for direct-to-home broadcasting, and only one-half of one for educational television. Expressed differently, such an antenna farm would be the equivalent of 77 WESTAR-type satellites. Such a set up could be the basis for an all-satellite broadcasting system that could fulfill every imaginable need.

Terrestrial DBS Applications. Since about 1976 a number of researchers have developed rather attractive satellite system concepts. Recently, Bekey (1979) and his co-workers, under contract with NASA, have developed a number of conceptualizations ranging from personal radio-telephone terminals the size of a wristwatch to holographic image transmission for teleconferencing via satellite and small rooftop antennas. Bekey's ideas are the result of the implications of the complexity-inversion technique, i.e., shifting from the past practice of small satellites and large, expensive earth terminals to the future direction of satellite technology using larger and more powerful satellites with very small earth antennas. The implications of these developments are impressive. Rather than necessitating "wired cities," this technique would create "wireless cities." DBS would then become a potentially very effective and affordable means for developing nations to participate in the forefront of satellite communication (Wigand, 1981a, 1980b). To explicate these developments three examples will suffice here: personal radio-telephone terminals, electronic transmission of mail, and the wide dissemination of educational television.

Personal radio-telephone terminals are part of the personal communication satellite system proposed by Bekey (1979). Its aims are to interconnect about 10 percent of the 1990 U.S. population, about twenty-five million people. This interconnection would become possible through wrist-sized radio-telephones, and communication would occur on a direct, from-user-to-user basis. Users could be in one particular location or mobile, and communication with anyone else would become possible via groundterminal entry point. Without going into highly technical details, suffice it to note that rechargeable batteries with enough energy to transmit at least five one-minute calls per day without recharging are considered adequate. The personal radio-telephone terminal features a microphone and loudspeaker, an antenna, a push-button dialer, an emergency override button, a transmit button, and a number display. This device would weigh no more than a large wrist watch. Bekey estimates that such a terminal could be mass produced for about $10. A satellite-based "discipline" would impose a call duration of one minute, and requests for longer calls would receive a lower priority in the order of calls received. Emergency calls would receive the highest priority. Bekey states that developments toward such a system could begin in 1980 and could readily permit commercial operation in 1990. The entire space system is estimated to cost $2.3 billion, as compared to its terrestrial equivalent of $20.7 billion. In comparison, and for the same number of channels, today's telephone system charges about $13.8 billion.

Such a satellite-based system allowing direct reception would enjoy a wider coverage than the present microwave/wire-based terrestrial systems. Bekey estimates that the total research and development, investments, and operations costs could be amortized within a ten-year period by charging its customers a mere $.005 per minute of conversation. The alternative terrestrial system would have to charge about $.054 per minute, while today's networks would charge $.036 per minute (Bekey, 1979). Costs for any terrestrial system would increase with increased long-distance calls. Long distance, once again, is no longer an issue for the satellite transmission of signals.

Bekey's electronic mail system would exchange first-class mail between business and government buildings via satellite. Direct home reception is not discussed in his conceptualizations. Such a system could deliver about fifteen million pieces of mail per year among 544,000 small terminals, each installed atop a separate office complex. Fifteen million pieces of mail reflects about 15 percent of the anticipated 1990 U.S. mail flow (Bekey, 1979). Initial users would be corporations with assets of more than $1 million. All messages would be digital and each would include a receiver-sender code number. Each terminal is designed to have a ten-minute buffer storage. The U.S. Postal Service (USPS), as well as its PTT counterparts in several European countries, have engaged in preliminary studies and experiments involving the transmission of electronic mail. These systems, however, are still dependent on the physical pickup and delivery of the mail piece. Bekey's proposed system requires at best an in-house distribution. A cost comparison revealed that the USPS hybrid system could deliver a letter for $.099 per letter, while the satellite-based system proposed by Bekey (1979) could do the same for $.026 per letter. The cost comparison alone would suggest that we rush ahead with a pure space-operated system. On the other hand, the various social implications are still difficult to foresee in their entirety. Policymakers will have to struggle with the job displacement of a large workforce and with retraining this workforce for other jobs. Still other problem areas are that the same organizational structure will have to remain for those individuals who cannot be reached by electronic mail. Such exclusions will occur by design, package delivery, other classes of mail, etc.

The educational television system proposed by Bekey would interconnect all 65,000 schools in the United States as well as their 16,000 district headquarters (or all 4,000 universities and colleges, with 250,000 remote

Direct Satellite Broadcasting

Table 8.2
User Cost Comparison for Educational Television

	Cost[a] per School per Year in Dollars	Cost per Classroom-Hour in Dollars	Cost per Pupil-Hour in Cents	Total[b] Twenty-Year Costs in Billions of Dollars
Space initiative	4,200	0.36	1.2	2.73
Ground alternative	20,800	1.78	5.9	13.53
Teachers	≈ 116,000	≈ 10.00	≈ 33.3	≈ 75.4

a. Average of ten classrooms per school equipped for educational television; six hours/day, five days/week, nine months/year; thirty pupils/classroom.
b. Ten-year research, development, training and equipment; ten-year operations and maintenance; all user equipment.

learning sites) with color television and interactive audio. Via the use of satellites, such a system would utilize small dish antennas on each school building to disseminate its own messages and programs. At the same time, programs could be shared between poor and rich districts throughout the United States. In order to make such an effort feasible, the satellite would have to transmit almost 1,500 television channels simultaneously through 600 beams, each covering an area of 80 by 160 km on earth. Such beams would be directed toward populated areas. A total of 634 simultaneous uplink channels would be required from the districts for program origination. The satellite would transmit its signals to 0.92-m-wide antennas installed at each school. Transmission from the schools would occur via antennas with a diameter of 3.05 m located on school district buildings. Bekey envisages three alternatives for program distribution for educational television: coaxial cables and program sharing between districts via fiber-optic cables as the ground option; a conventional educational system using teachers; and the space initiative already described. Bekey made a cost comparison on the basis of a six-hour day for instructional programming five days a week, nine months a year, with thirty students per class and half the classrooms (about ten rooms per school) equipped for educational television in each of the 65,000 schools in the United States. The space initiative proves by far to be the least expensive as reflected in Table 8.2. These figures are compared against the average cost for a teacher, which results in about $10 per hour. Assuming that the ten classrooms would have simultaneous instruction, the resulting cost of teachers per school per year would amount to at least $116,000, compared to $4,200 for the space initiative and $20,000 for the strictly terrestrial alternative.

POLICY IMPLICATIONS

Given virtually unlimited technical possibilities in DBS, it appears that the broadcast industry must actively participate in these technological developments. This point becomes important considering that broadcasters are told what they can do with the satellites post facto; they deserve an active part in these future developments. In a sense it becomes bothersome to note that the WARC 1979 conference in Geneva attempted to allocate the airwaves up to the year 2000. How can proper allocations be made that are functional when the various technological developments of satellite technology are not yet determined? Taylor (1978, p. 126) points out that this implies putting "technological development in a straightjacket for twenty years when we have no idea what services the next generation of viewers will want."

Satellites are at present the essential element to broadcast development until the year 2000. Some of the technological developments described earlier may appear today as science-fictionlike dreams. These developments, however, are good possibilities for the future. The technology in many instances already exists, but its implementation in many cases means a large-scale effort and there may be doubts as to whether these ideas are economically justified at the present time. There are other hurdles to be overcome, such as international agreements, national regulatory boards and agencies, as well as various governmental bodies. The advent of satellite broadcasting is a primary example of how technology has developed well before man is able to put it into proper use when considering the social, legal, and international implications.

A number of important questions will have to be answered that are in part based on the organizational control of the airwaves in various countries, i.e., the issuing of licenses to private operators by the government versus the functioning of a monopolylike organization in the form of the PTTs. For example, will the PTTs be competing with private communication companies? Will these companies possibly exploit the lucrative business otherwise needed by the PTTs to subsidize rural services, if and when they are allowed to compete? Will the European PTTs invest their funds in cable networks, etc. because of previous heavy investment efforts in terrestrial systems, even though a rooftop-to-rooftop, satellite-based system may be cheaper? Is the lack of competition in the satellite business the best route to go for PTTs, and is this in the best interest of the public? DBS may trigger a long-overdue reevaluation of the various social needs and gratifications and national purposes that television and radio serve. The needs differ from country to country, based largely on the level of several areas of development. The final test, however, will be whether numerous and diverse institutions from the private and governmental sectors for broadcasting, telecommunications, and satellites services can eventually cooperate and act in concert. Only when these institutions have adapted to this new technology can national broadcasting goals be achieved.

One of the main advantages of DBS is the possibility of reaching a worldwide television audience and thus enhancing worldwide understanding and cooperation, in addition to promoting and extending freedom of information and communication. This is not to say that this *audience* would be watching the same global television program at the same time. There are too many factors that would make such an effort infeasible: Language barriers and cultural differences would fragment a worldwide audience, and one-third of the world is asleep at any given point in time. There are only a few truly international events where such a network would benefit a worldwide audience: the Olympics, soccer championships, world crisis situations, space explorations, UN events, etc. This limited demand, however, can be met by interconnecting various national and regional broadcast satellite systems.

In developed and industrialized countries, DBS is likely to be incorporated into existing networks in an auxiliary role. This seems to be happening and will be the case for the very near future. In the case of the United States, the main interest in satellites has been to provide cheaper networking facilities in lieu of coaxial or microwave terrestrial connections. Especially in the case of Western Europe, today's frequency assignments do not make possible more than about four national television programs in each country. To date no Western European country has developed more than three channels (programs). Past television viewers' behavior in border areas, however, has demonstrated that viewers are willing to pay for sets and antennas that can receive programs from neighboring countries (Wigand, 1979). This behavior, then, may be an indication that the demand for additional programs has not been saturated. DBS could meet such a demand for Western Europe.

Efforts at the national and international levels are necessary to see what roles DBS can play in a given country's development process. In the past, developing countries designed their broadcast systems so that they would reach the people in major urban areas, the rich, the educated, whereas the accessibility to the media in many rural areas was limited (Wigand, 1976). The content and form of the messages are usually tailored for urbanites. Messages become dysfunctional when content and form do not agree with the cognitive structure of the recipient.

The advent and possibility of the widespread use of DBS gives policymakers another stab at examining the *structure* and *function* of their respective broadcast systems. Lucas describes an experience with instructional television, and one can observe similar examples in the field of health care delivery utilizing DBS. In part, Lucas makes the point that the problem lies in the design of the telecommunication service that quite frequently does not fit the pattern of instruction or health care. This implies that users must take the initiative to use DBS in their setting and shape it to their needs. Similarly, policymakers in most developing countries previously started and implemented broadcast policies with an overwhelming emphasis on structure. This means that broadcast systems typically were initiated in highly populated urban areas. These residents received radio and television content that was often ill suited for their local and national purposes. In addition, even when the content would have been well suited for the urban dweller, it may have been the case that the rural resident would have been in higher need of broadcasting services in terms of national development priorities. This did not occur due to structural constraints in terms of operating a national broadcasting system. It can be readily seen that a proper interplay between structure and function when designing a broadcast system did not occur in many developing countries, and a structural-functional approach was typically emphasized. In such a setting mass media are socializing agents in the development process. With the advent and possible widespread use of low-cost DBS even for developing countries, policymakers should emphasize a functional-structural approach; i.e., one should start with the functions of a broadcast system, from which the structure will emerge. DBS readily overcomes the previous structural hurdles with regard to transmitters, geographical problems, etc., since DBS can be available anywhere in a wireless world.

Increased flexibility, as well as increased television program offerings and diversity, can become a reality due to DBS. Some may argue that increased diversity and choice will merely mean more old movies, more detective stories, more superheroes, etc. on the television screen. These popular tastes and preferences are quite adequately catered to around the world, but they do not decrease the value of individual choices. Mass audience preferences cannot allow for programming for special interests and minority segments of an audience. Program diversification, then, will be a desirable development associated with DBS that can increase the quality of information, entertainment, and news, as well as the range of choices available to individual viewers (Wigand, 1981b).

A case in point is the Public Broadcasting Service (PBS) in the United States. PBS, comprised of a membership of over 260 public television station representatives from around the United States, recently established for its own purposes three "mini-networks" whose programs are delivered simultaneously via the WESTAR satellite. A fourth channel will be added later. One service carries the basic television programming featuring entertainment and cultural and public affairs shows. Another service carries educational programming, and the third features specialized programs of local or regional interest. Some PBS stations are also equipped to transmit their local programs and productions to the Washington, D.C. headquarters for later networkwide distribution. Satellite technology thus enables the network to transmit on several different lines rather than just one, as is the practice with commercial networks. In addition, PBS is now giving its local stations a choice of what to air. The economics are such that after the earth terminals are paid for, the annual operating costs of the four channels will be less than the cost of one terrestrial channel.

In summary, in developed and industrialized countries satellites allow broadcasters to operate as they have in the past. What is new is the added convenience, lower costs, the fact that geographical distance is no longer a concern, the increase in the number of broadcast sources, as well as the flexibility and immediacy of such operations. There is a widely-held belief that broadcasting via satellites will establish a new and more vital image of the medium of television. Especially in the case of less-developed countries, the possibility now exists of reaching large audiences at a low cost and with tailored programs essential to their future development and survival in a complex and everchanging world.

Many developing countries do not yet operate extensive television broadcast systems. The advent of DBS no doubt constitutes a potential of magnitude that is difficult to assess at the present time. At a relatively low cost entire national broadcast systems could be established without the high costs of terrestrial interconnections. Economic realities would at first not allow for direct-to-home reception, but community receivers are likely to be installed by the states' governments. It is obvious that in this situation, access to the system and control over programming are dependent on the country's government and subject to its priorities. In most developing countries, the education of their citizens ranks at the top of a priority list. Wigand (1976) and others have described the value of television programming for national development, providing education and information as well as a sense of national identity and unity. Past demonstration experiments have already shown that satellite broadcasting holds substantial promise of accelerating national development for educational purposes in such areas as literacy, family planning, health care, training in agricultural and mechanical skills, and others.

Decisions for the implementation of such systems, however, will have to compete with other priorities. Often the engineering and technical know-how will have to be imported for the design and operation of such systems. The old problem with regard to indigenous programming most likely will remain, and much of the software may have to be acquired abroad, just as in the past. If the latter prevails, translation and cultural differences of educational programs may reduce the communication effectiveness, if not constitute an even larger barrier.

These brief deliberations suggest that DBS may not necessarily provide a panacea to fulfill the educational and cultural needs of developing countries in the next few years. Bilateral, if not multilateral, cooperation, as well as regional or interregional efforts, will be necessary to accomplish these goals.

REFERENCES

Antwort der Bundesrepublik auf die kleine Anfrage der Abgeordneten Lenzer et al. — Drucksache 8/2842; Entwicklung und Nutzung eines Direkt-Fernseh-Satelliten (TV-SAT) — Drucksache 8/2910; May 30, 1979. Reprinted in *Media Perspektiven,* 1979, 7, 503-516.

Bargellini, P. L. *A synopsis of commercial satellite communication systems.* Unpublished paper, Comsat Laboratories, 1977.

Barna, B. Spreading the word and data. *Dun's Review,* 1979, *114*(2), 76-77.

Bekey, I. Big comsats for big jobs at lower user cost. *Astronautics & Aeronautics,* 1979, *17*(2), 42-56.

Belitz, M. Personal telephone conversation, July 26, 1979.

Blonstein, J. L. EUROSPACE: The seventh U.S.-European conference on "Space Business in the Eighties." *Satellite Communication,* 1978, *2*(12), 36-38.

Business communications: The new frontier. *Fortune,* October 9, 1978, 26-80.

Coates, J. F. Aspects of innovation: Public policy issues in telecommunications development. *Telecommunications Policy,* 1977, *1*(3), 196-206. (a)

Coates, J. F. *The future of telecommunications.* Paper presented to the International Telecommunications Exposition, Atlanta, Georgia, October 13, 1977. (b)

Commonwealth Government Task Force, *National communications satellite system: Report July 1978.* Canberra, Australia: Australian Government Publishing Service, 1978.

Dauses, M. A. Direct satellite broadcasting by satellites and freedom of information. *Journal of Space Law,* 1975, *3*(1 & 2), 59-72.

Disher, J. H. Space transportation, satellite services, and space platforms. *Astronautics & Aeronautics,* 1979, *17*(4), 42-51, 67.

Eastland, T. A. Satellite communications and related applications. In *Research and development.* Ottawa, Canada: Government of Canada, Department of Communications, 1977.

Edelson, B. I., & Morgan, W. L. Orbital antenna farms. *Astronautics & Aeronautics,* 1977, *15*(9), 20-28.

Engler, N., Strange, J., & Hein, G. *Compendium of applications technology satellite user experiments 1967-1973.* Cleveland, OH: NASA-Lewis, August 1976.

Federal Ministry of Posts and Telecommunications. *Telecommunications report.* Bonn, Federal Republic of Germany: Federal Ministry of Posts and Telecommunications, Commission for the Development of the Telecommunication System, 1976.

Friedman, M. Blair experiment in commercials distribution by satellite may lead to major commitment. *Television/Radio Age,* 1979, *26*(18), 40-41, 75-79.

Frutkin, A. W. Direct/community broadcast projects using space satellites. *Journal of Space Law,* 1975, *3*(1 & 2), 17-24.

Galloway, E. Direct broadcast satellites and space law. *Journal of Space Law,* 1975, *3*(1 & 2), 3-16.

The global communications satellite catalogue. *Satellite Communications,* January 1978, 27-30.

Golden, D. A. Personal correspondence. July 3, 1979.

Goodwin, C. J. Space platforms for building large space structures. *Astronautics & Aeronautics,* 1978, *16*(10), 44-47.

Grey, J., & Gerard, M. *A critical review of the state of foreign space technology.* New York: American Institute of Aeronautics and Astronautics, 1978, 9-24.

Hanell, S. Prospects for specialized satellite communications services in Europe in the 1980s. In *Multinational telecommunications.* Uxbridge, Middlesex, UK: Online Conferences, 1975.

Henderson, A. T. National Communications Satellite Evaluation Support Group, Australian Postal and Telecommunications Department. Personal correspondence, August 6, 1979.

Hill, A. CATV & satellites: The sky is the limit. *Satellite Communications,* 1978, *2*(12), 20-25.

Homet, R. S., Jr. Communications policy making in Western Europe. *Journal of Communication,* 1979, *29*(2), 31-38.

Hudson, H. E. Implications for development communications. *Journal of Communication,* 1979, *29*(1), 179-186.

International Telecommunication Union. *Final protocol: Space telecommunications,* July 17, 1971, [1972] 23 U.S.T., at 1573, n.1,-1574 (effective January 1, 1973).

Johansen, R. Social evaluations of teleconferencing. *Telecommunications Policy,* 1977, *1*(4), 395-419.

Kader, S. A. Secretary General, Arab States Broadcasting Union. Personal correspondence, July 7, 1979.

Kaiser, J. Wir brauchen sie nicht, aber wir kriegen sie: Fernsehdirektempfangssatelliten für die Bundesrepublik. Broadcast on Sender Freies Berlin, Berlin, Federal Republic of Germany, November 9, 1978.

Masmoudi, M. The new world information order. *Journal of Communication,* 1979, *29*(2), 172-185.

Mayer, R. Minister for Research and Technology, Federal Republic of Germany, Personal correspondence, July 17, 1979.

Messerschmitt-Bölkow-Blohm. Personal correspondence, July 6, 1979.

Molo, S. The challenge of satellite communications in direct broadcasting. *Proceedings of an EBU-ESA Symposium on Direct Satellite Broadcasting.* Dublin, Ireland, May 23-25, 1977, 139-148.

Nordenstreng, K., & Schiller, H. I. (Eds.). *National sovereignty and international communication.* Norwood, NJ: Ablex, 1979.

Parker, E. B. Communication satellites for rural development. *Telecommunications Policy,* 1978, *2*(4), 309-315.

Pikus, I. M. Legal implications of direct broadcasting technology. *Journal of Space Law,* 1975, *3*(1 & 2), 17-24.

Ploman, E. W. *Kommunikation durch Satelliten.* Mainz, Federal Republic of Germany: von Hase und Kohler, 1974.

Pool, I. de S. Direct broadcasting satellites and cultural integrity. *Society,* September/October 1975, 47-56.

Press, F. U.S. space policy — a framework for the 1980s. *Astronautics & Aeronautics,* 1979, *17*(7-8), 34-35.

Read, W. H. Information as a national resource. *Journal of Communication,* 1979, *29*(1), 172-178.

Rice, R. E., & Parker, E. B. *Cost and policy implications of communication satellite systems for rural telecommunications in developing countries.* Paper presented to the seventh Annual Telecommunications Policy Research Conference, Skytop, PA, April 29-May 1, 1979.

Robinson, G. O. (Ed.). *Communications for tomorrow: Policy perspectives for the 1980s.* New York: Praeger, 1978.

Sauve, J. *Communications satellites: The Canadian experience.* Unpublished paper, Montreal, Canada, 1978, p. 3.
SBS's services must fly this year. *Business Week,* January 25, 1982, *76,* 81.
Schendel, A. H. *Considerations on communications satellite activities in Europe.* Unpublished paper, no date.
Scott R. The challenge of communication by direct broadcast satellite: Viewers' needs and broadcasters' opportunities. *Proceedings of an EBU-ESA Symposium on Direct Satellite Broadcasting.* Dublin, Ireland, May 23-25, 1977, 149-154.
Tabussi, S. J. Personal correspondence, August 1, 1979.
Taylor, J. P. Satellite systems of the 1990s will operate from huge platforms orbiting in space. *Television/Radio Age,* 1978, *25*(24), 26-29, 124-126.
Thiele, R. Satelliten-Rundfunk: Anmerkungen zum gegenwärtigen Stand. *Media Perspektiven,* 1976, *6,* 405-418.
Topol, S. The growth and future of satellite communications. *Earth station symposium '78.* Atlanta, CA: Scientific Atlanta, 1978.
TV commercials via satellite: Who are the winners, losers? *Television/Radio Age,* 1979, *26*(20), 42-44, 90, 94.
United Nations. Report of the Legal Sub-Committee on the Work of its Eighteenth Session (12 March - 6 April 1979), April 10, 1979, A/AC.105/240.
Weintraub, B. Cable TV mogul sinks big money into 24-hour newscast program. *The Arizona Republic,* October 14, 1979, p. G-9.
Wigand, Rolf T. The process of mass communication: Mass media as agents of socialization in developing countries. *Konferenzprotokoll der Association Internationale des Etudes et Recherches sur l'Information,* 1976, *2,* 473-486.
Wigand, Rolf T. Mass media abundance: Selected developments and audience effects in the United States of America. *Communications — International Journal of Communication Research,* 1979, *5,* 2-3, 213-239.
Wigand, Rolf T. The Direct Satellite Connection: Definitions and Prospects. *Journal of Communication,* 1980a, *30*(2), 140-146.
Wigand, Rolf T. *The direct satellite connection: Its future and policy implications.* Paper presented to the session on "Dissemination Policy and Communication Research: Models and New Directions," International Communication Association annual convention, Acapulco, Mexico, May 21, 1980b.
Wigand, Rolf T. Satellitenkommunikation: Die heutige Situation in Nordamerika. *Media Perspektiven,* 1980c, *7,* 445-456.
Wigand, Rolf T. *The future of telecommunications.* Paper presented to the "Telecommunications in the Year 2000: National and International Perspectives" conference, New Brunswick, NJ, November 17-20, 1981a.
Wigand, Rolf T. *Local communication and communication research: An American perspective.* Paper presented at the Congress on "Local Communication and Communication Research," International Union for Research on Communication, Baden-Baden, Federal Republic of Germany, November 12-13, 1981b.

COMMUNICATION REVIEWS AND COMMENTARIES

9 ● Public Communication and Televised Presidential Debates

DENNIS K. DAVIS ● SIDNEY KRAUS
Cleveland State University

THE emergence of new media technology has created a resurgence of concern for the survival of democracy. Benjamin Barber (1982, p. 21) argued that "this may be our last opportunity to turn the technology of the new age into a servant of an old political idea: democracy. Democracy will have a difficult time surviving under the best of circumstances; with television as its adversary, it seems almost sure to perish." Although Barber has chosen to take an extreme position, his views are echoed by others. But not all scholars are pessimistic. In her book *Electronic Democracy,* Anne Saldich (1979) suggests that television has transformed the American political process, personalizing remote politicians and activating social groups. She celebrates the arrival of new technology that she believes will create the diversity on which democracy thrives (p. 91). But Barber tells us that this same technology will create a new tower of Babel: "The critical communication *between* groups that is essential to forging of a national culture and public vision will vanish" (1982, p. 23).

For over two decades the contribution to democracy of one form of televised communication has been studied. A critical reexamination of our efforts to make televised presidential debates serve democracy illustrates the practical problems we face whenever we try to make a new technology deliver an old message. Since their introduction in 1960, televised presidential debates have attracted widespread public attention while provoking controversy among scholars. Some critics (Auer, 1962; Bitzer & Rueter, 1980) labeled these debates as counterfeit. They argued that televised debates are deceptive because they do not provide a true confrontation between candidates in which clearly opposing positions on vital issues are presented. Other researchers (Chaffee, 1978; Kraus & Davis, 1982a) defend debates as a practical means of efficiently informing voters about

Correspondence and requests for reprints: Sidney Kraus, Department of Communication, Cleveland State University, Cleveland, OH 44115.

issues and candidates. Their arguments are based on those of other scholars and are grounded in recent survey research that demonstrates that debates do inform the public, including those segments that tend to be less interested in politics (Kraus, 1962, 1979).

Even defenders of modern political debates admit that debates can and should be restructured to make them more useful to voters. However, they argue that it will take considerable effort to convince politicians and political parties that restructured debates can serve their interests. Modern candidates think in terms of winning elections, not in terms of developing political institutions that will strengthen democracy (Kraus & Davis, 1982b). Parties seek ways of exploiting forms of communication such as advertising, which were developed for very different purposes, instead of developing new formats for political messages. When parties discovered that long political speeches failed to attract viewers, they turned to 60-second commercials. Candidates and parties agreed to debates only when they believed such debates would be advantageous to them, not because they felt compelled to serve democracy.

Though televised debates have occurred in three elections and are likely to occur in the future, we seem no closer to institutionalizing them in a way that would clearly improve our electoral process. We now have much empirical evidence concerning the consequences of past debates, but this evidence does not provide us with a definitive means of structuring ideal debates. The challenge we face involves adapting an ancient strategy for structuring public communication to make it fit a modern technology and modern needs. Planning for past debates has been haphazard, involving intense negotiations in very limited periods of time. Such planning has neglected the historical and philosophical grounding of debates. In this chapter we have sought to analyze the origin and development of debates in a way that could prove useful to future policy making. Our intent is to consider what debates might be expected to do for our society and to suggest how the best use might be made of them.

We also hope that this analysis of the potential contribution and hazards of televised debates can contribute to a broader understanding of how our new technology might be made to serve the best interests of democracy. A century of experience with mass media technology has demonstrated that there are no easy formulas for making new technologies serve political ideals. Although it has long been recognized that the way in which communication is structured in a society seems to be intimately associated with its political institutions (Siebert, Peterson, & Schramm, 1963), this relationship is not as simple as it has been portrayed by some theorists. Complete freedom of communication, even if it were technically, economically, and politically feasible, would not guarantee that a nation would become or remain a democracy. Nor does the imposition of specific restrictions on communication necessarily put a nation on the road to totalitarianism. Completely free communication can be chaotic and ineffective. We may like to believe that our own media system is completely free, but it is in fact controlled by a variety of economic, legal, and political restraints. On the other hand, scholars of Soviet mass communication have noted that completely centralized control of media has proved difficult to maintain (Markham, 1967). The Russians have been as puzzled about applying new technologies to serve political ends as have Americans. Development of new forms of communication that will strengthen democracy requires careful deliberation and research.

CLASSICAL DEMOCRATIC THEORY

The tradition of public communication that led to the development of debates began in fifth-century B.C. Greece. This was a period of radical social and political change in Greece as it evolved from a traditional, militaristic social order into a fledgling democracy. According to Harper (1979, p. 16) the Greeks created the first society in which various new forms of public communication were so well accepted that skill in public speaking became an important basis for acquisition and maintenance of political power. Debates were one of many ways that communication came to be structured in public situations. Protagoras of Abdera (481-411 B.C.) is credited with originating the debate format (Keefe, Harte, & Norton, 1982, p.2).

Persons who could not speak effectively sought to hire others to speak for them in the courts, legislative assemblies, and public ceremonies. This created a demand for persons educated as public speakers and spawned various schools of rhetoric. But the new forms of public communication were not well respected. The dominant Greek political philosophy, originated by Parmenides, viewed the social order as fundamentally static and argued that public communication produced only superficial changes. Morrall (1977, pp. 31-32) notes that "the denial by Parmenides and his school of the reality of change took the stuffing, as it were, out of the whole process of rational deliberation on future community policies, a process which lay at the heart of the newly emerged democracy." An irresolvable conflict arose between the traditional elites who dominated Greek democracy so that it served their interests and persons whose power derived largely from their skill as public communicators. Such persons were feared as potential demogogues, and care was taken to limit their power to communicate.

The Greeks never managed to fully integrate public communication into their political order. Although they demonstrated that such communication might provide a foundation for a creative and productive social order, they failed to adequately understand and control the new forms of communication. Greek society alternated between periods of relatively open public communication and periods of suppression. The new forms of public communication were often abused during periods of freedom. Demogogues arose, only to be suppressed. Morrall (1977, p. 23) attributes the collapse of Athenian democracy to the fact that Athens was not democratic enough. The exclusion of 50 percent or more of the population (women, slaves, resident foreigners) from citizenship "was a standing contradiction to its own premises of equality and freedom." It was argued by many Greek leaders and philosophers, however, that the inclusion of such persons would be impractical because it would be impossible to adequately educate them to responsibly participate in public gatherings.

THE SOPHISTS

Two important, competing schools of rhetoric developed that proposed very different roles for public communication in democracy. The earliest of these schools, the Sophists, was quite pragmatic in its approach to public communication. The Sophists focused on teaching skills for presentation of messages, but they did not teach how to critically evaluate the substance of messages. They were not concerned about the possible abuses of the skills they taught and so neglected the teaching of ethics. The students of the Sophists gained a reputation for unscrupulous and self-serving public communication. Harper (1979, p. 24) describes the Sophist approach:

> Rhetoric in the initial phase of the classical period, was thought of primarily as a technical skill. It consisted of a set of prescriptions for delivering public speeches in the courts, legislative assemblies, and other public gatherings. It consisted of rules for gathering materials, organizing them into messages, and delivering them orally to large groups of people.

Morrall (1977, p. 32) views the rise of the Sophists as a backlash against the Parmenidean school. He maintains they made "a gesture of despairing commonsense in protest against the inexorably static world picture which the Parmenidean philosophical orthodoxy sought to impose on the free-wheeling play of reason in political action which had become the Athenian ideal."

The Sophists served to advance public communication by formalizing the teaching of the techniques that enabled persons to communicate more effectively in public. They worked to promote the acceptance of public communication as a means of resolving political and social problems. But although many men educated by the Sophists rose to power in Greece, they failed to conclusively establish public communication as an inviolable basis for democracy.

THE SOCRATIC SCHOOL

The Socratic school developed, in part, as a reaction against the Sophists. Socrates, Plato, and their followers urged the necessity of developing a broad theory of public communication to provide ethical as well as technical guides to communication. They believed that well-structured public communication could be made to serve the public good. They spoke out against the willingness of the Sophists to teach techniques that served to arouse emotion and impede rational decision making. Reason was one of the primary virtues revered by the Socratic school. They believed that a just and good society must be ruled by men trained to reason objectively on the basis of factual information.

The Socratic school gradually developed an approach that emphasized communication rules and skills intended to encourage the development and application of reason. Their approach was based upon the format of the dialogue developed by Socrates and later perfected by Plato and Aristotle. They assumed that, if public communication is structured in ways which support rational decision making, then it will best serve the public good. Unfortunately, they did not equate the public good with democracy. Many members of this school were quite skeptical about democratic forms of government. One major source of their skepticism lay in their view that a quite complex theory was necessary to properly structure the use of public communication. Limited social and intellectual resources made it unlikely that this theory could be widely taught, understood, and applied. As an alternative they proposed educating a small elite, to whom Plato referred as philosopher kings, who would exercise political power for the public good. Aristotle served as the tutor of Alexander the Great and hoped that Alexander's military conquests would usher in a new age of reason. He appears to have been unconcerned about Alexander's suppression of public communication in Athens, believing it to be improperly structured and therefore not worth preserving. Aristotle believed that the best forms of public communication would only flourish under authoritarian rule, but he recognized that it would be difficult to find an enlightened dictator who was willing to risk the luxury of such communication.

The followers of Socrates shared his idealistic faith that public communication could be used to develop reason and gain knowledge of ideal truth. Once truth was discovered, then an ideal social order could be created. Socrates dared to pursue truth by asking embarrassing questions and pursuing dangerous lines of thought. His eventual execution as a traitor only served to intensify the commitment of his followers to his ideals.

The legacy of the Socratic school is an uncompromising commitment to the use of highly specialized forms of public communication to pursue the truth, but not necessarily to develop democracy. Democratic political institutions may be seen as irrelevant or even detrimental to this search. On the other hand, the Sophists were unswerving in their defense of democratic social orders that would permit them unrestricted practice of their public speaking skills. Neither school was able to develop a theory of public communication that would allow such communication to be used to advance democracy. It is not surprising that public communication came to be regarded by subsequent elites as an experiment that had failed.

THE ROMANS

The Romans borrowed many Greek ideas about rhetoric, but also failed to develop a truly practical theory. Meador (1979, p. 65) describes the decline of public communication in Rome:

> Though the Romans were familiar with Socratic theory, conditions in the new Empire were inimical to creative oratory: the length of speeches, number of advocates, and duration of court trials were reduced; orators ran the risk of crossing the Emperor in every speech they gave; the dynamic issues of the past were for the most part absent; the power of the monarchy steadily encroached on the self-governing bodies. The problem of reconciling the organizational requirements of empire and self-government based on free interchange of ideas proved too difficult for Rome.

The experience of the Greeks and Romans highlights several problems surrounding the introduction and use of any new forms of public communication. Ideal forms of public communication (such as highly structured and abstract philosophical debates) have few direct practical applications, and those forms of public communication that come to be widely practiced tend to involve the arousal of emotion and to entertain. The Greeks offer no simple answers to this dilemma. Instead, they suggest what can happen if no answer is found. Democracy based on abuse of public communication will fail, and it is unlikely that ideal forms of public communication will flourish in a dictatorship, no matter how benign.

The Greeks also illustrate the vital interrelationship between public education and public communication. People must be taught skills which enable them to communicate in public. Ideally, these skills should include ethical standards and critical abilities that enable them to use public communication wisely. The Greeks believed that some men possess the ability to think rationally and that certain forms of communication can aid in the development and exercise of reason. But they fail to demonstrate that all men can be educated to use their powers of reason. New forms of public communication cannot be expected to spontaneously create the educated audiences required if such communication is to be used effectively.

MEDIEVAL PUBLIC COMMUNICATION

The rise of Christianity coupled with the collapse of the Roman Empire created a totally new climate for public communication theory and skills. Christian leaders perceived no need for theories that would permit the use of reason to discover truth. They believed that the truth had already been revealed to them (Harper, 1979, pp. 70-71.) Some interest remained in certain practical skills, such as the structuring of letters and the delivery of sermons. Letters served as a primary means of communication between religious and political elites. Sermons communicated religious ideas and demands from elites to the lay audiences. Public communication ceased to be used as a means of defining and debating societal goals. Rather, it was subordinated to theology (Harper, 1979, pp. 76-77).

Another factor complicated the application of classical forms of public communication during the medieval period. Greek society was based on oral communication, but in medieval times the written word became paramount. Socratic and Sophist theories were not easily applied to written communication. One such attempt was made by St. Augustine in *On Christian Doctrine* (Harper, 1979, pp. 76-77). He carefully reinterpreted classical theories and demonstrated how their principles could be applied to the interpretation and the advancement of scripture. His writings enabled parts of the classical theories to be preserved, but essential ideas were discarded.

The classical debate format survived as a part of the curriculum of medieval education (Keefe, Harte, & Norton, 1982, pp. 3-4). Disputation was considered a means of teaching logic. Students were encouraged to develop their ability for abstract reasoning by debating topics drawn from logic and philosophy. Everyday-life issues and problems were avoided as topics. Debate became a means of educating a small elite and ceased to be a widely practiced form of public communication. The revival of debate as public communication awaited the decline of church authority and the revival of classical traditions.

POPULAR CHALLENGES TO CHURCH AUTHORITY

The transition from the medieval period to the modern era occurred gradually. Modern scholars now reject the notion that there was a sudden sharp break between the middle ages and the Reformation and Renaissance that followed. The authority of the medieval church was never completely consolidated. The church delegated temporal political authority to many competing kings and lords. These leaders provided protection from invaders in return for services and taxes. At the bottom of medieval society, the vast majority of persons subsisted as serfs and peasants. Their loyalty was often coerced or induced through elaborate public ceremonies and rituals.

The power of medieval political and religious leaders was eroded by a slow revival of classical values and ideas by intellectuals and by a series of widespread popular rebellions that mobilized the serfs and peasants against their superiors.

In the thirteenth and fourteenth centuries, several intellectuals drew the attention of elites to Roman law and Greek philosophy as alternate bases for political power. They advanced a variety of arguments that effectively undermined the temporal authority of the church (Ullmann, 1966, pp. 215-279). At the same time popular challenges to this authority appeared. Popular associations were created to demand control over specific aspects of daily life. Guilds and unions demanded control over jobs. Village organizations strengthened their ability to govern on the basis of populist traditions extending back to the barbarian era. A variety of heretical religious leaders were able to quickly mobilize large popular followings because the church did so little to effectively educate the masses against heresy. The church sought to control such heresy by establishing orders of friars to work directly with the lay people, but then faced the problem of controlling these orders.

Some of the most revolutionary ideas to be rediscovered from the classical period were those involving public communication. In particular the arguments of the Socratic school aroused interest and growing acceptance. Aristotle's synthesis of Socratic ideas was viewed as providing an alternate way of conceptualizing the temporal world. Although most scholars continued to accept the divinely ordained right of the church to define and control the supernatural, a minority began to argue that Aristotle's notions of natural laws discovered by reason provided a useful alternative for understanding and controlling the world of everyday life. Not surprisingly, these scholars found support for their arguments among political leaders who were looking for ways to avoid reliance on the church to justify their temporal authority. As Aristotle's views on natural law and reason gained acceptance, so did reverence for public communication as a means to these ends.

THE RENAISSANCE

As the centralized authority of the church diminished, the possibility of engaging in new forms of public communication increased. Renaissance intellectuals and small businessmen read and reinterpreted classical theories. They saw in these theories a justification for both intellectual and economic freedom. Freedom of thought and free trade could be viewed as natural rights, which were not to be impaired by religious or political authorities.

Some of the most vocal and effective support for public communication came from religious groups. Small Protestant sects that sprang up in the wake of the Reformation were subjected to political and religious persecution. They were forced to develop effective communication strategies in order to survive and grow. Successful Protestant leaders were highly skilled in the use of oral and written forms of public communication. Their right to use these forms of communication was constantly threatened. Some of the most astute leaders sought to defend their right to communicate, not just on religious grounds, but also on the basis of Aristotelian notions. The most famous of these defenses in the English language is found in *Areopagitica,* in which Milton argues that all men must have the right to use public communication to search for truth that can bring them closer to an understanding of God.

During the Renaissance the tradition of academic debates gained increasing favor. Debates were strongly associated with Greek and Roman ideals and thus were considered important to reviving these ideals. Disputations were central to the curriculum of secularized colleges and universities. Debating became an extracurricular and intercollegiate activity (Keefe, Harte, & Norton, 1982, p. 4). Debating was considered an essential part of a liberal education, which would create free men capable of using reason to make wise decisions.

But while the Renaissance brought new freedoms to elites, it made the daily lives of the majority more chaotic. New forms of public communication helped to spawn political, social, and intellectual movements that threatened traditional elites. Elites responded with armed force. Peasants and serfs were caught in the struggles between competing elites. Nations searched for ways of resolving conflict peacefully through the use of new forms of public communication, but most efforts failed. Thus the rise of modern public communication brought to Europe what had been experienced in Greece centuries earlier. Public communication did not automatically guarantee the peaceful emergence of democracy. Instead, it unleashed creative forces that made the reconception of democracy possible.

Richard Sennett (1974) describes how the development of new forms of public communication in sixteenth- and seventeenth-century Europe created a new man — one who was freed from traditional rules, but bound by codes generated through public communication. Sennett outlines the way in which such diverse forms of public communication as coffeehouse discussion, dramatic performances, and public meetings led to the institutionalization of arbitrary social roles that public men were expected to play. He maintains that these roles were not as rigid as the traditional roles they replaced. They could be adjusted to the personality of the individual and to the needs of an ever-changing social order. Public communication emerged as central to the development and maintenance of modern social orders. It was men socialized in this way who could conceive of practical forms of democracy and seek to implement them.

THE AMERICAN EXPERIMENT

In Europe the advocates of democracy found much resistance. Powerful elites resisted attempts to broaden political participation. Members of the emerging middle class were often satisfied with securing material success for themselves. The poor had been socialized to accept a highly structured class system in which all important political decisions were made for them.

In the American colonies these factors were not as strong. The possibility for experimentation with new political institutions was greater. Many of the persons who chose to immigrate to the colonies were seeking greater freedom to engage in forms of public communication they considered necessary.

The American revolutionaries were quite familiar with the arguments for democracy created by Europeans seeking to change their political orders. Our revolutionaries drew upon more than a century of philosophical and political debate in Europe to create a powerful synthesis of the strongest arguments for revolution and democratic government. Their writings make clear their debt to classical, medieval, and Renaissance thinkers. They conceived of man as ultimately responsible to God, but in his temporal life governed by natural laws and having certain natural rights: life, liberty, and the pursuit of happiness. From libertarian theorists like Milton, they borrowed the notion that uncontrolled public communication could serve as a means of pursuing both temporal and eternal truth and that such truth can and should serve as the basis for democratic political institutions. They believed that public communication can educate men to be rational, capable of making wise political decisions.

But, despite the idealism of the Founding Fathers, the new nation was plagued by many of the same problems that confounded earlier attempts at creating democracies. Public education proved difficult to achieve. The danger of illiterate masses electing demogogues seemed ever present. Uncontrolled public communication resulted in malicious verbal and printed attacks on political opponents. Ideal forms of public communication, such as electoral debates, did not develop spontaneously. Gradually, public communication was institutionalized. Laws limiting public communication were created and justified as necessary for national security or to preserve more important rights also guaranteed by the Constitution. Private commercial enterprises were permitted to control the new mass media technologies and to sell whatever forms of communication would make a profit.

MODERN DEBATES

One of the more constructive responses to the perceived necessity for making public communication more effective in serving democracy was the development of modern theories of argumentation and debate. These theories have always linked debate closely to democracy, assuming that, when properly structured, debate can make democratic political institutions function effectively (Mills, 1964, pp. 1-21). McBath (1963, pp. 19-25) traces the development of modern debate theory to literary and debating societies that flourished throughout the country following the revolution. These societies established rules to permit more efficient discussion of controversial issues. Following widely publicized collegiate debates between Harvard, Princeton, and Yale in the 1890s, debate leagues were organized across the country "along patterns already set up for athletic contests" (McBath, 1963, p. 25). A debate between Cornell and Pennsylvania produced one of the first published set of standards for debating. Forensic honor societies were organized in the early 1900s (Keefe, Harte, & Norton, 1982, p. 9). One of these societies, Pi Kappa Delta, has staged debate tournaments since 1926.

The academic debate tradition now provides a rich source of potential rules that can be imposed on televised debates to make them a more useful means of public communication. The purpose of most academic debates is to permit a balanced presentation of arguments and evidence on significant issues by evenly matched opponents. Keefe, Harte, and Norton (1982, pp. 30-38) list several apparent benefits of debate experience, including: (1) respect for academic research; (2) awareness of and knowledge about public issues; (3) critical thinking ability; (4) appreciation of systematic change as a basis for democratic action; and (5) the ability to communicate. Austin Freeley (1971, pp. 1-14) provides a cogent outline of the relationship between debate and rational decision making, concluding "that [debate] gives us our best or our only opportunity to reach rational conclusions [and] that it is in the national interest to promote debate." But, although there is evidence that students who debate well are also better critical thinkers (Brembeck, 1949; Gruner et al., 1971), we lack evidence that audiences who listen to debates are aided in developing their ability to make rational decisions.

The academic debate tradition is grounded in classical and Renaissance educational theories. This tradition assumes that rational thought can best be encouraged by presenting two polarized positions on issues. But on many issues there are more than two sides to be considered. Audiences may assume that it is necessary to choose between one of the two extremes. Debates do not serve to negotiate compromise positions, nor do they suggest the form such compromises might take. Audience participation in debates is prohibited. Audience members cannot choose issues, ask questions, or react. Debates are decided by highly trained critics, not by a democratic vote. Debate analysts have neglected the way in which debates serve to arouse and direct emotion as well as reason. Although it may be possible to train critics to avoid being swayed by emotional appeals, untrained audiences are likely to respond differently. Thus the modern debate format serves largely as a tool for educating debaters in how to engage in a highly structured form of communication to impress an expert observer. It is not designed as a vehicle for public education. Thus, although this tradition offers many different possibilities for structuring debates, it may be necessary to go beyond these formats in seeking to create rules for debates designed to serve the public.

ELECTION CAMPAIGN DEBATES

America lacks a tradition of election campaign debates. Though formally structured debate and argumentation are fundamental to the operation of many of our political institutions — most notably our legal system and our legislatures — they have not been widely used in election campaigns. When confrontations between candidates have occurred, they have tended to be loosely structured contests amounting to little more than joint appearances. If formal debates are in fact a useful way of structuring public communication to encourage rational decision making, then election campaigns should be an appropriate setting for them. There is wide agreement that candidates should be chosen carefully and objectively. Candidates who can present themselves and their views effectively demonstrate skills that should make them better leaders once in office.

A variety of factors has interfered with the institutionalization of election debates. Initially, problems of transportation and mass communication inhibited debates. Even if candidates could overcome transportation problems, only a relatively small audience could actually hear them. One reason why the Lincoln-Douglas debates were so successful may be that shorthand reporting techniques made it possible for the first time to print verbatim accounts. But although these problems have been largely overcome, political debates continue to be rare events. Incumbent candidates enter into them reluctantly, often as a last resort. It is argued that debates can only benefit unknown challengers who will be legitimized through their joint appearance with a well-known incumbent. These and other campaign strategy decisions have dictated the frequency and format of past debates.

It is not surprising that the debates arranged through political negotiations (Kraus & Davis, 1982b) have been criticized by scholars concerned about advancing and defending the debate tradition. But neither side has given sufficient attention to the interests and needs of the electorate. Debates need to be taken seriously as a means of educating the public. Such education will be vital to developing new political institutions that are more democratic. But, for debates to serve this purpose, they must first be institutionalized as a regular part of political campaigns at all levels of American government. This institutionalization must be accompanied by efforts to inform the public about using debates wisely. Ideally, strategies could be found for increasing public involvement in the planning of debates, especially in the selection of issues to be debated. Opinion polls might provide one means of enabling voters to directly influence how debates are conducted.

Elsewhere (Kraus & Davis, 1976) we have argued that new political institutions should facilitate transactions between citizens and government. Institutionalized debates could do this by permitting candidates and the public to respond to each other. Ideally, well-planned debates would increase public interest in politics, which in turn would lead to learning political information from sources other than the debates. An informed and motivated public should not only make better vote decisions, it should have a greater respect for the political institutions that make such decisions possible. Continually declining voter turnouts and rising political apathy are unacceptable in a vital democracy. Televised debates provide one of many possible strategies for increasing voter involvement through the use of new technology.

CONCLUSIONS

The history of public communication makes clear the importance of imposing carefully devised structures upon such communication to make it serve democracy effectively. The freedom to communicate publicly also entails the responsibility to communicate in ways that will serve democracy well. We cannot assume that certain forms of communication will necessarily accomplish the objectives we set for them, especially when we use new technologies to transmit such communication. We have the legacy of almost two and one-half centuries of efforts to structure public communication. But in that time no ideal forms of communication have been developed. We do not need to fear that new technologies will undermine perfect ways of communicating in public. But history does teach the importance of considering questions of public communication seriously. The manner in which our society realizes its lofty democratic goals may depend in large part upon the decisions we make in the next two decades concerning public communication. We must recognize that this technology requires innovative but not reckless use. We cannot continue to allow political self-interest and economic profits alone to dictate the format of public communication. A renewed commitment to using public communication to serve democracy must guide our efforts to plan the development and use of new technology.

REFERENCES

Auer, J. J. The counterfeit debates. In S. Kraus (Ed.), *The great debates.* Bloomington: Indiana University Press, 1962.

Barber, B. The second American revolution. *Channels of Communications,* 1982, *1*(6).

Bitzer, L., & Rueter, T. *Carter vs Ford: The counterfeit debates of 1976.* Madison: University of Wisconsin Press, 1980.

Brembeck, W. L. The effects of a course in argumentation on critical thinking ability. *Speech Monographs,* 1949, *16*(September).

Chaffee, S. H. Presidential debates: Are they helpful to voters. *Communication Monographs,* 1978, *45*(November), pp. 330-346.

Dahl, R. A. *A preface to democratic theory.* Chicago: University of Chicago Press, 1956.

Freeley, A. *Argumentation and debate: Rational decision making* (3rd ed.). Belmont, CA: Wadsworth.

Gruner, C. R., Huseman, R. C., & Luck, J. I. Debating ability, critical thinking and authoritarianism. *Speaker and Gavel,* 1971, *8*(March), 63-64.

Harper, N. *Human communication theory: The history of a paradigm.* Rochelle Park, NJ: Hayden, 1979.

Keefe, C., Harte, T. B., & Norton, L. E. *Introduction to debate.* New York: Macmillan, 1982.

Kraus, S. (Ed.). *The great debates.* Bloomington: Indiana State University Press, 1962.

Kraus, S. (Ed.). *The great debates: Carter vs. Ford, 1976.* Bloomington: Indiana State University Press, 1979.

Kraus, S., & Davis, D. K. *The effects of mass communication on political behavior.* University Park: Pennsylvania State University Press, 1976.

Kraus, S., & Davis, D. K. Political debates. In D. Nimmo & K. Sanders (Eds.), *The handbook of political communication.* Beverly Hills, CA: Sage, 1982. (a)

Kraus, S., & Davis, D. K. Televised political debates: The negotiated format. *Gamut: A Journal of Ideas and Information,* 1982, 5(Winter). (b)

Markham, J. W. *Voices of the red giants.* Ames: Iowa State University Press, 1967.

McBath, J. H. (Ed.). *Argumentation and debate: Principles and practices* (Rev. ed.). New York: Holt, Rinehart & Winston, 1963.

McBurney, J. H. *Argumentation and debate: Techniques of a free society.* New York: Macmillan, 1982.

Meador, P. A. Quintilian and the Institutio Oratoria. In N. Harper, *Human communication theory: The history of a paradigm.* Rochelle Park, NJ: Hayden, 1979.

Mills, G. E. *Reason in controversy: An introduction to general argumentation.* Boston: Allyn & Bacon, 1964.

Mitchell, L. M. *With the nation watching: Report of the Twentieth Century Fund task force on televised presidential debates.* Lexington, MA: D. C. Heath, 1979.

Morrall, J. B. *Aristotle.* London: George Allen & Unwin, 1977.

Morrall, J. B. *Political thought in medieval times.* Toronto: University of Toronto Press, 1980.

Pearce, W. B., & Cronen, V. E. *Communication, action, and meaning: The creation of social realities.* New York: Praeger, 1980.

Saldich, A. R. *Electronic democracy: Television's impact on the American political process.* New York: Praeger, 1979.

Siebert, F., Peterson, T., & Schramm, W. *Four theories of the press.* Urbana: University of Illinois Press, 1963.

Sennett, R. *The fall of public man: On the social psychology of capitalism.* New York: Vintage, 1974.

Ullmann, W. *Principles of government and politics in the Middle Ages.* New York: Barnes & Noble, 1966.

COMMUNICATION REVIEWS AND COMMENTARIES

10 • Social Judgment Theory

DONALD GRANBERG
University of Missouri—Columbia

HISTORICAL ORIGINS

FOR the theory of social judgment, to be described and assessed in this chapter, the book *Social Judgment* (Sherif & Hovland, 1961) is a key source. For present purposes, the subtitle of that volume, *Assimilation and Contrast Effects in Communication and Attitude Change*, is also instructive. The subtitle makes clear that this is a theory about the process of communication. I will use 1961 as a pivotal point in time, describing in this initial section events and developments in theory and research which preceded it. In subsequent sections I will describe the basic concepts and propositions in the theory and then attempt to relate empirical evidence reported since 1961 to the theory.

The central figure in the development of social judgment theory is Muzafer Sherif, a social psychologist who arrived from Turkey to do his graduate studies at Harvard and Columbia Universities. After spending most of World War II in Turkey, he returned to the United States and did research at Princeton University with Hadley Cantril and later at Yale University prior to becoming a professor of psychology at the University of Oklahoma. In 1965, he moved to Pennsylvania State University, where he is now an emeritus professor. These historical facts are significant for my purpose because while at Princeton, in addition to his work with Cantril (Sherif & Cantril, 1947), he also met his wife and long-time collaborator, Carolyn Wood Sherif. At Yale, he established a working relationship with Carl Hovland. The contribution of Hovland to the development of social judgment theory is difficult to determine. As director of the large communications research program at Yale, Hovland had many irons in the fire. It would probably be a mistake to suggest that social judgment theory was a focal interest of Hovland's or that he had made a major intellectual contribution to its development. On the other hand, he certainly facilitated its development, financially and administratively. It is also of interest that Hovland chose to focus on this theory to a considerable extent in the lecture he gave when receiving the Distinguished Scientific Contribution

Correspondence and requests for reprints: Donald Granberg, Center for Research in Social Behavior, University of Missouri, Columbia, MO 65211.

award in 1957 from the American Psychological Association (1959). If his contribution and interest in this theory were substantial, they were unfortunately limited to the early stages of the development of the theory, since Hovland died in 1961 at the age of 49. So for him the 1961 *Social Judgment* volume was published posthumously.

The contribution of Carolyn Sherif is even more difficult to assess. It is virtually impossible to separate out, with any confidence, the individual contributions of the members of this husband-and-wife team. For instance, primary credit for the classic Robbers' Cave experiment on intergroup relations usually goes to Muzafer Sherif (1956, 1958). This is indeed as it should be, given that he was the principal investigator. However, recently it was disclosed that it was Carolyn Sherif's idea that their theory of intergroup relations (Sherif & Sherif, 1953) be tested by using groups of boys in a summer camp setting (Sherif, 1976, p. 118). Not only is it impossible to effectively separate out their individual contributions from jointly authored works with any confidence, it is also not necessary. Rather, when I speak of social judgment theory in this chapter I will use the plural possessive form (Sherifs').

Their stay in Oklahoma was punctuated by several empirical studies that were of significance in the development of this theory, including those pertaining to race relations (Hovland & Sherif, 1952; Sherif & Hovland, 1953), prohibition (Hovland, Harvey, & Sherif, 1957; Sherif & Jackman, 1966), and elections (Sherif & Hovland, 1961; Sherif, Sherif, & Nebergall, 1965). In the context of these studies were developed the "method of ordered alternatives" and the "own categories procedure," theoretically relevant techniques for measuring attitudes.

Four developments occurred prior to 1961 that should not be ignored if one is to understand the emergence of social judgment theory. Here they are described briefly.

The "New Look" in Social Perception

In the 1930s several social psychologists began to examine the influence of internal factors, such as values, attitudes, and beliefs, on perception. Does a child's estimate of the size of a coin vary as a function of the socioeconomic status of the child? Is one's susceptibility to the Müller-Lyer illusion affected by growing up in a well-carpentered environment with a lot of straight lines and right angles? Is one's estimate of the national median family income affected by one's station in life? Do the connotations of skin color norms and preferences affect what one perceives in social situations? These are the kinds of questions the New Look people wanted to answer. They are questions of considerable relevance to psychological functioning in everyday life, but they are also completely alien to the study of basic perceptual processes as it had been developing. Psychophysics and the scientific study of perception grew out of philosophical concern over the relation between mind and matter and, more specifically, over the question of how changes in the world "out there" are linked with psychological experience. And how much change in the world out there does there need to be before it is experienced as different by the individual (i.e., what is a "just noticeable difference")?

In any event, Sherif was very much a part of the New Look movement, along with Gardner Murphy, Nevitt Sanford, Kenneth Clark, and, later, Donald Campbell (Bruner, 1957; Tajfel, 1969). In Sherif's (1935, 1936) dissertation research, people made estimates of how far a light moved, but the title of the dissertation was "A Study of Some Social Factors in Perception." (This was expanded and published in book form as *The Psychology of Social Norms*.) It was Sherif's strong impression, based on his extensive observation of social norms and social movements in different contexts, his reading of anthropology, as well as laboratory study, that basic psychological processes such as perception were influenced by internal factors and the cultural context. Furthermore one would have, at most, a partial account of these processes if these sociocultural factors were ignored, as they had been in much of psychology.

Thurstone's Assumption in the Method of Equal-Appearing Intervals

When Lewis Thurstone (1928) asserted that "attitudes can be measured," he meant measurement in a rather precise sense. Figuratively speaking, Thurstone wanted to put a ruler or yardstick up to a person's head or against a person's behavior and then say "There, at some point on the ruler, is where the person's attitude lies." The problem was, of course, how to derive words and numbers to put on the scale. Thurstone's solution is well known:

1. Select an issue and gather a large number of statements covering the entire range of possible positions on the issue.
2. Have "judges" sort the statements objectively into eleven categories depending solely on the degree of favorability or unfavorability implied in the statement.
3. Calculate a measure of central tendency and a measure of variation in the judges' sorting of each statement. Usually, the median and Q values are used, the former being taken as the scale value of the statement.
4. Select a set of statements for an attitude scale using two criteria: obtain statements with scale values at equal intervals along the scale (e.g., 1.0, 1.5, 2.0); if one has a choice where there are two or more statements with the desired scale value, select the one with the lower Q value (the one on which the judges showed more consensus).

Then one was ready to *measure* the person's attitude. Ask a person which of the set of statements (with known scale values) the person agrees with and calculate the median scale value of these items. *That* is where the person's attitude falls on that issue.

Thurstone recognized that the validity of his claims for this procedure depended on an assumption that in step 2 the judges could sort the statements objectively, and that the scale values that were derived would be independent of the identity of the judges and the sociohistorical web in which they were immersed. Now some assumptions in science are metaphysical or untestable. Others are testable or become testable. Thurstone's assumption was of the latter type. The initial tests of the assumption proved favorable (Hinckley, 1932; Pinter & Forlano, 1937). Scale values for attitude statements, derived from groups of judges with opposed attitudes on the issue under consideration, were very highly correlated. For twenty years (1932-1952), the conventional wisdom was that Thurstone's key assumption was valid.

Anchoring Effects in Psychophysical Scaling

Between 1920 and 1950 several articles in psychophysics collectively served to demonstrate the relativity of perception and judgment. This grew out of the Gestalt tradition. One of the central themes in Gestalt psychology is that stimulus items do not have absolute stimulating value, but rather are responded to on the basis of the context in which they appear (Granberg & Aboud, 1969). A light judged as somewhat bright in one stimulus series might be judged as somewhat dim in a different series. A stimulus item is perceived in relation to previous items in the series, the items present at the time, and the current contextual arrangement (see Helson, 1964).

In psychophysics, when one item or factor has a strong influence on how a second item is perceived, the first is said to *anchor* the perception of the second. More generally, any factor that is relatively important, at a given time, in the constellation of factors comprising an individual's frame of reference, is an anchor. Suppose we have a series of five weights, ranging between 75 and 150 grams and we ask people to judge them, using five categories from very light to very heavy, over a series of presentations. People develop an idea of what the series consists of and, because the differences among the stimuli are sufficient, make their judgments with considerable accuracy. Next we repeat the series, only this time just prior to each trial we ask people to lift a given weight. When that "anchoring" weight is at or just beyond the range of the stimulus series, there is a tendency for judgments of the items in the stimulus series to shift in the direction of the anchoring stimulus. That is called *assimilation*. As the distance between the stimulus series and the anchoring stimulus increases, the tendency is for judgments of the stimulus items to be distributed in the direction away from the anchoring stimulus. That is *contrast* (Sherif, Taub, & Hovland, 1958).

The experience of contrast is a common occurrence. If one has been lifting fifteen- to twenty-pound turkeys all day, an eight-pound turkey may seem exceptionally light. Nor is this type of effect confined to psychophysical judgments. Cohen (1957) asked people to judge how undesirable some moderately undesirable behaviors (MUBs) were. By *contrast*, the MUBs (e.g., picking flowers in a public park) were evaluated as less undesirable when they were judged in the context of very undesirable behaviors (VUBs) than when they were judged alone. The presence of VUBs (e.g., putting one's deformed child in a circus) anchored the judgments of the MUBs (see Pepitone & DeNubile, 1976).

All of this may seem very far removed from the study of attitudes and communication processes. However, to the Sherifs this branch of psychophysics seemed well developed and a source of ideas. Specifically, they were impressed with the evidence pertaining to the relativity of human judgment, the concept of an anchoring effect, and the dual kinds of anchoring effects that had been observed — namely, assimilation and contrast.

Ego-Involvement as
an Integrative Concept

Sherif was struck by the apparent contradiction between the New Look emphasis on the impact of attitudes on perception and the support of Thurstone's assumption of no effect. Sherif had long recognized that social movements and social issues are central in the lives of some people and matters of abiding concern. To a considerable extent a person's ego or self-concept can be closely bound to the success or failure of a particular group. Thus, it was expected that to the extent that an issue was important to the person, the person's own attitude would serve as an anchor in the psychological processes of perception and judgment of a communication.

Thus Sherif, in collaboration with Hovland, went back and scrutinized the studies that had appeared to support Thurstone's assumption. In particular, he noticed that Hinckley had excluded subjects from his study for two reasons: (a) having a neutral or nonextreme attitude and (b) being "careless" in the sorting task by placing thirty or more of the 114 statements in any one of the eleven categories. Sherif suspected, and produced evidence to indicate, that people who placed or displaced a large number of statements in the end categories did so not because of carelessness but because they had a high level of ego-involvement in the issue under consideration. These people's attitudes acted as anchors against which other statements were judged, and placing a large number of statements in the end categories reflected the way they really saw and categorized the domain.

It was primarily on the basis of these historical influences that the assimilation-contrast model of communication, or social judgment theory, emerged. People who took extreme positions on an issue and who were highly committed to and ego-involved in that position would engage in displacement effects when estimating the position being advocated by a communicator. If the actual position of the communicator was only a short distance from the subject's position, assimilation would occur. The communicator would be displaced or drawn toward the person's own attitude. The actual discrepancy would be underestimated. On the other hand, if the actual distance was large, contrast would occur in which the communicator would be displaced away from the person's own attitude. The actual discrepancy would be overestimated. Ego-involvement is the key here, in that the displacement effects were expected to occur as a function of ego-involvement. People for whom the issue was unimportant were not expected to show assimilation and contrast. In fact, it was in comparison to such people that assimilation and contrast on the part of the highly involved people could be demonstrated and inferred.

Assume, for instance, a scale represented by nine positions, A through I, which goes from one extreme position (A) through neutrality (E) to the other extreme (I). If a communicator takes some moderate position, say at position C, but the communicator is seen by different people as having taken different positions, then displacement has occurred. If people who are themselves at position A estimate the communicator to be advocating position B, that would be assimilation, while for people at position I to estimate the communicator's position as B would be contrast. If people at positions D and F estimated the communicator's position at C, that would be a veridical (accurate) placement judgment, indicative that neither assimilation nor contrast had occurred, since the actual discrepancy and the perceived discrepancy would be the same.

Thus we see that from the vantage point of social judgment theory, the crucial comparisons pertinent to Thurstone's assumption should have included people with moderate or neutral views, as well as people with relatively distinct and extreme views.

Incidentally, Thurstone's technique and his assumption are now largely of historical interest in the sense of what they led to in subsequent developments. For a variety of reasons, Thurstone's technique of attitude measurement involving equal-appearing intervals is not much used by social psychologists today. It is a cumbersome way to develop a measuring instrument, and it has not really been shown that the extra effort required results in greater precision or more predictive power. But another reason is that in the past twenty years, thanks initially to the research of Sherif and Hovland, the consensus among social psychologists has been that Thurstone's crucial assumption was incorrect. The only question remaining concerns the form and degree of incorrectness and an assessment of how devastating the incorrectness is on the validity of the technique.

For Sherif and Hovland the critique of Thurstone's procedure, based on the New Look emphasis in the psychology of perception, anchoring effects in psychophysics, and the integrating concept of ego-involvement, served as a major point of departure for the development of social judgment theory. What followed shortly were the development of some theoretically relevant measuring instruments and the expansion of what was being communicated from a simple brief statement for an attitude scale to a speech. Reactions to the speech could include displacement effects (assimilation and contrast), but they might also include changes in the recipient's attitude either in the direction of or away from the communicator's position. Although the theory has been refined and expanded, the rudiments were present in the 1950s and stemmed from the interaction of the four influences described in this section.

MAJOR FEATURES OF THE THEORY

In order to understand social judgment theory, it is necessary to characterize the central concepts of the theory, inasmuch as these concepts form the building blocks of the theory.

Attitude Structure

In this theory an attitude is conceived as an internal factor that is inferred from behavior in relation to some relatively specific object or set of objects. A person's attitude, however, is thought of not as some point on a continuum but as a series of three zones or latitudes. When one has an entire array of possible positions on some issue (e.g., whether there should be capital punishment) going from one extreme to the other, one can then describe the person's attitude based on that person's behavioral response to each position.

The *latitude of acceptance* consists of the alternatives regarded by the person as basically acceptable. Within the latitude of acceptance, there will be one position that represents the person's own position, the position that ideally expresses the person's outlook or is most acceptable in the sense of coming closest to such an expression. The *latitude of rejection* consists of the alternatives regarded as objectionable. Also, within this latitude there will be one position that is regarded as most objectionable or most undesirable. The *latitude of noncommitment* consists of items or alternatives that fall within neither the latitude of acceptance nor the latitude of rejection, items responded to in a noncommital way. This sounds complex or different from most ways of analyzing and measuring attitudes, but it is really not unusual. For instance, if we give people a twenty-item Likert-type scale, we could say that the items the person agrees with comprise the latitude of acceptance, the items disagreed with, the latitude of rejection, and the items to which the person responded by saying "don't know" or "undecided" would comprise the latitude of noncommitment.

The Sherifs, however, developed two rather innovative procedures for measuring attitudes in a way that seemed to follow from their theory. The "own categories procedure" developed as a consequence of the research, referred to in the previous section, demonstrating that in Thurstone scaling judges' attitudes did influence the way they sorted attitude statements on an issue. Sherif and Hovland (1953) believed that such a sorting task could be used to reveal certain qualities of the individual's attitude. But this would be especially true if the individual were allowed to choose the number of categories rather than impose a fixed number (usually eleven in the Thurstone procedure) for the person to use. It is undoubtedly easier and less cumbersome to score a procedure in which a fixed number of alternatives is used, as in the use of seven alternatives in the semantic differential (Osgood, Suci, & Tannenbaum, 1957). Sherif and Hovland, however, decided to develop what can be thought of as a more subjective or phenomenological procedure by allowing an individual to impose a structure on the domain. In their procedure, if one walks around with four categories in one's mind for dealing with possible positions on the issue of gun control, this should become evident if the person sorts statements pertaining to gun control using the own categories procedure. The steps that are followed in the own categories procedure are listed below.

1. The person whose attitude is being measured sorts a set of statements into piles or categories in such a way that the items within a category seem to belong together and are different from items in other categories. The person doing the sorting is told to use as many or as few categories as seems necessary or appropriate. The statements to be sorted should be a large number (e.g., sixty) and should include all gradations of possible positions on an issue, especially including some that are moderate and might be regarded as ambiguous.

2. Once the sorting task is completed, the person is asked which category or pile contains statements that are most acceptable or that come closest to the person's own position, and is asked to label any other categories that also contain statements the person accepts. Then he or she is asked to indicate which category contains statements that are most objectionable and any other categories that are also objectionable. By this means, one can learn the number of categories used and the size of the latitudes.

If a category is labeled as neither acceptable nor objectionable, the items in it would fall in the latitude of noncommitment. The three latitudes are reciprocally related and mutually exhaustive. That is, in a given study, the size of the three latitudes would add up to the same sum. For example, if researchers were using a set of sixty statements, and in one person's sorting there were twenty statements in the categories comprising the latitude of acceptance and fifteen in the latitude of noncommitment, this would necessarily mean that the size of the latitude of rejection would have to equal twenty-five. It is also possible to compute scale values for specific items using the own categories procedure, even though this is a bit cumbersome (Sherif et al., 1965; LaFave & Sherif, 1968).

Overall, the own categories procedure is a clever way of probing how an individual subjectively structures an issue. It is also somewhat subtle or indirect because during the sorting phase, it is not necessary for one to know that one's attitude is going to be revealed. Although theoretically interesting and relevant, this way of measuring people's attitudes on an issue is a difficult and painstaking process, and it has not been, and probably will not be, used on a mass level or in many studies.

The second procedure developed by the Sherifs to measure the latitudes comprising an attitude is the *ordered alternatives procedure*. This procedure is far more manageable for use on a mass scale. In it people are presented with a relatively small number of alternative positions (usually between seven and eleven, with nine being the standard number). The only requirements are that the statements be about the same issue, that they include all the major alternatives, and that they be capable of being ordered along a continuum from one extreme to another. Some believe the statements should also be scaled so as to have roughly equal intervals (Eagly & Telaak, 1972), but this is not part of the procedure recommended by the Sherifs (Sherif, 1979). On the Vietnam war issue, the extremes could have been defined, say in 1968, as follows:

   A. The United States should immediately withdraw all its troops from Vietnam and completely cease all military aid to the Republic of Vietnam, regardless of the consequences.

   I. The United States should do whatever is necessary to achieve a complete victory over its enemies in Vietnam, including the use of nuclear, chemical, and biological weapons if this is necessary to achieve such a victory.

Between statements A and I would be a series of statements that would gradually become less dovish and more hawkish.

In this procedure, people would be asked, successively, which position they regard as most acceptable, to indicate any other positions that are also acceptable, which position is most objectionable, and to indicate any other positions they regard as objectionable. (For a recent example of how this procedure has been adapted in an effort to improve on traditional ways of measuring family size preferences, see Granberg, 1982.)

Note that, again, people are not required to respond to all alternatives; thus, alternatives that are evaluated as neither acceptable nor objectionable comprise the latitude of noncommitment. It is the Sherifs' recommendation that the set of ordered alternatives be repeated four times on four separate pages, with the instructions asking people to indicate the statement that is the one most acceptable, others that are acceptable, most objectionable, and others that are objectionable on pages one through four, respectively. This may seem a redundant procedure and a waste of space or paper, but experimental research has shown that it does make a difference (Granberg & Steele, 1974). If the alternatives are presented only once with all the instructions, people are far more likely to respond to every alternative, leaving no latitude of noncommitment. In both the own categories and ordered alternatives procedures, the size of the latitude of rejection varies as a positive function and is the best single indicator of the level of ego-involvement in the issue under consideration. Thus if one were using an ordered alternatives procedure to choose people who were highly ego-involved in the issue, the probability of having a false positive (a person who appeared to be highly involved but really was not) could be minimized by using a four-page form rather than a one-page form (Granberg & Steele, 1974).

Once again, in the ordered alternatives procedure the sizes of the latitudes are mutually exhaustive. If there are nine alternatives and the person checks three as acceptable and four as objectionable, the latitudes of acceptance, rejection, and noncommitment would equal 3, 4, and 2, respectively. The ordered alternatives procedure has been used in a large number of studies in relation to a large variety of issues (Sherif & Sherif, 1967; Sherif, 1980) and it has considerable potential for use on a mass scale. It is also evident that if these two theoretically relevant measuring procedures are both valid measures of the concepts, the results one obtains from administering comparable measures to the same people should result in a high correlation between the two — for example, in the size of the latitude of rejection using the two procedures. Evidence on this point is limited, but there is some reason to think it holds up among people who are highly concerned about an issue (Rogers, 1978) but not among people who are unselected as to level of involvement.

Ego-Involvement

As indicated in the previous section, the concept of ego-involvement is a central, integrating concept in social judgment theory. A person's attitude on an issue anchors a person's experience and behavior in social relations and in response to social stimuli to the extent that the person is ego-involved in the issue. According to the theory, it is axiomatic that people who are highly ego-involved in an issue respond very differently to a communication about that issue than people who are not so involved. The underlying process is thought to work in such a way that attitudinal structure varies as a function of ego-involvement.

Specifically, it was expected that involvement lowers the threshold of rejection and thereby increases the size of the latitude of rejection. It was also expected that highly involved people would be undecided or noncommital toward fewer items in an issue domain, and that this would be reflected in a smaller latitude of noncommitment. This has been borne out rather consistently in research and has numerous real-life parallels. In cases of extreme ego-involvement and in times of social crisis, neutrality may be rejected altogether, the latitude of noncommitment is nonexistent, and the number of categories reduced to two. The statement attributed to Jesus, "He who is not with me is against me," the use by Martin Luther King, Jr., of an idea attributed to Dante that the hottest places in hell are reserved for those who try to maintain their strict neutrality in a time of moral crisis, the excoriation and opprobrium with which John Foster Dulles viewed and condemned "wicked neutralism," and the common observation that in reality there are no observers at a crucifixion or execution all serve to illustrate the kinds of social judgments that follow from extreme commitment and high levels of ego-involvement.

As implied previously, based on casual observation and anecdotal evidence, it was expected that as involvement increased, the number of categories used to evaluate and group communications about an issue would decrease. This has been systematically and consistently verified in research using the own categories procedure.

Another expectation was that ego-involvement would have the consequence of raising the threshold of acceptance so that the size of the latitude of acceptance and the level of ego-involvement would be inversely related. With a few exceptions, this prediction has not been borne out. Overall, ego-involvement seems to be related closest to the size of the latitude of rejection. But recall that the sizes of the three latitudes are reciprocally related, mutually exhaustive, and must add up to a fixed sum. Thus, if the size of the latitude of rejection increases, something has to give way. Generally, most research has indicated that it is the latitude of noncommitment rather than the latitude of acceptance that changes. The sizes of the latitudes of rejection and noncommitment are more closely correlated (inversely) than either is to the latitude of acceptance. The latter tends to stay relatively more or less constant in size regardless of extremity or level of ego-involvement.

Key Features of the Communication

One key concept social judgment theory uses is the *degree of ambiguity* or lack of structure in a communication. This again shows an influence of the Gestalt tradition on social judgment theory. Generally, it was the Sherifs' contention that one could observe evidence of intriguing processes only if the communication was at least moderately ambiguous — that is, lacking in structure or definition. Internal factors and conditions, such as attitudes and involvement, increase in importance in the individual's frame of reference as the degree of structure in the external stimulus situation decreases (Sherif & Sherif, 1956). Thus, their approach is very different from and perhaps nearly opposite to Thurstone's. Recall that Thurstone suggested that if one had a choice, one would choose the less ambiguous statement for use in the final stages of research. The Sherifs would advocate inclusion of some ambiguous statements that are subject to displacement tendencies — assimilation and contrast.

The importance of this is that ambiguity is a fact of life and a common feature of communications in the real world. For instance, when World War II began, General Douglas MacArthur, stationed in the Philippines, received numerous communications from Washington from which he inferred that help (reinforcements and supplies) was on its way. It was not. After the war, MacArthur reread those cables, finding that while they were positive in tone and encouraging, they never promised that help was on its way (Manchester, 1979). The ambiguity of the communications, together with MacArthur's strong preference and high involvement, made the assimilative inference possible.

When Robert Kennedy ran for President in 1968, one of the questions he was asked repeatedly was whether, as attorney general, he had authorized the wiretapping of the phones of Martin Luther King, Jr. Kennedy's answer was that he was forbidden by law from answering that question directly. OK, so far. But then he went on to say that he would not answer the question, even though to do so might increase his support and help his campaign. That was misleading and deceptive; misleading because it allowed and led liberals to conclude that he really had not authorized the wiretaps, and deceptive because it is now unambiguously clear, based on documents obtained through the Freedom of Information Act, that Kennedy did personally authorize the wiretapping of King's phones on several occasions (Garrow, 1981, pp. 73, 93).

Here are a few more examples which illustrate the importance of ambiguity in political communication:

1. "Let him say not one single word about his principles, or his creed — let him say nothing — promise nothing. Let no committee, no convention — no town meeting ever extract from him a single word, about what he

thinks now or what he will do hereafter. Let the use of pen and ink be wholly forbidden as if he were a mad poet in Bedlam." Advice of Nicholas Biddle, campaign manager of William Henry Harrison. (Shepsle, 1972)

2. "What you don't say can be more important than what you do say. What you leave unsaid then becomes what the audience brings to it. . . . Get the voters to like the guy, and the battle's two thirds won." (McGuinnis, 1969)

3. "When Bill Brock, the . . . Republican national chairman, ran for the Senate in 1970, his billboards read, 'Bill Brock believes.' His speeches were about as informative, and before long, he was being attacked for running an empty, issue-less campaign. So he promised he would spell out his message more fully before election day. And he kept that promise. With three weeks left in the campaign, the billboards blossomed with a new slogan: 'Bill Brock Believes What We Believe.'" (Broder, 1977)

4. "The Chief beneficiary of this lack of clarity at this very early stage of the campaign [February, 1976] appears to be Jimmy Carter, the former Georgia governor and newcomer to national politics, who has cultivated a startlingly high level of recognition and support from all types of Democrats." (Reinhold, 1976)

5. "Carter and Ford are hardly charismatic figures, but experience has taught politicians that it is unwise to sharpen the issues too much. Nixon said almost nothing in 1972 and got a landslide from McGovern, who tried to be specific; so did Stevenson and Goldwater — they got clobbered, too. Our system puts a premium on ambiguity." (TRB, 1976)

6. "[Treleavan] found that [George] Bush was 'an extremely likeable person,' but that 'there was a haziness about exactly where he stood politically.' This was perfect. . . . So there would be no issues in the race." (McGuinnis, 1969, pp. 38-39)

Ambiguity in communication is not limited to the political sphere. Romantically involved couples, engaged to be married or already married, do not always communicate directly or explicitly about their preferences, plans, and hopes for the future. With this degree of ambiguity in communication, it is altogether likely that each will attribute views to the other in such a way that perceived similarity will exceed actual similarity (cf. Byrne & Blalock, 1963). In our terms, assimilation will prevail — at least for the time being and so long as the romantic glow predominates in the relationship. Prior to "no-fault" divorce laws, one reason for divorce was "irreconcilable differences." From the vantage point of social judgment theory, one might suggest that many of these differences were irreconcilable and existed all along but went unrecognized due to inadequate and ambiguous communication.

Another variable, already alluded to, in social judgment theory is *discrepancy*. This is not a feature of the communication; rather it *refers* to the actual distance between a communicator's position and the position of the recipient of the communication along some scale. If one also knows the recipient's estimate of the communicator's position, then one is able to infer whether assimilation (actual discrepancy > perceived discrepancy), veridicality (actual discrepancy = perceived discrepancy), or contrast (actual discrepancy < perceived discrepancy) has occurred.

Identity of the communicator is another variable to which social judgment theory accords some attention. Here the stress would be on whether the communicator and recipient have shared and recognized membership and reference group ties, and whether the communicator has a reputation for credibility and expertise. Some studies stemming from or purporting to deal with social judgment theory have used the identity of the communicator as an independent variable (e.g., Manis, 1961b, Rhine & Severance, 1970), but most have not. Most such studies have examined how people respond to anonymous communicators. This is a limitation in the research; although, of course, anonymous communications are by no means absent or rare in the real world. This emphasis on anonymous communicators is probably traceable to the fact that social judgment theory grew out of studies dealing with problems in Thurstone scaling. In the case of the latter, it was customary that the communication statements be anonymous (but see Eiser, 1971).

In terms of outcome variables, social judgment theory focuses on assimilation and contrast, which have already been identified and defined, and attitude change. The displacement phenomena (assimilation and contrast) are analytically distinct from, and should not be confused with, attitude change, even though at times they have been so confused. *Positive attitude change* refers to the change of a person's attitude in the direction of a communication — that is, to some degree taking the advice of the communicator. *Negative attitude change,* also referred to in some places as a boomerang effect, occurs when a person changes an attitude in the direction away from a communicator.

Social judgment theory also has attended to some more directly and explicitly evaluative judgments, such as asking people whether or not the communication was biased, educational, or propagandistic, and so forth. This focus is relatively uninteresting and has not been a productive vein of research. It also has been pursued from other theoretical points of departure (e.g., Aronson, Turner, & Carlsmith, 1963; Bochner & Insko, 1966), so there is nothing special or unique about the interest in social judgment theory as to whether the recipient derides, belittles, or derogates a communicator.

Overall, the theory may be summarized as follows:

1. In order to understand an individual's reaction to a communication, it is necessary (or at least useful) to know the individual's evaluative and placement judgments of the communication.

2. The placement judgment of a communication and attitude change are part of the same process. Understanding of attitude change can be facilitated by relating it to the judgment process.
3. Placement of a communication is a function of discrepancy and ambiguity.
    a. In the case of a completely unambiguous communication, there will be no systematic displacement effects regardless of discrepancy.
    b. When the communication is moderately ambiguous, assimilation occurs when the discrepancy is small and the communication falls within the latitude of acceptance; but contrast occurs when the discrepancy is large and the communication falls within the latitude of rejection.
    c. When a communication is highly ambiguous, assimilation occurs and the amount of assimilation increases as discrepancy increases.
4. Positive attitude change occurs as a curvilinear, quadratic function of discrepancy. As discrepancy increases, positive attitude change increases up to a point and then decreases. At extreme discrepancies under a condition of high ego-involvement, negative attitude change occurs. In terms of producing positive attitude change, diminishing returns occur as the discrepancy increases to the point of getting into the person's latitude of rejection.
5. People who are higher in ego-involvement show less positive attitude change in response to a moderately or highly discrepant communication than do people who are not so involved. This is because people who are highly involved have larger latitudes of rejection, and therefore the communication is more likely to fall within their latitudes of rejection sooner and deeper than people who are less involved.
6. The occurrence of assimilation of a communication and positive attitude change in response to it are related to each other. Although the nature of this relationship is imprecisely specified, one possibility is for them to be negatively related when the discrepancy is small (as if they were alternatives) but positively related when the discrepancy is large (as if they were complementary).

ADDITIONAL EMPIRICAL EVIDENCE

Assimilation and Contrast

There is no doubt that assimilation and contrast occur in communications between individuals and groups of people. The questions that remain are whether the displacement occurs in systematic ways that can be discovered, discerned, and described succinctly, and whether such phenomena are merely some intriguing cognitive biases to keep academicians busy, or whether they might be of substantial practical importance.

The latter question must remain a matter of judgment, but certain examples can be cited if one were to mount an argument in this respect. It is an old, but still widely used adage in social psychology that what one defines as real in one's mind is real in its consequences. Thus, to predict my behavior, it may be just as consequential or important to know what I think you said as what you actually said.

In 1962, at the height of the Cuban missile crisis, U.S. officials received two different communications, one far more hostile in tone than the other. That combination created considerable anxiety and uncertainty about what had been communicated by the Soviets. The resolution of that crisis depended, in large measure, on the acceptance of Robert Kennedy's rather unusual advice to ignore the more hostile message and to concentrate on and respond on the basis of the more conciliatory message. That crisis may have been as close as the two superpowers have ever come to a nuclear war, and the communication process between the contending sides was highly significant in determining the outcome (Kennedy, 1969; Divine, 1971).

In the domain of electoral politics, there is strong and consistent evidence that how people respond to candidates, and how people vote, is related more to the degree of perceived similarity than to the actual similarity between the citizen and the politician (Shaffer, 1981). If this were not so, perceptions of positions taken by candidates would be of far less interest.

Whether displacement phenomena in communication, like assimilation and contrast effects, can be described and predicted through a few simple integrative principles is not so clear at this point. Hovland and Sherif's (1952) early study was of considerable heuristic value, in that it stimulated a large number of studies and experiments on social judgment processes. Not all the data that were produced were considered consistent with social judgment theory, and this led to the development of some alternative or rival theories, such as perspective theory (Upshaw, 1969) and accentuation theory (Eiser & Stroebe, 1972). The data that have accumulated on the old problem of Thurstone's assumption are legion and complex. There are no good grounds for optimism over the prospect of any single theory successfully integrating them.

A somewhat more specific research problem that has been addressed in several articles concerns the process in which citizens form impressions of the policy positions taken on issues by candidates. Following some early clues in the literature (Berelson, Lazarsfeld, & McPhee, 1954; Page & Brody, 1972; Sherrod, 1972), Granberg and Brent (1974) used social judgment theory to examine the placement judgments of Hubert Humphrey, Richard Nixon, and George Wallace on the Vietnam issue in 1968. Since then, several other papers have examined other issues and subsequent elections in the United States (Granberg & Seidel, 1976; Granberg & Jenks, 1977; Granberg, Harris, & King, 1981; Kinder, 1978; King, 1978; Granberg & Brent, 1980). Recently, Brent and Granberg (1982) attempted to summarize the cumulating evidence on this problem by a set of empirically derived propositions. They do not necessarily constitute a theory, but given that they summarize existing empirical evidence, one would not want to have a theory that implied something other than these propositions. They are given here to illustrate a research program on assimilation and contrast effects in communication in a rather specific and delimited area.

1. *People tend to assimilate the issue positions of a preferred candidate.* That is, they displace their estimates to make a preferred candidate's position appear closer to their own position than it actually is. The dynamics of the process leading to this outcome are not entirely clear. But the possibility that attraction leads to perceived similarity is at least as plausible as the alternative that perceived similarity leads to attraction (Page & Jones, 1979; Granberg & King, 1980). Note that if one were brave, this proposition, and others that follow, could easily be restated or recast at a somewhat more abstract level (e.g., people tend to assimilate in their estimates of the attitudes of a liked other).

2. *The assimilation of a preferred candidate is facilitated by a positive sentiment relationship to and, to a lesser extent, by a unit relationship with the candidate* (Heider, 1958; Kinder, 1978). Sentiment relationship refers to the individual's affective, attitudinal orientation, while unit relationship refers to having a characteristic in common, such as being a member of the same group (see Granberg et al., 1981).

3. *The degree of assimilation of a preferred candidate on an issue is positively related to the importance attached to that issue.* Although the studies in this series have not measured ego-involvement in the manner suggested by the Sherifs, issue importance has been measured in a couple of different ways, and the results point toward this conclusion.

4. *People who are very concerned about the outcome of an election assimilate in their estimates of a preferred candidate more than people who are not so concerned.* This is closely related to the preceding proposition, but here we are dealing with overall concern about the election rather than the importance attached to a given issue. That the results for importance and concern both point in the same direction suggests the possibility that ego-involvement with a candidate may be the underlying operating factor.

5. It is not necessary to vote for a candidate for assimilation to take place. *Nonvoters tend also to assimilate in their estimates of the position of a preferred candidate.* This finding is important because it points to the pervasiveness of this assimilation tendency. Nonvoters may have low interest and little concern and lack feelings of efficacy and a sense of citizen's duty to vote, but they still often do have a preference as to which candidate they would like to see win. And, apparently, this preference is sufficient to produce an assimilation in their placement judgments.

6. *People who cross party lines to vote for a preferred candidate do not assimilate the views of their preferred candidate more than people whose candidate preference and party identification are consistent.* On logical and theoretical grounds, one might have expected crossover voters to have especially strong motivation to avoid inconsistency between self and preferred candidate and thus to show more assimilation. However, research has shown that crossover voters are fairly weak partisans and low in political involvement, and this may be why they have generally shown a somewhat weaker assimilative tendency than people who are not crossover voters.

7. *When candidate O takes an extreme and unambiguous position on an issue, supporters of O assimilate O less on that issue than do supporters of other more moderate candidates in estimating the position of their respective preferred candidate.* This is a way of stating abstractly specific findings, such as on the issue of urban unrest in 1968, when people preferring Humphrey or Nixon assimilated their preferred candidate more than did the supporters of Wallace.

8. *When candidate O has a key issue on which O's campaign is centered and on which O takes an extreme and unambiguous position, O's supporters assimilate O on that issue less than on some other issue on which O's position is less well known.* For example, George Wallace's supporters in 1968 assimilated Wallace more on the Vietnam issue than on the issue of urban unrest. In 1972, George McGovern's supporters assimilated McGovern more on the urban unrest issue than on the issue of the Vietnam war.

9. *The tendency to contrast a nonpreferred candidate is not as strong or reliable as the tendency of people to assimilate a preferred candidate.* Actually, this finding is somewhat counterintuitive and was not originally expected. It was assumed that in politics people are more sure of what they are against than what they favor and that this would produce stronger contrast in placing a nonpreferred candidate than assimilation of a preferred candidate. However, the findings in this kind of comparison have been highly consistent and point toward the asymmetry of assimilation being stronger than contrast — at least in this context.

10. *Ambiguity may facilitate assimilation of a preferred candidate, but a lack of ambiguity may facilitate contrast of a nonpreferred candidate.* Related to the latter point is the fact that when contrast of a nonpreferred candidate occurs, the incumbent candidate (who is more familiar and thus less ambiguous) is more subject to contrast than is a candidate who challenges an incumbent. In 1976, Carter supporters contrasted Ford more than Ford supporters contrasted Carter. But in 1980, Reagan supporters contrasted Carter more than Carter supporters contrasted Reagan. More work needs to be done on developing ways of measuring ambiguity

in survey research and of operationalizing ambiguity in experimental research (Manis, 1961a; Granberg & Campbell, 1977).

Attitude Change

The prediction in social judgment theory, that positive attitude change increases as discrepancy increases up to a point but then decreases beyond that, has generally been supported in research. A review of the experimental literature on attitude change located over thirty studies in which discrepancy was a variable, and nearby all the evidence is compatible with the theoretical curve of social judgment theory (if one is willing to make certain extensions, assumptions, and extrapolations). The problem with the curvilinear hypothesis is that it provides such a big umbrella that almost any conceivable results can be sheltered beneath it. Whittaker (1964) even reported evidence of a cubic function and still interpreted it as consistent with the quadratic curvilinear hypothesis. Technically, about the only type of evidence on discrepancy as a factor in attitude change that would be inconsistent with social judgment theory would be if attitude change decreased as discrepancy increased down to a point of inflection but then increased beyond that with additional increments in discrepancy. No experiment in which discrepancy has been manipulated at three or more levels has reported such results.

Future research using discrepancy as a variable might very well utilize the implications of the concept of latitudes. That is, experiments using discrepancy as a variable have held the amount of discrepancy constant for each subject, although different subjects in different conditions get different degrees of discrepancy. A clear implication of social judgment theory is that if you want to be effective in producing positive attitude change, work within the person's latitude of acceptance or perhaps the latitude of noncommitment. Thus over time attitude change could be brought about more effectively, perhaps, by a series of messages at gradually increasing discrepancy from the person's original attitude. In other branches of psychology, this would be called producing change by a series of successive approximations. In the only experiment like this, Harvey and Rutherford (1958) reported that this gradual, shifting method was superior to the absolute and constant discrepancy in producing change in a well-formed or strongly held attitude.

There is also a need for more research to clarify where the point of inflection occurs in the curvilinear relationship between discrepancy and attitude change. Does it occur at the end of the individual's latitude of acceptance, within the latitude of noncommitment, or not until the message is within, or is judged to be within the latitude of rejection? That may seem like a technical point, but it shows the kind of refinement that is needed if social judgment theory is to develop more fully.

CONCLUSIONS

This last section contains an assessment of social judgment theory in relation to some criteria that are characteristics of a good scientific theory. First a good theory should be, at minimum, consistent with known facts. Ideally, it should synthesize and explain a given set of facts and events. In relation to this *veracity* criterion, social judgment theory stacks up quite well. From the start, it has been grounded in empirical data and succeeded in incorporating a substantial number of known facts. In fairness, it should be pointed out that this somewhat sanguine view has not been universally shared. On the one hand, Shaw and Constanzo (1970) interpreted extant data as supportive of, and consistent with, social judgment theory. On the other hand, Zimbardo and Ebbesen (1969, pp. 50-56) leveled a serious critique of the prohibition study (Hovland et al., 1957) which formed part of the empirical base of social judgment theory. Zimbardo and Ebbesen charged that the data had been presented in such a way as to exaggerate grossly the magnitude of assimilation and contrast effects, and in a way in which education and the respondent's own position were confounded.

This suggested the need for further studies of displacement effects in communication. Some of the ensuing studies are not necessarily inconsistent with the theory, but also it seems difficult to account adequately for some results within the parameters of the original theory. For instance, Manis and Moore (1978) reported an experiment dealing with the issue of national health insurance. People who rated a neutral message after hearing an extreme speech tended to contrast the neutral speech away from the extreme speech. But when a thirty-minute irrelevant task intervened, placements of the neutral speech were shifted toward the extreme speech (assimilation). Such effects are not necessarily inconsistent with social judgment theory, but the authors had to look elsewhere in order to devise some explanations of the results.

But is there evidence that directly contradicts a basic tenet of social judgment theory? That gets to another criterion for a good theory — namely, that of *disconfirmability*. A good theory should be sufficiently specific so that it cannot incorporate any conceivable result. The theory must be stated so that it is capable of being disproven. A theory that can explain everything is a no-risk theory, and in the same sense a theory that can explain everything, in fact, explains nothing.

In some respects social judgment theory may be, as implied in the discussion of discrepancy, a big umbrella, but there are at least some points at which it is clearly disconfirmable. For instance, if contrast occurred at a small discrepancy and assimilation at a large discrepancy, there would be no way of handling such an anomaly with the theory. Similarly, if there were a U-shaped function between discrepancy and opinion change, in response to a communication, there would be no way for the theory to incorporate such a set of data gracefully.

Although no set of data reported in the literature resembles the hypothetical disconfirming data in the preceding paragraph, one rather troublesome experiment was reported recently. Social judgment theory led to the prediction of a main effect of involvement in the issue, such that people with a high level of involvement would show less positive attitude change, in response to a discrepant communication, than would people with a low level of involvement. In most studies, this expectation has been sustained. If one examines the family of curves in social judgment theory relating involvement, discrepancy, and attitude change, it is possible for involvement and discrepancy to interact, but only in an ordinal fashion. Under no condition, according to the theory, should highly involved people show more positive attitude change than people who are less involved. Yet, Petty and Cacioppo (1979) found that in response to a communication making a strong argument, those who were highly involved did show more positive change. One could counter that the experimental manipulation they used did not produce anything more than low or moderate involvement in the transitory experimental situation, or that the kind of involvement studied in that experiment was substantially different from the kind of abiding ego-involvement in an issue the Sherifs were writing about. Nonetheless, it is not easy to see how the results of Petty and Cacioppo can be reconciled with social judgment theory as originally formulated.

Another criterion of a good theory is that it be *distinctive,* unique, or in some way different from other theories that purport to deal with the same phenomena. In this respect, we have something of a paradox. The most unique aspect of social judgment theory is that it posits a relationship between a person's judgment or placement of a communication and how the individual responds to the communication in terms of positive attitude change, attitude stability, or negative attitude change (Kiesler, Collins, & Miller, 1969). Yet this unique aspect has not been extensively explored (Harvey & Rutherford, 1958; Granberg & Campbell, 1977). This is due partly to the fact that what is called for is a rather unusual type of analysis in experimental research. For example, in an experiment on attitude change, one might experimentally manipulate the amount of involvement, discrepancy, ambiguity, and identity of the communicator as independent variables in order to look for their main and interactive effects on the dependent variables of placement judgments of the communication and attitude change. But what the unique aspect of social judgment theory calls for is an examination of the relationship between the dependent variables with different combinations of levels of the independent variables. Social judgment theory is not highly specific as to what the nature of the relationship between social judgment and attitude change should be, but it is clear that there should be some relationship. If it were observed that there were no relationship, or no consistent or coherent relationship, between these variables in a series of studies, this would be damaging to social judgment theory. Thus far not much evidence exists on that matter. Granberg and Campbell (1977) suggested that there might be a relationship with discrepancy as an intervening variable. In their interpretation, assimilation and positive attitude change might be inversely related when the discrepancy is small (as if they were alternatives) but positively related when the discrepancy is large (as if they were complementary). Their analysis was post hoc, however, so it should be considered highly tentative, at this time, and subject to additional examination.

Another criterion for evaluating theories is *parsimony* — that, of two *adequate* depictions of a phenomenon, the simpler is to be preferred. Note the emphasis on the word "adequate." Willie Sutton's erstwhile explanation of why he robbed banks (because that's where they keep the money) may be highly parsimonious, but it is not a very adequate or satisfying theory of crime. Social judgment theory would rate highly on the criterion of parsimony. It does not contain excess baggage in the form of irrelevant variables or unnecessarily complicated intervening motivational processes. In one sense, social judgment theory may be more of a descriptive theory, owing to its origins in psychophysics, than a dynamic motivational theory. This would be true especially in relation to balance theory or the theory of cognitive dissonance, which are more likely to attempt to explain why people did a certain thing. Social judgment theory observes and predicts that people who are high in involvement may respond to a highly discrepant communication by showing negative attitude change. But beyond pointing out that the communication fell deep within the person's latitude of rejection, no psychodynamic explanation is offered by social judgment theory as to why the observed response occurred.

With regard to the *scope* of the theory, one has to consider the major methods or situations that are used in research to study attitude change. In the first of these, a person receives an oral or written communication from a source pertaining to some attitude object. This is the type of research situation on which social judgment theory focused almost from the start. It has obvious relevance for that type of information processing situation, and thus it is well within its scope.

The second type of situation is one in which one is induced to engage in attitudinally discrepant behavior. This type of situation, sometimes called the "forced compliance" paradigm, has been a central focus in research stimulated by cognitive dissonance theory (Festinger, 1957; Festinger & Carlsmith, 1959) and later by self-perception theory (Bem, 1967). This type of role-playing or counterattitudinal behavior situation has been given only cursory treatment by people working from the perspective of social judgment theory (Sherif et al., 1965; Peterson & Koulack, 1969).

A third type of situation used to study communication processes and attitude change deals with what happens when the person has direct contact with the attitude object itself. This question relates to the attitudinal consequences of repeated exposure to a stimulus object and also to the vitally important question of what happens when people from different groups meet. We know now that the answer to the old question as to whether increased contact between groups produces more favorable attitudes is a case in point of posing the question in an inadequate way. The real question, or intervening variable, becomes "Contact under what conditions?" If the increased contact takes place under conditions of equal status, cooperative interdependence, and endorsement of the authorities, it is highly probable that attitudes will become more favorable. The Sherifs have contributed substantially to theory and research on intergroup relations and have attempted to integrate social judgment theory with the analysis of intergroup relations (Sherif, 1966, 1976). There is room for further development along that line. For instance, analyzing the perceptions, impressions, and communications that occur in the negotiation process would seem to be potentially within the scope of social judgment theory.

Finally, a good theory should have *heuristic value,* in the sense that it should stimulate research and lead to new discoveries; on this criterion, social judgment theory would be rated somewhere in the middle range. There is an active area of research stimulated by social judgment theory (for recent reviews of some of the published and unpublished research, see Sherif, Kelly, Rodgers, Sarup, & Tittler, 1973; Sherif, 1976, 1980). But in terms of *amount* of research, it is not in the same category as Festinger's theory of cognitive dissonance, which may have predominated in the 1960s, or Heider's balance — attribution theory — which may have predominated in the 1970s.

There are many reasons why people choose to work on research in a given topical area or from a particular theoretical perspective. Some social scientists prefer to work on leads or perspectives that are counterintuitive or not obvious. Social judgment theory does not have a high potential interest for people with such a preference. People who work on a counterintuitive lead run a considerable risk of its being a dead end, a trivial or inconsequential finding. Social judgment theory seems to have proceeded more from the idea of refining commonsense observations in a way that the theory will almost certainly have relevance to what goes on in everyday events. In closing, it is difficult to know what future fate has in store for social judgment theory. But there are several worthwhile concepts and ideas in this theory, and there are several paths that might be fruitful to explore in greater depth from the vantage point of this theory. There is also a need for a periodic stock-taking in which the cumulating evidence is reviewed and the theory expanded and, where necessary, revised.

REFERENCES

Aronson, E., Turner, J., & Carlsmith, J. Communicator credibility and communication discrepancy as determinants of opinion change. *Journal of Abnormal and Social Psychology,* 1963, *67,* 31-36.

Bem, D. Self-perception: An alternative interpretation of cognitive dissonance phenomena. *Psychological Review,* 1967, *74,* 183-200.

Berelson, B., Lazarsfeld, P., & McPhee, W. *Voting: A study of opinion formation in a presidential campaign.* Chicago: University of Chicago Press, 1954.

Bochner, S., & Insko, C. Communicator discrepancy, source credibility and opinion change. *Journal of Personality and Social Psychology,* 1966, *4,* 614-621.

Brent, E., & Granberg, D. Subjective agreement with the presidential candidates of 1976 and 1980. *Journal of Personality and Social Psychology,* 1982, *42,* 393-403.

Broder, D. Brock a good choice. *Columbia Daily Tribune,* February 2, 1977, p. 6.

Bruner, J. On perceptual readiness. *Psychological Review,* 1957, *64,* 123-152.

Byrne, D., & Blalock, B. Similarity and assumed similarity of attitudes between husbands and wives. *Journal of Abnormal and Social Psychology,* 1963, *67,* 636-640.

Cohen, E. Stimulus conditions as factors in social change. *Sociometry,* 1957, *20,* 135-144.

Divine, R. *The Cuban missile crisis.* Chicago: Quadrangle, 1971.

Eagly, A., & Telaak, K. Width of the latitude of acceptance as a determinant of attitude change. *Journal of Personality and Social Psychology,* 1972, *23,* 388-397.

Eiser, J. Enhancement of contrast in the absolute judgment of attitude statements. *Journal of Personality and Social Psychology,* 1971, *17,* 1-10.

Eiser, J., & Stroebe, W. *Categorization and social judgment.* New York: Academic Press, 1972.

Festinger, L. *A theory of cognitive dissonance.* Evanston, IL: Row, Peterson, 1957.

Festinger, L., & Carlsmith, J. Cognitive consequences of forced compliance. *Journal of Abnormal and Social Psychology,* 1959, *58,* 203-211.

Garrow, D. *The FBI and Martin Luther King, Jr.: From "solo" to Memphis.* New York: W. W. Norton, 1981.

Granberg, D. Family size preferences and sexual permissiveness as factors differentiating abortion activists. *Social Psychology Quarterly,* 1982, *45,* 15-23.

Granberg, D., & Aboud, J. A contextual effect in judgments of visual numerousness. *American Journal of Psychology,* 1969, *82,* 221-227.

Granberg, D., & Brent, E. Dove-hawk placements in the 1968 election: Application of social judgment and balance theories. *Journal of Personality and Social Psychology,* 1974, *29,* 687-695.

Granberg, D., & Brent, E. Perceptions of issue positions of presidential candidates. *American Scientist,* 1980, *68,* 617-625.

Granberg, D., & Campbell, K. Effect of communication ambiguity and discrepancy on placement and opinion change. *European Journal of Social Psychology,* 1977, *7,* 137-150.

Granberg, D., Harris, W., & King, M. Assimilation but little contrast in the 1976 U.S. presidential election. *Journal of Psychology,* 1981, *108,* 241-247.

Granberg, D., Jefferson, L., Brent, E., & King, M. Membership group, reference group and the attribution of attitudes to groups. *Journal of Personality and Social Psychology,* 1981, *40,* 833-842.

Granberg, D., & Jenks, R. Assimilation and contrast in the 1972 election. *Human Relations,* 1977, *30,* 623-640.

Granberg, D., & King, M. Cross-lagged panel analysis of the relation between attraction and perceived similarity. *Journal of Experimental Social Psychology*, 1980, *16*, 573-581.

Granberg, D., & Seidel, J. Social judgments on the urban and Vietnam issues in 1968 and 1972. *Social Forces*, 1976, *55*, 1-15.

Granberg, D., & Steele, L. Procedural considerations in measuring the latitudes of acceptance, rejection, and noncommitment. *Social Forces*, 1974, *52*, 538-542.

Harvey, O., & Rutherford, J. Gradual and absolute approaches to attitude change. *Sociometry*, 1958, *21*, 61-68.

Heider, F. *The psychology of interpersonal relations.* New York: John Wiley, 1958.

Helson, H. *Adaptation-level theory.* New York: Harper & Row, 1964.

Hinckley, E. The influence of individual opinion on construction of an attitude scale. *Journal of Social Psychology*, 1932, *37*, 283-296.

Hovland, C. Reconciling conflicting results derived from experimental and survey studies of attitude change. *American Psychologist*, 1959, *14*, 8-17.

Hovland, C., Harvey, O., & Sherif, M. Assimilation and contrast effects in reaction to communication and attitude change. *Journal of Abnormal and Social Psychology*, 1957, *55*, 242-252.

Hovland, C., & Sherif, M. Judgmental phenomena and scales of attitude measurement: Item displacement in Thurstone scales. *Journal of Abnormal and Social Psychology*, 1952, *47*, 822-832.

Kennedy, R. *Thirteen days: A memoir of the Cuban missile crisis.* New York: W. W. Norton, 1969.

Kiesler, C., Collins, B., & Miller, N. *Attitude change: A critical analysis of theoretical approaches.* New York: John Wiley, 1969.

Kinder, D. Political person perception: The asymmetrical influence of sentiment and choice on perceptions of presidential candidates. *Journal of Personality and Social Psychology*, 1978, *36*, 859-871.

King, M. Assimilation and contrast of presidential candidates' issue positions, 1972. *Public Opinion Quarterly*, 1978, *41*, 515-522.

LaFave, L., & Sherif, M. Reference scales and placement of items with the own categories technique. *Journal of Social Psychology*, 1968, *76*, 75-82.

Manchester, W. *American Caesar: Douglas MacArthur, 1880-1964.* Boston: Little, Brown, 1979.

Manis, M. The interpretation of opinion statements as a function of message ambiguity and recipient attitude. *Journal of Abnormal and Social Psychology*, 1961, *63*, 78-81. (a)

Manis, M. The interpretation of opinion statements as a function of recipient attitude and source prestige. *Journal of Abnormal and Social Psychology*, 1961, *63*, 82-86. (b)

Manis, M., & Moore, J. Summarizing controversial messages: Retroactive effects due to subsequent information. *Social Psychology*, 1978, *41*, 62-68.

McGuinnis, J. *The selling of the president 1968.* New York: Simon & Schuster, 1969.

Osgood, C., Suci, G., & Tannenbaum, P. *The measurement of meaning.* Urbana: University of Illinois Press, 1957.

Page, B., & Brody, R. Policy voting and the electoral process: The Vietnam war issue. *American Political Science Review*, 1972, *66*, 979-995.

Page, B., & Jones, C. Reciprocal effects of policy preferences, party loyalties and the vote. *American Political Science Review*, 1979, *73*, 1071-1089.

Pepitone, A., & DeNubile, M. Contrast effects in judgments of crime severity and the punishment of criminal violators. *Journal of Personality and Social Psychology*, 1976, *33*, 448-459.

Peterson, P., & Koulack, D. Attitude change as a function of latitudes of acceptance and rejection. *Journal of Personality and Social Psychology*, 1969, *11*, 309-311.

Petty, R., & Cacioppo, J. Issue involvement can increase or decrease persuasion by enhancing message-relevant cognitive responses. *Journal of Personality and Social Psychology*, 1979, *37*, 1915-1926.

Pinter, R., & Forlano, G. The influence of attitude upon scaling of attitude items. *Journal of Social Psychology*, 1937, *8*, 39-45.

Reinhold, R. Issues run second in campaign. *New York Times News Service,* February 21, 1976.
Rhine, R., & Severance, L. Ego-involvement, discrepancy, source credibility and attitude change. *Journal of Personality and Social Psychology,* 1970, *16,* 175-190.
Rogers, L. *The influence of ego-involvement on attitude structures for issues of varying degrees of personal relevance.* Unpublished doctoral dissertation, Pennsylvania State University, 1978.
Shaffer, S. Balance theory and political cognitions. *American Politics Quarterly,* 1981, *9,* 291-320.
Shaw, M. & Constanzo, P. *Theories of social psychology.* New York: McGraw-Hill, 1970.
Shepsle, K. The strategy of ambiguity: Uncertainty and electoral competition. *American Political Science Review,* 1972, *66,* 555-568.
Sherif, C. W. *Orientation in social psychology.* New York: Harper & Row, 1976.
Sherif, C. W. Social values, attitudes, and the involvement of the self. *Nebraska symposium on motivation,* 1980, *27,* 1-64. (Available from the University of Nebraska Press).
Sherif, C. W., & Jackman, N. Judgments of truth by participants in collective controversy. *Public Opinion Quarterly,* 1966, *30,* 173-186.
Sherif, C. W., Kelly, M., Rodgers, H., Sarup, G., & Tittler, B. Personal involvement, social judgment and action. *Journal of Personality and Social Psychology,* 1973, *27,* 311-328.
Sherif, C. W., Sherif, M., & Nebergall, R. *Attitude and attitude change: The social judgment-involvement approach.* Philadelphia: W. B. Saunders, 1965.
Sherif, M. A study of some social factors in perception. *Archives of Psychology,* 1935, *187.*
Sherif, M. *The psychology of social norms.* New York: Harper & Row, 1936.
Sherif, M. Experiments in group conflict. *Scientific American,* 1956, *195,* 54-58.
Sherif, M. Superordinate goals in the reduction of intergroup conflicts. *American Journal of Sociology,* 1958, *63,* 349-356.
Sherif, M. *In common predicament.* Boston: Houghton Mifflin, 1966.
Sherif, M., & Cantril, H. *The psychology of ego-involvements.* New York: John Wiley, 1947.
Sherif, M., & Hovland, C. Judgmental phenomena and scales of attitude measurement: Placement of items with individual choice of number of categories. *Journal of Abnormal and Social Psychology,* 1953, *48,* 135-141.
Sherif, M., & Hovland, C. *Social judgment: Assimilation and contrast effects in communication and attitude change.* New Haven, CT: Yale University Press, 1961.
Sherif, M., & Sherif, C. W. *Groups in harmony and tension.* New York: Harper & Row, 1953.
Sherif, M., & Sherif, C. W. *An outline of social psychology.* New York: Harper & Row, 1956.
Sherif, M., & Sherif, C. W. Attitude as the individual's own categories: The social judgment-involvement approach to attitude and attitude change. In C. W. Sherif & M. Sherif (Eds.), *Attitude, ego-involvement, and change.* New York: John Wiley, 1967.
Sherif, M., Taub, D., & Hovland, C. Assimilation and contrast effects of anchoring stimuli on judgments. *Journal of Experimental Psychology,* 1958, *55,* 150-155.
Sherrod, D. Selective perception of political candidates. *Public Opinion Quarterly,* 1972, *35,* 554-562.
Tajfel, H. Social and cultural factors in perception. In G. Lindzey & E. Aronson (Eds.), *Handbook of social psychology* (Vol. 3). Reading, MA: Addison-Wesley, 1969.
Thurstone, L. Attitudes can be measured. *American Journal of Sociology,* 1928, *33,* 529-554.
TRB. Gracious interval. *The New Republic,* November 13, 1976.
Upshaw, H. The personal reference scale: An approach to social judgment. In L. Berkowitz (Ed.), *Advances in experimental social psychology* (Vol. 4). New York: Academic Press, 1969.
Whittaker, J. Parameters of social influence in the autokinetic situation. *Sociometry,* 1964, *27,* 88-95.
Zimbardo, P., & Ebbesen, E. *Influencing attitudes and changing behavior.* Reading, MA: Addison-Wesley, 1969.

11 • Cognitive Schemata and Persuasive Communication: Toward a Contingency Rules Theory

MARY JOHN SMITH
University of Wyoming

THIS chapter is divided into four sections. First, a critique of the traditional theoretical paradigm in persuasion is presented. Next, an alternative contingency rules approach, based on cognitive schema theory, is described. Third, the chapter reports some preliminary data supporting the proposed theory, and finally, the advantages of the new theoretical model vis-à-vis the prevailing paradigm are discussed.

A CRITIQUE OF THE PREVAILING PARADIGM

Over the last decade, dissatisfaction with the traditional theoretical paradigm in persuasion has grown steadily. Criticism has focused on two related issues: (1) the pervasive reliance on "attitude" as a central analytical unit in persuasion theory, and (2) a continuing allegiance to the "Hovland tradition" in theory and research (see Hovland, Janis, & Kelley, 1953), entailing a variable-analytic, causal laws approach to the explanation of persuasive behavior.

The depth of discontent with the traditional "attitude-toward-object" construct is reflected in comments ranging from Abelson's (1976) acerbic charge that "the present state of attitude theory is frankly a mess" (p. 40), to Miller's (1980) conclusion that the construct has failed to yield any "useful advice regarding prediction and control in everyday persuasive transactions" (p. 321). Two primary objections underlie this disaffection. First, critics argue that "attitude" is a conceptually ambiguous construct,

---

Correspondence and requests for reprints: Mary John Smith, Department of Communication, University of Wyoming, Laramie, WY 82071.

leading to a plethora of different operationalizations and, therefore, to a variety of noncomparable "attitude change" findings (see Jaccard, 1981; Fishbein & Ajzen, 1975, 1972; and Greenwald, 1968a). To support this criticism, Fishbein and Ajzen (1972) reviewed attitude change research published over a two-year period and found more than 500 different operationalizations of the "attitude-toward-object" concept. Commenting on these conceptual and operational problems, Greenwald (1968a, p. 361) concludes that, given "the diversity of attitude definitions," many persuasion theorists have begun to "despair at finding consensus or justification for one definition as opposed to others."

Second, Miller (1980, 1967; Miller & Burgoon, 1978) and others (Wicker, 1971, 1969; Festinger, 1964) have questioned the reliability of attitude as a predictor of overt behavior, and considerable research documents the construct's predictive inefficiency (Wicker, 1971, 1969; Wrightsman, 1969; Berg, 1966; Miller & Hewgill, 1966; Carr & Roberts, 1965; Festinger, 1964; LaPière, 1934). Defenders of the attitude-behavior link have responded with numerous "other variables" explanations for the failure of attitude-toward-object measures to predict behavior. However, most of these accounts have been less than elegant, since they typically relate attitudes to behavior by taking into consideration multiple sources of situational and normative variance (Rokeach & Kliejunas, 1972; Ajzen & Fishbein, 1970; Warner & DeFleur, 1969), the attitude formation process (Regan & Fazio, 1977), properties of the attitude itself (Fazio & Zanna, 1978; Heberlein & Black, 1976; Norman, 1975), measurement problems (Weigel & Newman, 1976; Fishbein & Azjen, 1974; Tittle & Hill, 1967), and a number of related internal mediators such as competing attitudes, personality traits, habits, and so forth (Triandis, 1980; McArthur, Kiesler, & Cook, 1969; Ehrlich, 1969). Too often these "other variables" accounts offer the persuasion researcher multivariate predictive models that lack either parsimony, conceptual clarity, or both (see Wicker, 1971; for an example of a particularly cumbersome verbal formulation, see Rokeach & Kliejunas, 1972).

Citing these conceptual and predictive problems, a number of theorists have called for alternative approaches to the message-behavior relationship. Two classes of alternatives have been proposed. First, several writers (Miller, 1980; Miller & Burgoon, 1978; Larson & Sanders, 1975; Bem, 1972; DeFleur & Westie, 1963-1964; Campbell, 1963; Green, 1954) have urged that the cognitive or predispositional approach to persuasion be abandoned altogether in favor of a behavioral perspective. For example, Larson and Sanders (1975) argue that the function of persuasion is best viewed as behavior alignment to conform to contextual constraints, and Green (1954, p. 336) suggests that persuasion theory ought to focus on the alteration of "a defined behavior in a defined situation." Taking a different approach, other theorists have suggested that attitude be replaced by a more precise and behaviorally sensitive cognitive structure. Several writers (Jaccard, 1981; O'Keefe, 1980; Fishbein & Ajzen, 1975) advocate the use of "belief," or a subjective relationship probability, as the central analytical unit in cognitive theories of persuasion. Taking a related but broader perspective, Miller (1980, pp. 326-327) has proposed that "the *process* of information processing rather than the *construct* of attitude [might be] viewed as a set of related antecedent variables, which function to inhibit or facilitate behavior change. Such a theoretic posture," he argues, "is less likely to lead the persuasion student down blind alleys in search of some elusive solution to the attitude-behavior problem."

Taking this information-processing approach, several communication theorists (Smith, 1981, Cappella & Folger, 1980; Infante, 1980) have proposed that dynamic cognitive organizers such as "cognitive schemata" (see Taylor & Crocker, 1981), "scripts" (see Schank & Abelson, 1977; Abelson, 1976), or "plans" (see Schank & Abelson, 1977; Miller, Galanter, & Pribram, 1960) might profitably be viewed as mediators of overt persuasive effects. Noting that cognitive schemata are interrelated sets of "interpretative and behavioral rules containing pre-determined action sequences" Smith (1981) argues that, "relative to 'attitude,' 'schema' is conceptually unambiguous and incorporates an explicit link to overt human action." Despite over thirty years of arguments such as these for behavioral or cognitive alternatives to the traditional attitude construct, persuasion theorists, with very few exceptions (see Jaccard, 1981; O'Keefe, 1980; Hewes, 1980; Larson & Sanders, 1975; Fishbein & Ajzen, 1975, pp. 457-474) continue to rely heavily on attitude as a central analytical unit in persuasion theory and research (for recent examples, see Petty & Cacioppo, 1981; Cushman & McPhee, 1980).

The second major source of dissatisfaction with persuasion theory grows out of the epistemological posture most persuasion theorists assume when investigating social influence processes. Following the lead of social psychologists in the tradition of Carl Hovland and the Yale school theorists (see Hovland et al., 1953), communication scholars early on adopted a variable-analytic, probabilistic causal laws approach to the explanation of persuasive behavior. The laws approach, which the social psychologists borrowed from the physical and biological sciences, explains both message production and responses to messages by referring to causes or antecedent variables capable of producing some consequent effects (see Hume, 1902). Applied to persuasion, laws are general statements about the ways people will probably respond to certain types of message variables in specifiable kinds of communication environments (Miller, 1972, p.

28; also see Berger, 1977), and they take the general form: "Message strategy X will probably cause response Y, under specifiable boundary conditions $Z_1 \ldots Z_n$. A prototype statistical-inductive persuasion law derived from McCroskey's (1972) work states that: "Evidence in a persuasive message (X) will probably cause greater attitude change (Y) than a message containing no evidence, under the conditions that the source lacks credibility, the evidence is novel, the message is well-delivered, and the like $(Z_1 \ldots Z_n)$." Thus the prevailing laws epistemology assumes that message strategies are generative forces having the capacity of *cause* responses in human recipients. Applied to message production, this assumption implies that, given any well-defined communication environment, effective compliance-gaining strategies are predetermined, and, therefore, are to be "found" rather than "chosen."

In recent years critics from several disciplines, including the communication sciences (Smith, 1982; Reardon, 1981; Shimanoff, 1980), rhetorical theory (Bormann, 1980, 1978; Simons, 1980, 1978a, 1978b; Rosenthal, 1972), and social psychology (Jaccard, 1981; Buss, 1979, 1978; Eagly & Himmelfarb, 1974; Harré & Secord, 1972; Miller et al., 1960), have challenged this deterministic approach to persuasion on conceptual as well as practical grounds. Their objections fall into two related classes. First, several writers (see Smith, 1982, pp. 67-73; Shimanoff, 1980, pp. 204-205; Bormann, 1978, pp. 58-67; Simons, 1980, pp. 206-207, 1978a, pp. 28-41) argue that the laws approach is an inappropriate explanatory model for persuasion because the epistemological assumptions it entails are incompatible with the nature of the phenomena needing explanation; namely, human message production and responses to messages. In making this argument, most critics (see Smith, 1982; pp. 67-68; Pearce, 1976, pp. 18-19) concede that numerous persuasive communication behaviors, such as skills deficits, chronic psychological predispositions, and acute physiological arousal states, are in fact causally determined phenomena, and therefore, compatible with these laws assumptions. However, based on evidence accumulated over more than twenty years by communication specialists and cognitive psychologists (see Higgins, Herman, & Zanna, 1981; Pearce & Cronen, 1980, pp. 231-302; Schramm & Roberts, 1971, pp. 191-346; Bauer, 1964; Davison, 1959), these writers (see Smith, 1982, pp. 68-70; Simons, 1980, pp. 206-207) contend that much persuasive communicative behavior is embued with choice and thus is *purposive*, not causal, in nature.

Applied to persuasion theory, this analysis suggests that people are not constrained by antecedent conditions to select one compliance-gaining tactic over another when they desire to influence others. Nor are their responses to persuasive messages forced by antecedent message strategies. Rather the process of producing and responding to messages is a complex, cognitive activity wherein humans select from varying alternative courses of action those strategies best meeting their needs and desires. In doing so they normally produce and accept those persuasive recommendations promising benefits, and reject those threatening undesirable consequences. Based on this analysis, several writers (Smith, 1982, pp. 67-73; Shimanoff, 1980, pp. 200-205) have concluded that the laws assumptions: (1) that antecedent conditions *predetermine* message strategy selection, and (2) that message strategies, in turn, *cause* responses in people, are misleading accounts of the motivational dynamics underlying persuasive communication behaviors.

The second class of objections concerns the secondary consequences of applying causal assumptions, including a variable-analytic methodology, to the persuasion process. Several critics representing diverse theoretical persuasions (Smith, 1982; Jaccard, 1981; Delia, 1977; Eagly & Himmelfarb, 1974) argue that the prevailing laws paradigm has led to an unduly simplistic view of the persuasion process. This oversimplification is manifested in at least three ways. First, the assumption that message variables directly cause responses has encouraged many persuasion theorists to deemphasize the interpretative and memory reconstruction processes whereby receivers assign uniquely personal meanings to messages (see Delia, 1977, pp. 75-79). As a consequence, persuasion researchers following the Hovland tradition often treat uninterpreted message content as a critical variable mediating cognitive and behavioral outcomes (see Greenwald, 1968b, pp. 147-148; for a summary of some illustrative message research, see Burgoon & Bettinghaus, 1980, pp. 143-153), despite persuasive evidence that recipients respond to their idiosyncratic reconstructions of and cognitive responses to message content, in effect, to the messages they create for themselves (see Petty, Ostrom, & Brock, 1981; Petty & Cacioppo, 1981, pp. 225-250; Perloff & Brock, 1980; Greenwald, 1968b). Second, some critics (see Smith, 1982, p. 315) contend that the use of a causal paradigm to conceptualize and describe persuasion has been at least partially responsible for perpetuating the erroneous view of persuasion as undirectional process of influence, in which some active source induces change in one or more relatively passive receivers. As a result of this view, the dynamically developmental nature of the persuasion process has been obscured or ignored in much persuasion theory and research (see Miller, 1978, pp. 172-173).

Finally, several writers (Smith, 1982, p. 315; also see Reardon, 1981) argue that persuasion's historical association with causal laws has encouraged communication professionals and laypersons alike to view persuasion as a conceptually narrow, manipulative form of communication that is somehow set apart from other, more "worthy" or "socially significant" forms of human communicative interaction (for a related discussion, see Miller & Burgoon, 1978). Indeed professional writers in persuasion often perpetuate this equation of "persuasion" with "salesmanship" by including in their works "ethical" guidelines that imply persuasion is a dangerous, manipulative tool. Suggestions that persuaders should not "falsify or misrepresent evidence," that they should avoid "smear attacks" and "name-calling" and develop "expectations about ethics and morality," are not uncommon in contemporary persuasion textbooks (for a summary of ethical guidelines appearing in several popular texts, see Larson, 1979, pp. 248-275). Although ethical concerns undeniably are pertinent to all forms of communicative interaction, it is interesting that one rarely finds a similar preoccupation with ethics in works on interpersonal or relational communication, subdisciplines that traditionally have not been directly associated with a causal epistemology. As a result of this conceptually narrow view of social influence processes, the role of persuasion in all forms of human communication has been undeservedly trivialized, contributing to the declining interest in persuasion research that Miller and Burgoon (1978) spoke of in this volume five years ago.

Reflecting these concerns about the application of a causal epistemology to persuasion, several theorists representing divergent conceptual postures (Smith, 1982; Reardon, 1981; Jaccard, 1981; Bormann, 1980, 1978; Simons, 1978a; 1978b; Eagly & Himmelfarb, 1974) have called for new theoretical paradigms within which to explore persuasive communication. For instance, the social psychologist Jaccard (1981) has argued for development of "new frameworks and approaches" to replace "the Hovland tradition" in persuasion theory and research (p. 260). Reflecting a rhetorical perspective, Bormann (1978) has urged theorists to "abandon the Newtonian model and the influence of the old behaviorism" (p. 61). And the communication theorist Reardon (1981) argues for a "persuasion renaissance, the beginnings of which must be characterized by a loosening of the fetters that have bound the phenomenon to undeserved negative attributions" (p. 15). Finally, Smith (1982) summarized many of these concerns by calling for a "complete overhaul in ways of thinking and talking about persuasion," arguing that abandoning the traditional epistemology "should prompt professionals and laypersons alike to assume a more realistic view of the role of persuasion in all human communication" (pp. 314-317).

COGNITIVE SCHEMA THEORY AND CONTINGENCY RULES: TOWARD AN ALTERNATIVE THEORETICAL APPROACH

As a response to these criticisms, the contingency rules theory: (1) abandons the concept of "attitude" as the central mediator of overt persuasive effects in favor of the cognitive organizer "schema," and (2) adopts a purposive epistemological posture, holding that persuasive behaviors are governed antecedently by expectations about the consequences of alternative courses of action. Since it is grounded in cognitive schema theory, the contingency rules perspective represents an information-processing approach to persuasion theory and research.

Cognitive Schema Theory

Frederick Bartlett (1932) is credited with originating the construct "schema" as a reaction to the associationists' (Ebbinghaus, 1885) copy theory of perception and memory. Taking issue with the assumption that external stimuli and cognitive representations are isomorphic, he argued that perception and memory are not mere reproductive processes, but rather are reconstructive activities, guided by "an active organization of past reactions, or of past experiences" (Bartlett, 1932, p. 21). Bartlett's then-revolutionary cognitive schema theory of human information processing is now a commonly accepted account, and it rests on three related assumptions (see Hastie, 1981; Taylor & Crocker, 1981): (1) experiential phenomena, including external and internal stimuli, are dynamically different from cognitive representations thereof, (2) experiential phenomena, including self and other objects and actions, cannot be related cognitively without some self-organizing hypothesis by which the relationship is defined, and (3) human interpretative processes and action episodes are highly purposive, being driven by anticipatory assumptions about what the world means and how to go about enacting appropriate behaviors to reach desired goal states. These anticipatory assumptions about meanings and actions are termed "cognitive schemata."

More particularly, schemata are defined as hierarchically interrelated sets of expectancies or hypotheses, each of which relates either: (1) a self or other *object* to its presumed *attribute,* or (2) some specified *action* to its anticipated *consequences* (see Hastie, 1981; Taylor & Crocker, 1981; Tesser, 1978; Schank & Abelson, 1977; Markus, 1977; Abelson, 1976; Neisser, 1976; Minsky, 1975; Reed, 1973, 1972; Miller et al. 1960). "I am an honest person," "Politicians are crooks," "Crime doesn't pay," and "Virtue is its own reward" are clichéd examples of schemata, each representing an assumed relationship or cooccurrence between either self/other objects and their attributes or an action sequence and its anticipated consequences. Because schemata represent *anticipatory assumptions* about object-attribute and action-consequence covariations, they function as *contingency rules* that guide interpretation and structure action.

As this description suggests, a schematic set relevant to any area of experience consists of two functionally distinct types of contingency rules: interpretative and behavioral schemata.[1] *Interpretative contingency rules,* variously labeled prototype schemata (Tversky, 1977; Rosch & Mervis, 1975; Reed, 1972), template schemata (Norman & Bobrow, 1975), frames (Minsky, 1975), and thematic structures (Lingle, Geva, Ostrom, Leippe, & Baumgardner, 1979), impart meaning to self and other phenomena.[2] According to Tesser (1978, p. 290), an interpretative "schema contains the network of associations that is believed to hold among the attributes of the stimulus and thereby provides rules for thinking about the stimulus." Thus, when some self or other object is matched against interpretative schemata, the stimulus object "come[s] to be ordered in a manner that reflects the structure of the schema" (Taylor & Crocker, 1981, p. 97). Importantly, interpretative rules contain "default options," allowing one to "fill-in" pertinent information when "some relevant attribute is unavailable from the stimulus itself or is ambiguous or is unavailable from memory" (Tesser, 1978, p. 290). In sum, interpretative contingency rules are configurations of object/attribute hypotheses, arranged hierarchically by abstraction level, that impart meaning to a person's self and other worlds.

The second variety of schemata, *behavioral contingency rules,* variously called procedural schemata (Neisser, 1976), action schemata (Taylor & Crocker, 1981), scripts (Schank & Abelson, 1977; Abelson, 1976), and plans (Schank & Abelson, 1977; Miller et al., 1960), represent anticipatory assumptions about how some specified action or behavior sequence is related to its consequences. As a mental representation of a "predetermined, stereotyped sequence of actions" (Schank & Abelson, 1977, p. 41), behavioral contingency rules enable a person "to envision a state toward which he or she would like to move" (Taylor & Crocker, 1981, p. 112). Moreover, because they "are temporally-ordered," Taylor and Crocker (1981, p. 112) note that an "action schema also provides a basis for moving from a current state to an ideal state by specifying, at least roughly, what intermediate events are required. . . . This, in turn, provides a basis for selecting the appropriate behavior sequence." In sum, behavioral contingency rules are temporally ordered, anticipatory action/consequence associations that serve as cognitive guides for purposeful action.

Although interpretative and behavioral contingency rules serve different functions, the two cognitive structures are integrally related. Indeed it will be recognized that behavioral contingency rules subsume interpretative rules, since the evaluative meanings people attach to objects and actions at any one abstraction level define the goals they value and the actions they interpret as goal maximizing. Thus behavioral contingency rules represent cognitive reorganizations of interpretative schemata (for a related analysis, see Pearce & Cronen, 1980, pp. 141-144). Given this subsumptive relationship, the balance of this chapter will focus on behavioral contingency rules or action schemata as the generative forces responsible for persuasive communication behaviors.

A Contingency Rules Theory of Persuasion

The contingency rules theory equates "persuasive behavior" with the *strategic choices people make* when they: (1) select compliance-gaining message strategies from the alternatives available in specified social influence contexts, and (2) selectively respond to self- or other-generated persuasive messages in specified contexts. Persuasion, then, is viewed as a compliance-gaining and compliance-responding strategic activity. Given this conception, the contingency rules theory rests on three assumptions. First, the perspective assumes that persuasive behavior is *purposive,* being governed *antecedently* by its *anticipated consequences.* The anticipatory action/consequence relationships that guide action are contained in behavioral contingency rules or action schemata that take the general form: If consequence X, in context Y, then behavior Z. Thus the theory assumes that behavioral contingency rules govern the strategic choices people make when they produce and respond to persuasive messages. Being guided by these anticipatory assumptions, persuasive agents "can foresee the probable consequences of different actions and alter their behavior accordingly," permitting both "insightful and foresightful" action (Bandura, 1971, p. 3). As this description suggests, the contingency rules theory abandons the distinction many communication theorists draw between antecedent and consequent regulators of communicative behavior (see Reardon, 1981, p. 58, 109; Pearce & Cronen, 1980, pp. 164-165). Behavioral consequences, typically learned vicariously in the adult actor, are assumed to govern persuasive behavior antecedently by creating expectancies of similar consequences in similar contexts.

Second, the contingency rules theory assumes that persuasive behavior is largely *self-regulated.* (For related perspectives, see Cushman, Valentinsen, and Whiting's [1980] theory of the self concept as a cybernetic control system; Bandura's [1977, 1971] self-reinforcement theory; and Schwartz's [1974, 1973] personal norms model.) The notion that behavior is controlled by its anticipated consequences is often erroneously interpreted to mean that people are at the mercy of situational or external influences. This construction is unfortunate since, as many theorists have observed, "behavior can and is extensively self-regulated by self-produced consequences for one's own actions" (Bandura, 1971, pp. 27-28; also see Schwartz, 1973, p. 353), including the selection of compliance-gaining strategies and the strategic responses one makes to persuasive messages. People set goals or behavioral standards for themselves and respond to their actions in self-satisfied or self-critical ways, depending on whether the behavior conforms to or violates self-imposed norms (see Bandura, 1977, pp. 128-158, 1971, pp. 27-35; and Schwartz, 1973, 1968 for supportive evidence). Thus if I consider myself to be a kind, generous, and honest person, I have set three standards for evaluating my own behavior. If I consider using a persuasive strategy that might hurt important others unnecessarily, I will likely regard myself with disfavor. In contrast, if I expect to behave generously and honestly, I should be pleased with my intentions. As this analysis shows, it is the *anticipation* of self-imposed consequences that motivates people to keep their persuasive behavior in line with self-established standards or values.

Third and finally, the contingency rules perspective assumes that expectancies about the *external consequences* of persuasive behavior, both physical and social, are *subsumed* within human self-regulatory systems. From this view, expected positive and negative external contingencies such as social approval or environmental hazards serve only "as cues to elicit covert self-satisfaction or self-criticism" (Bandura, 1971, p. 33). Thus the expectancy of an external "reward" for selecting a particular persuasive strategy or responding to messages in certain ways is motivational only if the reward is congruent with one's personal standards. And anticipated social or environmental "punishment" for persuasive choices is meaningful only if it blocks the pursuit of personal goals.

To summarize, the contingency rules approach to persuasion theory assumes that: (1) persuasive behavior is purposive, being governed antecedently by its anticipated consequences in specified contexts, (2) persuasive behavior is extensively self-regulated by anticipated self-satisfaction and self-criticism, and (3) expectancies about the external consequences of persuasive behavior are meaningful only if the contingencies are relevant to self-established goals and standards for behaving.

Behavioral Contingency Rules: A Two-Factor Model

According to the contingency rules theory, persuasive behavior entailing message production and response is governed antecedently by one of two types of behavioral contingency rules: self-evaluative and adaptive schemata. *Self-evaluative rules* link persuasive behavior to self-established standards for behaving (including basic values and central beliefs about the self), in short, to the kind of person one perceives himself or herself to be (for similar constructs, see Cushman et al., 1980; Bandura, 1977, pp. 128-158, 1971, pp. 27-35; Schwartz, 1973, 1968; Fishbein, 1967; Katz, 1960, pp. 174-189). The contingency rules approach recognizes two categories of self-regulated consequences, and therefore, two varieties of self-evaluative rules. First, *self-identity rules* link persuasive behavior to personal characteristics and values, including moral or ethical standards, that constitute one's conception of the self (for related constructs, see Cushman et al., 1980; Schwartz, 1973, pp. 352-355). As such, they obligate a person to produce and respond to messages in ways that promote the establishment and maintenance of a desired *private* self-concept. Second, *image-maintenance rules* link persuasive behavior to self-presentational or impression-management concerns (see Schlenker & Reiss, 1979; Gaes, Kalle, & Tedeschi, 1978; Tedeschi, Schlenker, & Bonoma, 1971), and therefore, they compel one to produce and respond to messages in ways that facilitate the establishment and maintenance of a desired *public* self-identity.

Schemata such as "I am honest," "I am intelligent," "I am a feminist," and "I am not a racist," exemplify self-evaluative behavior standards that might variously serve either private self-identity or public image-maintenance functions. Some of these self-defining standards will be *idiosyncratic,* reflecting values peculiar to an individual, for example, "I am honest." Others will be linked to self-defining *reference groups,* reflecting either identification with admired generalized others, for example, "I am a feminist," or *differentiation* from disliked generalized others, as in the example, "I am not a racist." All self-evaluative rules, whether of the self-identity or self-presentational variety, link persuasive behavior to anticipated self-satisfaction and self-criticism for conforming to or violating one's self-imposed values and standards. Thus their *practical force* derives from expectations of self-administered consequences.

Adaptive rules, the second type of behavioral schemata, link persuasive behavior to extrinsic goal achievement, including the acquisition of valued environmental and social consequences and the avoidance of negative ones (for related constructs, see Bandura, 1977, pp. 97-128, 1971, pp. 20-27; Dulany, 1968, 1961; Katz, 1960, pp. 171-178; Smith, Bruner, & White, 1956, pp. 41-43). The contingency rules theory differentiates among three kinds of extrinsic consequences, and therefore, three types of adaptive rules. First, *environmental contingency rules* relate persuasive behavior to concerns for the health, safety, and general physical and mental well-being of the self and important particular others. Second, *interpersonal relationship rules* relate message production and responses to the maintenance of personally satisfying relationships with particular admired others, including the attainment of intimacy and approval and the avoidance of personal rejection. Finally, *social normative rules* link persuasive behavior with general societal and cultural norms defining what persuasive strategies one must or must not select and what strategic responses one must or must not make in specified social contexts to achieve extrinsic objects of desire, including economic benefits, political advantage, and social status. Because all three varieties of adaptive rules associate persuasive behavior with extrinsic goal achievement, their *practical force* derives from expectations of externally administered positive and negative consequences that are relevant to a person's self-regulatory system, including personal goals and standards of behaving.

In summary, the contingency rules perspective assumes that persuasive behavior is governed antecedently by one of two types of behavioral contingency rules: self-evaluative and adaptive expectancies. Thus the approach is a *two-factor theory* of persuasive communication.

The Nature and Role of Context

Like all schemata, behavioral contingency rules are context specific. Thus categories of anticipated consequences, whether self-evaluative or adaptive, are selectively activated by the persuasive contexts where social influence agents produce and respond to messages. The contingency rules theory differentiates between two dimensions of context: potential and actual; and regards an actual context (AC) as a function of persuasive behavior (B) in a potential context (PC). Stated equationally: $AC = f(B) PC$.[3]

A *potential context* consists of situational phenomena that, at the time, are not under the control of the communicating parties. Physiological antecedents such as the communicators' intelligence levels, acquired and dispositional skills such as each persuader's level of communication competence, chronic psychological states such as anxiety, self-esteem, dogmatism, and authoritarianism, temporary arousal states such as fear and anger, and situational exigencies such as each communicator's social and economic status all represent conditions people do not fully control. Yet each affects the limits of purposive action. For example, acute fear arousal or chronic anxiety inevitably will influence persuasive behaviors, including message production and responses aimed at ensuring one's health and safety. Similarity, high dogmatism, or a low self-esteem will affect one's aspiration levels as well as the range of available strategic actions that feasibly may be taken to fulfill objectives. In short, numerous contextual antecedents constituting the potential context influence the goals people value and the persuasive actions they will take in pursuit of those goals. Thus the contingency rules theory recognizes that all persuasive choice-making behavior takes place within boundaries that expand and contract as a function of a relatively fixed potential context.

An *actual context* is a function of human choice-making behavior within potential contextual boundaries. Drawing principally on research into the contextual features of compliance-gaining and compliance-resisting situations (see Cody & McLaughlin, 1980; McLaughlin, Cody, &

Robey, 1980; Cody, McLaughlin, & Jordan, 1980; Sillars, 1980; Fitzpatrick & Winke, 1979; Clark, 1979; Cody, 1978; Miller, Boster, Roloff, & Seibold, 1977; Roloff & Barnicott, 1978; Wish, 1975; Roloff, 1976; Forgas, 1976; Miller & Steinberg, 1975; Marwell & Schmitt, 1967), the contingency rules theory recognizes three dimensions of persuasive behavior that interact with the potential context to define actual persuasive contexts: (1) the nature of the actual or desired *relationship* between or among the persuasive communicators, (2) the persuasive *intentions* of the communicators, and (3) the communicators' *coorientations* toward the persuasive *issue* or topic.

Research by Cody and McLaughlin (1980), Miller (Miller et al., 1977; Miller & Steinberg, 1975), and others (see Forgas, 1976; Wish, 1975) suggests that the relationship between communicators may be differentiated along three contextual dimensions: *intimacy* (superficial/intimate, impersonal/personal, interpersonal/noninterpersonal); *resistance* (friendly/hostile); and *dominance* (equal power/unequal power). Again following Cody and McLaughlin's (1980) and Miller's (Miller et al., 1977) analyses, the persuasive intentions of communicators can be differentiated along two contextual dimensions: *personal benefits* (selfish/altruistic, benefits self/benefits others/mutual benefits); and *consequences* (short-range consequences/long-range consequences). Finally, the communicators' coorientations toward the persuasion topic may be differentiated along three contextual dimensions: *ego-involvement* (each involved/each uninvolved); *schematic complexity* (each has many beliefs about the issue/each has few beliefs about the issue); and *affective coorientation* (congruent/incongruent).

From the contingency rules perspective, these eight continuous variables operating within some potential context determine the operative behavioral rules, whether self-evaluative, adaptive, or both, in any persuasive transaction. For example, in contexts characterized by high intimacy and low resistance, interpersonal relationship rules will likely predominate, whereas social normative rules are often dominant in low-intimacy, high-resistance contexts (for relevant research, see McLaughlin et al., 1980; Cody et al., 1980; Sillars, 1980; and Miller et al., 1977). And when people are ego-involved with the persuasion topic, self-identity and image-maintenance associations undoubtedly are highly salient (for relevant research, see Clark, 1979). Finally, contexts characterized by self-benefit concerns will probably activate environmental contingency, as well as social normative rules, defining what one must or must not do to garner personal, economic, political, or social advantage (for relevant research, see Clark, 1979; Cody, 1978). In short, context determines the configuration of available action/consequence expectancies that govern people's persuasive behavior, including their selection of message strategies and the nature of their responses to messages. This deterministic quality of context confers on the contingency rules theory two essential requisites for an adequate theory, *necessity* and *generality* (see Cushman & Pearce, 1977, pp. 344-345). Regarding necessity, context lends predictability to the contingency rules perspective by defining the precise conditions under which one can expect certain types of behavioral schemata to recurrently govern persuasive action. Moreover, because context determines the operative rules in specified communication environments, one can expect the same contingency rules to govern behavior in similar contexts. Thus context enables the contingency rules theory to claim a reasonable measure of generality.

Contingency Rules and the Practice of Persuasion

According to the contingency rules theory, *persuasive communication involves the coordination of human choice-making behavior according to contextually determined rules.* Recall that persuasive choice-making behavior is equated with: (1) the types of message strategies people select when they desire to influence the self or some other person, and (2) the kinds of strategic responses they make to self- and other-produced messages, including compliance-resisting and accepting actions. Such choice-making behavior is governed by self-evaluative rules, including self-identity and image-maintenance schemata, and adaptive rules, encompassing environmental contingency, interpersonal relationship, and social normative associations.

Regarding the strategy selection dimension of choice-making behavior, the contingency rules theory construes a *message strategy* as a set of action/consequence linking statements, selected from the total pool of available contextual schemata, that the persuader regards as especially instrumental to his or her goals. As this analysis implies, the persuasive message has two functional components: *consequence specifications* and *action stipulations.* As to consequence specifications, persuasive messages make salient those *consequences* that are: (1) instrumental to the persuader's intentions, and (2) relevant to other features of the context, including coorientations toward the communication topic and the actual or desired relationship between the communicators. For example, messages intended to convey the hazards of cigarette smoking usually emphasize environmental contingencies such as personal health. And interpersonal messages, such as those a spouse might direct toward a partner in an effort to save a deteriorating marriage, undoubtedly will stress interpersonal relationship and self-concept consequences, including the loss of intimacy and self-identification as a "couple." Finally, commercial messages advertising products such as designer blue jeans, toothpaste, and so forth, often emphasize self-presentational contingencies, as well as the social normative consequences associated with the advertised products. Beyond specifying contingencies, persuasive messages stipulate those *actions* people must or must not take to achieve or avoid the specified consequencies. Thus antismoking messages ask smokers "to stop," unhappy marriage partners urge each other "to start" salvaging their relationship, and established advertisers ask consumers "to continue" purchasing their particular brands of goods and services.

The second aspect of persuasive choice-making behavior concerns the kinds of strategic responses people make to self- or other-produced messages. Such responses may range from acceptance of the action/consequence associations contained in messages to resistance and rejection (see McLaughlin et al., 1980, for research on the selection of compliance-resisting strategies). According to the contingency rules theory, behavioral responses to self- or other-generated persuasive messages are governed by those behavioral contingency rules that: (1) people believe are especially instrumental to their own personal goals and objectives, and (2) are otherwise consistent with the persuasive context, including people's coorientations toward the communication topic and their actual or desired personal relationships with other communicators involved in the persuasive transaction. As this analysis suggests, people typically respond favorably to goal-maximizing action/consequence associations and eschew goal-blocking ones. Thus successful persuasion, whether self-instigated or produced by an external agent, induces the self or others to follow behavioral contingency rules that are instrumental to the goals of the communicating parties within some specified actual context.

CONTINGENCY RULES AND PERSUASION: SOME PRELIMINARY SUPPORTIVE DATA

The preliminary data reported here are limited to: (1) people's responses to persuasive messages, one of two dimensions of persuasive behavior recognized by the contingency rules theory, and (2) people's orientations toward the persuasive issue, one of three contextual variables differentiated by the proposed theory. Thus, the research examined: (1) the extent to which self-evaluative and adaptive schemata govern people's responses to messages, and (2) the impact that orientation toward a persuasive issue, including ego-involvement, schematic complexity, and affective position, has on the types of schemata governing responses to messages. In addressing these issues the criterion construct "responses to messages" was equated with subjects' self-reported intentions to perform some recommended action. Additionally, no attempt was made to differentiate among the subclasses of the predictors, self-evaluative schemata, and adaptive schemata. Thus the contingency rules approach was operationalized as a simple, two-factor predictive model.

Beyond these primary concerns this research explored two secondary issues. First, the predictive efficiency of the two-factor theory was compared with two alternative models: the traditional "attitude mediates behavior" model, and one of the more prevalent "other variables" accounts, the "attitudes plus relevant social normative considerations determine overt behavior" model (see Rokeach & Kliejunas, 1972; Warner & DeFleur, 1969). Second, this research sought to determine whether the predictive efficiency of the two-factor model could be augmented by adding a third predictor, "ascription of personal responsibility," a variable drawn from Schwartz's personal norms theory (1974). This highly speculative question was prompted by Schwartz's (1974, 1973, 1968) repeated finding that a person's willingness to take personal responsibility for the consequences of his or her actions is a critical predictor of personal normative behavior. Thus it is possible that the additional variable might significantly enhance the predictive power of the contingency rules model. On the other hand, given the proposed theory's assumption that human behavior is extensively self-regulated, it is also possible that "ascription of personal responsibility" is isomorphic with the practical force of behavioral contingency rules, and is, therefore, a redundant factor. If this latter speculation is correct, then the addition of the variable should add little to the predictive power of the two-factor model.

Method

The 127 college students participating in this research were exposed randomly to one of the following nine persuasive issues: gay rights/homosexuality ($n = 14$); development of renewable energy resources ($n = 11$); abortion ($n = 14$); the Virginia gubernatorial election ($n = 12$); casual clothing preferences/fashion ($n = 15$); handgun control ($n = 13$); donation of body organs after death ($n = 16$); traditional versus nontraditional family relationships ($n = 16$); and charity/helping behavior ($n = 16$). This diverse set of social, political, and personal preference issues was selected based on pilot data taken from a sample of thirty-six subjects indicating that college students' views on these issues vary widely on the contextual dimensions of ego-involvement, schematic complexity, and affective orientation.

The required data were collected by asking each subject to respond to a two-part questionnaire on one of the nine issues. The first part measured their orientations toward the persuasive issues, including ego-involvement, schematic complexity, and affective stance, and assessed the criterion variable, behavioral intentions regarding the issue. The second part measured the assumed predictor variables, including self-evaluative schemata, adaptive schemata, the traditional attitude construct, relevant social normative considerations, and ascription of personal responsibility for the consequences of intended behaviors.

Measurement

The context variable, ego-involvement, was operationalized as the subjects' scores on a seven-point scale asking them to indicate the extent to which they felt "emotionally involved or very concerned personally" with the issue (very involved/not at all involved.)[4] Schematic complexity was measured by asking each subject, again on a seven-point scale, to assess "the number of personal beliefs I have about the issue" (a great many beliefs/very few beliefs).[5] The final context variable, affective stance, was equated with the traditional concept of attitude, and operationalized as each subject's likes and dislikes regarding the issues. Thus, subjects completed typical seven-point scales ranging from "strongly agree" to "strongly disagree" on central affective dimensions associated with each issue. Representative affective statements toward which subjects expressed likes and dislikes were: "Democrat Charles Robb would make a better governor of Virginia than Republican Marshall Coleman" and "Regarding fashion in casual clothing at this particular time, the 'preppy look' is preferable to other casual clothing styles."

The criterion variable was operationalized as each subject's self-reported intention to perform a recommended action regarding each of the nine issues. Some examples illustrating both the form and content of the recommendations included in this research are:

> If you were to vote (or could vote, in the case of out-of-state residents) in the upcoming state election, and given your knowledge and beliefs on the issue, do you believe you would cast your ballot for Democrat Charles Robb in the November Virginia gubernatorial election?

> The Virginia Driver's license, as well as those of many other states, has attached to it a *Uniform Donor Document*, authorized under Act 2, Chapter 8, Title 32.1 of the Code of Virginia. It states that the license holder may agree to make an "anatomical gift . . . to take effect upon my death" of "eyes and other needed organs or parts for purposes of transplantation, therapy, medical research, or education." Given your knowledge and beliefs on the issue, do you believe you would be willing to sign this (or a similar) legally binding document?

Following Fishbein and Ajzen's procedure (see Ajzen, 1971; Ajzen & Fishbein, 1970), subjects reported their behavioral intentions regarding such recommended actions on seven-point scales ranging from "definitely yes" to "definitely no."

Finally, the predictor variables represented each person's subjective beliefs about the generative forces prompting his or her self-reported behavioral intentions, and were measured on seven-point scales ranging from "definitely yes" to "definitely no." Self-evaluative schemata were measured by asking subjects whether their "intended actions on this issue reflect some important aspects of my self-concept — in other words, *the kind of person I perceive myself to be.*" This statement was followed by parenthetical instructions that "the kind of person you perceive yourself to be may include your *private* self-identity, including your basic values and personal standards; and your *public* self-image, including all the characteristics you want others to see in you." The second primary predictor, adaptive expectancies, was assessed by asking subjects whether their "intended actions on this issue reflect my desire to achieve some *favorable* (or avoid unfavorable) *consequences* — in other words, to achieve things I want for myself and other people I care about." Following this statement was the instruction that "the 'things' you want for yourself and others you care about may include *physical or environmental* consequences such as the health and safety of yourself and important others, *interpersonal* concerns, including a desire for acceptance and satisfying relationships with important others, and *social* consequences, such as financial benefits, social status, and personal recognition."[6]

Two of the secondary predictors, "attitude" and "social normative considerations," were measured on single scales asking subjects whether their intended actions reflect "my basic attitudes or general feelings of favorableness or unfavorableness toward this issue," and "my desire to be consistent with the views, actions, norms, and values of the people whose opinions I value most," respectively. The final secondary predictor, "ascription of personal responsibility for the consequences of intended actions," was operationalized as the sum of subjects' scores on two scales asking whether they would prefer that their intended actions "be quoted anonymously" or "attributed to me by name" if, for whatever reason, they were to be publicized in "the University news media" and in "my hometown news media."[7]

Results

A stepwise multiple regression analysis showed that the five predictors accounted for 38.7 percent of the variance in subjects' behavioral intentions toward the nine persuasive issues, $F(5, 121) = 39.87$, $p < .001$. Self-evaluative schemata entered the equation first and accounted for 27.6 percent of the explained variance, $F(1, 125) = 21.07$, $p < .001$, followed by adaptive schemata, accounting for a relatively small, but significant 4.7 percent, $F(2, 124) = 3.22$, $p < .05$. On step three the traditional attitude construct entered the equation and reliably explained 4.3 percent of the variance, $F(3, 123) = 2.98$, $p < .05$. Social normative considerations and ascription of personal responsibility were the fourth and fifth entries into the equation, and they accounted for an insignificant 1.8 percent and .3 percent of the variance, respectively ($Fs < 1$).

Thus, the two-factor contingency rules model accounted for 32.3 percent of explained variance in behavioral intentions, $F(2, 124) = 35.77$, $p < .001$, and the addition of "ascription of responsibility" failed to significantly enhance its predictive power. Of the remaining variance the traditional "attitude determines behavior" model explained only 4.3 percent, and "attitudes plus relevant social normative considerations" accounted for 6.1 percent, $F(2, 124) = 4.70$, $p < .05$. Finally, self-evaluative schemata were far more potent predictors across all nine persuasive issues than were adaptive expectancies, explaining almost seven times as much of the variance as did adaptive concerns.

Context

As Table 11.1 shows, when subjects were highly ego-involved with the persuasive issues (operationalized as subjects who scored six or seven on the seven-point involvement scale), self-evaluative rules accounted for the bulk of the explained variance, whereas adaptive schemata reliably explained a much smaller percentage. In contrast, adaptive considerations took on a greater importance when subjects were relatively uninvolved with the issues (scored one or two on the seven-point scale), although self-evaluative schemata remained the most potent predictor among uninvolved subjects. Regarding schematic complexity, Table 11.1 shows that adaptive rules accounted for slightly more variance in behavioral intentions than did self-evaluative schemata when subjects held many beliefs about the persuasive issues (operationalized as subjects who scored six or seven on the seven-point schematic complexity scale). In contrast, self-evaluative schemata were twice as important as adaptive considerations among subjects who held few beliefs about the persuasive issues (scored one or two on the seven-point scale).

Finally, Table 11.1 shows that affective orientations toward the persuasive issues had a marked impact on the explained variance in behavioral intentions. When subjects held favorable attitudes toward the issues (operationalized as subjects who scored five, six, or seven on the relevant seven-point attitude measure), self-evaluative rules accounted for nearly 60 percent of variance associated with intended actions, whereas adaptive schemata reliably explained a much smaller percentage. Among subjects

Table 11.1
Percentage of Variance in Behavioral Intentions Explained by the Two-Factor Model as a Function of Context

Context	n	Self-Evaluative	Adaptive	Total
All nine issues	127	27.6	4.7	32.3
High involvement	56	22.2	6.7	28.9
Low involvement	49	25.8	15.5	41.3
High complexity	54	17.5	20.3	37.8
Low complexity	53	14.7	7.6	22.3
Favorable	66	58.8	9.0	67.8
Unfavorable	48	5.4	2.4	7.8
Neutral	13	8.8	49.1	57.9
Mean variance/all contexts		21.9	15.8	37.7
Mean variance/minus unfavorable context		24.6	18.0	42.7

Note: All explained variance is statistically reliable at $p < .01$, with two exceptions: The variance associated with self-evaluative schemata in the unfavorable context is significant at $p < .05$; and the variance accounted for by adaptive schemata in the unfavorable context is not statistically reliable.

who were unfavorable toward the persuasive issues (scored one, two, or three on the relevant seven-point scale), neither variable accounted for a substantial amount of variance in behavioral intentions. Finally, adaptive rules accounted for almost 50 percent of the variance in behavioral intentions among subjects who reported neutrality on the issues (scored four on the relevant seven-point scale), whereas self-evaluative schemata reliably explained less than one-fifth as much.

Conclusions

This research established three general findings. First, it demonstrated that people's responses to persuasive messages can be predicted reliably by referring to relevant self-evaluative and adaptive contingency rule-structures. As Table 11.1 shows, the two-factor model accounted for about one-third of the variance in behavioral intentions across all nine persuasive issues. And except for the anomalous unfavorable issues context, self-evaluative and adaptive schemata explained from 22.3 to 67.8 percent of the variance in subjects' intended actions in varying contexts. Including the unfavorable issues context, the two-factor model still accounted for a mean variance in behavioral intentions of 37.7 percent. Thus this research provides considerable preliminary support for the proposed view that persuasive behavior is governed antecedently by self-evaluative and adaptive expectancies.

Second, the research established that context, including ego-involvement, schematic complexity, and affective orientation toward persuasive issues, has a marked impact on the types of behavioral contingency rules governing people's responses to messages. For instance, when people are highly ego-involved with a persuasive issue, private self-identity and public image-maintenance concerns predominate, whereas expectancies about extrinsic consequences are relatively unimportant. In contrast, extrinsic adaptive considerations take on an importance equal to self-evaluative concerns when people are relatively uninvolved with the persuasive issue. Regarding schematic complexity both adaptive and self-evaluative expectancies play major roles in mediating the persuasive behavior of individuals who have a great number of beliefs about the issue. However, when people are relatively uninformed on the issue, self-identity and image-maintenance concerns are highly salient, and extrinsic considerations become relatively inconsequential. Finally, people's affective orientations toward the persuasive issue have powerful effects on the types of schemata governing their persuasive behavior. When individuals positively evaluate the implications of a persuasive issue, self-identity and image-maintenance schemata are pervasive, and extrinsic adaptive concerns are relatively unimportant. In contrast, when people are affectively neutral toward an issue, the reverse pattern appears. Concerns for extrinsic consequences predominate and self-evaluative considerations are relatively nonsalient. And when people hold negativistic attitudes toward a persuasive issue, neither type of schemata appears to have a substantial impact on their persuasive behavior. However, even here, self-evaluative concerns account for a reliable percentage of the variance associated with intended actions.

This research, then, provides impressive preliminary support for the proposed view that the operative rules governing people's persuasive behavior are determined by the actual context in which persuasive transactions take place. Moreover, the research shows that, across a variety of contexts, self-evaluative schemata typically exert a more powerful influence on persuasive behavior than do adaptive expectancies. This finding supports the contingency rules view that concerns about extrinsic "rewards" and "punishments" are often subsumed within each persuasive agent's self-regulatory system. Even so, this research has confirmed the central prediction that the relative mix of the two types of schemata varies sharply as a function of the actual context where persuasive communicators interact.

Third and finally, this research documented the superiority of the two-factor contingency rules approach vis-à-vis two common alternative models: the traditional "attitude determines behavior" model, and a prevalent "other variables" account, holding that "attitudes plus relevant social normative considerations determine behavior." The two-factor model accounted for nearly seven times as much variance in behavioral intentions as did the traditional attitude formulation, and it explained over five times as much variance as did the "other variables" account. Moreover, the addition of "ascription of responsibility," a variable previously found to exert a powerful impact on personal normative behavior, failed to enhance the predictive power of the two-factor model, boosting explained variance by an insignificant three-tenths of 1 percent. Apparently, attribution of personal responsibility is isomorphic with the practical force of a person's self-regulatory system, and therefore, is a redundant predictor.

Thus this research has provided substantial preliminary support for the central assumptions guiding the contingency rules theory. These assumptions are that: (1) persuasive behavior is governed antecedently by self-evaluative and adaptive schemata, and (2) the actual context where persuasive agents interact determines the types of behavioral contingency rules that govern their persuasive behavior.

Limitations of This Research

Four important questions were left unanswered by this preliminary research. First, the relationship between *overt* behavior and the central constructs, self-evaluative and adaptive schemata, was not explored. Although considerable research (see Ajzen & Fishbein, 1974; Fishbein & Coombs, 1974; Ajzen, 1971; Darroch, 1971; Ajzen & Fishbein, 1970; Hornik, 1970; Holman, 1956), including investigations of the behavioral effects of persuasive messages (see McArdle, 1972), suggests that behavioral intentions bear a high positive correlation with overt behavior, the extent to which behavioral contingency rules as conceptualized in the proposed theory govern overt action is an unresolved question.

Second, the validity of the subclasses of self-evaluative and adaptive schemata recognized by the contingency rules theory was not established. Self-evaluative schemata are assumed to take the two forms, private self-identity and public image-maintenance expectancies; and adaptive schemata are divided into environmental contingency rules, interpersonal relationship concerns, and social normative rules. The preliminary data reported here made no attempt to differentiate the amount of variance attributable to each of these five categories of anticipatory assumptions. Thus additional research is required to confirm or discount the reasonableness of the sub-schemata presumed to govern people's responses to messages. Third, the validity and reliability of the instruments used to measure self-evaluative and adaptive schemata need additional scrutiny. Although the probable reliability of the relevant data was established as a part of this research (see footnote 6), and the two instruments are structurally similar to scales validated previously by others (see Schwartz's "personal norms" scale in Schwartz, 1973, p. 356; and Pearce & Cronen's "life-script-act" and "act-consequence" scales in Pearce & Cronen, 1980, pp. 251-252), confidence in the reported data would be enhanced by conducting additional reliability and validity checks.

Fourth and finally, the supportive research represented a limited test of the contingency rules theory on two counts. First, the data were limited to people's intended *responses* to persuasive messages, one of the two dimensions of persuasive behavior recognized by the two-factor model. Thus the extent to which people's compliance-gaining strategic choices are governed by self-evaluative and adaptive rules remains a crucial unexplored issue. Second, only one of the three contextual dimensions differentiated by the proposed theory was examined in the supporting research. Left unexplored were: (1) the separate effects of the contextual variables, *relationships* among communicators, and their persuasive *intentions,* and (2) the interactive effects of all three context variables operating in tandem. Moreover, the context variable included in the research, orientation toward the persuasive issue, differed operationally from its precise conceptualization in the contingency rules theory. Because of the nature of the present design, a single agent's orientation, rather than two or more communicators' coorientations, toward the persuasive issues was examined. Although there is little reason to suspect markedly different results, the impact that coorientations toward issues have on the rules governing persuasive behavior should be addressed.

Although these four unresolved questions restrict the generality of the present findings, they neither: (1) diminish the importance of the reported data that positively support the basic tenets of the contingency rules theory, nor (2) impugn the logical integrity of the proposed theoretical structure itself. Rather, they represent problems that *any* paradigm in its theoretical and methodological infancy inevitably experiences. Thus given a period for sustained research, methodological refinement and theoretical development, there is every reason to expect a satisfactory resolution of these issues.

THE CONTINGENCY RULES THEORY AS A NEW PERSUASIVE PARADIGM: AN APPRAISAL

Given its present state of development, the contingency rules theory has four principal features that recommend it as an alternative theoretical paradigm in persuasion. First, the approach resolves some of the more serious objections that both behavioral and cognitive theorists have to a reliance on attitude as the central analytical unit in persuasion theory. Compared to attitude, "schema" is relatively unambiguous conceptually, and therefore, lends itself to reasonably straightforward operational deductions. Moreover, behavioral schemata are, by definition, anticipatory assumptions about action/consequence sequences. Thus the proposed theory's central construct is linked explicitly to overt human action. Furthermore the contingency rules approach does not abandon outright the attitude construct. Rather, a person's affective orientation toward persuasive issues is treated as one of several dimensions of context. As a subclass of context, attitude is presumed to interact with other contextual variables to influence the types of behavior contingency rules governing persuasive action. Thus by adopting "behavioral schema" as the antecedent motivator of persuasive behavior, the contingency rules theory strikes a compromise between advocates of a strictly behavioristic approach to persuasion theory and cognitive theorists, even those who continue to emphasize the mediational role of attitude in message-behavior relationships.

Second, the contingency rules theory resolves some of the thornier differences between "laws" and "rules" approaches to the explanation of persuasive behavior. The basis for this resolution is found in the theory's conceptualization of "context." Recall that the proposed theory defines an actual context as a function of persuasive choice-making behavior in some relatively fixed potential context. Thus the approach explicitly recognizes that numerous causal antecedents, including physiological, psychological, and environmental forces operating in the potential context, influence the consequences people value and the types of actions they reasonably may take in pursuit of desired outcomes. From the contingency rules perspective, a laws analysis is required to adequately explain the impact of causal antecedents on persuasive behavior. In contrast, a purposive rules analysis is required to satisfactorily account for the strategic choices people make in potential contexts when they generate goal-oriented messages and make instrumental responses to messages. Thus the contingency rules theory regards laws and rules not as competing paradigms vying to explain the same domain of persuasive phenomena, but rather as complementary explanatory systems applicable to different areas of persuasive experience. When applied to its appropriate domain, each approach can yield equally valuable, although qualitatively different, information about the nature of persuasive behaviors. The two perspectives, then, should complement one another in the accumulation of knowledge about persuasive communication.

Third, the contingency rules theory has three features not possessed by the traditional theoretical paradigm that make it an especially meaningful framework for understanding persuasion as a *complex symbolic activity*. First, the approach makes *interpretation* or the assignment of *meaning* to messages a central cognitive activity in persuasion. Recall that behavioral contingency rules entail interpretative schemata or sets of hierarchically ordered object-attribute hypotheses that impart meaning to actions and their expected consequences. Thus the contingency rules theory assumes that message production and responses are functions of the meanings people attach to self- or other-produced messages. This emphasis on interpretation contrasts sharply with the "Hovland" theoretical paradigm that treats messages as stimuli having the capacity to cause responses either directly, or more typically, indirectly by arousing some internal psychological state such as "dissonance," "effectance," or "reactance." By making meaning a central mediator of persuasive behavior, the proposed theory suggests that persuasion theorists' foremost concern should be the explanation of *symbolic* social influence processes, not the explanation of multiple, sometimes peripheral, psychological phenomena related to symbolic social influence.

Second, the contingency rules approach makes *developmentalism* central to the process of persuasive communication. Unlike the concept of attitude, behavioral schemata by definition are temporally ordered phenomena. Thus one can expect the schemata governing people's persuasive behavior in specified contexts to evolve as the persuasive transaction progresses through time. For instance, as the relationships among communicators (including intimacy and relative power and dominance) change, the contingency rules governing their behavior should change as a function of the altered context. Likewise changes in people's persuasive intentions or coorientations toward persuasive issues will trigger evolutionary changes in the operative schemata. This developmental view of persuasive communication contrasts sharply with the traditional view of persuasion as a reasonably static, unidirectional process in which some powerful persuader induces attitude changes in relatively passive receivers.

Third and finally, the contingency rules theory makes *context* an integral part of the process of persuasion, assuming that the types of schemata governing people's persuasive behavior are contextually determined. In marked contrast, theorists in the "Hovland" mold typically regard context as a secondary concern, conceptualizing it in one of two ways: (1) as "unexplained variance" in message-behavior relationships, or (2) as one of several sets of boundary conditions attached to message-behavior relationships. Taking a radically different approach, the contingency rules theory systematizes the variable "context" as a central construct in *all* theoretical generalizations about message-behavior relationships. Thus the proposed perspective regards persuasive communication as a complex *social* phenomenon, affected profoundly by the situational milieu where persuasive behaviors are enacted. To summarize, the contingency rules approach, unlike the traditional paradigm, makes interpretation, developmentalism, and context central to the process of persuasion. As a result, the proposed theory explicitly recognizes the symbolic, processual, and social nature of persuasive communication.

The fourth and final quality of the contingency rules theory that recommends it as a viable alternative to the traditional paradigm concerns its *integrative* potential. Specifically, the contingency rules theory provides a coherent conceptual framework or theoretical umbrella for performing two important tasks: (1) integrating much diverse theory and research on the nature of persuasion as a subdiscipline in communication, and (2) integrating persuasion with other forms of human communicative interaction. Regarding the first function the contingency rules theory offers persuasion researchers a theoretical framework within which compliance-gaining and responding strategies can be explored systematically. Previously, research on compliance-gaining and compliance-resisting strategies has been essentially *atheoretical* (for example, see Cody & McLaughlin, 1980; McLaughlin, 1980; McLaughlin et al., 1980; Sillars, 1980; Miller et al., 1977; Marwell & Schmitt, 1967).[8] Indeed the dominant conceptual housing presently guiding such research consists of strategic taxonomies representing either: (1) a priori assumptions about the kinds of strategies people presumably use in compliance-gaining and responding situations (see Sillars, 1980; Miller et al., 1977; Marwell & Schmitt, 1967), or (2) categories of strategies that subjects themselves believe they use in compliance-gaining and responding situations (see Cody & McLaughlin, 1980; McLaughlin et al., 1980; Cody et al., 1980). Although useful, these typologies are *descriptive,* not explanatory, in nature. The contingency rules theory provides a coherent framework for integrating and explaining the diverse taxonomies derived from compliance-gaining and responding research. The proposed theory is particularly appropriate for this task because it: (1) describes persuasive behavior as a compliance-gaining and responding strategic activity, and (2) posits a systematic explanation for the strategic choices people make when they produce and respond to messages.

Second, the contingency rules theory provides a useful conceptual framework for integrating persuasion with other forms of human communication. Persuasion too often is viewed as a manipulative process, somehow set apart from other types of communicative interaction. The contingency rules theory rejects outright this dichotomy, regarding persuasion as a developmental, symbolic activity whose function is the coordination of human choice-making behavior according to contextually determined rules. If human communication as a general field of inquiry is concerned with the ways people manage their affairs by symbolic means, then persuasion as the proposed theory construes it is a central ingredient in all forms of human communicative interaction. Thus the conceptual stance taken by the contingency rules theory eliminates many of the negative attributions that have been attached to persuasive communication.

For that reason, the new perspective should prompt professionals and laypersons alike to assume a more realistic view of the role of persuasion in all human communication.

NOTES

1. Searle's (1969) notions of constitutive and regulative rules, adopted by many communication rules theorists (see Pearce & Cronen, 1980, pp. 141-144; Cushman & Whiting, 1972) are conceptually similar to interpretative and behavioral schemata, respectively. However, as cognitive schema theorists describe them (see Taylor & Crocker, 1981; Hastie, 1981; Tesser, 1978; Markus, 1977; Neisser, 1976), schemata are more general cognitive organizers than Searle's (1969) original conceptions. Accordingly, interpretative and behavioral schemata are construed as self-organizing expectancies guiding *all* psychological phenomena, including information processing and overt human action. In contrast, Searle's (1969) notions are more particularized, being especially suited to the analysis and explanation of linguistic behavior, including the syntactical and semantic choices people make when they create meaning.

2. Cognitive schema theorists typically classify "personal constructs" (Kelly, 1955), the central cognitive organizer in "constructivist" approaches to communication theory (see O'Keefe, 1980; Delia, 1977) as a subset of interpretative schemata. As a subset, "personal constructs" are thought to serve as "central tendency" prototypes for processing information about other people (for a pertinent discussion, see Hastie, 1981, p. 40).

3. In developing his theory of reciprocal determinism, Bandura (1977) uses the terms "potential and actual environments" in a manner similar to the present usage of "potential and actual contexts." However, his interpretation of the nature of the two constructs and their relationship to one another differs considerably from the conceptualizations developed in this chapter (for a discussion of Bandura's usages, see Bandura, 1977, pp. 194-213).

4. This operationalization of "ego-involvement" is taken from Smith (1978, p. 312; 1977, p. 200).

5. A separate study was conducted to validate this single-scale measure of schematic complexity. A sample of eighty-seven subjects was exposed randomly to the nine issues employed in this research and asked: (1) to complete the single-scale measure of schematic complexity used in this research, and (2) using Petty and Cacioppo's "thought-listing" procedure (see Perloff & Brock, 1980; Cacioppo & Petty, 1979), "to write out all the beliefs (you can think of) that you have about this issue." The two indices correlated positively ($r = .76$; $p < .01$) providing support for the validity of the simple index of schematic complexity used in this research.

6. Support for the stability of these two measures was found for computing standard errors of measurement for each (see Dick & Hagerty, 1971, pp. 39-40). The standard error for the scores on the self-evaluative scale was .31, indicating a 95 percent probability that the sample scores did not deviate from the population mean by more than plus or minus .60 of a single scale unit. The standard error for the scores on the adaptive scale was .11, indicating a 95 percent probability that the sample scores did not deviate from the population mean by more than plus or minus .21 of a single scale unit. These results appear

to confirm that the frequent problem of single-scale instability did not apply to either measurement.

7. This operationalization of "ascription of responsibility" differs from Schwartz's procedure (see Schwartz, 1973, p. 356). However, because the two scales used in this research tap both a person's awareness of consequences as well as his or her willingness to take public responsibility for them, the operationalization appears to be an adequate measure of Schwartz's original conception (see Schwartz, 1973, p. 353).

8. One notable exception is Sillars's (1980) use of a subjective expected utility (SEU) model to explain compliance-gaining strategy selection. However, Sillars limited the SEU model to an explanation of choice-making behavior as a function of a single variable, the nature of the relationship between communicating parties. As a consequence, its generality as a theoretical account for a variety of compliance-gaining and responding activities has not been established.

REFERENCES

Abelson, R. P. Script processing in attitude formation and decision-making. In J. S. Carroll & J. W. Payne (Eds.), *Cognition and social behavior*. Hillsdale, NJ: Lawrence Erlbaum, 1976.

Ajzen, I. Attitudinal vs. normative messages: An investigation of the differential effects of persuasive communication on behavior. *Sociometry*, 1971, *34*, 263-280.

Ajzen, I., & Fishbein, M. The prediction of behavior from attitudinal and normative variables. *Journal of Experimental Social Psychology*, 1970. *6*, 466-487.

Ajzen, I., & Fishbein, M. Factors influencing intentions and the intention-behavior relation. *Human Relations*, 1974, *26*, 1-15.

Bandura, A. *Social learning theory*. Morristown, NJ: General Learning Press, 1971.

Bandura, A. *Social learning theory*. Englewood Cliffs, NJ: Prentice-Hall, 1977.

Bartlett, F. C. *Remembering: A study in experimental and social psychology*. London: Cambridge University Press, 1932.

Bauer, R. A. The obstinate audience: The influence process from the point of view of social communication. *American Psychologist*, 1964, *19*, 319-328.

Bem, D. J. Self-perception theory. In L. Berkowitz (Ed.), *Advances in Experimental Social Psychology* (Vol. 6). New York: Academic Press, 1972.

Berg, K. R. Ethnic attitudes and agreement with a negro person. *Journal of Personality and social Psychology*, 1966, *4*, 216-220.

Berger, C. R. The covering law perspective as a theoretical basis for the study of human communication. *Communication Quarterly*, 1977, *25*, 7-18.

Bormann, E. G. Generalizing about significant form: Science and humanism compared and contrasted. In K. K. Campbell and K. H. Jamieson (Eds.), *Form and genre: Shaping rhetorical action*. Falls Church, VA: Speech Communication Association, 1978.

Bormann, E.G. *Communication Theory*. New York: Holt, Rinehart & Winston, 1980.

Burgoon, M., & Bettinghaus, E. P. Persuasive message strategies. In M. E. Roloff and G. R. Miller (Eds.), *Persuasion: New directions in theory and research*. Beverly Hills, CA: Sage, 1980.

Buss, A. R. Causes and reasons in attribution theory: A conceptual critique. *Journal of Personality and Social Psychology*, 1978, *36*, 1311-1321.

Buss, A. R. On the relationship between causes and reasons. *Journal of Personality and Social Psychology*, 1979, *37*, 1458-1461.

Cacioppo, J. T., & Petty, R. E. Attitudes and cognitive responses: An electrophysiological approach. *Journal of Personality and Social Psychology*, 1979, *37*, 2181-2199.

Campbell, D. T. Social attitudes and other acquired behavioral dispositions. In S. Koch (Ed.), *Psychology: A Study of a Science* (Vol. 6). New York: McGraw-Hill, 1963.

Cappella, J. N., & Folger, J. P. An information-processing explanation of attitude-behavior inconsistency. In D. P. Cushman and R. D. McPhee (Eds.), *Message-attitude-behavior relationship: Theory, methodology, and application.* New York: Academic Press, 1980.

Carr, L., & Roberts, S. O. Correlates of civil rights participation. *Journal of Social Psychology*, 1965, 67, 259-267.

Clark, R. A. The impact of selection of persuasive strategies on self-interest and desired liking. *Communication Monographs*, 1979, 46, 257-273.

Cody, M. J. *The dimensions of persuasive situations: Implications for communication research and assessments of taxonomy construction methodologies.* Unpublished doctoral dissertation, Michigan State University, 1978.

Cody, M. J., & McLaughlin, M. L. Perceptions of compliance-gaining situations: A dimensional analysis. *Communication Monographs*, 1980, 47, 132-148.

Cody, M. J., & McLaughlin, M. L., & Jordan, W. J. A multidimensional scaling of three sets of compliance-gaining strategies. *Communication Quarterly*, 1980, 28, 34-46.

Cushman, D. P., & McPhee, R. D. (Eds.). *Message-attitude-behavior relationship: Theory, methodology, and application.* New York: Academic Press, 1980.

Cushman, D. P., & Pearce, W. B. Generality and necessity in three types of theory about human communication, with special attention to rules theory. *Human Communication Research*, 1977, 3, 344-353.

Cushman, D. P., & Whiting, G. C. An approach to communication theory: Towards consensus on rules, *Journal of Communication*, 1972, 22, 217-238.

Cushman, D. P., Valentinsen, B., & Whiting, G. *Self-concept as a generative mechanism in interpersonal communication.* Presented at the International Communication Association Convention, Acapulco, 1980.

Darroch, R. K. *Attitudinal variables and perceived group norms as predictors of behavioral intentions and behavior in the signing of photographic releases.* Unpublished doctoral dissertation, University of Illinois, 1971.

Davison, W. P. On the effects of communication. *Public Opinion Quarterly*, 1959, 23, 343-360.

DeFleur, M. L., & Westie, F. R. Attitude as a scientific concept. *Social Forces*, 1963-1964, 42, 17-31.

Delia, J. G. Constructivism and the study of human communication. *Quarterly Journal of Speech*, 1977, 63, 66-83.

Dick, W., & Hagerty, N. *Topics in measurement: Reliability and validity.* New York: McGraw-Hill, 1971.

Dulany, D. E. Hypotheses and habits in verbal "operant conditioning." *Journal of Abnormal and Social Psychology*, 1961, 63, 251-263.

Dulany, D. E. Awareness, rules, and propositional control: A confrontation with S-R behavior theory. In D. Horton and T. Dixon (Eds.), *Verbal behavior and S-R behavior theory.* Englewood Cliffs, NJ: Prentice-Hall, 1968.

Eagly, A. H., & Himmelfarb, S. Current trends in attitude theory and research. In S. Himmelfarb and A. H. Eagly (Eds.), *Readings in attitude change.* New York: John Wiley, 1974.

Ebbinghaus, H. *Memory: A contribution to experimental psychology.* Leipzig, Germany: Duncker & Humblot, 1885.

Ehrlich, H. J. Attitudes, behavior, and the intervening variables. *American Sociologist*, 1969, 4, 29-34.

Fazio, R. H., & Zanna, M. P. Attitudinal qualities relating to the strength of the attitude-behavior relationship. *Journal of Experimental Social Psychology*, 1978, 14, 398-408.

Festinger, L. Behavioral support for opinion change. *Public Opinion Quarterly*, 1964, 28, 404-417.

Fishbein, M. Attitude and the prediction of behavior. In M. Fishbein (Ed.), *Readings in attitude theory and measurement.* New York: John Wiley, 1967.

Fishbein, M., & Ajzen, I. Attitudes and opinions. *Annual Review of Psychology*, 1972, 23, 487-544.

Fishbein, M., & Ajzen, I. Attitudes towards objects as predictors of single and multiple behavioral criteria. *Psychological Review,* 1974, *81,* 59-74.

Fishbein, M., & Ajzen, I. *Belief, attitude, intention and behavior: An introduction to theory and research.* Reading, MA: Addison-Wesley, 1975.

Fishbein, M., & Coombs, F. S. Basis for decision: An attitudinal analysis of voting behavior. *Journal of Applied Social Psychology,* 1974, *4,* 95-124.

Fitzpatrick, M. A., & Winke, J. You always hurt the one you love: Strategies and tactics in interpersonal conflict. *Communication Quarterly,* 1979, *27,* 3-11.

Forgas, J. P. The perception of social episodes: Categorical and dimensional representations of two different social milieus. *Journal of Personality and Social Psychology,* 1976, *34,* 199-209.

Gaes, G. G., Kalle, R. J., & Tedeschi, J. T. Impression management in the forced compliance situation: Two studies using the bogus pipeline. *Journal of Experimental Social Psychology,* 1978, *14,* 483-510.

Green, B. F. Attitude measurement. In G. Lindzey (Ed.), *Handbook of Social Psychology* (Vol. 1). Reading, MA: Addison-Wesley, 1954.

Greenwald, A. G. On defining attitude and attitude theory. In A. G. Greenwald, T. C. Brock, & T. M. Ostrom (Eds.), *Psychological foundations of attitudes.* New York: Academic Press, 1968. (a)

Greenwald, A. G. Cognitive learning, cognitive response to persuasion, and attitude change. In A. G. Greenwald, T. C. Brock, & T. M. Ostrom (Eds.), *Psychological foundations of attitudes.* New York: Academic Press, 1968. (b)

Harré, R., & Secord, P. F. *The explanation of social behavior.* Oxford: Basil Blackwell, 1972.

Hastie, R. Schematic principles in human memory. In E. T. Higgins, C. P. Herman, & M. P. Zanna (Eds.), *Social cognition: The Ontario symposium* (Vol. 1). Hillsdale, NJ: Lawrence Erlbaum, 1981.

Heberlein, T. A., & Black, J. S. Attitudinal specificity and the prediction of behavior in a field setting. *Journal of Personality and Social Psychology,* 1976, *33,* 474-479.

Hewes, D. E. An axiomatized, stochastic model of the behavioral effects of message campaigns. In D. P. Cushman and R. D. McPhee (Eds.), *Message-attitude-behavior relationship: Theory, methodology, and application.* New York: Academic Press, 1980.

Higgins, E. T., Herman, C. P., Zanna, M. P. (Eds.). *Social cognition: The Ontario symposium* (Vol. 1). Hillsdale, NJ: Lawrence Erlbaum, 1981.

Holman, P. A. Validation of an attitude scale as a device for predicting behavior. *Journal of Applied Psychology,* 1956, *40,* 347-349.

Hornik, N. A. *Two approaches to individual differences in an expanded prisoner's dilemma game.* Unpublished master's thesis, University of Illinois, 1970.

Hovland, C. I., Janis, I. L., & Kelley, H. H. *Communication and persuasion.* New Haven, CT: Yale University Press, 1953.

Hume, D. *Enquiries concerning human understanding.* Oxford: Clarendon Press, 1902.

Infante, D. A. Verbal plans: A conceptualization and investigation. *Communication Quarterly,* 1980, *28,* 3-10.

Jaccard, J. Toward theories of persuasion and belief change. *Journal of Personality and Social Psychology,* 1981, *40,* 260-269.

Katz, D. The functional approach to the study of attitudes. *Public Opinion Quarterly,* 1960, *24,* 163-204.

Kelly, G. *The psychology of personal constructs.* New York: W. W. Norton, 1955.

LaPière, R. T. Attitudes versus actions. *Social Forces,* 1934, *13,* 230-237.

Larson, C. U. *Persuasion: Reception and responsibility* (2nd ed.). Belmont, CA: Wadsworth, 1979.

Larson, C., & Sanders, R. Faith, mystery, and data: An analysis of "scientific" studies of persuasion. *Quarterly Journal of Speech,* 1975, *61,* 178-194.

Lingle, J. H., Geva, N., Ostrom, T. M., Leippe, M. R., & Baumgardner, M. H. Thematic effects of person judgments on impression organization. *Journal of Personality and Social Psychology,* 1979, *37,* 674-687.

Markus, H. Self-schemata and processing information about the self. *Journal of Personality and Social Psychology,* 1977, *35,* 63-78.

Marwell, C., & Schmitt, D. R. Dimensions of compliance-gaining behavior: An empirical analysis. *Sociometry,* 1967, *30,* 350-364.

McArdle, J. B. *Positive and negative communication and subsequent attitude and behavior changes in alcoholics.* Unpublished doctoral dissertation, University of Illinois, 1972.

McArthur, L. A., Kiesler, C. A., & Cook, B. P. Acting on an attitude as a function of a self-precept and inequity. *Journal of Personality and Social Psychology,* 1969, *12,* 295-302.

McCroskey, J. C. A summary of experimental research on the effects of evidence in persuasive communication. In T. D. Beisecker & D. W. Parson (Eds.), *The process of social influence.* Englewood Cliffs, NJ: Prentice-Hall, 1972.

McLaughlin, M. L., Cody, M. J., & Robey, C. S. Situational influences on the selection of strategies to resist compliance-gaining attempts. *Human Communication Research,* 1980, *7,* 14-36.

Miller, G. A., Galanter, E., & Pribram, K. H. *Plans and the structure of behavior.* New York: Holt, Rinehart & Winston, 1960.

Miller, G. R., A crucial problem in attitude research. *Quarterly Journal of Speech,* 1967, *53,* 235-240.

Miller, G. R. *An introduction to speech communication.* Indianapolis: Bobbs-Merrill, 1972.

Miller, G. R. The current status of theory and research in interpersonal communication. *Human Communication Research,* 1978, *4,* 164-178.

Miller, G. R. Afterword. In D. P. Cushman & R. D. McPhee (Eds.), *Message-attitude-behavior relationship: Theory, methodology, and application.* New York: Academic Press, 1980.

Miller, G. R., Boster, F., Roloff, M. E., & Seibold, D. Compliance-gaining message strategies: A typology and some findings concerning effects of situational differences. *Communication Monographs,* 1977, *44,* 37-51.

Miller, G. R., & Burgoon, M. Persuasion research: Review and commentary. In B. D. Ruben (Ed.), *Communication Yearbook 2.* New Brunswick, NJ: Transaction, 1978.

Miller, G. R., & Steinberg, M. *Between people: A new analysis of interpersonal communication.* Chicago: Science Research Associates, 1975.

Miller, G. R., & Hewgill, M. A. Some recent research in fear-arousing message appeals. *Speech Monographs,* 1966, *33,* 377-391.

Minsky, M. A framework for representing knowledge. In P. H. Winston (Ed.), *The Psychology of computer vision.* New York: McGraw-Hill, 1975.

Neisser, V. *Cognition and reality: Principles and implications of cognitive psychology.* San Francisco: W. H. Freeman, 1976.

Norman, D. A., & Bobrow, D. G. On the role of active memory processes in perception and cognition. In C. Cofer (Ed.), *The structure of human memory.* San Francisco: W. H. Freeman, 1975.

Norman, R. Affective-cognitive consistency, attitudes, conformity, and behavior. *Journal of Personality and Social Psychology,* 1975, *32,* 83-91.

O'Keefe, D. J. The relationship of attitudes and behavior: A constructivist analysis. In D. P. Cushman & R. D. McPhee (Eds.), *Message-attitude-behavior relationship: Theory, methodology, and application.* New York: Academic Press. 1980.

Pearce, W. B. The coordinated management of meaning: A rules-based theory of interpersonal communication. In G. R. Miller (Ed.), *Explorations in interpersonal communication.* Beverly Hills, CA: Sage, 1976.

Pearce, W. B., & Cronen, V. E. *Communication, action, and meaning: The creation of social realities.* New York: Praeger, 1980.

Perloff, R. M., & Brock, T. C. "And thinking makes it so": Cognitive responses to persuasion. In M. E. Roloff & G. R. Miller (Eds.), *Persuasion: New directions in theory and research.* Beverly Hills, CA: Sage, 1980.

Petty, R. E., & Cacioppo, J. T. *Attitudes and persuasion: Classic and contemporary approaches.* Dubuque, IA: William C. Brown, 1981.

Petty, R. E., Ostrom, T. M., & Brock, T. C., (Eds.), *Cognitive responses in persuasion.* Hillsdale, NJ: Lawrence Erlbaum, 1981.
Reardon, K. K. *Persuasion: Theory and context.* Beverly Hills, CA: Sage, 1981.
Reed, S. K. Pattern recognition and categorization. *Cognitive Psychology,* 1972, *3,* 382-407.
Reed, S. K. *Psychological process in pattern representation.* New York: Academic Press, 1973.
Regan, D. T., & Fazio, R. H. On the consistency between attitudes and behavior: Look to the method of attitude formation. *Journal of Experimental Social Psychology,* 1977, *13,* 28-45.
Rokeach, M., & Kliejunas, P. Behavior as a function of attitude-toward-object and attitude-toward-situation. *Journal of Personality and Social Psychology,* 1972, *22,* 194-201.
Roloff, M. E. Communication strategies, relationships, and relational changes. In G. R. Miller (Ed.), *Explorations in interpersonal communication.* Beverly Hills, CA: Sage, 1976.
Roloff, M. E., & Barnicott, E. F. The situational use of pro- and anti-social compliance-gaining strategies by high and low Machiavellians. In B. D. Ruben (Ed.), *Communication Yearbook 2.* New Brunswick, NJ: Transaction, 1978.
Rosch, E., & Mervis, C. B. Family resemblances: Studies in the internal structure of categories. *Cognitive Psychology,* 1975, *7,* 573-605.
Rosenthal, P. I. The concept of the paramessage in persuasive communication. *Quarterly Journal of Speech,* 1972, *63,* 15-30.
Schank, R. C., & Abelson, R. P. *Scripts, plans, goals and understanding.* Hillsdale, NJ: Lawrence Erlbaum, 1977.
Schlenker, B. R., & Riess, M. Self-presentations of attitudes following commitment to proattitudinal behavior. *Human Communication Research,* 1979, *5,* 325-334.
Schramm, W., & Roberts, D. F. (Eds.). *The process and effects of mass communication.* Urbana: University of Illinois Press, 1971.
Schwartz, S. H. Words, deeds, and the perception of consequences and responsibility in action situations. *Journal of Personality and Social Psychology,* 1968, *10,* 232-242.
Schwartz, S. H. Normative explanations of helping behavior: A critique, proposal, and empirical test. *Journal of Experimental Social Psychology,* 1973, *9,* 349-364.
Schwartz, S. H. Awareness of interpersonal consequences, responsibility, denial, and volunteering. *Journal of Personality and Social Psychology,* 1974, *30,* 57-63.
Searle, J. R. *Speech acts: An essay in the philosophy of language.* Cambridge: Cambridge University Press, 1969.
Shimanoff, S. B. *Communication rules: Theory and research.* Beverly Hills, CA: Sage, 1980.
Sillars, A. L. The stranger and the spouse as target persons for compliance-gaining strategies: A subjective expected utility model. *Human Communication Research,* 1980, *6,* 265-279.
Simons, H. W. The rhetoric of science and the science of rhetoric. *Western Journal of Speech Communication,* 1978, *42,* 37-43. (a)
Simons, H. W. In praise of muddleheaded anecdotalism. *Western Journal of Speech Communication,* 1978, *42,* 21-28. (b)
Simons, H. W. The forum: Simons on Bormann and Osborn. *Quarterly Journal of Speech,* 1980, *66,* 206-208.
Smith, M. B., Bruner, J. S., & White, R. W. *Opinions and personality.* New York: John Wiley, 1956.
Smith, M. J. The effects of threats to attitudinal freedom as a function of message quality and initial receiver attitude. *Communication Monographs,* 1977, *44,* 195-206.
Smith, M. J. Discrepancy and the importance of attitudinal freedom. *Human Communication Research,* 1978, *4,* 308-314.
Smith, M. J. *Cognitive schema theory and the perseverance and attenuation of unwarranted empirical beliefs.* Manuscript submitted for publication, 1981.

Smith, M. J. *Persuasion and human action: A review and critique of social influences theories.* Belmont, CA: Wadsworth, 1982.

Taylor, S. E., & Crocker, J. Schematic bases of social information processing. In E. T. Higgins, C. P. Herman, & M. P. Zanna (Eds.), *Social cognition: the Ontario symposium* (Vol. 1). Hillsdale, NJ: Lawrence Erlbaum, 1981.

Tedeschi, J. T., Schlenker, B. R., & Bonoma, T. V. Cognitive dissonance: Private raciocination or public spectacle? *American Psychologist,* 1971, *26,* 685-695.

Tesser, A. Self-generated attitude change. In L. Berkowitz (Ed.), *Advances in Experimental Social Psychology* (Vol. 11). New York: Academic Press, 1978.

Tittle, C. R., & Hill, R. J. Attitude measurement and prediction of behavior: An evaluation of conditions and measurement techniques. *Sociometry,* 1967, *30,* 199-213.

Triandis, H. C. Values, attitudes, and interpersonal behavior. In H. Howe & M. Page (Eds.), *Nebraska symposium on motivation* (Vol. 27). Lincoln: University of Nebraska Press, 1980.

Tversky, A. Features of similarity. *Psychological Review,* 1977, *84,* 327-352.

Warner, L. G., & DeFleur, M. L. Attitude as an interactional concept: Social constraint and social distance as intervening variables between attitudes and action. *American Sociological Review,* 1969, *34,* 153-169.

Weary, G. Self-serving attributional biases: Perceptual or response distortions? *Journal of Personality and Social Psychology,* 1979, *37,* 1418-1420.

Weigel, R. H., & Newman, L. S. Increasing attitude-behavior correspondence by broadening the scope of the behavior measure. *Journal of Personality and Social Psychology,* 1976, *33,* 793-802.

Wicker, A. W. Attitudes vs. actions: The relationship of verbal and overt behavioral responses to attitude objects. *Journal of Social Issues,* 1969, *25,* 41-78.

Wicker, A. W. An examination of the "other variables" explanation of attitude-behavior inconsistency. *Journal of Personality and Social Psychology,* 1971, *19,* 18-30.

Wish, M. *Role and personal expectations about interpersonal communication.* U.S.-Japan seminar on multidimensional scaling, San Diego, August 1975.

Wrightsman, L. Wallace supporters and adherence to "law and order." *Journal of Personality and Social Psychology,* 1969, *13,* 17-22.

II • INFORMATION SYSTEMS

12 ● Attitude Change and Attitudinal Trajectories: A Dynamic Multidimensional Theory

STAN A. KAPLOWITZ ● EDWARD L. FINK

Michigan State University ● University of Maryland—College Park

THE area of attitudes, beliefs, and persuasion is one of the most well-worked areas in social psychology. Not only have many different aspects of this problem been addressed, but many of these aspects are "blessed" with many different theories. We have theories regarding (1) the effect of source credibility on message acceptance (see Hass, 1981, for a review); (2) the relationship of preexisting cognitions to attitude change (these include various theories of cognitive consistency such as those of Heider, 1946, 1958; Osgood & Tannenbaum, 1955; Festinger, 1957), as well as theories dealing with resistance to persuasion, such as anchoring and inoculation (discussed by McGuire, 1964); (3) the relationship of message discrepancy to attitude change (see Sherif, Sherif, & Nebergall, 1965; Aronson, Turner, & Carlsmith, 1963; Laroche, 1977; Fink, Kaplowitz, & Bauer, 1980); (4) the effect of thought on attitude change (see Tesser, 1978, for a review of relevant literature); (5) the decay of attitude change over time (see Cook & Flay, 1978, for a review); and (6) the relationship among message repetition, content of various messages received, and attitude change (Himmelfarb, 1974; Saltiel & Woelfel, 1975; Anderson, 1974; see Sawyer, 1981, for a review of much of this literature).

While the work done in the above areas has established some regularities, we are still far from a general, integrated, scientific theory. There are several reasons for this. First, some of the theoretical principles make

AUTHORS' NOTE: This chapter was prepared for presentation at the meetings of the International Communication Association in Boston, May 1982. It is excerpted from a longer manuscript entitled "A Dynamic Multidimensional Theory of Attitude and Belief Change." The authors would like to thank G. Barnett, J. Woelfel, Y. Trope, G. B. Armstrong, D. D'Alessio, N. Doran, C. Corey, and K. Neuendorf for valuable comments on an earlier draft of, and/or the issues addressed in, this chapter.

Correspondence and requests for reprints: Stan A. Kaplowitz, Department of Sociology, Michigan State University, East Lansing, MI 48824.

indeterminate predictions. This is true, for example, of Festinger's (1957) original formulation of cognitive dissonance theory, which tells us that many different modes of dissonance reduction are possible, but gives us no general basis for predicting which mode will be employed.[1]

Second, most of the theoretical principles are stated in a nonmathematical form predicting the general direction of a relationship, but not its strength or functional form. This makes it very difficult to state any general laws in which a number of variables are related via a single equation. The development of such equations is also hindered by the unfortunate tendency to define social psychological variables operationally as if they were dichotomous or trichotomous (e.g., distinguishing low, medium, and high credibility sources) rather than manipulating them at many levels or measuring them precisely and relatively continuously.

Third, even theoretical work that conceives of variables as continuous and develops mathematical models often lacks a sense of process, and simply contains equations that fit certain observed regularities[2] (see McPhee & Poole, 1981, for an elaboration of this point).

Fourth, there is very little integration among the different theories and propositions. Each deals with its own sets of concepts, processes, and measuring instruments (see, for example, McGuire, 1969, p. 271; Fishbein & Ajzen, 1975, p. 52). Hence each has a limited and imprecisely known range of applicability, and when the different processes lead to seemingly contradictory predictions, such conflicts cannot generally be resolved by reference to a more general theory.

Fifth, McGuire (1960, pp. 345-346) points out that attitude change takes place gradually over time and some studies (Walster, 1964; Tesser & Conlee, 1975; Kaplowitz, Fink, & Bauer, 1980; Miller, 1980; Poole & Hunter, 1979, 1980) have shown gradual changes and, in some cases, oscillations. As we shall show later, understanding the time course of attitude change is vital for understanding any cognitive or social forces involved. As we shall also argue, such time courses have been dealt with inadequately on both a theoretical and an empirical level.

By contrast, with just three principles and two fundamental variables (length and time), Newton was able to explain phenomena as diverse as planetary motion, falling objects (either through the air or on an inclined plane), the motion of objects on a level plane after a collision, and the motion of a pendulum. We will present a theory that is mathematical and dynamic, and that allows for the integration of many disparate phenomena into a single framework built on a few assumptions. We do not claim that we have succeeded in doing for attitude change what Newton did for mechanics. But because our theoretical approach is mathematical and deterministic, it is highly testable. Hence if the evidence proves us wrong, it can also suggest possibilities for improving the theory (see Kac, 1969).

As Lave and March (1975) point out, a model allows for the derivation of predictions that are not obvious and that are testable. The model and the phenomenon to be modeled are isomorphic in some limited but powerful respects. We shall present a mechanistic model. The model is useful to the extent that it can (1) incorporate known empirical regularities; (2) generate predictions that may be evaluated precisely; (3) integrate seemingly disparate phenomena; and (4) do these things parsimoniously. Our model is mechanistic not because we are convinced that the laws of cognition are the same as the laws of physics. Rather, it is because models generally have been built on metaphors (see Leatherdale, 1974; cf. Mandler & Kessen, 1959; see Roedinger, 1980, for metaphors applied to memory) and mechanics has one of the best existing combinations of richness and precision.

Indeed, McGuire's (1969, p. 257) discussion of messages as impulses and of spatial and temporal inertia in attitude change (McGuire, 1981, pp. 303-304) are the results of the same kind of mechanistic analogy employed here, and Anderson (1974, p. 88) states that "simple physical mechanisms exist which may have psychological counterparts."

THE STRUCTURE OF BELIEFS AND ATTITUDES

Craig (1975) distinguishes between network and spatial models of attitudes and beliefs. Network models represent attitudes and beliefs as connections between concepts and attitudinal change as a change in these connections. Such models include Heider's (1946) balance theory and Phillips and Thompson's (1977) representation of cognitive relations.

Our own model, by contrast, starts with the assumption that each person's attitudes and beliefs can be represented as the relationship between concepts in a multidimensional space (see Woelfel & Saltiel, 1978; Woelfel, Cody, Gillham, & Holmes, 1980; Woelfel & Fink, 1980). There have been many such spatial models and they have been used for many different purposes, such as to understand attitude and belief structures (Jones & Young, 1972; Osgood, Suci, & Tannenbaum, 1957), person perception (Rosenberg, Nelson, & Vivekananthan, 1968), color and other aspects of sensory perception (Shepard, 1980; Wish, 1967), racial and national stereotypes (Bell & Robinson, 1980; Wish, 1971), and behavioral taxonomies (Pierce & Amato, 1980). In all of these models, it is assumed that distance corresponds to dissimilarity and that concepts may be represented in a space in which dimensionality may be empirically determined.

Woelfel and Fink (1980) state the following assumptions for their multidimensional model:

A.1: The more similar person P regards concepts A and B, the closer they will be in P's cognitive space.
A.2: The more P likes A, the closer A will be to the concept "Me" in P's cognitive space.
A.3: Change in attitudes or beliefs is equivalent to motion of concepts relative to each other in this space.

A corollary to A.2 is:

A.2.1 The more P thinks person Q likes A, the closer A and Q will be in P's cognitive space.

Evidence supporting A.2 can be found in Woelfel et al. (1980). We suggest and are testing a refinement of A.2:

A.2.1 alt.: P's perception that concept A is *similar* to him- or herself (or to Q) is indicated by the distance between A and the concept "Actual Me" (or "Actual Q").
A.2.2 alt.: P's *evaluation* (or P's view of Q's evaluation) of A is indicated by the distance between the concepts A and "My Preference" (or "Q's Preference") within P's cognitive space.

Note that this formulation is quite consistent with Heider's (1946) balance theory in two important respects. First, it deals with both sentiment and unit relations. Any unit relationship (e.g., A owning B) implies similarity, hence, closeness, on at least one dimension. Second, as long as the space has a Euclidean metric,[3] the usual balance effects must hold. For example, if the relationship between P and Q is positive and the one between Q and R is positive (i.e., P is close to Q, and Q is close to R) the relationship between P and R must also be positive. Moreover, consistent with Heider (1958), if P likes him- or herself, (P's "Actual Me" near "My Preference") P will like that which is similar to him- or herself. (In this case, the predictions of A.2 and A.2 alt. are very similar.)

While the spatial model has some important similarities to balance theory, it also has some advantages over that theory. First, relations are conceived of as continuous, rather than trichotomized into positive, negative, or neutral. Second, it is easier, in the spatial model, to represent asymmetric sentiment relationships — Q may be close to P's Preference without P being close to Q's Preference.

Our multidimensional approach has an obvious resemblance to the semantic space approach of Osgood et al. (1957), which measures at-

...des with responses to semantic differential scales. Our approach has, however, several operational advantages that have theoretical implications. First, unlike scales with a few discrete values, such as seven-point scales, our scales are continuous[4] and unbounded at one end. As Woelfel and Fink (1980) point out, physical science has almost always utilized such scales, and doing so is crucial for discovering the functional relationship among variables. That attitudes can be meaningfully measured on such a scale is shown by Hamblin (1974) and by work in psychophysics (see Baird & Noma, 1978).

Second, we make no a priori assumption that certain attributes are viewed as orthogonal by the subject. Indeed, there is some evidence that "activity" and "potency" are not viewed as orthogonal (see Woelfel & Fink, 1980, p. 79).

Third, rather than imposing a certain set of attributes on the phenomenon to be evaluated, we allow subjects to (implicitly) use any attributes they might consider, and to use as many dimensions as they wish. In fact, empirical evidence from multidimensional scaling (MDS) suggests that the attributes of evaluation, potency, and activity that form such an important part of Osgood et al.'s (1957) view of cognitive structure are not always the important dimensions to people (Wish, Deutsch, & Biener, 1972).[5] (Indeed, some dimensions may correspond to no obvious attributes at all.) Since attitude change that is along a dimension that the investigators have not considered will be undetected, this finding leads to serious questions about the usefulness of Osgood et al.'s approach, and about the general strategy of choosing only a few dimensions without evidence that these are the only dimensions involving theoretically important relations (Barnett & Woelfel, 1979).

The concepts in P's cognitive space may include complex concepts as well as single words. For example, the concepts "10% tuition increase" and "20% tuition increase" are separate concepts that may have separate locations. And for many students, the concept "20% tuition increase at my own university" may have a very different location from "20% tuition increase at some other university."

As implied earlier, P's beliefs about other people's beliefs and attitudes can also be incorporated in this model. Hence for each person Q, P's space may contain both the concepts of "Actual Q" and "Q's Preference." Furthermore, if P believes that A and B are quite similar, but believes that Q does not share that view, then P's view of A and/or B will be at different locations, in P's space, from P's view of Q's view (A_Q and B_Q) of those two concepts.

To understand when A and A_Q would be at different locations, let us consider the following cases. If P is six feet tall, and Q is five feet tall, P will see his or her "Actual Me" as close to "tall" and will see Q as far from "tall." But this need not cause P to believe that P's and Q's concepts of "tall" are different (i.e., have different locations). But suppose P knew that five-footer Q considered him- or herself closer than P to "tall." Then P would assume P's and Q's concept of tall were different.

One might object that our spatial model is unable to represent fully certain relations described in everyday language. For example, our spatial model contains no clear way to distinguish among "A likes B," "A and B are married," and "A is B's mother." But, while not everything that can be represented in ordinary language can be represented in MDS, the reverse is also true. MDS permits us to quantify the degree of similarity an individual sees among concepts and the amount of positive affect he or she feels toward them. We believe that being able to represent such information in a way that is precise and that makes meaningful comparisons possible is of great value in explaining and understanding attitude change.

DYNAMIC MODELS OF ATTITUDE CHANGE

The Need for Such Models

Thus far we have assumed that attitudes and beliefs can be represented as the spatial relationship among concepts and that attitude change involves motion of those concepts. We have also noted that McGuire has suggested that a message is like an impulse (a force lasting for a certain period of time). An advance in attitude change theory will result if we can learn more about these forces.

There have been many mathematical models of attitude change, but typically they only predict equilibrium values of the attitude change. However, if we assume that Newton's law (force = mass × acceleration) holds for cognitive systems, then these forces determine the time course (trajectory) of attitude change. By studying the time course, we may hope to uncover the forces involved.

Not only do most models predict only equilibrium values, but empirical research has also given inadequate attention to trajectories. Very few studies measure attitude more than once after the experimental treatments. Those that do generally have at least one of the following deficiencies: (1) they lack a theoretical structure for making predictions of the time course; (2) they measure time very crudely (e.g., "immediately after message" versus "later"); (3) they neither control for nor measure the other messages the subject receives between the various posttreatment measures.

Our aim is to develop a dynamic model that will deal with the process of attitude change as it proceeds in the absence of further external messages.[6] Instead of only being able to predict the equilibrium point of the process, such a model could make predictions at other points as well. Even more important, to describe the change of an attitude after receipt of a message requires positing various forces or processes governing this change. To the extent that we can develop a satisfactory model, these forces will be revealed.

Possible Attitude Change Trajectories

Assuming that attitude change is equivalent to the motion of concepts, we now examine a variety of conceivable trajectories. We will then examine some dynamic models and see which trajectories are consistent with each model.

One very simple trajectory has the concept, once set in motion by a message, continuing to move in that direction at a *constant rate* until receipt of another relevant message (Figure 12.1a). A more likely trajectory has the concept constantly moving in the same direction toward an asymptote. There are two different versions of such a trajectory: the *constantly decelerating asymptotic* trajectory (Figure 12.1b) and the *S-shaped asymptotic* trajectory (Figure 12.1c).

Additional possibilities have the attitude's motion change directions and be *pulled back part of the way* to its original value (Figure 12.1d; see Poole & Hunter, 1979, for such an example), *all of the way* back (Figure 12.1e), or even *past* its *original location*[7] (Figure 12.1f). Still more complex trajectories are continued *oscillations* (found by Kaplowitz et al., 1980), which may be *damped* or *undamped*. Such oscillatory trajectories can have an equilibrium value that is either equal to the original attitude (Figure 12.1g and Figure 12.1h) or different from it (Figure 12.1i and Figure 12.1j).

Still other conceivable trajectories are some discontinuous ones. If McGuire's dictum on the gradualness of attitude change is wrong, an *immediate instantaneous change* trajectory is possible (Figure 12.1k). This is a limiting case of the constantly decelerating aymptotic trajectory. And if attitude change takes place suddenly, after the completion of cognitive processing, we may imagine a *delayed instantaneous change* trajectory (Figure 12.1l). This is a limiting case of the S-shaped asymptotic trajectory.

Some Formal Models and Their Trajectories

All of the models below assume that force = mass × acceleration. They differ as to the nature of the mass and force involved. In addition, while the continuous models assume that the space is isotropic (i.e., all directions are equivalent) the discontinuous ones do not.

Attitude Change 371

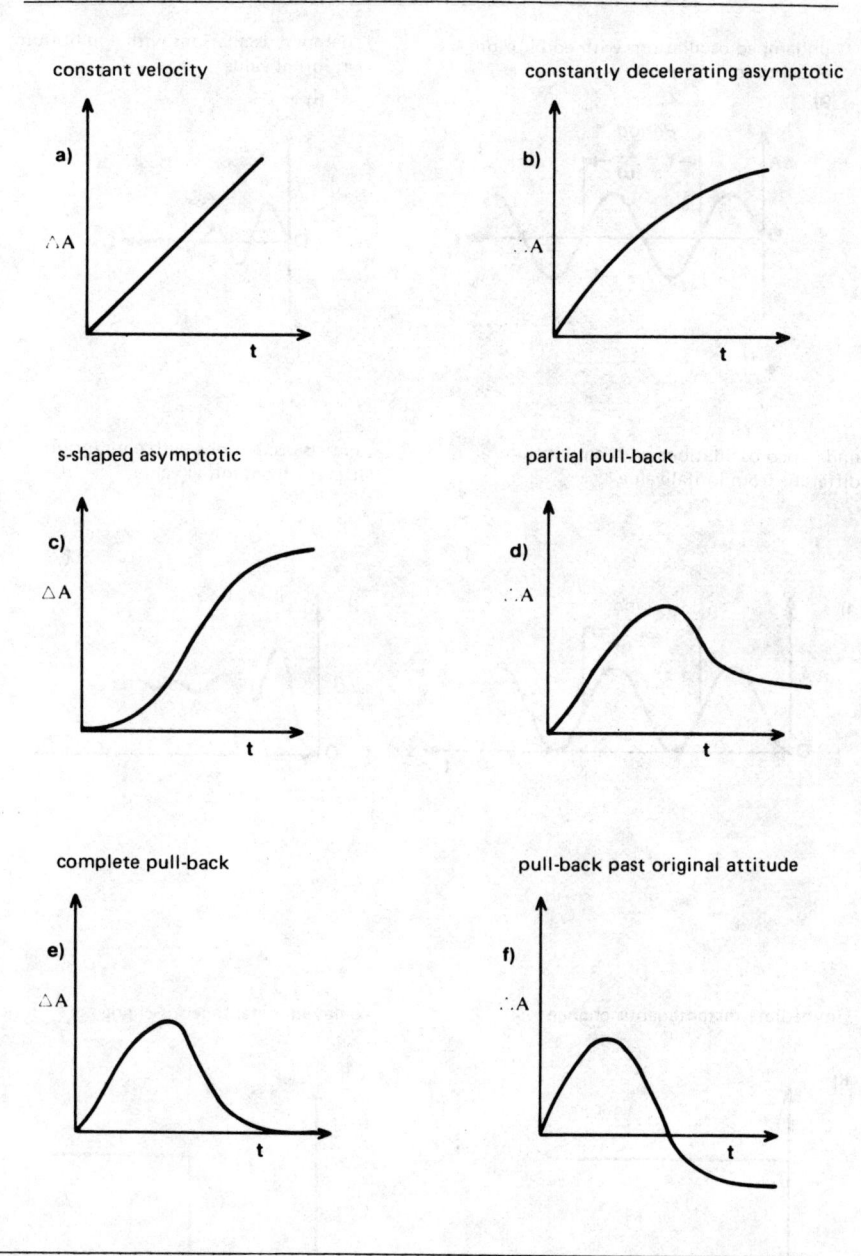

Figure 12.1. Possible attitude change trajectories. ΔA is change of location of concept A projected onto one dimension; positive values of ΔA represent movement in the initial direction; t is time from conclusion of message; t = 0 upon completion of the persuasive message.

undamped oscillations with equilibrium equal to initial value
g)

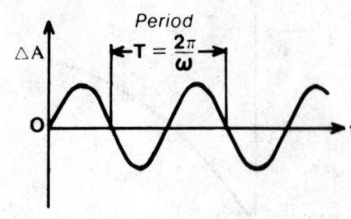

damped oscillations with equilibrium at initial value
h)

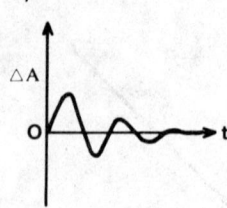

undamped oscillations with equilibrium different from initial value
i)

damped oscillations with equilibrium different from initial value
j)

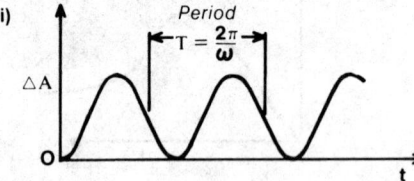

immediate instantaneous change
k)

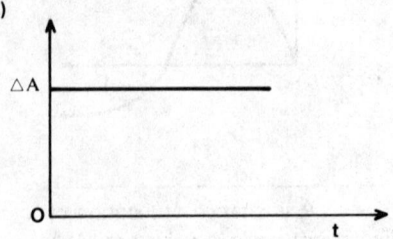

delayed instantaneous change
l)

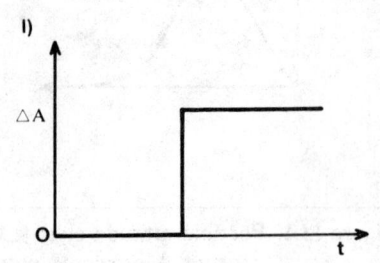

Attitude Change

Variable-Mass (VM) Impulse Models. These have been developed by Woelfel and his associates (Saltiel & Woelfel, 1975; Woelfel et al., 1980; Woelfel & Saltiel, 1978), and are based on the following assumptions:

VM.1: The message "A is like B" or "A is B" is a force pushing concepts A and B toward each other in P's cognitive space.

VM.2: Information acts like inertia or mass. The more messages P has received about a concept, the more resistant to acceleration that concept will be.

VM.1 is consistent with Woelfel et al. (1980). Indeed, Serota, Cody, Barnett, and Taylor (1977) have shown that one can use information about the configuration of concepts in a person's cognitive space to construct the message that will effectively move any given concept toward that person's "Me." VM.2 is supported by Danes, Hunter, and Woelfel (1978).

Woelfel does not specify the exact nature of the message force, but by doing so we can make predictions regarding the attitude trajectory. We assume the force is a brief impulse, which is completed at $t = 0$. If this is the only force, the concept, once set in motion, will continue to move with a constant velocity as in Figure 12.1a.

Since this is not very plausible, it is necessary to posit the existence of a force acting in the opposite direction to the motion. If we assume that, like friction, the magnitude of this force is proportional to the velocity, then in any dimension the motion satisfies the following equation:

$$m\ddot{x} + c\dot{x} = 0 \qquad [1]$$

where m is the mass of the concept, c is the coefficient of friction, x is the distance along dimension X, $\dot{x}$ is the first derivative with respect to time (velocity) and $\ddot{x}$ is the second derivative (acceleration). The solution to this equation is

$$x = a_1 + a_2 \exp(-(c/m)t) \qquad [2]$$

where a_1 and a_2 reflect initial conditions. If we set x to be initially zero, then at $t = 0$ we have $x = a_1 + a_2 = 0$ and $a_1 = -a_2$.
Hence equation 2 may be rewritten as

$$x = a_1 (1 - \exp(-(c/m)t)) \qquad [3]$$

and we see that x asymptotically approaches a_1, which we relabel ΔA, the change of position of concept A along dimension X. We also see that

$$\dot{x} = (\Delta A)\exp((-c/m)t) \qquad [4]$$

This model, therefore, predicts the constantly decelerating asymptotic trajectory in Figure 12.1b.

Fixed-Mass Spring Models. Like the variable-mass impulse model, this model assumes that the message "A is B" is a force pushing A and B together. The force is viewed as springlike in that at moderate displacements from equilibrium, $F_{restore} = -kx$, where $F_{restore}$ is the restoring force, x is the displacement from equilibrium, and k is the restoring coefficient. While the variable-mass impulse model views the information in the message as both an impulse and as contributing mass to the concept(s) implicated, the spring model is more parsimonious. It simply assumes that the information in the message is converted into energy to displace the springs so that they connect the concepts implicated. While the mass of a concept is not assumed to change, the model does predict that those concepts about which we have received much information, and are therefore well anchored to other concepts, will be more difficult to move.

Why do we conceive of these forces as being like springs rather than strings, braces, or gravity? A spring is superior to a string in that it resists both stretching and compression. A brace can be regarded as a special case of a spring, one with an extremely high restoring coefficient. As for a gravitational force, its strength depends on the inverse square of the distance between the bodies. It does not, therefore, give any special role to messages. Finally, as we shall show later, if the restoring coefficients of the springs are related appropriately to standard attitude change variables, this model is able to account for a wide variety of findings in the attitude change literature.

Let us now examine the trajectories predicted by this model. Suppose concept A is initially connected to concepts $C_1, \ldots, C_n$ by springs with coefficients $k_1, \ldots, k_n$, respectively, and is initially at equilibrium. Now, suppose a new message connects A to C_{n+1} with a spring of coefficient k_{n+1} (C_{n+1} need not be distinct from the previous C_i). This new spring is connected at $t = 0$, and suddenly changes the equilibrium point for A. A, however, is still at the old equilibrium point and is therefore being pulled or pushed toward the new one.

To determine A's trajectory, we use the standard equation of spring motion

$$m\ddot{x}^* + c\dot{x}^* + kx^* = 0 \qquad [5]$$

where x^* is the displacement of the spring from the new equilibrium, k is the effective restoring coefficient of the springs connected to A, c is its frictional or damping coefficient, and m is the mass of the moving system.[8] We are positing the existence of such friction because cognitive motion (cognitive processing) consumes cognitive energy (see Berger & Luckmann, 1967, p. 53). Since we are assuming the springs themselves to be massless and all concepts to have unit mass, m is equal to 1.

Attitude Change

If, as before, we set $x = 0$ at $t = 0$, and $x = \Delta A$ at equilibrium, then $x = x^* + \Delta A$. Substituting into equation 5 gives us

$$m\ddot{x} + c\dot{x} + kx = k\,\Delta A \qquad [6]$$

Assuming c and k constant with respect to time,[9] the general solution to equation 6 is

$$x = a_1 \exp(\lambda_1 t) + a_2 \exp(\lambda_2 t) + \Delta A \qquad [7]$$

where
$$\lambda_1 = \frac{-c}{2m} + \frac{(c^2 - 4km)^{1/2}}{2m}$$

$$\lambda_2 = \frac{-c}{2m} - \frac{(c^2 - 4km)^{1/2}}{2m}$$

and a_1 and a_2 reflect initial conditions.

This equation results in three distinct structural solutions of the differential equation (see Haberman, 1977; Petrovskii, 1969; Greenberg, 1980). If $c^2 > 4k$, the λs are real and unequal. Note, however, that since k is presumed positive, both λs must be negative. This is the *overdamped* case. From equation 7, at $t = 0$,

$$x = a_1 + a_2 + \Delta A = 0 \qquad [8]$$

Differentiating equation 7, we have

$$\dot{x} = a_1 \lambda_1 (\exp(\lambda_1 t)) + a_2 \lambda_2 (\exp(\lambda_2 t)) \qquad [9]$$

Since A is presumed at rest when the additional spring was connected, the velocity at $t = 0$ was zero. Therefore, at $t = 0$, we have

$$\dot{x} = a_1 \lambda_1 + a_2 \lambda_2 = 0 \qquad [10]$$

Combining equations 8 and 10 gives us

$$a_1 = \frac{\Delta A \lambda_2}{\lambda_1 - \lambda_2} \text{ and } a_2 = \frac{-\Delta A \lambda_1}{\lambda_1 - \lambda_2} \qquad [11]$$

and hence

$$x = \Delta A \left(\left(\frac{1}{\lambda_1 - \lambda_2} \right) (\lambda_2 \exp(\lambda_1 t) - \lambda_1 \exp(\lambda_2 t)) + 1 \right) \qquad [12]$$

To examine the trajectory we see, from equations 9 and 11 that

$$\dot{x} = \frac{\Delta A}{\lambda_1 - \lambda_2} (\exp(\lambda_1 t) - \exp(\lambda_2 t)) \qquad [13]$$

At $t=0$ and $t=\infty$, $\dot{x}$ is zero. Since $\lambda_1 > \lambda_2$ for $0 < t < \infty$, $\dot{x} > 0$. Hence this solution leads to the S-shaped asymptotic trajectory in Figure 12.1c.

If $c^2 = 4k$, the roots are real and equal. This is the *critically damped* case. (Since this requires exact equality of roots, it is usually not considered to occur except in idealized systems.) In this case,

$$x = (a_1 + a_2 t)\exp(\lambda t) + \Delta A \qquad [14]$$

As before, we assume $x = 0$, and $\dot{x} = 0$ at $t = 0$. Hence we have $a_1 = -\Delta A$. Since

$$\dot{x} = (a_2 + a_1 \lambda + a_2 \lambda t)(\exp \lambda t) \qquad [15]$$

$$\dot{x} = a_2 + a_1 \lambda = 0$$

Hence $a_2 = -a_1 \lambda = \Delta A \lambda$ and equation 14 can be rewritten as

$$x = \Delta A [(\lambda t - 1)(\exp(\lambda t)) + 1] \qquad [16]$$

Hence

$$\dot{x} = \lambda^2 (\Delta A) t \exp(\lambda t) \qquad [17]$$

As with the overdamped case, this describes an S-shaped asymptotic trajectory.

If $c^2 < 4k$, the λs are complex conjugates. This is the *underdamped* case. Defining

$$r = \frac{-c}{2m} \qquad [18]$$

and

$$\omega = \frac{(4km - c^2)^{1/2}}{2m} \qquad [19]$$

$$\lambda_1 = r + \omega i \text{ and}$$

$$\lambda_2 = r - \omega i.$$

The solution can then be written as

$$x = \exp(rt)(a_1 \sin(\omega t) + a_2 \cos(\omega t)) \qquad [20]$$

At $t = 0$,

$$x = a_2 = -\Delta A$$

Differentiating equation 20 we have

$$\dot{x} = \exp(rt)[\omega(a_1(\cos(\omega t) - a_2 \sin(\omega t)) + r(a_1 \sin(\omega t) + a_2 \cos(\omega t))]$$

At $t = 0$,

$$\dot{x} = a_1 \omega + a_2 r = 0$$

Hence,
$$a_1 = \frac{-ra_2}{\omega} = \frac{r\Delta A}{\omega}$$

and the solution can be written as
$$x = \Delta A \left[(\exp(rt))\left(\frac{r}{\omega}(\sin(\omega t)) - \cos(\omega t)\right) + 1\right] \quad [21]$$

This describes the oscillatory trajectories with an initial value of zero but a final equilibrium of ΔA (Figure 12.1i and Figure 12.1j; note that $2\pi/\omega$ is the period of oscillation). Whether the oscillations are damped or undamped depends on whether r is zero or negative.

More Complex Variants of the Spring Model. While the spring model we have presented is attractive for its parsimony, other more complex variants are possible and will be considered briefly. One such possibility is that messages both create springs and add mass to the concepts. If additional messages simply create additional springs, thereby increasing the effective spring coefficient, the period of oscillation will decrease but the rate of damping will remain the same (see equations 18 and 19). If the messages add mass to concept A, the period will increase but the rate of damping will decrease.

Another variant assumes that a message both produces an initial impulse and creates a spring. In this case, to find the resulting trajectory, we add a trajectory predicted by the impulse model (Figure 12.1a or Figure 12.1b) to one predicted by the fixed mass spring model (Figures 12.1g-12.1j).

Finally, it is possible that within the fixed-mass spring model the effective spring coefficient k is nonconstant. It is, for example, quite plausible that forgetting weakens the springs while self-generated messages (cognitive responses) strengthen them. Such changes in k would, as indicated above, cause the period of oscillation to be nonconstant.

Discontinuous Models. These can be modeled spatially through catastrophe theory (see Thom, 1975; Paulos, 1980). Such models assume that the space is anisotropic in that some dimensions are different from others and that it is possible, while moving on a surface, to reach a singularity (e.g., a "hole").

Summary

Many different trajectories of attitude change are possible and examination of trajectories should enable us to distinguish among a number of different conceptions of the forces involved in attitude change (i.e., dynamic models). From looking at the possible trajectories, however, it is clear that distinguishing among them requires that time from receipt of message be measured very precisely and that the attitude be measured at a very large number of different points.

FURTHER EXPLICATION OF THE FIXED-MASS SPRING (FMS) MODEL

This model is most useful if it can successfully account not only for the time course of attitude change, but also for the effect of standard social psychological variables on the equilibrium values of the attitudes. For the model to do so, we must describe further these springs and their restoring coefficients.

> FMS.1: If P receives a message from Source S linking concepts A and B, this sets up three springs. One links As and Bs (P's view of S's view of A and B, respectively). This we call the *message information spring*. A second spring is between As and A (where A is P's own view of A) and the third is between Bs and B. These latter springs are called the *differential perspective springs*, as they reflect the degree to which P sees S's view as relevant to his or her own view.

Consistent with Woelfel and Fink (1980), we regard a simple message as a statement linking two concepts. Communications that deal with a larger number of concepts are compound messages. These can be decomposed into simple messages. Each such simple message, we assume, creates its own set of springs. While the three springs created by the message will pull A toward B, this motion will be resisted by preexisting springs connecting A and B to other concepts. These springs we call the *anchoring springs*. The equilibrium location of A and B will be determined by the equilibrium length and restoring coefficients of the message springs and the anchoring springs. To derive the restoring coefficients of the various spring connections we present some further assumptions.

> FMS.2: The information derived from the message provides the energy necessary to perform the work of stretching or compressing a spring.
>
> FMS.3: In traversing cognitive distance, just as in traversing physical distance, energy is dissipated at a rate proportional to the amount of energy in the system.
>
> FMS.4: Over time energy dissipates out of the system at a rate proportional to the amount of energy in it (cf. Prigogine, 1978).

The Message-Information Spring

The equilibrium length of this spring is determined as follows:

> FMS.5: A message from source S saying "A and B are m units apart" creates a springlike connection with equilibrium length m between As and Bs.

Attitude Change

Ordinary messages do not, of course, specify such distances numerically. But, as Cliff (1959) has shown, our culture contains shared and quantifiable understandings of the intensity of adverbs such as "very," "slightly," etc. This suggests that verbal messages specifying the similarity between two concepts can also be quantified. We believe, moreover, that to the extent that people state their own beliefs and their interpretation of a message precisely, the ability to predict attitude change will be greater.

Information in the Message. We view the information contained in the message as information theorists view the information contained in an event — as the "surprise" in the message. That unexpected messages will have more impact than expected ones is well documented in social psychology. Aronson and Linder (1965), for example, found that unexpected positive or negative feedback has more impact than such feedback where it is expected. We define the information in the message H(m) as follows:

$$H(m) = (\sum_i (x_i - m)^2 p_i)^{1/2} \qquad [22]$$

where x_i is a possible value of the AB distance, m is the value specified (or implied) in the message, and p_i is the probability that P had previously assigned to S stating the value as x_i.[10] The equation above can be rewritten as

$$H(m) = (\sum_i ((x_i - \bar{d}(A_S, B_S)) + (\bar{d}(A_S, B_S) - m))^2 p_i)^{1/2}$$

$$= (\sum_i ((x_i - \bar{d}(A_S, B_S))^2 p_i) + \sum ((\bar{d}(A_S, B_S) - m)^2 p_i)$$

$$+ 2 \sum_i ((x_i - \bar{d}(A_S, B_S)) (\bar{d}(A_S, B_S) - m) p_i))^{1/2} \qquad [23]$$

where $\bar{d}(A_S, B_S)$ is P's expected value of S's view of the AB distance. The final summation in equation 23 equals

$$2 [(\bar{d}(A_S, B_S) - m) \sum_i (x_i - \bar{d}(A_S, B_S)) p_i]^{1/2}$$

By the definition of $\bar{d}(A_S, B_S)$, this equals zero. Since both m and $\bar{d}(A_S, B_S)$ are constant, the previous summation equals $(\bar{d}(A_S, B_S) - m)^2$. Hence,

$$H(m) = (\sum_i ((x_i - \bar{d}(A_S, B_S))^2 p_i) + (d(A_S, B_S) - m)^2)^{1/2} \qquad [24]$$

This, in turn, can be rewritten as

$$H(m) = (\sigma^2_{A_S B_S} + D^2)^{1/2} \qquad [25]$$

where $\sigma^2_{A_S B_S}$ is the variance or uncertainty of P's expectations of S's message[11] and D is the discrepancy between the expected and actual value of the message. $\sigma_{A_S B_S}$ is expected to be a function of P's perception of S's expertise, P's own expertise, the degree to which P perceives S and P as similar, and the degree to which P perceives a consensus on the meaning of concepts A and B. See Kaplowitz and Fink (1981) for a more detailed discussion.

Trustworthiness. The message from S contains a certain amount of information as to S's view of the A-B relationship and hence a certain amount of energy. En route some of this energy is lost, as if P is asking him or herself, "How much do I trust this information to reflect P's true view?" We assume that the perfectly trustworthy source is located at "My Preference" in P's space and that, to be used, the information (energy) must travel to this point. By assumption FMS.3, however, some of this energy is lost in transit and the loss is a negative exponential function:

$$E = \frac{\alpha}{2} H(m) \exp(-\mu(d(S,MP))) \qquad [26]$$

where E is the energy available for the A_S-B_S connection, H(m) is the information in the message, and d(S,MP) is the distance of S from P's "My Preference." Parameters α and μ are assumed constant within subjects.[12]

All of the following help us to regard a source as trustworthy: (1) similarity to us (Berscheid, 1966; Brock, 1965; Mills & Jellison, 1968), especially if those similarities imply similar interests, values, and perspectives; (2) character traits we respect (e.g., Heston,, 1973); and (3) our positive affect toward the communicator (e.g., Kelman, 1961). All of the above sources of trustworthiness would be reflected in S being close to "My Preference."

Message Discrepancy. To calculate the coefficient of the message information spring ($k_{A_S B_S}$), we add two more assumptions.

> FMS.6.1: The energy from the message is used to perform the work of displacing a spring of equilibrium length m (the A-B distance specified in the message) so that its ends just touch A_S and B_S.

By FMS.3, as the spring is displaced, energy is lost, following a negative exponential function with respect to the displacement.

FMS.6.2: The spring coefficient $k_{A_S B_S}$ has a value such that all of the energy that was in the original message and remains after losses for trustworthiness and displacing the spring is converted into the work of displacing it.

Physicists define the amount of work entailed in moving something a distance, D*, as

$$W = \int_0^{D^*} F dx$$

where F is the force and x is the distance. The force necessary to displace the spring is equal and opposite to the restoring force, which by Hooke's Law is $-kx$. Hence if D* is the displacement of the spring,

$$W = (1/2) k_{A_S B_S} (D^*)^2 \quad [27]$$

From equations 25 and 26 and assumptions FMS.6.1 and FMS.6.2, we have another equation for W:

$$W = \frac{\alpha}{2} (\sigma^2_{A_S B_S} + D^2)^{1/2} \exp(-\mu(d(S,MP))) \exp(-\beta D^*) \quad [28]$$

where β is another parameter that is assumed constant within individuals.

But what is D*? Suppose P had no prior uncertainty as to S's position (i.e., $\sigma_{A_S B_S} = 0$). In this case, the displacement, D*, would be simply D, the discrepancy between P's prior expectation of S and the value of the actual message (i.e., $D^* = D = \bar{d}(A_S, B_S) - m$).

But, in fact, there is always some uncertainty as to the message. Suppose D = 0. This means that the expected value of P's view of the A-B distance is m (the value of the message). But this does not mean that the spring of equilibrium length m need not be displaced. In view of the uncertainty about A_S and B_S, the distance between A_S and B_S could be either more or less than m. In either case displacement would be required, and the expected value of this displacement is

$$D^* = \sigma_{A_S B_S} = (\sigma^2_{A_S} + \sigma^2_{B_S})^{1/2}$$

More generally, the expected difference between m and d(As, Bs), which is equal to D, can be expressed by an equation we encountered earlier:

$$D^* = (\sum_i (x_i - m))p_i^{1/2} = (D^2 + \sigma^2_{A_S B_S})^{1/2} \qquad [29]$$

(see equations 22-25).

Combining equations 27, 28, and 29 gives us

$$k_{A_S B_S} = \frac{\alpha T \exp(-\beta D^*)}{D^*} \qquad [30]$$

where T (trustworthiness) is $\exp(-\mu(d(S,MP)))$.

Notice that less-discrepant messages, which have smaller D and hence smaller D^*, cause tighter springs. But, since $\sigma_{A_S B_S}$ is never zero, neither will D^* be, and the restoring coefficient will always be finite.

The Differential-Perspective Spring

As stated earlier, some of the original energy in the message is lost before it can be used in the message-information spring. What is left to affect P's cognitive space moves A_S and B_S. Some, but not all, of this energy is transmitted to move A and B. It is as if P is now deciding, "Given that I have received a certain amount of information as to what S thinks, to what degree is S's view relevant to my own judgment?"

The motion of A_S and B_S is transferred to A and B by the springs between A_S and A and between B_S and B (the differential perspective springs). The stiffer those springs, the more A and B will move with A_S and B_S.

These springs should have zero equilibrium length. The coefficients of these springs, k_{AA_S} and k_{BB_S}, should, like $\sigma_{A_S B_S}$, depend on the expertise of the source, similarity of source to receiver, and consensus in the meaning of A and B. See Kaplowitz and Fink (1981) for a fuller discussion.

The Anchoring Springs:
Time Decay and Cognitive Responses

The springs connecting A and B to other concepts are based predominantly on prior messages.[13] The strength of these springs should be related to the degree to which the prior messages are remembered. Ebbinghaus (1885/1964) has proposed a negatively accelerated curve of forgetting.

Such a curve follows from our theory. By FMS.4, energy loss fits the following equation:

$$E = E_o \exp(-\gamma t) \qquad [31]$$

where E_o is the initial energy, t is the time elapsed, and γ is another parameter. The work used in displacing a spring creates potential energy, and from equation 18 we see that this potential energy is proportional to the spring's restoring coefficient. Hence equation 31 implies that for any cognitive spring,

$$k = k_o \exp(-\gamma t) \qquad [32]$$

where k_o is the coefficient at $t = 0$, immediately after the receipt of the message. The decay of a spring, however, can be counteracted by additional messages that provide new information and energy to that connection.

The trajectory equations for the spring model were derived on the assumption that k was constant. But what if the spring decay (as in equation 32) causes a violation of this assumption? In this case, one can only generate an approximate solution to the differential equation. For time periods of ten minutes or less, however, we suspect that the decay should be small enough that k can be approximated as constant. Moreover, to the extent that decay is noticeable, its qualitative effects are regular. From equation 19 we can see that if the trajectory is initially underdamped, reducing k will first lengthen the period and eventually lead to an overdamped trajectory.

What is the role of counterarguments and other cognitive responses? There are three possible interpretations within the context of the spring model: (1) Such cognitive responses are a consequence of the oscillatory motion of the attitudes, but have no consequence themselves; (2) cognitive responses reflect attention to the topic and lack of attention increases the damping coefficient; or (3) cognitive responses are like external messages and strengthen springs. This last possibility is suggested by studies showing self-generated attitude change (for reviews, see Tesser, 1978; Petty, 1981) and the relationship of cognitive responses to attitude change (Petty, Wells, & Brock, 1976; Cacioppo & Petty, 1979a, 1979b; Petty & Cacioppo, 1977), as well as by the fact that we remember best those things we think about most.

If the first possibility above holds and cognitive responses have no effect, then the trajectory should be the same whether cognitive responses are encouraged or are made difficult through distraction. If the cognitive responses reduce the damping coefficient, then subjects who are encouraged to think will have trajectories with shorter periods of oscillation and slower rate of damping than will those who are distracted. Finally, if cognitive responses tighten springs, then, as predicted by the reduced damping formulation, cognitive responses should cause the period to be shorter and the damping to be slower. The differences from the reduced damping formulation is that this one suggests that cognitive responses can cause abrupt changes in the period. If, in addition, each time the subject's view is at an extremum in the oscillation cycle, a spring pulling the view back in the opposite direction is strengthened, this can keep changing the equilibrium position of the set of springs. By changing the equilibrium position, such cognitive responses may actually increase the amplitude of oscillation.

Predicting Attitude Change from Message Discrepancy,
Source Credibility, and Prior Commitment.

Having explained how discrepancy and other variables contribute to the spring coefficients, we will now demonstrate how the model relates the equilibrium value of the attitude change of these springs and variables. For ease of calculation and presentation, we make a few simplifying assumptions. First, we assume that all of the springs anchoring concept A can be represented as a single spring firmly anchored at one end to A's initial location, A_0, and at equilibrium prior to the message. This aggregate spring, the restoring coefficient of which we call k_{A_0}, must, therefore, have an equilibrium length equal to zero. We make an analogous assumption for B.

We now clarify the meaning of message discrepancy. We have defined discrepancy as the difference between the position advocated in the message and the expected value of source S's assertion. Traditionally, the literature has viewed discrepancy as the difference between the message and one's own view.

To understand the relationship between these different definitions we must distinguish two cases. In one case, P knows what some other sources think and can locate S relative to these other sources and him- or herself. In this case, P may be able to guess, "If I think A and B are x units apart, then given what others like S have thought, S will probably think A and B are less (or more) than x units apart." But suppose P has no prior clue as to the direction of S's bias? In this case, P's most likely guess as to $\bar{d}(A_S,B_S)$, the expected value of the distance between S's conceptions of A and B, respectively, is simply d(A,B), P's own conceptions of that distance. Hence in this case the two kinds of discrepancies are equal.

Attitude Change

Spring Coefficients

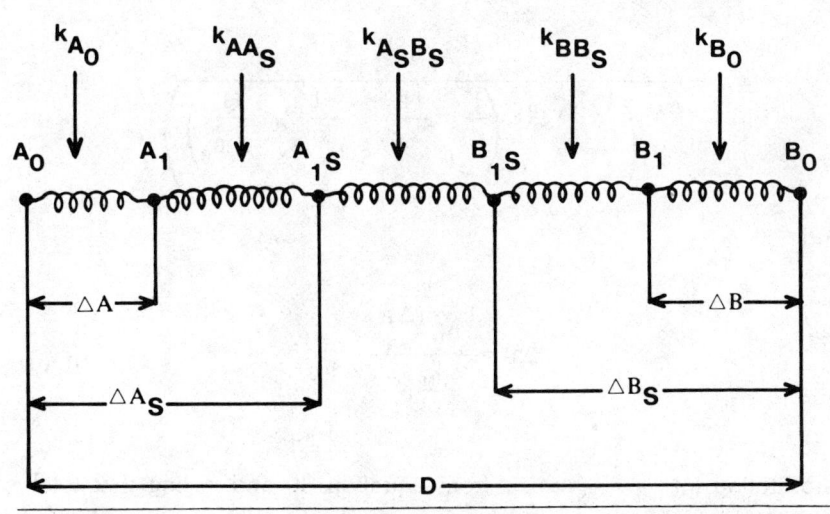

Figure 12.2. Springs and attitude changes as a result of a message from source S.

Let us now consider the situation shown in Figure 12.2. We assume that A has moved from its initial location, A_0, to its location after the message, A_1, a distance ΔA, and that A_S which initially had the same expected location as A is now at A_{1S} and is a distance $\Delta A_S - \Delta A$ from A. Moreover, as discussed earlier, we assume that the equilibrium length of the spring between A and A_S is zero. The situation for concept B is completely analogous. We have drawn Figure 12.2 as if the message is that the distance between A and B is zero. This simplifies the diagram by making D for the message equal to the original distance between A and B, $d(A_0, B_0)$. None of the equations below depends, however, on this assumption.

Since each concept is assumed in equilibrium, the sum of all forces acting directly on each is zero. Hence, looking at A_1, we have

$$k_{A_0} \Delta A_1 = k_{AA_S} (\Delta A_S - \Delta A_1) \qquad [33]$$

and looking at A_{1S} we have

$$k_{A_S B_S} (D - (\Delta A_S + \Delta B_S)) = k_{AA_S} (\Delta A_S - \Delta A) \qquad [34]$$

The analogous equations hold for B_1 and B_{1S}. Solving these equations gives us

$$\Delta A = \frac{k_{A_S B_S} D}{k_{A_0}\left(1 + k_{A_S B_S}\left(\frac{1}{k_{A_0}} + \frac{+1}{k_{AA_S}} + \frac{+1}{k_{BB_S}} + \frac{+1}{k_{B_0}}\right)\right)} \quad [35]$$

and

$$\Delta B = \frac{k_{A_0}(\Delta A)}{k_{B_0}} \quad [36]$$

Substituting for $k_{A_S B_S}$ from equation 30 and noting that total attitude change is $\Delta A + \Delta B$, we have

$$\Delta A + \Delta B = \frac{\alpha T(k_{A_0} + k_{B_0})\exp(-\beta D^*)D}{k_{A_0} k_{B_0} D^* + \alpha T(\exp(-\beta D^*))\left(\frac{1}{k_{A_0}} + \frac{+1}{k_{AA_S}} + \frac{+1}{k_{BB_S}} + \frac{+1}{k_{B_0}}\right)} \quad [37]$$

Examining equation 36 we see that it is consistent with many findings that a more trustworthy source (higher value of T) and a more expert source (higher value of k_{AA_S} and k_{BB_S}) will produce more attitude change. Since k_{A_0} and k_{B_0} reflect prior commitment, information, or ego-involvement, the equation is also consistent with findings that these variables inhibit attitude change (see Sherif et al., 1965; Zimbardo, 1960).

Finally, we see that attitude change is zero both when the discrepancy is zero and when it is infinite. Hence the theory predicts the nonmonotonic relationship between discrepancy and attitude change found by Aronson et al. (1963), Bochner and Insko (1966), Whittaker (1965), Brewer and Crano (1968), and Nemeth and Markowski (1972).

A BRIEF LOOK AT OTHER ASPECTS OF THE MODEL

A major strength of the model we have proposed is its ability to account not only for the findings discussed thus far but for many other important and seemingly unrelated phenomena in attitude change. While a detailed discussion of these is beyond the scope of this chapter, we will attempt to provide a further sense of the theory's possibilities. For a fuller discussion see Kaplowitz and Fink (1981).

Source-Object Congruity Effects

Most theories of the effect of message discrepancy (e.g., Aronson et al., 1963; Laroche, 1977; Fishbein & Ajzen, 1975) assume that while a source of low credibility can be very ineffective, he or she will not have a negative effect. But much evidence (e.g., Tannenbaum, 1953) supports Osgood and Tannenbaum's (1955) prediction that endorsement by a negatively evaluated source can be a "kiss of death" for an object.

Our own theory predicts that regardless of P's feelings toward the source, the distance between A_S and B_S (P's view of S's views of A and B) will move toward the view stated in the message. But this does not mean that if S endorses A, P will become more favorable to A. If S has endorsed A, the second concept, concept B, is "S's Preference" (SP), "good" or some other evaluative term. If B is SP, A_S and A (if A_S and A are tightly linked) both move toward SP_S (P's view of S's view of SP). If S is presumed to know his or her own preferences, SP_S is at the same location as SP. Since A is moving toward SP, P will become less favorable to A if the movement toward SP is also movement away from P's "My Preference" (MP). Assuming that S and SP are at the same location, P will become less favorable to A if S is located far from MP (see Figure 12.3).

Aside from predicting the usual source-object congruity effects, our theory is able to account for departures from this theory such as incredulity effects and the ability of a negatively evaluated source to be highly effective by arguing against his or her own interest (Walster, Aronson, & Abrahams, 1966).

Effects of Similarity of Source and Recipient

Consistent with experimental evidence, our model predicts that on matters of opinion similar sources will be more influential than dissimilar ones. For matters perceived as totally factual, we predict that similar and dissimilar sources will be equally effective in causing attitude change.

a. SP (and S) closer than A to MP: P becomes more favorable to A but less to S

A
↓
↑
SP,S

MP

b A closer than SP (and S) to MP: P becomes more favorable to S but less favorable to A

SP,S
↓
↑
A

MP

Figure 12.3. Source-object motion resulting from different configurations. We assume that S and SP are at the same location.

Effects of Message Repetition

Our model predicts: (1) Increased message repetition leads to greater message retention; and (2) if the messages occur when the concepts are at the equilibrium point, increased repetition will cause increased acceptance of the message. If, however, the repetitions all occur so close together that no noticeable decay of springs has taken place, the asymptotic value of the attitude change, as the number of repetitions increases, falls short of the change advocated by the message.

Persistence of Attitude Change

We predict that while a high credibility source will produce more initial attitude change, under most conditions this change will decay more rapidly than the change produced by a less credible source. Hence the amounts of attitude change will converge over time.

Cognitive Responses

While we have already discussed the possible effects of cognitive responses on the trajectory of attitude change, we will now briefly extend our discussion of them.

We see cognitive responses as being generated by a sudden increase in the restoring force of a preexisting spring. The increase in this restoring force, which we refer to as the "tension," is the product of the increased displacement of the spring and its restoring coefficient. Attention to an external message is viewed as resulting from expected increases in spring tension. When several external messages and potential cognitive responses are competing for attention within P's cognitive system, the "winner" is likely to be the one that has produced the greatest amount of actual or expected tension. This explains the role of distraction in inhibiting cognitve responses. Since concepts we care about greatly have the highest restoring coefficients in their anchoring springs, this also explains why cognitive responses and attention to external messages are most likely when a message deals with something we care about. In addition, the theory leads to the interesting prediction that messages that produce the greatest initial attitude change (moderately discrepant messages from highly credible sources) will produce the greatest counterarguing.

If we assume that self-generated counterarguments are like other messages and cause the stiffening of springs resisting the message, they not only result in final attitude change being less than initial change but also create resistance to further change from future persuasive messages. Hence, the theory predicts the inoculation effect found by McGuire (1964). Our view of cognitive responses is also consistent with evidence that memory is enhanced by repeating external messages (Cacioppo & Petty, 1979; Wilson & Miller, 1968), by rehearsing a message, and by linking its concepts to others (see, for example, Wingfield & Byrnes, 1981, for a brief discussion of each of these points).

Finally, the theory defines cognitive dissonance in terms of the tension in the cognitive springs and distinguishes dissonance from inconsistency. It also discusses conditions under which dissonance produces the most discomfort and translates dissonance-reduction strategies into the spring model.

CONCLUSION

We have examined the trajectory of attitude change by systematically varying the time interval from receipt of message to attitudinal response (see Kaplowitz et al., 1980). Our results gave modest but statistically significant support for a spring model with oscillations. To provide a more precise test, we plan a series of experiments in which computers will be used to measure the time interval precisely, and in which our procedures will exercise stronger control over extraneous variables.

Obviously, much empirical work remains to be done on this theory, and there is still room for theoretical elaboration. In view of the theory's ability to account for such a wide variety of known and seemingly disparate findings, and its ability to make precise predictions as to the time course of attitude change, it merits such testing and attention.

NOTES

1. Walster, Berscheid, and Barclay (1967) have, however, attempted to deal with this problem.

2. There are some exceptions to this criticism, such as Saltiel and Woelfel's (1975) and Hunter and Cohen's (1972) treatment of the discrepancy-attitude change problem. See also Abelson (1964), Taylor (1968), and Woelfel and Fink (1980).

3. A space with a Euclidean metric has the following properties: (If $d(i,j)$ is the distance from i to j, then (a) $d(i,i) = 0$; (b) $d(i,j) = d(j,i)$; (c) $d(i,k) \leq d(i,j) + d(j,k)$.

4. By a continuous scale, we mean a scale in which between any two values another is possible, assuming technology and observer precision permit this.

5. They found that important dimensions for judging nations were geography, population, culture/race.

6. Hunter and Cohen's (1972) "dynamic models," by contrast, assume that the actor is continuously receiving a particular external message. Hence these models confound the effect of time with the effect of message repetition.

7. Note that while such a trajectory is consistent with findings of a "boomerang effect" (see, for example, Worchel & Brehm, 1970), it is not required by such findings. It is quite possible that when a boomerang effect occurs, the initial motion of the attitude is opposite to the direction advocated by the message.

8. Equation 5 holds for each dimension in the space. If, however, the springs connected to A are not in a straight line, not only is the motion in more than one dimension, but the effective value of k in each dimension changes as A moves, thus complicating the mathematics.

9. Later we will see what happens to the trajectories if this assumption is relaxed.

10. Note that this formulation implies that x_i, a possible value of $d(A_S,B_S)$, could be negative, meaning that P distinguishes between A being in one or the other direction from B.

11. According to Attneave (1959), the information in an event of probability p is $\log_2(1/p)$. Therefore, if the probability distribution is normal, an event with deviation D from the expected value of the distribution has information value =

$$\text{value} = \frac{D^2 + (2\sigma^2)(\ln(\sigma\sqrt{2\pi}))}{2\sigma^2(\ln(2))}$$

12. It is possible that interpersonal scaling differences would make these parameters vary across subjects. The reason for the use of $\alpha/2$ will be apparent later.

13. Barnett (1977a), however, has found that words have connotations because they sound like other words, suggesting that words are linked, even if weakly, to their near homonyms.

REFERENCES

Abelson, R. P. Mathematical models of the distribution of attitudes under controversy. In N. Frederiksen & H. Gulliksen (Eds.), *Contributions to mathematical psychology*. New York: Holt, Rinehart & Winston, 1964.

Anderson, N. Cognitive algebra: Information theory applied to social attribution. In L. Berkowitz (Ed.), *Advances in experimental social psychology* (Vol. 7). New York: Academic Press, 1974.

Aronson, E., & Linder, D. Gain and loss of esteem as determinants of interpersonal attractiveness. *Journal of Experimental Social Psychology*, 1965, *1*, 156-171.

Aronson, E., Turner, J. A. & Carlsmith, M. Communicator credibility and communication discrepancy as determinants of attitude change. *Journal of Abnormal and Social Psychology*, 1963, *67*, 31-37.

Attneave, F. *Application of information theory to psychology: A summary of basic concepts, methods and results*. New York: Holt, Rinehart & Winston, 1959.

Baird, J. C., & Noma, E. *Fundamentals of scaling and psychophysics*. New York: John Wiley, 1978.

Barnett, G. A. Bilingual semantic organization: A multidimensional analysis. *Journal of Cross-Cultural Psychology*, 1977, *8*, 315-330. (a)

Barnett, G. A. Linguistic relativity: The role of the bilingual. In B. Ruben (Ed.), *Communication Yearbook 1*. New Brunswick, NJ: Transaction, 1977. (b)

Barnett, G. A., & Woelfel, J. On the dimensionality of psychological processes. *Quality and Quantity*, 1979, *13*, 215-232.

Bell, W., & Robinson, R. V. Cognitive maps of class and racial inequalities in England and the United States. *American Journal of Sociology*, 1980, *86*, 320-349.

Berger, P., & Luckmann, T. *The social construction of reality*. Garden City, NY: Doubleday, 1967.

Berscheid, E. Opinion change and communicator-communicatee similarity and dissimilarity. *Journal of Personality and Social Psychology*, 1966, *4*, 670-680.

Bochner, S., & Insko, C. A. Communicator discrepancy, source credibility and opinion change. *Journal of Personality and Social Psychology*, 1966, *4*, 614-621.

Brewer, M. B., & Crano, W. D. Attitude change as a function of discrepancy and source of influence. *Journal of Social Psychology*, 1968, 76, 13-18.

Brock, T. C. Communicator-recipient similarity and decision change. *Journal of Personality and Social Psychology*, 1965, 1, 650-654.

Cacioppo, J. T., & Petty, R. E. Attitudes and cognitive responses: An electrophysiological approach. *Journal of Personality and Social Psychology*, 1979, 37, 2181-2199. (a)

Cacioppo, J. T., & Petty, R. E. The effects of message repetition and position on cognitive response, recall, and persuasion. *Journal of Personality and Social Psychology*, 1979, 37, 97-109.

Cliff, N. Adverbs as multipliers. *Psychological Review*, 1959, 66, 27-44.

Cook, T. D., & Flay, B. R. The persistence of experimentally induced attitude change. In L. Berkowitz (Ed.), *Advances in experimental social psychology* (Vol. 11). New York: Academic Press, 1978.

Craig, R. T. *Models of cognition, models of messages, and theories of communication effects: Spatial and network paradigms.* Paper presented to the International Communication Association, Chicago, April 1975.

Danes, J. E., Hunter, J. E., & Woelfel, J. Mass communication and belief change: A test of three mathematical models. *Human Communication Research*, 1978, 4, 243-252.

Ebbinghaus, H. E. *Memory: A contribution to experimental psychology.* New York: Dover, 1964. (Originally published, 1885).

Festinger, L. *A theory of cognitive dissonance.* Stanford, CA: Stanford University Press, 1957.

Fink, E. L. Kaplowitz, S. A., & Bauer, C. L. *Multiple discrepant messages and attitude change: Experimental tests of some mathematical models.* Paper presented at meetings of the American Sociological Association, New York, 1980.

Fishbein, J., & Ajzen, I. *Belief, attitude, intention, and behavior: An introduction to theory and research.* Reading, MA: Addison-Wesley, 1975.

Greenberg, D. F. *Mathematical criminology.* New Brunswick, NJ: Rutgers University Press, 1980.

Haberman, R. *Mathematical models: Mechanical vibrations, population dynamics and traffic flow.* Englewood Cliffs, NJ: Prentice-Hall, 1977.

Hamblin, R. L. Social attitudes: Magnitude estimation and theory. In H. M. Blalock, Jr. (Ed.), *Measurement in the social sciences.* Chicago: Aldine, 1974.

Hass, R. G. Effects of source characteristics on cognitive responses and persuasion. In R. E. Petty, T. M. Ostrom, & T. C. Brock (Eds.), *Cognitive responses in persuasion.* Hillsdale, NJ: Lawrence J. Erlbaum, 1981.

Heider, F. Attitudes and cognitive organization. *Journal of Psychology*, 1946, 21, 107-112.

Heider, F. *Psychology of interpersonal relations.* New York: John Wiley, 1958.

Heston, J. *Ideal source credibility: Re-examination of the semantic differential.* Paper presented at meetings of the International Communication Association, Montreal, Canada, April 1973.

Himmelfarb, S. "Resistance" to persuasion induced by information integration. In S. Himmelfarb & A. H. Eagly (Eds.), *Readings in attitude change.* New York: John Wiley, 1974.

Hunter, J. E., & Cohen, S. H. *Mathematical models of attitude change in the passive communication context.* Unpublished manuscript, Michigan State University, 1972.

Jones, L. E., & Young, F. W. Structure of a social environment: Longitudinal individual differences scaling of an intact group. *Journal of Personality and Social Psychology*, 1972, 24, 108-121.

Kac, M. Some mathematical models in science. *Science*, 1969, 166, 695-699.

Kaplowitz, S. A., & Fink, E. L. *A dynamic multidimensional theory of attitude and belief change.* Unpublished manuscript, Michigan State University, 1981.

Kaplowitz, S. A., Fink, E. L., & Bauer, C. L. *Cognitive dynamics I: A model of the effect of discrepant information on unidimensional attitude change.* Paper presented at meetings of the Society for Mathematical Psychology, Madison, Wisconsin, August 1980.

Kelman, H. Processes of opinion change. *Public Opinion Quarterly*, 1961, 25, 57-78.

Laroche, M. A model of attitude change in groups following a persuasive communication: An attempt at formalizing research findings. *Behavioral Science*, 1977, 22, 246-257.

Lave, C. A., & March, J. G. *An introduction to models in the social sciences.* New York: Harper & Row, 1975.
Leatherdale, W. H. *The role of analogy, model, and metaphor in science.* Amsterdam: North Holland, 1974.
Mandler, G., & Kessen, W. *The language of psychology.* New York: John Wiley, 1959.
McGuire, W. J. Cognitive consistency and attitude change. *Journal of Abnormal and Social Psychology,* 1960, *60,* 345-353.
McGuire, W. J. Inducing resistance to persuasion: Some contemporary approaches. In L. Berkowitz (Ed.), *Advances in experimental social psychology* (Vol. 1). New York: Academic Press, 1964.
McGuire, W. J. The nature of attitudes and attitude change. In G. Lindzey & E. Aronson (Eds.), *The handbook of social psychology* (Vol. 3). Reading, MA: Addison-Wesley, 1969.
McGuire, W. J. The probabilogical model of cognitive structure and attitude change. In R. E. Petty, T. M. Ostrom, & T. C. Brock (Eds.), *Cognitive responses in persuasion.* Hillsdale, NJ: Lawrence J. Erlbaum, 1981.
McPhee, R., & Poole, M. S. Mathematical modeling in communication research. In M. Burgoon (Ed.), *Communication Yearbook 5.* Rutgers, NJ: Transaction, 1981.
Miller, R. L. *The temporal persistence of psychological reactance: A double boomerang.* Paper presented at meetings of the American Sociological Association, New York, August 1980.
Mills, J., & Jellison, J. M. Effects on opinion change of similarity between the communicator and the audience he addresses. *Journal of Personality and Social Psychology,* 1968, *9,* 153-156.
Nemeth, C., & Markowski, J. Conformity and discrepancy of position. *Sociometry,* 1972, *35,* 562-575.
Osgood, C. E., Suci, G. J., & Tannenbaum, P. H. *The measurement of meaning.* Urbana: University of Illinois Press, 1957.
Osgood, C. E., & Tannenbaum, P. H. The principle of congruity in the prediction of attitude change. *Psychological Review,* 1955, *62,* 42-55.
Paulos, J. A. *Mathematics and humor.* Chicago: University of Chicago Press, 1980.
Petrovskii, I. G. Ordinary differential equations. In A. D. Aleksandrov, A. N. Kolmogorov, & M. A. Lavrent'ev (Eds.), *Mathematics, its content, methods, and meaning* (S. H. Gould & T. Bartha, trans.). Cambridge: MIT Press, 1969.
Petty, R. E. The role of cognitive responses in attitude change processes. In R. E. Petty, T. M. Ostrom, & T. C. Brock (Eds.), *Cognitive responses in persuasion.* Hillsdale, NJ: Lawrence J. Erlbaum, 1981.
Petty, R. E., & Cacioppo, J. T. Forewarning, cognitive responding and resistance to persuasion. *Journal of Personality and Social Psychology,* 1977, *35,* 645-655.
Petty, R. E., Wells, G. L., & Brock, T. C. Distraction can enhance or reduce yielding to propaganda: Thought disruption vs. effort justification. *Journal of Personality and Social Psychology,* 1976, *34,* 874-884.
Phillips, J. L., & Thompson, E. G. An analysis of the conceptual representation of relations: Components in a network model of cognitive organization. *Journal for the Theory of Social Behaviour,* 1977, *7,* 161-184.
Pierce, P. L., & Amato, P. R. A taxonomy of helping: A multi-dimensional scaling analysis. *Social Psychology Quarterly,* 1980, *43,* 363-371.
Poole, M. S., & Hunter, J. E. Change in hierarchical systems of attitudes. In D. Nimmo (Ed.), *Communication Yearbook 3.* New Brunswick, NJ: Transaction, 1979.
Poole, M. S., & Hunter, J. E. Behavior and hierarchies of attitudes: A deterministic model. In D. P. Cushman & R. D. McPhee (Eds.), *Message-attitude-behavior relationships: Theory, methodology and application.* New York: Academic Press, 1980.
Prigogine, O. Time, structure, and fluctuations. *Science,* 1978, *201,* 777-785.
Roedinger, H. L., III. Memory metaphors in cognitive psychology. *Memory and Cognition,* 1980, *8,* 231-246.
Rosenberg, S., Nelson, C., & Vivekananthan, P. S. A multi-dimensional approach to the structure of personality impressions. *Journal of Personality and Social Psychology,* 1968, *9,* 283-294.

Saltiel, J., & Woelfel, J. Inertia in cognitive processes: The role of accumulated information. *Human Communication Research*, 1975, *1*, 333-344.

Sawyer, A. Repetition, cognitive response, and persuasion. In R. E. Petty, T., M. Ostrom, & T. C. Brock (Eds.), *Cognitive responses in persuasion*. Hillsdale, NJ: Lawrence J. Erlbaum, 1981.

Serota, K. B., Cody, M. J., Barnett, G. A., & Taylor, J. A. Precise procedures for optimizing campaign communication. In B. Ruben (Ed.), *Communication Yearbook 1*. New Brunswick, NJ: Transaction, 1977.

Shepard, R. N. Multidimensional scaling, tree-fitting and clustering. *Science*, 1980, *210*, 390-398.

Sherif, C. W., Sherif, M., & Nebergall, R. E. *Attitude and attitude change: The social judgment-involvement approach*. Philadelphia: W. B. Saunders, 1965.

Tannenbaum, P. H. *Attitude toward source and concept as factors in attitude change through communication*. Unpublished doctoral dissertation, University of Illinois, 1953.

Taylor, M. Towards a mathematical theory of influence and attitude change. *Human Relations*, 1968, *21*, 121-137.

Tesser, A. Self-generated attitude change. In L. Berkowitz (Ed.), *Advances in experimental social psychology* (Vol. 11). New York: Academic Press, 1978.

Tesser, A., & Conlee, M. C. Some effects of time and thought on attitude polarization. *Journal of Personality and Social Psychology*, 1975, *31*, 262-270.

Thom, R. *Structural stability and morphogenesis: An outline of a general theory of models*. Reading, MA: Benjamin, 1975.

Walster, E. The temporal sequence of post-decision processes. In L. Festinger (Ed.), *Conflict, decision, and dissonance*. Stanford, CA: Stanford University Press, 1964.

Walster, E., Aronson, E., & Abrahams, D. On increasing the persuasiveness of a low prestige communicator. *Journal of Experimental Social Psychology*, 1966, *2*, 325-342.

Walster, E. L., Berscheid, E., & Barclay, A. M. A determinant of preferences among modes of dissonance reduction. *Journal of Personality and Social Psychology*, 1967, *7*, 211-216.

Whittaker, J. B. Attitude change and communication attitude discrepancy. *Journal of Social Psychology*, 1965, *65*, 141-147.

Wilson, W., & Miller, H. Repetition, order of presentation and timing of arguments as determinants of opinion change. *Journal of Personality and Social Psychology*, 1968, *9*, 184-188.

Wingfield, A., & Byrnes, D. L. *The psychology of human memory*. New York: Academic Press, 1981.

Wish, M. A model for the perception of Morse Code like signals. *Human Factors*, 1967, *9*, 529-539.

Wish, M. Individual differences in perceptions and preferences among nations. In C. W. King & D. Taggart (Eds.), *Attitude research reaches new heights*. Chicago: American Marketing Association, 1971.

Wish, M., Deutsch, M., & Biener, L. Differences in perceived similarity of nations. In A. K. Romney, R. N. Shepard, & S. Nerlove (Eds.), *Multidimensional scaling: Theory and applications in the behavioral sciences* (Vol. 2). New York: Seminar Press, 1972.

Woelfel, J., Cody, M. J., Gillham, J. R., & Holmes, R. Basic premises of multi-dimensional attitude change theory. *Human Communication Research*, 1980, *6*, 153-167.

Woelfel, J., & Fink, E. L. *The measurement of communication processes: Galileo theory and method*. New York: Academic Press, 1980

Woelfel, J., & Saltiel, J. Cognitive processes as motions in a multidimensional space. In F. Casmir (Ed.), *International and intercultural communication*. New York: University Press, 1978.

Worchel, S., & Brehm, J. W. Effects of threats to attitudinal freedom as a function of agreement with communicator. *Journal of Personality and Social Psychology*, 1970, *44*, 18-22.

Zimbardo, P. G. Involvement and communication discrepancy as determinants of opinion conformity. *Journal of Abnormal and Social Psychology*, 1960, *60*, 86-94.

INFORMATION SYSTEMS

13 • An Unequal Speaking Linear Discrepancy Model: Implications for Polarity Shift

FRANKLIN J. BOSTER • JAN E. FRYREAR • PAUL A. MONGEAU
Arizona State University

JOHN E. HUNTER
Michigan State University

SCORES of experiments have been performed pursuing a satisfactory explanation of the phenomenon known as the polarity, or choice, shift. The quantity of polarity shift experiments is all the more remarkable given the consistency of the research. Put simply, there is little debate concerning certain crucial empirical generalizations. Achieving an understanding of the present theoretical stasis requires understanding the method by which polarity shift data are generated.

The majority of polarity shift experiments examine decisions made on choice dilemma items (Kogan & Wallach, 1964).[1] Each item involves a hypothetical situation in which one (or another for whom one is an advisor) is faced with two, mutually exclusive courses of action. One alternative is so constructed that, if taken and successful, it leads to the most desirable outcome, but if taken and unsuccessful, it leads to a very undesirable outcome. The other alternative is so constructed that, if taken, it results in a moderately rewarding outcome. Subjects are asked to judge the lowest odds, or probability, of the former alternative succeeding they would require before pursuing, or recommending that another pursue, that course of action.[2] Some examples are presented in the Appendix.

The usual procedure in a polarity shift experiment is to present Ss with a pretest on which they are asked to make a number of choice dilemma judgments. Subsequently, groups of Ss are composed and are instructed to discuss one or a number of item(s) until they reach consensus. Finally, Ss are given a posttest on which they are asked to make individual judgments on each choice dilemma item for a second time. The polarity shift is

Correspondence and requests for reprints: Franklin J. Boster, Department of Communication, Michigan State University, East Lansing, MI 48824.

defined as the difference between the mean individual pretest judgment and the group consensus, although occasionally the difference between the individual pretest judgment and the individual posttest judgment is used to define the polarity shift.

The results of polarity shift experiments are remarkably uniform. Following is a review of empirical generalizations drawn from this literature. This review is very selective; only generalizations pertinent to subsequent arguments developed in this chapter are considered.

First, choice dilemma items, and other dilemma experiments, consistently produce polarity shifts (for comprehensive reviews see Dion, Baron, & Miller, 1970; Myers & Lamm, 1976).[3] Some choice dilemma items consistently yield a risky shift. Other choice dilemma items consistently yield a cautious shift. Nevertheless, the shifts move toward one of the two poles: extreme risk or extreme caution.[4]

Moreover, the more extreme the mean pretest score, the larger the polarity shift. Thus, when discussing a choice dilemma item which consistently yields a risky shift, the more risky the mean pretest score, the larger the risky shift (Teger & Pruitt, 1967; Stoner, 1968). Similarly, when discussing a choice dilemma item which consistently yields a cautious shift, the more cautious the mean pretest score, the larger the cautious shift (Fraser, Gouge, & Billig, 1971).

Given the definition of the polarity shift, the group decision must be more polar than the mean individual pretest judgment in order to obtain a polar shift. Moreover, for a shift to be polar the mean individual pretest judgment must be on the same end of the continuum as the group decision, although obviously not as extreme. Since experiments consistently find polarity shifts, it follows that the group decisions must also be quite polar. In other words, these decisions must be either very risky or very cautious. Thus since risky items consistently produce risky shifts, and since cautious items consistently produce cautious shifts, risky items must produce risky decisions and cautious items must produce cautious decisions.

Explanations of these results have varied widely. Recent evidence supports the persuasive arguments theory (Burnstein & Vinokur, 1973, 1975; Burnstein, Vinokur, & Trope, 1973; Ebbeson & Bowers, 1974; Knowles, 1976; Vinokur & Burnstein, 1974; 1978). Proponents of this perspective argue that in a given culture, for any choice dilemma item there exists a pool of persuasive arguments in support of each alternative course of action. When the majority of arguments in this pool favor a particular direction, pretest judgments are skewed in the opposite direction. Thus, when the pool of arguments contains more risky than cautious arguments, the distribution of pretest scores is skewed in a cautious direction (positively). When the pool of arguments contains more cautious than risky arguments, the distribution of pretest scores is skewed in a risky direction (negative). The mean pretest judgment, in turn, reflects this tendency. Depending on the distribution of arguments among group members, the pool of arguments should affect the direction of the arguments that arise in group discussion; thus a predominantly risky pool produces more risky arguments in the discussion and a predominately cautious pool produces more cautious arguments in the discussion. If group decisions are affected by persuasive argumentation, then group decisions are expected to be more extreme than the mean pretest judgment. Therefore a polarity shift results.

Consistent with this explanation, Vinokur and Burnstein (1974) found that when choice dilemma items which commonly produce a risky shift are discussed, more risky arguments arise in the group discussion; and when choice dilemma items which commonly produce a cautious shift are discussed, more cautious arguments arise in the group discussion. The results of this experiment also revealed that for items which commonly produced a risky shift, risky arguments were perceived as more persuasive; and for items which commonly produced a cautious shift, cautious arguments were perceived as more persuasive. Furthermore, the results of several experiments show that risky shifts occur in groups in which the preponderance of arguments are risky (Ebbeson & Bowers, 1974; Silverthorne, 1971), and that cautious shifts occur in groups in which the preponderance of arguments are cautious (Ebbeson & Bowers, 1974; Silverthorne, 1971).

The results of these experiments indicate that it is fruitful to view the polarity shift phenomenon as a persuasion process. Although persuasive arguments theorists have not articulated this process precisely, Boster, Mayer, Hunter, and Hale (1980) have recently developed a model of the process by which groups reach a decision in polarity shift experiments. While the model is more precise than the persuasive arguments explanation in articulating the type of persuasion process that produces the polarity shift, it incorporates the central features of the persuasive arguments explanation. Following is a sketch of this model.

A LINEAR DISCREPANCY MODEL OF THE POLARITY SHIFT

Messages may be characterized as advocating some opinion. If opinions are arrayed on a continuum ranging from risky to cautious, then a message may be viewed as advocating some degree of risk or caution. Thus, messages and opinions may be scaled on the same continuum.

Since messages and opinions may be so scaled, it is meaningful to speak of persons comparing the messages they hear with their opinions.

The theory of communication discrepancy (French, 1956) asserts that this comparison process is central to group opinion change and hence to group decision making. Three postulates form the core of this theory. First, when persons speak in a group discussion, they advocate their opinion at that point in the discussion. Second, all group members listen to each message and change their opinion in the direction of the opinion advocated by the speaker's message. Third, the greater the discrepancy between the opinion advocated and the opinion held by the listener(s), the greater the listeners' opinion change.

More formally, if the opinion of group member i is denoted x_i, and if some other group member, j, is speaking, then the opinion change induced by j's message is

$$\Delta x_i = \alpha (m_j - x_i) \quad [1]$$

where m is the value of the message on the risky-cautious continuum. From the first postulate it follows that

$$m_j = x_j \quad [2]$$

Substituting 2 into 1 results in

$$\Delta x_i = \alpha (x_j - x_i) \quad [3]$$

Following, this model is generalized to a group discussion context. The model is generalized in two ways. First, it is assumed that all group members speak equally often. Second, this assumption is relaxed, and an unequal speaking model is developed.

Equal Speaking

If every group member speaks equally often, then the total impact of an average round of discussion is the sum of the change induced by each speaker. Thus,

$$\Delta x_i = \sum_{j=1}^{N} \alpha (x_j - x_i) \quad [4]$$

If the average opinion in the group is denoted $\bar{X}$,

$$\bar{X} = 1/N \sum_{i=1}^{N} x_i \quad [5]$$

By the linearity of the change operator it follows that

$$\Delta \bar{X} = 1/N \sum_{i=1}^{N} \Delta x_i \quad [6]$$

Boster et al. (1980, p. 167) show that from 6 it follows that

$$\Delta \bar{X} = 0 \quad [7]$$

Hence, if each group member speaks equally often, then the linear discrepancy model predicts that there will be no change in the mean group opinion.

Suppose that each person's opinion is compared to the group mean. Define a variable which is the discrepancy between a person's opinion and the group mean. Denote this discrepancy by D_i. Then,

$$D_i = x_i - \bar{X} \quad [8]$$

By linearity of the change operator, the change in D_i is given by

$$\Delta D_i = \Delta (x_i - \bar{X}) \quad [9]$$

$$= -N\alpha D_i \quad [10]$$

Therefore, D_i satisfies the following exponential decay equation,

$$D_{i,n} = (1 - N\alpha)^n D_{i,0} \quad [11]$$

Obviously, equation 10 converges to zero exponentially.

Therefore, if each group member speaks equally, then the linear discrepancy model predicts that (1) each group member's opinion converges to the group mean, and (2) the group mean does not change. That is, the linear discrepancy model predicts that the mean pretest opinion will be the group decision when group members all speak equally often. This model predicts that no polarity shift will occur, since the polarity shift is defined as $\bar{X} - G^*$, where G^* is the group decision, and the equal speaking model predicts that $G^* = \bar{X}$. Since experiments consistently demonstrate a polarity shift, this model must be false.

Unequal Speaking

Rarely do group members speak equally. Thus, in this section the assumption of equal speaking is relaxed. Suppose that a constant, f_i, is assigned to each person i, which measures the number of messages that i offers to the group in the average period of time required for everyone to have a chance to speak. Then, if j is speaking,

$$\Delta x_i = f_j \alpha (x_j - x_i) \quad [12]$$

In the course of a round of discussion the change in each member is the sum of each speaker's impact. Thus,

$$\Delta x_i = \sum_{j=1}^{N} f_j \alpha (x_j - x_i) \quad [13]$$

The mean of the messages heard in the group discussion is no longer the mean prediscussion opinion. Rather, it is a weighted mean; group members' prediscussion opinions being weighted by f_i. That is,

$$\bar{X}_f = \sum_{i=1}^{N} x_i f_i \qquad [14]$$

Boster et al. (1980) show that if group members emit a differential number of messages during a group discussion, the linear discrepancy model predicts that there will be no change in $\bar{X}_f$. Furthermore, Boster et al. (1980) show that each group member's opinion coverges to $\bar{X}_f$ according to the unequal speaking version of the linear discrepancy model. Thus, the unequal speaking model predicts that the weighted (by speaking frequency) pretest mean will be the group decision. This model predicts a polar shift when group members holding polar pretest opinions emit more messages in the group discussion than do those group members holding less extreme opinions. For example, consider a three-person group in which $x_1 = 1$, $x_2 = 2$, $x_3 = 6$, $f_1 = .50$, $f_2 = .25$, and $f_3 = .25$. In this case $\bar{X} = 3$ and $G^* = 2.55$. Thus, $\bar{X} - G^* = .75$. Scoring the response so that the lowest number indicates the most risky opinion, the model predicts a risky shift. Note, however, that if f_1 and f_3 are reversed, a shift toward caution is obtained, since the less polar group member spoke with greater frequency than the most polar group member.

A Prediction Concerning Variances

Both the equal speaking and the unequal speaking versions of the linear discrepancy model predict that variances decrease over time. Thus, in the typical polarity shift design the pretest variance for any given group is expected to be larger than the posttest variance for that group. Moreover, the extent to which the variances decrease may be derived from the linear discrepancy model. Boster et al. (1980) show that from equation 13 it follows that[5]

$$\sigma_n^2 = \beta^2 \sigma_0^2 \qquad [15]$$

where σ_n^2 is the posttest variance, σ_0^2 is the pretest variance, and $\beta = (1 - N\alpha)$. N is the number of persons per group.[6] The parameter, α, may be estimated using the ordinary least squares criterion by regressing posttest score onto pretest score and $\bar{X}_d$, where, $X_d = N\bar{X} - x_i/N - 1$. In this context, $\bar{X}$ is the mean of the pretest scores for a given group. Thus,

$\bar{X}_d$ is a score computed for each person i, which is the group mean of the remaining group members' pretest scores.

Speaking Time

Boster et al. (1980) developed a model of speaking frequency, f_i. They argue that each group member has some tendency to speak, and they denote this tendency T_i for group member i. They assert that this tendency is inversely proportional to the discrepancy between pretest opinion and the group mean. Formally,

$$T_i = K - |x_i - \bar{X}| \qquad [16]$$

where K is a constant chosen to make T_i positive.

The frequency with which i speaks is a function not only of i's tendency to speak but also of the tendencies of all group members to speak. Thus, Boster et al. postulate that

$$f_i = T_i / \sum_{j=1}^{N} T_j \qquad [17]$$

where the denominator is the sum of each group member's tendency to talk. Boster et al. did not measure actual speaking frequency and thus provide no test of this model. They do argue that the excellent fit of the unequal speaking model with their data, $r_{GG^*} = .83$, suggests that the speaking time model must have closely approximated actual speaking time.

The persuasive arguments theory advances a somewhat different model of speaking frequency: When discussing a risky item, persons with risky pretest opinions will speak more than persons with cautious pretest opinions. Thus, the persuasive arguments theory predicts an item X pretest opinion interaction.

Social comparison theory advances yet another model of speaking frequency. Reingen (1977) argues that social comparison theory implies that normative factors influence speaking frequency. Thus, the nature of group composition is expected to affect speaking frequency. If the majority of group members have risky pretest opinions, then these persons are expected to speak more than either persons with neutral pretest opinions or persons with cautious pretest opinions. If the majority of group members have cautious pretest opinions, then these persons are expected to speak more than either persons with neutral pretest opinions or persons with risky pretest opinions. In a group in which there is no majority, equal speaking would be expected.

The normative model suggests that groups will come to very different decisions, and hence shifts, compared to those implied by the persuasive arguments model. If the linear discrepancy model describes accurately the process by which groups make decisions, then the persuasive arguments theory implies that risky shifts, and risky group decisions, will arise whenever groups discuss risky items. Cautious shifts, and hence cautious decisions, arise whenever groups discuss cautious items. On the other hand, if the linear discrepancy model describes accurately the process by which groups make decisions, then the normative model suggests that risky shifts, and hence risky decisions arise whenever there is a risky group majority. Cautious shifts, and hence cautious decisions, arise whenever there is a cautious majority. These two views are clearly in conflict when either a risky majority discusses a cautious item or a cautious majority discusses a risky item.

Some data pertinent to this question exist. Vinokur (1969) analyzed data in which groups of subjects discussed either risky items or cautious items and were composed of either a risky majority, a cautious majority, or no majority (symmetric condition). He found that regardless of group composition, risky shifts were obtained on risky items and cautious shifts were obtained on cautious items, with the curious exception that groups composed of a cautious majority produced a risky shift when discussing cautious items.

Reingen (1977) had subjects discuss risky items in groups which were composed of either a strong risky majority, a slight risky majority, no majority, or a strong cautious majority. He found risky shifts in the former two conditions, no shift in the no majority condition, and a statistically nonsignificant cautious shift in the cautious majority condition.

These experiments produced somewhat different results in the risky item, cautious majority condition. Moreover, neither experiment addresses the informational influence (persuasive arguments theory) versus normative influence (social comparison theory) controversy at the level at which these theories make predictions. The theories are actually predictions concerning speaking frequency. The Vinokur and the Reingen experiments examine only mean shifts.

Thus, an experiment was designed to examine several issues. First, it was designed to be a more difficult test for the Boster et al. (1980) model. As those authors note, group composition was not controlled in their experiment. Only risky majorities discussed risky items, and only cautious majorities discussed cautious items. Whether the model is as successful predicting the results of discussions in which a risky (cautious) majority discusses a cautious (risky) item is not known. Moreover, an adequate test of the normative influence versus informational influence explanations requires that speaking frequency be measured and correlated with each type of influence. This experiment addresses both issues.

METHOD

Subjects

Experimental Ss were 108 students drawn from introductory communication courses at a large Southwestern university. An additional 143 Ss provided test-retest reliability data for choice dilemma items. Subjects participated in order to fulfill a course research participation requirement.

Design

The design of this experiment was a 2 × 3 independent groups design. A risky majority, a cautious majority, or a symmetrical group discussed an item which has been shown to yield either a consistent risky shift or a consistent cautious shift. Ss were nested within treatments.

Risky majorities were composed of two Ss who initially responded to the pertinent choice dilemma item in a risky manner and one S who responded in either a cautious or a neutral manner. A cautious majority was composed of two Ss who initially responded to the pertinent choice dilemma item in a cautious manner and one S who responded in either a risky or a neutral manner. Symmetrical groups were composed of one subject who initially responded to the pertinent choice dilemma item in a risky manner, one who initially responded in a cautious manner, and one who initially responded in a neutral manner.

The response scale for the choice dilemma items ranged from 1 to 10, with 1 being the most risky alternative and 10 being the most cautious alternative. A response of 1-4 was considered a risky response for the purpose of assigning Ss to treatments. Similarly, a response of 5-6 was considered a neutral response, and a response of 7-10 was considered a cautious response. The choice dilemma items were taken from Stoner (1968). Two of these items have consistently been shown to produce a risky shift (the latter two items in the Appendix), and two of these items have consistently been shown to produce a cautious shift (the former two items in the Appendix).

Procedure

Initially, subjects completed the choice dilemma questionnaire in class. Based on these pretest responses, they were solicited by telephone to participate in the experiment and were assigned to treatments by virtue of their availability and their pretest opinions.

Solicited subjects were instructed to report to a 15' x 18' soundproof laboratory room containing four one-way mirrors. Ss sat on chairs around a round table to which a microphone had been taped. A camera, videotape recorder, and monitor were in a room behind the one-way mirrors.

When all Ss in a given group had assembled in the laboratory, a second pretest was administered. This pretest was the same questionnaire completed by the Ss in class and served to ensure that Ss had understood the first pretest questionnaire. As several persons have noted, the choice dilemma items are often misunderstood (see Fraser et al., 1971, for a creative alternative to the normal choice dilemma format).

Following completion of this choice dilemma questionnaire, the experimenter distributed a second questionnaire, which contained demographic measures and measures of individual difference variables. Upon completion of this questionnaire, the experimenter read the following insructions to the group:

> The task that we have for you today is to engage in a discussion of an issue. The issue we want you to discuss is _____ (Ss were given a copy of the topic to keep during the discussion). You are to discuss the item and decide, as a group, what opinion is the best one. You must continue to discuss the issue until everyone has come to agreement. When you come to agreement, that is, where everyone in the group agrees as to the proper course of action, then knock on the window. I will then come in and give you another short task.
>
> We are going to videotape this discussion for our records. The camera is behind one of these mirrors; they are one-way mirrors. Please don't let that bother you. We are the only people who will see the tapes, so there is no need to be nervous.
>
> Are there any questions before we begin? If there are no more questions, then give me about a minute to turn on the recording equipment. I will knock on the window, and that will be your cue to begin discussing the issue.

Groups actually discussed two issues; one to warm up, followed by that referred to in the directions. Only the second discussion was videotaped.

Subjects discussed the second item to consensus, or until the end of a fifteen-minute period. If they did not reach consensus in fifteen minutes, the data were not considered. Following the discussions, Ss again filled out the choice dilemma items, thus providing individual posttest data.

Instrumentation

In addition to Stoner's (1968) choice dilemma items, measures of demographic characteristics, individual differences, and speaking time were obtained. Demographic measures included age, sex, grade point average, and so on. Individual difference measures included measures of self-esteem, Machiavellianism, dogmatism, communication apprehension, need for affiliation, and extroversion.[7] Several speaking frequency measures were taken. Two raters judged the videotaped discussions for individual speaking time, number of speaking turns, and number of arguments.

RESULTS

Fit of the Linear Discrepancy Model

For the equal speaking model the correlation between predicted and obtained group decision (and hence, shift), r_{GG*}, was found to be .73. For the unequal speaking model r_{GG*} = .84. The difference between these nonindependent correlations was statistically significant ($t = 2.62$; df = 33; $p < .05$). Therefore, the unequal speaking model provided a substantially better fit with the data. While the reliability of G* was not estimated, the reliability of G was found to be .90. Thus, correcting r_{GG*} for attenuation due to measurement error in G yielded a corrected correlation of .89. If $r_{GG} = r_{G*G*}$, then correcting for error of measurement in both G and G* yields a corrected correlation of .93.

A scatterplot of the relationship between G and G* for the unequal speaking model is presented in Figure 13.1. The regression of G onto G* appears to be linear from this graph. Estimating the regression coefficients by the method of ordinary least squares produces the following equation:

$$\hat{G} = 1.54G^* - 3.50$$

The intercept was found to be significantly smaller than zero ($t = -3.54$; df = 34; $p < .05$), and the slope was found to be significantly larger than one ($t = 3.19$; df = 34; $p < .05$). From Figure 13.1 it may be observed that the negative intercept and the steep slope are attributable to the presence of a small number of outliers. The average absolute value error in prediction was $|\bar{e}| = 1.51$ on a ten-point scale.

The decisions predicted by the unequal speaking model may be broken down by experimental treatments. The mean treatment scores predicted by the unequal speaking version of the linear discrepancy model are produced in Table 13.1. They may be compared with the obtained treatment means presented in Table 13.2. To facilitate comparison analyses of variance were performed on both predicted and obtained scores. These analyses are presented in Tables 13.3 and 13.4, respectively.

A comparison of Tables 13.1 and 13.2 illustrates the close fit of the model to the data. The correlation between the predicted means and the obtained means is .94. The absolute value of error in mean prediction is $|\bar{e}| = 1.08$. A comparison of Tables 13.3 and 13.4 shows that the model correctly predicts all statistical inferences. The size of the item effect is

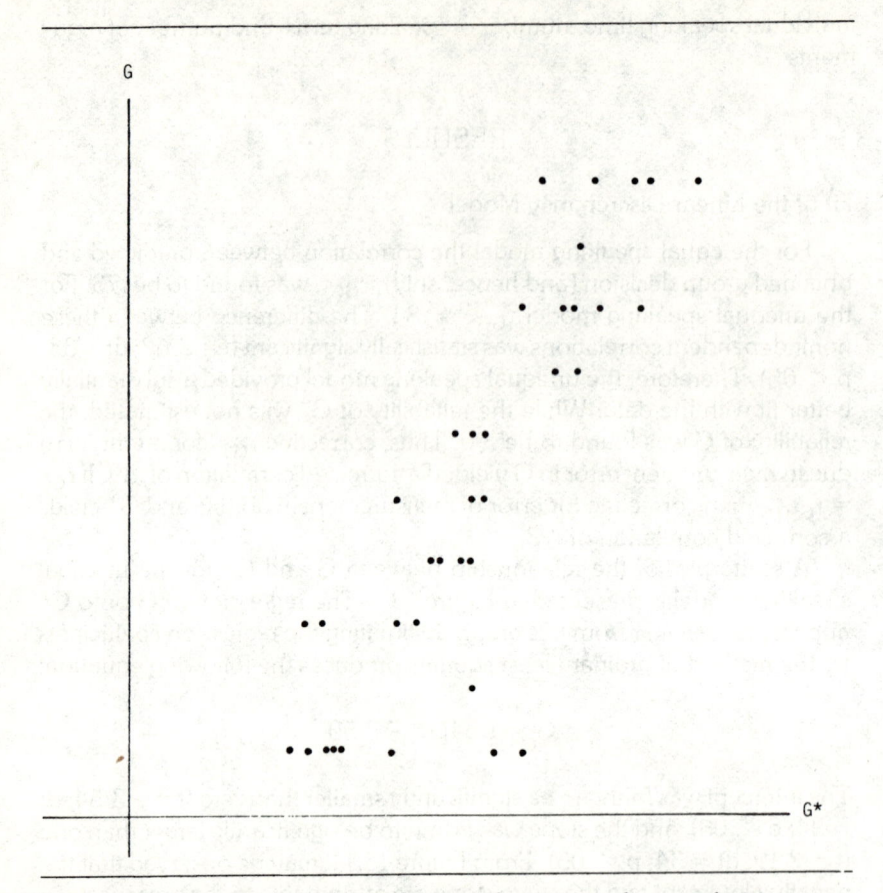

Figure 13.1. Scatterplot of obtained group decisions and group decisions predicted by the unequal speaking version of the linear discrepancy model.

slightly underestimated. The size of the majority effect is somewhat overestimated.

Predicted shifts are broken down by treatments and presented in Table 13.5. Obtained shifts are broken down by treatments and presented in Table 13.6. The analyses of variance performed on these data are presented in Tables 13.7 and 13.8, respectively.

The correlation between predicted shifts and obtained mean shifts is smaller than the correlation between predicted mean decisions and obtained mean decisions, $r = .74$. This result is attributable to the lower reliability of difference scores (shifts). Again, the predicted analysis of

Table 13.1
Group Decisions Predicted by the Unequal Speaking Version of the Linear Discrepancy Model, Broken Down by Item and Majority

	ITEM Risky	ITEM Cautious	
Risky	X = 3.30 S_x^2 = 0.40 S_x = 0.63 N = 7	X = 5.80 S_x^2 = 0.17 S_x = 0.41 N = 5	4.55
Symmetrical	X = 4.39 S_x^2 = 0.65 S_x = 0.81 N = 6	X = 5.97 S_x^2 = 1.58 S_x = 1.26 N = 4	5.18
Cautious	X = 6.06 S_x^2 = 0.37 S_x = 0.81 N = 6	X = 7.76 S_x^2 = 0.53 S_x = 0.72 N = 8	6.91
	4.58	6.51	5.55

(Rows labeled under MAJORITY)

Table 13.2
Obtained Group Decisions, Broken Down by Item and Majority

	ITEM Risky	ITEM Cautious	
Risky	X = 1.86 S_x^2 = .98 S_x = .99 N = 7	X = 5.60 S_x^2 = 6.64 S_x = 2.58 N = 5	3.42
Symmetrical	X = 2.83 S_x^2 = 1.81 S_x = 1.34 N = 6	X = 7.25 S_x^2 = 3.69 S_x = 1.92 N = 4	4.60
Cautious	X = 4.83 S_x^2 = 9.81 S_x = 3.13 N = 6	X = 8.50 S_x^2 = 1.50 S_x = 1.22 N = 8	6.93
	3.11	7.35	5.11

(Rows labeled under MAJORITY)

Table 13.3
Unweighted Means Analysis of Variance of the Effect of Item and Majority on Predicted Group Decision

Source	SS	df	MS	F	P	N^2	N
Item	3.46	1	3.46	7.36	<.05	.17	.41
Symmetry	2.42	2	1.21	2.57	>.05	.12	.35
Linear	.22	1	.22	<1.00	>.05	.01	.10
Quadratic	2.20	1	2.20	4.68	<.05	.11	.33
Item x Symmetry	.20	2	.10	<1.00	>.05	.01	.10
L x L	.00	1	.00	<1.00	>.05	.00	.00
L x Q	.20	1	.20	<1.00	>.05	.01	.10
Within	14.16	30	.47	—	—	.70	.84
Total	20.24	35	.58	—	—	1.00	—

Fmax = 4.00; df = 6.5; p < .05

Table 13.4
Unweighted Means Analysis of Variance of the Effect of Item and Majority on Obtained Group Decision

Source	SS	df	MS	F	P	N^2	N
Item	140.42	1	140.42	28.72	<.01	.41	.64
Symmetry	52.07	2	26.04	5.33	<.05	.15	.39
Linear	51.86	1	51.86	10.61	<.01	.15	.39
Quadratic	.21	1	.21	<1.00	>.05	.00	.03
Item x Symmetry	.26	2	.13	<1.00	>.05	.00	.03
L x L	.01	1	.01	<1.00	>.05	.00	.01
L x Q	.25	1	.25	<1.00	>.05	.00	.03
Within	146.58	30	4.89	—	—	.43	.66
Total	339.33	35	9.70	—	—	0.99	—

Fmax = 10.01; df = 6.5; p < .05

variance underestimates the item effect and overestimates the majority effect. These errors are somewhat larger for the shifts than for the group decisions.

The direction of both the group decisions and the group shifts are consistent with past research. Risky items yield both risky group decisions and risky shifts. Cautious items yield both cautious group decisions and cautious shifts. One feature of these data may be misleading. Past research shows that the magnitude of the polarity shift is a function of initial mean.

Table 13.5
Polarity Shifts Predicted by the Unequal Speaking Version of the Linear Discrepancy Model, Broken Down by Item and Majority

		ITEM		
		Risky	Cautious	
M A J O R I T Y	Risky	$X = 0.03$ $S_x^2 = 0.16$ $S_x = 0.40$ $N = 7$	$X = -0.73$ $S_x^2 = 0.21$ $S_x = 0.46$ $N = 5$	−0.35
	Symmetrical	$X = 0.67$ $S_x^2 = 0.59$ $S_x = 0.77$ $N = 6$	$X = -0.13$ $S_x^2 = 0.46$ $S_x = 0.68$ $N = 4$	0.27
	Cautious	$X = -0.01$ $S_x^2 = 0.64$ $S_x = 0.80$ $N = 6$	$X = -0.30$ $S_x^2 = 0.46$ $S_x = 0.54$ $N = 8$	−0.16
		0.23	−0.39	−0.08

Table 13.6
Polarity Shifts Obtained by the Unequal Speaking Version of the Linear Discrepancy Model, Broken Down by Item and Majority

		ITEM		
		Risky	Cautious	
M A J O R I T Y	Risky	$X = 1.47$ $S_x^2 = 1.08$ $S_x = 1.04$ $N = 7$	$X = -0.53$ $S_x^2 = 6.25$ $S_x = 2.50$ $N = 5$	0.47
	Symmetrical	$X = 2.22$ $S_x^2 = 1.50$ $S_x = 1.22$ $N = 6$	$X = -1.42$ $S_x^2 = 1.68$ $S_x = 1.30$ $N = 4$	0.40
	Cautious	$X = 1.22$ $S_x^2 = 9.70$ $S_x = 3.11$ $N = 6$	$X = -1.04$ $S_x^2 = 0.79$ $S_x = 0.89$ $N = 8$	0.09
		1.64	−1.00	0.32

Table 13.7
Unweighted Means Analysis of Variance of the Effect of Item and Majority on Predicted Polarity Shift

Source	SS	df	MS	F	P	N^2	N
Item	33.52	1	33.52	43.52	<.01	.36	.60
Symmetry	35.84	2	17.92	24.22	<.01	.39	.62
Linear	33.42	1	33.42	45.16	<.01	.36	.60
Quadratic	2.42	1	2.42	3.27	>.05	.03	.16
Item x Symmetry	1.27	2	.64	<1.00	>.05	.01	.12
L x L	.96	1	.96	1.30	>.05	.01	.10
L x Q	.31	1	.31	<1.00	>.05	.00	.06
Within	22.20	30	.74	–	–	.24	.49
Total	92.83	35	2.65	–	–	1.00	–

$F_{max} = 9.29$; df = 6.5; $p < .05$

Table 13.8
Unweighted Means Analysis of Variance of the Effect of Item and Majority on Obtained Polarity Shift

Source	SS	df	MS	F	P	N^2	N
Item	63.73	1	63.73	15.17	<.01	.33	.57
Symmetry	.98	2	.49	<1.00	>.05	.01	.07
Linear	.87	1	.87	<1.00	>.05	.00	.07
Quadratic	.11	1	.11	<1.00	>.05	.00	..02
Item x Symmetry	4.33	2	2.17	<1.00	>.05	.02	.15
L x L	.10	1	.10	<1.00	>.05	.00	.02
L x Q	4.23	1	4.23	1.01	>.05	.02	.15
Within	126.00	30	4.20	–	–	.65	.80
Total	195.04	35	5.57	–	–	1.01	–

$F_{max} = 12.26$; df = 6.5; $p < .05$

Thus it would be expected that a risky majority discussing a risky item would produce a larger risky shift than a symmetrical group discussing a risky item, which would produce a larger risky shift than a cautious majority discussing a risky item. Similarly, a cautious majority discussing a cautious item is expected to produce a larger cautious shift than a symmetrical group, which would produce a larger cautious shift than a risky majority. While the shifts reported in Table 13.6 appear to be inconsistent with such a prediction, these shifts are affected by the amount of possible shift. For example, a risky majority discussing a risky item is limited by the response

Unequal Speaking Linear Discrepancy Model

Table 13.9
Corrected Shifts as a Function of Item and Majority

		ITEM	
		Risky	Cautious
M A J O R I T Y	Risky	.63	−.11
	Symmetrical	.55	−.34
	Cautious	.24	−.41

scale. If the pretest opinion distribution is $x_1 = 1$, $x_2 = 2$, $x_3 = 5$, then the size of the risky shift can be no larger than 1.67. On the other hand, if the pretest opinion distribution is $x_1 = 3$, $x_2 = 5$, $x_3 = 7$, then the size of the risky shift can be as large as 4. Thus, the obtained shifts are divided by the potential amount of shift, and these results are presented in Table 13.9. From that table it may be observed that the order of the mean shifts is as predicted.

Equation 15 provides a prediction of the extent to which variances are expected to change from the pretest to the posttest. The estimate of β was found to equal .66. Thus, the unequal speaking model predicts that the posttest variance should be less than the pretest variance by a factor of .44. The data show that for each of the thirty-six groups formed in this study, the posttest variance was less than the pretest variance. The average decrease was by a factor of .22. Thus the model closely approximates the decreases in variance.

In these data the polarization phenomenon may be observed most clearly if the pretest means are compared with the group decisions, which in turn are compared with the posttest means. Thus, the pretest means are presented in Table 13.10 and the posttest means are presented in Table 13.11. From a comparison of these tables it may be observed that the group decisions are more polar than either the pretest or the posttest opinions. Moreover, the posttest opinions are more polar than the pretest opinions. The correlation between the pretest and posttest scores is .55, and when it is corrected for attentuation due to error of measurement, $r = .71$. Thus the polarization is fairly uniform.

The extent to which consensus, as opposed to compromise, was reached may be assessed by correlating posttest scores with predicted posttest scores. The predicted posttest score is the group decision. That is, if there were perfect consensus, then a subject's posttest score would equal the group decision. The correlation between the obtained posttest score and the predicted posttest score was .81. Since 51 percent of the subjects'

Table 13.10
Pretest Means Broken Down by Item and Majority

		ITEM		
		Risky	Cautious	
MAJORITY	Risky	$X = 3.33$ $Sx^2 = 0.48$ $Sx = 0.69$ $N = 7$	$X = 5.07$ $Sx^2 = 0.06$ $Sx = 0.25$ $N = 5$	4.20
	Symmetrical	$X = 5.06$ $Sx^2 = 0.28$ $Sx = 0.53$ $N = 6$	$X = 5.84$ $Sx^2 = 0.75$ $Sx = 0.87$ $N = 4$	5.45
	Cautious	$X = 6.06$ $Sx^2 = 0.35$ $Sx = 0.59$ $N = 6$	$X = 6.46$ $Sx^2 = 0.75$ $Sx = 0.86$ $N = 8$	6.76
		4.82	6.12	5.47

Table 13.11
Posttest Means Broken Down by Item and Majority

		ITEM		
		Risky	Cautious	
MAJORITY	Risky	$X = 2.33$ $Sx^2 = 0.79$ $Sx = 0.89$ $N = 7$	$X = 6.20$ $Sx^2 = 6.56$ $Sx = 2.56$ $N = 5$	4.27
	Symmetrical	$X = 3.33$ $Sx^2 = 2.15$ $Sx = 1.47$ $N = 6$	$X = 6.67$ $Sx^2 = 4.71$ $Sx = 2.17$ $N = 4$	5.00
	Cautious	$X = 4.95$ $Sx^2 = 4.95$ $Sx = 2.32$ $N = 6$	$X = 8.71$ $Sx^2 = 1.12$ $Sx = 1.06$ $N = 8$	6.83
		3.54	7.19	5.37

Unequal Speaking Linear Discrepancy Model

posttest scores equaled their predicted posttest scores, the regression of posttest opinion onto predicted posttest opinion yielded an intercept near zero (a = .90) and a slope near one (b = .80). Thus while some compromise existed, considerable amounts of persuasion undoubtedly occurred in these group discussions.

Speaking Frequency

Raters' judgments of each of the three speaking frequency measures — speaking time, turns, and arguments — were very reliable. The interrater correlations were .997, .97, and .93 for speaking time, turns, and arguments, respectively.

The three measures of speaking frequency are highly intercorrelated. The correlation between speaking time and turns was .67; between speaking time and arguments, .66; and between turns and arguments, .44. While the hypothesis of unidimensionality cannot be tested with only three measures, the reliability of this three item scale is $\alpha = .86$. Such a high coefficient α with so few items strongly suggests unidimensionality. Thus, these measures are treated as measures of an underlying construct, speaking frequency. It is the mean of these three measures that was used to estimate f_i for the unequal speaking model.

In order to assess the effect of normative influence and informational influence on speaking frequency, the majority × pretest opinion interaction and the item × pretest opinion interaction were formed. For the normative influence effect a new variable was constructed. If the majority was risky, then pretest opinions that were most risky were scored 10, and pretest opinions that were most cautious were scored 1. For a cautious majority the scoring was reversed. For a symmetrical group equal speaking was assumed. These scores were then converted into percentages for each group, so as to match the metric of speaking frequency. In order to assess the effect of informational influence, if the item being discussed was risky, then those persons with the most risky pretest opinions were given a score of 10, and those persons with the most cautious pretest opinions were given a score of 1. For a cautious item this scoring was reversed. Again the scores were converted into percentages for each group.

Both of these variables were correlated with speaking frequency. The correlation for normative influence was .00. The correlation for informational influence was .40. Thus regardless of majority, persons spoke with greater frequency if their pretest opinion matched the type of item being discussed. That is, persons with risky pretest opinions spoke with greater frequency than persons with cautious pretest opinions when discussing a risky item but less than persons with cautious pretest opinions when discussing a cautious item.

Moreover, individual difference variables and demographic characteristics were correlated with speaking frequency. Of these variables only communication apprehension correlated substantially with speaking frequency ($r = -.19$). Thus not surprisingly, high communication apprehensives tended to speak less frequently than low communication apprehensives.

If the effect of both informational influence and communication apprehension on speaking frequency is assessed, a multiple correlation, $R = .43$, is obtained. The standardized regression coefficients are .39 and .16 for information influence and communication apprehension, respectively. Correcting the correlation matrix among these variables for measurement error in communication apprehension and speaking frequency, a multiple correlation of $R = .47$ is obtained. The standardized regression coefficients are .42 and .18 for informational influence and communication apprehension, respectively. Thus these two predictors provide relatively accurate prediction of speaking frequency. Nevertheless, sufficient error of prediction exists to suggest that there are other important predictors of speaking frequency.

Reliability of the Choice Dilemma Items

An additional 143 subjects were administered pretest choice dilemma questionnaires and posttest choice dilemma questionnaires without the intervention of a group discussion. Both pretest and posttet item responses were radically skewed. That is, the risky items had a distribution of responses skewed in a cautious direction (the vast majority of responses being risky), and the cautious items had a distribution of responses skewed in a risky direction (the vast majority of responses being cautious). There were no mean differences between pretest scores and posttest scores for any of the four items used in this experiment, nor were there any significant differences in item variances.

Test-retest correlations were computed to estimate item reliability and ranged from .37 to .66. The average correlation was .55. Transforming these individual reliabilities into an estimate of the reliability of a three person group yielded a coefficient of .90.[8]

The effect of the majority was uniform on both risky items and on both cautious items. Moreover, there is no evidence that either the risky items or the cautious items interacted with majority. Finally, the pattern of correlations with other variables was the same for both risky items and for both cautious items. Thus the two risky items and the two cautious items are not considered as nested factors in the analysis of variance design.

DISCUSSION

These data are consistent with the unequal speaking version of the linear discrepancy model. Group decisions, group shifts, variances, the effect of treatments on group decisions, and the effect of treatments on group shifts are all predicted with considerable accuracy by this model. It is possible that error in prediction may be attributed exclusively to error of measurement. It would be difficult to reject this hypothesis, given these data.

Moreover, the data suggest that informational influence, as measured by the pretest opinion × item interaction, plays a key role in determining the extent to which a person speaks in a group discussion. Individual differences, as measured by communication apprehension, also exert an impact on speaking frequency. The discrepancy model built by Boster et al. (1980), demographic variables, and other individual difference variables proved not to correlate with speaking frequency. In addition, normative influence, as measured by the pretest opinion × majority interaction, was not an accurate predictor of speaking frequency. Advocates of this position might object that this experiment was an inadequate test of their position. Perhaps had groups composed of all cautious members discussed a risky item, or had groups composed of all risky members discussed a cautious item, more support for the normative influence position would have been obtained. Such arguments might be more persuasive had these data yielded a correlation between normative influence and speaking frequency that exceeded .00.

Although these results are encouraging, it would be premature to conclude that a satisfactory explanation of speaking frequency had been developed. The multiple correlation of informational influence and communication apprehension with speaking frequency, $R = .47$ when corrected for attenuation, illustrates that there is considerable error in prediction. Thus undoubtedly other variables are important determinants of speaking frequency. In order to develop an adequate explanation of speaking frequency, these variables must be discovered.

Taken together, these data paint a consistent picture of the polarity shift phenomenon, although it is a somewhat impressionistic painting. The nature of cultural values affects the pool of arguments favoring either risky or cautious alternatives for each choice dilemma item. The type of item then interacts with persons' pretest opinions to determine the extent to which they will speak, and hence the extent to which they will be influential, in a group discussion. The extent to which group members are apprehensive about communicating also plays a role in determining f_i. Pretest opinion and speaking frequency then combine to determine the group decision. The manner in which they combine is defined by the unequal speaking version of the linear discrepancy model. The group decisions, combined with the pretest group opinions, then define the direction and magnitude of the polarity shift.

This picture is similar to the one painted by Boster et al. (1980). That study examined only risky majorities discussing risky items and cautious majorities discussing cautious items. Thus, the fact that the model of speaking frequency did not predict large differences in speaking frequency, coupled with the fact that the equal speaking model fit the data well ($r_{GG^*} = .82$), produced a close fit of the unequal speaking model to the data. By measuring f_i, and by assessing the effect of several variables on f_i, this experiment extends the Boster et al. (1980) study.

NOTES

1. On the other hand, choice shifts have also been obtained in gambling situations and task difficulty choice experiments. These results have proved to be general across a variety of subjects as well (see Dion et al., 1970, pp. 308-309).

2. The nature of this judgment is different across experiments. In some studies Ss are requested to judge the odds, as contrasted with the lowest odds, of pursuing a given alternative. In some experiments Ss are to assume that they are the individuals faced with the choice. In other experiments they are to assume the role of advisor to the person faced with the choice. Fraser et al. (1971) show that these minor variations in procedure have a negligible effect on experimental results.

3. Similarly, experiments in which the polarity shift is measured as the difference between individual pretest judgments and individual posttest judgments typically find that the individual posttest judgments are more polar than the individual pretest judgments (e.g., Flanders & Thistlethwaite, 1967).

4. For a discussion of the characteristics of items that produce consistent risky shifts and cautious shifts see Clark (1971).

5. Equation 15 in this chapter corrects equation 21 in Boster et al. (1980).

6. If β is greater than 1, equation 15 predicts that the variance would increase over time. Such a result would mean that there was "overshoot." That is, Ss would change their posttest opinions in a more extreme direction than the group decision. Theoretically, such a result is most improbable.

7. Machiavellianism was measured by Christie and Geis's (1970) MACH IV scale. Dogmatism was measured by Troldahl and Powell's (1965) short form of the Rokeach (1960) dogmatism scale. Self-esteem was measured by Rosenberg's (1965) self-esteem scale. Eysenck's (1953) measure of extroversion was employed. The Personal Report of Communication Apprehension (PRCA) was used to measure communication apprehension (McCroskey, 1970). Need for affiliation items were gleaned from the Edwards Personal Preference Schedule.

8. This reliability is given by

$$\frac{V - [s_x^2 (1 - r_{xx})/3]}{3}$$

REFERENCES

Boster, F. J., Mayer, M. E., Hunter, J. E., & Hale, J. L. Expanding the persuasive arguments explanation of the polarity shift: A linear discrepancy model. In D. Nimmo (Ed.), *Communication yearbook 3*. New Brunswick, NJ: Transaction, 1980.

Burnstein, E., & Vinokur, A. Testing two classes of theories about group induced shifts in individual choice. *Journal of Experimental Social Psychology*, 1973, 9, 123-137.

Burnstein, E., & Vinokur, A. What a person thinks upon learning he has chosen differently from others: Nice evidence for the persuasive arguments explanation of choice shifts. *Journal of Experimental Social Psychology*, 1975, 11, 412-426.

Burnstein, E., Vinokur, A., & Trope, Y. Interpersonal comparison versus persuasive argumentation: A more direct test of alternative explanations for group induced shifts in individual choice. *Journal of Experimental Social Psychology*, 1973, 9, 235-245.

Christie, R., & Geis, F. L. *Studies in Machiavellianism*. New York: Academic Press, 1970.

Clark, R. D. III. Group-induced shift toward risk: A critical appraisal. *Psychological Bulletin*, 1971, 76, 251-270.

Dion, K. L., Baron, R. S., & Miller, N. Why do groups make riskier decisions than individuals? In L. Berkowitz (Ed.), *Advances in experimental social psychology* (Vol. 5). New York: Academic Press, 1970.

Ebbeson, E. B., & Bowers, R. J. Proportion of risky to conservative arguments in a group discussion and choice shift. *Journal of Personality and Social Psychology*, 1974, 29, 316-327.

Eysenck, H. J. *The structure of human personality*. New York: John Wiley, 1953.

Flanders, J. P., & Thistlethwaite, D. L. Effects of familiarization and group discussion upon risk taking. *Journal of Personality and Social Psychology*, 1967, 5, 91-97.

Fraser, C., Gouge, C., & Billig, M. Risky shifts, cautious shifts and group polarization. *European Journal of Social Psychology*, 1971, 1, 7-30.

French, J. R. P., Jr. A formal theory of social power. *Psychological Review*, 1956, 63, 181-194.

Knowles, E. S. Information weighting, familiarization and the risky shift. *Social Behavior and Personality*, 1976, 4, 113-119.

Kogan, N., & Wallach, M. A. *Risk taking: A study in cognition and personality*. New York: Holt, Rinehart & Winston, 1964.

McCroskey, J. C. Measures of communication-bound anxiety. *Speech Monographs*, 1970, 37, 269-277.

Myers, D. G., & Lamm, H. The group polarization phenomenon. *Psychological Bulletin*, 1976, 83, 602-627.

Reingen, P. H. Effects of skewness of initial choices on the risky shift: An experimental test with the use of consumer stimuli. *Psychological Reports*, 1977, 40, 95-101.

Rokeach, M. *The open and closed mind: Investigations into the nature of belief systems and personality systems*. New York: Basic Books, 1960.

Rosenberg, M. *Society and the adolescent self-image*. Princeton: Princeton University Press, 1965.

Silverthorne, C. F. Information input and the group shift phenomenon in risk taking. *Journal of Personality and Social Psychology*, 1971, 20, 456-561.

Stoner, J. A. F. Risky and cautious shifts in group decisions: The influence of widely held values. *Journal of Experimental Social Psychology*, 1968, 4, 442-459.

Teger, A. I., & Pruitt, D. G. Components of group risk taking. *Journal of Experimental Social Psychology*, 1967, 3, 189-205.

Troldahl, V. C., & Powell, F. A. A short-form dogmatism scale for use in field studies. *Social Forces*, 1965, 44, 211-214.

Vinokur, A. Distribution of initial risk levels and group decisions. *Journal of Experimental Social Psychology*, 1969, 13, 207-214.

Vinokur, A., & Burnstein, E. Effects of partially shared persuasive arguments on group induced shifts. *Journal of Personality and Social Psychology*, 1974, 29, 305-315.

Vinokur, A., & Burnstein, E. Depolarization of attitudes in groups. *Journal of Personality and Social Psychology*, 1978, 35, 872-885.

APPENDIX: Choice Dilemma Items

Mr. E is the president of a light metals corporation in the United States. The corporation is quite prosperous and has strongly considered the possibilities of business expansion by building an additional plant in a new location. The choice is between building another plant in the United States, where there would be moderate return on the initial investment, or building the plant in a foreign country. Lower labor costs and easy access to raw materials in that country could mean a much higher return on the initial investment. On the other hand, there is a history of political instability and revolution in the foreign country under consideration. In fact, the leader of a small minority party is committed to nationalizing, that is, taking over all foreign investments.

Imagine that you are advising Mr. E. Listed below are several probabilities, or odds, of continued political stability in the foreign country under consideration.

Please check the lowest probability that you would consider acceptable for Mr. E's corporation to build a plant in that country.

A man about to embark on a vacation trip experiences severe abdominal pains and must choose between disrupting his vacation plans in order to see a doctor or boarding an airplane for an overseas flight.

Imagine that you are advising the man. Listed below are several probabilities, or odds, that the pains will become more severe.

Please check the lowest probability that you would consider acceptable before you would advise the man to leave on his vacation as he had planned.

A recent medical-school graduate is choosing between two long-term projects. One is almost certain to be a success, and will help his career, but will not be of major importance. The other will be either a complete success or a complete failure; if successful, it will lead to a cure for a "crippling disease which leaves children blind and mentally retarded."

Imagine that you are advising the doctor. Listed below are several probabilities, or odds, that the uncertain project will be successful.

Please check the lowest probability that you would consider acceptable before you would advise the doctor to choose the uncertain project.

A person involved in an airplane accident must choose between rescuing only his child and attempting to rescue both his spouse and child, with the realization that both will be lost if the attempt is unsuccessful.

Imagine that you are advising this person. Listed below are several probabilities or odds that both the spouse and the child could be saved.

Please check the lowest probability that you would consider acceptable before you would advise the person to attempt to rescue *both* the child *and* the spouse.

INFORMATION SYSTEMS

14 ● Measuring Aspects of Information Seeking: A Test of a Quantitative/Qualitative Methodology

BRENDA DERVIN ● THOMAS L. JACOBSON ● MICHAEL S. NILAN

University of Washington

THE RESEARCH PROBLEM

INFORMATION has been a central concept in communication research since the early persuasion research period. The continuing importance of this concept is reflected in Schramm's (1973, pp. 38, 41) statement that information is "the stuff of communication" and that communication is "the ability to process information and share it with others."

Over the years a variety of specific definitions of information have been offered, ranging from the idea that information consists of "assertions as to the state of affairs at a given 'now'" (Berlo, 1977, p. 23), to the idea that information is the making of choices (see Krippendorf, 1977), to the idea that information is defined in terms of its potential for reducing cognitive uncertainty (Atkins, 1973, p. 205). Although there are variations among these definitions, virtually all are based on a single theoretic formulation developed by Shannon and Weaver (1949). Derived from research in the area of electrical engineering, the concept holds that information is that

AUTHORS' NOTE: This study was supported by the Demonstration/Education Project at the Puget Sound Blood Center, a National Research and Demonstration Center for the National Heart, Lung, and Blood Institute, under Grant HL 17365-06. The authors are indebted to Richard F. Carter of the University of Washington School of Communications for the contribution his theoretical work has made to this chapter.

Correspondence and requests for reprints: Brenda Dervin, School of Communications, University of Washington DS-40, Seattle, WA 98195.

which reduces uncertainty.[1] Since their formulation, information theory concepts have had a tremendous impact on conceptualization in the study of communication not only in the fields of electrical engineering and artificial intelligence, but in the behavioral sciences as well.

The information-theoretic approach has been and continues to be valuable, especially in its contributions to measurement and to understanding some systematic phenomena. At the same time, however, the approach has embedded in it three assumptions — some implicit, some explicit — that are unnecessarily restrictive when applied to human behavior.[2] These assumptions are that information is something that:

- exists *externally*, outside individual frames of reference;
- can potentially provide a *complete description* of reality; and
- is measurable on single, *quantitative, unidimensional* scales.

The External Information Assumption

The first assumption is that information is something that describes an external reality and that the observational activities in the human communication process therefore focus on external information sources. Information in this assumption is seen as an object or thing that is transferred from one place to another. The "black box" of human information processing is analyzed as if it were initiated by the "reception" or "effect" of something, understood conceptually as a "bit" of information. Metaphorically, the model of reception of bits of information is transformed into an equivalent of the reception of bricks tossed to or at someone. The focus of the research becomes this posited external information and the external reality it is assumed to describe. Information becomes something that exists outside the internal, subjectivity of individuals, outside the black box, as absolute and objective.

The Complete Description Assumption

The second assumption is that information is something that can potentially provide a complete description of external reality. This assumption is best illustrated by the mathematics of information theory, which allows for a complete reduction of uncertainty. Conceptually, the assumption is that the external reality is completely describable by information and that a complete description allows the individual to make a completely adaptive response to this reality. It is further assumed that adaptive responses are the only functional responses. In this context human information processing is again best seen as a transmission process, where concern is focused on how much of that external information the organism has been able to process.

The Quantitative Unidimensional Assumption

The third assumption is that this hypothetical external thing, information, is adequately quantified on a single, continuous, numerical scale. As in the two assumptions above, human use of information is measured by "amount" of uncertainty reduction. The scales or dimensions used are variations of simple bit measurement mathematics, and they are applied similarly to many varieties of behavior (see Berlo, 1977, for an example). Even when information theory mathematics is not being utilized directly, the measurements of information usually focus on amount of a message attended to, retained, and used. In this context measurements of uncertainty reduction remain independent of the meanings ascribed to messages by perceivers. In much of the research based on this assumption, the major portion of the conceptualization is often limited to defining the information-theoretic concepts and presenting the elegance of the associated mathematics, while considerably less attention is given to what kind of human behavior is involved (the subject of the model).[3]

It should be noted that not all approaches to information that have assumed externality and completeness have also assumed unidimensionality. But the unidimensional assumption is a common consequence of the other two assumptions. In effect it is assumed that an external, undescribed thing called information reduces uncertainty and potentially allows complete adaptation to reality, and that measurement of the obtaining of this thing (e.g., amount of information exposed to, learned, recalled) is automatically a measure of uncertainty reduction. In this perspective multidimensional measurement becomes unnecessary. Recent work has, however, introduced the idea of measuring different kinds of external information, such as information about ends versus means versus attributes for assessing means.[4] An important implication of the trend toward qualitative and multidimensional measurement of external information is that while some observers assume that qualitative approaches always focus on internal subjectivity, there is, in actuality, no necessary relationship.

THE RESEARCH CONSEQUENCES

All research starts with assumptions, of course, and all assumptions have research consequences. The three assumptions reviewed above have been applied with an almost unvarying consistency over a long period of time. Their consequences, therefore, are large, and they are becoming more and more apparent in recent attempts to reconceptualize approaches to researching human information use. More specifically, these assumptions have contributed to:

- a *disciplinary contradiction* in which human communication is posited as being cognitive while it is studied as noncognitive;
- *lack of progress;*
- *audience myths* created by the lack of attention to and retention of messages, resulting from barriers that members of the audience set up; and
- *the quantification confusion* that results from assertions that efforts to quantify human behavior are ipso facto antihuman.

The Disciplinary Contradiction

One result of the use of the information theory approach in behavioral communication research is that while the literature strongly indicates that communication behaviors are fundamentally cognitive behaviors, communication is seldom researched as cognitive.

In the most frequent research examples, a vaguely defined message assumed to be a container of information is hypothesized as having a certain impact on behavior. In this approach cognitive processes remain black box, and examination of cognition is logically excluded. In less frequent cases, communication is treated at best as quasi-cognitive.[5] The lower-order concepts used in such research vary considerably. In some cases single concepts such as feedback are applied, and in others, computers are used to "model" cognitive behavior. Common to them, however, is the notion of reduction of uncertainty and the language of applied cybernetics and information theory. Humans are seen basically as "processors" of information, and therefore, like machines they are gauged in reference to the ideal standard of "noiseless" signal transmission: perfect communication. Since such perfect transmission is nearly unheard of in human behavior, the dominant picture becomes that of humans as one variety of imperfect processors, essentially imperfect machines.

The Lack of Research Progress

A second result of the use of these assumptions about information is that while a great deal of communications research has been conducted, the power of the findings from the research is very limited. This result is illustrated by three clear trends in the literature. One is the continuing references to low levels of variance accounted for in traditional communication research (see Capella, 1977; Dervin, 1980, 1981; Dervin et al., 1981; Hewes & Haight, 1979). Another is the increasing acceptance of complex multivariate designs and the accompanying logic that only by the introduction of more and more variables will more variance be accounted for.[6]

The final illustration of this consequence is a reflection of the same concern for lack of research progress manifested in a different way. In this case it is the growing vocality of a countertrend that suggests that human communication and information use can be most productively analyzed holistically, nonquantitatively, and nonanalytically.[7]

The Creation of Audience Myths

A third consequence of the use of the information theory assumptions is the creation of a negative "bad guy" view of audiences. This view derives directly from the use of the assumptions. If an external, nonqualitative, and supposedly complete standard of information is used as the basis for assessing whether or not members of audiences have or have not received messages, clearly most members of the audience will have erred by not receiving. If in order to explain why the audience has erred the standard is maintained, then logically one must focus on the audience to explain the discrepancy.

It is in such a context that constructs such as the selectivity processes (selective perception, attention, retention) are developed. In this context, it is posited that members of the audience throw up barriers (e.g., resistance to change, emotional blocks) to information receipt.

The Quantification Confusion

A fourth consequence, related to the others, is the growing polarization between so-called quantitative and so-called nonquantitative researchers. Looking at the quantitative research, the qualitative researchers see a lack of emphasis on the human behavior behind the numbers and assume that quantification is the problem rather than the assumptions that guide conceptualization. Because of this, ironically, many qualitative researchers are making some of the same restraining assumptions about human behavior and the nature of information as quantitative researchers.

A prime example of this is the frequent reference in some qualitative work to various kinds of direct or mediated effects from contexts, structures, and messages (see, for example, Beltran, 1976; Carey, 1975; Cushman & Sanders, in press; Goffman, 1959; Habermas, 1979). In some of this work respondents are not asked to assess what they see to be the effects on themselves; in other examples respondents are asked, and their judgments are combined with observer assessments and those from other participants in a kind of convergent picture of effects with demarcations between various inputs not kept systematically clear.[8] As a result it becomes difficult to distinguish which conclusions derive from understandings of the subjective reality constructing of respondents, and which derive from the subjective reality constructing of observers.

The impact of this trend on qualitative research is that it becomes quasi-cognitive in the same sense as quantitative research based on information theory premises does. This is because both approaches share some of the same external information assumptions.

Despite the polarization of the qualitative and quantitative approaches, both are making progress in the difficult process of breaking away from past assumptions. Unfortunately, in the presence of polarization, the two approaches are seen as mutually exclusive and in competition and, thus, are not easily able to enrich each other.

AN ALTERNATIVE

There is widely available work in the field of information theory itself that addresses the problem of information theory's applicability to the study of human behavior. In essence these commentaries speak to the issue of whether measures of information as prescribed by information theory have anything to do with "meaning"(see, for example, Conant, 1979; McKay, 1969). While such recognition has led to changes in research approaches, these changes have mostly been variations on the concepts of information theory. They have not led to other promising, empirical approaches.

The study reported herein is an attempt to develop an alternative. This alternative arises from a different set of assumptions about the nature of information and information use. While there are a number of possible ways of presenting these alternative assumptions, we have chosen here to contrast them to the information-theoretic assumptions. For this purpose it can be said that in the alternative perspective information is seen as something that:[9]

- can provide only an *incomplete description* of reality;
- exists to a significant degree *internally,* as part of individual frames of reference; and
- is measurable in terms of *multidimensional qualities.*

The Incomplete Description Assumption

This assumption is pivotal for this alternative perspective. It postulates that there are fundamental and pervasive discontinuities or gaps in life and phenomena. In this theoretic formulation the gap condition is posited as generalizable (see Carter, 1980): It is seen as arising from the fact that all things are not connected and that things are constantly changing.

From this perspective information seeking and use cannot be posited only or even primarily as adaptive. The notion of adaptation implies a passive rather than an active response to the environment; it requires a completely connected, external reality to adapt to. Alternatively, external reality can be posited as never complete, forever imperfect, always filled with gaps. In this context information seeking and use are seen as activities individuals participate in in order to make personal sense in the presence of incomplete instruction from reality. Since life is inherently unmanageable, individuals are forever encountering instances where they need to make sense and where obtaining complete, exact pictures of reality is impossible.

The condition of gap is seen as applying not only to direct experience with reality, but to indirect experience attended to via messages and signals. The condition is seen as applying not only to specific unique moments in time-space, but to the very concepts of time and space themselves (see Ornstein, 1969).

In the presence of all this change and difference, it is assumed that the imperative human mode of information seeking and use for each individual is to create notions of information, time, and space that work personally. The important word here is *create*. Information seeking and use are assumed to be large constructive processes rather than adaptive ones.[10] The present theoretic approach refers to these constructive processes in general terms as "sense making" and specifically in terms of the gap condition as "gap-bridging."

The Internal Information Assumption

The idea that no amount of external information can provide a complete description of reality logically leads to the idea that each individual person must, therefore, be constructing some kind of useful personal sense. The idea that the process is constructive leads to the idea that an important locus of information is internal.

Considerable past research has shown that people perceive and interpret reality differently. Most of this work has interpreted the evidence as proof that humans are imperfect information processors, that they are incapable of getting the external information into themselves in correct ways. The alternative perspective assumes, in contrast, that comparing individual perceptions and interpretations to an external standard is a nonproductive way of dealing with human information seeking and use.

In the alternative perspective, it is assumed that the individual does attend to an external reality; can attend to this external reality at a given time from only one point in space; makes from this reality a sense that is some interaction of what is "really" there and the constructive sense he or she applied to that reality; constructs sense that is highly individual and highly influenced by the past; and, makes sense at a given moment in time-space that applies only to that moment in an everchanging time-space. It must be reiterated that the individuality of this process applies not only to given moments in time and space, but to the very concepts of time and space themselves and, therefore, to the concept of information. Therefore it is posited that as the individual moves through time-space, the very ways in which he or she sees gaps or information and his or her needs for it differ from those of other individuals. The conclusion is that information will be more usefully conceptualized as a user construct than as an observer construct.[11]

The Qualitative Multidimensional Assumption

The above two assumptions logically lead to the conclusion that different individuals will construct different kinds of gaps as they move through time-space and have the need for different kinds of gap-bridging and, thus, different kinds of information. In fact, for purposes of this chapter it is assumed that a relativistic approach taps all these differences and, therefore, must be qualitatively multidimensional.

A TEST OF THE ALTERNATIVE

The concepts presented in the discussion above — that human experience is relative and needs to be studied as relative — are not new in the behavioral sciences. A diverse set of scholars has emphasized the humanness of behavior and its dependence on contexts that are often individually specific and full of individualized meaning (see, for example, Dewey, 1963; Thompson, 1963 [on C.S. Peirce]; Bateson, 1972; Bronowski, 1969; Bruner, 1973; Stephenson, 1980).

Efforts to operationalize concepts derived from the relativity notion in communication research have, however been frustrated. Theorizing is one thing and conceptualizing fruitful research approaches is another. Methodologies addressing individually relative and qualitative behavior are obviously difficult. One specific purpose of this chapter is to present a methodology for studying qualitatively relativistic differences in information seeking.

A second specific purpose focuses on application. One of the *raison d'êtres* for communication research is to provide guidance for communication intervention in specific situations. The usual way of going about this has been to test the individual's performance or understanding resulting from expert-designed instructions based on absolute, external information assumptions. The discussion above, however, suggests that the qualitative differences in internally seen gaps should be the best place to start when considering information system designs that are to be responsive to individual needs. The applied purpose of this study, then, is to discuss the benefits of focusing on qualitatively relativistic differences in gaps as an approach to looking at information use in an applied setting.

A third specific purpose focuses on validating the proposed methodology and its application by testing relativistically qualitative differences in gap-bridging as predictors of a set of criterion measures of information seeing in a way that is congruent both with the purpose of presenting the proposed methodology and with the purpose of using it in an applied setting.

For the purposes of this chapter a set of different qualities of gap-bridging are the predictor variables. In addition it is assumed that it will be helpful in an applied setting to know: (1) how much emphasis people moving through the system place on different kinds of gaps, and (2) what success the individuals have in bridging different kinds of gaps. These two dimensions of information seeking are the criterion variables. The general hypotheses is that the different qualities of gap-bridging (i.e., the different kinds of gaps individuals see themselves as needing to bridge) will predict differences in information-seeking emphasis and success.

In review, the three specific purposes of this chapter are to:

1. present a methodology for looking at information seeking qualitatively and relativistically as differences in qualities of gap-bridging;
2. discuss the benefits of doing so in applied settings; and
3. validate the approach by using relativistic, qualitative differences in gap-bridging as predictors of a set of criterion measures of information seeking, emphasis, and success.

A METHODOLOGY FOR TESTING THE ALTERNATIVE

As mentioned above the general recognition of qualitative and relative differences in behaviors is not new, especially in qualitative modes of inquiry with a high priority on attentiveness to the individual. The purpose here, however, is simultaneously quantitative inquiry and qualitatitive sensitivity to the individual. The research problem, as always, is to tap the concrete reality and detail of particular situations, and at the same time produce generalizable, intersubjectively sharable, and systematic observations.

Such research has been especially difficult in the empirical behavioral sciences since qualitative aspects of behavior such as subjectivity have in the past been thought impossible to measure. A rift has been created between qualitative and quantitative research methods as a result. With the developments outlined in the sections above, however, it is now becoming clear that these two modes can be used in a complementary rather than mutually exclusive fashion. The question is thus primarily a methodological one: How to do the research while avoiding both the "mystique of quality" and the "mystique of quantity" (Kaplan, 1964, p. 207).

This task cannot be accomplished simply by choosing the right measurement tools alone. It must be addressed at the methodological level. In this sense methodology refers to a conceptual framework whereby variable validity is seen in light of specific theoretic or pragmatic research purposes (Kaplan, 1964).

It has been indicated that the very fact of individually different conceptions of time-space implies qualitatively different kinds of cognitive information processing or gap bridging. Time-space linearity or uniformity cannot be assumed since varying perceptions of it constitute some of the qualitative cognitions within which information seeking and use occur and that, thus, are the subject of the measurement. Therefore measurement tools that assume time-space equivalence of behaviors (and most in the behavioral sciences do) cannot suffice. What is needed is a methodology based specifically on individual differences in time-space perceptions and information seeking and use.

A methodology has been constructed for the present study that uses a flexible conception of time-space, allowing respondents to define time-space and information seeking for themselves relative to their own perceptions of things (see Atwood & Dervin, 1981; Dervin et al., 1980, 1981, for other applications of the same methodology).

The methodology relies on a survey interview method called the "time-line" approach. The actual survey method will be described in the methods section of this chapter. What is important at this point, however, are the ways in which the method allows each respondent to define relative to his or her own perspectives and in qualitative terms time, space, and information seeking. This is accomplished by having the respondent describe each of the time-space moments that he or she saw him- or herself as moving through in a situation with the respondent being free to chose what time-space moments to attend, how to attend them, how to order them, how to collapse and/or expand time-space in the ordering, and how to connect one time-space moment to another. Within this ordering of respondent-defined time-space moments, the respondent describes what gaps he or she saw him- or herself having to bridge. These gaps are operationalized as the questions the respondent had in his or her head. The criterion variables of information-seeking emphasis and success are then operationalized vis-à-vis these questions.

Several features of this methodological approach are worth noting. One is that the interview process is highly structured. The second is that it is nevertheless virtually content free. The interviewer provides the structure based on the assumed-to-be universal imperative of the human condition — movement through time-space (no matter how individualistically perceived). The respondent provides the content — the unique perceptions, the time-space moments, the gaps to be bridged, and the assessments of gap-bridging results.

It is important to note at this point that the above discussion uses four terms — *information seeking, sense making, gap-bridging,* and *question asking* — that may from one perspective seem interchangeable. However, each plays a different methodological role. Information seeking is the research domain, the arena of behavior that is the focus of this study. Sense making refers to a general conceptual approach, one that posits the human need to construct meaning in the absence of complete instruction from the environment. Gap-bridging is a metaphor used as a theoretic construct for purposes of this study to refer to a general set of cognitive behaviors required in sense making. Question asking is the specific operationalization of gap-bridging used in this study.

Methods

The time-line approach was developed specifically to tap human information seeking and use behaviors based upon the theoretic and methodological considerations outlined above. The hypotheses of this present study were tested using this approach in a blood donor retention setting, asking respondents how they saw and made sense out of their most recent donation experience.

The Sample. The sample frame was the blood donor roster of the Puget Sound Blood Center for a four-week period in March and April 1980. Only Seattle residents were included. Sampling was done randomly within eight strata, created with three stratification variables — age (young/old), sex (male/female), and donor status (new/repeat). A total of ten respondents was sought for each of the eight cells. In all, a total of 258 individuals were contacted with a maximum of four callbacks per individual to obtain eighty respondents.

The Questionnaire. In the actual field setting interviewers asked respondents to describe all the events (time-space moments) they recalled from their most recent blood donation as if they were showing cognitive photographs to the interviewer of everything they and others did and said as well as everything that just happened. For each event named (called a time-line step), respondents were asked what questions they had in their heads. Questions were described for respondents as "holes in understanding, things you needed to learn, find out, come to understand, make sense of, or unconfuse." The resulting questions, of course, differed in their natures and it is the qualities of these different questions that are the predictor variables for this study (the qualities of gap-bridging).

For each question named respondents were asked a series of closed-ended items, which form the criterion measures for this study. The items focus on information-seeking emphasis and success. Specifically, the respondent was asked how many times he or she asked a given question, how many other questions he or she asked at the same time-space moment, how difficult the respondent found getting an answer, and whether he or she was successful in getting an answer. The actual questionnaire included many other dimensions such as a more detailed description by respondents of how they saw given moments in time-space.

Interviewers. The questionnaires were administered by graduate students and advanced undergraduates trained for a minimum of ten hours. Interviewing quality was validated. The average interview took ninety-three minutes with the range being 50-130 minutes.

Unit of Analysis. The unit of analysis for this study was not the respondent, but the gap-bridging instance, the point in time-space when the respondent saw some kind of gap to be bridged. The eighty respondents for this study generated 481 questions asked, or gap-bridging instances, an average of 6.01 per respondent (for examples of the use of units of analysis other than the person, see Dervin et al., 1980, 1981; Grunig & Disbrow, 1977).

Predictor Variables. The conceptual predictor variables for this study are qualities of gap-bridging. They are specifically developed for this study in two different ways. The first is in terms of theoretically derived measures. Here the purpose was, in line with the discussion presented in sections above, to tap the specific time-space moments of the respondents in terms of some assumed-to-be fundamental time-space notions. Five content-analytic schemes were developed for this purpose (see Atwood & Dervin, 1981; Dervin et al., 1981). Each was applied to the questions asked by respondents using a dichotomous coding procedure — i.e., a given question either was or was not described by a specific category within a given scheme. The five conceptually derived schemes are presented in Table 14.1 with data on the frequency of their occurrence as well as their interjudge coding reliabilities. The five schemes tap in turn whether a respondent's question focused on the past, present, or future *(time focus);* what aspect of time-space the question focused on — entities, time and space concerns, or the connections between time and space *(5W focus);* whether a respondent's question indicated he or she was evaluating time-

Table 14.1
Outline of the Content Analysis Schemes Tapping Qualities of Gaps in Time-Space Bound Situations Indicated by Respondent Questions

Category	n[a]	%	Category Definitions[b]
Time Focus			
Past/present	241	50.1	Attempting to learn something about the present or past.
Future	240	49.9	Attempting to learn something about the future.
5 W Focus			
Who	63	13.1	Attempting to identify one or more humans—who they are, what they are like, what they think or feel.
What	159	33.1	Attempting to identify one or more nonhuman entities—objects or situational conditions.
When/where	92	19.1	Attempting to locate one or more entities in time or space.
Why	68	14.1	Attempting to determine the reasons, causes, and explanations of events.
How	99	20.6	Attempting to determine the means or procedures for moving from one point in time-space to another.
Valence Focus			
Bad	118	24.5	Attempting to determine if road was/is/will be a bad one.
Neutral	281	58.4	Attempting to bridge a gap where the question statement was neutral.
Good	82	17.0	Attempting to determine if road was/is/will be a good one.
Entity Focus			
Self	177	36.8	Attempting to bridge gap in which self is major focus.
Other	108	22.5	Attempting to bridge gap in which one or more others is major focus.
Object/situation	196	40.7	Attempting to bridge gap in which one or more objects and/or situations are major focus.
Movement Focus			
How I got here	89	18.5	Attempting to learn how self came to this point in time-space.
Where I am now	108	22.5	Attempting to learn about the point in time-space self is at now.
How I get there	181	37.6	Attempting to learn how to move from a current point in time-space to a future point.
Where I will be	103	21.4	Attempting to learn about the point in time-space self will be at in the future.

(continued)

Table 14.1 (Continued)

Category	n[a]	%	Category Definitions[b]
Descriptive Focus			
Pain	71	14.8	Attempting to learn about the pain and discomfort connected with donating and how self will react.
My body	34	7.1	Attempting to learn about own physical body—its characteristics and history.
Blood processing	29	6.0	Attempting to learn about the characteristics and how it is processed.
Donating objects	42	8.7	Attempting to learn about the objects associated with donating.
Donating process	143	29.7	Attempting to learn about the time and characteristics of the donating process and the reasons for things being done.
Eligibility	31	6.4	Attempting to learn about one's own eligibility and the eligibility rules.
Planning	40	8.3	Attempting to learn what is needed to plan for donating both at home and at the donating site.
Staff	24	5.0	Attempting to learn about the blood center staff—who they are, what they are like, what they think.
Self-control	14	2.9	Attempting to learn about one's own ability to cope with situation and how one will react.
Donating others	42	8.7	Attempting to learn about other donators—who they are, what they are like, what they think or feel.
After donating	11	2.3	Attempting to learn about events occurring after the donating process.

a. Total N = 481 questions asked. The percentages above are based on "the proportion of questions which fell into each of the nature of gap categories." Each section of the table consists of one conceptual scheme into which any given question could only be coded into a single category. Percentages may not add to exactly 100.0 within sections due to rounding error.
b. Interjudge coding reliabilities for the six schemes outlined above were: (using Stempel's [1955] percentage agreement index and Scott's [1955] adjustment respectively): time focus, 96 percent/92 percent; 5W focus, 87 percent/83 percent; valence focus, 93 percent/88 percent; entity focus, 94 percent/91 percent; movement focus, 96 percent/95 percent; descriptive focus, 98 percent/98 percent.

space *(valence focus)*; what kind of entity was focused on *(entity focus)*; and what aspects of movement through time-space the question focused on *(movement focus)*.

In addition to the conceptual schemes applied to respondent questions, a descriptive or inductively derived scheme was developed directly from responses with the intent of tapping the qualitative differences between gaps in a way salient to the specific applied setting. The descriptive scheme is also presented in Table 14.1 with data on the frequency of the occurrence of each category and interjudge coding reliabilities.

Criterion Variables. Two classes of information-seeking criterion variables were proposed for this study. One class, consisting of two measures, focuses on the amount of emphasis respondents placed on different questions. These two measures were tapped in the following ways:

- *Frequency of asking.* This measure is a straight count of the number of times a respondent asked a specific question. The mean frequency was 1.18, standard deviation, .48.
- *Proportionate emphasis.* This measure taps the extent to which a given question was at a given time-space moment the only question the respondent saw him- or herself as needing to answer. Quantitatively it was calculated by dividing one (the number of times a question was asked at a given moment in time-space) by the total number of questions asked at that moment and multiplying by 100. The mean proportionate emphasis was 69.23, standard deviation, 30.77.

The second class of criterion variables, consisting of two measures, focused on the success respondents reported in gap-bridging. These two measures were tapped in the following ways:

- *Ease of gap-bridging.* This measure taps the respondents' perceptions of the ease or difficulty of obtaining answers to their questions. The variable was tapped using a ten-point scale with one specified as hard and ten as easy. Mean ease was 7.37, standard deviation, 3.05.
- *Completeness of gap-bridging.* This measure taps respondents' perceptions of whether they got no answers, or the extent to which their questions were answered. The variable was tapped using a three-point scale from no answer (coded zero), partial answer (coded one), and complete answer (coded two). Mean completeness was 1.43, standard deviation, .81.

Statistical Analyses. The predictive purposes of this study were executed with one-way analyses of variance supplemented with Duncan's test for within-table mean comparisons. A total of twenty-four analyses of variance were performed, one for each of the six content-analytic templates applied to qualities of gap-bridging on each of the four criterion variables (all statistical analyses were done by computer using *Statistical Package for the Social Sciences;* Nie et al., 1975).

Results

Table 14.2 presents the results for the use of the six content-analytic templates as predictors for each of the four criteria. Results will be presented below by criterion variable across all predictors.

Frequency of asking. Results show significant analyses of variance on this criterion for five of the six content-analytic templates. In overview results show that certain kinds of questions were more frequently asked by respondents than others. A summary portrait shows that these were questions about the future, about where the respondent will be, and what kinds of situations or objects he or she will be having to face. This portrait is confirmed by the descriptive focus results, which show that questions about one's own self-control, pain, and specific questions about blood and the processing of blood were repeated significantly more often. The specific data points that support this portrait include:

- *time focus* — Questions about the "future" were asked significantly more often (mean of 1.26) than "past/present" questions.
- *5W focus* — "What" questions were repeated significantly more often (1.31) than questions in any of the other categories in this scheme — "who," "when/where," "why," and "how" (a high of 1.17).
- *entity focus* — Questions about "situations/objects" were asked significantly more often (1.33) than questions about "self" (1.12) or "others" (1.01).
- *movement focus* — Questions focusing on "where will I be" were asked significantly more often (mean of 1.40) than any of the other questions in this scheme — "where was I," "where am I," "how I get there" (high of 1.14).
- *descriptive focus* — Questions focusing on pain were the most frequently repeated (1.48) in this template. In a second group based on frequency, significantly higher than the very least frequently repeated questions but not different from all other categories were questions about "my self-control" (1.43) and "blood and processing" (1.28). Least emphasis was given to questions on "other and donating" (1.00); this finding was significantly lower than that for the three categories mentioned above.

Proportionate Emphasis. Results show significant analyses of variance for this criterion for all six predictor templates. In overview results show that certain kinds of questions were significantly more likely to be the sole gap-bridging focus at a given time-space moment. These questions were those focusing on the past and how one got to the present, those focusing on the whys and hows in and between time-space moments, those evaluating whether given time-space moments were positive, and those focusing on self rather than on others or situations and objects. In terms of descriptive focus questions on the requirements of and planning for donating

Table 14.2
Results of One-Way ANOVAs with Six Content-Analytic Templates Tapping Qualities of Gaps as Predictors of Information-Seeking Emphasis and Success

Predictor Variable Templates	n	Frequency of Asking (Emphasis)	Proportionate Emphasis	Ease of Gap-Bridging (Success)	Completeness of Answer
Time Focus					
Past/present	241	1.10[a]	72.30[b]	7.51[a]	1.30[a]
Future	240	1.26[b]	66.15[a]	7.23[a]	1.56[b]
p		<.001	<.05	n.s.	<.001
5W Focus					
Who	63	1.06[a]	62.63[a]	7.56[ab]	1.51[b]
What	159	1.31[b]	64.43[a]	6.88[a]	1.45[b]
When/where	92	1.17[a]	69.34[ab]	8.08[b]	1.52[b]
Why	68	1.09[a]	80.37[c]	6.81[a]	1.12[a]
How	99	1.10[a]	73.39[bc]	7.77[ab]	1.48[b]
p		<.001	<.001	<.01	<.01
Valence Focus					
Bad	118	1.23[a]	69.85[a]	6.61[a]	1.42[a]
Neutral	281	1.18[a]	66.03[a]	7.55[b]	1.41[a]
Good	82	1.11[a]	79.32[b]	7.84[b]	1.51[a]
p		n.s.	<.01	<.01	n.s.
Entity Focus					
Self	177	1.12[a]	73.79[b]	7.30[a]	1.48[a]
Other	108	1.01[a]	65.68[a]	7.53[a]	1.31[a]
Situation/object	196	1.33[b]	67.07[a]	7.35[a]	1.45[a]
p		<.001	<.05	n.s.	n.s.
Movement Focus					
How I got here	89	1.09[a]	76.80[c]	6.43[a]	1.05[a]
Where I am now	108	1.11[a]	65.85[ab]	7.59[b]	1.39[b]
How I get there	181	1.14[a]	71.42[bc]	8.09[b]	1.59[c]
Where I will be	103	1.40[b]	62.40[a]	6.68[a]	1.56[bc]
p		<.001	<.01	<.001	<.001
Descriptive Focus					
Pain	71	1.48[c]	62.99[ab]	6.55[a]	1.66[b]
My body	34	1.06[ab]	66.42[abc]	7.56[a]	1.53[b]
Blood and processing	29	1.28[bc]	53.22[a]	6.83[a]	1.00[a]
Donating objects	42	1.05[ab]	71.63[abc]	7.62[a]	1.31[ab]
Donating process	143	1.11[ab]	72.07[bc]	8.05[a]	1.44[ab]
Requirements of	31	1.19[ab]	80.65[c]	7.35[a]	1.45[ab]
Planning for	40	1.20[ab]	80.63[c]	7.20[a]	1.48[b]
Staff	24	1.17[ab]	70.83[abc]	6.63[a]	1.13[ab]
My self-control	14	1.43[bc]	71.67[abc]	5.64[a]	1.29[ab]
Others and donating	42	1.00[a]	60.30[ab]	7.36[a]	1.43[ab]
After donating	11	1.00[ab]	68.18[abc]	8.27[a]	1.73[b]
p		<.001	<.01	<.05	<.05

abc. In a vertical column within a section, the subscripts a through c indicate the use of Duncan's test for the significance of differences in subgroup means. Unlike subscripts indicate that the means were significantly different at $p < .05$.
n.s. = not significant.

received more proportionate emphasis, while questions about blood and blood processing received less. This portrait is supported by these specific data points:

- *time focus* — Questions about the "past/present" received significantly more proportionate emphasis (72.30 mean) than questions about the "future" (66.15).
- *5W focus* — "Why" questions received significantly more emphasis than all others with the average "why" questions being 80.37 percent of the questions asked at a given point in time-space. "How" questions also received more emphasis (73.39) although this differed significantly only from "why" and "what" questions and not from "when/where" questions.
- *valence focus* — Questions evaluating whether given time-space moments were "good" were significantly more emphasized (79.32) than either "bad" or "neutral" questions.
- *entity focus* — Questions focusing on "self" (73.79) were significantly more likely to receive proportionate emphasis than questions about "others" (65.69) or "situations/objects" (67.07).
- *movement focus* — Questions focusing on "how I got here" received more emphasis (76.80) than either "where am I now" or "where will I be" questions (65.85 and 62.40, respectively). Questions on "how to get there" were in the middle, but received significantly greater emphasis than "where am I now" and "where will I be" (71.42).
- *descriptive focus* — Most emphasized questions were those focusing on the "requirements of" and "planning for" donating (80.65 and 80.63, respectively), receiving significantly greater emphasis than three of the nine other descriptive categories. "Donating process" questions also received somewhat more emphasis (72.07), significantly greater than one other category. Least emphasis went to "blood and processing" (53.22), significantly less than to the three other categories.

Ease of Gap-Bridging. Results show significant analyses of variance on four of the six criterion-predictor templates. In overview results show that certain kinds of gaps were seen as harder to bridge. These gaps were those focusing on the whys and whats of time-space, attempts to evaluate the negative aspects of time-space, and attempts to bridge gaps dealing with understanding movement from the past to the present as well as the nature of the future. The following specific findings support this portrait:

- *5W focus* — "Why" questions and "what" questions were significantly more likely to be termed harder to get answers to (6.81 and 6.88, respectively) than "when/where" questions (8.08). "How" and "who" questions stood in between.
- *valence focus* — Questions evaluating time-space moments in terms of whether they were "bad" were significantly harder to get answers to

Measuring Information Seeking

(6.61) than either "neutral" or "good" questions (7.55 and 7.84, respectively).

- *movement focus* — Questions focusing on "how I got here" and "where I will be" were significantly harder to get answers to (6.43 and 6.68, respectively) than either "where am I now" and "how I get there" questions (7.59 and 8.09, respectively).
- *descriptive focus* — While the overall analysis of variance for this predictor was significant, the within-table mean comparison showed that none of the category means were significantly different.

Completeness of Gap-Bridging. Results show significant analyses of variance on four of the predictor templates. The overall portrait suggests that certain kinds of gaps were less likely to be completely bridged according to respondent reports. These gaps were those focusing on the past and movement from the past to present and those focusing on the why aspects of time-space. In terms of descriptive focus, questions about blood and its processing received the least complete answers, while questions about pain, the respondent's own body, the respondent's planning for donating, and what happens after donating were more likely to receive complete answers. The following specific findings support this portrait:

- *time focus* — "Past/present" questions were significantly less likely to be completely answered (1.30) than "future" questions (1.56).
- *5W focus* — "Why" questions were significantly less likely to be completely answered (1.12) than questions in all other categories — "who," "what," "when/where," and "how" (low of 1.45 to high of 1.51).
- *movement focus* — Questions focusing on "how I got here" were significantly less likely to get complete answers than those in all other categories in this scheme (1.05 compared to a low of 1.36). Questions about "where I am" were next (1.36), receiving significantly less complete answers than "how I got here" questions (at the high of 1.59). "Where I will be" questions fell in between.

Summary of Results

The results above can be summarized in two ways. One summary focuses on the portrait developed across predictor templates for each of the criterion variables. This portrait shows that:

- The *most frequently asked* questions focused on gaps the respondents saw as they faced the future — where they would be, what kinds of situations and objects they would meet, what kind of control over self they would have, and what kinds of technical process they would be involved in.

- The *most emphasized* questions (those that were most likely to represent the sole gap that respondents were attempting to bridge at a given time-space moment) were those dealing with the self and self-movement through time-space and the making of a coherent, cognitive whole of the process, understanding the hows and whys and the connections between different time-space moments.
- The *hardest* questions to answer focused on either those time-space points that were not yet at hand (the future) or those aspects of gap-bridging that indicated respondents were attempting to evaluate events, make connections between different time-space points, and understand underlying connections.
- The questions with *least complete answers* were those that focused on past events and underlying causes and reasons (the whys), while those with the most complete answers involved gaps that were bridged by the sheer movement of self through the experience. A notable exception here was questions about blood and its processing, which were least completely answered.

An alternative summary focuses on the portrait developed across criterion variables for given predictor variables. Three major findings emerge from this perspective:

- Questions that received more proportionate emphasis were also frequently those reported as less easy to answer and less likely to have received complete answers. Categories here include "why" questions, "past/present" questions, and "how I got here" questions — all focusing on gap-bridging involving the connections between different time-space moments.
- Those questions that were more likely to be asked more than once were also those that were asked in conjunction with other questions at the same moment in time-space (i.e., received lower proportionate emphasis). These questions tended to be those that our systems now term as more "factual," focusing, for example, on the nature of situations and objects and the whats of time-space moments. On the other hand, questions that were asked alone at given time-space moments tended not to be asked more than once. The questions tended to be those that our systems called more "subjective," dealing, for example, with the connecting of different time-space moments, the whys and hows, and the moving from one time-space to another.
- Questions about blood and its processing were less frequently asked and less emphasized than other descriptive focus categories. It is significant however, that they were also reported as least completely answered given that for this category blood center staff have a variety of alternative inputs that evidently did not provide for donors, or donors felt were inadequate for their gap-bridging.

CONCLUSIONS

This study had three specific purposes: (1) to present a methodology for studying qualitative relativistic differences in gap-bridging in systematic ways, (2) to examine the utility of the methodology as an approach to looking at information use in applied settings, and (3) to validate the methodology by using qualitative relativistic differences in gap-bridging as predictor variables to a set of criterion measures of information seeking. The first purpose was covered in the first part of this chapter; the second and third purposes are discussed in reverse order below.

The pivotal purpose is the third, of course, and the results above show strong support for the general hypothesis predicting differences in information-seeking emphasis and success between different qualities of gap-bridging. The power of the findings is most clearly shown by the single statement that of the twenty-four significance tests completed, nineteen or 79 percent were significant.

More important than significance per se, however, is the pattern of the findings. First, they are logical. This is shown by such findings as the greater proportionate emphasis on qualities of gap-bridging concerning self and self-movement through time and space and on understanding the hows and whys and connections between time-space moments. It is, after all, self that is the imperative focus of gap-bridging. The human need for constructing coherency and wholeness of understanding is also well established. Another example of the logical nature of the findings is the fact that among the hardest gaps to bridge were those in the future.

A second salient feature of the pattern of the findings is that they are system reflective. What this means is that if we take our information systems as they are currently designed with their emphasis on external, absolute information, we would expect people moving through these systems to have the most difficulty bridging gaps where the focus is now defined by systems as "subjective." Such gaps include those involving connections between different time-space moments and understandings of the whys behind events. Significantly, it was these kinds of gaps that received proportionately more emphasis from respondents, and yet were seen as harder to bridge and less likely to be bridged. It is also significant that these qualities of gap-bridging, which our systems now call more subjective, are the kinds of gaps that most clearly pertain to the generalized gap condition posited in earlier sections of this chapter. In essence, then, these qualities of gaps clearly deal with the connections between things and times and spaces, and thus, focus directly on the lack of connectedness posited by the discontinuity assumption.

A third characteristic of the findings is that the qualitative approach to information seeking made a difference in that not only the individual findings but the pattern of the findings vary across qualities. This is clearly shown in the two paragraphs immediately above, but deserves special mention.

The findings are themselves further supported by the strength of the implications that can be drawn from them for application to systems. These strengths can generally be subsumed under the term *intervention guidance* in that they suggest to the practitioner — in this case the individual concerned with communicating in a blood center setting — what kinds of information will be helpful to individuals intersecting with these systems. Three such strengths can be pinpointed.

The first application strength is the fact that the methodology applied provides a means of developing an index of the kinds of questions users of systems have as they move through these systems. In this study results show that the variety was not overwhelmingly large. This finding alone is encouraging for the practitioner in that it runs counter to the idea that if one looks at information seeking as individually determined, one will not be able to handle the diversity of results. Pertinent to this issue is the understanding that the methodology used here is one that allows uniqueness to emerge in the context of fundamental dimensions of human experience. The uniquenesses are gaps respondents see themselves as facing and their assessments of these gaps. The fundamental dimensions focus on movement through time-space, however uniquely defined. It is this focus on fundamentals that, it is suggested, allows the methodology to begin to allow order or systematic pattern to emerge from a relativistic, qualitative approach.

A second applied strength is that the application of the methodology allows the practitioner to track how important different kinds of information are to users and how successfully users are obtaining these kinds of information. These analyses provide the practitioner with specific guidelines for communication planning. In these data, for example, the results suggest that respondents were not bridging the gaps they had about blood and its processing to the extent they wanted to despite the fact that their experience took place at a site where relevant input was readily available.

Another example of such helpful guidance that appears in these data deals with the frequently mentioned issue of how to retain blood donors once they donate. Past literature has shown that the drop-out rate is large and that a good number of first donations result from various kinds of social pressure (see Hillman et al., 1975; Oswalt, 1977; Scherer, 1975 for reviews of studies on blood donating motivations). This finding is confirmed by the sense-making pattern in these data. Respondents reported a need to make sense of how they ended up donating and how all the time-space moments of donating connect to each other and form a coherent whole. Clearly, whatever reasons propelled them to the donating site did not supply them with sufficient sense making in these areas. Such findings suggest a lucrative area for communication planning. As one example it may be that committed donors should be on hand to talk with these obviously uncommitted donors and share their perspectives on how they move from never having donated to a first-time donation to a commitment to repeat.

The current study has a number of weaknesses, of course. Most obvious is that the various templates used to measure qualities of gap-bridging are only in the development stage and, further, that they are not mutually exclusive. Obviously, too, since the application of methodology is relatively new, repeated uses will be needed to unearth other difficulties that did not emerge in this test.

This test of the methodology does, however, suggest a fruitful approach for further exploration. Beyond the specific findings is the fact that powerful results were achieved with a methodology that was directed to aspects of information seeking previously ignored in quantitative research. The primary implication of the findings is that using quantitative empirical approaches to study relativistic qualitative aspects of information seeking is a viable enterprise, one that could be even more powerful with more development. This conclusion is not a condemnation of quantitative techniques but rather support of their use, especially in conjunction with qualitative and relativistic suppositions.

NOTES

1. A great number of researchers and theorists have worked on the development of methods to increase fidelity in signal transmission through the examination of redundancy, bits, and probabilities of control processes, and so on. Shannon and Weaver generalized these methods.

2. Several prior critical reviews of these assumptions are available, mostly subsumed under the general title "the absolute information approach" (see, in particular, Dervin, 1976, 1980, 1981; Dervin et al., 1980, 1981).

3. This tendency would seem to be an example of the "law of the hammer," where a powerful and convenient tool is used on everything in sight, not because it is appropriate but rather because of its convenience.

4. For examples of efforts using qualitative approaches to external, nonrelativistic information, see Ackoff (1958), Dervin and Greenberg (1972), Wade and Schramm (1969).

5. Examples of research in this class include efforts to develop a "cognitive evaluation theory" (Cusella, 1980; Deci, 1975) and the community of researchers promoting a "cognitive science" (Craig, 1979).

6. Support for this assertion comes from observations of the increased use of such sophisticated multivariate techniques as discriminant and factor analysis and multiple regression. It is telling that one of the consequences of conducting research without adequate conceptual guidance is that one then lacks adequate criteria for choosing among variables. As a result the number of the variables that must be addressed at one time increases.

7. The range of positions on this issue varies from condemnation of all quantitative approaches to acceptance of a complementary relationship between quantitative and qualitative approaches (for examples of works representing the range, see Blumer, 1969; Carey, 1975; Christians & Carey, 1981; Glaser & Strauss, 1967; Meyer, Traudt, & Anderson, 1980).

8. It is interesting to note that this convergent picture building serves in the qualitative approach much the same function as some statistical analyses do in quantitative approaches. Smith (1972) makes this point well.

9. Alert readers will notice that the information-theoretic assumptions are presented in a different order than the alternative assumptions. This is because each set of assumptions has its own internally consistent logical order (for comprehensive literature reviews relating to these alternative assumptions, see Dervin, 1976, 1980, 1981).

10. Bruner's (1973 in particular) work is most notable for its early emphasis on cognitive behavior as constructing behavior.

11. It should be noted that some researchers (e.g., Clarke & Kline, 1974; Edelstein, 1974) have made helpful advances by presenting operationalizations of information seeking that were user-based.

REFERENCES

Ackoff, R. K. Toward a behavioral theory of communication. *Management Science,* 1958, *4,* 218-234.

Atkins, C. Instrumental utilities and information seeking. In P. Clarke (Ed.), *New models for communication research.* Beverly Hills, CA: Sage, 1973.

Atwood, R., & Dervin, B. Challenges to socio-cultural predictors of information seeking: A test of race vs situation movement state. In M. Burgoon (Ed.), *Communication yearbook 5.* New Brunswick, NJ: Transaction, 1981.

Bateson, G. *Steps to an ecology of mind.* New York: Ballantine, 1972.

Beltran, L. R. S. Alien premises, objects, and methods in Latin American communication research. *Communication Research,* 1976, *3,* 107-134.

Bem, D. Constructing cross-situational consistencies in behavior. *Journal of Personality* 1972, *40,* 17-26.

Berlo, D. K. Communication as process: Review and commentary. In B. D. Ruben (Ed.), *Communication yearbook 1.* New Brunswick, NJ: Transaction, 1977.

Blumer, H. *Symbolic interactionism: Perspective and method.* Englewood Cliffs, NJ: Prentice-Hall, 1969.

Bronowski, J. *Nature of knowledge: The philosophy of contemporary science.* New York: Science Books, 1969.

Bruner, J. *Beyond the information given.* New York: W. W. Norton, 1973.

Cappella, J. N. Research methodology in communication: Review and commentary. In B. D. Ruben (Ed.), *Communication yearbook 1.* New Brunswick, NJ: Transaction, 1977.

Carey, J. W. A cultural approach to communication. *Communication,* 1975, *2.*

Carter, R. F. *Communication as behavior.* Paper presented at the annual meeting of the Association for Education in Journalism, Fort Collins, Colorado, 1973.

Carter, R. F. *A journalistic cybernetic.* Paper presented at the Conference on Communication and Control in Social Processes, University of Pennsylvania, Philadelphia, 1974.

Carter, R. F. *Elementary ideas of systems applied to problem solving strategies.* Paper presented at the annual meeting of the Far West Region of the Society for General Systems Research, San Jose, California, 1975.

Carter, R. F. *Discontinuity and communication.* Paper presented at the seminar on communication from eastern and western perspectives at the East-West Center, Honolulu, Hawaii, 1980.

Christians, C. G., & Carey, J. W. The logical and aims of qualitative research. In G. Stempel III and B. Westley (Eds.), *Research method in mass communications.* Englewood Cliffs, NJ: Prentice-Hall, 1981.

Clarke, P., & Kline, F. G. Media effects reconsidered: Some new strategies for communication research. *Communication Research,* 1974, *1,* 224-239.

Conant, R. C. A vector theory of information. In D. Nimmo (Ed.), *Communication yearbook 3.* New Brunswick, NJ: Transaction, 1979.

Craig, R. T. Information systems theory and research: An overview of individual information processing. In D. Nimmo (Ed.), *Communication yearbook 3.* New Brunswick, NJ: Transaction, 1979.

Cusella, L. P. The effects of feedback on intrinsic motivation: A propositional extension of cognitive evaluation theory from an organizational perspective. In D. Nimmo (Ed.), *Communication yearbook 4.* New Brunswick, NJ: Transaction, 1980.

Cushman, D. P., & Sanders, R. E. Rules theories of human communication processes: The structural and functional perspectives. In B. Dervin & M. Voigt (Eds.), *Progress in communication sciences* (Vol. 2), in press.

Deci, E. L. *Intrinsic motivation.* New York: Plenum Press, 1975.

Dervin, B. Strategies for dealing with information needs: Information or communication? *Journal of Broadcasting,* 1976, *20,* 324-333.

Dervin, B. Communication gaps and inequities: Moving toward a reconceptualization. In B. Dervin & M. Voigt (Eds.), *Progress in communication sciences* (Vol. 2). Norwood, NJ: Ablex, 1980.

Dervin, B. Mass communication: Changing conceptions of the audience. In W. Paisley & R. Rice (Eds.), *Public communication campaigns.* Beverly Hills, CA: Sage, 1981.

Dervin, B., & Greenberg, B. The communication environment of the urban poor. In G. Kline & P. Tichenor (Eds.), *Current perspectives in mass communication.* Beverly Hills, CA: Sage, 1972.

Dervin, B., et al. The human side of information: An exploration in a health communication context. In D. Nimmo (Ed.), *Communication yearbook 4.* New Brunswick, NJ: Transaction, 1980.

Dervin, B., et al. Improving predictions of information use: A comparison of predictor types in a health communication setting. In M. Burgoon (Ed.), *Communication Yearbook 5.* New Brunswick, NJ: Transaction, 1981.

Dewey, J. *How we think.* Boston: D. C. Heath, 1933.

Edelstein, A. S. *The uses of communication in decision making.* New York: Praeger, 1974.

Glaser, B., & Strauss, A. *Discovery of grounded theory.* Chicago: Aldine, 1967.

Goffman, E. *The presentation of self in everyday life.* Garden City, NY: Doubleday, 1959.

Grunig, J. E., & Disbrow, J. Developing a probabilistic model for communications decision making. *Communication Research,* 1977, *4,* 145-168.

Habermas, J. [*Communication and the evolution of society*] (T. McCarthy, trans.). Boston: Beacon Press, 1979.

Hewes, D., & Haight, L. The cross-situational consistency of measures of communicative behaviors. *Communication Research,* 1979, *6,* 243-270.

Hillman, R., et al. Report on the task group on blood donor recruitment. In S. M. Weiss (Ed.), *Proceedings of the National Heart and Lung Institute Working Conference on Health Behavior* (DHEW #76-868). Washington, DC: DHEW, 1975.

Kaplan, A. *The conduct of inquiry: Methodology for behavioral science.* New York: Chandler, 1964.

Krippendorff, K. Information systems theory and research: An overview. In B. Ruben (Ed.), *Communication yearbook 1.* New Brunswick, NJ: Transaction, 1977.

McKay, D. M. *Information, mechanism, and meaning.* Cambridge: MIT Press, 1969.

Meyer, T. P., Traudt, P. J., & Anderson, J. A. Non-traditional mass communication research methods: An overview of observational case studies of media use in natural settings. In D. Nimmo (Ed.), *Communication yearbook 4.* New Brunswick, NJ: Transaction, 1980.

Mischel, W. Toward a cognitive social learning reconceptualization of personality. *Psychological Review,* 1973, *80,* 252-283.

Nie, N. H., et al. *Statistical package for the social sciences.* New York: McGraw-Hill, 1975.

Ornstein, R. E. *On the experience of time.* Baltimore: Penquin Books, 1969.

Oswalt, R. M. A review of blood donor motivation and recruitment. *Transfusion,* 1977, *17,* 123-135.

Rotter, J. P., et al. *Application of a social learning theory to personality.* New York: Holt, Rinehart, & Winston, 1972.

Scherer, P. B. Blood donor motivation: A background paper. In S. M. Weiss (Ed.), *Proceedings of the National Heart and Lung Institute Working Conference on Health Behavior* (DHEW #76-868) Washington, DC: DHEW. 1975.

Schramm, W. *Men, messages, and media: A look at human communication.* New York: Harper & Row, 1973.

Scott, W. A. Reliability in content analysis: The case of nominal scale coding. *Public Opinion Quarterly,* 1955, *19,* 321-325.

Shannon, C. E., & Weaver, W. *The mathematical theory of communication.* Urbana: University of Illinois Press, 1949.

Smith, D. H. Communication research and the idea of process. *Speech Monographs,* 1972, *39,* 174-182.

Stempel, G. H. Increasing reliability in content analysis. *Journalism Quarterly,* 1955, *19,* 449-455.

Stephenson, W. Conspiring: A general theory for subjective communicability. In D. Nimmo (Ed.), *Communication yearbook 4.* New Brunswick, NJ: Transaction, 1980.

Thompson, M. *The pragmatic philosophy of C. S. Peirce.* Chicago: Chicago University Press, 1953.

Wade, S., & Schramm, W. The mass media as sources of public affairs, science, and health knowledge. *Public Opinion Quarterly,* 1969, *33,* 197-209.

III • INTERPERSONAL COMMUNICATION

15 ● Accuracy in Detecting Deception: Intimate and Friendship Relationships

MARK E. COMADENA

Illinois State University

SINCE 1940 a considerable amount of research has been conducted on the ability of observers to detect deceptions on the part of others (Fay & Middleton, 1941; Maier, 1966; Maier & Janzen, 1967; Maier & Thurber, 1968; Thackery & Orne, 1968; Shulman, 1973; Ekman & Friesen, 1974; Maier & Lavrakas, 1976; Bauchner, Brandt, & Miller, 1977; Geizer, Rarick, & Soldow, 1977; Littlepage & Pineault, 1978, 1979; Hocking, Bauchner, Kaminski, & Miller, 1979). This research, which has used a variety of procedures for operationalizing deception, indicates that under normal laboratory conditions, unaided by any mechanical equipment, untrained observers accurately identify previously unknown liars at, or slightly above, what would be expected by chance alone.

While much research has been conducted on the deception attribution process, few empirically based generalizations may be made because researchers have typically overlooked the many contextual elements that may influence both the performance and perception of deceptive acts (DePaulo & Rosenthal, 1979; Knapp & Comadena, 1979). One contextual element conspicuously missing in the majority of detection accuracy studies has been the nature of the relationship between subjects used as deceivers and deception detectors. Virtually no research exists that examines the ability of judges to detect deceptions from communicators with whom they have developed intimate relationships.

That social psychologists have overlooked the intimate dyad as a context for deception research is unfortunate. Aspects of the intimate relationship suggest several theoretically interesting questions relevant to the performance and evaluation of deception. The intimate dyad is a very

---

Correspondence and requests for reprints: Mark E. Comadena, Department of Communication, Illinois State University, Normal, IL 61761.

special social system, especially when viewed from a communication perspective. Some have suggested that intimates develop very efficient, smooth-flowing, and idiosyncratic (i.e., unique to the relationship partners) communication systems (Altman & Taylor, 1973; Gottman, 1979). Others have suggested that communications are transmitted and understood rapidly, accurately, and with great sensitivity in the intimate relationship (Rosenthal, Hall, DiMatteo, Rogers, & Archer, 1979). If intimates do indeed develop unique communication systems and a sensitivity to one another's communicative behaviors, what, then, are the implications for sending and receiving deceptive messages in such relationships? How accurate are individuals at detecting deception in their intimate partners? Are certain types of deception more accurately detected than others? Within the intimate dyad, is one sex more accurate than the other at detecting deceptions? Answers to these questions may provide a basis for generalizing about the ability of judges to detect deceptive communications.

In an attempt to answer such questions, the present study examined the relationship between observer sex, type of deception (i.e., factual versus emotional), level of familiarity between deceiver and deception detector, and observer accuracy in detecting deception. The following sections examine each of these contextual elements and discuss how observer accuracy is expected to relate to each.

FAMILIARITY AND DETECTION ACCURACY

The first study to note the effects of baseline (truthful) behavior on judges' accuracy in detecting deception was conducted by Ekman and Friesen (1974). In that study, some observers viewed deceivers' heads and faces only, while other observers viewed the communicators in a body-only condition. The researchers also had some observers view a videotaped sample of the communicators' truthful behavior prior to making judgments of truthfulness, while other observers received no such baseline information. Ekman and Friesen (1974) found that observers in the body-only condition were significantly more accurate (63.5 percent) than were observers in the face- and head-only conditions. This level of accuracy, however, was achieved only by those observers who viewed a videotaped sample of a communicator's honest behavior prior to judging the communicator's truthfulness.

Brandt, Miller, and Hocking (1980b) explored the effects of providing observers with added exposures to a baseline of truthful behavior on judgmental accuracy. In that study fifty undergraduate students observed videotaped excerpts of sixteen individuals as they lied and told the truth in an interview situation. Prior to rating the truthfulness of the sixteen interviewees, observers were exposed (via videotape) to various amounts of truthful baseline communication for each interview before rating his or her truthfulness.

The baseline manipulation in the Brandt et al. (1980b) study was engaged as follows. Observers in the high-familiarity condition received six repetitions of the sample behavior. Those in the moderate-familiarity received four, those in the low-familiarity received one, and those in the no-familiarity condition did not receive a baseline exposure. Results indicated that judgmental accuracy was greatest in the moderate-familiarity condition, which was significantly different from the no- and high-familiarity conditions, but not from the low-familiarity condition. In a similar study, Brandt et al. (1980a) found that familiarity (i.e., three repetitions) accounted for 29 percent of the variance in observers' accuracy scores.

While the Ekman and Friesen (1974) and Brandt et al. (1980a, 1980b) studies indicate judgmental accuracy may be enhanced with knowledge of a communicator's truthful behavior, the experimental procedures incorporated in these studies obviously do not permit generalizations to intimate and enduring relationships. Exposing an individual to one, two, or several repetitions of the same behavior segment does not adequately capture the level of familiarity achieved in an intimate relationship. In an intimate relationship, both partners have psychological information about the other and a baseline of truthful behavior based on communication over a wide variety of topics in a number of different emotional contexts.[1]

Only one study has explored the relationship between familiarity as afforded through relational intimacy and accuracy in detecting deception (Miller et al., 1981). In that study, subjects were twelve married couples, their close friends, and twelve strangers. Upon arrival at the experimental setting, one spouse was randomly selected as the communicator/deceiver and shown a set of videotaped presentations. After viewing the videotapes, the spouse selected as the communicator was interviewed by the *experimenter* concerning the content of the tapes and his or her feelings toward the subject of the videotapes. Spouses were randomly instructed to lie or tell the truth in response to selected question sets within the interview schedule. The interview was observed by the spouse's marital partner, friend, and stranger through a one-way mirror. The researchers observed that the degree of accuracy in judging deception concerning factual information did not differ significantly between spouses, friends, and strangers. Friends, however, were significantly more accurate than were spouses or strangers in judging deception involving emotional information. The authors suggested that friends may have been at a "discovery" stage in their relationships with the communicators and that this caused them to monitor behaviors more closely — picking up deviations from normal communications to which spouses no longer attended as closely.

A limitation in the Miller et al. study was that evaluations of communicator truthfulness were obtained from observers who were not involved in the interaction itself. Recall that observers rated communicators through a one-way mirror. Such a procedure may attenuate spouses' sensitivity to certain nonverbal information, such as voice pitch and subtle facial expressions, and cause them to be less accurate in their attributions. Thus, in a "live" rating condition, where the potential for deception is known, intimates may demonstrate greater accuracy than friends in detecting deceptions. The present research tests this notion.

DECEPTION TYPE

At the most basic level, there are essentially two types of deception. Since human communication has a dual function — to affect cognitive behavior and to affect emotional responses — deceptions may be operative in one or the other or both functions. That is, deceptions may concern factual information or they concern emotional information.

Little research exists which *compares* observers' abilites to detect factual and emotional deceptions. Recall that Miller et al. (1981) found no significant differences between spouses, friends, and strangers in their ability to detect factual messages. In the same study, however, friends were significantly more accurate than were spouses or strangers in judging deception involving emotional information. One would expect that as relationship development increases, partners' abilities to detect both types of deceptions would increase. This suggestion seems particularly true for emotional deception, since relationship development usually requires emotional involvement and disclosure. The present study addresses this contention.

SEX DIFFERENCES IN DETECTING DECEPTION

Surprisingly little research has explored sex differences in deception detection, and virtually no research has examined sex differences within the intimate dyad. A study by Shulman (1973) revealed no significant differences between unacquainted males and females in their ability to detect deceptive communication. Rosenthal and DePaulo (1979) found women were substantially and significantly more likely than men to interpret the deceptive encodings as the deceiver wanted them interpreted rather than as the deceiver really felt.

That women were "substantially" inaccurate in decoding deception in the Rosenthal and DePaulo (1979) study is rather surprising. Women, because of differential socialization processes, are typically held to be more sensitive to the social cues of others than are men (Broverman, Vogel, Broverman, Clarkson, & Rosenkrantz, 1972; Henley, 1977; Maccoby & Jacklin, 1974). In a review of seventy-five published articles that reported sex differences in ability to decode nonverbal communication, Hall (1978) concluded that more studies indicated a female advantage than would occur by chance alone. If the nonverbal behaviors of deceitful and truthful communicators differ, as research indicates they do (Knapp & Comadena, 1979), one would expect females to demonstrate a degree of accuracy in detecting deception that is higher than that of males. Furthermore, one would expect that in ongoing relationships, where partners have developed sensitivities to one another's communication behaviors, women should emerge as better deception detectors than men. The present research examines this notion.

A SUMMARY AND RESEARCH OBJECTIVES

A considerable amount of research has been conducted on the ability of observers to detect deception on the part of others. This research, however, has virtually neglected the influence that the relationship between actors used as deceivers and deception detectors may have on observers' perceptions of deception. Little empirical evidence exists concerning the ability of individuals to detect deception on the part of others with whom they have developed a relational history. The only study to explore the relationship between judgmental accuracy in detecting deception and relational history found friends to be significantly more accurate than either strangers or intimates in judging deception involving emotional information (Miller et al., 1981). In the same study (Miller et al., 1981), the degree of accuracy in judging deception concerning factual information did not significantly differ between the three groups.

The Miller et al. (1981) study possessed a major procedural limitation that should be eliminated in future studies of this type. The limitation concerns the experimenters' decision to have observers rate communicators through a one-way mirror. Not only does such a procedure make generalization to face-to-face interaction difficult, but also the procedure may have attenuated spouses' sensitivity to certain subtle nonverbal cues (e.g., pitch, tone of voice, facial cues), causing them to be less accurate than friends in their attributions. Friends may not monitor the same cues intimates monitor to distinguish truth from deception.

In summary, since intimates have both psychological information and knowledge of one another's communicative idiosyncracies through interaction with each other over a wide variety of topics in a number of different emotional situations, they should, when given the motivational cue that their partners may or may not be lying, be significantly more accurate than their friends in detecting both factual and emotional deceptions in their partner. Specifically, the following hypotheses were tested in this study:

H.1: Intimates will be significantly more accurate in judging factual deception than friends will be.

H.2: Intimates will be significantly more accurate in judging emotional deception than friends will be.

Research on gender differences in nonverbal decoding ability (Hall, 1978) indicates females have a slight advantage over males in interpreting the communicative cues of others. Thus, if the overt behavior of deceivers differs from that of truth tellers, as research indicates it does, females should be better than males at decoding deception. However, in studies designed to test such a notion, females have not demonstrated a marked superiority over males (Rosenthal & DePaulo, 1979; Shulman, 1973). Whether female sensitivity to nonverbal cues interacts with familiarity with another's behavioral repertoire to enhance judgmental accuracy is open to investigation. Accordingly, the following research questions were examined in this study:

RQ.2: Are females significantly more accurate than are males in detecting deception?

RQ.3: Is judgmental accuracy in detecting deception enhanced by the interaction of sex and familiarity?

METHODS

Subjects

A total of twenty-two intimate couples and their friends served as subjects for the study. Subject participation was solicited through the local and campus newspapers of a large midwestern university. Volunteers were offered five dollars for their services.

The average age of the intimate was 23.5 years; men averaged twenty-four years, while women averaged twenty-three years of age ($t = 1.39, p = .172$). The average age of the friend was twenty-five years; here men ($n = 13$) averaged twenty-seven years and women ($n = 9$) averaged

Table 15.1
Frequencies for Subjects' Education

	Friends	Intimates
Elementary	1	0
High school	1	3
Part of college	8	12
Bachelor's degree	6	15
Master's degree	5	13
Ph.D.	1	1
	22	44

twenty-four years of age ($t = 1.12$, $p = .285$). Overall the two subject groups did not differ significantly in age ($t = 1.42$, $p = .168$).

The educational levels represented in the two subject groups were very similar. Table 15.1 presents the variety and frequency of educational levels of subjects. A chi-square test of the data presented in Table 15.1 indicated that no significant differences in education existed between intimates and friends ($\chi^2 = .81$, $df = 3$).[2]

A third comparison between intimates and friends did reveal a significant difference. Intimates reported they knew their intimate partners an average of forty-six months. Twenty of the twenty-two intimate couples were married. The average length of marriage was 15.8 months. The two couples who were not married had been cohabitating for sixteen months.[3] Friends, on the other hand, reported they knew the spouses an average of 18.9 months. The reported histories of the two groups were significantly different ($t = 5.61$, $p = .001$).

Finally, the two subject groups were compared in terms of the perceived closeness of their relationships. An eleven-item questionnaire developed from Wheeless's (1976) measure of solidarity was completed by the spouses and employed to provide index for comparison. In this study, married partners perceived significantly more solidarity in their marital relationships ($\bar{X} = 67.43$) than in their relationships with their friends ($\bar{X} = 49.50$, $t = 7.86$, $p = .0001$). The eleven-item solidarity inventory had an internal reliability of .95 (Cronbach's alpha).

These data indicate the two subject groups (friends and intimates) were relatively homogeneous in age and education but significantly different in relational histories and perceived closeness in the relationships.

Independent Variables

Three independent variables were utilized in the present study: (1) communicative familiarity between deceiver and observer, (2) type of deception, (3) sex of the observer. The following sections outline the procedures used to operationalize the independent variables.

COMMUNICATIVE FAMILIARITY

Communicative familiarity is a sensitivity to the communicative style and idiosyncracies of another achieved through observing another in many emotional situations and, as such, is positively related to relational intimacy (Altman & Taylor, 1973). In the present study, the operational objective was to identify two distinct types of intimacy that would differentiate two levels of communicative familiarity. The two types of relationships studied were (1) intimates and (2) friends. A description of the specific procedures used to operationalize these relational types follows.

To participate as an intimate, the observer had to have been married to his or her spouse for not more than three years. The three-year marriage criterion was employed for two reasons. First, marriage provides one indication that the relationship was at least once characterized by a high degree of intimacy. Furthermore, marriage ensures the experimenter that the individuals have had the opportunity to familiarize themselves with one another's communicative idiosyncracies through discussion over a wide variety of topics in a number of different contexts. Second, the three-year criterion provides for a test of the familiarity hypothesis on individuals with different relational histories than have been studied before. Recall that Miller et al. (1981) failed to support the hypothesis using couples who were married for at least five years (and friends partners had known for at least one year).

Since marriage alone may not reflect how intimate a relationship is for two individuals, spouses qualified as intimates only if *both* partners reported they were adjusted in their marriage. The Marital Quality Inventory (MQI; Norton & Montgomery, 1980) was employed to provide an index of marital quality. The MQI measures a respondent's perceptions of his or her marital relationship along six dimensions. Three dimensions — happiness, satisfaction, and commitment — reflect the respondent's perceptions of self within a marital relationship, and three dimensions — stability, cohesion, and consensus — reflect the respondent's perceptions of the marriage as a unit. In the present study, the MQI had an internal reliability of .93 (Cronbach's alpha). In short, both members of a marital (intimate) relationship had to report a score of 85 or higher to be qualified as adjusted.[4]

To participate as a friend, an observer had to be selected by both spouses; that is, he or she had to be a friend of *both* spouses. In addition, he or she had to have known both spouses at least two months and to have engaged in face-to-face interaction with both spouses, on the average, at least once a week for the past two months. As spouses were contacted concerning participation in the study, they were told they would have to bring a friend with them, either male or female, who best met the above qualifications.

TYPE OF DECEPTION

Two types of deception were examined in the present study: (1) deception concerning factual information, and (2) deception concerning emotional information. Factual deception was operationalized as a response to an interview question in which the interviewee completely misrepresented the *facts* associated with an audio-videotape presentation he or she observed prior to the experimental interview.

Emotional deception was operationalized as a response to an interview question in which the interviewee completely misrepresented the *feelings* he or she experienced while observing an audio-videotape presentation prior to the experimental interview.

SEX OF OBSERVERS

The sex of observers, male and female, served as the third independent variable.

Dependent Variable

The dependent variable was observer accuracy in judging deception. Accuracy indexes were derived from the scales observers completed during the experimental interviews. The following scale was used to obtain observers' truthfulness ratings (adapted from Miller et al., 1981):

> If "0" represents lying and "10" represents telling the truth, to what degree do you believe _____ (name of communicator being observed) is telling the truth?

Observers responded to this scale following each of five sets of stimulus questions in the experimental interview schedule. Observers were led to believe that responses to any particular question set could be totally true, partly true, or totally false, thus permitting the use of an interval level scale to measure judgmental accuracy.

Since observers' truthfulness ratings did not reveal how accurate observers were in their evaluations, truthfulness ratings were adjusted to produce accuracy indexes. To produce an accuracy index, the number reported by an observer was subtracted from ten if the communicator he or she evaluated deceived, and added to zero if the communicator he or she evaluated told the truth. The adjusted scores for each type of deception (i.e., factual and emotional) were summed and divided by two to provide an average accuracy index for each observer. This adjusted accuracy score served as the dependent measure in the present study. These procedures were adopted from Miller et al. (1981).

Developing Deception-Inducing Stimulus Tapes

Two audio-videotape (cassette) presentations were developed (Tape A and Tape B) to create a situation in which observers evaluated "factual" and "emotional" messages that were of questionable veracity. The formats of the two cassette tapes were identical. Both contained five mini-presentations of approximately seventy-seven seconds in length. The titles and brief descriptions of each presentation of Tape A and Tape B appear in Tables 15.2 and 15.3. The first two recordings on each tape presented a small number of facts on topics familiar to most individuals. These recordings were used to operationalize factual deceptions. The third and fourth recordings on each tape were designed to arouse negative emotional responses in the observers and were used to operationalize emotional deceptions. The fifth recording on each tape was on a neutral topic and was incorporated to add a degree of ambiguity to the format of the tapes. As subjects observed Stimulus Tape A or B, they completed four bipolar adjective scales for each presentation: pleasant-unpleasant, positive-negative, factual-not factual, beautiful-ugly. These scales were used to record subjects' perceptions of the tapes primarily to determine the extent to which the third and fourth presentations of each tape successfully aroused negative emotional responses.

Procedures

Subjects met at the experimental setting in groups of three — two intimates and their mutual friend. Upon arrival at the laboratory, subjects were briefed on the purpose of the experiment and asked to complete several brief questionnaires independently. Spouses completed the following scales: (1) the eighteen-item MQI, (2) Snyder's (1974) self-monitor (SM) scale, (3) an eleven-item measure of interpersonal solidarity, and (4) several demographic items. Friends completed the following measures: (1) the SM scale, (2) several demographic items, and (3) two questions concerning his or her relational history with both spouses.

Once they completed their questionnaires, spouses were directed to separate rooms, where they viewed and evaluated one of the two stimulus tapes developed for the study. At the conclusion of this observation period, spouses were briefed on their roles in the three interviews to follow. In the

Table 15.2
Stimulus Tape A

1. *The Volkswagen Commercial* (54 seconds)
   This film outlined the salient features of the 1970 Volkswagen Van. Major innovations were emphasized.

2. *The World Food Problem* (53 seconds)
   This film presented a researcher who had been working on the world food problem. Hybrid grains and vegetables were discussed.

3. *Fetal Alcohol Syndrome* (80 seconds)
   This film showed a small boy suffering from fetal alcohol syndrome. The narrator described the boy's physical features and developmental limitations.

4. *Battered Women* (84 seconds)
   This film presented interviews with men who had physically abused their wives. Included were photographs of abused women and FBI statistics.

5. *Deer Family of North America* (75 seconds)
   This film presented members of the deer family found in North America.

first two interviews, spouses rotated in their roles as interviewer and interviewee. Interviewees attempted to deceive interviewers on the content and emotional reponses aroused by the presentations contained on the stimulus tapes. Interviewers attempted to detect any deceptions. In the third interview, the friend, who until this time was waiting in an adjacent room and isolated from the experimental activities, participated as an interviewer and attempted to detect deceptions on the part of one of the spouses.

The experimental interview schedule contained two major sections. Part I consisted of three warm-up questions that were always answered truthfully by the interviewee. These questions had a dual function: (1) they acclimated subjects to their interview roles, and (2) they provided interviewers with a sample of truthful behavior in the laboratory context that he or she could use to identify possible deceptions from his or her interviewee.

Part II of the experimental interview schedule contained five sets of stimulus questions. The first two sets concerned the facts or content of the first two presentations the interviewee observed on his or her stimulus tape. The first question of each set asked, "What was the first (second) presentation about?" and the second asked, "Are you really telling me the truth?" The third, fourth, and fifth question sets addressed the interviewee's emotional reactions to the third, fourth, and fifth presentations he

Table 15.3
Stimulus Tape B

1. *The Development of the Child* (90 seconds)
   This film presented a demonstration of the sensory capabilities of neonates.

2. *Foliage Plants for Interiors* (79 seconds)
   This film illustrated the ways in which foliage plants could be used to enhance interior environments.

3. *Early Infantile Autism* (90 seconds)
   This film showed a small girl suffering from early infantile autism. The girl's father described his reactions upon learning his child was suffering from autism.

4. *Neglected Children* (90 seconds)
   This film outlined the living conditions of neglected children. A father was shown being overly physical with his daughter.

5. *Water* (76 seconds)
   Water was shown as it moved from clouds, to earth, and then to streams.

---

or she observed on the stimulus tape. The first question in each of these sets asked, "What were your feelings toward the third [fourth/fifth] presentation you observed?" and the second question asked, "Are you really telling me the truth?"

Interviewers were instructed to ask only those questions contained on the interview schedule and not to probe responses. Interviewers were told that for any of the five stimulus question sets, an interviewee may be completely truthful, completely deceptive, or somewhere in between. In reality, interviewees always lied (to both questions) about (1) one of the two "factual" presentations and (2) one of the two "emotional" presentations he or she had observed prior to the interview. Interviewees always told the truth to those questions concerning the fifth ("neutral") presentation. Lie instructions were given to interviewees through "instruction slips" developed for the study. Specifically, four sets of instruction slips were created; each set represented one of four possible combinations of lie-truth manipulations involving the first four presentations of the stimulus tapes. Fifteen copies of each type of instruction slip were placed in small, unobtrusively coded containers. Subjects selected a slip from a container. With the experimenter's comments and multiple instruction slips in each container, the subjects were led to believe their instructions could require them to always lie, always tell the truth, or to lie to one question and tell the truth to the second question about a particular presentation observed.

Prior to each execution of the experiment, two of the coded containers were selected for use by random drawings.[5]

To minimize differences that might occur as a function of subjects' varying abilities in spontaneously planning what to say during deception, each subject was provided a brief description of a film he or she *could* claim to have seen and an emotional description he or she *could* claim to have experienced (Ekman & Friesen, 1974). These descriptions were also designed to reinforce the impression that the presentation sets varied in content and emotional qualities. Subjects were always encouraged to create their own deceptions.

The interviews proceeded by having one spouse — selected randomly via flip of a coin prior to each execution of the experiment — ask the other the set of ordered questions contained on the experimental interview schedule. Once this interview was completed, spouses exchanged roles and repeated the interview exercise. At the conclusion of this interview, one spouse — again selected randomly via a flip of a coin prior to each execution of the experiment — served as the interviewee for a final interview with his or her friend.

Prior to this interview, the friend was instructed on the expectations of the interviewer role. The instructions given to the spouses were also given to the friend. In addition, the spouse selected as interviewee chose a new instruction slip and was informed that if the new instruction slip required him or her to lie, he or she had to develop *new* lies. That is, factual lies had to involve content different from that used in the first interview. Emotional lies could not be easily changed, so the instruction slip the spouse selected always had him or her lie about the emotional presentations he or she told the truth about in the first interview. These procedures were implemented to minimize the effects practice may have on the behavioral manifestation of the deceptions.

To motivate subjects to perform well at their tasks (i.e., to deceive their partners and to detect deceptions in the partners), they were reminded that the results of their individual performances would be kept in strict confidence. In addition, subjects were led to believe that the best overall deceiver and deception detector would receive an additional ten dollars.

Audio-videotape recordings were made of all interviews. After all experimental interviews were completed for each subject group, subjects were independently interviewed by the experimenter and shown videotape recordings of their interviews. During these postexperimental interviews, subjects were asked (1) to reevaluate the truthfulness of his or her interviewee's responses, irrespective of the ratings given to those responses in the initial interview, and (2) to rate the extent to which seven nonverbal behaviors affected their truthfulness evaluations. The behavioral ratings were used in other research, but are reported here to document accurately the data-gathering procedures.

At the conclusion of the post experimental interviews, subjects were brought together and briefed on the exact nature of the experiment. The experimenter answered any questions subjects had concerning the project. Finally, subjects were given five dollars and thanked for their participation.

Data Analysis

Preliminary analyses were conducted (1) to determine which subjects qualified for data analysis, and (2) to assess subjects' responses to the stimulus tapes used to operationalize emotional deceptions.

To test the theoretical hypotheses and to provide answers to the research questions guiding this study, observers' judgmental accuracy scores were submitted to a 2 (friend/intimate) × 2 (female/male) × 2 (factual lie/emotional lie) analysis of variance with repeated measures on the third variable.

RESULTS

Selecting Subjects for Analysis

While twenty-two intimate couples and their friends participated in the experiment, the data obtained from all subjects were not used to test the theoretical hypotheses and to answer the research questions. Specifically, the data obtained from one intimate couple were excluded from analysis because that couple failed to meet the marital adjustment criterion used to define intimacy. The data from all friends were analyzed; all reported they meet the criteria established for inclusion in the study.

Subjects' Evaluations of Stimulus Tapes

Subjects' evaluations of the stimulus tapes, particularly the third and fourth presentations of each tape, were of special interest because these presentations were used to operationalize emotional deception. The third and fourth presentations of each tape were designed to elicit "negative" emotional responses in observers.

Subjects' evaluations of the third and fourth presentations of Tapes A and B appear in Tables 15.4 and 15.5, respectively. In general, the two tapes functioned as designed. Presentations 3 and 4 of each tape aroused negative emotional responses in observers. However, certain qualitative and quantitative differences among the four emotional presentations were

Table 15.4
Subjects' Evaluations of Stimulus Tape A

	Unpleasant-Pleasant	Negative-Positive	Not Factual-Factual	Ugly-Beautiful
Volkswagen Commercial	5.29[a]	5.05	5.14	4.00
World Food Problem	4.76	5.29	5.52	4.29
Fetal Alcohol Syndrome	2.48	3.52	6.00	2.67
Battered Women	1.57	2.76	6.14	1.57
Deer Family of North America	6.10	5.67	5.33	5.86

a. Indexes represent mean scores computed for all subjects on 1(-) to 7(+) scales.

noted. The impact these reported phenomenological differences had on subjects' deceptions concerning these tapes and the impact these differences had on observers' evaluations of deception are open to question. Perhaps subjects found deception about "Fetal Alcohol" and "Autism" less stressful and less difficult than deception about "Battered Women" and "Neglected Children" and appeared more "normal" or "relaxed" while perpetrating deceptions concerning the former presentations than the latter presentations. If deceptions concerning certain presentations were easier to perpetrate than others, perhaps observers' abilities to detect deceptions concerning the "easier" presentations were diminished because fewer nervous mannerisms were likely to appear with deceptions concerning the less difficult topics. Additional research is needed to assess accurately the impact subtle differences in emotional experiences have on communicators' ability to perpetrate deceptions about those experiences. Analyses in the present study proceed with the qualification that results concerning those aspects of the experiment addressing emotional deception must be interpreted in light of the differences noted in this section.

Primary Results

To test the theoretical hypotheses and to answer the research questions, observers' judgmental accuracy scores were submitted to a 2 × 2 × 2 repeated measures analysis of variance for unequal cell frequencies. The Biomedical Computer Program BMD-P2V was used to accomplish the ANOVA (Dixon & Brown, 1979). Table 15.6 provides a summary of this analysis. Table 15.7 presents the means and variances for the experimental

Table 15.5
Subjects' Evaluations of Stimulus Tape B

	Unpleasant-Pleasant	Negative-Positive	Not Factual-Factual	Ugly-Beautiful
Development of the Child	5.38[a]	5.76	5.91	4.76
Foliage Plants	5.00	5.43	4.91	4.95
Early Infantile Autism	2.90	3.38	5.52	3.71
Neglected Children	1.48	1.76	5.05	1.81
Water	6.14	5.67	4.76	5.71

a. Indexes represent mean scores computed for all subjects on 1(-) to 7(+) scales.

design. The two theoretical hypotheses were not supported. The main effect for familiarity was not significant ($F = 3.31$, $df = 1/60$, $p < .074$, power = .50), nor was the interaction between deception type and familiarity significant ($F = .01$, $df = 1/60$, $p < .907$, power = .08).

The two research questions asked (1) which sex was the better detector of deception and (2) whether sex interacted with familiarity to affect judgmental accuracy. The analysis of variance identified a significant sex × relationship interaction ($F = 4.34$, $df = 1/60$, $p < .05$, eta = .28). A simple effects analysis of observers' accuracy scores averaged across the two deception types revealed female spouses were significantly more accurate in detecting deception than were male spouses ($F = 4.04$, $df = 1/60$, $p < .05$). Male and female friends were not significantly different in their accuracy scores ($F = 1.21$, $df = 1/60$, $p > .05$). The sex × relationship interaction accounted for 8 percent of the variance in observers' accuracy scores. Figure 15.1 presents a graph of the sex × relationship interaction.

A test was also conducted to determine if order of evaluation affected intimates' accuracy scores. Subjects who evaluated communicators second may have learned to monitor a set of cues that aided them in their evaluations. Table 15.8 presents the means and variances for order of evaluation. A correlated sample t test performed on these data did not reveal a significant difference ($t = .12$, $df = 40$, $p > .05$). Thus order of evaluation did not affect intimates' accuracy scores.

Supplemental Analyses

In an attempt to explain further the pattern of results observed in the study, subjects' self-monitor (SM) scores (Snyder, 1974) were analyzed.

Table 15.6
Summary of Sex × Relationship × Deception Type
ANOVA of Accuracy Scores

	SS	df	MS	F	p
Between subjects					
Sex (A)	.498	1	.498	.09	.764
Relationship (B)	18.048	1	18.048	3.31	.074
A × B	23.636	1	23.636	4.34	.042
Error between	327.055	60	5.451		
Within subjects					
Deception type (R)	6.602	1	6.602	1.07	.304
R × A	9.761	1	9.761	1.59	.213
R × B	.085	1	.085	.01	.907
R × A × B	3.942	1	3.942	.64	.426
Error within	368.886	60	6.148	.64	.426

Table 15.7
Means and Variances for Experimental Design

	Deception Type	
	Factual	Emotional
Friends		
Females		
$\bar{X}$	3.33	4.83
s^2	2.81	3.69
Males		
$\bar{X}$	5.08	4.65
s^2	3.74	3.52
Intimates		
Females		
$\bar{X}$	5.48	6.12
s^2	7.11	2.52
Males		
$\bar{X}$	4.64	4.85
s^2	7.90	10.24

The high self-monitoring individual is particularly sensitive to the expression and self-presentation of others in social situations. Geizer, Rarick, and Soldow (1977) had high and low self-monitors judge excerpts from the television show *To Tell the Truth* and found high self-monitors to be significantly more accurate than low self-monitors in detecting deceivers.

Detecting Deception

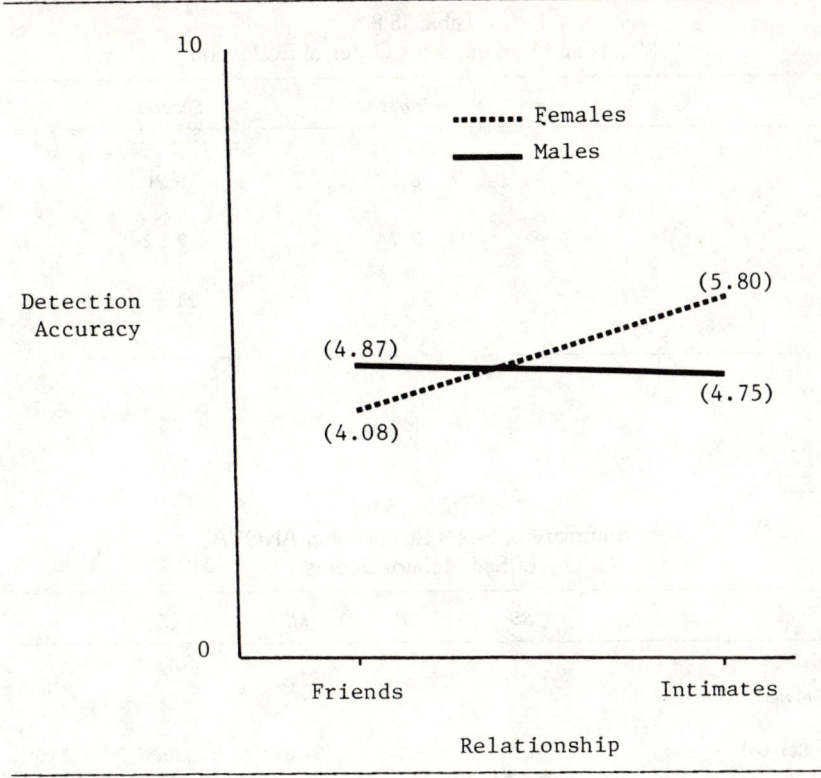

Figure 15.1. Graph of the sex × relationship interaction.

In a study by Brandt, Miller, and Hocking (1980a), subjects' SM ability accounted for approximately 18 percent of the variance in their judgmental accuracy scores. In the present study, subjects' SM scores correlated $-.126$ ($p = .162$) with factual accuracy and $-.002$ ($p = .495$) with emotional accuracy. A 2 (female/male) × 2 (friend/intimate) analysis of variance of SM scores revealed no significant differences (see Table 15.9). Table 15.10 presents descriptive statistics for subjects' self-monitoring scores. In conclusion, female spouses' accuracy in judging deception could not be accounted for in terms of their self-monitoring abilities. The SM scale had an internal reliability of .775 (Kuder-Richardson).

Analyses were also conducted to determine if observer accuracy in judging emotional deception was affected by the emotional experience about which a communicator either lied or told the truth. Recall from earlier analyses that the second emotional tape subjects observed was evaluated as more unpleasant than the first emotional tape. Table 15.11

Table 15.8
Means and Variances for Order of Evaluation

	First	Second
$\bar{X}$	5.32	5.20
s^2	3.74	2.82
n	21	21

Table 15.9
Summary of Sex × Relationship ANOVA
of Self-Monitor Scores

	SS	df	MS	F	p
Between subjects					
Sex (A)	51.677	1	51.677	2.55	.116
Relationship (B)	48.400	1	48.400	2.39	.128
A × B	47.714	1	47.714	2.35	.130
Error	1217.461	60	20.291		

presents the means and variances of observer accuracy scores for all stimulus question sets. An ANOVA (see Table 15.12) conducted on observer accuracy scores prior to averaging them into single factual and emotional indexes revealed no main effect for deception type; observers were, however, slightly more accurate judging communications concerning the more unpleasant of the two emotional presentations.

Finally, observer accuracy in judging deception during the stimulated-recall exercise of the postexperimental interviews was explored. This

Table 15.10
Means and Variances for Subjects' Self-Monitor Scores

Relationship	Females	Males
Friends		
$\bar{X}$	15.56	11.31
s^2	13.53	22.90
Intimates		
$\bar{X}$	15.33	14.76
s^2	14.73	26.90

Table 15.11
Means and Variances of Accuracy Scores Before Averaging

	Deception Type			
	Factual		Emotional	
	1	2	1	2
Friends				
Males				
$\bar{X}$	5.15	5.00	3.92	5.38
s^2	3.58	3.83	3.20	3.04
Females				
$\bar{X}$	2.11	4.56	4.44	5.22
s^2	2.62	2.83	3.57	3.38
Intimates				
Males				
$\bar{X}$	4.67	4.62	9.29	5.43
s^2	4.14	3.37	3.65	3.54
Females				
$\bar{X}$	6.00	4.95	6.09	6.14
s^2	3.85	3.58	3.02	2.85

analysis was conducted to determine if a second exposure to another's communications aids an observer in evaluating the truthfulness of the communications. Since only a small number of friends completed the stimulated-recall exercise because of time limitations encountered in the execution of the experiment, analysis was limited only to intimates. Table 15.13 presents the means and variances of intimates' judgmental accuracy scores obtained during the stimulated-recall exercise of the postexperimental interviews. A 2 (male/female) × 2 (factual/emotional)

Table 15.12
Summary of Sex × Relationship × Deception Type
ANOVA of Accuracy Scores Before Averaging

	SS	df	MS	F	p
Between subjects					
Sex (A)	.996	1	.996	.09	.769
Relationship (B)	36.099	1	36.099	3.31	.074
A × B	47.272	1	47.272	4.34	.042
Error between	654.117	60	10.902		
Within subjects					
Deception type (R)	36.491	3	12.164	.99	.398
R × A	29.618	3	9.873	.81	.493
R × B	22.347	3	7.449	.61	.611
R × A × B	331.037	3	10.346	.84	.472
Error within	2206.845	180	12.260		

ANOVA (see Table 15.14) performed on the accuracy scores revealed a significant main effect for deception type ($F = 5.42, df = 1/40, p < .025$). Intimates were significantly more accurate judging emotional deceptions than factual deceptions during the stimulated-recall exercise. No other tests were significant.

DISCUSSION

Summary of Results

This study examined the ability of male and female friends and intimates to detect deceptions concerning both factual and emotional information. The results provided support for the familiarity hypothesis. Intimates were better detectors of deception than were friends ($p < .074$). Furthermore, female spouses were observed to be significantly more accurate at detecting deception in general than were their male partners. Judgmental accuracy was not related to subjects' self-monitoring abilities. When given an opportunity to reevaluate their partners' truthfulness from videotapes, intimates were significantly more accurate judging emotional deceptions than factual deceptions.

Implications

The present study makes a significant contribution to the program of research aimed at identifying contextual factors that enhance observer

Table 15.13
Means and Variances for Analyses of Video Accuracy Scores

	Deception Type	
Sex	Factual	Emotional
Females		
$\bar{X}$	5.31	6.36
s^2	9.80	4.33
Males		
$\bar{X}$	4.74	6.05
s^2	5.95	5.95

accuracy in judging deception. Evidence was uncovered that indicates familiarity with another's communicative style and idiosyncracies may enhance judgmental accuracy. Intimates were better at detecting deception than were friends because they had a better idea of what was "normal" for their partners and could more easily perceive behavior that exceeded the boundaries of normality. The results indicate that (1) performance cues were available to aid observers in discriminating truth from deception, and (2) such cues were used by intimates to make relatively accurate attributions of truthfulness. In general, the results provide some support for the notion that relational partners develop greater sensitivity to one another's communicative behaviors as their relationship becomes more intimate (Altman & Taylor, 1973; Kelley & Thibaut, 1978; Knapp, 1978; Rosenthal et al., 1979).

While observer sex alone did not significantly affect judgmental accuracy, evidence was uncovered that indicated the interaction of sex and familiarity with another's communicative idiosyncracies significantly enhances observer accuracy in judging deception. Specifically, female spouses appear to be significantly more accurate than male spouses in judging both factual and emotional deceptions. This finding confirms the results of a number of studies that indicate women are more sensitive than men to social cues of others (Zukerman, Lipets, Koivumaki, & Rosenthal, 1975; Hall, 1978; Rosenthal et al., 1979).

Before comparing the results of the present study with the results of Miller et al.'s (1981) study, a couple of comments will be made concerning the emotional deceptions examined in this investigation. First, observers were more accurate (not significantly) judging communicator truthfulness when communicators discussed their reactions to the more "unpleasant" of two emotional presentations they had observed. Perhaps deceptions concerning extreme emotional experiences are more difficult to perpetrate

Table 15.14
Summary of Sex × Deception Type ANOVA
of Video Accuracy Scores

	SS	df	MS	F	p
Between subjects					
Sex (A)	4.07	1	4.07	.53	.469
Error between	305.23	40	7.63		
Within subjects					
Deception type (R)	29.17	1	29.17	5.42	.025
R × A	.36	1	.36	.07	.797
Error within	215.35	40	5.38		

than are deceptions concerning less emotionally arousing experiences. This difficulty may be a function of a reduced number of linguistic choices one has in describing extremes in emotion. Researchers interested in pursuing studies of the type outlined in this report should note that observer accuracy in judging emotional deception may be influenced by the type of emotional experience about which communicators are instructed to lie.

A second point worth noting about the emotional deceptions examined in this study is that during the stimulated-recall exercise intimates were significantly more accurate judging the truthfulness of one another's emotional messages than they were judging the truthfulness of factual messages. Why this pattern of results did not emerge in the experimental interviews is open to question. Obviously, the intimates saw and/or heard something the second time they viewed the messages that tipped them off to the deceptions. This finding points to a sensitivity intimates may have for their partners' emotional expressiveness and may support the notion that a person selects a mate whose experience and expression of emotion are similar to his or her own; i.e., partners may have similar thresholds for experiencing and expressing various emotions (Izard, 1977). Hence intimates may use knowledge of their own emotional experiences and expressions in validating emotional messages from their partners.

In contrasting the results of this study with the only other test of the familiarity hypothesis that used acquainted subjects (Miller et al., 1981), an interesting methodological issue emerges. Recall that Miller et al. (1981) observed a curvilinear relationship between relational history/communicative familiarity and judgmental accuracy. Friends, who had known spouses for at least one year, were significantly more accurate than were spouses and strangers in judging emotional deceptions. The degree of accuracy in judging factual deceptions did not significantly differ between spouses, friends, and strangers.

Miller et al. (1981) suggested friends were at a discovery stage in their relationship with the communicators and that this caused them to monitor behaviors more closely, possibly picking up deviations in normal communications to which spouses no longer attended as closely. However, friends in the present study knew spouses an average of 18.9 months — a relational history that would appear to place them in the "discovery" phase in their relationships with spouses, according to Miller et al.'s criteria — and they did not demonstrate a marked superiority in judging deceptions.

On the surface, the results of this study do not provide support for Miller et al.'s "monitoring attenuation" hypothesis. However, one must also examine methodological differences between the two studies to interpret the results accurately.

One major methodological difference between the present study and the experiment by Miller et al. involves the observational method by which observers evaluated communicators. Observers in the present study evaluated communicators during a live interview they conducted with the communicators. In Miller's study observers evaluated speakers through a one-way mirror as the speakers participated in an interview with a research assistant. This experimenter contends that the observational procedure in Miller et al.'s (1981) study artificially attenuated spouses' ability to detect deceptions. Friends and intimates may monitor different sets of cues to evaluate message truthfulness. Important cues not available to spouses in Miller's study include subtle aspects of gaze, temporal patterning of speech, and other paralinguistic cues.

In reality, observers in Miller's study did not evaluate their partners as they interacted with them; rather, observers evaluated their partners as they interacted with a relative stranger (the research assistant). Observers in the present study made evaluations of communicators as *they* engaged in an ongoing discussion with the communicators. Until research indicates that such a concern is unwarranted, future studies should have observers participate in the deceptive interactions they evaluate.

NOTES

1. While intimates might be sensitive to one another's communicative behavior — a skill that might aid them in detecting deception — they may not always demonstrate high levels of judgmental accuracy in their everyday interactions. Intimates may not always be motivated to detect deception in their partners. Some deception may be mutually acceptable to maintain a comfortable definition of a relationship. And if the relationship is characterized by a high degree of trust, partners may ignore cues that might otherwise create suspicion. In fact, some research suggests that social relationships may suffer when

people are too good at decoding messages they were not intended to receive (Rosenthal et al., 1979). Thus intimates may only demonstrate their detection skills in certain situations involving certain types of lies.

2. Before the chi-square test was computed, the "elementary" and "high school" categories were collapsed into one, as were the "master's" and "Ph.D." categories, to avoid cells with theoretical frequencies less than one (Dixon & Massey, 1969).

3. Individuals who had been cohabitating for at least one year and not more than three could participate as intimates, provided they met the relational adjustment criterion specified in the independent variable section.

4. This cutoff score was derived from the norms of another commonly used measure of marital adjustment in therapy research — the Locke-Wallace (1959) inventory. The Locke-Wallace inventory is a fifteen-item measure that assesses the "accommodation of a husband and wife to each other at a given time" (p. 251). Scores on this instrument may range from 2 to 158. A score of 100 (63 percent of the total score) on the Locke-Wallace inventory is typically used to discriminate "highs" from "lows" in marital adjustment (Gottman, 1979). Since eleven of the fifteen Locke-Wallace items are contained within the MQI (only those items perceived to have questionable content validity were eliminated) and since scores on the MQI could range from zero to 131, a score of 85 (65 percent of total score) was selected to "approximate" the Locke-Wallace cutoff score. For those couples classified as adjusted, males had an average MQI score of 110.57 (range = 89-129) and females had an average score of 112.29 (range = 90-120). With the cutoff score used and the average MQI scores observed, the couples selected for analysis, as a group, could be characterized as adjusted in their marriages.

5. Since spouses both perpetrated and evaluated deceptions, a major concern in the experimental procedures was instructing subjects on their roles without leaking information that might artificially aid them in their roles as interviewers. Each spouse had to realize that the stimulus tape he or she observed was different in content and emotional qualities from that observed by his or her partner. Postexperimental interviews conducted by the experimenter indicated the manipulations employed led spouses to believe their tapes were completely different in content and emotional qualities.

REFERENCES

Altman, I., & Taylor, D. A. *Social penetration: The development of interpersonal relations.* New York: Holt, Rinehart & Winston, 1973.

Bauchner, J. E., Brandt, D. R., & Miller, G. R. The truth/deception attribution: Effects of varying levels of information availability. In B. R. Ruben (Ed.), *Communication yearbook I.* New Brunswick, NJ: Transaction, 1977.

Brandt, D. R., Miller, G. R., & Hocking, J. E. Effects of self-monitoring and familiarity on deception detection. *Communication Quarterly,* 1980, *28,* 3-10. (a)

Brandt, D. R., Miller, G. R., & Hocking, J. E. The truth/deception attribution: Effects of familiarity on the ability of observers to detect deception. *Human Communication Research,* 1980, *6,* 99-108. (b)

Broverman, I. K., Vogel, S. R., Broverman, D. M., Clarkson, F. E., & Rosenkrantz, P. S. Sex-role stereotypes: A current appraisal. *Journal of Social Issues,* 1972, *29,* 59-78.

DePaulo, B. M., & Rosenthal, R. Telling lies. *Journal of Personality and Social Psychology,* 1979, *37,* 1713-1722.

Dixon, W. J., & Brown, M. B. (Eds.). *BMDP-79: Biomedical Computer Programs* (P-Series). Berkeley: University of California Press, 1979.

Dixon, W. J., & Massey, F. J. *Introduction to statistical analysis* (3rd ed.). New York: McGraw-Hill, 1969.

Ekman, P., & Friesen, W. V. Detecting deception from the body or face. *Journal of Personality and Social Psychology,* 1974, *29,* 288-298.

Fay, P. J., & Middleton, W. C. The ability to judge truth telling or lying from the voice as transmitted over a public address system. *Journal of General Psychology*, 1941, *24*, 211-215.

Geizer, R. A., Rarick, D. L., & Soldow, G. F. Deception and judgment accuracy: A study in person perception. *Personality and Social Psychological Bulletin*, 1977, *3*, 446-449.

Gottman, J. M. *Marital interaction: Experimental investigations.* New York: Academic Press, 1979.

Hall, J. A. Gender effects in decoding nonverbal cues. *Psychological Bulletin*, 1978, *85*, 845-857.

Henley, N. M. *Body politics: Power, sex, and nonverbal communication.* Englewood Cliffs, NJ: Prentice-Hall, 1977.

Hocking, J. E., Bauchner, J. E., Kaminski, E. P., & Miller, G. E. Detecting deceptive communication from verbal, visual, and paralinguistic cues. *Human Communication Research*, 1979, *6*, 33-46.

Izard, G. E. *Human emotions.* New York: Plenum Press, 1977.

Kelley, H. H., & Thibaut, J. W. *Interpersonal relations: A theory of interdependence.* New York: John Wiley, 1978.

Knapp, M. L. *Social intercourse: From greeting to goodbye.* Boston: Allyn & Bacon, 1978.

Knapp, M. L., & Comadena, M. E. Telling it like it isn't: A review of theory and research on deceptive communication. *Human Communication Research*, 1979, *5*, 270-285.

Littlepage, G., & Pineault, T. Verbal, facial and paralinguistic cues to the detection of truth and lying. *Personality and Social Psychological Bulletin*, 1978, *4*, 461-464.

Littlepage, G., & Pineault, T. Detection of deceptive factual statements from the body and the face. *Personality and Social Psychological Bulletin*, 1979, *5*, 325-328.

Locke, H., & Wallace, K. Short marital adjustment and prediction tests: Their reliability and validity. *Marriage & Family Living*, 1959, *21*, 251-259.

Maccoby, E. E., & Jacklin, C. N. *The psychology of sex differences.* Stanford, CA: Stanford University Press, 1974.

Maier, N. Sensitivity to attempts at deception in an interview situation. *Personnel Psychology*, 1966, *19*, 55-65.

Maier, N., & Janzen, J. The reliability of persons making judgments of honesty and dishonesty. *Perceptual and Motor Skills*, 1967, *25*, 141-151.

Maier, N., & Thurber, J. A. Accuracy of judgments of deception when an interview is watched, heard, and read. *Personnel Psychology*, 1968, *21*, 23-30.

Maier, R. A., & Lavrakas, P. J. Lying behavior and evaluation of lies. *Perceptual and Motor Skills*, 1976, *42*, 575-581.

Miller, G. R., Bauchner, J. E., Hocking, J. E., Fontes, N. E., Kaminski, E. P., & Brandt, D. R. ". . . and nothing but the truth": How well can observers detect deceptive testimony? In B. D. Sales (Ed.), *Perspectives in law and psychology. Volume II: The jury, judicial and trial process.* New York: Plenum Press, 1981.

Norton, R. W., & Montgomery, B. *Marital quality inventory.* Unpublished manuscript, Purdue University, 1980.

Rosenthal, R., & DePaulo, B. M. Sex differences in eavesdropping on nonverbal cues. *Journal of Personality and Social Psychology*, 1979, *37*, 273-285.

Rosenthal, R., Hall, J. A., DiMatteo, M. R., Rogers, P. L., & Archer, D. *Sensitivity to nonverbal communication: The PONS test.* Baltimore: Johns Hopkins University Press, 1979.

Shulman, G. *An experimental study of the effects of receiver sex, communicator sex, and warning on the ability of receivers to detect deception.* Unpublished master's thesis, Purdue University, 1973.

Snyder, M. The self-monitoring of expressive behavior. *Journal of Personality and Social Psychology*, 1974, *30*, 526-537.

Thackery, R. I., & Orne, M. Effects of the type of stimulus employed and the level of subject awareness on the detection of deception. *Journal of Applied Psychology*, 1968, *52*, 234-239.

Wheeless, L. R. Self-disclosure and interpersonal solidarity: Measurement, validation and relationships. *Human Communication Research,* 1976, *3,* 47-61.

Zuckerman, M., Lipets, M. S., Koivumaki, J. H., & Rosenthal, R. Encoding and decoding nonverbal cues of emotion. *Journal of Personality and Social Psychology,* 1975, *32,* 1068-1076.

16 ● The Affective Perspective-Taking Process: A Test of Turiel's Role-Taking Model

BRANT R. BURLESON
Purdue University

THE activity of role-taking figures prominently in many discussions of the communication process. For example, the role-taking process occupies a central place in the classic analyses of communication presented by Piaget (1926) and Mead (1934). More recently, the concept of role-taking has been employed to explain numerous communicative phenomena by writers from several different theoretical traditions, including those representing rules positions (Cushman & Craig, 1976), cognitive-developmental positions (Flavell, 1968), symbolic interactionist positions (Blumer, 1969), and constructivist positions (Delia, O'Keefe, & O'Keefe, in press). Although each of these theoretical viewpoints conceptualizes the nature of the role-taking process somewhat differently, all of them maintain that the possibility of coordinated social action depends on the individual's capacity to "take" (i.e., imaginatively construct) the perspective of others: One must be able to represent and anticipate the other's view of a situation in order to mesh one's line of action with that of the other (Feffer, 1970). More specifically, it has been proposed that role-taking serves a crucial function in such diverse communicative activities as effectively adapting the form and content of a message to an audience; managing the topic of a conversation; selecting the proper titles, honorifics, and forms of address; choosing the appropriate speech registers and sociolinguistic codes; and maintaining coherence in discourse (Delia & O'Keefe, 1979).

Although the process of role-taking thus occupies a central place in explanations of several significant communicative phenomena, many discussions of this process have been quite general and sometimes even

Correspondence and requests for reprints: Brant R. Burleson, Department of Communication, Purdue University, West Lafayette, IN 47907.

rather vague. This chapter reviews a detailed theoretical analysis of the role-taking process recently presented by Elliot Turiel (1977), and then reports a study designed to test two hypotheses derived from Turiel's analysis.

The process of role-taking is widely thought to occur through the application of an individual's cognitive structures to some social stimuli. Until recently, most researchers, particularly those in the cognitive-developmental research tradition, assumed that the cognitive activities of persons constituted "structured wholes"; that is, several cognitive-developmental theorists have maintained that persons' cognitive structures are so organized and so interdependent that very general modes of thought could be identified across diverse situations and over diverse domains of content (Kohlberg, 1969; Piaget, 1960; Selman, 1980). These theorists have further argued that cognitive structures and processes *evolve* as structured whole; hence, some researchers have sought to chart the emergence of very general stages of role-taking ability over the course of development (e.g., Selman, 1980). Because of the assumption regarding the "wholeness" or interdependence of cognitive activities, most researchers have adhered, at least tacitly, to two basic propositions regarding the nature of role-taking: (1) Role-taking skill represents a general cognitive capacity (proposition of generality); and (2) the role-taking process undergoes a series of qualitative transformations during the course of development (proposition of processural development).

The first of these propositions, that of generality, refers to the notion that the individual's capacity to take the role of another does not vary as a function of the *content* of the other's perspective. That is, if role-taking constitutes a general cognitive capacity, then equivalent levels of this capacity should be displayed over diverse contexts. For example, according to the proposition of generality, an individual should display at least roughly equivalent levels of role-taking ability whether asked to make inferences about another's perceptual perspective (what another is seeing) or another's affective perspective (what another is feeling).

The proposition that role-taking constitutes a general cognitive capacity has not been well supported by the empirical evidence. Most data offered in support of the generality proposition have been of a correlational nature. However, as Turiel (1978) argues, such evidence is not adequate to support the generality thesis, since positive correlations among different role-taking tasks may reflect nothing more than similarity in *rates* of development rather than some underlying conceptual interdependence among different domains of role-taking skill. Moreover, a host of recent studies have found levels of role-taking skill displayed in different domains of content (e.g., perceptual, cognitive, affective) to be either uncorrelated or only minimally correlated with one another (e.g., Kurdek, 1977; Kurdek & Rodgon, 1975; O'Connor, 1977; Rubin, 1978; see the reviews of Ford, 1979; and Shantz, 1975). Thus, role-taking skill seems to be far more domain-specific, and perhaps even task-specific, than suggested by the proposition of generality.

Several theorists (e.g., Hale & Delia, 1976; Turiel, 1977) have explained the nongenerality of role-taking skill by reference to a "partial-structure" or "domain-specific" view of cognitive development. The partial-structure hypothesis maintains that cognitive development proceeds within distinct subsystems of thought which are structurally independent of other subsystems. Because individuals' cognitive structures are differentially elaborated with respect to various domains of activity and involvement, persons may be expected to display different levels of role-taking skill that are consistent with the degree of structural elaboration in each content-based cognitive domain.

The partial-structure or domain-specific view of cognitive development also has important consequences for the proposition that the role-taking process *itself* undergoes qualitative transformations during the course of development (i.e., the proposition of processural development). Turiel (1977) forcefully distinguished between cognitive *structures* and cognitive *process*. Cognitive structures are the primary elements through which thought proceeds and is organized; cognitive processes are mental activities conducted *through* cognitive structures (for a similar analysis, see Delia, O'Keefe, & O'Keefe, in press). For example, what Kelly (1955) terms "personal constructs" can be viewed as the primary structures of thought, while mental activities like attribution, information integration, and role-taking can be viewed as cognitive processes conducted through these underlying structures.

Turiel (1977) specifically argues that what changes qualitatively with development are cognitive structures, not cognitive processes. For Turiel, the basic *nature* of the role-taking process involves an individual symbolically representing the perspective of another to him or herself, the *function* of this process being the determination of the other's internal states. These fundamental aspects of role-taking are held not to vary with development. Instead, Turiel suggests that it is more appropriate to view the cognitive structures underlying the role-taking process as the loci of developmentally related qualitative change; cognitive structures are thought to become progressively more elaborated and sophisticated over the course of development. Although qualitative changes in cognitive structures should lead to increasingly accurate role-taking as well as the manifestation of role-taking ability in increasingly complex situations, Turiel emphasizes that these changes in role-taking should be viewed as *quantitative* increases in ability, not as *qualitative* changes in the nature and function of the process itself.

Turiel's analysis of the role-taking process can neatly account for several empirical findings that are problematic when viewed from positions espousing the propositions of generality and processural development. For example, as was noted above, several studies have found individuals' levels of role-taking skill in different domains to be only weakly correlated. From Turiel's perspective this is a reasonable finding, since the cognitive structures that underlie persons' role-taking abilities are expected to be differentially elaborated in different domains of activity and involvement. Moreover, Turiel believes that his disinction between underlying cognitive structures (which change qualitatively with development) and cognitive processes (which do not change qualitatively) can account for the frequently replicated finding that young children manifest role-taking skill when confronted with a simple problem or stimulus array but fail to display role-taking skill when presented with a more complex problem or stimulus array: Older children supposedly possess more highly developed cognitive structures than do younger children which enable them to display a capacity to take others' roles in more demanding situations (see Turiel, 1977, pp. 104-106).

While this analysis of role-taking is useful in explaining otherwise anomalous findings, Turiel's model of the role-taking process has yet to be directly tested. The purpose of the present study was to test the notion that role-taking activity remains qualitatively invariant over the course of development, and that changes in role-taking ability are actually due to qualitative changes in underlying cognitive structures. Delia (1976) proposed that interpersonal constructs — dimensions for interpreting, evaluating, and anticipating the thoughts and behaviors of others — can be viewed as the basic social-cognitive structures underlying all social perception processes, particularly processes such as affective perspective-taking (the process of inferring how and why another *feels* as he does). Persons' systems of interpersonal constructs are known to undergo a number of qualitative changes during childhood and adolescence. Specifically, considerable research has shown that with advancing age, children's systems of interpersonal constructs become increasingly differentiated (i.e., contain a progressively greater number of elements) and abstract (i.e., contain elements that change from being concerned with specific physical and behavioral features of others to being concerned with psychologically centered traits, motives, and dispositions; see, for example, Barenboim, 1981; Delia, Burleson, & Kline, in press; Livesley & Bromley, 1973; Scarlett, Press, & Crockett, 1971). Following the logic of Turiel's position, it was hypothesized that while levels of both interpersonal construct system development and affective perspective-taking skill would be positively related to age, controlling for the influence of qualitative changes in interpersonal cognitive structures would have the effect of substantially diminishing the relationship between level of affective perspective-taking skill and chronological age.

A second question addressed by the present study was the extent to which different role-taking tasks tapping nominally the same domain of cognitive development would be positively intercorrelated. As noted above, many studies have found various assessments of role-taking skill in different domains to be unrelated to one another. However, if the capacity to take the affective perspective of another is chiefly a function of underlying developments in the interpersonal construct system, then different assessments of affective perspective-taking capacity should be positively intercorrelated even when controlling for the effect of age.

METHOD

Subjects

Participants in the study were ninety-six children attending a parochial school in a moderate-sized midwestern community. Six males and six females from each grade, one through eight, were randomly selected for participation in the study from class rosters supplied by school authorities. Data from one second-grade female and one sixth-grade female were lost due to equipment difficulties; thus data analyses were performed on a sample size of $N = 94$. All of the children were white and were from middle-class backgrounds.

Procedures

Each subject was individually interviewed by one of two trained experimental assistants. All interviews were tape recorded. Each interview was initiated with the subject stating his or her age and birthdate; this information was used to compute the subject's age in months. The subjects then completed an interview schedule composed of an interpersonal construct elicitation task and three affective perspective-taking tasks (several other tasks not germane to the present report were also completed during the interview session). The three affective perspective-taking tasks employed in this study were chosen because previous research had found performance on them to be positively associated with age at moderate to high levels of magnitude. The various tasks were presented in random order. Subjects' responses to all tasks were tape recorded. These recordings were transcribed and all codings were made from the transcriptions. Details concerning the nature and scoring of each task are reported below.

Interpersonal construct elicitation and assessments of construct system differentiation and abstractness. Subjects were asked to describe (1) a liked peer, (2) a disliked peer, and (3) themselves in as much detail as possible; probe questions were employed to elicit the maximum description of each figure. (See Delia, Burleson, & Kline [in press] for a more detailed description of this construct elicitation procedure.) Following the procedures of Crockett, Press, Delia, and Kenney (1974), each description was scored for the number of interpersonal constructs it contained. The total number of constructs used in describing the three figures was employed as the index of construct system differentiation (the extensive data supporting the reliability and validity of this method of assessing construct differentiation or "cognitive complexity" is reviewed by O'Keefe & Sypher, 1981). To determine coding reliability, two protocols from each of the eight grades were randomly selected and independently scored by two coders. Interrater reliability for the construct system differentiation codings, as assessed by Pearson correlation, was .96.

Each construct identified in the differentiation codings was also scored for abstractness within a four-level hierarchical system. Constructs pertaining to physical characteristics or appearance received one point; those referring to specific behaviors, abilities, and interests or those referring to social-role or demographic characteristics received two points; constructs providing a global evaluation of the other or referring to general interests and attitudes received three points; and constructs pertaining to psychological qualities such as dispositions, motivations, and traits received four points. (For a more detailed discussion of this scoring system see Burleson [1981]; the reliability and validity of this measure is documented in, e.g., Applegate & Delia [1980]; Barenboim [1981]; and Delia, Burleson, & Kline [1979].) Two independent codings of construct abstractness on the sixteen reliability assessment protocols yielded an interrater reliability coefficient of .94 as assessed by Pearson correlation. An index of mean construct system abstractness was employed in all subsequent analyses; this index was formed by dividing subjects' total abstractness scores by the number of constructs in their three impressions.

Rothenberg's Test of Social Sensitivity (RTSS). In this task, the child listened to four brief tape recordings of emotionally charged adult interactions and then was asked to identify the feelings displayed in the interactions and to explain the causes of these feelings. Children's responses were scored in terms of accuracy in identifying the projected feelings, and in terms of the psychological-centeredness of their explanations for the causes of these feelings. (For a detailed description of this task and its coding procedures, see Rothenberg [1970].) Interrater reliability for two independent codings of the sixteen reliability assessment protocols was .91 by Pearson correlation.

Social Perspectives Task (SPT). A second assessment of affective perspective-taking skill was obtained through a version of Hale and Delia's (1976) Social Perspectives Task adapted for use with children and adolescents by Delia, Burleson, and Kline (1979). Subjects were asked to think about two emotionally laden situations: (1) an actual instance in which someone the subject knew did something that hurt the subject's feelings or disappointed him or her, and (2) a hypothetical instance in which a classmate of the subject was having a party but had failed to invite the subject. For each situation the child was asked to explain why the offending party acted as he or she did and what the offending party was thinking and feeling about the situation. Children's responses to these questions were scored for the extent to which they reflected an ability to distance themselves from their own feelings about the situation and represent realistically the offending party's point of view. (Details on the administration and scoring of this task, as well as its reliability and validity, are reported in Burleson [1980].) Two independent scorings of the sixteen reliability evaluation protocols yielded an interrater reliability coefficient of .93 by Pearson correlation.

Comforting Message Rationales (CMR). A third assessment of affective perspective-taking ability was obtained by evaluating the quality of children's message choice justifications. Subjects were asked to imagine themselves confronting an emotionally distressed friend in four different situations. For each situation, subjects were instructed to state what they would say to make their friend feel better about the situation, and then were asked to explain *why* what they had said would tend to make their friend feel better. The children's rationales for their comforting message strategies were scored for the extent to which they reflected an explicit awareness of the distressed other's feelings and the choice of a strategy designed to cope with the specific other's feelings in the specific situation. (A detailed description of this task and its coding procedures are reported in Burleson [1980b].) Coding reliability, determined by having two independent judges score the sixteen reliability evaluation protocols, was .89, as assessed by Pearson correlation.

Affective Perspective-Taking Index (APT-Index). An index combining the children's performances on the three perspective-taking tasks was formed by transforming the children's scores on each task to standard scores (z-scores) and then summing these standard scores.

RESULTS

Table 16.1 reports the means, standard deviations, and intercorrelations of all variables included in the study. As expected, all of the social-cognitive indices were positively associated with age at moderate magnitudes. In particular, performance on the three affective perspective-taking tasks was associated with age (average $r = .65$), as was the index combining scores on these three tasks ($r = .71$; $r^2 = .50$). Also as expected, all of the social-cognitive assessments were positively correlated with one another, including the children's performances on the three affective perspective-taking tasks (average $r = .74$). More important, children's scores on the three perspective-taking tasks remained positively intercorrelated at moderate levels when controlling for the effect of age in months (average partialed $r = .56$). These latter results lend support to hypothesis two, which predicted that different assessments of affective perspective-taking capacity would remain substantially correlated when partialing out the influence of chronological age. It was suggested that performance on the perspective-taking tasks would remain intercorrelated when controlling for age because performance on these tasks is a function of underlying developments in interpersonal cognitive structures. This interpretation is supported by the significant age-partialed associations between construct differentiation and the three perspective-taking tasks (average partialed $r = .50$) and between construct abstractness and the three perspective-taking indices (average partialed $r = .29$).

Hierarchical regression analyses were conducted to assess the relative contributions of interpersonal construct system developments and chronological age to affective perspective-taking ability. Sex of subject (males = 0, females = 1) was always entered first into the regressions to control for the potentially confounding effects of this variable.[1] The cognitive structure indices (i.e., construct differentiation and construct abstractness) were entered at the second step of the regression analysis. These two indices were entered into the analysis simultaneously, since there was no rationale for ordering these variables with respect to one another. Age in months was entered into the regressions at the third and final step; chronological age was entered last since a central interest of the study was the proportion of variation in perspective-taking skill explained by age when controlling for qualitative developments in interpersonal cognitive structures.

Separate regression analyses were carried out for each of the three affective perspective-taking assessments as well as for the summary APT index. Very similar patterns of results were observed for all the perspective-taking measures. For the sake of brevity, then, only the analysis on the combined affective perspective-taking score (i.e., APT index) is reported here.[2]

The results of this analysis are summarized in Table 16.2. The three sets of predictors (sex, cognitive structure developments, and chronological

Table 16.1
Means, Standard Deviations, and Intercorrelations for All Variables

Variables	(2)	(3)	(4)	(5)	(6)	(7)	(8)	M	S.D.
(1) Age in months	−.04	.56	.52	.73	.58	.63	.71	126.57	27.51
(2) Sex	—	.08	.13	.12	.20	.18	.19	0.49	0.50
(3) Construct differentiation	.12	—	.35	.65	.65	.74	.75	26.00	13.93
(4) Construct abstractness	.18	.09	—	.50	.53	.55	.58	2.74	0.43
(5) RTSS	.22	.42	.20	—	.72	.73	.90	28.55	6.32
(6) SPT	.28	.48	.33	.52	—	.76	.91	9.23	2.97
(7) CMR	.26	.61	.33	.54	.62	—	.92	6.70	3.50
(8) APT Index	.30	.60	.35	.80	.86	.86	—	00.00	2.73

Note: N = 94; r ≥ .20, p < .05; r ≥ .27; p < .01. Correlations above the diagonal are zero-order; those below the diagonal are with the effect of age in months partialed out.

481

age) collectively explained 74.28 percent of the variability in APT index (adjusted $R^2 = .73$). Sex accounted for a very small and nonsignificant portion of the variance in affective perspective-taking skills (3 percent). In contrast, the indices of qualitative change in interpersonal cognitive structures jointly explained a large and highly significant portion of the variability in APT index (65 percent). Both construct system differentiation and construct abstractness significantly contributed to the prediction of affective perspective-taking ability, with construct differentiation being the more powerful predictor in this variable set. Entered last into the regression, age in months explained an additional 6 percent of the variance in APT index — a small but statistically significant increment. This latter result is particularly interesting because it indicates that chronological age *uniquely* explains only 6 percent of the variance in affective perspective-taking ability. In other words, controlling for the (negligible) influence of sex and the (quite substantial) influence of qualitative developments in interpersonal cognitive structures has the net effect of reducing the amount of variance in APT index explained by age from 50 percent to 6 percent (recall that between age and APT index, the zero-order $r = .71$; $r^2 = .50$).[3] These results lend strong support to hypothesis one, which predicted that controlling for the influence of interpersonal construct system developments would substantially diminish the relationship between level of affective perspective-taking skill and chronological age.

DISCUSSION

An underlying premise of this study has been that chronological age, like most demographic variables, is not itself a useful explanatory construct. At best, age is a summary index of other, more theoretically interesting variables (e.g., degree of social experience, qualitative developments in cognitive structures, level of intelligence, and extent of norm internalization). Consequently, one important goal of developmental research should be to identify those theoretically relevant underlying variables summarized by chronological age. The present study represents an effort to realize this goal in attempting to explain the age-related variation in one communicatively relevant process — affective perspective-taking — in more theoretically meaningful terms.

The present investigation found that chronological age, when considered in isolation, accounted for 50 percent of the variance in affective perspective-taking skills; however, when controlling for the effect of changes in cognitive structures, age uniquely explained only 6 percent of the variance in these skills. Thus, 88 percent of the age-related variation in

Table 16.2
Summary of Hierarchical Regression Analysis on APT Index

Variable	Step Entered	Beta at Step of Entry	R	R^2	R^2 Change	df	F	p
Sex	1	.19	.19	.03	.03	1,92	3.32	n.s.
Construct differentiation	2	.62*			#			
Construct abstractness	2	.35*	.83	.68	.65#	3,90	63.97	.001
Age in months	3	.34*	.86	.74	.06#	4,89	64.27	.001

Note: N = 91. (*) indicates predictor variables significantly contributing to the prediction of APT Index with p < .05. (#) indicates that a predictor variable or variable set accounts for a significant (p < .05) increase in the explained criterion variance.

483

affective perspective-taking skills can be explained by reference to qualitative changes in interpersonal cognitive structures.

These results strongly support Turiel's rejection of the proposition of processural development. That is, if the perspective-taking process underwent age-related change *not* a function of qualitative developments in underlying cognitive structures, then a substantial portion of the age-related variability in perspective-taking skills would remain intact when controlling for qualitative changes in these structures. But since the great proportion of age-related variability in affective perspective-taking can be more parsimoniously explained as a function of changes in underlying cognitive structures, there is little reason for believing that the affective perspective-taking process *itself* changes qualitatively with development. Other results of the present study also bear on Turiel's view of the perspective-taking process. For example, when controlling for the effect of sex, the two indices of interpersonal construct system development were found to explain 65 percent of the variability in APT index. Moreover, all of the perspective-taking assessments remained significantly correlated with both indices of construct system development when controlling for the influence of chronological age, and the two construct system predictors continued to account collectively for substantial variation in the perspective-taking assessments when controlling for *both* the effects of sex and age (for APT index, the second-order partial $R = .66$; $R^2 = .43$). These findings support Turiel's notion that it is qualitative developments in underlying cognitive structures that are responsible for variation in perspective-taking abilities. Turiel's position on this issue is further bolstered by the findings of other studies indicating that individual differences in affective perspective-taking abilities among persons of the same age group are moderately related to individual differences in indices of interpersonal construct system development (e.g., Hale & Delia, 1976).

The present findings also lend support to Turiel's domain-specific view of cognitive development. Considerable previous research has found that dimensions of cognitive development such as construct differentiation are not general traits (e.g., Burleson, Applegate, & Neuwirth, 1981; also see the review of O'Keefe & Sypher, 1981). That is, a given individual's constructs may be highly differentiated and abstract in one domain of activity and involvement, but quite undifferentiated and concrete in a different domain. Similarly, considerable research indicates that perspective-taking skill is not a highly general ability (see the review by Ford, 1979). In the present study, the three independent assessments of affective perspective-taking skill were found to remain moderately correlated when the effect of age was partialed out. Since each of the perspective-taking tasks had the children do rather different things, these moderate associations are probably not due to shared method variance.

Instead, the moderate-level, age-partialed associations among the perspective-taking assessments suggest that there is a domain of cognitive ability legitimately thought of as "affective perspective-taking skill." Moreoever, the age-partialed significant positive associations between each of the affective perspective-taking assessments and each index of interpersonal construct system development suggest that the varied types of affective perspective-taking tapped in the present study have a common base. That is, individual differences in the domain of interpersonal construct system development consistently underlie variation in the domain of affective perspective-taking skills, regardless of the specific manner in which these skills are manifested.

Since the assessments of construct system development and affective perspective-taking utilized in this study required extensive verbalization by the children, it might be thought that the positive relationships observed among these variables are due simply to the general verbal abilities of the children. However, several previous studies have found assessments of interpersonal construct differentiation and construct abstractness uncorrelated with both general verbal and intellectual abilities (e.g., Applegate & Delia, 1980; Burleson et al., 1981; Sypher & Applegate, in press; also see the review by O'Keefe & Sypher, 1981). Similarly, the indices of affective perspective-taking ability employed in this study have been found either uncorrelated or only weakly correlated with assessments of general intellectual and verbal skills (e.g., Delia et al., 1979; Rothenberg, 1970; Rubin, 1978). Thus it is unlikely that the relationships between construct system developments and perspective-taking skills observed in this study are due to some unassessed variable such as intelligence or verbal ability.

Although the predictors included here explained a large proportion of the variance in affective perspective-taking skills, over one-fourth of the variance remained unexplained. Thus it is likely that aspects of cognition other than qualitative developments in *interpersonal* cognitive structures play an important role in the affective perspective-taking process. For example, all of the affective perspective-taking tasks employed in this study required the children to engage in a recursive thinking process (see Devries, 1970; Miller, Kessel, & Flavell, 1970). Perhaps qualitative changes in the formal logical structures underlying the recursive thinking process can account for some of the unexplained variation in affective perspective-taking skills. Future research should analyze more specifically the component skills involved in the affective perspective-taking process and attempt to explain more completely its nature.

NOTES

1. Several researchers have reported small but statistically significant associations between sex and indices of social-cognitive development (e.g., Delia, Burleson, & Kline,

in press; Little, 1968). Where such relationships have been found, they have consistently been due to females outperforming males.

2. Separate analyses for each assessment of affective perspective-taking are available from the author on request.

3. It might be argued that the results of the hierarchical regression analysis reported above are somewhat misleading, since, as age was forced into the regression equation last, any variability in APT index jointly due to age and qualitative developments in cognitive structures was attributed to the cognitive variables. Since the cognitive structure variables are moderately correlated with age, this argument has some appeal; however, it ignores several important factors. First, a chief interest of this study was determining the portion of variability in perspective-taking skills accounted for by age when the effects of structural developments are partialed out; thus, the ordering of the independent variables was mandated by the focus of the study. Second, a series of hierarchical regression analyses *were* conducted in which the cognitive structure variables were entered subsequent to age; these analyses revealed that the cognitive structure variables, although entered into the regression equation last, still uniquely accounted for better than three times the amount of variation in affective perspective-taking skills than that uniquely explained by age (a detailed report of these analyses is available from the author on request). Finally, it is important to note that there is no mathematically acceptable way to partition the criterion variance in multiple regression so as to represent the "joint" or "common" effects of two or more independent variables. Although McPhee and Seibold (1979) suggest several procedures for determining joint or common effects, these procedures are regarded as illegitimate by most statisticians. For example, McPhee and Seibold recommend a formula given by Cohen and Cohen (1975, eq. 3.5.4) as their second method of deriving unique and common effects in multiple regression, but Cohen and Cohen (1975, p. 95) emphatically state that this very formula "cannot serve as a variance partitioning scheme." The merit of Cohen and Cohen's position is demonstrated by McPhee and Seibold's application of this formula (1979, p. 376) — an application yielding conceptually meaningless "negative variances." Cohen and Cohen strongly emphasize that the hierarchical model employed in the present study "is the *only* basis on which variance partitioning can proceed with correlated independent variables" (p. 98, italics in original). The hierarchical procedure necessarily eliminates the existence of joint or common effects; thus the order in which the independent variables are entered into the regression is crucial. Such ordering is always a conceptual matter, dependent on logical considerations and the particular research questions being addressed.

REFERENCES

Applegate, J. L. & Delia, J. G. Person-centered speech, psychological development, and the contexts of language usage. In R. St. Clair & H. Giles (Eds.), *The social and psychological contexts of language*. Hillsdale, NJ: Lawrence Erlbaum, 1980.

Barenboim, C. The development of person perception in childhood and adolescence: From behavioral comparisons to psychological constructs to psychological comparisons. *Child Development*, 1981, *52*, 129-144.

Blumer, H. *Symbolic interactionism: Perspective and method.* Englewood Cliffs, NJ: Prentice-Hall, 1969.

Burleson, B. R. *Task administration and coding procedures for the Social Perspectives Task (children's and adolescents' version).* Mimeo, Department of Rhetoric and Communication, State University of New York at Albany, 1980. (a)

Burleson, B. R. The development of interpersonal reasoning: An analysis of message strategy justifications. *Journal of the American Forensic Association*, 1980, *16*, 102-110. (b)

Burleson, B. R. *The influence of age, construct system developments, and affective perspective-taking skills on the development of comforting message strategies: A hierar-

chical regression analysis. Paper presented at the annual convention of the International Communication Association, 1981.

Burleson, B. R., Applegate, J. L., & Neuwirth, C. M. Is cognitive complexity loquacity? A reply to Powers, Jordan, and Street. *Human Communication Research*, 1981, 7, 212-225.

Cohen, J., & Cohen, P. *Applied multiple regression/correlation analysis for the behavioral sciences*. Hillsdale, NJ: Lawrence Erlbaum, 1975.

Crockett, W. H., Press, A. N., Delia, J. G., & Kenney, C. T. *The structural analysis of the organization of written impressions*. Mimeo, Department of Psychology, University of Kansas, 1974.

Cushman, D. P., & Craig, R. T. Communication systems: interpersonal implications. In G. R. Miller (Ed.), *Explorations in interpersonal communication*. Beverly Hills, CA: Sage, 1976.

Delia, J. G. A constructivist analysis of the concept of credibility. *Quarterly Journal of Speech*, 1976, 62, 361-375.

Delia, J. G., Burleson, B. R., & Kline, S. L. *Person-centered parental communication and the development of social-cognitive and communicative abilities: A preliminary longitudinal analysis*. Paper presented at the annual convention of the Central States Speech Association, 1979.

Delia, J. G., Burleson, B. R., & Kline, S. L. Developmental changes in children's and adolescents' interpersonal impressions. *Journal of Genetic Psychology*, in press.

Delia, J. G., & O'Keefe, B. J. Constructivism: The development of communication. In E. Wartella (Ed.), *Children communicating*. Beverly Hills, CA: Sage, 1979.

Delia, J. G., O'Keefe, B. J., & O'Keefe, D. J. The constructivist approach to communication. In F. E. X. Dance (Ed.), *Comparative theories of human communication*. New York: Harper & Row, in press.

Devries, R. The development of role-taking as reflected by behavior of bright, average, and retarded children in a social guessing game. *Child Development*, 1970, 41, 759-770.

Feffer, M. Developmental analysis of interpersonal behavior. *Psychological Review*, 1970, 77, 197-214.

Flavell, J. H. *The development of role-taking and communication skills in children*. New York: John Wiley, 1968.

Ford, M. E. The construct validity of egocentrism. *Psychological Bulletin*, 1979, 86, 1169-1188.

Hale, C. L., & Delia, J. G. Cognitive complexity and social perspective-taking. *Communication Monographs*, 1976, 43, 195-203.

Kelly, G. A. *The psychology of personal constructs* (2 vols.). New York: W. W. Norton, 1955.

Kohlberg, L. Stage and sequence: The cognitive-developmental approach to socialization. In D. A. Goslin (Ed.), *Handbook of socialization theory and research*. Chicago: Rand McNally, 1969.

Kurdek, L. A. Convergent validation of perspective-taking: A one-year follow-up. *Developmental Psychology*, 1977, 13, 177-173.

Kurdek, L. A., & Rodgon, M. M. Perceptual, cognitive, and affective perspective-taking in kindergarten through sixth-grade children. *Developmental Psychology*, 1975, 11, 643-650.

Little, B. R. Factors affecting the use of psychological vs. nonpsychological constructs on the Rep Test. *Bulletin of the British Psychological Society*, 1968, 21, 34.

Livesley, W. J., & Bromley, D. B. *Person perception in childhood and adolescence*. London: John Wiley, 1973.

McPhee, R. D., & Seibold, D. R. Rationale, procedures, and application for decomposition of explained variance in multiple regression analyses. *Communication Research*, 1979, 6, 345-384.

Mead, G. H. *Mind, self, and society: From the standpoint of a social behaviorist*. Chicago: University of Chicago Press, 1934.

Miller, P. H., Kessel, F. S., & Flavell, J. H. Thinking about people thinking about people thinking about . . .: A study of social cognitive development. *Child Development*, 1970, 41, 613-623.

O'Connor, M. The relationship of spatial and conceptual role-taking in young children. *Journal of Genetic Psychology,* 1977, *131,* 319-320.

O'Keefe, D. J., & Sypher, H. E. Cognitive complexity measures and the relationship of cognitive complexity to communication. *Human Communication Research,* 1981, *8,* 72-92.

Piaget, J. *The language and thought of the child* (M. Gabrin. trans.). London: Routledge & Kegan Paul, 1926.

Piaget, J. The general problem of the psychobiological development of the child. In J. M. Tanner & B. Inhelder (Eds.), *Discussions on child development: Proceedings of the World Health Organization study group on the psychobiological development of the child* (Vol. 4). New York: International Universities Press, 1960.

Rothenberg, B. B. Children's social sensitivity and the relationship to interpersonal competence, intrapersonal comfort, and intellectual level. *Developmental Psychology,* 1970, *2,* 335-350.

Rubin, K. H. Role-taking in childhood: Some methodological considerations. *Child Development,* 1978, *49,* 428-433.

Scarlett, H. H., Press, A. N., & Crockett, W. H. Children's descriptions of peers: A Wernerian developmental analysis. *Child Development,* 1971, *42,* 439-453.

Selman, R. L. *The growth of interpersonal understanding: Developmental and clinical analyses.* New York: Academic Press, 1980.

Shantz, C. U. The development of social cognition. In E. M. Hetherington (Ed.), *Review of child development research* (Vol. 5). Chicago: University of Chicago Press, 1975.

Sypher, H. E., & Applegate, J. L. Cognitive differentiation and verbal intelligence: Clarifying relationships. *Educational and Psychological Measurement,* in press.

Turiel, E. Distinct conceptual and developmental domains: Social convention and morality. In C. B. Keasey (Ed.), *Nebraska symposium on motivation, 1977: Social-cognitive development.* Lincoln: University of Nebraska Press, 1977.

Turiel E. Social regulations and domains of social concepts. In W. Damon (Ed.), *New directions for child development: Social cognition.* San Francisco: Jossey-Bass, 1978.

17 • Marital Interaction: Perceptions and Behavioral Implications of Control

DONAVAN EMERY
Concordia College—Moorhead

ONE assumption of many researchers is that communication influences the evolution of our relationships with others and is simultaneously influenced by the definitions we attribute to these relationships. As Bateson (1936) has cogently argued, communication via language is the primary vehicle through which our relationships are defined. Systems theorists have long understood the importance of viewing the whole system in a relationship, particularly the interdependence of the verbal messages we exchange. Rapaport (1968) and Lewin (1968), for example, both recognized that verbal language must be characterized in the way it works — namely, as interdependent linked messages.

Communication researchers interested in small groups and marital and family relationships have recently attempted to explain communication phenomena in similar terms. An interactional perspective, developed from the seminal work of Bateson (1936) and Watzlawick, Beavin, and Jackson (1967), has attempted to characterize those communicative phenomena which occur in everyday communication. Although researchers do not agree entirely, it is clear that underlying patterns of behavior embedded in the verbal messages characterize enduring relationships. Pearce and Conklin (1979) have recently suggested that not only are conversations coherent sequences of messages with an underlying structure, but that meaning in the conversation can best be understood when contextualized or framed by an episode.

One such episode thought to be particularly useful to explain how individuals define their relationships occurs when they are in conflict. The general area of conflict and relational disagreement has always been

Correspondence and requests for reprints: Donavan Emery, Department of Speech Communication, Concordia College, Moorhead, MN 56560.

central to relationship and family research and continues to be on the upswing (Barry, 1970). Three research strategies predominate the literature on conflict. One has been to correlate a variety of variables with the production of conflict. The most widely studied variable has been power (see, for example, Rollins & Bahr, 1976; Olson & Cromwell, 1975; Kolb & Straus, 1974; Olson & Rabunsky, 1972).

Nevertheless, power remains a confusing variable with little consensus on how it should be conceptualized and operationalized (Safilios-Rothschild, 1970). Other studies (e.g., Renne, 1970) found that variables such as race, socioeconomic status, physical health, and general level of happiness all influence conflict and disagreement. Numerous authors have identified relationships between conflict and sex, emotional balance, personality characteristics, communication skills, and relationship type (Barry, 1970; Fitzpatrick & Best, 1979). In short, this approach has generated a confusing maze of relationships with little hope for clarity.

A second research approach has been to note the effects of conflict on relationships. The most basic conclusion is that conflict can be constructive or destructive. It can promote open exchanges which facilitate problem solving and relational cohesion (Spanier, Lewis & Cole, 1975), or it can foster anxiety and dissatisfaction (Kolb & Straus, 1974). The third approach emphasizes the process of communication in the dyad. This is the perspective represented in this study; it recognizes the distinction between power and control patterns which develop in interaction (Bott, 1957; Rogers-Millar & Millar, 1979). The research strategy is to identify and describe how dyad members exchange relational control messages.

Observing language patterns of interaction during conflict is the primary purpose of this study. A parallel purpose, which should provide a fuller explication of conflict, is to compare individual predispositions toward control in a conflict situation in terms of internal or external locus of control.

Even a perusal of personality and social psychological journals reveals a high level of research interest in the predictive validity of locus of control. The locus of control construct stems from social learning theory and the work of Rotter (1966; Rotter, Chance, & Phares, 1972). According to social learning theory, people form relatively stable beliefs about the sources of the reinforcements they receive. These beliefs develop over time and are learned through social interaction. Some individuals associate the acquisition of reinforcements primarily with their own actions. These individuals develop generalized expectancies that reinforcements are personally controlled. Rotter (1966) argues that such individuals have an "internal" locus of control. Other individuals differ with respect to expectancies about the control to reinforcement. These individuals associate reinforcement with external events and the behavior of others. Reinforcements are believed to be controlled by external sources. These individuals, Rotter argues, have an "external" locus of control: They generally expect reinforcements to occur by virtue of chance, luck, fate, and the behavior of other people.

One reason for the increase in locus of control research in recent years is that the construct is versatile as a predictor. Two thorough reviews of this research have recently been published in book form (Phares, 1976; Lefcourt, 1976). Unfortunately, a great deal of research attempting to link locus of control to observable behavior does so in only a limited sense. That is, a typical research approach has been to examine the dependent measures. Few studies have investigated locus of control as a predictor of observable behaviors other than that of test-taking (see Phares, 1976; Lefcourt, 1976).

Beyond these attempts in the social psychological literature, an emerging theoretical and research perspective in the field of communication suggests a potentially significant theoretical *and observable* link between locus of control and behavior. This perspective, as suggested by Bateson (1936) and Watzlawick et al. (1967), has sought to identify the patterns of interaction in various types of relationships. More specifically, theoretical and research efforts by Sluczki and Beavin (1965), Rogers and Farace (1976), and others have attempted to explicate how verbal messages act to define the nature of the interaction. In support of this notion, Bateson has argued that every communication between people has a report and command dimension. One communicative consequence of their theoretical relationship between report and command suggests that the relational aspect of the verbal message (command) provides the information to interpret the content aspect (report) of the message.

As one individual offers a control statement to define the relationship (dominant, submissive, or equal) the second individual must accept, reject, or modify the definition offered. Further, as these differential attempts stabilize over time, larger relational patterns emerge. Out of this perspective, three predominant patterns have characterized this interaction research: complementary, symmetrical, and transitive patterns of interaction (Ellis, 1976; Rogers-Millar & Millar, 1979).

Briefly, complementary relationships are characterized by transactions where paired messages are dissimilar in control direction. Typically, one person attempts to structure (dominant) the relationship and the other accepts the control bid (submissive). Symmetrical relationships are inferred from paired messages with the same control type. Competitive symmetry, for example, typifies the struggle over which interactants will control the dominant position in the definition of the relationship. In contrast, submissive symmetry is characterized by each individual deferring control to the other, while equivalent symmetry indicates an attempt to define the relationship as equal. The third relational pattern, transitivity, also characterizes structure in the interaction. As the name implies, these relational patterns indicate a relationship with no clear definition. The verbal behavior described by these patterns overall can be systematically observed using one of several coding schemes designed to tap these relationship control patterns (Ellis, 1976; Rogers & Farace, 1976).

The conceptual link that needs to be made is that there is a relationship between individuals' locus of control and control as defined in their relationships. That is, locus of control should have observable pragmatic consequences, and a test would constitute a construct validation of considerable significance.

It seems theoretically reasonable to speculate that an individual expecting internal control and one expecting external control should differ with respect to the amount of control each typically tries to exert verbally in their relationship with another person. The expected pattern of relational control can be cast in terms of complementary and symmetrical patterns. The defining characteristics of internality and externality suggests that in a dyadic social influence situation, the pattern of interaction between an internal and an external should be complementary. The internal believes in and expects external control. The expectation and beliefs of each individual complement those of the other. If these complementary expectations are manifested through interaction, then we would expect that an internal will attempt to establish and maintain relational control in a social influence situation and that his or her external counterpart will complement and facilitate such attempts by deferring to them.

A similar argument can be made for the pattern of interaction between two internals, such that the interaction should be symmetrical. One might expect, for example, that both individuals would attempt to structure their interaction, and the result would be a prevalence of competitive symmetry. Each individual is confident in his or her ability to influence events and other people personally. Therefore, the verbal interaction of these individuals should be characterized by recurring patterns in which one person's definition of the relationship precipitates a similar definition on the part of the other person.

Sameness in locus of control would not necessarily predict symmetrical interaction patterns when two individuals disagree with each other and expect external control. In such a situation, we would expect an unclear or transitive structure of interaction. Each individual theoretically has generalized doubts about his or her ability to influence events and other people. Yet if each believes differences in opinion must be resolved through influencing the other, then interaction between the two should be characterized by both attempts to control and a willingness to defer. Attempts to control should stem from each person's interest in resolving differences of opinion to his or her own satisfaction. Therefore each external individual should periodically check his or her dominance in the relationship. However, the dominant position is one which theoretically the external does not typically occupy across relationships. The typical expectation of such a person in an influence situation is that the other person controls reinforcement. Therefore, with each external expecting the other person to control, each should periodically express a willingness to let the counterpart control the relationship. Thus no clear symmetrical or complementary structure of interaction should occur between two externals. The structure of the interaction should be highly transitive by virtue of the competing demands of defending one's own position versus the generalized expectations that the other person controls reinforcements. This study, then, is an attempt to describe the relationship between locus of control and relational control to explicate the nature of an individual's locus and its pragmatic consequences. The following exploratory and descriptive research questions were formulated.

1. What types of relational control patterns characterize the dyadic communication of internals interacting with externals? (The expectation was that the interaction patterns would be characterized by complementarity.)
2. What types of relational control patterns characterize the dyadic communication of internals interacting with internals? (The expectation was that the interaction would be characterized by competitive symmetry.)
3. What types of relational control patterns characterize the dyadic communication of externals' interaction with other externals? (The expectation was that the interaction would be characterized by transitive patterns.)

METHODS

Sample

The Rotter Internal-External Locus of Control Scale (Rotter, 1966) was initially administered to fifty-two pairs of married couples enrolled in various communication classes at a large midwestern university. The mean score on this test was 9.47. The split-half reliability (.88) and the Kuder-Richardson 20 (.81) were somewhat higher than those obtained elsewhere (see Rotter, 1966; Lefcourt, 1976; Emery, 1981). The criterion for selection of internals and externals was based on locus of control scores falling approximately one standard deviation above and below the mean. Thus subjects 6 or less were classified as internal and those scoring 14 or more were classified as external. Couples were retained in the study on this basis and were assigned to dyads such that ten dyads were composed of an internal and an external, ten dyads were composed of two internals, and ten dyads were composed of two externals.

Data Collection and Procedure

In order to stimulate interaction between members of each dyad, the subjects were asked to complete the Revealed Differences Questionnaire developed by Strodtbeck (1951). After the subjects completed this questionnaire, each dyad was requested, through standardized instruction, to discuss and "work through" those issues on the revealed differences questionnaire on which they disagreed. These instructions were provided by trained interviewers who were present during the ensuing discussion. The interviewers followed standardized guidelines to be unobtrusive and to intervene in the discussion *only as a facilitator* and not as a participant. The interaction between dyadic members was audiotaped for coding purposes.

Coding

The audiotaped interaction was submitted to interaction analysis using a coding scheme developed by Ellis (1976). This coding scheme consisted of mutually exclusive and exhaustive categories to code verbal interaction. The coding scheme is an extension of the system used by Rogers and Farace (1972). Three dimensions were considered in the coding scheme: speaker identification, grammatical format, and relation to previous comment (response style). The interaction was coded into either control bids (↑), which were attempts to dominate or structure the relationship; deference (↓), which symbolized submissiveness to another; or equivalence (→), which was a bid for mutual identification. Typically, the scheme also codes intensity. This research, however, used the three-code classification, since intensity did not discriminate.

Data Analysis

The observational data were subjected to lag sequential analysis. Briefly, the basic unit of the lag sequential analysis is the act. An act is defined as one instance of verbal behavior regardless of length. An act terminates when it is interrupted by another individual's act or when category functions are crossed. Nearly all units of the analysis comprised uninterrupted comments of a single member.

The interact, each contiguous pair of acts, also served as a unit of analysis. For example, individual A emits an act which is followed by an act from individual B. A's act then becomes the antecedent for B's subsequent act. Both A's antecedent act and B's subsequent act comprise a single interact matrix then displaying the categorized units as both rows- (antecedent acts) and columns- (subsequent acts) generated interact frequencies. The frequency data from each matrix were then submitted to a transition probability analysis explained in detail in Attneave (1959). Initially, the frequency analysis of single acts results in state possibilities that report the simple probability occurring within some parameter of behavior. For the purposes of this study each interaction category was defined as one of the states. The model then generated transition probabilities, or the probability of entering a specific state given the last state occupied. The three-state model in this research produced a 3 × 3 interact matrix containing nine possible one-step transitions. The transition matrices traced the transition probabilities from state to state over a period of time. The likelihood ratio compared specific states in each matrix to the composite matrix. We have, then, (1) a single statement about the significance of each group matrix and (2) a test for the specific sources of variance generated by individual states. The statistic was distributed as a likelihood ratio.

After describing the transitions among the interactions and comparing them to the group interaction, it was important to test whether or not a specific transition (matrix cell) occurred more often than one would expect by chance. If the interaction states were independent, then the probability of a one-up (↑) following a one-up (↑ , or ↑ ↑), for example, would be no different from the probability of a ↑ anywhere. The difference between observed and predicted values were determined with the binomial Z test (Bakeman & Dabbs, 1976):

$$Z = (x - NP) / N\sqrt{NPQ}$$

This tested whether or not the probability of one act following another was greater than the probability of the act anywhere. The x = the joint frequencies of the events in question. NP was the predicted joint frequency (N = frequency of one event; P = probability of the other). NPQ was the variance of the difference between predicted and observed ($Q = 1 - NP$). Since the data were problematic with respect to statistical significance, the Z score was treated as an index with a p value assigned to it. A Z score of 2.0 was minimal before a sequence was considered acceptable.

The lag sequential analysis mapped the characteristic patterns to suggest a flow of behavior implicit in the interaction. The lag implied the number of steps a particular behavior is removed from a criterion behavior. A max lag of five was the largest sequential step of interest to be investigated.

RESULTS

This section reports the results of the study as they relate to the specific research questions. These are concerned with the descriptive nature of the types of control patterns characteristic of each group. A measure of significant differences and the amount of certainty in each group of dyads is reported to indicate the appropriateness of analyzing the data using lag sequential analyses. The results for each group are then reported to indicate predominant structural patterns.

Reliability

The Scott's pi test for reliability on a sample of the interaction yielded high reliability. The average reliability among all coders was .91. This surpassed levels of reliability as reported in similar data in earlier studies. In addition, disagreements in coding were satisfied. An important measure of structure overall was the distribution of data.

In order to account for this distribution, the likelihood statistic, a conservative test for homogeneity was used to compute differences within each group. The obtained likelihood ratios for each group included external-external (L. R. = 159.09, 60 df, $p < .01$); external-internal (L. R. = 129.85, 60 df, $p < .01$); internal-internal (L. R. = 134.79, 60 df, $p < .01$). These indicate that significant differences occurred for each group.

Stereotypy

Beyond the notion of significant structural differences in the data, it is important to indicate the amount of structure ranging from zero to one (redundancy). Stereotypy initially measured the amount of structure in the communication pattern for the dyads in each group. Essentially, stereotypy as a measure of uncertainty indicated the amount of redundancy or constraint that existed in the group of dyads at a particular level of complexity. In this study, zero-order (act), first-order (interact), and second-order (double interact) stereotypy are graphed in Figure 17.1.

These results indicate that each type of dyad gains in predictable structure from the act to the interact level and slightly less predictable structure is gained in moving to the double interact. In general, this analysis provides the evidence that the appropriate level of analysis is the interact. This conclusion is consistent with past research (Altmann, 1965).

Lag Sequential Analysis

INTERNAL-EXTERNAL DYADS

The lag sequential analysis of data from the internal-external dyads is depicted in Figure 17.2. A max lag of five is reported in Z scores for each

Marital Interaction 497

```
1.0

 .8

 .6

 .4                                    SECOND-ORDER
                                       FIRST-ORDER

 .2
                                       ZERO-ORDER
  0
     INTERNAL-    INTERNAL-   EXTERNAL-
     INTERNAL     EXTERNAL    EXTERNAL
```

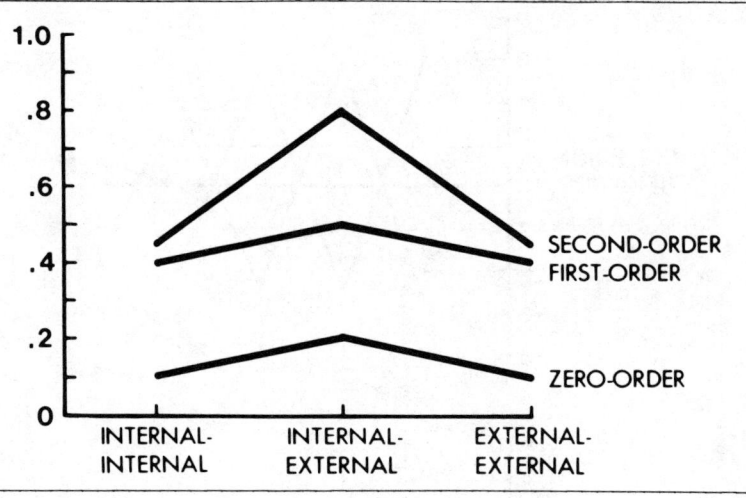

Figure 17.1. Stereotypy.

criterion. Given a one-up (↑) as the criterion, the following sequence structured the interaction: ↓, ↑, ↓, ↑, ↓. That is, the predominant pattern of interaction structured as complementarity. Inspection of the coded interaction between internals and externals indicated that the most characteristic utterance of internals is that of dominance (↑) and that the likely relational response of externals is deference (↓).

A similar structure characterized the interaction with a one-down (↓) as the criterion. In this case, the structure of the interaction is (↓) ↑, ↓, ↑, ↓, ↑. Complementarity also characterized the interaction when a one across (→) is the criterion, such that a ↑→, ↓, ↑, ↓, ↓ sequence of relational codes followed. Overall, these results indicate reciprocal complementarity. When an internal attempts to impose structure (↑), the external cooperates by deferring (↓). This precipitates a subsequent one-up (↑) and the completion of the cycle (↑ ↓ ↑). This sequence chained predictably to five lags.

INTERNAL-INTERNAL DYADS

The second group of dyads, internal-internal, was also characterized by a particular structure in the interaction. Figure 17.3 portrays the lag sequential data for the internal dyads. When a one-up (↑) is the criterion, for example, the most likely subsequent behavior at the interact level (lag 1) is another one-up (↑), indicating competitive symmetry. The most probable behavior at lags 2, 4, and 5 are ↓, ↓, and →, respectively.

Submissive symmetry characterizes the interaction of internal dyads at lag 1 when a one-down (↓) is the criterion, resulting in a (↓) followed by

498 INTERPERSONAL COMMUNICATION

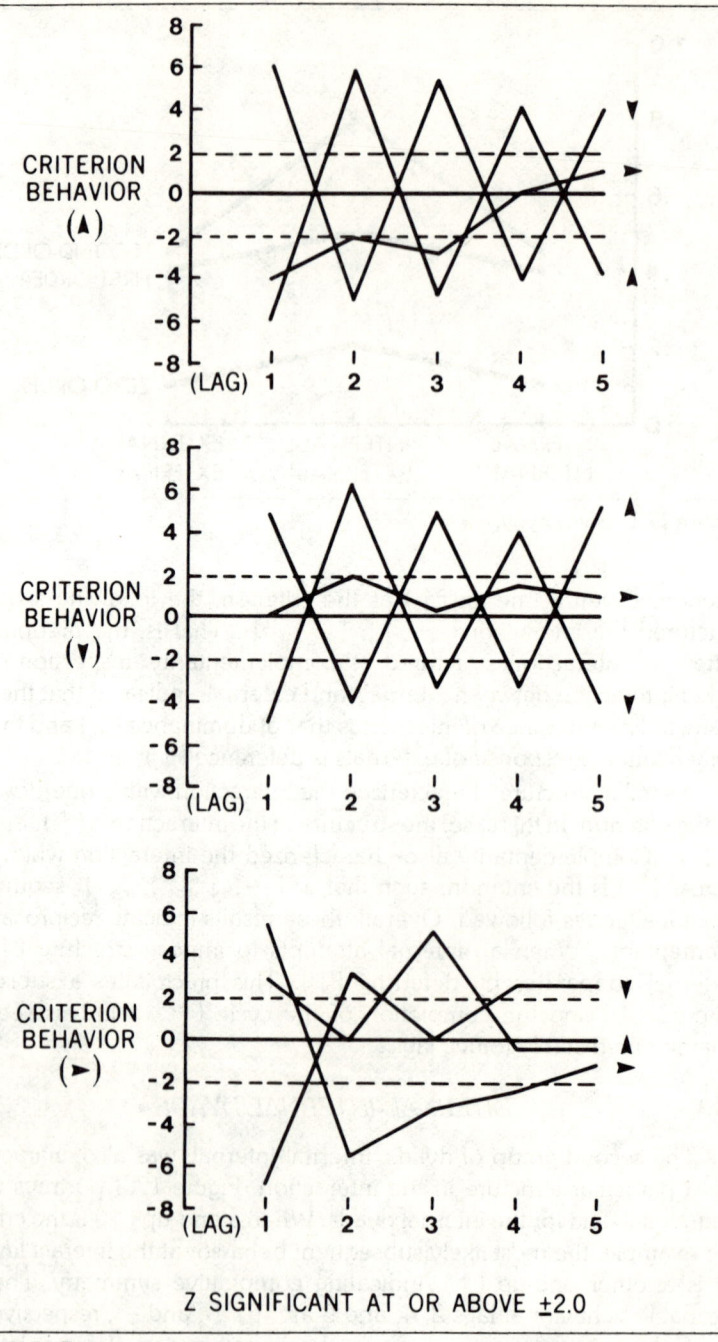

Figure 17.2. Lag sequential analysis.

Z SIGNIFICANT AT OR ABOVE ±2.0

Marital Interaction

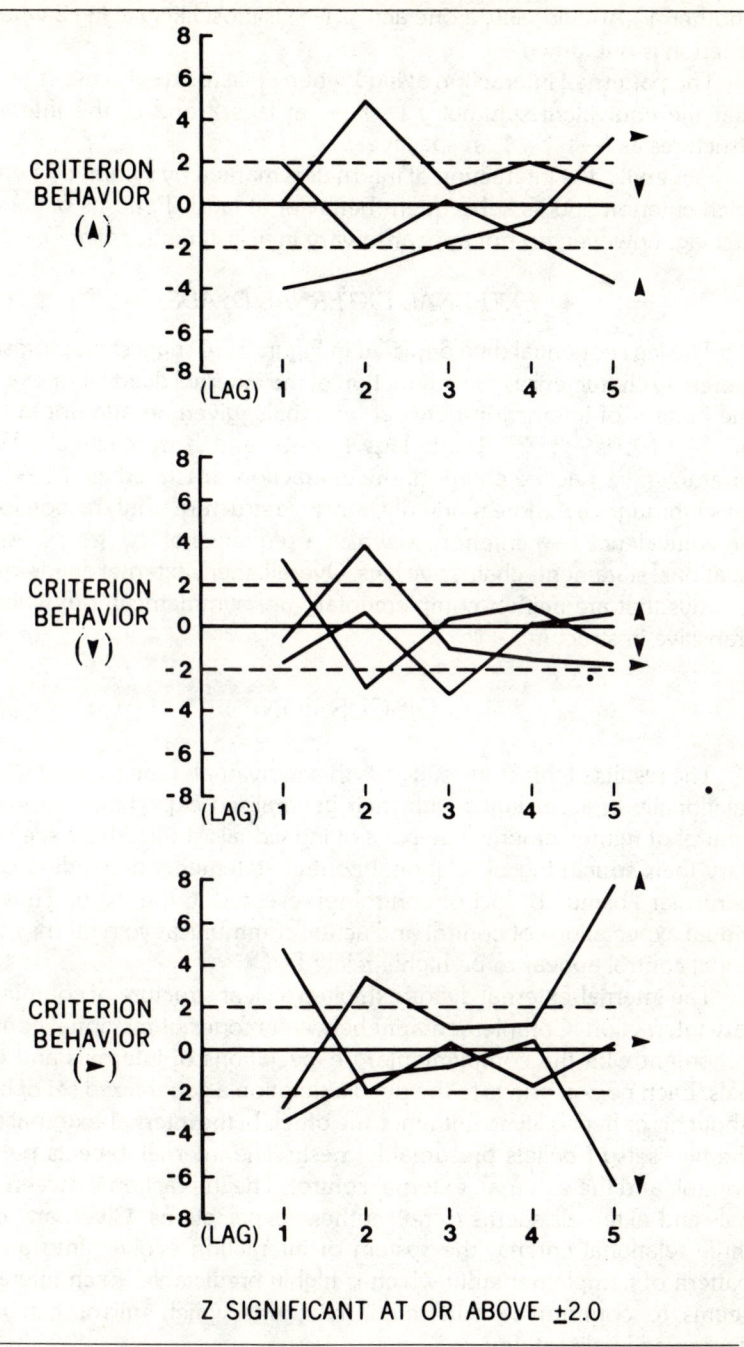

Z SIGNIFICANT AT OR ABOVE ±2.0

Figure 17.3. Lag sequential analysis.

another ↓. Additionally, a one across (→) is most likely at lag 2 when the criterion is one down.

The pattern of interaction at lag 1 when an across (→) is the criterion is that the equivalent symmetry (→) →; at lags 2 and 5, the interaction structures as (→) ↑, ↑, respectively.

Generally, the interaction of internals is marked by symmetry between each criterion and its subsequent behavior at lag 1. Patterns beyond the first lag, however, do not appear to vary in a systematic manner.

EXTERNAL-EXTERNAL DYADS

The lag sequential data depicted in Figure 17.4 suggest that transitivity generally characterizes the interaction of the external dyads. For example, the pattern of interaction between externals, given an attempt at dominance (↑), is →, ↑, ↓, ↑ lags 1, 2, 3, and 5, respectively. With a one-down (↓) as the criterion, the interaction structured as ↑, →, → at lags 1 through 3. A more markedly transitive structure of interaction follows an equivalence (→) criterion, in which a sequence of ↓, ↓, ↑, →, ↓ → relational statements chains five lags. Overall, then, external dyads interact in ways that are neither complementary nor symmetrical, but which are transitive in structure.

DISCUSSION

The results of this study suggests that individuals tend to communicate relationally in accordance with their generalized expectations about the control of reinforcement. The pairs of individuals studied here seemed to vary their structuring of relational control statements depending on the particular "blend" of loci of control represented in the dyad. Thus individual expectations of control and actual communicative patterns of relational control appear to be highly related.

The internal-external dyads exhibited a clear structure of complementary interaction. Complementarity between modes of relational control is congruent with the complementary expectations of internals and externals. Each person brings to the dyadic situation a generalized set of beliefs about his or her ability to influence the other. In the internal-external dyad, the two sets of beliefs presumably mesh: The internal expects personal control, and the external, external control. The interaction between internals and externals seems to reflect these expectations. Given any of the three relational criteria, the system of interaction evolves into a stable pattern of complementarity which is highly predictable. Each interactant seems to communicate in relational terms which mirror his or her generalized belief state.

Z SIGNIFICANT AT OR ABOVE ±2.0

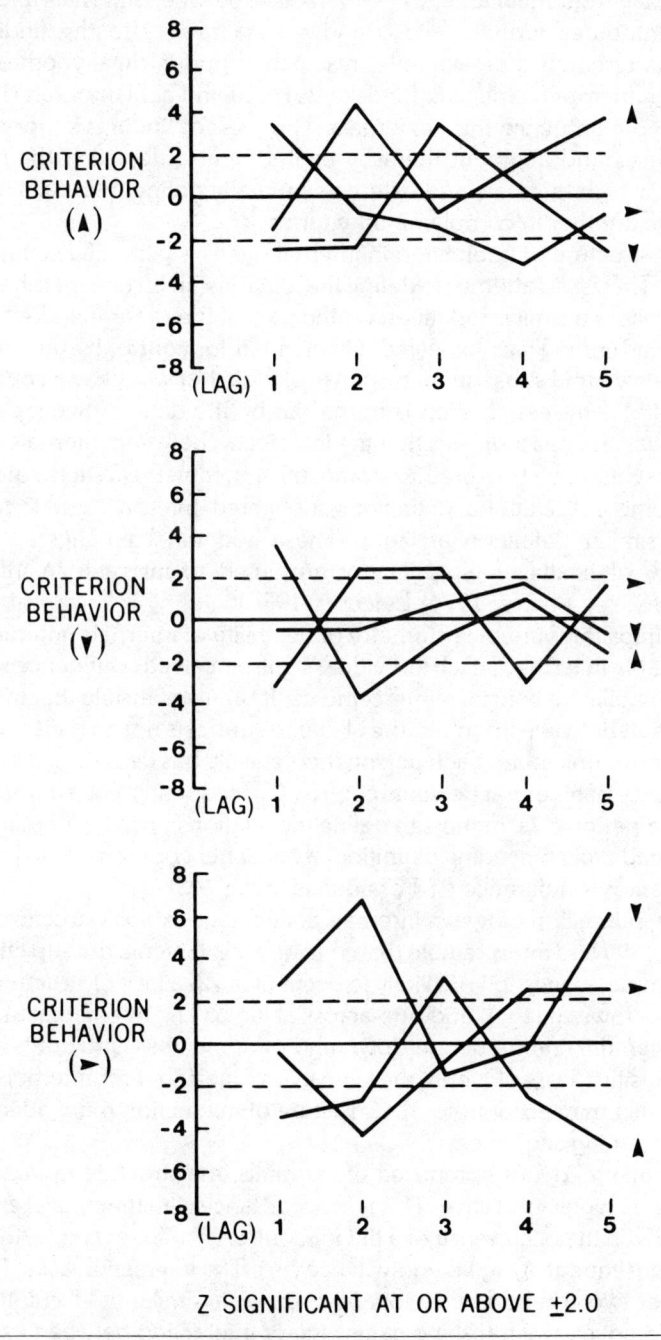

Figure 17.4. Lag sequential analysis.

The lag sequential analysis of interaction between internals and externals contributes further validity and generalizability to the findings of previous research. For example, research supports the hypothesis that internals attempt (Capage & Lindskold, 1973) and actually exert (Phares, 1966) more influence than externals. The present findings support these hypotheses and augment them by capturing and depicting the *process* through which internals and externals mutually define their relationships with one another in complementary terms.

The structure of interaction in internal dyads is generally symmetrical at lag 1. That is, an attempt to define the relationship by one member tends to precipitate a similar definition on the part of the other member. In one sense, this finding was expected. Given a bid for control by one internal, the expected and subsequent response of the other would be a counterbid for control. This expectation is borne out by the data. However, the lag sequential analysis indicates that the interaction between internals at lag 1 is not exclusively structured as competitive symmetry. When equivalent and submissive relational definitions are offered, internals tend to reciprocate a similar definition at lag 1. These additional findings suggest a property of flexibility typically not attributed to internals in influence situations (see Phares, 1976; Lefcourt, 1976).

Perhaps this variable symmetry or flexibility of internals' interaction is explainable in terms of each individual's self-perceived confidence in his or her own ability to control reinforcements. It seems plausible that in dyadic interaction between internals, the ability to control is not an issue for either of the communicators. Each person theoretically has generalized beliefs in the efficacy of his or her personal control. Consequently, each internal may exhibit a periodic willingness to define the relationship in terms that match the immediately preceding definition of his or her counterpart, even when the criterion is deference (↓) or equivalence (→).

The interaction between internals at later lags exhibits structure that is theoretically less interpretable than that at lag 1. Given a one-up criterion, for example, a one-down is likely to occur at lag 2, a lack of structure at lag 3, a one-down at lag 4, and one-across at lag 5. The interaction at longer lags, given the criteria of one-down and of one-across, structures in similarly transitive ways. Overall these results suggest that for internal dyads, the interact may account for the structure of interaction more adequately than longer lag sequences.

For marital dyads composed of externals, the structure of interaction tends to be highly transitive. This is in accordance with theoretical expectations. Given the occurrence of a bid for control (↑), for example, the most likely consequent at lag 1 is equivalence (→). The interaction at lag 1, given the other two criterion behaviors of ↓ or →, is similarly difficult to interpret. Moreover, the transitive patterning of interaction between externals seems most interpretable when the interactants' loci of control are taken into account. Externals who find themselves in disagreement should each be somewhat reluctant to "take charge" of the discussion. However, if each individual hopes to resolve the disagreement to his or her satisfaction, there should be a certain number of attempts to dominate on the part of both interactants because of the situation. Their interaction is characterized by communication in which stable relational patterns are short-lived. The interactants seem to engage in a substantial amount of verbal experimentation, each apparently "searching" for ways to reconcile the need to influence and the generalized expectation to be influenced, hence the transitive patterning of interaction between externals.

SUMMARY

This study represents an initial attempt to examine some communicative consequences of locus of control. The data reported here suggest that individuals' expectations for control have a bearing on the way in which they interact with others in dyadic settings, and that the structuring of dyadic interaction varies systematically with compositional changes in loci of control. Overall this study demonstrates both the value and a means of examining the behavioral consequences of personality variables. The methodology employed here enriches the findings of previous research. This study connects an important trait (locus of control) and state (relational control), which more fully explicates the relationship between power and control in a conflict situation. This study, as well as an earlier study which examined similar questions in acquaintance dyads, suggests that psychological variables can be expanded to the dyadic level and increase our understanding of communication in a variety of communicative contexts. It also suggests that communication scholars explore the communicative behavior in marital and family relations. They include those predispositions (including locus) that impinge on the repertoire of behaviors that are accessible to each individual. Future research needs to examine further the ways in which locus of control translates to observable behavior across various interpersonal contexts. This research has been a step in that direction.

REFERENCES

Altmann, S. A. Sociobiology of rhesus monkeys. II. Stochastics of social communication. *Journal of Theoretical Biology*, 1965, *8*, 490-522.

Attneave, F. *Applications of information theory to psychology*. New York: Holt, 1959.

Ayres, J. *Relational communication patterns in stranger and friend interactions*. Paper presented at the annual convention of the Western Speech Communication Association, Phoenix, Arizona, November 1977.

Bakeman, R., & Dabbs, M., Jr. Social interaction observed: Some approaches to the analysis of behavioral streams. *Personality and Social Psychology Bulletin,* 1976, *2,* 335-345.

Barry, W. Marriage research and conflict: An integrative review. *Psychological Bulletin,* 1970, *73,* 41-54.

Bateson, G. *Naven.* Stanford: Stanford University Press, 1936.

Bott, E. *Families and social networks.* London: Tavistock, 1957.

Capage, J., & Lindskold, S. Locus of control, sex, target accommodation, and attempts at influence. *Proceedings of the 81st Annual Convention of the APA* (Montreal, Canada), 1973, *8,* 297-298.

Cromwell, R. E., & Olson, D. H. *Power in families.* New York: John Wiley, 1975.

Ellis, D. *An analysis of relational communication in ongoing group systems.* Unpublished doctoral dissertation. University of Utah, 1976.

Ellis, D. *A social system model of relational control in two ongoing group systems.* Paper presented at the annual convention of the Speech Communication Association, Washington, D.C., December 1977.

Ellis, D. Trait predictors of relational control. In B. Rubin (Ed.), *Communication yearbook 2.* New Brunswick, NJ: Transaction, 1978.

Ellis, D., & Drecksel, G. *Relational stability and change in women's consciousness-raising groups.* Paper presented at the annual convention of the International Communication Association, Chicago, Illinois, 1978.

Ellis, D., & Fisher, B. Phases of conflict in small group development: A Markov analysis. *Human Communication Research,* 1975, *1,* 195-212.

Ellis, D., & Skerchock, L. Relational control sequences in sex-typed and androgynous groups. *Western Speech Journal* 19, *44,* 35-49.

Emery, D. *An investigation of perceptions and subsequent interaction in locus and relational control.* Paper presented at the annual convention of the Speech Communication Association, Anaheim, California, 1981.

Ericson, P. M. *Relational communication: Complementarity and symmetry and their relation to dominance and submission.* Unpublished doctoral dissertation, Michigan State University, 1972.

Fisher, B. Decision emergence: Phases in group decision making. *Speech Monographs,* 1970, *37,* 53-66.

Fisher, B. A., & Beach, W. A. *Content and relationship dimensions of communicative behavior.* Paper presented to the annual convention of the Speech Communication Association, Washington, D.C., December 1977.

Fisher, B. A., Glover, T. W., & Ellis, D. G. The nature of complex communication systems. *Communication Monographs,* 1977, *44,* 231-240.

Fitzpatrick, M. A., & Best, P. Dyadic adjustment in traditional, independent, and separate relationships: A validation study. *Communication Monographs,* 1979, *46,* 167-178.

Kolb, T., & Straus, M. Marital power and marital happiness in relation to problem-solving ability. *Journal of Marriage and the Family,* 1974, *36,* 756-766.

Kullback, S., Kupperman, M., & Ku, H. H. Tests for contingency tables and Markov chains. *Technometrics,* 1962, *4,* 573-608.

Lefcourt, H. *Locus of control: Current trends in theory and research.* New York: Halsted Press, 1976.

Lewin, K. Feedback problems of social diagnosis and action. In W. Buckley (Ed.), *Modern systems research for the behavioral scientist.* Chicago: Aldine, 1968.

Olson, D. H., & Cromwell, R. E. Power in families. In R. E. Cromwell & D. H. Olson (Eds.), *Power in families.* Beverly Hills, CA: Sage, 1975.

Olson, D. H., & Rabunsky, C. Validity of four measures of family power. *Journal of Marriage and the Family,* 1972, *34,* 224-234.

Phares, E. Internal-external control as a determinant of amount of social influence exerted. *Journal of Personality and Social Psychology,* 1966, *2,* 642-647.

Phares, E. *Locus of control in personality.* Morristown, NJ: General Learning Press, 1976.

Pearce, W. B., & Conklin, F. Hierarchical meanings in coherent conversations. *Communication Monographs,* 1979, *46,* 75-87.

Rapaport, A. The promises and pitfalls of information theory. In W. Buckley (Ed.), *Modern systems research for the behavioral scientist.* Chicago: Aldine, 1968.

Renne, K. Correlates of dissatisfaction in marriage. *Journal of Marriage and the Family,* 1970, *32,* 54-67.

Rogers, L. E., & Farace, R. V. Relational communication analysis: New measurement procedures. *Human Communication Research,* 1976, *1,* 222-239.

Rogers-Millar, E. *Symmetry and complementarity: Evolution and evaluation of an idea.* Paper presented at the ICA/SCA Asilomar conference on Human Communication from the Interactional View, Asilomar, California, February 1979.

Rogers-Millar, L. E., & Millar, F. E. *A transactional definition and measure of power.* Paper presented at the annual convention of the Speech Communication Association, Washington, D.C., December 1977.

Rogers-Millar, L. E., & Millar, F. E. Domineeringness and dominance: A transactional view. *Human Communication Research,* 1979, *5,* 238-246.

Rollins, B., & Bahr, S. A theory of power relations in marriage. *Journal of Marriage and the Family,* 1976, *38,* 619-627.

Rotter, J. Generalized expectancies for internal versus external control of reinforcement. *Psychological Monographs,* 1966, *80* (Whole No. 609).

Rotter, J., Chance, J., & Phares, E. *Applications of a social learning theory of personality.* New York: Holt, Rinehart & Winston, 1972.

Safilios-Rothschild, C. The study of family power structure: A review, 1960-1969. *Journal of Marriage and the Family,* 1970, *32,* 539-552.

Sluczki, C., & Beavin, J. Simetria y complementaridad: Una definicion operacional y una tipologia de parejas [Symmetry and complementarity: An operational definition and typology of pairs]. *Acta Psiquatricia y Psiocologica de American Latina,* 1965, *11,* 321-330.

Spanier, G., Lewis, R., & Cole, C. Marital adjustment over the family life cycle: The issue of curvilinearity. *Journal of Marriage and the Family,* 1975, *37,* 263-275.

Strodtbeck, F. Husband-wife interaction over revealed differences. *American Sociological Review,* 1951, *16,* 468-473.

Watzlawick, P., Beavin, J. H., & Jackson, D. D. *Pragmatics of human communication: A study of interactional patterns, pathologies, and paradoxes.* New York: W. W. Norton, 1967.

18 • Reciprocity of Self-Disclosure: A Sequential Analysis

KATHRYN DINDIA
University of Wisconsin—Milwaukee

IT has been hypothesized that self-disclosure is reciprocal (cf. Altman, 1973; Altman & Taylor, 1973; Chaikin & Derlega, 1974b; Chelune, 1978; Cozby, 1973; Derlega & Chaikin, 1975; Jourard, 1971; Pearce & Sharp, 1973). Despite the fact that more than fifty studies have examined the proposition that self-disclosure is reciprocal, it remains a hypothesis. The proposition is unconfirmed because the studies that attempted to test the hypothesis failed to employ an operational definition of reciprocity that was consistent with the conceptual definition.

This chapter reviews the conceptual and operational definitions of reciprocity. The inconsistency between the conceptual and operational definitions in previous research aimed at testing the reciprocity hypothesis is examined. The inadequacy of relationship analysis and difference analysis as statistical tests of the reciprocity hypothesis is demonstrated, and it is argued that the most appropriate test of the reciprocity hypothesis is sequential analysis. This study employs sequential analysis as a test of the reciprocity hypothesis.

RECIPROCITY DEFINED

Reciprocity of self-disclosure is defined conceptually as mutually contingent self-disclosure. This means that A's self-disclosure to B causes B's self-disclosure to A, and vice versa. Jourard (1959) originated the idea that self-disclosure is reciprocal. He coined the term "dyadic effect" to represent the idea that "disclosure begets disclosure" (Jourard, 1971, p. 66).

Reciprocity has been defined operationally in several ways, including a positive relationship between, or a similarity in, A and B's self-disclosure, and a positive effect of A's self-disclosure on B's self-disclosure. These

AUTHOR'S NOTE: The author wishes to thank Malcolm R. Parks for his consultation and other assistance with this study.

Correspondence and requests for reprints: Kathryn Dindia, Department of Communication, University of Wisconsin, Milwaukee, WI 53201.

operational definitions are not consistent with the conceptual definition of reciprocity. A and B's self-disclosure may be positively related or similar without being contingent. A's self-disclosure may have a positive effect on B's self-disclosure without this effect being mutual. What needs to be demonstrated is that A's self-disclosure has a positive effect on B's self-disclosure, and vice versa.

PREVIOUS TESTS OF RECIPROCITY

A review of the literature relevant to this hypothesis reveals an inconsistency in the conceptual and operational definitions of reciprocity. Table 18.1 summarizes the research aimed at testing the reciprocity hypothesis. These studies employed three types of data analysis: relationship analysis, difference analysis, and sequential analysis.

Relationship Analysis

Interclass and intraclass correlations have been employed to test reciprocity of self-disclosure. A positive and significant correlation between A and B's self-disclosure has been interpreted as reciprocity. These studies are two types: nonexperimental designs employing questionnaire data and nonexperimental designs employing observational data.

Questionnaire Data. Questionnaire studies rely on data obtained from self-disclosure questionnaires that attempt to measure the extent of a subject's past self-diclosure to and from another person(s) in the context of social and familial relationships. These studies examine what has been labeled "perceived reciprocity" and/or what has been labeled "actual reciprocity." "Perceived reciprocity" is the correlation between a subject's report of his or her self-disclosure to another person and the same subject's report of the other person's self-disclosure to the subject. This correlation represents intrasubjective perceptions of reciprocity. "Actual reciprocity" is the correlation between a subject's report of his or her self-disclosure to another person and the other person's report of his or her self-disclosure to the subject. This correlation represents intersubjective perceptions of reciprocity (Rubin & Shenker, 1978).

Significant relationships were found between the input and output of a subject's self-disclosure to another person (Jourard, 1959; Jourard & Landsman, 1960; Jourard & Richman, 1963; Levinger & Senn, 1967; Panyard, 1973; Pearce, Wright, Sharp, & Slama, 1974; Rubin, Hill, Peplau, & Dunkelschetter, 1980; Rubin & Shenker, 1978). This finding was consistent for "perceived reciprocity" (Jourard & Richman, 1963; Levinger & Senn, 1967; Panyard, 1973; Pearce et al., 1974; Rubin et al., 1980; Rubin & Shenker, 1978), and for "actual reciprocity" (Jourard,

Table 18.1
Summary of Empirical Results Relevant to Reciprocity of Self-Disclosure

Study	D	M	Criterion	Operationalization	A	Results
Archer & Berg, 1978	E	O	Intimacy	postrated	D	+
	E	O	Amount	number of words	D	+, +/−
Becker & Munz, 1975	E	O	Intimacy	postrated	D	+
	E	O	Amount	duration	D	+
Brewer & Mittelman, 1980	E	O	Intimacy	postrated	D	∅
Certner, 1973	E	O	Intimacy	prescaled	R	+
Chaiken et al., 1975	E	O	Intimacy	postrated	D	+ (normals)
	E	O	Intimacy	postrated	D	+, +/− (neurotics)
Cozby, 1972	E	Q	Intimacy	willingness to self-disclose	D	∅
Dalto et al., 1979 (1)	E	Q	Intimacy	intent to self-disclose	D	∅
(2)	E	Q	Desirability	intent to self-disclose	D	∅
	E	O	Intimacy	prescaled	D	∅
	E	O	Desirability	prescaled	D	+
Davis, 1976	N	O	Intimacy	prescaled	R	½
					S	+
Davis, 1977	N	O	Intimacy	prescaled	R	½
					S	+
Davis, 1978	N	O	Intimacy	prescaled	R	½
					S	+
Davis & Skinner, 1974	E	O	Intimacy	postrated	D	+
Davis & Sloan, 1972	E	O	Intimacy	postrated	D	+
DeForest & Stone, 1980	E	Q	Intimacy	willingness to self-disclose	D	+
Derlega, Chaikin, & Herndon, 1975	E	O	Intimacy	postrated	D	+
	E	O	Amount	duration	D	+
Derlega, Harris, & Chaikin, 1973	E	Q	Intimacy	intent to self-disclose	D	+
	E	Q	Amount	intent to self-disclose	D	+
Derlega, Walmer, & Furman, 1973	E	Q	Intimacy	willingness to self-disclose	D	+
	E	Q	Amount	willingness to self-disclose	D	+

508

Derlega, Wilson, & Chaikin, 1976	E	O	Intimacy	postrated	+
	E	O	Amount	duration	∅
	E	O	Intimacy	postrated	+ (strangers)
	E	O	Intimacy	postrated	∅ (strangers)
	E	O	Intimacy	postrated	+ (friends)
	E	O	Intimacy	postrated	∅ (friends)
Dion & Dion, 1978	E	Q	Intimacy	intent to self-disclose	+
Ebersole et al., 1977	E	O	Intimacy	postrated	∅
	E	O	Amount	number of words	+
Ehrlich & Graeven, 1971	E	O	Intimacy	postrated	∅
	E	O	Topic	postrated	+
Feigenbaum, 1977	E	O	Intimacy	postrated	+
	E	O	Intimacy	number of self-referrent words	+
Gary & Hammond, 1970	E	O	Intimacy	prescaled	+
Johnson & Dabbs, 1976	E	O	Amount	duration	+
Jourard, 1959	N	O	Amount	actual reciprocity	+
Jourard & Friedman, 1970	E	O	Amount	duration	+
Jourard & Jaffe, 1970	E	O	Amount	duration	+
	E	O	Amount	duration	+
	E	O	Amount	actual reciprocity	½
Jourard & Landsman, 1960	N	O	Intimacy	S's ratings confirmed by partner	+
Jourard & Resnick, 1970	N	O	Amount	perceived reciprocity	+
Jourard & Richman, 1963	N	O	Amount	number of self-disclosing statements	∅
Kohen, 1975	N	O	Amount	number of self-disclosing statements	D (rate-matching)
Levin & Gergen, 1969	E	Q	Amount	check list of statements	+, +/−
Levinger & Senn, 1967	N	Q	Amount	perceived reciprocity	+
	N	Q	Amount	actual reciprocity	+
Lynn, 1978	E	O	Intimacy	intent to self-disclose	+
Mann & Murphy, 1975	E	O	Amount	number of self-disclosing statements	+/−
Morgan & Evans, 1977	N	Q	Amount	number of self-disclosing statements	+
Panyard, 1973	N	Q	Amount	perceived reciprocity	+
	N	Q	Amount	actual reciprocity	+

(continued)

Table 18.1 (Continued)

Study	D	M	Criterion	Operationalization	A	Results
Pearce et al., 1974	N	Q	Amount	perceived reciprocity	R	+
Powell, 1968	N	Q	Amount	actual reciprocity	R	+
Rubin, 1975 (1)	E	O	Amount	rate of self-references	D	+
(2)	E	O	Intimacy	postrated	D	+
	E	O	Amount	number of words	D	+
	E	O	Intimacy	postrated	D	+/−
Rubin et al., 1980	N	Q	Amount	number of words	D	+
	N	Q	Amount	perceived reciprocity	R	+
Rubin & Shenker, 1978	E	Q	Amount	actual reciprocity	R	+
	E	Q	Amount	perceived reciprocity	R	+
Savicki, 1972	E	O	Intimacy	actual reciprocity	D	+
	E	O	Amount	prescaled	D	+
Sermat & Smyth, 1973 (1)	E	O	Intimacy	duration	D	+
(2)	E	O	Intimacy	postrated	D	∅
	E	O	Intimacy	postrated	D	+
Strassberg et al., 1976	N	O	Self-disclosing statements	S's report of own intimacy	S	+
Tognoli, 1969	E	Q	Intimacy	intent to self-disclose	D	+
Vondracek, 1969	E	O	Intimacy	postrated	D	+
Vondracek & Vondracek, 1971	E	O	Amount	duration	D	+
Woolfolk, 1979	E	O	Amount	frequency	D	+
	E	Q	Intimacy	willingness to self-disclose	D	∅
Worthy et al., 1969	N	O	Intimacy	prescaled	R	+
					D	+

D = Design; E = experimental; N = nonexperimental; M = Measure: Q = questionnaire; O = observational; A = Analysis; R = relationship; D = difference; S = sequential. Results: + indicates reciprocity; ∅ indicates null results; +/− indicates curvilinear results; ½ indicates one-way effect.

1969; Jourard & Landsman, 1960; Levinger & Senn, 1967; Panyard, 1973; Pearce et al., 1974; Rubin et al., 1980; Rubin & Shenker, 1978).

Only one study was found that tested the difference between "perceived reciprocity" and "actual reciprocity" correlations. The "perceived reciprocity" correlations were significantly higher than the "actual reciprocity" correlations (Pearce et al., 1974). However, several studies measured both "perceived reciprocity" and "actual reciprocity" and the values for "perceived reciprocity" substantially exceeded the corresponding values for "actual reciprocity" (Levinger & Senn, 1967; Panyard, 1973; Pearce et al., 1974; Rubin et al., 1980; Rubin & Shenker, 1978). The higher degree of "perceived reciprocity" has been attributed to problems of a response set and other sources of bias (Levinger & Senn, 1967; Rubin & Shenker, 1978).

Several researchers have claimed that "perceived reciprocity" findings exaggerate the degree of reciprocity as evidenced by "actual reciprocity" findings. However, "actual reciprocity" may not measure actual reciprocity any more than "perceived reciprocity." The labels "perceived reciprocity" and "actual reciprocity" are misleading. Both are based on perceptions of self-disclosure and, technically, both are perceptions of reciprocity. In questionnaire research, the actual behavior of the subject is not measured and hence not known. Consequently, the credibility of the results rests on the questionnaire's ability to predict actual self-disclosure. The postdictive, concurrent, and predictive validity of self-disclosure questionnaires has not been demonstrated by research (Chelune, 1978; Cozby, 1973; Goddstein & Reinecker, 1974). Thus generalizations from either "perceived reciprocity" or "actual reciprocity" are unwarranted.

Observational Data. In nonexperimental, observational research, two or more subjects, typically strangers, engage in a structured or unstructured interaction in a dyad or small group. Self-disclosure is measured by observing the intimacy and/or amount of the subject's self-disclosure. Reciprocity is tested by the correlation between the subject's self-disclosure to his or her partner or the other group members and the partner's or other group members' self-disclosure to the subject.

All five observational studies surveyed found a positive relationship between the self-disclosure of dyadic and small group members. This finding was consistent for intimacy of self-disclosure (Certner, 1973; Davis, 1976, 1977, 1978; Worthy, Gary, & Kahn, 1969) and the amount of self-disclosure (Kohen, 1975).

These studies provide evidence that there is a positive relationship between A and B's reported and observed levels of self-disclosure. They do not provide evidence that A's self-disclosure has a positive effect on B's self-disclosure, and vice versa. Correlation indicates that A and B's self-disclosure are related but not contingent. This is because A and B's self-disclosure may be related for a number of reasons, only one of which is reciprocity.

They may be related due to a one-way effect. A's self-disclosure has a positive effect on B's self-disclosure, but B's self-disclosure does not have a positive effect on A's self-disclosure, or vice versa (correlation does not indicate the direction of the relationship). Jourard and Resnick (1970) paired high and low disclosers and found that high disclosers had a positive effect on the self-disclosure of low disclosers, but low disclosers had no effect on the self-disclosure of high disclosers. Davis (1976, 1977, 1978) found a positive relationship between dyadic members' self-disclosure and through subsequent analysis discovered that it was due to a one-way effect.

Another variable, C, may cause A and B's self-disclosure to be related. For instance, A and B's self-disclosure may be related due to similar personality traits or predispositions to self-disclose (e.g., both A and B are typically high or low disclosers). In questionnaire studies, dyads are not randomly assigned but preexist in the form of social and familial relationships. A subject's self-disclosure to another person may be related to the other person's self-disclosure to the subject because of hereditary or environmentally acquired personality traits in familial relationships and because "like attracts like" in social relationships.

There is a second, analogous way to express this point. Correlation measures the covariation of self-disclosure within dyads relative to the total variation of self-disclosure across dyads. As the relative similarity of self-disclosure within dyads increases, the value of R or r increases. As the relative dissimilarity of self-disclosure across dyads increases, the value of R or r increases (cf. Haggard, 1958). Dyads with a high level of self-disclosure could be distributing these behaviors noncontingently throughout a discussion. The same could be true for dyads with low levels (or any level) of self-disclosure. In this case, a positive correlation would be due to different base rates (i.e., a large variation) of self-disclosure across dyads (Gottman, Markman, & Notarius, 1977; Gottman, Notarius, Markman, Bank, Yoppi, & Rubin, 1976). Partners' self-disclosure may be similar without being contingent. Gottman (1979, p. 65) makes the point this way:

> It is easier to see this if we consider nonsocial behaviors, such as eating or typing. A husband may eat or type at a rate similar to his wife's without any contingency between these two activities; they may, for example, have similar physical tempos. In this case, we would merely report that eating or typing took place at similar rates, not that they were reciprocal. If a mother smiles at a rate similar to her infant, their interaction may, nonetheless, be totally unconnected and noncontingent; the mother's smiling and her infant's smiling would be considered reciprocal only if they were somehow connected in the probability change sense.

DIFFERENCE ANALYSIS

The second major approach employed to test reciprocity of self-disclosure has relied on t-test and analysis of variance and covariance. This type of data analysis has been applied in both nonexperimental and experimental designs.

Nonexperimental Designs

Difference analysis was employed in a nonexperimental design in a rate-matching test of reciprocity. Kohen (1975) used the t-test to study differences in opposite-sex, dyadic partners' amount of self-disclosure. Kohen hypothesized that partners' self-disclosure would be similar. Difference analysis was used to test whether the mean of the males' self-disclosure was different from the mean of the females' self-disclosure. The results indicated that the two groups differed significantly from each other in the number of statements disclosed. Kohen interpreted this finding as indicating that the number of disclosures was not reciprocated.

There are two problems with this use of difference analysis as a test of the reciprocity hypothesis. First, had the mean of the two groups' self-disclosure been similar, this would not mean that the dyadic partners' self-disclosure was similar. The mean of the two groups could be similar, and there still could be large discrepancies in self-disclosure within dyads. Aggregate data do not indicate the amount of similarity/dissimilarity between members of a particular dyad. As Cappella (1981) has indicated, some dyads may be compensating while others are reciprocating. When analyzed in the aggregate, differences may cancel each other. Second, even if each dyad were similar, this would not mean that self-disclosure was reciprocal. The point is the same as the one that states that the analysis of correlations is an inadequate test of the reciprocity hypothesis.

Experimental Designs

In experimental designs, a confederate's or experimenter's self-disclosure is manipulated and the effect of such self-disclosure on a subject's self-disclosure is estimated. The difference between the mean of the subject's self-disclosure for the different experimental groups is tested for significance. Significant values of t and F are interpreted as reciprocity.

The independent and dependent variables include the intimacy and amount of self-disclosure. Generally, the dependent measure is the observation of a subject's self-disclosure. However, there are several exceptions where the dependent measure is a subject's report of his or her willingness or intention to self-disclose.

Questionnaire Data. Subjects are exposed to the oral or written self-disclosure of another (sometimes alleged) person. Questionnaires are used to measure a subject's report of what he or she hypothetically would be willing to self-disclose to the other person or his or her intention to self-disclose to the other person at some future time.

With two exceptions (Derlega, Harris, & Chaikin, 1973; Woolfolk, 1979), a confederate's self-disclosure had a positive effect on a subject's self-disclosure (Cozby, 1972; DeForest & Stone, 1980; Derlega, Harris, & Chaikin, 1973; Derlega, Walmer, & Furman, 1973; Dion & Dion, 1978; Lynn, 1978; Tognoli, 1969).

The criticism leveled against the validity of self-report measures of self-disclosure also applies to these studies. The predictive validity of these measures has not been demonstrated by research, and thus generalizations from self-report measures of self-disclosure to actual behavior are unwarranted.

Observational Data. The experimental studies surveyed here employed an observational measure of a subject's self-disclosure as the dependent measure of self-disclosure. This procedure consists of the prerated intimacy of the topics a subject chooses to disclose, the postrated intimacy of a subject's self-disclosure, the number of words or statements a subject discloses, or the frequency, duration, or rate of a subject's self-disclosure.

The majority of these studies found that a confederate's or experimenter's self-disclosure had a positive effect on a subject's self-disclosure (Archer & Berg, 1978; Becker & Munz, 1975; Chaikin, Derlega, Bayma, & Shaw, 1975; Davis & Skinner, 1974; Davis & Sloan, 1972; Derlega, Chaikin, & Herndon, 1975; Derlega et al., 1973; Derlega, Wilson, & Chaikin, 1976; Ehrlich & Graeven, 1971; Feigenbaum, 1977; Gary & Hammond, 1970; Johnson & Dabbs, 1976; Jourard & Friedman, 1970; Jourard & Jaffee, 1970; Levin & Gergen, 1969; Morgan & Evans, 1977; Powell, 1968; Rubin, 1975; Savicki, 1972; Sermat & Smyth, 1973; Vondracek, 1969; Vondracek & Vondracek, 1971; Worthy et al., 1969). However, there were several exceptions to this finding (Archer & Berg, 1978; Brewer & Mittelman, 1980; Chaikin et al., 1975; Dalto, Ajzen, & Kaplan, 1979; Derlega et al., 1976; Ebersole, McFall, & Brandt, 1977). Several studies indicated that a confederate's self-disclosure had a curvilinear effect on a subject's self-disclosure (Archer & Berg, 1978; Cozby, 1972; Levin & Gergen, 1969; Lynn, 1978; Mann & Murphy, 1975; Rubin, 1975). As the intimacy or amount of a confederate's self-disclosure increased, the intimacy or amount of a subject's self-disclosure rose proportionately less.

The review of experimental studies reveals mixed results. In general, a confederate's or experimenter's self-disclosure had a positive effect on a subject's reported and observed self-disclosure. However, the generalizability of these findings may be rather limited. Extreme manipulations were used in most of these studies. Superficial, perfunctory remarks have been used in the low-disclosure conditions and explicit, personal comments on highly private topics (e.g., sexual behavior or mental deviance) for the high-disclosure conditions. While the manipulations may be effective, they may not be representative of the range of self-disclosure typically encountered outside the laboratory. If the results of these studies are to be generalizable beyond the experimental conditions, the manipulations of self-disclosure must be representative of conditions typically found in first encounters (Chelune, 1978).

Regardless of the generalizability of these studies, they do not provide evidence that self-disclosure is reciprocal. Difference analysis, as applied to experimental studies, provides evidence that A's self-disclosure has a positive effect on B's self-disclosure. Difference analysis does not provide evidence that B's self-disclosure *also* has a positive effect on A's self-disclosure. Difference analysis provides information about one-way causality. It cannot provide information about the mutual influence that interacting partners may have on each other's self-disclosure.

SEQUENTIAL ANALYSIS

Interaction can be thought of as a sequence of behaviors between two or more individuals that continues across time. What can be observed and tested is the manner in which A's present self-disclosure affects B's future self-disclosure, and vice versa. Sequential analysis can be employed as a test of the reciprocity hypothesis, testing whether A's self-disclosure has a positive effect on B's subsequent self-disclosure, and vice versa. It can test for causality as opposed to relatedness (i.e., relationship analysis) and for mutual causality as opposed to one-way causality (i.e., difference analysis). Four studies have used sequential analysis to test the reciprocity hypothesis.

Davis (1976) studied pairs of statements in dyads. A "reciprocity index" was obtained for each subject by computing the rank-order correlation between the intimacy-scale values of his or her self-diclosures and the immediately preceding disclosures of his or her partner. A significant negative intraclass correlation between partners' scores on the index indicated an asymmetrical effect; the more A's present self-disclosure was positively related to B's previous self-disclosure, the more B's present self-disclosure was negatively related to A's previous self-disclosure. According to Davis, one person returned the other person's self-disclosure, while the other person did not. Similar results were found in two other studies (Davis, 1977, 1978).

In spite of the use of sequential analysis, Davis's studies as tests of the reciprocity hypothesis are problematic. Davis's work is flawed because he has failed to extract the individual trends toward greater intimacy in each person before doing his correlational analysis. His results can be explained by two independent trends, both increasing in time (Cappella, personal communication).

Strassberg, Gabel, and Anchor (1976) explored the sequential pattern of self-disclosure in discussion groups. Rather than selecting pairs of statements, they examined the sequence of all statements among group members. The one-sample runs test was applied to the pattern of self-disclosing and non-self-disclosing comments in the groups to determine whether the obtained sequences could be attributed to chance. The pattern of self-disclosing and non-self-disclosing statements observed in the groups was found to be nonrandom. The results indicated that self-disclosing statements tended to occur together in the group discussion, and these series were embedded in runs of non-self-disclosing statements. That is, a self-disclosing statement tended to be preceded and/or followed by another self-disclosing statement more frequently than would occur by chance. Similarly, non-self-disclosing statements tended to cluster together more frequently than would occur by chance. Unfortunately, this study fails to provide conclusive evidence of reciprocity because the authors did not take into account who was self-disclosing. The analysis revealed a significant tendency for self-disclosing statements to occur contiguously. However, the significant pattern could be due to some pattern other than reciprocity (e.g., a one-way effect).

Unfortunately, none of the sequential analyses reviewed adequately tested reciprocity of self-disclosure, and consequently none of them provide information about reciprocity of self-disclosure. This is not an inherent problem in sequential analysis as a test of reciprocity as is the case with relationship and difference analysis. Rather, it involves the inappropriate application of these statistics as tests of reciprocity.

Summary

The studies cited in this review have relied on inadequate statistical tests of the reciprocity hypothesis. These studies provide overwhelming evidence that the reported self-disclosure of members of family and social relationships is related, that the observed self-disclosure of strangers interacting in dyads and small groups is related, and that an experimenter's or confederate's self-disclosure has a positive effect on both a subject's reported willingness or intent to self-disclose and on his or her observed self-disclosure. These and other findings have been interpreted as evidence of reciprocity of self-disclosure. However, this review of the literature indicates that the reciprocity hypothesis remains untested and that there has been no evidence produced indicating that self-disclosure is reciprocal. The following study was conducted to provide such a test.

METHOD

Subjects

Subjects in the study were eight volunteers enrolled in a large lecture, introductory speech communication course. Four of the subjects were women, four were men. Six were Caucasian, two were Asian. The subjects were paid $25.00 for their participation in the study.

Procedures

Subjects were informed that this was a study of the acquaintance process. They were told that they would be assigned three partners and participate in three dyadic conversations, one conversation with each partner. They were also told that they would repeat this procedure, with the same three partners, at one-week intervals for four weeks.

Subjects were randomly assigned three partners: a same-sex partner, an opposite-sex partner, and another same-sex partner (someone other than the first partner). All dyadic partners were strangers. Subjects participated in nine dyadic conversations, three with each of three partners, one conversation with each partner each week, for three weeks. Each week each subject talked to the same three people. Only the order of the conversations was changed. Subjects thought they would participate in a fourth conversation with each partner on the fourth week, but instead they completed questionnaires and were debriefed.

Overall, there were thirty-six dyadic conversations. All the conversations were unstructured; no tasks or topics were assigned or provided. All conversations were tape recorded and lasted approximately one-half hour.

This particular design was selected for several reasons. The repeated conversations with the same partner were employed to avoid the "stranger on the train" phenomenon, where the reciprocation of intimate self-disclosure is hypothesized to be commonplace but not generalizable to more typical situations where the possibility of a future encounter exists (Altman, 1973). The repeated-conversations procedure was also employed to assess the effect of relational development on reciprocity of self-disclosure. It has been hypothesized that the stage of a relationship is a factor that mediates reciprocity of self-disclosure (Altman, 1973). The subjects conversed with three (as opposed to one) partners so that the effect of personal factors (individual difference variables) and dyadic composition on reciprocity of self-disclosure could be assessed. Altman (1973) has also hypothesized that personal factors and group composition affect reciprocity of self-disclosure.

Subjects were seated in a face-to-face position in comfortable chairs, approximately three feet apart, in a small room. A microphone was placed in the middle of a table between them. At the beginning of each conversation, the experimenter turned on the tape recorder and left the room. After thirty minutes, the tape recorder automatically turned off and soon afterward the investigator returned to the room.

Coding System

Two trained coders, one male and one female, who were seniors and majors in the Department of Speech Communication, continuously coded the conversations in real time directly from the tape recordings using the MORE (Microprocessor Operated Recording Equipment), a hand-held, solid-state device with a numerical keyboard. This device provided a sequential record of the codes and the duration of each code.

Coders rated the verbal content according to a two-digit coding system. The first digit represented who was speaking, the second digit represented self-disclosure or non-self-disclosure. The unit coded was the complete thought or independent clause (Dollard & Mowrer, 1947). If an utterance did not contain a complete thought, it was coded as non-self-disclosure.

Self-disclosure was operationally defined as a self-reference (Rogers, 1960; Powell, 1968; Chelune, 1978). A self-reference was defined by Rogers (1960) as "a verbal response by S which describes him in some way, tells something about him, or refers to some affect he experiences." Chelune (1978) defined a self-reference as a thought unit that is descriptive of some quality or aspect of the speaker. The specific coding rules are reported elsewhere (Dindia, 1981). In general, the observers coded as self-disclosure all statements of fact about the self, as well as explicit affective and evaluative statements. Everything else was coded as non-self-disclosure.

RESULTS

Reliability

Each observer was randomly assigned half of the data to code. Interrater reliability was assessed by having both observers code a random sample of 15 percent of the eighteen hours of tape. Intercoder agreement was checked for three one-hour periods at the beginning, middle, and end of data coding. Cohen's Kappa (1960) was employed as an index of observer agreement on six thirty-minute conversations. The proportion of agreement after chance agreement was removed from consideration was: $k = .911, .916, .924, .923, .858, .676$. The mean Kappa computed for all six conversations was $k = .871$. Agreement was checked on a second-by-second basis. The conversation with the lowest agreement was thought to be due to a lack of synchrony, one coder's response time being slower than that of the other coder. Therefore, Cohen's Kappa was recalculated for this conversation on a plus-or-minus, one-second basis. The recalculated Kappa was $k = .942$, making the mean Kappa for all six conversations $k = .912$.

Lag Sequential Analysis

The data were analyzed using Lag Sequential Analysis (Sackett, 1978). Lag Sequential Analysis counts the number of times a behavior of interest (e.g., A's self-disclosure) follows a selected behavior (e.g., B's self-disclosure) at various lag steps removed in the ordered data and compares this number with the number of occurrences of the behavior of interest in the data as a whole.

Lags are defined as the number of event or time units between sequential behaviors. Both event and time units were employed in this study. However, only the results for the event analysis are reported here. The results for the time analysis were similar and are reported elsewhere (Dindia, 1981). The event was the utterance, a continuous flow of verbal communication by a dyadic member to the point at which he or she terminated verbal output or was interrupted by the other dyadic member.

The event lag analysis was performed for the effect of B's self-disclosure on A's subsequent self-disclosure for A's following five utterances, and vice versa. The frequency of A's self-disclosure following B's self-disclosure, and vice versa, was counted for each utterance. The frequency data were transformed into lag conditional probabilities by dividing the frequency of A's self-disclosure following B's self-disclosure by the total number of occurrences of B's self-disclosure, and vice versa. Next, the conditional probabilities of A's self-disclosure following B's self-disclosure were compared with the unconditional probability of A's self-disclosure, that is, the probability of the occurrence of A's self-disclosure in the data as a whole.

The method for assessing the statistical significance of conditional lag probabilities is to test them against unconditional probabilities. This method proceeds under the null hypothesis that A's self-disclosure will follow B's self-disclosure randomly. That is, A's self-disclosure following B's self-disclosure will occur no more frequently than A's relative frequency in the data as a whole. A nonchance relationship would be assumed if a Z score was significant using the unconditional probability as the expected value and the conditional probability as the observed value (Sackett, 1979).

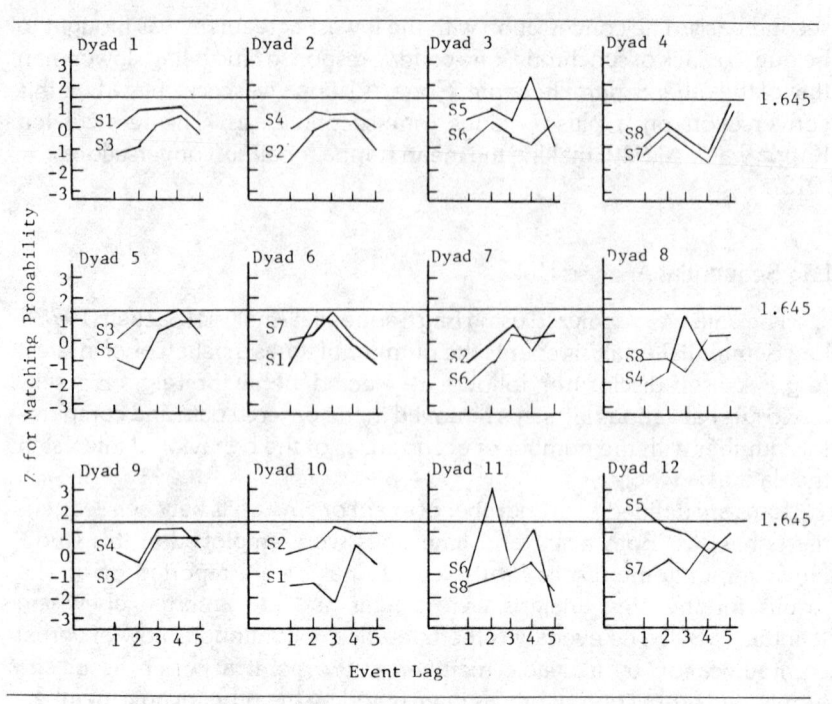

Figure 18.1. Lag sequential analysis of first conversation.

Since 360 conditional lag probabilities were computed (one for A's self-disclosure following B's self-disclosure, and vice versa, for five utterances over thirty-six conversations), some significant conditional lag probabilities were expected to occur by chance. To control for Type I errors, it is necessary to show that more significant conditional probabilities occurred than would be expected by chance (Sackett, 1980).

Reciprocity was operationally defined such that B's self-disclosure significantly increases the probability of A's self-disclosure above its unconditional probability, and vice versa. Lag Sequential Analysis was used to estimate and test the degree of (lagged) dependence of A's self-disclosure on B's self-disclosure, and vice versa.

Each dyad's Z scores for the lag sequential analysis are displayed in Figures 18.1 through 18.3. The figures plot the Z scores for the event data for five utterances for the three rounds of conversations, respectively.

Each graph represents a dyadic conversation. The vertical axis of the graphs reports the Z scores for the effect of each subject's self-disclosure on his or her partner's self-disclosure. The effect of a given subject's self-disclosure on his or her partner's self-disclosure is indicated by a line preceded by the number of the subject. (Subjects are numbered from one

Reciprocity of Self-Disclosure

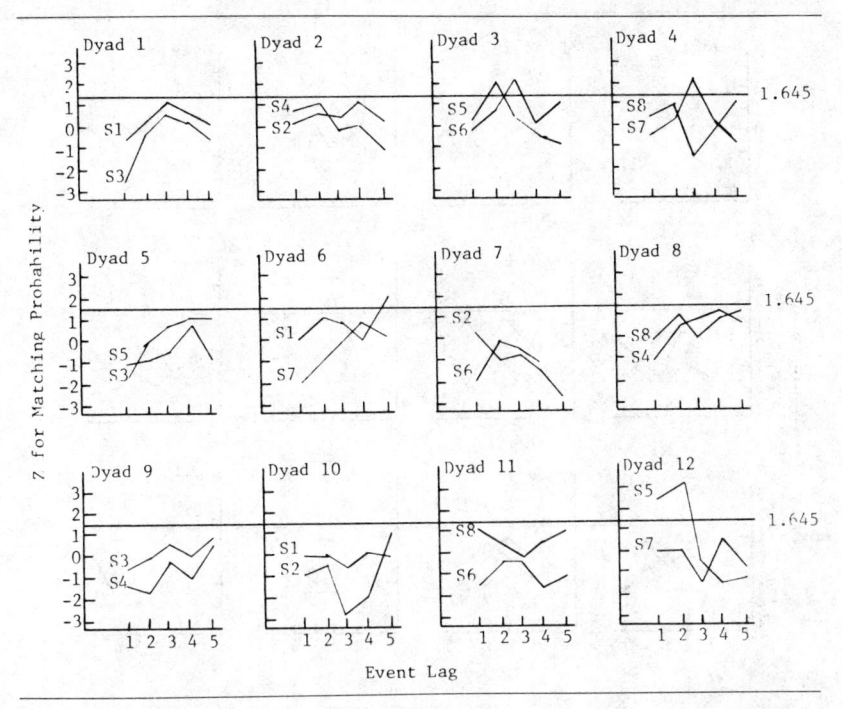

Figure 18.2. Lag sequential analysis of second conversation.

to eight, i.e., S1 - S8.) The horizontal axis reports the event lag or subsequent utterance in which a particular Z score occurred. A Z score above 1.645 (one-tailed, $p \leq .05$) indicated that the subject's self-disclosure significantly increased the probability of his or her partner's self-disclosure. Z scores below 1.645 are not significant. If both subjects have Z scores above 1.645, then reciprocity is present since each person's self-disclosure significantly increased the probability of the other person's self-disclosure. A significant Z score for only one person in the dyad would indicate a one-way effect but would not be evidence of reciprocity of self-disclosure.

In fact, no evidence of reciprocity was found. In all, 3 percent, or twelve of the 360 computed Z scores, were significant. This many significant Z scores are likely to have occurred by chance. The magnitude of the significant Z scores was quite small; all were less than a Z score of four. The greatest number of significant Z scores occurred at lag one where 5 percent, or four out of 72 computed Z scores (one for each person for each conversation) were significant. This result is also likely to have occurred by chance.

There was only one instance of a mutual effect, that is, both persons' self-disclosure increased the probability of the other person's self-

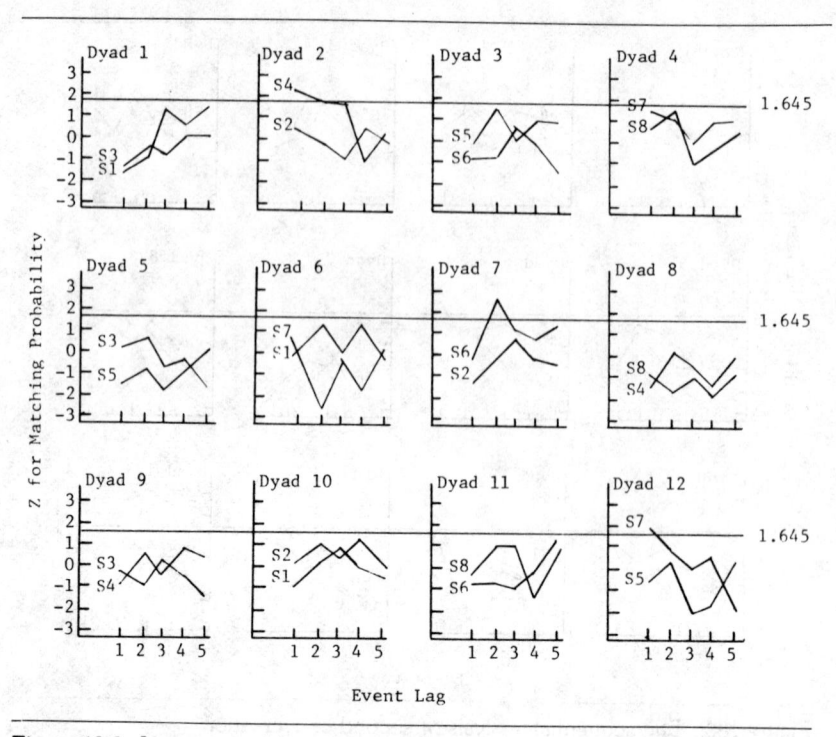

Figure 18.3. Lag sequential analysis of third conversation.

disclosure in any of his or her following five utterances. There were nine instances of a one-way effect, that is, one person's self-disclosure increased the probability of the other person's self-disclosure in one or more of the other person's following five utterances, but the other person's self-disclosure did not affect the first person's self-disclosure in any of the first person's following five utterances. The possibilty that this one-way effect was significant was tested. In all, 5½ percent, or ten of 180 computed Z scores (one for the effect of one person's self-disclosure on his or her partner's self-disclosure for the following five utterances, for each conversation) were significant. This result is also likely to be due to chance.

In sum, the lag conditional probabilities for B's self-disclosure following A's self-disclosure, computed for event data for B's following five utterances, and vice versa, were not markedly different from what would be expected by chance. The event analysis did not find evidence of reciprocity of self-disclosure. In addition, the event analysis did not find evidence of a one-way effect of A's self-disclosure on B's self-disclosure or vice versa.

Intraclass Correlation

A post hoc analysis of the relationship between dyadic partners' self-disclosure was performed. Dyadic partners engaged in conversation on three separate occasions. Therefore, an overall R was calculated for all thirty-six conversations. Additionally, R was calculated separately for each occasion. The difference between the correlations for the three occasions could not be tested for significance due to the small sample size (Steiger, 1980). R was computed on the percentage of the duration of self-disclosure, an index of self-disclosure computed by the formula, duration of self-disclosure divided by the duration of talk (i.e., self-disclosure and non-self-disclosure). This controls for the different speaking durations of partners (Chelune, 1978). Similar measures of self-disclosure have been employed in other studies of self-disclosure where the length of a subject's response is not fixed (cf. Chelune, 1975). The overall R for all thirty-six conversations was significant ($R = .48, p \leq .05$). The intraclass correlations for the first, second, and third conversations were, respectively, $R(12) = .16$, NS; $R(12) = .75, p \leq .005$, one-tailed; and $R(12) = .54, p \leq .05$, one-tailed.

The interpretation of these correlation coefficients is not straightforward. At each point in time each subject engaged in three dyadic conversations, so the dyadic conversations are not independent. This dependence decreases the total variance of self-disclosure across dyads, which decreases the value of the denominator in the R equation and inflates the obtained value of R. On the other hand, the small sample size limited the power of the test to detect significant results. Nonetheless, these coefficients seem to indicate that dyadic members' self-disclosure was related, at least in the second and third conversations. Hence, there was no evidence of reciprocity of self-disclosure, but there was some evidence of a positive relationship between dyadic partners' self-disclosure.

DISCUSSION

A comparison of the results of the present study with the results of the studies listed in Table 18.1 indicates several things. First, the majority of the nonexperimental studies reviewed found a positive relationship between dyadic partners' and small group members' self-disclosure. In the present study, self-disclosure was positively related but not reciprocal. It is possible that the previous studies that found a positive relationship between dyadic partners' and small group members' self-disclosure might not have found reciprocity had they tested for it.

Self-disclosure may be related but not reciprocal. Something other than A's self-disclosure eliciting B's self-disclosure, and vice versa, may cause A and B's self-disclosure to be positively related. This is especially true for self-disclosure being positively related in social and familial relationships, where subjects are not randomly assigned to dyads. This is less plausible for the nonexperimental, observational studies that randomly assign subjects to dyads or small groups.

The majority of the nonexperimental, observational studies reviewed found a positive relationship between dyadic partners' and small group members' self-disclosure in a brief encounter between strangers. In the present study, self-disclosure was related in the second and third conversations between dyadic partners, but not in their initial interaction. The question arises, why wasn't self-disclosure related in their first conversation? The reason the positive relationship did not reach significance in the first conversation may be due in part to the small sample size and, consequently, the low power to detect significance. This sample size was much smaller than the sample sizes employed in the other nonexperimental, observational studies reviewed.

Nonetheless, the relationship between A and B's self-disclosure increased substantially from the first to the second conversations. There are no studies with which to compare this result. No other studies have analyzed the relationship between dyadic members' self-disclosure on more than one occasion. However, Kohen (1975) divided dyadic conversations into a five-minute unstructured acquaintance period and a ten-minute discussion period. For purposes of analysis, the ten-minute discussion period was further divided into two five-minute periods. The correlation between dyadic members' number of self-disclosures over the total interaction was significant. The correlations for each time-period were significant, with a substantial increase in the correlations with each time-period. So the increase in correlations from the first conversation to the second conversation is similar to Kohen's findings.

This increase in correlations, both in the present study and in Kohen's study, may be due to an increase in the variation of self-disclosure across dyads as the dyads became better acquainted and more varied in their self-disclosure. Correlation is a ratio of covariance of self-disclosure within dyads to total variance of self-disclosure across dyads. A nonsignificant correlation could be due in part to similar base rates (i.e., a small variation) of self-disclosure across dyads. Because all dyads start out as strangers, self-disclosure levels may be similar at first across dyads. But as relationships develop at different rates, the level of self-disclosure across dyads may differ. Small sample size and small variability of self-disclosure across dyads in initial interactions may explain the lack of a positive relationship in dyads' first conversations and why there was a substantial increase in correlations in dyads' second conversations.

A comparison of the results from the present study with the results of the experimental studies reviewed reveals another anomaly. Most of the experimental studies found a one-way effect of an experimenter's or confederate's self-disclosure on a subject's self-disclosure. However, this study did not find a one-way effect of a person's self-disclosure on another person's self-disclosure, let alone a two-way effect. This may be due to the more naturalistic situation employed in the present study than in the typical experimental study. In this study, subjects engaged in unstructured interaction. They did not choose their partners, they were tape recorded, and they talked for thirty minutes in each conversation. This is, however, far less restrictive and a more realistic simulation of true conversational self-disclosure than the frequent experimental study where strangers (seen, unseen, or imagined) disclose (in writing or in person) nothing, superficial information, or intimate information. Without extreme manipulations, the effect of one person's self-disclosure on another person's self-disclosure may not be significant.

Another explanation for the lack of reciprocity found in this study is that almost all the other observational studies aimed at testing the reciprocity hypothesis involved strangers as subjects. These strangers interacted briefly (if at all) and knew they would never see each other again. This is true for both nonexperimental studies where two or more strangers interact in a dyad or small group and for the experimental studies where a confederate or experimenter "interacts" with a subject. Many researchers have commented on the lack of generalizability of this situation, likening it to the "stranger on the train" phenomenon. It has been hypothesized that such situations yield maximum reciprocity (Altman, 1973). In this study, subjects knew (or at least thought) they would interact with their partners on an individual basis in the near future. Perhaps self-disclosure is reciprocal only among strangers who know they will never see each other again and not for subjects who know they will see each other again.

In sum, there is no empirical evidence supporting reciprocity of self-disclosure. In fact, this study, although limited in generalizability by its small sample size, provided evidence indicating that self-disclosure is not reciprocal. Replications of this study are needed to provide confirmatory evidence of this result.

REFERENCES

Altman, I. Reciprocity of interpersonal exchange. *Journal for the Theory of Social Behavior,* 1973, *3*, 249-261.

Altman, I., & Taylor, D. A. *Social penetration: The development of interpersonal relationships.* New York: Holt, 1973.
Archer, R. L., & Berg, J. H. Disclosure reciprocity and its limits: A reactance analysis. *Journal of Experimental Social Psychology,* 1978, *14,* 527-540.
Becker, J. F., & Munz, D. C. Extraversion and reciprocation of interviewer disclosures. *Journal of Consulting and Clinical Psychology,* 1975, *43,* 593.
Brewer, M. B., & Mittelman, J. Effects of normative control of self-disclosure on reciprocity. *Journal of Personality,* 1980, *48,* 89-102.
Cappella, J. N. Mutual influence in expressive behavior: Adult-adult and infant-adult dyadic interaction. *Psychological Bulletin,* 1981, *89,* 101-132.
Certner, B. C. The exchange of self-disclosures in same-sexed groups of strangers. *Journal of Consulting and Clinical Psychology,* 1973, *40,* 292-297.
Chaikin, A. L., & Derlega, V. J. Liking for the norm-breaker in self-disclosure. *Journal of Personality,* 1974, *42,* 117-129. (a)
Chaikin, A. L., & Derlega, V. J. *Self-disclosure.* Morristown, NJ: General Learning Press, 1974. (b)
Chaikin, A. L., Derlega, V. J., Bayma, B., & Shaw, J. Neuroticism and disclosure reciprocity. *Journal of Consulting and Clinical Psychology,* 1975, *43,* 13-19.
Chelune, G. J. *Studies in the behavioral and self-report assessment of self-disclosure.* Doctoral Dissertation, University of Nevada, 1975.
Chelune, G. J. Nature and assessment of self-disclosing behavior. In P. McReynolds (Ed.), *Advances in Psychological Assessment IV.* San Francisco: Jossey-Bass, 1978.
Chelune, G. J. Measuring openness in interpersonal communication. In G. J. Chelune et al. (Eds.), *Self-disclosure: Origins, patterns and implications of openness in interpersonal relationships.* San Francisco: Jossey-Bass, 1980.
Cohen, J. A coefficient of agreement for nominal scales. *Educational and Psychological Measurement,* 1960, *20,* 37-46.
Cozby, P. C. Self-disclosure, reciprocity and liking. *Sociometry,* 1972, *35,* 151-160.
Cozby, P. C. Self-disclosure: A literature review. *Psychological Bulletin,* 1973, *79,* 73-91.
Dalto, D. A., Ajzen, I., & Kaplan, K. J. Self-disclosure and attraction: Effects of intimacy and desirability on beliefs and attitudes. *Journal of Research in Personality,* 1979, *13,* 127-138.
Davis, J. D. Self-disclosure in an acquaintance experience: Responsibility for level of intimacy. *Journal of Personality and Social Psychology,* 1976, *33,* 787-792.
Davis, J. D. Effects of communication about interpersonal process on the evolution of self-disclosure in dyads. *Journal of Personality and Social Psychology,* 1977, *35,* 31-37.
Davis, J. D. When boy meets girl: Sex roles and the negotiation of intimacy in an acquaintance exercise. *Journal of Personality and Social Psychology,* 1978, *36,* 684-692.
Davis, J. D., & Skinner, A. E. Reciprocity of self-disclosure in interviews: Modeling or social change. *Journal of Personality and Social Psychology,* 1974, *29,* 779-784.
Davis, J. D., & Sloan, M. L. Interviewer facilitation of interviewee self-disclosure — reciprocity or modeling. *Bulletin of the British Psychological Society,* 1972, *25,* 150.
DeForest, D., & Stone, G. L. Effects of sex and intimacy level on self-disclosure. *Journal of Counseling Psychology,* 1980, *27,* 93-96.
Derlega, V. J., & Chaikin, A. L. *Sharing intimacy: What we reveal to others and why.* Englewood Cliffs, NJ: Prentice-Hall, 1975.
Derlega, V. J., Chaikin, A. L., & Herndon, J. Demand characteristics and disclosure reciprocity. *The Journal of Social Psychology,* 1975, *97,* 301-302.
Derlega, V. J., Harris, M. S., & Chaikin, A. L. Self-disclosure reciprocity, liking and the deviant. *Journal of Experimental Social Psychology,* 1973, *9,* 277-284.
Derlega, V. J., Walmer, J., & Furman, G. Mutual disclosure in social interactions. *The Journal of Social Psychology,* 1973, *90,* 159-160.
Derlega, V. J., Wilson, M., & Chaikin, A. L. Friendship and disclosure reciprocity. *Journal of Personality and Social Psychology,* 1976, *34,* 578-582.
Dindia, K. A. *Reciprocity of self-disclosure: A sequential analysis.* Doctoral dissertation, University of Washington, 1981.

Dion, K. K., & Dion, K. L. Defensiveness, intimacy, and heterosexual attraction. *Journal of Research in Personality*, 1978, *12*, 479-487.

Dollard, J., & Mowrer, O. H. A method of measuring tension in written documents. *Journal of Abnormal and Social Psychology*, 1947, *42*, 3-32.

Ebersole, P., McFall, M., & Brandt, C. Imitation and prior classroom contact as determinants of reciprocal self-disclosure. *Psychological Reports*, 1977, *41*, 87-91.

Ehrlich, J. H., & Graeven, D. B. Reciprocal self-disclosure in dyads. *Journal of Experimental Social Psychology*, 1971, *7*, 389-400.

Feigenbaum, W. M. Reciprocity in self-disclosure within the psychological interview. *Psychological Reports*, 1977, *40*, 15-26.

Gary, A. L., & Hammond, R. Self-disclosure of alcoholics and drug addicts. *Psychotherapy: Theory, Research and Practice*, 1970, *7*, 142-143.

Goodstein, L. D., & Reinecker, V. M. Factors affecting self-disclosure: A review of the literature. In B. A. Maher (Ed.), *Progress in experimental personality research* (Vol. 7). New York: Academic Press, 1974.

Gottman, J. M. *Marital interactions: Experimental investigations.* New York: Academic Press, 1979.

Gottman, J., Markman, H., & Notarius, C. The topography of marital conflict: A sequential analysis of verbal and nonverbal behavior. *Journal of Marriage and the Family*, 1977, *39*, 461-477.

Gottman, J., Notarius, C., Markman, H., Bank, S., Yoppi, B., & Rubin, M. E. Behavior exchange theory and marital decision making. *Journal of Personality and Social Psychology*, 1976, *34*, 14-23.

Haggard, E. A. *Intraclass correlation and the analysis of variance.* New York: Dryden Press, 1958.

Johnson, C. F., & Dabbs, J. M., Jr. Self-disclosure in dyads as a function of distance and the subject-experimenter relationship. *Sociometry*, 1976, *39*, 257-263.

Jones, E. E., & Archer, R. L. Are there special effects of personalistic self-disclosure? *Journal of Experimental Social Psychology*, 1976, *12*, 180-193.

Jourard, S. M. Self-disclosure and other cathexis. *Journal of Abnormal and Social Psychology*, 1959, *59*, 428-431.

Jourard, S. M. The effects of experimenters' self-disclosure on subjects' behavior. In C. Speilberger (Ed.), *Current topics in community and clinical psychology*. New York: Academic Press, 1969.

Jourard, S. M. *Self-disclosure: An experimental analysis of the transparent self.* New York: Wiley-Interscience, 1971.

Jourard, S. M., & Friedman, R. Experimenter-subject "distance" and self-disclosure. *Journal of Personality and Social Psychology*, 1970, *15*, 278-282.

Jourard, S. M., & Jaffe, P. E. Influence of an interviewer's disclosure on the self-disclosing behavior of interviewees. *Journal of Counseling Psychology*, 1970, *17*, 252-257.

Jourard, S. M., & Landsman, M. J. Cognition, cathexis, and the "dyadic effect" in men's self-disclosing behavior. *Merrill Palmer Quarterly*, 1960, *6*, 178-186.

Jourard, S. M., & Resnick, J. L. The effect of high-revealing subjects on the self-disclosure of low-revealing subjects. *Journal of Humanistic Psychology*, 1970, *10*, 84-93.

Jourard, S. M., & Richman, P. Disclosure output and input in college students. *Merrill Palmer Quarterly*, 1963, *9*, 141-148.

Kohen, J. A. Liking and self-disclosure in opposite sex dyads. *Psychological Reports*, 1975, *36*, 695-698.

Levin, F. M., & Gergen, K. J. Revealingness, ingratiation, and disclosure of self. *Proceedings of the 77th Annual Convention of the American Psychological Association*, 1969, *4*, 447-448.

Levinger, G., & Senn, D. J. Disclosure of feelings in marriage. *Merrill Palmer Quarterly*, 1967, *13*, 237-249.

Lynn, S. J. Three theories of self-disclosure exchange. *Journal of Experimental Social Psychology*, 1978, *5*, 466-479.

Mann, G., & Murphy, K. C. Timing of self-disclosure, reciprocity of self-disclosure, and reactions to an initial interview. *Journal of Counseling Psychology*, 1975, *22*, 304-308.

MORE (Microprocessor Operated Recording Equipment). Available from Observational Systems, Inc., 1103 Grand Ave., Seattle, WA 98122.

Morgan, R. N., & Evans, J. F. Comparison of reinforcing and modeling techniques for promoting self-disclosure. *Psychological Reports,* 1977, *40,* 363-371.

Panyard, C. M. Self-disclosure between friends: A validity study. *Journal of Counseling Psychology,* 1973, *20,* 66-68.

Pearce, W. B., & Sharp, S. M. Self-disclosing communication. *Journal of Communication,* 1973, *23,* 409-425.

Pearce, W. B., Wright, P. H., Sharp, S. M., & Slama, K. M. Affection and reciprocity in self-disclosing communication. *Human Communication Research,* 1974, *1,* 5-15.

Powell, W. J. Differential effectiveness of interviewer interventions in an experimental interview. *Journal of Consulting and Clinical Psychology,* 1968, *32,* 210-215.

Rogers, J. M. Operant conditioning in a quasi-therapy setting. *Journal of Abnormal and Social Psychology,* 1960, *60,* 247-252.

Rubin, Z. Disclosing oneself to a stranger: Reciprocity and its limits. *Journal of Experimental Social Psychology,* 1975, *11,* 233-260.

Rubin, Z., Hill, C. T., Peplau, L. A., & Dunkelschetter, C. Self-disclosure in dating couples: Sex roles and the ethic of openness. *Journal of Marriage and the Family,* 1980, *42,* 305-317.

Rubin, Z., & Shenker, S. Friendship, proximity, and self-disclosure. *Journal of Personality,* 1978, *46,* 1-22.

Sackett, G. P. Measurement in observational research. In G. P. Sackett (Ed.), *Observing behavior. Volume II: Data collection and analysis methods.* Baltimore: University Park Press, 1978.

Sackett, G. P. The lag sequential analysis of contingency and cyclicity in behavioral interaction research. In J. D. Osofsky (Ed.), *Handbook of infant development.* New York: John Wiley, 1979.

Sackett, G. P. Lag sequential analysis as a data reduction technique in social interaction research. In D. B. Sawin et al. (Eds.), *Exceptional Infant 4: Psychosocial risks in infant-environmental transactions.* New York: Brunner/Mazel, 1980.

Savicki, V. E. Outcomes of nonreciprocal self-disclosure strategies. *Journal of Personality and Social Psychology,* 1972, *23,* 271-276.

Sermat, V., & Smyth, M. Content analysis of verbal communication in the development of a relationship: Conditions influencing self-disclosure. *Journal of Personality and Social Psychology,* 1973, *26,* 332-346.

Steiger, J. H. Tests for comparing elements of a correlation matrix. *Psychological Bulletin,* 1980, *87,* 245-251.

Strassberg, D. S., Gabel, H., & Anchor, K. N. Patterns of self-disclosure in parent discussion groups. *Small Group Behavior,* 1976, *7,* 369-378.

Tognoli, J. J. Response matching in interpersonal information exchange. *British Journal of Social and Clinical Psychology,* 1969, *8,* 116-123.

Vondracek, F. W. The study of self-disclosure in experimental interviews. *Journal of Psychology,* 1969, *72,* 55-59.

Vondracek, S. I., & Vondracek, F. The manipulation and measurement of self-disclosure in preadolescents. *Merrill Palmer Quarterly,* 1971, *17,* 51-58.

Woolfolk, A. E. Self-disclosure in the classroom: An experimental study. *Contemporary Educational Psychology,* 1979, *4,* 132-139.

Worthy, W., Gary, A. L., & Kahn, G. M. Self-disclosure as an exchange process. *Journal of Personality and Social Psychology,* 1969, *13,* 59-63.

IV • MASS COMMUNICATION

19 ● International Mass Communication Research: A Critical Review of Theory and Methods

K. KYOON HUR
University of Texas—Austin

THE literature in international communication has reached almost landslide proportions in recent years. A resurgence in international communication research has been marked by the publication of more specialized books and journals and the growth of professional organizations and meetings particularly during the 1970s. While the field of international communication has received continuous attention from scholars of various disciplines, the renewed interest in this field has come at a time when communication scholars are focusing on the need for revision of the existing communication theories — not only in international communication research, but in communication research as a whole (Rogers, 1976, 1978; Dervin, 1980; Chaffee, 1977; Halloran, 1981). This renewed interest has also come at a time when scholars as well as policymakers concerned with communication are focusing on the need to restructure existing international communication systems that are faced with ever-increasing transfer of both communication hardware and software across national boundaries (Nordenstreng & Schiller, 1979; Gunter, 1978; Masmoudi, 1979).

Despite the plethora of research in international communication, however, there have been few systematic attempts to reflect accurately the state

AUTHOR'S NOTE: This chapter was submitted to the Mass Communication Division at the annual convention of the International Communication Association, Boston, May 1-5, 1982. The author wishes to thank Rita Atwood of the University of Texas—Austin for her help and valuable suggestions.

Correspondence and requests for reprints: K. Kyoon Hur, Department of Radio-TV-Film, University of Texas, Austin, TX 78712.

of the art in research and theory in pertinent areas of the field. The ability of scholars in the field to monitor the literature has lagged behind for reasons other than sheer magnitude, and the attempt of scholars to provide synthesizing overviews of the literature has been lacking for reasons other than specialization. As a result, international communication as a field of study remains largely undefined and fragmented across different disciplines, e.g., anthropology, cross-cultural psychology, international and comparative politics and sociology, and intercultural and international communication.

Certainly, a number of areas fall within the broad rubric of international communication. In a trend analysis of international communication research in the United States between 1950 and 1970, Mowlana (1973) categorizes international communication research into the following aspects: (1) communication systems studies discussing the structure and operations of media systems in specific cultures and/or geographical areas of the world; (2) theoretical studies in international communication and various applications studies, including communication and foreign policy, public opinion and propaganda, cross-cultural communication, communication and development in general, and diffusion of innovations in particular; and (3) studies of channels in international communication, such as international news communication, international communicators and foreign correspondence, communication and technology, and laws and regulations in international communication. This list of the variety of areas in international communication research even before the proliferation of the literature during the 1970s suggests that the literature in the field may be too large and too eclectic to be synthesized into single reviews. Yet the need for research solutions to shed light on the characteristics of crucial issues in current international communication research, as well as for policy solutions to solve some of the disturbing problems of imbalance in communication flows, ownership structures, and cultural homogenization trends, makes a research overview of pertinent areas of international communication very important.

The purpose of this chapter is to provide a critical review of international mass communication research, focusing on the relationship between theory and methods that have been explored in past research in the field. The major questions posed in this investigation are: How appropriate are various methods employed in international mass communication research in relation to basic assumptions of the research questions for which they have been utilized? How appropriate or inappropriate are linkages made between concepts and operationalization, as well as linkages of both with the kinds of inferences that were made based on obtained research results? Within this context, the scope of this investigation will be limited to the parameters established by the definition of international mass communication research set forth here. International mass communication research includes those studies that involve examinations of media systems of the world, processes and effects of international mass communications. This includes such subject areas as media systems, comparative media analysis, the flow of news, information, and cultural materials between and across national or cultural boundaries, and the effects of international mass communication. This can be contrasted with, but not entirely separated from, such distinctive subject areas as "intercultural communication," which emphasizes interpersonal communication across cultures both within and across national boundaries, and "communication and development," which emphasizes both the theoretical and practical utilization of communication hardware and software in developmental processes mainly in developing countries. For a practical limitation, however, this chapter will not include studies that deal exclusively with intercultural communication and communication and development; intercultural communication research rarely incorporates mass communication, and the bulk of the literature in communication and development is concerned with applications as well as implications of communications technology in the developmental process of Third World countries.

Instead, this chapter will focus on the characteristics of international mass communication research that can only be considered in light of issues that pervade all of communications research. More specifically, an attempt will be made to distinguish between theory and corresponding methods of analysis for examining international mass communication research questions.

The central controversy in the past decade of international mass communication research stems from challenges to conventional research approaches that originated in developed Western nations and have been perpetuated in developing nations, and even adopted by researchers from developing nations. These challenges include the assertion that Western models of mass communication research have been too capitalistic and oriented toward marketing objectives with the intent of furthering the political, economic, and cultural hegemony of developed Western nations (Beltran, 1975). Another challenge is that Western models of international mass communication research are primarily concerned with theoretical issues, and that they ignore the pragmatic communication problems and issues in developing nations.

Recently, several scholars in international mass communication research have attempted to posit what they believe is a more useful perspective for examining the diverse advocacy positions for future research directions. For example, Lang (1979) argues that various approaches to communication research are not as distinctively different as those that confuse ideological differences with theoretical differences. Halloran (1981) suggests that the main problem in the debate over future directions in international mass communication research is not the imposition of adoption of research models from developed nations, but rather the fact that such research models have resulted in "bad research, bad social science." Atwood (1980) supports this notion by identifying several important conceptual issues that limit the utility of mass communication research conducted in developing nations, regardless of cultural or ideological orientation. Dervin (1980) also contends that challenges to Western models of international communications are challenges of a practical nature, but argues that such challenges have little utility unless they are accompanied by philosophical, theoretical shifts in the way researchers conceive of communication processes.

While these researchers vary to some extent in the degree and nature of the confrontations they advocate, they agree on the immediately crucial need to sort out the useful research findings that can guide the investigation of international mass communication systems and their related environments. It is not difficult to find rigidifying perspectives occurring in the field of international communication as the literatures become too large and too eclectic. By bringing different perspectives into a literature overview, however, we can do more than find characteristics of major approaches to international mass communication studies; we can also search for the divergences and convergences in the directions taken in international mass communication research. This requires an analysis of the relationships of different perspectives to research and theory in pertinent subject areas of international mass communication. The following section, therefore, examines the research literature in two main subject areas: mass media systems analysis and the process and effects of international mass communication.

MASS MEDIA SYSTEMS ANALYSIS

The proliferation of the literature in mass media systems can be noted particularly during the last thirty years, not only with regard to those studies conducted by U.S. researchers, but also those by foreign researchers. For example, Mowlana (1973) shows that communication systems studies constituted more than 50 percent of the total international communication research studies published from 1950 through 1970 in the United States. This growth continued during the 1970s with more emphasis on media systems of developing countries and regions (Katz & Wedell, 1979; UNESCO, 1975; Lent, 1979). Thus the plethora of study and research in mass media systems offers a growing body of information, although familiarity with the characteristics of "other" mass media systems, both for pedagogical and policy reasons, is a totally different question.

Since it is not difficult to find the literature in mass media systems analysis through the available bibliographies, this section will discuss several issues and problems associated with approaches and methods in media systems analysis, rather than evaluate specific studies per se. Here particular attention will be paid to the evaluation of mass media systems research focusing on the problem of research paradigms in comparative media systems studies on a cross-national basis.

First, a review of studies on mass media systems suggests that there is an uneven amount of research focus on specific cultures and geographical areas, with more attention paid to Western European and North American systems. Except for a few general, descriptive studies on the world media systems (Emery, 1969; Dizard, 1966; Merrill, Bryan, & Alisky, 1970) and on the Soviet Union's and China's media systems (Inkles, 1956; Markham, 1967; Yu, 1964), only a small proportion of media systems studies began to appear during the 1970s about such regions as Africa (Hachten, 1971; Head, 1977), Asia (Lent, 1971, 1978; Lerner, 1976), Eastern Europe (Paulu, 1974), the Middle East (Mowlana, 1971, 1977), and the developing countries as a whole (Katz & Wedell, 1979). This is not surprising when we consider the historical world power structure dominated primarily by the Western industrialized societies and the Soviet Union as well as Communist China. However, it is still interesting to note that only a handful of communication scholars have expressed concern about this uneven research focus on different cultural and geographical areas (Mowlana, 1973, 1976; Dinh, 1979).

Aside from the issue of ethnocentric bias in approaches and methods used in these studies, the mere lack of literature in media systems analysis in developing countries and regions appears to have the alarming result of ignorance about the characteristics of these media systems. An understanding of specific nations' and regions' media systems depends on the availability of literature in these areas. This also raises the question of access to the available literature. Although there are a great number of foreign research studies on the relevant media systems readily available in almost every foreign culture (often included in bibliographies), the access to these materials is largely limited due to the number of these works translated. Furthermore, there is a tendency in the international communication research community to consider foreign publications and reports as less reliable sources of "scientific" research information. Though not explicitly stated, this is certainly one of the factors that contributes to the ideological debates occurring in international mass communication research.

Second, there is the lack of divergences and convergences in approaches and methods used in the study of mass media systems. Theoretically, the major approaches and methods in media systems studies constitute a systems approach, in which various case studies follow a structural and functional approach covering history, policy, organizational structure, finance, programming, relations with other media and external/foreign influences, and audiences of the media. However, most of the past research in media systems analysis has concentrated on the historical description of a single system on a country-by-country basis or on a media basis (Emery, 1969; Dizard, 1966; Head, 1977; Paulu, 1967, 1974; Lent, 1971; Merrill et al., 1970; Hachten, 1971; Markham, 1967; Hopkins, 1970; Liu, 1971; Yu, 1964; Smith, 1973; Pool, 1972a). While the contributions made by these researchers are of great significance to the growing body of information on various media systems of the world, these studies primarily rely on the methodology of case studies and thus often result in uneven depths of analysis due to variations among the systems and the availability of data. In other words, there is the lack of functional analyses in the sense that these studies have focused on the media systems of countries or regions as a whole, when analyses of media systems, processes, and effects received should be studied concurrently. Furthermore, the specific value of case studies — to provide the distinctive nature of any given period in history — often becomes obsolete in the constantly changing media policies covering the structure and operations of a system.

There is no readily available solution to these problems associated with mass media systems studies, but a promising sign in the field is the recent trend in international mass communication research to bring a variety of mass media systems analyses together with updated information. In recent years there have been a number of major publications and symposia that provide not only up-to-the-minute examinations of a variety of mass media systems in the world but also different foci on media systems analysis. For example, a symposium on Western European broadcasting in the *Journal of Communication* (1978) shows how the Western European broadcasting systems have changed since Paulu's (1967) major work in this area. Specifically, as Grandi (1978) well summarizes, Western European broadcasting systems have undergone enormous changes in terms of relaxation of government control, public participation in the system accountability, decentralization of broadcasting monopolies and introduction of advertising. This particular example suggests that the study of media systems cannot rely solely on the historical description; the structure and operations of media systems of the world are undergoing continuous changes influenced by both domestic and international socioeconomic, political, and cultural factors, as outlined by Davison and George (1954) almost three decades ago. Furthermore, the current changes in communications technology have constantly modified the economic and political parameters of the existing communication system. These changes should be accounted for carefully in media systems analyses. Such analyses also involve policy research in mass media systems in the changing context of world communications structure (Gerbner, 1977). As Pool (1974) points out, good policy research has to take account of all factual and normative variables operating in the system. Both in theory and methods, this means a multidisciplinary approach to media systems analysis, incorporating findings from sociology, economics, political science, psychology, organization theory, and engineering, as well as humanities and cultural values research. There are fallacious arguments in the current theoretical debates that one research approach is by nature less empirical and more theoretical than another, and that one is not so much the cold determination of the facts as it is philosophical and conceptual deliberation. No single approach or finding is decisive in mass media systems analysis.

The recent collaborated works of various disciplines as related to specific regional media systems provide significant insight into the dynamics of those systems. Examples include case studies of mass media in the Third World (Lent, 1979), broadcasting in Asia and the Pacific (Lent, 1978), analysis of various communication media channels and usage in Asia (Lerner, 1976) and in the Pacific (Lerner & Richstadt, 1976), and structural analysis of information systems related to rural development in Latin America (McAnany, 1980). The major strength of these studies is that they not only include a variety of national communication systems as cases for investigation, but they also approach systems analysis using diverse methods, including economic and political structural analysis, communication channels analysis, content analysis, and audience analysis.

There is the problem of lack of focus in this type of edited work, but this is a technical problem rather than a theoretical one. If an edited volume lacks a good overview of the domain under investigation, it is a limitation imposed on the editor, not on the reader. The reader, within a context of the work, can search for divergences and convergences when specific research is brought together. Indeed, bringing literature together seems to be the first major task in international mass communication research (Mahan, 1981), which can then be followed with a "state of the art" review to provide synthesis and interpretation (for examples of this kind of work, see McAnany, Schnitman, & Janus, 1981; Shore, 1980; Pool, 1974).

A current survey of the international communication literature shows that there are a number of individual research studies focused on different aspects of mass media systems, but most of them are scattered throughout major journals and reports and have not been brought into a systematic collection. A few examples of such studies include those on media policy (Miller, 1973; Lent, 1975; Hachten, 1979; Fagen, 1974; Boyd, 1975; Howell, 1979; Toogood, 1972, 1978), media advertising as related to economic and cultural conditions (Fejes, 1980; de Cardona, 1975; Janus, 1981; Marquez, 1975), media content and broadcast programming analyzed for educational and/or cultural implications (Chu & Alfian, 1980; Robinson, 1974), media channels and their usage (Whiting & Stanfield, 1972; Powell, 1975-1976; Mowlana, 1977), and communicator as well as audience attitudes toward the mass media (Giffard, 1976; Brown & Lee, 1977; Martin, Chaffee, & Izcaray, 1979). This list, which can certainly be extended, suggests the immediate need for both literature collection and synthesis in the field in a tradition similar to that of Schramm's (1964) pioneering work in mass media and national development. One good example of such work may be found in Katz and Wedell (1979), in their examination of broadcasting in the Third World. In this work the authors provide not only the historical development of Third World broadcasting systems through structural analysis, but also critical examinations of the performances of these systems through programming and audience analysis. Certainly, more works of this type are needed in the study of mass media systems.

Third, in mass media systems studies, aside from the lack of comparisons between and among systems, there is a stalemate in comparative media research, partly due to ideological conflict and the resultant lack of coordination and partly due to theoretical and methodological limitations that have not been explored fully in mass media research.

In a broader sense, there are two schools of thought as to approaches and methods used in comparative media research. One school consists of those providing detailed descriptions of a variety of media systems on a regional or worldwide basis, as discussed in the section above. This is not exactly comparative media research, but rather case studies through which comparison between media systems are offered. The other school consists of those concerned with theory construction in comparative mass media systems and thus in providing theoretical discussions of systems typology, often with empirical data on various systems elements (Siebert, Peterson, & Schramm, 1956; Loevinger, 1967; Nixon, 1960, 1965; Namurois, 1964).

It is natural to find that the methodological traditions of these two camps are in conflict, as the former is primarily descriptive and evaluative while the latter is empirical and scientific. There has been growing criticism in recent years addressed to the social science approach to comparative mass media analysis (Mowlana, 1976; Toogood, 1980). One of the criticisms that appears to go beyond ideological debates is that the systems typology and index developed and used in comparative media analysis is culture-bound and thus inadequate as it has been linked to political ideology. For example, the classification developed in *Four Theories of the Press* (Siebert et al., 1956) and later redesigned in terms of systems control and ownership (Namurois, 1964; Wells, 1974) was based on political systems model and ideology (e.g., democracy versus communism). Another example includes comparative studies of press freedom of various media systems in which the index of press freedom is directly linked with democratic concepts of press freedom (Nixon, 1960, 1965; Lowenstein, 1970). Certainly, then, comparing mass media systems in terms of the relationship between media and government is susceptible to ideological bias and ignores other socioeconomic and cultural factors that influence the structure and operations of the media system.

Another criticism of the social science approach to the comparative study of communication systems is that often the systems have been analyzed in the context of socioeconomic and political development (Lerner, 1958; Pye, 1963; Fagen, 1964; Schramm, 1964). The critical arguments here are that (1) mass media systems cannot be compared on traditional communications development measurements (e.g., radio and television sets per 1,000 people, newspaper circulations) and that (2) communications development cannot be examined in relation to other socioeconomic and political development because they are not necessarily correlated to each other. This criticism has been well taken in recent years as both developmental concepts and the role of communication in development are being reassessed (Rogers, 1976; Schramm & Lerner, 1976; Eisenstadt, 1976).

These critical arguments raise theoretical and methodological questions not only for comparative study of mass media systems but also for any other social inquiry in which researchers are concerned with the adequacy and validity of concepts, variables, and data and measurements. It is true that comparative mass media analysis has had "its share of poorly defined terms, vague and ambiguous concepts, and culture-bound variables" (Mowland, 1976, p. 482) that have resulted in its remaining a largely unfruitful research area. This, however, should not obscure the significant task of comparative media research to build theory with data collection and analysis. The contribution made by Lerner (1958) is not the applicability of his theory of media and development to modern concepts of development and mass media analysis, but that it provides a context within which data gathering and analysis was achieved in a truly comparative setting. Precisely for this reason, his model or theory could have been explicated and revised to create a "better" theory (Frey, 1972).

Comparative methods widely used in the field of comparative politics and other social sciences have shown that the behavior of social systems and of people within these systems can be compared systematically and interchangeably both at system and individual levels (Holt & Turner, 1970; Merritt, 1971; Przeworski & Teune, 1970; Gillespie & Nesvold, 1971). As proposed by Mowlana (1976) and independently researched by individual scholars, there are four kinds of data that provide theory in comparative mass media analysis. The first is aggregate data, which provide the kind of statistical data on media ownership, number of media, budget, and the economics of production and distribution. This kind of data analysis is widely reported in various case studies. The second kind is sample survey data concerning media control (Lowenstein, 1970) and the audiences' media usage and preference patterns (Robinson, 1972; Shore, 1980). The third type is content analysis data, which describe the messages in a comparative setting. Examples include those studies reporting on television programming by different categories (Head, 1977; Lee, 1980; Shaheen, 1979) and those studies exclusively concerned with either newspaper content or television news programs (I will review these in the following section). Finally, there are the cultural data, which, according to Mowlana, can close the gaps between the aggregate and survey data. Except in a few studies (Farace, 1966; Farace & Donohew, 1965), however, cultural data have not been included and examined in comparative media analysis; their use has been confined mainly to other anthropological and cultural studies.

In summary, then, review of the literature in mass media systems analysis, particularly from a comparative perspective, reveals the types of research areas that have been neglected as well as the theoretical and methodological problems associated with mass media systems studies. The fact that study of mass media systems and comparative mass media systems utilizes a systems approach suggests analysis of these systems in terms of the interrelationships among "forcings (something being done to the system)," "the properties of the system," and "responses (in turn the system doing something)" (Trimmer, 1950, pp. 1-3). The systems analysis in mass media thus includes examinations of the physical nature of the medium (technology), the historical circumstances of its emergence and development, its economy, the social controls of the medium, and the effects of the medium. Methodologically, this requires both macrolevel and microlevel analyses in which different types of data can be obtained through various research techniques. Despite the plethora of research in mass media, the systems approach to the field has not yet been explored fully.

INTERNATIONAL COMMUNICATION PROCESSES AND EFFECTS ANALYSIS

As noted above, the bulk of the literature in international mass communications has dealt with the specific or comparative conditions of media structure and operations in terms of media productions, dissemination, and media usage. Because of the nature of case studies and the comparative methods employed, most of these studies have not been concerned with mass media systems analysis in the context of international mass communication structure and processes. There has been, however, considerable research in recent years focused on the structure and process of international mass communications and their effects on domestic cultures and social systems, including the mass media system. This includes studies dealing with the international mass communication network structure, distribution of media products across national and cultural boundaries, and the effects of imported messages on domestic cultural and social systems, as well as on individuals in those systems. These types of studies have become, in fact, a basis for the current debates on "media imperialism" or "cultural imperialism," and the resultant call for the new world information order.

Structure and Flow of International Mass Communications

Past research in this area can be divided into two categories by media content; news and information versus entertainment and cultural materials. The available literature will therefore be reviewed accordingly.

The area of news flow and the structure of international news has probably received the greatest attention in international mass communication research. In his pioneering survey of the world's press in international news coverage, later reported in his examination of mass media and national development, Schramm (1960, 1964) notes that "the flow of news among nations is thin, that it is unbalanced, with heavy coverage of a few highly developed countries and light coverage of many less developed nations, and that, in some cases, it tends to ignore important events and to distort the reality it represents" (Schramm, 1964, p. 65). He further points out that the flow of news between nations is governed by three basic realities: the ownership of the great avenues of news exchange agencies, the ownership of long-distance telecommunication facilities, and the concentration of wealth, technology, and power in a few highly developed nations. Perhaps the greatest contribution made by Schramm here is his delineation of major theoretical concepts and approaches to the study of international news communication, namely, the patterns of international news flow, the coverage of international news and the accuracy of the coverage, and the factors influencing international news flow, including international news organizational structure. Consequently, later studies concerned with international news communication fall, by and large, into one or more of these areas.

The most voluminous research in international news processes has dealt with the coverage of international news by various media of the world; from this research, a set of hypotheses on international news flow has also been presented. Here the unit of analysis is international news items reported in media output (which becomes the level of analysis) on a specific national, regional, or worldwide basis. Examples include international news coverage in the world's press (Gerbner & Marvanyi, 1977), the major news wire agencies (Weaver & Cleveland, 1980; Stevenson & Cole, 1980), the U.S. media in general (Lent, 1978; Kaplan, 1979) and U.S. television in particular (Larson, 1977, 1979), the Pacific region (Nnaemeka & Richstadt, 1980), Asia (Schramm, 1980), and Latin America (McNelly, 1979), and in specific countries' media, such as Japanese television (Iwao, 1981), the Swedish press (Thoren, 1968), the Korean press (Nam, 1970), and Finland's dailies (Starck, 1968). More specialized studies deal with the coverage of foreign news focused on specific countries or events mostly by the U.S. media and international news agencies, including coverage of Canada by the U.S. media and vice versa (Sparkes, 1977; Hart, 1968), the coverage of Africa (Pratt, 1980; Charles, Shore, & Todd, 1979), Asia (Lent & Rao, 1979; Mujahid, 1970), and the Middle East (Belkaoui, 1978) by U.S. newspapers and/or magazines, and the coverage of Latin America (Hester, 1974) and Africa (Bishop, 1975) by the major news agency or agencies.

By and large, these studies confirm the earlier findings by Schramm (1960, 1964) that the flow of news between and among these countries is unbalanced and that the coverage of international news reflects distortion, with emphasis on negative events, although there is variation in the amount and type of international news coverage by the media under investigation. Despite the abundant evidence of the imbalance in international news flow, however, there is no readily discernible pattern of elaborate character in the data that has led to the theoretical formulation of international news flow patterns.

Several important theoretical hypotheses related to international news flow have been proposed (Hester, 1971, 1973), but most of these have remained unsupported empirically. The obvious reason for this failure is not theoretical but methodological. Although studies of international news flow and those of international news coverage clearly require different research techniques, in most cases they have been treated interchangeably. In methodological terms, the former is flow or transaction analysis, which is concerned with the volume of message, whereas the latter is content analysis, which is concerned with the type of message. Yet most international news flow studies do not employ well-formulated transactional analytical techniques (Deutsch, 1956; Savage & Deutsch, 1960); rather, they employ content analytical techniques to explain international flow processes. Although these two approaches are different ways of bringing evidence to bear on the same questions concerning international news flow, content analysis involves broader theoretical concepts; it is concerned not only with the patterns of international news flow, but also with news selection processes and news values in international news communications.

When these methodological issues are delineated, there are significant research results bearing on international news flow processes. Using a rather well-founded theoretical and methodological ground established by gatekeeping studies (White, 1950; Donahue, Tichenor, & Olien, 1972), a number of researchers have attempted to theorize the process of international news coverage and flow by various media (Ostagaard, 1965; Galtung & Ruge, 1965; Rosengren, 1976, 1977; Hester, 1971, 1973). Aside from general features, the major criteria they identified as conducive to international news selection or values were socioeconomic proximity between nations, wealth or power of the nations, saliency of elite people, and the negativity of the event (Galtung & Ruge, 1965). While a particular hypothesis in this framework has been supported in one case and rejected in another, there is some evidence in this direction supplied more recently by other studies (Bergsma, 1978; Nnaemeka & Richstadt, 1980). Though the generality of the proposed set of hypotheses here requires more comparative studies of this kind across different media systems, the past findings, which show a remarkable consonance of media content related to international news values, suggest that research findings are quite amenable to synthesis and interpretation.

In contrast to the voluminous research in international news flow, study of the flow of entertainment and cultural materials in international mass communication research is a relatively recent phenomenon. The pioneer study in this area was conducted by Nordenstreng and Varis (1974), who analyzed the international inventory of television program structure and the flow of television programs between nations based on a fifty-country survey. In this survey two well-founded trends emerged in the international flow of television programs: a one-way traffic from the big exporting countries to the rest of the world and the domination of entertainment materials in the flow of television programs.

Although this study, along with another pioneering study by Guback (1969) of international film structure and flow, has received perhaps the greatest attention in the current discussion of cultural imperialism in international communication and has resulted in various studies specifically concerned with television flow between and among countries (Read, 1976; Pool, 1977), the systematic data collection method and the theoretical approach to account for the factors affecting international television program flow employed in this study have not been explicated. The only exceptions are found in the current and forthcoming studies from the International Television Flows Project (Chapman, 1980) and in the UNESCO project in Egypt (Rachty & Sabat, 1980).

This trend thus shows that much of the effort in television and/or film flow studies is directed outside the United States and suggests that the available research findings are unlikely to enhance our knowledge of the process of international television and film flows unless there is more research attention directed to this area by communication scholars, particularly by those in the United States following the traditional social science approach. For example, Nordenstreng and Varis (1974) proposed a number of hypotheses indicating that the flow of television programs across nations is influenced by the wealth and power of the nation, economic and demographic characteristics of the television audience of the nation, and tariffs imposed on programming importation by the nation. This set of proposed hypotheses (which Nordenstreng and Varis did not test empirically) was not examined in detail in later studies and thus was left largely unexplained. These are certainly crucial research questions that need to be studied, in light of the fact that one of the theoretical arguments occurring in the cultural imperialism debate as related to international television flow concerns the question of whether the degree of television program importation exhibited by many developing nations is due to audience demands or to the international television marketing structure dominated by developed nations (Nordenstreng & Schiller, 1979; Katz & Wedell, 1979). Without more hard data on economic and demographic characteristics of international television audiences, such questions are not likely to be answered.

There is ample evidence for the worldwide sprawl of television and film entertainment products, especially those produced in the United States, Great Britain, France, and West Germany, and for the economic impact of these products on the receiving countries' television and film industries. Ever since the publication of Schiller's (1969) pioneering study, well-founded findings by Guback (1969, 1974), Schiller (1976), Read (1976), Tunstall (1977), Wells (1972), and McAnany et al. (1981) have indicated that television and film products shown in many parts of developing nations evoke a remarkable degree of cultural homogenization trends and international marketing practices dominated by Western media. Based on the notion of political economy theorists that the dominant culture in a society is that of the class that wields the dominant material power in that society, these trends have enhanced in recent years the notion of "cultural imperialism" or "media imperialism." The contributions made by these studies are of great significance, to the point that their findings have become a base for policy solutions calling for the "the new world information order," for actual introduction of protective measures against economic domination and cultural homogenization (Katz & Wedell, 1979; Schnitman, 1981), and for research direction linking communication aspects to economic aspects (Jussawalla, 1979).

However, what is lacking in these studies is the inclusion of other useful research alternatives, although this should not be interpreted as a denial of the importance of the findings of these studies. Largely because of their roots in political economy approaches, these studies have concentrated on the basic structural and economic foundations and constraints of society, and thus have ignored the useful assumptions made in social science studies that have examined the ways in which individuals seek and use information within the structural context of media systems. There is the need to link individual communication behaviors to systems purposes, functions, and impacts. Simply looking at structural constraints in international mass communication does not go far enough in confronting the most important controversies in international mass communication research. What is also needed is the so-called social science approach — looking at the social and cultural effects of mass communication in cross-national settings. The following section will discuss the findings and the problems associated with international mass communication effects studies, particularly from an audience analysis perspective.

Effects of International Mass Communication

As noted above, the bulk of the literature in international mass communication research has dealt with the specific conditions of media production and dissemination in world media systems and their interaction processes. In other words, this is a systems approach that concentrates on both communicator and communication channel variables rather than on effects variables. Such a focus is in direct contrast to the central focus in so much of the literature of communication research, that is, the focus on the effects of mass communication. In international mass communication research, therefore, relatively little is known about the social and cultural effects of international mass communication products on the receiving cultures. In this sense, it is worth noting the following argument made by

McCombs (1977, p. 72) in his proposal for assessing the impact of international communication:

> Both the concern behind the evaluative statements and the single-variable descriptive research (in international communication) are linked to the fear and assumption that large doses of foreign popular culture and foreign-prepared news and information have sizable and undesirable effects on local populations.... But for the most part this assumption of undesirable effects remains implicit in both the evaluative and empirical treatments of cultural imperialism. The connotation of effects comes through in even a casual perusal of these statements, but there is little specification of just what these effects might be.

McCombs (1977, p. 72) thus proposed "a detailed explication of the social effects of mass communication, partially evaluative and partially empirical."

A search of the international mass communication research literature shows that there are a limited number of studies that take such an approach, with emphasis on the effects of American television and/or film on local populations in terms of their cognitive, attitudinal, and behavioral orientations toward the American culture as well as their own (Sparkes, 1977; Payne, 1980; Tsai, 1970; Jorgenson & Karlin, 1980; Pingree & Hawkins, 1981). Although there is some variation among findings of these studies, they have generally supported the notion of limited or few media effects in that exposure to American television and film content by local populations has few cognitive and attitudinal effects, much less behavioral effects. For example, Sparkes (1977) noted that there was little attitudinal effect associated with watching American television news in the Canadian population. Payne (1980) also noted that there was no significant relationship between viewing of American television and attitudes toward the United States among Icelandic children. He found that viewing American television neither increased knowledge about the United States nor led to any significant psychological identification with the United States. Pingree and Hawkins (1981) recently found similar evidence in Australian children. They found that Australian children were not likely to base their conceptions of what life was like in the United States on their viewing of U.S. television programs. In line with these findings of limited mass media effects, Jorgenson and Karlin (1980) found that Romanian children and adolescents learned specific kinds of information from American films and television programs, but that the characteristics seen in American media appeared to be accepted to the degree that they conformed to already existing beliefs of the viewers. Tsai (1970) also found that the exposure to American television programs by Formosan children did not influence their outlook on their own culture, but their specific attitudes toward the U.S. culture.

The findings of these studies suggest that the effects of U.S. television and film content, if any, are at best cognitive, rather than attitudinal or behavioral. Such findings are not unfamiliar in effects studies of international mass communication. A series of studies examining the effects of *All in the Family* in a cross-national setting, namely, the United States and Canada, have indicated that the primary effect of the series was to reinforce existing beliefs, irrespective of the cultural setting (Vidmar & Rokeach, 1974; Surlin & Tate, 1976; Tate & Surlin, 1976). There are, however, numerous problems associated with such findings that can be attributed to "bad research, bad social science." Without exception, these studies fell short of a rigorous social science approach to theory building based on "accuracy, parsimony, generality, and causality" (Przeworski & Teune, 1970, p. 20). There are problems of reliability and validity for estimates of various effects measures, analytical techniques for measuring effects, and representative samples of populations under investigation. In almost all cases, effects measures employed in these studies dealt with individual reports of exposure and perception of U.S. television/film content without specifying particular types, themes, and formats of U.S. television programs. In almost all cases, effects of these programs were measured in "one-shot" surveys, with no examination of cumulative and cultivating effects. In almost all cases, samples surveyed in these studies were not representative of the total populations, thus making inferences to the cultural background of populations very doubtful.

In this sense, the available findings of research on international mass communication effects need to be reevaluated, particularly in light of increasing research evidence that supports the notion of "powerful mass media" (Noelle-Neumann, 1973; Robinson, 1974). Especially in cross-cultural media research, there is evidence that spectacular events have a profound impact on national and international images (Deutsch & Merritt, 1965; Pool, 1972b) and that significant social dramas, both in news and entertainment formats, mediated through television and transmitted across national and cultural boundaries have some significant social and cultural impact on individuals (Katz, 1980; Hur, 1981, in press). Furthermore, there is new evidence that U.S. television programs have social and cultural "cultivation" effects on importing societies in terms of social reality construction (Pingree & Hawkins, 1981). All of this evidence calls for a new research direction in effects studies to examine the long-term, cumulative impact of alien mass communication products in the socialization process of individuals in local cultures. Pingree and Hawkins (1981, p. 97) sum up such a new direction as follows:

> One of the most promising approaches to studying the influence of television on culture starts with the hypothesis that information learned from the mass media is incorporated into individuals' conceptions of

social reality and presumably guides further learning and behavior. If a careful analysis finds a relationship between television viewing and these conceptions, then we can begin to make a case for television's contribution to our shared values and assumptions.

CONCLUSION

An attempt has been made in this chapter to bring together the literature of international mass communication to reflect the state of the art in research and theory in pertinent subject areas of the field. The intent was not only to provide an overview of international mass communication research in pertinent subject areas, but also to synthesize the existing research, which can, in return, present new directions for future investigation. It appears, however, that this attempt has had only modest success. This review shows that, despite the growing body of information on systems, processes, and effects of international mass communication, relatively little knowledge has emerged on what can be called "theories" of international mass communication. Even the need for building such theories has been a point of argument in the debate over research approaches to international mass communication studies (Toogood, 1980). The lack of existing theoretical assumptions and propositions makes synthesis of theories in the field difficult and premature, even after almost a generation of international mass communication research productivity. As discussed in this chapter, the problems associated with such difficulties are numerous, but they can be boiled down to the divergences in approaches and methods in international mass communication research and the conflicts existing in the divergences.

In light of these existing divergences and conflicts in the field, then, the following summary points can be made for future direction in international mass communication research.

First, a detailed explication of systems approach is needed in mass media systems and comparative mass media analysis. Theoretically, this means an examination of all the factual and normative variables operating both within and across systems of the mass media. Methodologically, this means the utilization of different data-gathering and data-analytical techniques, including case study methods, content analysis, and audience survey analysis.

Second, a distinction has to be made between content analysis and flow analysis in accounting for the process of international mass communications. Study of the flow of news, information, and cultural materials across national/cultural boundaries should be concerned with both the volume and the type of the flow, but theoretical linkages between the two should involve great care with inferential connections.

Third, a rigorous standard in survey studies looking at the social and cultural effects of international mass communication is needed. The inadequacy of effects measures and sampling of populations in local cultures does not warrant inferences made in past research related to the impact of alien mass communication products on local cultures from individual reports of communication behaviors. Particularly, the long-term cultivation effects should be ascertained in this type of research.

Finally, there is a need to link findings made by systems studies and processes and effects analysis of international mass communication. It is true that findings available in systems analysis and processes and effects analysis are fundamentally related, despite the differences of research focus and research technique in past international mass communication research.

REFERENCES

Atwood, R. Communication research in Latin America: Cultural and conceptual dilemma. Paper presented to the Intercultural Communication Division, the International Communication Association Annual Convention, Acapulco, Mexico, May 1980.

Belkaoui, J. M. Images of Arabs and Israelis in the prestige press, 1966-1974. Journalism Quarterly, 1978, 55, 732-738.

Beltran, L. R. Research ideologies in conflict. Journal of Communication, 1975, 25, 187-193.

Bergsma, F. News values in foreign affairs on Dutch television. Gazette, 1978, 24, 207-222.

Bishop, R. How Reuters and AFP coverage of independent Africa compares. Journalism Quarterly, 1975, 52, 654-662.

Boyd, D. A. Development of Egypt's radio: Voice of the Arabs under Nasser. Journalism Quarterly, 1975, 50, 645-653.

Brown, R. G., & Lee, J. The Japanese press and the 'people's right to know.' Journalism Quarterly, 1977, 54, 477-482.

Chaffee, S. H. Mass media effects: New research perspectives. In D. Lerner & L. M. Nelson (Eds.), Communication research: A half-century appraisal. Honolulu: University of Hawaii Press, 1977.

Chapman, G. P. International television flows project: Information statement. Cambridge: University of Cambridge, 1980.

Charles, J., Shore, L., & Todd, R. The New York Times coverage of Equatorial and Lower Africa. Journal of Communication, 1979, 29, 148-155.

Chu, G., & Alfian, M. Programming for development in Indonesia. Journal of Communication, 1980, 30, 50-57.

Davison, P. W., & George, A. An outline for the study of international political communication. In W. Schramm (Ed.), The process and effects of mass communication (1st ed.). Urbana: University of Illinois Press, 1954.

de Cardona, E. Multinational television. Journal of Communication, 1975, 25, 122-127.

Dervin, B. Communication gaps and inequities: Moving toward a reconceptualization. In B. Dervin & M. J. Voight (Eds.), Progress in communication sciences (Vol. 2). Norwood, NJ: Ablex, 1980.

Deutsch, K. W. International communication: The media and flows. Public Opinion Quarterly, 1956, 19, 143-160.

Deutsch, K. W., & Merritt, R. L. Effects of events on national and international image. In H. C. Kelman (Ed.), *International behavior.* New York: Holt, Rinehart & Winston, 1965.

Dinh, T. V. Nonalignment and cultural imperialism. In K. Nordenstreng & H. I. Schiller (Eds.), *National sovereignty and international communication.* Norwood, NJ: Ablex, 1979.

Dizard, W. P. *Television: A world view.* Syracuse, NY: Syracuse University Press, 1966.

Donohue, G. A., Tichenor, P. J., & Olien, C. N. Gatekeeping: Mass media systems and information control. In F. G. Kline & P. J. Tichenor (Eds.), *Current perspectives in mass communication research.* Beverly Hills, CA: Sage, 1972.

Eisenstadt, S. N. The changing vision of modernization and development. In W. Schramm & D. Lerner (Eds.), *Communication and change: The last ten years — and the next.* Honolulu: University of Hawaii Press, 1976.

Emery, W. B. *National and international systems of broadcasting.* East Lansing: Michigan State University Press, 1969.

Fagen, P. The media in Allende's Chile: Some contradictions. *Journal of Communication,* 1974, *24,* 59-70.

Fagen, R. R. Relations of communication growth to national political systems in the less developed countries. *Journalism Quarterly,* 1964, *41,* 87-94.

Farace, V. R. Mass communication and national development. *Journalism Quarterly.* 1966, *43,* 305-313.

Farace, V. R., & Donohew, L. Mass communication in national social systems: A study of 43 variables in 115 countries. *Journalism Quarterly,* 1965, *42,* 253-261.

Fejes, F. The growth of multinational advertising agencies in Latin America. *Journal of Communication,* 1980, *30,* 36-49.

Frey, F. W. Communication and development. In I. S. Pool et al. (Eds.), *Handbook of communication.* Chicago: Rand NcNally, 1972.

Galtung, J., & Ruge, M. H. The structure of foreign news. *Journal of Peace Research,* 1965, *2,* 64-91.

Gerbner, G. *Mass media policies in changing cultures.* New York: John Wiley, 1977.

Gerbner, G., & Marvanyi, G. The many worlds of the world's press. *Journal of Communication,* 1977, *21,* 52-66.

Giffard, A. C. South African attitudes towards news media. *Journalism Quarterly,* 1976, *53,* 653-660.

Gillespie, J. V., & Nesvold, B. A. (Eds.). *Macro-quantitative analysis.* Beverly Hills, CA: Sage, 1971.

Grandi, R. Western European broadcasting in transition. *Journal of Communication,* 1978, *28,* 48-51.

Guback, T. *The international film industry.* Bloomington: Indiana University Press, 1969.

Guback, T. Film as international business. *Journal of Communication,* 1974, *24,* 90-101.

Gunter, J. An introduction to the great debate. *Journal of Communication,* 1978, *28,* 141-156.

Hachten, W. A. *Muffled drums: The news media in Africa.* Ames: Iowa State University Press, 1971.

Hachten, W. A. Policies and performance of South African television. *Journal of Communication,* 1979, *29,* 62-72.

Halloran, J. D. The context of mass communication research. In E. McAnany, J. Schnitman, & N. Janus (Eds.), *Communication and social structure.* New York: Praeger, 1981.

Hart, J. The flow of news between the U.S. and Canada. *Journalism Quarterly,* 1968, *45,* 516-521.

Head, S. W. *Broadcasting in Africa: A continental survey of radio and television.* Philadelphia: Temple University Press, 1977.

Hester, A. An analysis of news flow from developed and developing nations. *Gazette,* 1971, *17,* 29-43.

Hester, A. Theoretical considerations in predicting volume and direction of international information flow. *Gazette,* 1973, *19,* 238-247.

Hester, A. The news from Latin America via a world news agency. *Gazette,* 1974, *20,* 82-89.
Holt, R. T., & Turner, J. E. (Eds.). *The methodology of comparative research.* New York: Macmillan, 1970.
Hopkins, M. W. *Mass media in the Soviet Union.* New York: Pegasus, 1970.
Howell, W. J. Ireland's second TV channel: Seeking national culture and viewer choice. *Journalism Quarterly,* 1979, *56,* 77-86.
Hur, K. K. *The cultural impact of TV entertainment about the other culture.* Paper presented at the Conference on Culture and Communication, San Diego, 1981.
Hur, K. K. Roots in Britain: A uses and gratifications analysis. *Journalism Quarterly,* in press.
Inkles, A. *Public opinion in Soviet Russia: A study of mass persuasion.* Cambridge, MA: Harvard University Press, 1956.
Iwao, S. Study of the international TV news in Japan. *KEIO Communication Review,* 1981, *2,* 3-17.
Janus, N. Z. Advertising and the mass media in the era of global corporation. In E. G. McAnany, J. Schnitman, & N. Z. Janus (Eds.), *Communication and social structure.* New York: Praeger, 1981.
Jorgenson, R., & Karlin, A. L. *The influence of American films and television programs on the adolescents of a Romanian community.* Paper presented at the International Communication Association Annual Convention, Acapulco, Mexico, May 1980.
Jussawalla, M. *Bridging global barriers. Two new international orders: NIEO, NICO.* Paper presented to the 1979 Advanced Seminar on International Communication Policy and Organizations, East-West Center, Honolulu, 1979.
Kaplan, F. L. The plight of foreign news in the U.S. media. *Gazette,* 1979, *25,* 233-243.
Katz, E. *Television diplomacy: Sadat in Jerusalem.* Paper presented to the Conference on World Communications: Decisions for the 1980s, Annenberg School of Communication, University of Pennsylvania, Philadelphia, 1980.
Katz, E., & Wedell, G. *Broadcasting in the Third World.* Cambridge, MA: Harvard University Press, 1979.
Lang, K. The critical functions of empirical communication research. *Media Culture, and Society,* 1979, *1,* 83-96.
Larson, J. International affairs coverage on network television news: A study of news flow. *Gazette,* 1977, *23,* 241-256.
Larson, J. International affairs coverage on U.S. network TV. *Journal of Communication,* 1979, *29,* 136-147.
Lee, C. C. *Media imperialism reconsidered.* Beverly Hills, CA: Sage, 1980.
Lent, J. A. *The Asian newspapers, reluctant revolution.* Ames: Iowa State University Press, 1971.
Lent, J. A. Government policies reshape Malaysia's diverse media. *Journalism Quarterly,* 1975, *50,* 663-669.
Lent, J. A. *Broadcasting in Asia and the Pacific.* Philadelphia: Temple University Press, 1978.
Lent, J. A. (Ed.). *Third World mass media: Issues, theory and research.* Philadelphia: Temple University Press, 1979.
Lent, J. A., & Rao, S. A content analysis of national media coverage of Asian news and information. *Gazette,* 1979, *25,* 22-30.
Lerner, D. *The passing of traditional society.* New York: Macmillan, 1958.
Lerner, D. (Ed.). *Asian communication: Research, training, planning.* Honolulu: East-West Center, 1976.
Lerner, D., & Richstadt, J. (Eds.). *Communication in the Pacific.* Honolulu: East-West Center, 1976.
Liu, A. P. *Communication and national integration in Communist China.* Berkeley: University of California Press, 1971.
Loevinger, L. The lexonomics of telecommunications. *Journal of Broadcasting,* 1967, *11,* 285-311.

Lowenstein, R. L. Press freedom as a political indicator. In H.-D. Fischer & J. C. Merrill (Eds.), *International communication: Media, channels, functions.* New York: Hasting House, 1970.

Mahan, E. *International communication: Access to the literature.* Paper presented to the Twenty-Sixth Seminar on the Acquisition of Latin American Library Materials, Tulane University, April 1981.

Markham, J. W. *Voices of the red giants: Communications in Russia and China.* Ames: Iowa State University Press, 1967.

Marquez, F. T. The relationship of advertising and culture in the Philippines. *Journalism Quarterly,* 1975, *52,* 436-442.

Martin, R., Chaffee, S. H., & Izcaray, F. Media and consumerism in Venezuela. *Journalism Quarterly,* 1979, *56,* 296-304.

Masmoudi, M. The new world information order. *Journal of Communication,* 1979, *29,* 172-185.

McAnany, E. G. (Ed.). *Communications in the rural Third World.* New York: Praeger, 1980.

McAnany, E. G., Schnitman, J., & Janus, N. Z. (Eds.). *Communication and social structure.* New York: Praeger, 1981.

McCombs, M. E. Assessing the impact of international communication. In J. Richstadt (Ed.), *New perspectives in international communication.* Honolulu: East-West Center, 1977.

McNelly, J. International news for Latin America. *Journal of Communication,* 1979, *29,* 156-163.

Merrill, J. C., Bryan, C. R., & Alisky, M. *The foreign press.* Baton Rouge: Louisiana State University Press, 1970.

Merritt, R. L. *Systematic approaches to comparative politics.* Chicago: Rand McNally, 1971.

Miller, R. E. The CRTC: Guardian of the Canadian identity. *Journal of Broadcasting,* 1973, *17,* 189-200.

Mowlana, H. Mass media systems and communication behavior. In M. Adams (Ed.), *The Middle East: A handbook.* London: Antony Blond, 1971.

Mowlana, H. Trends in research on international communication in the United States. *Gazette,* 1973, *14,* 79-90.

Mowlana, H. A paradigm for comparative mass media analysis. In H.-D. Fischer & J. C. Merrill (Eds.), *International and intercultural communication.* New York: Hasting House, 1976.

Mowlana, H. Technology versus tradition: Communication in the Iranian revolution. *Journal of Communication,* 1977, *29,* 107-112.

Mujahid, S. Coverage of Pakistan in three U.S. news magazines. *Journalism Quarterly,* 1970, *47,* 126-130.

Nam, S. The flow of international news into Korea. *Gazette,* 1970, *16,* 14-26.

Namurois, A. *Problems of structure and organization of broadcasting in the framework of radiocommunication.* Geneva: European Broadcasting Union, 1964.

Nixon, R. B. Factors related to freedom in national press systems. *Journalism Quarterly,* 1960, *37,* 13-28.

Nixon, R. B. Freedom in the world's press: A fresh appraisal with data. *Journalism Quarterly,* 1965, *42,* 3-14.

Nnaemeka, T., & Richstadt, J. Structured relations and foreign news flow in the Pacific region. *Gazette,* 1980, *26,* 235-258.

Noelle-Neumann, E. Return to the concept of powerful mass media. *Studies of Broadcasting,* 1973, 66-112.

Nordenstreng, K., & Schiller, H. I. (Eds.). *National sovereignty and international communication.* Norwood, NJ: Ablex, 1979.

Nordenstreng, K., & Varis, T. *Television: A one-way traffic?* Paris: UNESCO, 1974.

Ostagaard, E. Factors influencing the flow of news. *Journal of Peace Research,* 1965, *2,* 39-63.

Paulu, B. *Broadcasting on the European continent.* Minneapolis: University of Minnesota Press, 1967.

Paulu, B. *Radio and television broadcasting in Eastern Europe.* Minneapolis: University of Minnesota Press, 1974.
Payne, D. E. *U.S. TV in Iceland: A synthesis of studies.* Paper presented at the International Communication Association Annual Convention, Acapulco, Mexico, May 1980.
Pingree, S., & Hawkins, R. U.S. programs on Australian television: The cultivation effects. *Journal of Communication,* 1981, *31,* 97-105.
Pool, I. S. Communication in totalitarian societies. In I. S. Pool et al. (Eds.), *Handbook of communication.* Chicago: Rand McNally, 1972. (a)
Pool, I. S. Public opinion. In I. S. Pool et al. (Eds.), *Handbook of communication.* Chicago: Rand McNally, 1972. (b)
Pool, I. S. The rise of communication policy research. *Journal of Communication,* 1974, *24,* 31-42.
Pool, I. S. The changing flow of television. *Journal of Communication,* 1977, *27,* 139-149.
Powell, D. Television in the USSR. *Public Opinion Quarterly,* 1975-1976, *39,* 287-299.
Pratt, C. N. The reportage and image of Africa in six U.S. news and opinion magazines. *Gazette,* 1980, *26,* 31-45.
Przeworski, A., & Teune, H. *The logic of comparative social inquiry.* New York: John Wiley, 1970.
Pye, L. W. (Ed.). *Communications and political development.* Princeton, NJ: Princeton University Press, 1963.
Rachty, G., & Sabat, K. *Importation of films for cinema and television in Egypt.* Paris: UNESCO, 1980.
Read, W. Global TV flow: Another look. *Journal of Communication,* 1976, *26,* 69-73.
Robinson, G. Mass media and ethnic strife in multinational Yugoslavia. *Journalism Quarterly,* 1974, *51,* 490-497.
Robinson, J. P. TV's impact on everyday's life: Some cross-national evidence. In E. Rubinstein et al. (Eds.), *Television and social behavior* (Vol. 4). Washington, DC: U.S. Government Printing Office, 1972.
Robinson, J. P. The press as kingmaker. *Journalism Quarterly,* 1974, *51,* 589-594.
Rogers, E. (Ed.). *Communication and development: Critical perspectives.* Beverly Hills, CA: Sage, 1976.
Rogers, E. The rise and fall of the dominant paradigm. *Journal of Communication,* 1978, *28.*
Rosengren, K. International news: Time and type of report. In H.-D. Fischer & J. C. Merrill (Eds.), *International and intercultural communication.* New York: Hasting House, 1976.
Rosengren, K. Four types of tables. *Journal of Communication,* 1977, *27,* 67-75.
Savage, I. P., & Deutsch, K. W. A statistical model of the gross analysis transaction flows. *Econometrica,* 1960, *28,* 551-572.
Schiller, H. I. *Mass communication and American empire.* Boston: Beacon Press, 1969.
Schiller, H. I. *Communication and cultural domination.* White Plains, NY: International Arts and Sciences Press, 1976.
Schnitman, J. Economic Protectionism and Mass Media Development. Film Industry in Argentina. In E. G. McAnay, J. Schnitman, & N. Z. Janus (Eds.), *Communication and social structure.* New York: Praeger, 1981.
Schramm, W. *One day in the world's press.* Stanford, CA: Stanford University Press, 1960.
Schramm, W. *Mass media and national development.* Stanford, CA: Stanford University Press, 1964.
Schramm, W. Circulation of news in the Third World: A study of Asia. In G. Wilhoit & H. de Bock (Eds.), *Mass Communication Review Yearbook* (Vol. 1). Beverly Hills, CA: Sage, 1980.
Schramm, W., & Lerner, D. (Eds.). *Communication and change: The last ten years — and the next.* Honolulu: East-West Center, 1976.
Shaheen, J. G. Television programming in selected Middle East nations: Lebanon, Bharain and Quartar. J. A. Lent (Ed.), *Case studies of mass media in the Third World.* Philadelphia: Temple University Press, 1979.

Shore, L. Mass media for development: A reexamination of access, exposure and impact. In E. G. McAnany (Ed.), *Communications in the rural Third World.* New York: Praeger, 1980.

Siebert, F. S., Peterson, T., & Schramm, W. *Four theories of the press.* Urbana: University of Illinois Press, 1956.

Smith, A. *The shadow in the cave.* Urbana: University of Illinois Press, 1973.

Sparkes, V. TV across the Canadian border: Does it really matter? *Journal of Communication,* 1977, *27,* 40-47.

Starck, K. The handling of foreign news in Finland's daily newspapers. *Journalism Quarterly,* 1968, *45,* 516-521.

Stevenson, R. L., & Cole, R. R. *Patterns of world coverage by the major Western agencies.* Paper presented at the International Communication Association Annual Convention, Acapulco, Mexico, May 1980.

Surlin, S. H., & Tate, E. *All in the Family:* Is Archie funny? *Journal of Communication,* 1976, *26,* 61-68.

Tate, E., & Surlin, S. H. Agreement with opinionated TV characters in cultures. *Journalism Quarterly,* 1976, *53,* 199-203.

Thoren, S. The flow of foreign news into the Swedish press. *Journalism Quarterly,* 1968, *45,* 516-521.

Toogood, A. Politics and the Canadian Broadcasting Corporation. *Quarterly Journal of Speech,* 1972, *58,* 184-190.

Toogood, A. Commericial television is alive and well and public in Britain. *Public Telecommunications Review,* 1978, *6,* 6-13.

Toogood, A. *The problem of the paradigm in comparative communications systems studies.* Paper presented at the International Communication Association Annual Convention, Acapulco, Mexico, May 1980.

Trimmer, J. D. *Response of physical systems.* New York: John Wiley, 1950.

Tsai, M. K. Some effects of American television programs on children in Formosa. *Journal of Broadcasting,* 1970, *14,* 229-238.

Tunstall, J. *The media are American: Anglo American media in the world.* New York: Columbia University Press, 1977.

UNESCO. *National communication systems: Some policy issues and options.* Paris: Author, 1975.

Vidmar, N., & Rokeach, M. Archie Bunker's bigotry: A study in selective perception and exposure. *Journal of Communication,* 1974, *24,* 64-69.

Weaver, D., & Cleveland, W. *Foreign news coverage in two U.S. wire services.* Paper presented at the International Communication Association Annual Convention, Acapulco, Mexico, May 1980.

Wells, A. *Picture tube imperialism.* Maryknoll, NY: Orbis Books, 1972.

Wells, A. (Ed.). *Mass communications: A world view.* Palo Alto, CA: Mayfield, 1974.

White, D. M. The gatekeeper: A case study in the selection of news. *Journalism Quarterly,* 1950, *27,* 383-390.

Whiting, G. C., & Stanfield, D. J. Mass media use and opportunity structure in rural Brazil. *Public Opinion Quarterly,* 1972, *36,* 56-68.

Yu, F. T. C. *Mass persuasion in Communist China.* New York: Praeger, 1964.

MASS COMMUNICATION

20 • Television Rules of Prepartum New Families

THOMAS R. LINDLOF • GARY A. COPELAND
Pennsylvania State University • University of Alabama—Tuscaloosa

IT has become axiomatic of studies of media audience behavior to assume or document the ways that people do *not* act on mediated communications as a mass. While the aggregate circulation for media outlets may show some predictability, audience responses to the media, and the consequences of those responses, vary enormously among individuals, social groups, and social settings. As a departure point for understanding the dynamics of media use, it is still useful to consider the claim of Freidson (1971, p. 207) that "an adequate concept of the audience must include some idea of its social character, some idea that being a member of a local audience is a social activity in which interaction with others before, during and after any single occasion of spectatorship has created definite shared expectations and predisposing definitions."

Television viewing for most persons is, in fact, an activity linked to various ongoing social goals and may show rhythms of use distinctive to changes in the life span (Dimmick, McCain, & Bolton, 1979). Such change-points — e.g., entry into adolescence, marriage, or parenthood — often manifest changes in family structure and familial role. Surprisingly little research has examined changes in media use that attend changes in life-span role. Among the reasons for this lack of systematic investigation could be problems in applying the appropriate processual methods (Smith, 1972; Meyer, Traudt, & Anderson, 1980), as well as the lack of theoretical models other than functionalism (McQuail & Gurevitch, 1974).

The present study attempts in an exploratory manner to assess the prospective uses of television in the new family setting among couples expecting their first child. In making this population a specific focus of

AUTHORS' NOTE: This research was funded in part by the Office for Research, College of Liberal Arts, Pennsylvania State University. We would like gratefully to acknowledge the assistance of James Dupree and Lynne Kelly (graduate students in the Department of Speech Communication, Penn State University, at the time of this study), as well as the cooperation of the State College, Pennsylvania, chapter of the Childbirth Education Association. This investigation, a series of assumptions is made: (1) predominant communication patterns within families contribute significantly to children's developing uses of and interpretive schemes applied to television; (2) family communication patterns change over time due in part to changing family composition and the developmental states and needs of family members; and (3) family communication patterns may be profitably conceptualized as rule governed in many situations involving television as a social object, with such rules undergoing negotiation and redefinition at certain points in time. Each assumption is not without its problematic aspects, and will be examined in turn.

BACKGROUND OF FAMILY USES OF TELEVISION

The first stage of systematic social research of family uses of television, begun when the medium was diffusing into the general population in the late 1940s, was concerned with mapping the demographic and social class attributes of adopters as well as some features of family control of disciplinary procedures regarding set operation. For example, McDonagh (1950) found early television-owning families to have higher-status occupational classifications and more children than non-television households; the television families reported declines in reading, family conversation, and various outside activities after acquisition of a set. Social class was found to be positively related to permissiveness and inversely related to obedience demands (Blood, 1961; Maccoby, 1954), while Hess and Goldman (1962) found no significant differences among social statuses on parental evaluation of children's patterns of televiewing. In a more recent study, Martin and Benson (1970) reported no significant differences among educational levels for parental viewing "rules," although differences in application of rules between fathers and mothers in the lower-class category (defined as semiskilled and unskilled workers) did appear. Lower-class fathers were less likely than lower-class mothers to establish such rules as setting time limits for viewing and segregating set use from children's homework obligations. Lower-class parents indicated that regulations of television set use often occurred as rewards for good behavior; by contrast, upper-middle-class parents reported much less willingness to permit exceptions to their televiewing policies, with exceptions permitted only for the appearance of

---

chapter was first presented to the Mass Communication Division of the International Communication Association annual conference, Boston, May 1-5, 1982.

Correspondence and requests for reprints: Thomas R. Lindlof, Department of Speech Communication, Pennsylvania State University, University Park, PA 16802.

"special" programs that would benefit their children. Thus while the upper-middle-class parents manage family viewing carefully, albeit flexibly, lower-class parents "tend to intervene in a personalistic, rather than an ideological fashion. That is, competition between the husband-father and others for control of the TV is apt to be resolved in his favor, and disapproval of a program the children are watching tends to be expressed by direct manipulation of the set itself or by simple personal command" (Blood, 1961, p. 221). Clearly the dynamics of family interaction regarding television use as revealed by the early nonprogrammatic research show a complexity that cannot be explained by sole reference to social class attributes. (Moreover, the varying definitions of social class among such studies cause great difficulties in generalizing their results.) At the same time, the evidence suggests communicative elaborations in television households that modify early notions of family televiewing as "parallel" rather than interactive communication (Maccoby, 1951).

Recent research has considered family influences of various types as *conditional* modifiers of such effects as social learning, consumer behavior, and interpretational skills (see Messaris & Sarett, 1981, for a review of parent-child interactions regarding television). In the area of political socialization, the impact of important televised political events such as presidential debates for altering children's agendas is also subject to the influence of parental perceptions (Anderson & Avery, 1978); in some cases, therefore, family communication about the meanings of televised portrayals can *intervene* to modify children's attitudes. The "conditional-influence" hypothesis assumes that television often operates in the home as a locus of conversation, used deliberately or inadvertently as a source of exemplars for regulating action either inside or outside the immediate televiewing context. As a routine activity that cannot be blithely separated from other routines occurring in the home, family televiewing and its interactional components (program choice, conversational flow, social partitioning, etc.) can be seen as a manifestation of more general modes of communication. Treating the televiewing phenomenon as an inseparable part of ongoing communication patterns not only provides a more substantial foundation for proceeding theoretically, but also avoids the tendency to examine television to the exclusion of other media. Such an approach is also much more amenable to naturalistic case study (Traudt, 1979), and ethnographic (Lull, 1976) methods that attempt to document in descriptive fashion the actual sequences of communication that attend media use. More specifically, the effects of "social class" will probably be unknown to the child whose communication behavior is being investigated; social class is a social scientific construct with a usually taken-for-granted validity. On the other hand, a child could be expected to report on some aspects of family communication, perhaps eventuating in an account of the construction of a particular social reality.

Many studies of television-related family communication have resulted in descriptive typologies of television rules or uses (e.g., Barcus, 1968; Lull, 1980), including the substantial work done by Chaffee, McLeod, and their associates (Chaffee, McLeod, & Atkin, 1971; McLeod & Chaffee, 1972; McLeod & Brown, 1976) in identifying prominent family communication patterns that have tested reliably among samples and appear to be associated with indexes of political knowledge, media use, and aggressive tendencies among children and adolescents. Their instrument, the Family Communication Pattern (FCP) scales, has differentiated families that stress harmonious relationships and resist or avoid discussion of extrapersonal topics *(socio-oriented)* from those families that encourage discussion of extrapersonal or controversial topics and respect expressions of opinion from their children *(concept-oriented)*. One distinct advantage of their construct is its alternative explanation of the common assumption that media effects occur mainly through children's direct modeling of program content. Rather, the family's communicative environment exerts an indirect influence on children's exposure to and interpretations of media content; that influence seems most apparent in the child's modeling of home communication norms, as suggested by the findings derived from applications of the FCP scales. Such modeling may have consequences for children's communicative predispositions outside the family context and, as Chaffee, McLeod, and Atkin (1971, p. 29) note, "help guide the child in his 'cognitive mapping' of situations he encounters outside the immediate family context, e.g., at school, in relation to public affairs issues, and mass media use."

Use of the Family Communication Pattern scales has become increasingly widespread among researchers interested in the family-media interact. Abel (1976) found that among socio-orientation families, there was a high correlation between the mother's indications of what should be her child's television viewing preferences and the child's own content preferences. Children of low socio-orientation backgrounds, on the other hand, were *more accurate* in their perceptions of their mother's actual programming preferences. Lull (1980) tested the relationships between the FCP scales and a six-part typology of social uses of television, and found socio-oriented parents to be reluctant to use TV set operation for punitive purposes, although they did draw on it as a conversational resource and as a way of maintaining "an actively interdependent communicative environment" (p. 331). Concept-oriented families reported less reliance on the medium for social cohesion, but did make greater use of television for facilitating arguments, clarifying values, and making fantasy/reality distinctions for their children. Put simply, concept-oriented families do not seem to accept television as readily into their lives as a background or concomitant to their activities, but instead prefer to use it *purposively* for commenting on larger issues. Unfortunately, the degree of agreement between spouses — in terms of their family communication backgrounds, salience of television's presence in the home, information sources about television, and procedures for regulating its operation and content — has received limited attention.

THE RULES CONCEPT

Much recent theoretical and empirical effort concerning family interactions with television as a social object has been organized around rules-governed perspectives (Fry & McCain, 1980; Lull, 1981; Messaris & Starett, 1981; Reid, 1979). A rules approach presumably became a more congenial grounding for communications researchers because its assumptions often portray behavioral regularities as deriving from social actors' intentions and cultural definitions rather than from universal or externally imposed causes. The notion of rules seems especially useful for describing many types of communication events since rules are context-sensitive, attempt to consider the meaning-structure of the social actor, and rely on *sequences* of behavior for their empirical referents. For some rules theorists, verbalizations of social actors are unsatisfactory data for establishing operative rules (see Sigman, 1980). In other words, social actors are often unaware of or give self-delusory explanations for behavioral productions that are observed to occur in certain contexts and are subject to breakdowns due to mistaken rule perceptions among participants. As Fry and McCain (1980) observed, much of what actually occurs in the televiewing environment is implicit or taken for granted, making problematic the uncritical acceptance of respondents' accounts of their "rule" use. Apparently, verbal reports may be admissible in probing the extensive limits of purported rules where breaching procedures are introduced into routine activities. The other view of this issue (Harre & Secord, 1973; Collett, 1977) regards rules as conscious productions, deployed for tactical purposes, thus requiring some criterion of rule articulation by the social actor.

Of the several investigations of television rule use in families, few have given criteria for the identification of rules or even attempted to determine the extent to which the researcher's definition of a rule is congruent with that of the respondent's. Generally, "rules" are meant to imply the exercise of social controls regarding television operation or content by one or more family members. Recently, there have been attempts to refine categories of television rules. Fry and McCain (1980) factor analyzed twenty-one

Likert-type items (dealing with time, content, and context of viewing) and arrived at a three-factor solution of predominant family viewing rules: *restrictiveness* (primarily proscriptive statements regarding content and viewing time); *content discussion* (primarily relating to parent-child discussions); and *social control* (items relating to use of television as a punitive or reward device). In a regression analysis, FCP scales were found to be related to content discussion and social control, but not to restrictiveness; as might be expected, highly concept-oriented parents showed more content discussion rules than their low-concept counterparts. The twenty-one items, however, were presumably generated from earlier research, not from the respondents, and contained items (e.g., "We have a very strict policy about how much TV _____ watches") that were not constructed in rule form.

Lull (1981) attempted to bring the disparate TV-related interactions noticed anecdotally and in the research literature under the purview of "three essential heuristic themes which emerge from each typology or review of communication rules" (p. 7). The first rule type is called *habits,* which are distinguishable by their nonnegotiable, obligatory character; failure to comply with habitual rules usually invokes negative sanctions. Habitual rules — an example of which is a set bedtime with no exceptions — are usually applied to children, for whom any articulation or justification of the rule need not be given. The second rule type — *parameters* — specifies a range of appropriate behavior in a given context, where knowledge or articulation of the specific rule-governed action is possible. A prominent case of parametric rules, according to Lull, is the program choice activity where some system of discretionary decision making, such as turn taking or allowing the child his or her "special night," provides family members with an informal code for exercising their options. As Lull notes, parametric rules can be negotiated, although they too are usually authoritatively enforced and would appear to be devised on an ad hoc basis. Finally, *tactical* rules are undertaken by social actors in order to achieve a result extrinsic to the immediate context; a tactical rule — such as when a parent presents his or her child with a TV-viewing "bonus" (e.g., staying up late) as a reward for future conduct — is a means/ends strategy "devised by individuals, dyads, or groups in order to gain some objective that is typically more important and abstract than are the conditions and rewards of the situations at hand" (Lull, 1981, p. 14). This type fulfills the wholly conscious, intentional rule-following model where failure to follow does not necessarily invoke sanctions; it is often stated in syllogistic form (Cushman & Whiting, 1972): viz., in context X, Y is required or permitted to happen.

In the sense that rules are usually considered prescriptive, followable, and dependent on context for recognition and performance (Shimanoff,

1980), rules — as explanatory models — are in fact descriptions of social actors' mental constructs for purposive action. In what might appear to be a habitual rule sequence — e.g., a mother sending her child to bed at the regular hour — the controlling parent may actually be operating tactically to satisfy the expectations of the other parent; the child in this sequence, unable to recognize or articulate the parent's rule, may be following a separate tactical rule ("compliance") for attaining an abstract end (the "good will" of his or her mother). If habitual rules are simply indexed by the criterion of overt behavior, without some interrogative measure of the actors' perspectives, then concept of rule is divorced from the phenomenological awareness of intentions of the social actors. Parametric rules seem to be expressive of *norms* — i.e., the ranges within which a social actor may profitably activate his rules. As Jackson (1965, p. 12) notes, "The norm is a setting or baseline on which family behavior is measured and around which it varies to a greater or lesser degree." A functioning family unit will therefore "enforce" its norms by invoking behaviors that Jackson (1965, p. 13) calls homeostatic mechanisms, "which delimit the fluctuations of other behaviors along the particular range where the norm is relevant." Part of a family member's articulation of a rule-governed behavior may well be directed toward maintenance of a norm. In fact, the rules followed by different persons in similar circumstances *will vary in relation to their roles* vis-à-vis the others implicated in the situation.

The foregoing discussion highlights the difficulties posed by (a) assuming that all or most behavioral regularities are rule-governed, and (b) ascribing a conscious intent or plan on the part of the social actor whose "rule-governed" behavioral productions are being observed. Collett (1977) suggests a hypothetical situation in which the social actor is ignorant of a conventional rule — knowing which piece of cutlery to select at a polite dinner party — and yet performs adequately through imitation of a more knowledgeable guest. To the naive observer the social actor appears to possess the requisite rule-governed actions, although they are actually based on a more superordinate norm. That is, "Presumably what happens is that the imitator forms an inductive hypothesis about the rule and then tests this against subsequent instances until he arrives at an hypothesis that resists disconfirmation" (Collett, 1977, p. 16). Transferred to the family televiewing setting, a child gradually learns the "implicit" rules for using the medium or interpreting its content through similar inductive processes. In Collett's illustration authoritative texts on etiquette could have saved the hypothetical actor from his or her imitative efforts, but in the case of a child's accommodative efforts at learning appropriate rules for interpretations of televised narrative sequences, secondary coding schemes do not exist and must be inferred through periods of trial and error (Messaris & Sarett, 1981, p. 229).

In learning the rules of TV set operation and its social milieu, however, the child may often be informed in a more deductive mode — i.e., first learning the rule by name, before understanding its outer bounds through consequences of its infractions. Although some families may take on the task of *prescribing* interpretations of program content (or using questioning techniques for value clarification), interpretations are usually left open ended. Prescriptive rules for *interactively* negotiating television use (which might include prescriptive interpretations for certain program bits used as conversational examplars) do incorporate standards of "correctness" since "the members of the community which uphold the rule will . . . reserve for themselves the right to evaluate the performance of those individuals for whom they take to fall within its jurisdiction" (Collett, 1977, p. 8). There is, therefore, the expectation that social actors know the rules they perform, given the evaluations and possible sanctions that are forthcoming by interactants who uphold those rules.

RESEARCH QUESTIONS

The development of family viewing — and sets of rules for negotiating specific interactions — is undoubtably a gradual process, representing the reorganization of priorities and time budgeting caused by the needs of a first child. Dealing sensibly with television may be an issue of low salience for the first few years of a new family. As the child begins to function independently and acquires a repertoire of favorite programs and characters — by the age of three for most American children (Singer & Singer, 1981) — parents may be expected to have begun devising strategies for not only monitoring their child's exposure patterns, but also for organizing their own daily activities more efficiently. The objective of the present line of research is to investigate the origins of these strategies and their instantiations, as tactical rules.

Because there is no direct precedent in the literature from which to construct hypotheses in a deductive fashion, research questions have been articulated and operationalized from some of the issues addressed in this introduction. It is assumed that the period prior to the birth of a first child is one of anticipation and preparation; thus, expectant parents will evince differential patterns of information exposure regarding the role of television in the family setting. Likewise, the extent of interspouse discussion of television's role in child rearing — and more global discussions of media impact — should vary. Sources of this variance might be found in the occupational and educational statuses of the prospective parents, ascribed salience of television use, current media use, and each partner's background of family communication style. The latter possible source is intriguing, but problematic: new parents may resort to solutions recalled from their individual family's televiewing practices, or they may deliberately try to avoid tactics that they perceive to have failed or been counterproductive when they were growing up.

If rules are conceptualized as "relationship agreements" that prescribe and organize interactions within a stable system (Jackson, 1965), then the onset of an ambiguous situation — such as the establishment of viewing rules in the new family setting — might show some instability of agreement. As McLeod and Chaffee (1972, p. 94) remark, "Changes in the person's role at critical junctures of his life force the person to solve problems anew, to reorder priorities, and to seek information relevant to the decisions he must make." Prior research has often focused on the mother as the chief arbiter of children's viewing choices and exposure patterns, as indicated by studies whose data derive from in-depth interviews with mothers (e.g., Barcus, 1968) or correlations between mothers' and children's estimates of viewing time (Rossiter & Robertson, 1975). As noted earlier, however, research suggests that only at lower-class levels do fathers show less interest than mothers in establishing TV rules. Fathers are also perceived as being more influential in program choice by other family members (Lull, 1978), but when triadic relations (mother/father/child) are involved in televiewing, the mother appears to assume an "overseer" or managerial role (Brody, Stoneman, & Sanders, 1980) while the father engages more in play with the child.

Accordingly, this study intends to probe the following questions:

1. What types of rules are likely to emerge from prospective parents in response to some structured, prototypical family viewing problems? It is expected that some responses may be advocated by spouses that will *not* be followed later during actualities. By structuring a role-playing situation, it is expected that *ideal rule statements* will emerge, giving some indications of their global predispositions as well as an attitudinal baseline to be checked against follow-up observations.

2. What will be the effects of interspouse variance in family communication backgrounds on rule formulation and other areas of related interest, such as exposure to media sources of information about children and TV and the extent of interspouse discussions about future regulation of family televiewing? It is expected that the lower the differences in interspouse family communication backgrounds, the less discussion

about future family televiewing will have taken place during the period of expecting a child.

METHODS

Sample and Conditions of Administration

Data collection was conducted in a city of approximately 35,000 in the Northeast where a large state university is located. It was decided that the most efficient way of identifying members of the expectant parent population and obtaining their cooperation would be through an agency offering regularly scheduled natural childbirth classes. (Other methods of identifying members — e.g., soliciting participation through notices posted at gynecological/obstetrical clinics — were discarded because of anticipated impracticality and undesirable response bias.) This method of securing respondents had the following benefits:

1. The full cooperation and support of the sponsoring organization's board of directors, instructor coordinator, and individual instructors enhanced the legitimacy and the value of the research effort.

2. Because few of the participating couples knew each other prior to the start of the courses, intact group response sets were avoided. Moreover, the researchers were assured by the instructor-coordinator that discussion of television-related issues was not a part of the curriculm and was not likely to be discussed informally.

3. All participants received the same set of appeals for participation and research instrument directions, reducing the possibility that different respondents would perceive different task demands.

Although comparable characteristics of noncooperating couples or prospective parents who did not attend childbirth preparation classes were unknown, reliance on cooperating participants probably resulted in a sample of some degree of unrepresentativeness. The sponsoring organization, however, estimated that 75 percent of women giving birth at the regional hospital had completed a formal childbirth preparation course. The rate of compliance among the prospective parents from whom cooperation was sought was 79 percent. Therefore, although the sampling scheme was not conducted on a randomized basis, there is reason to believe a relatively representative sample was obtained, given the exigencies of gaining access to this rather special population. Tables 20.1-20.5 provide the age, educational level, occupational, television ownership, and television usage characteristics of the sample. Among the forty-three participating couples (eighty-six respondents in all), one respondent reported a child by a previous marriage. All other respondents (mean length

Table 20.1
Sample Characteristics: Age

Range	n	Percentage of Total
20-24	30	35
25-29	37	43
30-34	16	19
Over 34	3	3

Table 20.2
Sample Characteristics: Educational Level

Level	n	Percentage of Total	Cumulative Percentage
Less than high school degree	2	2	2
High school degree	22	26	28
Some college	19	22	50
Bachelor's degree	20	23	73
Some graduate school	5	6	79
Master's degree (or equivalent)	7	8	87
Advanced work beyond master's	11	13	100

Table 20.3
Sample Characteristics: Occupation

Classification	n	Percentage of Total
Professional	23	27
Housewife	11	13
Clerical/secretarial	9	11
Student	8	9
Skilled labor	7	8
White-collar/managerial	6	7
Unskilled labor	6	7
Self-employed	4	5
Farm/ranch	3	4
Clergy	3	4

Table 20.4
Sample Characteristics: Television Set Ownership (by couple)

	Set 1 n	Set 1 %	Set 2 n	Set 2 %	Set 3 n	Set 3 %
Room						
Living room	33	77	1	2	0	
Bedroom	1	1	8	19	0	
Den	5	12	1	2	0	
Recreation room	2	5	0		0	
Type						
Color	30	70	3	7	0	
Black and white	11	26	10	23	0	

Table 20.5
Sample Characteristics: Television Services (by couple)

Service	n	Percentage of Total
Antenna only	8	19
Basic cable	23	53
Pay cable (HBO)	12	28

of marriage: 3.36 years) were expecting their first child. All of the women in the sample were, at the time of survey administration, between their fifth and ninth month of term.

The organization sponsoring the natural childbirth classes set the following ground rules for administration of the study: (1) participation of class member would be wholly voluntary, with assurances that noncooperation would not affect their class standing, (2) the researchers' appeals for cooperation could be done during the third week of each eight-week course, although administration could not be done during regular class meetings; and (3) the instrument could be administered the week following the in-class appeal, immediately before or after the scheduled class meetings. To ensure independence of response from each spouse, respondents were not permitted to jointly discuss items of the research instrument during its administration, nor were they permitted to complete the instrument away from the supervision of the researchers. All data were collected during a forty-five-day period in July and August of 1981.

Research Instrument

The items comprising the self-administered interview schedule were sequentially grouped as follows:

1. hypothetical family televiewing situations, eliciting from respondents open-ended rule statements and exception statements;
2. five socio-orientation and five concept-orientation items from the FCP scales, adapted from Chaffee and Tims (1976);
3. two questions eliciting the "TV programs currently on the air that you would especially encourage your five-year-old child to watch," and "TV programs currently on the air that you would especially discourage your five-year-old child from watching" (respondents were allowed up to five open-ended responses per question);
4. an array of demographic and media use items; and
5. measures of joint discussion between spouses during the period of expecting a child about "how do you plan to regulate or treat your child's TV viewing in the future" (with responses ranked as follows: three or more times; once or twice; and none), and media information sources and topics regarding any material dealing with children and television that each spouse had been exposed to during the period of expectation.

The construction of the three hypothetical situation problems deserves special attention since these problems attempt to elicit from the prospective parents those procedures (labeled "rule statements") employed for negotiating the problems and any unusual circumstances (labeled "exceptional statements") that would temporarily suspend or qualify their normal application of those procedures. The open-ended responses to these hypotheticals constitute dependent measures of projected rule use by which the effects of interspouse agreement on the Family Communication Pattern scales can be analyzed. The three hypotheticals, and the instructions to respondents for answering them, were written as follows:

The next three situations are ones you might encounter in your family in the future. Each situation involves a parental decision or action. *Answer them in terms of how you would act in each situation.* Provide as much information as you can. Also, explain any circumstances that might lead you to make an *exception* to that action.

1. If my spouse and I were going out for the evening and were leaving our five-year-old child with a babysitter (whom we do not know prior to that evening), *I would give the babysitter these instructions concerning our child's TV viewing:*
2. If I learned that my five-year-old child has been watching TV programs that I disapprove of at a friend's house, without telling me, *I would* (please complete):
3. If I were watching my favorite TV program at home in the evening and my five-year-old child asked to change the channel to watch another show, *I would* (please complete):

The first hypothetical asks the respondent to state admissible televiewing rules for their child in their absence; by instructing a surrogate (the babysitter), it was hoped that the prospective parent would frame his or her answer in terms of *ideal-type* rule statements. The other two hypotheticals represent everyday situations that could conceivably occur to any of the couples — the second hypothetical chosen for its assumption of operative content rules, the third for its assumption of operative rules regarding TV receiver control. Respondents' rule statements for the second and third hypotheticals should reveal the specific form of parental communicative responses to these ambiguous situations. Each hypothetical was accompanied by the query — "Would you make any *exceptions* to the above? (If yes, please explain)" — affording respondents the opportunity to qualify their rule statements with the conditional circumstances that might legitimately breach them.

Although the hypotheticals embody the rudiments of context, encourage prescriptive statements, and are presumed to be followable by the responding spouse, the responses are labeled "rule statements" primarily for convenience rather than for purposes of construct validation. It should be obvious that a *rule*— as the construct was treated in the introductory section — requires a criterion of behavioral regularity. Although such evidence is by no means sufficient for establishing the presence of rule-governed behavior, there must be evidence that a social actor knows the rule such that it can be phrased in syllogistic form. Despite these caveats, the construction and use of the hypothetical situation problems are justified on the grounds that anticipated roles imply anticipated actions, and that "role-playing experiments" of the type described here are consistent with a rules approach to human action (Harre & Secord, 1973, p. 313-317).

FINDINGS

Hypotheticals: Rule Statements and Exception Statements

Since the hypothetical situation problems asked for open-ended responses — and were positioned at the front of the instrument, obviating responses "conditioned" by exposure to other items — a wide range of respondent-generated answers was obtained. Categories were established for each set of rule and exception statements according to the semantic similarity of the statements under each hypothetical heading, and the statements were then content analyzed for membership in the categories. Appendix A lists the labels for each rule and exception statement category, along with their frequencies. Three rule statements and one exception statement were coded for each respondent's hypothetical problems; as can be seen in Appendix A, very few respondents articulated as many as three rule statements per hypothetical. Only a very small minority of cases mentioned more than one exception; thus, one exception statement per hypothetical was coded. Each coding category was carefully defined to clearly differ from all other categories under the hypothetical. The rule statements were coded into the three response slots for each hypothetical in the order in which the respondents wrote them. (It should be noted that some respondents *listed* statements in their verbatim accounts in such a way that order was irrelevant, while others constructed decision-making "scenarios" in which one or more statements were contingent on the first. Lacking a coding or data entry scheme that could consider this distinction, the authors resorted to an enumeration of statements into response slots that assumed independence of statements from each other.)

As a check on the reliability of the content analysis procedure, two communications graduate students (naive to the subject and purposes of the study) coded the hypothetical responses of the entire sample according to the coding categories. Using the index of intercoder agreement developed by Scott (1955) — a conservative test that takes account of the observed frequency distribution in all possible categories of a variable — coefficients of intercoder agreement were calculated for the rule and exception statements of each hypothetical. Coefficients for the rules statements under the three hypotheticals were .76, .90, and .81, respectively. Coefficients for the exception statements under the three hypotheticals were .73, .68, and .76, respectively. The intercoder agreement levels were judged adequate for assuming reliable content categories.

By incorporating a surrogate report device as a pretext for answering hypothetical 1, it was hoped that the most salient rules for management of television would be gleaned. Concerns about the appropriateness of specific program content emerged as the dominant rule statements — both in terms of *prescriptive* instructions (i.e., designating educational, child-suitable, or family-suitable programming) or *proscriptive* instructions (i.e., designating programs that could not be watched by the child — such as those involving violent or "immoral" elements). Interestingly, only three respondents would prohibit the child from viewing pay cable programming specifically, while a sizable percentage of the sample (28 percent) subscribes to the local pay cable service, Home Box Office. The next group of rule statements mentioned most frequently centered on time limitations on viewing. Limitations on amount of viewing, usually specifying exact amounts of permissable viewing time, were cited by twenty-two respondents. A designated bedtime — indicating the latest hour at which their child could watch TV — was cited by twenty respondents, although this rule statement appeared more often as a secondary or tertiary instruction. The widespread assumption among the respondents was that there *would* be television viewing permitted in their absence. Few respondents ($f = 6$) ruled out televiewing altogether (due partly to three respondents reporting not owning a television), or would have the babysitter encourage the child to engage in other activities — play, reading, etc. — instead of TV viewing ($f = 4$), with these statements entirely written as secondary and tertiary instructions. Conversely, unrestricted televiewing by the child was proposed by only four respondents, suggesting that — at least in the context of this hypothetical construction — some degree of televiewing management is important to the couples. Spouse differences were minimal for all rule statements, except for limitations on amount of viewing; seventeen of the twenty-two respondents citing this instruction were female. Seventy-one percent of the sample would not make exceptions to their instructions, although some interesting sex differences did occur among the two most-cited exceptions statements. Of the sixteen content prescriptions, twelve were written by female spouses; of the five content proscription exceptions, all were given by male spouses. While generalizations must remain tentative, given the low frequency of response, these results tend to suggest that prospective mothers may give greater weight to actively designing their child's television use and perception rather than simply prohibiting certain content areas.

While making no assumptions about types of disapproved programs, hypothetical 2 does include the premise of an extant rule against certain programs. Given this premise, all but seven respondents formulated responses for the hypothetical situation. The predominant responses, by far, among the prospective parents were to *further articulate* the rule and its rationale to either the child ($f = 38$ for primary response; $f = 45$ among all responses) or to the friend's parents ($f = 12$ for primary response; $f = 26$ for all responses). Recourses to direct action were mostly secondary or not considered. The rule statement, "Restrict a child's visits to friend's house," was cited by twenty-one respondents, although most cited it as a secondary or tertiary response. In other words, scenarios were frequently constructed in which rule articulation was attempted first, followed by another rule elaboration — e.g., restricting the child's visits — *if* the effects of the prior response were unsatisfactory. Similarly, other direct actions, such as exercising disciplinary action on the child or giving the friend's parents instructions about the child's viewing behavior, were either not frequently cited or contingent on other responses. Very few exceptions ($f = 8$) were given for the rule statements, with all appearing to hinge on context-specific details of the infraction. There were no sex differences among the exception statements.

Hypothetical 3 presented a dilemma designed to highlight the communicative environment of the family, with television as the focus. Two interesting aspects of the response distributions to this hypothetical should be noted. First, very few secondary and tertiary responses were given compared with the other two hypotheticals; apparently, most respondents felt that one response would suffice to cover the situation, with little need for contingent or elaborated responses. Also, a greater frequency and wider range of exceptions were produced, indicating that context is highly important in evaluating the hypothetical request. Changing the channel only for an approved program was, by far, the leading response to this situation. Two other very frequently mentioned rule statements — "Discuss concepts of 'sharing'/'turn taking'" ($f = 17$) and "Refuse to change channels" ($f = 16$) — presented polar orientations to resolving the situation. Another rule statement, that of negotiating with the child ($f = 9$), covered a variety of tactical solutions, from rewards for good behavior to letting the child stay up past the designated bedtime. One response, telling the child to watch his or her show on another set, is interesting for its implications of the communicative environment and the implicit values therein; the situation is "solved" by pursuing individual viewing separately. The exceptions centered predominantly on the nature of the child's program and its suitability or potential benefits for the child; no sex differences were noted for the application of exceptions.

FCP Scales and Interspouse Differences

Table 20.6 displays the mean scores for each item of the Family Communication Pattern scales, in addition to the mean summed scores for the concept-orientation subscales and the socio-orientation subscales. Consistent with the suggestion that some instability might be manifested when new roles are anticipated, differences in family communication background between spouses could have some bearing on their responses to questions involving family television viewing. Such differences could predict interpretations of family conflicts involving their children's media use or orientations to action. To assess these possible effects, a procedure was conducted to separate couples with low or moderate interspouse differences on concept-orientation items from those couples with high interspouse differences on the items; the same procedure was carried out with the socio-orientation items. The summed scores for each spouse on the socio- and concept-orientation subscales were subtracted, yielding two absolute difference scores for each of the subscales. Each male and female spouse would, therefore, have one difference score on the concept-orientation subscales (labeled DIFFCON) and one difference score on the socio-orientation subscales (labeled DIFFSOC). Since the kurtosis coefficient indicated a relatively normal distribution for the difference scores, the cut-off for high versus low interspouse differences on the subscales was determined to be one standard deviation from the mean of the difference

Table 20.6
Family Communication Pattern Scales[a]

	Item Means
Concept Orientation Subscales	
1. How often did your parents say that you should always look at both sides of an issue?	3.588
2. How often did your parents admit that children know more about some things than adults do?	2.176
3. How often did your parents talk at home about things like politics or religion, where one family member takes a different side from others?	2.976
4. How much did your parents emphasize that getting your ideas across is important even if others don't like it?	3.224
5. How much did your parents emphasize that every member of the family should have some say in family decisions?	3.082
Subscale mean	14.837
Socio-Orientation Subscales	
1. How often did your parents say that their ideas are correct and you shouldn't question them?	2.869
2. How often did your parents answer your arguments by saying something like "You'll know better when you grow up"?	2.706
3. How often did your parents emphasize that you shouldn't argue with adults?	3.200
4. How often did your parents say that you should give in on arguments, rather than making people angry?	2.188
5. How much did your parents emphasize that the best way to stay out of trouble is to keep away from it?	3.435
Subscale mean	14.198

a. Items were accompanied by five-point interval scales.

scores. (For the concept-orientation subscales, the mean of the interspouse difference scores was -0.929, with a standard deviation of 4.298. For the socio-orientation subscales, the mean of interspouse difference scores was -0.119, with a standard deviation of 5.002.) Those couples with *low* DIFFCON and *low* DIFFSOC classifications had difference scores within one standard deviation of the sample means. *High* DIFFCON and *high* DIFFSOC couples had difference scores falling outside

Table 20.7
Interspouse Difference Classifications

	DIFFCON n	DIFFSOC n
Low	64	56
High	22	30

one standard deviation of the sample means. Table 20.7 displays the breakouts of respondents into low and high DIFFCON and DIFFSOC classifications.

Interspouse differences on socio- and concept-orientation subscales, classified by the scheme outlined above, were associated with the rule statements for each of the hypotheticals. Appendix B exhibits the contingency tables for these relationships. For hypothetical 1, the low DIFFCON group was much more likely to list both content prescription and content proscription rule statements ($p < .05$; 9 df) — i.e., take an active interest in the specific programming to which the child would be exposed in their absence. The low DIFFSOC group was also more likely to state content prescription rules ($p < .05$; 10 df).

For hypothetical 2, no significant differences between the high and low DIFFCON groups appeared for the rule statements. The low DIFFSOC group, though, appeared to put more emphasis on encouraging the child and/or friend to watch TV at home, as well as attempting to determine the child's reasons for watching the disapproved programs (rule statement 4). Because of the low cell frequencies for those rules, no chi square test for significance was performed. An intuitive interpretation of the results, however, might be that the interspouse agreement on harmonious relations implied in the socio-orientation subscales might well result in desires to avoid direct confrontation over the issue.

For hypothetical 3, there was a significant difference between the groups on rule statement 8 (refusal to change channels), with the high DIFFCON group more likely to propose refusal to the child's request ($p < .05$; 8 df). Low DIFFCON respondents showed a nonsignificant tendency to change the channel for an approved program vis-á-vis the high DIFFCON group. No differences among the DIFFSOC groups appeared for this hypothetical, with the exception of a slight tendency among low DIFFSOC respondents to suggest another activity to the child; low cell frequencies prevented the assessment of statistical significance.

Patterns of Media Information Exposure and Interspouse Discussion

As indicated in Tables 20.8 and 20.9, the extent to which the respondents viewed on television, heard on radio, or read in magazines or

Table 20.8
Media Information Source

Media	n	Percentage of Total
Television	18	21
Magazines	26	30
Newspapers	4	5
Radio	5	6
Other	5	6

Table 20.9
Topics about Children and Television from Media Sources

Topic	n
Children's viewing habits and practices	13
Children's programming	2
Television effects on children—general	5
Television effects on children—violence	20
Television effects on children lifestyle content (including pornography, morality, sexual content)	4

newspapers material related to the subject of children and television during the time they had been expecting a first child varied widely by medium. The topics converged around the subjects of "children's viewing habits and practices," and "television effects on children-violence." In order to determine the possible relationship between interspouse differences in family communication background and their media information exposure about children and television, respondents' DIFFCON and DIFFSOC scores were correlated with their exposure to *any* media source on any topics concerning children and television. (In other words, respondents reporting at least one media source were assigned "1" for media exposure; respondents reporting no media sources were assigned "0.") The Pearson correlation coefficient for DIFFCON and media exposure was only .03. DIFFSOC and media exposure, however, correlated at .18 ($p < .05$), showing a moderate relationship between larger differences in interspouse socio-orientation background and greater likelihood of exposure to media information concerning children and television.

Discussion of future plans for regulating or treating their expected child's television viewing among spouses was found to be rather minimal. Thirty-seven respondents (43 percent of the sample) reported no discussions of that type during the period of expectation. Four respondents reported "one or two" discussions, while only nine respondents had had "three or more" such discussions with their spouses. Rank ordering the levels of discussion from greatest to lowest frequency, respondents' DIFFCON and DIFFSOC scores were correlated with discussions of children's future televiewing using the Kendall tau procedure. Only the correlation between DIFFCON and discussions approached statistical significance ($\tau = -0.14$; $p = .055$); thus, a weak correlation between greater differences in concept-orientation background and fewer discussions appeared in this sample, contrary to expectations. In light of the low correlations obtained, no relationship between communication background differences among spouses and their discussions of future family viewing practices can be inferred.

Programs Encouraged and Discouraged

Those programs that respondents would either encourage their child to view or discourage from viewing are ranked by frequency in Table 20.10. Among all respondents, 29 (34 percent of the total sample) would not encourage their child to watch any programs, while 27 (31 percent) would not discourage their child from watching any programs. These responses, possibly reflecting some undetermined agenda such as "social desirability," might be considered in light of the prescriptive and proscriptive statements of the hypotheticals. To further investigate the relationship between spouses' family communication background and their projected viewing policies, Pearson correlations were computed between the summed FCP subscales and the number of encouraged and discouraged programs. While the correlations for encouraged programs were too weak to be statistically significant, the coefficients for the summed concept subscale and summed socio subscale with discouraged programs were -.23 ($p < .05$) and .17 ($p = .056$), respectively. These relationships meet the expectations that individuals whose prior family experiences stressed norm maintenance and closure on extrapersonal argument might also tend toward a prohibitive stance regarding program selection, particularly where verbal interpretation of morally ambiguous content could prove difficult.

CONCLUSIONS

The use of the hypothetical situations was intended to involve the prospective parents in some arguably realistic situations (without suggesting a priori rules), and therefore widen rather than narrow the range of

Table 20.10

Program (ranked by frequency)	n	Percentage of Total
Programs Encouraged for Child Viewing		
Sesame Street	39	33
Captain Kangaroo	10	8
Educational (generic)	8	7
Electric Company	8	7
Mister Roger's Neighborhood	6	5
National Geographic specials	4	3
Little House on the Prairie	4	3
Those Amazing Animals	3	3
Nova	3	3
Programs Discouraged for Child Viewing		
Dallas	18	15
Charlie's Angels	17	14
Soap operas (generic)	7	6
Dukes of Hazard	6	5
Pay cable (generic)	5	4
Movies (generic)	5	4
Incredible Hulk	4	3
Situation comedies (generic)	4	3
Three's Company	4	3

possible responses. To the extent that rich, often unique accounts of rule formulation were obtained, the purpose of the method was accomplished; the authors recommend the design of similar role-playing probes for inquiries where conscious, goal-directed scenarios are desired, rather than forced-choice measures of subject reaction. One problem, of course, lies with the reduction of these data for analysis. In transforming the original, qualitative accounts to a data language adaptable to aggregate analysis, much of the textual grain and narrative structure are lost. One way of alleviating the problem, unexplored here because of space limitations, would be parallel qualitative and quantitative analyses.

From the analysis of the relationship of interspouse communication background differences and rule formulation, a picture emerges of couples with wide differences in concept orientation (i.e., differences in their perceptions of their family's willingness to discuss extrapersonal topics openly and frequently) to be somewhat inflexible in their rule formulations. Couples with low differences in concept orientation seemed more concerned with taking a direct hand in guiding their child's exposure to programming. If interspouse differences do indeed portend some instability of agreement when entering on a new role, then one recourse to ambiguous situations might be to respond inflexibly or even dogmatically — as the high DIFFCON group appeared to do, especially in hypothetical 3.

Across all three hypotheticals couples low in socio-orientation differences tended to use suasive tactics for getting the child to conform to family goals. This would be expected of spouses with *high* socio-orientation scores, although the syndrome in this case seemed to operate among couples relatively congruent in their socio-orientation, without regard for the *magnitude* of socio-orientation. It may be that couples experiencing the same degree of stress on harmonious relations in their upbringing will, over time, tend to agree on rules that have the effect of enforcing social norms within the household. These conclusions are very tentative, given (1) the many rule statements on which there seemed minimal differences between the groups, (2) the small sample size and the slightly atypical character of the sample of prospective parents (due to the atypicality of the university-based community), and (3) the risks involved in applying an instrument, the FCP scales, differently than it has been used in the past. Regarding the latter issue, the FCP scales have typically been administered to children and adolescents for rating their current family communicative environment. By asking mature respondents to rate their past family communication modes, the results obtained may be more an artifact of attributions about the items rather than reports of or reactions to ongoing interactions. The instrument may, however, be producing results valid to the objectives of the study in that attributions about previous family communication patterns may be most relevant at that point where a new familial role is assumed. Those attributions may be functioning as exemplars for approaching their own emergent roles.

Rules theory has yet to be seriously developed beyond its present status as a promising heuristic for conceptualizing the interactive methods of television users. It may eventually provide an alternative to the uses and gratifications approach, although the rules approach, too, must avoid becoming constrained in its explanatory power by tautological assumptions. This chapter is an initial abductive step in a longitudinal study of the development of families' procedures for negotiating television as a social object. Using a subsample of this study's families, the *analytic induction* model of doing research will "permit the direct identification of time order, covariance, and rival causal factors" (Denzin, 1978, p. 27) among the emergent variables. Because the model identifies and explains negative cases that refute propositions established over a long-term observational period, the theoretical framework remains incomplete until the propositions cover all cases, thus accounting for rival hypotheses. The possible influences of prior family communication style on the development of television-related interaction will be among the areas of interest that can be usefully investigated through such a model.

Appendix A
Responses to Hypothetical Problems:
Rule Statements

Hypothetical 1: "If my spouse and I were going out for the evening and were leaving our five-year-old child with a babysitter (whom we do not know prior to that evening), I would give the babysitter the following *instructions* concerning our child's TV viewing":

Rule Statements	Response 1	Response 2	Response 3	Total
0. No response.	4	44	75	123
1. No instructions/No restrictions on TV viewing.	4	0	0	4
2. No TV viewing.	6	0	0	6
3. Child must be in bed by designated time.	8	9	3	20
4. Time limitations on amount of TV viewing.	15	6	1	22
5. Eating limitations during TV viewing.	0	0	1	1
6. Content proscriptions.	17	11	1	29
7. Content prescriptions.	24	9	4	37
8. No pay cable programs.	2	1	0	3
9. Encourage other activities for child besides TV.	0	3	1	4
10. Allow child to watch programs the family normally watches.	4	1	0	5
11. Babysitter's judgment.	2	2	0	4
	86	86	86	258

Hypothetical 2: "If I learned that my five-year-old child has been watching TV programs that I disapprove of at a friend's house, without telling me, I would (please complete)":

	Response 1	Response 2	Response 3	Total
0. No response.	3	44	77	124
1. Explain or talk to child about disapproval of behavior.	38	7	0	45
2. Exercise displinary action.	5	3	0	8
3. Restrict child's visits to friend's	8	12	1	21
4. Determine child's reactions/reasons for watching programs.	7	2	0	9
5. Explain feelings/thoughts about subject to friend's parents.	12	11	3	26
6. Give friend's parents instructions about child's TV viewing.	7	5	4	16
7. Encourage child and/or friend to watch TV at my home.	2	2	1	5
8. Don't know.	4	0	0	4
	86	86	86	258

Appendix A (Continued)

Hypothetical 3: "If I was watching my favorite TV program at home in the evening and my five-year-old child asked me to change the channel to watch another show, I would (please complete)":

Rule Statements	Response 1	Response 2	Response 3	Total
0. No response.	6	69	84	159
1. Change channel only for an approved program.	35	2	0	37
2. Change channel after negotiating with child.	7	2	0	9
3. Change channel if my show is a rerun or not a special.	1	0	0	1
4. Change channel (no qualification).	5	0	0	5
5. Discuss concepts of "sharing"/"turn taking" in viewing time or choice.	12	5	0	17
6. Suggest that child watch my program.	1	3	0	4
7. Refuse to change channels.	14	2	0	16
8. Tell child to watch his/her show on other TV.	3	2	0	5
9. Suggest another activity to child.	2	1	2	5
	86	86	86	258

Responses to Hypothetical Questions: Rule Exceptions

Exception Statements	Responses
Hypothetical 1	
0. No exceptions.	61
1. Content prescriptions.	16
2. Content proscriptions.	5
3. Babysitter's judgment for viewing.	3
4. Weekends.	1
	86
Hypothetical 2	
0. No exceptions.	78
1. If friend was unaware of disapproval.	3
2. Depends on exact situation.	2
3. Give child a chance to explain.	2
4. If child or friend's parents give reasons for watching programs.	1
	86

(continued)

Appendix A (Continued)

Hypothetical 3

0. No exceptions.	42
1. "Special" program for children.	12
2. Low interest in my program.	5
3. Viewing interests of those watching my program.	2
4. Punishment.	2
5. Depends on my mood.	2
6. Depends on advisability/benefit of either show for child.	19
7. Depends on time period of the programs.	2
	86

Appendix B
Contingency Tables: DIFFCON/DIFFSOC by Rule Statements

Rule Statement	High DIFFCON	Low DIFFCON	High DIFFSOC	Low DIFFSOC
Hypothetical 1				
0.	32	91	47	76
1.	2	2	2	2
2.	4	2	4	2
3.	5	15	7	13
4.	7	15	7	15
5.	0	1	0	1
6.	5	24	9	20
7.	6	31	9	28
8.	1	2	1	2
9.	2	2	1	3
10.	1	4	1	4
11.	1	3	1	3
Hypothetical 2				
0.	28	96	48	76
1.	13	32	16	29
2.	1	7	2	6
3.	5	16	8	13
4.	3	6	1	8
5.	9	17	8	18
6.	5	11	6	10
7.	1	4	0	5
8.	1	3	1	3

(continued)

Appendix B (Continued)

		Hypothetical 3		
0.	39	120	59	120
1.	8	29	12	25
2.	1	8	2	7
3.	1	0	1	0
4.	0	5	1	4
5.	4	13	6	11
6.	3	1	1	3
7.	8	8	6	10
8.	1	4	2	3
9.	1	4	0	5

REFERENCES

Abel, J. D. The family and child television viewing. *Journal of Marriage and the Family,* 1976, 331-335.

Anderson, J. A., & Avery, R. K. An analysis of changes in voter percetion of candidates' positions. *Communication Monographs,* 1978, 45, 354-361.

Barcus, F. E. Parental influence on children's television viewing. *Television Quarterly,* 1968, 8, 63-73.

Blood, R. O. Social class and family control of television viewing. *Merrill-Palmer Quarterly of Behavior and Development,* 1961, 7, 205-222.

Brody, G. H., Stoneman, Z., & Sanders, A. K. Effects of television viewing on family interactions: An observational study. *Family Relations,* 1980, 29, 216-220.

Chaffee, S. H., McLeod, J. M. & Atkin, C. K. Parental influences on adolescent media use. In F. G. Kline & P. Clarke (Eds.), *Mass communication and youth.* Beverly Hills, CA: Sage, 1971.

Chaffee, S. H., & Tims, A. R. Interpersonal factors in adolescent television use. *Journal of Social Issues,* 1976, 32(4), 98-115.

Collett, P. The rules of conduct. In P. Collett (Ed.), *Social rules and social behavior.* Totowa, NJ: Rowman & Littlefield, 1977.

Cushman, D., & Whiting, G. C. An approach to communication theory: Toward consensus on rules. *Journal of Communication,* 1972, 22, 217-238.

Denzin, N. K. *The research act* (2nd ed.) New York: McGraw-Hill, 1978.

Dimmick, J. W., McCain, T. A., & Bolton, W. T. Media use and the life span. *American Behavioral Scientist,* 1979, 23, 7-31.

Freidson, E. Communications research and the concept of the mass. In W. Schramm & D. Roberts (Eds.), *The process and effects of mass communication.* Urbana: University of Illinois Press, 1971.

Fry, D. L., & McCain, T. A. *Controlling children's television viewing: Predictors of family television rules and their relationship to family communication patterns.* Paper presented to the Association for Education in Journalism Annual Conference, Boston, 1980.

Harre, R., & Secord, P. F. *The explanation of social behavior.* Totowa, NJ: Littlefield, Adams, 1973.

Hess, R. D., & Goldman, H. Parents' views of the effect of television on their children. *Child Development,* 1962, 33, 411-426.

Jackson, D. D. The study of the family. *Family Process,* 1965, 4, 1-20.

Lull, J. *Mass media and family communication: An ethnography of audience behavior.* Unpublished doctoral dissertation, University of Wisconsin, 1976.

Lull, J. Choosing television programs by family vote. *Communication Quarterly,* 1978, *26*(4), 53-57.

Lull, J. The social uses of television. *Human Communication Research,* 1980, *6,* 197-209. (a)

Lull, J. Family communication patterns and the social uses of television. *Communication Research,* 1980, *7,* 319-334. (b)

Lull, J. *The rules of mass communication.* Paper presented to the International Communication Association Annual Conference, Minneapolis, 1981.

Maccoby, E. Television: Its impact on school children. *Public Opinion Quarterly,* 1951, *15,* 421-444.

Maccoby, E. Why do children watch television? *Public Opinion Quarterly,* 1954, *18,* 239-244.

Martin, C. A., & Benson, L. Parental perceptions of the role of television in parent-child interactions. *Journal of Marriage and the family,* 1970, 410-414.

McDonagh, E. C. Television and the family. *Sociology and Social Research,* 1950, *35,* 113-122.

McLeod, J. M., & Brown, J. The family environment and adolescent media use. In Ray Brown (Ed.). *Children and television.* Beverly Hills, CA: Sage, 1976.

McLeod, J. M., & Chaffee, S. M. The construction of social reality. In James T. Tedeschi (Ed.). *The social influence process.* Chicago: Aldine, 1972.

McQuail, D. & Gurevitch, M. Explaining audience behavior: Three approaches considered. In Jay G. Blumler & Elihu Katz (Eds.), *The uses of mass communications.* Beverly Hills, CA: Sage, 1974.

Messaris, P., & Sarett, C. On the consequences of television-related parent-child interactions. *Human Communication Research,* 1981, *7,* 226-244.

Meyer, T. P., Traudt, P. J., & Anderson, J. A. Non-traditional mass communication research methods: Observational case studies of media use in natural settings. In D. Nimmo (Ed.), *Communication yearbook 4.* New Brunswick, NJ: Transaction, 1980.

Reid, L. N. Viewing rules as mediating factors in children's responses to commercials. *Journal of Broadcasting,* 1979, *23,* 15-26.

Rossiter, J. R., & Robertson, T. S. Children's television viewing: An examination of parent-child consensus. *Sociometry,* 1975, *38,* 308-326.

Scott, W. A. Reliability of content analysis: The case of nominal scale coding. *Public Opinion Quarterly,* 1955, *19,* 321-325.

Shimanoff, S. *Communication rules.* Beverly Hills, CA: Sage, 1980.

Sigman, S. J. On communication rules from a social perspective. *Human Communication Research,* 1980, *7,* 37-51.

Singer, J. L., & Singer, D. *Television, imagination, and aggression.* Hillsdale, NJ: Lawrence J. Erlbaum, 1981.

Smith, D. H., Communication research and the idea of process. *Speech Monographs,* 1972, *39,* 174-182.

Traudt, P. J. *Television and family viewing: An ethnography.* Unpublished master's thesis, University of Utah, 1979.

MASS COMMUNICATION

21 • Contextual Age and Television Use: Reexamining a Life-Position Indicator

REBECCA B. RUBIN • ALAN M. RUBIN
Kent State University

> Johan Johansson, 57, a widower with no children who lives in a small Brooklyn apartment on a $521 monthly disability check, walked with the aid of leg braces as he came to claim his $2.25 million prize in the New York state lottery. "I want my health. Money or no money, that's the most important thing in life," said Johansson. . . . He said he intends to stay in the apartment where his wife died and where he said he now mostly watches television. (*Cleveland Press,* September 20, 1981, p. 2)

THIS somewhat stereotypic portrait of a frail, aging person's reliance on television has been the concern of communication study in recent years. In actuality, the focus of research interest has been twofold. On one hand, the stereotype of overwhelming affinity with the television medium has led to research investigating media use by older persons. Second, researchers have been concerned with progressing beyond chronological measures of aging to ascertain life-position indicators that may be indicative more of the aging process than the number of years a person has lived. The present investigation seeks to explore more fully one life-position indicator — *contextual age* — with a population of both aged and nonaged adults in order to develop the construct and to examine the relationship between contextual age and television use for an adult sample with a broad age range.

Research on aging has studied the concept of age in relation to a variety of human processes. However, past reliance on the chronological age measure in social gerontology and communication research has been recognized as insufficient by several researchers. Kaluger and Kaluger (1979), for example, argue that biological processes of aging are often

---

Correspondence and requests for reprints: Rebecca B. Rubin, School of Speech, Kent State University, Kent, OH 44242.

tempered by individual, social, economic, and environmental differences. Hurlock (1975) adds the possible effects of health, living conditions, social and marital status, education level, and gender on the aging process. Pfeiffer (1977) attributes aging differences to adjustments in changing lifestyles that are typical in later years — loss of spouse, decrease in mobility, loss of opportunity for recognition, reduction in social relationships, and so on. Thus, alternatives to chronological age might include physical, social, economic, and personality conditions, as well as an individual's ability to adjust to changes.

Wilson (1974) has developed a programmed perspective on aging based on reactions to changes in the environment. The inability to accept change, according to Wilson, may speed up the aging process. Even the acceptance or rejection of the notion of aging is an ingredient in psychological aging. Other researchers (Havighurst, 1968; Knapp, 1977; Neugarten, 1972; Neugarten, Havighurst, & Tobin, 1968) argue that personality factors can be used to explain aging patterns and to predict associations between life satisfaction and activity. This activity theory of aging asserts that older persons have the same psychological and social needs as those who are middle aged, but social norms (e.g., forced retirement) or physiological declines block the fulfillment of these needs. The disengagement theory of aging (Cummings, 1963; Cummings & Henery, 1961; Henery, 1965) views aging as a period of mutual withdrawal where the individual's decline in social participation is functionally advantageous to both the individual and society; individuals who decrease their interactions with others become more preoccupied with themselves and experience satisfaction in this process, since the pressure of emotional investment in others is lessened.

One additional construct alternative to chronological age has been "functional age" (McFarland, 1973). This concept was developed as a measure of physiological age — the ability of individuals to perform their jobs and adapt to the normal stresses found within them. This view suggests that age is more dependent on an individual's physiological and psychological position in life than on chronological age.

This recent emphasis on life-position indicators of aging has received attention in the communication literature as well. Graney and Graney (1974) suggest that use of the mass media performs an important function in the lives of the elderly; when social contacts with others diminish in later life, the media are used to maintain social psychological satisfaction. Schramm (1969) and Cassata (1967) support this notion that increased media use functionally counteracts the sense of alienation often experienced in later years. Swank (1979) notes that it is the less mobile, older individual who relies more on television than any other form of social activity or media channel.

Inclusion of social activity, living arrangement, health, economic status and education as sociological and biographical factors affecting television use has received additional attention in the literature. Wenner (1976) proposed that television viewing patterns are linked to elements of life-position. His factor-analytic study identified three types of viewers. Type 1 viewers were discriminating; they were socially mobile, oriented toward information programming, and married. Type 2 viewers used television for companionship and preferred not to watch alone; they were socially isolated, widowed, and lived alone. Type 3 viewers used television for companionship, as a time-killer, and as a topic for conversation; they lived alone or in retirement homes. In addition, in his extensive review of the television and aging literature, Kubey (1980) rejects the notion proposed in past investigations that the link between higher television viewing levels and low income and education is a function of changes which accompany aging. He contends that these findings are partly the result of long-standing social class variables and that today's elderly just happen to have less formal education and fewer financial resources. The tone of his argument implies that nonaged persons, experiencing similar lifestyle conditions, may also rely extensively on television use.

The importance of including communication behavior along with the social and psychological attributes of aging hinges on the idea that communication needs interact with the aging process. The "life-span position" concept developed by Dimmick, McCain, and Bolton (1979) has been proposed as an alternative to chronological age and was used to explain human development and media use. However, a more recent investigation (Rubin & Rubin, 1981) suggests a functional relationship between age and context, including the communication channels, social interaction, and psychological conditions of an individual's environment. This "contextual age" construct purports that the context in which one lives — comprising communication, social, psychological, physiological, and economic dimensions — is a more accurate indicator of individuals' life-positions.

A subsequent study (Rubin & Rubin, 1982) has shown that contextual age components — physical health, interpersonal interaction, mobility, life satisfaction, social activity, and economic security — are heuristically useful for explaining sociodemographic characteristics, television viewing patterns, and television use motivations of aging and aged persons. For example, socially active, self-reliant elders were found to display little affinity with television, while the opposite was true for the less mobile and less healthy elderly. Also, individuals who lived alone and were less satisfied with their lives used television as a means of escape and had a greater affinity with the television medium. Economic security, life satisfaction, and self-reliance were also found to be negatively linked with escapist and companionship uses of television. The findings of this prior study suggest, then, that conditions of life satisfaction, mobility, physical health, social activity, and economic security tend to interact with television use and affinity.

Differences in mobility, life satisfaction, physical health, social interaction, and economic security, however, are not limited to older persons. Younger persons could viably have similar contextual age characteristics and associated communication behaviors as the older population. The purpose of the present investigation, then, is to develop further the contextual age construct by examining these life-position indicators in an adult group with a broader age range. The investigation seeks to refine the contextual age construct as a life-span position measure distinct from chronological aging, and to discover similarities and dissimilarities in television use, viewing behaviors, television affinity, and contextual age factors across the broader age sample and in relation to the older age sample in the prior study (Rubin & Rubin, 1982).

METHODS

Questionnaires were administered to 300 persons, aged seventeen to eighty-three, in two Wisconsin counties by twelve trained interviewers from a communication research class at a midwestern university. Data collection took place during a one-week period in November 1980 and was restricted to Tuesdays through Saturdays so that prior weekday television viewing levels could be assessed.

The instrument utilized in the present investigation was identical to the one employed in the prior study (Rubin & Rubin, 1982). It assessed a number of variables: component dimensions of contextual age; television viewing patterns, including daypart and daily viewing levels, program type viewing, and television affinity; television viewing motivations; and sociodemographic characteristics.

Contextual Age Factors

Five statements were included for each of six initial contextual age categories — physical health, interpersonal interaction, mobility, life satisfaction, social activity, and economic security. Along with five television affinity measures, the items were alternately presented to respondents, who indicated their level of agreement with each statement on a five-point scale ranging from "strongly agree" (5) to "strongly disagree" (1). Table 21.1 summarizes the contextual age statements, their initial categories, means, and standard deviations.

Responses to the thirty contextual age items were subjected to principal factor analysis with iterations. Recognizing from the prior study of the

Table 21.1
Initial Contextual Age Sets

Initial Contextual Age Categories and Statements	Mean	Standard Deviation
Physical Health		
1. I usually feel in top-notch physical condition.	3.40	0.96
2. Healthwise, I am no worse off than anyone else my age.	3.87	0.92
3. I have a great deal of trouble hearing other people.*	1.99	0.99
4. I have a great deal of trouble with my eyesight which prevents me from doing things.*	1.62	0.77
5. I have serious medical or health problems.*	1.71	0.90
Interpersonal Interaction		
1. I have as much contact as I would like with somebody I can trust and confide in.	3.45	1.08
2. I get to see my friends as often as I would like.	3.39	0.98
3. I often feel lonely.*	2.06	0.97
4. I spend enough time communicating with my family or friends by telephone or mail.	3.28	1.03
5. I have ample opportunity for conversations with other people	3.96	0.83
Mobility		
1. I stay at home most of the time.*	2.51	1.10
2. I usually drive my own car or use the city bus to get around.	4.12	0.90
3. I have to rely on other people to take me places.*	1.65	0.92
4. I usually don't travel more than a few blocks from my home each day.*	1.85	0.97
5. I have trouble keeping up with others when going shopping or on trips.*	1.81	0.90
Life Satisfaction		
1. I find a great deal of happiness in life.	3.79	0.77
2. I've been very successful in achieving my aims or goals in life.	3.43	0.83
3. I am very content and satisfied with my life.	3.57	0.84
4. My life could be happier than it is now.*	3.07	1.07
5. Compared to other people, I get down in the dumps too often.*	1.97	0.94
Social Activity		
1. I often travel, vacation, or take trips with others.	3.04	1.12
2. I often visit with friends, relatives, or neighbors in their homes.	3.29	0.97
3. I often participate in games, sports, or activities with others.	3.36	1.10
4. I often go out shopping or to the movies.	2.98	1.04
5. I often participate in the meetings or activities of clubs, lodges, recreation centers, churches or other organizations.	2.93	1.15

(continued)

Table 21.1 (Continued)

Initial Contextual Age Categories and Statements	Mean	Standard Deviation
Economic Security		
1. I have no major financial worries.	3.20	1.11
2. After I pay my basic living expenses each month, I have little money left over to buy anything else.*	2.85	1.09
3. When buying a product, I usually buy the best, even if it costs more.	2.74	0.92
4. I have enough money to buy things I want, even if I don't really need them.	2.96	1.06
5. I live quite comfortably now and have enough money to buy what I need or want.	3.27	1.01

Note: Response options ranged from "strongly disagree" (1) to "strongly agree" (5) with each statement. Statements from each category were alternately presented to the respondents. In other words, an economic security statement followed a social activity statement which followed a life satisfaction statement, and so on. The polarity of starred items was subsequently reversed for further analyses.

older age sample that these life-position statements were interrelated, oblique rotation procedures were utilized. The factor solution explained 44.3 percent of the total variance. A scree test was employed to determine factor retention, resulting in the identification of four principal contextual age factors. Table 21.2 summarizes the factor solution. In order to construct the four contextual age variables employed in subsequent analyses, factor scores were computed.

Factor 1, *life satisfaction*, has an eigenvalue of 5.04 and accounts for 38.0 percent of the common variance. Four of the five initial life satisfaction statements, as well as an interpersonal interaction statement concerning loneliness, load on this factor. The items reflect an individual's life contentment and happiness. The factor is quite similar to the life satisfaction factor in the prior study.

Factor 2, *physical health*, has an eigenvalue of 2.20 and accounts for 16.6 percent of the common variance. Three statements which indicate a perception of one's physical health (especially a sense of having medical problems) and a mobility item (concerning the ability to keep up with others) load substantially on this factor. This factor is related to the self-reliance factor in the prior study; however, self-reliance incorporated more of the mobility items and fewer of the physical health items.

Factor 3, *economic security*, has an eigenvalue of 1.40 and accounts for 10.5 percent of the common variance. Similar to the economic security factor of the prior study, four of the five original economic security state-

Table 21.2
Contextual Age Oblique Rotated Factor Matrix

	Contextual Age Factors			
Contextual Age Items	Life Satisfaction (Factor 1)	Physical Health (Factor 2)	Economic Security (Factor 3)	Social Activity (Factor 4)
Physical health (1)	.06	.05	.02	.02
Interpersonal interact (1)	.12	.04	−.06	.02
Mobility (1)	.01	.26	.02	.22
Life satisfaction (1)	.59	.27	.05	.04
Social activity (1)	−.03	−.18	.12	.45
Economic security (1)	.06	−.04	.62	.16
Physical health (2)	−.08	.15	.14	−.05
Interpersonal interact (2)	.21	.10	.01	.30
Mobility (2)	.01	−.06	.04	−.02
Life satisfaction (2)	.32	−.14	.22	.01
Social activity (2)	.10	−.03	.02	.59
Economic security (2)	.00	.04	.63	.18
Physical health (3)	−.10	.52	.04	.11
Interpersonal interact (3)	.46	.27	.00	.25
Mobility (3)	.19	.26	−.02	−.02
Life satisfaction (3)	.71	−.11	.05	−.07
Social activity (3)	−.05	.07	−.10	.06
Economic security (3)	.05	.01	.03	−.01
Physical health (4)	.11	.41	−.09	−.09
Interpersonal interact (4)	−.03	.03	−.01	.01
Mobility (4)	−.04	.28	−.05	.13
Life satisfaction (4)	.56	.08	.13	.01
Social activity (4)	−.16	.04	.06	.23
Economic security (4)	−.03	.07	.70	−.11
Physical health (5)	.02	.56	−.06	−.02
Interpersonal interact (5)	.09	.01	.02	.07
Mobility (5)	.06	.57	.09	−.08
Life satisfaction (5)	.42	.26	.00	.07
Social activity (5)	.04	−.03	.07	.05
Economic security (5)	.08	−.03	.85	−.17

Note: The factor solution explained 44.3 percent of the total variance. Factor 1 had an eigenvalue of 5.04 and accounted for 38.0 percent of the common variance. Factor 2 had an eigenvalue of 2.20 and accounted for 16.6 percent of the common variance. Factor 3 had an eigenvalue of 1.40 and accounted for 10.5 percent of the common variance. Factor 4 had an eigenvalue of 1.28 and accounted for 9.7 percent of the common variance. The fifth through ninth factors in the unrotated solution had eigenvalues of 0.88, 0.80, 0.63, 0.58, and 0.47 and accounted for 6.7 percent, 6.0 percent, 4.7 percent, 4.4 percent, and 3.5 percent of the common variance, respectively. Item identifications and numbers in parentheses refer to the initial contextual age statements and categories in Table 21.1.

ments load highly on this factor. The items reflect a perceived state of economic sufficiency and well-being.

Factor 4, *social activity,* has an eigenvalue of 1.28 and accounts for 9.7 percent of the common variance. Statements with high loadings concern a person's activity and interaction, particularly taking trips and visiting friends. The factor resembles the prior study's interaction factor; however, the interaction factor contained additional interpersonal interaction elements for the older sample and accounted for a greater proportion of the common variance in that study's factor solution.

Television Viewing Patterns

Daypart and Daily Viewing Levels. Daypart viewing and amount of daily viewing were assessed by presenting six three-hour dayparts to respondents and asking them to specify the number of hours they had watched television in each of those prior-day time peiods — 7 a.m. to 10 a.m., 10 a.m. to 1 p.m., and so on. These weekday dayparts reflect Central Time. This structured recall procedure has worked well in previous research and seems to provide more reliable data than requesting a singular, generalized recall of all previous-day television viewing. Within each of the dayparts, responses ranged from zero to three hours of previous-day viewing. A cumulative amount of daily viewing index was obtained by summing the responses to the six dayparts, with a potential range of zero to eighteen hours. The average amount of television viewing for the previous weekday was 3.05 hours. This was considerably less than the 4.76 average viewing hours for the older sample in the prior study. Similar to the findings of the prior study, though, the most frequently viewed time periods were the prime time and late afternoon/early evening dayparts, with over two-thirds of all respondents watching television between 7 p.m. and 10 p.m., and nearly one-half of the respondents viewing between 4 p.m. and 7 p.m.

Program Type Viewing. Respondents were asked to indicate how often they typically watched each of fourteen television program types on a five-point scale ranging from "always" (5) to "never" (1) watch. The program types and their mean responses are as follows: news, 3.51; documentary-magazine, 3.49; sports, 3.25; movies, 3.10; drama, 2.92; situation comedy, 2.87; general comedy, 2.76; talk-interview, 2.51; music-variety, 2.45; action-adventure, 2.35; game show, 2.20; children's program, 2.00; daytime serial, 1.84; and religion, 1.38. Computation of a Kendall's Coefficient of Concordance reveals that the present investigation's broader age sample and the prior study's older age sample differ with regard to the ordering of their frequency of viewing the several program types ($W = .79$, ns). In particular, the older sample members more often watched music-variety, game, and talk-interview programs and less often watched sports, movies, and situation comedies as compared to the present sample members.

Television Affinity. A five-point concordance scale was also used in asking individuals to respond to five television affinity statements (e.g., "Watching television is one of the most important things I do each day," "If the television set wasn't working, I would really miss it"). Responses were coded so that a 5 reflects a high level and a 1 indicates a low level of television affinity. The interitem correlation of the five-item affinity index was .50 with a .82 reliability coefficient. The mean affinity score for the sample was 2.05. By contrast, the mean affinity score for the past study's older sample was 2.83, which is obviously greater than that of the present sample, yet not overwhelmingly positive.

Television Viewing Motivations

Respondents were also asked to indicate their agreement with each of fourteen television viewing motivation statements. Response options were presented on a five-point scale ranging from "strongly agree" (5) to "strongly disagree" (1) with the statement (e.g., "I watch television because it helps me to learn how to act with other people or in different situations," "I watch television because it gives me something to talk about with others"). The viewing motivation and television affinity measures were adapted from items used earlier by Rubin (1979, 1981).

The viewing motivations included in the statements and their mean responses are: information-learning, 3.77; entertainment, 3.53; relaxation, 3.22; economics-inexpensive, 3.13; convenience, 3.17; companionship, 2.79; pass time, 2.65; arousal-excitement, 2.63; escape-forget, 2.33; habit, 2.27; topic for communication, 2.25; behavioral guidance, 2.02; social interaction, 1.79; and product advertising, 1.73. While several of the mean responses were more salient for the prior study's older sample, a Kendall's Coefficient of Concordance indicates a substantial consistency in the ordering of the salience of viewing motivations across the prior and present studies' different age samples ($W = .97$, $p < .001$).

Sociodemographic Characteristics

Sociodemographic data gathered from the respondents and the manner of data coding are as follows: chronological *age* (ranging from seventeen to eighty-three years); *sex* (male = 0, female = 1); *education* (ranging from a low level of one for grade school to a high level of six for graduate school); *family size* (ranging from one to eight persons); monthly spendable *income* (ranging from a low level of one for $100 or less to a high level of nine for $801 or more); and *occupation* (ranging from a low

Table 21.3
Contextual Age Factor Correlation Matrix

	Life Satisfaction	Physical Health	Economic Security	Social Activity
Life satisfaction	—			
Physical health	.22	—		
Economic security	.28	−.04	—	
Social activity	.24	.21	.25	—

$r = .12$, $p < .05$; $r = .16$, $p < .01$; $r = .20$, $p < .001$ (two-tailed).

occupational prestige level of one to a high level of thirteen, based on the Troldahl [1967] "Occupational Prestige Scale").

The mean age of the sample members was 40.6 years. The sample was 47 percent male and 53 percent female. The median education level was just below "some college." The mean family size was 3.5 persons. The median monthly spendable income level was just above the "$301-$400" income category.

Statistical Analysis

Pearson product-moment and partial correlations, controlling for chronological age, were computed in order to identify the relationships of contextual age factors with sociodemographics, viewing patterns, and viewing motivations. T-tests for sex differences were also computed but did not reveal significant changes from the relationships located in the correlation procedures. As depicted in Table 21.3, contextual age factors were intercorrelated, indicating the need to utilize multivariate procedures to determine associations within and between several categories of variables.

Canonical correlation analysis was therefore employed to examine the relationships of the set of contextual age factors with the sets of sociodemographics, viewing patterns, and viewing motivations. Within the Pearson and partial correlation procedures, assessment of relationships focused on those associations significant at or beyond the .001 level. Interpretation of canonical roots and variates focused, as is usual practice, on coefficients of .30 and greater.

RESULTS

The results of the investigation are systematically presented below. Examined first are the sociodemographic correlates of the contextual age factors, then the television viewing pattern correlates of contextual age, and finally the viewing motivation correlates of contextual age. Within each section the initial analysis level assessed univariate relationships between contextual age and the other variables, while the subsequent analysis considered the multivariate associations between the set of the contextual age factors and the sets of the other three categories of variables. The partial correlations, controlling for chronological age, of the initial analysis are presented in Table 21.4. Correlates that are significant at or beyond the .001 level are italicized in the table.

Contextual Age and Sociodemographics

Only a few significant (at the .001 level) correlates of contextual age are evident from the data in Table 21.4. Age is negatively related to physical health and positively associated with economic security. Income is also a positive correlate of economic security. The latter relationship was also evident in the prior study of the older age sample (Rubin & Rubin, 1982). Younger respondents indicate a more favorable state of physical health, while older respondents and those with more available income perceive a greater sense of economic well-being. It would appear that across a broader age range, physical health and perceived economic security life-position sets provide improved indicators of a person's chronological age.

Several of the sociodemographic sets show no substantial relationship to contextual age factors. In particular, gender, education, family size, and occupation do not appear to be strongly related to contextual age for this broader age sample. Similar to the prior study of the older age group, though, physical health is marginally related to education level and economic security is marginally related to occupational prestige. In contrast to the prior study, in the present investigation family size (which was generally smaller for the older group) is not related to either life satisfaction or physical health, and the gender of the respondent is not associated with economic security.

In order to assess the interaction within and between these sets of contextual age and sociodemographic variables, canonical correlation procedures were employed. This analysis is summarized in Table 21.5. Two significant canonical roots were located.

Root 1 explains 26 percent of the variance. Set 1 indicates a negative relationship between economic security and physical health. Set 2 reflects positive relationships between age, income, and possibly family size. Comparisons across the sets reveal that economically secure but less healthy individuals tend to be older persons who have more available money.

Root 2 explains 11 percent of the variance. Set 1 includes a positive relationship between economic security and physical health and possible

Table 21.4
Partial Correlates of Contextual Age Factors
Controlling for Chronological Age

Correlates	Life Satisfaction	Physical Health	Economic Security	Social Activity
Sociodemographics:				
Age	.11	−.25	.30	−.02
Gender	−.04	.15	.01	.13
Education	.03	.16	.15	−.05
Family size	−.03	.04	−.10	−.06
Income	.12	.01	.31	−.05
Occupation	.00	.10	.16	−.03
Daypart Viewing:				
7 a.m.-10 a.m.	−.02	−.15	.03	−.08
10 a.m.-1 p.m.	−.08	−.24	.06	−.03
1 p.m.-4 p.m.	.01	−.14	−.05	−.09
4 p.m.-7 p.m.	−.04	−.15	−.13	−.03
7 p.m.-10 p.m.	−.15	−.12	−.11	−.03
10 p.m.-1 a.m.	−.08	−.07	−.05	−.09
Amount of Daily Viewing	−.13	−.24	−.11	−.10
Program Type Viewing:				
News	.10	−.05	.01	.02
Documentary-magazine	.02	−.08	.07	.08
Sports	.04	−.10	−.10	.02
Movies	−.19	−.16	.01	−.07
Drama	−.07	−.03	−.03	−.01
Situation comedy	.00	−.11	−.12	−.05
General comedy	−.09	−.14	−.14	−.03
Talk-interview	.05	.05	−.02	.22
Music-variety	−.02	−.13	.00	−.02
Action-adventure	−.05	−.19	−.13	.03
Game show	−.04	−.10	−.12	.14
Children's programs	.03	−.10	−.11	−.03
Daytime serial	−.10	.00	−.01	.06
Religion	−.10	−.08	.04	.02
Television Affinity	−.24	−.37	−.04	−.16
Viewing Motivations:				
Information-learning	.05	−.02	.04	.10
Entertainment	−.06	−.17	−.04	.04
Relaxation	−.03	−.24	.03	−.08
Economics-inexpensive	−.08	−.22	−.23	−.13
Convenience	−.12	−.18	−.04	−.13
Companionship	−.21	−.23	.00	−.10
Pass time	−.23	−.32	.00	−.09
Arousal-excitement	−.12	−.28	−.04	−.08
Escape-forget	−.27	−.28	.00	.00
Habit	−.21	−.28	−.05	−.07
Topic for communication	−.07	−.17	−.09	.02
Behavioral guidance	−.04	−.27	.00	.00
Social interaction	−.15	−.29	−.13	−.09
Product advertising	−.01	−.29	−.02	.03

Income: r = .13, p < .05; r = .17, p < .01; r = .21, p < .001 (two-tailed).
All other variables: r = .12, p < .05; r = .16, p < .01; r = .20, p < .001 (two-tailed).

Table 21.5
Sociodemographic Canonical Correlates of Contextual Age Factors

	Root 1	Root 2
Canonical correlation	.51	.33
Eigenvalue	.26	.11
Bartlett's chi-square	105.93	33.86
Degrees of freedom	24	15
Significance	$p < .001$	$p < .01$

Set 1: Contextual Age Factors

Life satisfaction	-.24	-.32
Physical health	.38	.96
Economic security	-.85	.57
Social activity	.29	-.20
Redundancy coefficients	.07	.04

Set 2: Sociodemographics

Age	-.48	-.32
Gender	.15	.52
Education	.07	.58
Family size	.30	-.06
Income	-.63	.31
Occupation	-.10	.31
Redundancy coefficients	.03	.02

negative associations between these factors and life satisfaction. Set 2 includes positive associations among education and gender, in particular, and with income and occupation to a lesser extent, and slight negative relationships between these four variables and age. Across the sets, comparisons reflect that healthy and economically secure persons (who are less satisfied with their lives) are (younger) females with higher levels of education (income, and occupational prestige). Parentheses used above and subsequently identify interpretable variables with more marginal loadings in the canonical solutions.

Contextual Age and Viewing Patterns

Table 21.4 also reports the daypart and daily viewing level, program type viewing, and television affinity correlates of the contextual age factors. The only strongly significant association obvious among the contextual age factors and daypart or daily viewing levels is that less healthy persons watch increased amounts of television, particularly during the 10 a.m.-1 p.m. daypart.

A few significant correlates can be noted for program type viewing and television affinity. Socially active persons more regularly view talk-interview shows. Aside from two more marginal negative relationships between life satisfaction and movie viewing and between physical health and action-adventure program watching, no other substantial associations are evident with regard to program type watching. The program findings provide a contrast to the prior study which located several additional program viewings associated with the contextual age factors for the older age group. Television affinity, however, is related to several contextual age factors as a significant negative correlate of physical health and life satisfaction, as well as social activity to a lesser degree. Less healthy, life-dissatisfied, and socially inactive persons indicate that television plays a more important role in their lives.

Canonical correlation analysis was also utilized to assess the interactions within and between these sets of contextual age and viewing pattern variables. Following from both the methodology of the prior study and the current lack of substantial daypart associates of contextual age, daypart viewing was omitted from the analysis. This canonical correlation analysis is summarized in Table 21.6 Three significant canonical roots were observed.

Root 1 explains 25 percent of the variance. Set 1 includes a positive relationship between physical health and social activity and a negative association between these factors and economic security. Set 2 indicates a negative association between television affinity and talk-interview program viewing. Comparisons across the sets indicate that healthy (and somewhat socially active) but economically insecure persons exhibit a lack of affinity with television and more regularly watch talk-interview programs. In particular, and also in accordance with the partial correlation findings, healthy persons regard television to be unimportant in their lives.

Root 2 explains 15 percent of the variance. Set 1 includes positive associations between economic security and physical health and negative relationships between these variables and life satisfaction and social activity. Set 2 depicts a positive variate for movie viewing and negative associations between movie viewing and action-adventure, children's, and, to a lesser extent, game show watching. Across the sets, comparisons reflect that economically secure, healthy persons who are less satisfied with their lives and less socially active more often watch movies, but they also view action-adventure, children's (and game show) programming less frequently.

Root 3 exlains 11 percent of the variance. Set 1 indicates a positive relationship between life satisfaction and economic security. Set 2 includes

Table 21.6
Viewing Pattern Canonical Correlates of Contextual Age Factors

	Root 1	Root 2	Root 3
Canonical correlation	.50	.39	.32
Eigenvalue	.25	.15	.11
Bartlett's chi-square	185.76	102.42	56.52
Degrees of freedom	64	45	28
Significance	$p < .001$	$p < .001$	$p < .01$

Set 1: Contextual Age Factors

Life satisfaction	.24	−.58	.78
Physical health	.77	.68	−.12
Economic security	−.35	.82	.51
Social activity	.31	−.46	−.15
Redundancy coefficients	.05	.06	.02

Set 2: Viewing Patterns

News	.02	−.16	.45
Documentary-magazine programs	−.10	−.01	.10
Sports	−.07	−.29	−.18
Movies	−.16	.41	−.38
Drama programs	.14	.25	−.16
Situation comedies	.01	−.22	−.05
General comedies	.12	−.10	−.41
Talk-interview programs	.33	−.17	−.01
Music-variety programs	−.23	.08	.41
Action-adventure programs	−.05	−.47	.00
Game shows	.08	−.31	.06
Children's programs	.08	−.39	.11
Daytime serials	.10	.11	−.31
Religious programs	−.16	.05	−.13
Amount of viewing	−.03	−.21	−.15
Television affinity	−.85	.12	−.09
Redundancy coefficients	.02	.01	.01

a positive association between news and music-variety program watching and negative connections between these programs and viewing general comedies and movies, as well as daytime serials to a lesser degree. In other words, those who more regularly view news and music-variety programs avoid watching general comedies and movies (a pattern that was evident for the older viewers in the prior study's sample). The small redundancy coefficients of .02 and .01 make comparisons across the two sets inadvisable.

Contextual Age and Viewing Motivations

The television viewing motivation correlates of the contextual age factors are also summarized in Table 21.4. These data indicate several significant relationships. The life satisfaction factor is negatively related to several viewing motivations, especially escape, pass time, habit, and companionship. Those persons who are less satisfied with their present life condition indicate that they use television in order to forget their problems, to pass the time of day, out of habit, and as a means of companionship. Escape, companionship, and pass time were also negatively related to life satisfaction for the older sample in the prior study.

The physical health factor is also negatively linked to several television use motivations, including pass time, social interaction, product advertising, escape, habit, arousal, behavioral guidance, relaxation, companionship, and economics. Less healthy persons rely on television for a variety of reasons, especially to pass the time of day, as a means of social interaction when friends are visiting, to seek out product information, as a vehicle of escape from problems, out of habit, for excitement, to seek out information as to how they should act with others, as a means of relaxation, for companionship, and because it is inexpensive to watch. In particular, those who experience poor health and immobility rely extensively on television. Escape, product advertising, and companionship were also significant negative correlates of the "self-reliance" (physical health and mobility) contextual age factor for the prior study's older age sample.

In contrast, the social activity factor fails to produce any substantial viewing motivation correlates, while the economic security factor is significantly linked (at the .001 level) to only one television use reason — economics. Those who are less economically secure watch television because it is an inexpensive means of communication. This finding is consistent with the results of the prior study for the older sample. However, that older age group's responses produced several positive relationships between the "interaction" (social activity and interpersonal interaction) contextual age factor and viewing motivations (e.g., arousal, topic for communication, economics, relaxation) in the prior study's sample.

In order to determine the interactions within and between these sets of contextual age and viewing motivation variables, canonical correlation analysis was once again employed. This analysis is summarized in Table 21.7. Two significant canonical roots were found.

Root 1 explains 25 percent of the variance. Set 1 depicts a positive variate for physical health. Set 2 indicates a negative variate for pass time viewing, in particular. Across the two sets, the canonical loadings indicate that those persons who experience physical health problems utilize television principally as a means of passing the time of day.

Table 21.7
Viewing Motivation Canonical Correlates of Contextual Age Factors

	Root 1	Root 2
Canonical correlation	.50	.38
Eigenvalue	.25	.15
Bartlett's chi-square	161.49	80.65
Degrees of freedom	56	39
Significance	$p < .001$	$p < .001$

Set 1: Contextual Age Factors

Life satisfaction	.21	.85
Physical health	.92	−.49
Economic security	.11	.02
Social activity	.00	.35
Redundancy coefficients	.06	.04

Set 2: Viewing Motivations

Information-learning	.02	.15
Entertainment	.10	.19
Relaxation	−.12	.49
Economics-inexpensive	−.18	.15
Convenience	−.01	−.17
Companionship	.16	−.17
Pass time	−.38	−.07
Arousal-excitement	−.28	−.23
Escape-forget	−.18	−.65
Habit	−.19	−.11
Topic for communication	.04	.05
Behavioral guidance	−.25	.36
Social interaction	−.17	−.31
Product advertising	−.19	.62
Redundancy coefficients	.01	.02

Root 2 explains 15 percent of the variance. Set 1 reflects a positive association between life satisfaction and social activity and negative relationships between these factors and physical health. Set 2 includes positive associations between product advertising, relaxation, and behavioral guidance motivations and negative relationships between these television viewing reasons and escapist viewing and, to a lesser extent, the social interaction motivation. Comparisons across the sets indicate that those persons who are satisfied with their lives and socially active but in poorer physical health watch television to seek out product information, as a means of relaxation, and for behavioral guidance, but not to escape from life's problems (or as a vehicle of social interaction). It may be of interest to note that in contrast to the initial canonical root, pass time viewing did not emerge as a significant variate in the second root. In other words, once the condition of physical health is tempered by increases in life satisfaction and social activity, other viewing motivations are more salient than simply using the medium to pass time.

DISCUSSION

The main purpose of this investigation was to consider the utility and heuristic potential of the contextual age construct as a life-position indicator of television use for adults in a broad age distribution. In order to proceed with this assessment, the relationships between the contextual age factors and chronological age, television viewing patterns, and viewing motivations require closer inspection.

Several chronological age associations were evident across the broader age, adult sample. Chronological age was related negatively to family size and education level and positively to spendable income. It was also initially noted that chronological age was a significant positive associate of economic security but a negative correlate of physical health. However, an examination of the first multivariate set of results indicates that the relationships between chronological age, other sociodemographic traits, and contextual age are more complex than what appears on the surface of the univariate correlation results. Economically secure and less healthy persons were observed to be older adults with more spendable income. Those who are economically secure and healthy, though, were found to be younger females with higher education levels and possibly less life satisfaction. Consequently, the physical health and economic security dimensions of contextual age are salient components of the construct and seem to work in opposite directions in relation to sociodemographic traits, although their effects may be tempered by other contextual age dimensions, such as life satisfaction.

In addition, family size does not appear to be associated with life satisfaction or physical health and mobility, and the person's gender seems unrelated to economic security for the present investigation's broader age sample. These two results contrast substantially with the prior study, in which it was found that those elder persons who lived with others exhibited an increased sense of life satisfaction and self-reliance, while males were observed to be more economically secure than females in the older age sample. Younger persons in the prior sample were also more self-reliant and economically secure. Certain sociodemographic conditions (e.g., family size, gender), would seem to play a unique role in contributing to the life-position of chronologically older persons, but without apparent applicability to a broader age group of adults.

For the present sample, chronological age was linked positively to viewing music-variety, news, and religious programs and negatively to watching situation comedies and daytime serials. With the exception of a positive association between social activity and watching talk-interview shows, connections between contextual age factors and television program type viewing were not as obvious. Chronological age was also a positive correlate of television affinity, and television affinity was a negative associate of physical health and life satisfaction. Once again, physical health seems to be an important aspect of these relationships. In particular, less healthy persons were found to watch more television and exhibit increased affinity with the television medium.

The canonical analyses, however, suggest that physical health functions in conjunction with other life-position factors in providing a more accurate portrait of these relationships. So, for example, less healthy, socially inactive, economically secure persons exhibit salient affinity levels. To the contrary, no connection with television affinity is evident for less healthy persons who are economically insecure, socially active, and satisfied with their lives. These findings compare favorably with the results of the prior study in which those elder persons with higher levels of life satisfaction and self-reliance (physical health and mobility) displayed less television affinity than did those who were less content with their lives and less mobile and less healthy.

However, salient viewing pattern and contextual age connections were more obvious for the older age sample, particularly with regard to television program type viewing. Perhaps the elder audience has developed more clearly defined programming likes and dislikes than has the broader age adult audience. A comparison between the mean viewing pattern scores across the two studies would seem to support the notion that the older audience has more salient viewing levels and program preferences. In addition, the program preferences across the two age samples are somewhat divergent, as noted previously.

By contrast, a comparison between the present data and those of the prior study indicate that while the broader age and older samples are partial to different types of programming, they watch television for similar reasons. Information, entertainment, relaxation, economics, convenience, and companionship are rather consistent and fairly salient viewing motivations across the two age samples. In fact, chronological age had only one fairly substantial viewing motivation correlate — a positive link with behavioral guidance.

Once again, however, an examination of the associations between viewing motivations and contextual age factors indicates several additional, and some interrelated, connections. Similar to the prior study, the economically insecure watched television because it was an inexpensive means of communication. Those persons dissatisfied with their lives used television for a number of compensatory reasons, including escape, pass time, habit, and companionship. The less physically healthy relied on television to pass time, to view when friends visited, to escape, out of habit, for excitement, to learn about interacting with others, to relax, for companionship, to seek out product information, and because it was inexpensive. In other words, the physically frail exhibited numerous motivations for using television, among which to pass the time of day seemed to be most important. Life satisfaction and social activity, however, seem to interact with the state of one's health to alter viewing motivation patterns somewhat. Increases in life satisfaction and social activity seem to compensate for the level of physical health, so that television is used for other reasons (such as for relaxation, behavioral guidance, and to seek product information) instead of just to pass time. It would be interesting to ascertain if the self-learning or product information sought by these adults is related to the individual's physical infirmity. The notion of a life-dissatisfied, physically infirm individual using television as a companion also compares favorably to a past investigation (Rubin & Rubin, 1981) conducted in the confined context of a hospital.

Several similarities and differences in the contextual age factor solutions of the present and past studies were noted earlier. In particular, the factor structures for the older age and broader age groups were largely consistent. Each contained four similar, principal factors of contextual age. However, for the older age sample the interaction factor incorporated several interpersonal interaction items in addition to social activity items, and explained a substantially greater percentage of the common variance in the prior study's factor solution than the social activity factor did for the current investigation. Also, the self-reliance factor for the older sample included additional mobility items and fewer physical health items, but it explained a smaller percentage of the common variance in the factor solution of the prior study than the physical health factor did in the present investigation. As was also evident in the prior study, not all of the total variance was explained by the contextual age factor solutions. What was suggested then, and now, is the search for additional life-position components which may be useful for explaining individual differences in television use. In particular, lifestyle, self-concept, psychological health, alienation, efficacy and life control, and fulfillment of interpersonal needs may be additional viable constructs worth pursuing.

The results of the present and prior investigations do suggest, however, that chronological age alone does not provide a truly accurate framework for explaining communication behavior. The emergence of the multivariate associations among physical health, economic security, life satisfaction, chronological age, and other sociodemographic traits reflect that although declines in physical health are obviously indicative of advanced chronological age, factors other than merely biological ones are also important components in any meaningful conception of the relationship between aging and communication behavior.

REFERENCES

Cassata, M. *A study of the mass communication behavior and the social disengagement of 177 members of the Age Center of New England.* Unpublished doctoral dissertation, Indiana University, 1967.

Cummings, E. Further thought on the theory of disengagement. *International Social Science Journal*, 1963, *3*, 377-393.

Cummings, E., & Henery, W. E. *Growing old: The process of disengagement.* New York: Basic Books, 1961.

Dimmick, J. W., McCain, T. A., & Bolton, W. T. Media use and the life span. *American Behavioral Scientist*, 1979, *23*, 7-31.

Graney, M. J., & Graney, E. E. Communications activity substitutions in aging. *Journal of Communication*, 1974, *24*(4), 88-96.

Havighurst, R. J. A social-psychological perspective on aging. *The Gerontologist*, 1968, *8*, 67-71.

Henery, W. E. Engagement and disengagement: Toward a theory of adult development. In R. Kastenbaum (Ed.), *Contributions to the psychology of aging.* New York: Springer-Verlag, 1965.

Hurlock, E. B. *Developmental psychology* (3rd ed.). New York: McGraw-Hill, 1975.

Kaluger, G., & Kaluger, M. F. *Human development* (2nd ed.). St. Louis: C. V. Mosby, 1979.

Knapp, M. R. The activity theory of aging. *The Gerontologist*, 1977, *17*, 553-559.

Kubey, R. W. Television and aging: Past, present, and future. *The Gerontologist*, 1980, *20*, 16-35.

McFarland, R. A. The need for functional age measurements in industrial gerontology. *Industrial Gerontology*, 1973, *19*, 1-19.

Neugarten, B. L. Personality and the aging process. *The Gerontologist*, 1972, *12*, 9-15.

Neugarten, B. L., Havighurst, R. J., & Tobin, S. S. Personality and patterns of aging. In B. L. Neugarten (Ed.), *Middle age and aging.* Chicago: University of Chicago Press, 1968.

Pfeiffer, E. Psychopathology and social pathology. In J. E. Birren & K. W. Schaie (Eds.), *Handbook of the psychology of aging.* New York: Van Nostrand Reinhold, 1977.

Rubin, A. M. Television use by children and adolescents. *Human Communication Research*, 1979, *5*, 109-120.

Rubin, A. M. An examination of television viewing motivations. *Communication Research*, 1981, *8*, 141-165.

Rubin, A. M., & Rubin, R. B. Age, context and television use. *Journal of Broadcasting*, 1981, *25*, 1-13.

Rubin, A. M., & Rubin, R. B. Contextual age and television use. *Human Communication Research*, 1982, *8*, 228-244.

Schramm, W. Aging and mass communication. In M. W. Riley, J. W. Riley, & M. E. Johnson (Eds.), *Aging and society, volume 2: Aging and the professions.* New York: Russell Sage, 1969.

Swank, C. Media uses and gratifications. *American Behavioral Scientist,* 1979, *23,* 95-117.
Troldahl, V. *Occupational prestige scale.* Unpublished manuscript, Department of Communication, Michigan State University, 1967.
Wenner, L. Functional analysis of TV viewing for older adults. *Journal of Broadcasting,* 1976, *20,* 77-88.
Wilson, D. L. The programmed theory of aging. In M. Rockstein (Ed.), *Theoretical aspects of aging.* New York: Academic Press, 1974.

MASS COMMUNICATION

22 • Children's Realities in Television Viewing: Exploring Situational Information Seeking

RITA ATWOOD • RICHARD ALLEN • RALPH BARDGETT • SUSANNE PROUDLOVE • RONALD RICH

University of Texas—Austin

A DOMINANT trend in past research involving children and television viewing has been to treat children as passive consumers of television content, particularly vulnerable to and victimized by the negative influences of television. A multitude of studies have examined the influence of television advertising, the impact of televised violence and sex, and a wide array of other content-related variables assumed powerful in shaping children's lives. In addition, traditional approaches to studying the effects of children's exposure to television content have expanded to include the mediating or causal role of other personal attributes and environmental forces.[1]

CONCEPTUAL FRAMEWORK

Challenges to these traditional modes of examining the impact of television messages on children have proliferated in recent years. These challenges address problems associated with inappropriate conceptualizations and inferences, as well as inadequate methods of data collection evident in traditional research.

Alternative Perspectives Emerging

One thrust of the various challenges confronting traditional research on children and television focuses on the need to conceptualize children as

Correspondence and requests for reprints: Rita Atwood, Department of Radio-TV-Film, University of Texas, Austin, TX 78712.

active consumers of television content and the need to query them regarding the uses and gratifications linked to their television consumption (Brown et al., 1974; Lee & Browne, 1981; Greenberg, 1974; von Feilitzen, 1976; Lometti et al., 1977; Rubin, 1977).

Another arena of challenge involves researchers who agree that children must be viewed as active consumers of television, but argue that the uses and gratifications literature is hampered by reliance on quantitative approaches. These researchers advocate a more qualitative orientation that pays attention to the processes and conditions of television message consumption in natural environments (Anderson & Meyer, 1974; Donohue et al., 1977; Meyer & Hexamer, 1980; Lull, 1978, 1980; Traudt, 1981; Wolf et al., 1981).

A third source of challenge to traditional mass media effects literature has not centered attention on children and television viewing. However, conceptual implications stemming from this third challenge have direct relevance to the controversies being presented here. For example, the researchers offering this challenge suggest that all people should be viewed as active information seekers and users. In addition, they argue for the need to examine such information seeking and use behavior in situational contexts from the perspective of those engaged in the search and utilization process (Atwood & Dervin, 1981; Atwood, 1980; Dervin et al., 1976, 1980, 1981).

Convergence of Alternative Perspectives

The three different types of challenges to traditional concepts and methods used in past studies of children and television viewing converge on at least two important issues:

1. *Children are active consumers of messages from their environments, including television message environments.* This view is a considerable departure from the notion of the child as a vacuous entity, passive and malleable by the causal forces existing in television messages.

2. *Understanding how children experience television viewing necessitates taking their perceptions of that experience into consideration.* Researchers must converse with and ask children about their television viewing experiences in order to gain access to their perceptions. Researchers should not depend solely on their own observations of and inferences about the connections between television content and children's lives.

Within the context of agreement on these issues, there are degrees of difference. Furthermore, there are other issues that distinguish the three areas of challenge to traditional approaches. Although it is not possible to provide a complete sorting out of the divergent arguments within the scope of this chapter it will be useful to describe how the situational sense-making approach differs from the first two types of challenges presented.

Divergence of Alternative Perspectives

The nature of the situational sense-making attempt to examine issues raised by researchers with a uses and gratifications orientation and those with a qualitative, process orientation consists primarily of three basic assumptions. These three assumptions depart from one or the other or both types of challenges preceding them:

1. *All information seeking and use is active, constructive behavior, regardless of different levels of time or energy expended in achieving exposure to various sources.* The conceptualization of information seeking and use supporting this assertion is that people pose questions in their message environments, create answers from the raw informational material available, and put such answers to use in ways most relevant to their information needs. However, this view contends that the choice of message environment or the sources turned to for raw informational material are choices often associated with system constraints.[2]

2. *All people, including children, seek and use information in the situational contexts of their movement through time and space — and the constantly changing information needs related to such movement.* The notion of people moving uniquely through time and space, encountering gaps or discontinuities in that movement, and seeking and using information to bridge gaps has been articulated by a number of researchers. These researchers suggest that information seeking and use can most usefully be studied in the situational contexts where they are taking place.[3]

3. *The constructive process people engage in when they connect to data in their message environments and create information useful for their situational needs can be studied most productively from their self-reports.* The actors involved in connecting to their message environments and constructing useful bridges for their situational gaps can provide the most useful insight into differences and commonalities of such processes.

PURPOSE, PROBLEM, AND RESEARCH QUESTIONS

Numerous researchers have provided evidence for the utility of examining situational variables related to information seeking and use (Capella, 1977; Clarke & Kline, 1974; Davis, 1977; Donohue et al., 1975; Edelstein, 1974; Grunig & Disbrow, 1977; Mischel, 1973; Tichenor et al., 1973). Others have indicated more specifically the growing concern about focusing on children's perspectives of their television consumption (Haynes, 1978; Loughlin et al., 1980; Morrison et al., 1979; Reeves, 1978; Rubin, 1977; Sheikh & Moloski, 1977). However, there has been little research that has combined an emphasis on the self-reports of children in their situational contexts of television viewing. More importantly, there has been no previous effort to examine situational sense-making variables alongside more-traditional content variables assumed to impact children. Although this study does not claim to undertake a direct comparative test of these two types of variables, the purpose is to investigate the potential for pursuing such comparisons.

Therefore the problem confronted in this study is one of selecting both traditional content variables and situational variables to be incorporated as predictors of children's information seeking and use associated with television messages, as well as identifying criterion measures of information seeking and use.

Traditional Predictor Variable

Among the numerous types of variables that have been used to predict the impact of television viewing on children, the nature of the television program has received widespread attention. A number of researchers have developed distinctions for different kinds of content within a given television program,[4] and other researchers have constructed various category schemes for classifying types of television programs (Eastman & Liss, 1980a, 1980b; Hofstetter & Buss, 1981; Rubin, 1977; Webster & Coscarelli, 1979). Based on the different category schemes used in several of these studies, program type is the traditional predictor variable of children's information seeking and use selected for this study.

Situational Predictor Variable

Researchers who have centered attention on situation-bound measures of information seeking and use suggest that one of the most useful variables for predicting such behavior is one that represents the kinds of gaps people face as they move through time and space — gaps that can be bridged only by information seeking and use. Based on this gap notion, a variable called "situation movement state" has been developed as part of a programmatic research effort (Atwood & Dervin, 1981; Dervin et al., 1976, 1980, 1981). The variable of situation movement state is the situational predictor selected for this study.

Criterion Measures of Information Seeking and Use

The concept of information seeking guiding this study departs from past approaches that have equated information seeking with sources people turn to or are exposed to. Instead, this study is guided by a view of information seeking as purposive activity designed to cope with discontinuities or bridge gaps encountered in movement through time and space. This concept of information seeking is operationalized in this study as the nature of questions children ask in order to bridge the gaps they encounter while viewing television. Among the various typologies that have been developed for examining the nature of questions, the five Ws variable is the criterion measure of information seeking chosen for this study (Atwood, 1980; Atwood & Dervin, 1981).

Several other criterion measures related to information seeking are included in this study. A criterion measure called "how asked" represents the way children report asking their questions. Although prior studies have looked at children's question-asking activity (Wolf et al., 1981), no research to date has considered the questions that children ask just in their own heads and do not articulate aloud. This study also includes criterion measures representing children's reports of when their questions were answered and the sources they turned to — the variables called "when answered" and "source of answer." The notion of source of answer here differs from previous studies in that sources are seen as providing the raw material for answer construction, but children are seen as ultimately responsible for that construction activity (Atwood & Dervin, 1981).

Finally, information use is conceptually defined in this study as the utilities derived from successful gap bridging — in other words, the way obtaining raw material from the message environment and constructing bridges with that material helps people continue their movement. Researchers using the same conceptual definition of information use have developed a criterion measure called "helps," which represents the utilities people report from constructing answers to their questions (Dervin et al., 1980, 1981). This helps variable has been adaped as the criterion measure of information use for this study.

Consistent with the preceding discussion of the purpose and problem guiding this study, the following research questions can be posited:

1. How useful is a variable such as program type in predicting the criterion measures of information seeking and use?
2. How useful is a variable such as situation movement state in predicting the criterion measures of information seeking and use?
3. What specific relationships exist among the predictor variables of program type and situation movement state and the criterion measures of information seeking and use?

METHOD OF DATA COLLECTION

Sample

The population of children for this study was selected within the context of several constraints. First, the interview procedures require that children be able to spend as much as 45 minutes to an hour with interviewers, and this negated the possibility of interviewing children in public school settings. Because of time and transportation limitations it was not feasible to interview children in their homes. For these reasons the Extend-A-Care after-school program for children in Austin, Texas, was contacted. It agreed to participate in this study.[5] The Extend-A-Care staff made parent lists available for all the children enrolled in the program at two different school sites. Letters of consent required by the Extend-A-Care program, as well as explanations of the research purpose and interview method, were sent to 114 homes. On-site interviews were completed with 55 children whose parents had returned consent forms. These 55 children represent a diverse sample in terms of age, sex, and ethnic background, although most were from lower-or middle-income families headed by working parents, single parents, and parents attending the University of Texas.

Questionnaire

The questionnaire used in this study was adapted from questionnaires previously used to investigate adult self-reports of information seeking and use (Atwood & Dervin, 1981; Dervin et al., 1976, 1980, 1981). The questionnaire was structured to elicit reports from children regarding how they situationally perceive television content and how they seek and use information in those situational contexts.

The interview session started with an interviewer explaining to a child that the purpose of the interview was to learn more about children's television viewing experiences. The child was asked to name several television shows he or she had watched in the past several days and then to name the television show best remembered or most important.[6] The child was then asked to describe the program on a time-line, as though the child had a camera and took pictures during the program. When the time-line description was completed, the interviewer went back over each situation reported and asked the child to report any questions he or she had asked aloud or silently; when each question was answered; and the source turned to for the answer. The interviewer then explained that people sometimes see answers to questions as helping them in some way and asked the child if and how the answer to a particular question helped — or would have helped had the question been answered. The interviewers then asked several questions relating to demography and terminated the interview.

Fielding

The interviewers were all graduate students enrolled in a course on survey research methods in the Radio-TV-Film Department of the University of Texas, Austin. All interviewers received extensive training in appropriate techniques for eliciting respondents perspectives and specific problems that might be encountered while interviewing children. The interviews were conducted in empty classrooms at the school sites in order to minimize distractions and interruptions, and all interviews were completed during a two-week period during March 1981. Children were advised that they could terminate the interview at any time they felt they needed to, but were encouraged to try to complete it. Special care was taken in coordinating with Extend-A-Care staff members in order to make the children feel as comfortable and secure as possible.

METHOD OF CONTENT ANALYSIS

There are essentially two phases of analysis involved in this study: (1) the content analysis of open-ended reports from children regarding program type, situation movement state, five Ws nature of questions asked, and helps derived from constructing answers to their questions; (2) statistical analysis of the coded responses. Both phases revolve around the unit of analysis selected in accord with the research questions posited in this study.

The unit of analysis chosen for this study is the question reported by the child at each situation step of describing the program. Given that the purpose is to examine criterion measures of information seeking and use, only those program types and situation movement steps associated with questions asked can be considered in light of their predictive capabilities. Similarly, the other criterion measures of information seeking and use pivot around the presence or absence of questions being asked. Therefore, the actual n for this study is constituted by a total of 128 questions asked by the 55 children interviewed, with missing data reported only for criterion measures depending on whether questions were eventually answered.

The process of content analysis focused on in this section includes the calculation of intercoder reliability percentages for the different content analysis schemes. These intercoder reliability figures were obtained by the proportion of agreement method suggested by Holsti (1969), and percentages are subsequently reported along with content analysis scheme descriptions for each variable.

Program Type

Based on several studies that have categorized television content by program type (Eastman & Liss, 1980a, 1980b; Hofstetter & Buss, 1981; Rubin, 1977), this study proposes three basic categories for the predictor variable of program type and describes them in Table 22.1.

Table 22.1
Definition and Description of Program Types
Used as Predictors in Analysis of Variance

Label	Definition	Example	n^a	%
Cartoon/sit-com programs	Animated programs shown on a regular basis or as specials. Nonanimated programs with comedy as primary intent.	*Bugs Bunny, Drack Pack, Charlie Brown, Happy Days, Three's Company, Taxi*	57	45
Reality programs	Programs of an educational or informational nature. Entertaining variety shows, talk shows, music shows, game shows. Shows sensationalizing real life.	*Sesame Street, Electric Company, Mister Rogers, Carol Burnett, John Davidson, Tic-Tac-Dough, Real People, Those Amazing Animals, That's Incredible*	31	24
Action/drama programs	Serious narrative fiction. Fast action, mystery oriented. Includes frightening, futuristic, supernatural and imaginary. Can be serial, movie, or special.	*Dallas, Eight Is Enough, White Shadow, Dukes of Hazard, Dirty Harry, Hart to Hart, Sunday Movie*	40	40

a. n = with no missing data.

Children's Realities in TV Viewing

The category of cartoon/situation comedy program type represents both animated and nonanimated programs with a primarily humorous orientation and purpose.[7] The majority of programs reported by children during their time-line interviews fell into this category, with fifty-seven programs or 45 percent coded into the cartoon/situation comedy program type.[8]

The second category of program type is labeled reality programs and is constituted by programs of an educational or real-life nature, including programs geared specifically for children's educational development and programs presenting real-life characters rather than actors. This category has thirty-one programs (24 percent).

The third category of program type includes all television shows of an action/adventure nature. This category was reserved for programs involving serious drama, action, or mystery. The children reported forty programs or 40 percent coded into this category.

The proportion of agreement indicating interjudge coder reliability for content analysis of program type was 95 percent. The variable in its final form was used as a three-category nominal predictor with $n = 128$ and no missing data.

Situation Movement State

Table 22.2 describes the four categories which constitute the predictor variable of situation movement state. This variable represents the nature of gaps children reported while watching a television program.

The arrival/observing state is one in which children report that television characters have reached a desired goal or are observing and understanding something. Of all the time-line steps associated with a question being asked, twenty situation movement states, or 15.6 percent, were coded into the arrival/observing state.

The traveling/drifting state was coded for those situation movement states in which the children reported that television characters were moving under their own control toward a known or unknown destination. The category contained sixty-three situation movement states, or 49.2 percent.

The barrier state is one in which children report that characters are traveling down a road in control of their movement, when suddenly their road is blocked by some obstacle or disappears. Barrier states were coded for twenty-two situation movements states, or 17.2 percent of all those reported.

The problematic state involves those situation movement states where the characters are reported to be on a road not of their own choosing and are not in control of their own movement. The state had coded into it twenty-three situation movement states, or 18.0 percent.

Table 22.2
Definition and Description of Situation Movement State Variables
Used as Predictors in Analysis of Variance

Label	Definition	Example	n[a]	%
Arrival/observing state	Reaching desired goal. Perceiving, watching, recognizing, understanding, thinking, trying to find things out. Speculation.	They found the dog. They won the tournament. The men were watching illegal aliens. They heard a telephone.	20	15.6
Traveling/drifting state	Moving under control toward goal of known or unknown origin.	Harry walks away. Dorothy and Toto skip down a yellow brick road.	63	49.2
Barrier state	Walking down road under control and road is blocked or washed away.	Richard fell off his bike. The lion in the jungle scares Dorothy.	22	17.2
Problematic state	On road not of own choosing. Not in control of situation or road is out of control. Clear indication that road was not desirable.	Fonzie got married by accident.	23	18.0

a. n = 128 with no missing data.

Interjudge coding reliability for content analysis of situation movement state was 89 percent agreement. The variable was used as a four-category nominal predictor with $n = 128$ and no missing data.

Five Ws Nature of Questions

Table 22.3 describes the content analysis scheme used to code questions reported by children in their time-line interviews. This scheme, called the five Ws nature of questions, distinguishes among questions in terms of how people ask questions to bridge the gaps in their movement. In other words, questions are not coded on the literal grammatical use of what, why, where, who, and how; rather, questions are coded on the basis of whether they are asking for descriptions, explanations, etc.

The what/who category was reserved for questions children asked in order to construct descriptions, clarify something, or find out what is going on. Of the total number of questions reported by children, fifty-seven or 44.5 percent were coded into the what/who category.

Questions asking for reasons or explanations were coded into the why category. The children reported forty questions, or 31.3 percent, coded into the why category.

The how/where category involved questions asking how something or someone moves through space, or where something or someone moves through or is located in space. The category received thirty-one questions, or 24.2 percent.

Interjudge coding reliability for content analysis of five Ws nature of questions was 96 percent agreement. For the purpose of using this variable as a criterion measure in analysis of variance, each category was re-created as a dummy variable. An example of this process is the what/who category, which was originally coded as one in a three-category nominal variable. The what/who category and the other two categories were recoded as dichotomous variables that asked, for example, whether the child's question was a what/who question. The result of this transformation was a set of three dummy variables representing the five Ws nature of questions with $n = 128$ and no missing data.

Helps

The helps variable represents the criterion measure of information use. As Table 22.4 illustrates, the children reported various utilities derived or anticipated from answers to their questions.

The good feelings category includes those helps related to receiving pleasure, enjoyment, excitement, and encouragement. Eighteen of the helps reported by children, or 22.2 percent, were coded into the good feelings category.

Table 22.3
Definition and Description of Five Ws Nature of Questions Used as
Criterion Variables in Analysis of Variance

Label	Definition	Example	n^a	%
What/who?	Respondent is asking for description of entities or conditions on the road. A respondent may want to clarify objects or to ask what is going on or what is going to happen (how things will turn out); also may ask whether things could have been different. This also includes asking how someone feels.	Wonder who was on the phone? What does it look like? What is he going to do? Was he nervous? Will he get killed?	57	44.5
Why?	Respondent is asking for reasons to explain being on road, or reasons for road conditions.	Why did he get married? Why just the boys dancing? How come they were stealing? What's the reason?	40	31.3
How/where?	Respondent is asking how to move through space on road, or where to move or locate in space on road. Any type of recipe knowledge or directions would be included.	How did they put out light? How can the monster plant talk? Where was the noise coming from? How did they make the noise?	31	24.2

a. $n = 128$ with no missing data.

Table 22.4
Definition and Description of Helps Used as Criterion Variables in Analysis of Variance

Label	Definition	Example	n^a	%
Good feelings	Helped by giving pleasure, enjoyment, excitement, happiness, encouragement.	Made me feel better. Helped me enjoy it. Made me laugh.	18	22.2
Skills/knowledge	Helped by teaching how to do something or avoid doing something. Gave skills or advice (planning for future events in real life). Helped by teaching something new about self, others, objects, events. Helped by giving knowledge, teaching or satisfying curiosity.	If I got a splinter it would help me not to say ouch. So if my brother got hit he wouldn't hurt himself. I learned that an alien is someone from another planet.	29	35.8
Clarify/reality	Helped by explaining past events, situations, or current events. Helped by describing or explaining what would happen next or in the future—what consequences or resolutions would be. Helped by finding out something is real or true or possible.	Wanted to find out how many other times he had been lonely. Would have known if it was the monster or the man. Let me know innocent boy wasn't going to get his brains blown out.	34	42.0

a. $n = 81$ with 47 missing cases due to no helps reported.

Children's reports of being helped by learning how to do something or by acquiring new skills or knowledge were coded into the skills/knowledge category. Twenty-nine of the helps reported, or 35.8 percent, were coded into this category.

The clarify/reality category was reserved for children's reports of being helped by receiving explanations of past, present, or future events or by being able to find out that something was real or possible. The clarify/reality category was coded for thirty-four helps, or 42.0 percent of the total helps reported.

Interjudge coding reliability for content analysis of the helps scheme was 86 percent agreement. Each category of the helps variable was re-created as a dichotomous dummy variable, resulting in a set of three dummy variables with $n = 81$ and 47 missing cases due to no helps derived or anticipated from answers.

Other Criterion Measures

The criterion measure of how a question was asked was derived from children's reports as to whether they asked a question out loud or in their own heads. It is interesting to note that, of the 128 questions reported, children stated that only 26 questions, or 20.3 percent, were asked out loud, whereas 102 questions, or 79.7 percent, were asked just in their own heads. The criterion measure of how asked consisted of two dichotomous variables with $n = 128$ and no missing data.

The criterion measure of when a question was answered was obtained by providing children with three alternative responses: never, when asked, and later. Sixty-seven questions, or 52.3 percent, were never answered; twenty-five questions, or 19.5 percent, were answered when they were asked; and thirty-six questions, or 28.1 percent, were answered at some later time. This criterion measure of when answered consisted of three dichotomous variables with $n = 128$ and no missing data.

While the measures of how asked and when answered did not require content analysis, the open-ended reports of source of answer did. This was a fairly straightforward process of identifying only three different types of sources reported by children, and no interjudge coder reliability calculations were deemed necessary. Of the three sources reported, thirty-six, or 59.0 percent, were TV as source; nine, or 14.7 percent, were own thinking as source; and sixteen, or 26.2 percent, were mother as source.

The criterion measure of source of answer was converted to a set of three dichotomous variables with $n = 61$ and 67 missing cases due to questions never answered.

METHOD OF STATISTICAL ANALYSIS

One-way analyses of variance were conducted to provide evidence relevant to the research questions posed in this study. These research questions dictated the need for a test of the significance of program type as a predictor of the criterion measures of information seeking and use, and a test of the significance of situation movement state as a predictor of the criterion measures of information seeking and use. In addition, specific relationships between predictor and criterion measures were examined by using Duncan's test for significance of mean differences. All analyses were conducted using the *Statistical Package for the Social Sciences* (Nie et al., 1975).

RESULTS

The results of one-way analyses of variance and applications of Duncan's test for significance of mean differences are summarized in this section in relation to the two predictor variables of program type and situation movement state.

Program Type

Table 22.5 presents the results of one-way analysis of variance testing the utility of program type as a predictor of the criterion measures of information seeking and use.

1. *Five Ws nature of questions:* Program type nears significance as a predictor of children asking what and why questions, but is not a significant predictor of children asking how questions.
2. *How asked:* Program type is not a significant predictor of whether children reported asking questions out loud or just in their own heads.
3. *When answered:* Program type nears significance as a predictor of children reporting that their questions were never answered, but program type is not a significant predictor of children reporting that their questions were answered when questions were asked or at some later time.
4. *Source of answer:* Program type is significant at $p < .05$ in predicting that children report turning to television as a source of raw material for answer construction, but program type is not a significant predictor of children turning to their own thinking or to their mothers. More specifically, children report turning to television most often during action/

Table 22.5
One-Way Analysis of Variance for Program Types
as a Predictor for All Criterion Measures

Criterion Measure	Cartoon/ Sit-Com	Reality	Action/ Drama	F Ratio	df	p
Questions						
What	.38[a]	.65[b]	.53	2.721	2	ns (<.10)
Why	.37[b]	.10[a]	.26	2.981	2	ns (<.10)
How	.24	.25	.26	0.060	2	ns
How Asked						
Out loud	.18	.30	.16	0.842	2	ns
In own head	.80	.70	.84	0.649	2	ns
When Answered						
Never	.52	.70[b]	.32[a]	2.945	2	ns (<.10)
When Q asked	.18	.10	.32	1.547	2	ns
Later	.27	.20	.37	0.697	2	ns
Source of Answer						
TV	.22[a]	.30	.53[b]	3.663	2	<.05
Own thinking	.08	.00	.00	1.626	2	ns
Mother	.13	.00	.16	1.616	2	ns
Helps						
Good road	.11	.25	.16	1.304	2	ns
Skill/knowledge	.21	.30	.21	0.359	2	ns
Clarify	.28	.10	.37	1.989	2	ns

Note: Unlike horizontal superscripts indicate cell means significantly different from each other at $p < .05$ using Duncan's test for mean differences.
Ns = Program Types. Cartoon/Sit-com—89 questions asked
Reality/Info/Variety—20 questions asked
Action/Drama/Sci Fi—19 questions asked

drama programs and least often during cartoon/situation comedy programs, with reality programs falling in between.

5. *Helps:* Program type is not a significant predictor of children reporting helps from having constructed answers to their questions.

Situation Movement State

The results of one-way analysis of variance testing the utility of situation movement as a predictor of the criterion measures of information seeking and use are portrayed in Table 22.6.

1. *Five Ws nature of questions:* Situation movement state is a significant predictor at $p < .01$ of children asking why and how questions, but is not significant in predicting what questions. Examination of within cell mean

Children's Realities in TV Viewing

Table 22.6
One-Way Analysis of Variance for Situation Movement State as a Predictor for All Criterion Measures

Criterion Measure	Arrival	Travel	Barrier	Problem	F Ratio	df	p
Questions							
What	.50	.51	.27	.39	1.391	3	ns
Why	.10[a]	.29[a]	.32	.57[b]	3.985	3	<.01
How	.40[b]	.21	.40[b]	.04[a]	4.058	3	<.01
How Asked							
Out loud	.25	.19	.14	.22	0.308	3	ns
In own head	.75	.81	.86	.70	0.750	3	ns
When Answered							
Never	.75	.46	.55	.43	1.980	3	ns
When Q asked	.10	.21	.18	.22	0.421	3	ns
Later	.15	.32	.27	.26	0.712	3	ns
Source of Answer							
TV	.15	.37	.27	.17	1.755	3	ns
Own thinking	.05	.06	.05	.04	0.063	3	ns
Mother	.05	.10	.14	.22	1.154	3	ns
Helps							
Good road	.35[b]	.17[a]	.18	.09[a]	3.529	3	<.05
Skill/knowledge	.30	.19	.32	.17	0.824	3	ns
Clarify	.25	.29	.27	.22	0.141	3	ns

Note: Unlike horizontal superscripts indicate cell means significantly different from each other at $p < .05$ using Duncan's test for mean differences.

Ns = SMS. Arrival—20 questions asked
Travel—63 questions asked
Barrier—22 questions asked
Problem—23 questions asked

differences reveals that children reported asking why questions significantly more often in problematic states than children who reported asking why questions in either arrival/observing or traveling/drifting states, with those reporting why questions for barrier states falling between. In addition, children reported asking how question most frequently in arrival/observing states and barrier states than in problematic states, with how questions asked in traveling/drifting states falling between.

2. *How asked:* Situation movement state is not a significant predictor of whether children reported asking questions out loud or in their own heads.

3. *When answered:* Situation movement state is not a significant predictor of children reporting when or if their questions were answered.

4. *Source of answer:* Situation movement state is not a significant predictor of children reporting that they turned to different sources for answer construction assistance.

5. *Helps:* Situation movement state is significant at $p < .05$ in predicting that children reported good road helps from obtained or anticipated answers to their questions. Situation movement state was not a significant predictor of children reporting either skills/knowledge helps or clarify/reality helps. More specifically, children reported significantly more good road helps associated with arrival/observing states than with traveling/drifting states or with problematic states, with barrier states falling between.

Research Questions Examined

The results of this study provide evidence that situation movement state offers stronger promise than does program type for being a useful predictor of the five Ws nature of questions and of the helps related to answer construction. In addition, the results indicate that program type may offer greater utility than situation movement state as a predictor of source of answer.

An examination of specific relationships suggests that why questions are asked most frequently in problematic states and somewhat less often in barrier states. How questions are asked most often in barrier states and in arrival/observing states. The findings indicate that children report turning to television for answer construction assistance most often while viewing action/drama programs and somewhat less frequently during reality programs.

DISCUSSION AND SUMMARY

The results of this exploratory study have provided some useful insights regarding the current controversies surrounding research endeavors concerned with children and television viewing. On one level the results of this study contribute to the challenges that children are active consumers of television messages and that understanding the process of their consumption necessitates taking their perspectives into account. On yet another level the findings presented in this study suggest that situational self-reports from children provide useful ways to examine predictor and criterion measures of information seeking and use.

Significance and Interpretation of Findings

While the findings of this study must be considered in light of the limitations that will be specified, there are several noteworthy contributions resulting from this research.

On a purely descriptive level, the evidence revealing that almost 80 percent of the questions reported by children were asked in their own heads indicates that previous studies have failed to tap into the information seeking behavior of children because they have examined only articulated questions. This inadequacy in prior research approaches may account, in part, for continued adherence to the notion of children as passive consumers of television content and a sense of distrust regarding their ability to self-interrogate and report honestly their information seeking.

Evidence stemming from one-way analysis of variance using program type and situation movement state as predictors of criterion measures of information seeking and use suggests that situation movement state is a stronger predictor of the five Ws nature of questions and helps, and program type is a stronger predictor of the sources of answers. These findings are consistent with previous studies that indicate that situational perception of gaps encountered are closely associated with the nature of questions asked and the helps derived from constructing answers to those questions. In addition, these findings corroborate prior evidence that system constraints may be linked to sources turned to for answer construction assistance — in the case of this study, television is turned to as a source most often when children are watching action/drama programs. There may be other system constraints, such as availability of parents, not tapped by this study.

Limitations of the study

There are several important limitations relating to this study that have implications for future research. The lack of random sampling and the relatively small number of children limit the type of statistical analysis that can be performed and also restrict the inferences that can be made from the results of analysis.

More importantly, the questionnaire design used in this study required that children report a time-line narrative of a television program without tapping into their situational connectedness with that program or the situational relevance of that program to their own lives.[9] This limitation suggests more appropriate methods for future studies of this kind.

Suggestions for Future Research

Future studies should use a questionnaire design that allows the child the opportunity to distinguish between a time-line of his or her own activities and a time-line account of the television program that has been viewed as part of those activities. In addition, future studies should incorporate different types of variables representing the way the child perceives situational connectedness or relevance between the television content and his or her own life.

The results of this exploratory study into the realities of children and their television viewing offers promise that future research using similar methods and guided by similar concepts will yield valuable insight into the process of situational information seeking and use.

NOTES

1. For a useful critique of children being treated as passive consumers of television and a discussion of inadequacies in the children and television effects literature, see Wolf et al. (1981). For a comprehensive bibliography of this literature, see Murray (1980).

2. Empirical evidence supporting the notion of people turning to sources associated with system constraints can be found in Atwood and Dervin (1981). In addition, evidence supporting the notion that information is self-constructed can be found in Carter (1974, 1975, 1977), Davis (1977), Dervin et al. (1981), Dervin et al. (1980), Grunig (1979), Stamm and Grunig (1977).

3. For a more complete discussion of the idea of people moving uniquely through time and space and encountering discontinuties or gaps in that movement, see Atwood and Dervin (1981), Carter (1977), and Dervin (1979).

4. For example, a number of researchers have examined prosocial versus antisocial types of television content, including Ahammer and Murray (1979), Collins (1975), Sprafkin and Rubenstein (1979), Sprafkin et al. (1980), Stein and Friedrich (1975). Others, such as Dominick et al. (1979), have classified content into aggressive versus assertive categories. Researchers have also looked at real versus fantasy content, violent versus nonviolent content, and informational versus entertainment content.

5. Extend-A-Care is a nonprofit organization founded in 1969 in Austin, Texas. The purpose of Extend-A-Care is to provide after-school care for the children of working parents whose incomes are in the lower and mid-range brackets. The Extend-A-Care program now serves over 800 children in Austin, with 44 percent being white; 36 percent being Black; and 20 percent being Hispanic.

6. Part of the purpose of this study was to allow the children the opportunity to report on television programs that were relevant to them. It should also be noted that previous studies have asked people about their own life situations, not specifically their media use. This study, therefore, is considered exploratory.

7. On the basis of children's descriptions of cartoons, the authors of this study decided that the majority of cartoons were of a comic or humorous nature and combined them with situation comedies to form one category of program type.

8. The unit of analysis being questions asked by the children dictated that a program be identified for each situation step at which a question was asked. If the child had been used a unit of analysis, the n for program type would have been: cartoon/situation comedy = 31; reality = 9; and action/drama = 15.

9. For studies that have examined children's perceptions of the reality of television and the relation of television content to their own lives, see Donohue (1977), Krull and Husson (1979), Reeves (1978), and Rubin (1977).

REFERENCES

Ahammer, I. M., & Murray, J. P. Kindness in the kindergarten: The relative influence of role playing and prosocial television in facilitating altruism. *International Journal of Behavioral Development,* 1979, *2,* 133-157.

Anderson, J. A., & Meyer, T. P. *Man and communication.* Washington, DC: College University Press, 1974.

Atwood, R. *Communications research in Latin America: Cultural and conceptual dilemmas.* Paper presented to the Intercultural Division, International Communication Association, Acapulco, Mexico, 1980.

Atwood, R., & Dervin, B. Challenges to socio-cultural predictors of information seeking: A test of race vs. situation movement state. In M. Burgoon (Ed.), *Communication yearbook 5.* New Brunswick, NJ: Transaction-International Communication Association, 1981.

Brown, J. R., Cramond, J. K., & Wilde, R. J. Displacement effects of television and the child's functional orientation to media. In J. G. Blumler & E. Katz (Eds.), *The uses of mass communications: Current perspectives on gratifications research.* Beverly Hills, CA: Sage, 1974.

Capella, J. N. Research methodology in communication: Review and commentary. In B. D. Ruben (Ed.), *Communication yearbook 1.* New Brunswick, NJ: Transaction-International Communication Association, 1977.

Carter, R. F. *Toward more unity in science.* Unpublished paper, School of Communications, University of Washington, 1974.

Carter, R. F. All manner of soft collisions. *Clio,* 1975, 4(1), 10-16.

Carter, R. F. *Theory for researchers.* Paper presented to the Theory and Methodology Division, Association for Educators in Journalism, August 1977.

Clarke, P., & Kline, F. G. Media efforts reconsidered: Some new strategies for communication research. *Communication Research,* 1974, 1(2), 224-240.

Collins, W. A. The developing child as a viewer. *Journal of Communication,* 1975, 25(4), 35-43.

Davis, D. K. Assessing the role of mass communication in social process. *Communication Research,* 1977, 4(1), 23-24.

Dervin, B., Zweizig, D., Banister, M., Gabriel, M., Hall, E., & Kwan, C. with Bowes, J., & Stamm, K. *The development of strategies for dealing with the information needs of urban residents: Phase I — Citizen study.* Final report on Project No. L0035JA to Office of Libraries and Learning Resources, Office of Education, U.S. Dept. of Health, Education and Welfare, 1976.

Dervin, B., Harlock, S., Atwood, R. & Garzona, C. The human side of information: An exploration in a health communication context. In D. Nimmo (Ed.), *Communication yearbook 4.* New Brunswick, NJ: Transaction-International Communication Association, 1980.

Dervin, B., Nilan, M., & Jacobson, T. Improving predictions of information use: A comparison of predictor types in a health communication setting. In M. Burgoon (Ed), *Communication yearbook 5.* New Brunswick, NJ: Transaction-International Communication Association, 1981.

Dominick, J. R., Richman, S., & Wurtzel, A. Problem solving in television shows popular with children. *Journalism Quarterly,* 1979, 56(3), 455-463.

Donohue, G. A., Tichenor, P. J., & Olien, C. N. Mass media and the knowledge gap: A hypothesis reconsidered. *Communication Research,* 1975, 2(1), 3-23.

Donohue, T. R. Favorite TV characters as behavioral models for the emotionally disturbed. *Journal of Broadcasting,* 1977, 21(3), 333-345.

Donohue, T. R., Meyer, T. P., & Anderson, J. A. *Television's role in the family interaction process.* Unpublished grant application, 1977.

Eastman, H. A., & Liss, M. B. Ethnicity and children's television preferences. *Journalism Quarterly,* 1980, 57(2), 277-280. (a)

Eastman, H. A., & Liss, M. B. Television preferences of children from four parts of the United States. *Journalism Quarterly,* 1980, 57(3), 488-491. (b)

Edelstein, A. S. *The uses of communication in decision-making.* New York: Praeger, 1974.

Greenberg, B. S. Gratifications on television viewing and their correlates for British children. In J. Blumler & E. Katz (Eds.), *Annual review of communication.* Beverly Hills, CA: Sage, 1974.

Grunig, J. E. Time budgets, level of involvement and use of the mass media. *Journalism Quarterly,* 1979, 56(2), 248-262.

Grunig, J. E., & Disbrow, J. Developing a probablistic model for communications decision making. *Communication Research,* 1977, 4(2), 145-168.

Haynes, R. B. Children's perception of "comic" and "authentic" cartoon violence. *Journal of Broadcasting,* 1978, 22(1), 63-69.

Hofstetter, C. R., & Buss, T. F. Motivation for viewing two types of TV programs. *Journalism Quarterly,* 1981, 58(1), 99-103.

Holsti, O. R. *Content analysis for the social sciences and humanities.* Reading, MA: Addison-Wesley, 1969.

Krull, R., & Husson, W. H. Children's attention: The case of TV viewing. In E. Wartella (Ed.), *Children communicating.* Beverly Hills, CA: Sage, 1979.

Krull, R., & Husson, W. Children's anticipatory attention to the TV screen. *Journal of Broadcasting,* 1980, *24*(1), 35-47.

Lee, E. B., & Browne, L. A. Television uses and gratifications among black children, teenagers, and adults. *Journal of Broadcasting,* 1981, *24*(2), 203-208.

Lometti, G. E., Reeves, B., & Bybee, C. R. Investigating the assumptions of uses and gratifications research. *Communication Research,* 1977, *4*, 321-338.

Loughlin, M., Donohue, T. R., & Gudykunst, W. B. Puerto Rican children's perceptions of favorite television characters as behavioral models. *Journal of Broadcasting,* 1980, *24*(2), 159-171.

Lull, J. T. *Ethnomethods and television viewers.* Paper presented to the Mass Communication Division, Internation Communication Association, Chicago, April 1978.

Lull, J. T. The social uses of television. *Human Communications Research,* 1980, *6*, 197-209.

Meyer, T. P., & Hexamer, A. Student's understanding of television: Getting to the child's frame of reference. In C. Corder-Bolz (Ed.), *Television and youth.* Austin, TX: Southwest Educational Development Laboratory, 1980.

Mischel, W. Toward a cognitive social learning reconceptualization of personality. *Psychological Review,* 1973, *80*(4), 253-283.

Morrison, P., McCarthy, M., & Gardner, H. Exploring the realities of television with children. *Journal of Broadcasting,* 1979, *23*(4), 453-463.

Murray, J. P. *Television and youth.* Boys Town, NB: Boys Town Press, 1980.

Nie, N. H., Hull, C. H., Jenkins, J. G., Steinbrenner, K., & Bent, D. H. *Statistical package for the social sciences* (2nd ed.). New York: McGraw-Hill, 1975.

Reeves, B. Perceived TV reality as a predictor of children's social behavior. *Journalism Quarterly,* 1978, *55*(4), 682-689; 695.

Rubin, A. M. Television usage, attitudes, and viewing behaviors of children and adolescents. *Journal of Broadcasting,* 1977, *21*(3), 355-369.

Sheikh, A. A., & Moleski, M. Children's perception of the value of an advertised product. *Journal of Broadcasting,* 1977, *21*(3), 347-354.

Sprafkin, J. N., & Rubenstein, E. A. Children's television viewing habits and prosocial behavior: A field correlational study. *Journal of Broadcasting,* 1979, *23*(3), 265-276.

Sprafkin, J. N., Silverman, L. T., & Rubinstein, E. A. Reactions to sex on television: An exploratory study. *Public Opinion Quarterly,* 1980, *44*(3), 303-315.

Stamm, K. R., & Grunig, J. E. Communication situations and cognitive strategies in resolving environmental issues. *Journalism Quarterly,* 1977, *54*(4), 713-720.

Stein, A. H., & Friedrich, L. K. Impact of television on children and youth. In E. M. Hetherington (Ed.), *Review of child development research* (Vol. 5). Chicago: University of Chicago Press, 1975.

Tichenor, P., Rodenkirchen, J. M., Olien, C. N., & Donohue, G. A. Community issues, conflicts, and public affairs knowledge. In P. Clarke (Ed.), *New models for mass communications research.* Beverly Hills, CA: Sage, 1973.

Traudt, P. *Qualitative research on television and the family: Phenomenological approaches to mass communication and social behavior.* Unpublished doctoral dissertation, College of Communication, University of Texas, 1981.

von Feilitzen, C. The functions served by the media. In R. Brown (Ed.), *Children and television.* Beverly Hills, CA: Sage, 1976.

Webster, J. G., & Coscarelli, W. C. The relative appeal to children of adult versus children's television programming. *Journal of Broadcasting,* 1979, *23*(4), 437-450.

Wolf, M. A., Abelman, R., & Hexamer, A. Children's understanding of television: Some considerations and a question-asking model for receivership skills. In M. Burgoon (Ed.), *Communication yearbook 5.* New Brunswick, NJ: Transaction-International Communication Association, 1981.

V • ORGANIZATIONAL COMMUNICATION

23 • Communicative Strategies in Organizational Conflicts: Reliability and Validity of a Measurement Scale

LINDA L. PUTNAM • CHARMAINE E. WILSON
Purdue University • University of Washington

MOST organizational researchers treat conflict as an inevitable and pervasive aspect of organizational life (Perrow, 1979; Pondy, 1967; Katz & Kahn, 1978). Although communication scholars acknowledge this claim by including a chapter on conflict in their texts (Koehler, Anatol, & Applbaum, 1981; Goldhaber, 1979; Huseman, Logue, & Freshley, 1977), researchers in our field have typically ignored the role of communication in organizational conflict. Outside our field organizational researchers have focused on role conflicts (House & Rizzo, 1972; Johnson & Stinson, 1975), supervisor-subordinate disagreements (Burke, 1970; Renwick, 1977), interdepartmental disputes (Lawrence & Lorsch, 1967; Walton & Dutton, 1969), and interorganizational conflicts (Assael, 1969; Sebring, 1977), in addition to a wealth of information on labor-management conflicts (Walton & McKersie, 1965). The breadth and depth of these topics underscore the significance of conflict research for organizational communication (Putnam & Jones, 1982).

An area that has received considerable attention in the past decade is conflict management styles. Even though conflict styles are primarily interpersonal variables, researchers have examined them within the contexts of supervisor-subordinate and interdepartmental conflicts. Conflict

AUTHORS' NOTE: The authors would like to express appreciation to Janet Jordon, Patrice Buzzanell, Mark Cox, Connie Bullis, Patricia Geist, and Sandy Herrod, whose class projects on the OCCI contributed significantly to this research. Also, we thank Mary Ann Samad for her assistance with computer analysis.

Correspondence and requests for reprints: Linda L. Putnam, Department of Communication, Purdue University, West Lafayette, IN 47907.

styles are actually communicative behaviors. Although organizational researchers rarely link the two, conflict theorists treat communication as the critical variable in the manifest stage of conflict (Thomas, 1976; Pondy, 1967; Katz & Kahn, 1978). Communication "is the means by which conflicts get socially defined, the instrument through which influence is exercised" (Simons, 1974, p. 3). As Frost and Wilmot (1978, p. 10) note, "It is through communicative behaviors that conflicts are recognized, expressed, and experienced." Current research on conflict styles ignores the vital role of communication in both the design and the measurement of ways to handle disagreements. In the measurement of conflict styles, self-report instruments in current use demonstrate moderate to low reliability and questionable content validity. This study addresses these concerns by (1) presenting the need for a communicative-based conflict strategies scale, (2) discussing the theoretical and conceptual foundation of this scale, (3) presenting results of item analysis and internal reliability of the scale, and (4) summarizing findings from construct and predictive validity of the instrument.

REVIEW OF RELEVANT LITERATURE

Conflict Management Styles

Research on conflict management styles grew out of general disillusionment with value-ladden approaches to the study of conflict. Early research in this area treated conflict as a contagious disease that should be eliminated from an organization. In the decade of the 1960s theorists and practitioners changed their orientation to a positive view; conflict promoted intragroup cohesiveness (Coser, 1956), maintained a balance of power between opponents (Blake, Shepard, & Mouton, 1964), generated creative approaches to problem solving (Hall, 1969), and facilitated organizational change (Litterer, 1966). In effect, conflict was potentially constructive — if it was managed effectively. This orientation led to a flurry of studies on effective and ineffective strategies for managing conflicts (Deutsch, 1973; Blake et al., 1964; Burke, 1970; Kilmann & Thomas, 1977; Renwick, 1977).

Blake and Mouton (1964) were the first researchers to propose a five-category scheme for the management of organizational conflict. Consistent with a managerial perspective, the five styles represented two dimensions, concern for self and concern for others (Rahim & Bonoma, 1979). These dimensions differed in their evaluative (good versus bad) and their dynamic (active versus passive) qualities. Two studies conducted by Ruble and Thomas (1976) supported this two-dimensional theory and concluded that the competitive-cooperative dichotomy, which evolved from game theory research, did not capture the range of alternatives for conflict participants. When the two dimensions were graphed onto a matrix, they yielded five styles: forcing, confronting, smoothing, avoiding, and compromising (Blake & Mouton, 1964). *Forcing* resulted from production-oriented management styles and signified the use of competitive behaviors to win one's position, even if it meant ignoring the needs of the opponent. Forcing was linked to the use of power, particularly expert or legitimate power, in winning an argument. *Confronting,* also called problem solving, collaborating, and integrating, consisted of facing a conflict directly, evaluating causes, and examining possible solutions. To reach creative solutions, participants had to exchange information and to integrate alternative points of view. *Smoothing,* also called accommodating, referred to behaviors that glossed over, concealed, or played down differences by emphasizing common interests. *Avoiding* was physical withdrawal, refusal to discuss the conflict, or the tendency to sidestep the situation. Smoothing styles aimed to cover up the conflict, while avoiding strategies exemplified physical or psychological withdrawal. *Compromising* behaviors aimed at "splitting the difference" or finding a middle-ground alternative. Compromisers were individuals who looked for easy solutions by finding the midpoint between the opposing viewpoints.

Previous research on these five styles aimed to identify which ones were most effective, most constructive, and most important to an organization. The first group of studies operated from the assumption that individuals differed in their characteristic modes of conflict management. For example, several investigators reported that supervisors who used confrontation and forcing handled conflict more effectively than managers who used other styles (Burke, 1970; Lawrence & Lorsch, 1967). Effectiveness, in this sense, referred to bringing a resolution to the conflict. But supervisors who used forcing and avoiding were rated as the least constructive in their approaches to conflict management (Burke, 1970), while those who confronted disagreements directly or smoothed over problems were perceived as the most constructive managers of conflict (Burke, 1970; Renwick, 1977). But even though smoothing satisfied interpersonal needs, it also hindered goal achievement and interfered with productivity (Lawrence & Lorsch, 1967). In effect, confrontation emerged as the most constructive, most effective, and most important mode of handling conflict. Smoothing was seen as desirable but not necessarily effective, while forcing was viewed as effective but not desirable. Supervisors who avoided conflicts received the lowest scores on satisfaction and climate measures.

Other organizational variables mediated these findings and raised doubts as to whether conflict strategies were trait- or state-based behaviors. Specifically, female subordinates, in comparison with their male counterparts, perceived their supervisors as more likely to avoid, smooth over, or compromise in conflict situations (Renwick, 1977). This observation, however, was confounded by the sex of the supervisor and by a subordinate's level of commitment to the organization. Both male and female subordinates were less likely to withdraw from a conflict if their supervisors were women. Male supervisors appeared to inhibit confrontation styles for both male and female subordinates (Zammuto, London, & Rowland, 1979). In addition, subordinates who scored high on organizational commitment were least likely to smooth, to avoid, or to compromise, especially when they reported to a female manager. One explanation for this finding might be that the feeling-oriented cognitive systems of female supervisors were conducive to integration and cooperation (Kilmann & Thomas, 1975). Another explanation is that male supervisors forced resolutions in order to maintain a semblance of harmony.

Despite the prolific nature of this research, investigations of conflict management styles are plagued by conceptual and methodological problems. The first one stems from the assumption that individuals have a characteristic mode of conflict management behavior. While this assumption may hold for some people, it may not be true for a majority of subjects. Since each individual receives scores on all five modes, respondents can score in the upper quartile on at least three different styles.[1] Research on organizational commitment and sex of supervisor suggests that conflict management styles follow models of situational leadership in that they characterize an individual's choice of behavior across a variety of situations. The conflict situation, in turn, is defined by the amount of conflict, the organizational structure, and the personal-cultural factors of the individual (Rahim & Bonoma, 1979). A contingency theory, then, appears more suitable than a trait model for studying the effectiveness of conflict styles across organizational circumstances.

A second problem with previous research is ambiguity in the definition of conflict. Most studies either fail to state a definition of conflict or define it in broad, vague terms like "opposing actions of individuals." A third shortcoming is the failure to specify a source or target of conflict; that is, individuals direct their conflict strategies at a target. Researchers who fail to specify a target and a context obtain only gross insights about conflict management behaviors. A fourth difficulty with this research is the tools used to measure conflict styles. In the studies cited above, conflict resolution styles are measured with one-item scales (Renwick, 1977), a set of aphorisms (Lawrence & Lorsch, 1967; Burke, 1970), Blake and Mouton's managerial grid (Zammuto et al., 1979; Bernardin & Alvarez, 1976), and a forced-choice questionnaire (Kilmann & Thomas, 1977). These instruments vary from the absence of any tests on reliability and validity to statistics that indicate low levels of reliability.

Development of the Organizational Communication Conflict Instrument (OCCI)

The Organizational Communication Conflict Instrument (OCCI) is developed to meet standards of reliability and validity for the measurement of interpersonal strategies in conflict management. Unlike previous questionnaires, the development of this scale rests on the assumption that conflict strategies are those communicative behaviors, both verbal and nonverbal, that provide a means for handling conflict. Conflict, then, involves strategic or planned interaction; that is, participants make choices about alternative behaviors by considering their own goals and the anticipated goals of the other person (Schelling, 1960). Conflict strategies represent the behavioral choices that people make rather than a person's characteristic style. In addition to examining strategies, this scale focuses on a particular phase of conflict — disagreements (i.e., differences of opinion that occur in interdependent relationships). Disagreements are generally content-oriented conflicts that can develop into incompatible goals and interests (Bernard, 1965; Rapoport, 1965). Disagreements, while similar to misunderstandings, entail deep-seated latent differences rather than surface misinterpretations or semantic quibbles. In the semantic model of conflict, misunderstandings can be managed with full and open communication (Pondy, 1967; Tompkins, Fisher, Infante, & Tompkins, 1974). But when disagreements uncover underlying incompatibilities, the potential for escalation is stronger and open communication exacerbates rather than reduces tensions. Essentially, if disagreements are not managed effectively, they can escalate into irreconcilable situations.

A final assumption underlying the OCCI is that the decision to use a particular conflict strategy is largely governed by situational rather than personality constraints, particularly such variables as the nature of the conflict, the relationship between participants (role specialization and position), organizational structure (differentiation and integration), and environmental factors (Lawrence & Lorsch, 1967). This assumption posits that there is no magic formula or "best way" to handle conflict. Confrontation, while deemed constructive and effective in previous studies, may *not* be a beneficial strategy when the conflict is trivial and when quick decisions are required. Avoidance may be quite effective for handling less important and highly volatile conflicts, and forcing may be appropriate for crisis situations or for "unpopular courses of action" (Rahim & Bonoma, 1979). The OCCI, then, is designed to tap choices about conflict strategies in a variety of organizational contexts. The long-range goal of this research is to identify factors that affect decisions to use particular strategies and to test the evolution of these strategies across conflict episodes.

Consistent with these three assumptions, the OCCI was designed to assess an employee's use of communicative strategies across conflict situations. Three forms of the scale were constructed and tested with 820 subjects: 451 employees of banks, insurance firms, and newspaper organizations; 49 teaching assistants; 145 juniors and seniors in supervision and management classes; and 175 students in an introductory communication course. Of the 451 employees in nonuniversity settings, 140 were in the banking industry (two different banks), 283 represented members of a large insurance firm, and 28 were employees of a small-town newspaper chain. The 820 subjects were employed in stages of testing for item analysis, internal reliability, social desirability, and concurrent-predictive validity. This study presents the results of these stages and summarizes three predictive validity investigations that support the discriminatory and predictive power of the OCCI.

ITEM DEVELOPMENT AND ANALYSIS

In the first stage of item analysis, the researchers critically analyzed previous conflict management scales (Thomas & Kilmann, 1978; Kilmann & Thomas, 1977; Hall, 1969; Blake & Mouton, 1964; Lawrence & Lorsch, 1967). The inadequacies of previous scales were reviewed in Kilmann and Thomas's report (1977) on the MODE instrument (Management of Differences Exercise). They cite the following deficiencies: failure to measure psychometric properties of the scales, nonipsative scoring for the Lawrence and Lorsch scale, low internal reliabilities and unstable scores for some of the five styles, inconsistencies in defining the smoothing mode, and potential social desirability effects for all scales. As an attempt to rectify these problems, Thomas and Kilmann developed the MODE instrument, a forced-choice questionnaire with thirty pairs of statement that depicted the five styles of conflict management. A statement that represented each *style* was compared with statements linked to the other four *modes* an equal number of times; however, the same items were not repeated in each comparison, and only twelve items were used to score each mode.

Even though the MODE instrument improved on the reliability and the social desirability problem apparent in other scales, this questionnaire presented researchers with other critical problems. First, no efforts were made to verify the existence of five distinct styles of conflict management; that is, no efforts were made to analyze the item structure of the scale. Second, internal reliabilities of the five modes did not meet the .80 standard of acceptability as established by Nunnally (1978). Third, information on item analysis is nonexistent. Since each item contributed different amounts of variance to all five subscales, paired comparison confounded the measurement of any one style, particularly since subjects were forced to choose among alternatives that might *not* reflect their own behavior. In effect, the content validity, item information, and factor structure of the MODE instrument were problematic.

Unlike previous questionnaires, the OCCI was constructed to measure communicative choices in the management of organizational conflict. Form A of OCCI consisted of thirty items drawn from a pool of sixty-five items designed to tap communicative dimensions of Blake and Mouton's (1964) five styles. Each item followed a seven-point Likert response format that ranged from "strongly agree" to "strongly disagree," and each item met the criteria of simplicity in wording, clarity, and use of only one statement. As a test of content validity, five graduate students employed a modified Q-sort procedure to sort the sixty-five items into the five conflict management styles; the thirty items (six per style) with the best overall interrater reliability (above .80 using simple agreement) were selected for Form A. Form A was administered to 175 undergraduate students in a large introductory communication course and received internal reliabilities that varied from .62 on avoidance to .68 on compromise. Item-total correlations ranged from .48 to .71; elementary linkage analysis (McQuitty, 1957) suggested that the five styles were highly intercorrelated. In general, items on Form A did not meet standards of discriminatory power, item consistency, and internal reliability.

Form B of the OCCI was developed from the items on Form A that best characterized the five styles. Form B consisted of thirty-five items (see Table 23.1), ten of which were drawn from Form A. Form B was completed by 360 subjects: 168 members of three organizations, forty-nine teaching assistants at a large university, and 143 juniors and seniors in supervision and management classes. Subjects were asked to indicate the behaviors they would typically use in a specified type of organizational conflict. Factor analysis with an orthogonal varimax rotation revealed a three-factor solution, as determined by the scree test for number of factors (Cattell, 1966). The three factors accounted for 58 percent of the common variance; thirty of the thirty-five factors loaded above .42 on one dimension. Table 23.1 lists the items, the factor loadings, the eigenvalues, and common variances for the three factors. A five-factor solution, while desirable to support Blake and Mouton's model, resulted in multiple low-level loadings on the fourth and fifth dimensions, made little conceptual sense, and accounted for only an additional 9 percent of the total variance; hence a three-factor solution was adopted.

Table 23.1
Factor Analysis of Form B of the OCCI

	Nonconfrontation	Solution-Orientation	Control
Form B items			
27. I sidestep disagreements when they arise.	.77	−.17	.03
2. I shy away from topics that are sources of disputes.	.74	−.18	−.01
15. I keep quiet about my views in order to avoid disagreements.	.74	−.16	−.10
35. I ease conflict by claiming our differences are trivial.	.74	−.04	.01
5. I steer clear of disagreeable situations.	.74	−.06	.01
8. I avoid a person I suspect of wanting to discuss a disagreement.	.71	−.14	.13
26. I withdraw when someone confronts me about a controversial issue.	.71	−.22	.04
28. I try to smooth over disagreements by making them appear unimportant.	.68	.01	.10
33. I make our differences seem less serious.	.66	.12	−.01
34. I hold my tongue rather than argue.	.64	.07	−.08
17. I downplay the importance of a disagreement.	.64	.19	.05
18. I reduce disagreements by saying they are insignificant.	.60	.11	.05
19. I meet the opposition at a midpoint of our differences.	.25	.66	.05
23. I try to use everyone's ideas to generate solutions to problems.	−.20	.64	−.25
4. I suggest solutions that combine a variety of viewpoints.	−.24	.64	−.27
16. I frequently give in a little if the other person will meet me halfway.	−.18	.61	.07
22. I suggest we work together to create solutions to disagreements.	−.29	.61	−.23
12. I will go fifty-fifty to reach a settlement.	.32	.60	−.01
14. I offer creative solutions in discussions of disagreements.	−.30	.60	−.16
10. I integrate arguments into a new solution from issues raised in a dispute.	−.39	.59	−.14
6. I give in a little on my ideas when the other person also gives in.	.21	.58	−.08

Table 23.1 (Continued)

	Nonconfrontation	Solution-Orientation	Control
24. I offer tradeoffs to reach solutions in a disagreement.	−.01	.56	.05
1. I blend my ideas with others to create new alternatives for resolving a conflict.	−.18	.51	−.14
21. I dominate arguments until the other person understands my position.	.03	−.29	.73
25. I argue insistently for my stance.	−.08	−.29	.73
20. I assert my opinion forcefully.	−.23	.04	.60
13. I raise my voice when trying to get another person to accept my position.	.11	−.01	.55
3. I insist my position be accepted during a conflict.	.04	−.28	.55
29. I stand firm in my views during a conflict.	−.19	.14	.50
11. I stress my point by hitting my fist on the table.	.01	−.13	.50
Loadings below .48			
7. I look for middle-of-the-road solutions.	.35	.43	−.05
9. I minimize the significance of a conflict.	.42	.32	.03
30. I take a tough stand, refusing to retreat.	.30	−.38	.28
31. I settle differences by meeting the other person halfway.	.31	.21	.29
32. I am steadfast in my views.	.14	.11	.24
Additional items from Form C			
31. I frequently shift topics to avoid "touchy subjects."	.66	.18	−.06
32. I joke and laugh to downplay the severity of a disagreement.	.53	−.18	.05
33. I rarely reveal my true feelings during a controversy.	.51	−.28	.01
34. I back down when another person confronts me about a problem.	.46	−.10	.08
% of common variance	29	17	10
Eigenvalues	8.00	5.76	2.96
Fourth factor eigenvalue	1.53		

Note: Item wording was adapted to fit the type of conflict used for the study. The words "peer," "supervisor," "member of systems or accounting department" were added to fit the respective conflict under study.

Table 23.2
Descriptive Statistics for Dimensions of Conflict Strategies
Form B of OCCI

Conflict Strategy	Mean	SD	Range	1 SD Below Mean	1 SD Above Mean
Nonconfrontation (12 items)	55 Mode = 70	17.7	Low = 10 High = 84	10-37 N = 44	73-84 N = 48
Solution-oriented (11 items)	36 Mode = 37	10.1	Low = 16 High = 73	16-26 N = 51	45-73 N = 44
Control (6 items)	32 Mode = 34	8.7	Low = 10 High = 49	10-23 N = 51	40-49 N = 49

Note: The scales were scored with 1 = always and 7 = never. Low scores represent frequent use, while high scores indicate infrequent use.

The three factors were *nonconfrontation* (avoidance and smoothing as indirect strategies for dealing with conflict), *solution-orientation* (direct confrontation, open discussion of alternatives, and acceptances of compromises), and *control* (direct confrontation that leads to persistent argument and nonverbal forcing). Conceptually, these three factors paralleled Horney's (1945) typology of moving away from (nonconfrontation), moving toward (solution-orientation), and moving against (control) the opposing party. In essence, interitem correlations and factor analysis of the OCCI demonstrated that smoothing and avoiding were similar types of communication; both represented an escape from conflict and an absence of direct confrontation. Problem solving correlated positively with compromising; both types of communication involved open discussion of disagreements and the search for mutually acceptable solutions. In one orientation, alternative solutions evolved from integrating diverse views, while in the other perspective the solutions emerged from concessions made by both parties. Another explanation for intercorrelations between these communicative strategies was that compromising behaviors might lead to integrative solutions. The willingness to compromise, as signaled by "giving in" or making concessions, might result in the discovery of integrative solutions.

Table 23.2 presents the mean scores, standard deviations, ranges, and numbers of subjects who scored one standard deviation above and below the mean for each of the three dimensions. It was apparent from the range of scores that the nonconfrontation scale was used less frequently than were the other two styles; however, the number of respondents who scored one standard deviation above and below the mean were equivalent for the three modes. Intercorrelations between the three scales yielded nonsignificant coefficients, with the exception of $r = .33$ between control and nonconfrontation (see Table 23.3). Since the two scales were conceptually discrete, this coefficient suggested a possible social desirability bias in item responses. The use of PIAS (Purdue Instrument Analysis System; Porter, 1975) to analyze the items revealed that each factor met standards for high internal reliability and high discriminatory power. Moreover, item analysis identified items 31 and 32 as failing to increase reliability and as failing to discriminate between high and low scores. Items 7, 11, and 30 were also eliminated from summated scores, because they differed significantly with greater than 50 percent of the other items.[2] This process resulted in twelve items for the nonconfrontation scale, with a .93 Cronbach alpha; eleven items for solution-orientation, with a .88 alpha reliability; and six items for control, with a .82 alpha. Thus, item analysis demonstrated that the OCCI was a reliable instrument with high discriminatory power. But discrepancies between the mean and the mode for the nonconfrontation scale and intercorrelations between nonconfrontation and control indicated a possible response bias in the measurement of this scale.

Form C of the OCCI was developed to minimize potential social desirability of the nonconfrontation scales. Table 23.1 presents the items from Form C that emerged high in interitem reliability and discriminatory power; these items loaded above .40 on at least one dimension. Other items included on Form C also loaded on one of the dimensions but failed to meet item analysis standards.[3] Form C added four nonconfrontation items to Form B. As a test for social desirability of the OCCI, fifty-two junior and senior students in the upper-level supervision and management classes completed Form C in two stages, two weeks apart. In the first stage, one class was asked to indicate the degree of favorableness or desirability of the behavior; the other class was asked to indicate which item represented their own probable behaviors. In the second stage, the pattern was reversed. Correlations between the ratings were computed as indices of social desirability. The correlations were in the moderate range, .48 for nonconfrontation, .11 for control, and .28 for solution-orientation. The correlations between nonconfrontation and control strategies were negative ($r = -.13$). While some social desirability continued to influence item responses, it did not account for 80 percent of the variance found in previous questionnaires (Thomas & Kilmann, 1975). Since items on the OCCI tapped communicative behaviors, the desirability that individuals should discuss their differences might be reflected in these correlations.

Table 23.3
Correlations Between the OCCI and
Other Conflict Instruments

	OCCI Scales		
Conflict Management Styles[a]	Nonconfrontation	Solution-Orientation	Control
Forcing			
L&L[b]	.18	−.23*	.38**
MODE[c]	−.23	−.31**	.44**
Smoothing			
L&L	.15	.24*	−.08
MODE	.22*	.02	.01
Confrontation—L&L	−.08	.48**	−.27*
Avoiding—MODE	.41**	−.06	−.19
Compromise—MODE	−.03	.26*	−.29*
Nonconfrontation—OCCI		−.01	−.04
Solution-orientation—OCCI			.33*

a. The five Blake and Mouton styles are also referred to as smoothing = accommodation, forcing = competition, and confrontation = collaboration.
b. L&L: Lawrence and Lorsch Aphorism Instrument.
c. MODE: The Thomas-Kilmann Management of Difference Exercise.
* $p < .01$
** $p < .001$

VALIDITY

Construct Validity

Tests of construct validity were conducted to determine if scales on the OCCI correlated positively with similar constructs and negatively with dissimilar ones. Two questionnaires, the Lawrence and Lorsch (1967) Aphorism Scale and the Kilmann and Thomas (1977) MODE instrument, were administered concurrently with Form B of the OCCI to ninety-three graduate management students at a large university. Subjects were given the same instructions for all three questionnaires; the order of the instruments was systematically rotated to control for order effects. Since Lawrence and Lorsch (1967) recommended the use of only three scales, this study computed three scores for this instrument, five scores on the MODE, and three scores for the OCCI. Table 23.3 presents coefficients for intercorrelations among these eleven scales. Even though the coefficients were only moderately high, they provided support for both the convergent and discriminant validity of the OCCI. As expected, control strategies correlated above the $p < .001$ level with the forcing scales on both instruments.

Moreover, control received a low but significantly negative correlation with confrontation and with compromise, suggesting both convergent and discriminant validity. Solution-orientation was negatively correlated with forcing on both instruments and received a .48 coefficient with confrontation on the Aphorism Scale and .15 on the MODE. Nonconfrontation correlated positively with avoiding and smoothing on the MODE instrument and negatively with confrontation. In general, then, correlations with scores from the three questionnaires demonstrated construct validity for the OCCI.

Predictive Validity

While internal reliability and construct validity are important characteristics of a questionnaire, the acid test of the usefulness of any instrument is predictive validity. Tests of predictive validity should evolve from the conceptual framework that gives rise to the scale — in this case, the organizational contingencies that potentially influence the use of conflict strategies. One contingency that affects the choice of communicative strategies is organizational structure, especially structural characteristics of differentiation (Lawrence & Lorsch, 1967). Pondy (1967) addresses differentiation in both his bureaucratic and his systems models of conflict. Bureaucratic conflicts occur along the vertical dimension of differentiation — disagreements between supervisors and subordinates. Bureaucratic conflicts concern authority relationships, particularly such issues as autonomy, power, and control. In organizations, control is enacted through the use of impersonal rules, formalized procedures, and leadership persuasion. Moreover, levels of the hierarchy may influence the management of bureaucratic conflicts: Middle managers often become trapped between the control demands of their supervisors and their subordinates. Even when hierarchical levels are examined, the unit of analysis is the supervisor-subordinate dyad. The ease in identifying these relationships has led conflict researchers to concentrate their attention on the bureaucratic model (Pondy, 1967).

Two predictive validity studies were designed to test the bureaucratic model of organizational conflict. In the first study 283 employees of a large insurance firm completed two versions of Form C of the OCCI: one version for peer-related conflicts and another for supervisor-subordinate disagreements. Each subject received only one version of the questionnaire plus a request for demographic data on employee position, level of supervisory role, length of time in the organization, sex, age, and educational background. The first study examined the effects of position level (subordinates, first-line supervisors, and middle-upper managers) and type of conflict (peer or supervisor) on choices of communicative strategies for handling disagreements. Based on Pondy's bureaucratic model and studies by Burke (1970) and Renwick (1977), we hypothesized:

H.1: Subordinates would use more nonconfrontation strategies than would managers, particularly in supervisory conflicts.

H.2: Managers would use more control strategies, especially in conflicts with subordinates.

H.3: Middle and upper managers would use fewer solution-oriented and more control strategies than would first-line supervisors.

The first two hypotheses were consistent with previous research findings; the third emanated from Pondy's (1967) prediction that upper managers would identify less with the rank and file, would be more differentiated from the lower levels than are first-level supervisors, and would consequently manage conflict through the use of formalized procedures rather than through problem-solving communication.

The majority of the 283 respondents were female (63 percent) with a high school education (69 percent). Managerial roles were held by fifty-eight (20 percent) of the respondents; thirty were first-line supervisors and twenty-eight were middle and upper managers. The number of subjects who completed the questionnaire for each type of conflict was generally balanced: 160 for the peer conflict and 123 for supervisor disagreement. A 2 × 3 (type of conflict by organizational level) ANOVA was used to test for main and interaction effects for the three types of strategies. Significant differences were examined with a Newman-Keuls post hoc test. As predicted, subordinates selected nonconfrontation strategies more frequently than did either managerial group ($F = 5.17, df = 2,227, p < .004$, sub. = 38.47, first-line $M = 46.23$; upper $M = 56.84$; lower means = more frequent use). All managers used more control strategies than did subordinates ($F = 6.08, df = 2,227, p < .003$, sub. = 41.99, first-line $M = 37.53$, upper $M = 38.47$; low means = high frequency). Consistent with H.3, first-line supervisors used more solution-oriented strategies than did upper-level managers and subordinates ($F = 4.91, df = 2,227, p < .008$, sub. = 20.92, first-line $M = 17.9$, upper $M = 19.62$). These differences suggested that first-line supervisors in conflict situations engaged in more problem-solving communication than did upper managers.

But conflicts that filtered into the upper echelon were typically handled with the use of control. This finding might also reflect the arbitrator role that upper managers play in settling lower-level disputes (Lawrence & Lorsch, 1967). Contrary to predictions, no interaction effects were found between position level and type of conflict. Unexpectedly, respondents employed more nonconfrontation and controlling strategies in peer-related than in supervisor conflicts (nonconfrontation, $F = 11.28, df = 1,227, p < .001, P$

= 58.53, S = 62.16; Control, F = 8.67, df = 1,227, $p < .004$, P = 38.00, S = 40.66; low means = high frequency). This finding indicated that employees had a broader repertoire of communicative strategies to manage peer-related as opposed to supervisor conflicts. Since employees interacted on a daily basis more frequently with peers, many disagreements might arise, some that merited attention and others that were too trivial for the potential risk and expended energies of confrontation. That is, it was plausible that the realm of communicative strategies deemed appropriate for conflict with a supervisor was more restricted than the realm of strategies linked to peer-related conflicts (Wilson, 1981).

The second predictive validity study also examined the bureaucratic model of conflict management but employed three specific conflict situations as examples of upward, downward, and horizontal communication. The subjects were forty-nine teaching assistants (TAs) in the departments of English, psychology, political science, and physical education at a large university. Twenty-four of the subjects were female; twenty-five were male; all had full responsibility for the courses they were teaching. Three conflict situations were developed; each pertained to an evaluation incident. In one situation (a supervisor conflict), the TAs had to choose communicative strategies for managing a disagreement about TA teaching performance with the course supervisor. In the second situation (peer conflict), the TA had to select strategies for managing a disagreement with a fellow graduate student whose apathetic performance was affecting a group grade on a class project. In the third situation (subordinate conflict), the TA had to decide how to handle a disagreement with a B-average student who was suspected of plagiarizing a written assignment. These three situations were rated by fifteen communication graduate students as being consistently high in importance, similar in content areas, moderate in intensity, and high in believability.

Based on Pondy's (1967) bureaucratic model, we posited the following hypotheses:

H.1: TAs will use more controlling strategies in subordinate conflicts than they will in disagreements with their supervisors.

H.2: TAs will use more nonconfrontation strategies in supervisor disagreements than they will in conflicts with subordinates and with peers.

Each TA completed Form B of the OCCI for all three situations; the order of the situations was systematically rotated to control for order effects. A repeated-measures, one-way ANOVA with a BMD-P2v computer program was used to test for differences across the levels. Assumptions of homogeneity of variance were met on all three conflict situations prior to running ANOVA. Data analyses yielded a significant difference on all three

Table 23.4
Mean Differences for Conflict Strategies:
TA Study

Conflict Strategy	Course Supervisor	Fellow TA	Student
Nonconfrontation	65.18**	66.18**	72.34
Solution-orientation	36.22**	36.47**	45.81
Control	34.61	32.41	31.14*

Note: The scales were scored with 1 = always and 7 = never. Low scores represent frequent use, while high scores indicate infrequent use.
* $p < .01$
** $p < .001$

types of strategies. Further analyses with a post hoc Newman-Keuls procedure revealed that TAs were more likely to choose solution-oriented communicative strategies ($F = 13.21$, $df = 2,47$, $p < .001$; see Table 23.4) and nonconfrontation approaches ($F = 11.36$, $df = 2,47$, $p < .001$) in supervisor and peer disagreements than they were in subordinate conflicts. In contrast, TAs were more likely to use control strategies in disagreements with subordinates than they were in conflicts with supervisors ($F = 6.18$, $df = 2,47$, $p < .01$).

The second investigation generally supported the two hypotheses. In a situation where TAs had access to formalized procedures, the "imposition of rules defined the authority relationship" (Pondy, 1967, p. 315) and led to the use of control strategies. But in peer and supervisor conflicts, TAs relied on strategies designed to gain autonomy or to avoid confrontation. Of relevance to the first investigation was the finding that *nonconfrontation* strategies were used frequently in the peer as well as in the supervisor situations.

The third predictive validity study followed Pondy's (1967) systems model — lateral conflicts among employees who had horizontal working relationships. Lateral conflicts, like bureaucratic ones, focused on issues of differentiation, but the primary type of differentiation was coordination rather than control. Previous research on lateral conflicts revealed that the sources of disputes were goal differentiation, scheduling problems, and quality-control issues that resulted from functional interdependence (Dutton & Walton, 1966; Walton & Dutton, 1969; Seiler, 1963). In the third validity study, the issue of quality-control and procedural coordination were apparent in a conflict between the systems and the accounting departments of a large metropolitan bank. The subjects for this study were

120 employees, sixty within each department. Of the 120 employees, thirty from each department were males and thirty were females; hence sixty males and sixty females completed the questionnaires. The length of employment for respondents was one year or less for twenty-five subjects, one to three years for twenty-nine employees, three to five years for thirty-six subjects, and over five years for thirty employees.

Employees received two conflict scenarios, one intradepartmental situation and one interdepartmental incident. The researchers developed the scenarios from critical incidents elicited in an interview with a bank executive. The incidents, then, exemplified actual conflicts that had occurred or were occurring in both departments. The scenario for the interdepartmental conflict concerned an inherent need for structure in the design of computer programs (the systems department) and the accounting department's persistence in making changes by building flexibility into their designs. The systems employees, in their frustration with the changes made by the accounting department, frequently returned incorrect output, rather than make the never-ending changes. Respondents were asked to complete Form B of the OCCI by describing how their respective departments typically handled these situations. The two intradepartmental conflicts also emphasized procedures and quality-control issues. In the systems department, the scenario pitted the designers' creativity in developing computer programs against the programmers' need for workability. The accounting department scenario contrasted the need for information disclosure with the requirement for confidentiality of financial data.

Each respondent received both an interdepartmental and an intradepartmental scenario and two copies of the OCCI. The order of the scenarios was rotated within each department. From research findings reported by Lawrence and Lorsch (1967), we predicted that employees would report more controlling strategies in the management of interdepartmental as opposed to intradepartmental conflicts. This study also examined the role of sex and length of employment on communication strategies, but no predictions were made regarding these differences. Three unidimensional $2 \times 2 \times 4$ (type of conflict $\times$ sex $\times$ term of employment) repeated-measure ANOVAs were run on the three conflict strategies. Data were examined for homogeneity of variances prior to running statistical tests. As predicted, interdepartmental disagreements were handled with more controlling strategies ($F = 5.12$, $df = 1,119$, $p < .03$, inter = 32.93, intra = 33.92; low means = high frequency) and fewer nonconfrontation strategies ($F = 46.12$, $df = 1,119$, $p < .001$, inter = 63.39, intra = 58.61) than were intradepartmental conflicts. These findings suggested that employees were more inclined to withdraw from an intradepartmental than from an interdepartmental dispute. Perhaps employees were more selective in confronting co-workers about their controversies than they were in confronting colleagues from another department. Working on a daily basis in close quarters might lead to avoidance rather than to solution-orientation or controlling tactics.

Moreover, sex and length of service interacted to affect the use of communicative strategies. During the first year of an employee's work, females used more nonconfrontation strategies than did males ($F = 3.45$, $df = 3,117, p < .02, f = 55.11, m = 64.68$; low means = high frequency). But this pattern reversed itself for employees who had been with the bank for more than five years ($f = 66.65, m = 57.62$). As females became socialized into the organization, they relied less on avoidance strategies and increased, to a small degree, their use of solution-oriented communication ($F = 2.35, df = 3,117, p < .07$, 1 yr. $f = 38.50$, 5 yr. $f = 36.00$). Males, in contrast, employed more withdrawal tactics after five years of employment than they did during the first year on the job (1 yr. $m = 64.68$, 5 yr. $= 57.62$). They also decreased the frequency of their use of solution-oriented communication (1 yr. $m = 32.43$, 5 yr. $m = 39.50$). Thus length of employment socialized females to use more solution-oriented approaches and socialized males to rely more on nonconfrontation tactics (Bullis, Cox, & Herrod, 1981).

These three predictive validity studies supported the power of the OCCI to predict the communicative strategies employees might use in bureaucratic and systems conflicts. Several findings were consistent across all three investigations. Employees preferred nonconfrontation strategies for handling peer-related and intradepartmental conflicts. In effect, it was more difficult for an employee to confront a co-worker, friend, or departmental colleague about a conflict than to clash directly with subordinates, interdepartmental peers, or supervisors. But respondents were controlling and forceful in their positions when managing conflicts with representatives from other departments or with subordinates. First-level supervisors, however, used more problem-solving strategies with subordinates than did middle and upper managers. Surprisingly, no consistent pattern emerged for handling disagreements with supervisors. Perhaps the choice to collaborate on solutions or to avoid a conflict hinged on other organizational factors, namely, the degree of trust in the relationship, the duration and importance of the conflict, or the way previous conflicts were handled.

DISCUSSION

This program of research examines the role of verbal and nonverbal strategies in the management of organizational conflict. In particular, it focuses on communicative behaviors that represent planned interaction or strategic choices. Conflict, in this sense, refers to disagreements that arise from or can lead to incompatible goals, values, and behaviors. This study operates from the assumption that conflict is beneficial to an organization, but inappropriate management of it can have deleterious effects. Moreover, the appropriateness of a particular strategy hinges on the contingencies that affect conflict situations rather than on an individual's personality traits or on the presumed desirability of any one strategy.

This study reports on the Organizational Communication Conflict Instrument (OCCI), a scale developed from communicative-based items designed to tap the five conflict styles proposed by Blake and Mouton (1964). Repeated testing with two forms of the OCCI reveals a three-factor, instead of a five-dimension, structure. The three factors are:

(1) Nonconfrontation: indirect strategies for handling a conflict; choices to avoid or withdraw from a disagreement; such communicative behaviors as silence, glossing over differences, and concealing ill feelings.

(2) Solution-orientation: direct communication about the conflict; behaviors that aim to find a solution, to integrate the needs of both parties, and to give in or compromise on issues.

(3) Control: direct communication about the disagreement; arguing persistently for one's position, taking control of the interaction, and advocating one's position.

Factor analysis with Forms B and C demonstrate only three discrete dimensions; smoothing and avoiding represent overlapping behaviors and confrontation-compromise load onto one dimension. Coefficients from the construct validity study reinforce these findings. Nonconfrontation correlates significantly with both smoothing and avoidance modes, while solution-orientation correlates positively with compromise and confrontation styles. The unexpected link between compromise and collaborative communication may stem from the fact that both strategies aim for an acceptable solution; in one approach the conflicting parties settle for "splitting the difference," and in the other approach the parties focus on an integrative or collaborative solution. These three dimensions exemplify lose-lose (nonconfrontation), win-lose (controlling), and win-win (solution-orientation) approaches to conflict management.

The fact that this research uncovers three discrete factors does not discount subtle differences within each type of strategy. Elementary linkage analyses (McQuitty, 1957) on the three scales suggest smaller clusters of items within both the solution-orientation and the nonconfrontation scales. In effect, compromise and smoothing may indicate typal strategies that fall within the larger scope of solution and nonconfrontation communication. Moreover, as a conflict develops over time, one set of strategies may evolve into another. Initial choices to withdraw from a disagreement may lead to glossing over differences, especially when the other person is confrontative. Similarly, efforts at collaborative solutions may end in compromise, when participants exhaust plausible courses of action or when conflict escalates to a potentially destructive state.

This process orientation adheres to Pondy's (1967) contention that conflict is a dynamic episode, a sequence of events rather than a single occurrence. Both Pondy (1967) and Thomas (1976) describe evolutionary stages of conflict that move cyclically from latent to aftermath phases. Research on communicative strategies falls into the manifest or the enacted stage of conflict development. However, the way a conflict evolves from stage to stage affects the strategies used in responding to a felt difficulty. The OCCI could be used to test a process model of conflict. Do different communicative strategies correspond to different stages of conflict episodes? Is the choice to avoid a disagreement contingent on the way a conflict evolves? Through time series analyses, researchers could track the evolution of communicative strategies during the development of a conflict episode. This design might also reveal the subtle relationships that exist among the types of strategies. In effect, the OCCI could be used to test a developmental as well as a contingency model of conflict.

Predictive validity results support a contingency orientation toward conflict in organizations. More specifically, these studies substantiate Pondy's (1967) description of bureaucratic and systems models. One type of contingency, differentiation, as operationalized through control-autonomy struggles in vertical conflicts and through coordination disputes in lateral conflicts, affects the perceived use of communication strategies. Subordinate conflicts, disagreements with supervisors that typically center on issues of autonomy and independence, are managed with controlling tactics, while peer-related conflicts are handled with nonconfrontation approaches. Controlling strategies, while representing power relationships, could also support Lawrence and Lorsch's (1967) contention that many organizational disputes are passed up the hierarchy; hence managers, who frequently function as arbitrators, may employ persistence and forcing as ways of handling arbitrated disputes. Interdepartmental conflicts are also managed with controlling strategies of communication. As Lawrence and Lorsch (1967, p. 217) point out, "Members in specialized organizational roles in highly differentiated organizations tend to see their organizational surroundings in terms of that role." When representatives from different departments have disagreements, they forget the inevitability of specialization and operate as if their own "role perspective" is the only world view in the organization. The user, locked into a role bias, might feel justified in employing controlling tactics as a way to handle an "impossible department."

The link between peer conflicts and nonconfrontation strategies across all three studies is an unexpected finding. In fact, it contradicts Jamieson and Thomas's (1974) observation that nonconfrontation strategies are used primarily in supervisor-subordinate conflicts. One plausible explanation for reliance on nonconfrontation strategies in conflicts between peers is the emotional and personal risk involved in confronting a colleague. Since peers have frequent interactions and often form closer friendships than do supervisors and subordinates, the use of avoidance and smoothing minimizes the ill effects of a potentially destructive situation. If the conflict escalates, it could have damaging effects on personal as well as professional relationships. Hence it may involve greater long-term risk to confront a peer than to discuss a disagreement with a supervisor or with a representative of another department. This finding may also stem from a design limitation; that is, the use of the word "supervisor" refers to one person, while the term "peer" refers to many employees. Future studies should attempt to sort out this potential effect.

As a whole, reliability and validity research on the OCCI demonstrate that the instrument has high discriminatory power, moderate construct validity, and strong predictive validity. Even though this research is limited by its exclusive reliance on self-report measures, the use of multiple studies makes a convincing argument that situational factors have an effect on communicative strategies in conflict management. Future studies should test the OCCI with behavioral measures of communicative strategies and should use interviews, quasi-experimental designs, and nonobtrusive measures to test the power of the OCCI to predict behaviors. Future investigations should also examine the links between conflict strategies and other communicative behaviors, namely, compliance gaining (Miller, Boster, Roloff, & Seibold, 1977; McLaughlin, Cody, & Robey, 1980; Sillars, 1980), communicator style (Norton, 1978), and relational control (Rogers & Farace, 1975). Communication researchers can play a significant role in discovering appropriate and effective ways to handle organizational conflicts. Heretofore this domain has remained largely untapped by organizational communication scholars. We need research that identifies the unique characteristics of conflict episodes and tests for the impact of these characteristics on communication strategies in different phases of conflict development. The practical and theoretical significance of such work is evident in Lawrence and Lorsch's (1967, p. 224) comment: "An effective conflict resolution system is really the same thing as an effective decision-making system — rather central to organizational performance."

NOTES

1. To support our contention that individuals do *not* necessarily have a characteristic mode of conflict management, we isolated the scores in the upper third and the scores

above the normative mean on two or more modes of the OCCI. Of the 360 subjects who completed Form B, twenty-nine of them received scores in the upper one-third range on *all three* conflict styles, and nineteen of these respondents scored one standard deviation above the mean on the three scales. The following breakdown shows the number of respondents who scored in the upper third on two scales:

Conflict Strategies	Upper third	1 SD above mean
Nonconfrontation-solution orientation	54	21
Nonconfrontation-control	49	31
Solution-orientation and control	41	22

Scores on the three scales do not identify a characteristic style of conflict management for 144, or 40 percent, of the respondents (using upper third scores).

2. Additional support for the reliability of the scales stemmed from coefficients for average item-total score correlations and coefficients for average interitem correlations.

Conflict Strategies	Item-total score r	Interitem r
Nonconfrontation	.74	.51
Solution-orientation	.62	.34
Control	.66	.37

3. While fifteen additional items were added to Form C, only four of them met standards of reliability and discriminatory power. The majority of the bad items were written to be reverse-scored, but this procedure did not result in highly reliable items. Other items were high in reliability but differed in content with at least 50 percent of the other items.

REFERENCES

Assael, H. Constructive role of interorganizational conflict. *Administrative Science Quarterly,* 1969, *14,* 573-582.

Bernard, J. Some current conceptualizations in the field of conflict. *American Journal of Sociology,* 1965, *70,* 442-454.

Bernardin, H. J., & Alvarez, K. The managerial grid as a predictor of conflict resolution method and managerial effectiveness. *Administrative Science Quarterly,* 1976, *21,* 84-92.

Blake, R. R., & Mouton, J. S. *The managerial grid.* Houston: Gulf, 1964.

Blake, R. R., Shepard, H., & Mouton, J. S. *Managing intergroup conflict in industry.* Houston: Gulf, 1964.

Bullis, C. B., Cox, M. C., & Herrod, S. L. *Organizational conflict management: The effects of socialization, type of conflict, and sex on conflict management strategies.* Unpublished manuscript, Purdue University, Department of Communication, 1981.

Burke, R. J. Methods of resolving superior-subordinate conflict: The constructive use of subordinate differences and disagreements. *Organizational Behavior and Human Performance,* 1970, *5,* 393-411.

Cattell, R. B. The scree test for the number of factors. *Multivariate Behavioral Research,* 1966, *1,* 245-276.

Coser, L. A. *The functions of social conflict.* New York: Macmillan, 1956.
Deutsch, M. *The resolution of conflict: Constructive and destructive processes.* New Haven, CT: Yale University Press, 1973.
Dutton, J. M., & Walton, R. E. Inter-departmental conflict and cooperation: Two contrasting studies. *Human Organization,* 1966, *25,* 207-220
Frost, J. H., & Wilmot, W. W. *Interpersonal conflict.* Dubuque, IA: William C. Brown, 1978.
Goldhaber, G. M. *Organizational communication* (2nd ed.). Dubuque, IA: William C. Brown, 1979.
Hall, J. Conflict management survey: A survey of one's characteristic reaction to and handling of conflicts between himself and others. Monroe, TX: Teleometrics International, 1969.
Horney, K. *Our inner conflicts.* New York: W. W. Norton, 1945.
House, R. J., & Rizzo, J. R. Role conflict and ambiguity as critical variables in a model of organizational behavior. *Organizational Behavior and Human Performance,* 1972, *7,* 467-505.
Huseman, R. C., Logue, C. M., & Freshley, D. L. (Eds.). *Readings in interpersonal and organizational communication* (3rd ed.). Boston: Holbrook Press, 1977.
Jamieson, D. W., & Thomas, K. W. Power and conflict in the student-teacher relationship. *Journal of Applied Behavioral Science,* 1974, *10,* 321-336.
Johnson, T. W., & Stinson, J. E. Role ambiguity, role conflict, and satisfaction: Moderating effects of individual differences. *Journal of Applied Psychology,* 1975, *60,* 329-333.
Katz, D., & Kahn, R. L. *The social psychology of organizations* (2nd ed.). New York: John Wiley, 1978.
Kilmann, R. H., & Thomas, K. W. Interpersonal conflict-handling behavior as reflections of Jungian personality dimensions. *Psychological Reports,* 1975, *37,* 971-980.
Kilmann, R. H., & Thomas, K. W. Developing a forced-choice measure of conflict-handling behavior: The mode instrument. *Educational and Psychological Measurement,* 1977, *37,* 309-325.
Koehler, J. W., Anatol, K. W. E., & Applbaum, R. L. *Organizational communication* (2nd ed.). New York: Holt, Rinehart & Winston, 1981.
Lawrence, P. R., & Lorsch, J. W. *Organization and environment.* Boston: Harvard University, Graduate School of Business Administration, 1967.
Litterer, J. A. Conflict in organizations: A re-examination. *Academy of Management Journal,* 1966, *9,* 176-186.
McLaughlin, M. L., Cody, M. J., & Robey, C. S. Situational influences on the selection of strategies to resist compliance-gaining attempts. *Human Communication Research,* 1980, *7,* 14-36.
McQuitty, L. L. Elementary linkage analysis for isolating orthogonal and oblique types and typal relevancies. *Educational and Psychological Measurement,* 1957, *17,* 207-229.
Miller, G., Boster, F., Roloff, M., & Seibold, D. Compliance-gaining message strategies: A typology and some findings concerning effects of situational differences. *Communication Monographs,* 1977, *44,* 37-51.
Norton, R. W. Foundation of a communicator style construct. *Human Communication Research,* 1978, *4,* 99-112.
Nunnally, J. C. *Psychometric theory* (2nd ed.). New York: McGraw-Hill, 1978.
Perrow, L. R. *Complex organizations.* Glenview, IL: Scott, Foresman, 1979.
Pondy, L. R. Organizational conflict: Concepts and models. *Administrative Science Quarterly,* 1967, *12,* 296-320.
Porter, D. T. *Purdue instrument analysis system manual.* Buffalo: State University of New York, 1975.
Putnam, L. L., & Jones, T. S. The role of communication in bargaining. *Human Communication Research,* 1982, *8,* 262-280.
Rahim, A., & Bonoma, T. V. Managing organizational conflict: A model for diagnosis and intervention. *Psychological Reports,* 1979, *44,* 1323-1344.

Rapoport, A. *Fights, games, and debates.* Ann Arbor: University of Michigan Press, 1965.

Renwick, P. A. Effects of sex-differences on the perception and management of conflict: An exploratory study. *Organizational Behavior and Human Performance,* 1977, *19,* 403-415.

Rogers, L. E., & Farace, R. V. Relational communication analysis: New measurement procedures. *Human Communication Research,* 1975, *1,* 222-239.

Ruble, T. L., & Thomas, K. W. Support for a two-dimensional model of conflict behavior. *Organizational Behavior and Human Performance,* 1976, *16,* 143-155.

Schelling, T. C. *The strategy of conflict.* Cambridge, MA: Harvard University Press, 1960.

Sebring, R. The five million dollar misunderstanding: A perspective on state government-university interorganizational conflicts. *Administrative Science Quarterly,* 1977, *22,* 505-523.

Seiler, J. A. Diagnosing interdepartmental conflict. *Harvard Business Review,* 1963, *41,* 121-132.

Sillars, A. L. The stranger and the spouse as target persons for compliance-gaining strategies: A subjective expected utility model. *Human Communication Research,* 1980, *6,* 265-279.

Simons, H. W. Prologue. In G. R. Miller & H. W. Simons (Eds.), *Perspectives on communication in social conflict.* Englewood Cliffs, NJ: Prentice-Hall, 1974.

Thomas, K. W. Conflict and conflict management. In M. Dunnette (Ed.), *Handbook of industrial and organizational psychology.* Chicago: Rand McNally, 1976.

Thomas, K. W., & Kilmann, R. H. The social desirability variable in organizational research. *Academy of Management Journal,* 1975, *18,* 741-752.

Thomas, K. W., & Kilmann, R. H. Comparison of four instruments measuring conflict behavior. *Psychological Reports,* 1978, *42,* 1139-1145.

Tompkins, P. K., Fisher, J. Y., Infante, D. A., & Tompkins, E. V. Conflict and communication within the university. In G. R. Miller & H. W. Simons (Eds.), *Perspectives on communication in social conflict.* Englewood Cliffs, NJ: Prentice-Hall, 1974.

Walton, R. E., & Dutton, J. M. The management of interdepartmental conflict: A model and review. *Administrative Science Quarterly,* 1969, *14,* 73-84.

Walton, R. E., & McKersie, R. B. *A behavioral theory of labor negotiations.* New York: McGraw-Hill, 1965.

Wilson, C. E. *The influence of role relationship and organizational position on perceived conflict strategies.* Unpublished master's thesis, Purdue University, 1981.

Zammuto, R. F., London, M., & Rowland, K. W. Effects of sex on commitment and conflict resolution. *Journal of Applied Psychology,* 1979, *64,* 227-231.

24 ● The Compliance Interview: Negotiating Across Organizational Boundaries

JAMES A. GILCHRIST

Western Michigan University

FOR many large organizations, significant resources are committed to receiving and processing large quantities of information obtained in small quantities from large numbers of clients. Insurance companies, banks, government revenue departments, and licensing departments are overwhelmed by data accumulating in small amounts from each of thousands — sometimes millions — of customers. The processing of premium payments, mortgage payments, property tax payments, and radio licenses is work that is essential for providing income, or in the case of government agencies, is the reason for the organization's existence.

In most cases this influx of information is handled by automated data processing equipment. The use of these computerized systems necessarily limits the forms and formats of allowable inputs. Such large information processing systems must sort information into a finite set of categories using predetermined criteria, then aggregate, update, and otherwise manipulate the information, also according to predetermined rules. These systems can handle exceptions, but only if the exception is predictable enough to be sorted and processed according to identifiable rules. Other "exceptions" are "kicked out" of the system and must be resolved by highly effective, but relatively inefficient, humans. In order to maintain an optimum flow of information and income and to reduce costs of unex-

AUTHOR'S NOTE: This chapter is based on the author's doctoral dissertation, supervised by Larry D. Browning of the University of Texas—Austin. The research was supported in part by Intergovernmental Personnel Act Grant 78TX09 from the U.S. Civil Service Commission. John Waite Bowers, of the University of Iowa, was a consultant to the grant project.

Correspondence and requests for reprints: James A. Gilchrist, Department of Communication Arts and Sciences, Western Michigan University, Kalamazoo, MI 49008.

pected variety, organizations demand — and usually receive — compliance from their clients as to when, in what kind of envelope, with what kind of check, and with what documents transactions will occur.

This study is concerned with what happens when clients do not comply and when usual, often automated, procedures (form letters, for example) fail to bring compliance. At some point, an employee will often contact the client directly, seeking both immediate and long-term compliance. These compliance interviews involve the negotiation of compliance across organizational boundaries. They are potentially very costly in employee time, public relations, and delayed receipt of information and/or income.

GOALS OF THE COMPLIANCE INTERVIEW

A primary characteristic distinguishing interviews from other communication exchanges is that they are "entered into for a specific task-related purpose associated with a particular subject matter" (Downs, Smeyak, & Martin, 1980, p. 5). In the compliance interview, there are three specific purposes most relevant to the organization:

1. to obtain immediate compliance from the client;
2. to obtain long-term compliance from the client;
3. to obtain a cooperative relationship with the client.

Identifying the client's goals in these interviews is, however, problematic. A client strongly motivated toward the same goals would likely comply upon simple notification of noncompliance. There would be little need for the compliance interviewer to persuade or negotiate terms of complaince. This research is directed, however, to circumstances in which clients resist, for whatever reasons, the interviewer's efforts to obtain compliance.

THE COMPLIANCE INTERVIEW AS STRATEGIC INTERPERSONAL PERSUASION

Because the interview is directed toward specific purposes (or at least should be), analysis of these interviews should be viewed from a strategic perspective. Cegala (1979, p. 10) described a strategic model consisting of three elements:

A competent persuader must possess
1. a fair amount of knowledge about the rules of social behavior that are pertinent to the context. . . .
2. a repertoire of strategies for adapting to various contexts. . . .

3. motivation to engage in covert and overt behavior that is intended to achieve desired objectives.

Folger (1979, pp. 7-8) listed four categories toward which these persuasive efforts may be directed:

1. messages which influence the distribution of resources that are shared in a relationship. . . .
2. attempts to influence one's beliefs or attitudes. . . .
3. attempts to change the behavior or conduct of another. . . .
4. influence over the communicative interaction which occurs between the members of a relationship.

The compliance interviewer, then, makes choices of messages on the basis of his or her knowledge of context, repertoire of message strategies, and the specific objectives of the interview. These objectives may be achieved through bargaining, messages intended to change client attitudes, direct requests for behavior compliance, and attempts to control the course of interaction in the interview.

For competent interviewers, these choices should not be random, but should reflect an overall strategy organized into an interview agenda. The objective of this research was to discover the strategies employed by compliance interviewers and to construct, from observation of such interviews, descriptions of the agendas actually employed.

(A note on ethical issues: An important issue is concerned with whether the compliance demand is justified ethically as well as pragmatically. In the specific interviews studied, I do believe an ethical interest was served by being interested in strategy from the standpoint of the interviewer. Bowers [1974] provides examples of compliance demands in which the client's perspective would be more appealing to my personal sense of justice.)

THEORETICAL ASSUMPTIONS

In addition to the strategic perspective outlined above, the research was guided by two specific theoretical positions. These positions are described here since the analysis of data necessarily reflects the analyst's assumptions about the observed phenomena.

In *The Strategy of Conflict,* Thomas C. Schelling was concerned with the study of communication in circumstances where one or both parties possessed significant coercive power, a circumstance often obtaining in compliance interviews. In coercive settings, Schelling notes that the study of communication strategy is "not concerned with the *application* of force but with the *exploitation of potential force"* (1960, p. 5) This study involves communication *about* coercion but does not extend to considerations regarding the carrying out of coercive acts. The research focuses on symbolic acts intended to influence the outcomes of a compliance conflict.

The second theoretical position, also articulated by Schelling, is that "most conflict situations are essentially bargaining situations" (p. 5). Moreover, following the research of Watzlawick, Beavin, and Jackson (1967), Walton and McKersie (1965), Goffman (1967, 1971), and Morris (1978), negotiation may involve not only the distribution of economic rewards but also the definition of roles, the saving of "face," and the negotiation of rules for future interaction. Immediate behavioral compliance is only one of the issues subject to bargaining.

RESEARCH METHODOLOGY

Subjects and Context

Subjects were state tax enforcement officers whose job was to conduct compliance interviews with delinquent taxpayers. Ten subjects participated in the first study; fifty-seven subjects participated in the second. Each of these studies is described below.

As a part of their job, the compliance officers initiated interviews after receiving computer-generated assignments from a headquarter's office. Most of these assignments required contacting owners of small to medium-sized businesses who had failed to file quarterly sales tax returns, who had filed incorrectly, who had filed a return but did not pay, or whose check had been returned for insufficient funds. Assignments were received after mailed notices generated no response.

In most of these interviews, the amount of money involved was small, usually less than $1,000 and often less than $50. However, the totals are quite large given the large volume of compliance assignments, usually over 100 per month per officer. In fiscal year 1979, 320 compliance officers collected over $154 million, a four-to-one return on compliance expenditures.

The compliance officers have significant coercive powers at their disposal, including assessing interest penalties of up to 20 percent, filing tax liens, freezing bank accounts, levying assets, seizing cash on hand, seizing and selling off business inventories, and criminal penalties. All of these sanctions, however, impose significant costs in employee time and public relations. As a result, agency policy directs that officers attempt to obtain compliance through interviews before imposing costly penalties.

As a further effort to reduce cost, the officers are encouraged to conduct initial interviews by telephone. Visits to the client's home or business are scheduled only when necessary. A significant consequence of this policy is that client compliance cannot actually occur during the telephone interview. The officer's objective, then, becomes that of seeking a credible verbal commitment to comply by mail or a later visit.

Study One

The first study was an observational field study of actual compliance interviews. The subjects for this study were selected because of established reputations for success at obtaining compliance, and for favorable relationships with clients. One hundred interviews were observed. Nearly two-thirds were telephone interviews, during which the researcher listened on another telephone, with the subject's consent. The remainder were "field" visits to the taxpayer's home or place of business. In these visits, the researcher was introduced as a "fellow employee" — a statement that accurately reflected the researcher's employment as a management trainer at the time. The compliance officers were told that the conversations were being observed because the researcher was working on developing training programs and needed to learn as much as possible about the work. This explanation was also true.

The study yielded two types of data: descriptions of compliance interviews and interviewers' accounts of the interviews (Harré & Secord, 1973). The accounts were obtained by interviewing the subjects following each call or visit to elicit (1) explanations and interpretations of the taxpayer's behavior, (2) explanations of an interviewer's decisions about how to conduct the conversation, and (3) verification of the researcher's description of what was said in the interview.

These data were analyzed using Glaser and Strauss's (1967) constant comparison method for generating grounded theory. These analytical procedures have been described in greater detail elsewhere (Bowers, Gilchrist, & Browning, 1980).

The data obtained were rich in detail and interpretation and provided a reasonable cross-section of client behavior. The data base was limited, however, to only a few compliance officers, making generalizations about interviewer strategy difficult. The findings from the study were most useful in constructing a normative theory (Bowers, Gilchrist, & Browning, 1980) and in establishing a base for the simulations used in study two.

Study Two

Fifty-seven compliance officers were subjects in study two. These subjects participated in the study as part of the requirements to attend a two-day training session intended to improve their skills at conducting compliance interviews. Organization policies prohibited random selection of subjects, but the subject pool was found not to differ significantly from the total population in distribution of age (median = 31.6), sex (15 female, 42 male), ethnicity (40 white, 9 black, 8 Mexican-American), or years experience in the job (Mean = 5.3).

On the basis of the first study, two research assistants were trained to play the roles of delinquent taxpayers in twelve cases used for simulations. The training included observing actual compliance interviews and practice sessions with compliance officers. The taxpayer/confederates called the subjects two weeks before the training course to inform them that simulation tapes would be made for use as stimulus materials in the training. There was no deception — the tapes were used for this purpose. The subject was then given information normally available before conducting a compliance interview: a fictional taxpayer name, address, type of business, type of assignment, prior record of compliance, specific details on the assignment, etc.

The subject then called a telephone number he or she had been given, asked to speak to the taxpayer (using the name provided), and continued to speak to the confederate as though it were an actual compliance interview. These conversations were taped for analysis. Each subject made two tapes, one with each of two confederates using different types of simulation cases.

The cases and instructions to the confederates represented the range of client behaviors observed in the first study. In some cases confederates were provided with evasive excuses; in others, with blunt arguments. In some cases, confederates were instructed to stammer and sound confused. Confederates also varied their willingness (or unwillingness) to commit themselves to early compliance.

Analysis of these data also followed the general strategies outlined by Glaser and Strauss (1967). The procedure required initial coding of tapes using a very concrete coding system of 114 categories — separate categories for subject and confederate messages. An iterative procedure was then used to successively reduce the typology to a smaller set of categories. The reductions were based on (1) observed patterns in interact matrices (similar messages types should occur in similar patterns); (2) theoretical findings in prior research on communication and conflict, bargaining, persuasion, and interviewing; and (3) conclusions reached on the basis of analysis of data from study one. (A more detailed description of these procedures has been reported in Gilchrist, 1980.)

Two secondary analyses were then performed on the coded data. First, the reduced coding typology was employed to construct a client-interviewer interact matrix showing the contingent relationship between client messages and interviewer response. Second, subject profile scores

The Compliance Interview

Table 24.1
Interviewer Message Categories

Category	Frequency	Percentage of Utterances
Informative Messages		
1. Informs	835	35.7
2. Questions	108	4.6
3. Seeks Confirmation	305	13.1
Persuasive Messages		
4. Argues Critically	106	4.5
5. Acknowledges	93	4.0
6. Describes Sanctions	262	11.2
7. Assures Cooperatively	257	11.0
Bargaining Messages		
8. Proposes	369	15.8
9. Requests Proposal	166	7.1
10. Accepts Proposal	64	2.7
11. Rejects Proposal	57	2.4
12. Confirms Proposal	639	27.4
"Other" Messages		
13. Clarifies Role	40	1.7
14. Assumes Fault in Other	17	0.7
15. Responds Courteously	161	6.9
	3479	148.9

Total Number of Utterances: 2336

were computed reflecting the proportion of each message type expressed by each subject. Correlationlike measures were then used to discover patterns of message preferences across subjects (see Appendix B for a more detailed explanation).

FINDINGS

This report combines the major conclusions from both the observational study and the simulation study. Tables 24.1 and 24.2 present the reduced coding system developed in the simulation study. As noted, these categories were derived from more concrete categories on the basis of observed patterns in interact matrices. The percentages in these tables exceed 100 percent because more than one message type was often present in an utterance.

Table 24.2
Interviewee Message Categories

Category	Frequency	Percentage of Utterances
Informative Messages		
1. Informs	327	14.0
2. Questions	306	13.1
3. Confirms Information	184	7.9
4. Gives Sales Figures	42	1.8
Persuasive Messages		
5. Accounts	506	21.7
6. Responds Incoherently	87	3.7
Bargaining Messages		
7. Proposes	220	9.4
8. Requests Proposal	28	1.2
9. Accepts Proposal	42	1.8
10. Rejects Proposal	24	1.0
11. Commits Indefinitely	136	5.8
12. Confirms Proposal	462	19.8
"Other" Messages		
13. Agrees to Benefit	42	1.8
14. Expresses Ability to Get Loan	14	0.6
15. Clarifies Roles	62	2.7
16. Responds Courteously	98	4.2
17. Silence, First Move	72	3.1
	2735	117.3

Total Number of Utterances: 2336

The distinctions between informative, persuasive, and bargaining messages are significant to the interpretation of findings from both studies. The informative messages convey, solicit, or clarify the definition of the situation. These messages have no necessary implications for what ought to occur or what will occur, but focus instead on what has occurred or what is occurring. These messages establish the factual base from which the interview can proceed.

Persuasive messages, by contrast, are directed toward what *ought* to occur. These messages reflect interpretations of past, present, and future behavior by the communicators. The persuasive messages are concerned with both ethical and pragmatic judgments regarding what should happen in a relationship between the client and the organization.

Bargaining messages are directed toward what *will* occur. These messages represent proposals and requests for proposals regarding the timing of compliance behaviors. By use of these messages, possible outcomes are expanded, limited, or discovered.

The fourth type of messages — "other" messages — are of little theoretical significance. These messages occurred in no consistent pattern or served technical purposes unique to the context of the study.

These three general message types can be used to describe adequately the overall agenda observed in both studies. This agenda involved a progression from informative messages to persuasive messages to bargaining messages. At the conclusion of a successful bargain, the interviews ended. Within this general framework, there were some significant deviations that will be described below.

The "Ideal" Interview Agenda

Analysis of the observational study provided the first indications that the interview followed a reasonably consistent agenda. The first objective appeared to be establishing the necessary factual base. Almost all of the interviewers began with a self-introduction, confirmation of the interviewee's identity, and a brief description of the reason for the call or visit. For example:

ER: Is this Mrs. Johnson?
EE: Yes, it is.
ER: My name is E_____ S_____ and I'm with the state comptroller's department. I'm calling because according to our records we haven't received your April sales tax return yet. Have you sent that in?

In most instances there is a reasonable chance that the agency records are inaccurate. There is also the possibility that the taxpayer complied after the assignment was issued to the compliance officer, but before the interview. Only in the case of "hot check" assignments is the situation certain — the officer will have the actual check in hand. This opening pattern was also observed in the simulation study, in which 90.3 percent of initial interviewer utterances stated the nature of the problem and 40.3 percent sought confirmation.

The interviewee's response to the opening questions was considered critical to the success of the interview. Subjects reported that their judgments regarding the taxpayer's willingness to cooperate were based almost entirely on these first exchanges. The following response types were most typical:

1. A direct answer asserting that compliance had occurred.
2. A direct answer acknowledging that compliance had not occurred.
3. An excuse or complaint apparently intended to justify noncompliance.

4. A confused response indicating uncertainty or ignorance.
5. A combination of any of these, including combinations that might appear illogical, such as both #1 and #3.

The interviewers preferred, not unexpectedly, a direct answer that was also accurate. If the taxpayer asserted that he or she had complied, the interviewer then asked questions necessary to bring agency records up to date: When was it filed? How much was the payment? What were total sales figures? Often, the answers to these questions revealed that the assertion of compliance was not accurate.

Similar questions were asked if the person acknowledged noncompliance. The questions provided necessary information for establishing how much tax was owed, a step which should precede discussion regarding when payment would be made.

After this information was established, those officers observed in the first study usually requested a proposal from the interviewee or presented a proposal of their own:

- Can you mail me a check for that today?
- When can you send in that return with payment?

This marked the initiation of the bargaining phase of the interview. This phase was marked by an exchange of offers and counter-offers from both parties, although the interviewers were generally more active in initiating bargaining. In the simulation study, interviewers averaged over three proposals per tape.

The bargaining phase concluded with a proposal being accepted by both parties. This conclusion was marked by negotiating precise details of the agreement:

ER: So, you can pay tomorrow. Is that correct?
EE: Yes.
ER: Can you bring the check to my office?
EE: Yes.
ER: Do you know where it is?
EE: No.
ER: [gives address] What time will you be here?

The interview concluded with these exchanges.

This, however, is an "ideal" agenda. It accurately describes many conversations of the experienced, successful officers working with reasonably cooperative taxpayers. The deviations from this agenda are interesting, for they shed light on the interviewees' perspective and indicate the range of strategies used by the compliance officers. Also interesting are

The Compliance Interview

the strategies used by the interviewers to keep the conversation on the agenda they prefer.

Agenda Control

As noted above, one way taxpayers often responded to initial questions was to present an excuse or complaint apparently intended to justify noncompliance. These messages were coded as "accounts" in the simulation study. The accounts blamed sick cats, snowstorms, road construction, red tape, personal illness, deaths, tornadoes, and poverty for preventing compliance. Many of the observed accounts were incoherent. As a consequence, the taxpayer/confederates offered similar accounts in the simulation study.

These accounts met with one of the following interviewer responses:
1. Critical Arguments:
    A. "Sermons": A comment on the ethics of the taxpayer. "You collected that money from your customers, so it's not your money."
    B. "Logical Argument": A comment on the validity of the excuse. "Last week's weather doesn't explain why you didn't send in your payment two months ago."
    C. "Put Down": A comment on the taxpayer's competence. "If you kept records daily like you're supposed to, you would have the information."
2. Acknowledgments:
    "Yes, this weather has been bad . . ."
    "I'm sorry the construction has hurt your business . . ."
3. Cooperative Assurances:
    "Well, I'm sure we can get this taken care of . . ."
4. Ignoring the account: The interviewer's response did not comment on the account.
5. A combination of these.

In the simulation study, interviewees' accounts were followed by

- an acknowledgment in 16.8 percent of the cases
- a critical argument in 11.9 percent
- a cooperative assurance in 11.9 percent
- an informative message in 41.1 percent
- a proposal or request for proposal in 38.3 percent

This distribution differed from that observed in the first study that included those officers with reputations for success. These subjects responded with an acknowledgment-question or acknowledgment-proposal sequence in almost every interview. In both studies, the acknowledgment-question or the acknowledgment-proposal pattern was observed to give the interviewer greater control over the agenda. To explain this finding, consideration must be given to understanding the interviewee's perspective, particularly his or her reason for offering accounts.

A theoretical explanation for these accounts is provided by Goffman's (1971) model of remedial processes. Goffman was concerned with circumstances in which one person violates general social norms and is confronted with this fact by another. According to Goffman, the violator will often assume that others place the worst possible interpretations on the reasons for the violation. To overcome this fear the offender will present an excuse offering a more favorable interpretation. If this excuse is honored, the breach caused by the violation can be closed and the interaction can continue without undue concern over how "awful" or "evil" one might appear. However, if the account is not accepted, the offender's fears are confirmed, making interaction painful. The offender will likely repeat excuses or offer new ones until the situation appears completely hopeless or until an account is at least minimally accepted. This pattern of excuses has also been observed by Morris (1978) in interaction between college teachers and students who have missed assignments or tests. This interpretation of excuses, though not expressed in the theoretical language used above, was frequently offered by the subjects in the observational study.

The patterns of interaction observed in this research support this explanation. Those subjects who responded with acknowledgments presented relatively fewer persuasive messages than did those whose responses rejected the interviewees' accounts. When the accounts were rejected, interviewees offered new ones or extended previous ones and became less willing to cooperate. These interviewers continued to argue over excuses, more frequently presented information regarding coercive penalties, presented more proposals, and were less likely to obtain favorable commitments. Interviewers' preferences for "critical arguments" were correlated with "sanctions" and the length of bargaining. Critical arguments appeared to fuse the relational issues with the substantive (compliance) issue, resulting in protracted and difficult bargaining. Those interviewers who acknowledged the accounts and then returned to the "ideal" agenda received quicker cooperation and more favorable commitments to comply.

Bargaining Strategy and the Use of Coercion

As noted earlier these interviews were conducted in a setting giving considerable coercive power to the representatives of the organization.

These sanctions ranged from interest penalties, to padlocking businesses, to criminal charges. Some penalties were cheap to apply because the penalty could be carried out by computer. Thus interest penalties were automatic, as were computer-generated notices of tax liens. The other penalties required extensive amounts of employee time. The more threatening penalties were also more expensive to carry out, and thus officers were encouraged to use them judiciously.

These penalties were frequently referred to during bargaining exchanges, presumably to encourage better solutions. At first it may appear that there would be little to bargain about. Indeed, *whether* the interviewee would pay and the total amount to be paid were not subject to negotiation. The timing of compliance was negotiable: today, tomorrow, or next week. The method was negotiable: by mail, at the interviewee's office, or the interviewer's office. It was also possible to make several payments over a period of time — up to six months.

In the observational study the data were analyzed to identify the strategic rules that appeared to be used by the interviewers in the presentation of coercive information and in the exchange of proposals. These rules are summarized here.

Rule One: Begin by requesting immediate compliance. Most subjects, in both studies, initiated bargaining by requesting immediate compliance from the interviewee. By making the first offer, interviewers could set the expectation that clients would comply quickly. The subjects in study one usually did not ask for a proposal until after presenting a proposal of their own.

Not all forms of opening offers were observed to be equally effective. The most experienced subjects expected immediate compliance but communicated this expectation in ways that allowed themselves to make subsequent concessions and that offered some flexibility to the interviewees. Two examples of this approach are:

- Can you bring your check today, or would you rather mail it?
- Do you want to send a check or pay in cash?

These two examples violate the principle:

- This payment *must* be made today.
- The full amount *must* be paid this afternoon or we'll seize your business.

The first two examples request immediate compliance and place greatest emphasis on the limited set of choices available to the interviewee. The latter examples force the interviewer into an untenable position should subsequent concessions be required. The interviewer must either hold to the commitment, thereby reducing the probability of a reasonable agreement, or concede anyway, thereby losing credibility. Moreover, the rigid interviewer demand often results in equally rigid demands from the interviewee. The most experienced and successful subjects appeared to communicate "toughness" by making concessions slowly, often by repeating the same proposal several times, rather than by using "demanding" language. Then, when it became necessary to quit bargaining, the interviewers often did use "demanding" language that increased credibility by the shift from a more flexible position.

Rule Two: Make concessions slowly. This strategic rule was not as consistently followed, but appeared to characterize the behavior of the more experienced subjects in the observational study as well as most of those in the simulation study. This rule recommends that interviewers begin by asking for full, immediate compliance and avoid making concessions until specific offers have been received from interviewees. This rule is consistent with the findings of Bartos (1970) on the relative success of "tough" bargainers.

Violations of this strategic rule were most frequent among the most inexperienced subjects included in the simulation study. These subjects frequently began bargaining by describing a variety of ways in which the interviewee could comply, including mention of possible extended payout plans. The alternatives were described before receiving proposals from interviewees. The confederates playing taxpayer roles, instructed to try to get the best deal they could, consistently said they wanted the most lenient proposal mentioned. The interviewers then returned to the proposal for immediate compliance and attempted, usually without success, to bargain from that position. The ineffectiveness of this bargaining strategy was attested to in the accounts obtained in the observational study. Those subjects reported that any mention of more lenient proposals acceptable to the interviewee led to a commitment to that proposal by the interviewee. Listing alternatives was taken to be a list of proposals. When interviewers returned to a demand for immediate compliance, they violated the general bargaining norm that offers, once made, reflect the bargainer's good faith and are not subject to capricious withdrawal (Rubin & Brown, 1975).

Rule Three: Strategically disclose information on coercive sanctions. The subjects in the observational study, and a majority of those in the simulation study all appeared to manage carefully the disclosure of information on coercive sanctions. Because this information, no matter how tactfully presented, is potentially threatening to "face," strategically successful interviewers used it only to the extent necessary. These interviewers used the information not so much with an intent to coerce as with an intent to inform. This association was indicated by subjects' accounts obtained in the observation study and by a strong correlation between subjects' preference for informative messages and for "describes sanctions" messages in the simulation study.

This rule was followed by first ordering the sanctions according to degree of severity from interest penalties to seizure of inventories. (Possible criminal penalties were not mentioned in any of the interviews.) During the bargaining phase, these penalties were described in order to convince interviewees that it would be to their benefit to comply. Usually, the description of a penalty was followed by a proposal or a request for a proposal in the same utterance. The most extreme penalties were mentioned only after repeated efforts to elicit acceptable proposals had failed.

There were two deviations from this rule. Among some of the most inexperienced officers, there was a tendency to describe *all* potential penalties early in the interview. This strategy left the interviewers with few choices for influencing interviewees during protracted bargaining. As one experienced officer stated in the observation study, "Once you've brought out the big gun of seizure and sale, all of the other penalties are about as effective as a water pistol."

A second deviation from this rule was often carried out by those subjects who also tended to employ critical arguments in response to interviewee accounts. This was indicated by a strong relationship, among some, between preference for critical arguments and messages describing penalties. These subjects appeared to adopt a radically different view when compared to those who offered acknowledgments and strategically managed coercive information. These "arguers" seemed to feel it was important to "let the taxpayer know" that he was "wrong," "irresponsible," or that "he is breaking the law." The taxpayer, in their view, should feel guilty.

Not surprisingly, these subjects obtained few such admissions from taxpayer/confederates trying to save face. Accounts from the observation study indicated similar responses in actual conversations. It is also not surprising that these subjects further attempted to punish recalcitrants with coercive threats, usually with little success.

CONCLUSIONS

This study generated evidence that compliance interviewers conduct their interviews using reasonably predictable interview agendas. Interviewers with the strongest reputations for success used strategies consistent with current theory and research in communication, conflict, and bargaining. This last finding is particularly valuable since little of that theory has been based on observation of professional conflict negotiators (Miller & Simons, 1974).

APPENDIX A: INTERACT MATRIX

The interact matrix (Table A24.1) shows the frequency of joint message choices on client-interviewer interacts. The rows of the matrix identify interviewer messages; the columns, client messages. The first number in each cell is a frequency count of the number of interacts in which the combination occurred. For example, there were thirty-seven interacts in which an interviewee's *informs* message was followed by a subject's *questions* message. The second number is a *row* percentage; the third, a column percentage. As shown, 24.9 percent of interviewers' *questions* messages occurred in response to an *informs* message, and clients' *informs* messages were followed by *questions* in 11.3 percent of the interacts in which the client offered such a message. In interpreting the matrix, the reader should keep in mind that the opening move has been excluded.

APPENDIX B: PATTERNS OF MESSAGE PREFERENCES

Table A24.2 shows correlationlike measures indicating patterns of message performance. This table must be read with caution, however, because it does not have the properties usually associated with a "correlation matrix." Most importantly, the table lacks symmetry; that is, the entries above the diagonal are correlations between different quantities than those below the diagonal. For example, consider the row variable, *questions,* and the column variable *informs.* The *questions-informs* correlation was .22. But this correlation was not based on the same quantities as its counterpart, the *informs-questions* correlation. That correlation is .11.

This difference occurred because of how the row and column variables were calculated. The row quantities were calculated by counting, for each subject, the number of times a message was coded into each category, then dividing that count by the total number of coded messages. Thus the row variable *informs* is the proportion of *all* messages uttered that were coded *informs;* the row variable *questions* is the proportion of *all* messages uttered that were coded *questions.* The remaining row variables were calculated in the same manner. One consequence of these procedures is that the row measures are not independent of each other, since the sum of these quantities for each subject is defined to be 1.

The column variables were calculated differently and represent different quantities in each row. For example, consider the *informs-questions* correlation. In this case, the *questions* variable was calculated using three measures: (1) the frequency of *questions,* (2) the frequency of *informs,* and (3) the total number of coded messages. The *questions* variable for this correlation was a proportion, the numerator of which was the frequency of *questions* messages. The denominator was the total number of messages *minus* the number of messages coded *informs.* Thus, the *informs-questions* correlation is between the proportion of informing to *all* uttered messages and the proportion of questioning messages to all *other* messages uttered. The remaining column variables were similarly calculated for the *informs* row. Thus the column variables for each row are not independent. Each quantity is a proportion calculated with the same denominator, and the sum of the quantities for each subject is 1. The column quantities are, however, independent of their associated row variables.

Further, consider the *seeks confirmation-questions* correlation. The *questions* variable in this correlation is not the same quantity as that in the *informs-questions* correlation. In this case, the numerator is the same (the frequency of messages coded as questions), but the denominator is different: the total number of coded messages minus the number coded as *seeks confirmation* messages. Although calculated differently, the *questions* variable in the *informs* row and the *questions* variable in the *seeks confirmation* row are not mathematically independent, since both quantities use the same numerator.

As a consequence of these considerations, the reader should not consider the table to be a "correlation matrix." The entries are presented in a matrixlike format for convenience only. Each row should be taken as a separate table, a separate set of correlations. The table should be read by rows rather than by columns since the column quantities change across the rows. The property that makes these correlations useful is that each row variable is independent of its associated column variables. Since the other relationships are not independent, however, tests of significance are inappropriate. This points analysis toward identifying patterns in the correlations that generate substantive theory.

(Tables A24.1 and A24.2 begin on next page)

Table A24.1
Interviewer-Interviewee Interact Matrix

	Informs	Questions	Confirms information	Gives sales figures	Accounts	Responds incoherently	Proposes	Requests proposal	Accepts proposal	Rejects proposal	Commits indefinitely	Confirms proposal	Clarifies roles	Agrees to benefit	Expresses ability to get loan	Responds courteously
Informs	119 / 16.2 / 36.5	257 / 34.9 / 84.3	53 / 8.6 / 34.2	24 / 3.3 / 57.1	208 / 28.3 / 41.1	40 / 5.4 / 46.0	51 / 6.9 / 23.2	13 / 1.8 / 46.4	31 / 2.9 / 16.8	6 / 0.8 / 25.0	20 / 2.7 / 14.7	41 / 5.6 / 8.9	29 / 3.9 / 90.6	11 / 1.5 / 26.2	2 / 0.3 / 14.3	4 / 0.5 / 4.6
Questions	37 / 24.9 / 11.3	9 / 8.5 / 3.0	18 / 17.0 / 9.8	1 / 9 / 2.4	27 / 25.5 / 5.3	5 / 4.7 / 5.7	6 / 5.7 / 2.7	2 / 1.9 / 7.1	4 / 3.8 / 3.2	0 / 0 / 0	9 / 8.5 / 6.6	7 / 6.6 / 1.5	0 / 0 / 0	0 / 0 / 0	1 / 0.9 / 7.1	2 / 1.9 / 2.3
Seeks confirmation	59 / 23.2 / 18.1	22 / 8.7 / 7.2	53 / 20.9 / 28.8	17 / 6.7 / 40.5	82 / 32.3 / 16.2	19 / 7.5 / 21.8	3 / 1.2 / 1.4	3 / 1.2 / 10.7	5 / 2.0 / 4.0	2 / 0.8 / 8.3	5 / 2.0 / 3.7	6 / 2.4 / 1.3	8 / 3.1 / 25.0	2 / 0.8 / 4.8	1 / 0.4 / 7.1	0 / 0 / 0
Argues critically	12 / 11.7 / 3.7	5 / 4.9 / 1.6	8 / 7.8 / 4.3	0 / 0 / 0	60 / 58.3 / 11.9	9 / 8.7 / 10.3	7 / 6.8 / 3.2	0 / 0 / 0	2 / 1.9 / 1.6	4 / 3.9 / 16.7	2 / 1.9 / 1.5	7 / 6.8 / 1.5	1 / 1.0 / 3.1	5 / 4.9 / 11.9	1 / 1.0 / 7.1	0 / 0 / 0
Acknowledges	6 / 6.5 / 1.8	1 / 1.1 / 0.3	4 / 4.3 / 2.2	0 / 0 / 0	85 / 91.4 / 16.8	1 / 1.1 / 1.1	2 / 2.2 / 0.9	2 / 2.2 / 7.1	1 / 1.1 / 0.8	0 / 0 / 0	1 / 1.1 / .7	3 / 3.2 / 0.6	0 / 0 / 0	4 / 4.3 / 9.5	0 / 0 / 0	2 / 2.2 / 2.3
Describes sanctions	44 / 17.4 / 13.5	48 / 19.0 / 15.7	24 / 9.5 / 13.0	13 / 5.1 / 31.0	79 / 31.2 / 15.6	12 / 4.7 / 13.8	34 / 13.4 / 15.5	4 / 1.6 / 14.3	8 / 3.2 / 6.4	4 / 1.6 / 16.7	8 / 3.2 / 5.9	21 / 8.3 / 4.5	1 / 0.4 / 3.1	7 / 2.8 / 16.7	2 / 0.8 / 14.3	0 / 0 / 0

670

Assures cooperatively	49 19.3 15.0	15 5.9 4.9	19 9.5 10.3	5 2.0 11.9	98 38.6 19.4	12 4.7 13.8	25 9.8 11.4	1 0.4 3.6	13 5.1 10.4	3 1.2 41.7	16 6.3 22.8	31 12.2 6.7	1 0.4 3.1	11 4.3 26.2	7 2.8 50.0	4 1.6 4.5
Proposes	71 19.9 21.8	19 5.3 6.2	37 10.4 20.1	6 1.7 14.3	122 34.2 24.1	13 3.6 14.9	61 17.1 27.7	14 3.9 50.0	13 3.6 10.4	10 2.8 41.7	31 8.7 22.8	34 9.5 7.4	1 0.3 3.1	7 2.0 16.7	4 1.1 28.6	3 0.8 3.4
Requests proposal	20 12.3 6.1	7 4.3 2.3	11 6.7 6.0	1 0.6 2.4	72 44.2 14.2	5 3.1 5.7	18 11.0 8.2	2 1.2 7.1	13 8.0 10.4	5 3.1 20.8	24 14.7 17.6	16 9.8 3.5	0 0 0	0 0 0	1 0.6 7.1	0 0 0
Accepts proposal	3 4.7 0.9	0 0 0	0 0 0	0 0 0	2 3.1 0.4	0 0 0	34 63.1 15.5	3 4.7 10.7	3 2.7 2.4	1 1.6 4.2	7 10.9 5.1	22 34.4 4.8	0 0 0	0 0 0	0 0 0	0 0 0
Rejects proposal	2 3.5 0.6	1 1.8 0.3	1 1.8 0.5	0 0 0	17 29.8 3.4	2 3.5 2.3	38 66.7 17.3	0 0 0	0 0 0	3 5.3 12.5	4 7.0 2.9	4 7.0 0.9	0 0 0	0 0 0	1 1.8 7.1	0 0 0
Confirms proposal	52 8.2 16.0	26 4.1 8.5	23 3.6 12.5	2 0.3 4.8	42 6.6 8.3	5 0.8 5.7	94 14.8 42.7	5 0.8 17.9	62 0.7 49.6	5 0.8 20.8	47 7.4 34.6	327 51.4 70.8	0 0 0	16 2.5 38.1	3 0.5 21.4	8 1.3 9.2
Assumes fault in other	0 0 0	0 0 0	0 0 0	0 0 0	1 50.0 0.2	1 50.0 1.1	0 0 0	0 0 0	0 0 0	0 0 0	0 0 0	0 0 0	0 0 0	0 0 0	0 0 0	0 0 0
Responds courteously	3 2.0 0.9	3 2.0 1.0	4 2.6 2.2	2 1.3 4.8	1 0.7 0.2	0 0 0	1.3 1.3 0.9	0 0 0	0 0 0	0 0 0	3 2.0 2.2	75 49.7 16.2	0 0 0	1 0.7 2.4	0 0 0	73 48.3 83.9

Interviewer Messages

671

Table A24.2
Patterns of Message Preference

Dependent Measures

Independent Measures	Informs	Questions	Seeks confirmation	Argues critically	Acknowledges	Describes sanctions	Assures cooperatively	Proposes	Requests proposal	Accepts proposal	Rejects proposal	Confirms proposal	Clarifies role	Assumes fault	Responds courteously
Informs	—	.11	.35	−.11	.05	.18	.10	.06	−.25	−.10	−.31	−.11	−.04	.00	.25
Questions	.22	—	.56	−.12	−.02	−.18	−.28	−.17	−.10	−.27	−.11	.02	−.03	−.03	−.04
Seeks confirmation	.35	.50	—	−.10	−.07	−.10	−.14	−.23	−.11	−.37	−.12	−.07	.26	−.20	−.15
Argues critically	−.09	−.13	−.11	—	−.06	.28	.38	.23	−.02	−.04	.40	−.44	.16	.17	.03
Acknowledges	.05	−.04	−.08	−.07	—	.03	.04	−.22	−.01	−.03	−.16	.11	−.02	.05	.18
Describes sanctions	.19	−.22	−.13	.28	.04	—	.32	.05	−.03	.18	.02	−.33	−.11	.06	−.11
Assures cooperatively	−.02	−.30	−.11	.38	.09	.34	—	.23	.04	−.08	.17	−.31	−.11	−.07	.06
Proposes	−.12	−.24	−.27	.1	−.21	.00	.15	—	−.11	.16	.33	.02	.12	.01	.18
Requests proposal	−.25	−.11	−.11	−.02	.00	−.03	.01	.13	—	.30	.43	.07	.17	.19	−.12
Accepts proposal	−.11	−.23	−.40	−.05	−.03	.16	−.09	.16	.30	—	.30	.24	−.34	.10	−.16
Rejects proposal	−.32	−.13	−.14	.39	−.16	−.01	.14	.33	.41	.30	—	−.15	.05	.02	−.24
Confirms proposal	−.09	−.03	−.03	−.41	−.18	−.23	−.28	.18	.16	.34	−.09	—	−.04	−.03	.32
Clarifies role	−.04	−.05	.26	.16	−.02	−.12	−.12	.11	.16	−.36	.04	−.07	—	.12	.01
Assumes fault	−.02	−.04	−.21	.15	.05	.06	−.07	.01	.18	.10	.02	−.05	.12	—	.10
Responds courteously	.15	−.10	−.20	.00	.16	−.17	−.04	.13	−.15	−.18	−.24	.18	.00	.10	—

REFERENCES

Bartos, O. J. Correlates and consequences of "toughness" in bargaining. In P. G. Swingle (Ed.), *The structure of conflict.* New York: Aldine, 1970.

Bowers, J. W. Communication strategies in conflicts between institutions and their clients. In G. R. Miller & H. W. Simons (Eds.), *Perspectives on communication in social conflict.* Englewood Cliffs, NJ: Prentice-Hall, 1974, 125-152.

Bowers, J. W., Gilchrist, J. A., & Browning, L. D. Communication training for high-powered bargainers: Development and effects. *Communication Education,* 1980, *29,* 10-20.

Cegala, D. J. *An explication and test of a model of interpersonal persuasion.* Paper presented at the annual meetings of the Speech Communication Association. San Antonio, TX: 1979.

Downs, C. W., Smeyak, G. P., & Martin, E. *Professional interviewing.* New York: Harper & Row, 1980.

Folger, J. P. *Sorting power, control, dominance: A conceptual model.* Paper presented at the annual meetings of the Speech Communication Association. San Antonio, TX: 1979.

Gilchrist, J. A. *A grounded theory model for developing a typology of message strategy.* Paper presented at the annual meetings of the Speech Communication Association. New York, 1980.

Glaser, B., & Strauss, A. *The discovery of grounded theory: Strategies for qualitative research.* Chicago: Aldine, 1967.

Goffman, E. *Interaction ritual: Essays in face-to-face behavior.* Chicago: Aldine, 1967.

Goffman, E. *Relations in public.* New York: Harper & Row, 1971.

Harré, R., & Secord, P. F. *The explanation of social behavior.* Totowa, NJ: Littlefield, Adams, 1973.

Miller, G. R., & Simons, H. W. *Perspectives on communication and social conflict.* Englewood Cliffs, NJ: Prentice-Hall, 1974.

Morris, G. H. *The remedial process: A negotiation of rules.* Unpublished master's thesis, University of Texas — Austin, 1978.

Rubin, J. Z., & Brown, B. R. *The social psychology of bargaining and negotiation.* New York: Academic Press, 1975.

Schelling, T. C. *The strategy of conflict.* Cambridge, MA: Harvard University Press, 1960. (Republished, New York: Oxford University Press, 1963.)

Walton, R. E., & McKersie, R. B. *A behavioral theory of labor negotiations: An analysis of a social interaction system.* New York: McGraw-Hill, 1965.

Watzlawick, P., Beavin, J. H., & Jackson, D. D. *Pragmatics of human communication.* New York: W. W. Norton, 1967.

25 ● Office Technology: A Report on Attitudes and Channel Selection from Field Studies in Germany

ARNOLD PICOT ● HEIDE KLINGENBERG ●
HANS-PETER KRÄNZLE

Universität Hannover

THE purpose of this chapter is to explore possible impacts new technologies of office communication might have on the structure of organizational communication.[1] Rapid progress in microelectronics has produced a variety of new technical communication channels for office use. Some of them, such as viewphone, video conferencing, integrated text, and fax services, are expected to enter the commercial arena of office communication in the distant future. Currently, other new channels are being implemented or are about to be introduced, such as telecopy services (fax, facsimile), telephone conferencing, computer conferencing, electronic messaging, and videotext. Their diffusion, however, is not yet much advanced.

Our research focuses on some new technologies of this latter group, mainly on new electronic channels for written (text) communication. These new media will enrich the spectrum of existing channels in organizational communication (face to face, telephone, classic mail, telex, and sometimes telecopy contacts).

Availability of more facilities allowing electronic mediation of information will change the patterns of organizational communication. These changes and their possible consequences deserve scientific attention. Most people spend a remarkable proportion of their lifetime working and communicating in organizations or communicating with organized institutions. It is widely accepted that our construction of social reality as well as the

Correspondence and requests for reprints: Arnold Picot, Universität Hannover, Lehrgebiet E für Betriebswirtschaftslehre (Unternehmensführung und Organisation) Wunstorfer Str. 14, D-3000 Hannover 91, West Germany.

modes of relating to each other depend to a substantial extent on communication experiences made in everyday life (Berger & Luckmann, 1966). Therefore, possible structural changes in organizational communication patterns caused by new office communication technologies could affect persons' way of life. Furthermore, quality of social life also depends on the effectiveness and efficiency of organizations. As far as those are affected by new office technology, indirect impacts on the way of life may occur.

MAJOR PROPOSITIONS ON IMPACTS OF NEW OFFICE COMMUNICATION TECHNOLOGY

To simplify, speculations about expected consequences the availability of new text-oriented electronic media would produce can be divided into three contrasting groups. They represent different schools of thought about functions of technologies and organizations in society.

Proposition I: Revolutionary and Advantageous Changes in Office Communication

According to this position new electronic text media would not only replace the old text communication channels mail and telex and thus enable written organizational communication to become faster and more efficient, but this technological development would also substitute the new media for a large proportion of oral communication in organizations, especially of telephone and face-to-face contacts regarded as particularly time-consuming and costly. Assuming a task-oriented, rational perspective on organizational communication, a diminution of face-to-face and oral communication in favor of telecommunication and written information is believed desirable, since most verbal communication tends to be a prolix nuisance.

> The phone also shares a problem with all speech communication: the information density of speech is very low. Generally, the electronic transmission of speech requires about 60,000 bits per second. These 60,000 bits of speech carry about the same information as 15 characters of written text. . . . But you can transmit 15 characters directly as text by transmitting only 120 bits of information, rather than 60,000 bits of speech. If you insist on transmitting speech you are transmitting 500 times too many bits. And these bits have to be paid for. In a very fundamental sense, speech is not an economic medium of communication. (Marill, 1980, p. 185; see also Merrihue, 1960, p. 179; Turoff, 1973)

New electronic text media seem to share all the desirable properties necessary to overcome the shortcomings of oral communication. They are fast, they document the information content, they are asynchronous, and they provide these qualities at low cost and over almost any distance between sender and receiver (e.g., Uhlig, Farber, & Bair, 1979; Panko, 1980).

New structural configurations for innovative organizational decision making could emerge (Witte, 1976; Szyperski, 1979, p. 161ff). By means of new communication technologies, decentralized autonomous groups could pursue their work effectively without risking organizational disintegration (Witte, 1977, 1980). Thus organizational functioning could become more independent of location restrictions (Goddard, 1971), even including "working at home" (Goldmark, 1972). Ultimately, the technological development would lead to a more effective reconciliation of individual needs and organizational demands.

Such prospects are, of course, attractive. They nourish expectations of a rapid development of market demand for new communication technologies.

Proposition II: Modest Changes of
Organizational Communication

However, one quickly thinks of an analogue to the above predictions. The Management Information System (MIS) euphoria of the 1960s and early 1970s made many similar promises which, for the most part, remained unfulfilled. That movement was also driven by a rational approach trying to match demand and supply of information in organizations with the help of upcoming new information technology (Argyris, 1971; Kirsch & Klein, 1977; Feldman & March, 1981). Therefore, one hesitates to accept fully the view of a technological revolution of office communication.

Skepticism derives from two interrelated sources. Social psychological and related research underline the functional importance of nonverbal aspects in face-to-face communication. Developing a "social meaning" and establishing social relations would require face-to-face contacts (Watzlawick, Beavin, & Jackson, 1967; Argyle, 1969). In organizational communication requirements of that kind are manifold — for example, developing trusting relationships among members, coordinating the information for performance of complex and dynamic tasks, creatively solving complex problems, motivating members, and evaluating performance.

On the other hand, recent economic theory of organization shows that firms are concerned mainly with situations heavily involving these functions and, thereby, with sensitive communication problems. The emergence of business organizations can be explained by market failure considerations. Those economic exchanges (transactions) are carried out within the firm which would be too complex and too expensive for market coordination (Arrow, 1974; Williamson, 1975; Picot, in press). Market exchange principally demands the possibility of codifying goods, services, and conditions involved. Whenever this is not feasible (or only at extremely high costs), and if the intended exchange should still take place, the parties involved integrate and build some kind of (hierarchical) organization (firm). Thus, the internal organization of business firms handles the more complicated transactions of an economy. Typically, these internal transactions call for an information exchange which only to a lesser degree can be translated into, for example, written codes. Consequently, symbolic interaction and social presence — that is, oral and face-to-face communication — are inevitable and most important requisites for successful goal achievement in organizational communication. In the field of communication with other locations and organizations, the new technologies could also replace the old text media which, according to this theory, cover a larger proportion of the whole external communication. Thus transactions with the environment could be facilitated.

Given this picture, and assuming that at present channels are selected according to their specific strengths, the second proposition would expect that new communication technologies will substantially replace existing text communication channels (mail and telex) and will only marginally affect channels of oral communication (telephone, face to face). However, to that extent organizational communication could become faster and better organized. Taking the organization as a whole, these changes would be incremental rather than revolutionary. In addition, development of future markets will be relatively slow.

Proposition III: Social and Economic Hazards

Yet one may also have reason to argue that there are dangers involved with the upcoming new communication technologies. The business world could widely adopt the first proposition's expectations, hoping for a more rational control of organizational behavior. It could design organizational communication systems, making extensive use of the new technologies and permitting transmission of task-oriented information almost exclusively through new technical channels. Consequences could be harmful in several respects: Coordination of complex tasks and solving of difficult problems would decline. Even if a Tayloristic redesign of jobs had been undertaken in advance, adaptability to external change would decrease while an increase of external control over individuals could be expected. In any case social structure of organization and need fulfillment of members would suffer, since there would be less chance of developing trusting social relations. That is why isolation of individuals could increase. Similar arguments are advanced by Weizenbaum (1980a, 1980b) regarding social impacts of information technology. Furthermore, depending on accessibility of the new communication technologies, one could fear a widening gap between information rich and information poor within large organizations and among industries or countries (Katzman, 1974).

RESEARCH QUESTIONS

In order to explore the empirical justification of expectations delineated above in more depth, one should try to answer the following questions.

1. What general attitudes do managers show toward new office technologies in general? Answers to this question could point to problems or changes new office communication technology will face when entering organizations.
2. What determinants influence the choice of communication channels? In concordance with Pye and Young, we believe the "next step forward in the hierarchy of predictive methodologies is to take individual selection acts and seek the empirical determinants of choices" (Pye & Young, 1980, p. 7). Improving our empirical knowledge about channel decisions will result in a better understanding of to what extent new channels will replace old ones. Reflecting our earlier discussion of socioemotional and rational functions of organizational communication, it seems useful to subdivide this problem into two components (Communication Studies Group, 1975, p. 18):

    2a. Cognitive (rational) determinants of channel selection

    2b. Affective (emotional) determinants of the selection act.

    Answers to these questions will help us in clarifying what task-oriented as well as affective conditions channels — in particular new text-oriented electronic media — are likely to be accepted as a communication tool in organizations. Only then we can tackle the following question:

3. What potential for substitution between channels can be observed in organizational communication, and what changes in communication patterns do people demand?

Having shed some empirical light on these questions we will, finally, be able to draw some general conclusions with respect to the above propositions about impacts of new organizational communication technologies.

SHORT DESCRIPTION OF THE FIELD STUDIES

The above research questions are included in a larger research program sponsored by the German Department of Research and Technology. This project aims at an assessment of impacts of new office communication technology on organizational structure and job characteristics evaluating the new teletex technology in several field experiments (Picot & Reichwald, 1979).

Teletex Technology

Teletex as a new electronic communication service of Western European and many overseas countries will be officially opened during the next three years, starting in 1982. The teletex system belongs to the family of electronic mail or electronic messaging systems. It integrates features of electronic information and word-processing devices with an advanced and comfortable electronic telex machine. Main characteristics are listed below.

— by means of electronic storage (mail basket) and automatic dialing, the functions of word-processing (typewriting) and text communication operate independently.

— accessability and compatibility to the nationwide and worldwide well-established telex system, increasing the new service's attractiveness as a communication tool for the business world and for public administration.

— high transmission speed: 2400 bit/sec., more than thirty times faster than the old telex system; transmission of a keyboard's standard repository of symbols.

— simple standard layout (CCITT standards) with a mandatory printer and a modest storage capacity so that the device could be affordable on a large scale (quick market penetration and surmounting critical mass limits); screen and other additions only optional.

Sample

The field consists of four suborganizations in two large private companies (insurance and electrical manufacturing) with some thirty locations throughout West Germany and West Berlin. Eighty teletex stations (preliminary versions of the teletex-technology allowing internal organizational use only between one organization's stations) were installed in this field, supplemented by telecopy (facsimile) facilities.

Participants in the investigations are 640 users having access to these stations, of whom 40 percent are technical and scientific personnel and 60 percent hold positions in business, finance, and other administrative functions. A breakdown by hierarchical level shows that approximately 50 percent are lower-level managers, 40 percent middle-level managers, and 10 percent high-level managers. Included in the study are 150 operators, especially secretaries.

Method

In order to answer our questions and to control other factors as exactly as possible, we had to develop a rather complex package of research instruments containing some twenty different tools. These range from expert interviews and various questionnaires for managers and secretaries over simply structured self-report measures (checklist-crossing in order to assess certain frequencies of information and communication) up to objective measures (counting of mail, telex, and teletex contacts, etc.). More detailed information about the research instruments is available on request.

RESULTS

The following results represent some first analyses of the data collected in the field. As collection of data was completed only very recently, the preliminary character of the reported findings should be stressed.

Attitudes Toward New Office Technology in General

Based on attitudinal questionnaire data (n = 629 users and 147 operators) we found an interesting tension between a favorable general attitude toward technological innovations in offices (Proposition I) and a skeptical view of the specific personal consequences to be faced when technological change in offices occurs (Proposition III).

On one hand, a large majority of managers and secretaries (80 percent) articulate a positive opinion on new office technology in general, especially on its contribution to more effective task performance. A majority (52 percent) do not fear substitution of their labor or major dequalifications of jobs. At the same time, higher educational requirements to be met in order to cope with technological changes are expected (70-80 percent).

On the other hand, there exists a widespread fear of unfavorable consequences for respondents' own work situation. Most (60 percent) are afraid of increasing impersonal work atmosphere, augmentation of written communication, and growing bureaucratic structures, all caused by new office technology.

These findings seem valid, since they were obtained in an organizational environment already well equipped with decentralized office technology allowing individuals to base their judgments on analogous experiences.

Following the first preliminary results from a factor-analysis (PCA with VARIMAX-rotation) no clear attribution was to be found whether the expectation of increasing written communication would be related to the expectation of increasing impersonal cooperation or to the expectation of better task performance. (The preceding factor-analysis as well as all following were computed by the SPSS subroutine "FACTOR." Further details about these analyses are available on request.)

Choice of Communication Channels

COGNITIVE DETERMINANTS OF CHANNEL SELECTION

In a first step we put together a list with possible work-related problems faced by organizational communication. These requirements had been collected from textbooks and discussions with practitioners. The list was extensively pretested, leaving twenty-one items which seem to have general significance as criteria shaping the process of organizational communication.

Then we asked managers to evaluate each requirement's general work related importance on a three-point scale. Figure 25.1 shows the results.

Unambiguity, speediness, exact wording, and reaching somebody seem to be the most important criteria to be met in order to solve communication problems in organizations. On the other hand, confidentiality and protection from faking do not play the role one would expect when following public debates in Europe.

In a next step we asked users to rate the six channels available to them (telephone, face to face, mail, telex, telefax, teletex) on a six-point scale ("1" being the highest rating) considering each channel's ability to fulfill the requirements mentioned above. First and still preliminary factor analyses (PCA and VARIMAX-rotation) of the data for each channel show that there might be four major factors involved when evaluating task-oriented functions of communication channels:

> Factor A: *Promptness* comprising items "speediness," "comfort," "capability of quick response," "transmission of small information volume"
>
> Factor B: *Complexity* comprising items "resolving disagreements," "transmission of unambiguous content," "transmission of difficult content," "certainty of reaching the wanted receiver"
>
> Factor C: *Confidence* comprising items "confidentiality," "protection from faking," "identification of sender"
>
> Factor D: *Accuracy* comprising items "exact wording," "capability of documentation," "easy processing by receiver," "transmission of large information volume"

These factors explain between 90 and 100 percent of the answer variance depending on the type of channel. Their order of contribution to variance explanation changes from channel to channel. Factor C, however, never exceeded a third rank.

```
very
important      1,0


               1,1   unambiguous understanding of content

               1,2   speediness

               1,3   certainty of exact wording/certainty of
                     information reaching the wanted receiver

               1,4   availability of channel/capability of quick respon-
                     se/capability of quick feed-back/transmission of
                     difficult content/short composition time

               1,5   easy processing by receiver/short transmission
                     time/resolving disagreement/capability of docu-
                     mentation

               1,6   identification of sender/transmission costs

               1,7   comfort/circular letters/transmission of small
                     information volume

               1,8   transmission of large information volume/
                     protection from faking

               1,9   confidentiality

less
important      2,0



un-
important      3,0
```

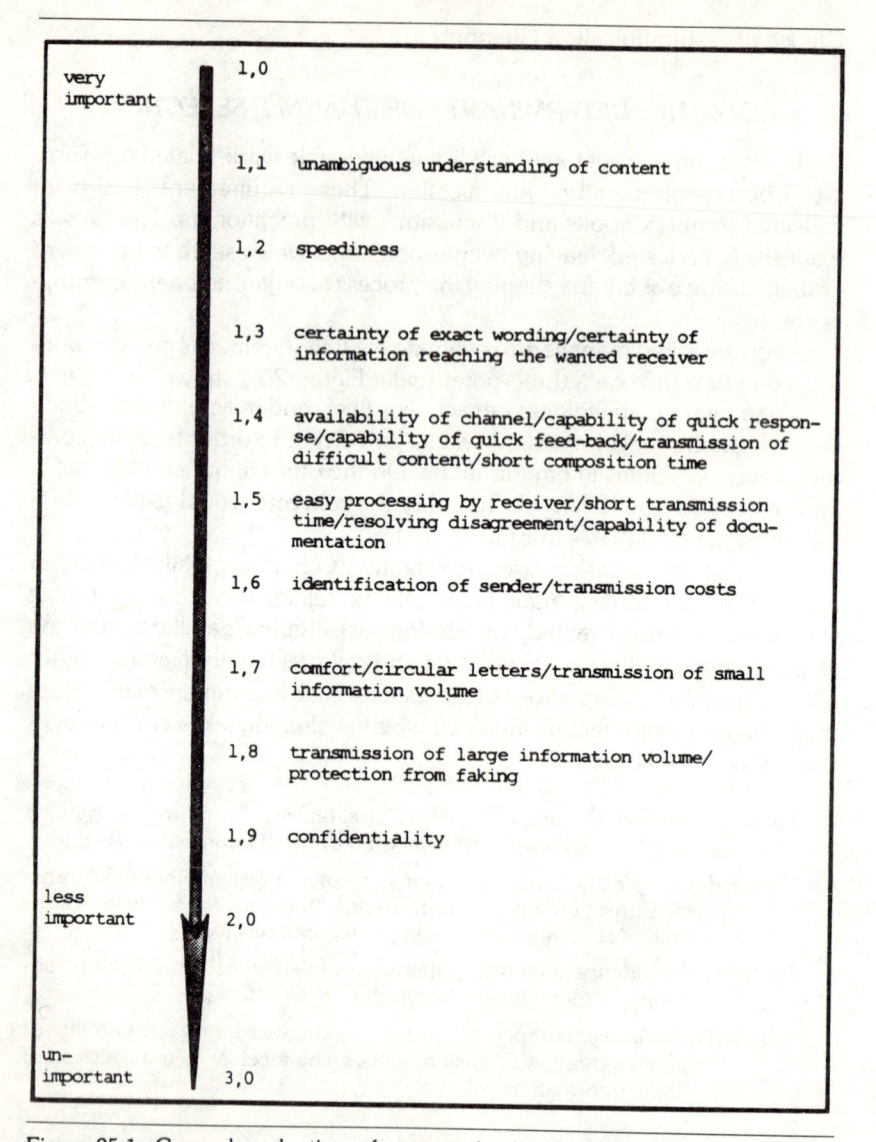

Figure 25.1. General evaluation of communication requirements by users (n = 477).

It is our contention that managerial promptness, semantic complexity, interpersonal confidence, and administrative accuracy represent four basic problems to be overcome by organizational communication. According to these factors we listed the communication requirements and their mean ratings with regard to each channel. This should allow us to find out possible channel preferences with respect to the four basic dimensions.

Office Technology

Table 25.1
Task-Oriented Evaluation of Communication Channels

Item Factor			Telephone (n = 326)	Face-to-Face (n = 316)	Mail (n = 337)	Telex (n = 328)	Fax (n = 332)	Teletex (n = 324)
Speediness			1.3	4.1	4.2	2.2	2.1	2.2
Comfort			1.4	3.6	3.5	3.0	2.6	2.9
Transmission of small information volume			1.7	4.7	3.5	2.0	2.4	2.5
Capability of quick response			1.4	2.9	4.5	2.5	2.5	2.5
Short composition time			1.3	3.4	3.9	2.8	2.7	3.0
Short transmission time			1.6	4.4	4.2	2.4	2.4	2.3
A	Promptness	weighted average	1.4	3.8	4.0	2.5	2.4	2.6
		rank	1	5	6	3	2	4
Resolving disagreement			2.1	1.2	4.0	4.0	3.8	3.7
Unambiguous understanding of content			2.6	1.6	2.6	3.2	2.7	2.8
Transmission of difficult content			3.0	1.5	2.8	3.8	3.0	3.1
Certainty of reaching the wanted receiver			1.6	1.3	2.9	3.1	3.1	3.0
B	Complexity	weighted average	2.3	1.4	3.1	3.5	3.1	3.1
		rank	2	1	3	6	3	3
Confidentiality (during transmission)			2.9	1.3	2.3	4.4	4.2	4.1
Protection from faking (during transmission process)			3.6	2.2	2.1	3.2	2.5	2.8
Identification of sender			2.8	1.5	1.9	3.0	2.5	2.7
C	Confidence	weighted average	3.1	1.7	2.1	3.5	3.1	3.2
		rank	3	1	2	6	3	5
Capability of documentation			5.1	4.9	1.5	2.1	1.6	1.7
Certainty of exact wording			4.0	3.2	1.6	2.2	1.7	1.7
Easy processing by receiver			4.3	4.2	2.0	2.4	2.1	1.8
Transmission of large information volume			4.3	3.2	2.2	3.3	3.1	2.2
D	Accuracy	weighted average	4.4	3.9	1.8	2.5	2.1	1.8
		rank	6	5	1	4	3	1

Scale: 1 = very good; 6 = very bad.

Table 25.1 condenses the results, also showing what order of channel preference was found if communication problems associated with one of the factors occur. When looking at the rankings the distances represented by the differences of the means should be kept in mind.

These rankings reflect managers' perceived effectiveness of channels with respect to each of the four basic communication issues. Tasks whose complexity or social characteristics (e.g., leadership) demand clarification and development of interpersonal relationships (Factors B and C) seem to require face-to-face contacts. In situations involving urgency, comfortable transmission, and less complex contents (Factor A), the telephone is preferred, followed at some distance by electronic text media and face-to-face contact. In communication situations where the information is well defined and subject to more or less programmed documentation or processing on the receiver's side (Factor D), text media are preferred, followed by face-to-face contact and telephone.

Though these results are produced by quite deviating methods, they are consistent with other theoretical and empirical literature of the field (Short, Williams, & Christie, 1976, p. 62ff; Johansen, Vallée, & Collins, 1978, p. 390f; Schulman & Steinman, 1978; Johansen, Vallée, & Spangler, 1979, p. 21ff; Rice, 1980).

AFFECTIVE DETERMINANTS OF CHANNEL SELECTION

The affective side of channel selection was covered by a pretested list of sixteen adjectives facing affective as well as cognitive components of attitudes. We asked managers to rate each of the six channels with respect to these items on a five-point scale, and we asked them to fill in the questionnaire in an emotional, affective way. After analyzing the data in factor analyses (PCA with VARIMAX-rotation), we came up with the following results — almost identical for all suborganizations investigated.

There are five basic factors (dimensions) describing and guiding emotional judgments of communication channels in organizations. These factors are the same for all channels, explaining between 87 and 100 percent of the answer variance. Their order of contribution to variance explanation changes from channel to channel.

Factor I: *Stimulation* comprising items "active," "creative," "happy," "energetic"

Factor II: *Comfort* comprising items "simple," "quick," "comfortable"

Factor III: *Dependability* comprising items "exact," "secure," "reliable"

Factor IV: *Formality* comprising items "standardized," "bureaucratic," "regular"

Factor V: *Privacy* comprising items "confidential," "personal," "secret"

We suggest that these factors represent relevant, mainly affective aspects of channel evaluation.

Table 25.2
Affective Evaluation of Communication Channels
(n = 241)

Factors		Channel					
		Telephone	Face-to-Face	Mail	Telex	Fax	Teletex
I Stimulation	weighted average	2.6	2.3	3.1	3.3	3.5	3.1
	rank	(2)	(1)	(3)	(5)	(6)	(3)
II Comfort	weighted average	1.4	2.4	3.3	2.4	2.1	2.3
	rank	(1)	(4)	(6)	(4)	(2)	(3)
III Dependability	weighted average	2.5	2.1	1.9	2.0	1.9	1.9
	rank	(6)	(5)	(1)	(4)	(1)	(1)
IV Formality	weighted average	4.0	4.1	2.9	3.1	3.2	3.2
	rank	(5)	(6)	(1)	(2)	(3)	(3)
V Privacy	weighted average	2.3	1.5	2.0	3.8	3.9	3.3
	rank	(3)	(1)	(2)	(5)	(6)	(4)

Scale: 1 = appropriate; 5 = by no means appropriate.

Table 25.2 shows weighted averages of the mean ratings of related items for each factor. For instance, the value of 3.3 for mail in Factor II (Comfort) is the weighted average of the values this channel received for the adjectives simple, quick, and comfortable in both organizations. With a value of 3.3 this channel is perceived to be somehow "not comfortable," as on our five-point scale, where five represents the lowest value (not appropriate) and one the highest value (appropriate). Thus values indicate to what extent related emotional aspects are attributed to communication channels. The circled figures indicate the ranking of a channel with respect to the evaluation features represented by a factor.

Whereas face-to-face communication ranks highest associated with Stimulation and Privacy, the telephone is highly preferred for Comfortable communication. Text-media score highest when Dependability and For-

Table 25.3
Breakdown by Channel and Communication Partner
(percentages)

Contacts	Channel					Total
	Telephone	Face-to-Face	Mail	Telex	Fax	
Intradepartmental	22	73	5	0	0	100%
Interdepartmental	53	28	15	3	1	100%
External	46	11	32	10	1	100%

mality are involved. Note the remarkable distance between text-oriented media and oral media on factors Stimulation and Formality, and also the by far leading position of the telephone on factor Comfort.

Finally, users were asked for an overall affective judgment on a six-point scale (one ranking highest) how much they liked using each channel regardless of the task or situation involved.

In all organizations popularity expressed for telephone and face-to-face contacts rank highest, with an overall mean value of 1.6 and 2.0, respectively. There is a remarkable affective gap between these two channels and the group of text-oriented channels, the first being mail (4.0) followed by fax (4.1), teletex (4.2), and telex (4.6).

It is interesting to note that the telephone ranks highest above face-to-face contacts. This may be due to its easy availability combined with its effectiveness for promptly carrying out a great variety of day-to-day communication (see also the importance of the telephone when situations with Factors A or II are involved).

Potential of and Demand for Substitution

In order to assess the potential of substitution between channels in organizations, we first need information about the distribution of channel use. Using a self-reporting measure, we studied some 16,000 contacts. Roughly, we found the following structure:

- average number of contacts per day: 30
- external/internal contacts:
  - 43% intradepartmental
  - 45% interdepartmental
  - 12% external
- distribution over channels (before implementation of teletex):
  - 39% telephone, 42% face to face, 16% mail, 3% telex/telefax
- contacts perceived as urgent: 40%

A breakdown by channel and communication partner for one suborganization is given in Table 25.3; other suborganizations show similar patterns.

These findings underline the enormous relative and absolute significance of oral communication in organizations, also reported by Mintzberg (1973, p. 38ff) and Weinshall (1979, p. 3). If the high proportion of telephone and face-to-face communication indicates that within the organization handling of the more difficult communication problems prevails, the findings seem consistent with Proposition II.

However, according to Proposition I, the high volume of oral communication could also point to a high potential of substitution if a large proportion of tasks, currently handled by oral channels, were efficiently replaceable by new text media (i.e., strongly related to Factor D). We therefore investigated possibilities of substitution between channels.

We asked managers experienced with new office communication technologies to give detailed judgments on possible replacement of their current use of oral and mail channels by electronic text and/or telefax, assuming that their communication partners disposed of the current technologies as well. They had to describe a number of recent communication events chosen randomly, and they had to give substantial reasons for their judgments. Results are presented in Figure 25.2.

Managers' judgments show that new electronic text communication media could replace about 4 percent of business trips, 9 percent of face-to-face contacts, nearly 20 percent of telephone contacts, and up to 60 percent of mail contacts. Thus new text-oriented channels could play a major role in replacing telephone contacts — especially if the high absolute volume of phone contacts is kept in mind — and in replacing traditional mail.

The main reasons managers mention for strictly denying the substitution of electronic text media for face-to-face contacts and business trips are: discussion needed, group meeting necessary, exchange of difficult ideas, and acquisition of background knowledge.

A comparison of perceived actual use of communication channels and wanted use can serve as an indicator of managers' demand for substitution. As Figure 25.3 shows, respondents still want more face-to-face contacts. They want the same decrease of telephone communication before and after experience with the new media. They demand a remarkable decrease of classic mail communication and an increase in use of fast new electronic text media. The latter reflects some good experience with the new channels, which offer relief from clumsy mail services and from the discomforts of other channels.

DISCUSSION

Watzlawick et al. (1967) show convincingly that any human communication process addresses aspects of information content *and* aspects of social relations between sender and receiver. Proportions of content-

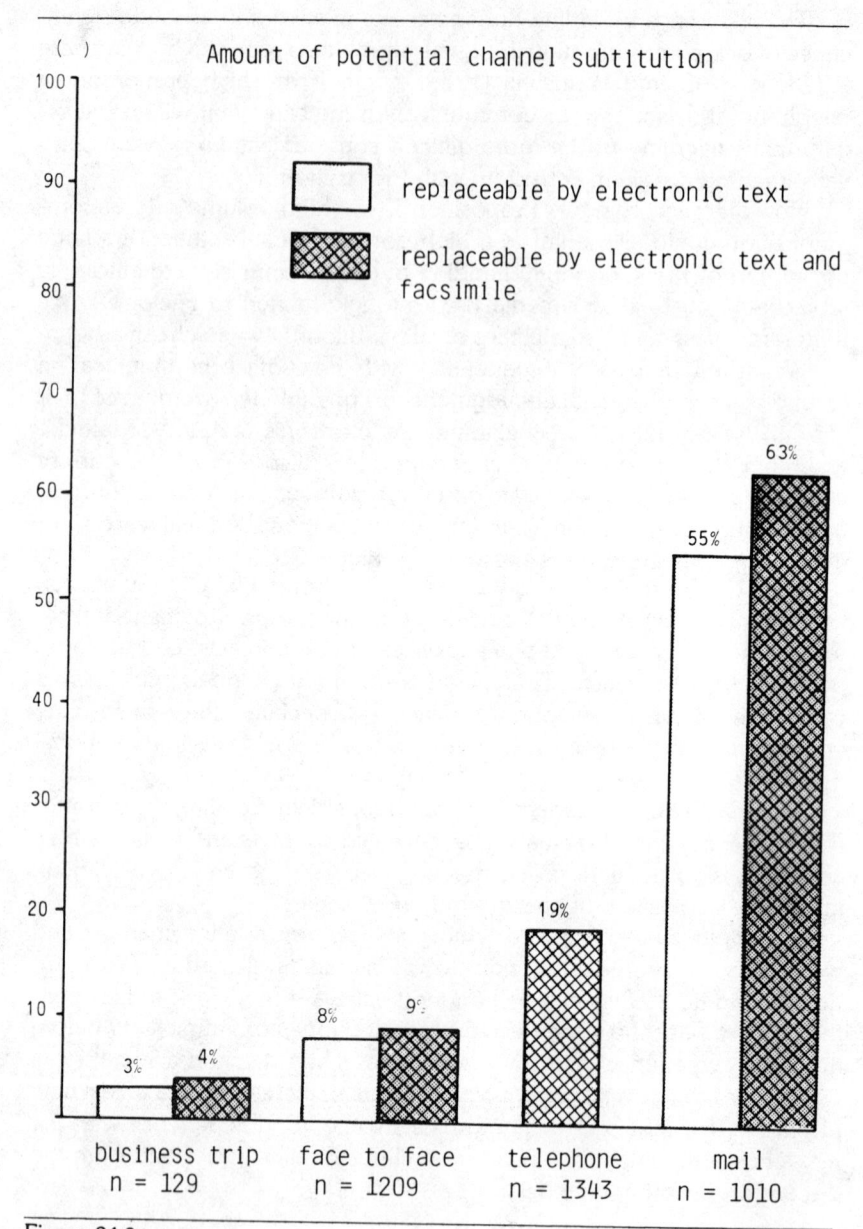

Figure 24.2.

oriented (task) problems and of relation-oriented (interpersonal) issues vary depending on contingencies. The authors further discern between two basic modes of communication: digital (coded) communication, mainly using languages and writing as tools, and analogous (symbolic)

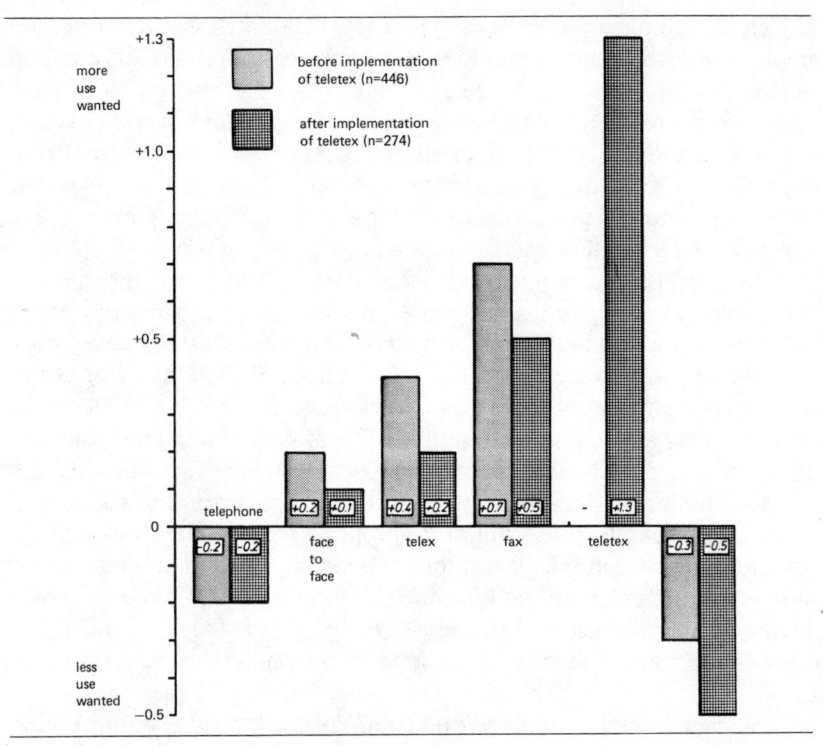

Figure 25.3 Mean differences between actual and wanted use of communication channels.

communication, working with nonverbal signals as means of message transmission, such as gestures, facial expressions, voice modulation, physical and environmental symbols, and other associative analogues ("metacommunication").

Whereas many matters of content (though not all) can be transmitted by coded communication, most aspects of interpersonal relationship (again, not all) require analogous communication. Coded (digital) information can be telecommunicated in cases where contents are not too complicated in the sense of social, value-oriented interpretation. Analogous communication eludes telecommunication for the most part and thus demands the social and physical presence of partners.

Looking at our research experience we believe these concepts provide a good basis for interpreting our results. Our findings about choice and substitution of channels seem to support assumptions underlying the above authors' as well as other authors' views (see Short et al., 1976; Baird, 1977). Referring to these theoretical and empirical foundations, one can predict impacts of new electronic text media confronting socioeconomic needs of organizational communication.

Telecommunication technology in general and new text-oriented media in particular can primarily take over those transfers of information which can be coded and whose content is not too complex. New technologies can carry out those communication problems faster, cheaper, and probably more reliably than channels previously used for that purpose. Hence they could replace old text-oriented channels (mail, telex). As far as telephone and face-to-face contacts were used for handling some of that kind of information exchange, they could also be replaced.

However, theory suggests, and our data indicate, that this type of information exchange does not prevail in organizational communication. The core of intraorganizational activity comprises processes heavily concerned with complicated contents or/and with social relations — for example, coordinating complicated tasks, solving complex problems, developing innovative strategies, monitoring and evaluating hardly tangible performances, and motivating people. Those and similar activities involve complex contents. Moreover, they affect and require trusting social relations. Consequently, they cannot be properly maintained by using telecommunication technology. In this context it is worth noting that in Japanese companies whose efficiency is, inter alia, attributed to a high degree of mutual trust and to the sharing of beliefs (e.g., Ouchi, 1980) face-to-face communication is reported to be remarkably high (Pascale, 1978).

Thus, the new text-oriented and technically powerful communication technologies will only partly keep promises — initially expressed in Proposition I — because much of the work-related information supply cannot be properly handled by the new media.

Our data on general attitudes toward new office technology show that some fears of the kind suggested in Proposition III exist. Overenthusiastic deployment of the new technologies, without taking account of the social character of organizational structure and performance, could be harmful. This would not only hinder individuals' need satisfaction, but in many cases the organization's viability would be endangered due to the social lifelessness of its communication structure and to its inability to adapt to change.

Underestimation of these problems can be avoided if an open, participatory planning and implementation strategy of new communication technology for organizations is adopted. Favorable attitudes toward new office technology as such seem to guarantee a fruitful process of communication development.

To sum up, Proposition II seems to provide a good description of possible impacts new communication technologies might produce. The extent of channel substitution outlined above will surely lead to improved organizational coordination and performance. The organization's information-processing capacity increases, thereby facilitating growth and regional expansion of activities. Some characteristics of office jobs will change along with the changes in text-oriented communication technology and its integration with EDP. However, as far as communication technology is concerned, and if the social and economic needs mentioned above are considered, there will be evolutionary rather than revolutionary impacts on people's way of life.

NOTE

1. This chapter was presented as a paper at the 32nd Annual Conference of the International Communication Association, Organizational Communication Division, Boston, May 2-7, 1982. It is a revised version of a paper presented at the EEC Conference on "The Information Society: Information Technology — Impact on the Way of Life," Dublin, November 18-20, 1981. This chapter draws upon a larger, ongoing, empirical project on office communication *(Bürokommunikation)* sponsored by the German Department of Research and Technology (Bundesminister für Forschung und Technologie). The research team for that study consists of two groups, one at Hochschule der Bundeswehr München, headed by Ralf Reichwald, the other at Hannover, headed by Arnold Picot. Cooperation with and support from the participating organizations (Allianz-Versicherung, Olympia/AEG/T & N, Siemens) are gratefully acknowledged.

REFERENCES

Argyle, M. *Social interaction.* London: Methuen, 1969.
Argyris, C. Management information systems: The challenge to rationality and emotionality. *Management Science,* 1971, *17,* B275-B292.
Arrow, K. J. *The limits of organization.* New York: W. W. Norton, 1974.
Baird, J. E., Jr. *The dynamics of organizational communication.* New York: Harper & Row, 1977.
Berger, P. L., & Luckmann, T. *The social construction of reality.* Garden City, NY: Doubleday, 1966.
Communication Studies Group. *The effectiveness of person-to-person telecommunications systems: Research at the Communications Studies Group, University College, London.* Long Range Research Report 3, 1975.
Feldman, M. S., & March, J. G. Information in organizations as signal and symbol. *Administrative Science Quarterly,* 1981, *26,* 171-181.
Goddard, J. B. Office communications and office location: A review of current research. *Regional Studies,* 1971, *5,* 263-280.
Goldmark, P. C. Tomorrow we will communicate to our jobs. *The Futurist,* 1972, April, 55-58.
Johansen, R., Vallée, J., & Collins, K. Learning the limits of teleconferencing: Design of a teleconference tutorial. In M. C. J. Elton, W. A. Lucas, & D. W. Conrath (Eds.), *Evaluating new telecommunications services.* New York: Plenum Press, 1978.
Johansen, R., Vallée, J., & Spangler, U. *Electronic meetings: Technical alternatives and social choices.* Reading, MA: Addison-Wesley, 1979.
Katzman, N. The impact of communication technology. *Ekistics,* 1974, 125-130.
Kirsch, W., & Klein, H. *Management-Informationssysteme II.* Stuttgart: W. Kohlhammer, 1977.
Marill, T. Time to retire the telephone? *Datamation,* 1980, August, 185ff.
Merrihue, W. V. *Managing by communication.* New York: McGraw-Hill, 1960.

Mintzberg, H. *The nature of managerial work.* New York: Harper & Row, 1973.
Ouchi, W. G. Markets, bureaucracies and clans. *Administrative Science Quarterly,* 1980, 25, 129-141.
Panko, R. R. The EMS revolution. *Computerworld,* August 25, 1980, pp. 1-12.
Pascale, R. T. Communication and decision making across cultures, Japanese and American companies. *Administrative Science Quarterly,* 1978, 23, 91-110.
Picot, A. Transaktionskostenansatz in der Organisationstheorie: Diskussionsstand und Aussagewert. *Die Betriebswirtschaft,* in press.
Picot, A., & Reichwald, R. *Untersuchungen der Auswirkungen neuer Kommunikationstechnologien im Büro auf Organisationsstruktur und Arbeitsinhalte — Phase 1: Entwicklung einer Untersuchungskonzeption, Eggenstein-Leopoldshafen.* Fachinformationszentrum Energie, Physik, Mathematik GmbH, 1979.
Pye, R., & Young, J. *Do current electronic office system designers meet user needs?* Paper presented at the Stanford University "International Symposium on Office Automation," March 26-28, 1980.
Rice, R. E. Impacts of computer-mediated organizational and interpersonal communication. In M. Williams (Ed.), *Annual review of information science and technology* (Vol. 15). White Plains, NY: Knowledge Industry Publications, 1980.
Short, J., Williams, E., & Christie, B. *The social psychology of telecommunications.* New York: John Wiley, 1976.
Schulman, A. D., & Steinman, J. I. Interpersonal teleconferencing in an organizational context. In M. C. J. Elton, W. A. Lucas, & D. W. Conrath (Eds.), *Evaluating new telecommunications services.* New York: Plenum Press, 1978.
Szyperski, N. Computer-conferencing — Einsatzformen und organisatorische Auswirkungen. In O. Grün & J. Rössl (Eds.), *Computergestützte Textverargeitung.* München: R. Oldenbourg, 1979.
Turoff, M. Human communication via data networks. *Computer Decisions,* 1973, pp. 25-29.
Uhlig, R. P., Farber, D. J., & Bair, J. H. *The office of the future. Communication and computers.* Amsterdam: North-Holland, 1979.
Watzlawick, P., Beavin, J. H., & Jackson, D. D. *Pragmatics of human communication: A study of interactional patterns, pathologies, and paradoxes.* New York: W. W. Norton, 1967.
Weinshall, T. D. General introduction. In T. D. Weinshall (Ed.), *Managerial communication: Concepts, approaches and techniques.* New York: Academic Press, 1979.
Weizenbaum, J. Where are we going?: Questions for Simon. In T. Forester (Ed.), *The microelectronics revolution.* Oxford, England: Basil Blackwell, 1980. (a)
Weizenbaum, J. Once more, the computer revolution. In T. Forester (Ed.), *The microelectronics revolution.* Oxford, England: Basil Blackwell, 1980. (b)
Williamson, O. E. *Markets and hierarchies: Analysis and antitrust implications.* New York: Free Press, 1975.
Witte, E. Die bedeutung neuer Kommunikationssysteme für die Willensbildung im Unternehmen. In H. Alback & D. Sadowski (Eds.), *Die Bedeutung gesellschaftlicher Veränderungen für die Willensbildung in Unternehmen.* Schriften des Vereins für Socialpolitik, Neue Folge, Bd. 88. Berlin: Duncker & Humblot, 1976.
Witte, E. Organisatorische Wirkungen neuer Kommunikationssysteme. *Zeitschrift für Organisation,* 1977, 46, 361-367.
Witte, E. Kommunikationstechnologie. In E. Grochla (Ed.), *Handwörterbuch der Organisation.* Stuttgart: C. E. Poeschel, 1980.

VI • INTERCULTURAL COMMUNICATION

INTERCULTURAL COMMUNICATION

26 • The Television Environment in Black and White

RICHARD L. ALLEN • BENJAMIN F. TAYLOR
University of Michigan—Ann Arbor

THE American public conceives of television in ambiguous terms. Television has received increasing attention over the years, but has been accorded decreasing esteem. People watch it more but enjoy it less. Many of its most adamant critics often fail to act in accord with their words. Television tends to hold its detractors with the same tenacity as it retains its admirers.

As opposed to the other media, television has most often been selected for examination because it receives the greatest share of people's free time (Baker & Ball, 1969) and because it plays the dominant role in the mass communication of ideas in the United States today (U.S. Commission on Civil Rights, 1977). As Comstock (1980) cogently points out, television has changed the way Americans spend their time. Generally, television is consumed as a medium, and the selection of what to watch is typically overshadowed by the decision to watch. That is, television is television first, programs second.

A considerable degree of passivity characterizes the television audience. However, this should not be interpreted as suggesting a homogeneous reaction to programming. Not only do amount of viewing and orientation toward the medium differ by social structural variables, but also the audience consists of distinguishable population segments (e.g., racial groupings). Television, it has been argued, might play a more important role in connection with various activities among blacks than for other groups. One reason, as often reported, is that blacks rely more on televi-

AUTHORS' NOTE: We would like to thank Dr. Howard Schuman for granting us access to the data from the 1977 Detroit Area Study. Also, we extend our gratitude to Dr. Duane Alwin for his useful advice and helpful comments. The authors assume sole responsibility for the contents of this chapter.

Correspondence and requests for reprints: Richard L. Allen, Department of Communication, University of Michigan, Ann Arbor, MI 48109.

sion for leisure and information and hold more favorable opinions toward the medium than do Americans as a whole (Bower, 1973; Greenberg & Atkin, 1978). Based on a considerable amount of impressionistic research but few empirical studies, television has been charged with having an effect on black self-esteem and, on a societal level, with intensifying social disturbances in the black community (e.g., Allen, 1968; Clark, 1972; Kerner Commission, 1968).

The comparison of the communication environment of blacks with that of whites has a long, if sporadic, research tradition. These studies may be usefully classified along several different dimensions (see Comstock, Chaffee, Katzman, McCombs, & Roberts, 1978): media exposure, or use of and attitudes toward the media, with media exposure receiving the most research attention.

Focusing on media exposure variables in general, the research has portrayed blacks and whites as relating differentially to the media (Bogart, 1972; Sharon, 1974). For example, Bogart (1972) analyzed a national sample of more than 15,000 adults, comparing the media exposure of whites and nonwhites. He found that the differences in newspaper and radio exposure between the two groups were primarily due to *differences* in social position and geography, but that television played a rather different role. In this instance, nonwhites were more frequent viewers of nonprime time television than were whites. During prime time, nonwhites and whites viewed television with approximately the same frequency. Bower (1973) found the same relationship when he compared blacks with nonblacks.

Concerning the dimension of attitudes and motives, again, most of the studies have indicated that media content preferences of blacks and whites differ. Generally, it has been found that blacks rely more on television as a source of information than do whites (Allen, 1968; Block, 1970; Greenberg & Dervin, 1972; Poindexter & Stroman, 1981).

Underlying the uses and gratification approach (motives for watching) is the assumption that a given medium has a particular normative character defined by what people expect from it. Although there are many qualifications, each medium's uses, and the gratifications derived from those uses, are different. This is so despite the fact that in individual circumstances any medium and any kind of content may serve almost any use or gratification.

The question may be posed: What is television's central character in our society? What is expected from it? Despite television being highly rated as a news source, its principal role as identified by the public is to provide entertainment and relaxation (Comstock et al., 1978). It has also been reported to be related to various demographic factors (particularly education) and to be differentially related to certain population groups.

Although the uses of or motives for attending to the media form an active area of research, seldom have black-white differences in the gratifications sought from the media been investigated. The overwhelming majority of the recent research in this area has confined itself to individuals' orientation toward political content in the media.

In summary, the commonly held notion that blacks have a substantially different exposure pattern and orientation toward television has generally been supported by the research studies. Nonetheless, several important issues have not been dealt with or have been dealt with poorly.

The available literature has been of limited comprehensiveness and has contained rather striking methodological shortcomings. The comparisons seldom have controlled for the lower socioeconomic position of blacks. Typically, the media behaviors and attitudes of a group of low-status blacks are compared to those of a group of whites undifferentiated on socioeconomic variables. Moreover, the majority of the studies *have* analyzed a limited range of media behaviors and attitudes (Lyle, 1967; Sargent & Stempel, 1968). Finally, most of the studies have not gone beyond description (Comstock & Cobbey, 1978).

Aside from the methodological shortcomings of much of the past literature, several important issues need attention. First, various measures of the media environment have been viewed as representing themselves or given a nominal definition which often leads to confusion. An alternative approach would be to treat these concepts as hypothetical constructs, only partially reflected in the operationalization. This would entail a theoretical definition of the different aspects of the television environment, thus providing meaning. It would be useful to set boundaries on these concepts so that a sense of shared meaning may be obtained. Moreover, when the various aspects of the television environment are viewed as several theoretical constructs, one is alerted to the possibility that several indicators may be used to tap its various segments. These indicators or operationalizations of the theoretical constructs permit measurement concerns to be more adequately addressed.[1]

In a similar vein, the issue of measurement error needs to be considered explicitly (see Allen, 1981; Allen & Taylor, 1981). That is, we need to discover the extent to which the various indicators are useful measures of the construct. Measurement error has not received a great deal of attention. Investigators have overlooked unreliability and other sources of error in their measurement instruments and, therefore, have not taken them into account in their analyses. Random measurement error can create grave problems in terms of parameter estimates. Errors of measurement in one variable have an influence on what item is related to another (Wheaton, Muthén, Alwin, & Summers, 1977). These measurement problems and their effect on estimates of substantive relationships are exacerbated in the case of comparative studies of media environments, where the possibility exists that they have a differential effect on the different groups. For example, it may turn out that the constructs have different meanings for the two groups, as reflected in the error structure of the constructs for the two groups. This may, therefore, distort the substantive relationships of these constructs with their predictors for either or both groups.

These issues may be formulated into the following research problem: What are the reliabilities of each of the indicators of the various latent constructs of the television environment? Are there different error structures of these latent constructs for the two groups (i.e., do these constructs have the same meaning for the two groups)? A corollary issue is whether important social structural variables have a significant influence on the television environment of the two groups, when measurement error is taken into account. *And* do the same patterns of relationship exist for the two groups? Even if they do, it may turn out that the strength of the relationship is different for the two groups. That is, do the different racial groups relate to television differently? Is there a race effect?

This study attempts to extend the thinking on black-white differences in their television environments by avoiding the limitations embodied in past research, which have militated against obtaining an adequate picture of these differences or similarities. The two dimensions of the television environment — exposure, and attitudes and motives — may be conceptualized as composed of three constructs. Television exposure is thought of as embodying total television and public affairs exposure. On the other hand, attitudes and motives are thought of as embodying gratification sought from that content.

While some researchers have viewed the concept of television exposure as addiction to television (Salomon & Cohen, 1978), television exposure is defined here as a social situation factor involving choice behavior. Thus the concept is defined in terms of the total content consumed (time-spent measure), without regard to the specific content — or, stated differently, as a medium-specific measure. Similarly, public affairs exposure is viewed as a choice among activities, but also as a choice among messages. To be exposed, then, is to be in a situation in which a decision is made, either directly or indirectly, to watch television instead of engaging in some other activity and to watch a particular type of *content* (Allen & Taylor, 1981). Public affairs exposure is viewed as a content-specific, medium-specific concept. Moreover, it is thought to be an essentially purposive behavior. As Levy (1978) pointed out concerning television news — one aspect of public affairs exposure — many people are "actively" oriented to the news. They consciously choose between competing newscasts, schedule their activities so as to be near a television set at news time, and pay close, although selective, attention to the program.

Gratification sought, a central variable in the uses and gratification approach, is defined as orientation of the audience members with respect to specific content. This concept is also content-specific and medium-specific and implies purposive behavior.

SOCIAL STRUCTURAL VARIABLES AND MEDIA ENVIRONMENT

Studies of large social systems have shown that there are small but persistent differences among socioeconomic status levels across a considerable range of variables. The problems of operationally defining and measuring socioeconomic status have occupied the attention of researchers much more than the question of why socioeconomic status is an important variable. In response to this trend, Rossi and Blum (1968) distinguished three major conceptual positions: (1) classes as subcultures defined by distinctive value patterns and differential association, (2) stratification as the differential distribution of resources and income, and (3) stratification as the distribution of prestige. Moreover, these three positions are generally assessed by a common set of indicators: occupation, income, and education. Furthermore the authors idientified three broad class processes considered to have varying, but important, implications for the generation of socioeconomic status-related attitudes and behavior. First, by definition, socioeconomic status levels differ with respect to income, occupation, and education, which have important, conceptually distinct effects on behavior and attitudes. Rossi and Blum called these processes the "direct effects of socioeconomic variables." The second set of processes, which they called "reactions to class position," were said to arise in reaction to the hierarchical and evaluational aspects of social stratification. Finally, they distinguished processes that tend to maintain and reinforce status differences, which they called, appropriately, "processes that maintain class differences." It is within the first basic, explanatory framework that we will operate in relating social structural variables to the media environment of blacks and whites.

The conception of the audience as individuals who relate to the media as members of groups influenced by their social environment has commanded considerable attention (McLeod & Becker, 1974). A long tradition exists in communication research of establishing the relationship between various social categories (socioeconomic status and background variables such as age and sex) and media environment, albeit not with respect to black-white differences. According to DeFleur and Ball-Rokeach (1975), the basic assumption informing this tradition is that people located similarly in the social structure have similar modes of orientation, which will predict their behavior toward the mass media. That is, members of a particular social category are conceived to have a more or less similar communication environment. This position, however, has not been thought to apply to blacks, especially with regard to media exposure.

Comstock (1980) noted that television exposure has always been greater among those with lower incomes and, particularly, lower education. Blacks, he stated, tend, on average, to view more television than whites when socioeconomic status is equivalent. The question still remains, however, whether the relationships of education and income to television exposure show the same pattern when the two groups are analyzed simultaneously. Allen and Bielby (1979) shed some light on this issue. While using only a black population, they found that the lower the education and the lower the socioeconomic status (the composite of occupation, income, and perceived social class), the greater the total television viewing (measuring television exposure over two points in time). Although there have been various operationalizations of the social structural variables with reference to television exposure as a time-spent measure, this same pattern has typically been found for blacks and the population taken as a whole.

In reference to public affairs exposure, Weaver and Buddenbaum (1980) reported, after an extensive review, that, in general, people with higher education and higher incomes tend to watch various informational programs more often than those with less education and lower incomes. Several other studies have reported that the older tend to watch more evening news (Comstock et al., 1978). Similarly, Allen and Taylor (1981), using a nationwide sample (hence a relatively small number of blacks), found that age was the only predictor of public affairs exposure.

Allen and Bielby (1979), using a sample of black adults, reported that those with higher education tend to view more public affairs programming, the relationship being much stronger for public affairs programming pertaining to blacks. But the strongest relationship was found between age and public affairs exposure: Those of an older age tended to view more often.

The difference in these relationships may be due to the differences in the way the concept of public affairs exposure has been conceptualized or operationalized. For example, in the Allen and Taylor study public affairs exposure was operationalized with respect to exposure to political content (a content-specific measure), whereas the Weaver and Buddenbaum (1980) review of public affairs measures focused on informational programs associated with network news and strictly public affairs programs (e.g., *Face the Nation, Issues and Answers*). Indeed, this is the more common approach to identifying public affairs exposure — one that does not refer to any specific content, such as politics. The measures used in this study are more attuned to this approach. Thus it may be concluded from past research that, with respect to public affairs as informational programming, whites who are older, have higher education, and receive higher income tend to watch more often. For blacks, however, the income variable does not seem to have an effect.

Although the uses and gratifications approach to communication is a flourishing research area, with gratification sought being a crucial variable, there have been no published studies investigating black-white differences in gratifications sought from television in general. Using only a sample of blacks and focusing on a content-specific area, politics, Stroman and Becker (1978) reported that highly educated blacks were more likely to use television to be reminded of their candidates' strengths, while low SES blacks were more likely to use television for interpersonal communication.

These studies on black-white differences in the gratification sought from such content at least suggest that social structural variables may have an influence. The exact influence of the variables for each group is yet to be determined.

Based on the above discussion, the following two major hypotheses may be presented:

H.1: For both blacks and whites, those who are older, those of a lower education, and those of a lower income will watch television more often, when measurement error is taken into account.

H.2a: For blacks, those who are older and those with a higher education will tend to watch public affairs programming more often, when measurement error is taken into account.

H.2b: For whites, those who are older, those with a higher education, and those with a higher income will tend to watch public affairs programming more often, when measurement error is taken into account.

The first hypothesis suggests that the pattern of the relationships for the two groups is the same; however, it does not refer to the issue of whether these relationships are significantly different across groups. That is, it is assumed that the same social structural variables influence the amount of time spent with television for both blacks and whites. Although not hypothesized, due to major methodological shortcomings of previous research, it has been suggested that the magnitude of these relationships will be different for the two groups.

On the other hand, the second hypothesis suggests that there are both similarities and differences. Most notably, the significance of income is hypothesized to vary across groups. Just as income does not seem to have an influence on blacks' views on major social issues (Caplan, 1970), research also suggests that it does not influence their informational use of the media.

For both of these hypotheses, it is assumed that the various constructs of television exposure have the same meaning for blacks and whites. Substantively, this implies that there is conceptual equevalence between the two groups concerning what constitutes exposure and gratification. There is evidence suggesting that certain communication constructs have quite different meanings for blacks and whites. For example, the comparison of black and white samples on their responses to the two-dimensional model of family communication patterns (FCP) revealed that the meanings of the items making up the scale were different for the two groups (Allen & Chaffee, 1977). Since these measures are much less associated with cultural antecedents, it seems reasonable to assume that the meanings of these concepts will not differ significantly.

The research problem may be viewed, partly, as an issue pertaining to error in measurement. With the recent development of confirmatory factor analysis and the more general model for the analysis of covariance structures, referred to as LISREL (Long, 1976), the measurement issues may be easily handled. These technical developments permit a separation of the structural equation model, which links the variables at the conceptual level, from the measurement model, which operationalizes the variables and provides empirical content with allowance for measurement error (Alwin, 1973). As a result of this separation, (1) measurement error can be minimized by estimating the true relationships among the conceptual variables, and (2) a relatively small number of structural models can account for a variety of relationships between the social structural variables and the various measures of the televison environment.

Different causal models may be in operation for blacks and whites. For example, television exposure may, in fact, result from different sources (social structural antecedents for blacks and for whites may be different and may have a stronger effect on the television environment of each group). To identify such differences, it is important to analyze each group separately and to make comparisons across groups (Madgison, 1979). The LISREL approach for performing simultaneous analyses across multiple groups is well suited to handling this problem.

RESEARCH DESIGN

The survey data were collected as part of the 1977 Detroit Area Study (DAS). The sample consisted of two independent samples of persons eighteen years of age and older in the Detroit, Michigan, SMSA. One sample was an area probability sample of housing units; the other was a probability sample of residential telephones. The sample of housing units used a subsample of the segments drawn in the 1976 DAS two-stage probability sample of housing units. The sample of residential telephone numbers was selected by a random digit-dialing procedure. The respondents, in both samples, were randomly selected from persons eighteen years of age and older in the household. The interviewing period extended from late April 1977 to July 1977. A total of 678 interviews were gathered — 325 in the housing unit sample and 353 in the telephone sample — constituting an overall response rate of 67 percent — 75 percent in the housing unit sample and 61 percent in the telephone sample. There were 139 black respondents and 523 white respondents.[2]

The social structural factors were (1) age — respondent indicated age at last birthday; (2) education — respondent indicated the highest level of education (in years attained); (3) income — respondent indicated the family income for the previous year; (4) sex — sex of respondent by observation; (5) perceived social class — an index of subjective social class based on responses to a series of items; and (6) occupational status — respondent indicated the kind of job or work performed for a living, coded according to Duncan's socioeconomic index.

There were three constructs — total television exposure, public affairs exposure, and gratification sought from television — representing the television environment. Television exposure was composed of the following indicators: (1) extent of television viewing — on a four-point scale, respondent indicated the degree of attraction toward television watching (y_1); (2) time spent with television — on a four-point scale, respondent indicated the amount of time spent watching television from 8 to 11 p.m. during weeknights (y_2). Public affairs exposure was composed of the following two indicators: (1) attention paid to public affairs information — on a four-point scale, respondent indicated amount of attention to public affairs in the media (y_3); (2) extent of watching news — on a four-point scale, respondent indicated the degree of attraction toward watching national news (y_4).

Finally, gratification sought was composed of the following three measures: (1) degree of watching television to relax — on a four-point scale, respondent indicated degree of watching evening television to relax (y_5); (2) degree of watching television for entertainment — on a four-point scale, respondent indicated the degree to which evening television was watched for entertainment (y_6); (3) degree of watching television for company — on a four-point scale, respondent indicated the degree to which evening television was watch for company (y_7).

Intercorrelations among the indicators along with their means and standard deviations are presented in Table 26.1.

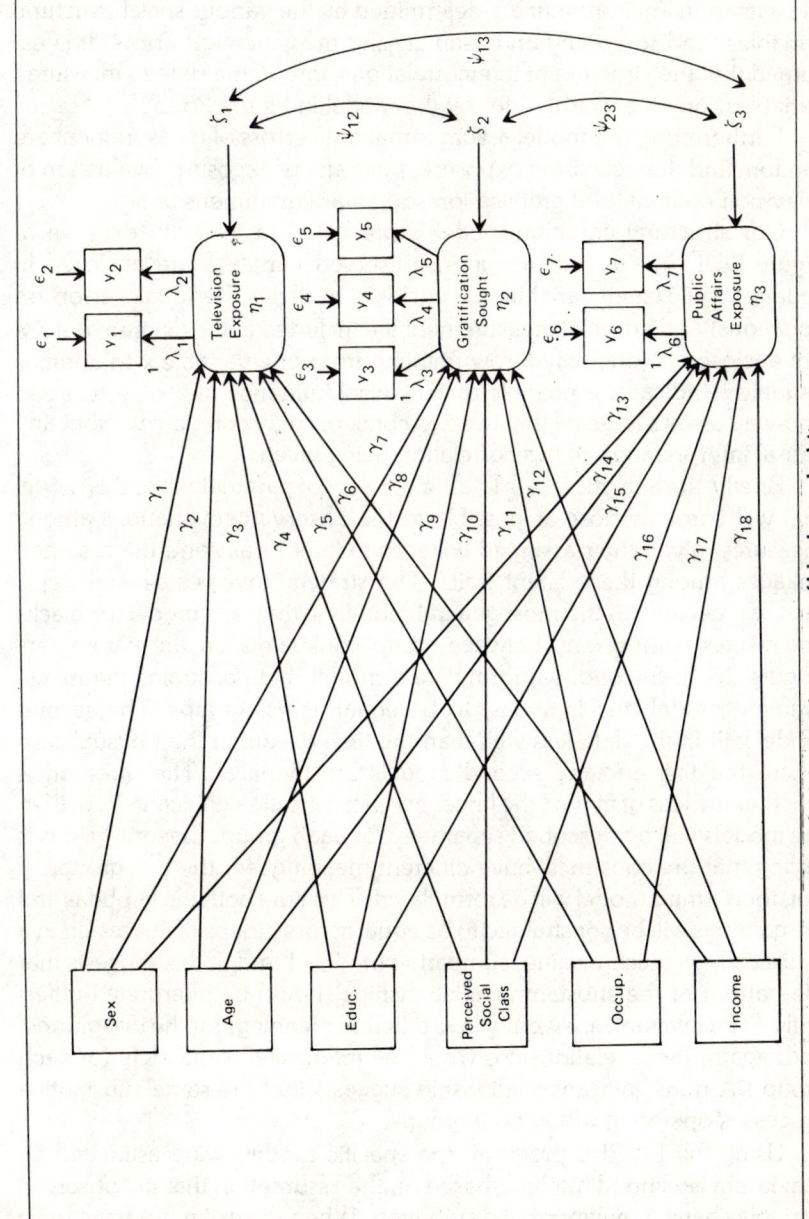

Figure 26.1 Model for the study of the television environment of blacks and whites.

ANALYSIS

A model was constructed to represent the process whereby variables of the television environment are determined by the various social structural variables, and to specify and estimate the measurement errors. It is assumed that the structure of intercorrelations among the sixteen measured variables can be accounted for by the model in Figure 26.1.[3]

Furthermore, the model assumes that only errors of measurement are random and that television exposure, pulic affairs exposure, evaluation of television content, and gratification sought are unidimensional.

Our structural equation model is presented in the path diagram of Figure 26.1. In this path diagram, observed variables are enclosed in squares, while latent variables are enclosed in circles. Residuals (errors on equations) and errors of measurement are included in the diagram but are not enclosed. A one-way arrow pointing from one variable x to another variable y indicates a possible direct causal influence of x on y. Curved two-way arrows indicate that the two concepts may correlate without any causal interpretation of this correlation being given.

Briefly, the analytic task is to estimate a set of parameters for this model that will come as close as possible to the observed covariations among measures, given their assumed linkages to latent traits and the assumed linkages among these latent traits. The strategy involves several steps. First, we begin with the most general model — that is, a model for blacks and whites without any between-group constraints on the parameters (Figure 26.1). Second, we formulate a model that constrains the measurement model (the lambdas) to be equal across groups. The second model will fit the data less well than the first, except in the unusual case where the first and the second models are identical. The question is whether the loss of fit (i.e., the larger χ^2) is statistically significant. If so, then the models will be described separately for each group. Essentially, this is saying that the constructs have different meanings for the two groups. If not, then a third model will be formulated. This time both the lambdas and the gammas will be constrained to be equal across groups. If this results in a statistically significant value, comparing models 1 and 3, this suggests that the pattern of the substantive relationships should be interpreted differently. (The relationships would have different meanings for the two groups, and, again, these relationships would be interpreted separately for each group.) A nonsignificant relationship suggests that the same substantive process is operating within both groups.

Using the LISREL program, the specific models were estimated by maximum likelihood method, based on the assumption that the observed variables have a multinormal distribution. When the estimates have been obtained, the information is used to determine standard errors for the

Table 26.1
Zero-Order Correlations, Means, and Standard Deviations for Indicators of Demographics and Television Exposure

	Variables	X_1	X_2	X_3	X_4	X_5	X_6	X_7	X_8	X_9	X_{10}	X_{11}	X_{12}	X_{13}
X_1	TV exposure 1	—												
X_2	TV exposure 2	.330	—											
X_3	Gratification 1	.316	.283	—										
X_4	Gratification 2	.364	.286	.455	—									
X_5	Gratification 3	.318	.331	.404	.396	—								
X_6	Public affairs 1	.022	.058	.044	−.023	.011	—							
X_7	Public affairs 2	.112	.287	.097	.136	.222	.448	—						
X_8	Sex	−.085	.074	−.012	−.031	.126	−.045	.136	—					
X_9	Age	.035	.179	.022	.001	.115	.291	.372	.048	—				
X_{10}	Education	−.073	−.153	.058	−.137	−.220	.062	−.145	−.068	−.377	—			
X_{11}	Perceived class	.039	.023	.020	−.058	.021	.072	−.018	.049	−.060	.350	—		
X_{12}	Occupation	−.009	−.023	−.034	−.216	−.104	.114	−.007	−.051	−.024	.475	.340	—	
X_{13}	Income	−.093	−.119	−.008	−.093	−.132	.001	−.194	−.149	−.262	.426	.320	.291	—
Mean		2.498	2.709	2.788	2.776	2.647	3.169	2.693	1.558	39.906	12.291	3.716	6.202	5.926
(SD)		(.749)	(1.057)	(.997)	(.795)	(1.096)	(.927)	(1.141)	(.497)	(16.532)	(2.851)	(1.592)	(2.710)	(2.091)

estimated parameters. The overall fit of the model may be assessed means of a χ^2 test (Jöreskog and Sörbom, 1978). LISREL can easily analyze data from several groups simultaneously, with some or all parameters constrained to be equal over groups (McGaw & Jöreskog, 1971; Sörbom, 1974, 1975).

RESULTS

It is assumed that the structure of intercorrelations among the thirteen measured variables can be accounted for by the model in Figure 26.1. It is assumed implicitly by this initial model that the structure of intercorrelations is completely accounted for by the impact of three latent constructs (television exposure, gratifications sought, and public affairs exposure) on their respective indicators and by the correlations among the latent constructs. Furthermore, the model assumes there is only random measurement error and that the various measures of the television environment are unidimensional.

The hypothesized model must provide an accepted fit to the data before the parameter estimates may be interpreted. Several judgments go into the determination of the adequacy of fit of any model: (1) the calculation of a χ^2 measure of goodness of fit; (2) the observation of the residual matrix (e.g., subtracting the observed correlation from the correlation reproduced by the parameter estimates); (3) the significance of χ^2 test of the null hypotheses that the observed and reproduced correlations depart within the range of chance variations; and (4) a helpful guide is denoted by the closeness of the χ^2 value to the degrees of freedom (see Kleugel, Singleton, & Starnes, 1977; Long, 1976; Maruyama & McGarvey, 1980). but as Jöreskog (1969) has pointed out, the ultimate criteria for goodness of fit of any model depends are its usefulness and the results it produces.

Table 26.2 presents the results from the analysis of our initial hypothetical model. For the white sample, the indicators for each of the respecitve latent constructs — television exposure, gratifications sought, and public affairs exposure — share a moderate amount of common variance, and each indicator is statistically significant. The component of each measure related to a common dimension varies considerably. Two of the latent constructs — total television exposure and public affairs exposure — show a wide range of shared variance. For the former the estimates are .57 and .67; for the latter they are .53 and .82. This suggests that the indicators are not equally useful as reflectors of the constructs.

Looking at the structural portion of the model, one notes that those who are older, those with a higher perceived social class, and those with smaller incomes all tend to watch television more often. Education, a

Table 26.2
Maximum Likelihood Estimates for Blacks and Whites
(model without constraints on any of the parameters)

Parameters	Blacks	Whites
λ_1	.567 (—)	.567 (—)
λ_2	.399 (4.059)*	.665 (8.148)*
λ_3	.639 (—)	.639 (—)
λ_4	.710 (5.792)*	.632 (9.949)*
λ_5	.641 (5.517)*	.633 (9.958)*
λ_6	.530 (—)	.530 (—)
λ_7	.883 (3.356)*	.818 (7.466)*
γ_1	−.126 (−.847)	−.025 (.433)
γ_2	.104 (.640)	.124 (1.935)
γ_3	−.259 (−1.495)	−.098 (−1.273)
γ_4	.265 (1.812)	.143 (2.178)*
γ_5	.077 (.524)	.046 (.680)
γ_6	−.097 (−.631)	−.137 (−2.039)*
γ_7	−.163 (−1.507)	.080 (1.481)
γ_8	.127 (1.085)	−.030 (−.508)
γ_9	−.145 (−1.168)	−.139 (−1.93)
γ_{10}	.027 (.263)	.163 (2.685)*
γ_{11}	−.131 (−1.239)	−.017 (−.269)
γ_{12}	.077 (.701)	−.096 (1.551)
γ_{13}	.088 (.908)	.099 (2.006)*
γ_{14}	.335 (2.521)*	.525 (6.566)*
γ_{15}	−.072 (−.649)	.155 (2.341)*
γ_{16}	.083 (.879)	.061 (1.124)
γ_{17}	.059 (.626)	.006 (.101)
γ_{18}	−.128 (1.242)	.087 (−1.559)
ψ_{12}	.835 (4.183)*	.734 (7.165)*
ψ_{13}	.454 (2.469)*	.215 (3.158)*
ψ_{23}	.300 (2.308)*	.145 (2.421)*
$\theta_{\epsilon 1}$	.532 (4.168)*	.717 (12.759)*
$\theta_{\epsilon 2}$	.768 (7.149)*	.610 (10.066)*
$\theta_{\epsilon 3}$	.592 (6.403)*	.592 (11.707)*

(continued)

Table 26.2 (Continued)

Parameters	Blacks	Whites
$\theta_{\epsilon 4}$	.497 (5.486)*	.601 (11.877)*
$\theta_{\epsilon 5}$	.589 (6.379)*	.599 (11.850)*
$\theta_{\epsilon 6}$	.793 (7.129)*	.699 (12.382)*
$\theta_{\epsilon 7}$	.428 (2.572)*	.284 (3.234)*
ζ_1	1.292 (2.922)*	.812 (5.020)*
ζ_2	.872 (3.530)*	.950 (6.660)*
ζ_3	.564 (2.227)*	.789 (5.511)*
χ^2 = 189.420		
df = 70		
p = .000		

Note: All estimates are standardized; t ratios are in parentheses.
—parameters fixed by program
* Statistically significant at $p < .05$.

variable hypothesized to have an inverse effect on television exposure, approaches but does not quite obtain statistical significance. As hypothesized, age and income do have an effect in the predicted direction; however, perceived social class has an effect not hypothesized.

For gratifications sought from television, only one social structural variable has a statistically significant effect: Those of a higher perceived social class tend to seek relaxation, company, and entertainment from television more often.

Finally, public affairs exposure is predicted by sex, age, and education. That is, males, those who are older, and those of a higher education are more likely to expose themselves to public affairs. Age and education show relationships as predicted, whereas, income does not. Instead, education looms as an important predictor.

The model accounts for 8 percent of the variance in television exposure, 5 percent in gratifications sought, and 26 percent in public affairs exposure. With the modest exception of public affairs exposure, these social structural variables do not seem to explain a substantial portion of the variance in these constructs of the television environment of whites.

Let us turn to the black sample.[4] As with the white sample, the indicators of this group's latent constructs share a considerable variance. Again, they are all statistically significant, with two of the same latent constructs showing a wide range in indicator estimates. The two indicators of total television exposure show a seventeen-point gap; those of public affairs exposure show a thirty-five-point gap.

An examination of the structural model shows that none of the exogenous variables has a statistically significant relationship with any of the latent constructs, save public affairs exposure. Here, age shows a strong relationship. Those who are older tend to expose themselves more often to public affairs programming. Although many of the relationships show substantial standardized estimates, the lack of statistical significance may be due to the relatively large standard errors — a function of the small sample size.

Before this model can be accepted, it is necessary to examine its fit, which is determined by the judgments outlined earlier. Calculating the χ^2 measure of goodness of fit, the value is 189.420 ($df = 70, p = .000$). The model, therefore, suggests a poor fit. The failure to reproduce the data, however, may be more of a matter of large sample size than of a substantial difference between the observed and the estimated models. A second measure of how well the model fits the data uses the difference between the correlations among the indicators (i.e., the S matrix) and the estimate of what these are for a particular model. Although not shown here, the data indicated a moderately good model, but one that could be improved on. The closeness of the χ^2 value to the degrees of freedom suggested that the model was adequate.[5]

Another question that needs to be addressed is whether a model that constrains the indicators of the latent constructs to be equal across groups will provide an adequate fit. This model implies that the constructs have the same meaning for both groups. It is assumed that there is conceptual equivalence across groups with respect to the television environment under investigation.

When we compare the change in χ^2 from model 1 to model 2, the difference is:

$$\chi^2 = \chi^2{}_2 - \chi^2{}_1 = 193.371 - 189.402 = 3.869$$

meaning that the difference in χ^2 due to respecification with four degrees of freedom is statistically nonsignificant. Thus it suggests that because it provides more information and an adequate fit, it is an improvement on model 1. It can, therefore, be concluded that the latent constructs, indeed, have the same meaning for the two groups.

As a further extension of the measurement issues, both the indicators of the latent constructs and the substantive relationship between the exogenous and endogenous variables are constrained to be equal across groups. This third model (Table 26.3) represents the issue not only of whether the two groups respond to the latent constructs similarly, but also of whether the patterns of the substantive relationships (the gammas) are

Table 26.3
Maximum Likelihood Estimates for Blacks and Whites
(model with constraints on the lambdas and gammas
to be equal for both groups)

Parameters	Blacks	Whites
λ_1	.567 (—)	
λ_2	.587 (9.324)*	
λ_3	.637 (—)	
λ_4	.651 (11.380)*	
λ_5	.632 (11.237)*	
λ_6	.522 (—)	
λ_7	.840 (7.913)*	
γ_1	−.059 (−1.083)	
γ_2	.122 (1.990)*	
γ_3	−.131 (−1.849)	
γ_4	.175 (2.908)*	
γ_5	.049 (.775)	
γ_6	.135 (−2.164)*	
γ_7	.014 (.299)	
γ_8	.017 (.321)	
γ_9	−.156 (−2.522)*	
γ_{10}	.129 (2.474)*	
γ_{11}	−.040 (−.732)	
γ_{12}	−.040 (−.738)	
γ_{13}	.097 (2.258)*	
γ_{14}	.478 (6.837)*	
γ_{15}	.100 (1.820)	
γ_{16}	.075 (1.626)	
γ_{17}	.022 (.461)	
γ_{18}	−.100 (−2.059)*	
ψ_{12}	.726 (4.417)*	.789 (7.822)*
ψ_{13}	.438 (3.136)*	.221 (3.137)*
ψ_{23}	.327 (2.724)*	.144 (2.481)*
$\theta_{\epsilon 1}$	.696 (12.130)*	
$\theta_{\epsilon 2}$	.638 (11.255)*	
$\theta_{\epsilon 3}$	.593 (12.036)*	

Table 26.3 (Continued)

Parameters	Blacks	Whites
$\theta_{\epsilon 4}$	.589 (11.816)*	
$\theta_{\epsilon 5}$	.610 (12.226)*	
$\theta_{\epsilon 6}$	.713 (12.794)*	
$\theta_{\epsilon 7}$	.250 (2.800)*	
ζ_1	.885 (3.226)*	.928 (5.471)*
ζ_2	1.026 (4.839)*	.944 (7.114)*
ζ_3	.604 (3.002)*	.796 (5.729)*

χ^2 = 212.431
df = 92
p = .000

Note: The lambdas, gammas, and theta epsilons are only presented for blacks, since the values are the same as those presented for whites. This is a result of specifying these to be equal across groups. All estimates are standardized; t ratios are in parentheses.
—parameters fixed by program
* Statistically significant at $p < .05$.

the same. Nothing is being said here about the possible difference in magnitude of estimates across groups, which may, indeed, be large and statistically significant. Rather, the attention is being placed on the similarity in the patterns of the substantive relationship across groups.

Before interpreting the estimates, the task of investigating fit is in order. Comparing model 1 (the one with no constraints on the parameters) and model 3 (the one with equality constraints for the lambdas and the gammas), we find the difference in the ratio, χ^2/df, for two models to be: χ^2 = 33.01 with 22 df, which is statistically nonsignificant. This suggests that there is no improvement in fit from the nonconstrained to the constrained model. The constrained model provides more information to examine our hypotheses; therefore, it is to be preferred. That is, it minimizes the effect of difference in the standard errors.

Although this model is preferred over the previous models, it is useful to determine whether it provides a good fit in and of itself. The chi square shows a value of 212.430 (df = 90, p = .000), which suggests that the model does not completely reproduce the S matrix. Especially with the large samples, this measure should be used primarily as a guide rather than a rule (Maruyama & McGarvey, 1980). Focusing on the other criteria of goodness of fit, a different picture is depicted. A second measure of how well the model fits the data uses the difference between the actual correlations (i.e., the S matrix) and estimation of what these are for this model.

Table 26.4
Estimated Reliabilities of Television Environment Measures

	Model 1	Model 3
Whites		
Extent of TV viewing	.28	.32
Time spent with TV	.39	.35
Attention paid to public affairs	.30	.29
Extent of watching news	.72	.75
Watching TV to relax	.40	.40
Watching TV for entertainment	.40	.42
Watching TV for company	.40	.39
Blacks		
Extent of TV viewing	.46	.33
Time spent with TV	.30	.34
Attention paid to public affairs	.21	.22
Extent of watching news	.57	.61
Watching TV to relax	.41	.43
Watching TV for entertainment	.50	.46
Watching TV for company	.59	.43

Inspection of these correlations (not shown) indicates a good fit. Virtually all of the correlations between the empirical measures are accounted for. Moreover, a useful guide is denoted by the closeness of the χ^2 value to the degrees of freedom. This ratio is 2.2 — substantially below the ratio of 5 suggested by Wheaton et al. (1977) as adequate.

As with model 1, the indicators of the latent constructs show considerable shared variance, each indicator being statistically significant (see Table 26.2). Unlike model 1, only the public affairs construct shows substantial variability in the shared variance between indicators; the range is .522 to .840. This is also reflected in the reliability of these indicators. With the exception of one of the measure of public affairs exposure (extent of watching news), none of the indicators is highly reliable. Table 26.4 shows that the change in the reliabilities from model 1 to model 3 is greater for the black sample; moreover, the reliabilities of the indicators for both groups are quite similar. This is, of course, partly a function of the indicators being constrained to be equal, but it also reflects the similarity in the size of the residuals (errors) of the indicators for both groups, which were not constrained to be equal.

Since the gammas are constrained to be equal across groups, the interpretation of these relationships applies to both groups. Table 26.2 indicates that those who are older, those with lower incomes and those with a higher perceived social class are more likely to expose themselves to television. This is the same relationship found for whites in model 1. Again, the age and income relationships were predicted, but education did not show the hypothesized relationship. And as predicted, this relationship is found for both blacks and whites.

Focusing on gratification sought, those with less education and those with a higher perceived social class tend to seek relaxation, company, and entertainment from television. No relationships were hypothesized for the construct, that is, there was little basis for making predictions. No significant relationship was found for the black sample, but the importance of perceived social class was found for the white sample in model 2. For model 3, however, perceived social class had a significant relationship with education — a variable that did not have an effect on this construct for any of the previous models.

Males, those who are older, and those with less income tend to watch more public affairs programming. The relationships found for this model are the same exhibited for the white sample in model 1 (age was the only statistically significant relationship found for the black sample).

The amount of variance explained is still minimal, with, again, the greater portion of the variance being explained in the public affairs construct for both groups (26 percent for blacks and 24 percent for whites). Eight percent of the variance is explained in the television exposure construct for both groups. Five percent of variance in gratification sought is explained for the white sample and 4 percent for the black sample. The similarity in the size of the estimates of explained variance is partly due to the equality constraints on the indicators of the hypothesized constructs, but it also indicates the similarity in the size of the residuals of the unobserved dependent variables (zetas).

When one looks at the reliability of the indicators for both samples, it may be observed that the indicators for both groups show only moderate reliability, with considerable variability. This indicates that some measures are clearly better indicators than others of their latent traits, and this varies from one group to the other. For both groups and for each latent construct, the findings suggest that the indicators are not equally useful.

More information may be extracted from the available data that would have a direct bearing on whether there is a race effect on the proferred television environment variables, as reported by past research. Also, it would be useful to examine whether the magnitudes of the relationship — in addition to the patterns — are the same across groups.

In order to deal with the above issue, LISREL with structured means was employed — a general method for studying differences in factor means and factor structure between groups. To get at the issue of whether there is a race effect, the intercepts of the dependent variables for the two groups are examined.

By specifying the intercepts for the white sample to be fixed and the intercepts for the black group to be free, it is possible to determine whether

Table 26.5
Maximum Likelihood Estimates for Blacks and Whites (general model)

Variable	Constant	Sex	Age	Education	Perceived Social Class	Occupation	Income
Whites							
TV exposure	.000[f]	.043*	.020	-.006	-.033	-.001	.044*
Gratifications sought from TV	.000[f]	-.068	.032	.130	-.148*	.018	.093
Public affairs exposure	.000[f]	-.087	-.539*	-.177*	-.062	-.007	.082
Blacks							
TV exposure	.087*	.029	-.017	.033	-.041	-.010	-.002
Gratifications sought from TV	.510*	.174	-.174	.147	-.047	.127	-.066
Public affairs exposure	.447*	-.077	-.379*	.057	-.098	-.058	.112

$\chi^2 = 397.564$
$df = 126$
$p = .000$

Note: All estimates are standardized.
f = fixed parameters.
* Statistically significant at $p < .05$.

Table 26.6
Maximum Likelihood Estimates for Blacks and Whites
(model with constraints on the betas to be equal for both groups)

Variable	Intercept	Sex	Age	Education	Perceived Social Class	Occupation	Income
Whites							
TV exposure	.000[f]	-.025	-.139*	.128	-.115	-.043	.084
Gratifications sought from TV	.000[f]	-.009	-.006	.160*	-.131*	.037	.040
Public affairs exposure	.000[f]	-.078	-.507*	-.112*	-.080	-.023	.088
Blacks							
TV exposure	.087*	-.025	-.139*	.128	-.115	-.043	.084
Gratifications sought from TV	.510*	-.009	-.006	.160*	-.131*	.037	.040
Public affairs exposure	.447*	-.078	-.507*	-.112*	-.080	-.023	.080

χ^2 = 411.686
df = 144
p = .000

Note: All estimates are standardized.
f = fixed parameters.
* Statistically significant at $p < .05$.

the television environment for blacks and whites differ and, if so, in what direction. First, by looking at Table 26.5 it may be observed that the fit per degree of freedom (χ^2/df) indicates that the model provides a good fit and, thus, that the estimates may be usefully interpreted. The table shows that there is, indeed, a statistically significant race effect. Blacks tended to watch more total television and more public affairs programming than whites. Moreover, blacks were more likely than whites to watch television for relaxation, for entertainment, and for company. In other words, for all the television environment variables there existed a difference between blacks and whites.

To get at the question of possible magnitude differences in the substantive relationships, we modified the above model by constraining the betas to be equal across groups. Put another way, we constrained the slopes to be equal across groups. Table 26.6 shows the results of this model specification.

Comparing this model with the previous one, the difference is: $\chi^2 = 411.686 - 397.564 = 14.122$ ($df = 18$). The χ^2 differences are statistically nonsignificant. This indicates that the magnitude of the differences in the pattern of relationships are not different across groups. That is, the slopes are essentially the same.

Summarizing the findings derived from the models using structured means, it was found that there was a race effect on all the television environment variables. Furthermore, the effects of the exogenous variables on the endogenous variables were the same for both groups. There were no interaction effects.

CONCLUSIONS

Several major issues were raised in this chapter. Before discussing the substantive issues, mention needs to be made of LISREL. It has provided insights into some of the methodological problems of prior work. Due to the limitations of our secondary data we were not able fully to exploit the capacities of LISREL; however, the results suggest the value of LISREL as a statistical procedure for examining our model of the television environment of blacks and whites.

While we have not extensively dealt with the measurement error problem with our indicators, the findings indicated that the incorporation of measurement error is valuable. First, we were able to determine, by observation of the measurement model, the amount of error in each indicator and also the reliability of each indicator. Second, we were able to estimate the amount of error in our theoretical variables, thereby getting an idea how well they were measured.

Another advantage of LISREL is that it forced us to clarify the concep-

The Television Environment

tual reasons for interrelating measures. Using this technique, we have identified and defined latent variables that represent the "true" variables, which were only imperfectly measured by our indicators.

Furthermore, LISREL afforded us the opportunity to analyze the television environment of blacks and whites simultaneously. This was done while various parameters were assumed to be equal. In addition, we were able to have a single model that analyzed the relationships of various social structural variables to various television environment variables, rather than having to use a model for each theoretical construct.

A major finding of this study is that, for both blacks and whites, the same social processes leading to particular televison attitudes and behavior seem to be operating. In the case of the more complex or evaluative assessment of the television environment, this similarity may not exist as reflected in several past studies. Moreover, for the more basic attitudes and behavior toward other media and for different operationalizations of the television environment, these findings may not apply. If this turns out to be the case, it would be of considerable utility. It would set the boundaries on the findings and may assist in subsequent theory construction regarding either the strength or the direction of the underlying true relationship.

Income was related to public affairs exposure, but in the opposite direction, and in the same direction as found for total television exposure. Moreover, income seems to have a relationship with public affairs exposure for both blacks and whites; however, it was hypothesized for only whites. The interpretation presented for total television exposure also seems appropriate here. Since these findings run counter to the bulk of past research, support for this notion awaits further empirical verification.

In summary, the relationships predicted for television exposure have been essentially supported and other insights have been revealed. For the more specific exposure construct, public affairs exposure, only one of the predicted relationships received support. Because these hypotheses were based on past research that did not take into account measurement error, the possibility exists that the proferred relationships are a better approximation of the "true" relationship. As Andrews (1977) pointed out, without adequate knowledge of the error composition of one's measures, an observed statistic provides no really dependable information.

Contrary to the hypothesis, education did not have an inverse relationship with total television exposure. No obvious explanation may be given, since most studies, using similar if not identical measures, have found the hypothesized relationship. Although not hypothesized, a relationship was found between perceived social class and television exposure. This may be due to the fact that this variable is rarely employed in this area of research.

Also, counter to our predication, education was not related to the informational use of television. Sex, on the other hand, was not hypothesized, yet it showed a relationship to public affairs exposure. This variable has been used in several previous studies, including a few national studies, and generally has not yielded any relationship.

For both exposure variables, age showed the strongest relationship in the predicted direction. This is consistent with previous findings using only a black sample and a study with a nationwide sample for various exposure constructs variously defined (Allen & Bielby, 1979; Allen & Taylor, 1981). The findings suggest that older people expose themselves to more television no matter what the content may be. This is in keeping with the observation that older people tend to spend more time at home and to have more disabilities that curtail their opportunities to do other things. Since the exposure measures used represent more sporadic viewing, it may be the case that older people have the television on while confined to the house, perhaps, without paying much attention to the offerings. It is noteworthy that age showed no relationship to an individual going to television for relaxation, company, or entertainment, which, given what has just been said, seems to apply more to those who are older.

Our findings provided some support for our hypotheses. Those who are older and those of lower income tend to expose themselves to television more often, as predicted. This suggests that television viewing might be considered an activity most frequently engaged in by people who have less capability to entertain alternatives or exploit their leisure time.

Not only were the patterns of the relationships between social structural variables and the television environment the same, but the magnitudes were also the same for blacks and whites. Moreover, the amount of total television, the amount of public affairs exposure, and the degree to which certain gratifications were sought from television differed across the two groups. Rarely have social structural and race effects been examined simultaneously. The results of this research indicate that location in the social structure and race both have an effect on orientations toward television.

A caveat must be stated. Because the white sample is considerably larger than the black sample, the standard errors are larger for the black group. This translates into the white sample having a greater influence on the estimates. The possibility exists that different relationships may be obtained when the sample sizes are more equal. It should be kept in mind, however, that most of the past studies have reported findings based on quite different sample sizes for blacks and nonblacks. Future research should take into account the problem of different sample sizes.

NOTES

1. Explicitly treating the various notions of the television environment as abstract concepts that are fundamentally unobservable carries with it a challenge to confront problems of measurement error directly, since abstract variables may be measured only indirectly. By measuring an abstract concept with several empirical indicators, one can

gain information from the relationships among these indicators that forms the basis for various measurement models. Adequately specified models permit estimates of relationships between concepts to be "corrected" for both random and nonrandom measurement errors, which may be easily tested by maximum likelihood estimation techniques, provided they are identified (Sullivan & Feldman, 1979).

2. The response rates by race are only available for the personal interviews. Here the interviewer's observations of the race of the persons refusing interviews were used to measure the race of the potential respondent for the noninterview addresses. The response rate for whites (76 percent) was higher than for blacks (69 percent), a result that corresponds to the city-suburb response rate differential, since blacks in the sample reside almost exclusively in the city of Detroit.

3. In estimating model parameters, the values of one of the paths from the various latent traits to their respective indicators have been fixed at 1.0. This specification is necessary for purposes of identification and is implicit in analyses with constructs containing single indicators.

4. Since the sample of blacks is comparatively small, the coefficients for blacks will be comparatively unstable. Thus if there are not differences between the groups, it is difficult to determine whether this is because of the differential contribution of the larger group to the estimates or because in fact no differences exist. Conversely, when differences exist it is likely that the differences will be larger with equally weighted samples (i.e., samples with approximately the same sample size).

5. The fit per degree of freedom (X^2/df) is probably a better indicator of overall fit. The ratio of 5 has been suggested by Wheaton et al. (1977) as minimally adequate.

REFERENCES

Allen, J. H. Mass media use patterns in a Negro ghetto. *Journalism Quarterly*, 1968, 45, 525-531.

Allen, R. L. The reliability and stability of television exposure measures. *Communication Research*, 1981, 8, 233-256.

Allen, R. L., & Bielby, W. Blacks' attitudes and behaviors toward television. *Communication Research*, 1979, 6, 437-562.

Allen, R. L., & Chaffee, S. H. Racial differences in family communication patterns. *Journalism Quarterly*, 1977, 54, 8-13; 57.

Allen, R. L., & Taylor, B. F. *The reliability and stability of media public affairs exposure.* Paper presented at the annual meeting of the International Communication Association, Minneapolis, May 1981.

Alwin, D. F. Making inferences from attitude-behavior correlations. *Sociometry*, 1973, 36, 253-278.

Andrews, F. M. *Estimating the valid and erroneous components of survey measures.* Ann Arbor: University of Michigan, Institute for Social Research.

Baker, R. K., & Ball, S. J. *Mass media and violence: Staff report to the National Commission on the Causes and Prevention of Violence.* Washington, DC: U.S. Government Printing Office, 1969.

Block, C. E. Communicating with the urban poor: An exploratory inquiry. *Journalism Quarterly*, 1970, 47, 3-11.

Bogart, L. Negro and white media exposure: New evidence. *Journalism Quarterly*, 1972, 49, 15-21.

Bower, R. T. *Television and the public.* New York: Holt, Rinehart & Winston, 1973.

Caplan, N. The new ghetto man: A review of recent empirical studies. *Journal of Social Issues*, 1970, 26, 59-73.

Clark, C. Race, identification, and television violence. In E. A. Rubinstein and J. P. Murray (Eds.), *Television and social behavior.* Washington, DC: U.S. Government Printing Office, 1972.

Comstock, G. *Television in America.* Beverly Hills, CA: Sage, 1980.

Comstock, G., Chaffee, S., Katzman, N., McCombs, M., & Roberts, D. *Television and human behavior.* New York: Columbia University Press, 1978.

Comstock, G., & Cobbey, R. E. *Research directions for the study of television and ethnicity: Methodological considerations.* Paper presented to the Conference on Television and the Socialization of the Minority Child, Los Angeles, April 1978.

DeFleur, M., & Ball-Rokeach, S. *Theories of mass communication.* New York: David McKay, 1975.

Greenberg, B. S., & Atkin, C. K. *Learning about minorities from television.* Paper presented at the annual meeting of the Association for Education in Journalism, Seattle, August 1978.

Greenberg, B. S., & Dervin, B. *Use of the mass media by the urban poor.* New York: Praeger, 1972.

Jöreskog, K. G. A general approach to confirmatory maximum likelihood factor analysis. *Psychometrika,* 1969, *34,* 183-202.

Jöreskog, K. G., & Sörbom, D. *LISREL IV: Analysis of linear structural relationships by the method of maximum likelihood.* Chicago: National Education Resources, 1978.

Kerner Commission. *Report of the National Advisory Commission of Civil Disorders.* New York: Bantam, 1968.

Kluegel, J. R., Singleton, R., & Starnes, C. E. Subjective class identification. *American Sociological Review,* 1977, *42,* 599-611.

Levy, M. R. *The audience experience with television news.* Lexington, KY: Association for Education in Journalism, 1978.

Long, J. Estimation and hypothesis testing in linear models containing measurement error. *Sociological Methods Research,* 1976, *5,* 157-206.

Lyle, J. The Negro and the news media. In J. Lyle (Ed.), *The news in megalopolis.* San Francisco: Chandler, 1967.

Madgison, J. New models for group comparisons. In J. Madgison (ed.), *Advances in factor analysis and structural equation models.* Cambridge, MA: Abt, 1979.

Maruyama, G., & McGarvey, B. Evaluating causal models: An application of maximum likelihood analysis of structural equations. *Psychological Bulletin,* 1980, *87,* 502-512.

McGaw, B., & Jöreskog, K. G. Factorial invariance of ability measures in groups differing in intelligence and socioeconomic status. *British Journal of Mathematical and Statistical Psychology,* 1971, *24,* 154-168.

McLeod, J. M., & Becker, L. B. Testing the validity of gratification measures through political effects analysis. In J. G. Blumler and E. Katz (Eds.), *The uses of mass communications.* Beverly Hills, CA: Sage, 1974.

Poindexter, P. M., & Stroman, C. A. Blacks and television: A review of the research literature. *Journal of Broadcasting,* 1981, *25,* 103-122.

Rossi, P. H., & Blum, Z. D. Class, status, and poverty. In D. P. Moynihan (Ed.), *On understanding poverty.* New York: Basic Books, 1968.

Saloman, G., & Cohen, A. A. On the meaning and validity of television viewing. *Human Communication Research,* 1978, *4,* 265-270.

Sargent, L. W., & Stempel, G. H. Poverty, alienation, and mass media use. *Journalism Quarterly,* 1968, *45,* 324-326.

Sharon, A. T. Racial differences in newspaper readership. *Public Opinion Quarterly,* 1974, *37,* 611-617.

Sörbom, D. A general method for studying differences in factor means and factor structures between groups. *British Journal of Mathematical and Statistical Psychology,* 1974, *27,* 229-239.

Sörbom, D. Detection of correlated errors in longitudinal data. *British Journal of Mathematical and Statistical Psychology,* 1975, *28,* 138-151.

Stroman, C. A., & Becker, L. B. Racial differences in gratification. *Journalism Quarterly,* 1978, *55,* 767-771.

Sullivan, J. L., & Feldman, S. *Multiple indicators.* Beverly Hills, CA: Sage, 1979.

U.S. Commission on Civil Rights. *Window dressing on the set.* Washington, DC: U.S. Government Printing Office, 1977.

Weaver, D. H., & Buddenbaum, J. M. Newspapers and television. In G. C. Wilhoit & H. deBock (Eds.), *Mass communication yearbook* (Vol. 2). Beverly Hills, CA: Sage, 1980.

Wheaton, B., Muthén, B., Alwin, D. G., & Summers, G. F. Assessing reliability in panel models. In D. R. Heise (Ed.), *Sociological methodology.* San Francisco: Jossey-Bass, 1977.

27 • Attribution Theory: Implications for Intercultural Communication

PETER EHRENHAUS
Rutgers University

IN his seminal book, *The Psychology of Interpersonal Relations,* Fritz Heider (1958) presents the conceptual foundations of attribution theory, and he details the factors required for a causal analysis of the perceptual process: It is "through perception we come to cognize the world around us, a world made up of things and people and events" (p. 20). Heider is concerned with the factors comprising the perceptual experiences of people, particularly those experiences concerned with social perception, interaction, and relationships. Attribution theory has been described as the study of commonsense psychology, the study of how people perceive, organize, and assign significance to the objects and events in their phenomenal worlds. Several questions that attribution research addresses are significant for the study of intercultural communication. While the perceptual process per se is tangential, the consequences of social perception are crucial to the quality of intercultural interaction.

The purpose of this chapter is to present an overview of several issues in the attribution literature that pertain to the study of intercultural communication. The chapter will be developed in four sections. First, I will briefly explain Heider's causal analysis, discuss subsequent formalizations of Heider's views, and review some of the issues that have since been the subject of inquiry. Second, I will note some discussions of attribution processes in the intercultural literature. Third, I will indicate uses of attribution theory in building an explanatory system for intercultural interaction. And finally, I will discuss the implications of our current knowledge of attribution processes for intercultural training.

Correspondence and requests for reprints: Peter Ehrenhaus, Department of Communication, Rutgers University, New Brunswick, NJ 08903.

AN OVERVIEW OF ATTRIBUTION THEORY

Heider's Causal Analysis

Heider's theory is concerned with the entire stream of information processing that underlies the organization of social behavior, from social perception through the causal analysis of phenomenal percepts. His analysis of the causal stream begins with the distal stimulus in the environment. The perceiver cannot directly experience the stimulus; mediation of some form is required. This mediation may be basic sensory input or a report about the stimulus through an outside party or through direct communication with the stimulus (in the case of social interaction). Consequently, the perceiver directly experiences a proximal stimulus and forms a phenomenal percept. In communicative interaction, the perceiver and the other are causally linked through the mediation of communication. Once this linkage has occurred, the constructive, inferential phase of attribution follows.

The inferential phase can occur immediately upon apprehension of the proximal stimulus; causal information may be in the proximal stimulus, which enables the inference to occur concurrently with perception. The social consequence of the phenomenal percept is often immediately identifiable; the environment, just as quickly, becomes comprehensible and predictable (if not controllable). The inferential phase of attribution can also occur subsequent to perception, developing in a linear and rational manner. Novel and uncertain proximal stimuli often initiate controlled information processing by the perceiver. Familiarity with the percepts allows automatic processing. The result of this processing enables the continuation of organized social behavior.

Heider is concerned with the causal analysis of person perception and the process of interpersonal relations. Causal attribution is a fundamental human process upon which much of social perception and action rests.

Formalizing Heider's Conception

Jones and Davis's (1965) theory of correspondent inferences was a major effort to present Heider's ideas in a more formal manner. As Regan (1978, p. 209) articulates their viewpoint, "Making attributions is seen as a largely rational activity in which the perceiver integrates two kinds of information in arriving at an estimate of the locus of causality for an action: the particular behavior of the actor, and the surrounding circumstances."

Jones and Davis differentiate the attribution process into those pieces of information that are overtly observable and those that are only inferable. All we can observe is an action and its effects; from these data we make inferences. Inferences begin about the actor's knowledge of some

Attribution Theory

topic or event and about the actor's ability to act on that knowledge. Based upon these inferences, we assume an intention underlying the observed action. From the assumed intention, we can infer back to dispositional characteristics — causal traits — of the person.

The properties we must infer are analogous to courtroom evidence and inferences of ability, opportunity, intention, and causal responsibility. The analogy is limited, however, in that the social inference phase of attribution is based upon information that we perceive as salient and that satisfies our judgmental requirements; the rules of evidence we employ in the attribution process are far looser than those of the courtroom.

Kelley's (1967) formalization draws an analogy between the trained scientist's method of inquiry and that of the layperson, concluding that the causal inference process is performed similarly by both. His model views attribution as the end product of a rational process; the cause of an event or behavior is inferred following an analysis of the covariation of an effect and its potential causes.

The analysis of covariation is based on three factors: consistency, distinctiveness, and consensus. Consistency concerns the occurrence of the event in question across time or location. Distinctiveness concerns the absolute probability of the event. And consensus concerns the production of the event by other persons. Consider the following example. X says, "I loved that movie!" Is X likely to say this on many occasions and in many contexts? Is X likely to say this about other films? Are others who have seen the film equally enthusiastic? The attributor's own answers to these questions will isolate the apparent causal factors and the proper attribution will be made (i.e., the movie is exceptional; it is only X's opinion).

Unlike the Jones and Davis model, the Kelley explanation assumes that the attributor will base attributions upon accumulated normative data, as the scientist gathers aggregate data to make inferences about factorial influences in analysis of variance designs. Research has found support for Kelley's explanation (Kelley, 1972a, 1972b; McArthur, 1972, 1976), and contrary evidence exists to support the Jones and Davis explanation (see Taylor & Fiske, 1978, for one example). These differences will be discussed in subsequent portions of this chapter.

Actor/Observer Differences

Jones and Nisbett (1972, p. 80) argue that "there is a pervasive tendency for actors to attribute their actions to situational requirements, whereas observers tend to attribute the same actions to stable personal disposition." Observers are quite inclined to take behavior at face value, reflecting stable personal characteristics, while actors are "much more likely than observers to see those actions constrained by the situation" (p. 83).

Two explanations are offered for these differences. First, the information available to actors and observers may differ; differing data may entail different subsequent causal attributions. Second, the difference may be a result of the manner in which the information is perceived and subsequently processed; different facets of the event or behavior may be salient for actors from those that are salient for observers.

The first explanation rests upon the assumption that the actor has better and more information about his or her emotions, intentions, and personal history than does the observer. The unequal access to privileged information makes the actor better able to assess all of the causal forces underlying the behavior. The second explanation rests on differences between the actor's and observer's focus of attention. The observer sees the actor as the dynamic agent against a stable situational field. The actor, while in the situational field, does not see this, but rather looks out upon the action in which he or she is situated.

Experimentation has produced a number of results that support both explanations (Calder, Ross, & Insko, 1973; Snyder, Stephen, & Rosenfield, 1976; Storms, 1973; Taylor & Fiske, 1975). As Monson and Snyder (1977) point out, researchers should more properly investigate the circumstances under which actors and observers will diverge in their attributions of what is often called the "fundamental attribution error" (see Ross, 1977).

Inferential Processes

Several of the questions raised about actor/observer differences are resolved by focusing upon influences in the inferential phase of attribution. Following the Jones and Davis explanation of inference making, Taylor and Fiske (1978) find that attributors repeatedly violate the normative requirements of information that underlie Kelley's (1967) explanation. Frequently, attributors will cease searching for information once a personally relevant and reasonable causal explanation of the event in question is possible — once information is identified as salient.

The perceived salience of information is critical to determine how it will be used by attributors. Taylor and Fiske find support for the focus of attention explanation of actor/observer differences, noting that different information is vivid for perceivers depending upon where their attention is focused. Vivid information is distinctive, and the more distinctive the information, the more useful or salient it appears to be, whether or not it actually provides a valid explanation of the causal forces underlying the event in question.

Two important intuitive strategies attributors use to reduce complex inferential tasks to simple social judgments have been discussed by

Tversky and Kahneman (1974). Availability concerns how attributors estimate the frequency of a class, or the probability of an event, by their ability to recall a specific instance. A particular causal explanation is more likely to be given if it is available to recall; considering attributors' attraction to vivid information, this finding is not surprising. The principle of representativeness states that attributors identify an event as a member of a class of events because of superficial resemblances; these features are viewed as critical features, and therefore as salient. Again the result is that information derived in social perception will be used to make inferences resulting in causal explanations that are not valid.

The final inferential error I shall mention is the principle of negativity. Kanouse and Hanson (1972) find that attributors have a strong and reliable tendency to overemphasize negative information about the individuals being judged. Negativity biases are ubiquitous; negative information is perceived to carry greater weight than positive information because it is salient, a result of standing in contrast to standards of behavior and expections that emphasize the positive.

How can attributors stray so far from valid standards of inference making at times, and employ them so well at other times? This discrepancy appears to be contingent upon the mode of information processing (Schneider & Shiffrin, 1977; Shiffrin & Schneider, 1977). If the proximal stimulus contains the causal information, then attribution occurs as an automatic process, seemingly concurrent with perception. This mode of processing is consistent with the Jones and Davis (1965) correspondent inferences model of attribution; the inferential stage of attribution may result in a valid explanation, but it contains the seed of misattribution as well.

Consider the consequences of processing in the "wrong" manner. If a phenomenal percept seems familiar, we process automatically, applying our causal schemata — an organized set of categories that provides a framework for attributing causes to people and situations, and for making judgments about acceptable behavior — and we take inferential shortcuts. If the assumption of familiarity is unwarranted, inferential errors are bound to result. When we are aware of the uncertainties and difficulties in making attributions, we are more likely to proceed with inference making carefully, applying the normative approach described by Kelley (1967).

Attributors see what they expect to see (Zadny & Gerard, 1974). If they expect to encounter a familiar stimulus, they will take inferential shortcuts, selectively searching for salient causal information in the proximal stimulus, concurrent with perception. Misattribution of cause is a likely consequence under these circumstances. Attributors will identify salient features and make causal inferences based upon those features regardless of their actual utility.

Ongoing Behavior

Attribution researchers have largely ignored the question of how behavioral sequences are perceptually organized. As the weight of the literature indicates, the major focus is upon inferential processes in general, and with the differences actors and observers seem to demonstrate in their processing.

The inferential phase of attribution occurs subsequent to social perception, and as Heider (1958) indicates, causal information may be in the proximal stimulus. The perceiver may apprehend information about how to organize behavioral sequences concurrent with direct perception — prior to any rational, sequential inferential process.

Newtson's (1973, 1976) research indicates that causal information is available in the perceptual unit employed by the observer. Further, the units of perception an attributor uses influence the subsequent inferential process. These conclusions are provocative; they indicate that we make sense of ongoing behavior in apprehending the flow of behavior. If we segment the flow of behavior differently, our inferences about actors' intentions, expectations, and causal capabilities may differ.

In an early study Heider and Simmel (1944) demonstrated that identifying motive is a crucial goal in attributions of ongoing behavior. Motives are attributable upon perceiving changes — or break points — in the flow of activity. The meaning given to ongoing behavior is constructed by inferring reasons for the changes in activity from one break point to the next.

Ehrenhaus (1982) contends that causal information is available in conversation, the proximal stimulus, to the extent that norms constrain communicative options in the conversation. Attribution of cause (we may say that intentions cause conversational behavior) occurs concurrently with perception. As constraints lessen upon communicative options, causal inferences must be made. In this circumstance, actors and observers engage in the constructive process in divergent fashion, assigning different meanings to the ongoing conversational behavior they witness.

ATTRIBUTION PROCESSES IN THE INTERCULTURAL COMMUNICATION LITERATURE

The study of attribution processes and the study of intercultural communication are both relatively recent developments. While little research about intercultural communication has been based in attribution theory, the theory can provide explanations for information already gathered about intercultural interaction.

Detweiler's (1975, 1978) research examines the influence of culture on attribution. His work draws upon Jones and Davis's theory of correspondent inferences and upon Pettigrew's (1958) work in the uses of categories for classifying social judgments. The Jones and Davis model assumes that observers know the meanings of the behaviors they are observing; this assumption becomes more questionable in intercultural exchanges. The attribution process is also dependent upon the category width of the attributor. Broad categorizers are more likely to realize that one behavior may have multiple interpretations, and consequently, they will place less confidence in the attributions they make. Narrow categorizers are less likely to accept discrepant interpretations of seemingly recognizable behaviors.

Detweiler (1975) finds the inference process is influenced by whether an observer judges an actor as culturally similar or dissimilar. Narrow categorizers see culturally dissimilar actors as intending and responsible for negative outcomes; broad categorizers see the same actions as unintended. In general, narrow categorizers make stronger judgments about culturally dissimilar actors than do broad categorizers; both types judge from their own cultural viewpoint. The cultural dimension is central to this attributional effect.

In more recent work, Detweiler (1978) systematically investigates the possible relationships among culture, category width, and attributions. The conclusion here is that culture influences the attributor's category width, which in turn influences attributions. Specifically, when only behavioral data about an actor is available to observers, their cultural orientation has a major influence upon their attributions about the actor. As individual disposition information about the actor becomes available, the observers' approach to categorizing (narrow, moderate, wide) becomes an increasingly significant factor in the subsequent attributions.

Pettigrew (1978) writes about the relationship of ethnicity to distortions in the attribution process. He asserts that the variable of ethnicity magnifies the effect of the fundamental attribution error — that observers systematically underestimate situational and social constraints upon actors and overestimate their personal dispositions as causing actors' behaviors. Citing Duncan's (1976) attribution study, which found whites attributed negative acts to personal traits when the actor was black and to situational factors when the actor was white, Pettigrew indicates that for across-group perceptions, undesirable behavior will be attributed to the actor's dispositions, ignoring role requirements. Positive acts will be attributed to situational factors, to motivation (versus disposition), or to the exceptional characteristics that distinguish the person from his or her group. Pettigrew also draws upon the work of Tversky and Kahneman (1974) to explain stereotyping. Their work, mentioned previously, concerns the methods attributors use to reduce complex inferential tasks to simple social judgments.

Brislin (1981) also recognizes the importance of attribution processes. He echoes Pettigrew's observation that the cultural factor in attribution processes (personal causality of negative outcomes, situational factors in positive outcomes) explains interethnic bias. He further asserts that negative information is considerable more influential than positive information in attributing traits to individuals and groups.

Citing from Kelley (1967), Brislin states that the categories used to make attributions will be unstable, and thus susceptible to influence (which may result in stereotyping), to the extent that the individual (1) has little social support, (2) has poor or ambiguous information for making attributions, and (3) is confronted with problems that appear unmanageable. The implications for intercultural contact are clear. When uncertainty is high due to the poor fit of our cultural categories for attributions, we must seek out new stable and useful categories. We seek to reduce the complexity of inferences to simple choice judgments. Distinctive, unusual features are readily identifiable, become overrepresented, and are readily available to recall.

EXPLAINING INTERCULTURAL PROCESSES WITH ATTRIBUTION THEORY

What should this theoretical perspective suggest to scholars concerned with intercultural communication? First, it should suggest that the attribution process is ubiquitous, fundamental to the organization and interpretation of social life. Second, human information processing is a complex operation, spanning an environmental reality to higher-level psychological constructive processes of intention, expectation, and causal agents and agencies. Third, people demonstrate faults in their inference making in regular and reliable fashion. Fourth, knowing how and under what circumstances attributors are likely to err in their attributions, we can begin to identify those circumstances as they occur in intercultural interaction.

In this portion of the chapter I will try to answer the following questions: What can we safely say we know about attribution processes in intercultural communication contexts? What can we speculate about attribution processes in intercultural communication? What questions do we need to ask about how attribution processes occur in intercultural interaction?

Since attribution theory has only recently been applied to questions of intercultural social perception, we can say there is little we know firmly. However, what we do know is quite significant. Detweiler (1975, 1978) provides evidence that culture has a crucial impact upon the process of causal inference; the perceived presence of cultural dissimilarity will likely reverse the attributor's assessment of causal factors. What we need to determine with far greater accuracy at this point is what constitutes perceived cultural similarity or dissimilarity. Are certain constant criteria drawn upon by attributors in reaching such decisions, or do these criteria vary in some regular and reliable fashion? Further, should the question of cultural similarity be considered as a discrete or continuous variable when we investigate attribution in intercultural contexts?

Duncan's (1976) research indicates that attributors are much more likely to have their inferences influenced by the negativity effect given perceived cultural dissimilarity. Negative information about dissimilars will be overestimated in reaching conclusions about those dissimilars' intentions and causal dispositions. Perhaps ethnocentrism does not simply influence higher cognitive processes; it may be a factor operating directly in social perception.

As Brislin (1981) and Pettigrew (1978) note, the problems associated with inferential error are likely to be operating in intercultural interaction; these problems have been thoroughly tested only within the dominant North American cultural group. These factors are perceived salience of information, the availability of certain information in memory, and the perceived representativeness of certain social objects and events to a classification based upon superficial characteristics. Rather than accepting these problems as equally valid across cultures, such a proposition demands testing. All cultural groups may not be equally likely to make these inferential errors.

Some cultures may be less likely to make the fundamental attribution error, for example. Role-taking skill may play a key part. As Regan and Totten (1975, p. 855) indicate, empathizing may be a function of altering the "overall perspective of the observer, highlighting the causal salience of situational cues and making his perspective in general more similar to that of the target." If a certain culture stresses the value of role taking, we should examine experimentally whether their attribution-related skill of inference making reflects this preferred mode of interpersonal contact.

We do have other suggestive evidence that certain categories of classification are valid across culture. Ekman's (1971a, 1971b) studies of labeling facial expressions conclude that certain physical features are identifiable universally. This suggests the universal use of certain simple causal schemata. Certain classification schemes used to make other attributions may also occur universally. We need to explore what categories for inference making occur cross-culturally and to investigate the use of those categories. Even if certain categorization schemes are part of our genetic inheritance in cognitive processing, the application of such capabilities is likely to be culturally mediated.

Hall (1977) asserts that certain cultures are high-context cultures and others are low-context cultures. What might be the influence of this variable upon the use of category schemes or upon the identification of salient features of the environment? We might speculate that in high-context cultures, the role of salience is particularly exaggerated since social cues are embedded in the context. Furthermore we might speculate that individual deviation from prescribed behavior in high-context cultures would be overattributed to personal causality, since the context seems to provide such a wealth of cues regarding the proper social script to follow.

We have no information about the attribution process in ongoing intercultural communication. Newtson's (1973, 1976) work indicates that differing units of perception can be applied by observers to the same social object, and that this will have implications for the directions the inferential phase of attribution will take. If units of perceptions vary with a culture, then they are likely to vary as well between cultures.

A number of questions become significant for intercultural communication scholars. Are certain cultures more homogeneous in their application of perceptual units in the analysis of ongoing behavior? Might Hall's distinction of high and low context be an explanation? What difficulties are likely to arise when intercultural communicators use different units of perception in conversation? How will they attribute different intentions to each other's behavior? How will they misattribute the causal factors at work? Will these problems produce an identifiable class of dyadic communication dysfunctions distinctly intercultural in nature?

Finally, what are the particular difficulties associated with empathizing in intercultural communication? Is it simply a matter of the observer shifting the overall perspective to the actor's in order to appreciate better the situational causal forces upon the actor? Detweiler's work may provide significant clues about intercultural empathy. Broad categorizers recognize important differences between themselves and culturally dissimilar individuals; they make less certain attributions as a result. By trying to empathize, these broad categorizers would find situational forces impinging upon the dissimilar individual, but they would not be able to assess their significance with any degree of certainty. Narrow categorizers, who fail to make adaptations to cultural differences, would assess the actor's situational constraints by using ethnocentric criteria. Neither type of categorizer would actually be empathizing with the culturally dissimilar actor. Contending with this type of problem suggests training in intercultural communication, the topic of the final section of this chapter.

ATTRIBUTION THEORY AND INTERCULTURAL TRAINING

An intercultural training approach that acknowledges the importance of attribution processes in intercultural communication is the Culture Assimilator (Albert & Adamopoulos, 1976; Fiedler, Mitchell, & Triandis, 1971; Mitchell, Dossett, Fiedler, & Triandis, 1972). Using many of the findings of attribution research as starting assumptions about potential sojourners, the Culture Assimilator training program sets the following goals: to provide opportunities for persons to assess critically dyadic intercultural exchanges, to have persons make conscious attributions about the feelings of interactants (one of their own culture and one of the host culture), and to compare their own attributions with those made by host nationals. The eventual goal of the program is to allow sojourners to develop the cultural sensitivity to make attributions as the host nationals do.

The program uses brief stories that highlight cultural differences in the reasons for action and that represent scripts the sojourners are likely to encounter. The stories purport to have a best solution from the host culture's perspective, and this is the basis for assessing the quality of the trainees' judgments.

A major criticism of this approach is that many problems do not have one correct solution; the training program implicitly encourages trainees incorrectly to simplify their analyses of complex issues. The program happens to make legitimate the inadvertent tendency to reduce complex inferential tasks to simple social judgments. The host culture's criteria for inference making may be internalized by the trainees, but they are just as likely to take the inferential shortcuts offered by salience, vividness, representativeness, and negativity.

Brislin (1981) speaks to these shortcomings by suggesting that trainers relate trainees' causal schemata — the categories they use for making inferences about people and situations — to stereotypes and the subsequent inferential problems they cause. Stereotypes focus upon conspicuous differences between classes of objects; Brislin relates this facet of stereotyping to the problems caused by vividness. Stereotypes overrely upon the familiar aspects of social objects; this relates to the heuristic of representativeness. Stereotypes rely on sharp distinctions between desirable and undesirable personal traits; negativity of information and actor/observer differences in making dispositional attributions contribute to this facet of stereotyping. And stereotypes develop from attributors' using personally relevant information as salient to the judgment at hand; the problems of salience are clearly reflected here.

The Culture Assimilator approach can be used to develop intercultural causal schemata, or categories; trainees can be sensitized to the situational and social constraints on host nationals' behavior and to downplay assessment of traits causing hosts' behavior. The training program concerns the process of intercultural social perception, and not content about the host culture. Detweiler (1980) believes this approach is essential. Trainees must be led to focus on how they process information and upon how their expectations will influence what they perceive.

Specifically, Detweiler believes that trainees should attend to whether their causal schemata are narrowly or broadly based. Broad categorizers are likely to benefit from content discussion of cultural differences since they are more accepting of the position that the appearance of a behavior may mean different things. Narrow categorizers are likely to have greater difficulty, unless they can first accept and appreciate pluralism in social perception and social cognition. Perhaps most important, trainers must be concerned with the quality of the information they convey. Accurate information includes the caveat that people vary in their motives, their expectations, and in their inferential processes, individually, intraculturally, and interculturally.

Knowledge of attribution processes can be used to teach potential sojourners what perceptual and inferential pitfalls they may face and the need for vigilance in this regard. Unless properly constructed, intercultural training programs will just give trainees new information, which they will use to make the same perceptual, inferential, and behavioral mistakes, but in places and with people where the stakes are much greater.

CONCLUSION

My purpose in this chapter has been to introduce the major issues in attribution theory to an audience concerned with intercultural communication. While little contextual research using attribution theory has been conducted, the potential is great for pursuing such research and for using the results to improve the quality of intercultural interaction. Only recently do we find communication researchers appropriating the perspective of attribution theory (see Newman, 1981; Sillars, 1980). It is likely that its adaptation by communication scholars will grow in the coming years, now that the integral role of attribution processes in the process of communication is being appreciated.

Heider's (1958) articulation of the attribution process gives us a sense of the elegance of the faculties humans have for uniting the activities of perceiving, cognizing, and behaving into one moment, one experience. While attribution is a theoretical perspective that is eminently researchable, we must proceed cautiously, taking care not to fall prey to faulty inferential leaps that assume attribution will function in highly complex social interaction as it does in rather basic judgmental situations. Attribution processes seem to be central to our appreciation of intercultural interaction. Our understanding of intercultural communication can only be enhanced by pursuing careful inquiry into these processes.

REFERENCES

Albert, R., & Adamopoulos, J. An attributional approach to cultural learning: The culture assimilator. *Topics in Culture Learning*, 1976, *4*, 53-60.

Brislin, R. W. *Cross-cultural encounters*. New York: Pergamon Press, 1981.

Calder, B. H., Ross, M., & Insko, C. A. Attitude change and attitude attribution: Effects of incentive, choice, competence, and consequences. *Journal of Personality and Social Psychology*, 1973, *25*, 84-99.

Detweiler, R. A. On inferring the intentions of a person from another culture. *Journal of Personality*, 1975, *43*, 591-611.

Detweiler, R. A. Culture, category width, and attributions: A model-building approach to the reasons for cultural effects. *Journal of Cross-Cultural Psychology*, 1978, *9*, 259-284.

Detweiler, R. A. Intercultural interaction and the categorization process: A conceptual analysis and behavioral outcome. *International Journal of Intercultural Relations*, 1980, *4*, 275-293.

Duncan, B. L. Differential social penetration and attribution of intergroup violence: Testing and lower limits of stereotyping of blacks. *Journal of Personality and Social Psychology*, 1976, *34*, 590-598.

Ehrenhaus, P. *Actors, observers, and the attribution of intent in conversation.* Paper presented at the annual meeting of the International Communication Association, Boston, 1982.

Ekman, P. Constants across cultures in the face and emotion. *Journal of Personality and Social Psychology*, 1971, *17*, 124-129. (a)

Ekman, P. Universals and cultural differences in facial expression of emotion. In J. Cole (Ed.), *Nebraska symposium on motivation*. Lincoln: University of Nebraska Press, 1971. (b)

Fiedler, F., Mitchell, T., & Triandis, H. Culture assimilator: An approach to cross-cultural training. *Journal of Applied Psychology*, 1971, *55*, 95-102.

Hall, E. T., *Beyond culture*. Garden City, NY: Doubleday, 1977.

Heider, F. *Psychology of interpersonal relations*. New York: John Wiley, 1958.

Heider, F., & Simmel, M. Experimental study of apparent behavior. *American Journal of Psychology*, 1944, *57*, 243-259.

Jones, E. E., & Davis, K. From acts to dispositions: The attribution process in person perception. In L. Berkowitz (Ed.), *Advances in experimental social psychology* (Vol. 2). New York: Academic Press, 1965.

Jones, E. E., & Nisbett, R. E. Actor and the observer: Divergent perceptions of the causes of behavior. In E. E. Jones, D. E. Kanouse, H. H. Kelley, R. E. Nisbett, S. Valins, & B. Weiner (Eds.), *Attribution: Perceiving the causes of behavior*. Morristown, NJ: General Learning Press, 1972.

Kanouse, D. E., & Hanson, L. R. Negativity in evaluations. In E. E. Jones, D. E. Kanouse, H. H. Kelley, R. E. Nisbett, S. Valins, & B. Weiner (Eds.), *Attribution: Perceiving the causes of behavior*. Morristown, NJ: General Learning Press, 1972.

Kelley, H. H. Attribution theory in social psychology. In D. Levine (Ed.), *Nebraska symposium on motivation*. Lincoln: University of Nebraska Press, 1967.

Kelley, H. H. Attribution in social interaction. In E. E. Jones, D. E. Kanouse, H. H. Kelley, R. E. Nisbett, S. Valins, & B. Weiner (Eds.), *Attribution: Perceiving the causes of behavior.* Morristown, NJ: General Learning Press, 1972. (a)

Kelley, H. H. Causal schemata and the attribution process. In E. E. Jones, D. E. Kanouse, H. H. Kelley, R. E. Nisbett, S. Valins, & B. Weiner (Eds.), *Attribution: Perceiving the causes of behavior.* Morristown, NJ: General Learning Press, 1972. (b)

McArthur, L. Z. How and why of what: Some determinants and consequences of causal attribution. *Journal of Personality and Social Psychology,* 1972, *22,* 171-193.

McArthur, L. Z. Lesser influence of consensus than distinctiveness information on causal attributions: A test of the person-thing hypothesis. *Journal of Personality and Social Psychology,* 1976, *33,* 733-742.

Mitchell, T., Dossett, D. L., Fiedler, F. E., & Triandis, H. C. Culture training: Validation evidence for the culture assimilator. *International Journal of Psychology,* 1972, *7,* 97-104.

Monson, T. C., & Snyder, M. Actors, observers, and the attribution process. *Journal of Experimental Social Psychology,* 1977, *13,* 89-111.

Newman, H. M. Interpretation and explanation: Influences on communicative exchanges within intimate relationships. *Communication Quarterly,* 1981, *29,* 123-131.

Newtson, D. Attribution and the unit of perception in ongoing behavior. *Journal of Personality of Social Psychology,* 1973, *28,* 28-38.

Newtson, D. Perception of ongoing behavior. In J. H. Harvey, W. Ickes, & R. F. Kidd (Eds.), *New directions in attribution research* (Vol. 1). Hillsdale, NJ: Lawrence J. Erlbaum, 1976.

Pettigrew, T. F. Measurement and correlates of category width as a cognitive variable. *Journal of Personality,* 1958, *26,* 532-544.

Pettigrew, T. F. Three issues in ethnicity: Boundaries, deprivations, and perceptions. In J. M. Yinger & S. J. Cutler (Eds.), *Major social issues.* New York: Free Press, 1978.

Regan, D. T. Attributional aspects of interpersonal attraction. In J. H. Harvey, W. Ickes, & R. F. Kidd (Eds.), *New directions in attribution research* (Vol. 2). Hillsdale, NJ: Lawrence J. Erlbaum, 1978.

Regan, D. T., & Totten, J. Empathy and attributions: Turning observers into actors. *Journal of Personality and Social Psychology,* 1975, *32,* 850-856.

Ross, L. Intuitive psychologist and his shortcomings: Distortions in the attribution process. In L. Berkowitz (Ed.), *Advances in experimental social psychology* (Vol. 10). New York: Academic Press, 1977.

Schneider, W., & Shiffrin, R. Controlled and automatic human information processing: I. Detection, search, and attention. *Psychological Review,* 1977, *84,* 1-66.

Shiffrin, R., & Schneider, W. Controlled and automatic human information processing: II. Perceptual learning, automatic attending, and a general theory. *Psychological Review,* 1977, *84,* 127-190.

Sillars, A. L. Attributions and communication in roommate conflicts. *Communication Monographs,* 1980, *47,* 180-200.

Snyder, M., Stephen, W. G., & Rosenfield, D. Egotism and attribution. *Journal of Personality and Social Psychology,* 1976, *33,* 435-441.

Storms, M. D. Videotape and attribution process: Reversing actors' and observers' points of view. *Journal of Personality and Social Psychology,* 1973, *27,* 165-175.

Taylor, S., & Fiske, S. Point of view and perceptions of causality. *Journal of Personality and Social Psychology,* 1975, *32,* 439-445.

Taylor, S., & Fiske, S. Salience, attention, and attribution: Top of the head phenomena. In L. Berkowitz (Ed.), *Advances in experimental social psychology* (Vol. 11). New York: Academic Press, 1978.

Tversky, A., & Kahneman, D. Judgment under uncertainty: Heuristics and biases. *Science,* 1974, *185,* 1124-1131.

Zadny, J., & Gerard, H. Attributed intentions and informational selectivity. *Journal of Experimental Social Psychology,* 1974, *10,* 34-52.

VII • POLITICAL COMMUNICATION

POLITICAL COMMUNICATION

28 ● News Media Use in Adolescence: Implications for Political Cognitions

STEVEN H. CHAFFEE ● ALBERT R. TIMS
Stanford University ● Indiana University—Bloomington

NEWS about politics and government deals with a reality that is quite remote from the day-to-day world of the typical American child. Yet the opportunity to assimilate political symbols and labels is presented daily: the face of the president, the names of the parties, and the issue catch phrases can only be evaded with difficulty in the media environment of today's growing child. By preadolescence or adolescence, most youngsters have sufficient experience with political information for it to play a significant role in their cognitive orientations. Recent reviews (Chaffee, 1978; Kraus & Davis, 1976) have suggested the important role mass media play as agents of political socialization. As communication researchers it is equally important for us to specify the process by which young people learn to use the news media.

The central question addressed in this chapter is whether there is a systematic developmental progression in news media use patterns during adolescence. In addressing this question we will first seek to establish a prima facie case for such a model. We will then examine (1) possible antecedent factors, (2) other communication behaviors that might be functionally related, and (3) specific effects in the area of political cognition, all of which can help in evaluating the validity of the overall hypothesis that there is a functional ordering of news media use proceeding medium-to-medium in a cumulative fashion.

AUTHORS' NOTE: This research was supported by a grant to the first author from the Vilas Estate Trust and by a grant from the National Science Foundation for data collection: "Election Campaigns and Preadult Political Socialization," NSF Grant SES-7913435. Coprincipal investigators are Jack Dennis (Department of Political Science, University of Wisconsin—Madison) and David O. Sears (Department of Psychology, University of California—Los

ORDERING THE MEDIA USE LEVELS IN ADOLESCENCE

A statistical ordering of media has been noted for some years in studies of adult voters in national elections. Campbell, Converse, Miller, and Stokes (1966) emphasize that the flow of political information varies from election to election, from major to minor offices, and especially from one person to another. They also comment that these latter, individual differences form a regular pattern that approximates a Guttman scale. Most voters are exposed to campaign information via radio, and television is the next most common medium. Successively fewer people are reached via newspapers and magazines. The relationship between media tends to be cumulative, in that those who are reached by the print media are mostly reached by the broadcast channels as well.

We suspect that this empirical ordering among adults grows out of both functional and probabilistic factors that operate during the developmental period of late childhood and adolescence. Following the lead of child psychologist Piaget (1962), a number of communication researchers have theorized that the development of media skills during adolescence involves a progression from the "concrete operations" to the "formal operations" stage of cognitive development (Wackman & Wartella, 1977). Salomon (1979) has focused particularly on the importance in this period of the acquisition of the sophisticated cognitive capabilities that are involved in reading. Reliance on broadcast media, he hypothesizes, in effect deprives an adolescent of the opportunity to practice the mental skills necessary to utilize print media fully. A consequence may be that some adolescents reach adaptation at the early levels in the cumulative progression across the various media, so that personal development does not proceed beyond radio and television as channels for political communication. Other adolescents, those who master the requisite reading skills, are able to extend their contacts with the political world further through the use of newspapers and magazines.

There are also clear differences between these two classes of media in the extent to which a person must be involved in order to attend to them. Radio and television exposure require little effort on a child's part, and they usually provide news in small, easily digested capsules. Many youngsters are often exposed to news via the broadcast media simply because it

---

Angeles). The authors thank Donald F. Roberts (Institute for Communication Research, Stanford University) for his thoughtful comments on an earlier draft of this chapter.

Correspondence and requests for reprints: Steven H. Chaffee, Department of Communication, Stanford University, Stanford, CA 94305.

"comes on" occasionally (a common situation for radio) or because "someone else turns it on" (typical for television). The use of printed media, by contrast, requires some degree of motivated and specific attention, and newspapers and magazines cover many news topics in much greater detail than the novice reader can comprehend. The earlier stages in a developmental progression, then, may in many cases be limited to broadcast media. Television, which is the most nearly universal of the media in terms of widespread public use, is the logical candidate for early news exposure. Radio, although an important source of news for many adolescents, is too variable in most people's opportunity for regular exposure to hold a predictable role in an invariant progression. We can consider radio functionally equivalent to television in terms of ease of consumption and simplicity of content. (Some theorists might argue that radio, as a single-channel medium, is more difficult to utilize than television, which transmits via both visual and auditory channels.) We might expect radio to predominate in use among those youngsters who have not yet developed regular patterns of television news consumption, or among those adolescents whose activities take them outside the home as they grow older.

Later stages in a hypothetical progression beyond broadcast media would consist of acquisition of the habit of reading a daily newspaper with some regularity, and perhaps of reading magazine articles about politics, too. The newspaper-magazine ordering is more likely to be found empirically than the reverse ordering (i.e., magazine-newspaper), even if for probabilistic reasons alone. Some three-fourths of households that contain young people receive a daily newspaper, while only about one-fourth receive a weekly news magazine. Whether the cognitive operations are more demanding for one print medium or the other is impossible to specify, as magazines vary from very simple to highly complex presentations of news and politically relevant content.

Our overall hypothesized ordering of radio-television-newspaper-magazine, then, can be broken down into two bodies of reasoning. First, there is an overriding expectation of a developmental broadcast-print sequence based on the assumption that print requires a higher level of cognitive skill and involvement, in addition to a fairly extensive knowledge base, for a person to establish a pattern of regular use. Second, within both the broadcast media and the print media there are empirical probabilities that encourage us to expect sequential dominance of specific media. Within the sphere of broadcast media use, television is the more ubiquitous medium and should be the first one most youngsters come to use regularly; those who do not should, in a sense by default, become more reliant on radio. For those who achieve the more advanced level, where sophisticated reading skills and a wider public affairs knowledge base have been added to the competences needed for broadcast news consumption, we would expect the newspaper to be the more common "entry" medium. Newspapers are more widely available and are received more often; their content also probably resembles that of radio and television somewhat more than does magazine content, making the broadcast-to-print transition that much easier. Of course, there will be cases where the "newspaper level" is bypassed (such as in families that do not subscribe to a newspaper), so that a transition may be made directly from broadcast media to magazine reading during adolescence.

Our conceptual model is cumulative in that attainment of each succeeding level presupposes mastery of those that precede it. Each of these can be thought of as a level that represents a stable pattern of behavior in itself. This means that a person at any given level may or may not be progressing to a higher level and should exhibit a pattern of associated behaviors that are appropriate to that specific level. In adulthood, we should find more mature adaptation behaviors at each of these levels, whereas many of those in adolescence should still be progressing toward a higher level, with some up-and-down fluctuations over time and by specific news topics.

SOCIAL DETERMINANTS AND COGNITIVE CONSEQUENCES

Our concern with news media use levels, while of inherent interest to the communication field itself, is greatly heightened by the implications it carries for the development of political cognitions (Becker, McCombs, & McLeod, 1975). Democratic political theory presumes a reasonable degree of citizen awareness and knowledgeability, and political information can seem imposingly complex to an adolescent. Beyond simple "itemized" cognitions such as the names of political actors or parties, there are a number of relations to be learned. These include associations between actors (e.g., candidates) and their parties, and the more enduring associations between parties and their established symbols and policy positions (Kennamer & Chaffee, 1982). In proposing a developmental progression of broadcast to print media, we are implicitly assuming that it is the regular use of print media that is more likely to enable a person to acquire and maintain these cognitive associations between the various elements of the political scene.

While these cognitive consequences will represent the immediate dependent variables in our analyses, the long-range effects of differential levels of media use can of course extend much farther; more deeply into the cognitive and affective realms, more broadly out into the society as one becomes politically active, and longitudinally into the person's future development. Our focus here will be on the validation of a progressive model of development of media use in adolescence and its immediate cognitive consequences. The full range of potential social and political impact is a much larger topic reserved for other studies.

Media use patterns do not simply "happen" to a person. They can be traced to social determinants that are rooted in both organismic variables (e.g., age) and structural factors, such as the family's socioeconomic status or parents' educational levels and patterns of news media use. Adolescent news media use is one among a number of interconnected elements of a person's daily communication behaviors, and these too can be divided between those that reside mainly in the adolescent and those traceable to factors in the social environment. Organismic behaviors grow directly out of active communication efforts on the part of an adolescent; among those that are more environmental in nature are parental initiation, facilitation, or encouragement of communication experiences for the adolescent. Both classes of communication, whether initiated by the adolescent or within the surrounding social environment, can involve either interpersonal or mediated forms of communication. From the viewpoint of the developing adolescent, the conventional academic distinction between mass and interpersonal communication makes little difference.

SURVEY DESIGN AND SAMPLE

The population for this study was defined as adolescents aged ten to seventeen in the state of Wisconsin. In early 1980 a random sample was contacted, using random-digit dialing techniques, by the Wisconsin Survey Research Laboratory. Following the adolescent interviews, which were conducted with approximately one hundred persons at each of the age levels from ten to seventeen, one parent of each was randomly sampled and interviewed by telephone. Of 782 adolescents interviewed, second-stage telephone interviews were completed with 718 parents; the final sample for the analyses that follow consists of those 718 parent-adolescent pairs for which we have full interview data (N = 1,436 individuals).

Geographical distribution was spread proportionately across the state by the random-digit dialing method. Sex ratios were also approximately representative, with 52 percent of the adolescent sample being males and 57 percent of the interviewed parents being mothers. (Within two-parent homes parents were selected randomly; single-parent homes mostly consist of the mother and children, which accounts for the predominance of mothers in the total sample.) Conduct of interviews by telephone produced some attrition, both in making contacts and in securing the cooperation of both parent and adolescent; the resultant sample is of somewhat higher socioeconomic status than the general population. Of the parents interviewed, 32 percent had attended college and another 53 percent had completed high school. Parents' ages ranged from twenty-seven to sixty-nine, the median being forty-one years.

Questions asked of the adolescent and parent subsamples were, insofar as possible, worded identically to permit parallel data analyses. Details of question-wording and statistical procedures are explained below in connection with each succeeding phase of the analysis.

GUTTMAN SCALE ANALYSIS OF NEWS MEDIA USE

Scalogram analysis, introduced by Guttman and others (Stouffer et al., 1950), is a method of constructing a cumulative scale that incorporates a test of unidimensionality. Three measures of news media exposure provided the raw data for this basic scaling exercise: the number of days within the past week that the person had watched network evening news on television or had read a daily newspaper, and the number of magazine articles about national politics the person had read in the past week. After experimenting with various cutting points in preliminary analyses, we cut these at a minimum of two days per week watching TV news, three days per week reading a newspaper, and three magazine articles read. These were assumed to represent successively higher levels of media use that a given person might or might not have reached.

To test whether this set of news media use levels represents a cumulative, unidimensional scale, we performed separate Guttman scale analyses for the adolescent and parent subsamples. The results, summarized in Table 28.1, are quite supportive of our assumptions. For both subsamples, the resulting scales reach or exceed the conventional minimum levels of reproducibility (.90) and scalability (.60). While error types could occur because, for example, a person might no longer follow the news via television after reaching a higher level on the scale, error types are in fact relatively rare. One might expect by chance that only two out of five persons scored at levels 1 or 2 on the scale would be scale types, because only two of the five possible combinations of scores fit into the logic of the scale (see note to Table 28.1). Overall, though, five of every six cases at these two levels were a scale type. In terms of internal validity, then, the scalogram representing the hypothesized progression in news media use has passed its first test.

Preliminarily at least, we will label each successive level on this scale according to the medium we presume to predominate at that level: Level 0 is (by default) labeled "Radio," Level 1 "Television," Level 2 "Newspaper," and Level 3 "Magazine." Are these labels justifiable on an empirical basis?

Table 28.1
Scalogram Analyses of News Media Use of Adolescents and Parents

Media Use Scale Properties					Adolescents	Parents
Scale score	TV news 2 days/wk	Newspaper 3 days/wk	Magazines 3 articles	Type of case	No. of cases	No. of cases
0	0	0	0	Scale type	98	39
1	X	0	0	Scale type	229	107
1	0	X	0	Error type	62	51
1	0	0	X	Error type	4	1
2	X	X	0	Scale type	258	406
2	0	X	X	Error type	11	9
3	X	X	X	Scale type	56	105
					718	718
			Total error types		77	61
			Percentage scale types[a]		86%	88%
			Coefficient of Reproducibility		.90	.94
			Coefficient of Scalability		.67	.63

a. Scale types as a percentage of all cases were calculated only for those with scale scores of 1 and 2, since there could not be error types for scale scores of 0 or 3. The first entry on this line means, for instance, that 86 percent of all adolescents scored as 1 or 2 on the Guttman scale were scale types, and the other 14 percent were error types. For comparison, by chance these percentages would be expected to be about 40 percent and 60 percent respectively, since there are two possible scale types and three possible error types for scores of 1 or 2 on the scale.

Table 28.2 provides an approximate response to that question, examining at each level of the scale the medium from which people say they get most of their news. (For Table 28.2 and our subsequent analyses, we have retained the error types as well as the scale types from Table 28.1. This in effect treats them as random error rather than specific error, making our validity tests of the general logic of our scale somewhat conservative.)

Radio is clearly the dominant source of news, especially among the parents, for those who have been classified in our scalogram analysis at level 0 in news media use in Table 28.2 Two one-way analyses of variance have been performed for each line in Table 28.2, one representing the linear relationship between our Guttman scale and reliance on a given medium, and a second one representing the quadratic component, which can be visualized as a simple symmetrical curve. For both the parents and the adolescents, the linear components are highly significant with regard to radio as a news source. Use of radio drops off continuously as the person's scale score increases. For the parents (only) there is also a component of curvilinearity in the relationship that we did not anticipate but that reflects

News Media Use in Adolescence

Table 28.2
Reliance on Different Media for News, by Media Use Scale Score

		Media Use Scale Score				Analysis of Variance (F-ratios)	
		0 (Radio)	1 (Television)	2 (Newspaper)	3 (Magazine)	Linear	Quadratic
Relies for news mainly on:							
Radio:	Parents	62%	21%	11%	13%	43.0***	33.0***
	Adolescents	38%	22%	19%	7%	20.0***	(< 1.0)
Television:	Parents	33%	67%	58%	39%	3.3	21.7***
	Adolescents	52%	67%	64%	54%	(< 1.0)	8.6**
Newspaper:	Parents	0%	12%	27%	30%	20.0***	(< 1.0)
	Adolescents	5%	8%	14%	27%	20.0***	2.5
(N)	Parents	(39)	(159)	(415)	(105)		
	Adolescents	(98)	(295)	(269)	(56)		

**p < .01
***p < .001

the sharp decline in radio reliance for persons above level 0 on the news media use scale.

Curvilinearity would, on the other hand, be the appropriate relationship to hypothesize for television as a news source, since we should expect this medium to predominate at level 1 of the scale — preliminarily labeled "Television." Inspection of Table 28.2 indicates that this is indeed the case for both subsamples. In more formal terms, the quadratic component is significant (and in the hypothesized direction) for both parents and adolescents, whereas the linear relationship is not significant in either subsample.

Reliance on newspapers as one's principal source of news is linearly, not curvilinearly, related to the news media use scale (Table 28.2). Newspaper reliance is practically nonexistent among parents and adolescents classified at level 0 on our scale; it is reported about 10 per cent of the time at level 1, 20 per cent at level 2, and nearly 30 per cent at level 3. This very regular progression, which is found with about equal strength for both subsamples, would not literally support our label of "Newspaper" for level 2, considering that more people at level 3 rely principally on newspapers for their news. But it is a finding consistent with our assumption that within the higher scale levels involving print media use, newspapers will predominate because they are more commonly available for reading. Self-reports that one relies mainly on magazines for news are so rare that the data cannot be analyzed sensibly in Table 28.2, although those few such reports as do occur are of course found at the higher levels of the news media use scale.

ANTECEDENTS OF ADOLESCENT MEDIA DEVELOPMENT

With the foregoing evidence to support further exploration of the cumulative media use scale, we turn next to the question of antecedent conditions that might explain why some adolescents are found at higher levels than others. In this preliminary exploration we will examine only a few major factors rather than probe all the conceivable antecedent variables. One obvious explanatory variable is simply age. Our sample covers a wide range of ages, ten through seventeen, and they represent a period in which many kinds of personal maturation normally occur. Closely correlated with age, of course, is grade in school ($r = .95$). Of these two measures, we chose grade rather than age as marginally the clearer locator of a person's level of cognitive development in adolescence. In our later analyses we will routinely enter grade as a first predictor or control variable when examining other antecedents, correlates, or effects of the adolescent level of media use.

Figure 28.1 shows the developmental trends in the level of adolescent media use and compares these levels to those of the adult population represented by the parent sample. These distributions suggest that as the adolescent matures, his media use patterns do in fact change in a manner consistent with the notion of a cumulative developmental progression: The proportions of individuals at our levels called "radio" and "television" steadily decline, while the proportion of individuals at the "newspaper" and "magazine" levels steadily increases with age. Despite these trends, it is clear that not all individuals are destined to reach the top of the scale. More than one-fourth of the parents remain at the two lower levels.

Other antecedent variables that might account for adolescent news media use development can be readily identified in the family environment. Perhaps the most obvious is the parents' own level of news media use, as measured here on the same Guttman scale as the adolescents' (see Table 28.1). We could reasonably expect a parent-adolescent correlation based on youngsters learning from the parental model, or simply due to parents providing more media in the home if they themselves are using them. For example, adolescents whose parents do not read newspapers or magazines, and who therefore do not subscribe to them for their families, clearly enjoy less opportunity to develop news-reading habits than do adolescents in media-rich homes. Similarly, parents who regularly turn on television news programs are likely to expose their youngsters, perhaps inadvertently, to public affairs content the latter would not seek. It is further possible that a parent-adolescent media use correlation could occur because an adolescent's media consumption stimulates that of the parent in approximately the reverse of the forms of influence described here. Evi-

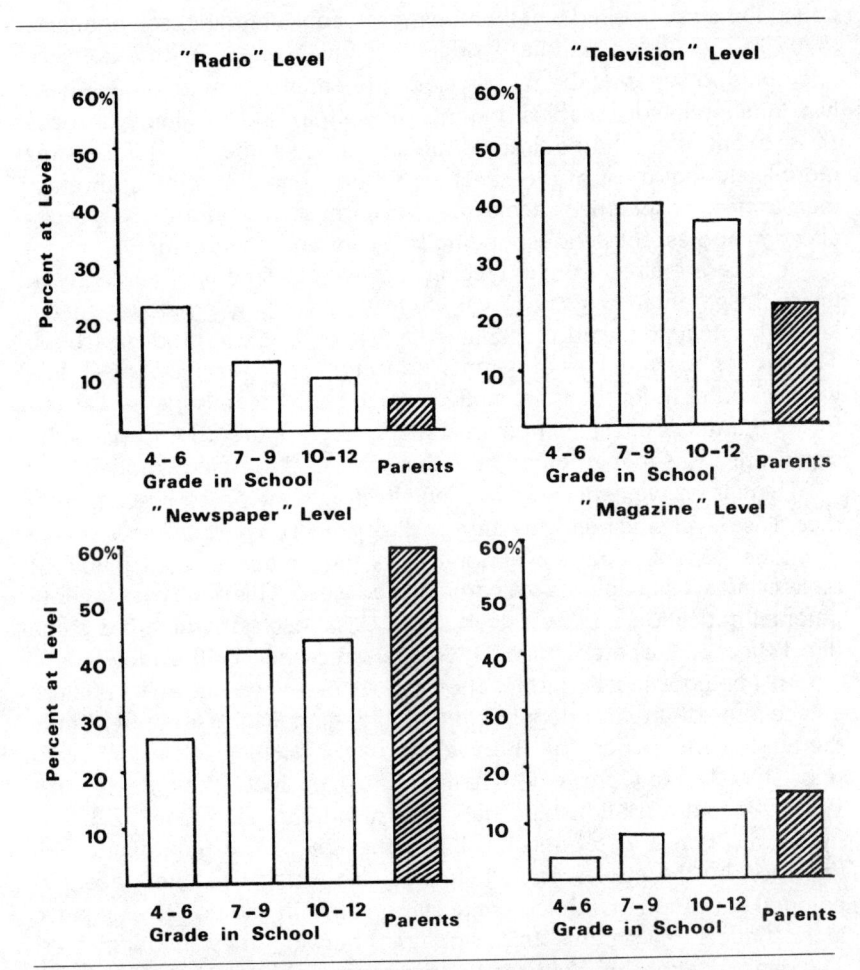

Figure 28.1. Percentage of total sample at each level of news media use scale, by grade in school and compared to parent sample.

dence of this "reverse influence" from adolescent to parent has been found for television viewing (Chaffee, McLeod, & Atkin, 1971).

If parental news media use is a factor affecting adolescent news media use in the same family, to what in turn can parental news media use be traced? As in the case of the adolescent, we should expect a parent's own education to have an important effect; many surveys show that an adult's years of schooling is one of the most reliable predictors of reading, especially of newspapers (Chaffee & Choe, 1981). Related to one's education is an additional variable, that of perceived socioeconomic class. One question in this survey asked whether the person considered himself or herself to be in the upper, middle, working, or lower class. A further probe attempted to separate the middle class into additional gradations. These two family-related variables, parents' education and the family's social class, might affect the adolescent media use level directly. But it seems more likely that most of the effect would be indirect, operating through their impact on parents' media use, which in turn would more directly affect an adolescent's corresponding behavior and development.

To separate direct from indirect effects, we peformed path analyses in which the parental media use level was treated as an endogenous variable leading directly to the adolescent media use level, as was grade in school. The exogenous variables of parents' education and perceived social class were tested both for their direct effects on the adolescent's media use and for their indirect effects via parents' media use. Figure 28.2 displays the significant paths that emerged from this analysis ("trimmed" model).

There is, as we expected, a strong effect of grade on adolescent news media use level, and nearly as strong a direct effect on parents' news media use. The possible effects of prior factors, however, are explainable as indirect effects that operate via parental media use. This is the case for both parental education and perceived social class, each of which has some direct effect on the parent but no additional direct effect on the adolescent.

An analogous path model (not shown here) was used to analyze antecedents of another dependent variable, namely, the amount of time the adolescent spends "on the average day" watching television. As in prior studies (see Comstock, Chaffee, Katzman, McCombs, & Roberts, 1978), we found relationships that contrast with those in Figure 28.1. The higher the grade in school, the lower the amount of time spent with television by the adolescent. There was also a negative direct effect of parental education on adolescent television time, in addition to a negative indirect effect (via parents' television time) between these two variables. The direct relationship between the time spent with television by parent and child was positive, whereas that between parental news media use and adolescent television time was negative; both of these parent-adolescent relationships were low but significant in path analysis.

Overall, we were able to explain with these variables more variation in our news media use scale ($R^2 = .11$) than we were in the analogous analyses of time spent watching television ($R^2 = .07$), although the latter is one of the more popular measures of mass communication behavior in the empirical literature (Comstock et al., 1978; Gerbner, Gross, Morgan, & Signorielli, 1980). This suggests that our scale is a comparatively reliable one. While we would not claim to have examined all of the major potential antecedents of this scale, we have accounted for a significant amount of its variance and established that it is related to antecedent factors in ways that

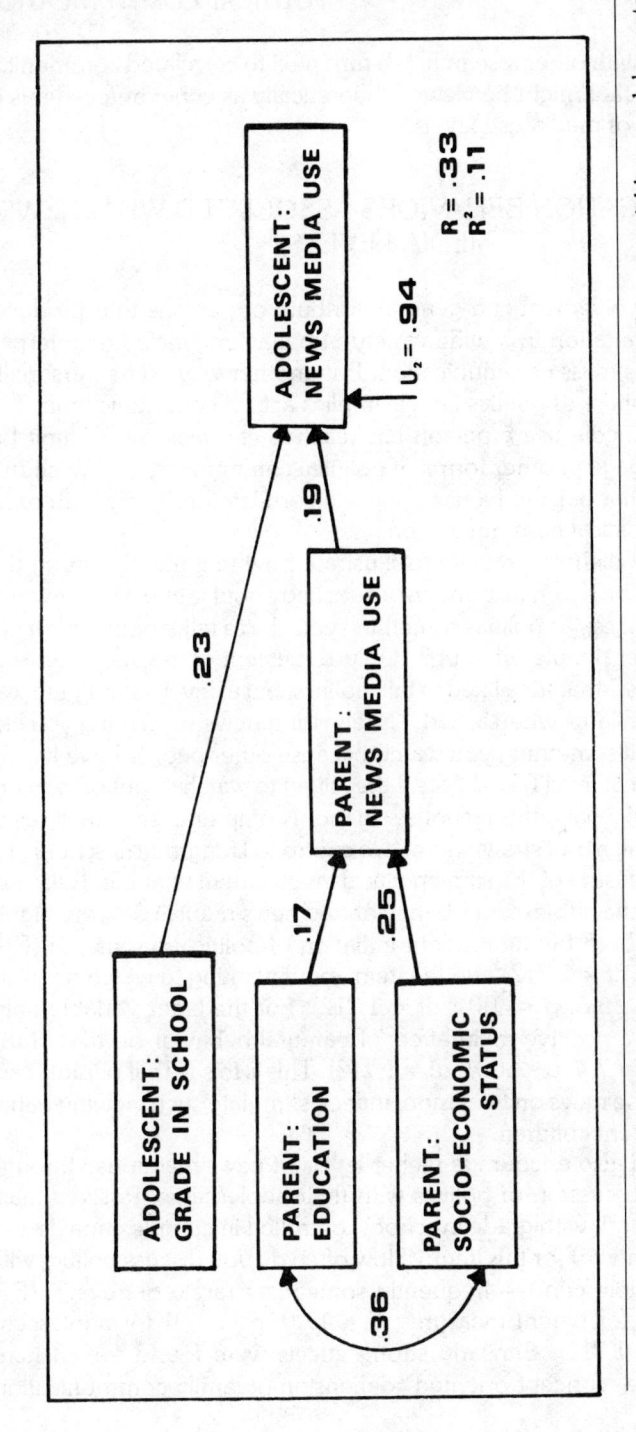

Figure 28.2. Path model of significant (p < .01) direct and indirect effects of antecedent and parental influence variables on adolescents' news media use scale score.

are consistent with other research. We turn next to correlated communication behaviors that might be viewed theoretically as either antecedents or consequences of media use levels.

COMMUNICATION BEHAVIORS ASSOCIATED WITH NEWS MEDIA LEVELS

Political involvement is a general attribute of persons that produces considerable variation in a wide variety of behaviors, including interpersonal as well as mass communication. Put another way, to be personally active in the sphere of politics largely implies acts of communication. The level of news media use a person has reached can facilitate or limit the capacity to engage in other forms of political communication. We should expect, then, that our media use scale will correlate positively with other measures of political communication.

Two simple dichotomous items illustrate how remarkably strong this correlation can be. Each respondent was asked about interest in conversations about politics: "Is politics something you like to talk about, or is it just something other people bring up?" Only 12 percent of the adolescents at level 0 said "yes," that they liked to talk politics, but at level 3 this figure was 64 percent. Similarly, when asked: "Is television news something you like to watch, or is it something you watch because other people have it on?" only 14 percent at level 0 said "yes," they liked to watch it, but 67 percent of those at level 3 gave this response. In more comprehensive analyses of these relationships (not shown here), we controlled for grade in school and the parental measure of the same political involvement variable. Relationships between the adolescent's behavior and news media use were highly significant, for both the item about initiation of political discussion ($F = 40.1$, $p < .001$, $df = 1,712$) and the item about wanting to watch news on television ($F = 26.6$, $p < .001$, $df = 1,712$). For the latter variable only, there was also a positive main effect of parental behavior on that of the adolescents ($F = 7.4$, $p < .001$, $df = 1,712$). This is to say that parents can, by turning on the news on television, indeed stimulate such viewing habits in their adolescent children.

Parents can also encourage higher levels of news media use through interpersonal discussion of politics with their adolescents. Positive main effects were found, with grade in school controlled in complex analyses of variance (not shown) for this item: "How often do you discuss politics with your (parent/adolescent) — frequently, sometimes, rarely, or never?" ($F = 12.6$, $p < .001$ for parent measures, $F = 17.0$, $p < .001$ for adolescent measure, $df = 1,711$). Similarly strong effects were found for an item representing the "concept-oriented" dimension of family communication

News Media Use in Adolescence

patterns (McLeod & Chaffee, 1972): "How often (do you tell your children/do your parents tell you) to question other people's beliefs about politics — frequently, sometimes, rarely, or never?" ($F = 12.1, p < .001$ for parent measure, $F = 16.0, p < .001$ for adolescent measure, $df = 1,700$).

These univariate analyses suffice to establish that a variety of other communication behaviors, both of the adolescent and of the parent, are involved in the development of news media use. Parental influence is clearer where direct participation is involved, either through discussion of politics with the adolescent or through semi-inadvertent influences such as turning on the TV news when the adolescent is also present.

As we have suggested, development of news media use might be viewed as part of a more global process of acquiring habits of active political communication behaviors of all types. To test this assumption we entered the four correlates already described in this section and seven other variables of the same general character into a single discriminant analysis. The criteria for including a discriminating variable were that it should (1) have to do with active communication behavior, either mass or interpersonal, and (2) deal with political or news content. The variables entered are described in Table 28.3, which also shows the results of the discriminant analysis.

Given the homogeneity of items, we should expect that a single function should dominate the discrimination among the four groups. This is indeed the case in Table 28.3 where Function 1 explains nearly 90 percent of the variance. All eleven items correlate positively with Function 1, but three items — particularly the one that refers specifically to newspaper use — are more strongly associated with Function 2, which is also statistically significant.

More important in Table 28.3 is the ordering of the four levels of media use on these two discriminating dimensions. For this analysis, the four levels were simply treated as different groups, not in any particular order. The discriminant analysis identifies those dimensions that separate these four groups maximally from one another, without regard to their nature. If this rather "indiscriminate" analysis were to reorder the groups in their presumed developmental sequence, we would have quite strong evidence to support our assumption that the scale is a unidimensional one. Examination of the group centroids at the bottom of Table 28.3 shows that this is the case. On the first, and major function, the four groups are spaced far apart in precise 0-1-2-3 order, separated by about equal intervals. On Function 2 the 0-1-2-3 order is also found, although the space between groups 0 ("Radio") and 1 ("Television") is not great. This makes sense, in that Function 2 is mainly a matter of attention to political news in the newspaper and so should not be expected to discriminate much between broadcast levels of media use.

Table 28.3
Canonical Discriminant Functions for News Media Use Scale and
Discriminating Communication Variables (adolescent sample, N = 718)

Discriminating Variable	Function 1	Function 2
Attention to news about politics on television	.89[a]	−.10
Information-seeking about things in the news	.50[a]	−.07
Frequency of discussing things in the news with others	.38[a]	.18
Initiation of discussions about politics with others	.27[a]	.15
Frequency of watching news specials on television	.27[a]	.20
Frequency of watching late evening news on television	.27[a]	.22
Frequency of discussing politics with different kinds of people	.23[a]	.19
Frequency of discussing politics with parents	.19[a]	.11
Attention to news about politics in newspapers	.21	.89[a]
Intentionally watching news on television	.12	.26[a]
Attention to news about politics on the radio	.07	.19[a]
Percentage of variance explained by function	89%	8%
Canonical correlation	.66***	.26***
Group centroids:		
Scale score 0 (Radio)	−1.57	−.55
Scale score 1 (Television)	−.14	−.45
Scale score 2 (Newspaper)	.48	.44
Scale score 3 (Magazines)	1.14	1.13

a. Entries in upper portion of table are correlations between the listed variable and the rotated canonical discriminant functions; superscripts indicate strongest correlation for each variable. Only significant functions are shown.
***$p < .001$.

Overall, these communicatory correlates provide strong validation of our assumptions about the progressive, cumulative nature of media use in adolescence, and about its systemic character in relation to general political involvement. They also give us a clearer picture of the role played by parents in fostering this development. For our final analyses, we turn to examination of some effects of media use development on political cognitions.

POLITICAL KNOWLEDGE AS A FUNCTION OF NEWS MEDIA USE

There has been a growing emphasis in recent years on political cognitions as the appropriate criterion measure for assessing effects of the news media (Becker, McCombs, & McLeod, 1975). Composite indices of public affairs knowledge have proved to be reliable outcomes of news media exposure in adolescence (Chaffee, Ward, & Tipton, 1970), as well as among adults. In most studies, though, there is little if any distinction among categories of political cognition that might differ in cognitive complexity or abstraction. One exception is the work of Jennings and Niemi (1974) on young adults. They found fairly strong intergenerational, within-family correlations on evaluations of political leaders and parties, but little or no correlation regarding more abstract political concepts. One explanation for this lack of parent-child correlation could be that young people do not absorb sophisticated political cognitions as readily as do older adults who have some years of experience to build upon.

Four categories of successively more complex or abstract political information were defined for our effects analyses. The first of these was simply knowledge of the names of the various candidates running for president in early 1980, an unaided recall item with repeated probes: "Do you happen to remember the names of any of the people who are running for president? Anyone else? Anyone else?" etc. Scores (number of correct names) ran as high as eleven names, with a mean of about 4.5 for the parents and 3.5 for the adolescents. Table 28.4 presents complete descriptive statistics and correlations among knowledge and news media use scales.

A second measure consisted of knowledge of the party affiliations of eight major candidates: "I am going to read you the names of some of the candidates who are running, and for each one I want you to tell me if you think of him as a Democrat, or as a Republican. First, Jimmy Carter." (This question was repeated for Ronald Reagan, Edward Kennedy, John Connally, George Bush, Gerald Ford, Jerry Brown, and Howard Baker.) The parent-adolescent gap on this candidate-party association measure was a bit higher than on the simple candidate-name recall index, with means of about 5.1 for parents and 3.5 for adolescents.

A more abstract association measure was created by summing correct responses to fourteen items asking about the party represented by various symbols, former leaders, and enduring political interests: e.g., elephant, donkey, Abraham Lincoln, Franklin D. Roosevelt, big business, working class. The parent sample greatly outdistanced the adolescents on this index, with a mean of 8.1 compared to the youngsters' 5.4.

The most difficult items were four party-issue association measures. After being asked their own positions on the four issues (increased funding for military, decreased funding for health and education, expanded development of nuclear power, and greater access to jobs for minority groups), each respondent was asked which of the two major parties was more in favor of the policy. This measure is, of course, debatable, although a clear majority of the parents identified the Republicans as favoring the

Table 28.4
Pearson Correlations, Means, and Standard Deviations for the News Media Use Scale and Measures of Political Knowledge

		(1)	(2)	(3)	(4)	(5)	(6)	(7)	(8)	(9)	(10)
News media use scale: adolescents	(1)	—									
News media use scale: parents	(2)	.23	—								
Candidate recall: adolescents	(3)	.32	.15	—							
Candidate recall: parents	(4)	.17	.36	.31	—						
Candidate party knowledge: adolescents	(5)	.28	.10	.58	.19	—					
Candidate party knowledge: parents	(6)	.20	.34	.29	.65	.23	—				
Party symbol knowledge: adolescents	(7)	.13	.07	.31	.06	.47	.06	—			
Party symbol knowledge: parents	(8)	.12	.34	.21	.51	.13	.72	.08	—		
Party position knowledge: adolescents	(9)	.08	-.03	.16	-.01	.30	.08	.38	.06	—	
Party position knowledge: parents	(10)	.06	.16	.09	.25	.06	.36	.02	.44	.07	—
Mean		1.39	1.82	3.41	4.84	3.47	5.50	5.37	8.63	1.69	1.76
Standard deviation		.82	.74	1.88	1.80	2.43	2.36	3.07	3.55	1.20	1.21

Note: Entries on the first ten lines of this table are the Pearson product-moment correlation coefficients between the listed variables.

first three and the Democrats the fourth, and these differences were eventually written into the platforms adopted by the parties later in the year. However valid the measure, neither group did especially well in the aggregate, with mean scores of less than two "correct" items out of the four among both the parents and the adolescents. This kind of party-issue measure clearly requires a more sophisticated level of political comprehension than do the simpler indices of candidate knowledge, candidate-party associations, and party-symbol associations.

Overall, each of these four knowledge indices was significantly correlated with news media use, for both the adolescents and their parents. Table 28.5 shows the group means at each level; the correlation coefficients are reported in Table 28.6. For every index, the news media use scale as a whole (comparing levels 0 and 3 in Table 28.5, right-hand column) accounts for larger differences among the parents than among the adolescents. This may be due to the fact that these habitual levels of use are less longstanding in the lives of younger people, who have had less opportunity to absorb mediated information at any level. The parent-adolescent difference is most marked for the measure of political party symbol knowledge, where news media use makes almost four times as much difference for parents. That this, the most enduring body of knowledge among our four criterion variables, should be the one most affected by parents' individual differences in news media use accords with our suggestion that it is the amount of *prior*, cumulative news media exposure that explains the greater differentials for parents than for adolescents in Table 28.5.

Another way of interpreting Table 28.5 is in terms of the parent-adolescent differences, or intergenerational knowledge gaps, at each level of news media use. These net differences are reported within the columns, separately for each knowledge index. There is a clear pattern of interaction in the data, in that the intergenerational gap widens as news media use levels increase. While this interactive pattern is found to some extent for each of the four knowledge indices, it is most obvious regarding knowledge of enduring symbols of the political parties. For this measure, the gap between parents and adolescents widens from less than one item mean difference at level 0 to more than two items difference at level 1, more than three at level 2, and more than four at level 3.

These findings further underscore our conception of political cognitions of this party-association character as being cumulative in nature. Although some adolescents have reached levels of news media use equivalent to those of their parents, they have presumably not been at those levels nearly as long. They can do almost as well, when news media use is controlled, at answering "current events" questions about candidates in the 1980 presidential race, but their store of information falls when party-oriented questions are asked. This is less the case with "current" candidate-party information than with long-term candidate-symbol in-

Table 28.5
Political Knowledge by News Media Use of Parents and Adolescents

Knowledge Index	News Media Use Scale Score 0	1	2	3	Net Difference (Level 3-Level 0)
Recall of names of presidential candidates (range = 0-11)					
Parents	3.1	4.2	5.0	5.8	+2.7
Adolescents	2.1	3.2	4.0	4.1	+2.0
Net difference (parents-adolescents)	+1.0	+1.0	+1.0	+1.7	
Knowledge of candidates' political parties (range = 0-8)					
Parents	3.7	4.5	5.8	6.5	+2.8
Adolescents	2.3	3.1	4.0	4.8	+2.5
Net difference (parents-adolescents)	+1.4	+1.4	+1.8	+1.7	
Knowledge of political party symbols (range = 0-14)					
Parents	5.7	7.2	9.0	10.3	+4.6
Adolescents	4.9	5.1	5.7	6.1	+1.2
Net difference (parents-adolescents)	+.8	+2.1	+3.3	+4.2	
Knowledge of political party issue positions (range = 0-4)					
Parents	1.4	1.5	1.8	2.1	+.7
Adolescents	1.6	1.6	1.8	2.0	+.4
Net difference (parents-adolescents)	-.2	-.1	0	+.1	

Note: Entries indicate the mean number of correct responses.

formation. Familiarity with parties transcends the events of a single election year, and parents with longstanding high levels of news media use are likely to have accumulated party-oriented information over a much longer period of years than their adolescent offspring.

The extent of the effect of news media use on political knowledge is addressed most directly in Table 28.6, which summarizes the results of a series of hierarchical multiple regression analyses. For each knowledge index we present the zero-order correlation between knowledge and news media use, then the standardized regression coefficient representing this relationship from an equation in which a person's educational attainment is controlled, and finally the regression coefficient that survives when all direct effects on news media use (from Figure 28.2) are controlled. Although our causal ordering of variables is to some extent arguable (i.e.,

Table 28.6
Indices of Political Knowledge, by News Media Use and Controlling for Education and Other Antecedent Variables

Knowledge Index	Zero-Order Correlation (r)	Standardized regression coefficient (beta) controlling for: Education	Both Antecedents[a]
Recall of names of presidential candidates			
Parents	.36***	.32***	.23***
Adolescents	.32***	.26***	.25***
Knowledge of candidates' political parties			
Parents	.34***	.25***	.22***
Adolescents	.28***	.23***	.22***
Knowledge of political party symbols			
Parents	.34***	.22***	.20***
Adolescents	.13***	.06	.06
Knowledge of political party issue positions			
Parents	.16***	.11**	.09**
Adolescents	.08*	.04	.06

a. In hierarchical regression, a person's years of education was entered as a single control variable in one equation. In the second equation both significant antecedents to news media use were entered as controls. For the parents the antecedents were the years of school completed (education) and perceived social class. For the adolescents, the antecedents were grade in school (education) and parents' news media use scale score.
*$p < .05$
**$p < .01$
***$p < .001$

knowledge can facilitate news media use, as well as the reverse), statistically this is a very stringent test of the strength of the bivariate relationship.

Generally speaking, the media-knowledge correlation appears to be quite robust in Table 28.6, although it declines for the more sophisticated knowledge measures and among the adolescents. Looking first at the parent sample, the correlations are uniformly strong across the first three indices and stand up well when controlled for antecedent variables; the fourth index, the four-item measure of party-issue knowledge, is also significantly correlated with news media use, even with controls, for the parent subsample. There is, however, a clear downward trend among the adolescents in the media-knowledge correlations as we move in Table 28.6 from the simplest to more complex types of knowledge. The regression coefficient with all controls is slightly higher among adolescents (.25 versus

.23 for parents) for candidate knowledge, and equal (.22 for both groups) for candidate-party associations. But for the more sophisticated types of knowledge (party-symbol and party-issue associations), the raw correlations are markedly lower and the regression coefficients nonsignificant among the adolescents.

Nevertheless, one's news media use level is an important determinant of political knowledge. It is especially impressive that this relationship holds up, at least for candidate-related information, even when we have controlled for the adolescents' education level. Our sample spans a long period in adolescent development, the ages of ten through seventeen (ranging from fourth grade to college sophomores at the extremes), and one would expect this great variation in the extent of educational experience to explain a large proportion of concomitant variation in public affairs knowledge.

News media use level, which holds up as a strong predictor of knowledge even when grade level is controlled, appears to be a powerful additional source of political information beyond the contributions of school and family. In adolescence, its main role is to familiarize people with the events and political personalities of the day. In adulthood, to judge from the parental data, the accumulation of a continuing supply of current information builds into a base of more sophisticated and enduring kinds of political knowledge. It is quite possible that the attainment of reading skills that enable a developing adolescent to advance to a higher level of news media use constitutes a necessary, if not sufficient, condition in the long-term process of differentiating the more from the less knowledgeable sectors of the political community.

SUMMARY AND DISCUSSION

We have proposed that there is in adolescence a developmental sequence in the use of news media, in which the use of broadcast news media (television and radio) precedes the reading of print news media (newspapers and magazines). Further, because of probabilistic differences in the availability of media, there is a four-level cumulative scale in which the media are ordered within these two different modes of presentation. Reliance on radio is most common among those who have not adopted regular use of the other media. At the other extreme, magazine use is characteristic of those who also use all the other media. This radio-television-newspaper-magazine ordering corresponds to the findings of previous adult surveys and to our analyses of the parents of the adolescents in our study.

The cumulative nature of news media use skills does not mean that broadcast media are abandoned once print media skills are acquired. Use of newspapers and magazines, which carry much richer bodies of political news than do the broadcast media, is usually associated with continued use of the broadcast media as well. But reliance on radio and/or television for one's news tends to be a matter of limitation; it is not a choice among all media, but rather a condition of default in that in most cases the news in print media is not easily accessible to the person. Studies that attempt to relate, say, exposure to television news to knowledge or other criterion measures obscure the critical difference between reliance on television alone and use of television as a supplement to other news media. A young person who has the skills to follow the news via print media may nevertheless limit his or her attention to television on topics that arouse relatively little interest. We would expect some fluctuation over time, then, in the actual use of various media, in that some who have attained higher levels at one time might not maintain those high levels constantly; the cognitive potential for use of print media remains, even though *behaviorally* the person might later appear to be operating at a lower level. Developmentally, on the other hand, we expect the progression of cognitive *capabilities* to increase, so that some youngsters will eventually move from lower to higher levels as a consequence of maturation.

News media use is not a behavior that simply occurs in the process of adolescent development. It depends partly on one's education and on the news media habits of one's parents. The latter habits are, in turn, the product of educational attainment and socioeconomic status, to some extent. These structural factors do not, however, "explain away" the impact of news media use levels on the development of political cognitions. Even when personal and family background variables are controlled, there are strong statistical relationships between a person's news media use and the amount of political knowledge held. Among adolescents this relationship holds mainly for current political events; for their parents it extends to the accumulation of enduring associations of symbols with political parties. We presume that this difference reflects the longer time the parents have had to acquire party-associated knowledge via the media.

The total picture is far from complete, of course. We have identified a number of strong correlates of news media use, including both mediated and interpersonal forms of purposive political communication. Causal relationships are quite likely reciprocal, in that news media use may build knowledge and stimulate further communication, and the latter may in turn lead one to more extensive use of the media. News media use, which appears from both scalogram analysis and multiple discriminant function analysis to be a unidimensional progression, is a central factor in the general process of the development of cognitive skills related to political activity. Regular use of print media, which involves skills that are not acquired by all — in adolescence or in adulthood — appears to be a particularly important achievement. With longitudinal exploration we may in the future be able to clarify further the roles played by different factors in this developmental progression.

REFERENCES

Becker, L. B., McCombs, M. E., & McLeod, J. M. The development of political cognitions. In S. H. Chaffee (Ed.), *Political communication: Issues and strategies for research*. Beverly Hills, CA: Sage, 1975.

Campbell, A., Converse, P. E., Miller, W. E., & Stokes, D. E. *Elections and the political order*. New York: John Wiley, 1966.

Chaffee, S. H. The mass media as agents of political socialization. *International Journal of Political Education*, 1978, *1*, 127-142.

Chaffee, S. H., & Choe, S. Y. Newspaper reading in longitudinal perspective: Beyond structural constraints. *Journalism Quarterly*, 1981, *58*, 201-211.

Chaffee, S. H., McLeod, J. M., & Atkin, C. K. Parental influences on adolescent media use. *American Behavioral Scientist*, 1971, *14*, 323-340.

Chaffee, S. H., Ward, L. S., & Tipton, L. P. Mass communication and political socialization. *Journalism Quarterly*, 1970, *47*, 647-659, 666.

Comstock, G., Chaffee, S., Katzman, N., McCombs, M., & Roberts, D. *Television and human behavior*. New York: Columbia University Press, 1978.

Gerbner, G., Gross, L., Morgan, M., & Signorielli, N. The "mainstreaming" of America: Violence profile no. 11. *Journal of Communication*, 1980, *30* 10-29.

Jennings, M. K., & Niemi, R. *The political character of adolescence*. Princeton, NJ: Princeton University Press, 1974.

Kennamer, J. D., & Chaffee, S. H. Communication of political information during early presidential primaries: Cognition, affect, and uncertainty. In M. Burgoon (Ed.), *Communication yearbook 5*. New Brunswick, NJ: Transaction, 1982.

Kraus, S., & Davis, D. K. *The effects of mass communication on political behavior*. University Park, PA: Pennsylvania State University Press, 1976.

McLeod, J. M., & Chaffee, S. H. The construction of social reality. In J. Tedeschi (Ed.), *The social influence processes*. Chicago: Aldine, 1972.

Piaget, J. *Play, dreams and imitation in childhood*. New York, W. W. Norton, 1962.

Salomon, G. Shape, not only content: How media symbols partake in the development of abilities. In E. Wartella (Ed.), *Children communicating: Media and development of thought, speech, understanding*. Beverly Hills, CA: Sage, 1979.

Stouffer, S. A. et al. *Measurement and prediction: Studies in social psychology during World War II* (Vol. 4). Princeton, NJ: Princeton University Press, 1950.

Wackman, D. B., & Wartella, E. A review of cognitive development theory and research and the implication for research on children's responses to television. *Communication Research*, 1977, *4*, 203-224.

29 ● Public Opinion, Communication Processes, and Voting Decisions

CARROLL J. GLYNN ● JACK M. McLEOD
University of Wisconsin—Madison

POLITICAL communication research has had as much trouble as other social science fields in developing appropriate concepts at the social system level. The concept of "public opinion" serves as a case in point. Public opinion has been treated conceptually as if it were some kind of "superorganic" being that expresses its view upon various issues as they arise. Despite this mysterious collective-system-level conceptual definition, operational definitions of public opinion have been restricted to statements about what percentage of individuals interviewed hold what views — e.g., 60 percent of U.S. adults think the president is doing a good job.

The assumption implicit in estimates of the state of public opinion is that it will lead to various types of societal outcomes; a given candidate will be reelected, for example. Unfortunately, the evidence for the validity of this assumption is not strong. Public sentiment seems elusively changeable and the connection between an individual's opinion and subsequent behavior has been shown to be weak (LaPiere, 1934; DeFleur & Westie, 1963; Festinger, 1964; Wicker, 1969; Seibold, 1975). One reason offered for the opinion behavior discrepancy is that "significant others" will be displeased (DeFleur & Westie, 1958; Schuman & Johnson, 1976). Adding a dynamic quality to the perceptions of others is the fact that such judgments can be inaccurate (Newcomb, 1953; Laing, Phillipson, & Lee, 1966; Scheff, 1967; Chaffee & McLeod, 1973). Fields and Schuman (1976) for example, found discrepancies between perceptions of neighbors' opinions and the expressed opinions of those neighbors.

Perceptions of individuals regarding more *generalized* others — judgments about the opinions of various publics — has not been adequately researched. Although studies of "pluralistic ignorance" (Schanck, 1932;

Correspondence and requests for reprints: Carroll J. Glynn, Mass Communication Research Center, University of Wisconsin, Madison, WI 53706.

Newcomb, 1961; Lipset, 1971; O'Gorman & Gerry, 1976) have analyzed the patterned misjudgment of public opinion, they have failed to investigate the sensitivity of the public to *changes* and *trends* in public opinion. A notable exception can be found in the work of Noelle-Neumann (1973, 1974), who in studies of the climate of public opinion in West Germany, has analyzed the process of public opinion formation and change through the individual's observation of the social environment.

Noelle-Neumann defines public opinion as "the dominating opinion which compels compliance of attitude and behavior in that it threatens the dissenting individual with isolation." She assumes that fear of isolating oneself (fear of separation or doubt about one's capacity for judgment) is an integral part of all processes of public opinion. Individuals estimate when they would isolate themselves or fall out of social favor by (1) observing their social environment, (2) assessing the distribution of opinions for or against their ideas, and (3) evaluating the strength, the urgency, and chances of success of certain proposals and viewpoints. These behaviors are important in changeable circumstances where people are caught in a struggle between conflicting positions and have to consider where they stand. An election campaign is a case in point.

When adapted to the study of election campaigns, Noelle-Neumann's "spiral of silence" theory bears some resemblance to the classical conception of the "bandwagon effect" where "the propagandist attempts to convince us that all members of a group to which we belong are accepting his program and that we *must therefore* follow our crowd and 'jump on the bandwagon'" (Lee & Lee, 1939). Voting behavior analysts disagree about the existence of such an effect, however. Lane (1958) alluded to "some evidence of the force of bandwagon sentiment," while Pool (1965) concluded there was "little evidence that such an effect plays a significant part in American elections" and that "the counteracting underdog effect is at least as large." Neither author provided specific evidence. More recent summaries (Weiss, 1969) have confined their evidence to null findings regarding the effects of computer projections of early returns on the voting behavior of people in later time zones (Lang & Lang, 1965; Mendelsohn, 1965; Miller, 1965). Other researchers accept the bandwagon effect, but place some important constraints on its operation. Patterson (1980) cites evidence of its operation in primary elections but implies that it would hold only when there is a lack of strong sentiment generally and where there is a clear favorite.

While there is agreement between the spiral of silence formulation and the bandwagon effect in the benefits accruing to the front-running candidate, there are important conceptual differences between them regarding the processes by which they are manifested. First, Noelle-Neumann casts her theory in terms of the negative avoidance of public disclosure about being on the losing side whereas the bandwagon effect focuses on the positive benefits of being on the winning side. Second, the bandwagon effect is seen as a late campaign effect while the spiral of silence should be stronger earlier in the campaign. Both perspectives, however, imply the necessity of going beyond the individual's own opinions to measure his or her perceptions of what others in the society or community are thinking.

An important, if briefly mentioned, distinction in the Noelle-Neumann research is that between the "hardcore" opinion holders and the rest of society. The hardcore are "not prepared to conform, to change their opinions, or even to be silent in the face of public opinion" (Noelle-Neumann, 1973). She believes the hardcore group gets accustomed to isolation and may support their own opinions by selecting out persons to confirm their views. We would expect the hardcore respondents to make greater use of interpersonal sources in the campaign than would other voters.

The spiral of silence theory also implies other communication outcomes. We would expect that those nonhardcore people who see their chosen candidate as losing would be extremely low in both use of mass media and interpersonal communication in the campaign. Because the mass media contain polling and other information pertinent to their assessment of the climate of opinion, nonhardcore voters generally should use the mass more than would the hardcore.

STUDY DESIGN

The purpose of the study was to analyze Noelle-Neumann's climate of opinion hypotheses as they relate to "hardcore" and "nonhardcore" individuals in a U.S. election. Interviews were conducted using a panel of ninety-six respondents at three time points — two prior to and one after the 1976 presidential election. The first and third interviews were conducted by telephone; the second wave used personal interviews. The first interview was conducted prior to the initial Carter-Ford September debate, the second in late October, and the third in the week after the November election. The second and third waves also included a replenishment sample of 209 additional respondents not previously interviewed.

The samples were drawn from telephone numbers selected by random digit dialing procedures using proportionate random sampling stratified according to the number of private telephone lines at each exchange. Respondents were screened at each selected number according to their eligibility to vote in the city of Madison, Wisconsin.

The major dependent variables were voting preferences in the September and October waves and the stated vote in the postelection-day interviewing. The amount of campaign discussion reported in September and October and the perceptions of changes in public support for the candidates served as additional dependent variables.

Two types of climate of public opinion variables constituted the major independent variables of the study. These were operationalized by taking the perceptions of which candidate was winning in September and October and by whether each candidate was seen as gaining support, staying the same, or losing support at the time of the first two waves of interviews. Perceptions were measured by the questions: (1) "Among the presidential candidates, Ford, Carter and others, what percentage of the vote do you think Ford will get (and Carter, and others)?" and (2) "Do you think Ford (Carter) is gaining, staying the same or losing support now?"

To control for selective perception — the possibility that partisan voters would distort their estimates of public opinion — party affiliation was used as a control variable. That is, the relationship between perceptions of public opinion and vote preference was evaluated controlling for the relatively enduring aspects of party affiliation. In keeping with the arbitrary assignment of high scores given to voting preferences for Carter, strong identification with the Democratic party was given a 7, moderate Democrats a 6, independent Democrats a 5, independents a 4, etc.

In our analyses of changes in vote preferences, vote preferences from previous waves of interviewing were used as controls. Tests for the contribution of the climate of opinion variables were then based on the increments they added to the variance accounted for in the hierarchical regression analyses used.

Separate analyses were conducted within groups of respondents divided as to their being either "hardcore" or "nonhardcore" voters. This distinction was made on the basis of vote preference consistency through the three waves of interviewing. Those who unequivocally preferred a given candidate in September and October and who reported voting for that same candidate in November were classified as "hardcore" ($n = 31$); all other voters were designated as "nonhardcore" ($n = 64$). For the cross-section sample analyses, the respondents were coded according to the consistency of their October preferences and November vote and their reports of having changed since September. This less exact method of estimating September preferences produced a somewhat higher proportion of "hardcore" than was present in the panel.

RESULTS

Vote preferences for the nonhardcore respondents shifted gradually from a preference for Ford in September (40 percent versus 31 percent

Table 29.1
Vote Preferences in September, October, and November Vote
Among Nonhardcore and Hardcore Panel Respondents (in percentages)

	Nonhardcore (n = 64)			Hardcore (n = 31)			All Respondents (N = 95)		
	Sept.	Oct.	Nov.	Sept.	Oct.	Nov.	Sept.	Oct.	Nov.
Carter	31	41	56	52	52	52	38	45	55
Ford	40	40	29	48	48	48	42	42	35
Neither	29	19	15	—	—	—	20	13	10
	100	100	100	100	100	100	100	100	100

Carter), to a deadlock in October, to a strong Carter vote in November (56 percent versus 29 percent Ford). The hardcore show a slight Carter preference (52 percent to 48 percent) that, by definition, continues over the three time points (see Table 29.1). The Carter margin in November (20 percent) for the total sample approximates the actual 1976 vote in Madison.

The hardcore and nonhardcore groups differed in ways other than their propensity to change preferences. In results not shown in the tables, we found that the hardcore tended to be older than other respondents. A majority of them were over thirty-five compared to only one-fourth of the nonhardcore. Not surprisingly, the hardcore were more politically partisan (74 percent affiliated with a party versus 49 percent for the nonhardcore), although the relative distribution of sentiment between the two major parties was similar for the two groups. The hardcore also were more likely to be politically interested, but were somewhat *less* knowledgeable about the names of candidates for various offices than were other respondents. The hardcore had slightly lower levels of education as well.

As shown in Table 29.2, the means for perceptions of what proportions the candidates would receive tended to be stable across the two groups and over time with Ford being 2 percent higher in all but one comparison. In terms of support, however, it is clear that the strong tendency to see Ford as gaining declined considerably from September to October (64 percent to 49 percent in the total sample). Differences between groups can be seen in the greater tendency for the hardcore to see the candidates as staying the same (averaging 44 percent versus 32 percent for nonhardcore); however, they were more likely than others to change their September perceptions that Ford was gaining while Carter was losing. Group difference also can be seen in the autocorrelations of the two groups between the September and October waves (data not shown in tables). The hardcore's autocorrela-

Table 29.2
Estimates of Candidates' Vote Percentages and Support Change Among Nonhardcore and Hardcore Panel Respondents (in percentages)

	Nonhardcore (n = 64)		Hardcore (n = 31)		All Respondents (N = 95)	
	Sept.	Oct.	Sept.	Oct.	Sept.	Oct.
Estimated Percentage—Mean						
Carter	46	45	48	45	46	45
Ford	48	47	47	47	48	47
Other	6	8	5	8	6	8
Support: Carter						
Gaining	28	25	3	26	20	25
Staying the same	36	37	52	45	41	39
Losing	36	38	45	29	39	36
Support: Ford						
Gaining	64	52	63	42	64	49
Staying the same	27	27	33	45	29	33
Losing	9	21	4	13	7	18

tions for candidate proportions averaged .86 compared to .56 for the nonhardcore; a slight reversal was found for candidate support where the testretest correlations averaged only .23 for the hardcore as opposed to .30 for the others.

Regression analyses were used to estimate the contribution of the climate of opinion variables to voting preferences. In the first set of analyses, September perceptions of public opinion were used to predict September vote preferences while the October estimates were used to predict both October preferences and November vote (see Table 29.3). Among all eighty-two panel respondents, the four perceptions of public opinion variables account for significant amounts of vote preference variance in both September (25.2 percent) and October (13.1 percent). They fail to predict significant amounts of variance in the November vote, however (5.6 percent). At least part of the decline in predictive power in November is attributable to the restricted variance in the dependent variable. A three-point scale (Carter-neither-Ford) was used in November compared with the earlier vote preference measures that used a five-point scale breaking down preferences for each candidate into "sure" and "not sure."

Inspection of the uncontrolled simple correlation and the beta coefficients for the total sample reveals a consistent pattern in the direction predicted from the Noelle-Neumann formulation. People prefer the candidate they see as winning and gaining support in the campaign. Perception of winning seems to be a more powerful predictor than does perception of changes in support (average simple correlation of .42 versus .22 for support), but this may reflect in part the restricted variances in the three-point support measures. Although the substantial intercorrelations of the climate of opinion measures destabilizes the betas, it does appear that perception of Ford's proportion is the strongest predictor among the four perception variables.

Comparison of the nonhardcore and hardcore groups indicates marked differences in the role played by the climate of opinion variables (see Table 29.3). For the nonhardcore, the four perception variables account for significant amounts of residual variance in September (49.1 percent) and October (24.6 percent); this declines to nonsignificant levels in the November vote (7.5 percent). In sharp contrast, the hardcore climate of opinion variables account for nonsignificant levels of vote preference variance in both September (4.6 percent) and October (3.0 percent). In both September and October, the differences in variance accounted for by the perception variables between the nonhardcore and hardcore groups is statistically significant.

The reasons for this difference between groups cannot be attributed to the simple correlations between the climate of opinion variables and vote preference. Among the nonhardcore, these average to .35 in September and .27 in October; the corresponding coefficients are higher for the hardcore, averaging to .46 and .44, respectively. What does seem to account for the group differences is the combination of a stronger correlation between party affiliation and vote preference in the hardcore group (.87 versus .30 and .62) *and* a stronger association between party affiliation and the climate of opinion variables (hardcore — .44 in September and .39 in October — versus .12 in September and .16 in October for the nonhardcore). Thus it appears that the perceptual processes of the more changeable nonhardcore respondents are more free of partisan commitments.

Because the number of respondents in the panel analyses was so small, as many as possible of the Table 29.3 panel analyses were replicated with the larger cross-section sample of 291 in Table 29.4. The results are similar to those of the panel. For the total sample the climate of opinion variables account for significant amounts of variance in vote preferences over and above that contributed by party affiliation. The larger sample allows the 4.1 percent of the November vote variance to be statistically significant. Differences between the nonhardcore and hardcore groups again surface in the October analyses where the four perception variables account for 16.8 percent of the residual variance among the nonhardcore compared with only 5.5 percent for the hardcore. The difference between these pro-

Table 29.3
Vote Preferences in September, October, and November Vote Regressed on Party Affiliation and Estimates of Candidates' Vote Percentages and Support Change (panel)

	Nonhardcore (n = 52)			Hardcore (n = 30)			All Respondents (N = 82)		
	Simple r	Beta	Incr. R^2	Simple r	Beta	Incr. R^2	Simple r	Beta	Incr. R^2
September Vote Preference									
Party affiliation	.30[a]	.40[a]	.088[a]	.87[a]	.82[a]	.761[a]	.62[a]	.53[a]	.389[a]
Estimated percentage (September)									
Carter	.57[a]	.30	—	.48[a]	−.18	—	.52[a]	.12	—
Ford	−.54[a]	−.40[a]	—	−.52[a]	−.24	—	−.53[a]	−.35[a]	—
Support (September)									
Carter	.23	.30[a]	—	.40[a]	.12	—	.25[a]	.24[a]	—
Ford	−.05	−.06	.491[a]	−.43	.00	.046	−.20	−.04	.252[a]
October Vote Preference									
Party affiliation	.62[a]	.60[a]	.383[a]	.87[a]	.77[a]	.761[a]	.76[a]	.65[a]	.571[a]
Estimated percentage (October)									
Carter	.29[a]	.12	—	.42[a]	−.04	—	.35[a]	.05	—
Ford	−.48[a]	−.40[a]	—	−.60	−.21	—	−.53[a]	−.33[a]	—
Support (October)									
Carter	.23	.16	—	.31	.05	—	.25[a]	.08	—
Ford	−.07	.09	.246[a]	−.35	.01	.030	−.18	.02	.131[a]
November Vote									
Party affiliation	.51[a]	.45[a]	.258[a]	Same as October vote preference data			.67[a]	.59[a]	.447[a]
Estimated percentage (October)									
Carter	.05	−.04	—				.20	−.03	—
Ford	−.19	−.23	—				−.36[a]	−.23[a]	—
Support (October)									
Carter	.27	.27	—				.27[a]	.15	—
Ford	−.06	.11	.075				−.16	.04	.056

Note: No November data for the hardcore group are shown because their vote preferences did not change. October climate of opinion estimates are used for both October vote preference and November vote analyses.
a. $p < .05$

Table 29.4
Vote Preference in October and November Vote Regressed on
Party Affiliation and Estimates of Candidates' Vote Percentages
and Support Change (cross-section sample)

	Nonhardcore (n = 139)			Hardcore (n = 152)			All Respondents (N = 291)		
	Simple r	Beta	Incr. R^2	Simple r	Beta	Incr. R^2	Simple r	Beta	Incr. R^2
October Vote Preference									
Party affiliation	.56[a]	.57[a]	.310[a]	.77[a]	.66[a]	.591[a]	.71[a]	.63[a]	.497[a]
Estimated percentage (October)									
Carter	.32[a]	.36[a]	—	.25[a]	.21[a]	—	.26[a]	.26[a]	—
Ford	−.12	−.24[a]	—	−.40[a]	−.22[a]	—	−.28[a]	−.23[a]	—
Support (October)									
Carter	.00	−.08	—	.31[a]	.06	—	.20[a]	.04	—
Ford	−.16	−.13	.168[a]	−.27[a]	.07	.055[a]	−.22[a]	−.00	.089[a]
November Vote									
Party affiliation	.39	.39	.150[a]	Same as October vote preference data			.63[a]	.58[a]	.393[a]
Estimated percentage (October)									
Carter	.14	.14	—				.19[a]	.17[a]	—
Ford	.02	.09	—				−.19[a]	−.15[a]	—
Support (October)									
Carter	.17	.11	—				.20	.09	—
Ford	.04	−.06	.028				−.14	.06	.041[a]

Note: No November data for the hardcore are shown because their vote preferences did not change. October climate of opinion estimates are used for both October vote preference and November vote analyses. Definitions of nonhardcore and hardcore differ from those in the panel in that the separation here depends on recall of change only.
a. $p < .05$.

767

portions is statistically significant. Again the greater connection between party affiliation and perception helps to account for the group differences.

There is obvious ambiguity in the casual time ordering of the climate of opinion and vote preference variables. The spiral of silence theory proposes the climate of opinion as being the independent variable; however, it is also possible that people bring their perceptions into line with their previous vote choices. Our panel allows us to analyze changes as well as levels of our critical measures among the nonhardcore group. In the regression analyses of October vote preferences, for example, September vote preference was introduced as the first block, thus making the analysis of subsequent variables to be equivalent to studying *changes* in vote preference (Table 29.5).

When the September perception variables are used in the analysis of October vote preference, they fail to account for a significant amount of variance (2.9 percent in Table 29.5) among the nonhardcore. This is in sharp contrast to the strong prediction by the climate of opinion variables as measured in October (18.2 percent in the second analysis in Table 29.5). Indices of changes in the four perceptual variables also predict a significant amount of the variance in October vote preference change (17.0 percent). The failure of the September levels of the perceptual variables to predict change is not solely due to the introduction of either the September vote preference or party affiliation. The simple correlations of September perceptual variables with October vote preference average to only .09. This does not mean that vote preferences must be affecting perceptions; it does indicate that the two processes were changing together during the September-to-October period.

Changes in the November vote from late October vote preferences also reveal some ambiguous results (see Table 29.6). The October perception variables account for a nonsignificant 5.1 percent of the incremental variance for the nonhardcore. None of the individual simple correlations coefficients is significant and the average is only .07 taking direction into account. Changes in the climate of opinion variables from September to October account for 7.9 percent of the changes in the November vote, but this does not reach significant levels. Further, there is a significant *negative* beta coefficient for changes in Carter's percentage relative to Ford.

One of Noelle-Neumann's key points is that those removed from the influence of the spiral of silence would find reinforcement from like-minded others. There is some support for this in the panel data that shows that the hardcore were more likely to discuss the election with others (Table 29.7). The differences are statistically significant for the September wave and in the right direction but at nonsignificant levels in October. The September differences held up when controls for political interest were introduced (not shown in tables).

Table 29.5
Vote Change: October Vote Preference Regressed on September Vote Preference, Party Affiliation, and Estimates of Candidates' Vote Percentages and Support Change Among Nonhardcore Respondents
(N = 43)

	Simple r	Beta	Incr. R^2
October Vote Preference			
September vote preference	.50[a]	.35[a]	.255[a]
Party affiliation	.59[a]	.48[a]	.209[a]
Estimated percentage (September)			
Carter	.25	.15	—
Ford	−.14	.09	—
Support (September)			
Carter	−.04	−.15	—
Ford	−.01	−.17	.029
October Vote Preference			
September vote preference	.50[a]	.15	.255[a]
Party affiliation	.59[a]	.55[a]	.209[a]
Estimated percentage (October)			
Carter	.31[a]	.12	—
Ford	−.49[a]	−.38[a]	—
Support (October)			
Carter	.17	.16	—
Ford	−.00	.13	.182[a]
October Vote Preference			
September vote preference	.50[a]	.58[a]	.255[a]
Party affiliation	.59[a]	.38[a]	.209[a]
Estimated percentage (September to October)			
Carter gain relative to Ford	.19	.41[a]	—
Support (September to October)			
Carter	.17	.28[a]	—
Ford	.00	.16	.170[a]

a. $p < .05$.

The greater role of interpersonal communication among the hardcore is shown in a different way in analyses of support for the two candidates (Table 29.8). Among the hardcore interpersonal communication (as indexed by the extent of discussion and reliance on others for campaign information) accounts for significant amounts of variance in Carter support (11.2 percent in September, 19.2 percent in October) and Ford support (37.9 percent in September, 25.5 percent in October). None of the proportions of variance accounted for by interpersonal communication is significant for the nonhardcore (Carter 5.5 percent, 0.4 percent; Ford, 2.9

Table 29.6
Vote Change: November Vote Regressed on October Vote Preference,
Party Affiliation, and Estimates of Candidates' Vote Percentages
and Support Among Nonhardcore Respondents (N = 43)

	Simple r	Beta	Incr. R^2
November Vote			
October vote preference	.60[a]	.47[a]	.364[a]
Party affiliation	.51[a]	.18	.270[a]
Estimated percentage (October)			
Carter	.03	−.16	—
Ford	−.20	−.11	—
Support (October)			
Carter	.13	.10	—
Ford	.07	.10	.051
November Vote			
October vote preference	.60[a]	.56[a]	.364[a]
Party affiliation	.51[a]	.21	.270[a]
Estimated percentage (September to October)			
Carter gain relative to Ford	−.13	−.26[a]	—
Support (September to October)			
Carter	−.00	−.20	—
Ford	.03	−.05	.079

a. $p < .05$.

percent, 0.5 percent). All four of the comparisons between variances accounted for by the two groups are statistically significant.

It was also suggested that the need to audit the climate of opinion would lead the nonhardcore respondents to use the media heavily during the campaign. Television should play a particularly heavy role in this process. Some support is shown for this in the September data in Table 29.8. For the nonhardcore, the television use index (including frequency, attention, and reliance) accounted for significant proportions of variance in candidate support in September (16.2 percent Carter, 20.6 percent Ford). The corresponding proportions for the hardcore were considerably less (10.7 percent Carter, 1.3 percent Ford). October comparisons showed nonsignificant increments for both groups for both candidates. Newspaper use failed to show consistent differences between the two groups in its influence on perceptions of candidate support. In September, newspaper use was much stronger in the hardcore in accounting for Carter support (37.9 percent versus 2.0 percent), but the reverse held for Ford support (5.1 percent hardcore versus 9.5 percent nonhardcore). In the October data, newspaper use was slightly stronger in the hardcore group for both

Table 29.7
Amount of Political Discussion in September and October
Among Nonhardcore and Hardcore Panel Respondents (in percentages)

Political Discussion	Nonhardcore (n = 65)	Hardcore (n = 32)	All Respondents (N = 97)
September			
A lot	31	49[a]	37
A little	55	48	52
None	14	3	11
October			
A lot	39	49	42
A little	57	45	53
None	4	6	5

a. $p < .05$ for difference between Nonhardcore and Hardcore, Mann-Whitney U test.

candidates (6.2 percent versus 5.9 percent Carter; 9.7 percent versus 2.2 percent Ford).

CONCLUSIONS

Our research goal was to test Noelle-Neumann's climate of opinion hypotheses in the context of an American election. Support was found for the first of her hypotheses that perceptions of public opinion — judgments of what others believe — would affect public behavior. Perceptions of the proportion of the vote the candidates would get and of the gain or loss in their support added significant increments to the prediction of vote preferences in September and October. This held even after controls for party affiliation were applied.

While we can say that there is a sizable association between the perceived climate opinion and expressions of voting intention, we cannot say from the available evidence that the perceptions lead to changes in voting. Analyses over time in our panel provide ambiguous findings. October climate-of-opinion measures predicted changes in vote preference from September to October, but September measures of the perception measures did not. Without panel designs with shorter time lags we cannot make stronger statements about casual ordering. About all we can say is that changes in perceptions of public opinion and changes in vote preference occurred in compatible directions during the September-October period.

A second aspect of Noelle-Neumann's work, the distinction between a "hardcore" of opinion holders relatively immune to the "spiral of silence"

Table 29.8
Changes in Candidate Support in September and October Regressed on Party Affiliation and Communication Variables: Variance Accounted for Among Nonhardcore and Hardcore Panel Respondents

	Nonhardcore (n = 52)		Hardcore (n = 30)	
	Sept.	Oct.	Sept.	Oct.
Carter Support				
Party affiliation	.018	.042	.089	.044
Interpersonal communication	.055	.004	.112	.192[a]
Newspaper use	.020	.022	.379[a]	.097
Television use	.162[a]	.014	.107	.148
Ford Support				
Party affiliation	.045	.000	.162[a]	.098
Interpersonal communication	.029	.055	.379[a]	.255[a]
Newspaper use	.095	.059	.051	.062
Television use	.206[a]	.065	.013	.108

a. $p < .05$.

and the majority of "nonhardcore" citizens, provided some marked contrasts in the sample examined here. Noelle-Neumann predicts that the hardcore will use interpersonal communication heavily to bolster their opinions. In September at least, our hardcore respondents showed higher levels of interpersonal discussion than did the nonhardcore. Even more impressive were the differences between groups in the extent to which interpersonal communication was involved in making judgments about the changes in support for Carter and Ford. In both September and October, the hardcore had much higher proportions of variance in perceptions of support accounted for by interpersonal communication. The expectation that the nonhardcore would show greater influences of television use was given mixed support in our data.

One further hypothesis from Noelle-Neumann will be examined in future analyses. That is, within the nonhardcore group, those seeing their chosen candidate as losing should exhibit avoidance behavior by being extremely low in interpersonal discussion during the campaign. This analysis will be reported in a revision of this chapter.

It is also relevant to ask whether our evidence is compatible with the traditional bandwagon effect. To the extent that vote preferences tended to vary with perceptions of which side was gaining and winning, there is supportive data. But if the bandwagon were operating as it is usually described, its effects would grow as election night draws near. Our data indicate quite the opposite. The September results are much stronger than those of October and November. It may be said, too, that the 1976 election lacked a clear favorite, a condition said to make the bandwagon effect less likely (Patterson, 1980).

The treatment here of perceptions of public opinion may be regarded as a small step toward developing communication-related concepts appropriate to the social system level of analysis. Opinions held by individuals may well affect overt behavior, but so do perceptions of what other people believe. In fact individuals may feel more free to express their perceptions of public opinion than they do about their own private opinions when the latter are socially unacceptable.

For this and other reasons, it may be useful to change our definitions of "public opinion" away from a collection of individual expressions to the summation of perceptions about what others in the society believe.

REFERENCES

Chaffee, S. H., & McLeod, J. M. *Interpersonal perception and communication.* Beverly Hills, CA: Sage, 1973.
DeFleur, M., & Westie, F. Verbal attitudes and overt acts. *American Sociological Review,* 1958, 23, 667-673.
DeFleur, M., & Westie, F. Attitude as a scientific concept. *Social Forces,* 1963, 42, 17-31.
Festinger, L. Behavioral support for opinion change. *Public Opinion Quarterly,* 1964, 28, 404-417.
Fields, J., & Schuman, H. Public beliefs about the beliefs of the public. *Public Opinion Quarterly,* 1976, 40, 427-488.
Lane, R. *Political life.* Glencoe, IL: Free Press, 1958.
Lang, K., & Lang, G. E. *The impact of expectations and election day perceptions on voting behavior.* Paper presented at the American Association for Public Opinion Research meetings, 1965.
Laing, R. D., Phillipson, H., & Lee, A. R. Interpersonal perception: A theory and a method of research. New York: Springer, 1966.
LaPiere, R. Attitude vs. actions. *Social Forces,* 1934, 13, 230-237.
Lee, A. L. & Lee, E. B. The devices of propaganda. *The fine art of propaganda.* New York: Harcourt, Brace, 1939.
Lipset, S. M. Youth and politics. In Robert K. Merton & Robert Nisbet (Eds.), *Contemporary social problems* (3rd. ed.). New York: Harcourt, Brace, 1971.
Mendelsohn, H. A. *Exposure to election broadcasts and terminal voting decisions.* Paper presented at the American Association for Public Opinion Research meetings, 1965.
Miller, W. E. *Analysis of the effect of election night predictions on voting behavior.* Unpublished report, University of Michigan, Survey Research Center, Political Behavior Program, 1965.
Newcomb, T. M. An approach to the study of communicative acts. *Psychological Review,* 1953, 60, 393-404.
Newcomb, T. M. *The acquaintance process.* New York: Holt, Rinehart & Winston, 1961.
Noelle-Neumann, E. Return to the concept of powerful mass media. *Studies in Broadcasting,* 1973, 12, 68-105.
Noelle-Neumann, E. Spiral of silence. *Journal of Communication,* 1974, 24(2), 43-51.
O'Gormann, H. J., & Garry, S. L. Pluralistic ignorance — A replication and extension. *Public Opinion Quarterly,* 1976, 40, 449-458.
Patterson, T. E. *The mass media election.* New York: Praeger, 1980.
Pool, I. S., Abelson, R. P., & Popkin, S. *Candidates, issues and strategies.* Cambridge: MIT Press, 1965.

Schanck, R. L. A study of a community and its groups and institutions conceived of as behaviors of individuals. *Psychological Monographs*, 1932, *43*, 221-224.

Scheff, T. J. Toward a sociological model of consensus. *American Sociological Review*, 1967, *32*, 32-46.

Schuman, H., & Johnson, M. P. Attitudes and behaviors. In Alex Inkeles (Ed.), *Annual review of sociology* (Vol. 2). Palo Alto, CA: Annual Reviews. 1976.

Seibold, D. R. Communication research and the attitude-verbal report-overt behavior relationship: A critique and theoretic reformulation. *Human Communication Research*, 1975, *2*(1), 3-32.

Weiss, W. Effects of mass communication. In *The handbook of social psychology*. Reading, MA: Addison-Wesley, 1969.

Wicker, A. W. Attitude vs. action: The relationship of verbal and overt behavioral responses to attitude objects. *Journal of Social Issues*, 1969, *25*(4), 41-78.

POLITICAL COMMUNICATION

30 • The Successful Communication of Cognitive Information: A Study of a Precinct Committeeman

DAVID A. BOSITIS • ROY E. MILLER

George Washington University • Southern Illinois University

THE systematic study of the effects of local political party campaign activities has been a somewhat neglected area in the literature concerning political campaigns. This relative lack of attention seems particularly unfortunate given the extremely large number of local political offices that are sought each year at a campaign cost of many millions of dollars and countless thousands of person-hours of volunteer labor. Accordingly, the present report is offered as an extension of earlier work that in its overview attempts to comment on the effectiveness of grassroots campaign activities (see Miller & Robyn, 1975a, 1975b; Miller & Richey, 1980; Miller, Bositis, & Baer, 1981; Baer, Bositis, & Miller, 1981; Miller, 1981). More specifically, the subject of this particular chapter is the precinct committeeman's role in the transmission of cognitive information in local-level elections. There are two important reasons why the communication of cognitive campaign information at the grassroots level is such an important subject of study. In general, they both have to do with the fact that one of the primary functions of political party activity is to persuade undecided voters to support their candidates (Crotty, 1971; Blydenburgh, 1971).

First, when analyzing the effectiveness of persuasive appeals it is important to take note of the role of cognitive information in attitude change. The steps leading to attitude change from persuasive appeals can be roughly indicated as follows: (1) attention to the communication, (2) comprehension of its contents, and (3) yielding to what is comprehended (McGuire, 1969). The successful communication of cognitive information

Correspondence and requests for reprints: David A. Bositis, Department of Political Science, George Washington University, Washington, DC 20052.

subsumes steps 1 and 2 above. Therefore the successful communication of cognitive information is a necessary condition for attitude change to occur as a result of persuasive appeals. It is not a sufficient condition (Hovland, Lumsdaine, & Sheffield, 1949; Bogart, 1957), but it is a necessary one.

Second, the general nature of campaign appeals in many if not most local elections is such that in a very real sense cognitive information is the persuasive appeal. The circuit judge candidate who advertises that he has never been overturned by a higher court is conveying both a cognitive datum as well as the persuasive implication that "I am so knowledgeable about the law that higher courts never question my judgments and therefore I deserve your support."

In sum, the communication of cognitive information is important to study because without the ability to effectively communicate such information, the local party machinery is incapable of much persuasion — a campaign function that is seemingly of growing importance given the expanding number of "independents" in the electorate.

SOME RELEVANT LITERATURE

What does the literature suggest about the communication of cognitive information? There are two sets of literature relevant to these concerns. The first set examines partisan political campaigns and the second examines public information and propaganda campaigns. There is no consensus among the scholars working in these areas about the parameters of the effective communication of cognitive information. Also, unfortunately, there is little comparability among the studies.

The studies most directly applicable to the concerns of this chapter are a field experimental study of a direct mailing during the campaign of a U.S. congressman (Miller & Robyn, 1975a, 1975b), a field experimental study of the effects of a precinct-level literature "drop" on several local races (Miller & Richey, 1980; Miller, 1981), and the study of a precinct committeeman's canvassing efforts in a primary election — of which the present work is an extension (Baer, Bositis, & Miller, 1981).

The Miller and Robyn study investigated the impact of a direct mailing on information levels in a U.S. congressman's campaign. The mailing emanated from the candidate and the letter was nonpersonalized. The authors concluded that there were no statistically significant information increases attributable to the mailing even though the observed differences were consistent with that interpretation. However, this was a campaign for a national-level office (member of Congress); the candidate in question was a well-known public figure (an ex-lieutenant governor of Illinois), and there was considerable mass media advertising in the campaign. In a very real sense this was a high-salience and high-information campaign and thus there was less chance that any single stimulus, such as the mailing, was going to be effective (Miller & Robyn, 1975a, 1975b).

The Miller and Richey study examined the effects upon voters of a precinct committeeman's literature "drop." The dropped literature concerned races for state's attorney, circuit judge, and county coroner — three campaigns that could best be characterized as low-interest and low-salience. The authors concluded that the literature drop did in fact increase both name recognition and professional information levels to a significant degree (Miller & Richey, 1980; Miller, 1981).

In the study by Baer, Bositis, and Miller (1981), it was found that the canvassing activities of a precinct committeeman were effective in increasing the cognitive information levels of the voters with respect to the candidates for the office of state's attorney. Again the race in question was a low-salience one as it was a primary election in which none of the candidates was either the incumbent or very well known in the county.

On the basis of the most relevant partisan political campaign literature, it would seem that effective communication of cognitive information is certainly possible. However, it is probably most likely to occur in campaigns that are of the low-salience and low-information genre.

Looking now at the literature concerning public information and propaganda campaigns, we again find that sometimes they are effective in increasing cognitive information levels and sometimes they are not. For example, Hovland, Lumsdaine, and Sheffield (1949) studied the effects of army indoctrination and propaganda films and concluded that information was indeed being successfully communicated by the films. Similarly, Bogart (1957) concluded that information was successfully transmitted during the U.S. government propaganda campaign in Greece during the Cold War. Westerstahl, Sarlvik, and Jansen (1961) have reported on a successful campaign in Sweden to raise public information levels regarding civil defense. Douglas, Westley, and Chaffee (1970) have reported on a public information campaign in Connecticut that successfully increased information levels regarding mental retardation, and Salcedo, Read, Evans, and Kong (1974) found increased information levels attributable to a targeted mass media campaign on pesticide safety.

On the other side of the coin, Star and Hughes (1950) have reported on an unsuccessful media-based campaign to increase public information levels concerning the United Nations. Likewise, Gruenhagen (1969) found no discernible effects due to a month-long information campaign in Virginia on pesticide use and safety.

Regardless of outcome, there seem to be several general points of agreement that can be extracted from the literature on public information campaigns. First, a certain threshold of "interest" in the subject matter is required in order to ensure that information will be attended to (Hyman & Sheatsley, 1947; Star & Hughes, 1950; Douglas, Westley, & Chaffee, 1970; Mendelsohn, 1973). Second, information is more likely to be attended to by persons for whom the information is congenial with their own positions (Hyman & Sheatsley, 1947). And third, information campaigns may show their greatest effects vis-à-vis those persons who initially have low information levels on the subject in question (Douglas, Westley, & Chaffee, 1970).

Accordingly, it would seem quite reasonable to ask whether or not these apparent constraints upon effective public information campaigns also function as parameters partially delineating conditions under which precinct commiteemen may expect to successfully transmit cognitive information in a partisan political campaign. In addition, the suggestion that attempts by political parties to communicate cognitive information are likely to be most successful in low-salience and low-information campaigns (Miller & Richey, 1980; Miller, 1981; Baer, Bositis & Miller, 1981) is certainly deserving of a more explicit test than what is has received to date. Thus it is the intent of the present work to investigate the role of these several possible constraining factors within the context of a campaign for a local political office.

DESIGN OF THE STUDY

In order to prepare a data base that would provide the most internally valid answers to many questions regarding the effectiveness of the precinct committeeman in local political campaigns, field experiments were conducted in the seventh precinct of Carbondale, Illinois, during both the 1980 primary and general elections. During both elections the potential respondent pool consisted of all registered voters in the precinct. Using random assignment procedures all potential respondents were assigned to one of several experimental groups. The many experimental groups differed in terms of whether they received a letter, a phone call, or a personal visit from the precinct committeeman, whether that contact was made "early" or "late" vis-à-vis election day, and whether they were contacted only once or twice. These differences are of no import to the present work, but they do allow for investigation of channel, timing, and multiple-contact effects (for example, see Baer, Bositis, & Miller, 1981; Miller, Bositis, & Baer, 1981). For present purposes, all of the treatment groups have been collapsed into one regardless of the number, timing, or channel of contact(s) by the precinct committeeman. All postelection interviews were conducted over the telephone, a process that yielded 185 completed interviews after the primary election and 167 completed interviews after the general election.

One particular design feature of this overall study merits special attention. A subset of the subjects in these two field experiments actually comprise a field experimental panel, i.e., the same subjects were observed in both the spring and the fall of 1980. The presence of this field experimental panel allows us to specifically address the question of whether or not the contextual differences between the primary and the general election affect the consequences of the precinct committeeman's efforts. In particular is the precinct committeeman better able to effectively transmit information in the lower-salience environment of the primary election than in the more highly charged atmosphere of the general election? It should be noted that this design feature will allow much more definitive information to be brought to bear on the above question than has been the case in any previous literature. The reason for this is that the results cannot possibly be affected by demographic, contextual differences as is possible when comparing the results to two studies done in two different locations (the entire study was done in a single precinct). Nor could any results be an artifact of comparing activities by two different precinct committeemen (the same person was filling that role throughout the study). In addition, the fact that the study, including the panel, was carried out using an experimental design, rules out a variety of other possible threats to the validity of any study conclusions.

One other aspect of the study design deserves some comment. Insofar as the present report is concerned, the experimental stimulus consisted of a contact between the subjects and the Democratic precinct committeeman in which various information was conveyed regarding one or more local campaign races, in particular, circuit judge, county coroner, and/or state's attorney. Noteworthy is the fact that there was no Republican committeeman in the precinct under study, and therefore conditions were probably near optimal for experimental treatment effects to manifest themselves.

EMPIRICAL EXPECTATIONS

It will be recalled that the earlier literature review suggested several factors that were likely to affect the successful communication of information in information campaigns in general. Those factors included the message recipient's degree of interest in the subject matter of the communication, their initial information level regarding that subject matter, and whether or not they were sympathetic to the content of the information. In addition, it was suggested that the character of the information environment would affect the effectiveness of information stimuli. In particular in a low-salience and low-information environment an information stimulus should cause a greater information gain than the same stimulus would in a high-information environment. These general suggestions regarding some important prerequisites of information gain give rise to a variety of empirical expectations regarding the effectiveness of a precinct committeeman in successfully communicating information specifically in local political campaigns.

1. The greater the individual's interest in local politics, the greater the information gain from being contacted by a precinct committeeman.
2. A contact by a precinct committeeman will be more effective in increasing the information level of individuals with initially low levels of information than of those with initially high levels of information.
3. A contact by a precinct committeeman will be most effective in increasing the information level of individuals who are highly interested and who have initially low levels of information.
4. A contact by a precinct committeeman will be least effective in increasing the information level of highly interested individuals with initially high information levels.

This last hypothesis deserves some amplification. Highly interested individuals with initially high levels of information will probably live in an environment with numerous informational stimuli, and given the type of motivation that these individuals have, i.e., high interest, they will likely attend to a great many of them. Thus a single additional stimulus, such as a contact by a precinct committeeman, can only be expected to have little or no effect.

No attempt will be made to postulate expectations regarding the other two combinations of interest and initial information level. The primary reason for this is because there seem to be no good a priori bases for assigning a weighting to the relative importance of interest versus information level. In other words there are not good reasons to expect that less interested individuals with initially low levels of information would gain more or less from a contact by a precinct committeeman than less interested individuals with initially high levels of information.

When one considers the role that having a sympathetic viewpoint plays in facilitating effective communication, the situation in political campaigns becomes somewhat cloudy. In particular in the general election context, party identification can be viewed as being related to both the interest and information dimensions previously discussed. On the one hand Democratic identifiers and, to a lesser extent, Independents are probably more interested in information about local Democratic candidates than are Republican identifiers. And given that individuals seek and are more receptive to information that is congenial to their already predetermined positions, Democratic identifiers and Independents would tend to seek and be more receptive to information about Democratic candidates than

Communication of Cognitive Information

would Republican identifiers (Hyman & Sheatsley, 1947; Becker, McCombs, & McLeod, 1975). On the other hand, if Republican identifiers tend to seek and be more receptive to information about the Republican candidates then their knowledge of the Democratic candidates should probably be lower, and, as we have seen, this lower level of information suggests that they should gain more from an informational stimulus about the Democratic candidates than individuals with high information levels.

Given this conflicting reasoning, the following two hypotheses are our most reasonable statements of expectations in this area. In these statements, and throughout the remainder of this work, Democratic identifiers and Independents will be referred to as "sympathetics" (since the informational stimuli are from the Democratic precinct committeeman). Likewise Republican identifiers will be referred to as "unsympathetics."

5. The information gained from an informational contact by a Democratic precinct committeeman will be greater for sympathetics with initially low levels of information than for unsympathetics or sympathetics with initially high levels of information.

6. The information gained from an informational contact by a Democratic precinct committeeman will be greater for unsympathetics with initially low information levels than for either sympathetics or unsympathetics with initially high information levels.

However, in the context of a primary election it must be remembered that those individuals actually voting in the Republican primary have no particular reason to take cognizance of information about the Democratic candidates since those candidates will not be on the ballot that they are voting. Therefore given this lack of salience of the Democratic candidates to Republican primary voters, the following expectation is in order.

7. During a primary campaign, the information gained from a contact by the Democratic precinct committeeman will be greater for persons who either do not vote at all or vote in the Democratic primary than for persons who vote in the Republican primary.

Since the primary campaign is usually a lower-interest and lower-information environment than the general election campaign, it is natural to expect that a single informational contact would probably have a greater impact in the primary campaign. In fact given the advantageous communications environment in the primary, the differences between the two elections should be considerable.

8. The effectiveness of an informational contact by a Democratic precinct committeeman in inducing information gain will be greater in a primary election than in a general election.

Having specified a variety of empirical expectations regarding several factors that affect the ability of a precinct committeeman to successfully communicate cognitive information in local-level campaigns, we are now almost ready to proceed to an actual test of those hypotheses. Before doing so, however, we must first deal briefly with some measurement considerations.

MEASUREMENT CONSIDERATIONS

Critical to a complete understanding of the forthcoming data analyses is a firm realization that conceptually they involve three different data bases (the primary election data set, the general election data set, and the panel data set), and that different data bases will be used as required in the tests of different hypotheses. Accordingly, the generic dependent variable in all analyses (information score) actually exists in three slightly different specific forms.

The information score for the primary election data set (INFORMp) consists of the number of correct responses to seven questions regarding the candidates in the race for Jackson County State's Attorney. The information score for the general election in all nonpanel analyses (INFORMg) consists of the number of correct responses to eight questions concerning the candidates for both circuit judge and county coroner as well as state's attorney. The information score for the general election in all panel analyses (INFORMp-g) consists of the number of correct responses to the four questions concerning the race for state's attorney that were asked both in the spring and fall. In other words the panel data concerns the race for only one office — Jackson County State's Attorney. It goes without saying, of course, that the answers to all information questions were included in the contact by the precinct committeeman.

The measurement of the independent factors that may affect the success of informational communication in local campaigns was fairly straightforward. Our subjects' level of interest was measured by dichotomizing their responses to the question "How much interest would you say that you have in Jackson County politics — a great deal of interest, some interest, little interest, or no interest at all." Their sympathetic status was indicated by their self-assessed party identification, which was measured by a standard party identification question with a response continuum ranging from strong Democrat to strong Republican. Finally, given that we had longitudinal data for our panel respondents, we were able to use their primary information scores (INFORMp) as a measure of their initial information levels vis-à-vis the general election campaign.

Table 30.1
Comparison of Contact Effects on Information Levels
by Level of Interest in Local Politics
for the Primary and General Elections

	Primary Election Data Base (INFORM$_P$)		General Election Data Base (INFORM$_G$)	
	High Interest	Low Interest	High Interest	Low Interest
Contacted group	E$\bar{x}$ = 1.60 (N = 85)	E$\bar{x}$ = 0.84 (N = 61)	E$\bar{x}$ = 4.00 (N = 59)	E$\bar{x}$ = 2.06 (N = 54)
Control group	C$\bar{x}$ = 0.64 (N = 17)	C$\bar{x}$ = 0.35 (N = 17)	C$\bar{x}$ = 3.59 (N = 32)	C$\bar{x}$ = 2.31 (N = 13)
Gain ratio (E$\bar{x}$/C$\bar{x}$)	2.50	2.40	1.11	.89

DATA FINDINGS

Before proceeding to an empirical test of the hypotheses previously discussed, a word is in order regarding the nature of the analytical evidence to be presented. First, throughout this work all comparisons will be made on the basis of the ratio of the mean information score of the contacted group to the mean information score of the relevant control group. Hereafter this will be referred to as a "gain ratio," although it must be remembered that in none of the analyses is this in fact a ratio involving actual gain scores. Second, throughout the analyses attention will be focused on the macro patterns of comparative relationships, which together constitute the evidence bearing on the total set of theoretical expectations that have been advanced. Accordingly, the concern will be with the direction and magnitude of relationships as they contribute to such patterns. The questions of statistical significance will be reserved for the overall findings, rather than for each individual comparison that might be made.

The first hypothesis suggests that individuals who are more interested in local politics should experience greater information gain from a contact by their precinct committeeman regarding local candidates than those individuals who are less interested. The evidence in Table 30.1 generally supports this hypothesis.

From Table 30.1 we see that in the primary election there is a slightly greater contact effect for the more highly interested individuals than for the lesser interested ones. The experimental group of the high-interest subjects had an average information level 2.5 times higher than that of the comparable control group. On the other hand, for the low-interest individuals the experimental group had an average information level a slightly lower 2.4 times higher than the information level of the comparable control group.

Looking now at the general election, examination of the data in Table 30.1 again suggests that the more highly interested individuals gained more from the informational contact than the less-interested individuals. There was a small but positive gain in information for the more highly interested individuals (11 percent gain), while for the individuals with a low degree of interest there was no information gain at all (in fact, the control group's mean was greater than the mean for the treatment group).

It is important here to say a few words regarding the gain ratio of .89 for the low-interest individuals in the general election. The fact that this value is less than 1.0, of course, indicates that the control group's mean information score was greater than that of the contacted group. At first blush this may be somewhat curious. Why would the control group have a higher mean? There would seem to be two alternative explanations for this phenomenon. First, it could merely be statistical artifact resulting from the random assignment procedures. Were this the preferred interpretation, one would assume the statistical equivalence of the two groups (a gain ratio of 1.0) and proceed with the analysis. On the other hand, it could be reasoned that for this particular experimental group the contact by the precinct committeeman triggered some unknown psychological processes that resulted in the diminished ability to retrieve certain information from long-term memory, i.e., the "forgetting" of information. Were this the preferred interpretation, one would take the gain ratio of less than unity as representing a "negative gain" (i.e., an information loss) and proceed with the analysis. To us the statistical artifact interpretation seems to be the more plausible. Regardless, and most importantly, neither interpretation alters the data pattern observed in Table 30.1, that being that in both elections individuals with a high interest showed a greater information gain from the precinct committeeman's contact than did low-interest individuals.

The second hypothesis suggests that information gain will be greater for individuals with low initial levels of information than for persons with high initial levels of information. To operationalize low versus high initial levels of information, the dichotomized primary information score (INFORM$_P$) was used as the measure of information levels at the beginning of the general election. This was then followed by an analysis of the contact effects on the panel information scores (INFORM$_{P-G}$) in each of these two groups, and is reported in Table 30.2

An inspection of the gain ratios in Table 30.2 for the high versus the low initial information groups shows that the data are consonant with the second hypothesis. The initially low information group gained about 25

Table 30.2
Comparison of Contact Effects on Information Levels (INFORM$_{P-G}$)
by Initial Information Level
(Panel Data Base)

	Low Initial Information	High Initial Information
Experimental group	E$\bar{x}$ = 1.31 (N = 26)	E$\bar{x}$ = 2.33 (N = 15)
Control group	C$\bar{x}$ = 1.05 (N = 20)	C$\bar{x}$ = 2.73 (N = 15)
Gain ratio (E$\bar{x}$/C$\bar{x}$)	1.25	.85

percent from the contact by the committeeman, while the initially high information group registered no gain whatsoever compared with its control group. In fact this is another instance where the contacted group had a lower mean than the comparable control group. Again this is probably a statistical artifact of the random assignment procedures, but might be interpreted as an average information loss. In either case the second hypothesis is clearly supported by the data.

The third and fourth hypotheses will be examined together because of their related phrasing and content. The third hypothesis states that a contact by a precinct committeeman will be most effective in increasing the information level of highly interested individuals with initially low levels of information. By implication, the term "most effective" here means more effective than any other combination of level of interest and initial information level. Similarly, the fourth hypothesis states that an informational contact will be least effective in increasing information levels of highly interested individuals with initially high information levels. Again by implication "least effective" here means less than any other combination of level of interest and initial information level.

The data in Table 30.3 clearly support both of these hypotheses. The contact effects among the high-interest but low-initial-information individuals (gain ratio = 1.82) were greater than for any other combination of those two criterion variables. Likewise the contact effectiveness was least for the high-interest but high-initial-information individuals (gain ratio = .80). As expected the gain ratios for the remaining two combinations of these criterion variables fell in between these extreme values.

The fifth hypothesis states that in the general election, sympathetics (Democratic identifiers and Independents) with initially low information levels should gain more from an informational contact about Democratic

Table 30.3
Comparison of Contact Effects on Information Levels (INFORM$_{P-G}$)
by Level of Interest and Initial Information Level
(Panel Data Base)

	High Interest	Low Interest
Low Initial Information		
Experimental group	E$\bar{x}$ = 2.18	E$\bar{x}$ = 0.71
	(N = 11)	(N = 14)
Control group	C$\bar{x}$ = 1.20	C$\bar{x}$ = 0.60
	(N = 15)	(N = 5)
Gain ratio (E$\bar{x}$/C$\bar{x}$)	1.82	1.18
High Initial Information		
Experimental group	E$\bar{x}$ = 2.45	E$\bar{x}$ = 2.0
	(N = 11)	(N = 4)
Control group	Cx = 3.08	Cx = 1.33
	(N = 12)	(N = 3)
Gain ratio (E$\bar{x}$/C$\bar{x}$)	.80	1.50

candidates than either unsympathetics (Republican identifiers) or sympathetics with initially high levels of information. The data presented in Table 30.4 tend to support this hypothesis also.

The sympathetics with initially low information levels are the only combination of party identification and initial information level where the contacted group has a higher mean than the comparable control group. The individuals in this group had on the average a 64 percent higher information score than the individuals in the comparable control group. The evidence in support of this hypothesis is even the more convincing when one considers that for all other combinations of party and initial information levels the contacted subjects registered at best no gain from the contact compared with their comparable control groups.

The sixth hypothesis states that the unsympathetics (Republican identifiers) with initially low information levels will gain more from the informational contact than either sympathetics or unsympathetics with initially high information levels. While the data is compatible with this hypothesis, the degree of support is certainly marginal. Although none of the three combinations of party and initial information level that are of immediate concern showed any positive gain in the contacted group over the comparable control group, it is the case that the gain ratio for unsympathetics with initially low information levels (.81), albeit less than 1.0, is still slightly

Table 30.4
Comparison of Contact Effects on Information Levels (INFORM$_{P \cdot G}$)
by Party Identification and Initial Information Level
(Panel Data Base)

	Sympathetics	Unsympathetics
Low Initial Information		
Experimental group	E$\bar{x}$ = 1.64	E$\bar{x}$ = 0.92
	(N = 14)	(N = 12)
Control group	C$\bar{x}$ = 1.00	C$\bar{x}$ = 1.14
	(N = 13)	(N = 7)
Gain ratio (E$\bar{x}$/C$\bar{x}$)	1.64	.81
High Initial Information		
Experimental group	E$\bar{x}$ = 2.0	E$\bar{x}$ = 2.8
	(N = 9)	(N = 5)
Control group	C$\bar{x}$ = 2.9	C$\bar{x}$ = 3.5
	(N = 11)	(N = 2)
Gain ratio (E$\bar{x}$/C$\bar{x}$)	.69	.80

greater than that for any of the more highly informed individuals — either sympathetic or unsympathetic.

The seventh hypothesis states that the information gain from the contact by a Democratic precinct committeeman in the primary campaign will be greater for persons who either vote in the Democratic primary or do not vote at all than for Republican primary voters. The evidence presented in Table 30.5 supports this hypothesis quite strongly.

Among those who either voted in the Democratic primary or did not vote at all, there was a 212 percent higher information level for the contacted individuals than for the comparable control subjects. However, this gain was not anywhere near as large for the voters in the Republican primary. Those voters improved their information levels by only 50 percent over their comparable control group.

The eighth and last hypothesis states that an informational contact by a Democratic precinct committeeman will have a greater effect on informational gain in a primary election than in a general election. This in fact was the case as is clearly indicated in Table 30.6

From Table 30.6 we can see that the subjects who were contacted by the precinct committeeman during the primary election had an average information score 156 percent higher than that of the control group in the

Table 30.5
Comparison of Contact Effects on Information Levels (INFORM$_p$)
by Primary Voting Behavior
(Primary Election Data Base)

	Voted in the Democratic Primary or Did Not Vote	Voted in the Republican Primary
Experimental group	$E\bar{x} = 1.31$ (N = 98)	$E\bar{x} = 1.08$ (N = 46)
Control group	$C\bar{x} = 0.42$ (N = 25)	$C\bar{x} = 0.72$ (N = 9)
Gain ratio ($E\bar{x}/C\bar{x}$)	3.12	1.5

primary. On the other hand, during the general election the contact by the precinct committeeman seems to have had no overall positive effect whatsoever.

CONCLUDING THOUGHTS

The findings of this research can be viewed from three different perspectives. First, the empirical findings are generally quite consistent with past literature. Second, the findings were totally consonant with the theoretical expectations that were developed. Third, and perhaps most important to many, the empirical findings are quire satisfying from the precinct committeeman's perspective.

From the perspective of past literature, the present study found strong contact effects in the primary (as did Baer, Bositis, & Miller, 1981) but no overall effects in the general election (similar to Miller & Robyn, 1975a, 1975b). On the other hand, Miller and Richey (1980) found statistically significant effects in a general election. However, the Miller and Richey study did not involve any work in the primary by the precinct committeeman, and the information levels of the subjects in the present study quite plausibly could have been raised to a level sufficiently high enough in the primary to make any more information gain in the general election extremely difficult (recall that the primary treatments raised information levels and those with higher information levels in the general election experienced less information gain than those with low information levels).

Table 30.6
Comparison of Contact Effects on Information Levels
in the Primary and General Elections

	Primary Election Data Base (INFORM$_P$)	General Election Data Base (INFORM$_G$)
Experimental group	E$\bar{x}$ = 1.28 (N = 147)	E$\bar{x}$ = 3.04 (N = 114)
Control group	C$\bar{x}$ = 0.50 (N = 34)	C$\bar{x}$ = 3.26 (N = 46)
Gain ratio (E$\bar{x}$/C$\bar{x}$)	2.56	.93

Additionally, the control groups in the earlier study could have been exposed to fewer informational stimuli from outside sources than the control group in this experiment because the local races in this election (1980) were much more hotly contested than in the earlier study (1976).

From the perspective of the theoretical bases of analysis the findings were in every case consonant with the empirical expectations. This gives us strong reason to believe in the credibility of the total set of theoretical assumptions. In fact if there was no substance to the theoretical assumptions underlying these analyses, then the probability that the empirical results would by chance alone be directionally consistent with eight out of eight hypotheses based upon those assumptions is only 1/256 or .004 $[\binom{8}{8}/2^8]$. It is quite likely, therefore, that chance has little or nothing to do with our total set of findings.

From the perspective of the precinct committeeman, it should be useful to know that informational contacts are much more likely to be effective during primaries rather than general elections (low- rather than high-information campaigns). This is probably the case because as the number of informational stimuli increases in a political campaign, the effect of any single informational stimulus decreases. Second, although there were no across-the-board information effects in the general election, the data suggest that the precinct committeeman can be successful in communicating information to the group probably most important to the precinct committeeman in his work — namely, sympathetics with initially low information levels. It is in this activation of marginal supporters that the precinct committeeman clearly can be the most effective in his attempts to communicate campaign information.

REFERENCES

Baer, D. L., Bositis, D. A., & Miller, R. E. A field experimental study of a precinct committeeman's canvassing efforts in a primary election. In M. Burgoon (Ed.), *Communication yearbook 5*. New Brunswick, NJ: Transaction, 1981.

Becker, L. B., McCombs, M. E., & McLeod, J. M. The development of political cognitions. In S. H. Chaffee (Ed.), *Political communication*. Beverly Hills, CA: Sage, 1975.

Blydenburgh, J. C. A controlled experiment to measure the effects of personal contact campaigning. *Midwest Journal of Political Science*, 1971, *15*, 365-381.

Bogart, L. Measuring the effectiveness of an overseas information campaign: A case history. *Public Opinion Quarterly*, 1957, *21*, 475-498.

Crotty, W. J. Party effort and its impact on the vote. *American Political Science Review*, 1971, *65*, 439-450.

Douglas, D., Westley, B. H., & Chaffee, S. H. An information campaign that changed community attitudes. *Journalism Quarterly*, 1970, *47*, 479-487.

Gruenhagen, R. H. *The effects of a planned communication program on change of attitudes and knowledge of the urban dweller toward chemicals and pesticides*. Virginia Cooperative Extension Service, Virginia Polytechnic Institute, 1969.

Hovland, C. I., Lumsdaine, A. A., & Sheffield, F. D. *Experiments on mass communication*. Princeton, NJ: Princeton University Press, 1949.

Hyman, H., & Sheatsley, P. Some reasons why information campaigns fail. *Public Opinion Quarterly*, 1947, *11*, 412-423.

McGuire, W. J. The nature of attitudes and attitude change. In G. Lindzey & E. Aronson (Eds.), *The handbook of social psychology* (Vol. 3, 2nd ed.). Reading, MA: Addison-Wesley, 1969.

Mendelsohn, H. Some reasons why information campaigns can succeed. *Public Opinion Quarterly*, 1973, *37*, 50-61.

Miller, R. E. *Literature drops in county-level political campaigns: What do they accomplish?* Paper delivered at the annual meeting of the Southwestern Political Science Association, Dallas, March 26-28, 1981.

Miller, R. E., & Richey, W. M. The effects of a campaign brochure "drop" in a county level race for state's attorney. In D. Nimmo (Ed.), *Communication yearbook 4*. New Brunswick, NJ: Transaction, 1980.

Miller, R. E., & Robyn, D. L. A field experimental study of direct mail in a congressional campaign: What effects last until election day? *Experimental Study of Politics*, 1975, *4*, 1-37. (a)

Miller, R. E., & Robyn, D. L. *A field experimental study of direct mail in a 1974 congressional primary campaign: Immediate effects*. Paper delivered at the Annual Meeting of the Political Communications Division of the International Communication Association, Chicago, April 23-26, 1975. (b)

Miller, R. E., Bositis, D. A. & Baer, D. L. A field experimental study of a precinct committeeman's efforts at stimulating voter turnout in a primary election: Telephone vs. mail vs. face-to-face appeals. *International Political Science Review*, 1981, *2*, 445-460.

Salcedo, R. N., Read, H., Evans, J. F., & Kong, A. C. A successful information campaign on pesticides. *Journalism Quarterly*, 1974, *51*, 91-95, 110.

Star, S. A., & Hughes, H. A report on an educational campaign: The cincinnati plan for the United Nations. *American Journal of Sociology*, 1950, *55*, 389-400.

Westerstahl, J., Sarlvik, B., & Janson, E. An experiment with information pamphlets on civil defense. *Public Opinion Quarterly*, 1961, *25*, 236-248.

VIII • INSTRUCTIONAL COMMUNICATION

31 ● Teacher Communication and Student Learning: The Effects of Perceived Solidarity with Instructor and Student Anxiety Proneness

GREGORY S. ANDRIATE
University of Bridgeport

THIS investigation focuses on teacher communication behaviors that affect student perceptions of the teacher-student relationship in the learning environment. Specifically, perceptions of interpersonal solidarity with the instructor are examined with respect to student anxiety traits, anxiety states, and classroom learning. While educational researchers have demonstrated that effective orientations toward subject (e.g., Crosswhite, 1972), school (e.g., Lunn, 1969; Shepps & Shepps, 1971), self (Brookover, Thomas, & Paterson, 1964), and even specific instructional units (cf. Bloom, 1976) are related to student learning processes, only recently has the concept of "affect toward instructor" received attention (e.g., Scott & Wheeless, 1977). Investigations of the relationship implied in teacher-student interactions should specify ways in which teachers contribute to student orientations and motivations toward learning and generate specific criteria for establishing professionally appropriate classroom relationships.

Solidarity and Learning

Brown (1965) originally conceptualized solidarity in terms of the psychological distance separating individuals: "Solidarity is often talked about in terms of being close or remote, near or far, the in-group versus the

AUTHOR'S NOTE: This chapter is based on the first of two studies in a doctoral dissertation directed by Professor Lawrence R. Wheeless, West Virginia University.

Correspondence and requests for reprints: Gregory S. Andriate, Department of Speech Communication, University of Bridgeport, Bridgeport, CT 06602.

out-group" (p. 57). Building on this definition, Wheeless (1976) suggested that "solidarity relationships refer to those in which closeness derived from similarity finds expression in sentiments, behaviors, and symbols" (p. 3). According to Wheeless (1978), solidarity relationships are "generally symmetrical" and typically derived through (1) similarities in personal characteristics; (2) closeness in physical and social space; (3) pleasant, affective sentiments such as liking, attraction, and trust; (4) cooperative, self-disclosive behaviors; and (5) symbolic expressions of intimacy and closeness.

The conceptually comprehensive reflection of the affective domain of interpersonal relationships provided by the solidarity construct has prompted instructional communication researchers to examine the relationship between solidarity and learning. Andersen (1978, 1979) investigated student perceptions of teacher-student solidarity with respect to teacher immediacy and student learning. Her findings indicated that the addition of solidarity slightly improved the predictive model between teacher immediacy and student affect, behavioral commitment, and cognitive learning. (Solidarity was also significantly and negatively correlated with cognitive learning, while immediacy was unrelated.) The multiple regression model also indicated that teacher-student solidarity and teacher immediacy were associated with decreases in short-term cognitive learning.

Nussbaum and Scott (1979) found perceived solidarity with instructor to be a significant predictor of student learning. Solidarity was a main contributor to the instructor communication variate in a significant canonical correlation between teacher self-disclosure, teacher communicator style, teacher-student solidarity, and three dimensions of student learning. While the addition of solidarity to this model did enhance the overall canonical relationship, this increase was not enough to statistically differentiate the canonical models with and without solidarity.

Andersen, Norton, and Nussbaum (1979) examined the relationship of teacher immediacy, teacher-student solidarity, and teacher communicator style to student perceptions of teacher effectiveness and student learning. Although not directly assessed, results appeared to indicate that perceived solidarity with instructor was positively associated with student affective and behavioral learning as well as student perceptions of teaching effectiveness. A direct test of the relationship by Nussbaum and Scott (1980) indicated that perceived solidarity with instructor was indeed differentially related to three domains of student learning. The use of three separate one-way analysis of variance procedures employing three levels of solidarity to predict each of the three domains of learning suggested that solidarity was not uniformly related to overall classroom learning: While perceived solidarity was positively associated with student affect and behavioral intentions, there were no significant differences between moderate or high perceptions of solidarity with instructor on either of these measures; also, students perceiving moderate solidarity with the instructor demonstrated significantly more cognitive learning than students perceiving either high or low solidarity. These results suggest that with respect to overall classroom learning, moderate perceptions of solidarity with the instructor may be the most functional.

Findings reported by Andersen (1978, 1979), Andersen et al. (1979), and Nussbaum and Scott (1979, 1980) suggest that perceptions of interpersonal solidarity with the instructor may be differentially related to the separate domains of student learning. While positive perceptions of the instructor are directly related to affective and behavioral-learning, there is no clear relationship with cognitive learning. Positive perceptions of the instructor appear to be either negatively related or unrelated to cognitive learning processes, an interpretation that has led some instructional communication researchers to speculate that high affect for the teacher may come at the expense of cognitive learning (e.g., Andersen, 1979; Elliot, 1979; Nussbaum & Scott, 1979, 1980).[1]

Perceived Threat and Classroom Performance

The relationship between student affective orientations and cognitive learning has been examined in investigations of the effects of perceived threat on cognitive performance (see Sarason, 1975; Spielberger, 1966, 1972, 1975). Such investigations have typically examined the relationships among stress conditions, anxiety, and performance in the learning environment.

Stress, defined as the "nonspecific response of the body to any demand made upon it" (Selye, 1976, p. 20), has been generally operationalized in either physical (e.g., threat of shock) or psychological (e.g., threat of failure; ego threat) terms (see Hodges, 1968; Spielberger, 1975). Anxiety, on the other hand, has been conceptualized as a process involving a "complex sequence of cognitive, affective and behavioral events that is evoked by some form of stress" (Spielberger, 1975, p. 137). Spielberger (1966) has argued that much of the confusion in stress, anxiety, and learning research has arisen through the use of the term "anxiety" in at least two senses: (1) an emotional state and (2) a personality trait. State anxiety (A-State) refers to "subjective, consciously-perceived feelings of tension, apprehension, and nervousness accompanied by or associated with activation of the autonomic nervous system" (Spielberger, 1975, p. 137), whereas trait anxiety (A-Trait) refers to "relatively stable individual differences in anxiety proneness; i.e., to differences among people in the disposition or tendency to perceive a wide range of situations as threatening and to respond to these situations with differential elevations in state anxiety" (Spielberger, 1975, p. 137).

While educational researchers have investigated the effects of various instructional variables on anxiety and student learning, such as the use of behavioral objectives (Tobias & Duchastel, 1974), instructional modes (Dowaliby & Schumer, 1973), alternative response modes (Tobias & Abramson, 1971), learner control (cf., Hedl & O'Neil, 1977), and computer-assisted instruction (see O'Neil & Richardson, 1977), the instructor as a potential source of threat has received little attention. Research investigating stress, anxiety, and learning indicates that it may not be anxiety proneness per se which produces differences in the performance of cognitive tasks, but rather the interaction of trait-like anxiety proneness with state perceptions of the learning environment, including the teacher (Heckhausen, 1975; Weiner, 1966).

Perceived Threat in Teacher-Student Relationships

Educational researchers have examined teacher-student communication as a dependent measure in studies of variables such as initiation of communication with teacher, receipt of communication from teacher, attention to teacher's communication with others, and behavioral interactions with teacher (Wine, 1972). However, the teacher-student relationship as an independent variable predicting state anxiety of students and its subsequent effects on learning has been only indirectly examined. For example, Kearney and McCroskey (1980) examined teacher communication style and communication apprehension of teacher and student with respect to student affect and behavioral commitment. Results indicated that student perceptions of teacher communication style were significantly related to state apprehension and student's affect and behavioral commitment. Concerning this indirect relationship between teacher communication style and student learning, they noted that students with positive perceptions of the teacher were less apprehensive about classroom interaction with him or her. Further, "students' trait communication apprehension was also a predictor of their own state apprehension" (Kearney & McCroskey, 1980, p. 549).

Although Kearney and McCroskey (1980) did not directly test the teacher-student relationship, their results suggest an interesting relationship among perceptions of the instructor, anxiety, and student learning. Evidently, both trait anxiety and perceptions of the teacher contribute to student anxiety states in the classroom, a position supported by the conceptual relationship between trait and state anxiety in human interaction.

In a review of the research on stress, anxiety, and learning, Spielberger (1975) concluded: "Persons who are high in anxiety proneness are disposed to perceive greater danger in relationships with other people that involve threats to self-esteem and to respond to these ego threats with greater elevations in state anxiety or drive than persons low in anxiety proneness" (p. 137).

The role relationship between teacher and student represents a potential threat to student self-esteem and therefore represents a source of psychological stress. In this way, the mere presence of the teacher might signal a potentially stressful situation, evoking perceptions of ego-threat manifested in elevated anxiety states. This is particularly problematic with respect to highly anxious students: Anxiety-prone students would be more likely to perceive any teacher as a source of threat to self-esteem. To the extent that the relational component of teacher communication behaviors reflects the degree of threat posed by any specific teacher-student relationship, student perceptions of this relationship should affect the degree of state anxiety experienced in the instructional environment.

Hypotheses

Teacher-student relationships were examined with respect to instructor communication behaviors that affect student anxiety and concomitant student learning. Specifically, student anxiety proneness and perceptions of interpersonal solidarity with instructor were investigated with respect to their effects on three separate aspects of the learning environment: (1) student affect and behavioral intent; (2) student classroom anxiety states; and (3) short-term cognitive learning. Hypothesis 1 concerned the first aspect, hypotheses 2 and 3 concerned the second, and hypothesis 4 concerned the third.

- H1: A linear combination of student anxiety proneness and perceived solidarity with instructor is significantly related to student affect and behavioral intent.
- H2: Perceptions of solidarity with the instructor are significantly and negatively related to state anxiety in the classroom.
- H3: A linear combination of anxiety proneness and perceived solidarity with the instructor is more predictive than anxiety proneness alone in explaining state anxiety in the classroom.
- H4: There are significant differences in cognitive learning among three levels of student state anxiety and three levels of perceived solidarity with the instructor, such that moderate levels of state anxiety and perceived solidarity are associated with greater cognitive learning than low levels

of state anxiety and perceived solidarity or high levels of state anxiety and perceived solidarity.

METHOD

Subjects

The subject pool consisted of 330 undergraduate students enrolled in a basic course in interpersonal communication at a large eastern university during the spring semester of 1980. The course was multisectioned, utilized six different instructors, and had a highly structured course content — that is, teaching outline, learning objectives, and standardized testing procedures for all course content were uniform among all sections.

Procedures

Subjects completed self-report instruments measuring trait anxiety proneness on the first day of class. Approximately seven weeks into the semester, a thirty-minute guest presentation over relevant course material was delivered in all sections by confederates trained in interpersonal distancing techniques. Students were informed that the material to be covered was from an instructional unit being developed for eventual incorporation into their course. They were also told that the units would involve a presentation of course content followed by a project designed to help prepare them for the next course examination. Immediately following the thirty-minute guest presentation subjects completed a self-report instrument measuring state anxiety and the unit project (a thirty-item fill-in-the-blank measure testing recall of information covered in the presentation) for either a pass/fail grade or a project grade of A, B, C, D, or F. Following completion of the unit project, subjects completed self-report instruments measuring perceived solidarity with the guest instructor and student affect and behavioral intent toward the instructional unit presented. Subjects were told that the purpose of the data collection was to provide feedback concerning the instructional unit only, and that evaluation responses would be kept confidential and not used to assess their performance in class.

Design

The stress associated with the cognitive performance situation was manipulated using two grading conditions normally employed within the framework of the course. Students completed the recall measure for either a pass/fail grade or a letter grade. Students completing the recall measure for a pass/fail grade were required to provide any response to each of the thirty items in order to receive a grade of pass. Students completing the recall measure in the graded condition were evaluated on the basis of the percentage of correct responses they provided using a standard grading criterion. The pass/fail condition was considered to represent a low stress condition, while the graded condition was considered to represent high stress.

Instructor communication behaviors reflecting interpersonal distance from students were manipulated to indicate varying degrees of interpersonal solidarity between instructor and students. Perceptions of interpersonal solidarity were induced through manipulating verbal and nonverbal status-solidarity cues previously suggested to reflect close versus distant interpersonal relationships (e.g., Andersen, 1978, 1979; Brown, 1965). Interpersonal distance reflected in classroom communication behaviors was manipulated to induce three conditions of solidarity with instructor in this study.[2]

The low solidarity condition was characterized by status-solidarity cues reflecting maximal status differential, formality, and interpersonal distance between teacher and student. Instructors in this condition employed the following verbal and nonverbal classroom behaviors: (1) formal dress (i.e., business attire); (2) formal modes of address with students (i.e., title and last name only); (3) avoidance of any self-disclosive statements; (4) lecture delivered in standing position from behind classroom podium; (5) little movement or animation while delivering lecture; (6) no smiling; (7) no direct eye contact with students; (8) no verbal feedback to student responses; (9) examples indicating lack of identification with student concerns (e.g., denigrated student mores and university sports), and (10) use of third person plural pronouns in classroom vocabulary, while avoiding all use of first person plural pronouns.

The moderate solidarity condition was characterized by status-solidarity cues reflecting normal professional distance in teacher-student relationships. The instructors in this condition employed the following verbal and nonverbal communication behaviors: (1) professional dress standards (i.e., neat shirt and slacks or skirt); (2) conventional modes of address (first and last name); (3) moderately disclosive, normal background information to students; (4) presentation delivered while seated at front desk; (5) normal bodily movement during presentation; (6) occasional smiles where appropriate; (7) sweeping eye contact and continuous shifting gaze among all areas of the classroom; (8) positive but impersonal feedback to student response; (9) normal classroom examples expressing professional orientations toward students and university programs; and (10) normal classroom vocabulary, emphasizing the use of second person plural pronouns in all classroom examples and discussions.

The high solidarity condition was characterized by status-solidarity cues reflecting similarities, peer relationships, and reduced interpersonal distance between teacher and student. Instructors in this condition employed the following verbal and nonverbal classroom behaviors: (1) informal dress (i.e., jeans and pullover shirt); (2) informal mode of address with students (provided first name only to students); (3) highly disclosive, extensive background information to students; (4) presentation delivered from in front of the desk, getting as physically close to students as possible; (5) continuous movement during presentation (i.e., used entire front of classroom with animated gestures and bodily motions); (6) continuous smiling; (7) prolonged eye-contact with individual students; (8) positive, personal feedback to every student response; (9) examples demonstrating obvious identification with student concerns; and (10) use of first person plural pronouns in all classroom examples and discussion.

Instruments

Anxiety Proneness. Anxiety proneness was conceptualized as the tendency to respond with increased anxiety states under conditions of stress, and was operationally defined as the score received on the A-Trait subscale of the State-Trait Anxiety Inventory (STAI) developed by Spielberger, Gorsuch, and Lushene (1970). The A-Trait subscale is designed to measure individual proneness to experience state anxiety, or the extent to which such anxiety states are characteristic of an individual. The A-Trait scale, a non-factor-based, twenty-item self-report instrument designed to measure general feelings of anxiety, has been demonstrated to have internal reliability estimates ranging from .83 to .92 (Spielberger et al., 1970). In the present study, the A-Trait scale had a split-half reliability estimate of .86 (Nunnally, 1978, formula 6-19).

State Anxiety. State anxiety was conceptualized in terms of feelings of anxiety and associated autonomic arousal at a particular moment in time and was operationalized using the A-State subscale of the STAI developed by Spielburger et al. (1970) and modified to employ a seven-step scale in order to create greater variability in scores and thereby increase its usefulness as a dependent measure. The A-State scale is a twenty-item self-report instrument designed to measure feelings of anxiety and autonomic arousal in particular situations. In this study, the A-State scale was targeted to determine feelings of student anxiety immediately following the presentation made by the guest instructor (confederate). The A-State scale had a split-half reliability estimate of .96 (Nunnally, 1978, formula 6-19).

Interpersonal Solidarity. Interpersonal solidarity was conceptualized in terms of perceptions of psychological closeness with the instructor and was operationally defined as the score received on a revised version (Andersen, 1978) of the scale developed by Wheeless (1976) to assess solidarity in interpersonal relationships. The modified Likert-type self-report instrument has been employed in applied research in the classroom (Andersen, 1978, 1979; Nussbaum & Scott, 1979, 1980) and has consistently reported unidimensionality and internal reliability estimates ranging from .88 to .96.

The interpersonal solidarity measure employed in this study was recast in the conditional verb tense in order to apply more appropriately to a relationship based on only thirty minutes of interaction with an instructor. Principle components factor analysis confirmed previously reported unidimensionality for perceptions of solidarity in an instructional setting. Examination of the unrotated factor structure (Table 31.1) revealed that all items had their highest loadings on the first unrotated factor. All twenty items were retained for inclusion in the present investigation. Unidimensionality was confirmed by an eigenvalue of 10.04 for the first factor, with all subsequent eigenvalues below 1.0. The twenty-item unidimensional solidarity measure had a split-half reliability of .94 (Nunnally, 1978, formula 6-19) in the present study.

Student Affect and Behavioral Intent. Student affect was operationalized using measures of student attitudes toward three aspects of the instructional environment: (1) content/subject matter of the instructional unit; (2) communication practices suggested in the unit; and (3) the guest instructor (confederate). Behavioral intentions toward two areas were also measured: (1) likelihood of engaging in communication practices suggested in the unit and (2) likelihood of enrolling in a future course offered by the guest instructor. Each specified affect and behavioral intention was measured using four seven-step semantic differential-type scales. This set of bipolar adjectives has consistently provided a valid index of student affect in the instructional environment (Scott & Wheeless, 1975), demonstrating internal reliability coefficients ranging from .88 to .95. In the present study, the semantic differential scales assessing each affect and behavioral intention yielded the following internal consistency coefficients: (1) .85 for content/subject matter; (2) .93 for communication practices suggested; (3) .93 for guest instructor; (4) .94 for likelihood of engaging in communication practices suggested; and (5) .97 for likelihood of enrolling in a future communication course offered by the guest instructor (Nunnally, 1978, formula 6-18).

In order to determine the appropriateness of combining measures of affect and behavioral intent into a single criterion measure of student affect, the three affect and two behavioral intent measures were subjected to a principle components factor analysis procedure employing orthogonal rotation. This procedure produced a single factor solution, indicating unidimensionality. The split-half reliability estimate of this combined measure

Table 31.1
Unrotated Factor Solution (principal components)
for Solidarity Instrument

	Factor 1
We could be very close to each other.	0.83260
This person would have a great deal of influence over my behavior.	0.73607
I would trust this person completely.	0.62857
We would feel very differently about most things.	−0.60813
I would willingly disclose a great deal of positive and negative things about myself, honestly and fully (in depth) to this person.	0.64753
We would not really understand each other.	−0.71467
This person would willingly disclose a great deal of positive and negative things about him/herself, honestly and fully (in depth) to me.	0.48042
I would distrust this person.	−0.56898
I would like this person much more than most people I know.	0.69644
I would seldom interact/communicate with this person.	−0.68461
I could really understand this person and who he/she really is.	0.67771
I would dislike this person.	−0.71481
I would interact/communicate with this person much more than with most people I know.	0.73657
We would not be very close at all.	−0.77965
We would share a lot in common.	0.78535
We would do a lot of helpful things for each other.	0.76442
I would have little in common with this person.	−0.73013
I could feel very close to this person.	0.81977
There would be a great deal of hostility and aggression between us.	−0.68259
I feel no interpersonal desire for friendship with this person.	−0.78248

of overall student affect was .91 in the present investigation (Nunnally, 1978, formula 6-19).

Cognitive Learning. Cognitive learning was conceptualized in terms of short-term student information acquisition and was operationally defined as the score received on a measure assessing recall of course content covered by the guest instructor (confederate). This cognitive learning measure, a thirty-item fill-in-the-blanks instrument developed from the scripted lecture delivered by all guest instructors, required students to supply key terms (nouns, adjectives, and adverbs) that had been systematically omitted from the script of the lecture delivered in class. Terms selected for omission were all associated with critical concepts designated as cognitive objectives in the course and slated to appear on the subsequent course examination. In the present investigation, the thirty-item instrument has a split-half reliability estimate of .91 (Nunnally, 1978, formula 6-19).

Statistical Analyses

The first hypothesis was tested using a multiple regression procedure. The second hypothesis was tested using a simple regression procedure. The third hypothesis was tested using a multiple regression procedure. The fourth hypothesis was first tested using a two-way analysis of variance procedure employing two levels of induced stress and three levels of induced solidarity to predict short-term cognitive learning. The generalizability of the experimental induction was also assessed using student self-reports: An additional two-way analysis of variance procedure, employing three levels of state anxiety and three levels of perceived solidarity, was utilized to predict short-term cognitive learning. Levels of both state anxiety and solidarity were created using a mean and standard deviation criterion for each self-report measure. Students scoring below one standard deviation from the mean were assigned a "low" designation, students scoring above one standard deviation from the mean were assigned a "high" designation, and students scoring at or between one standard deviation below and one standard deviation above the mean were assigned a "moderate" designation. The alpha level for all tests of statistical significance was set at .05.[3]

RESULTS

The first hypothesis, predicting that a linear combination of anxiety proneness and perceived solidarity with the instructor is significantly related to overall student effect and behavioral intent, was confirmed. The multiple regression procedure produced a significant model ($F = 105.20$, $df = 2/235, p < .05$), accounting for 47.24 percent of the total variance in overall student affect. While trait anxiety was a significant predictor in the partial model, it failed to achieve significance in the sequential model. This indicated possible multicolinearity between the predictor variables. Consequently, commonality analysis was employed to decompose R^2 into both unique and common components of predictor variables (Siebold & McPhee, 1975). The unique variance explained by student anxiety was 1.56 percent, while the unique variance explained by perceived solidarity with instructor was 47.05 percent. Common variance explained jointly by predictors was −1.38 percent, indicating a suppressor effect when both variables were employed to predict overall student affect toward learning.

The second hypothesis, predicting that perceived solidarity with instructor is significantly and negatively related to state anxiety, was confirmed. Perceived solidarity with instructor was correlated −.36 with state anxiety. The simple regression procedure produced a significant model ($F = 41.43$, $df = 1/277$, $p < .05$), accounting for 12.96 percent of the variance.

The third hypothesis, predicting that a linear combination of student anxiety proneness and perceived solidarity with instructor is more predictive than anxiety proneness alone in explaining variance in state anxiety, was also confirmed. The multiple regression procedure employing a linear combination of trait anxiety and perceived solidarity to predict state anxiety produced a significant model ($F = 26.22$, $df = 2/276$, $p < .05$), accounting for 15.97 percent of the variance. Commonality analysis indicated that trait anxiety uniquely explained 3.01 percent of the variance in the state anxiety, while perceived solidarity uniquely explained 14.82 percent of the variance. Trait anxiety and perceived solidarity jointly explained −1.86 percent of the total variance.

Investigation of the fourth hypothesis — examining relationships among levels of state anxiety, perceived solidarity with instructor, and cognitive learning — revealed meaningful differences in short-term recall of information due to these variables. The two-way analysis of variance procedure employing two levels of induced stress and three levels of status-solidarity cues to predict short-term recall revealed a significant interaction between state anxiety and perceived solidarity in explaining short-term recall ($F = 7.32$, $df = 2/282$, $p < .05$) accounting for 26.04 percent of the total variance. Under conditions of low solidarity, there was no significant difference in short-term recall between the high and low stress inductions ($t = 1.78$, $df = 88$), while under conditions of moderate solidarity, short-term recall was significantly greater in the high stress induction than in the low stress induction ($t = 2.05$, $df = 99$, $p < .05$, $eta^2 = 0.041$). Similarly, under conditions of high solidarity, short-term recall was significantly greater in the high stress than in the low stress induction ($t = 3.48$, $df = 92$, $p < .05$, $eta^2 = .116$). Moreover, under conditions of low stress, there was significantly greater short-term recall in the moderate solidarity induction than in either the low solidarity ($t = 4.68$, $df = 102$, $p < .05$, $eta^2 = 177$) or the high solidarity inductions ($t = 4.39$, $df = 94$, $p < .05$, $eta^2 = .170$). There was no significant difference in short-term recall between the high and low solidarity inductions ($t = 0.07$, $df = 86$). Under conditions of high stress there was significantly greater short-term recall in the moderate solidarity induction than in either the low ($t = 7.95$, $df = 85$, $p < .05$, $eta^2 = .426$) or the high solidarity inductions ($t = 2.95$, $df = 97$, $p < .05$, $eta^2 = .082$). However, when stress was high, short-term recall was significantly greater in the high solidarity induction ($t = 5.40$, $df = 94$, $p < .05$, $eta^2 = .237$) than it was in the low solidarity inductions (see Table 31.2). These results demonstrate that the moderate solidarity induction was consistently better for short-term recall of classroom information.

Table 31.2
Mean Short-Term Cognitive Learning
by Induced Stress and Status-Solidarity Cue Condition

		Solidarity		
Stress	Low	Moderate	High	TOTALS
Low	17.75 N = 48	22.86 N = 56	17.83 N = 40	19.76
High	15.67 N = 42	25.13 N = 45	21.83 N = 54	21.05
TOTALS	16.78	23.87	20.13	

When the fourth hypothesis was examined using student self-reports of state anxiety and perceived solidarity, no significant interaction was observed between these variables in predicting short-term recall of classroom information. The two-way analysis of variance procedure employing three levels of state anxiety and three levels of perceived solidarity to predict short-term recall revealed only a significant main effect for perceived solidarity ($F = 3.95$, $df = 2/282$, $p < .05$), with no significant main effect for state anxiety ($F = 2.55$, $df = 2/282$) and no significant interaction effect ($F = 1.72$, $df = 4/280$). Examination of the partial model for unequal cell sizes revealed that the main effect for perceived solidarity with instructor accounted for 3.53 percent of the total variance in short-term recall. Examination of the pattern of means indicated that short-term recall increased with the level of perceived solidarity with instructor. Use of t-tests for between-cell comparison of means indicated that short-term recall was significantly less with low levels of perceived solidarity than with either moderate ($t = 3.13$, $df = 249$, $p < .05$) or high ($t = 2.35$, $df = 95$, $p < .05$) levels of perceived solidarity. However, there was no significant difference in short-term recall between moderate and high levels of perceived solidarity with instructor ($t = 0.23$, $df = 140$). Therefore, the results of this analysis also demonstrated that moderate levels of perceived solidarity with instructor were consistently better for short-term recall of classroom information than low perceptions of solidarity with instructor. Also, high perceptions of solidarity were not significantly better than moderate perceptions for explaining variance in short-term cognitive learning outcomes.

DISCUSSION

Results of this study indicate that perceived solidarity almost exclusively accounted for the variance explained in student affect and behavioral intentions. Student anxiety proneness explained little, if any, of this variance. These results suggest that the rationale leading to the first hypothesis must be seriously reexamined. While it seems intuitively appealing that student anxiety proneness should be related to perceptions of psychological distance in teacher-student relationships, no empirical evidence of such a relationship was revealed in this investigation. Despite Spielberger's (1975, p. 137) assertion that high anxiety prone individuals are "disposed to perceive greater danger in relationships with other people that involve threats to self-esteem," this tendency was not manifested in terms of increased psychological distance between teacher and student.

At least two interpretations of this finding are plausible. The first may be that individuals do not necessarily respond to perceived interpersonal threats by increasing psychological distance between self and other. However, research investigating the relationship between perceived solidarity and interpersonal trust (e.g., Wheeless, 1978) suggests that perceived threats are indeed related to feelings of interpersonal closeness. A second interpretation might be that students do not generally perceive the teacher-student relationship as a source of potential threat to self-esteem. Perhaps the teacher role is so well defined that students do not interpret instructor communication behaviors as a source of interpersonal threat. Empirical investigation of this possibility would provide insights into the ways the teacher-student relationship affects student affective learning in the instructional environment.

The results of this investigation provided clear support for the second hypothesis, which predicted that perceptions of interpersonal solidarity with instructor are significantly and negatively related to student anxiety states in the classroom. Perceived solidarity accounted for 13 percent of the variance in student classroom anxiety states. This finding suggests that perceived solidarity with instructor provides a meaningful predictor of classroom anxiety states.

The importance of the observed relationship tested in hypothesis 2 was further emphasized by investigation of the third hypothesis, which predicted that a linear combination of student anxiety proneness and perceived solidarity with instructor would be more predictive than anxiety proneness alone in explaining variance in state anxiety. Inclusion of perceived solidarity improved the predictability of anxiety proneness in explaining variance in state anxiety and provided a better estimate of state anxiety than trait anxiety proneness. Commonality analysis of the regression model employed revealed little multicolinearity in the variance in state anxiety explained by anxiety proneness and perceptions of solidarity with instructor: Measures of student anxiety proneness and perceived solidarity with instructor tap separate areas in the domain of classroom anxiety states. Also, the finding that perceived solidarity provided a better estimate of state anxiety than trait anxiety proneness suggested that situationally specific perceptions of interpersonal closeness in the teacher-student relationship may provide a better estimate of student classroom anxiety states than measures of trait anxiety proneness.

The results of the two-way analysis of variance procedures employed to examine the fourth hypothesis demonstated that levels of perceived solidarity were significantly related to short-term cognitive learning. The analysis of variance procedure employing levels of induced stress and status-solidarity cues as predictors of short-term recall of information demonstrated a significant interaction between these variables in explaining cognitive learning outcomes. However, when levels of self-reported state anxiety and levels of perceived solidarity were employed to predict short-term recall of information, only the main effect for perceived solidarity was significantly related to short-term cognitive learning, accounting for 3.53 percent of the total variance. These results indicate that perceptions of solidarity with instructor were more meaningfully related to short-term cognitive learning than were the anxiety states experienced in the classroom.[4]

Results of analyses examining the level of interpersonal solidarity with instructor indicated that, for both status-solidarity cues and perceived solidarity, moderate to high perceptions of interpersonal solidarity generally produced greater short-term recall than did low perceptions of solidarity. Moreover, when perceptions of solidarity were induced through manipulation of instructor status-solidarity cues reflecting interpersonal distance from students, moderate levels of induced solidarity produced greater short-term recall than either high or low levels of induced solidarity. These results suggested that teachers engaging in status-solidarity cues reflecting moderate interpersonal distance from students may produce increased short-term recall of classroom information by students.

Perceptions of the teacher-student relationship provided a better estimate of classroom anxiety states than the measure of student anxiety proneness examined. This suggested that teacher behaviors reflecting interpersonal closeness with students were a meaningful predictor of anxiety states experienced by students in the classroom. Further, moderately high perceptions of interpersonal solidarity with instructor were associated with increased short-term recall of classroom information, while extremely low or extremely high perceptions of solidarity were associated with decreased short-term recall. Therefore, teachers whose classroom communication behaviors reflected moderately close interpersonal relationships with students apparently optimized student learning with respect to short-term recall of classroom information, while simultaneously reducing anxiety states experienced in the instructional environment. Consequently, teachers practicing classroom communication behaviors such as professional dress standards, moderate self-disclosure, spontaneous smiling, sweeping eye contact, positive feedback to student responses, and relaxed bodily postures may optimize student learning with respect to at least three separate learning outcomes.

The notion that the teacher plays an important role in creating positive orientations toward the learning experience is also reflected in contemporary conceptualizations of student achievement. For example, Bloom (1976) conceptualized the degree to which a student achieves in any given learning environment in terms of three independent factors: (1) cognitive entry behaviors, (2) affective entry behaviors, and (3) quality of instruction. Moreover, Bloom (1976) indicated that cognitive entry behaviors have been demonstrated to account for up to 50 percent of the variance in final cognitive achievement of students, while affective entry behaviors can account for as much as 25 percent of this variance. Further, due to some shared variance between measures of cognitive and affective entry behaviors, the combination of these factors can account for up to 65 percent of the overall variance in final student achievement (Friedrich, 1978).

Bloom (1976) has suggested, in more common terms, that only about two-thirds of a student's final cognitive achievement in the classroom can be predicted through assessing how "smart" that individual is and how "positively" he or she felt on entering the learning environment. The remaining variance in student achievement is obviously a function of the "quality of instruction" encountered in that learning environment. Further, Bloom's (1976) conceptualization suggested that quality of instruction variables interact with both cognitive and affective components of student learning behaviors. That is, the trait-like learning characteristics a student brings into the instructional environment interact with state-like quality of instruction variables in the subsequent development of new cognitive and affective learning behaviors.

Friedrich (1978) reconceptualized Bloom's learning model from a communication perspective. He suggested that the learning experience can be conceived in terms of student ability, student motivation, and quality of classroom communication. This model suggests that cognitive abilities and affective predispositions of students are directly mediated by the communication processes operating in the classroom environment. Such processes are a cofunction of the communication behaviors of both teacher and students. From this perspective, the quality of instruction (Bloom, 1976) might properly be understood in terms of communication transactions between teacher and student (see Hurt, Scott, & McCroskey, 1978). Further, teacher effectiveness might then be understood in terms of the appropriateness of the teacher-student relationship for conducting communication transactions within the learning environment.

The findings of the present investigation are consistent with the models of student learning suggested by Bloom (1976) and Friedrich (1978). The variables examined in this study suggest that classroom communication processes mediate both affective and cognitive components of student learning. While there was no direct empirical evidence of a causal relationship provided within this investigation, it appears plausible that instructor communication behaviors may lead to positive perceptions of the teacher, which may lead to decreased anxiety states experienced in the instructional environment, which may in turn lead to increased cognitive learning. Path models employing appropriate path analysis techniques might be constructed to investigate this potential causal relationship. If more cognitive learning is directly derived from classroom interactions with teachers displaying moderately close relationships with students, then effective teaching may involve adjustments in classroom communication behaviors to achieve optimal levels of "closeness" in teacher-student interactions.

NOTES

1. Conflicting evidence for the tradeoff between affective and cognitive student learning exists: When student motivation is low, teacher enthusiasm (which relates to positive perceptions of the teacher) has been found to produce increased cognitive learning (Naftalin, Ware, & Donnelly, 1973; Ware & Williams, 1975; Williams & Ware, 1977).

2. Six confederates, all graduate students with teaching experience as basic course instructors in speech communication, were employed in the solidarity inductions. The confederates were selected on the basis of the following criteria: (1) certification for teaching basic interpersonal communication and (2) not currently serving as an instructor in the basic course in interpersonal communication.

Confederates attended a common two-hour training session in which they were briefed as to the overall design of the study and apprised of the necessity of inducing variability in student perceptions of solidarity with instructor. The concept of interpersonal distancing behaviors, as developed by Brown (1965) and Andersen (1978), was briefly summarized in terms of status, formality, and psychological perceptions. The three solidarity conditions were then approached from the perspective of ten verbal and nonverbal classroom communication behaviors derived from Brown's (1965) consideration of status and solidarity and Andersen's (1978) Behavioral Indicants of Immediacy (BII) measure. Each confederate was provided with an instruction sheet summarizing the status-solidarity cues to be employed in all three solidarity conditions. Two confederates, one male and one female, were assigned to each solidarity condition.

3. Examination of the table of correlation coefficients suggested that traditional assumptions regarding the relationships among measurement instruments employed did not appear to hold up in this study. Specifically, the A-Trait and A-State subscales of the STAI failed to meet the specified alpha criterion level of .05 and were therefore not significantly related in this study. Since the A-Trait scale is conceptualized as a measure of an individual's tendency to experience anxiety states, the absence of a significant relationship between these measures was problematic.

Test of skewness and kurtosis of measurement instruments employed in Study I revealed that all measures fell within the range of acceptable limits for a normal distribution. Consequently, all tests of hypotheses and research questions reported in this section employed the raw data collected through use of student self-report instruments.

The a priori power of the analysis of variance decision model for detecting large effects in hypothesis testing was .99. The power of the decision model for detecting medium effects was .99, while the power for detecting small effects was .51. The power of the multiple regression model for detecting large effects in hypothesis testing was .99. The power for detecting medium effects was .99, while the power for detecting small effects was .48 (Cohen, 1977).

4. This interpretation is also supported by the interval data relating perceived solidarity, self-reported state anxiety, and short-term cognitive learning. Examination of the simple correlations coefficents revealed that while both state anxiety ($r = -.18$) and perceived solidarity ($r = .28$) were significantly related to short-term recall of information, perceived solidarity explained more of the variance in short-term cognitive learning processes. This suggests that measurement of perceived solidarity provides a better estimate of short-term recall than measurement of the state anxiety reported by students in the instructional environment.

REFERENCES

Andersen, J. F. *The relationship between teacher immediacy and teaching effectiveness.* Unpublished doctoral dissertation, West Virginia University, 1978.

Andersen, J. F. Teacher immediacy as a predictor of teaching effectiveness. In D. Nimmo (Ed.), *Communication yearbook 3.* New Brunswick, NJ: Transaction, 1979.

Andersen, J. F., Norton, R. W., & Nussbaum, J. F. *Three investigations exploring relationships among perceived communicator style, perceived teacher immediacy, perceived teacher-student solidarity, teaching effectiveness, and student learning.* Paper presented at the annual convention of the American Educational Research Association, San Francisco, 1979.

Bloom, B. S. *Human characteristics and school learning.* New York: McGraw-Hill, 1976.

Brookover, W., Thomas, S., & Paterson, A. Self-concept of ability and school achievement. *Sociology of Education,* 1964, *37,* 271-278.

Brown, R. *Social psychology.* New York: Free Press, 1965.

Cohen, J. *Statistical power analysis for the behavioral sciences.* New York: Academic Press, 1977.

Crosswhite, F. Correlates of attitudes toward mathematics. In J. W. Wilson & E. G. Begle (Eds.), *National longitudinal study in mathematics achievement.* Report 5, No. 20. Palo Alto, CA: School Mathematics Study Group, 1972.

Dowaliby, F. J., & Schumer, H. Teacher-centered versus student-centered mode of college classroom instructions related to manifest anxiety. *Journal of Educational Psychology,* 1973, *64,* 125-132.

Elliot, S. M. Perceived homophily as a predictor of classroom learning. In D. Nimmo (Ed.), *Communication yearbook 3.* New Brunswick, NJ: Transaction, 1979.

Friedrich, G. W. *Effects of teacher behavior on the acquisition of communicator competencies.* Paper presented at the annual convention of the American Educational Research Association, Toronto, 1978.

Heckhausen, H. Fear of failure as a self-reinforcing motive system. In I. G. Sarason & C. D. Spielberger (Eds.), *Stress and anxiety* (Vol. 2). New York: John Wiley, 1975.

Hedl, J. J., Jr., & O'Neil, H. F., Jr. Reduction of state anxiety via instructional design in computer-based learning environments. In J. E. Sieber, H. F. O'Neil, Jr., & S. Tobias (Eds.), *Anxiety, learning, and instruction.* New York: John Wiley, 1977.

Hodges, W. F. Effects of ego threat and threat of pain on state anxiety. *Journal of Personality and Social Psychology,* 1968, *8,* 364-372.

Hurt, H. T., Scott, M. D., & McCroskey, J. C. *Communication in the classroom.* Reading, MA: Addison-Wesley, 1978.

Kearney, P. K., & McCroskey, J. C. Relationships among teacher communication style, trait and state communication apprehension, and teacher effectiveness. In D. Nimmo (Ed.), *Communication yearbook 4*. New Brunswick, NJ: Transaction, 1980.

Lunn, J. The development of scales to measure junior high school children's attitudes. *British Journal of Educational Psychology*, 1969, *39*, 64-71.

Naftalin, D. H., Ware, J. E., & Donnelly, F. A. The Dr. Fox lecture: A paradigm of educational seduction. *Journal of Medical Research*, 1973, *48*, 630-635.

Nunnally, J. C. *Psychometric theory*. New York: McGraw-Hill, 1978.

Nussbaum, J. F., & Scott, M. D. Instructor communication behaviors and their relationship to classroom learning. In D. Nimmo (Ed.), *Communication yearbook 3*. New Brunswick, NJ: Transaction, 1979.

Nussbaum, J. F., & Scott, M. D. *Student learning as a relational outcome of teacher-student interaction*. Paper presented at the annual convention of the International Communication Association, Acapulco, Mexico, 1980.

O'Neil, H. F., Jr., & Richardson, F. C. Anxiety and learning in computer-based learning environments: An overview. In J. E. Sieber, H. F. O'Neil, Jr., & S. Tobias (Eds.), *Anxiety, learning, and instruction*. New York: John Wiley, 1977.

Oosthoek, H., & Ackers, G. The evaluation of an audio-taped course (II). *British Journal of Educational Technology*, 1973, *4*, 55-73.

Sarason, I. G. Anxiety and self-preoccupation. In I. G. Sarason & C. D. Spielberger (Eds.), *Stress and anxiety* (Vol. 2). New York: John Wiley, 1975.

Scott, M. D., & Wheeless, L. R. Communication apprehension, student attitudes, and levels of satisfaction. *Western Journal of Speech Communication*, 1975, *41*, 188-198.

Scott, M. D., & Wheeless, L. R. Instructional communication: An overview of theory and research. In B. D. Ruben (Ed.), *Communication yearbook 1*. New Brunswick, NJ: Transaction, 1977.

Siebold, D. R., & McPhee, R. D. Commonality analysis: A method for decomposing explained variance in multiple regression analyses. *Human Communication Research*, 1975, *5*, 355-365.

Selye, H. *The stress of life*. New York: McGraw-Hill, 1976.

Shepps, F. P., & Shepps, R. R. Relationships of study habits and school attitudes in mathematics and reading. *Journal of Educational Research*, 1971, *65*, 71-73.

Spielberger, C. D. Theory and research on anxiety. In C. D. Spielberger (Ed.), *Anxiety and behavior*. New York: Academic Press, 1966.

Spielberger, C. D. Anxiety as an emotional state. In C. D. Spielberger (Ed.). *Anxiety: Current trends in theory and research* (Vol. 1). New York: Academic Press, 1972.

Spielberger, C. D. Anxiety: State-trait-process. In C. D. Spielberger & I. G. Sarason (Eds.), *Stress and anxiety* (Vol. 1). New York: John Wiley, 1975.

Spielberger, C. D., Gorsuch, R. L., & Lushene, R. E. *Manual for the state-trait anxiety inventory*. Palo Alto, CA: Consulting Psychologist Press, 1970.

Tobias, S., & Abramson, T. The relationship of anxiety, response mode, and content difficulty to achievement in programmed instruction. *Journal of Educational Psychology*, 1971, *62*, 357-364.

Tobias, S., & Duchastel, P. C. Behavioral objectives, sequence, and anxiety in CAI. *Instructional Science*, 1974, *3*, 231-242.

Ware, J. E., & Williams, R. G. The Dr. Fox effect: A study of lecture effectiveness and ratings of instructor. *Journal of Medical Education*, 1975, *50*, 149-156.

Weiner, B. The role of success and failure in the learning of easy and complex tasks. *Journal of Personality and Social Psychology*, 1966, *3*, 339-344.

Wheeless, L. R. Self-disclosure and interpersonal solidarity: Measurement, validation, and relationships. *Human Communication Research*, 1976, *3*, 47-61.

Wheeless, L. R. A follow-up study on the relationships among trust, disclosure, and interpersonal solidarity. *Human Communication Research*, 1978, *4*, 143-157.

Williams, R. G., & Ware, J. E. An extended visit with Dr. Fox: Validity of student satisfaction with instruction ratings after repeated exposure to lecturer. *American Educational Research Journal*. 1977, *14*, 449-457.

Wine, J. *Cognitive-attentional approaches to test anxiety modification*. Paper presented at the annual meeting of the American Psychological Association, Honolulu, September 1972. (Cited in J. E. Sieber, H. F. O'Neil, Jr., & S. Tobias [Eds.], *Anxiety, learning, and instruction*. New York: John Wiley, 1977.)

INSTRUCTIONAL COMMUNICATION

32 ● Sugar or Spice: Teachers' Perceptions of Sex Differences in Communicative Correlates of Attraction

CYNTHIA STOHL
Purdue University

THIS study examines the relationship among teachers' perceptions of communicator style, children's sex, and social attractiveness to peers and teachers. This investigation was undertaken in response to the many reactions received when presenting the results of an earlier study (Stohl, 1981). In that paper a relationship was reported between children's communicator style and their social attractiveness to peers and teachers. Teachers were more attracted to children they perceived to have a style of communication that is attentive, relaxed, and friendly, whereas children preferred peers who communicate in a more contentious, impression-leaving, dramatic, animated, and open style.

The first set of reactions to these findings seemed to be based upon an assessment of teachers' superior, conservative attitudes. "Of course, how typical... teachers only like kids who are quiet, nonassertive, conforming ... teachers like kids who will pay attention and do whatever they say ... children who don't have a mind of their own ... kids like other kids who are exciting, active, etc."

The second set of reactions seemed to be based upon sex-typed expectations. "That's why the teacher's pet is always a girl ... little girls are socialized to be just what the teacher wants ... lots of sugar, little of spice. ... Boys are too aggressive, nonconforming, too assertive ... full of spiders and snails."

I wondered. Were these reactions only a residual of our "fondest" school memories in which the teacher did not like us because we were too knowing, too assertive, too dramatic, perhaps too tomboyish, but the kids

Correspondence and requests for reprints: Cynthia Stohl, Department of Communication, Purdue University, West Lafayette, IN 47906.

thought we were great? Or were these responses consistent with research findings?

Previous research suggests that there was more to the reactions cited above than simply stereotypic overreaction to our own school experiences. In support of the first set of reactions Feshbach (1969) found that teachers prefer rigid, conforming, orderly, dependent, passive, and acquiescent children over flexible, nonconforming, active, and assertive children. Kelly (1958) reported that teachers gave higher grades to students characterized as conforming, compulsive, and rigid, and Good and Grouws's data (1972) showed male and female teachers prefer compliant and cooperative children and reject assertive and active students. These variables also seemed to be related to the sex role expectations voiced in the second set of reactions.

Several studies have shown that both male and female teachers are more favorably disposed toward girls and stereotypic "female" qualities than toward boys and "male" qualities (see Brophy & Good, 1974; Fagot, 1981). Kaplan (1952) found aggressive boys were most annoying to three-fourths of school teachers in his study and that the teachers most preferred the less aggressive children. Kremer (1965) found the "good female" students were appreciative, calm, conscientious, considerate, cooperative, mannerly, poised, sensitive, dependable, mature, and obliging whereas the "good male" students were active, adventurous, aggressive, assertive, curious, energetic, enterprising, frank, independent, and inventive. Most interestingly, however, his data suggest that teachers gave the highest grades *only* to the female students who approached the ideal type. Teachers tended to reject the male students who exhibited the characteristics of the "good male" student as being too assertive or too aggressive and gave them lower grades. It seems that "to the extent that a teacher's grading is influenced by sex-typing in her students, she is more likely to be positively disposed toward a 'normally sex-typed girl' than towards a 'normally sex-typed boy' " (Brophy & Good, 1974, p. 204).

Other studies also confirm teachers' preference for qualities usually associated with the female sex role. Sears (1963) found that teachers preferred children who were achieving well, who posed no discipline problem, and who gave evidence of needing them, i.e., were dependent.

Clearly, the two sets of reactions were integrally related. The evidence suggests *teachers prefer those children who exhibit behaviors usually associated with the female role.* This proposition raised three basic issues that had not been investigated in the original study of communicator style and perceptions of attraction.

1. Do teachers report a significant sex difference in the manifestations of the subconstructs of the communicator style measure and in their attraction to these children?

2. Are the style variables related to teachers' perceptions of attractiveness consistent with female sex-typed expectations for both males and females?
3. Are the style variables related to peers' perceptions of attractiveness consistent with appropriate sex-role expectations?

Communicator style is "the way an individual verbally and paraverbally interacts to signal how literal meaning should be taken, interpreted, filtered or understood" (Norton, 1978, p. 99), and is measured on the following subconstructs: (1) impression leaving, (2) contentious, (3) open, (4) dramatic, (5) dominant, (6) relaxed, (7) friendly, (8) attentive, and (9) animated. These nine variables have been previously considered in studying young children's behavior (Piaget, 1926; Stott, 1962; Kohn, 1977). The nine style variables were also used in the original study of children's communicator style and perceptions of attraction (Stohl, 1981). In a study of adults Norton and Pettegrew (1977) found the best predictors of attraction were friendly, attentive, and relaxed.

This chapter is divided into four parts. In the following section a clearer explication of the "female" qualities that researchers suggest are more appropriate and thereby more desirable in the classroom setting is developed. At the end of this section, six specific research questions derived from the three basic issues cited above are formulated. In the second part, the methods, procedures, and analyses are explained. In the third part the results and discussion are presented. In the last section the implications for future research and the limitations of the study are discussed.

REVIEW OF PERTINENT LITERATURE

The general consensus from either a behavioral or a perceptual perspective seems to be that from early childhood on, males are more active and instrumental and females have greater affiliative and social needs (Fitzpatrick & Bochner, 1981). Eakins and Eakins (1978, p. 19) suggest that this tendency of males/females is related to the male's "view of the world as something requiring conquest or manipulation through competitive skills and resources whereas a female is socialized to view the world as something requiring placation and cultivation through nurturance and cooperation and hence females tend to have a passive attitude." Some researchers, however, suggest there are biological differences that explain the most variance between males and females (see Maccoby & Jacklin, 1974). Whatever the etiology of sex differences, for the purpose of this chapter it is only important that such differences are believed and perceived to exist.

Sex differences in communication patterns and styles have been extensively researched (see, e.g., Henley, 1977; Eakins & Eakins, 1978;

Maccoby & Jacklin, 1974). Many of the findings of sex differences in both verbal and nonverbal behavior of adults are consistent with sex differences found in the communication of children. Fitzpatrick and Bochner (1981) report that males are more instrumental, active, and verbally aggressive whereas females are more expressive and accommodating. Montgomery and Norton (1981) found that dominant style was the best predictor of a good male communicator and friendly style the best predictor for females. They also found significant mean differences for males and females on the animated, precise, and friendly styles.

With young children the prevailing view is that boys are more aggressive verbally and behaviorally than girls. Boys are rated by peers and teachers as significantly more aggressive than girls in overt physical and verbal aggression (Brodzinky, Messer, & Tur, 1979) and a highly significant sex difference is reported in observational studies of peer-directed physical and verbal aggression of children six years and under (Maccoby & Jacklin, 1980). Tauber (1979) found that boys are more active and aggressive in play whereas females are more nurturant and sedentary. The types of games and activities boys play are associated with high levels of aggression (Carpenter & Huston-Stein, 1980).

Females seem to have a more sensitive awareness to nonverbal behavior and are more socially competent both verbally and nonverbally at a younger age. Post and Hetherington (1974) found that between the ages of four and six, girls showed a more rapid growth than boys in social sensitivity to both proxemic and eye-contact cues. One reason girls may do better on nonverbal recognition tasks, however, is simply because they are looking more. Ashear and Snortum (1971) found significant sex differences in eye contact of listeners for preschool children and children in grades two, five, and eight. Levine and Sutton-Smith (1973) found significant sex differences in gazing occurring by age four and again females tended to look more than males. This tendency continues throughout adulthood (Henley, 1977).

In general boys are reported to be more aggressive behaviorally and verbally, more physically active, and more interested in the manipulation of objects, whereas females are reported to be more conforming, quieter, and more interested in verbal and symbolic activities. Specifically, the characteristics that continually emerge to be associated with young females are: accommodation, sendentariness, quietness, interest in verbal activities, more eye gaze, and greater communicative awareness. The characteristics associated with young males include: competitiveness, verbal and behavioral aggressiveness, great activity, noisiness, interest in manipulation of objects, less eye contact, and less sensitivity and/or awareness of nonverbal behavioral cues.

Let us now look more closely at the proposition that teachers prefer female sex-typed behaviors. In the context of schooling this does not seem surprising. With twenty or more children within the classroom there needs to be some emphasis on listening skills, attention, quiet activity, order, cooperativeness, and nonaggression. Given the goals of most school teachers, there is a great deal of overlap between behaviors associated with females and those related to school performance, but very little overlap between behaviors associated with males and the behaviors important for successful school performance. Brophy and Good (1974) explain the tendency of girls to outperform boys in early elementary grades especially in reading and other verbal skill activities by this relative compatibility of sex role expectations and student role expectations. They suggest that "the behavior expected of students in early elementary grades is much more compatible with the 'nice-litte-girl' stereotype than it is with the attributes and behavior expected of boys in our society" (Brophy & Good, 1974, p. 201). To the extent that boys have difficulty adjusting to school and teachers in early grades, they believe the problem results from conflict between the role of the pupil and the male sex roles as defined by our society (Brophy & Good, 1974). Even within experimental settings, when adults are asked to play the role of the teacher with child confederates, the teacher prefers the child who is more responsive, has greater eye contact, and is less assertive and more conforming (Keller & Bell, 1979; Bates, 1976, Teyber, Messe, & Stollack, 1977; Cantor & Gelfand, 1977).

This review implicitly suggests that although girls are reinforced for appropriate sex-typed behaviors, boys are rewarded (directly through grades, indirectly through affective behavior) for cross-sexed behavior. Fagot (1981) confirms that both experienced male and female teachers tend to prefer and reinforce both sexes for feminine-preferred activities. In contrast, peers reinforce children for sex-typed behavior. Fagot (1981) reported that preschool male peers reinforce male stereotypes. Hartup, Glazer, and Charlesworth (1967) also found peers reinforcing gender-appropriate behaviors. Lamb and Rooparine (1979) present observational data that clearly demonstrate that from at least three years of age, peers reinforce (punish) one another for sex-appropriate (-inappropriate) activities.

Outside the classroom context, however, things are somewhat different. Brophy and Good (1974) review studies that suggest the least attractive children are those who do not conform to expectations. Langlois and Downs (1980) test and affirm the proposition that parents reward children for sex-appropriate behaviors and punish them for sex-inappropriate behaviors. Feinman's research (1981) strongly confirms the intuitively popular notion that cross-sex-role behavior is less approved for boys than for girls "in contemporary American culture." This review indicates that Feinman needs to put in a qualifier "except in the case of teachers in contemporary American classrooms."

These findings suggest that there is a relationship among children's sex, teachers' perceptions of communicator style, and the attractiveness of children to peers and teachers. Such relationships are analyzed by specifically addressing six research questions. At this point no formal hypotheses were designed. It was generally expected, however, that significant sex differences would emerge in communicator style variables that would be consistent with previous research and that teachers would be attracted to those children who displayed "feminine-sex-typed" styles regardless of sex. Table 32.1 lists the research questions utilized in this study.

METHOD

Subjects

The subjects in this study were fifty-two children of mixed socioeconomic status who attended a day care center in Lafayette, Indiana, during the winter of 1980. The twenty-six boys and twenty-six girls ranged in age from three years to five years, five months.

Procedure

Each of the seven teachers at the day care center was randomly given communicator style/attractiveness questionnaires for twenty-two children (two teachers received twenty-three measures). All of the teachers were equally familiar with all of the children. After an explanatory meeting with the researcher instructions for filling out the measure were given. The teachers, not knowing the purpose of the study, filled out these questionnaires separately and within one week returned them to the investigator. Each child thereby received three independent ratings of communicator style, physical attraction, social attraction to other children, and personal attraction to the teacher. Subsequent to the receipt of the measures an assistant met with each of the fifty-two children individually and administered a picture sociometric interview.

Measures

Nine style variables, as well as communicator image, were used in this study. The short form of the communicator style measure was adapted, with "child" replacing "person" in the description of each subconstruct. A measure of attractiveness was also included in the questionnaire. On a seven-point scale each teacher was asked to evaluate the child on personal social attractiveness to the individual teacher.

The picture sociometric interview (PSI) used to assess a child's peer attractiveness was the technique first proposed by Moore and Updegraff (1964) and later used by Hartup, Glazer, and Charlesworth (1967) and Gottman, Gonso, and Rasmusen (1975). To administer the PSI each child

Table 32.1

Research Questions Related to Sex Differences in Style

1. Do teachers report a significant sex difference in the manifestation of the subconstructs of the communicator style measure?
    a. Are these differences consistent with previous findings of communicative differences between boys and girls?
    b. Are these differences consistent with the findings of sex differences in the communicator style of adults?
2. Do specific styles or combination of style variables discriminate between males and females?

Research Questions Related to Sex Differences in Attraction

3. Do teachers differentially report attraction to males and females?
4. Do peers differentially report attraction to males and females?
5. What style variables or combinations of style variables best predicts an attractive female and an attractive male for teachers?
    a. Are these styles consistent with sex-typed expectations?
6. What style or combination of style variables best predicts an attractive female and an attractive male for preschool children?
    a. Are these styles consistent with sex-typed expectations?

---

was seated directly in front of a board on which was mounted individual 3 × 5, black-and-white, head-and-shoulder photographs of all the children in that child's age group.

To introduce the tasks the assistant called attention to the pictures by having the child find his or her own photograph and then asked to name (or helped him or her name) all the other children. The assistant then said, "Now I want you to look over the pictures very carefully and find someone you would like to play with most." If the child was hesitant he or she was told he or she could point to the picture. Following this choice the child was asked the same question two more times. After a total of three spontaneous choices were made, the child was asked with whom would he or she like to play the least (in some cases the research said, "Who don't you want to play with?). After a total of three spontaneous negative choices were made, the child was thanked and returned to free play. A child received three points each time he or she was chosen first among spontaneous positive choices, two points when chosen second, and one point when chosen third. Three points were deducted each time the child was chosen first in negative choices and so on. The child's total score is referred to as his or her peer attractiveness ratings.

UNITS OF ANALYSIS

Attractiveness Stratifications

A teacher attractiveness score was obtained by first standardizing the personal attractiveness ratings on the questionnaire and then averaging them for each child. A peer attractiveness score was assessed from the combined results of the sociometric interview. In both cases a schematic summary (Tukey, 1972) was used to determine levels of attractiveness. The lower and upper percentiles constituted the extreme positions. These stratifications resulted in three groups of children for both peer and teacher attractiveness. The low peer attractiveness group consisted of those children whose scores ranged between 1 and 3 ($n = 16$), the moderately attractive group scored between 4 and 7 ($n = 20$), and the highly attractive group scored between 8 and 16 ($n = 16$). The low teacher attractiveness group scored between -2.69 and $-.70$ ($n = 15$), the moderately attractive group scored $-.42$ through $.44$ ($n = 21$), and the high teacher attractiveness group scored between $.72$ and 2.29 ($n = 16$).

Analyses

All style variables and three teacher attractiveness ratings were standardized. Style differences between males and females were investigated using two types of analyses. First, two 2×3 analyses of variance were utilized to examine central tendency differences (two levels of sex, three levels of attractiveness). The first analysis of variance used the teacher attractiveness stratification; the second used the peer attractiveness stratification. A discriminant analysis was employed to determine if some linear combination of style variables could be found that would discriminate between males and females.

To investigate whether style variables related to the attractiveness of children for teachers and peers are consistent with sex-typed expectations, 2×3 analyses of variance were utilized, and stepwise multiple regression equations were used to isolate the best predictors of attraction for males and females. A total of four regression equations were generated; two for each sex for both teacher and peer attractiveness.

RESULTS

It is evident from the results of these analyses that teachers perceive sex differences in the manifestation of the communicator style constructs and these perceived differences are consistent with the sex role expectations presented earlier. The differences are also consistent with past research findings of sex differences in communication.

Table 32.2
Z Score Differences Between Sexes for Style Variables

Style	Males	Females	F
Impression leaving	.3574	−.3581	7.50
Contentious	.3943	−.3940	9.40
Dramatic	.4628	−.4630	19.97
Dominant	.3479	−.3484	7.04
Animated	.4427	−.4427	12.48

Note: $p < .005$.

In answering research question 1, the results reported in Table 32.2 present evidence that males are perceived to be more active and assertive in their style of communication. Males were reported to be significantly more impression leaving, contentious, dramatic, dominant, and animated in style than females. There was no main sex effect for any style variable in which females were more highly rated. Only on the attentive style did females have a higher mean score than males (females, $X = .19$; males, $X = -.20$; $F = 1.52$) but these differences did not reach statistical significance.

In answer to research question 2, the discriminant analysis provides a more global approach to the study of sex differences. It was computed to determine if application of some linear combination of the style variables could discriminate between the sexes. Such an equation would take into account the interrelationships among the variables.

Tables 32.3 and 32.4 presents the standardized discriminate function coefficients. Application of this linear equation classified 74.5 percent of the children correctly ($\chi^2 = 14.35$; $p < .002$). The best discriminating variables were dramatic, dominant, and attentive, accounting for 67 percent of the unique variance. The results of these two analyses suggest not only that young children are perceived to manifest individual subconstructs of the communicator style measure that are consistent with sex role expectations, but also that young children demonstrate differences on the energy expenditure dimension of the communicator style measure identified by Norton (1978). This dimension represents the cluster of style variables — relaxed, dominant, dramatic, and animated.

Research questions 3, 4, 5, and 6 address the relationship among perceptions of attraction, sex role expectations, and sex differences in communicator style. A preliminary analysis did not uncover any direct sex bias on the part of the teachers in regard to attractiveness. Of the children in the high attractiveness stratification, 56 percent were male; in the middle stratification 50 percent were male; and in the lowest stratification 44 percent were male. Chi square analysis found none of these to be greater

Table 32.3
Standardized Discriminant Function Coefficients

Step Number	Variable	Coefficient	Coefficient	Percentage of Variance Explained
1	Dramatic	1.02	−1.09	41%
2	Dominant	−.38	.45	17%
3	Attentive	−.30	.24	9%

Note: $\chi^2 = 14.535$; $p < .002$.

Table 32.4
Classification Results

	N	Predicted Group Membership	
		1	2
Group 1 (males)	26	19 (73.1%)	7 (26.9%)
Group 2 (females)	26	6 (23.1%)	20 (76.9%)

Note: Percentage of grouped cases correctly classified = 74.5.

or less than expected by chance alone. Children (both males and females), however, did predominately choose those from their own sex group for the top three places. Of the group, 32 percent were consistent in all three choices, an additional 60 percent chose at least two out of the three from the same sex group, 5 percent chose only one from their own sex, and only one female chose all three top choices as males. Overall, however, there was no significant sex difference in any of the stratifications ($\chi^2 = 3.56$).

In answering research questions 5 and 6 two forms of analyses were undertaken. First, the analyses of variance were examined to see if there were any interaction effects between sex and levels of attractions. Although there were no significant interaction effects, the results suggest interesting trends and possibilities. In Figures 32.1 and 32.2 the graphed results of the mean scores for males and females are presented in the two extreme positions for peer and teacher attractiveness, respectively.

It can be seen that for peer attractiveness the only style variable in which the mean z score for females is higher is attentive ($X = .45$). It is important to note that this score is for the most attractive females. The other mean scores are as follows: high males, $X = .09$; low males, $X =$

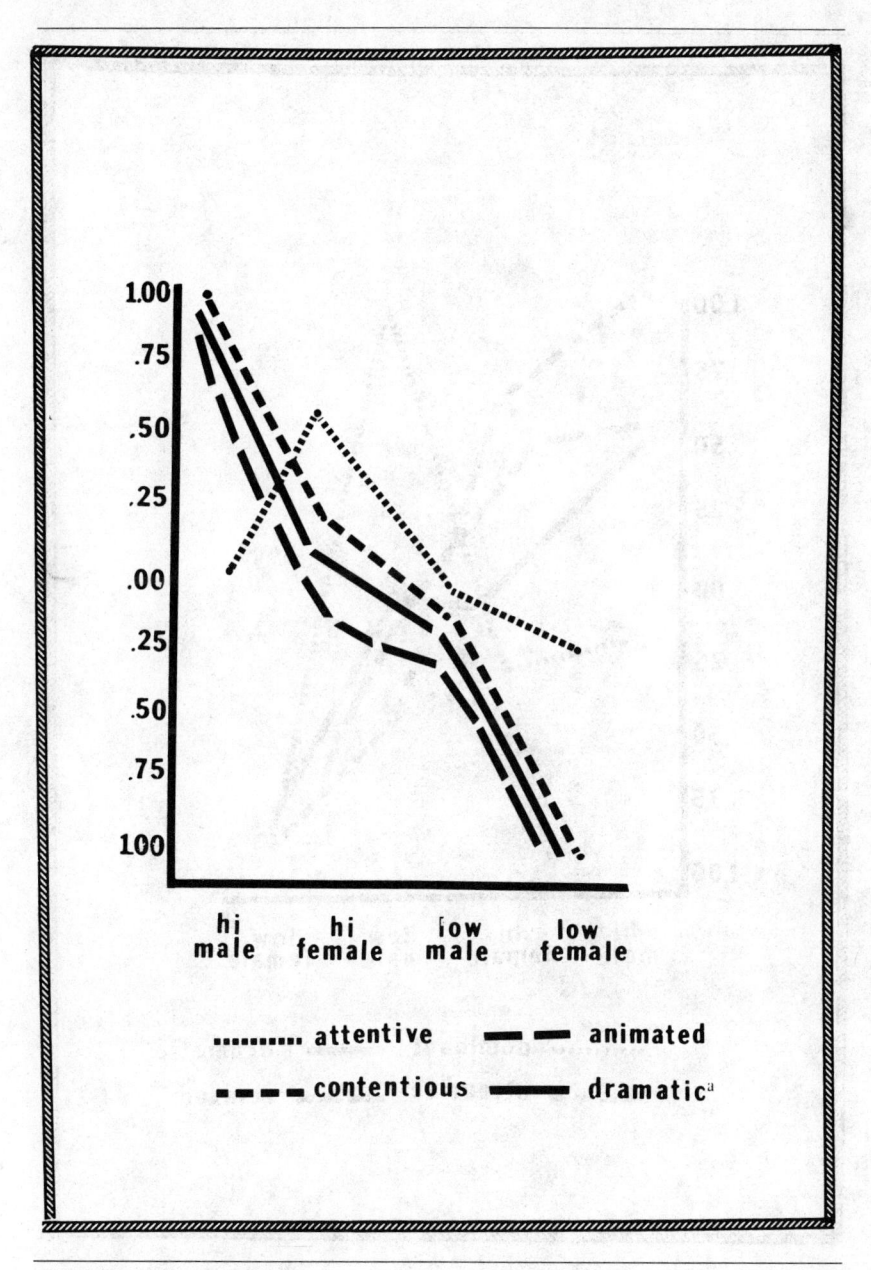

Figure 32.1. Peer attraction.
a. All other style variables follow a similar pattern.

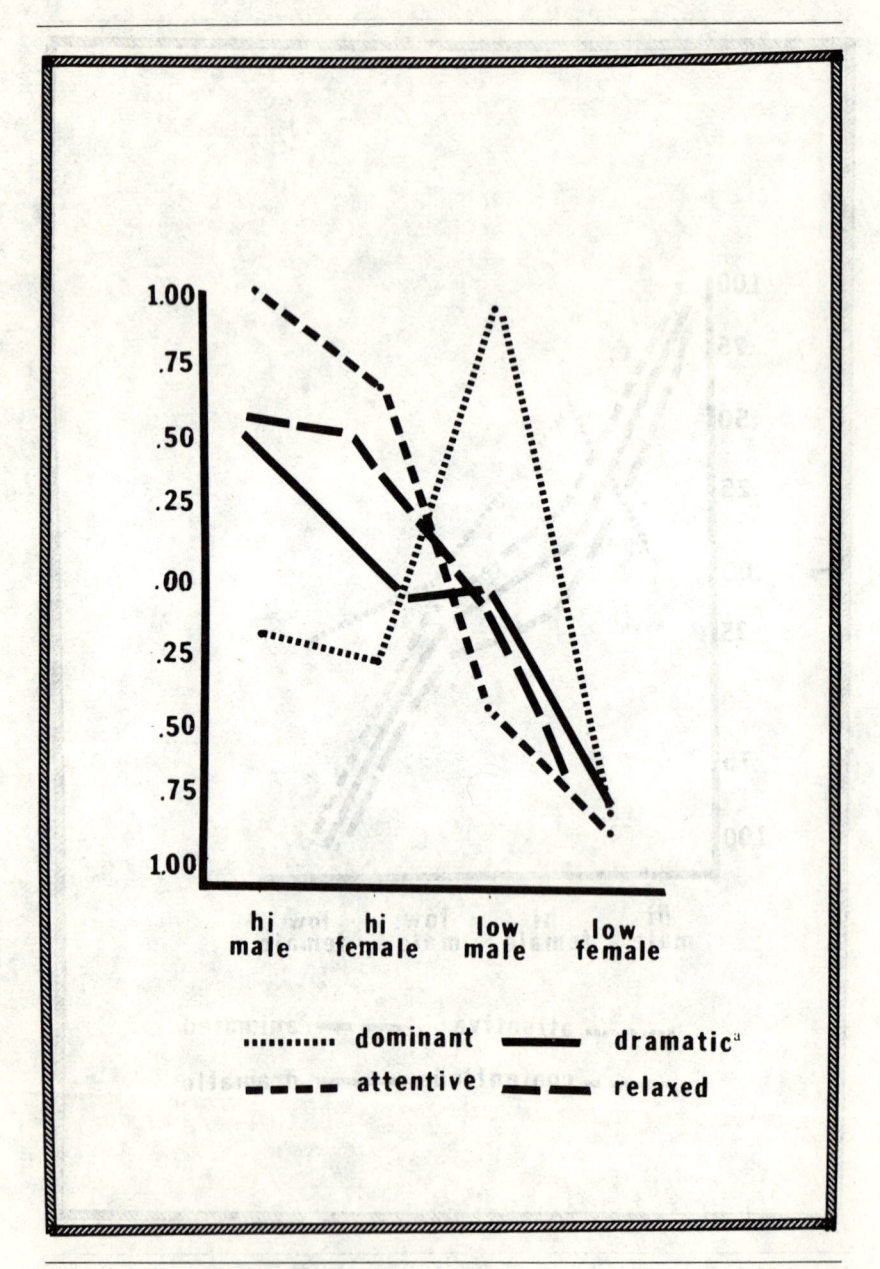

Figure 32.2. Teacher attraction.
a. All other style variables follow a similar pattern.

−.16; low females, $X = -.31$. Attentive is a style consistent with female sex role expectations and the most attractive females scored highest on this style, the least attractive females, the lowest. For the males the scores for both high and low are more similar.

The highest mean score for peer attractive males is in the contentious style, $X = .85$. Although highly popular girls are rated relatively low on the contentious style, $X = -.12$, it is still the second highest score. It may be that peers are more attractive to those children who are contentious in style relative to others within the same sex. It is the most contentious females who are the most attractive girls, even though they are equal in contentious style to the least popular boys.

For attractiveness to teachers, dominant, a style closely related to male sex typed expectations, is the only style variable in which the highest mean score is in the *least* attractive group. Least attractive males have a mean score of .98, least attractive females, $X = -.51$. The mean for the most attractive males was $X = -.12$, and for the most attractive females, $X = -.27$. It is the unattractive males who exhibit the highest degree of the male sex-typed behavior.

Most interestingly, it is the most attractive males who are perceived to manifest the greatest degree of attentiveness. The mean score for highly attractive males is .87, not only the highest score for within that style but the highest score across all styles. High attractive females have a mean score of .55, the least attractive males, $X = -.53$, the least attractive females, $X = -.81$.

The four regression analyses were computed to determine the ability of the communicator style variables to predict peer and teacher attraction for males and females separately. In the original work no sex comparison was made. The best predictors of teacher attraction were attentive, friendly, and relaxed. The results of this present analysis suggest that different style profiles will predict attractiveness for males and females.

Tables 32.5, 32.6, 32.7, and 32.8 present the results of the stepwise multiple regressions. For females, the only predictor, albeit a very powerful one, was attentive ($F = 21.16$; $p < .0001$). Attentive alone accounted for 47 percent of the unique variance.

For males, friendly was the most powerful predictor in the model of teacher attractiveness ($F = 20.65$; $p < .001$) accounting for 46 percent of the variance. Two other variables enter the model as significant predictors. At step 2 dominant accounts for an additional 10 percent of unique variance. The regression model for teachers' attraction to males was represented as follows: Y (teacher attraction) = friendly (.53) + dominant (−.53) + impression leaving (.68). The regression model accounted for 69 percent of the variance, an extremely strong effect.

Table 32.5
Stepwise Multiple Regression: Teacher Attraction—Females

Step	Variable	Beta Weight	R^2	Stepwise F	Significance
1	Attentive	−.74	.47	21.16	.0001

Table 32.6
Stepwise Multiple Regression: Teacher Attraction—Males

Step	Variable	Beta Weight	R^2	Stepwise F	Significance
1	Friendly	.531	.46	20.65	.0001
2	Dominant	−.528	.56	14.60	.0001
3	Impression leaving	.678	.69	16.80	.0001

The results in Table 32.6 demonstrate that for females an open style of communication was by far the most powerful predictor of peer attractiveness ($F = 4.53; p < .04$), accounting for 40 percent of the unique variance. Animated and contentious were also significant predictors. The regression equation Y (peer attractiveness) = open (3.66) + animated (−2.16) + contentious (−1.25) accounted for 53 percent of the variance.

In Table 32.7 the results are presented for peer attraction to males. Impression leaving is the best predictor accounting for 36 percent of the variance ($F = 13.38; p < .0001$). Attentive is the next best predictor, accounting for an additional 13 percent of variance explained, and open adds another 3 percent. The regression model is Y (peer attraction) = impression leaving (5.03) + attentive (−1.67) + open (−2.06). The entire regression equation accounts for 50 percent of the variance in the sample.

Research questions 1a, 1b, and 2 are answered positively. Teachers report significant sex differences in the manifestation of communicator style subconstructs. Males were perceived to be significantly more impression leaving, contentious, dramatic, dominant, and animated than females. These styles of communication are consistent with the male sex-typed characteristics presented in the first part of this chapter: aggressiveness, activity, noisiness, nonconformity. There was a trend for females to be more attentive, consistent with the female sex-typed characteristics of quietness, attentiveness, more eye contact, and greater communication awareness. The results of the discriminant analysis also give support to this issue. The best discriminating variables for males and females were dramatic, dominant, and attentive. These findings are somewhat different

Table 32.7
Stepwise Multiple Regression: Peer Attraction—Females

Step	Variable	Beta Weight	R^2	F	Significance
1	Open	3.66	.40	4.53	.04
2	Animated	−2.16	.48	3.42	.05
3	Contentious	−1.35	.53	2.82	.06

Table 32.8
Stepwise Multiple Regression: Peer Attraction—Males

Step	Variable	Beta Weight	R^2	F	Significance
1	Impression leaving	.50	.36	13.38	.001
2	Attentive	−1.67	.47	10.10	.001
3	Open	−2.06	.50	7.35	.001

than those of Montgomery and Norton (1981). They found significant mean differences in the self-reports of male and females on the animated, precise, and friendly styles. Possible causes of these differences and explanations will be presented in the discussion section.

In this study the teachers did not differentially report attraction to males and females. However, the results are consistent with the research that suggests teachers are more positively disposed to those children who exhibit female sex-typed behaviors. The results suggest that teachers are attracted to males who manifest less extreme male sex-typed behavior (lower dominant scores) and the greatest degree of female sex-typed behavior (attentiveness). The best predictors of teacher attraction for both males and females were styles that are both associated with female sex-typed behaviors (attentive and friendly). Although dominant and impression leaving do enter the regression equation for males, they contribute far less variance than the original 46 percent explained by friendly style.

DISCUSSION

This study found significant sex difference in teacher's perceptions of children's communicator style that are consistent with previous research findings of differences in young children's communication and sex role expectations. Males are perceived to be more contentious, impression leaving, dramatic, dominant, and animated. All five variables are highly visible, active, and energetic, clearly related to those "male" characteristics of aggressiveness and high activity level. In comparison, the only style in which females were more highly rated was attentive, a style suggestive of many "female" characteristics.

Although these styles do seem to be highly related to sex-typed behavior it is interesting to note that these are not the styles that Montgomery and Norton (1981) found to differ significantly between the sexes. In their study those styles were precise, animated, and friendly.

There are at least two major reasons, however, for such a difference emerging. The most obvious, but the least helpful, is that their data were from self-report measures whereas these data come from other report. It is possible that as individuals we focus on different important differences when reporting on ourselves rather than on someone else.

More important, however, is the second difference between the studies. Montgomery and Norton (1981) focus on college students, whereas this study is concerned with preschoolers. For young children, sex differences most probably first arise for the more overt styles. The styles that show significant differences between the sexes are the most noticeable, active styles. These are the same styles that have previously been shown to exhibit *no* significant age differences among 3-, 4-, and 5-year olds (Stohl, 1981). It is not surprising that they are among the first style variables all children process and react to (i.e., this is appropriate/not appropriate for me) since much of a child's manner is developed through imitation (Piaget, 1923; Keenan, 1974) and these styles are most distinctive.

There is some support for the proposition that peer attractiveness is related to consistency between sex and style behavior, although the interpretation of the results is difficult. The variables found to be related to peer popularity for females are attentive, open, animated, and contentious. For males the related variables are contentious, impression leaving, attentive, and open. It will be necessary for future research to develop indices related to childrens' perceptions of style in general and specific behavioral correlates of male and female styles before this relationship can be understood.

The results of the attraction dimension of this study do not support previous research that suggests that teachers are more favorably disposed toward females (Brophy & Good, 1974; Fagot, 1981). Rather, teachers seem to be most attracted to children who manifest female sex-typed communicative behaviors no matter what the child's sex. Indeed teachers, unlike peers, tend to reward cross-sex behavior of boys and not girls even though there seems to be a higher status afforded to male behaviors in our culture in general (Feinman, 1981). The reasons for such preference, however, seem to rest in the school as an institution rather than in the sexism of the teachers. It is the context that determines the "attractive" qualities.

Schools function to teach large numbers of children at the same time in the most efficient manner. As such, the attentive, friendly, and open styles will maximize the educational process, whereas children who communicate in styles that are contentious, impression leaving, dominant, dramatic, and animated may often interfere with the smooth functioning of the classroom. Teachers do enter classrooms with certain preconceived notions about the differences between males and females but their viewpoints and behaviors are largely controlled by the expectations of the school. It may be that dramatic and animated style are related to adults' perceptions of attractiveness in contexts other than the school. The more preschool and day care teachers see themselves in the role of preparing the children for "regular school," however, the more likely it is that they will prefer the feminine sex-typed behaviors. These are the behaviors we have all learned as more appropriate for successful school performance, and teachers are concerned with achievement.

If future research, however, does support the proposition that teachers prefer children with certain styles of communication, the importance of this phenomenon will reach far beyond any measure or concern with school achievement and sex differences. Cowen, Pederson, Babigan, and Trost (1973) have found that the best predictor of mental health problems as an adult is an individual's third-grade sociometric standing. There is a vast amount of evidence strongly indicating children's lack of attractiveness to peers and teachers frequently results in poor performance and personal unhappiness (e.g., Algozzine & Curan, 1979; Roff, Seels, & Golden, 1972; Stengel, 1971).

The findings of this study do not necessarily imply that variation in style causes variation in perceived attractiveness, which in turn causes variation in achievement and social development. Neither does it imply that "effeminate" boys will be more preferred than "macho" boys by teachers and less preferred by peers. Rather, the findings are highly suggestive of potential causal interactions that need to be investigated further.

The findings do clearly indicate, however, that context must be considered in any future study of the communicative correlates of attraction for adults as well as for children. Situational determinants of perceived attractive and appropriate behaviors are quite important. Indeed many aspects of communicative competence may also be strongly context bound.

The findings of this study seem to suggest that teachers' attitudes and behaviors toward children are influenced by the expectations and restrictions of the school setting. Rather than trying to change teachers' "sexist" attitudes so that they will be more accepting and appreciative of the less conforming and more active child, the focus of change needs to be on the structure and functioning of the classroom and the school. It is only in this way that the boys and girls with the more overt and active communicator styles will be more accepted by the teachers and thereby participate in a most positive educational and developmental context.

Limitations of the Study

Any further research done in this area, however, must deal with the limitations of the present investigation. The most obvious problem is in relating children's perceptions of attractiveness with measures of communicator style based on teacher observations. It is possible that children are perceiving and interpreting the communicative behaviors in ways other than adults. In other words, before we can be certain that children's perceptions of attraction are related to sex-typed style expectations, we need to develop some behavioral indices as to what children ascribe to female and male style behaviors.

A second major limitation of this study is the lack of control for children's physical appearance. Physical attraction has been shown to be highly related to social attraction (Langlois & Downs, 1980; Langlois & Stephan, 1977; Dion, Bersheid, & Walster, 1973) and it is quite possible that there is an interaction between physical attraction and social attractiveness. Appearance also has other dimensions that may influence perceptions of attraction. For example, female sex-typed behaviors may be desirable in the school setting for a rather masculine-looking child but such behaviors by an effeminate male will subject him to ridicule and/or concern. Redundancy in this case may be detrimental to social standing.

Despite these shortcomings this research report presents evidence that warrants further investigation. Is it instructional to be aware of the development of style differences and their relationship to sex differences, and the pragmatic importance of social attraction is far reaching; indeed the importance cannot be overemphasized. Children spend almost half their waking hours within a school setting. With the increasing number of children now enrolled and continuing to be enrolled in preschool and day care centers, the schools will have an even greater impact on the social and cognitive development of children. It is of upmost importance that we understand the phenomenon of social attractiveness in the classroom.

REFERENCES

Algozzine, B., & Curan, T.J. Teachers' predictions of children's school success as a function of their behavioral tolerances. *Journal of Educational Research*, 1979, 72, 344-348.

Ashear, V., & Snortum, J. Eye contact in children as a function of age, sex, social and intellectual variables. *Developmental Psychology*, 1971, *4*, 19-31.

Bates, J. E. Effects of children's nonverbal behavior upon adults. *Child Development*, 1976, *47*, 1079-1088.

Brodzinsky, D., Messer, S., & Tur, J. Sex differences in children's expression and control of fantasy and overt aggression. *Child Development*, 1979, *50*, 372-379.

Brophy, J., & Good, T. L. *Teacher-student relationships: Causes and consequences.* New York: Holt, Rinehart & Winston, 1974.

Cantor, N., & Gelfand, D. Effects of responsiveness and sex of children on adults' behavior. *Child Development*, 1977, *48*, 232-238.

Carpenter, C., & Huston-Stein, A. Activity structure and sex-typed behavior in preschool children. *Child Development*, 1980, *51*, 862-872.

Cowen, E. L., Pederson, A., Babigan, J., Izzo, L. D., & Trost, N. A. Long-term follow up of early detected vulnerable children. *Journal of Consulting and Clinical Psychology*, 1973, *41*, 438-446.

Dion, K. K., Bersheid, E., & Walster, E. What is beautiful is good. *Journal of Personality and Social Psychology*, 1973, *44*, 562-568.

Eakins, B., & Eakins, R. *Sex differences in human communication.* Boston: Houghton Mifflin, 1978.

Fagot, B. Male and female teachers: Do they treat boys and girls differently? *Sex Roles*, 1981, *7*, 263-273.

Feshbach, N. Student teacher preferences for elementary school pupils varying in personality characteristics. *Journal of Educational Psychology*, 1969, *60*, 126-132.

Feinman, S. Why is cross-sex-role behavior more approved for girls than for boys? A status characteristic approach. *Sex Roles*, 1981, *7*, 289-300.

Fitzpatrick, M., & Bochner, A. Perspectives on self and other: Male-female differences in perception of communicative behavior. *Sex Roles*, 1981, *7*, 523-535.

Good, T., & Grouws, D. *Reaction of male and female teacher trainees to descriptions of elementary school pupils.* Report 62, Center for Research in Social Behavior, 1972.

Gottman, J. M., Gonso, J., & Rasmunsen, B. Social interaction, social competence and friendship in children. *Child Development*, 1975, *46*, 709-718.

Hartup, W. W., Galzer, J. A., & Charlesworth, R. Peer reinforcement and sociometric status. *Child Development*, 1967, *38*, 1017-1024.

Henley, N. *Body politics: Power, sex and nonverbal communication.* Englewood Cliffs, NJ: Prentice-Hall, 1977.

Kaplan, L. The annoyances of elementary school teachers. *Journal of Educational Research*, 1952, *45*, 649-655.

Keller, B., & Bell, R. Q. Child effects on adults' method of eliciting altruistic behavior. *Child Development*, 1979, *50*, 1004-1009.

Kelly, E. A Study of consistent discrepancies between instructor grades and term-end examination grades. *Journal of Educational Psychology*, 1958, *49*, 328-334.

Keenan, E. Conversational competence in children. *Journal of Child Language*, 1974, *1*, 163-183.

Kohn, M. *Social competence, symptoms and underachievement in childhood: A longitudinal perspective.* New York: John Wiley, 1977.

Kremer, B. *The adjective checklist as an indicator of teachers' stereotypes of students.* Unpublished doctoral dissertation, Michigan State University, 1965.

Lamb, M., & Rooparine, J. Peer influences on sex-role development in preschoolers. *Child Development*, 1979, *50*, 1912-1922.

Langlois, J. H., & Downs, A. C. Peer relations as a function of physical attractiveness: The eye of the beholder or behavioral reality? *Child Development*, 1979, *50*, 409-418.

Langlois, J., & Stephan, C. The effects of physical attractiveness and ethnicity on children's behavioral attributions and peer preferences. *Child Development*, 1977, *48*, 1694-1698.

Langlois, J., & Downs, A. C. Mothers, fathers and peers as socialization agents of sex-typed play behaviors in young children. *Child Development*, 1980, *51*, 1237-1247.

Levine, M., & Sutton-Smith, B. Effects of age, sex, and task on visual behavior during dyadic interaction. *Developmental Psychology*, 1973, *9*, 400-405.

Maccoby, E., & Jacklin, C. *The psychology of sex differences*. Stanford, CA: Stanford University Press, 1974.

Maccoby, E., & Jacklin, C. Sex differences in aggression: A rejoinder and reprise. *Child Development*, 1980, *51*, 964-980.

Moore, S. G., & Updegraff, R. Sociometric status of preschool children related to age, sex, nurturance-giving and dependency. *Child Development*, 1964, *35*, 519-524.

Montgomery, B., & Norton, R. Sex Differences in Communicator Style. *Communication Monographs*, 1981, *48*, 121-132.

Norton, R., & Pettegrew, L. S. Communication style as an effect determinant of attraction. *Communication Research*, 1977, *4*, 257-282.

Norton, R. Foundation of a communicator style construct. *Human Communication Research*, 1978, *4*, 99-112.

Piaget, J. *The language and thought of the child*. New York: Harcourt Brace, 1926.

Post, B., & Hetherington, E. Sex differences in the use of proximity and eye contact in judgments of affiliation in preschool children. *Developmental Psychology*, 1974, *11*, 881-888.

Roff, M., Sells, S., & Golden, M. *Social adjustment and personality adjustment in children*. Minneapolis: University of Minnesota press, 1972.

Sears, P. *The effect of classroom conditions on the strength of achievement motives and work output of elementary school children*. Cooperative Research Program OE873. Washington, DC: HEW, 1973.

Stengel, E. *Suicide and attempted suicide*. Middlesex, England: Penguin, 1971.

Stohl, C. Perceptions of social attractiveness and communicator style: A developmental study of preschool children. *Communication Education*, 1981, *30*, 367-376.

Stott, L. H. Personality at age four. *Child Development*, 1962, *33*, 287-311.

Tauber, M. Parental socialization techniques and sex differences in children's play. *Child Development*, 1979, *50*, 225-234.

Teyber, E., Messe, L., & Stollack, G. Adult responses to child communications. *Child Development*, 1977, *48*, 1577-1582.

Tukey, J. W. *Exploratory data analysis*. Reading, MA: Addison-Wesley, 1977.

IX • HEALTH COMMUNICATION

33 ● Coping with Occupational Stress: Relational and Individual Strategies of Nurses in Acute Health Care Settings

TERRANCE L. ALBRECHT
University of Washington

You entered nursing because it was a good opportunity to use your natural nurturing skills. ... you could serve people in a worthwhile career that wouldn't cost too much initially, would allow some freedom, enough money to travel and perhaps a chance to pursue a career with leadership options. ... But it didn't work out that way. It's a tough life being a nurse. Your professional and personal life has become so stressful you find it hard to cope. Now the caregiver needs care. (Vachon, 1980a, p. 28)

Most research in the field of stress has been carried out within the philosophical framework of an epistemology rooted in the experience of science and most conveniently summarized as positivism. This is a doctrine that has been much under attack in recent years and the attacks raise the possibility that more adequate intellectual frameworks exist for solving the problems of research in this field. (Payne, 1978, p. 259)

THE juxtaposition of the two statements above illustrates the frustration of stress researchers and practitioners alike: that while social scientific endeavors in the area of occupational stress (particularly on how people cope) have been theoretically weak (Kanner, Kafry, & Pines, 1978) and methodologically inadequate,[1] those in the

AUTHOR'S NOTE: The author gratefully acknowledges the cooperation of the hospital nurses and administrators who participated in the study and provided encouragement and facilities for data collection. The author would also like to thank Professors Malcolm Parks and Loyd Pettegrew and the Division 8 readers for their helpful suggestions and comments, and Lynda Prendergast and Rosanne McCaughey for assistance with data reduction.

Correspondence and requests for reprints: Terrance L. Albrecht, Department of Speech Communication, University of Washington DE-05, Seattle, WA 98195.

world of work continue at the same time to experience very real, painful consequences of prolonged and acute stress levels.

Newman and Beehr (1979, p. 2) have emphasized that our understanding of the job stress process is "incomplete," in part due to a dearth of evaluation research. Simply, there have been few studies on the effectiveness of many relational and self-improvement coping strategies commonly advocated in workshops, popular press articles, etc. Until more research findings are accumulated, practitioners have "little more than their common sense and visceral instincts" on which to base their attempts to develop stress management programs (Newman & Beehr, 1979, p. 35).

The purpose of this study was to investigate the role of relational/communicative strategies in coping with stress. Current work on the suggestion that social support has a moderating effect on occupational stress has been encouraging (Katz & Kahn, 1978; Newman & Beehr, 1979; House, 1981; Kahn, 1981; Albrecht, Irey, & Mundy, in press). Given that job stress is inevitable (Vredenburgh & Trinkaus, 1981, p. 1), the present study was an effort to extend previous literature on the role of communication in the domain of job-related stress (cf. Pettegrew, Thomas, Costello, Wolf, Lennox, & Thomas, 1980). Specifically, this was an investigation of the perceived use and effectiveness of relational versus self-oriented coping strategies, and whether these configurations of strategies differed for those experiencing lower as opposed to higher stress levels.

Citing previous research problems, Payne (1978, p. 282) has argued for more "contextual" stress research involving smaller, detailed studies:

> Since we have demonstrated that the large scale cross-sectional study has not been very helpful in predicting individual reactions to stressors then this cannot be counted too negatively. Indepth, clinical and processual studies of the kind implied by pragmatism stand at least a chance of helping the individual case. Good and lasting solutions to such individual problems will surely have a reasonable chance of working in similar contexts.

This exploratory study on occupational stress in nursing was designed to be descriptive and detailed in order to answer some initial questions about the perceived use and effectiveness of various coping behaviors.

Vredenburgh and Trinkaus (1981) noted that nurses represent a particularly appropriate target population for study. Stress in their work is unavoidable. As professionals working in structured, bureaucratic organizations, they often experience such stressors as (1) role conflict; (2) unmet role expectations; (3) interpersonal conflict with other status groups (doctors, administrators, patients); (4) low pay and difficulty of working irregular hours and weekends; (5) the feeling of low status and respect, yet tremendous responsibility for critical patients; and (6) work overload (manifested by emotional and physical symptoms) due to frequent staff shortages, absenteeism, and turnover.[2] In the absence of formal organizational stress intervention programs, an important question is how nurses handle chronic job stress, either by themselves or through their relationships with others, in order to provide continually high-quality patient care.

CONCEPTUAL FRAMEWORK

Stress and Burnout in Nursing

"Burnout" has been defined as a reaction to daily stress on the job; it is a "wearing out" due to heavy demands (Maslach, 1976; Maslach & Jackson, 1980). The experience of reacting to job and work environment stress is a complex progression (Albrecht et al., in press). Daley (1979, p. 375) conceptualized burnout of those in the "helping" professions as a dynamic process with identifiable stages of development. Freudenberger (1977) cautioned that the phases may be so slow that some people may be oblivious to the symptoms or even deny there is a problem. Certainly, many authors have noted how psychological and physical exhaustion causes the nurse, the hospital, and the patients to suffer (Vachon, Lyall, & Freeman, 1978; Vachon, 1979; Hoffman, 1981).

Lazarus, Cohen, Folkman, Kanner, and Schaefer (1980) have shown that how people cope in reacting to stress has functional or dysfunctional consequences on their adaptation outcomes. Kahn (1981), drawing from the model of French, Rodgers, and Cobb (1974, p. 104), argued that adaptation occurs when an individual selects behaviors that increase his or her "personality-environment (P-E) fit." However, with limited empirical research it is unclear how the strategies nurses use to cope relate to their relative reaction levels (i.e., burnout levels) to stress.

Relational Coping Strategies

There is evidence that integration in supportive communication networks relates to the amount of work-related stress perceived by role incumbents. Involvement in a support network of people (in or outside the workplace) who communicate with and help each other may protect against stress and strain (Katz & Kahn, 1978).

Albrecht et al. (in press) used network analysis techniques in a study of social workers and found that those embedded in small network groups in the agency reported lower stress reaction than did more isolated individuals. In a comprehensive review of the social support literature, House (1981, p. 26) found consistent evidence that "social support" (the flow of emotional concern, instrumental aid, information, and/or appraisal information relevant to self-evaluation) is a buffer to strain.

As House (1981, p. 27) noted, most researchers have asked respondents to rate how much support they receive from others, resulting in a measure of "perceived support." He argued that this method is most appropriate in early efforts to understand the phenomenon, because support is likely to be effective only to the extent that it is perceived.

For nurses, support may come from a variety of relational sources, Vachon (1980b) emphasized that it is important for nurses to have caring relationships with peers and supervisors as well as with friends and family outside the hospital.

In contrast to seeking social support, withdrawal from others at work is a second type of relational behavior. This strategy may help in some cases (Newman & Beehr, 1979). However, House (1981) argued this by citing research on the negative health consequences of social isolation. Vachon (1980b) advocated that nurses avoid feelings of isolation as a way to cope with anxiety. Kahn et al. (1964) found that while withdrawal may be effective in the short term, the long-range avoidance of others increases the probability of conflict.

Finally, religious orientation has been speculated to have positive effects by several authors.[3] Selye (1976, p. 443) emphasized religious faith and "contemplation" of something "infinitely greater" as a way to reduce daily frustrations. Reinard and Crawford (1981, p. 24) suggested prayer as a "superior mechanism," and Vachon (1979) recommended prayer groups as a source of support for nurses working with terminally ill patients.

Self-Oriented Strategies

Most individual mechanisms concern modifying one's physical well-being, altering one's mental/emotional state, or changing one's environment. For example, physical fitness is typically recommended as a way to improve one's physical health (and subsequent mental outlook) to withstand stress on the job better (Newman & Beehr, 1979; Vachon, 1980b). In contrast, some individuals have engaged in dysfunctional behaviors associated with poor diet (undereating, overeating) leading to nutritional deficiencies (Selye, 1976; Vachon, 1980b).[4]

Acts associated with altering one's mental/emotional state may also have functional or dysfunctional consequences. For example, responding to stressful work situations by rationalizing the problem and oneself has been called healthy (Selye, 1976; Bridger, 1978; Newman & Beehr, 1979; Vachon, 1980b). Denial of a problem or ignoring the situation has been seen as appropriate for cancer care nurses on a limited basis (Vachon, 1980b). Vachon (1980b) also acknowledged the controlled use of alcohol as a way for some nurses to defuse job stress.[5] Selye (1976, p. 176) cited increased consumption as a "flight reaction" and a sign of distress.

Finally, occupational change or withdrawal has been suggested as a way to change a stressful environment (Newman & Beehr, 1979; Vachon, 1980b). Taking time off, however, has been discussed as a less drastic action and precludes the costs of job turnover for the individual and the organization (Vachon, 1980b; Reinard & Crawford, 1981).

Desired Strategies

It is possible that a difference exists between what individuals feel they can do to cope and what they wish they could do. Such a perceived discrepancy could, in turn, become a stressor. For example, Cherniss (1979) identified barriers that often prevent social welfare professionals from forming supportive relationships, implying that even if they wanted to seek out others they would be unable to do so. Hence, a discrepancy between actual and desired strategies could provide insight into the contextual nature of the perceived personal and work environments of respondents.

Research Framework

Based on the state of previous findings, opinion, and the exploratory nature of this study, the following research questions were formulated to guide the research effort:

RQ.1: How effective do nurses perceive relational and self-oriented strategies for reducing stress to be?

RQ.2: How do desired coping strategies relate to perceived levels of burnout?

RQ.3: Will high- and low-burnout nurses be discriminated on the basis of a configuration of relational and self-oriented strategies?

RQ.4: Will low-burnout respondents perceive supportive relationships with others in the hospital to be significantly more effective?

METHOD

The study was conducted in a large, 325-bed metropolitan hospital. The nonprofit institution has a national reputation for its specialty health care facilities and research.

Permission for the study was obtained from the chief hospital administrator, the assistant administrator for nursing services, and the nursing administration council. Study procedures were approved by the hospital's human subjects review committee.

Respondents

Participants in the study were 101 registered nurses and licensed practical nurses in five units of the hospital: respiratory therapy, oncology (cancer care), medical-surgical/primary care, cardiac care, and intensive care. Respondents included staff nurses, nursing care coordinators, and unit supervisors.

Research Procedures

Data were gathered using interview and field survey research techniques. Nondirective interviews (thirty to forty minutes each) were conducted with administrators and unit supervisors. These provided background information for questionnaire construction and scaling methods, and insight for later data interpretation.

Survey data were collected using a two-wave panel design with a two-week interval between administrations. Data were collected from nurses on the day, evening, and night shifts. Small groups of mixed staff filled out the surveys during scheduled times throughout working hours on hospital premises. These procedures were used for gathering both data waves.

Measurement

Burnout. The perception of the amount of chronic daily stress experienced on the job was measured using a modified version the Maslach Burnout Inventory (MBI), a two-scale instrument developed by Maslach and Jackson (1980). The fifty-two items were designed for measuring the *perceived frequency* which an individual experienced any of the stress symptoms listed and the *perceived intensity* of the feeling when it occurred. The items relate to three dimensions of burnout: emotional and physical exhaustion, depersonalization and psychological distancing of oneself from one's patients and work, and a decreased sense of personal accomplishment. Perceptions of frequency were rated on a seven-point scale ranging from "never" to "daily." Perceptions of intensity were rated on a seven-point scale ranging from "very mild" to "very strong."

Stress Coping Strategies. Respondents were asked to consider each of fifteen major relational and self-oriented coping strategies. They were asked first to describe on a six-point scale *how often* they used the strategy (ranging from "never" to "every day"). Second, they were asked to indicate the *perceived effectiveness* of the strategy by describing their level of agreement with the statement, "I feel better when I do this," on a seven-point scale ranging from "strongly disagree" to "strongly agree."

The items associated with relational strategies included seeking out co-workers (in the same unit), seeking out the supervisor, talking to others in the hospital (though not in the same unit), talking with spouse or roommates, talking with friends or family (not living with respondents), withdrawal from others at work, going out and partying more, and prayer.

The items associated with individual strategies included exercise, ignoring problems and just doing one's work, rationalizing oneself and the problems, having a drink after duty, thinking seriously about changing occupations, trying to take extra time off, and overeating.

In addition, respondents were asked to list on an open-ended section other strategies they used to cope with work stress. (Results are not included here.)

Desired Strategies. Respondents were asked how often they "wished" they could use each of twelve strategies to cope with stress. Frequency of these perceptions were measured on a six-point scale with the endpoints, "never wished I could do this" and "I always wish this."

Desired relational strategy items included seeking out co-workers (in the same unit), seeking out the supervisor, talking to others in the hospital (though not in the same unit), talking with spouse or roommates, talking with friends or family (not living with respondents), desire to be left alone at work (withdrawal), going out and partying more and ability to pray and receive more comfort.

Desired individual items were more time for exercise, ability to rationalize oneself and the problems better, change jobs, and take more time off work.

Again, respondents were asked to list on an open-ended section other strategies they wished they could use to cope with work stress (not included here).

RESULTS

Description of the Sample

Professional Profile. Nearly all respondents were staff nurses (95 percent), most working full time (69 percent). Most had been employed at the hospital less than five years ($s = 5.21$), though in nursing almost nine years ($s = 7.68$). The average length of time in present hospital position was about two and one-half years ($s = 2.48$). Educationally, 44 percent were RNs, 38 percent were RNs with bachelor's degrees, 15 percent were LPNs, and only 3 percent held master's degrees. About half reported they worked forty to fifty hours per week; 33 percent worked less than thirty hours per week; and 19 percent worked at least seventy hours per week.

Personal Profile. Most respondents were white females (96 percent); the average age was 32 ($s = 9.05$). About half were married (most for four years or less). Seventy-five percent did not have children living with them. Approximately 83 percent reported a specific religious commitment.

Response Rates. The total number of respondents in wave 1 was 101 (72 percent); ninety-six nurses participated in wave 2 (68 percent).[6]

Table 33.1
Response Rates for Each Unit and Shift
of Respondents Participating in Both Waves

Unit	Day	Evening	Night
Respiratory care	.89	.50	1.00
Oncology	.57[a]	—	—
Medical-surgical	.71	.73	.80
Cardiac care	.83	.75	.80
Intensive care	.47	.56	.38

a. Due to scheduling procedures on this unit, all shifts were combined for the response rate analysis.

Eighty-six respondents were in both waves (61 percent). Response patterns are in Table 33.1.[7]

Validity and Reliability of Measures

Validity. Following Maslach and Jackson (1980), discriminant validity of the MBI was first assessed by correlating it with the work satisfaction scale of the Job Descriptive Index (Smith, Kendall, & Hulin, 1969). The Pearson correlation coefficient was −.60 for the frequency scale and −.45 for the intensity scale. Second, the MBI was correlated with the Social Desirability Scale (Crowne & Marlowe, 1972) to determine whether the MBI scores were biased by a self-presentation response set.[8] The result for the frequency scale was .03 (n.s.) and .11 (n.s.) for the intensity scale.

While the lack of a relationship between the MBI and social desirability was consistent with Maslach and Jackson's (1980) results, the correlation with work satisfaction found in these data was stronger than their reported findings. However, their correlations were between satisfaction and subscales of the MBI. Factor analysis of the MBI in this study did not confirm their factor structure; hence the larger scales were left intact. Burnout as measured in this study, then, was judged to have a low level of redundancy with job dissatisfaction; the amount of variance accounted for in the relationship was 36 percent and 20 percent, respectively.

Reliability. The internal consistency and test-retest reliabilities were assessed for all indices. The results are in Table 33.2. The coefficients were generally acceptable. However, the test-retest was low for the intensity scale. A possible reason was that while respondents were fairly consistent in their frequency recall of stressful symptoms, these symptoms were not experienced to the same degree each time they occurred and thus could not be reliably measured.

Test-retest correlations were used to determine the reliability of the single-item coping strategies. The results are in Table 33.3. In general,

Table 33.2
Reliability Coefficients for All Indices

Measure	Cronbach alpha Wave 1	Wave 2	Test-retest r
MBI (frequency scale)	.86	.89	.83*
MBI (intensity scale)	.81	.96	.44*
Work satisfaction (JDI)	.79	.81	.84*
Social Desirability Scale	(not applicable)		.82*

*$p < .001$.

responses regarding the frequency of use did not fluctuate as much as judgments of their effectiveness. The most consistent responses for both actual and desired strategies were perceptions of the act of prayer and serious consideration of changing jobs.

Analysis of Results

Research Question 1. The perceived effectiveness of the coping strategies were first assessed by correlating the frequency of use with the perceived effectiveness measure (see Table 33.4).

The strategies perceived most effective with greater use were prayer, talking with friends and family, and seeking out others in the hospital (not in the same unit). The self-oriented strategy of exercise was also seen as effective. The least effective strategies were withdrawal, taking time off from work, and overeating.

The strategies were further evaluated by correlating each with the frequency and intensity of burnout. It could be expected that the most effective coping mechanisms would be those that had a negative relationship to the experience of stress symptoms (concerning use and perceived effectiveness of using the strategy). This would provide some evidence that increased use was adaptive in managing stress. These results are in Table 33.5.

The act of prayer and seeking out the supervisor and co-workers negatively correlated with both dimensions of burnout. Exercise and rationalization were associated with decreased intensity of burnout symptoms.

In contrast, higher stress levels were associated with interaction with spouse/roommates, "partying," social withdrawal at work, serious consideration of changing jobs, and overeating.

Research Question 2. It was also an aim of the study to investigate the relationship between job stress and desired (as opposed to actual) strategies for coping. Initial correlations are reported in Table 33.6.

Table 33.3
Test-Retest Correlation Coefficients for Coping Strategy Items

Strategy	Frequency	Effectiveness
Actual coping strategies		
Prayer	.85	.73
Withdrawal from others at work	.68	.35
Going out, partying more	.67	.53
Talking with spouse, roommates	.62	.57
Seeking out others in hospital (not in same unit)	.66	.63
Talking with friends, family	.63	.51
Seeking out co-workers (same unit)	.59	.46
Seeking out supervisor	.46	.47
Think seriously about changing occupation	.88	.68
Drink after getting off duty	.88	.66
Overeating	.81	.67
Exercise	.73	.46
Rationalizing self and problems	.63	.66
Ignoring problems and just doing the work	.59	.45
Try to take extra time off	.35	.53
Desired coping strategies		(not applicable)
Pray and receive more support	.77	
Go out and party more	.70	
Withdrawal from others at work	.66	
Seek out others in hospital (not in unit)	.64	
Talk with friends and family	.62	
Seek out co-workers (same unit)	.61	
Talk with spouse, roommates	.61	
Seek out supervisor	.59	
Change jobs	.80	
More time for exercise	.75	
Take time off from work	.72	
Rationalize self and situation better	.65	

Note: All coefficients significant at $p < .001$.

The nurse respondents most often wished they could take time off, have more time for exercise, rationalize situations better, and seek out co-workers in the same unit. Greater perceived frequency and acuteness of burnout were associated with increases in the following strategies: desire to change jobs, withdrawal from others at work, taking time off, "partying," talking with friends and family, exercise, and talking with spouse or roommates.

Research Questions 3 and 4. Stepwise discriminant analysis was used to test whether high- and low-burnout nurses differed according to the coping strategies they perceived to be most effective in reducing stress.[9] It was expected that a linear combination of the relational and self-oriented

Table 33.4
Descriptive Statistics and Correlations Between Perceived
Use and Effectiveness of Each Strategy

Strategy	r	Frequency	Effectiveness
Relational			
Prayer	.69*	2.43(1.69)	4.88(1.85)
Talking with friends, family	.65*	3.07(1.34)	5.25(1.43)
Seeking out others in hospital	.62*	2.39(1.34)	4.77(1.73)
Seeking out supervisor	.57*	2.49(1.04)	4.76(1.85)
Talking with spouse, roommates	.48*	4.12(1.37)	5.62(1.30)
Seeking out co-workers (same unit)	.45*	4.33(1.29)	5.79(1.04)
Going out and partying	.40*	2.90(1.23)	4.15(1.78)
Withdrawal	.25**	2.28(1.08)	3.19(1.61)
Self-oriented			
Exercise	.65*	3.40(1.50)	5.53(1.40)
Ignoring problems	.57*	2.84(1.45)	3.32(1.50)
Thinking of changing occupation	.53*	2.80(1.45)	4.06(1.73)
Rationalization	.47*	4.11(1.26)	5.34(1.21)
Drink after duty	.46*	2.58(1.41)	4.47(1.60)
Try to take time off	.36*	2.06(0.79)	5.43(1.46)
Overeat	.10	3.36(1.74)	2.68(1.90)

Note: Values = means (standard deviations in parentheses).
*$p < .001$.
**$p < .05$.

behaviors would differentiate the high and low groups. The stepwise method was used to identify the strategies perceived as effective and also as having the best discriminating power (see Nie, Hull, Jenkins, Steinbrenner, & Bent, 1975).

As shown in Tables 33.7 and 33.8, different subsets of the reported strategies contributed significantly ($p < .05$, change in Rao's V) to the discrimination between the high and low groups. Taken as a linear combination, the relational and self-oriented strategies were comparable in differentiating the high-frequency from the low-frequency groups. A more micro-level analysis of the strategies showed significant *t* results for talking with co-workers and drinking after work. As could be expected, those who experienced stress symptoms less frequently tended to perceive talking with co-workers as a more effective strategy than did the high-stress group. Also, the high-stress group reported drinking after work to be significantly more effective than did the low-burnout nurses.

Only one relational strategy emerged in the linear function differentiating the high- and low-intensity groups: talking with the supervisor. The low-stress group perceived three strategies as more effective in reducing the stress symptoms (and the analysis shows these related to the intensity

Table 33.5
Correlations Between Burnout (frequency and intensity) and
Reports of Coping Behaviors (frequency and perceived effectiveness)

Strategy	MBI frequency		MBI intensity	
Relational				
Prayer	−.15[a]	−.36*[b]	−.20**[a]	−.34*[b]
Talking with friends, family	.02	−.11	.16	−.01
Seeking out others in hospital	.08	−.05	.12	.02
Seeking out supervisor	−.24**	−.39*	−.18**	−.38*
Talking with spouse, roommates	.29**	−.10	.44*	−.05
Seeking out co-workers (same unit)	.01	−.30*	.02	−.24**
Going out and partying	.23**	.04	.30	.04
Withdrawal	.34*	.01	.35*	.05
Self-oriented				
Exercise	−.03	−.15	−.16	−.28**
Ignoring problems	.18	.03	.07	.08
Thinking of changing occupations	.56*	.28**	.45*	.29**
Rationalization	.13	−.12	.01	−.27**
Drinking after duty	.18	.15	.13	.12
Trying to take time off	.01	−.07	.08	.04
Overeating	.23**	−.11	.19	.02

a. correlations with frequency of strategy use.
b. correlations with effectiveness of strategy when it was used.
*$p < .001$.
**$p < .05$.

of feeling): talking with the supervisor, rationalizing the problem, and (unexpectedly) overeating. The micro-level *t* values show that talking with the supervisor, rationalization, and seriously considering occupation change were each perceived to have significantly different levels of effectiveness by the two groups.

General discriminant analysis results show that approximately 78 percent of the cases were correctly classified in the burnout-frequency analysis ($\chi^2 = 32.9, p < .001$); approximately 77 percent of the cases were correctly classified when the strategies were used to differentiate the high- and low-intensity groups ($\chi^2 = 23.8, p < .001$). The combined linear function accounted for about 53 percent of the variance in differentiating between the high- and low-frequency groups. Slightly less (47 percent) was accounted for by the combined function in discriminating the two intensity-level groups.

DISCUSSION AND IMPLICATIONS

The study reported here was an initial step in understanding how expectations for various responses to stress, particularly those of a rela-

Table 33.6
Correlations Between Burnout and Desired Coping Strategies

Strategy	X(SD)[a]	MBI frequency r	MBI intensity r
Relational			
Seeking out co-workers (same unit)	3.31(1.21)	.17	.06
Talk with friends, family	3.22(1.42)	.31**	.30**
Talk with spouse, roommates	3.22(1.42)	.24**	.28**
Seek out supervisor	2.90(1.05)	.15	.01
Pray	2.39(1.38)	.04	−.04
Go out and party more	2.29(1.16)	.33*	.30**
Withdrawal	2.26(1.09)	.36*	.33*
Seek out others in hospital	2.15(1.07)	.13	.21**
Self-oriented			
Take time off	4.01(1.33)	.37*	.33*
More time for exercise	3.62(1.39)	.24**	.09
Rationalize better	3.45(1.30)	−.01	−.03
Change jobs	2.86(1.32)	.58*	.47*

a. Descriptive statistics for coping strategies.
*$p < .001$.
**$p < .05$.

tional nature involving communication, related to the reported experience of occupational stress of nurses. The study examined (1) the relative functional or dysfunctional character of different coping mechanisms (found in the literature and modified by interview data), and (2) whether individual differences in stress levels could be predicted based on expectation levels for the effectiveness of various strategies.

Clearly, the relational strategies that related most to effectiveness were prayer, talking with friends and family (outside the hospital), and talking with others in the hospital (but not in the same unit). The least effective strategy was withdrawal. As might be expected, exercise emerged as the strategy most functional at a self-oriented level; overeating was unrelated to effectiveness. It is important to note that the strategies reported to be the most effective were not the ones necessarily used most often.

It was also found that increased perceptions of burnout were most strongly related to increased desires to change occupations; take time off; talk with friends, family, spouse, or roommates; "party"; and withdraw. It is not surprising that these desired strategies are those that together imply an "escape" from the hospital setting. The desire to separate one's professional and personal roles has been described as an initial developmental phase in burnout (Daley, 1979).

Table 33.7
Group Means, t Values, and Standardized Discriminant Function Coefficients for Burnout-Frequency[a]

Strategy	X Low	X High	Coefficient	t[b]
Talking with co-workers in unit	6.33	5.45	−.94	2.42**
Seeking out others in hospital	4.62	4.70	.33	n.s.
Partying	3.76	4.34	.41	n.s.
Seeking out family, friends	5.33	5.24	.29	n.s.
Rationalization	5.86	5.03	−.67	n.s.
Overeating	2.62	2.24	−.37	n.s.
Drinking	3.71	4.83	.46	−1.76***
Taking time off	5.38	5.07	−.24	n.s.

a. Low group $n = 21$ (some cases missing due to missing data); high group $n = 29$ (some cases missing due to missing data); discriminant function eigenvalue = 1.11; canonical correlation = .73; Wilks lambda = .47.

b. t tests were run on all strategies for the two groups. Two other factors were significant, although they did not contribute significantly to the overall discriminant function. They were (1) effectiveness of seeking out the supervisor ($t = 3.68, p < .001$; X low = 5.36, X high = 3.75), and (2) effectiveness of prayer ($t = 3.35, p < .001$; X low = 5.81, X high = 4.30).

**$p < .05$ (two-tailed test).
***$p < .05$ (one-tailed test).

Our results also showed that individual differences in reported stress levels could be explained somewhat by the perceived effectiveness of various strategies. That is, high- and low-stress respondents had differing expectations for a number of key relational and self-oriented strategies. Moreover, given that reacting to stress is a complex phenomenon, these strategies combined in different ways to predict the frequency and intensity of stress.

Specifically, the results suggested that a variety of relational and self-oriented strategies (both job- and nonjob-related) combined to differentiate high- and low-burnout respondents. Factors loading most heavily were talking with co-workers in the unit, rationalization, and drinking after work.

In contrast to the variety of strategies that predicted high and low frequency of stress, a restricted set of primarily self-oriented mechanisms emerged to differentiate the high- and low-intensity groups. However, the strongest coefficient contributing to the function was the relational factor of seeking support from the supervisor.

The results of the more micro-level analysis of the strategies showed the high- and low-frequency groups differed on the following: talking with co-workers in the unit, seeking out the supervisor, prayer, and drinking. That is, nurses experiencing burnout symptoms less frequently tended to have higher expectations for the effectiveness of seeking support from work relationships and prayer, but lower expectations for drinking.

Table 33.8
Group means, t Values, and Standardized
Discriminant Function Coefficients for Burnout-Intensity[a]

Strategy	X Low	X High	Coefficient	t[b]
Talking with supervisor	5.43	3.71	−.78	3.00**
Rationalization	5.90	5.00	−.74	2.82**
Changing jobs	3.67	4.62	.36	−2.22**
Overeating	2.57	2.38	−.50	n.s.
Ignoring stressors	3.10	3.43	.35	n.s.

a. Low group n = 21 (some missing data); high group n = 21 (some missing data); discriminant function eigenvalue = .89; canonical correlation = .69; Wilks lambda = .53.
b. t test results also show differences for two other strategies: (1) the effectiveness of prayer (t = 2.27**; X low = 5.59, X high = 4.48), and (2) effectiveness of exercise (t = 2.29**; X low = 5.94; X high = 5.24).
**$p < .05$ (two-tailed test).

The high- and low-intensity groups exhibited the following differences: talking with the supervisor, rationalization, serious consideration of changing occupations, prayer, and exercise. Again, these results were what we would expect: that low-intensity nurses reported significantly higher expectations for talking with the supervisor, rationalization, prayer, and exercise; they had lower expectations for the benefits of changing occupations.

These findings provide initial, tentative answers to the research questions. Configurations of strategies based on perceived effectiveness are useful discriminators in assessing occupational health. These data show some evidence for the role of social support as a moderator of stress. We do not infer a causal relationship here between social support and reduced stress, only that our findings are consistent with a mounting body of current evidence (cf. Blau, 1981; House, 1981; Albrecht et al., in press), which is a necessary first step in establishing causal patterns.

However, these findings need to be considered in light of measurement problems in the study — in particular, the low reliabilities of the MBI-intensity scale (.44) and some of the strategies (mostly associated with the perceived effectiveness measures). These specific problems relate to a larger methodological limitation of the study: the difficulty of associating self-reports of stress and coping. Certainly House's (1981) point is well taken: that self-reports are an appropriate means of tapping social support because it is something that must be perceived by the respondent. However, these measures should be used in an initial phase of a research project. Clearly, the argument by Payne (1978) for smaller, detailed longitudinal studies applies here. On-site observation of behavior across time would yield patterns of stress and the use of coping mechanisms. The tracking of this covariation would provide a more reliable indicator of these influences. Also such "triangulation" of methods (self-report with observation) could help in assessing convergent validity (Jick, 1979).

Despite these problems, the ways the relational strategies emerge here give us grounds for arguing for future studies to use a social network perspective in considering occupational stress and coping. These results show linkages to immediate peers and the supervisor at the workplace to be integral to the quality of work life. We suggest future study of the nature of work and personal social ties and how these relate to emotional and physical health. In addition, these findings prompt us to ask questions concerning the nature of stress shared by members of a system. That is, is a "contagion" effect produced (Ray, 1981; Cherniss, 1980), given that one uses relationships to talk about one's stresses?

Finally, the findings have some practical implications for intervention. Several strategies clearly were more effective than others, and some seemed to tie more with the frequency of stressor occurrence rather than stressor intensity, and vice versa. It was clear that high- and low-stress nurses tended to have differing expectations for which strategies would be effective. Unfortunately, some of these for the high-stress group could be termed dysfunctional for the individual, the hospital, and the nursing profession. An understanding of the nature of social support in the work environment through training and intervention methods could be helpful. In addition, the advice of Selye (1976) is implicit in the results of the personal strategies. That is, adopting a "philosophy of life" can be reinforcing and strengthening in coping. Such a philosophy, if well developed, can serve an orienting function for one's ability to rationalize situations and even build relationships.

NOTES

1. See, for example, criticisms by several authors in the edited text by Cooper and Payne (1978).

2. Vredenburgh and Trinkaus (1981) mentioned some of these stressors. Selye (1976, p. 375) characterized "conscientious nursing of difficult patients" as highly distressful. Nursing was also identified as a profession affected by burnout in an article by Bishop (1980), "The Personal and Business Costs of 'Job Burnout.'"

3. During interviews respondents identified prayer as a relational act; it was therefore included in this cluster.

4. In the interviews respondents felt this was often manifested by "overeating" but that perceptions of this behavior are relative. Selye (1976) explained that overeating serves as a diversion from the stressor and shifts the blood flow to decrease brain circulation and create a "tranquilized" effect.

5. This was also included on the basis of interview data. Perceptions of drinking (often socially) were that it was a deliberate act for coping.

6. The analyses reported here were based on the 101 cases in the wave 1 data: t-test analyses were run to determine whether significant differences existed between those who participated in the wave 2 collection and those who did not. No differences in response patterns were found.

7. Several of these response rates were low (.38, .47, .50, .56, .57). These rates were mostly associated with intensive care and oncology. In general, it appeared that this was

often due to high patient loads and staff shortages during the periods of data collection. This also made it difficult for the nurses present to leave to fill out the survey. Also, given the voluntary nature of the study, some chose not to participate. Unfortunately, there is no way to discern whether some potentially extreme (high or low) burnout cases were missed as a result.

8. Maslach and Jackson (1980, p. 11) noted this was a possibility, since many items refer to feelings "contrary to professional ideals" of those in the helping professions. Based on our results, we did not feel the burnout scores were biased by the social desirability factor.

9. The burnout frequency scores and the intensity scores were each arrayed on a continuum from highest to lowest levels. The sample was then divided into thirds, with the remaining analyses performed on the highest and lowest groups.

Analyses of the two groups in each set showed they generally represented a comparable mixture of respondents, i.e., a cross-section of all five units, all shifts, levels, and demographics (length of time in job, number of hours worked per week, etc.). The only significant t-test result was for a difference in age between the high- and low-intensity groups (X low = 35.82, X high = 30.21, t = 2.36, two-tailed $p < .05$). Furthermore, while a nonsignificant chi-square result was found for the distribution of respondents from each unit in the high- and low-intensity groups, a difference in distributions was found for the high- and low-frequency groups ($\chi^2 = 14.71$, $df = 4$, $p < .05$). The differences were mostly associated with more respondents from respiratory therapy and intensive care represented in the high-frequency group than in the low group, and more respondents from oncology and medical-surgical represented in the low group than in the high group.

REFERENCES

Albrecht, T. L., Irey, K. V., & Mundy, A. Integration in communication networks as a mediator of stress: The case of a protective services agency. *Social Work*, in press.

Bishop, J. E. The personal and business costs of "job burnout." *Wall Street Journal* (Western ed.), November 11, 1980, Section 2, p. 31.

Blau, G. An empirical investigation of job stress, social support, service length, and job strain. *Organizational Behavior and Human Performance*, 1981, 27, 279-302.

Bridger, H. The increasing relevance of group processes and changing values for understanding and coping with stress at work. In C. L. Cooper & R. Payne (Eds.), *Stress at work*. New York: John Wiley, 1978.

Cherniss, C. *Institutional barriers to social support among human service staff*. Paper presented at the Symposium on Burnout in the Helping Professions, Kalamazoo, Michigan, 1979.

Cherniss, C. *Staff burnout: Job stress in the social services*. Beverly Hills, CA: Sage, 1980.

Cooper, C. L., & Payne, R. (Eds). *Stress at work*. New York: John Wiley, 1978.

Crowne, D., & Marlowe, D. The social desirability scale. In R. Robinson & P. Shaver (Eds.), *Measures of social psychological attitudes*. Ann Arbor: Institute for Social Research, 1972.

Daley, M. R. Burnout: Smoldering problem in protective services. *Social Work*, 1979, 24, 375-379.

French, J. R. P., Jr., Rodgers, W. L., & Cobb, S. Adjustment as person-environment fit. In G. Coelho, D. Hamburg, & J. Adams (Eds.), *Coping and adaptation*. New York: Basic Books, 1974.

Freudenberger, H. Burnout: The organizational menace. *Training and Development Journal*, 1977, 31, 26-27.

Hoffman, R. Stress and the critical care nurse. *Supervisor Nurse*, August 1981, 20-23.

House, J. S. *Work stress and social support*. Reading, MA: Addison-Wesley, 1981.

Jick, T. Mixing qualitative and quantitative methods: Triangulation in action. *Administrative Science Quarterly*, 1979, 24, 602-611.

Kahn, R. L. *Work and health*. New York: John Wiley, 1981.

Kahn, R. L., Wolfe, D., Quinn, R., & Snoek, J. *Organizational stress: Studies in role conflict and ambiguity.* New York: John Wiley, 1964.
Kanner, A. D., Kafry, D. K., & Pines, A. Conspicuous in its absence: The lack of positive conditions as a source of stress. *Journal of Human Stress,* 1978, *4,* 33-39.
Katz, D., & Kahn, R. L. *The social psychology of organizations.* New York: John Wiley, 1978.
Lazarus, R. S., Cohen, J. B., Folkman, S., Kanner, A., & Schaefer, C. Psychological stress and adaptation: Some unresolved issues. In H. Selye (Ed.), *Selye's guide to stress research* (Vol. 1). New York: Van Nostrand Reinhold, 1980.
Maslach, C. Burned-out. *Human Behavior,* 1976, *5,* 16-20.
Maslach, C., & Jackson, S. E. *The measurement of experienced burnout.* Unpublished manuscript, University of California, Berkeley, Department of Psychology, 1980.
Newman, J. E., & Beehr, T. A. Personal and organizational strategies for handling job stress: A review of research and opinion. *Personnel Psychology,* 1979, *32,* 1-43.
Nie, N. H., Hull, C. H., Jenkins, J. G., Steinbrenner, K., & Bent, D. H. *Statistical package for the social sciences.* New York: McGraw-Hill, 1975.
Payne, R. Epistemology and the study of stress at work. In C. L. Cooper & R. Payne (Eds.), *Stress at work.* New York: John Wiley, 1978.
Pettegrw, L. S., Thomas, R. C., Costello, D. E., Wolf, G. E., Lennox, L., & Thomas, S. Job related stress in a medical center organization: Management of communication issues. In D. Nimmo (Ed.), *Communication yearbook 4.* New Brunswick, NJ: Transaction, 1980.
Ray, E. B. *A communication perspective on burnout in a human service organization.* Unpublished doctoral dissertation, University of Washington, 1981.
Reinard, J. C., & Crawford, J. E. *Communication and stress management: Lessons from a program on coping strategies to event and message stressors.* Paper presented at the annual meeting of the Western Speech Communication Association, San Jose, 1981.
Selye, H. *The stress of life.* New York: McGraw-Hill, 1976.
Smith, P., Kendall, L., & Hulin, C. *The measurement of satisfaction in work and retirement: A strategy for the study of attitudes.* Chicago: Rand McNally, 1969.
Vachon, M. L. S. Staff stress in the care of the terminally ill. *Quality Review Bulletin,* May 1979, 13-17.
Vachon, M. L. S. Care for the caregiver. *Canadian Nurse,* October, 1980, 28-33. (a)
Vachon, M. L. S. *Losses and gains: Some comments of staff stress in oncology.* Paper presented at the Cancer Nursing Symposium, Fred Hutchinson Cancer Research Center, Seattle, 1980. (b)
Vachon, M. L. S., Lyall, W. A. L., & Freeman, S. J. J. Measurement and management of stress in health professionals: Working with advanced cancer patients. *Death Education,* 1978, *1,* 265-375.
Vredenburgh, D. J., & Trinkaus, R. J. *Job stress among hospital nurses.* Paper presented at the annual meeting of the Academy of Management, San Diego, 1981.

34 ● The Advertising and Alcohol Abuse Issue: A Cross-Media Comparison of Alcohol Beverage Advertising Content

T. ANDREW FINN ● DONALD E. STRICKLAND
Washington University

IT is estimated that the costs of alcohol abuse and alcoholism, including health care, motor vehicle and other accidents, and lost productivity, may exceed $40 billion per year (NIAAA, 1978). The role of alcohol beverage advertising in the genesis of alcohol problems has received considerable public attention in recent years, including editorials in national and local media, regulatory proposals,[1] and congressional hearings.[2] Criticisms of alcohol beverage advertising have included the concerns that (1) alcohol advertising has undesirable *effects,* especially on subgroups of the population that are assumed to be particularly susceptible to mass media influences and/or alcohol abuse, (2) such advertising is *targeted* specifically and disproportionately at these subgroups, such as women, blacks, and youth, (3) alcohol advertising is a major component in mass media portrayals of alcohol beverage consumption as *normative,* and (4) that a large percentage of alcohol advertisements include objectionable thematic *content* as well as inappropriate role models for certain population subgroups.

In the intense public debate, these criticisms frequently have been regarded as a cumulative indictment of alcohol advertising, instead of as distinct and testable research questions requiring empirical evidence. A number of claims about the content of alcohol beverage advertising were

AUTHORS' NOTE: This research was supported by a grant from the United States Brewers Association to Washington University, St. Louis, a grant from the National Institute on Alcohol Abuse and Alcoholism to the University of Washington—Seattle (Grant 5-T32-AA07171-03), and general research support from the Social Science Institute, Washington University, St. Louis. We would like to thank Dow Lambert for his original contribution to the collection and made during the 1976 Hathaway Subcommittee hearings on media images of alcohol, but only anecdotal evidence was introduced to substantiate these statements.[3] The major hypothesized linkage between the content of beverage alcohol advertising and alcoholism and alcohol abuse outcomes involves three analytically distinct processes: (1) that alcohol advertising, through appeals to so-called lifestyle themes (wealth, affluence, success, achievement, hedonistic pleasure) or through more psychologically oriented themes (conformity, individuality, self-indulgent reward), entices nondrinkers to drink or encourages moderate drinkers to consume more; (2) that the use of particular kinds of human models in alcohol beverage advertising, who function as role models for drinking behavior, operate through processes of identification to induce increased alcohol consumption, especially among population subgroups alleged to be susceptible to alcohol problems; and (3) that certain techniques used in alcohol advertising suggest inappropriate activities associated with alcohol consumption or imply positive sanctions for excessive consumption.

A review of the literature by Pittman and Lambert (1978) failed to uncover any studies devoted to examining the content of commercial messages for alcohol beverages. Since Pittman and Lambert's review, a number of studies have looked at the content of alcohol beverage advertising in several media (Eveslage, Ostman, & Trager, 1978; Breed & DeFoe, 1979; DeFoe & Breed, 1979; Atkin & Block, 1980; Marstellar & Karnchanapee, 1980). A critical review of these studies can be found in Strickland, Finn, and Lambert (in press). This review suggests that these studies present an incomplete and inadequate picture of the structure and content of alcohol beverage advertising. Each of these studies is flawed by some or all of the following analytic shortcomings: (1) small or overly selective samples of advertisements, (2) failure to standardize or, in some cases, report categories used in the analysis of content, (3) inadequate treatment of category reliabilities (in most cases, reliabilities are unreported), (4) limitations in scope that prevent useful between-media comparisons, (5) reliance on anecdotal or illustrative evidence to support an interpretive framework, and (6) unsupported causal attribution based solely on content findings.

This chapter reports the results of a large-scale, systematic effort to assess the prevalence and content of alcohol beverage advertisements in

---

analysis of the magazine data, Angelica O'Donnell for her assistance in the preparation of the manuscript, and Vera Whisman for her help in coding the ads and pretesting the instrument.

Correspondence and requests for reprints: Donald E. Strickland, Department of Sociology, Washington University, St. Louis, MO 63130.

national circulation magazines and on television. Following a discussion of the methodology employed in the study, cross-media comparisons in three content areas are presented: (1) themes and appeals, (2) the use of human models, and (3) techniques of presentation. While the larger study from which this research is derived analyzed a variety of content dimensions, this chapter is focused on those elements of content relevant to the debate over the role of the content of alcohol advertising in the creation and maintenance of alcoholism and alcohol problems. Finally, a more structural analysis of alcohol beverage advertising by type of beverage, by marketers, and by media is presented along with an assessment of sampling adequacy.

METHOD

Magazine Sample

A total of forty-two magazines were chosen as the source of alcohol advertisements for this analysis of content (a complete list of magazines is found in Appendix A). Of these, nineteen were chosen because they are among the largest circulation magazines in the United States. The remaining twenty-three were included to ensure that there were sufficient numbers of magazines in each of the following subgroups: sports, news, black-oriented, men's, women's (home-oriented), women's (fashion/beauty-oriented), youth, and other special interest magazines. Since much of the criticism of print media advertising involves such target groups as youth, women, and blacks, this sampling strategy was most appropriate. Magazines with the largest circulation within each category were chosen for analysis.

For monthly publications, all twelve issues from 1978 were included in the sample. For weeklies, one issue per month was selected at random. A total sample of 504 magazines was identified for the study. Ten issues, four from *Hustler,* three from *Playgirl,* and one each from *Essence, Newsweek,* and *Rolling Stone,* could not be located, resulting in a final sample of 494 magazines. Since the eight issues of *Hustler* that were obtained had no alcohol ads, and the nine issues of *Playgirl* carried only four ads, these missing issues probably would have had little effect on the results described below.

For each magazine selected, each issue was searched and all alcohol advertisements were removed and assigned an identifying number. A total of 3,131 alcohol beverage ads were found in the 494 issues. As each ad was removed from the magazine, it was coded on a variety of what are here called "structural" characteristics. These included the magazine name, the number of pages and month for that issue, the size of the ad, and, of course, the beverage marketer and brand advertised. The total sample of 3,131 ads was found to contain 640 unique advertisements.

Television Sample

For a period of nine months, from October 1979 to June 1980, alcohol ads were videotaped from the five commercial television stations in the St. Louis market. The periods monitored were chosen systematically because of an expected concentration of alcohol advertising. These included late night, prime time, weekend, and sports programming. For the week of May 11, 1980, to May 18, 1980, the three network affiliates in St. Louis were continuously monitored for five hours per day, including the prime-time hours. The two independent stations in St. Louis provided information about scheduled alcohol ads for this same week, and all alcohol ads aired during prime time were taped. Together these procedures resulted in the videotaping of over 700 alcohol ads. Of these, 131 were unique ads: 114 different beer commercials and 17 wine advertisements.

Content Analysis Instrument

The two samples of unique ads were then content analyzed. The analysis covered three broad areas: themes and appeals, portrayals of human models, and techniques of presentation. The thematic content of each unique advertisement was assessed independently by two extensively trained coders as to the presence or absence of each of twenty-two themes or types of appeal. Themes were included on the basis of a review of related literature, a priori categories of substantive interest, and previous criticisms of alcohol beverage advertising content. The themes and appeals include product-oriented and human-model-oriented themes, appeals based on social as well as psychological motivations, and themes involving situation and process appeals. In addition, several themes emerged during extensive pretesting of the original thematic framework.[4] A complete list of the twenty-two themes and their definitions can be obtained from the authors.

For the human models analysis two trained coders counted the total number of human models in each ad, as well as the total number of women, blacks, couples, and celebrities. In addition, for the television ads, the coders counted the number of "primary models" in each category. Since some television ads used literally dozens of models, a definition of primary models was constructed during the pretesting and used to differentiate between "extras" and models central to the ad. A primary model was defined as a human model who (1) spoke during the ad, (2) appeared in the foreground during more than one scene, or (3) appeared in the foreground for more than one-half of the ad. For all models in the magazine ads, and for all primary models in the television ads, the coders estimated age in addition to coding race and sex.

The final section of the content analysis examined various techniques of presentation used in the ads. These included the structural characteristics of each ad (size or length), displays of the products (including the numbers of beverage containers and drinks portrayed), and the various settings and activities depicted in the ad. This section of the analysis also included identification of promotional techniques and suggested uses of the products. Finally, the coders examined the use of comparative advertising, claims of product purity, naturalness, or caloric content, and suggestions of how much to drink, including moderation messages.

Intercoder Reliability

The issue of the reliability of content analysis categories is of crucial importance in assessing the results of content analyses. Unfortunately, more often than not, no intercoder reliability is reported. A recent review of 127 content analysis studies appearing in over sixty social science journals in the last two decades found that more than two-thirds of the articles reported no intercoder reliability measure; in fact, the majority of these studies relied on only one coder for the entire analysis (Strickland & Finn, 1981).

In the present study, intercoder reliability was assessed using Krippendorff's (1980) refinement of Scott's (1955) pi. Unlike percent agreement, most often used when reliability coefficients are reported, Krippendorff's algorithm controls for the degree of agreement expected by chance. Although at least two independent judgments are needed to assess the degree of intercoder reliability, all other descriptive analyses require that the data be reduced to one set of results for reporting purposes. While this is sometimes done by averaging the judgments of the coders, the approach used here was to use a third trained coder to analyze each ad for which the original coders disagreed on the presence or absence of a particular theme; this third coder's decision on that theme was used in the frequency tabulations. Thus in the sections that follow the arbitrated frequencies are used in all analyses except the analysis of intercoder reliabilities. Since the coding of the structural characteristics of the ads was considered a process of tabulation rather than a judgment task, no intercoder reliability was computed, although consistency checks were made on a subsample of the ads.

RESULTS

Thematic Content

Major concern has been voiced over the themes and appeals used in alcohol beverage advertising. Much of this concern has been directed at the alleged disproportionate focus of alcohol ads on consumption and lifestyle appeals as opposed to information and product-oriented content. In particular, it is claimed that emotional lifestyle ads are often used that promise success (whether wealth, status, romance, or sex) through use of the product. In addition, the presence of such psychologically oriented themes as individuality, conformity, or self-indulgent reward, objectionable because of the alleged susceptibility of youth and other "high-risk" drinkers to such appeals, is seen as a major thrust of alcohol beverage advertising.

Table 34.1 presents the frequency of occurrence of the twenty-two themes for the magazine and television samples as well as the intercoder reliabilities for both samples.[5] The most frequent themes found in the magazine ads are *quality* of the product (29.1 percent), *tradition/heritage* of the product or processes (19.8 percent), product-related *information* (17.0 percent), associations of the product with *foreign settings* (11.4 percent), and suggestions that the product is appropriate for *special occasions* (10.8 percent). In the sample of television commercials the seven themes occurring in more than 10 percent of the ads are *camaraderie* or sociability (69.5 percent), change of state *relaxation* (40.5 percent), attempts at *humor* (38.2 percent), *quality* of the product (29.8 percent), leisure *physical activity* or sports and recreation (25.2 percent), product-related *information* (16.8 percent), and *tradition/heritage* (12.2 percent).

Several points about the nature and distribution of the most frequently occurring themes in each medium warrant elaboration. If the themes are divided into human-models-oriented appeals, or those largely centered on human values, attitudes, or activities, and product-oriented appeals, or those primarily related to the characteristics of the product, clear cross-media differences emerge. In magazine advertising, with the exception of *special occasions,* the most frequently occurring themes are product-related, involving product information, history, quality, or location of production. *Special occasions,* occurring in over 10 percent of the magazine ads, contains elements of both kinds of themes: gift-giving, product-oriented appeals as well as celebratory appeals involving social activities. In contrast, four of the five most frequently occurring themes in television commercials for beverage alcohol involve the human-models-

Table 34.1
Comparison Across Media of the Presence of Twenty-Two Themes
in Alcohol Beverage Advertisements:
Frequency and Intercoder Reliability

	Magazine Advertisements			Television Advertisements		
Theme/Appeal	Frequency (N = 640) N	%	Intercoder Reliability	Frequency (N = 131) N	%	Intercoder Reliability
Wealth/affluence	18	2.8	.45	5	3.8	.89
Achievement/success	20	3.1	.61	13	9.9	.84
Conformity	29	4.5	.63	3	2.3	.49
Medicinal benefits	0	0.0	—[a]	0	0.0	—[a]
Self/reward	12	1.9	.58	2	1.5	1.00
Information	109	17.0	.63	22	16.8	.84
Foreign settings	73	11.4	.69	6	4.6	.92
Humor	32	5.0	.66	50	38.2	.87
Close friendship	27	4.2	.61	9	6.9	.83
Tradition/heritage	127	19.8	.79	16	12.2	.89
Camaraderie	38	5.9	.57	91	69.5	.88
Quality	186	29.1	.58	39	29.8	.77
Religious symbolism	25	3.9	.85	5	3.8	.89
Sexual connotations	43	6.7	.71	8	6.1	.73
Hedonism	1	0.2	.50	6	4.6	.69
Relaxation	24	3.7	.45	53	40.5	.86
Impress others	13	2.0	.51	0	0.0	—[a]
Love/romance	22	3.4	.75	5	3.8	.79
Special occasions	69	10.8	.81	3	2.3	.34
General success	29	4.5	.41	1	0.8	.39
Individuality	30	4.7	.41	3	2.3	.85
Physical activity	22	3.4	.46	33	25.2	.71

a. No intercoder reliabilities are computed for themes not found in any of the ads.

oriented themes of *camaraderie, relaxation, humor,* and *physical activity*. Only *quality*, the standard component of competitive advertising of most products, is predominantly product-related. While product-related themes are apparently secondary in television commercials, the remaining themes occurring in more than 10 percent of the ads are product-related, *information* and *tradition/heritage*.

The preeminence of human-models-related themes in televised alcohol beverage commercials and the salience of these themes to the current regulatory debates necessitates additional analysis. Within the human-models-related themes, several subgroups deserve comment. Lifestyle themes (including *wealth/affluence, success/achievement, gen-*

eral success, and *hedonism*) occur relatively infrequently, appearing, on the average, once in every thirty-seven magazine ads and once in every twenty-one television commercials. As Table 34.1 shows, the controversial group of psychologically oriented or psychodynamic motivational appeals such as *conformity, individuality,* and indulgent *self-reward* occur equally infrequently in each medium. However, the most commonly occurring human models themes in each medium are a group of themes oriented toward sociability and conviviality (*camaraderie,* change of pace *relaxation,* and *humor*); in fact, while these themes occur only slightly more often than other human models themes in magazines (an average of once in sixteen ads) they are the three most frequently occurring of all the themes in alcohol advertising on television, found, on the average, in 50 percent of the commercials.

Clearly, the foregoing analysis indicates that alcohol beverage advertising differs in prevalence by medium and that considerable variation exists by the specific content of these themes. While human-models-oriented themes dominate television advertising, the more objectionable appeals based on status aspirations, lifestyle, and psychological motivations appear infrequently. When we examine the additional controversial appeals suggesting sexual and romantic enhancement with alcohol use, we find that, on the average, they appear in almost equal proportions in magazine and television alcohol advertising, in roughly 5 percent of the ads. In sum, this evidence provides little suport for much of the criticism of the content of beverage alcohol advertising.

The distribution of themes by medium also shows interesting structural contrasts: while five themes each appear in more than one-fourth of all televised alcohol beverage ads (with one theme appearing in over two-thirds of the ads), only one theme appears as frequently in magazine ads. On balance, the distributions within each medium suggest a relative homogeneity of television content not found in magazine advertising. This higher degree of thematic similarity in alcohol beverage ads on television is a consequence of several factors. First, differences in the products advertised partly account for such distributional differences. Although the voluntary advertising codes of both the Distilled Spirits Council of the United States (DISCUS) and the National Association of Broadcasters (NAB) prohibit advertising distilled spirits in the electronic media, there are no such global restrictions on product categories in the print media. In our analysis, thirty different product brands were advertised by sixteen different producers in the television sample, while 172 different brands from thirty-two producers were found in the magazine sample.

The smaller number of products advertised in televised alcohol ads only partly explains the similarity of content. Thirty different brands could entail thirty different ad campaigns. In spite of this, it could be argued that there is a prototypical beer advertisement constructed around one basic format and, since malt beverage advertising accounts for 87 percent of the television ads in our sample, the result is homogeneity of content. The typical beer ad depicts a group of males engaged in some work or recreational activity who then break for a beer in the context of a social gathering, where relaxing and humorous banter occur. No such pattern of occurrence was found in wine or distilled spirits advertising, which constitutes more than 95 percent of alcohol advertising in magazines.

Finally, differences in two more structural characteristics of the media result in a homogeneity of alcohol advertising on television relative to that in magazines. First, since magazines tend to be specialized in content and readership, often appealing to differentiated population subgroups (e.g., women, blacks, youth, males, sports enthusiasts), corresponding differences in advertising content are likely. Television, on the other hand, while certainly programmed for different audience and market segments, is unlikely to achieve such viewer differentiation, and advertising must appeal to a relatively more heterogeneous audience. Second, the action nature of television as a communication medium, with a corresponding emphasis on dynamic elements of content, results in the focus on human-models-oriented themes, whereas magazines, and print media in general, are limited to no more than stationary "slices" of such action. As a result, visual displays of inanimate objects (often product logos) and catchy text and phrasing occupy prominent roles in magazine advertising of beverage alcohol. Such inanimate content is rare in television commercials, even for similar products. The following analysis of the use of human models, crucial to the recently emerging emphasis on the social learning of both appropriate and inappropriate drinking and the current concern over content, reinforces many of these observations.

Human Models

In the last two decades, the shift away from direct effects/persuasion models of mass media influence and the increased use of social learning orientations have resulted in a more important role assigned to human model portrayals in the mass media. This is because one of the basic elements of social learning theory postulates vicarious learning through imitation of and identification with people that serve as role models for various behaviors. When human models in alcohol beverage ads are viewed as role models, the characteristics of these models, and the behaviors they display, take on special importance. Public discussions and previous studies based on anecdotal evidence have expressed concern over the use of models in alcohol ads that may serve as role models, especially for subgroups that share certain characteristics with the models (e.g., race, age, sex).

Since television is much better suited to portrayals of human behavior sequences than are the print media, it is not surprising that the thematic content of the television sample was dominated by human-models-related appeals, while the magazine sample was dominated by product-oriented appeals. Consistent with the nature of the themes, Table 34.2 shows that over 90 percent of the television ads in the present study contained one or more models, with a mean of over six models per ad. In contrast, less than 40 percent of all the magazine ads employed human models, and the average number per ad was less than one. Since human models are so much more prevalent in the television ads than in the magazine ads, it is reasonable that this difference is maintained across the subgroups of human models listed in Table 34.2. In addition to presenting the percentage of all sampled ads containing human models in each subgroup, Table 34.2 also shows the number of ads portraying models from various subgroups as a percentage of those ads using human models.

Females are represented in nearly two-thirds of the magazine ads with models, and over one-half of the televised ads with models. Males, however, appear in over 80 percent of the magazine ads with models, and in nearly all of the television ads with models (98.3 percent). While the total number of males in the magazine sample is somewhat higher than the number of females, males outnumber females five to one in the television sample. This predominance of males enhances the "macho" overtones of many of the televised beer ads. The frequent duplication of the "typical" format for beer ads, coupled with repetitions in the types of male models portrayed (working men, ranch hands, amateur "man next door" athletes, adventurous sportsmen, and retired football players), results in a striking degree of similarity in the types of models used in televised beer ads. Approximately 54 percent of the television beer ads featured male models cast in the mold of one of these macho images. Many other beer ads, while not designed around a strictly male image, nevertheless included a group of males enjoying the beer and each other's company. Taken together, the vast majority of these ads present beer drinking as a pastime to be enjoyed by males in the company of other males. Most of the females in the televised beer ads were portrayed as waitresses, rather than as consumers of the advertised product. The televised wine ads were much more likely to depict females as drinkers. Similarly, the magazine ads for distilled spirits and wine were more likely to portray female drinkers than were magazine ads for beer.

The breakdown of human models by race indicates that roughly 20 percent of the magazine and 30 percent of the television ads with models contained black models. On the other hand, nearly 80 percent of the magazine ads with models, and all of the television ads with models, contained one or more white models. On the surface this suggests little

Table 34.2
Comparison Across Media of the Presence of Human Models
in Alcohol Beverage Advertisements:
Frequency and Intercoder Reliability[a]

Ads with One or More	Magazine Advertisements			Television Advertisements		
	% of Total Ads (N = 640)	% of All Ads with Models (N = 251)	Intercoder Reliability (N = 640)	% of Total Ads (N = 131)	% of All Ads with Models (N = 118)	Intercoder Reliability (N = 131)
Human models	39.2	100.0	1.00	90.1	100.0	.99
Male models	32.8	83.7	.99	88.5	98.3	
Female models	25.2	64.1	1.00	47.3	52.5	.95
Black models	8.0	20.3	.93	26.7	29.7	.98
White models	30.8	78.5	.96	90.1	100.0	
Celebrity models	8.1	20.7	.88	19.1	21.2	.90
Models < 25 years of age[b]	0.8	2.0	.91	5.3	5.9	.72

a. There are no intercoder reliabilities reported for males and whites in television advertisements because the figures for males were derived by subtracting the number of females in each add from the total number of models in each ad, and the figures for whites were the result of subtracting the number of blacks from the total number of models.

b. While age judgments were made about all models in the magazine ads, only "primary models" were coded for age in the television sample. This was done because models were so much more numerous in the television ads, and many of them appeared so briefly that it was considered too difficult to estimate age reliably.

difference in the way blacks are portrayed in the alcohol ads of the two media. However, while 19.1 percent of the magazine ads containing models portrayed only black models, there was not one all-black ad in the television sample, although there were several ads in which blacks were more numerous than whites. In addition, televised alcohol ads were much more likely to portray blacks and whites together: While 29.7 percent of the television ads with models contained models of both races,[6] only three magazine ads, or 1.2 percent of the magazine ads with models, did the same. The most obvious explanation for these differences involves the audience characteristics of the media involved. While television content is generally designed for a rather broad, undifferentiated audience, most magazines are published for more narrow, specialized audiences. A closer look at the magazines in which alcohol ads with black models appeared provides support for this interpretation. Over three-fourths of the ads with black models appeared in one of the four black-oriented magazines sampled; less than 2 percent of the alcohol ads in the other thirty-eight magazines depicted black models.

Table 34.2 indicates that 19.1 percent of the televised ads used celebrity models, whereas only 8.1 percent of the magazines did so. The definition of a celebrity model included two very different types of celebrities. The first was pictures of or verbal references to recognizable celebrities, found in 2.5 percent of the magazine ads and in 19.1 percent of the television ads. The second type of celebrity was found in ads attempting to create "pseudocelebrities" by giving names and other personalizing information about the models portrayed. While not found in any of the television ads in our sample, this type of celebrity was found in 5.6 percent of the magazine ads, and accounted for over two-thirds of the magazine ads judged to contain celebrities. In addition, while almost all of the legitimate celebrities in the magazine sample were entertainment personalities, most of the celebrities in the televised alcohol ads were retired sports figures. The appearance of athletes, albeit retired athletes, in televised beer commercials is considered by some to be more objectionable than the use of other types of celebrities on the basis that professional athletes, possibly more than any other group, serve as role models for young people.

The final dimension of human models compared in Table 34.2 is the use of models under the age of twenty-five. In view of the recent increase in public awareness of alcohol problems among teenagers and young adults, and in light of long-standing concern over mass media effects on these groups, the issue of role modeling is particularly salient here. While 5.9 percent of the televised ads with models contained models judged to be under the age of twenty-five, only 2 percent of the magazine alcohol ads with models contained models that young. If role models are assumed to share characteristics with the subgroups for whom they are models, very few ads in the present samples provide role models for young people near or below the legal drinking age. Such a view of role models may be too strict, since models of any age, race, or sex could serve as role models for any individual's sense of appropriate behavior. Yet, without going beyond the content of the sample and attempting to infer advertiser intent, it is not possible to know whether individual human models in alcohol ads were chosen for their value as role models for particular population groups, or whether these groups identify them as such.

Techniques of Presentation

Table 34.3 compares the television and magazine samples on dimensions relevant to alcohol consumption and health considerations. Not surprisingly, the advertised product was displayed in nearly all the ads. An average of 2.5 bottles, cans, or glasses of the product were found in the magazine ads, while an average of seven containers of the product were pictured in the television ads. As with differences in thematic content, the greater use of human models in televised alcohol ads is the primary reason more product containers are found in the television ads, since most models

Table 34.3
Comparison Across Media of "Techniques of Presentation"
in Alcohol Beverage Advertisements:
Frequency and Intercoder Reliability[a]

Technique	Magazine Advertisements % of Total Ads (N = 640)	Intercoder Reliability	Television Advertisements % of Total Ads (N = 131)	Intercoder Reliability
Product displayed	93.9	.96	97.7	.88
Food pictured	9.4	.85	19.1	.86
Purity/naturalness claim	5.5	.85	17.6	.71
Heavy or frequent consumption	0.9	.66	0.8	—
Moderation message	2.7	.97	0.0	—
Hazardous/exotic activities	2.8	.55	16.0	.92

a. For convenience of presentation, the frequencies and percentages for all these variables are based on a dichotomy of present or absent. However, the reliability coefficients for most of these items were computed on a set of categories that included more than two choices. For example, it is reported here that food of some sort was pictured in 19.1 percent of the ads. The coders further broke this down into "full meal" or "snacks," so the reliability coefficient was computed on the basis of a three-category variable. Only one coder was used to code heavy or frequent consumption in the television sample; thus no reliability is reported.

are pictured with a drink in alcohol ads. Twice as many televised alcohol ads displayed food along with the advertised product as did ads in the magazine sample (19.1 versus 9.4). Insofar as the consumption of food reduces the intoxicating effects of alcohol, televised alcohol ads seem to be promoting this aspect of responsible drinking more than magazine ads. Claims about the naturalness of the product or the purity of the ingredients were made in 17.6 percent of the televised ads but in only 5.5 percent of the alcohol ads found in magazines. While no product category dominated purity claims in the magazine sample, most of the purity claims in the television sample were found in beer ads and were references to either the process or the water used.

Ads judged to contain suggestions of heavy or frequent consumption constituted less than 1 percent of both the magazine and television samples. Two magazine ads suggested use of the product "any time," while three other magazine ads made references to "stocking up" or serving enough to guests. While the former references were attempts to change the image of "after dinner" drinks and the latter references were to group consumption, only one magazine ad and one television ad were judged to imply heavy consumption on an individual level.

Diametrically opposed to suggestions of heavy or frequent consumption are messages of moderation. Table 34.3 indicates that while no moderation messages were found in the televised alcohol ads, 2.7 percent of the magazine ads contained messages of moderation. These included phrases such as "enjoy our quality in moderation," "concentrate on the eats," and "remember to take it easy." This suggests that on this dimension, alcohol ads in magazines promote moderate drinking more directly than do televised ads, largely a result of advertising campaigns of a few distillers.

Finally, Table 34.3 indicates that hazardous or exotic activities were depicted much more frequently in the televised ads than in the magazine ads (16.0 percent versus 2.8 percent). Examples of activities judged to be hazardous or exotic include portrayals of work situations such as log rolling and the use of explosives, and portrayals of recreational activities such as mountain climbing, hang-gliding, and skydiving. The claim made during the Hathaway hearings that some ads imply mixing hazardous activities and alcohol beverages was based on certain magazine advertisements (e.g., the portrayal of speedboat racing and a bottle of the advertised product in the same ad). Because the hazardous activity and the advertised product appear on the same page of a magazine ad, some obsevers have regarded this as suggesting that one mix alcohol consumption and hazardous activities. While it is usually not possible to determine the temporal sequence of events in a magazine ad, this is not a problem with television content. In every televised alcohol ad depicting hazardous activities, the models first engaged in the activity and were later portrayed in a drinking scene. In fact, even the televised ads with nonhazardous, ordinary work or recreational activities always portrayed the drinking scene as separate from and subsequent to the activity portrayed.

Structural Characteristics of the Samples

In this final analytic section, we present a more structural analysis of the distributional characteristics of the samples of magazine and television ads by product type and marketer as well as a comparison of these distributions with other measures of alcohol advertising to assess sampling adequacy. Table 34.4 ranks distilled spirits, wine, and beer advertisers by 1978 expenditures on magazine advertising[7] and presents the breakdown of magazine ads in our sample by product type and marketer. For this analysis we have used the total sample of 3,131 magazine ads rather than the 640 unique ads used in the content analysis; this larger sample of ads provides a more logical basis for comparison with advertising expenditures. Several things should be noted from this table. First, the figures for expenditures indicate that alcohol advertising in magazines is a $200 million a year business in the United States. Second, there is reasonable correspondence between a marketer's advertising expenditures and the number of its ads that were found in our magazine sample. Discrepancies are due to (1) the fact that we did not sample all magazines published, (2) differential costs of ads due to format used, the size of the ad, and the time of year it appeared, and (3) differential advertising rates by magazine. A comparison of the percentage columns in Table 34.4 shows, with few exceptions, the percentages of total advertising expenditures are similar to the percentages for the number of ads in the present sample.

By beverage class, 88 percent of the ads analyzed in the magazine sample were for distilled spirits products, and the percentage of total dollars expended on distilled spirits advertising in magazines was 90.7. The percentages for expenditures and frequency of sampled ads for both beer and wine marketers are also closely related. This suggests that since the present sample of 3,131 ads is apparently representative of producers/importers who use magazines to advertise their products, the sample is likely to be representative of the universe of magazine alcohol ads on other dimensions as well.

Table 34.5 presents a breakdown by individual beer and wine marketers of all locally placed and network television advertisements aired between April 7, 1980, and July 15, 1980, in the St. Louis television market. The list of network ads was compiled from weekly Broadcast Advertisers Reports, while the information about the locally placed ads was collected using the program logs of the St. Louis television stations.[8] Of the total of 4,375 alcohol beverage ads aired during this fourteen week monitoring period, 55 percent were aired by local stations and 45 percent were carried on the network feeds. By beverage type, almost 86 percent were ads for beer while just over 14 percent were wine ads. Notice, however, the difference between local and network wine advertisements: While less than 10 percent of the locally placed ads were for wine, over 20 percent of the network ads were wine advertisements.

Among beer producers, the largest (Anheuser-Busch) was, not surprisingly, also the largest advertiser, placing 20 percent of all alcohol beverage ads during the period monitored. One regional producer (Olympia) ranked second in the proportion of ads placed (13.5 percent). The second largest brewer, Miller, followed with 13.1 percent of the ads and the third largest brewer in 1980, Schlitz, ranked last among beer marketers (5.6 percent of the ads). Among the wine marketers, Gallo, Schenley, and Seagram placed the highest proportions of ads (2.4 percent, 2.3 percent,

Table 34.4
Selected Liquor Marketers Ranked by Magazine Advertising Expenditures for Distilled Spirits, Wine, and Beer in 1978

		Advertising Expenditures $	%	Ads in Present Sample N	%
	Distilled Spirits				
1	Seagram	70,196,485	35.2	886	28.3
2	Heublein	15,003,556	7.5	348	11.1
3	Hiram Walker	13,396,582	6.7	218	7.0
4	Liggett Group	12,447,213	6.2	215	7.0
5	Brown-Forman	10,008,422	5.0	183	5.9
6	Schenley	9,059,792	4.5	98	3.1
7	National	7,589,523	3.8	150	4.8
8	Somerset	7,182,013	3.6	71	2.3
9	Renfield	5,194,237	2.6	89	2.8
10	Buckingham	5,074,436	2.5	74	2.4
11	Puerto Rican Rum Prom.	5,012,266	2.5	77	2.5
12	Glenmore	3,296,385	1.7	77	2.5
13	Kobrand	2,329,087	1.2	16	0.1
14	Bacardi	2,155,040	1.1	41	1.3
15	Foremost-McKesson	1,950,980	1.0	43	1.4
16	James Beam	1,730,323	0.9	42	1.3
17	Schieffelin	1,676,955	0.8	33	1.2
	All others	7,742,458	3.9	94	3.0
Total distilled spirits		$181,045,753	90.7	2755	88.0
	Wine				
1	Seagram	2,252,563	1.1	44	1.4
2	National	1,999,982	1.0	40	1.3
3	Heublein	1,840,409	0.9	54	1.7
4	Schenley	964,580	0.5	28	0.9
5	Gallo	780,582	0.4	6	0.2
6	House of Banfi	557,902	0.3	15	0.5
7	Buckingham	319,551	0.2	11	0.4
8	Schieffelin	241,763	0.1	3	0.1
9	Brown-Forman	219,030	0.1	7	0.2
10	Liggett Group	212,297	0.1	3	0.1
11	Guild	202,554	0.1	5	0.15
12	Kobrand	197,468	0.1	2	0.05
13	Sebastiani	154,922	0.1	7	0.2
	All others	1,469,262	0.7	9	0.3
Total wine		$11,412,865	5.7	234	7.5

(continued)

Table 34.4 (Continued)

		Advertising Expenditures $	%	Ads in Present Sample N	%
		Beer			
1	Anheuser-Busch	2,346,600	1.2	57	1.8
2	Van Munching (Heinekin)	1,508,000	0.7	14	0.45
3	Molson	758,300	0.4	1	0.03
4	Iroquois Brands	325,300	0.2	22	0.7
5	Philip Morris (Miller)	318,800	0.15	10	0.32
6	Olympia	94,500	0.05	23	0.7
	All others	1,848,900	0.9	15	0.5
Total beer		$7,200,400	3.60	142	4.5
Total liquor		$199,659,018	100.0	3131	100.0

and 2.2 percent, respectively), yet significantly fewer ads than any malt beverage marketer. The distribution of wine ads shows an interesting pattern with respect to the placement of the ads: All but two wine marketers placed their advertising with either local stations or the networks, but not both.

The far right columns in Table 34.5 detail the breakdown, by marketer, of the 131 alcohol beverage commercials sampled in the content analysis. Not only do the totals for beer and wine ads closely parallel the total percentages of beer and wine advertisements aired during the period monitored, but most individual marketers are represented in the content analysis sample in roughly equal proportion to their total advertising. Almost 86 percent of the ads aired were beer ads and 87 percent of the ads in our content analysis were beer commercials. This suggests that the sample of television ads analyzed is reasonably representative of the total population of televised alcohol beverage advertisements, at least in one large urban market.

CONCLUSIONS

The present analysis of the content of alcohol beverage advertising in magazines and on television has attempted to explore some of the major controversies over the nature of the appeals and the portrayal of human models in such advertising. The results suggest that the extent of objectionable and controversial content in alcohol beverage advertising, in either medium, has been exaggerated by reliance on anecdotal evidence and that related criticisms of advertising for using young adult models under the age of majority to provide peer models for youth and adoles-

Table 34.5
Selected Beer and Wine Marketers[a] Ranked by
Total Number of Televised Beverage Alcohol Ads Aired
in the St. Louis Market, April 7, 1980-July 15, 1980

	Local N	Local %	Network N	Network %	Combined N	Combined %	Ads in Content Analysis Sample N	Ads in Content Analysis Sample %
Beer								
Anheuser-Busch	397	16.4	478	24.5	875	20.0	32	24.4
Olympia	473	19.5	118	6.1	591	13.5	15	11.4
Miller	71	2.9	501	25.7	572	13.1	22	16.8
Coors	396	16.3	44	2.3	440	10.1	9	6.9
Stroh	254	10.5	90	4.6	344	7.9	8	6.1
Pabst	294	12.1	53	2.7	347	7.9	4	3.1
Heileman	267	11.0	26	1.3	293	6.7	7	5.3
Schlitz	7	.3	240	12.3	247	5.6	16	12.2
Owens-Illinois[b]	47	1.9	—	—	47	1.1	1	0.8
Beer total	2206	90.9	1550	79.5	3756	85.9	114	87.0
Wine								
Gallo	—	—	106	5.4	106	2.4	5	3.8
Schenley	101	4.2	—	—	101	2.3	1	0.8
Seagram	—	—	97	5.0	97	2.2	4	3.1
Monsieur Henri	69	2.8	—	—	69	1.6	—	—
Banfi	—	—	61	3.1	61	1.4	2	1.5
Brown-Forman	—	—	53	2.7	53	1.2	1	0.8
Coca-Cola	—	—	46	2.4	46	1.0	2	1.5
Heublein	14	.6	31	1.6	45	1.0	—	—
Schieffelin	24	1.0	6	.3	30	.7	—	—
Paterno Imports	11	.5	—	—	11	.3	—	—
Other[c]	—	—	—	—	—	—	2	1.5
Wine total	219	9.1	400	20.5	619	14.1	17	13.0
Total	2425	100.0	1950	100.0	4375	100.0	131	100.0

a. The name of some of these marketers are not as well known as their products. Some of the less familiar wine marketers and their advertised products include: Schenley (Cruz Garcia Real Sangria), Seagram (Paul Masson), House of Banfi (Riunite), Monsieur Henri (Yago Sangria), Brown-Forman (Cella), Coca-Cola (Taylor), Heublein (Lancer's, Harvey's Bristol Cream), Schieffelin (Blue Nun), and Paterno Imports (Corvo).
b. Owens-Illinois, a glass-bottle manufacturer, placed ads that portrayed a group of beer drinkers around a piano singing, "The good, good taste of beer, buy it in bottles." By almost any standard, we believe this to be a promotional announcement for beer.
c. Two other wine ads (for Giacobazzi and Colony Chilled Light Burgundy) were videotaped for the content analysis prior to April 7, 1980, the date for which program log and BAR monitoring began. These products were not advertised in the St. Louis television market between April 7, 1980, and July 15, 1980; consequently there are no entries under the columns for local, network, or combined advertising.

cents is unsupported by the empirical evidence. We have also shown that the content of beverage alcohol advertising varies systematically by the medium used, with product-related themes dominating magazine advertising and human-models-related themes paramount in television advertising. These findings raise a larger set of issues with respect to the complexity surrounding advertising content and alcohol abuse.

First, a thorough understanding of the role played by alcohol beverage advertising in the creation and maintenance of alcohol problems must *begin* with an accurate description of the content of that advertising. The previous literature to the contrary, content analysis techniques are not appropriate for inferring advertiser motivation and intent, on the one hand, or causal attribution, on the other. Rigorous content analysis can inform a portion of the current debate, although it is not tantamount to knowledge of the impact of that advertising, whatever its content. Our goals in this research have been more modest: to delineate the contours of alcohol beverage advertising across media so as to specifically inform one of the components of the present debate that is too often blurred in the intensely emotional atmosphere aroused by such serious issues.

A second issue raised by the present research is the concern that alcohol advertising creates normative attitudes toward drinking, in general, and excessive or inappropriate consumption, in particular. While advertising is a major element in the ubiquitous media portrayals of drinking as a normative behavior in many settings, reflecting the reality of contemporary American drinking patterns, little support is found for the notion that excessive drinking is promoted, endorsed, or positively sanctioned by such advertising. In fact, not only do other forms of mass media communication (including television programming, cinema, radio programming, newspaper comics, novels, short stories, musical lyrics, and the routines of some of our most celebrated entertainers) equally portray moderate consumption as normative, but they often portray excessive drinking, intoxication, and alcohol-related problems in a humorous light. As a result, if only because of indifference, such nonadvertising portrayals seem to us to be open to far more serious indictment.

Third, one of the assumptions underlying the history of mass media regulation seems questionable given the present findings. If the U.S. experience with distilled spirits advertising and cigarette advertising is any indication, it is likely that any regulatory restrictions would be applied exclusively to the electronic media. The popular logic, based on the early persuasion models of the electronic mass media, is that television and radio have direct, persuasive effects and that their audiences are passive receivers, more easily manipulated by electronic media than by other communication media. While current mass media researchers are moving away from such received wisdom, policymakers continue to focus on the pernicious influences of mass media (interestingly, while the bulk of the concern in the recent Hathaway hearings was with television advertising, most of the argument by example involved print media advertising). The results presented herein, while indicating clear media differences in content, in general, show equally infrequent occurrences of the more objectionable elements of alcohol beverage advertising. Thus the philosophical stances underlying differential advertising regulation of different media are not supported by content differences along those controversial dimensions; whether such philosophies are sustained by differential media impact of alcohol beverage advertising remains to be demonstrated.

Finally, we share the view of a number of other alcohol and mass media researchers that a preoccupation with alcohol beverage advertising may divert attention from the real problem of alcohol abuse and alcoholism. The results of increased control of alcohol beverage advertising are unclear; there is the danger, however, that such action will lull us into a false sense of security that one of America's leading health problems is being dealt with adequately.

(Appendix A appears on page 870)

Appendix A
Sampled Magazines Rank Ordered by Number of Alcohol Advertisements in the Sample

Rank	Magazine	Number of Ads	% of Ads
1	Playboy	357	11.4
2	Psychology Today	250	8.0
3	Cosmopolitan	245	7.8
4	Penthouse	207	6.6
5	Ebony	160	5.1
6	New Yorker	153	4.9
7	Scientific American	129	4.1
8	People	124	4.0
9	Esquire	106	3.4
10	Apartment Life	104	3.3
11	Sports Illustrated	102	3.3
12	Newsweek	98	3.1
13	Glamour	95	3.0
14	Time	94	3.0
15	Field & Stream	92	2.9
16	Black Enterprise	88	2.8
17	Vogue	88	2.8
18	Essence	79	2.5
19	Better Homes & Gardens	72	2.3
20	Mechanix Illustrated	59	1.9
21	Mademoiselle	49	1.6
22	Rolling Stone	46	1.5
23	Oui	42	1.3
24	Jet	39	1.2
25	US News & World Report	39	1.2
26	Ladies' Home Journal	37	1.2
27	Redbook	34	1.1
28	National Lampoon	25	0.8
29	Nation's Business	24	0.8
30	Hot Rod	22	0.7
31	McCall's	21	0.7
32	Good Housekeeping	18	0.6
33	TV Guide	16	0.5
34	Family Circle	11	0.4
35	Playgirl	4	0.1
36	Reader's Digest	1	0.0
37	Woman's Day	1	0.0
38	Boys' Life	0	0.0
39	Hustler	0	0.0
40	National Geographic	0	0.0
41	Seventeen	0	0.0
42	'Teen	0	0.0

NOTES

1. The Bureau of Alcohol, Tobacco and Firearms (BATF) issued a Notice of Proposed Rulemaking in December 1980 dealing with the advertising and labeling of alcoholic beverages. These proposals address a number of advertising issues, including procedures for comparative taste tests, the prohibition of active athletes, the use of subliminal stimuli, and the use of terms such as "light," "natural," and "refresh."

2. Most notably, the 1976 "Hathaway hearings." See U.S. Congress, Senate (1976). A number of possible changes in federal regulation of alcohol advertising have been mentioned. These include a partial or complete ban on the advertising of alcohol beverages and disallowance of alcohol beverage advertising expenditures as tax deductions. The 96th Congress saw the introduction of two bills dealing with this last point (H.R. 97 and H.R. 1800). As of December 1981 these bills were pending before the House Ways and Means Committee.

3. The Hathaway hearings included testimony by Robert Hammond, Executive Director of the American Business Men's Research Foundation, that some alcohol advertisements encourage heavy consumption, implicitly suggest mixing hazardous activities and alcohol consumption, use sex to sell the product, suggest alcohol use for solving problems, and appeal specifically to youth, nondrinkers, and heavy drinkers (U.S. Congress, Senate, 1976, pp. 187-194). Testimony by Richard Herzog, Assistant Director of the Federal Trade Commission, also made reference to subgroups of the population as particularly vulnerable to alcohol advertising (p. 134). The Christian Life Commission's Representative, Phil Strickland, testified that certain alcohol ads promote excessive consumption (p. 311). In addition, Michael Looney (California Polytechnic State University) maintained that "with the legalization [sic] of marijuana, the alcohol industry is feeling some pressure to really push alcohol as the 'drug of choice' to young people." He also testified that the "alcohol industries attempt to sell their beverages with implications of sexuality, wealth, happiness and health" (p. 315).

4. Since the original goal was to use the same set of themes and appeals to analyze televised alcohol ads as well as those appearing in magazines, ads from both media were used to pretest the preliminary list of seventeen themes and their definitions. In the course of pretesting these themes and simultaneously training the coders, five new themes were added and the definition of each theme was revised and refined. A total of fifty televised alcohol ads and over 300 magazine ads were used in developing and refining the themes and training the coders. The final configuration of thematic descriptors is thus designed to accommodate the content of both the print and electronic media.

5. The average intercoder reliability across all themes is .62 for the magazine sample and .78 for the television sample. The relatively lower thematic reliabilities for the magazine ads deserve some comment. As noted, the vast majority of content analysis studies report no intercoder reliabilities, thus standards of comparison are few. Among those reporting reliabilities, many studies report only a single average reliability coefficient for all categories used in the analysis, often reporting an inflated value due to averaging over more objective structural categories (which are not included in our computations). Additionally, our use of a conservative coefficient, which includes an adjustment for chance agreement based on the coders' marginal distributions of judgments, tends to be affected more by disagreement among coders when the marginals are highly skewed, as in the case of relatively infrequently occurring themes. For example, given a hypothetical distribution such that the two coders agreed on the 90 percent of the ads in which a particular theme was absent but each judged a different half of the remaining 10 percent to contain the theme, the percent agreement coefficient would be .90, whereas the coefficient adjusted for chance agreement would be only .05! The average percent agreement coefficient computed for the twenty-two themes in the magazine sample is above .95.

6. The presence of blacks and whites together in 29.7 percent of the televised alcohol ads with models is an interesting contrast to a recent study that found that blacks and whites seldom appear together in prime-time programming or advertising. Weigel, Loomis, and Soja (1980) found that only 5.1 percent of all advertising time with human models included black-white interactions. The frequent use of retired athletes, often black athletes, in televised beer ads probably accounts for this difference.

7. The source for distilled spirits advertising expenditures was *The Liquor Handbook* (Gavin-Jobson Associates, 1979a). The source for beer and wine advertising expenditures was *The Wine Marketing Handbook* (Gavin-Jobson Associates, 1979b).

8. Broadcast Advertisers Reports, Inc. (BAR) prepares weekly reports on all network advertising. The data in Tables 34.4 and 34.5 are based on BAR monitoring of the ABC, CBS, and NBC network feeds originating in New York. To compile a list of local alcohol beverage advertisements the authors enlisted the cooperation of the five commercial television stations in St. Louis.

REFERENCES

Atkin, C., & Block, M. *Content and effects of alcohol advertising.* Report submitted to Bureau of Alcohol, Tobacco and Firearms, Federal Trade Commission, National Institute on Alcohol Abuse and Alcoholism, Department of Transportation, 1980.

Breed, W. & DeFoe, J. Themes in magazine alcohol advertisements: A critique. *Journal of Drug Issues,* 1979, *9,* 511-522.

Broadcast Advertisers Reports. *Network TV: Brand, product and parent company schedule detail.* New York: Author, 1980.

DeFoe, J., & Breed, W. The problem of alcohol advertisements in college newspapers. *Journal of the American College Newspaper Association,* 1979, *21,* 195-199.

Eveslage, T., Ostman, R., & Trager, R. *Liquor advertisements: A peek into the black box of strategy.* Paper presented at the Eighth Annual Popular Culture Association Convention, Cincinnati, Ohio, 1978.

Gavin-Jobson Associates, Inc. *The liquor handbook.* New York: Author, 1979. (a)

Gavin-Jobson Associates, Inc. *The wine marketing handbook.* New York: Author, 1979. (b)

Krippendorff, K. *Content analysis: An introduction to its methodology.* Beverly Hills, CA: Sage, 1980.

Marsteller, P., & Karnchanapee, K. The use of women in the advertising of distilled spirits 1956-1979. *Journal of Psychedelic Drugs,* 1980, *12,* 1-10.

National Institute on Alcohol Abuse and Alcoholism (NIAAA). *Third special report to the U.S. Congress on alcohol and health.* Washington, DC: U.S. Government Printing Office, 1978.

Pittman, D., & Lambert, M. D. *Alcohol, alcoholism and advertising: A preliminary investigation of asserted associations.* St. Louis, MO: Social Science Institute, Washington University, 1978.

Scott, W. Reliability of content analysis: The case of nominal scale coding. *Public Opinion Quarterly,* 1955, *17,* 281-287.

Strickland, D., & Finn, T. A. *A review of the use of intercoder reliability coefficients in social science content analysis articles: 1960-1980.* St. Louis, MO: Social Science Institute, Washington University, 1981.

Strickland, D., Finn, T.A., & Lambert, M.D. A content analysis of alcohol beverage advertising, Part I: Magazines. *Journal of Studies on Alcohol,* in press.

U.S. Congress, Senate. *Media images of alcohol: The effect of advertising and other media on alcohol abuse.* Hearings before the Senate Subcommittee on Alcoholism and Narcotics. Washington, DC: U.S. Government Printing Office, 1976

Weigel, R., Loomis, J., & Soja, M. Race relations on prime time television. *Journal of Personality and Social Psychology,* 1980, *39,* 884-893.

X • HUMAN COMMUNICATION TECHNOLOGY

35 • Teleconferencing, Concern for Face, and Organizational Culture

GLEN HIEMSTRA
University of Washington

THE combining of advanced telecommunication and computer technologies is ushering in what many believe will be a new age of communication, destined to alter culture in significant ways (Amara, 1981; Bell, 1979; O'Neill, 1981; Toffler, 1980). What efforts are being made to assess the effects of this revolution in information technology? In particular, what are the effects in organizations that are now rushing to join the communication revolution? Hulin (1981) reports that a survey of ten years of organizational research literature found (1) no questions about work in the year 2001 as affected by information technology, (2) no questions about the cost and benefits of working in a "group" via computerized conferencing, and (3) no questions about leadership when leader-follower contact is mediated through telecommunication.[1] Campbell (1981) surveyed "human resource development reports and planning documents" and interviewed managers in order to "glean" the research needs as appropriate from an industry viewpoint. Among the perceived needs was the need for research on the impact of microelectronic information processing on clerical and management personnel.

The need for research on the impact of information technology on the communication between people in organizations is evident. A central question to be addressed in such research is whether or not communication which is mediated via information technologies may alter the "culture" of the organization. Culture is defined by Schneider (1976) as a "system of symbols and meanings" which, together with norms or rules, make up the social reality of members of a culture. Since information technologies are designed specifically to affect the transmission of symbols and meanings, the revolution in information technology has the potential to alter the culture of an organization profoundly. The research problem is how to go about observing and testing any such effects. This chapter proposes the

---

Correspondence and requests for reprints: Glen Hiemstra, Department of Speech Communication, University of Washington DL-15, Seattle, WA 98195.

use of an approach to inquiry characterized as "linguistic ethnography" (Hymes, 1977). A specific interpretive framework is suggested here as amenable to such an inquiry method. The interpretive framework is an analysis of politeness strategies utilized by communicators in order to show regard for "face" (Brown & Levinson, 1978). This framework has shown promise in a pilot study as one avenue of assessment of the cultural impact of the information technology/communication revolution.

The research program suggested here is aimed at "interactive technologies," those technologies designed to facilitate and augment human-to-human communication. Other information technologies emphasize intramachine, machine-machine, or human-machine interaction and are the subject of other research efforts (e.g. Flannigam, 1981; Harkins & Joseph, 1980; Robey, 1980; Pateman, 1981). Interactive technologies are referred to most generally as teleconferencing and include three primary modes: computer conferencing, audio teleconferencing, and video teleconferencing.[2] The key feature of the interactive technologies is that they are intended to supplement or supplant communication that is now conducted by face-to-face, telephone, or hard-copy written interaction. They are selected as the focus because of their potential role in shaping organizational culture and because of their increasing use. For example, Hilton (1981a) points out that 84 percent of the Fortune 500 companies have "imminent plans for installing teleconferencing systems." Lowndes (1981) describes the installation or testing of teleconferencing systems at organizations such as ARCO, Westinghouse, Digetal Equipment Corp., IBM, Texas Instruments, Exxon, Proctor & Gamble, and Montgomery Ward. Services offered by outside vendors, such as AT&T's "picturephone meeting service," Holiday Inn's "Hinet" video conference facilities, computer conference networks such as the Electronic Information Exchange System (EIES), and numerous others are also leading to increased use of teleconferencing.

The remainder of this chapter will (1) review research to date on the social impacts of interactive technologies, (2) describe the alternative approach known as linguistic ethnography and outline the interpretive framework which focuses on "concern for face," (3) suggest specific research steps, and (4) briefly report the results of a pilot study using this framework.

RESEARCH ON INTERACTIVE TECHNOLOGIES

There has been an effort over the last decade to assess and predict the social impact of information technologies, particularly interactive technologies. The research to date has generally focused on questions of effectiveness of teleconferencing for particular tasks, acceptance by and attitudes of users, and some measures of the communication differences between teleconferencing modes and between teleconferencing and face-to-face interaction. As noted by Hulin (1981), the research tends not to appear in academic literature associated with organizational communication and behavior. Instead, published material is scattered throughout information science, engineering, computer science, futuristics, communication, sociology, psychology, and business trade publications. Since much reported research is unpublished, conceptual and literature reviews are useful and increasingly available.[3]

For this study representative literature was surveyed and categorized according to type of study, media used, independent variables other than media, dependent variables, and methods. The results of this review for thirty-three studies are displayed in Table 35.1. A central question asked regarding each study was "In what way, if any, did the study approach questions regarding the impact of teleconferencing on the intersubjective process of communication?"

Laboratory experiments represent the most common type of study. The typical format is to use teleconference media and face-to-face conferences as independent variables, and to have subjects converse in pairs or in groups in order to complete some task. Additional independent variables may also be included in the design. Most common is to use a variety of tasks or problems for subjects to complete (e.g., Christie & Holloway, 1975; Hiltz, Johnson, Aronovitch, & Turoff, 1980; Korzenny & Bauer, 1979; Krueger & Chapanis, 1980). Additional independent variables have included varying the size of vocabulary available for use (Kelly, 1976), varying the previous acquaintance level of subjects (Christie & Holloway, 1975; Kohl, Newman, & Tomey, 1975), varying group size (Krueger & Chapanis, 1980), and testing subjects over successive days (Kelly, 1976; Krueger & Chapanis, 1980). Fine technical variations may be added, such as varying camera angle and monitor height (Duncanson & Williams, 1973) or positioning of speakers (Kohl et al., 1975).

In addition to laboratory studies, there have been a variety of field research efforts. These have included one-shot case studies of actual teleconferencing users (Ferguson, 1977; Spelt, 1977), field studies involving either long-term analysis of a group of actual users (Duncanson & Williams, 1973; Kohl et al., 1975) or more broad-based surveys of many groups of users (Israelski, 1979; Johansen & DeGrasse, 1979), and field experiments which involve observation of groups of users who are experimenting with particular media and are not engaged in long-term use or who participate in a single experimental activity (Hiltz, 1978b; Spang, McNeal, & Vian Spangler, 1979). These various field research efforts have investigated each of the teleconferencing modes, as have the laboratory

Table 35.1
Research Interactive Technologies

(First author & year only)	Duncanson, 1973	Chapanis, 1975	Christie, 1975	Kohl, 1975	Vallee, 1975	Chapanis, 1976	Kelly, 1976	Ryan, 1976	Stoll, 1976	Albertson, 1977	Featheringham, 1977	Ferguson, 1977	Hiltz, 1977	Spelt, 1977	Uhlig, 1977	Hiltz, 1978a	Hiltz, 1978b	Hiltz, 1978c	Johansen, 1978	Kochen, 1978	McKendree, 1978	Strickland, 1978	Turoff, 1978	Williams, 1978	Korzenny, 1978	Israelski, 1979	Korzenny, 1979	Johansen, 1979	Spang, 1979	Hiltz, 1980	Krueger, 1980	Fowler, 1980	Rice, 1980
Type of Study																																	
Lab experiment	×	·	×	×	·	·	×	×	×	·	·	·	·	·	·	×	·	×	·	·	·	×	·	·	·	·	×	·	·	×	×	·	·
Field experiment	·	·	·	·	·	·	·	·	·	·	·	·	·	·	·	·	×	·	·	·	·	·	·	·	·	·	·	·	×	·	·	·	·
Field study	·	·	·	×	·	·	·	·	·	·	·	×	·	×	·	·	·	·	×	·	·	·	·	·	·	×	·	×	·	·	·	·	·
Case study	×	·	·	·	·	·	·	·	·	·	·	·	·	·	·	·	·	·	·	×	·	·	·	·	·	·	·	·	·	·	·	·	·
Concept. review	·	×	·	·	·	×	·	·	·	×	·	·	×	×	·	·	·	·	·	·	·	·	·	×	×	·	·	·	·	·	·	·	·
Lit. rev./anal.	·	·	·	·	×	·	·	·	·	·	×	·	·	·	·	·	·	·	·	·	·	·	·	·	·	·	·	·	·	·	·	·	·
Theory anal.–proposal	·	·	·	·	·	·	·	·	·	·	·	·	·	·	×	·	·	·	·	·	·	·	×	·	×	·	·	·	·	·	·	×	×
Application	·	·	·	·	·	·	·	·	·	·	·	·	·	·	·	·	·	·	·	·	·	·	·	·	·	·	·	·	·	·	·	·	·
Future forecast	·	·	·	·	·	·	·	·	·	·	·	·	·	·	·	·	·	·	·	·	·	·	·	·	·	·	·	·	·	·	·	·	·
Media																																	
Computer conf.	·	×	·	·	×	×	×	×	×	·	×	×	×	×	×	×	×	×	×	×	×	·	×	×	×	·	×	×	×	×	×	·	×
Audio teleconf.	·	×	×	×	·	×	·	×	×	×	·	·	·	·	·	·	×	·	×	·	·	×	·	×	×	×	×	·	·	·	×	×	·
Video teleconf.	×	×	×	×	·	×	·	×	×	·	·	·	·	·	·	×	·	·	×	·	·	×	·	×	×	·	×	·	·	×	×	×	·
Face-to-face	·	×	·	·	·	×	·	×	·	·	·	·	·	·	·	·	·	·	·	·	·	·	·	×	×	·	×	·	·	·	×	·	·
Other	·	·	·	·	·	·	·	·	·	·	·	·	·	·	·	·	·	·	·	·	·	·	·	·	·	·	·	·	·	·	·	·	·

877

Table 35.1 (Continued)

(First author & year only)	Duncanson, 1973	Chapanis, 1975	Christie, 1975	Kohl, 1975	Vallee, 1975	Chapanis, 1976	Kelly, 1976	Ryan, 1976	Stoll, 1976	Albertson, 1977	Featheringham, 1977	Ferguson, 1977	Hiltz, 1977	Spelt, 1977	Uhlig, 1977	Hiltz, 1978a	Hiltz, 1978b	Hiltz, 1978c	Johansen, 1978	Kochen, 1978	McKendree, 1978	Strickland, 1978	Turoff, 1978	Williams, 1978	Korzenny, 1978	Israelski, 1979	Korzenny, 1979	Johansen, 1979	Spang, 1979	Hiltz, 1980	Krueger, 1980	Fowler, 1980	Rice, 1980
Ind. Variables																																	
Other than Media																																	
Diff. problems	·	·	×	·	·	·	×	·	×	·	·	·	·	·	·	·	·	·	·	·	·	·	·	·	·	·	×	·	×	×	×	·	·
Size vocabulary	·	·	·	×	·	·	×	·	·	·	·	·	·	·	·	·	·	·	·	·	·	·	·	·	·	·	·	·	×	·	·	·	·
Technical variable	×	·	×	×	·	·	·	·	·	·	·	·	·	·	·	·	·	·	·	·	·	·	·	·	·	·	·	·	·	·	·	·	·
Acquaint. level	·	·	·	·	·	·	·	·	·	·	·	·	·	·	·	·	·	·	·	·	·	·	·	·	·	·	·	·	·	·	×	·	·
Group size	·	·	·	×	·	·	×	×	×	·	·	·	·	·	·	·	·	·	·	·	·	·	·	·	·	·	·	·	·	·	×	·	·
Successive days	·	·	·	·	·	·	·	·	·	·	·	·	·	·	·	·	·	·	·	·	·	·	·	·	·	·	·	·	·	·	×	·	·
Other	·	·	×	·	·	·	·	·	×	·	·	·	·	·	·	·	·	·	·	·	·	·	·	·	·	·	×	·	·	·	·	·	·
Dep. Variables																																	
User acceptance	×	·	×	×	·	·	·	·	·	·	·	·	·	·	·	·	·	·	·	·	·	·	·	·	·	·	·	×	·	·	×	·	·
Participation/usage rate	×	·	·	×	·	·	·	·	·	·	·	·	·	×	·	×	×	×	·	·	·	·	·	·	·	×	·	×	·	·	×	·	·
User attitudes	×	·	·	×	·	·	·	×	·	·	·	×	·	×	·	×	×	×	×	·	·	×	·	·	·	×	·	×	·	·	×	·	·
Decis. quality	·	·	·	·	·	·	·	·	·	·	·	·	·	×	·	·	×	×	·	·	·	×	·	·	·	×	·	·	·	·	×	·	·
Time to Decis.	·	·	·	·	·	·	·	·	·	·	·	×	·	×	·	·	×	×	·	·	·	×	·	·	·	·	·	·	·	·	×	·	·
Message types	·	·	·	·	·	·	·	·	·	·	·	·	·	·	·	·	·	×	·	·	·	·	×	·	·	×	·	·	×	·	·	·	·
No. of words	·	·	·	·	·	·	·	·	·	·	·	·	·	·	·	·	·	·	·	·	·	·	·	·	·	·	·	·	·	·	·	·	·
Cost	·	·	×	×	·	·	×	·	×	·	·	·	·	·	·	·	·	×	·	·	·	·	·	·	·	·	·	·	·	·	×	·	·
Other behaviors	·	·	·	·	·	·	·	·	·	·	·	·	·	·	·	·	·	·	·	·	·	·	·	·	·	·	·	·	·	·	·	·	·
Bales's IAS	·	·	·	·	·	·	·	·	·	·	·	·	·	·	·	·	·	·	·	·	·	·	·	·	·	·	·	·	·	×	·	·	·
Other	·	·	·	·	·	·	·	·	·	·	·	·	·	·	·	·	·	·	·	·	·	×	·	·	·	×	×	·	·	·	·	·	·

Method	Duncanson, 1973	Chapanis, 1975	Christie, 1975	Kohl, 1975	Vallee, 1975	Chapanis, 1976	Kelly, 1976	Ryan, 1976	Stoll, 1976	Albertson, 1977	Featheringham, 1977	Ferguson, 1977	Hiltz, 1977	Spelt, 1977	Uhlig, 1977	Hiltz, 1978a	Hiltz, 1978b	Hiltz, 1978c	Johansen, 1978	Kochen, 1978	McKendree, 1978	Strickland, 1978	Turoff, 1978	Williams, 1978	Korzenny, 1978	Israelski, 1979	Korzenny, 1979	Johansen, 1979	Spang, 1979	Hiltz, 1980	Krueger, 1980	Fowler, 1980	Rice, 1980
Groups	×	·	·	×	·	·	·	·	×	·	·	·	·	·	·	·	·	·	·	·	·	×	·	·	·	·	×	·	·	×	×	·	·
Pairs	·	·	·	·	·	·	×	×	·	·	·	×	·	×	·	·	×	·	·	·	·	·	·	·	·	×	·	×	·	·	·	·	·
Multipoint	·	·	·	×	·	·	·	·	·	·	·	×	·	·	·	·	×	·	·	·	·	·	·	·	·	×	×	×	·	·	×	·	·
User survey	×	·	×	·	·	·	·	×	·	·	·	·	·	·	·	·	×	·	·	·	·	×	·	·	·	×	·	×	·	·	·	·	·
Interviews	·	·	·	·	·	·	×	·	·	·	·	·	·	×	·	·	·	×	·	·	·	·	·	·	·	·	·	·	×	×	·	·	·
Content anal.	·	·	·	·	·	·	·	·	·	·	·	·	·	×	·	·	×	·	·	·	·	·	·	·	·	·	·	×	·	·	·	·	·
Message types	·	·	·	·	·	·	·	·	·	·	·	·	·	·	·	·	·	·	·	·	·	·	·	·	·	·	·	×	·	·	·	·	·
Total wd. counts	·	·	·	·	·	·	·	·	·	·	·	·	·	·	·	·	·	·	·	·	·	·	·	·	·	·	·	·	·	·	·	·	·
Categ. wd. counts	·	·	·	·	·	·	·	·	×	·	·	·	·	·	·	·	·	·	·	·	·	·	·	·	·	·	·	·	·	·	×	·	·
Other	×	·	·	×	·	·	·	·	·	·	·	·	·	·	·	·	·	·	·	·	·	·	·	·	·	·	·	·	·	·	×	·	·

(First author & year only)

studies, with the modes sometimes studied singly, sometimes in comparison.

Dependent measures fall into several general categories. The central thrust of the research effort has been to determine the advantages and disadvantages of the different communication media in terms of their effectiveness for performing certain tasks and in terms of the subjective and objective responses of the users. A comparison of advantages and disadvantages has formed the organization of literature reviews (e.g., Fowler & Wackerbarth, 1980; Johansen, Vallée, & Spangler, 1978).

On task effectiveness, while there is some variation among studies, the general conclusion most often reached is that as band width narrows (available channels decrease from face-to-face to computer conference interaction) the media are seen to be satisfactory for more simple communication tasks, such as information exchange, but less satisfactory for more complex, more interpersonally involving communication tasks, such as getting to know someone or managing conflict (e.g., Fowler & Wackerbarth, 1980; Hiltz, 1978a). These presumed differences in task effectiveness are usually based on the perceptions of subjects or users when these perceptions are solicited via questionnaire or interview rather than an independent measure of task effectiveness. When independent measures are used, the effects become more mixed. For example, Kelly (1976) found that different modes did not influence the ability to solve problems and complete tasks, but they did alter time needed for completion. Hiltz et al. (1980) found no difference in the "quality" of solution between two modes. Krueger and Chapanis (1980) found no difference in independent judgments regarding the "equivalence" of solutions reached via different media.

Objective measures of user responses have typically included some test of verbal productivity. For example, Chapanis (1976) summarizes several laboratory studies which found voice modes much wordier than modes without voice and face-to-face wordier than voice-only modes when measured by total word counts and words per unit time. Chapanis (1975) notes that persons using voice modes deliver eight times as many messages, eight times as many sentences, five times as many words, and twice as many different words than persons using teletypewriting. Others have found similar results (Krueger & Chapanis, 1980; Strickland, Guild, Barefoot, & Paterson, 1978). Stoll, Hoecker, Krueger, and Chapanis (1976) compared use of six linguistic classes of words as well as total words and found no significant difference between media in the former. The time needed for a pair or group to complete a task has also been used as an objective measure. Voice modes have consistently been found to be faster than computer conferencing for reaching decisions (Chapanis, 1976; Hiltz, 1978c; Krueger & Chapanis, 1980). When voice modes are compared, results are mixed; Chapanis (1975, 1976) reports little difference between audio and face-to-face. However, Krueger and Chapanis (1980) found audio nearly 40 percent faster than face-to-face, and Kohl et al. (1975) found in a long-term field trial that audio teleconference meetings were generally 30-35 percent shorter than the prior face-to-face meetings.

Field tests have added to measures of verbal productivity additional measures of usage rates or participation. These have included how often teleconference facilities are used, duration of each use, time of day for peak use, average length of message, and the like (e.g., Duncanson & Williams, 1973; Ferguson, 1977; Hiltz, 1978b; Kohl et al., 1975; Spelt, 1977).

Subjective user responses have also been collected in most laboratory and field studies. Measurement techniques have included relatively simple attitude response questionnaires (Duncanson & Williams, 1973; Hiltz, 1978a, 1978b; Spelt, 1977). Other researchers have used more complex measures of attitudes. Kohl et al. (1975) compared reactions using a semantic differential and found differences among media loaded around enjoyment, general evaluation, trust, complexity of group discussion, and confidentiality. Ryan (1976) also compared media using a semantic differential and found differences in aestheticism, evaluation, privacy, and potency.

Subjective user responses have also been solicited in the form of user descriptions of various media. There is consistency in such descriptions. Krueger and Chapanis (1980) provide a typical example. They compared face-to-face, audio, and teletype modes in a lab setting. Face-to-face conferencing was described as "informal, personal, relaxed, spontaneous"; audio conferencing as "quick, fast, efficient, effortless, fun, relaxing"; and teletype as "new, interesting, challenging, fun, clear, concise, logical, direct, businesslike, to the point." Johansen and DeGrasse (1979) studied users of computer-based message systems in the field and concluded that in "exchange conferences" communications "were usually functional and businesslike." When one surveys the broader teleconferencing literature, it is typically concluded that as band width narrows the communication is likely to be described as less friendly, emotional, and personal and more serious, businesslike, depersonalized, and task oriented (e.g., Fowler & Wackerbarth, 1980; Williams, 1978).

Research such as that reviewed here seems to suggest differences in communication mediated by information technology, differences that may lead to, and result from, alterations in the "system of symbols and meanings" or intersubjective processes that comprise a culture. Literature and conceptual reviews cited here also suggest cultural impacts. Several examples illustrate.

Johansen et al. (1979) note that "when someone chooses to hold an electronic meeting, the old unconscious rules for [in-person] meetings need revision" (p. 17). Albertson (1977) argues that research focused on effectiveness of mediated communication does not debate whether using technologically mediated communication "over long periods of time might also have behavioral or social consequences" (p. 33). Williams (1978) suggests that teleconferencing may substitute for "no communication" more than it actually replaces current face-to-face interaction, which would lead to additional implications. Fowler and Wackerbarth (1980) agree with Ritter and Stephenson that comparisons of audio and face-to-face communication may be based on incomplete understanding of the elements of face-to-face interaction, and that the lack of physical presence and visual cues in audio conferencing leads to "depersonalized, task-oriented discussions."

Researchers have described computer conferencing as an "altered state of communication" (Vallée, Johansen, & Spangler, 1975) and as a form that "can change the psychology and sociology of the communication process itself" (Turoff, 1978). Uhlig (1977) reviews several years of experience with a computer-based message system and notes several effects: Interaction does not have to be conducted in real time; the electronic network becomes a "place" in the minds of users; there is an increase of written as opposed to oral communication in the organization; communication rules are altered; decisions are speeded up; the ease of use of the system combined with the loss of "nuances of speech" and nonverbal cues can "lull the user into thinking he is having more interaction than he really is" (p. 123).

Kochen (1978, p. 23) suggests that "the form of linguistic communication used in computerized conferencing may be neither conversational speech nor formal writing, but a new linguistic entity with its own vocabulary, syntax, and pragmatics." Hiltz and Turoff (1978) observe that communication in a computer conference is more organized, more well thought out, and "richer" than natural conversation.

Reviewers have also lamented the inability of the research conducted so far to illuminate alterations in communicative processes. Johansen et al. (1979) note that sources for exploring such impacts are limited, both in terms of actual users to study and in "tests" to apply. In the most comprehensive review of research on computer-mediated communication to date, Rice (1980) concludes that despite a wide range of reported research, "it would be fruitful to determine just what it is that people do when they interact via computer" (p. 238). Chapanis (1975) wonders whether and how one can go about investigating the problem of how meanings are conveyed in conversation.

It becomes clear that much of the research on teleconferencing has not aimed at investigating the cultural world if its users are at an intersubjective level. This is a level which involves "intercommunication and language" and depends for understanding on an analysis of the intersubjective use of language (Shutz, 1977). In order to understand the impact of mediated communication on this intersubjective process more fully, research is needed which focuses on the interaction itself rather than on task effectiveness, user attitudes, or simple objective measures of communicative differences. A possible approach is described in the next section.

CULTURAL ANALYSIS, FACE NEEDS, AND LINGUISTIC ETHNOGRAPHY

Recognizing that each interactive information technology is satisfactory for certain tasks, and that a variety of communication responses is possible in each mode, the research so far points toward a general conclusion: As band width narrows from face-to-face interaction to computer terminal interaction, the communication is likely to be experienced as less friendly, emotional, and personal and more serious, businesslike, depersonalized, and task oriented. A question that may be raised is whether these differences in perception result from purely surface differences, such as in the number of words, or from a difference that may be described, metaphorically at least, as existing in the deep structure of the language characteristic of mediated interactions. Brown and Levinson (1978) suggest that the motivations which lead to particular language usages are "powerful enough to pass deep into language structure," and they further suggest that part of the motivation is social and includes "processes like face-risk minimization" (p. 99).

Investigating whether such deeper differences exist in language structure is appropriate to an effort to assess the cultural impact of information technology in organizations. Pacanowsky (1979) argues for an "organizational culture perspective" that emphasizes an understanding of "how organizational life is accomplished communicatively," rather than how communication variables influence organization effectiveness. Among the specific targets of an organizational culture perspective is investigating the structure of language use. "By acquiring the categories of a language we acquire the structural 'ways' of a group, and along with the language, the value implications of those ways" (Pettigrew, 1979, p. 575).

Several different lines of analysis offer utility for a cultural perspective that focuses on language. Mishler's (1979) emphasis on context, Mehan's (1978) call for a "constitutive ethnography," or a more purely linguistic discourse analysis (Sinclair & Coulthard, 1975) are examples. Another useful alternative, as yet not applied to mediated communication, would be a rules analysis (Shimanoff, 1980).

However, among the most intriguing possibilities is a hybrid approach involving the application of Brown and Levinson's (1978) extension of the concept of "face work." Following an explanation of this analytic framework, it will be suggested that the framework represents a means of conducting a "linguistic ethnography" (Hymes, 1977).

Goffman (1967) has proposed that concern for face, the "positive social value a person effectively claims for himself by the line others assume he has taken during a particular contact," is a factor in the structuring of social interaction (p. 5). Concern for one's own face and the face of others may act as both a motive for particular communicative strategies and, in Goffman's words, as a "condition for interaction" (p. 12). When concern for face is operating, the social actor behaves in ways that protect his or her own face and the face of others and that enable others to do the same.

Any social interaction carries a possible threat to face, and Goffman maintains that by appealing to face a person knows how to act in interaction. Concern for face may be demonstrated in both direct personal interaction and in mediated (written) interaction according to Goffman, but he maintains that "during direct personal contacts . . . unique information conditions prevail and the significance of face becomes especially clear" (p. 33). That is, spoken interaction should heighten concern for face and therefore increase the use of strategies designed to maintain face. The aim in interaction is to save face by structuring talk; the effect is to create the social situation or social structure.

There are several implications of this view for current knowledge regarding interactive information technologies. Since there have been reasonably consistent findings that as band width narrows perceptions of friendliness and personalness decrease while perceptions of task orientation, terseness, impersonalness, and the like increase, the question may be raised whether this is because of a decrease in concern for face or a shift in the ways in which face concerns are demonstrated.

A second implication relates to the issue of social presence. Williams (1978) notes that as band width narrows from face-to-face to video and audio teleconferencing, a "feeling of contact" termed "social presence" decreases. Korzenny (1978) has hypothesized, but so far has not supported (Korzenny & Bauer, 1979), that as band width narrows in mediated communication there will be a decrease in "psychological propinquity," the psychological distance or degree of perceived closeness of the interactants. The social psychological literature on "co-presence" and individual and group performance suggests that under certain conditions the physical presence of others, especially co-acting others, will be physiologically and psychologically arousing (see Davis, 1969). Goffman's suggestion that spoken interaction in direct personal contact heightens concern for face raises a question in regard to social presence. Does technologically mediated communication, with fewer channels and physically separated interactants, decrease behaviors which show concern for face and thereby further decrease a sense of social presence?

Hiltz and Turoff (1978) address the issue of concern for face in computer conferencing and conclude that computer conferencing reduces or eliminates the influence of this concern. Computer conference participants are said to "almost immediately drop the usual 'face work' or maintenance of 'front' that would occur in face-to-face meetings" (p. 94). The evidence for this conclusion may be questioned, however, since it consists of observation of the nonverbal behavior of participants while they sit at their computer terminals, and reports from participants regarding their delight at not having to worry about what to wear, eating and drinking, and the like. The evidence does not include the actual language interaction of computer conference participants, where concern for face may be demonstrated.

The role of concern for face in structuring social interaction has been fully developed by Brown and Levinson (1978). Their theoretical system is founded on three primary assumptions: that social actors have a want for *positive face*, a want for *negative face*, and a *rational capacity* to select a strategy that will achieve the face wants. The want for positive face is the want of a person for his or her self-image, personality, and wants to be desirable to others. The want for negative face is the want of a person that his or her actions or territory be unimpeded by others. Positive face is the desire to be approved of; negative face, the desire not to be imposed on. Rational capacity is the ability to choose from among alternative strategies.

Any interaction has the potential to be a face-threatening act (FTA). In an FTA to positive face, a speaker (S) shows a lack of caring about a hearer's (H) feelings, wants, and so on. In an FTA to negative face, S impedes or shows intent to impede H's freedom of action. When a potentially face-threatening act is contemplated, S will select a communication strategy depending on the contextual factors of relative power of the interactants, psychological distance between the interactants, and the riskiness of the FTA. The strategy selection process may be either conscious or unconscious. S may choose to do the FTA or not to do the FTA. If S chooses to do the FTA, S may decide to do it "on record" and "baldly," in a straightforward way. Or S may decide to engage in a particular "politeness strategy," either going "off record" with the FTA (becoming ambiguous) or using some form of redressive action, either positive politeness or negative politeness. These choices form the basic framework of a model of possible politeness strategies presented by Brown and Levinson.

The model, or hierarchy of strategies consists of four "superstrategies," "higher-order strategies" for each superstrategy, and a set of "output strategies" or linguistic means designed to achieve the higher-order goals. Although Brown and Levinson present these strategies in a series of treelike diagrams, they are careful to point out that they do not represent decision trees or flow diagrams, but instead are a catalog of available choices.

A list of superstrategies, higher-order strategies, and output strategies is presented in Table 35.2. Each of the strategies is designated with a number that may be used as a code when interaction is analyzed. Each of the strategies is thoroughly defined and illustrated by Brown and Levinson. Only definitions of superstrategies will be offered here.

Superstrategy 1, Bald on Record (BOR), involves speaking in conformity with "Grices's Maxims," which are "guidelines for achieving maximally efficient communication" (Brown & Levinson, 1978, p. 100). There are four maxims:

1. *Maxim of Quality:* be nonspurious (speak the truth, be sincere)
2. *Maxim of Quantity:* don't say *more* than is required; don't say *less* than is required
3. *Maxim of Relevance:* be relevant
4. *Maxim of Manner:* be perspicuous; avoid ambiguity or obscurity.

While these maxims define the 'basic set of assumptions underlying every talk exchange," utterances do not generally or even frequently meet these conditions. "Indeed, the majority of natural conversations do not proceed in such a brusque fashion at all" (p. 100). However, even when the maxims are departed from, they are seen as remaining in operation at a deeper level. The strategy of Bald on Record, which may be seen as a nonpoliteness strategy, will be selected by a speaker when S wants to do an FTA with *maximum efficiency* more than S wants to satisfy the face wants of him- or herself or those of H. For example, S is likely to choose BOR to warn "Your pants are on fire!" rather than adding a polite redress, "I hate to bother you, but your pants are on fire."

Brown and Levinson also suggest that BOR is likely to be selected when there is channel noise, or when communication difficulties exert pressure to be efficient. A bad phone connection is suggested as an example. It seems possible that the technology of teleconferencing, the knowledge that minutes on a teleconference system often mean dollars spent, and, in the case of computer conferencing, the relative slowness of interaction may all combine to encourage use of BOR in technologically mediated communication.

Table 35.2
Politeness Strategies

Superstrategy	Higher-Order Strategy	Output Strategy	
1. Bald on Record	1.1 Nonminimization of face threat		
	1.2 FTA-oriented BOR use		
2. Positive Politeness	2.1 Claim common ground	2.1.1	Notice, attend to H
		2.1.2	Exaggerate interest, approval, sympathy
		2.1.3	Intensify interest to H
		2.1.4	Use in-group identity markers
		2.1.5	Seek agreement
		2.1.6	Avoid disagreement
		2.1.7	Presuppose/raise/assert common ground
		2.1.8	Joke
	2.2 Convey that S & H are cooperators	2.1.9	Assert, presuppose S's knowledge, concern for H's wants
		2.1.10	Offer, promise
		2.1.11	Be optimistic
		2.1.12	Include S & H in activity
		2.1.13	Give (or ask for) reasons
		2.1.14	Assume, assert reciprocity
	2.3 Fulfill H's wants for some X	2.1.15	Give gifts to H
3. Negative Politeness	3.1 Be direct	3.1.1	Be conventionally indirect
	3.2 Don't presume/assume	3.2.2	Question, hedge
	3.3 Don't coerce H	3.3.3	Be pessimistic
		3.3.4	Minimize imposition
		3.3.5	Give deference
	3.4 Communicate S's want not to impinge on H	3.4.6	Apologize
		3.4.7	Impersonalize S and H
		3.4.8	State FTA as general rule
		3.4.9	Nominalize
	3.5 Redress other wants of H	3.5.10	Go on record as incurring debt
4. Off Record	4.1 Invite conversational implicature (inference)	4.1.1	Give hints
		4.1.2	Give association cues
		4.1.3	Presuppose
		4.1.4	Understate
		4.1.5	Overstate
		4.1.6	Use tautologies
		4.1.7	Use contradiction
		4.1.8	Be ironic
		4.1.9	Use metaphors
		4.1.10	Use rhetorical questions
	4.2 Be vague or ambiguous	4.2.11	Be ambiguous
		4.2.12	Be vague (about FTA, about object of FTA)
		4.2.13	Overgeneralize
		4.2.14	Displace H
		4.2.15	Be incomplete, use ... (ellipses)

Note: This list is compiled from Brown and Levinson (1978), who define and describe each of the strategies.

Superstrategy 2, Positive Politeness (PP), is redress directed at H's positive face. S shows that his or her wants are similar to H's wants, at least partly. Positive politeness is representative of intimate behavior, where interest in and approval of each other is important. Positive politeness is distinguished from routine intimate language behavior by an element of exaggeration. Positive politeness strategies are usable as a kind of "social accelerator," indicating that S desires to "come closer" to H (Brown & Levinson, 1978, p. 108). Examples of PP may include preceding a request with a compliment, as in "What a beautiful garden. Could I have some lettuce?" or using familiar address forms, as in "Say mate, that's my seat."

Superstrategy 3, Negative Politeness (NP), is redress directed at H's negative face, H's want to be unhindered, unimpeded. Negative politeness is the heart of what we usually see as showing respect for another. It is more specific and focused than positive politeness and more conventionalized. Negative politeness strategies may be used as a "social brake," as a "distancer" between people (1978, p. 135). Examples of NP may include adding qualifiers to requests, such as *"Could you please* pass the salt," or *"Is there any chance* you could help me change this tire?"

Superstrategy 4, Off Record (OR), is a communicative act "done in such a way that it is not possible to attribute only one clear communicative intention to the act" (1978, p. 216). If an actor wishes to do an FTA but wants to avoid responsibility, he or she can do it off record, leaving it up to the hearer to make the desired interpretation. For example, instead of asking H to close the window, S may say, "It's quite drafty in here," leaving it up to H to decide whether this is a request to close the window. Off-record utterances are "essentially indirect uses of language" which rely on H to draw the intended inference (p. 216). Importantly, Brown and Levinson note that off-record strategies "are amongst the very most pervasive in all the social interactions we have studied" (p. 218).

Brown and Levinson see in their theoretical framework "an ethnographic tool of great precision for investigating the quality of social relationships in any society" (p. 62). They hope "by this means to be able to characterize to some extent the 'ethos' of a culture or subculture, and . . . the affective quality of social relationships" (p. 64). That is, on analysis a culture may be discovered to be a "positive politeness culture," as exemplified perhaps by the "back-slapping Western U.S.A.," a "negative politeness culture," as exemplified perhaps by the "stand-offish British," or perhaps a non-face-oriented "efficiency culture," for which Brown and Levinson offer no example (p. 250).

As a tool for conducting what Hymes (1977) has called "linguistic ethnography" the Brown and Levinson framework offers the possibility of examining interaction at the point where social structure and the "internal systematics of interaction" overlap, where "structure informs and determines interaction and where interaction creates or recreates social structure" (1978, p. 246). Hymes suggests that a linguistic ethnography would "study the relationship among linguistic elements in the service of speech styles" (1977, p. 168). This kind of study seems possible using Brown and Levinson's politeness strategies. Such an analysis offers the possibility of examining the structuring activities of a teleconference microculture, a way of moving toward an understanding of the "system of symbols and meanings" of that microculture, and hence toward understanding whether the microculture so created is any different from the larger culture in which it is embedded. Such an analysis seems to go beyond and to a deeper level of social structure than the research conducted to date on interactive information technologies.

Hymes describes the linguistic inquiry involved as *"the interpretation of codes"* (p. 171). The research focus is on the discovery of contrastive relevance rather than repetition, "showing that a particular change or substitution or choice counts as a difference within a larger frame of reference" (p. 172-173). The kind of contrastive relevance of importance exists in *"discourse grammar,"* or natural conversation, rather than *"resource grammar,"* or base grammatical structure. The search for contrastive relevance involves the attempt to "discover what changes of form have consequences for meaning, what choices of meaning lead to changes of form." One "moves back and forth between form and meaning" in order to "discover the individual devices and the codes of which they are a part" (p. 174). The ultimate goal of this kind of language inquiry is not just to determine consequences for linguistic structure, but to "discover something of the *resonance and consequence* of this instance of a genre within cultural worlds" (p. 174).

Brown and Levinson see their system of politeness strategies as a useful tool for conducting a hybrid method of inquiry such as Hymes's linguistic ethnography. They note that work in social theory and the study of interaction has tended to concentrate either on social structure or on the "internal systematics of interaction." Work in the ethnography of speaking is seen as an example of a third area where these domains overlap. Brown and Levinson argue that if work in the third area is to succeed, then "the fine-grained analysis of . . . communication behavior . . . cannot be ignored" (p. 246). The politeness strategy framework for examining face work is seen as providing such a fine-grained analysis, at a point where the two domains of social structure and interaction systematics overlap. As such it seems especially useful as a means for conducting a linguistic ethnography.

RESEARCH QUESTIONS SUMMARIZED

Out of the convergence of current knowledge regarding mediated communication, and the concept of concern for face, the following general research questions have emerged:

1. Does concern for face, as indicated by the use of politeness strategies, appear in communication mediated by interactive information technologies?
2. If concern for face appears, to what degree does it appear, and what output strategies are used?
3. Do the media differ in evidence of concern for face?
4. Is there a correspondence between the apparent ethos created by the use of politeness strategies and user's views of mediated communication?
5. Do the politeness strategies used in mediated communication seem to differ in comparison to the general organization use of politeness strategies?
6. How might the media be altering the organizational culture?

METHOD

The ultimate aim of this program of research is to enable a comparison between teleconferencing modes and their influence on concern for face and use of politeness strategies. However, each medium may also be studied independently in terms of its impact on organizational culture.

Data Collection

Selection of conferences or organizations that are using one or more of the interactive technologies will be sought. These are likely to be larger rather than smaller organizations. For the computer mode either a full computer conference system or a computer-based message system with conference capabilities will be satisfactory. Criteria for selection of a particular conference will include the following:

1. The conference will be a working meeting, not a simple test of the system or a one-time experiment.
2. The conference must include at least three, preferably more, participants.
3. In the case of a computer conference, the conference must include both synchronous and asynchronous interaction, and access to private messages if possible.
4. The conference must be of reasonable length for analysis.

Observation. Both the organization as a whole and specific conferences will be observed via two basic methods. Specific conferences will be observed using a "nonparticipant-unstructured" observation style (Lawler, Nadler, & Cammann, 1980). The researcher does not exert control over or participate in the communication. Communication is observed as it occurs, and any interaction in which the researcher participates is left out of the analysis. Observations will be recorded via field notes and will concentrate on context and the politeness atmosphere. For a computer conference, an effort to observe a single participant engaging in a synchronous session and in asynchronous contact will be included. For the purposes of comparison, face-to-face as well as mediated conferences will be observed, involving as many of the same participants as possible.

The second observation method for specific conferences emphasizes retrievability of data (Mehan, 1978). For computer conferences this involves collection of the automatically maintained transcript. For audio conferences it will involve transcription of an audio tape, and for video and face-to-face conferences transcription of audio or video tape. Resulting transcripts will be analyzed using the method outlined in the analysis section.

Interviews. Following data collection regarding specific mediated conferences, conference participants will be interviewed. Interviews will be conducted face-to-face or, in the case of geographically distant participants, by telephone. The interview approach to be used is characterized as "structured open-ended" (Lawler et al., 1980). In this style the interviewer begins with a set of preplanned questions, but the respondent is free to answer the questions in any manner. The interviewer is also free to follow up or prompt further responses. The preplanned questions will include the following:

1. How would you compare "mediated" meetings and face-to-face meetings?
2. How would you characterize or describe the interaction that takes place in a mediated conference?
3. Has the use of the medium changed (a) the way you work, (b) your view of those with whom you work, (c) your view of the organization?
4. Do you have any other reactions to or feelings about the teleconferencing medium?

Interviews will be tape recorded and transcribed for later comparative analysis.

A potentially useful interview comparison may be obtained if a "group focus interview" can be arranged involving participants in a previous mediated conference (Calder, 1980). This method involves gathering the group of participants for a "more or less open-ended discussion of their work" (p. 403). A discussion moderator (the researcher) may guide discussion to assure that specific topics are discussed, but essentially the conversation is open-ended, with no question-answer format.

The goal is to achieve as natural an interaction as possible. Focus group sessions last about two hours. The moderator solicits discussion regarding both the general impact of information technology on organizational life and specific reactions to interactive technologies.

The focus group session is tape recorded and transcribed. Calder suggests analysis on two levels — a content analysis of group-related topics and an analysis of "verbatim topical quotes" to look for patterns and associations, the "implicit logic inherent in the everyday thought of employees" (p. 405). An additional analysis would be intriguing for the research proposed here; an analysis of the focus group interview for its politeness atmosphere or concern for face. An analysis of politeness strategies displayed in the group interview would afford a comparison to the mediated conference in which the interviewees had previously participated.

There is an obvious problem in using a focus group interview in the proposed study, beyond the expected problem of people giving two hours of their time. Interactive information technologies assume geographically dispersed participants. Hence convening a group interview may be logistically difficult or impossible. If this problem can be overcome, the focus group interview may provide a useful base for comparison. In cases where a focus group interview was possible, individual interviews would continue to be used as well.

Data Analysis. The analysis of data involves four basic phases. First is a content analysis of the transcripts of mediated and face-to-face meetings to determine whether concern for face is shown through the use of politeness strategies. Second is a qualitative analysis of observation and interview data for the purpose of comparison to conclusions suggested by the content analysis. Third, as data on various media are collected, a comparison between media can be made. Finally, the issue of whether interactive technology is affecting the "ethos of the culture or subculture" can be addressed. As will be demonstrated, the analysis involves both qualitative and quantitative features.

Context Description. The units of description suggested by Hymes (1972) will be used in order to set the context of each conference as clearly as possible. These units include the basic social units of speech community, speech situation, speech event, speech act, speech styles, and ways of speaking. They also include a list of speech act components. Various media and various situations may highlight other context variables. The central goal of this thorough description of context is to avoid the "context stripping" common to other research methods (Mishler, 1979).

Content Analysis. Three issues are key for the content analysis of the transcripts of mediated and face-to-face meetings. These are the units of analysis, the steps in the application of the Brown and Levinson politeness strategies framework, and the mix of qualitative and quantitative analysis.

Selecting a unit of analysis that is appropriate for the observation of politeness strategies and that may afford some legitimate comparison between media is a major problem. Goffman (1967) suggests the "move" and the "interchange" as the appropriate analytical units when considering face work. The move is "everything conveyed by an actor during a turn at taking action" (p. 20). The interchange involves two or more moves between two or more interactants in which they maintain a "single moving focus of attention" (p. 35). Other discourse analysis systems have used units such as the "utterance" (Albrecht & Cooley, 1980), the "turn" (Sinclair & Coulthard, 1975), the "message" (Rogers, 1972; Rogers & Farace, 1975), the sentence (Sillars & Folger, 1978), ten-second speech intervals (Hawes, 1972), and the "speech act" (Hymes, 1972). The key consideration in selecting units of analysis is that they allow the coding system to be functional for the particular communication event and flexible (Ayers & Miura, 1981).

The problem of an appropriate unit of analysis is compounded by the unique nature of the computer conference. Here interaction may be synchronous or asynchronous, messages are sent in the form of "entries," several consecutive entries by one author may all focus on one issue, or one long entry by an author may reply to several previous entries by several other authors.

Because of the need to interpret interaction in context, a unit of analysis similar to Goffman's "interchange" is needed first. Of course the entire organizational setting, entire conference, and, in the case of computer conferences, the synchronous and asynchronous sequences provide broad contexts. However, an intermediate unit between these large parameters and the single utterance or entry is seen as desirable.

An arbitrary decision to pair consecutive utterances into "interacts" (Hawes, 1972) or "transactions" (Rogers, 1972) is unsatisfactory for computer conferences because of the existence of consecutive entries by the same author and because a specific response to a particular initiation may come several entries after the initiative entry. The concept of the "double interact," a unit of initiation-response-feedback to response, has more theoretical attractiveness. It is seen to be the fundamental unit of organizing (Weick, 1979) and of social interaction (Sinclair & Coulthard, 1975).

The double interact also has practical attractiveness, in that it should appear in all the mediated and face-to-face conference modes.

Experience in the pilot study of a computer conference showed that many entries fit the definition of the double interact, others were shortened to initiation-response, or the interact, while others received no response and hence stood alone. For entries which stood alone, interpretation was based on overall context. In some cases a series of four or more entries strung together into larger transactions. So while the double interact is seen as an ideal for establishing context, flexibility is needed to allow for simple interacts, isolated entries, and longer transactions.

The utterance, or entry in a computer conference, provides the next and most important unit of analysis. The utterance is verbal material bounded by another's verbal material (Sinclair & Coulthard, 1975). It is analogous to the "turn" (Albrecht & Cooley, 1980). In the case of a computer conference, each individual entry will be counted as an utterance. Others have treated consecutive entries by one author as a single utterance (Spang et al., 1979). However, experience in the pilot showed that consecutive entries may involve two entirely unrelated transactions and were better treated as separate utterances.

A smaller unit than the utterance is also desired, since an utterance may consist of anything from a word to many sentences. The "speech act" (Hymes, 1972) is a possibility, because politeness strategies illustrated by Brown and Levinson consistently are carried out in identifiable speech acts. The speech act is the smallest free unit, typically one free clause plus subordinate clauses, and occasionally consisting of single words. However, as Brown and Levinson note, since face-threatening acts "do not necessarily inhere in single acts . . . some strategies for FTA-handling are describable only in terms of sequences of acts or utterances" (p. 238). Hence a somewhat larger unit than the act but still smaller than the utterance is desired.

Sinclair and Coulthard (1975) note that within an utterance a shift to a new exchange or topic may occur. They identified this point and the speech unit it bounded as the "move." A move may consist of a word, a clause, a sentence, or several sentences that mark a shift in exchange, topic, or emphasis. After experimenting in the pilot with the speech act, it was decided that the "move" was more useful for interpretive purposes, and each entry was divided into moves using slash marks.

The units of analysis then will be, in descending order of magnitude, the double interact or other transaction, the utterance (or entry), and the move. The first step in analysis of a conference transcript will be to identify and mark these units. The central purpose of identifying these units is not to establish any expected theoretic connection to face work, but rather to establish as clear a context as possible in which to interpret possible politeness strategies. In the pilot study, for example, moves served best as warning flags that indicated potential shifts in politeness output strategy. While new moves did not always lead to new politeness strategies, shifts in politeness strategy within a single utterance usually coincided with new moves.

Application of the Framework. Once the contextualizing units have been marked, a conference transcript can be analyzed for the existence of concern for face and politeness strategies. Based on experience in the pilot study, the following general format will be implemented.

The conference transcript will be read straight through several times for familiarization. Lines will be drawn to connect double interacts and other transactions. Isolated utterances will be noted. Each utterance will be marked with slashes to indicate where move boundaries seem to occur. In a computer conference synchronous and asynchronous segments will also be marked off.

Next, working gradually through the transcript, each utterance will be read, following the lines designating interaction sequences. A basic decision algorithm will be used for each utterance, and each utterance will be coded using the numerical system embedded in Table 35.2. The decision algorithm follows this ideal format:

A. Is there an FTA and resultant politeness strategy present?
Yes No
↓
B. Identify and code the *superstrategy used*.
BOR(1) PP(2) NP(3) OR(4)
C. Identify *higher-order strategy* and code.
D. Identify *output strategy* and code.

This ideal decision algorithm will be applied in a flexible way. In practice, a reverse or back-and-forth procedure will often be used. For example, a possible output strategy will be noticed in the language first, then the utterance and its context will be examined for the existence of an FTA, and a tentative decision regarding both super and output strategies will be recorded. With this procedure the higher-order strategy (step C) will be decided by default. In the pilot only rarely did identifying a higher-order strategy aid in specifying an output strategy. Since the same language behavior might fulfill more than one strategy given a different context, interpreting the context for the kind of FTA present and the type of superstrategy present will usually be necessary before a final determination can be made. The transcript will be worked through several times in this fashion until the researcher is satisfied with the consistency of the decisions.

When an utterance consists of several moves which show a single line of politeness output strategy throughout, it will be coded for only one politeness output strategy (e.g., 2.1.4; see Table 35.2). When an utterance consists of several moves and shows one or more shifts in politeness output strategy, each output strategy will be coded, with the shifts indicated by an arrow (e.g., 2.1.2→1.1). When an utterance which consists of one or more moves seems to involve a combination of output strategies designed to accomplish a single line of politeness behavior rather than a true shift in behavior, the output strategies will be coded separately and connected by a plus sign (e.g., 2.1.8 + 2.1.4). Brown and Levinson describe the first of these strategy mixtures, the shift, as a situation in which a speaker and addressee move "back and forth between approaching and distancing in their interaction," while they see the second kind of mixed strategy as a "kind of hybrid" (pp. 235-236).

Quantitative Analysis. Hymes (1977) has suggested that a linguistic ethnography approach would involve both qualitative and quantitative analysis. In such an approach the "study of language is inseparable from the study of social life, and . . . quantitative differences are inseparable from qualitative effects" (p. 169). The use of qualitative and quantitative analysis enables "triangulation," or the use of multiple methods to study a phenomenon (Jick, 1979). The approach used in the proposed study provides both a level of "between-methods" triangulation through a mix of observation, content analysis involving both qualitative and quantitative interpretation, and interviews. A level of "within-method" triangulation is provided through the comparison of groups. The quantification of qualitative results, which describes the process to be used in the content analysis of transcripts, is seen by Jick as a "primitive triangulating device." However, the total mix of methods provides a higher level of sophistication in triangulation.

Quantitative analysis will primarily involve comparison between numbers of politeness *super*strategies. For a particular transcript, after utterances are coded, the total number of output strategy displays will be counted and compared to the number of utterances and moves. The proportional use of *super*strategies will be compared next. Utterances that display a single output strategy will be recorded under the appropriate *super*strategy. Utterances displaying a shift in or combination of output strategies but which remain within a single *super*strategy will be counted as one instance of the appropriate *super*strategy. Utterances which display a shift in or combination of output strategies *and super*strategies will be counted separately as "mixed *super*strategy" utterances. Utterances that involve no FTA and display no politeness strategy will be counted separately, as will utterances that are uninterpretable.

Using these totals, utterances displaying a single line of one of the *super*strategies, or a mixed *super*strategy, can be compared to the total number of utterances and to the totals for each of the other *super*strategies. The sheer number of times *super*strategies are used may also be compared to each other.

It is possible that the impact of utterances with mixed strategies will be dominated either by the initial strategy (a primacy effect) or by the ending strategy (a recency effect). A test will be conducted to determine if there is a difference between beginning and ending *super*strategies in mixed entries for particular conferences.

The chi-square test for one sample will be used to test the significance of comparisons between politeness strategies (Siegel, 1956). In cases involving one degree of freedom, Yates's correction will be used (Minium, 1970). As data are collected on conferences in different media, cross-group comparisons of the numbers and types of politeness strategies will be made using a chi-square test for independent samples (Siegel, 1956).

Interpretive Framework or Coding Scheme? Cross media comparisons raise the issue of whether the politeness strategy list provided by Brown and Levinson should be used as an interpretive framework intended to guide analysis or as a coding scheme subject to tests of interrater reliability. The authors themselves do not make an argument either way, referring consistently to their conceptualization as a "tool — for example, as "an ethnographic tool of great precision" (p. 62).

Treating the politeness strategies as a simple coding scheme creates considerable problems. Brown and Levinson list four superstrategies, twelve higher-order strategies, and forty-two output strategies. Such a large number of choices obviously complicates the likelihood of achieving high interrater reliability. Moreover, it creates a difficult training problem if the coders are to become fully versed in the politeness framework. Finally, there is a danger that using the politeness strategy list as a simple and inviolable coding scheme in order to achieve a statistical level of interrater reliability will cause it to lose its flexibility and thereby damage its ability to capture the "ethos" of a culture.

There are also, however, the problems of establishing the reliability of the findings regarding a particular conference and of conducting comparisons across media. Interpretive scholars have suggested that the test of an interpretive account lies in its sensibleness rather than in an appeal to statistical correspondence (Hawes, 1978; Simons, 1978). Since the proposed analysis involves statistical comparisons between politeness strategies and between media, and since the key comparison will focus on the more simple set of four politeness *super*strategies, it is feasible to test interrater reliability statistically on these four *super*strategies.

Hence, conference transcripts subject to politeness strategy analysis will be coded by two independent coders in addition to the researcher and tested for interrater reliability. "Unitizing reliability" is not seen as an issue (Hawes, 1972). The larger and smaller analysis units, the double interact and the move, are seen as useful mainly for establishing context for interpretation. Only utterances are meaningful in establishing how much concern for face is demonstrated, and their delineation is by definition straightforward and not subject to interpretation. For this reason the analysis units will be preestablished by the researcher. "Categorizing reliability," or "the proportion of units of behavior which the coders [classify] similarly," will be tested between coders for politeness superstrategies only (Hawes, 1972, p. 95). The test of reliability will be by Guetzkow's formula, with a significance level of .05 (Hawes, 1972).

Ethos Analysis and Comparisons. The final research question was "How might the media be altering the organizational culture?" Any conclusions regarding this question depend on understanding the ethos of mediated communication as indicated by concern for face and politeness strategies. Also needed are an understanding of the general organizational ethos and a sense of how the organization members view the mediated communication technology. The final analysis step involves a comparative account of these issues.

Several sources of data were proposed: naturalistic observation of the organization and of mediated conferences, naturalistic observation of face-to-face meetings, politeness strategy analysis of comparable face-to-face meetings, and structured open-ended interviews of participants in mediated conferences. Each of these sources will yield interpretive data, as well as a means of quantitative comparison in the case of politeness strategy comparisons.

The central issue in this final analysis step is cultural "ethos," which Brown and Levinson define as "the quality of interaction characterizing groups . . . in a particular society" (p. 248). Ethos refers specifically to "interactional quality" and depends on variation in several dimensions, including the nature and distribution of politeness strategies and the general level of weightiness of face-threatening acts in a culture. Weightiness of FTAs is a function of relative power, distance, and risk. Other factors in interactional quality include the extent to which all acts are FTAs and which acts are FTAs, the varying values and differing sources of assessment of power, distance, and risk, and finally the sets of persons who an actor wants to pay him or her positive face (Brown & Levinson, 1978, p. 249-250).

One may learn, for example, from a comparison of interview data to politeness strategy analysis of mediated communication that organization members describe mediated communication as impersonal, with a confirmatory finding that the ethos of the conference is dominated by bald on record and negative politeness strategies that are likely to emphasize social distance. The interview data may also show that participants attribute their impressions to inexperience rather than to alterations in communication behavior. Hilton (1981b) in fact describes a video teleconference involving six participants at two locations. One participant responds, "It was a new experience for us, so we were a little stilted and formal with each other, I think. Frankly I missed the camaraderie" (p. 12).

One may also find from observation in the organization and in face-to-face meetings that concern for face and the resultant ethos is quite different from that observed in mediated conferences. Should the ethos of mediated conferences not differ from other organizational settings, different conclusions would be drawn. It is this kind of comparative and interpretive analysis that is likely to form the most significant conclusions in the research program.

RESULTS OF A PILOT STUDY OF A COMPUTER CONFERENCE

The transcript of a computer conference was analyzed using the politeness strategy framework as a trial of this interpretive approach. The results are briefly summarized here; a full report is available (Hiemstra, 1982).

The conference studied involved four active participants who made seventy-one entries (utterances) over a forty-three-day period. The first thirty-three entries involved synchronous interaction, while the remainder of the conference was asynchronous. The purpose of the conference was the joint production of a research report. The conference was an actual working activity, not an experimental test of the computer system. Two of the active participants appeared to be experienced with computer conferencing, while two did not.

The first step in the research was to divide the transcript of public comments into analysis units. As proposed in this chapter, these units were the double interact, or other transaction, the utterance, and the move. Of these units, the move proved to be the most problematic, involving a difficult interpretation of whether a change in emphasis or topic had occurred in a particular utterance. Where doubt occurred, a move boundary was usually established. The move was very useful as a contextualizing unit, since the move often acted as a warning flag of a shift in politeness strategy.

There were three significant findings in the analysis. First, concern for face was strongly evident in the language of the conference. Almost every utterance was interpreted to involve a face-threatening act. More than 75 percent of the utterances were interpreted as either positive politeness, negative politeness, or a mix of politeness strategies. The remaining utterances which were seen as FTAs (21 percent) used the strategy bald on record. This finding runs contrary to the contention of Hiltz and Turoff (1978) that participants in computer conferences drop the usual maintenance of face.

Second, a pattern of politeness strategies emerged that seemed to indicate a particular ethos for the computer conference. When the politeness strategy seen by Brown and Levinson as a social distancer, negative politeness, is combined with the strategy bald on record, a social neutral at best and more likely a social distancer, they were used twice as often as positive politeness. Positive politeness is seen as a social magnet by Brown and Levinson. From this observation it was concluded that it was not lack of concern for face which created the ethos of this conference. Concern for face was high. Rather, it was the choice of politeness strategies which created an ethos that seemed one of relative coolness and distance.

Third and most striking, the politeness strategy observed by Brown and Levinson as perhaps the most pervasive in natural conversation, off record, was observed only once, in a mixed utterance. This lack of off-record strategies was seen as the most significant way in which the computer conference may alter the intersubjective process of communication. Alternative explanations for the disappearance of this strategy were proposed, including a pressure exerted by the computer medium toward efficiency, the lack of nonverbal cues needed to interpret indirect or off-record utterances, and a task-related emphasis on efficiency.

Comparisons to conclusions drawn from other observations and from the reactions of conference participants were not made in this initial study, since only the transcript was available. There were also no comparisons to other coders' interpretations of the transcript. This initial study did demonstrate the feasibility of using the Brown and Levinson framework of politeness strategies as a tool for analysis. One addition to their list of output strategies was made, and the complexity of the framework necessitated several iterations of the analysis, but it did prove to be practically applicable. The study indicated that the concept of concern for face and the framework of politeness strategies has significant potential as an interpretive method for observing structural changes in the "system of symbols and meanings" of a cultural setting, and for indicating the ethos of that setting.

CONCLUSION

Few cultural phenomena are more subject to conjecture than the shift from the industrial society to the information society. Few technological movements are entering society more swiftly or more completely than the whole range of information technologies. A fundamental difference between information technologies and other technologies expected to have significant impact on culture (e.g., bioscience technologies, robotics, energy technologies) is that the information technologies are here, they are usable now, and they are generally economical now. Innovations and improvements will continue at a rapid pace, but the machinery of the information-communication revolution is in place or in production lines, and organizations are rushing to join up. Indeed, one could say that a "great experiment" in organizational communication has begun.[4] If the information technologies are indeed going to alter culture and its organizations, it is important that research be undertaken which focuses on possible alterations in the intersubjective process by which culture is created. The research program proposed here is one effort in that direction.

NOTES

1. Hulin did a content analysis of 460 studies published from 1971 to 1979 in the *Journal of Applied Psychology, Organizational Behavior & Human Performance, Administrative Science Quarterly, Academy of Management Journal,* and *Personnel Psychology.*

2. *Computer conferencing* involves interaction through written words via computer terminals, key features of which are that "meetings" do not have to be conducted in synchronous time, and an automatic transcript is maintained.

Audio teleconferencing involves essentially a conference phone call, which may include built-in mikes and speakers, facsimile transmission, and "electronic blackboards" (pressure-sensitive boards that simultaneously transmit writing and figures to other locations).

Video teleconferencing involves multisite television or videophone transmission/reception, which may include transmission of visual aids and may involve either wide-band picture transmission or slow scan picture transmission which changes at intervals.

3. Among reviews of information technology issues are *Electronic Meetings: Technical Alternatives and Social Choices* (Johansen et al., 1979), *Network Nation* (Hiltz & Turoff, 1978), *Electronic Communication: Technology and Impacts* (Henderson & MacNaughton, 1980), and *The Computer Age: A Twenty Year View* (Dertouzos & Moses, 1979).

4. The term "great experiment" in organizational communication was coined by Bonnie Johnson in a private conversation with the author.

REFERENCES

Albertson, L. A. Telecommunication as a travel substitute: Some psychological, organizational, and social aspects. *Journal of Communication,* 1977, *27,* 32-43.

Albrecht, T. L., & Cooley, R. E. Androgyny and communicative strategies for relational dominance: An empirical analysis. In D. Nimmo (Ed.), *Communication yearbook 4*, New Brunswick, NJ: Transaction, 1980.

Amara, R. Management in the 1980's. *Technology Review*, 1981, *83*, 76-82.

Ayers, J., & Miura, S. Y. Construct and predictive validity of instruments of coding relational control communication. *Western Journal of Speech Communication*, 1981, *45*, 159-171.

Bell, D. The social framework of the information society. In M. L. Dertouzos & J. Moses (Eds.), *The computer age: A twenty year view*. Cambridge: MIT Press, 1979.

Brown, P., & Levinson, S. Universals in language usage: Politeness phenomena. In E. N. Goody (Ed.), *Questions and politeness*. Cambridge: Cambridge University Press, 1978.

Calder, B. J. Focus group interviews and qualitative research in organizations. In E. E. Lawler, D. A. Nadler, & C. Cammann (Eds.), *Organizational assessment: Perspectives on the measurement of organizational behavior and the quality of work life*. New York: John Wiley, 1980.

Campbell, J. P. Research needs appropriate for human resource development as gleaned from corporate planning documents and management interviews. Paper presented at Innovations in Methodology Conference, Center for Creative Leadership, Greensboro, North Carolina, March 1981.

Chapanis, A. Interactive human communication. *Scientific American*, 1975, *232*, 36-42.

Chapanis, A. *Human factors in teleconferencing systems: Final report*. Baltimore, MD: Johns Hopkins University, 1976. (ERIC Document Reproduction Service No. ED 163902)

Christie, B., & Holloway, S. Factors affecting the use of telecommunications by management. *Journal of Occupational Psychology*, 1975, *48*, 3-9.

Davis, J. H. *Group performance*. Reading, MA: Addison-Wesley, 1969.

Dertouzos, M. L., & Moses, J. (Eds.). *The computer age: A twenty year view*. Cambridge: MIT Press, 1979.

Duncanson, J. P., & Williams, A. D. Video conferencing: Reactions of users. *Human Factors*, 1973, *15*, 471-485.

Featheringham, T. R. Computerized conferencing and human communication. *IEEE Transactions on Professional Communication*, 1977, *PC-20* (4), 207-213.

Ferguson, J. A. PLANET: A computer conferencing system and its evaluation through a case study. *Behavior Research Methods & Instrumentation*, 1977, *9*, 92-95.

Flannigam, R. R. Computers and communication. Paper presented to the Northwest Communication Association Convention, Coeur D'Alene, Idaho, 1981.

Fowler, G. D., & Wackerbarth, M. E. Audio teleconferencing versus face-to-face conferencing: A synthesis of the literature. *Western Journal of Speech Communication*, 1980, *44*, 236-252.

Goffman, E. On face work. In E. Goffman, *Interaction ritual*. Garden City, NY: Doubleday, 1967.

Harkins, A. M., & Joseph, E. C. Ethnotronics and human learning futures. In K. M. Redd & A. M. Harkins (Eds.), *Education: A time for decisions*. Washington, DC: World Future Society, 1980.

Hawes, L. C. Development and application of an interview coding system. *Central States Speech Journal*, 1972, *23*, 92-99.

Hawes, L. C. The reflexivity of communication research. *Western Journal of Speech Communication*, 1978, *42*, 12-20.

Henderson, M. M., & MacNaughton, M. J. (Eds.). *Electronic communication: Technology and impacts*. Boulder, CO: Westview Press, 1980.

Hiemstra, G. E. *Saving face in a computer conference: An empirical and cultural analysis*. Paper presented to the Western Speech Communication Association Convention, Denver, February 1982.

Hilton, J. Adjusting to office television. *Wall Street Journal*, January 12, 1981, p. 18. (a)

Hilton, J. Face to camera at an actual teleconference. *Wall Street Journal*, July 13, 1981, p. 12. (b)

Hiltz, S. R. Computer conferencing: Assessing the social impact of a new communication medium. *Technological Forcasting and Social Change*, 1977, *10*, 225-238.

Hiltz, S. R. The computer conference. *Journal of communication,* 1978, *28,* 157-163. (a)
Hiltz, S. R. The human element in computerized conferencing systems. *Computer Networks,* 1978, *2,* 421-428. (b)
Hiltz, S. R. Controlled experiments with computerized conferencing: Results of a pilot study. *Bulletin of the American Society for Information Science,* 1978, *4,* 11-12. (c)
Hiltz, S. R., Johnson, K., Aronovitch, C., & Turoff, M. *Face-to-face vs. computerized conferences: A controlled experiment.* Research Report Number 12. Newark: New Jersey Institute of Technology, Computerized Conferencing & Communications Center, August 1980.
Hiltz, S. R. & Turoff, M. *The network nation: Human communication via computer.* Reading, MA: Addison-Wesley, 1978.
Hulin, C. L. *Representative questions from 10 years of research articles.* Paper presented at Innovations in Methodology Conference, Center for Creative Leadership, Greensboro, North Carolina, March 1981.
Hymes, D. Models of the interaction of language and social life. In J. J. Gumperz & D. Hymes (Eds.), *Directions in sociolinguistics.* New York: Holt, Rinehart & Winston, 1972.
Hymes, D. H. Qualitative/quantitative research methodologies in education: A linguistic perspective. *Anthropology and Education Quarterly,* 1977, *8,* 165-176.
Israelski, E. W. A user study of the Bell Systems video teleconferencing system: Applications and attitudes. *Ergonomics,* 1979, *22,* 743.
Jick, T. D. Mixing qualitative and quantitative methods: Triangulation in action. *Administrative Science Quarterly,* 1979, *24,* 602-611.
Johansen, R., & DeGrasse, R. Computer-based teleconferencing: Effects on working patterns. *Journal of Communication,* 1979, *29,* 30-41.
Johansen, R., Vallée, J., & Spangler, K. Electronic meetings: Utopian dreams and complex realities. *The Futurist,* October 1978, *12,* 313-319.
Johansen, R., Vallée, J., & Spangler, K. *Electronic meetings: Technical alternatives and social choices.* Reading, MA: Addison-Wesley, 1979.
Kelly, M. J. Studies in interactive communication: Limited vocabulary natural language dialogue (Doctoral dissertation, Johns Hopkins University, 1975). *Dissertation Abstracts International,* 1976, *36,* 3647B. (University Microfilms No. 76-1518)
Kochen, M. Long-term implications of electronic information exchanges for information science. *Bulletin of the American Society for Information Science,* 1978, *4,* 22-23.
Kohl, K., Newman, T. G., Jr. & Tomey, J. F. Facilitating organizational decentralization through teleconferencing. *IEEE Transactions on Communications,* 1975, *COM-23* (10), 1098-1103.
Korzenny, F. A Theory of electronic propinquity: Mediated communication in organizations. *Communication Research,* 1978, *5,* 3-23.
Korzenny, F., & Bauer, C. *A preliminary test of the theory of electronic propinquity: Organizational teleconferencing.* Paper presented at the annual meeting of the International Communication Association, Information Systems Division, Philadelphia, May 1979.
Krueger, G. P., & Chapanis, A. Conferencing and teleconferencing in three communication modes as a function of the number of conferees. *Ergonomics,* 1980, *23,* 103-122.
Lawler, E. E., Nadler, D. A., & Cammann, C. (Eds.). *Organizational assessment: Perspective on the measurement of organizational behavior and the quality of work life.* New York: John Wiley, 1980.
Lowndes, J. C. Teleconferencing systems expected to reduce costs. *Aviation Week & Space Technology,* June 8, 1981 pp. 322-333.
McKendree, J. D. Project and crisis management applications of computerized conferencing. *Bulletin of the American Society for Information Science,* 1978, *4,* 13-15.
Mehan, H. Structuring school structure. *Harvard Educational Review,* 1978, *48,* 28-60.
Minium, E. W. *Statistical reasoning in psychology and education.* New York: John Wiley, 1970.
Mishler, E. G. Meaning in context: Is there any other kind? *Harvard Educational Review,* 1979, *49,* 1-19.
O'Neill, G. K. 2081. *Omni,* May 1981, pp. 52-55, 95-96. (From G. K. O'Neill, *The year 2081,* forthcoming.)

Pacanowsky, M. E., & Berky, F. *An analysis of organizational culture: A theoretical overview.* Paper presented at the annual meeting of the International Communication Association, Philadelphia, March 1979.

Pateman, T. Communicating with computer programs. *Language and Communication,* 1981, *1,* 3-12.

Pettigrew, A. M. On studying organizational cultures. *Administrative Science Quarterly,* 1979, *24,* 570-581.

Rice, R. E. The impacts of computer-mediated organizational and interpersonal communication. *Annual Review of Information Science and Technology,* 1980, *15,* 221-249.

Robey, D. Computers and management structure: Some empirical findings reexamined. In D. Katz, R. L. Kahn, & J. S. Adams (Eds.), *The study of organizations.* San Francisco: Jossey-Bass, 1980.

Rogers, L. E. *Dyadic systems and transactional communication in a family context.* Unpublished doctoral dissertation, Michigan State University, 1972.

Rogers, L. E., & Farace, R. V. Analysis of relational communication in dyads: New measurement procedures. *Human Communication Research,* 1975, *1,* 222-229.

Ryan, M. G. The influence of teleconferencing medium and status on participants' perception of the aestheticism, evaluation, privacy, potency, and activity of the medium. *Human Communication Research,* 1976, *2,* 225-261.

Schneider, D. Notes toward a theory of culture. In K. R. Basso & H. A. Selby (Eds.). *Meaning in anthropology.* Albuquerque: University of New Mexico Press, 1976.

Shimanoff, S. B. *Communication rules: Theory and research.* Beverly Hills, CA: Sage, 1980.

Shutz, A. Concept and theory formation in the social sciences. In F. R. Dallmayr & T. A. McCarthy (Eds.), *Understanding and social inquiry.* London: University of Notre Dame Press, 1977. (Reprinted from M. Natanson [Ed.], *Collected papers,* Vol. 1, 1967.)

Siegel, S. *Nonparametric statistics.* New York: McGraw-Hill, 1956.

Sillars, A. L., & Folger, J. B. *A second look at relational coding assumptions.* Paper presented at the annual meeting of the International Communication Association, Chicago, 1978.

Simons, H. W. In praise of muddleheaded anecdotalism. *Western Journal of Speech Communication,* 1978, *42,* 21-36.

Sinclair, J. M., & Coulthard, R. M. *Towards an analysis of discourse.* Oxford, England: Oxford University Press, 1975.

Spang, S., McNeal, B., & Vian Spangler, K. *Interactive group modeling: Part 4. Some preliminary tests of the HUB system.* Menlo Park, CA: Institute for the Future, 1979. (ERIC Document Reproduction Service No. ED 182 791)

Spelt, P. F. Evaluation of a continuing computer conference on simulation. *Behavior Research Methods & Instrumentation,* 1977, *9,* 78-91.

Stoll, F. C., Hoecker, D. G., Krueger, G. P., & Chapanis, A. The effects of four communication modes on the structure of language used during cooperative problem solving. *Journal of Psychology,* 1976, *94,* 13-26.

Strickland, L. H., Guild, P. D., Barefoot, J. C., & Paterson, S. A. Teleconferencing and leadership emergence. *Human Relations,* 1978, *31,* 583-596.

Toffler, A. *The third wave.* New York: William Morrow, 1980.

Turoff, M. The EIES experience: Electronic information exchange system. *Bulletin of the American Society for Information Science,* 1978, *4,* 9-10.

Uhlig, R. P. Human factors in computer message systems. *Datamation,* May 1977, pp. 120-126.

Vallée, J., Johansen, R., & Spangler, K. The computer conference: An altered state of communication. *The Futurist,* June 1975, *9,* 116-121.

Weick, K. E. *The social psychology of organizing* (2nd ed.). Reading, MA: Addison-Wesley, 1979.

Williams, E. Teleconferencing: Social and psychological factors. *Journal of Communication,* 1978, *28,* 125-131.

36 • Computer-Mediated Communication: A Network-Based Content Analysis Using a CBBS Conference

JAMES A. DANOWSKI
University of Wisconsin—Madison

COMPUTER-MEDIATED communication (CMC) systems such as private messaging, public conferencing, bulletin boards, and several variations in between are proliferating. Researchers are increasingly interested in measuring and evaluating CMC. On the one hand, some of the features of CMC provide a testbed for theoretical propositions about human communication. CMC provides a highly controlled, time-sensitive, and automatically audited environment. This not only enables testing of hypotheses about CMC in relation to other variables, but also enables testing of more general propositions about human communication that are not dependent on the type of medium used. On the other hand, the implementation of CMC systems in organizations can benefit from practically guided formative and summative evaluation research.

Based on these dual research needs, the objective of this chapter is to develop and present a methodology for both theoretically and practically oriented research that is particularly attuned to the nature of CMC. This methodology integrates communication *network* analysis perspectives and procedures, performs *content analysis* on the relationships among

AUTHOR'S NOTE: The author acknowledges the research assistance of Joanne Taeuffer in development of the methodology and of Ilya Adler, Rosa Elizondo, Charles Steinfield, and Eric Wendler for data gathering and processing. This research was supported by the National Science Foundation, Division of Information Science and Technology, IST-801088. Views expressed do not necessarily reflect those of NSF.

Correspondence and requests for reprints: James A. Danowski, School of Journalism and Mass Communication, University of Wisconsin, Madison, WI 53706.

concepts in message pairs, represents the aggregate message content relationships with a *distance* model, and enables derivation of *optimal communication management strategies* over time. Application of the methodology is illustrated with data obtained from a public computer conference, a CBBS in Boston.

SPECIAL FEATURES OF CMC

As Rice and Danowski (1981) discuss, the research techniques generally appropriate for evaluating CMC are no different from those appropriate for evaluating most other human activity. Depending on the stakeholders involved and their perspectives, an adequate mix of methods can be chosen from a well-stocked master toolkit of social science and evaluation methods. Why, then, propose a special CMC methodology? Some important CMC features point to research needs not easily met by "off the shelf" methods. This chapter shows that several aspects of existing methods may be linked, resulting in an enhanced research capability. This methodology, however, is not intended to replace others. In contrast, it may be one element of a larger methodological constellation. Four key features of CMC motivate the development of the enhanced method.

(1) *Communication networks.* It is widely known that a network perspective analyzes the structure of message exchange among a set of nodes — for example, individuals or groups. Separate network analyses can be performed by topics, by media used, by strength of links, and by other factors. Given the general value of network perspectives, one may wonder why network aspects of CMC are singled out as a basis for further methodological development. The main reason is that network traffic can be efficiently gathered on most systems. This reduces some of the barriers to network analysis of other communication behaviors, such as those via face-to-face modes, for which data are typically difficult to obtain, hard to code and clean, and filled with error. In contrast, conference network traffic can be captured in an automated fashion, at low cost, virtually error-free, with time-sensitivity, and without extensive manual coding and data entry. One particular approach to this will be discussed shortly.

(2) *Message content.* It can be argued that the most central aspects of human communication processes are the *messages* people exchange and the meanings they attach to symbolic message elements. Although networks of message traffic are important, they may be viewed as the accumulated traces of repeated message *content* exchange. In addition, even though the medium used is important, the main reason for its use is typically to exchange message content. And, while participants' individual differences are often significant, it is message content that communicates and bridges these differences.

Perhaps CMC message content has enhanced importance for several reasons. Each message typically has a standard header including such things as sender, receiver, time, date, and subject. These fixed formats may heighten user content awareness. Furthermore, CMC messages are visible, retrievable, and controllable by users, more so than with media such as newspapers, letters, and memos. Moreover, CMC messages are typically more personal than those in mass media. In short, for both general theoretical and specific CMC-related reasons, an appropriate methodology should focus on message content.

(3) *Time-sensitivity.* Users comment that some forms of CMC, particularly public conferencing, seem to have different "life-cycles." Speaking metaphorically, a conference can be viewed as wiggling, stumbling, and crawling about at first, then growing rapidly, experiencing identity crises, later maturing, and finally dying. While measurement of change over time in human processes is generally thought to be important, given these life-cycle notions, methods for CMC analysis should be particularly time-sensitive.

(4) *Leadership.* CMC participants have often commented that leadership is especially important. This may be because of greater coordination needs than for face-to-face communication, arising from asynchronous communication, users' reduced sensory engagement, their greater diversity, and other factors. These point to the need for a methodology that will enhance leaders' control over the course of conferences.

In sum, the methodology presented in this chapter is responsive to the four CMC features just described. It integrates *network* analysis perspectives and procedures, performs *content* analysis on the relationships among concepts in message pairs, represents the aggregate message content *relationships* with multidimensional scaling techniques, and enables derivation of *optimal communication management strategies* over time. The scope of application of the method is briefly discussed in the next section.

Scope

The utility of the current method ranges from basic communication research applications to practical conference management. It can address questions about and enable testing of scientific questions and hypotheses about change over time in CMC and related variables. For example: "How is change in the message content exchanged associated with change in the communication network structure?" Or, "What are the major life-stages of conferences and to what extent are these fixed by external factors?"

More practical conference management evaluations require two general kinds of applications. One is *formative* in nature: "How can the course of a computer conference be shaped as it occurs?" The second application is more *summative*. After a conference has lived out a normal life, one may ask: "How well did it accomplish its objectives?" Our methods enable these practical evaluation applications as well.

Basic Procedures

This CMC methodology has the following major components:

1. segmentation of communication activity by communication *network* structure
2. segmentation of communication activity by *time*
3. identification of message *content* elements; that is, *concepts*
4. identification of stimulus and response *message pairs*
5. tabulation of concept co-occurrence within message pairs, aggregated across all message pairs in a segment
6. multidimensional scaling of the aggregated co-occurrence matrix to identify the overall pattern of *relationships* among message elements

If derivation of communication strategies for changing the course of the CMC is desired, then additional steps follow:

7. identification of which concepts should be moved closer to or further from other concepts
8. derivation of *optimal messages* (combinations of concepts) to achieve the desired change
9. *entry* of optimal change messages into the conference

After step 7, the process begins again with step 1. Comments about some of the above steps are in order.

Segmentation. For many decades, it has been known that different social groups communicate differently. Because of this, communication participants, typically mass communication audience members, have been divided into subsets homogeneous within but different across. The first segmentations, starting in the 1930s, were based on *demographic* or structural locator variables such as income, education, age, sex, race, and so on. During the 1960s and 1970s, however, as communication participants appeared to develop increasing lifestyle and attitudinal differences that cut across demographic factors, *psychographic* segmentation gained prominence.

An even more refined *infographic* segmentation (Danowski, 1976) can be performed according to actual communication behaviors. A range of these may be used, including such things as the *network* structure of communicators, the *media* used, *message* variables, and *information processing styles*.

In a particular research situation, the choice of specific demographic, psychographic, or infographic segmentation strategies should depend on the evaluation objectives. For example, the more a communication program is concerned with disseminating information, the more useful *infographic* segmentation is. If participants are grouped and analyzed according to their information exposure, processing styles, and subsequent "second stage" dissemination potential, then it is more likely that overall program objectives will be achieved. In evaluating CMC, infographic segmentation according to communication network variables appears particularly useful. Most CMC systems enable users to engage in series of overlapping dyadic relationships. These define a dynamic communication network among users.

An additional segmentation variable with particular relevance to CMC is *time*. Along with conference "life-cycle" aspects, reasons for time segmentation include the more general value placed on "over time" analysis in the social sciences. Measuring variables over time can reveal underlying causal sequencing among variables and more accurately reflect *processual* dynamics. CMC presents unique possibilities to segment both by time and network variables because CMC software codes each message entry according to time, sender, and receiver.

Message Content Parsing. Content analysis of message concepts is a focal point of our methodology. Particular approaches to isolating message concepts can be tailored to the research objectives. Various computerized and manual procedures exist for performing textual content analysis.

Concept Co-occurrence. Unlike traditional content analysis, our method does not simply identify the atomistic occurrence of concepts, that is, treat concepts as independent and separate. Rather, it maps the *relationships* among concepts by indexing the *co*-occurrence of concept *pairs*. Moreover, rather than selecting messages as the units within which to observe concept pairs, we select *pairs* of messages. This choice is based on the assumption that communication requires at least two participants, and that a communication event is constituted by a message sent and the response it triggers.

Consider the following hypothetical message pair. User A enters a public conference message about an upcoming user group meeting and offers a new software package he wrote. Subsequently, User B responds by asking User A to send him or her the software, but also requests information about User A's disk drives. There are two concepts in message A of the pair: (1) user group meeting information, and (2) offer of software. Two additional concepts are in message B: (3) request for software, and (4) request for hardware information.

Message A   Message B

Concept 1 (c1)   Concept 3 (c5)
Concept 2 (c2)   Concept 6 (c6)
Concept 3 (c3)   Concept 7 (c7)
Concept 4 (c4)
Concept 5 (c5)

CO-OCCURRENCE MATRIX

	c1	c2	c3	c4	c5	c6	c7
c1	0	0	1	0	0	1	1
c2		0	1	0	0	1	1
c3			1	1	1	1	1
c4				0	0	1	1
c5					0	1	1
c6						0	1
c7							0

Figure 36.1. An illustration of computation of message concept co-occurrence. The example analysis is for a single message pair. Note that the co-occurrence scoring is performed for each pair of messages from person A to person B and an aggregate matrix is created across the entire network or network segment within a time segment.

Consider the co-occurrence of these concepts across the two messages in the pair. Concept 1 co-occurs with concept 3 and concept 4; concept 2 likewise co-occurs. Each of these concept pairs (1-3, 1-4, 2-3, 2-4) receives a co-occurrence score of 1. If these pairs co-occur in other message pairs in the conference segment, their scores would be incremented accordingly. Note that co-occurrence of concepts within one message is not counted. If it were, then individual-level content structures, rather than group-level structures, would be measured. Figure 36.1 graphically presents the basic co-occurrence procedure with another, more abstract message pair.

Concept co-occurrence mapping, aggregated across message pairs, represents two aspects of the communication process. One, it reveals the manifest conversational structure among participants as it appears to an external observer. Second, to some extent it indirectly represents the collective cognitive structure among participants. This second aspect merits further discussion. First, the concepts co-occurring are not necessarily those in direct response to concepts initiated in the first message of a pair. This is exemplified by concept 4 in the earlier example. User B added the concept "disk drives." The ability of our methodology to measure these indirect relations presents opportunities to observe aspects of the underlying psychological structure among participants.

Consider that over a number of message pairs, the appearance of the same concept co-occurrences, even if at first glance they seem unrelated, indicates that a regularity exists in participants' underlying psychological processes. On one hand, there may be a kind of facilitative semantic trigger effect; one concept tends to positively elicit another concept. Alternatively, there may be a kind of compensatory trigger effect; one concept appears in response to another because the first does not create sufficient positive feelings. Hence, seemingly unrelated concepts emerge as the participants change an undesirable subject to a more pleasant one. Such underlying psychological processes can be investigated by linking the present methodology with self-report-based cognitive mapping.

MDS. Multidimensional scaling (MDS) of concept co-occurrence matrices, aggregated across message pairs in a segment, effectively represents the overall relationships among concepts. There are numerous nonmetric and metric scaling algorithms from which to choose (Kruscal & Wish, 1978). If, however, an evaluation objective is for leaders to extract optimal messages, as indicated earlier by steps 7-9, then it is advisable to use one particular kind of metric scaling procedure known as GALILEO (Woelfel & Fink, 1980). This approach has the Automatic Message Generator (AMG) algorithm programmed to select optimal combinations of concepts for inclusion in subsequent messages. Application of AMG will be illustrated shortly.

ILLUSTRATION OF THE CMC EVALUATION METHODOLOGY: BOSTON CBBS CASE

CBBS

The CMC system we chose to study as an illustration of the methodology is a public computer conference operating in the Boston area using a Computerized Bulletin Board System (CBBS) conferencing software

```
#1 Terminal need nulls?  Hit control-N while this types:

              ***  Welcome to CBBS/Boston  ***
      *** New Englands 1st Computerized Bulletin Board System ***
                   [System up since 12/2/78]

----> Control characters accepted by this system:

    CTL-H/DEL  Erases last character typed. (And echos it)
    CTL-C      Cancel current printing
    CTL-K      'Kills' current function, returns to menu
    CTL-N      Send 5 nulls after CR/LF
    CTL-R      Retypes current input line (after DEL)
    CTL-S      Stop/start output (for video terminal)
    CTL-U      Erases current input line

Problems?  Try calling the following numbers:
  Ward Woiwich:  (61 ) 752-97 5 Rm. #317, 26  5576,  26-5032
  Scot Marcus:   (61 ) 906-57 8, 8 3  7o2

Bulletins: Last updated 04/28/79, 14 lines.
(Hit multiple control-c's to skip this...)
]--> 04/28/79 Thanks to CBBS user LEO KENEN for solving a perplexing
              CPM problem... We now are running 48K CP/M!
]--> 03/26/79 New IDS modem installed, while other IDS modem is
              out being repaired...
]--> 03/10/79 CBBS phone numbers moved into messages and out of
              Bulletins (were too long..)
]--> 02/24/79 Second Shugart SA800 now online.. We'll now be able
              to handle up to 540 online messages!
]--> 01/25/79 Now running with SD Systems 48K ExpandoRAM.
]--> 01/09/79 We thank Tarbell Electronics for their donation of a
              disk controller.
Note: When we say C/R, we mean your return or newline key!

Y/N: IS THIS YOUR FIRST TIME ON THE SYSTEM?N
What is your first name?ROSA

Logging name to disk...
Next msg # will be 228
You are caller #  3234

FUNCTION: B,C,D,E,G,H,K,N,P,Q,R,S,W,X (OR ? IF NOT KNOWN)
```

Figure 36.2. Boston CBBS sample transcript: log-on and commands.

package (Christensen & Suess, 1978). CBBS systems are basically very similar to other conferencing systems such as EIES (Hiltz & Turoff, 1978), CONFER (Parnes, 1980), and others. Users log into the conference and read earlier entries, make entries, list summary header information on prior ones, search for and retrieve them. Sample CBBS transcripts appear in Figures 36.2 and 36.3.

Computer-Mediated Communication

MSG 115 IS 08 LINE(S) ON 03/04/79 FROM ROLF ROSENGREN TO ALL
ABOUT BACKGAMMON FOR N.S. OR SOL 20

PLEASE SEND FOR A FLYER BACKGAMMON FOR N,S.OR SOL-20 TO:
RR ELECTRONICS P.O. BOX 384 PARK RIDGE N.J. 07656
WILL RUN ON A CRT OR PRINTER DELUX GAME
PLACE YOUR CHIPS ANYWHERE YOU WANT UP TO 50.
THE COMPUTER PLAYS AGAINST YOU.
THE COMPUTER OR YOU CAN RULE THE DICE
MANY FEATURES THANK YOU FOR YOUR INTEREST.

MSG 116 IS 04 LINE(S) ON 03/06/79 FROM ROGER MAAS TO ALL
ABOUT WANT GIRLFRIEND

DESPERATELY LONELY mathematician 33 wants compatible woman
18-35. No smoking, minimal drinking. call 41-???-??-?? or
write to Roger Maas, PO BOX ???, Stanford, CA 9???

MSG 117 is 02 LINE(S) ON 03/07/79 FROM CHARLIE STROM TO ALL
ABOUT EXIDY SORCERER

I AM INTERESTED IN EXCHANGING EXPERIENCES, IDEAS, ETC.
WITH USERS OF THE EXIDY SORCERER.

MSG 118 is 10 LINE(S) ON 3/9/79 FROM STEVE BROWN TO APPLE
USERS ABOUT PROGRAMS & IDEAS

    WE ARE A SMALL GROUP OF APPLE USERS IN LITTLE ROCK
ARKANSAS. WE ARE ABOUT 15 STRONG NOW. WE ARE INTERESTED
IN IDEAS & PROGRAM EXCHANGE. WE ARE NOT INTERESTED IN
PIRATING PROGRAMS.
CONTACT: ???
             %DATACORE
             ??-??-????
             ??? A W ?? ?? STREET
             LITTLE ROCK, ARKANSAS ?????
MENTION THE BULLETIN BOARD

MSG 119 IS 06 LINE(S) ON 3/9/79 FROM ALDWEN OF THYMESWOOD TO
ROGER MAAS ABOUT GIRLFRIEND

Aren't you looking a bit far from home for the love of your
life? You might have better luck if you look in California...
Of course, there is the case of the two computer hackers who
were married via computer (over the ONTYME network) by this
weirdo

Figure 36.3. Boston CBBS sample transcript: message entries.

Most CBBSs use "Ward and Randy's" software, which is available for approximately $50. Ward and Randy's Bulletin Board, located in Chicago, was the first CBBS operating in the United States. It is still the largest and serves as a sort of informal national headquarters for over 200 CBBSs around the country. Most of the latter are accessed mainly by users in their local telephone dialing area, because calling CBBSs in other areas requires long-distance telephone charges.

The hardware necessary to operate a CBBS is quite basic: a small "home computer" with a dual floppy disk drive, a modem, and a normal telephone line. These simple requirements have aided CBBS proliferation. Someone with a home computer and the software package who wants to start a conference simply announces their telephone number, and anyone can call in and begin conferencing. The only cost to users is for the phone call. Some CBBSs are operated by user groups and other organizations, others by individuals, and yet others by computer-related merchandisers who use the CBBSs as a promotional vehicle. The message content varies some across CBBSs, but overall there is high similarity. We observed this as we read the entries on all the conferences operating at the time we designed this research, late in 1978.

There are several specific reasons that we selected a CBBS conference for the present research.

(1) *CBBS conferences represent "natural" forces in the developing "information society."* One reason is that users have no particular occupational or organizational affiliation motivating their participation. Conferencers are primarily hobbyists, the rapidly growing home computer user segment. They are motivated by personal interest. Another reason for naturalness is that CBBS use is essentially free, particularly if users reside in the local telephone calling areas of the conference; there is no "artificial" use stimulation or dampening such as might occur with systems funded by government agencies or dedicated to in-house organizational or corporate use.

(2) *Multiple conferences are occurring using the same CBBS software.* This enables rich possibilities for studying sets of conferences rather than solely individual users within a particular conference. Investigators can treat each CBBS conference, currently numbering more than 200 across the United States, as a distinct unit of analysis. There is sufficient sample size to make system-level generalizations and also to study regional and other variations in use. In contrast, most other CMC occurs on "one of a kind" systems. Many factors of these are often unique: operating software and user interfaces, dedicated purposes, cost structures, user characteristics, and so on. This makes generalizing evaluation results particularly troublesome, although less so with CBBS.

(3) *CBBSs are public conferences.* This is advantageous for the current research. We are able to access conference entries without privacy prob-

lems. Other situations may require negotiation with users before capturing their message content. Furthermore, it is not even necessary to contact the CBBS conference managers to obtain access. There are therefore reduced chances for researchers to contaminate the CMC system.

Boston CBBS

For the current research application, we chose a Boston-area CBBS. We selected this particular one because we recognized the highly developed information infrastructure in the Boston area. As a result, we expected this conference to have a sufficiently high message content diversity for a challenging test of the methodology. At the same time, our observation of all other CBBS conferences operating when data were gathered in 1978 and 1979 revealed that the Boston CBBS was representative. Another reason we chose it is that it had recently begun operation. We could therefore capture the conference in its earliest "life-stage." At the outset, message content diversity is probably higher before more routine message patterns develop. Moreover, conference managers would have undertaken less message packing, i.e., deletion of messages from the conference records.

On CBBSs, most packing appears to occur on the basis of a time criterion. For example, messages are deleted offering equipment for sale that has subsequently been sold, or announcing dates and times for user meetings that have already been held. To represent the actual, in contrast to the packed version of the conference, we logged in daily and recorded messages. Messages later packed were thus retained for our analysis, thus circumventing the packing process. Nevertheless, interesting research questions about packing processes abound with respect to alternative editing rules, message "throwaways," and other aspects.

Procedures

In analyzing the Boston CBBS, we executed the methods as follows:

(1) *Network segmentation*. Because the main purpose of the present research is to illustrate the kernel procedures — the content analysis and co-occurrence scaling — we analyzed the aggregate network structure rather than separate network groups. Moreover, network patterns were important to the identification of message pairs, as discussed in (3) below.

(2) *Time segmentation*. We selected the first 161 messages entered into the Boston conference. These began with its first operation on December 2, 1978; the 161st message was entered on February 23, 1979. Thus we had a bit more than the first ten weeks of the conference life. Again, because of our initial objective, we chose to first test the technique with one time segment.

(3) *Message pair identification.* To identify message pairs, we took each message, beginning with the last message in the series, then searched backward through the earlier 160 messages to see if the message was a response to a prior stimulus message. If so, then these two messages met a necessary but not sufficient condition to be a pair for further analysis. The identification of a potential stimulus message resulted under two conditions. One, a response message, person A's, was explicitly addressed to a particular person B. If so, we searched back and located the prior message that person B had sent that triggered A's response. Two, person A may have responded to a message person B had addressed to all conference users, not specifically to person A.

Once a potential message pair was so located, an additional sufficiency criterion was applied, namely that the two message pair candidates had to have at least one common concept. This fits conceptual definitions that for communication to occur there must be some minimal commonality in the code participants use. Moreover, it also makes the analysis of conference CMC, in contrast to private mail CMC, possible. Consider the conference situation in which an earlier message is addressed to all or a group of users rather than to a specific person. If person A's message did not reference a specific earlier sender, then without the common concept criterion, all of the generally addressed messages would be paired with person A's message. Many concept co-occurrences would be identified in error, and the resulting analysis would be highly misleading. Generally addressed messages would therefore have to be eliminated from such an analysis. Yet this is the very kind of message that distinguishes conferencing from private messaging.

In the Boston CBBS twenty-two message pairs were identified among the first 161 messages. Thirty-eight different messages were involved in these twenty-two pairs. This may seem to be a rather low degree of "networking," i.e., of users responding to the messages entered by others. Perhaps this is because this was the first series of messages entered. As a conference matures, the proportion of networking may increase up to a peak during the mid-life of the conference, then decline as it approaches the latter part of its life-cycle. These notions suggest interesting hypotheses for future research.

(4) *Identification of message concepts.* Because this is the first application of our procedures, we thought it best to use human coders in identifying concepts within messages. A coder read each of the thirty-eight messages in the twenty-two message pairs and partitioned them into the smallest meaningful concept units. A second coder repeated this process, and agreement was above 90 percent. Forty-three distinct concepts appeared.

Computer-Mediated Communication

Table 36.1
Message Concept Elements

1. CBBS procedures
2. Modems/couplers
3. Request help/information
4. Give help/information
5. Offer information at future date
6. Greetings/salutations
7. Give name/address/phone number
8. Computer software
9. Discuss user groups
10. Offer computer-related service/software free
11. Computer games
12. Leave message on computer bulletin board (this or other)
13. Refer to earlier message
14. Computer for the blind
15. Express interest
16. Source listing
17. Computer system (other than CBBS)
18. Hard copy
19. Thank you
20. Acknowledge receipt of message
21. Discuss problems with own computer
22. Delete this message
23. Fantasy
24. Ask for participation in discussing topic
25. Will send information by other means (telephone, mail)

(5) *Computation of concept co-occurrence.* The concepts identified created a 43 × 43 concept matrix. Each cell of the matrix represents a particular concept pair. In filling the matrix, a coder took each of the twenty-two message pairs one at a time and tabulated co-occurrence scores for concept pairs within it. Each time a concept pair co-occurred in a message pair, a value of 1 was added to that concept pair's cell in the master matrix. Again, Figure 36.1 illustrates this process.

After we formed the 43 × 43 aggregate matrix, we packed it. This was necessary because the MDS program we used was limited to thirty-nine concepts. Hence we were required to remove the lowest-frequency concepts. We examined the matrix rows and columns on a concept-by-concept basis, rather than a concept pair basis, and looked for concepts that had only one co-occurrence with only one other concept. There were sixteen such concepts. These were removed, resulting in a revised 25 × 25 concept matrix. The twenty-five concepts appear in Table 36.1.

Before factoring the aggregate matrix, we reversed the cell scores so that higher numbers meant less co-occurrence and smaller numbers

Table 36.2
Distances Among Pairs of Message Concepts

	1	2	3	4	5	6	7	8	9	10	11	12	13	14	15	16	17	18	19	20	21	22	23	24	25
1																									
2																									
3	49	64																							
4	64	64	25																						
5	64	64	64																						
6	49	64	01	64																					
7		49	25	64		16																			
8			64			36	04																		
9			49				36	49																	
10			36			64	16	64	64																
11			04			16	04	49	36	36															
12			09			49	25	64	64	64	09														
13			64							64	64														
14							49	36	64																
15		64	64			49	36	64	64			64		64											
16			25			25	16					64	64												
17			64			49		64	49			25	64												
18			64			49							64												
19			64			49					04		64												
20	64	64	64			49		64					64		64		64								
21	49	64	36	64		25	64	64	49	49	64	49	64		49	64	64	64	64	64					
22			49			64	64	64	64	64	64	64						64		64	64				
23			64			64												64		64	64	64			
24			64			64															64	64	64		
25			49												64							64	64	64	

Note: Cells with a value of 640, indicating no co-occurrence, are left blank for presentational convenience. The actual matrix scaled, however, includes the appropriate 640 cell values.

Table 36.3
Coordinates of Message Concepts on Three Dimensions

Concept	Dimension 1	Dimension 2	Dimension 3
1	125.5	6.6	−137.5
2	77.0	198.4	−52.3
3	−79.2	−140.9	5.7
4	−37.7	−56.4	87.0
5	380.0	−77.5	−9.6
6	157.5	−99.9	−109.7
7	−226.1	233.3	119.7
8	−3.0	282.1	137.4
9	−251.2	−59.1	213.4
10	−159.1	−298.6	12.7
11	−282.5	−62.6	258.4
12	−306.7	13.1	−46.5
13	146.0	−127.7	355.0
14	−59.4	188.0	−89.2
15	7.7	393.3	−162.4
16	−238.2	−29.7	201.5
17	260.9	−147.8	63.4
18	407.4	−121.8	107.9
19	260.2	−59.4	120.3
20	335.0	165.5	−31.8
21	−120.7	137.9	−69.0
22	−264.7	−170.3	−184.4
23	−95.0	−290.9	−324.4
24	−31.4	−189.9	−334.7
25	−2.2	314.4	−130.9

higher co-occurrence, just as in physical distance measurement. After reversal, the highest co-occurrence score, originally an 8, was converted to 1 and the original 1 became 8. At this point we made a further transformation by squaring the scores. We noted that in physics the mutual attraction of two objects (of equal mass) is related to the square of the distance between them. We think a parallel concept attraction function is plausible, particularly because we used a distance model. After squaring, a score of 1 remained 1, while the highest score became 64.

The final data preparation step was to assign a very large number to the pairs not co-occurring at all, those having zero cell values before transformation. Finding no standard yet accepted in the literature, we chose a rule: Multiply the highest cell entry times ten and assign this number to the unrelated pairs. In the current data, this resulted in cell values of 640 for the unrelated concepts. This transformed co-occurrence matrix, which was then multidimensionally scaled, appears in Table 36.2.

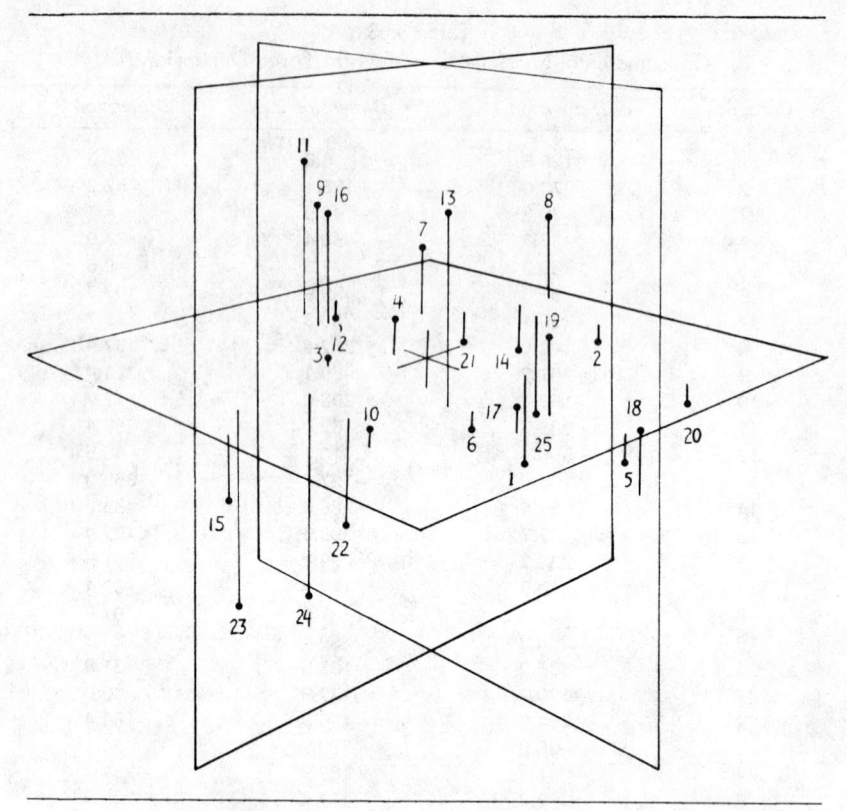

Figure 36.4. Plot of message concepts in three dimensions.

(6) *Multidimensional scaling.* We factored the matrix using the GALILEO metric multidimensional scaling procedure referenced earlier. Three dimensions accounted for meaningful variance. The coordinate projections of each of the twenty-five concepts are represented in Figure 36.4. It shows the x-y, x-z, and y-z planes and the twenty-five concepts positioned within these dimensions. The names of these concepts are listed in Table 36.1. More detailed MDS results are available from the author upon request.

(7) *Optimal message generation.* As discussed earlier, for some evaluation objectives it is useful to formatively evaluate communication management strategies to enable conference leaders to shape the course of subsequent conferencing, bringing it more closely in line with purposes and objectives. To illustrate application of the present method for this purpose, we used the Automatic Message Generator (AMG) function of the GALILEO multidimensional scaling program. AMG works according

to standard vector algebra procedures, determining the length and direction of the resultant vector for the concept to be moved as vectors of additional concepts are added. The program determines the efficiency of each possible combination so that users can select the particular combination with the highest likelihood of repositioning the concept within the larger concept space. The details as to how the algorithm operates are well documented in Woelfel and Fink (1980).

To apply AMG, the investigator first selects a focal concept to move and a target toward which to move it. An informal analogy as to how AMG works is the game of billiards. A player selects a ball to move toward a target, usually a pocket. Then he or she considers alternative angles and forces with which to strike the focal ball with other balls. The player then selects the most likely combination and executes.

Because the current research is illustrative, the choice of concepts to be moved and target concepts is arbitrary. We selected as the target the concept closest to the centroid of the space. This was *giving information*. The most central concept was selected as the target because it may often be the case that conference leaders wish to move a concept closer to the center of discussion. Nevertheless, movement of concepts away from targets is just as easily analyzed. We chose *user groups* as the concept to move closest to the center. Many CBBS conferences are operated by user groups, and there may be advantages to increasing the centrality of discussion about user group concepts.

We instructed AMG to select the best two-concept AMG message set. The two optimal message concepts the AMG routine selected were *offer information* and *source listing*. After entry of the optimal messages, including these two concepts with *user groups*, the actual effects could be measured by performing steps 1-6 with the next time segment. Furthermore, experimentation could then determine how many repetitions of the message are needed to achieve the desired movement of a concept toward or away from the target.

DISCUSSION

Paths to Refining the Methodology

The present case illustration demonstrates that the CMC evaluation methodology's core network analysis, content analysis, and multidimensional scaling procedures can be meaningfully applied to actual CMC. There are now several directions for refinement and elaboration. One is to extend the present analysis to the time-series case. A stream of conference messages can be segmented into time intervals based on when messages are entered. Then a series of content analyses and multidimensional scaling routines can be performed. The results can reveal change over time in the conceptual space of the conference.

These procedures enable the conduct of refined field experiments that can serve a range of basic questions, hypotheses, and practical applications. For example, does increasing message content diversity lead to a less densely connected communication network structure? Might the reverse be the case depending on the kind of content (Danowski, 1980)? A more practical example would be that if one were interested in the effects of leaders' use of optimal (AMG) messages or other messages in a conference, one could systematically enter these messages and observe their effects over time on the conference content space.

Consider another example that ties the current method to a survey method: If one were interested in experimenting with the effects of message content on the cognitive structures of users, one could apply our methodology to the conference messages, survey users to directly measure cognitive structures with self-report concept proximities data, and then analyze these using the same MDS program. In so doing, one could examine the effects of changing message content on users' direct conceptual structures over a time-series.

As we discussed earlier, our procedures alone, without self-report surveys, measure the *underlying* conceptual structure to the extent that psychological dynamics are translated into overt messages. This may be a major portion of cognitive structure. But there may be interesting aspects of it that do not get translated into overt messages to others — for example, perceived attributes of a computer or conferencing system as a whole. Users may have many attitudes and cognitions that they have no motive to express unless asked by someone, yet these psychological factors may indirectly affect other variables of interest.

A second, future extension of the method also concerns segmentation, but of a different sort. Distinct communication network groups can be identified according to structural criteria — for example, nodes who share a majority of links among themselves compared to the total set of nodes in the conference. If separate network groups exist, then the basic methodology presented here can be used within each segment. Such *infographic* segmentation can be useful for a variety of evaluation purposes. One example is a possible need to develop different optimal communication management strategies for the various network groups. Or at a more basic theory level, one might hypothesize that within network groups varying in structural features — for example, in internal density or connectivity or in the diversity of environmental linkage — different patterns of message content may be exchanged.

A third extension of the methodology, one we are currently exploring, is to use automated content analysis procedures. Once an appropriate program is selected and tested, the application of the present methodology could be extended to virtual real time application. To do this, all that would be required is for the user to read prior CMC messages into a file, select the segments for which separate analyses are desired, then call up the content analysis program and the multidimensional scaling program. At that point the statistical analysis would be complete. The user could observe the graphic and/or tabular results of the MDS on his or her terminal, perhaps select the AMG optimal message option and identify the optimal message, log back into the conference, and enter the message. After entering optimal messages for a time, the user could then repeat the analysis in the same way to see what effects the optimal messages have actually had on the overall concept space of the conference. A program called CATPAK™ (Woelfel & Holmes, 1982), developed after the current research was done, seems useful for such purposes.

Issues

The nature of the CMC evaluation methodology may raise some critical issues. One issue concerns the social control aspects of the optimal message applications. Some may view the techiques as too "Orwellian." Privacy per se, of course, is not technically an issue, provided that one applies the methodology as we have here to *public* conferences, not to private electronic mail. Still, some may feel that the analysis, selection, and entry of optimal messages is excessively manipulative. Nevertheless, a counter-argument can be raised that people naturally attempt to influence the course of their communication with others, regardless of whether it is face-to-face communication, telephone communication, computer communication, and so on. Attempting to influence the course of computer conferencing is qualitatively no different from influencing day-to-day communication as it has been occurring for millenia. Furthermore, people expect control to be exercised by their leaders, provided it is not excessive and in their best interests.

Nevertheless, such techniques could be made available to anyone who wished to use them in a conference. Yet some have informally suggested that this may result in "message wars" among communicators, each of whom is analyzing and entering optimal messages. While the images this suggests may be entertaining, message wars are unlikely to become day-to-day practice. One may expect that the degree of message-optimizing that might go on would be similar to what occurs for other kinds of communication within a particular social community. The basic personalities of people govern the overall contours of communication experiences.

All things considered, the method is merely a tool for measuring CMC, one tool in a large assortment. Its uses and implications depend fully on the research or evaluation stakeholders, their objectives, their applications in conjunction with other methods, and their results in achieving these objectives. In short, the method presented here is an enhanced set of procedures linking together several bodies of methods — network analysis, content analysis, and multidimensional scaling — in such a way that these are responsive and sensitive to CMC's special features.

REFERENCES

Christensen, W., & Suess, R. Hobbyist computerized bulletin board. *Byte,* November, 1978, pp. 150-157.

Danowski, J. A. An infographic model of media access for elderly advocate organizations. In P. A. Kerschner (Ed.), *Advocacy and age.* Los Angeles: University of Southern California Press, 1976.

Danowski, J. A. Group attitude uniformity and connectivity of organizational communication networks for production, innovation, and maintenance content. *Human Communication Research,* 1980, 299-308.

Hiltz, S. R., & Turoff, M. *Network nation: Human communication via computer.* Reading, MA: Addison-Wesley, 1978.

Kruscal, J. B., & Wish, M. *Multidimensional scaling.* Beverly Hills, CA: Sage, 1978.

Parnes, R. *The CONFER conferencing system.* Paper presented at the conference on Evaluating Computer Conferencing, Newark, New Jersey, 1980.

Rice, R. E., & Danowski, J. A. Issues in computer conferencing evaluation and research. In S. R. Hiltz and E. B. Kerr (Eds.), *Studies of computer mediated communication: A synthesis of findings.* Final Report in the National Science Foundation, NSF IST-801077, 1981.

Woelfel, J., & Fink, E. *The measurement of communication processes: Galileo theory and method.* New York: Academic Press, 1980.

Woelfel, J., & Holmes, R. *CATPAK™ demonstration.* Paper presented at the meeting of the International Communication Association, Boston, 1982.

/ HUMAN COMMUNICATION TECHNOLOGY

37 • Communication Networking in Computer-Conferencing Systems: A Longitudinal Study of Group Roles and System Structure

RONALD E. RICE

Annenberg School of Communications
University of Southern California

ORGANIZATIONAL communication is becoming increasingly facilitated by computers. Computer-mediated communication systems such as electronic mail, computer conferencing, automated offices, and the like (see Keen & Scott-Morton, 1978; Panko, 1980; Rice, Johnson, & Rogers, 1982) are becoming commonplace in businesses and research communities. Associated with these developments are a variety of policy and research issues, including (1) impacts and benefits, (2) fertile sources of communication data for researchers, and (3) the patterns of use and intercommunication among individual and group users. Each of these aspects is considered below.

RESEARCH ISSUES CONSIDERED

Social and Organizational Impacts
of Computer-Mediated Communication

A review of the prior research in this area is beyond the scope of this chapter; comprehensive reviews and overviews of impacts can easily be

AUTHOR'S NOTE: Partial support for preparation of the network data analyzed herein was provided by National Science Foundation Grant NSF-MCS-77-27813. Conclusions reported here are not necessarily those of NSF. I thank Dr. Roxanne Hiltz for her support and Dr. Peter Marsden for his advice.

Correspondence and requests for reprints: Ronald E. Rice, Annenberg School of Communications, University of Southern California, Los Angeles, CA 90007.

found in Bair (1979), Hiltz and Kerr (1981), Hiltz and Turoff (1978), Johansen (1977), Kling (1980), Moss (1981), Rice (1980a, 1980b, 1982), Rice and Case (1981), and Uhlig, Farber, and Bair (1979). The main points of much prior research are that these systems can be very appropriate for some kinds of communication tasks; that their impacts on organizational structure depend to a large extent on the organization's goals, management philosophy, and environment; that users typically increase their satisfaction and comfort with a system with increased use; that reported benefits are not necessarily due to increased use; and that organizational communication networks increase in size and span when facilitated by such systems. Of note here is simply that the potential benefits and impacts of using computer-mediated communications is an important concern for communication researchers, users, organizational managers, vendors, and system designers.

Analytical Opportunities from
Computer-Monitored Data

There are several distinct gains for evaluators and researchers in using the kinds of data accessible by a computer that can monitor the usage of the services it provides. Overviews of evaluations using computer-monitored data are available in Penniman and Dominick (1980), Rice and Danowski (1981), Rouse (1975), and Svoboda (1976). Only a few of these issues need be mentioned here.

In computer-messaging systems designed to collect such data, there is typically little or no response bias, and a full census of users is possible. Computer-monitored data are accurate, in that the data can consist of usage measures, who messaged whom, when, for how long, and so on, although content is usually inaccessible to protect the confidentiality of the user. (This is *not* to argue that such data are *complete* descriptions of the events analyzed.) This facility is quite important, considering the wealth of recent research indicating that, in general, respondents' reports of their communication activities diverge widely from their actual communication behavior as observed or monitored (see Berger & Roloff, 1980; Bernard, Killworth, & Sailer, 1980; Nisbett & Wilson, 1977; Shweder, 1980; among others). Although the controversy continues concerning the extent, form, and generalizability of these kinds of divergence, one recent study (Bernard et al., 1981) is very convincing. An experiment administered through the main computer of a computer-conferencing system asked users typical sociometric questions, and compared these data to the communication behavior recorded by the computer. The results not only reaffirmed the typical presence of large discrepancies between reported and actual communication behavior (in both forgetting and inventing recipients of messages), but also showed this discrepancy even in reports collected within minutes of a respondent's sending the message.

Another, related aspect of computer-monitored data is that these accurate census data allow us to investigate the communication networks of groups of users. Rogers and Kincaid (1981, p. 346) define communication networks as consisting of *relations* among "interconnected individuals who are linked by patterned flows of information." These networks embed organizations and user groups in their environments (Farace, Monge, & Russell, 1977; Katz & Kahn, 1966; Rogers & Agarwala-Rogers, 1976; Weick, 1969) and are, in fact, one picture of an organization's or group's structure. Finally, the servicing computer can capture extensive *longitudinal* network data so that researchers avoid the ungrounded assumption of much cross-sectional research that the system under study is at some equilibrium state.

Group Information Exchange and Network Roles in a System

This chapter is concerned primarily with a few specific questions at the analytical level of the multigroup network, concerning groups as they interrelate within the system. Not discussed here are a variety of questions and results at the individual or group-specific level.

In a computer-conferencing system involving formally constituted groups of geographically dispersed members, the nonverbal aspects of human communication are largely missing, so the emphasis in interaction shifts to the exchange of information. Flows of information into groups, out of groups, and within groups become important attributes of system and group structure.

As with Blau's (1977) exchange theory, group members who have low status attempt to provide information to and attract recognition of members of high status, thereby gaining increased status themselves. However, users of computer-mediated communication systems often are freer to search for those information exchanges that provide satisfactory resorces in return than they would be in tyical organizations or communication contexts. Users making initial searches must find rewarding reciprocal exchanges early on, or the time and energy in continual unreciprocated messaging will deplete their physchological and material resources. Indeed, individuals and groups that have early access to information may continue to "occupy" their information-rich or reciprocal positions and thereby function better or have more power than those who have later access to information flows within the system.

At the group level, whether a group is constituted to perform a task or is organized for more undirected reasons also plays a part in cross-group information exchanges. Members of a nontask group are freer to explore their informational environment, because their activities are not necessarily detractions from the group's sense of cohesiveness or interferences with an ongoing task; a group can prosper by "scouting" the environment for useful information. A task group, as a unit, on the other hand, is unlikely to interact with the wider system or environment as long as they are stable, because the task focuses internal group communication exchanges and cohesion.

From this brief overview of the information environment of groups within a computer-mediated communication system, the following analyses based on computer-monitored, accurate, longitudinal communication data will attempt to analyze group communication networks, to assess:

1. the information-based attributes that adequately describe the system-wide communication network;
2. the importance of reciprocity in cross-group networks;
3. the information-based network roles that groups occupy, and whether task orientation is a factor; and
4. longitudinal occupancy of these roles.

THE SYSTEM, USERS, AND DATA ANALYZED

The data represent the "private messaging" behavior of members of eight formal and two other "user groups" during twenty-four months on the Electronic Information Exchange (EIES) computer-conferencing system, sponsored by the National Science Foundation. The EIES system, history, user groups, and research context are described in several sources, including Bamford and Savin (1978), Hiltz (1981), Hiltz and Turoff (1978), and Rice (1980b). Only private messaging data are analyzed here. *Private Messages* (representing 70 percent of all items sent) can be sent to any individual or list of individuals, and confirmation of delivery is provided. There are alternate means of EIES communication, not discussed here.

The user consultants and the system monitor personnel were combined in the analysis to form analysis group zero ($N = 17$). This group consisted of experienced users who earned extra system time by providing help to other users, and of New Jersey Institute of Technology systems personnel who maintained and improved the system. Thus, this group was a "service" entity.

A *task* group is a group that has an explicit task to perform, with or without deadlines, around which the group organizes itself. A *nontask* group is a group that does not have an explicit task to perform, but rather is constituted to enable communication to happen; implicit or informal tasks may arise from this communication activity, but the group as a whole is not designed to perform these informal tasks. For our purposes, we classify groups 1 ($N = 45$), 5 ($N = 56$), 6 ($N = 25$), 7 ($N = 30$), and 8 ($N = 76$) as *task* groups, and groups 2 ($N = 32$), 3 ($N = 46$), and 4 ($N = 67$) as *nontask* groups, in order to explore differences in group communication structure based on the task/nontask distinction.

Group 9 comprised all those accounts of other (very small) groups, and unaffiliated separate individuals. Thus group 9 was not a formal EIES group, but can be taken to represent, loosely, a random collection of individuals that may be used as a control group against which behavior in formal EIES groups may be compared.

RESULTS

We consider two related aspects of system structure: what attributes of information flow best describe the system-level interaction of EIES groups and what information-based roles those groups occupy. We are also interested in changes in each of these aspects over time.

Method and Definitions for Analyzing System Structure

The role of a group can be defined in terms of outward and inward information flow, as well as flow strictly within the boundaries of the group. Group networks, then, are indicators of social structure based simply on information flows. In particular, we here use Marsden's (1981a, 1981b) definitions of network roles, as presented in Table 37.1.

We also utilize Marsden's (1981a, 1981b) GENMRG3D program to analyze the multigroup network. The program fits log-linear models of which information attributes characterize the system to an $I \times I \times 2$ (outflow by inflow by internal group communication flows for a system with I groups) contingency table with varying constraints in the fitting of the three-variable interaction term. Constraints are fitted by entering a "design matrix" that specifies into which "level" (much as in analysis of variance) of the design a given cell of the contingency table is placed. Then the models are tested against the data by means of an iterative proportional scaling algorithm.

This method has several distinct advantages over other network analysis methods for the purposes of the present analyses (see also Marsden, 1981a, 1981b): (1) Unlike network role characterizations as described by Burt (1978), Harary, Norman, and Cartwright (1965), or

Table 37.1
Possible Roles Based Upon Dimension of
Information Flow

Sign of Group's Modeled Parameters with Respect to
the Average Information Flow Values, Within a System,
for Dimensions of a Group's Flows:

In	Out	Roles Based on Two Dimensions*	Within	Roles Based on Three Dimensions*
+	+		+	1. Primary
		Carrier		
+	+		−	2. Broker
+	−		+	3. High-status clique
		Receiver		
+	−		−	4. Snob
−	+		+	5. Low-status clique
		Transmitter		
−	+		−	6. Sycophant
−	−		+	7. Isolate clique
		Isolate		
−	−		−	8. Isolates

Source. Marsden (1981a).

Richards and Rice (1982), Marsden's method allows for role distinctions based on all three dimensions of information flow. (2) Participation levels are defined probabilistically, relative to average information flow levels, and thus take into account the communication volume and size of both the system and its constituent groups. (3) The program can take into consideration the total amount of links possible. (i.e., two matrices are usually entered as data: one of actual communication links, and one of linkages absent; this last matrix is the difference between potential linkage amount within and across groups, and actual linkage amount). (4) Perhaps the method's most rigorous attribute is that roles defined are subject to statistical testing. That is, roles imposed by the method can be tested against the data for their adequacy rather than accepted arbitrarily. This ability is particularly necessary in light of Burt and Bittner's (1981) article, which emphasizes (1) how few studies have tested the fit of the roles analyzed, and (2) how analyses can be misleading, when, with complex data, several alternative role categorizations are possible but not tested against each other.

Thus this method allows for the detection and testing of group attributes: inflow, outflow, internal relations, and selected cross-group relations. The general model is:

$$\log([m(i, j, 1)] / [m(i, j, 2)]) = t + a(i) + b(j) + g(i, j)$$

where m is the maximum likelihood estimate using the "absent" link matrix (1) and the "actual" link matrix (2), "t is the unweighted conditional log-odds on the presence of a relation (based on the overall network communication volume), a(i) is the (above- or below-average) increment given that the potential sending actor is in category i, b(j) is the (above - or below-average) increment given that the potential receiving actor is in category j, and g(i, j) is an (above- or below-average) interaction effect of the log-odds given that the potential sending actor is in category i and the receiving actor is in category j" (Marsden, 1981a).

Several models will be tested for their utility in describing the information-flow-based role structure of the 10 EIES user groups, considered as a system, over 24 monthly periods. In the Independence model (2), only inputs and outputs are considered, not relations within or across particular groups. This model is used as the baseline explanatory model for tests of the following models. The Reciprocity model (3) tests the tendency of different pairs to communicate reciprocally, while within-group relations may differ across groups. The Constant Inbreeding model (4) tests the tendency for all groups to communicate within themselves equally while not making distinctions among outside groups. The Differential Inbreeding model (5) tests the tendency for all groups to communicate within themselves differentially, while treating out-groups the same. The Strict Reciprocity model (6) tests the tendency of different pairs of groups to communicate reciprocally, while within-group preferences are similar across groups.

A nonsignificant G square (i.e., the model "fits" the data) for model 2 or 4 establishes the validity of the fourfold role categorization of Table 37.1, while a nonsignificant G square for model 3, 5, and 6 establishes the validity of the eightfold role categorization (because groups under these three models have different in-group preferences). The general test is

$$G \text{ square} = 2(\times[i, j]*\log[\times(i, j)/m(i, j)])$$

distributed as the chi-square distribution. One can test the significance of the *difference* between a more general model and a less general model contained within the first model. Model 2 versus 3, 5, or 6 tests within-group or reciprocal effects over the independence model of no within-group or reciprocal effect. Model 4 versus 5 tests if there are within-group preferences that vary across groups, given equal out-group preferences. Model 4 versus 6 tests if there are reciprocal out-group preferences, given equal within-group preferences. Model 3 versus 5 tests for the tendency of groups to communicate reciprocally, over and above within-group preferences that vary across groups. Model 6 versus 3 tests for within-group preferences, given reciprocal out-group preferences.

The degrees of freedom used in these tests are shown in Table 37.2 (and thus will not be reported later). "I" is the number of EIES groups

Table 37.2
Degrees of Freedom Available for
Simple and Conditional Model Tests

Model	2	3	4	5	6
2	$(I-1)^2$	$\dfrac{I(I-1)}{2}$	1	1	$\dfrac{(I-2)(I-1)}{2}$
3		$\dfrac{(I-2)(I-1)}{2}$			
4			$I(I-2)$	$I-1$	$\dfrac{I(I-3)}{2}$
5		$\dfrac{I(I-3)}{2}$		I^2-3I+1	
6		$I-1$			$\dfrac{I(I-1)}{2}$

Note. Off-diagonals are degrees of freedom for the conditional tests of a column model over a row model; diagonals are degrees of freedom for simple model significance tests, where I is the number of groups in the system.

involved in the monthly analysis. Because some groups became part of the system in different months, or during some months had very little activity, each month's analysis will not necessarily contain all ten groups. Thus, Table 37.4, below, will not show results for every group in every month.

System Structure

The results from the simple and conditional model tests as shown in Table 37.3 are fairly straightforward and concern two issues: (1) How is EIES structure best characterized? That is, which attributes of information exchange are statistically significant aspects of how groups interact internally and externally in a given month? (2) How does this structural description change over time?

In month 2 we see that models 3, 5, and 6 complete as "best fits" to the data, all with nearly perfect fits to the data, each with a $p > .990$. If we had used only one of these models to test against the data, we would have a structural description that does not differ significantly from the data and thus would be valid.

But we can do better. It is clear that in the beginning of the EIES system life, reciprocal relations are important, but so are group differences. We are

Table 37.3
Summary of Simple and Conditional Model Tests

Mo.	Simple Tests: Model 2	3	4	5	6	Conditional Tests: Models 2-3	2-4	2-5	2-6	4-5	5-3	6-3	4-6
2	79[a]	2 .993[b]	76	7 .999	3 .999	77	2 .9	72	77	71	5 .89	.2 .999	76
3	241	28 .02	162	64	29 .1	213	79	178	213	98	36	.7 .999	133
4	417	8 .93	87	24 .74	9 .98	408	329	392	408	63	88	1 .983	78
5	949	38	275	126	38 .01	910	673	822	910	149	88	0 .999	237
6	1265	19 .25	239	128	19 .5	1246	1026	1137	1246	111	109	0 .999	220
7	1382	14 .5	235	88	15 .87	1368	1147	1295	1368	148	73	0 .999	221
8	866	13 .6	165	51	13 .89	853	701	816	853	114	38	0 .999	152
9	1214	7 .96	283	73	7 .999	1207	931	1141	1207	210	67	0 .999	276
10	886	14 .52	238	61	14 .85	872	648	825	872	177	47	0 .999	224
11	1036	32	288	127	32 .07	1005	749	909	1005	161	95	0 .999	256
12	1330	24 .6	636	149	26 .85	1305	694	1181	1304	487	124	2 .975	610
13	1795	15 .6	815	140	15 .8	1780	981	1656	1780	675	125	0 .999	800
15	1549	20 .80	782	138	20 .98	1529	767	1411	1529	644	118	0 .999	762
16	2068	36 .25	815	242	36 .47	2032	1252	1826	2032	574	205	0 .999	779
17	1979	28 .60	685	171	28 .8	1951	1294	1808	1951	514	143	0 .999	657
18	1864	30 .35	671	219	33 .6	1834	1193	1645	1831	452	189	3 .9	731
19	2188	19 .90	792	194	23 .95	2169	1397	1994	2165	596	175	4 .85	769
20	2045	13 .99	747	123	16 .995	2033	1299	1923	2029	634	110	3 .9	731
21	1750	18 .99	719	119	17 .999	1742	1041	1631	1733	600	119	0 .999	702
22	2144	16 .995	878	244	20 .999	2128	1267	1900	2124	634	228	4 .85	858
23	2968	20 .975	1183	201	24 .999	2948	1785	2767	2944	982	181	9 .5	1159
24	3352	15 .995	1049	207	19 .999	3337	2303	3145	3333	842	192	4 .95	1030
25	1007	15 .975	423	105	15 .995	991	584	902	992	318	90	0 .999	408

a. rounded G square
b. p levels (blank if < .001)

able to test to see which is a *better* structural description. If we test the model of reciprocity with group differences against the model of no reciprocity but with group differences (model 3 versus model 5), G square is 5, with $p > .89$. There is no significant difference between these structural descriptions. Thus, the significant fit of the reciprocity model with group differences is due solely to the group differences aspect of the model, when these two models are compared. But we test model 6 (strict reciprocity) against model 3 (reciprocity) and also find no significant improvement, indicating that the significant fit of model 6 is due solely to the reciprocity aspect of the model. For month 2, there are simply two equally satisfactory structural descriptions: group differences with no reciprocity, and reciprocity with no group differences.

We could turn to the test of model 4, with the baseline model 2, which, for the only month out of the twenty-four, shows no significant difference ($p > .9$), indicating that similar group preferences is *not* a valid attribute of the data. Because similar within-group preferences do not constitute a good descriptor of the data, and because model 6 includes this descriptor along with reciprocity, we can argue that model 5, differential inbreeding with no reciprocity, is actually the best description of the data for month 2. The major point of this ambiguous (or multiple!) result is that system structure is not yet "simple" or uniquely formed; i.e., there are several tendencies in the data for month 2. Our best statement is that reciprocity has not staked a claim as a clear attribute of systemwide interactions in the first month, but that differential group preferences have.

In month three, every model was significantly different from the data (model 6 has a $p < .1$, which is not very convincing). Even though model 6 is not a convincing fit, it is significantly better than model 3, indicating that the apparently significant aspect of group differences is actually an artifact of the strong reciprocity aspect. In any event, we can say that there was no significant system structure based on information flows as proposed by the various models for month 3.

The implication of this result, along with the result for month 2, is that there is unstructured information flow in the early stages of system development, due, hypothetically, to the lack of conclusions across the groups about satisfactoriness of any particular set of information exchanges. Groups are still seeking out relations.

In month 4, as in month 2, models 3, 5, and 6, all fit the data well and thus compete as characterizations of system structure. Here, however, model 3 (reciprocity) *is* significantly better than model 5 (differential inbreeding; G square is 88, $p < .001$), so we know that reciprocity is a valid descriptor of system structure. We can go further and say that only reciprocity, and not group differences, is the best descriptor of cross-group preferences. So, reciprocity has emerged as a significant aspect of system-wide interaction by month 4, but we are unsure whether group differences persist as a significant aspect.

But system stability has yet to emerge. Month 5 displays the same lack of structural description as did month 3, but here without even a hint of significance from model 6. Taken with the results from the first three months, this result emphasizes that structure is still emerging, as neither reciprocality nor group preferences has yet to become a clear-cut attribute of information exchange.

However, month 6 begins a string of five months of well-defined system structure, which seems to become more stable until month 10. In each of these months, models 3 and 6 are good fits to the data, indicating that reciprocity has emerged as an important factor in exchange relations among the EIES groups. As in every month, the additional descriptive power of model 3 over model 6 is not significant, indicating that group differences are not a strong aspect of system structure but reciprocity is. The decline in the fit of the two models in month 10 prophesizes the result for month 11, as the short stability in system structure ends.

Indeed, we see that the results for month 11 are the same as for month 3: no model is a good fit, although model 6 barely approaches such a fit. The implication here is that although structural stability emerged (in the sense that a model of network structure based on information flows achieved and maintained significant fit with the data) in months 6 through 9, stability declined in month 10 and degenerated into a lack of structure (as defined by the models) in month 11. The early satisfaction of the groups with the information exchanges in month 6 was not permanent. Four months was either not long enough to forge permanent information exchange relations, or four months was long enough for the majority of exchanges to enable the groups to perform their inter- and intragroup tasks, and then move on.

For the rest of the system's analyzed life, the description that held in months 6 through 9 served as a valid characterization of the EIES system-wide information interactions. The early months, then, are characterized by unstable system structure, as reciprocity, group differences, and combinations of the two compete among themselves as valid descriptions of the system while also dropping out altogether in several months as significant aspects of systemwide interaction. After the early instability, reciprocity emerges as a primary aspect of information exchanges, as hypothesized, except for some instabilities in months 10, 11, 16, and 18.

However, because both reciprocity models increase in fit, it is unclear whether groups *increase* their in-group preferences over time or *decrease* those preferences. The miniscule differences in the chi-square values

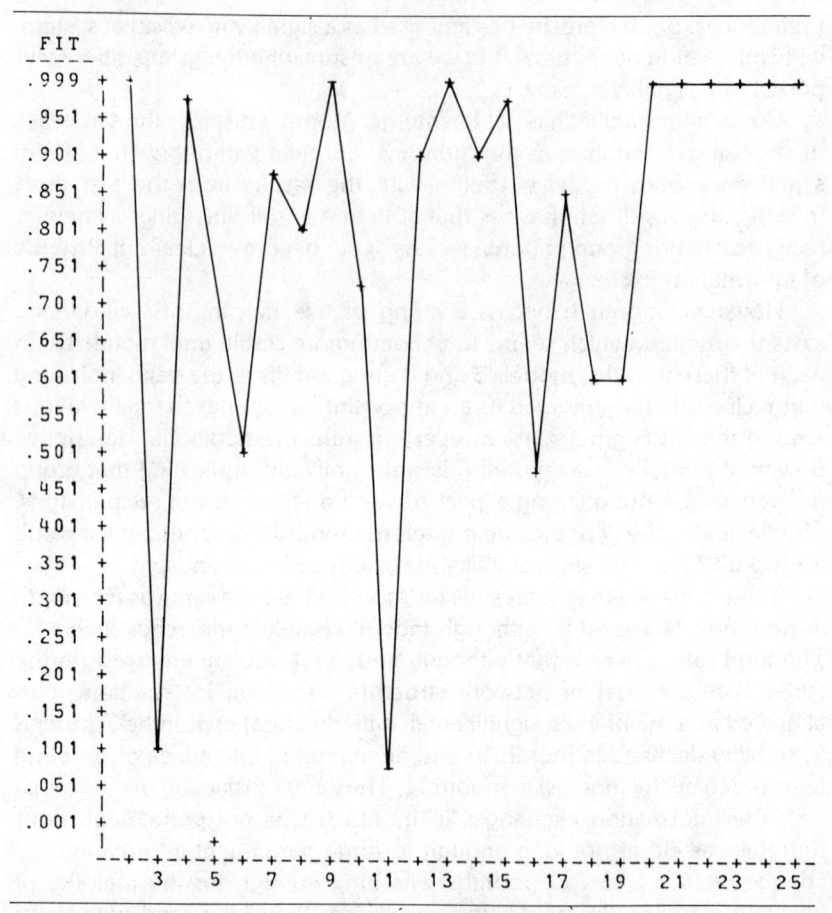

```
FIT
.999 +    +              +              +                   +--+--+--+--+
     |   /|             /|\            /|\                 /
.951 + / |            / | \          / | \               /
     |/  |           /  |  \        /  |  \             /
.901 +   |          /   |   +      /   |   \           /
     |   |         /    |    \    /    |    \         /
.851 +   |        /     |     \  /     |     \       /
     |   |       /      |      \/      |      \     /
.801 +   |      /       |      /       |       \   /
     |   |     /        |     /        |        \ /
.751 +   |    /         |    /         |         +
     |   |   /          |   /          |        /|
.701 +   |  /           |  +           |       / |
     |   | /            | /            |      /  |
.651 +   |/             |/             |     /   |
     |   +              +              |    /    |
.601 +                                 |   /     +--+--+
     |                                 |  /
.551 +                                 | /
     |                                 |/
.501 +           +                     +
     |          /|
.451 +         / |
     |        /  |
.401 +       /   |
     |      /    |
.351 +     /     |
     |    /      |
.301 +   /       |
     |  /        |
.251 + /         |
     |/          |
.201 +           |
     |           |
.151 +           |
     |           |
.101 +--+        +
     |
.051 +
     |
.001 +
     |   +
     --+--+--+--+--+--+--+--+--+--+--+--+--+--+--+--+--+--+--+--+--+--+--+--+
        3   5   7   9  11  13  15  17  19  21  23  25
```

Figure 37.1. Goodness of fit of strict reciprocity model by month. Higher *p* level indicates better fit of model to date.

between the models lead us to conclude that in-group preferences are the same. A visual portrayal of the increase in reciprocity as an attribute of systemwide relations appears in Figure 37.1, which shows the rise in the fit of model 6 to the data, over time.

Inspection of the residuals (a full discussion of this is beyond the scope of this chapter) resulting from the matching of the estimated cell frequencies of the strict reciprocity model to the actual cell frequencies reveals that the reciprocity models do a good job of describing the patterns of communication interaction among groups, and that any particular group relationships over and above those defined by model 6 emanate largely from the two special groups, 0 and 9. This is not too surprising, and no further consideration of residuals is necessary.

Computer-Conferencing Systems

Strong cross-group (the third dimension of information flow) parameters reveal which specific groups participated in reciprocal or unreciprocal exchanges. That analysis, beyond the scope of this chapter, showed a tendency of highly reciprocating groups (such as group 4) also to have higher average "success" scores as reported by their members (see Hiltz, 1981, p. 110).

Role Occupancy by Groups Within the EIES System

This section describes how each group is categorized into an information-based role, depending on the sign of the inward, outward, or within-group parameters that Marsden's program estimates.

Using the numbers for the various roles defined in Table 37.1, based on above- or below-average information flows as explained above, Table 37.4 portrays role occupancy of each EIES user group over twenty-four months.

As a brief aid to the reader, here we show how a group is characterized into one of the eight types of roles defined in Table 37.1, based on the three dimensions of information flow. The values for the parameters from the strict reciprocity model's computer output, for each dimension of flow (in-, out-, and within-group) are used to categorize each group (except as noted below). For example, in month 4, the inflow parameter for group 0 is 1.500, the outflow parameter is 2.559, and the within-group-choice parameter is .520. Thus, all three dimensions have positive parameter values, and from Table 37.1 we classify group 0 as a Primary Position, sending, receiving, and internally processing higher-than-average information flows. In addition, the inflow and outflow parameters are greater than 1.00, so we can say that group 0 is strongly defined on the inward and outward information flow parameters. As we see in Table 37.4, group 0 for month 4 is labeled 1I0, taking the 1 from Table 37.1 and capitalizing the I and O for the strong parameters.

In the EIES system, roles defined as "snobs" (role 4 in Table 37.1, greater-than-average receivers who do not communicate much internally or externally), "sychophants" (role 6, those who only communicate at above-average levels outwardly) or "isolates" (role 8, those who minimally communicate in any direction) were never occupied. Thus, below-average within-group information flows occurred only for groups that had above-average inward *and* outward flows. It seems as if a group with imbalanced inputs and outputs at least had to maintain a strong group preference; complementarily, only a rich information-based role (the "carrier" of Table 37.1) — occupied by groups 0 and 9 — was able to maintain weak within-group flows. The following paragraphs summarize longitudinal role occupancy for sets of similar groups.

Table 37.4
Role Occupancy of EIES User Groups Over Time

Month	EIES User Group 0	1**	2	3	4	5**	6**	7**	8**	9
* 2	1IO	7I W		3iO	1i W	7				2 o
3	2IO	7IOW	7	7 oW	7	7I W				2
4	1IO	7 OW	7I	3 W	7 o	7IOW				1I
* 5	1IO	7IO	7I	7 W	7I	7 OW				2I
6	1IO	7IOW	5IO	5	5 o	7IOW				1I
7	1IO	7IO	1 O	7I W	7	7IOW				2I W
8	1IO	7IO	7IoW	5	5I	7IOW				1I
9	1 O	7 OW	1i	7	5	7I W				3I
10	2IOw	7io	7	7I W	5 o	7IOW				1I
*11	1IO	7IOW	5	7	7	7I W				1Io
12	2IO		5 o	7IOW	7 o	7IOW	1I W	7IOW	1IO	1 W
13	2IO		1	7	7 o	7IOW	7IOW	7IOW	1	2I
14	2IO		1	7	7IO	7IOW	7IOW	7 W	1IO	2
15	2IO		1 o	7	3	7IOW	7	7IOW	7 W	2IO
16	1IO		1	1	7	7IOW	7 W	7IOW	7	1 W
17	1IOW		3	1 O	7	7IOW	7 W	7IOW	7	1 W
18	1IOW		1	1 O	7	7IOW	7i	7IOW	7 W	1 w
19	1IOW		7	1i	3i	7	7	7IOW	7	1
20	1IOW		1	1	7	7IOW	7i	7IOW	7IO	1
21	2IO	7	1IO	7 W	1	7 OW	7IOW	7IOW	7	1IO
22	2IO	7IOW	1	7 W	1	7 OW	7 W	7IOW	7IO	1
23	2IO	7IOW	1	1	1	1	7 W	7IOW	7	1IO
24	2I	7	1	1io	3	7I W	7IOW	7IOW	7	1
25	2IO		7IOW	7	7I	3	7	7	7	2IO

Note:
- I   i   input
- O (strongly)   o (weakly) defined   output parameter
- W   w   group

*Months when symmetry/reciprocity model did not show a significant fit, although it was significantly better than any other model. The eight-fold role typology is used for these months, even though it does not provide a significant fit to the data, for four reasons: 1) in each month, elements of the eight-fold typology still show conditionally improved fits; 2) in these months, of all groups, only groups 0 and 9 are differentiated when a four-fold typology would not differentiate them; 3) it is a useful heuristic to allow comparisons across months; and 4) roles are collapsed downward again for a pooled analysis (see Table 37.1).
**These groups are considered "task" groups.

User Consultants and the "Random" Group. Group 0 (the user consultants) began as a strong primary group (thirteen of the twenty-four weeks) but shifted over time to its role as a service, or broker, passing information in and out but not primarily within. Group 9 showed variance in role occupancy as it vacillated between primary and broker status, settling into its primary role by month 17. The shift to primary status possibly indicates that many of the "random" group members had been established members of EIES yet were free of group constraints, so they could pass information on to members of other groups of which they had become aware in their existence as "floaters" throughout EIES. Simultaneously, without allegiance to specific groups, they were able to communicate with other "floaters" who also had experience with EIES.

Nontask Groups. The three groups roughly categorized as nontask groups — groups 2, 3, and 4 — all showed a fair amount of variance in role occupancy, generally drifting from isolate or low-status cliques to primary or high-status cliques over time. The progression over time of these groups in and out of roles reveals a shift from groups preoccupied with internal relations only to groups that interact widely with their electronic environment. Group members begin to relate externally and establish reciprocal exchanges. The lack of a strongly motivating groupwide task (relative to task-based groups) not only allows group members to do this, but in fact forces them to do so if they are to continue as viable members of the system.

Task Groups. Task groups — groups 1 and 5 through 8 — on the other hand, continue to occupy the isolate clique role even if there is a slight tendency to enter the system in the primary role. These groups are task-bound, and to survive, their communication structure must be inward-focused. Because of the importance of the group's task orientation to role occupancy, it would be difficult to argue that the inability of these groups to remain in their initial primary position or to exit from their isolate status is indeed a sign of an early role-occupancy advantage by nontask groups. An additional clue as to the importance of a group's task orientation is provided by the fact that all the task groups remained almost totally in the isolate clique role, regardless of whether they entered EIES in month 2 or month 12.

Transitions in Network Role Occupancy

The groups are too few, and their role occupancy too consistent, to perform Markov analysis on their transitions from occupying a particular role in one month to occupying a particular role in the next month. For a brief and nonrigorous insight into general transition patterns, however, roles were collapsed across the third dimension to reduce the many empty transition cells. (Three of the four [+ or −] in-group parameter distinctions never occurred, and the three-dimensional role categorization is not justified in months 2, 5, and 11 anyway, because of the lack of fit of any model to the data in those months.) Under this reduced fourfold role typology (see Table 37.1), groups 0 (service) and 9 (random) are consistently information carriers; task groups generally remain isolate groups after perhaps a few periods as carriers or receivers, while nontask groups shift from isolate roles through transmitters to carriers or receivers. Transitions of groups from one of these four roles from month to month were then pooled over the twenty-four months, as shown in Table 37.5.

Table 37.5
Fourfold Rle Transition Probabilities

From Role	To Role Carrier	Receiver	Transmitter	Isolate	Totals
C	61 (a)	2	1	8	72
	.85 (b)	.03	.01	.08	
	.87 (c)	.29	.01	.04	
	.32 (d)	.01	.01	.04	
R	1	0	1	4	6
	.17	.00	.17	.66	
	.01	.00	.08	.04	
	.01	.00	.01	.02	
T	2	0	5	8	15
	.13	.00	.33	.53	
	.03	.00	.42	.08	
	.01	.00	.03	.04	
I	6	5	5	79	95
	.06	.05	.05	.83	
	.09	.71	.42	.80	
	.03	.03	.03	.42	
Totals	70	7	12	99	188

Note. Cells are (a) = cell frequency; (b) = proportion of outward transitions; (c) = proportion of inward transitions; (d) = proportion of all matrix transitions.
$\chi^2 = 133.47; p < .001$.

Table 37.5 shows that the most frequent transition was to remain an isolate (42 percent of all transitions). The next most frequent transition was to remain a carrier (32 percent). Remaining in either of the other two roles (receiver or transmitter) was infrquent (0.0 percent and 0.03 percent, respectively).

A group was most likely to become a receiver by first being an isolate (.71 transition rate) and most likely to become a transmitter by first being an isolate or a transmitter (.42); once either a receiver or a transmitter, the likely transition was to an isolate (.66, .53) where a group tended to remain (although a transmitter had some chance, .33, of maintaining its role). So there was a general overall trickle into the isolate role (total inward transition to outward rate is 1.04, while the rate for the carrier role is .97), with three (transmitter, receiver, and isolate) roles making transitions primarily into the isolate role but with slight intermediary transitions.

Thus, a group had a reasonable chance overall of occupying the information-rich "carrier" role but for practical purposes faced a struggle against systemwide tendencies, which drew most groups into the isolate role and kept them there. This general flow in role occupancy also represents a hierarchy of roles based on the amount and direction of information passing through a group. That hierarchy begins with the carrier role, moves down through the transmitter and then the receiver, and ends with the isolate.

To illustrate these relationships and critical transitions graphically, the pooled transition matrix of raw frequencies was first iteratively doubly standardized. The resultant matrix (with each row and each column summing to 1.00) was then clustered based on strong components. Links between i and j are added in the same order as the magnititude of transition frequency between the roles. A threshold value is the transition frequency at which two or more components are linked together into a larger component. Figure 37.2 presents the threshold values, critical links, and graphical clustering of the roles into components.

The cluster results repeat, in a different form, the verbal analysis above. The carrier role was the most difficult to which to make a transition from another role, as indicated by the very large gap between any other connecting threshold. The receiver role was clustered quite close to the isolate role but quite far from the transmitter role. Indeed, in this cluster analysis the transmitter role is closer to being joined with the carrier role than with the other two. Again this visual portrayal indicates a hierarchy of roles based on an active-passive scale of a group's information flow.

Considering this hierarchy with respect to reciprocity, it appears that a group does not become primarily a receiver by first transmitting a lot of information, but is motivated to become a transmitter by first receiving above-average levels of messages (when, of course, occupying either role does not lead directly to becoming an isolate, the likely outcome). A strongly transmitting group that escapes immediate isolate status clearly tends to continue transmitting, but this does not seem to generate above-average inward flows. There is a small (.13) tendency for a transmitting group to become a carrier. The upshot of these transitions is that to achieve an information-rich role, a group must (1) continue to exchange information in all directions, and (2) be aware that the other groups in the system must perceive the group as an appropriate receiver of above-average information flows.

SUMMARY

This chapter has reported on research results concerning the development of a communication network involving research groups as they

Component Nodes	Threshold	Critical Link
R, I	.424401	R —>I
R, T, I	.277514	T —>I
C, R, T, I	.222737	R —>C

Hierarchical Clustering Based Upon Critical Link Thresholds

```
Threshold:  41.2        39.3 //28.3      26.5      24.7      22.8
Role      ..+....+....+....+..//..+....+....+....+....+....+.

R     —+
      |——————————//——————+
I     —+
                         |——————————————————+
T     ———————————————//——————+              |
                                             |
C     ———————————————//——————————————————————+
```

Figure 37.2. Clustering of roles by transitions, with standardized threshold values and critical links. Scale attenuated between threshold values of 39 and 28.

communicate over a two-year period via a nationwide computer-conferencing system.

The major results of this analysis are summarized here. First three information flows — into a group, from a group, and within a group — along with the added constraint of reciprocal relations between pairs of groups, are significant attributes of the systemwide network structure. Second, this description of the network becomes quite stable over the twenty-four months, after some early vacillation. Third, the groups occupy well-defined information-based network roles, with task groups remaining isolates, nontask groups becoming information-rich, and the service/random groups remaining carriers or brokers of information.

There are implications for managers and users of such systems. Reciprocity among groups is an important attribute of communication, as users attempt to achieve stable, equal information exchanges. Nontask groups seem more likely to be able to change their role. While task groups seem less likely to transact with their environment. If the task group requires information from an unstable environment, the manager will need to support specific individuals "scouting" the environment. For a group to remain in an information-rich network role takes constant effort. Becoming a transmitter only or a receiver only is a sign of imminent isolation with respect to systemwide information exchanges. However, a leader of a task group in a stable environment may well *prefer* receiver or isolate status for the group, in order to focus exchanges within the group. Finally, evaluations of usage behaviors should not be based on early periods of use.

For researchers, one implication is that computer-monitored, accurate, longitudinal network data provide rich insights that are not likely forthcoming from cross-sectional self-report data. In addition, a new network analysis approach has been shown to be useful and rigorous in investigating multigroup networks. This method has revealed some of the principles of computer-mediated human communication networks.

REFERENCES

Bair, J. Communication in the office of the future: Where the real payoff may be. *Business Communications Review,* 1979, *9*(1), 3-11.

Bamford, H., & Savin, W. Electronic information exchange: The National Science Foundation's developing role. *Bulletin of the American Society for Information Science,* 1978, *18,* 12-13.

Berger, C., & Roloff, M. Social cognition, self-awareness and interpersonal communication. In B. Dervin & M. Voigt (Eds.), *Progress in communication sciences* (Vol. 2). Norwood, NJ: Ablex, 1980.

Bernard, H., Killworth, P., & Sailer, L. Informant accuracy in Social Network Data IV. *Social Networks,* 1980, *2,* 191-218.

Bernard, H., Killworth, P., & Sailer, L. *Informant accuracy in Social Network Data V.* Paper presented to the Sunbelt Social Networks Conference, Tampa, Florida, 1981.

Blau, P. *Inequality and heterogeneity: A primitive theory of social structure.* New York: Macmillan, 1977.

Burt, R. *Interests in a social topology: Foundation for a structural theory of action.* (Paper No. 8). Berkeley: University of California, Survey Research Center, 1978.

Burt, R., & Bittner, W. A note on inferences regarding network subgroups. *Social Networks,* 1981, *3,* 71-88.

Farace, R., Monge, P., & Russell, H. *Communicating and organizing.* Reading, MA: Addison-Wesley, 1977.

Harary, F., Norman R., & Cartwright, D. *Structural models.* New York: John Wiley, 1965.

Hiltz, S. R. *The impact of a computerized conferencing system on scientific research communities.* Final report to the Information Science and Technology Division, National Science Foundation (NSF-MCS-77-27813). East Orange, NJ: Upsala College, 1981.

Hiltz, S. R., & Kerr, E. *Studies of computer-mediated communications systems: A synthesis of the findings.* Final report to the Information Science and Technology Division, National Science Foundation (IST-8018077). East Orange, NJ: Upsala College, 1981.

Hiltz, S. R., & Turoff, M. *The network nation: Human communication via computer.* Reading, MA: Addison-Wesley, 1978.

Johansen, R. Social evaluations of teleconferencing. *Telecommunications Policy,* 1977, *1*(5), 395-415.

Katz, D., & Kahn, R. *The social psychology of organizations.* New York: John Wiley, 1966.

Keen, P., & Scott Morton, M. *Decision support systems.* Reading, MA: Addison-Wesley, 1978.

Kling, R. Social analyses of computing: Theoretical perspectives in recent empirical research. *Computing Surveys,* 1980, *12*(1), 61-110.

Marsden, P. Methods for the characterization of role structures in network analysis. In L. Freeman, & A. Romney (Eds.), *Research methods in social networks analysis.* Berkeley: University of California Press, 1981. (a)

Marsden, P. Models and methods for characterizing the structural parameters of groups. *Social Networks,* 1981, *3,* 1-27. (b)

Moss, M. (Ed.). *Telecommunications and productivity.* Reading, MA: Addison-Wesley, 1981.

Nisbett, R., & Wilson, T. Telling more than we can know: Verbal reports on mental processes. *Psychological Review,* 1977, *84,* 231-259.

Panko, R. The EMS revolution: A survey of electronic message systems. *Computerworld,* 1980, *14,* 34; 45-56.

Penniman, W., & Dominick, W. Monitoring and evaluation of on-line information system usage. *Information Processing and Management,* 1980, *116,* 17-35.

Rice, R. E. Computer conferencing. In M. Voigt & B. Dervin (Eds.), *Progress in communication sciences* (Vol. 2). Norwood, NJ: Ablex, 1980. (a)

Rice, R. E. The impacts of computer-mediated organizational and interpersonal communication. In M. Williams (Ed.), *Annual review of information science and technology* (Vol. 15). White Plains, NY: Knowledge Industry Publications, 1980. (b)

Rice, R. E. *Human communication networking in a teleconferencing environment.* Unpublished doctoral dissertation, Stanford University, 1982.

Rice, R. E., & Case, D. Electronic mail in the university. *American Society for Information Science Proceedings,* 1981, 228-230.

Rice, R. E., & Danowski, J. Issues in computer conferencing evaluation and research. In S. R. Hiltz, & E. Kerr (Eds.), *Studies of computer-mediated communications systems: A synthesis of the findings. Final report to the Information Science and Technology Division, National Science Foundation* (IST-8018077). East Orange, NJ: Upsala College, 1981.

Rice, R. E., Johnson, B., & Rogers, E. The introduction of new office technology. In J. Sutton (Ed.), *American Federation for Information Processing Societies Office Automation Conference Proceedings,* 1982.

Richards, W., Jr., & Rice, R. E. NEGOPY network analysis program. *Social Networks,* in press.

Rogers, E. M., & Agarwala-Rogers, R. *Communication and organizations.* New York: Macmillan, 1976.

Rogers, E. M., & Kincaid, L. *Communication network analysis.* New York: Macmillan, 1981.

Rouse, W. Design of man-computer interfaces for on-line interactive systems. *Proceedings of the IEEE,* 1975, *63*(6), 847-857.

Shweder, R. (Ed.). *New directions for methodology of behavioral science: Fallible judgment in behavioral research.* San Francisco: Jossey-Bass, 1980.

Svoboda, L. *Computer performance measurement and evaluation methods.* New York: Elsevier, 1976.

Uhlig, R., Farber, D., & Bair, J. *The office of the future: Communications and computers.* New York: Elsevier, 1979.

Weick, K. *The social psychology of organizing.* Reading, MA: Addison-Wesley, 1969.

AUTHOR INDEX

Abel, J. D., 558, 581
Abelman, R., 606, 609, 624, 626
Abelson, R. P., 330, 332, 336, 337, 357, 361, 390, 391, 760, 773
Abrahams, D., 387, 394
Abramson, T., 795, 810
Ackers, G., 810
Ackoff, R. K., 441, 442
Adamopoulos, J., 731, 733
Agarwala-Rogers, R., 927, 944
Ahammer, I. M., 624
Ajzen, I., 331, 332, 346, 351, 357-359, 365, 387, 392, 508, 514, 526
Akert, R. M., 77, 88
Albert, R., 731, 733
Albertson, L. A., 877-879, 882, 901
Albino, J. W., 38, 62
Albrecht, T. L., 833, 834, 846, 848, 893, 894, 902
Alfian, M., 538, 549
Algozzine, B., 827, 828
Alisky, M., 535, 536, 552
Alkema, F., 94, 115, 132
Allen, A., 168
Allen, J. H., 695, 719
Allen, R. L., 696, 697, 699, 701, 718, 719
Altman, I., 116, 118, 132, 135, 207-209, 211, 216, 218, 224, 225, 232, 233, 235, 238, 240-244, 249, 447, 453, 467, 470, 506, 517, 525, 526
Altman, S. A., 496, 503
Alvarez, K., 632, 650
Alwin, D. F., 696, 701, 712, 719, 720
Amara, R., 874, 902
Amato, P. R., 366, 393
Anatol, K. W. E., 629, 651
Anchor, K. N., 510, 515, 528
Andersen, J., 64, 82, 88, 137, 143, 168, 169, 793, 794, 798, 800, 808, 809
Andersen, P. A., 137, 168
Anderson, J. A., 442, 444, 555, 557, 581, 582, 606, 624, 625
Anderson, N. H., 115, 134, 364, 366, 391
Andrews, F. M., 717, 719
Applbaum, R. L., 629, 651
Applegate, J. L., 478, 484-488
April, C., 79, 89
Archer, D., 77, 79, 88, 91, 447, 467, 470, 471

Archer, R. L., 508, 514, 526, 527
Ardrey, M., 211, 244
Argyle, M., 64, 79, 88, 90, 94, 115, 116, 132, 218, 238-240, 242, 244, 676, 691
Argyris, C., 676, 691
Arntson, P. H., 141, 169, 207, 218, 247
Aronovitch, C., 876, 880, 903
Aronson, E., 317, 327, 364, 379, 386, 387, 391, 394
Arrow, K. J., 677, 691
Ashear, V., 814, 829
Assael, H., 629, 650
Atkin, C. K., 558, 581, 695, 720, 745, 758, 851, 872
Atkins, C., 419, 442
Attneave, F., 391, 495, 503
Atwood, R., 428, 430, 442, 534, 549, 606, 608-610, 624, 625
Auer, J. J., 289, 302
Ausubel, D. P., 44, 60
Avery, R. K., 58, 61, 557, 581
Ayres, J., 503, 893, 902

Baars, B. J., 58, 62
Babigan, J., 827, 829
Backlund, P. M., 166, 169
Baddeley, A., 67, 68, 74, 85, 88
Baer, D. L., 775-778, 788, 790
Bahr, S., 490, 505
Bair, J. H., 676, 692, 926, 943, 944
Baird, J. C., 368, 391
Bakeman, R., 495, 504
Baker, R. K., 694, 719
Bales, R. F., 104, 116, 120, 132
Ball, S. J., 694, 719
Ball-Rokeach, S., 699, 720
Bamford, H., 928, 943
Bandura, A., 338, 339, 340, 356, 357
Banister, M., 606, 608, 610, 625
Bank, S., 512, 527
Banks, C., 225, 246
Barber, B., 289, 302
Barbour, A., 166, 169
Barclay, A. M., 390, 394
Barclay, J. R., 43, 60
Barcus, F. E., 558, 563, 581
Barefoot, J. C., 880, 904
Barenboim, C., 476, 478, 486
Bargellini, P. L., 274, 286

945

Barna, B., 272, 273, 286
Barnett, G. A., 368, 373, 391, 394
Barnicott, E. F., 342, 361
Baron, R. A., 237, 247
Baron, R. S., 396, 416, 417
Barry, W., 490, 504
Barthes, R., 192, 198, 204
Bartlett, F. C., 336, 357
Bartos, O. J., 666, 673
Bates, J. E., 815, 829
Bateson, G., 426, 442, 489, 491, 504
Bauchner, J. E., 80, 88, 446, 448-450, 454, 455, 467-471
Bauer, C. A., 876, 884, 903
Bauer, C. L., 364, 365, 370, 390, 392
Bauer, R. A., 333, 357
Baum, A., 212, 237, 238, 240, 244
Baumgardner, M. H., 337, 359
Bayma, B., 508, 514, 526
Beach, W. A., 504
Beaty, M. J., 168
Beavin, J. H., 489, 491, 505, 656, 673, 676, 687, 692
Becker, J. F., 508, 514, 526
Becker, L. B., 698, 700, 720, 739, 750, 758, 781, 790
Beehr, T. A., 833, 835, 836, 849
Behnke, R. R., 168
Beighley, K. C., 84, 88
Bekey, I., 279, 280, 281, 286
Belitz, M., 272, 286
Belkaoui, J. M., 542, 549
Bell, D., 874, 902
Bell, R. Q., 815, 829
Bell, W., 366, 391
Beltran, L. R. S., 423, 442, 533, 549
Bem, D. J., 168, 326, 327, 331, 357, 422, 442
Benson, L., 556, 582
Bent, D. H., 619, 626, 842, 849
Berardo, F. M., 219, 244
Berelson, B., 319, 327
Berg, J. H., 508, 514, 526
Berg, K. R., 331, 357
Berger, C. R., 75, 88, 107, 108, 110, 111, 116, 117, 119, 122, 132, 333, 357, 926, 943
Berger, P., 374, 391, 675, 691
Bergsma, F., 543, 549
Berkowitz, L., 116, 132
Berky, F., 883, 904
Berlo, D. K., 173, 204, 419, 421, 442
Berlyne, D. E., 228, 244
Bernard, H., 926, 943
Bernard, J., 633, 650
Bernardin, H. J., 632, 650
Bernstein, B., 53, 60
Berscheid, E., 380, 390, 391, 394, 828, 829

Best, P., 490, 504
Bettinghaus, E. P., 120, 132, 334, 357
Bielby, W., 699, 718, 719
Biener, L., 368, 394
Billig, M., 396, 404, 416, 417
Bishop, J. E., 847, 848
Bishop, R., 542, 549
Bittner, W., 930, 943
Bitzer, L., 289, 302
Black, J. S., 331, 359
Blake, R. R., 630-632, 634, 635, 640, 647, 650
Blalock, B., 316, 327
Blalock, H. M., 95, 107, 108, 132
Blau, G., 846, 848
Blau, P., 927, 943
Block, C. E., 695, 719
Block, M., 851, 872
Blonstein, J. L., 251, 286
Blood, R. O., 556, 557, 581
Bloom, B. S., 792, 807-809
Bloomfield, L., 40, 60
Blum, Z. D., 698, 720
Blumer, H., 442, 473, 486
Blydenburgh, J. C., 775, 790
Bobrow, D. G., 337, 360
Bochner, A., 813, 814, 829
Bochner, S., 317, 327, 386, 391
Bogart, L., 695, 719, 776, 777, 790
Bolton, W. T., 555, 581, 585, 603
Bond, M. H., 237, 244
Bonoma, T. V., 340, 362, 630, 632, 633, 651
Boomer, D., 76, 88, 103, 132
Borgatta, E. F., 104, 132
Bormann, E. G., 333, 335, 357
Bositis, D. A., 775-778, 788, 790
Boster, F. J., 342, 355, 360, 397, 399-402, 415-417, 649, 651
Bostwick, L., 212, 213, 226, 227, 246
Bourhis, R., 38, 39, 61
Bower, G. H., 67, 89
Bower, R. T., 695, 719
Bowers, J. W., 36, 37, 41, 60, 242, 244, 655, 657, 673
Bowers, R. J., 396, 397, 417
Bowes, J., 606, 608, 610, 625
Bowles, D., 237, 244
Boyd, D. A., 538, 549
Bradac, J. J., 36, 37, 41 42, 60, 242, 244
Bradley, P. H., 38, 60
Brandt, C., 509, 514, 527
Brandt, D. R., 446-450, 454, 455, 463, 467-471
Bransford, J. D., 43, 60, 64, 75, 89
Breed, W., 851, 872
Brehm, J. W., 390, 394
Brembeck, W. L., 300, 302
Brent, E., 319, 320, 327

Author Index

Brewer, M. B., 386, 392, 508, 526
Bridger, H., 835, 848
Brislin, R. W., 728, 729, 731, 733
Broadcast Advertisers Reports, 864, 872
Brock, T. C., 334, 356, 360, 361, 380, 383, 392, 393
Broder, D., 316, 327
Brody, G. H., 563, 581
Brody, R., 319, 328
Brodzinsky, D., 814, 829
Bromley, D. B., 476, 487
Bronowski, J., 426, 442
Brookover, W., 792, 809
Brooks, W. D., 116, 125, 132
Brophy, J., 812, 815, 826, 829
Broverman, D. M., 450, 470
Broverman, I. K., 450, 470
Brown, B. B., 233, 235, 238, 249
Brown, B. R., 666, 673
Brown, J., 85, 89
Brown, J., 558, 582, 606, 625
Brown, M. B., 460, 470
Brown, P., 51, 52, 53, 60, 875, 883-889, 893, 894, 896-900, 902
Brown, R., 792, 798, 808, 809
Brown, R. G., 538, 549
Browne, L. A., 606, 626
Browning, L. D., 657, 673
Bruneau, T., 145, 168, 239, 244
Bruner, J. S., 37, 60, 306, 327, 340, 361, 426, 442
Bryan, C. R., 535, 536, 552
Buber, M., 189, 204
Buda, M. A., 235, 245
Buddenbaum, J. M., 699, 720
Bugental, D. E., 79, 89, 115, 132
Bukoff, A., 237, 245
Buller, D. B., 237, 239, 244
Bullis, C. B., 646, 650
Burdick, H., 108, 135
Burgess, P., 79, 88, 115, 132
Burgoon, J. K., 64, 70, 71, 78, 80, 89, 91, 93, 97, 98, 111, 132, 141, 168, 207, 218, 237, 239, 242, 244
Burgoon, M., 37, 60, 331, 334, 335, 357, 360
Burk, K., 84, 89
Burke, R. J., 629-632, 642, 650
Burleson, B. R., 476-479, 484-487
Burnstein, E., 396, 397, 417
Burt, R., 929, 930, 943
Business Week, 270, 271, 286
Buss, A. H., 143, 144, 155, 168
Buss, A. R., 333, 357
Buss, T. F., 608, 611, 625
Bybee, C. R., 606, 626
Byrne, D., 316, 327
Byrnes, D. L., 390, 394

Cacioppo, J. T., 324, 328, 332, 334, 356, 357, 360, 361, 383, 390, 392, 393
Calabrese, R. J., 75, 88, 107, 108, 116, 119, 122, 132
Calder, B. H., 724, 733
Calder, B. J., 891, 892, 902
Calhoun, J. B., 211, 217, 244
Cambra, R. E., 145, 168, 169
Camden, C. T., 58, 62
Cammann, C., 891, 903
Campbell, A., 737, 758
Campbell, D. E., 212, 232, 249
Campbell, D. T., 331, 357
Campbell, J. P., 874, 902
Campbell, K., 322, 324, 325, 327
Cantor, N., 815, 829
Cantril, H., 304, 329
Capage, J., 502, 504
Caplan, N., 701, 719
Cappella, J. N., 63, 89, 332, 358, 422, 442, 513, 516, 526, 607, 625
Carbone, T., 38, 60
Carey, J. W., 423, 442, 443
Carlsmith, J. M., 239, 245, 317, 326, 327
Carlsmith, M., 364, 387, 391
Carlston, D., 77, 90
Carpenter, C., 814, 829
Carr, L., 331, 358
Carroll, J. M., 228, 229, 244
Carter, L. F., 104, 132
Carter, R. F., 424, 442, 443, 624, 625
Cartwright, D., 929, 943
Case, D., 926, 944
Cassata, M., 584, 603
Cattell, R. B., 635, 650
Cegala, D. J., 654, 673
Certner, B. C., 508, 511, 526
Chaffee, S. H., 289, 302, 531, 538, 549, 552, 558, 563, 567, 581, 582, 695, 699, 701, 719, 736, 739, 746, 749, 750, 758, 759, 773, 777, 778, 790
Chaikin, A. L., 207, 208, 211, 226, 233, 237, 242, 244, 245, 506, 508, 509, 514, 526
Chance, J., 490, 505
Chapanis, A., 876, 877-882, 902, 903, 904
Chapin, F. S., 218, 219, 227, 244
Chapman, G. P., 544, 549
Charles, J., 542, 549
Charlesworth, R. 815, 816, 829
Charney, E. J., 239, 244
Chelune, G. J., 506, 511, 515, 518, 523, 526
Chemers, M. M., 235, 244
Cherniss, C., 836, 847, 848
Chipman, A., 93, 121, 124, 135
Choe, S. Y., 745, 758
Chomsky, N., 46, 59, 60

Christensen, W., 912, 924
Christians, C. G., 442, 443
Christie, B., 684, 689, 692, 876-879, 902
Christie, R., 416, 417
Chu, G., 538, 549
Civikly, J. M., 38, 62
Clark, C., 695, 719
Clark, E. V., 41, 60
Clark, H. H., 41, 60
Clark, R. A., 342, 358
Clark, R. D., III, 416, 417
Clarke, C. F. O., 229, 244
Clarke, P., 442, 443, 607, 625
Clarkson, F. E., 450, 470
Cleveland, W., 542, 554
Clevenger, T., Jr., 139, 140, 168
Cliff, N., 379, 392
Coates, J. F., 286
Cobbey, R. E., 696, 720
Cobbs, S., 834, 848
Cody, M. J., 58, 61, 341, 342, 344, 355, 358, 360, 366, 373, 394, 649, 651
Cohen, A. A., 71, 72, 89, 697, 720
Cohen, E., 308, 327
Cohen, J., 518, 519, 526
Cohen, J. B., 834, 849
Cohen, P., 486, 487
Cohen, S. B., 212, 249
Cohen, S. H., 390, 392
Cole, C., 490, 505
Cole, R. R., 542, 554
Coleman, G., 240, 247
Collett, P., 559, 561, 562, 581
Collins, A. M., 64, 89
Collins, B., 324, 328
Collins, K., 684, 691
Collins, W. A., 624, 625
Comadena, M. E., 446, 450, 471
Comer, R. J., 92, 133
Communication Studies Group, 678, 691
Communication, C., 968
Comstock, G., 694-696, 699, 719, 720, 746, 758
Conant, R. C., 424, 443
Condon, W. S., 120, 133
Conezio, J., 72, 91
Conklin, F., 489, 505
Conklin, K. R., 207, 208, 210, 211, 214, 244
Conlee, M. C., 365, 394
Constanzo, P., 323, 329
Converse, P. E., 737, 758
Cook, B. P., 331, 360
Cook, M., 109, 110, 134, 244
Cook, T. D., 364, 392
Cooley, R. E., 893, 894, 902
Coombs, F. S., 351, 359
Cooper, C. L., 237, 244, 847, 848
Coscarelli, W. C., 608, 626

Coser, L. A., 630, 651
Costello, D. E., 833, 849
Couch, A. S., 104, 133
Coulthard, R. M., 883, 893, 894, 904
Council of State Governments, 229, 244
Courtright, J. A., 36, 37, 60, 242, 244
Coward, R., 192, 204
Cowen, E. L., 827, 829
Cox, M. C., 646, 650
Cozby, P. C., 117, 118, 133, 506, 508, 511, 514, 526
Craig, R. T., 366, 392, 441, 443, 473, 487
Craik, F., 67, 70, 73, 74, 89
Cramond, J. K., 606, 625
Crano, W. D., 386, 392
Crawford, J. E., 835, 836, 849
Crocker, J., 332, 336, 337, 356, 362
Crockett, W. H., 476, 478, 487, 488
Cromwell, R. E., 490, 504
Cronen, V. E., 303, 333, 337, 338, 352, 356, 360
Crosswhite, F., 792, 809
Crotty, W. J., 775, 790
Crowne, D., 839, 848
Cummings, E., 584, 603
Cummings, H. W., 39, 61
Curan, T. J., 827, 828
Cusella, L. P., 441, 443
Cushman, D. P., 332, 338-340, 343, 356, 358, 423, 443, 473, 487, 560, 581

Dabbs, J. M., Jr., 495, 504, 509, 514, 527
Dahl, R. A., 302
Daley, M. R., 834, 844, 848
Dallinger, J., 138, 170
Dalto, D. A., 508, 514, 526
Daly, J. A., 137, 140, 142, 156, 168, 169
Danes, J. E., 373, 392
Daniels, T. D., 44, 61
Danowski, J. A., 906, 908, 922, 924, 926, 944
Dauses, M. A., 253, 286
Davis, D. E., 211, 244
Davis, D. K., 85, 91, 289, 290, 301, 303, 607, 624, 625, 736, 758
Davis, F., 122, 133
Davis, J. D., 508, 511, 512, 514, 515, 526
Davis, J. H., 885, 902
Davis, K., 721, 723-725, 727, 733
Davison, P. W., 536, 549
Davison, W. P., 333, 358
Dean, J., 218, 238-240, 244
de Cardona, E., 538, 549
Deci, E. L., 441, 443
De Fleur, M. L., 331, 345, 358, 362, 699, 720, 759, 773
DeFoe, J., 851, 872
DeForest, D., 508, 514, 526
DeFusco, P., 240, 247

Author Index

DeGrasse, R., 876, 881, 903
de la Zerda Flores, N., 38, 61
Deleuze, G., 192-195, 200, 201, 204, 205
Delia, J. G., 35, 61, 182, 205, 334, 356, 358, 473, 475, 476, 478, 479, 484-487
Denes, P. B., 64, 89
DeNubile, M., 308, 328
Denzin, N. K., 577, 581
DePaulo, B. M., 446, 449-451, 470, 471
Derlega, V. J., 207, 208, 211, 226, 233, 237, 242, 244, 245, 506, 508, 509, 514, 526
Dertouzos, M. L., 901, 902
Dervin, B., 422, 428, 430, 441-443, 531, 534, 549, 606, 608-610, 624, 625, 695, 720
Desor, J. A., 211, 212, 217, 245
Deturck, M. A., 237, 239, 244
Detweiler, R. A., 727, 728, 730, 732, 733
Deutsch, K. W., 543, 547, 549, 550, 553
Deutsch, M., 368, 394, 630, 651
Devoe, S., 97, 98, 135
Devries, R., 485, 487
Dewey, J., 25, 26, 33, 188, 189, 204, 426, 443
Dibner, A. S., 94, 133
Dick, W., 356, 358
Diehl, C. F., 84, 89
DiMatteo, M. R., 79, 91, 447, 467, 470, 471
Dimmick, J. W., 555, 581, 585, 603
Dindia, K. A., 518, 519, 526
Dinh, T. V., 535, 550
Dion, K. K., 509, 514, 527, 828, 829
Dion, K. L., 396, 416, 417, 509, 514, 527
Disbrow, J., 430, 443, 607, 625
Disher, J. H., 276, 278, 286
Dittmann, A. T., 76, 89
Divine, R., 319, 327
Dixon, W. J., 460, 470
Dizard, W. P., 535, 536, 550
Dollard, J., 518, 527
Dominick, J. R., 624, 625
Dominick, W., 926, 944
Donnelly, F. A., 808, 810
Donohew, L., 540, 550
Donohue, G. A., 543, 550, 607, 625, 626
Donohue, T. R., 606, 607, 624-626
Dosey, M. A., 211, 212, 226, 245
Dossett, D. L., 731, 734
Douglas, D., 777, 778, 790
Dowaliby, F. J., 795, 809
Downs, A. C., 815, 828, 829
Downs, C. W., 654, 673
Drecksel, G., 504
Duchastel, P. C., 795, 810
Dulany, D. E., 340, 358
Duncan, B. L., 727, 729, 733
Duncan, S., Jr., 239, 245

Duncanson, J. P., 876-879, 881, 902
Dunkelschetter, C., 507, 510, 511, 528
Dutton, J. M., 629, 644, 651, 652

Eagly, A. H., 312, 327, 333-335, 358
Eakins, B., 813, 829
Eakins, R., 813, 829
Eastland, T. A., 277, 286
Eastman, H. A., 608, 611, 625
Ebbesen, E. B., 237, 246, 323, 329, 396, 397, 417
Ebbinghaus, H., 336, 358, 382, 392
Ebersole, P., 509, 514, 527
Eco, U., 197, 204
Edelson, B. I., 276, 278, 286
Edelstein, A. S., 442, 443, 607, 625
Edney, J. J., 211, 215, 234, 235, 239, 245
Ehrenhaus, P., 726, 733
Ehrlich, H. J., 331, 358
Ehrlich, J. H., 509, 514, 527
Eibl-Eibesfeldt, I., 239, 245
Eichelman, W., 211, 225, 245
Eisenstadt, S. N., 539, 550
Eiser, J., 317, 319, 327
Ekman, P., 73, 89, 93, 98-103, 111, 120, 121, 133, 239, 245, 446-448, 458, 470, 729, 733
Elliot, S, M., 794, 809
Ellis, D. G., 58, 61, 491, 492, 494, 504
Ellis, J., 192, 204
Ellsworth, P., 239, 245
Elman, D., 237, 245
Emery, D., 493, 504
Emery, W. B., 535, 536, 550
Emmert, P., 116, 125, 132
Engler, N., 274, 286
Erickson, F., 239, 245
Ericson, P. M., 504
Ernst, M. L., 229, 245
Ertle, C. D., 168
Esser, A. H., 211, 212, 236, 243, 245
Evans, G. W., 211, 225, 237, 245
Evans, J. F., 510, 514, 528, 777, 790
Eveslage, T., 851, 872
Eysenck, H. J., 208, 245, 416, 417
Eysenck, M. W., 67, 89
Eysenck, S. B. J., 208, 245

Fagen, P., 538, 550
Fagen, R. R., 539, 550
Fagot, B., 812, 815, 826, 829
Fairbanks, G., 84, 89
Farace, R. V., 491, 492, 494, 505, 540, 550, 649, 652, 893, 904, 927, 943
Farber, D. J., 676, 692, 926, 944
Farrell, T. B., 58, 61
Fay, P. J., 446, 471
Fazio, R. H., 331, 358, 361
Featheringham, T. R., 877-879, 902

Feffer, M., 473, 487
Feigenbaum, W. M., 509, 514, 527
Feinman, S., 815, 826, 829
Fejes, F., 538, 550
Feldman, M. S., 676, 691
Feldman, S., 719, 720
Felipe, N., 237, 238, 245
Ferguson, J. A., 876-879, 902
Ferguson, L., 93, 121, 124, 135
Ferris, S. E., 115, 134
Ferris, S. R., 79, 90
Feshbach, N., 812, 829
Festinger, L., 108, 133, 225, 245, 326, 327, 331, 358, 364, 365, 392, 759, 773
Fiedleer, F., 731, 733, 734
Fields, J., 759, 773
Fink, E. L., 364-368, 370, 378, 380, 382, 387, 390, 392, 394, 911, 921, 924
Finn, T. A., 851, 854, 872
Firestone, I. J., 211, 240, 243, 246
Fishbein, J., 365, 387, 392
Fishbein, M., 331, 332, 339, 346, 351, 357-359
Fisher, B. A., 35, 61, 504
Fisher, J. Y., 633, 652
Fiske, S., 723, 724, 734
Fitzpatrick, M. A., 342, 359, 490, 504, 813, 814, 829
Flanders, J. P., 416, 417
Flannigam, R. R., 875, 902
Flavell, J. H., 473, 485, 487
Flay, B. R., 364, 392
Flexser, A., 70, 82, 90
Foa, U. G., 104, 133
Folger, J. P., 63, 73, 74, 83, 89, 91, 332, 358, 655, 673, 883, 904
Folkman, S., 834, 849
Fontes, N. E., 122, 133, 448-450, 454, 455, 467-469, 471
Ford, M. E., 475, 484, 487
Forgas, J. P., 342, 359
Forlano, G., 307, 328
Fortune, 274, 286
Foss, C., 233, 235, 238, 249
Foucault, M., 192, 194-197, 204
Foulke, E., 84, 90
Fowler, G. D., 877-882, 902
Fox, M. N., 115, 132
Franks, J. J., 43, 60
Fraser, C., 51, 52, 53, 60, 396, 404, 416, 417
Freedman, N., 73, 90
Freeman, S. J. J., 834, 849
Freidson, E., 555, 581
Fremouw, W. J., 162, 169
French, J. R. P., 398, 417, 834, 848
Frentz, T. S., 58, 61

Freshley, D. L., 629, 651
Freudenberger, H., 834, 848
Frey, F. W., 540, 550
Friedman, M., 275, 286
Friedman, R., 237, 246, 509, 514, 527
Friedrich, G. W., 807-809
Friedrich, L. K., 624, 626
Friesen, W. V., 73, 89, 93, 98-103, 111, 120, 121, 133, 446-448, 458, 470
Frijda, N. H., 102, 133
Fromm-Reichmann, F., 108, 133
Frost, J. H., 630, 651
Frutkin, A. W., 253, 286
Fry, D. L., 559, 581
Fujimoto, E. K., 94, 95, 133
Funder, D. C., 168
Furman, G., 509, 514, 526

Gabel, H., 510, 515, 528
Gabriel, M., 606, 608, 610, 625
Gadamer, H. G., 188, 191, 204
Gaes, G. G., 340, 359
Galanter, E., 332, 333, 336, 337, 360
Galloway, E., 253, 286
Galtung, J., 543, 550
Galzer, J. A., 815, 816, 829
Gardner, H., 607, 626
Garrison, J. P., 137, 168
Garrow, D., 315, 327
Garry, S. L., 760, 773
Gary, A. L., 120, 135, 509, 510, 511, 514, 527, 528
Garzona, C., 606, 608-610, 624, 625
Geertz, C., 31, 33
Gehring, R. E., 72, 90
Geis, F. L., 416, 417
Geizer, R. A., 446, 462, 471
Gelfand, D., 815, 829
Geller, J., 97, 98, 135
George, A., 536, 549
Gerard, H., 725, 734
Gerard, M., 251, 287
Gerbner, G., 537, 542, 550, 746, 758
Gerety, T., 229, 245
Gergen, K. J., 509, 514, 527
Geva, N., 337, 359
Giddens, A., 204
Giffard, A. C., 538, 550
Gilchrist, J. A., 657, 658, 673
Giles, H., 38, 39, 54, 61
Gilkinson, H., 139, 148, 169
Gillespie, J. V., 540, 550
Gillham, J. R., 366, 373, 394
Gilmour, R., 94, 115, 132
Ginsburg, H. J., 237, 245
Glaser, B., 107, 133, 442, 443, 657, 658, 673

Author Index

Glass, D.C., 214, 245
Glover, T.W., 504
Goddard, J.B., 676, 691
Goffman, E., 92, 117, 121, 133, 218, 226, 233-235, 239, 241, 245, 423, 443, 656, 664, 673, 884, 885, 893, 902
Gold, C., 75, 91
Golden, D.A., 258, 259, 287
Golden, M., 827, 830
Goldhaber, G.M., 629, 651
Goldman, H., 556, 581
Goldmark, P.C., 676, 691
Gonso, J., 816, 829
Good, T.L., 812, 815, 826, 829
Goodstein, L.D., 511, 527
Goodwin, C.J., 276, 278, 287
Gorsuch, R.L., 799, 810
Goss, B., 39, 61
Gottman, J.M., 447, 470, 471, 512, 527, 816, 829
Gouge, C., 396, 404, 416, 417
Gouldner, A.W., 116, 133
Graeven, D.B., 509, 514, 527
Graham, A., 64, 90
Granberg, D., 307, 313, 319, 320, 322, 324, 325, 327, 328
Grandi, R., 536, 550
Graney, E.E., 584, 603
Graney, M.J., 584, 603
Green, B.F., 331, 359
Greenberg, B.S., 441, 443, 606, 625, 695, 720
Greenberg, C.I., 211, 212, 238, 240, 244, 246
Greenberg, D.F., 375, 392
Greenwald, A.G., 331, 334, 359
Gregory, M.J., 58, 61
Grey, J., 251, 287
Grice, H.P., 49, 61
Gross, L., 746, 758
Grossberg, L., 171, 172, 182, 189, 192, 196, 203, 204
Grouws, D., 812, 829
Gruenhagen, R.H., 777, 790
Gruner, C.R., 300, 302
Grunig, J.E., 430, 443, 607, 624-626
Guattari, D., 192-195, 200, 201, 204, 205
Guback, T., 543, 544, 550
Gudykunst, W.B., 607, 626
Guild, P.D., 880, 904
Gunter, J., 531, 550
Gurevitch, M., 555, 582
Guttman, N., 84, 89

Haber, R.N., 72, 91
Haberman, R., 375, 392

Habermas, J., 423, 443
Hachten, W.A., 535, 536, 538, 550
Hagerty, N., 356, 358
Haggard, E.A., 512, 527
Haight, L., 422, 443
Hailey, J.L., 156, 168
Hale, C.L., 475, 479, 484, 487
Hale, J.L., 237, 239, 242, 244, 397, 399-402, 415-417
Hall, E., 606, 608, 610, 625
Hall, E.T., 211, 212, 220, 233, 237, 246, 730, 733
Hall, J., 630, 634, 651
Hall, J.A., 79, 91, 447, 450, 451, 467, 470, 471
Hall, S., 22, 33
Halliday, M.A.K., 48, 49, 55, 57, 61
Halloran, J.D., 531, 534, 550
Hamblin, R.L., 368, 392
Hammond, R., 509, 514, 527
Hanell, S., 287
Haney, C., 225, 246
Hanley, T.D., 38, 62
Hansford, B.C., 145, 169
Hanson, L.R., 724, 733
Harary, F., 929, 943
Harkins, A.M., 875, 902
Harlock, S., 606, 608-610, 624, 625
Harper, N., 291, 292, 295, 302
Harper, R.G., 78, 90
Harre, R., 333, 359, 559, 568, 581, 657, 673
Harris, M.S., 508, 514, 526
Harris, W., 319, 327
Harrison, R.P., 71, 89, 93, 111, 133
Hart, J., 542, 550
Harte, T.B., 291, 295, 297, 299, 302
Hartup, W.W., 815, 816, 829
Harvey, O., 305, 322, 323, 324, 328
Hasan, R., 48, 49, 55, 57, 61
Hass, R.G., 364, 392
Hastie, R., 75, 77, 90, 336, 356, 359
Hastorf, A., 93, 94, 106, 122, 124, 134
Hattie, J.A., 145, 169
Havighurst, R.J., 584, 603
Hawes, L.C., 58, 61, 182, 204, 893, 898, 902
Hawkins, R., 546, 547, 553
Hayduk, L.A., 237, 238, 240, 246
Hayes, D.P., 146, 169
Haynes, R.B., 607, 625
Head, S.W., 535, 536, 540, 550
Heape, C., 142, 143, 170
Heberlein, T.A., 331, 359
Heckhausen, H., 795, 809
Hedl, J.J., 795, 809
Heidegger, M., 30, 33, 190, 191, 196, 204

Heider, F., 107, 133, 320, 326, 328, 364, 366, 367, 392, 721, 726, 732, 733
Hein, G., 274, 286
Heise, D. R., 95, 107, 133
Heise, G. A., 64, 90
Helson, H., 307, 328
Henderson, A. T., 251, 287
Henderson, M. M., 901, 902
Henery, W. E., 584, 603
Henley, N. M., 237, 239, 246, 450, 471, 813, 814, 829
Henning, J. H., 139, 169
Henson, A., 239, 245
Herman, C. P., 333, 359
Herndon, J., 508, 514, 526
Herrod, S. L., 646, 650
Hess, R. D., 556, 581
Hester, A., 542, 543, 550, 551
Heston, J., 380, 392
Hetherington, E., 814, 830
Hewes, D. E., 63, 66, 75, 87, 90, 91, 332, 359, 422, 443
Hewgill, M. A., 331, 360
Hexamer, A., 606, 609, 624, 626
Hiemstra, G. E., 899, 902
Higgins, E. T., 333, 359
Hill, A., 268, 287
Hill, C. T., 507, 510, 511, 528
Hill, R. J., 331, 362
Hillman, R., 440, 443
Hilton, J., 875, 899, 902
Hiltz, S. R., 876-882, 885, 900-902, 912, 924, 926, 928, 937, 943
Himmelfarb, S., 333-335, 358, 364, 392
Hinckley, E., 307, 308, 328
Ho, E., 64, 82, 91
Hockett, C., 59, 61
Hocking, J. E., 446-450, 454, 455, 463, 467-471
Hodges, W. F., 794, 809
Hoecker, D. G., 880, 904
Hoffman, R., 834, 849
Hofstetter, C. R., 608, 611, 625
Holloway, S., 876, 902
Holman, P. A., 351, 359
Holmes, R., 366, 373, 394, 923, 924
Holsti, O. R., 611, 626
Holt, R. T., 540, 551
Homans, G. C., 117, 133
Homet, R. S., Jr., 287
Hope, M. L., 237, 245
Hopkins, M. W., 536, 551
Hopper, R., 38, 55, 59, 61
Horney, K., 638, 651
Hornik, N. A., 351, 359
House, J. S., 833-835, 848, 849
House, R. J., 629, 651

Hovland, C. I., 304, 305, 308, 310, 311, 319, 323, 328, 329, 330, 332, 359, 776, 777, 790
Howard, R. B., 237, 245
Howell, W. J., 538, 551
Hudson, H. E., 287
Hughes, H., 777, 778, 790
Hulin, C., 839, 849, 874, 876, 901, 903
Hull, C. H., 619, 626, 842, 849
Hume, D., 332, 359
Hunter, J. E., 365, 370, 373, 390, 392, 393, 397, 399-402, 415-417
Hur, K. K., 547, 551
Hurlock, E. B., 584, 603
Hurt, H. T., 807, 809
Huseman, R. C., 300, 302, 629, 651
Husson, W. H., 624, 626
Huston-Stein, A., 814, 829
Hyde, T. S., 67, 90
Hyman, H., 778, 781, 790
Hymes, D. H., 875, 884, 888, 889, 892-894, 896, 903

Infante, D. A., 332, 359, 633, 652
Inkleles, A., 535, 551
Insko, C. A., 317, 327, 386, 391, 724, 733
International Telecommunication Union, 254, 287
Irey, K. V., 833, 834, 846, 848
Israelski, E. W., 876-879, 903
Ittelson, W. H., 207, 209, 216, 248
Iwao, S., 551
Izard, C. E., 102, 133, 468, 471
Izcaray, F., 538, 552
Izumi, K., 234, 246
Izzo, L. D., 827, 829

Jaccard, J., 140, 168, 169, 331-335, 359
Jacklin, C. N., 450, 471, 813, 814, 830
Jackman, N., 305, 329
Jackson, D. D., 489, 491, 505, 561, 563, 581, 656, 673, 676, 687, 692
Jackson, S. E., 49, 58, 61, 834, 837, 839, 848, 849
Jacobs, S., 49, 58, 61
Jacobson, T., 606, 608-610, 624, 625
Jaffe, P. E., 509, 514, 527
Jamieson, D. W., 649, 651
Janis, I. L., 330, 332, 359
Janson, E., 777, 790
Janus, N. Z., 537, 538, 544, 551, 552
Janzen, J., 446, 471
Jefferson, G., 49, 50, 61, 62
Jefferson, L., 320, 327
Jellison, J. M., 380, 393, 842, 849
Jenkins, J. G., 619, 626
Jenkins, J. J., 67, 90

Author Index

Jenks, R., 319, 327
Jennings, M. K., 751, 758
Jick, T., 846, 848
Jick, T. D., 896, 903
Johansen, R., 267, 287, 684, 691, 876, 881-882, 901, 903, 904, 926, 943
Johnson, B., 925, 944
Johnson, C. A., 223, 246
Johnson, C. F., 509, 514, 527
Johnson, K., 876, 880, 903
Johnson, M. K., 64, 75, 89
Johnson, M. P., 759, 774
Johnson, T. W., 629, 651
Johnson-Laird, P., 63, 90
Jones, C., 320, 328
Jones, E. E., 107, 108, 133, 527, 721, 723-725, 727, 733
Jones, L. E., 366, 392
Jones, S. B., 80, 89
Jones, T. S., 629, 651
Jordan, W. J., 342, 358
Joreskog, K. G., 706, 720
Jorgenson, R., 546, 551
Joseph, E. C., 875, 902
Jourard, S, M., 116, 118, 133, 207, 208, 224, 226, 227, 237, 242, 246, 506, 507, 509, 511, 512, 514, 527
Jussawalla, M., 545, 551

Kac, M., 366, 392
Kader, S, A., 251, 287
Kafry, D. K., 832, 849
Kahn, G. M., 120, 135, 510, 511, 514, 528
Kahn, R. L., 629, 630, 651, 833-835, 848, 849, 927, 943
Kahneman, D., 228, 246, 725, 727, 734
Kaiser, J., 287
Kalle, R. J., 340, 359
Kaluger, G., 583, 603
Kaluger, M. F., 583, 603
Kaminski, E. P., 122, 133, 446, 448-450, 454, 455, 467-471
Kane, M. J., 58, 61
Kanner, A., 834, 849
Kanner, A. D., 832, 849
Kanouse, D. E., 107, 108, 133, 724, 733
Kaplan, A., 428, 443
Kaplan, B., 212, 249
Kaplan, E. A., 80, 88
Kaplan, F. L., 542, 551
Kaplan, K. J., 508, 514, 526
Kaplan, L., 812, 829
Kaplowitz, S. A., 364, 365, 370, 380, 382, 387, 390, 392
Karlin, A. L., 546, 551
Karlin, M. B., 67, 89
Karnchanapee, K., 851, 872

Kartus, S., 237, 248
Kaswan, J. W., 79, 89, 115, 132
Katz, D., 339, 340, 359, 629, 630, 651, 833, 834, 849, 927, 943
Katz, E., 534, 535, 538, 544, 545, 547, 551
Katz, J. J., 42, 61
Katzman, N., 695, 699, 719, 746, 758
Kearney, P. K., 795, 810
Keefe, C., 291, 295, 297, 299, 302
Keen, P., 925, 943
Keenan, E., 826, 829
Keller, B., 815, 829
Kelley, H. H., 107, 108, 117, 133, 135, 330, 332, 359, 467, 471, 723-725, 728, 733, 734
Kelly, E., 812, 829
Kelly, G. A., 356, 359, 475, 487
Kelly, M., 326, 329
Kelly, M. J., 876-880, 903
Kelman, H., 380, 392
Kelvin, P., 207, 208, 217, 222, 223, 226, 227, 246
Kelz, J. W., 93, 94, 107, 122, 134
Kendall, L., 839, 849
Kendon, A., 76, 90, 116, 120, 132, 133
Kennamer, J. D., 739, 758
Kennedy, R., 319, 328
Kenney, C. T., 478, 487
Keppel, G., 127, 133
Kerner Commission, 695, 720
Kerr, E., 926, 943
Kessel, F. S., 485, 487
Kessen, W., 366, 393
Kiesler, C., 324, 328, 331, 360
Killworth, P., 926, 943
Kilmann, R. H., 630, 632, 634, 639, 640, 651, 652
Kimble, G. A., 72, 82, 90
Kincaid, L., 927, 944
Kinder, D., 319, 320, 328
King, M., 319, 320, 327, 328
Kira, A., 214, 227, 234, 238, 246
Kirsch, W., 676, 691
Kirsner, K., 68, 90
Kleck, R., 93, 94, 106, 107, 122, 124, 133, 134
Klein, H., 676, 691
Klein, R. H., 142, 143, 170
Kliejunas, P., 331, 345, 361
Kline, F. G., 442, 443, 607, 625
Kline, S. L., 476, 478, 479, 485, 487
Kling, R., 926, 943
Klopf, D. W., 145, 168, 169
Kluegel, J. R., 706, 720
Knapp, M. L., 55, 61, 78, 90, 446, 450, 467, 471

Knapp, M. R., 584, 603
Knowles, E. S., 218, 237, 238, 246, 248, 396, 417
Kochen, M., 877-879, 882, 903
Koehler, J. W., 629, 651
Kogan, N., 395, 417
Kohen, J. A., 509, 511, 513, 524, 527
Kohl, K., 876-879, 881, 903
Kohlberg, L., 474, 487
Kohn, M., 813, 829
Koivumaki, J. H., 467, 472
Kolb, T., 490, 504
Konecni, V. J., 237, 246
Kong, A. C., 777, 790
Korzenny, F., 876-879, 884, 903
Koulack, D., 326, 328
Kramer, B., 812, 829
Kraus, S., 289, 290, 301-303, 736, 758
Krippendorff, K., 108, 134, 419, 443, 854, 872
Kristeva, J., 192, 198, 205
Krueger, G. P., 876-881, 903, 904
Krull, R., 624, 626
Kruskal, J. B., 911, 924
Ksionzky, S., 101, 104, 105, 106, 112, 113, 134
Ku, H. H., 504
Kubey, R. W., 585, 603
Kuhn, T., 203, 205
Kuiken, D., 242, 246
Kullback, S., 504
Kupperman, M., 504
Kurdek, L. A., 475, 487
Kwan, C., 606, 608, 610, 625

Labov, W., 54, 61
Lacan, J., 198, 205
LaFave, L., 312, 328
Laing, R. D., 759, 773
Lalljee, M., 109, 110, 134
Lamb, M., 815, 829
Lambert, M. D., 851, 872
Lamm, H., 396, 417
Lampel, A. K., 115, 134
Landsman, M. J., 507, 509, 511, 527
Lane, R., 760, 773
Lang, G. E., 760, 773
Lang, K., 533, 551, 760, 773
Langer, E. J., 239, 245
Langlois, J. H., 815, 828, 829
LaPiere, R. T., 331, 359, 759, 773
Laplanche, J., 204, 205
Larimer, M. W., 110, 111, 132
Laroche, M., 364, 387, 392
Larson, C., 331, 332, 359
Larson, C. E., 166, 169
Larson, C. U., 335, 359

Larson, J., 542, 551
Laslett, B., 207, 209, 211, 223, 226, 249
Latin, H., 212, 213, 226, 227, 246
Laufer, R. S., 207, 224, 246, 249
Lave, C. A., 366, 393
Laver, J. D. M., 103, 132
Lavrakas, P. J., 446, 471
Lawler, E. E., 891, 903
Lawrence, P. R., 629, 631-634, 640-642, 645, 648, 649, 651
Lazarsfeld, P., 319, 327
Lazarus, R. S., 834, 849
Leatherdale, W. H., 366, 393
Lee, A. L., 760, 773
Lee, A. R., 759, 773
Lee, C. C., 540, 551
Lee, E. B., 606, 626, 760, 773
Lee, J., 538, 549
Lefcourt, H., 491, 493, 502, 504
Leibman, M., 212, 246
Leippe, M. R., 337, 359
Lennox, L., 833, 849
Lent, J. A., 534-538, 542, 551
Lerner, D., 535, 537, 539, 551, 553
Levin, F. M., 509, 514, 527
Levine, M., 814, 830
Levinger, G., 507, 511, 527
Levinson, S., 875, 883-889, 893, 894, 896-900, 902
Levy, M. R., 697, 720
Lewin, K., 231, 246, 489, 504
Lewis, A., 38, 39, 61
Lewis, O., 234, 246
Lewis, R., 490, 505
Leyhausen, P., 211, 218, 238, 247
Libuser, L., 237, 246
Lichten, W., 64, 90
Lieman, L. A., 41, 42, 60
Light, L., 82, 90
Lin, N., 35, 61
Linder, D., 379, 391
Lindsay, P. H., 65, 90, 91
Lindskold, S., 502, 504
Lingle, J. H., 337, 359
Lipets, M. S., 467, 472
Lippmann, L., 229, 247
Lippmann, W., 23, 24, 33
Lipset, S. M., 760, 773
Liss, M. B., 608, 611, 625
Litterer, J. A., 630, 651
Little, B. R., 486, 487
Little, K. B., 237, 247
Littlepage, G., 446, 471
Liu, A. P., 536, 551
Livesley, W. J., 476, 487
Locke, H., 470, 471
Lockhart, R. S., 67, 70, 89

Author Index

Loevinger, L., 538, 551
Loftus, E. F., 65, 89
Logue, C. M., 629, 651
Lomas, C. W., 139, 169
Lometti, G. E., 606, 626
London, M., 632, 652
Long, J., 701, 706, 720
Longabaugh, R., 105, 134
Loo, C., 237, 247
Loomis, J., 871, 872
Lorr, M., 104, 134
Lorsch, J. W., 629, 631-634, 640-642, 645, 648, 649, 651
Loughlin, M., 607, 626
Love, L. R., 79, 89, 115, 132
Lowenstein, R. L., 539, 540, 552
Lowndes, J. C., 875, 903
Luck, J. I., 300, 302
Luckmann, T., 374, 391, 675, 691
Lull, J., 58, 61, 557-560, 563, 582, 606, 626
Lumsdaine, A. A., 776, 777, 790
Lunn, J., 792, 810
Lushene, R. E., 799, 810
Lustig, M., 141, 169, 207, 218, 247
Lyall, W. A. L., 834, 849
Lyle, J., 696, 720
Lyman, L. M., 213, 236, 241, 242, 247
Lynn, S. J., 509, 514, 527

MacNaughton, M. J., 901, 902
Maccoby, E. E., 450, 471, 556, 557, 582, 813, 814, 830
Mach, R. S., 239, 247
Madgison, J., 701, 720
Mahan, E., 537, 552
Mahl, G. F., 102, 134
Maier, N., 446, 471
Maier, R. A., 446, 471
Maines, D. R., 240, 247
Manchester, W., 315, 328
Mandler, G., 366, 393
Manis, M., 317, 322, 323, 328
Mann, G., 510, 514, 527
Mansfield, E., 239, 247
March, J. G., 366, 393, 676, 691
Marill, T. H., 675, 691
Marinelli, R. P., 93, 94, 107, 122, 134
Markel, N., 64, 90
Markham., J. W., 291, 303, 535, 536, 552
Markman, H., 512, 527
Markowski, J., 386, 393
Markus, H., 336, 356, 360
Marlowe, D., 839, 848
Marquez, F. T., 538, 552
Marsden, P., 929-931, 937, 943, 944

Marshall, N. J., 210, 213, 220, 221, 233, 234, 247
Marsteller, P., 851, 872
Martin, C. A., 556, 582
Martin, E., 654, 673
Martin, R., 538, 552
Maruyama, G., 706, 711, 720
Marvanyi, G., 542, 550
Marwell, C., 342, 355, 360
Maslach, C., 834, 837, 839, 848, 849
Masmoudi, M., 287, 538, 552
Massey, F. J., 470
Matarazzo, J. D., 78, 90, 116, 119, 134
Matthews, R. W., 237, 247
Mayer, M. E., 397, 399-402, 415-417
Mayer, R., 287
McAnany, E. G., 537, 544, 552
McArdle, J. B., 351, 360
McArthur, L. A., 331, 360
McArthur, L. Z., 723, 734
McBride, G., 218, 247
McBurney, J. H., 299, 303
McCain, T. A., 555, 559, 581, 585, 603
McCall, G., 75, 90
McCarrell, N. S., 43, 60
McCarter, R., 102, 135
McCarthy, M., 607, 626
McCauley, C., 240, 247
McClelland, P. D., 96, 134
McCombs, M. E., 546, 552, 695, 699, 719, 739, 746, 750, 758, 781, 790
McCroskey, J. C., 136-138, 140, 143, 146-148, 153, 154, 162, 168, 169, 333, 360, 416, 417, 795, 807, 809, 810
McDonagh, E. C., 556, 582
McFall, M., 509, 514, 527
McFarland, R. A., 584, 603
McGarvey, B., 706, 711, 720
McGaw, B., 706, 720
McGuinnis, J., 316, 328
McGuire, M., 58, 61
McGuire, W. J., 364-366, 369, 370, 389, 393, 775, 790
McKay, D. M., 424, 444
McKendree, J. D., 877-879, 903
McKersie, R. B., 629, 652, 656, 673
McLaughlin, M. L., 58, 61, 341, 342, 344, 355, 358, 360, 649, 651
McLeod, J. M., 558, 563, 581, 582, 698, 720, 739, 745, 749, 750, 758, 759, 773, 781, 790
McMahan, E. M., 79, 90, 96, 134
McNeal, B., 876, 894, 904
McNeill, D., 41, 61
McNelly, J., 542, 552
McPhee, R. D., 332, 358, 365, 393, 486, 487, 802, 810

McPhee, W., 319, 327
McQuail, D., 555, 582
McQuitty, L. L., 635, 647, 651
Mead, G. H., 473, 487
Meador, P. A., 294, 303
Mehan, H., 883, 891, 901
Mehrabian, A., 37, 62, 64, 79, 90, 94, 101, 104-106, 112, 113, 115, 134, 135, 237, 239, 241, 247, 249
Meisels, M., 211, 212, 226, 245
Meltzer, L., 146, 169
Mendelsohn, H. A., 760, 773, 778, 790
Merrihue, W. V., 675, 691
Merrill, J. C., 535, 536, 552
Merritt, R. L., 540, 547, 550, 552
Merton, R. K., 217, 218, 247
Mervis, C. B., 337, 361
Messaris, P., 557, 559, 562, 582
Messe, L., 815, 830
Messer, S., 814, 829
Messerschmitt-Bolkow-Blohm, 261, 287
Meyer, T. P., 442, 444, 555, 582, 606, 624-626
Michlin, M., 39, 62
Middleton, W. C., 446, 471
Milgram, S., 217, 247
Millar, F. E., 490, 491, 505
Miller, A., 229, 247
Miller, D. T., 38, 61
Miller, G. A., 38, 41, 43, 61, 63, 64, 90, 332, 333, 336, 337, 360
Miller, G. B., 80, 88
Miller, G. R., 37, 60, 98, 108, 117, 118, 122, 133, 134, 330-332, 334, 335, 342, 355, 360, 446-450, 454, 455, 463, 467-471, 649, 651, 667, 673
Miller, H., 390, 394
Miller, M. D., 137, 168
Miller, N., 324, 328, 396, 416, 417
Miller, P. H., 485, 487
Miller, R. E., 538, 552, 775-778, 788, 790
Miller, R. L., 365, 393
Miller, W. E., 737, 758, 760, 773
Mills, G. E., 297, 299, 303
Mills, J., 380, 393
Minium, E. W., 897, 903
Minsky, M. A., 336, 360
Mintzberg, H., 691
Miron, M. S., 84, 89
Mischel, W., 422, 444
Mishel, W., 607, 626
Mishler, E. G., 883, 893, 903
Mitchell, L. M., 303
Mitchell, T., 731, 733, 734
Mittelman, J., 508, 526
Miura, S. Y., 893, 902
Moleski, M., 607, 626

Molo, S., 287
Monge, P., 927, 943
Monson, T. C., 724, 734
Montgomery, B., 453, 471, 814, 825, 826, 830
Moore, J., 323, 328
Moore, S. G., 816, 830
More, 518, 528
Morgan, M., 746, 758
Morgan, R. N., 510, 514, 528
Morgan, W. L., 276, 278, 286
Morrall, J. B., 291, 292, 303
Morris, D. 237, 247
Morris, G. H., 656, 664, 673
Morrison, P., 607, 626
Mortensen, C. D., 141, 169, 174, 205, 207, 218, 247
Morton, H., 237, 246
Morton, T. L., 242, 247
Moses, J., 901, 902
Moss, M., 926, 944
Motley, M. T., 58, 61, 62
Mouton, J. S., 630-632, 634, 635, 640, 647, 650
Mowlana, H., 532, 534, 535, 538-540, 552
Mowrer, O. H., 40, 62, 518, 527
Mujahid, S., 542, 552
Mulac, A., 38, 62
Mullens, S., 238, 240, 248
Mumford, L., 22, 33
Mundy, A., 833, 834, 846, 848
Munz, D. C., 508, 514, 526
Murphy, K. C., 510, 514, 527
Murray, J. P., 624, 626
Muthen, B., 696, 712, 720
Myers, D. G., 396, 417

Nadler, D. A., 891, 903
Naftalin, D. H., 808, 810
Nam, S., 542, 552
Namurois, A., 538, 539, 552
Naremore, R. C., 38, 62
Nassiakou, M., 105, 135
Nebergall, R., 305, 312, 326, 329, 364, 386, 394
Neisser, V., 336, 337, 356, 360
Nelson, C., 366, 393
Nemeth, C., 386, 393
Nesvold, B. A., 540, 550
Neugarten, B. L., 584, 603
Neuwirth, C. M., 484, 485, 487
Newcomb, T. M., 759, 760, 773
Newman, H. M., 732, 734
Newman, J. E., 833, 835, 836, 849
Newman, L. S., 331, 362
Newman, T. G., Jr., 876, 881, 903

Author Index

Newton, D., 726, 730, 734
Nicholson, H., 79, 88, 115, 132
Nie, N. H., 433, 444, 842, 849
Nie, N. N., 619, 626
Niemi, R., 751, 758
Nilan, M., 606, 608-610, 624, 625
Nisbett, R., 73, 90, 107, 108, 133, 723, 733, 926, 944
Nitsch, K., 43, 60
Nixon, R. B., 538, 539, 552
Nnaemeka, T., 542, 543, 552
Noelle-Neumann, E., 547, 552, 760, 761, 764, 768, 771-773
Nofsinger, R. E., Jr., 178, 205
Noma, E., 368, 391
Nordenstreng, K., 287, 531, 543, 544, 552
Norman, D. A., 65, 90, 91, 331, 337, 360
Norman, R., 331, 360, 929, 943
Norton, L. E., 291, 295, 297, 299, 302
Norton, R. W., 453, 471, 649, 651, 793, 794, 809, 813, 814, 819, 825, 826, 830
Notarius, C., 512, 527
Nunnally, J. C., 635, 651, 799, 800-802, 810
Nussbaum, J. F., 793, 794, 800, 809, 810

O'Connor, M., 475, 488
O'Gormann, H. J., 760, 773
Ogston, W. D., 120, 133
O'Hara, J. O., 237, 244
O'Keefe, B. J., 182, 205, 473, 475, 487
O'Keefe, D. J., 182, 205, 332, 356, 360, 473, 475, 484, 485, 488
Olien, C. N., 543, 550, 607, 625, 626
Olson, D. H., 490, 504
O'Neil, H. F., 795, 809, 810
O'Neill, G. K., 874, 903
Ono, H., 93, 94, 106, 122, 124, 134
Oosthoek, H., 810
Orne, M., 446, 471
Ornstein, R. E., 425, 444
Orr, D. B., 84, 91
Ortony, A., 64, 65, 66, 69, 70, 80, 82, 86, 88, 91
Osgood, C. E., 40, 62, 104, 134, 135, 311, 328, 364, 366, 367, 368, 387, 393
Osmond, H., 236, 247
Ostagaard, E., 543, 552
Ostman, R., 851, 872
Ostrom, T. M., 334, 337, 359, 361
Oswalt, R. M., 440, 444
Ouchi, W. G., 690, 692

Pacanowsky, M. E., 883, 904
Page, B., 319, 320, 328
Paivio, A., 68, 72, 91
Palmer, S. E., 64, 91

Panko, R. R., 676, 692, 925, 944
Panyard, C. M., 507, 510, 511, 528
Park, L. D., 92, 134
Parker, E. B., 250, 287
Parnes, R., 912, 924
Parr, A. E., 228, 247
Pascale, R. T., 690, 692
Pastalan, L. A., 228, 230, 247
Pateman, T., 875, 904
Paterson, A., 792, 809
Paterson, S. A., 880, 904
Patterson, A. H., 235, 247
Patterson, M. L., 237-240, 247, 248
Patterson, T. E., 760, 763, 773
Paul, G. L., 148, 170
Paulos, J. A., 377, 393
Paulu, B., 535, 536, 552, 553
Paulus, P. B., 211, 237, 247, 248
Payne, D. E., 546, 553
Payne, R., 832, 833, 846-849
Pearce, W. B., 303, 333, 337, 338, 343, 352, 356, 358, 360, 489, 505, 506, 507, 510, 511, 528
Pederson, A., 827, 829
Pellegrino, J., 82, 90
Penniman, W., 926, 944
Pepitone, A., 308, 328
Peplau, L. A., 507, 510, 511, 528
Perloff, R. M., 334, 356, 360
Perrow, L. R., 629, 651
Peterson, T., 290, 303, 538, 539, 554
Petrovskii, I. G., 375, 393
Petterson, P., 326, 328
Pettigrew, A. M., 883, 904
Pettigrew, L. S., 813, 830, 833, 849
Pettigrew, T. F., 727-729, 734
Petty, R., 324, 328, 332, 334, 356, 357, 360, 361, 383, 390, 392, 393
Pfeiffer, E., 584, 603
Phares, E., 490, 491, 502, 504, 505
Philipsen, G., 58, 62
Philipszoon, E., 102, 133
Phillips, G. M., 140, 162, 170, 207, 218, 248
Phillips, J. L., 366, 393
Phillipson, H., 759, 773
Piaget, J., 473, 474, 488, 737, 758, 813, 826, 830
Piche, G. L., 39, 62
Picot, A., 677, 678, 692
Pierce, P. L., 366, 393
Pikus, I, M., 253, 287
Piliavin, J. A., 92, 133
Pilkonis, P. A., 142, 143, 170
Pineault, T., 446, 471
Pines, A., 832, 849
Pingree, S., 546, 547, 553

Pinter, R., 307, 328
Pitkin, H.F., 29, 33
Pittman, D., 851, 872
Planalp, S., 63, 66, 75, 87, 90, 91
Plant, J., 226, 227, 248
Ploman, E.W., 287
Poindexter, P.M., 695, 720
Pollman, V.A., 237, 245
Pondy, L.R., 629, 630, 633, 641-644, 648, 651
Pontalis, J.B., 204, 205
Pool, I.S., 287, 536, 537, 544, 547, 553, 760, 773
Poole, M.S., 365, 370, 393
Popkin, S., 760, 773
Popper, K., 125, 134
Porter, D.T., 639, 651
Post, B., 814, 830
Powell, D., 538, 553
Powell, F.A., 416, 417
Powell, W.J., 510, 514, 518, 528
Powers, W.G., 39, 62
Pratt, C.N., 542, 553
Press, A.N., 476, 478, 487, 488
Press, F., 276, 278, 287
Pribram, K.H., 332, 333, 336, 337, 360
Prigge, D.Y., 38, 62
Prigogine, O., 378, 393
Prisbell, M., 138, 170
Proshansky, H.M., 207, 209, 216, 224, 246, 248
Pruitt, D.G., 396, 417
Przeworski, A., 540, 547, 553
Putnam, L.L., 629, 651
Pye, L.W., 539, 553
Pye, R., 678, 692

Quillian, M.R., 65, 91
Quine, W.V., 131, 132, 135
Quinn, R., 835, 849

Rabunsky, C., 490, 504
Rachty, G., 544, 553
Rahim, A., 630, 632, 633, 651
Ramsey, S.J., 214, 241, 248
Rao, S., 542, 551
Rapaport, A., 216, 248, 489, 505, 633, 652
Rarick, D.L., 446, 462, 471
Rasmunsen, B., 816, 829
Ratner, D., 212, 213, 226, 227, 246
Ray, C., 237, 248
Ray, E.B., 847, 849
Read, H., 777, 790
Read, W.H., 287, 544, 553
Reardon, K.K., 333-335, 338, 361
Redding, C.W., 139, 170

Redmond, M.K., 166, 169
Reed, H., 115, 134
Reed, S.K., 336, 337, 361
Reeves, B., 606, 607, 624, 626
Regan, D.T., 331, 361, 721, 729, 734
Reichwald, R., 678, 692
Reid, L.N., 559, 582
Reinard, J.C., 835, 836, 849
Reinecker, V.M., 511, 527
Reingen, P.H., 401, 402, 417
Reinhold, R., 316, 329
Renne, K., 490, 505
Renshaw, S.L., 39, 61
Renwick, P.A., 629-632, 642, 652
Resnick, J.L., 509, 512, 527
Rhine, R., 317, 329
Rice, R.E., 250, 287, 684, 692, 877-879, 882, 904, 906, 924, 925, 926, 928, 930, 944
Richards, W., 930, 944
Richardson, F.C., 795, 810
Richardson, S.A., 93, 130, 135
Richey, W.M., 775-778, 788, 790
Richman, P., 507, 509, 527
Richman, S., 624, 625
Richmond, V.P., 136, 138, 140, 143, 146-149, 153, 154, 168, 169, 170
Richstadt, J., 537, 542, 543, 551, 552
Riess, M., 237, 244, 340, 361
Rivlin, L.G., 207, 209, 216, 248
Rizzo, J.R., 629, 651
Roberts, D.F., 333, 361, 695, 699, 719, 746, 758
Roberts, S.O., 331, 358
Robertson, T.S., 563, 582
Robey, C.S., 58, 61, 342, 344, 355, 360, 649, 651
Robey, D., 875, 904
Robinson, G.O., 287, 538, 553
Robinson, J.P., 540, 547, 553
Robinson, R.V., 366, 391
Robyn, D.L., 775-777, 788, 790
Rodenkirchen, J.M., 607, 626
Rodgers, H., 326, 329
Rodgers, W.L., 834, 848
Rodgon, M.M., 475, 487
Roedinger, H.L., III, 366, 393
Roff, M., 827, 830
Rogers/Rogers-Millar, L.E., 313, 329, 490-492, 494, 505, 649, 652, 893, 904
Rogers, E., 531, 539, 553, 925, 927, 944
Rogers, J.M., 518, 528
Rogers, P.L., 79, 91, 447, 467, 470, 471
Rogers, W.T., 64, 91
Rokeach, M., 331, 345, 361, 416, 417, 547, 554
Rollins, B., 490, 505

Author Index

Roloff, M. E., 342, 355, 360, 361, 649, 651, 926, 943
Romano, J., 238, 240, 248
Rommetveit, R., 179, 187, 190, 205
Rooparine, J., 815, 829
Rorty, R., 18, 23, 24, 26, 33
Rosch, E., 337, 361
Rosenberg, M., 416, 417
Rosenberg, S., 75, 91, 366, 393
Rosenfeld, H.M., 116, 120, 135
Rosenfeld, L.B., 237, 248
Rosenfield, D., 724, 734
Rosengren, K., 543, 553
Rosenkrantz, P.S., 450, 470
Rosenthal, P.I., 333, 361
Rosenthal, R., 79, 91, 446, 447, 449-451, 467, 470-472
Ross, L., 73, 90, 724, 734
Ross, M., 724, 733
Rossi, P., 698, 720
Rossiter, J.R., 563, 582
Rothenberg, B.B., 478, 485, 488
Rothkopf, E.Z., 68, 91
Rotter, J.P., 422, 444, 490, 493, 505
Rouse, W., 926, 944
Rowland, K.W., 632, 652
Rubenstein, E.A., 624, 626
Rubin, A.M., 585, 586, 591, 593, 602, 603, 606-608, 611, 624, 626
Rubin, D., 39, 62
Rubin, J.Z., 666, 673
Rubin, K.H., 475, 485, 488
Rubin, M.E., 512, 527
Rubin, R.B., 585, 586, 593, 602, 603
Rubin, Z., 507, 510, 511, 514, 528
Rubinow, S., 97, 98, 135
Ruble, T.L., 630, 652
Rueter, T., 289, 302
Ruge, M.H., 543, 550
Rumelhart, D., 64, 65, 90, 91
Russell, H., 927, 943
Rutherford, J., 322, 324, 328
Ryan, M.G., 877-879, 881, 904

Sabat, K., 544, 553
Sackett, G.P., 519, 520, 528
Sacks, H., 49, 62
Safilios-Rothschild, C., 490, 505
Sahin, H., 85, 91
Sailer, L., 926, 943
Saine, T.J., 78, 89, 93, 97, 98, 111, 132, 239, 244
Salcedo, R.N., 777, 790
Saldich, A.R., 289, 303
Salomon, G., 697, 720, 737, 758
Salter, V., 79, 88, 115, 132
Saltiel, J., 364, 366, 373, 390, 394

Sanders, A.K., 563, 581
Sanders, R., 331, 332, 359, 423, 443
Sarason, I.G., 794, 810
Sarett, C., 557, 559, 562, 582
Sargent, L.W., 696, 720
Sarlvik, B., 777, 790
Sarte, J.P., 190, 205
Sarup, G., 326, 329
Saslow, G., 116, 119, 134
Satellite Communications, 251, 286, 287, 288
Satz, P.H., 84, 89
Sauve, J., 276, 288
Savage, I.P., 543, 553
Savicki, V.E., 510, 514, 528
Savin, W., 928, 943
Sawyer, A., 364, 394
Scarlett, H.H., 476, 488
Schachter, S., 108, 135
Schaefer, C., 834, 849
Schanck, R.L., 759, 773
Schank, R.C., 332, 336, 337, 361
Scheff, T.J., 759, 774
Scheflen, A.E., 120, 135, 233, 239, 248
Schegelof, E.A., 49, 62
Schelling, T.C., 633, 652, 655, 657, 673
Schendel, A.H., 288
Schenkein, J., 50, 61
Scherer, K.R., 54, 61
Scherer, P.B., 440, 444
Schiller, H.I., 287, 531, 544, 552, 553
Schlenker, B.R., 340, 361, 362
Schmitt, D.R., 342, 355, 360
Schneider, D., 874, 904
Schneider, W., 725, 734
Schneirla, T.C., 218, 248
Schnitman, J., 537, 544, 545, 552, 553
Schramm, W., 290, 303, 333, 361, 419, 441, 444, 538, 539, 541-543, 554, 584, 603
Schulman, A.D., 684, 692
Schulte, D.C., 237, 245
Schuman, H., 759, 773, 774, 795, 809
Schutz, A., 188, 189, 205
Schutz, W.C., 208, 248
Schwartz, A.U., 229, 245
Schwartz, B., 219, 233, 234, 248
Schwartz, S.H., 338-340, 345, 352, 357, 361
Scott-Morton, M., 925, 943
Scott, L., 55, 61
Scott, M.B., 213, 236, 241, 242, 247
Scott, M.D., 162, 169, 792-794, 800, 807, 809, 810
Scott, R., 288
Scott, W.A., 432, 444, 569, 582, 854, 872
Searle, J.R., 37, 62, 356, 361

Sebring, R., 629, 652
Sechrest, L. B., 238, 248
Secord, P. F., 333, 359, 559, 568, 581, 657, 673
Sedlak, A., 75, 91
Seibold, D., 342, 355, 360, 486, 487, 649, 651, 759, 774, 802, 810
Seidel, J., 319, 328
Seiler, J. A., 644, 652
Seligman, M. E., 157, 170
Sells, S., 827, 830
Selman, R. L., 474, 488
Selye, H., 794, 810, 835, 847, 849
Senn, D. J., 507, 511, 527
Sennett, R., 298, 303
Sermat, V., 117, 118, 135, 510, 514, 528
Serota, K. B., 373, 394
Severance, L., 317, 329
Shaffer, S., 319, 329
Shaheen, J. G., 540, 553
Shannon, C. E., 419, 441, 444
Shantz, C. U., 475, 488
Shapiro, J. G., 95, 135
Sharon, A. T., 695, 720
Sharp, S. M., 506, 507, 510, 511, 528
Shaw, J., 508, 514, 526
Shaw, M., 323, 329
Sheatsley, P., 778, 781, 790
Sheffield, F. D., 776, 777, 790
Sheikh, A. A., 607, 626
Shenker, S., 507, 510, 511, 528
Shepard, H., 630, 650
Shepard, R. N., 72, 91, 366, 394
Shepps, F. P., 792, 810
Sheps, R. R., 792, 810
Shepsle, K., 316, 329
Sherif, C., 305, 311, 312, 313, 315, 326, 329, 364, 386, 394
Sherif, M., 304-306, 308, 310-313, 315, 319, 323, 326, 328, 329, 364, 386, 394
Sherrod, D., 319, 329
Shiffrin, R., 725, 734
Shils, E., 207, 208, 228, 248
Shimanoff, S. B., 333, 334, 361, 560, 561, 582, 884, 904
Shiraishi, D., 237, 244
Shore, L., 537, 540, 542, 549, 554
Short, J., 684, 689, 692
Shulman, G., 446, 449, 451, 471
Shutz, A., 883, 904
Shweder, R., 926, 944
Siebert, F. S., 290, 303, 538, 539, 554
Siegel, S., 897, 904
Sigman, S. J., 559, 582
Signorielli, N., 746, 758
Sillars, A. L., 342, 355, 357, 361, 652, 732, 734, 883, 904

Siller, J., 93, 121, 124, 135
Silverman, L. T., 624, 626
Silverthorne, C. F., 397, 417
Simmel, G., 207, 208, 218, 223, 226, 231, 248
Simmel, M., 726, 733
Simmons, J. L., 75, 90
Simons, H. W., 333, 335, 361, 630, 652, 667, 673, 898, 904
Sinclair, J. M., 883, 893, 894, 904
Singer, D., 562, 582
Singer, J. E., 214, 245
Singer, J. L., 562, 582
Singleton, R., 706, 720
Skerchock, L., 504
Skinner, A. E., 508, 514, 526
Slama, K. M., 507, 510, 511, 528
Sloan, M. L., 508, 514, 526
Sluczki, C., 491, 505
Smetana, J., 237, 247
Smeyak, G. P., 654, 673
Smith, A., 536, 554
Smith, D. H., 442, 444, 555, 582
Smith, M. B., 340, 361
Smith, M. J., 332-335, 356, 361
Smith, P., 839, 849
Smith, R. E., 229, 248
Smith, R. J., 237, 248
Smyth, M., 117, 118, 135, 510, 514, 528
Snider, J. G., 104, 135
Snoek, J., 835, 849
Snortum, J., 814, 829
Snyder, M., 455, 461, 471, 724, 734
Soja, M., 871, 872
Soldow, G. F., 446, 462, 471
Sommer, R., 212, 216, 233, 235, 237, 238, 245, 248
Sorbom, D., 706, 720
Spang, S., 876-879, 894, 904
Spangler, K., 880, 882, 901, 903, 904
Spangler, U., 684, 691
Spanier, G., 490, 505
Sparkes, V., 542, 546, 554
Spelt, P. F., 876-879, 881, 904
Spielberger, C. D., 122, 135, 149, 168, 170, 794-796, 799, 805, 810
Sprafkin, J. N., 624, 626
Stacks, D. W., 80, 89
Stamm, K., 606, 608, 610, 624-626
Standing, L., 72, 91
Stanfield, D. J., 538, 554
Star, S. A., 777, 778, 790
Starck, K., 542, 554
Starnes, C. E., 706, 720
Stea, D., 234, 235, 248
Steele, L., 313, 328
Steiger, J. H., 523, 528

Stein, A. H., 624, 626
Steinberg, M., 98, 108, 117, 118, 134, 342, 360
Steinbrenner, K., 619, 626, 842, 849
Steinman, J. I., 684, 692
Stempel, G. H., 432, 444, 696, 720
Stengel, E., 827, 830
Stephan, C., 828, 829
Stephen, W. G., 724, 734
Stephenson, W., 426, 444
Stevenson, R. L., 542, 554
Stewart, J., 39, 62
Sticht, T. G., 84, 90
Stinson, J. E., 629, 651
Stivale, G., 204, 205
Stohl, C., 811, 813, 830
Stokes, D. E., 737, 758
Stokols, D., 211, 212, 226, 236, 237, 238, 240, 248
Stoll, F. C., 877-880, 904
Stollack, G., 815, 830
Stone, G. L., 508, 514, 526
Stoneman, Z., 563, 581
Stoner, J. A. F., 396, 403, 404, 417
Storms, M. D., 724, 734
Stott, L. H., 813, 830
Stouffer, S. A., 741, 758
Strange, J., 274, 286
Strassberg, D. S., 510, 515, 528
Straus, M., 490, 504
Strauss, A., 442, 443, 657, 658, 673
Strickland, D., 851, 854, 872
Strickland, L. H., 877-880, 904
Strodtbeck, F., 494, 504
Stroebe, W., 319, 327
Stroman, C. A., 695, 700, 720
Sturtevant, E. H., 103, 135
Suci, G. J., 40, 62, 104, 134, 311, 328, 366-368, 393
Suess, R., 912, 924
Sullivan, A., 39, 62
Sullivan, J. L., 719, 720
Summers, G. F., 696, 712, 720
Sundene, B., 104, 135
Sundstrom, E., 236-240, 243, 248
Sundstrom, M. G., 236-238, 249
Surlin, S. H., 547, 554
Sutton-Smith, B., 814, 830
Suziedelis, A., 104, 134
Svoboda, L., 926, 944
Swank, C., 584, 604
Sypher, H. E., 478, 484, 485, 488
Szyperski, N., 676, 692

Tabussi, S. J., 271, 288
Tajfel, H., 306, 329

Tannenbaum, P. H., 40, 62, 104, 134, 311, 328, 364, 366-368, 387, 393, 394
Tardy, C. H., 41, 42, 60
Tate, E., 547, 554
Taub, D., 308, 329
Tauber, M., 814, 830
Taylor, B. F., 696, 697, 699, 701, 718, 719
Taylor, C., 20, 21, 33
Taylor, D. A., 116, 118, 132, 135, 224, 242, 244, 447, 453, 467, 470, 506, 526
Taylor, D. M., 54, 61
Taylor, J. A., 373, 394
Taylor, J. P., 277, 278, 282, 288
Taylor, M., 390, 394
Taylor, S., 723, 724, 734
Taylor, S. E., 332, 336, 337, 356, 362
Tedeschi, J. T., 340, 359, 362
Teger, A. I., 396, 417
Telaak, K., 312, 327
Television/Radio Age, 275, 288
Tesser, A., 336, 337, 356, 362, 364, 365, 383, 394
Teune, H., 540, 547, 553
Teyber, E., 815, 830
Thackery, R. I., 446, 471
Thibaut, J. W., 117, 135, 467, 471
Thiele, R., 288
Thistlethwaite, D. L., 416, 417
Thom, R., 377, 394
Thomas, K. W., 630, 632, 634, 639, 640, 648, 649, 651, 652
Thomas, R. C., 833, 849
Thomas, S., 792, 809, 833, 849
Thompson, E. G., 366, 393
Thompson, M., 426, 444
Thomson, D., 81, 82, 91
Thoren, S., 542, 554
Thurber, J. A., 446, 471
Thurstone, L., 306-310, 315, 319, 329
Tichenor, P. J., 543, 550, 607, 625, 626
Tims, A. R., 567, 581
Tipton, L. P., 750, 758
Tittle, C. R., 331, 362
Tittler, B., 326, 329
Tobias, S., 795, 810
Tobin, S. S., 584, 603
Todd, R., 542, 549
Toffler, A., 874, 904
Toglia, M. P., 72, 90
Tognoli, J. J., 510, 514, 528
Tomey, J. F., 876, 881, 903
Tomkins, S. S., 102, 135
Tompkins, E. V., 633, 652
Tompkins, P. K., 633, 652
Toogood, A., 538, 554
Topol, S., 276, 288
Totten, J., 729, 734

Tracy, K., 63, 91
Trager, R., 851, 872
Traudt, P. J., 442, 444, 555, 557, 582, 606, 626
TRB, 316, 329
Triandis, H. C., 105, 135, 331, 362, 731, 733, 734
Trimmer, J. D., 540, 554
Trinkaus, R. J., 833, 847, 849
Troldahl, V. C., 416, 417, 592, 604
Trope, Y., 396, 417
Trost, N. A., 827, 829
Trudgill, P., 38, 39, 61
Tsai, M. K., 546, 554
Tukey, J. W., 818, 830
Tulving, E., 64, 65, 67, 70, 73-75, 81-83, 89-91
Tunstall, J., 544, 554
Tur, J., 814, 829
Turiel, E., 474-476, 488
Turner, J. A., 317, 327, 364, 387, 391
Turner, J. E., 540, 551
Turoff, M., 675, 692, 876-880, 882, 885, 900, 901, 903, 904, 912, 924, 926, 928, 943
Tversky, A., 337, 362, 725, 727, 734

Uhlig, R. P., 676, 692, 877-879, 882, 904, 926, 944
Ullmann, W., 296, 303
UNESCO, 534, 554
United Nations, 252, 288
Updegraff, R., 816, 830
Upshaw, H., 319, 329
U. S. Commission on Civil Rights, 694, 720
U. S. Congress, 229, 249
U. S. Congress, Hearings before the Senate Subcommittee on Alcoholism and Narcotics, 871, 872

Vachon, M. L. S., 832, 834-836, 849
Valentinsen, B., 338, 339, 340, 359
Valins, S., 107, 108, 133
Vallée, J., 684, 691, 877-880, 882, 901, 903, 904
VandeCreek, L., 95, 135
Vann, D. H., 93, 121, 124, 135
Varis, T., 543, 544, 552
Vassiliou, V., 105, 135
Vian Spangler, K., 876, 894, 904
Vidmar, N., 547, 554
Vinokur, A., 396, 397, 402, 417
Vinsel, A., 233, 235, 238, 249
Vivekananthan, P. S., 366, 393
Vogel, S. R., 450, 470
Von Feilitzen, C., 606, 626
Vondracek, F. W., 510, 514, 528
Vondracek, S. I., 510, 514, 528

Vredenburgh, D. J., 833, 847, 849

Wackerbarth, M. E., 880-882, 902
Wackman, D. B., 737, 758
Wade, S., 441, 444
Wallace, K., 470, 471
Wallach, M. A., 395, 417
Walmer, J., 509, 514, 526
Walster, E. L., 365, 387, 390, 394, 828, 829
Walton, R. E., 629, 644, 651, 652, 656, 673
Wapner, S., 212, 249
Ward, S. L., 750, 758
Ware, J. E., 808, 810
Warner, L. G., 331, 345, 362
Warnick, B., 58, 62
Warren, C., 207, 209, 211, 223, 226, 249
Wartella, E., 737, 758
Washburn, S. L., 211, 249
Watkins, J. T., 95, 135
Watkins, M., 64, 81, 82, 91
Watzlawick, P., 489, 491, 505, 656, 673, 676, 687, 692
Wauson, M. S., 237, 245
Weary, G., 362
Weaver, D., 542, 554, 699, 720
Weaver, W., 419, 441, 444
Webster, J. G., 608, 626
Wedell, G., 534, 535, 538, 544, 545, 551
Weick, K. E., 893, 904, 927, 944
Weigel, R. H., 331, 362, 871, 872
Weiner, B., 107, 133, 795, 810
Weiner, M., 241, 249
Weinshall, Th. D., 692
Weintraub, B., 268, 288
Weiss, W., 760, 774
Weizenbaum, J., 677, 692
Wells, A., 539, 544, 554
Wells, G. L., 383, 393
Wenner, L., 485, 604
Westerstahl, J., 777, 790
Westie, F. R., 331, 358, 759, 773
Westin, A., 207-209, 216, 219, 220, 225-228, 240, 242, 249
Westley, B. H., 777, 778, 790
Wheaton, B., 696, 712, 720
Wheeler, L., 118, 135
Wheeless, L. R., 143, 169, 472, 792, 793, 800, 805, 810
White, D. M., 543, 554
White, R. C., 84, 89
White, R. W., 340, 361
Whitehead, J. L., 38, 62
Whiting, G. C., 63, 91, 338-340, 356, 359, 538, 554, 560, 581
Whitman, R. F., 44, 61

Author Index

Whittaker, J. B., 322, 329, 386, 394
Wicker, A. W., 331, 362, 759, 774
Wiener, M., 37, 62, 79, 90, 97, 98, 101, 115, 134, 135
Wiens, A. N., 78, 90, 116, 119, 134
Wigand, R. T., 250, 252, 254, 261, 264, 267, 268, 273, 276, 279, 283-285, 288
Wilde, R. J., 606, 625
Willems, E. P., 212, 232, 249
Williams, A. D., 876, 881, 902
Williams, E., 684, 689, 692, 877-879, 881, 882, 884, 904
Williams, F., 38, 62, 104, 135
Williams, M., 64, 79, 88, 90, 115, 132, 239, 247
Williams, R. G., 38, 62, 808, 810
Williamson, O. E., 677, 692
Willis, F. N., 237, 249
Wilmot, W. W., 630, 651
Wilson, C. E., 643, 652
Wilson, D. L., 584, 604
Wilson, M., 509, 514, 526
Wilson, T., 926, 944
Wilson, W., 390, 394
Wine, J., 795, 810
Wingfield, A., 390, 394
Winke, J., 342, 359
Wish, M., 342, 362, 366, 368, 394, 911, 924
Witte, E., 676, 692
Woelfel, J., 364, 366-368, 373, 378, 390-392, 394, 911, 921, 923, 924

Wohlwill, J. F., 228, 249
Wolf, G. E., 833, 849
Wolf, M. A., 606, 609, 624, 626
Wolfe, D., 835, 849
Wolfe, M., 207, 224, 246, 249
Woodall, W. G., 64, 70, 71, 73, 74, 80, 83, 85, 89, 91
Woolfolk, A. E., 510, 514, 528
Worchel, S., 390, 394
Worthington, M. E., 93, 94, 106, 122, 135
Worthy, M., 120, 135
Worthy, W., 510, 511, 514, 528
Wright, P. H., 507, 510, 511, 528
Wrightsman, L., 331, 362
Wurtzel, A., 624, 625

Yoppi, B., 512, 527
Young, F. W., 366, 392
Young, J., 678, 692
Yu, F. T. C., 535, 536, 554

Zadny, J., 725, 734
Zammuto, R. F., 632, 652
Zanna, M. P., 331, 333, 358, 359
Zeleny, M., 203, 205
Zetterberg, H. L., 95, 135
Zimbardo, P. G., 142, 145, 170, 208, 225, 246, 249, 323, 329, 386, 394
Zuckerman, M., 467, 472
Zweizig, D., 606, 608, 610, 625

SUBJECT INDEX

Actor/observer inferences, 723-724
Adaptors, 103
Advertising, 850; alcohol abuse sanctions in, 851; lifestyle themes in, 851, 855-858; role models in, 851, 858-861
Affect displays, 102
Affective perspective taking, 476-477; index of, 476-477, 479
Affiliation, 112-113, 115-132
Aging: activity theory of, 584; disengagement theory of, 584
Alcohol: abuse, 850; advertising, 852-872
Alcohol advertising, 852-872; in magazines, 852-853; on television, 853; presentation techniques of, 861-863; role models in, 858-861; themes in, 855-858
Ambiguity, 315-317
Anonymity, 220
Anxiety proneness, 799
Artifacts, 233-239
Assimilation, 318-322
Attire, 240-241
Attitude, 364; decay of, 382-384, 389; structure of, 366-369; trajectories, 364, 367-377
Attitude change, 364-416; dynamic models of, 369-391, 395-416
Attribution theory, 721-733; actor/observer differences, 723-724; correspondent inferences, 722-723; inferential error and, 729; inferential phase of, 722, 726; inferential processes, 724-726; intercultural training using, 731; intercultural communication and, 726-733; perceived similarity and, 727-729; role taking and, 729; stereotyping, 728, 731
Audience anxiety, 144

Bandwagon effect, 760, 773
Beliefs, structure of, 366-369
Blacks: media exposure and, 695-719; media motives of, 695; media usage and, 695-696; public affairs programming and, 699
Burnout, 834-835, 844-847

Cable television, 266-268

Channel selection, 681-690; affective determinants of, 684-686; cognitive determinants of, 681-684; substitution in, 686-690
Children: as active consumers of television, 605-606; as information seekers, 606-624; news media exposure and, 737-739; television and, 605-626
Chronemics, 238
Codes, 53-55, 97
Cognitive information, 775-789
Cognitive responses, 389-390
Cognitive schema, 332, 335-338
Cognitive structures, 366-369, 395-398, 474-485
Communication as action, 28-33
Communication networks, 905, 908, 915, 927-941
Communication apprehension, 136-167; distribution of, 145-146; effects of, 162-167; expectations and, 157-160; generalized context, 147-148; pathological, 151-153; person-group, 148-149; situational, 149-156; traitlike, 147; treatment of, 160-162
Compliance interviewing, 653-669; agenda control, 663-664; agendas of, 661-663; as interpersonal persuasion, 654-655; coercion in, 664-665; goals of, 654; rules for, 665-667
Comprehension, 65-68
Computer-mediated communication, 875-901, 905, 925; analytical opportunities of, 926-927; evaluation of, 907-911, 921-924, 929-941; features of, 906-907; organizational impact of, 925-926; social impact of, 925-926
Computerized bulletin board system, 911-927
Conflict management: compliance interviewing as, 653-669; styles of, 630-633
Context, 36-39, 42-44, 51, 66-67, 75, 179, 341-343, 348-351; components of, 585, 586-590; sociodemographics and, 593-598; television usage and, 583; viewing motivations and, 598-600; viewing patterns and, 595-597
Contingency rules, 335, 338-356

Subject Index

Contrast, 318-322
Correspondent inferences, 722-723
Critical school, 18-33, 532-538

Debates: history of, 291-301; presidential, 289-302; televised, 289-291, 300-302
Deception, 447-470; emotional, 449, 454; factual, 449, 454
Deception detection, 80, 447-470; deception type and, 454, 459-470; familiarity and, 447-470; gender and, 454, 459-470
Deconstruction of interpersonal relationships, 196-199
Deductive theory, 95
Democratic theory, 291-302; the American experiment, 298-299; medieval public communication, 295-297; the Renaissance, 297-298; Romans, 294-295; the Socratic school, 293-294; and Sophists, 292-293
Depth of processing, 67-68, 72
Descartes, Rene, 19-21
Dewey, John, 22, 25, 26-28
Direct mailing, 776
Direct satellite broadcasting, 250-268; and cable television, 266-268; defined, 253-254; direct to home, 259; future of, 268-281; international application, 260-266; policy implications, 282-286; uses of, 254-259, 268
Discontinuous models, 377
Discrepancy, 380-382, 395-416
Discursive description, 193-202
Dominance, 79, 491-493
Dramaturgic perspective, 218-219
Dynamic models, 369-416

Ego-involvement, 308-310, 313-314, 384-386
Electronic text, 675-676, 679, 687-690; teletex, 679
Emblems, 101
Empirical school, 538-540
Enlightenment, 19-22
Environment, 233-237
Expectations, 157-160
Expressivism, 19-22

Face needs 883-885
Face-threatening acts, 885
Facsimile transmission, 271
Family communication, 555-581; patterns in, 556-558, 571-581; prepartum families and, 555-581; television usage in, 556-559, 575
Field, 55-56

Fixed-mass spring model, 373-391

Habits, 560
Handicapped persons and communication, 92-132
Haptics, 237-238
Hermeneutic approach, 18, 184-187
Hovland, Carl, 304-305

Illustrators, 102
Incongruency, 113
Inference making, 77
Inferential processes, 724-726
Information, 378-380, 419-441, 606-624
Information theory, 420-424; assumptions of, 420-421; critique of, 421-424
Information seeking model, 424-441, 606-624; assumptions of, 424-426
Integration, 71-77
Intentionality, 98-100
Interactional approach, 179-180
Interactional perspective, 489-503
Interactive technologies, 875-901
Intercultural communication, 721, 726-733; attribution theory and, 726-733; stereotyping and, 728; training in, 731
International communication, 531-549
Interpersonal construct, 478-485
Intersubjectivity, 187-190
Intimacy, 118, 208, 209, 221, 242
Introversion, 208

Kinesics, 239-240

Language intensity, 36-37, 41-43, 242
Latitude of acceptance, 310-313
Latitude of noncommitment, 311-313
Latitude of rejection, 310-313
Laws approach, 332-333
Learning, 792-797, 801-822; anxiety and, 794-797; solidarity and, 792-794, 805-808; threat and, 794-795
Lexical items, 39-45
Linear discrepancy model, 395-416; equal speaking, 398; unequal speaking, 399-416
Lippman, Walter, 22-26

Marital interaction, 489-503
Mass communication, 532-549; comparative approach to, 538-540; descriptive approach to, 532-538; effects of, 545-548; flow of, 541-545; mass media systems analysis, 534-540; policy research, 537-538; structure of,

541-545; Third World broadcasting, 538
Mass media, 18-28; public opinion and, 22-28
Mathematical models, 373-391, 395-416
Meaning, 40, 172-203; behavioral approach to, 40-44; effects model of, 172-173; mentalism, 174-175; phenomenological, 182-183
Memory, 65, 69-71; retrieval, 80-84; semantic network model, 66; recognition failure, 81-83
Mode, 57-58

Negotiation, 653-669
News media use, 726, 737-758; adolescence and, 737-758; cognitive consequences of, 739-758; political communication and, 726, 748-758; school grade and, 745-746; social determinants of, 739-748; political knowledge and, 750-756
Nonverbal communication, 63, 93-94, 97-100, 101-124
Nursing: burnout in, 834-835, 844-847; stress in, 833-847

Objectivism, 19-22
Occupational stress, 832-847; burnout because of, 834, 837, 844-847; in nursing, 833-835, 844-847; strategies for coping with, 834-835, 837-838, 844-847
Office technology, 674-690; and organizational communication, 674, 676-690; changes in, 675-677; problems with, 677
Organizational communication conflict instrument, 633-650
Organizational conflict, 629-650; compliance interviewing and, 653-669; management of, 629-650; management style and, 629-633
Organizational culture, 864

Perceived similarity, 727
Persuasion, 343-348, 351-356
Phenomenological approach, 182-184
Physical appearance, 240-241
Polarity shift, 395-416
Policy research, 537-538
Politeness strategies, 885-890
Political campaigns, 775-789
Political communications, 289-302, 319-322, 726-758; adolescence and, 737-758; candidate contact, 777; contact by candidate and, 777-789;

exposure to, 737-739, 775-789; news media and, 726, 748-749; political campaigns and, 775-789; public opinion and, 759-773; voting behavior, 759-773
Power, 490-494
Predispositions toward verbal behavior, 141-142, 207
Prior commitment, 384-386
Privacy, 206-243; defined, 208-210; dimensions of, 210-232; informational, 228-231; physical, 210-216; psychological, 223-228; social, 216-223; strategies for, 232-243
Proxemics, 237-238
Psychophysical scaling, 306-308
Public opinion, 759-773

Radical structures, 193
Reciprocity, 116-124, 506-523; experimental designs and, 513-514; nonexperimental designs and, 513; perceived, 511
Recognition failure, 81-83
Reduction of uncertainty, 96, 107-124
Regulators, 102
Relational control, 489-503; coding of, 494-500; locus of, 490-494
Repetition, 389
Reticence, 140, 207
Retrieval, 80-84
Retroactive uncertainty, 108
Rhizomes, 193-196, 199-202
Risky shift, 397-416
Role taking, 473-485; attribution theory and, 729; cognitive capacity and, 474-485; domain specific, 475; partial structure, 475; Turiel's model of, 475-476
Root structures, 193
Rules: contingency, 335, 338-356; television viewing, 559-581

Satellite communication, 250-286; history of, 250-253
Self-disclosure, 242, 506-523; coding of, 518; self-report of, 514; sequential analysis and, 516, 519-522
Semantic network model, 66
Sherif, Carolyn, 305
Sherif, Muzafer, 304-306
Shyness, 142-143, 208
Signs, 97
Similarity, 387
Situation movement state, 613-618
Situational approach, 51
Social judgment theory, 304-327

Subject Index

Social perspectives task, 479; dimensions of, 104-107
Solidarity, 792-794, 797-799, 805-808; learning and, 792-794, 805-808
Source credibility, 384-386
Spiral of silence theory, 760-773
Stage fright, 139-140
Structural approach, 45-51, 178-179
Student anxiety, 792-808
Student-teacher relationships, 795-797, 805-808
Submissiveness, 79, 491-493
Symbols, 97
Synchrony, 70-71, 76

Teleconferencing, 875-901, 907-924; framework for analysis, 892-901; task effectiveness and, 876-880; unit of analysis, 893-895; verbal productivity and, 880-881
Television, 439, 542-549, 555-581, 583-603, 605, 694-719; children and, 605-626; contextual age and, 583-603; discussion patterns and, 573; exposure patterns, 573; family uses of, 556-559; family communication patterns and, 556-559, 573; gratification and, 695-698, 700-719; interpretation of, 556-557; public affairs exposure and, 695-719; race and, 694-719; social class and, 557; social learning and, 557
Tenor, 56-57
Territory, 212-213, 215
Transcendental approach, 181
Trustworthiness, 380
Turiel's model of role taking, 475-476

Uncertainty, 107-124
Unwillingness to communicate, 141, 207
Uses and gratifications, 605-606

Variable mass impulse model, 373
Variable analytic approach, 35; critique of, 35-45, 333-335
Verbal immediacy, 37-38
Violations: of expectations, 80; of privacy, 215, 217
Vocalics, 239-240
Voting behavior, 759-773

ABOUT THE EDITOR

MICHAEL BURGOON is Professor of Communication at Michigan State University, where he received his Ph.D. in communication in 1970. He is the author of numerous journal articles in communication, speech, psychology, journalism, and management. He has also authored and edited several communication books. He has been an active member of the International Communication Association, serving as Director of Placement Services, Chairperson of the Finance Committee, Chairperson of the Convention Site Committee, and Chairperson of the Instructional Communication Division. In addition, he has served on the editorial boards of a number of scholarly journals in the communication discipline. Professor Burgoon is an active consultant and researcher for industry, and has been funded by the Gannett newspaper group and the American Society of Newspaper Editors in the past few years to study the communication behavior of consumers and producers of news.

REF P. 87 .C5974 v.6

For Reference

Not to be taken from this room